HAMMOND®
NEW
CONTEMPORARY

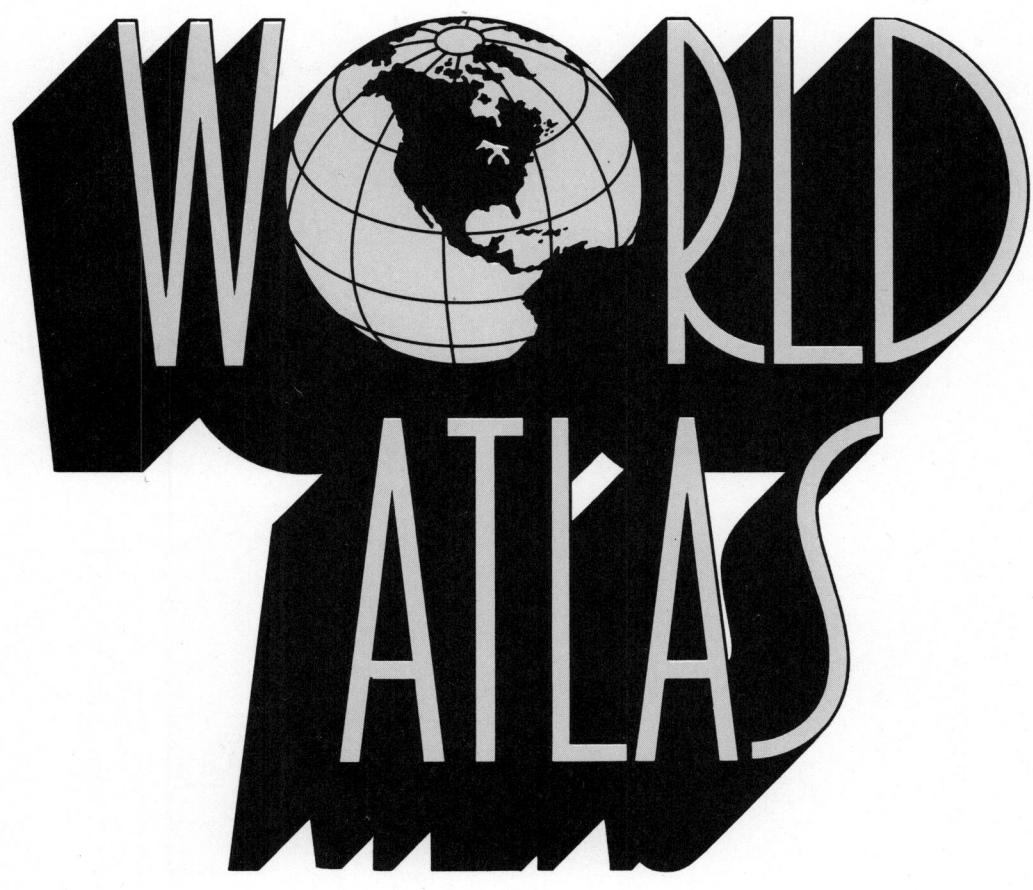

WORLD ATLAS

NEW PERSPECTIVE EDITION

INCLUDING ZIP CODES

DOUBLEDAY and COMPANY, Inc.   GARDEN CITY, NEW YORK

Hammond Publications Advisory Board

GAZETTEER-INDEX OF THE WORLD

This alphabetical list of grand divisions, countries, states, colonial possessions, etc., gives page numbers and index references on which they are shown on the largest scale as well as area and population of each unit. The index reference shows the square on the respective map in which the name of the entry may be located.

Country	Page No.	Index Ref.	Area (Sq. Miles)	Population
*Afghanistan	70	A 2	250,000	17,078,263
Africa	54, 57	......	11,682,000	345,000,000
Alabama, U.S.A.	130	......	51,609	3,444,165
Alaska, U.S.A.	133	......	586,412	302,173
*Albania	43	E 5	11,100	2,126,000
Alberta, Canada	114	......	255,285	1,838,037
*Algeria	54	F 6	919,591	16,776,000
American Samoa	89	J 7	83	27,159
Andorra	31	G 1	175	19,000
*Angola	57	K14	481,351	6,761,000
Antarctica	88	......	5,500,000	....
Antigua & Dependencies	125	G 3	171	73,000
*Argentina	93	H10	1,072,070	23,983,000
Arizona, U.S.A.	134	......	113,909	1,772,482
Arkansas, U.S.A.	139	......	53,104	1,923,295
Ascension	5	G 8	34	1,154
Asia	58	......	17,032,000	2,043,997,000
*Australia	86	......	2,967,741	12,630,000
*Austria	38	B 3	32,374	7,419,341
*Bahamas	124	C 1	4,404	168,838
*Bahrain	60	F 4	231	207,000
*Bangladesh	70	F 3	55,126	70,000,000
*Barbados	125	G 4	166	253,620
*Belgium	25	......	11,779	9,660,154
Belize	122	C 2	8,867	122,000
*Benin	54	G10	43,483	3,200,000
Bermuda	125	H 3	21	52,000
*Bhutan	70	G 3	18,000	1,034,774
*Bolivia	90	G 7	424,163	4,804,000
*Botswana	57	L16	224,764	700,000
*Brazil	90	K 6	3,284,426	90,840,000
British Columbia, Canada	117	......	366,255	2,466,608
British Indian Ocean Terr.	58	L10	29	1,400
Brunei	83	E 4	2,226	130,000
*Bulgaria	43	G 4	42,829	8,501,000
*Burma	81	B 2	261,789	31,240,000
*Burundi	57	M12	10,747	4,100,000
California, U.S.A.	140	......	158,693	19,953,134
*Cambodia	81	E 4	69,898	8,110,000
*Cameroon	54	J10	183,568	6,600,000
*Canada	96-97	......	3,851,809	23,388,100
Canal Zone	123	H 6	647	44,650
*Cape Verde	5	F 9	1,557	302,000
Cayman Islands	124	B 3	100	10,652
*Central African Empire	54	K10	236,293	1,800,000
Central America	122-123	......	197,575	20,500,000
*Ceylon (Sri Lanka)	70	E 7	25,332	12,300,000
*Chad	54	K 8	495,752	4,178,000
Channel Islands	11	E 8	74	128,000
*Chile	93	F10	292,257	8,834,820
*China (mainland)	77	......	3,691,506	740,000,000
China (Taiwan)	77	K 7	13,948	14,577,000
*Colombia	90	F 3	439,513	21,117,000
Colorado, U.S.A.	145	......	104,247	2,207,259
*Comoros	57	P14	719	266,000
*Congo	57	J12	132,046	1,400,000

*Members of the United Nations.

Library of Congress Cataloging in Publication Data
Hammond Incorporated.
  Hammond New contemporary world atlas.
  Includes indexes.
  1. Atlases.   I. Title.   II. Title: New contemporary world atlas.
G1021.H274   1979   912   78-31957
ISBN: 0-385-12895-9

GAZETTEER-INDEX OF THE WORLD

Country	Page No.	Index Ref.	Area (Sq. Miles)	Population
Connecticut, U.S.A.	146		5,009	3,032,217
Cook Islands	89	K 7	91	20,000
*Costa Rica	122	E 5	19,575	1,800,000
*Cuba	124	B 2	44,206	8,553,395
*Cyprus	64	E 5	3,473	649,000
*Czechoslovakia	39	C 2	49,370	14,497,000
Delaware, U.S.A.	181	R 3	2,057	548,104
*Denmark	19		16,614	4,912,865
District of Columbia, U.S.A.	180	F 5	67	756,510
Djibouti	55	P 9	8,880	250,000
Dominica	125	G 4	290	70,302
*Dominican Republic	124	D 3	18,704	4,011,589
*Ecuador	90	E 4	109,483	6,144,000
*Egypt	54	M 6	386,659	37,900,000
*El Salvador	122	C 4	8,260	3,418,455
England, U.K.	11		50,516	46,417,600
*Equatorial Guinea	57	H11	10,831	320,000
*Ethiopia	54, 55	O 9	471,776	27,946,000
Europe	6		4,063,000	652,000,000
Faerøe Islands, Denmark	19	B 2	540	38,000
Falkland Islands	93	H14	6,198	1,950
*Fiji	89	H 8	7,015	519,000
*Finland	16		130,128	4,706,000
Florida, U.S.A.	148		58,560	6,789,443
*France	26		212,841	50,770,000
French Guiana	90	K 3	35,135	48,000
French Polynesia	89	L 8	1,544	109,000
*Gabon	57	J12	103,346	526,000
*Gambia	54	C 9	4,127	524,000
Georgia, U.S.A.	152		58,876	4,589,575
*Germany, East (German Democratic Republic)	20		41,814	17,117,000
*Germany, West (Fed. Rep. of)	20		95,959	61,194,600
*Ghana	54	F10	92,099	9,900,000
Gibraltar	31	D 4	2	27,000
Gilbert Islands	89	J 6	354	47,711
*Great Britain and Northern Ireland (United Kingdom)	8		94,399	56,076,000
*Greece	43	F 6	50,548	8,838,000
Greenland	94	O 2	840,000	55,000
*Grenada	125	G 4	133	96,000
Guadeloupe and Dependencies	124	F 3	687	360,000
Guam	89	E 4	212	84,996
*Guatemala	122	B 3	42,042	5,200,000
*Guinea	54	D 9	94,925	4,500,000
*Guinea-Bissau	54	C 9	13,948	517,000
*Guyana	90	J 2	83,000	763,000
*Haiti	124	D 3	10,694	4,867,190
Hawaii, U.S.A.	155		6,450	769,913
*Holland (Netherlands)	25		13,958	13,077,000
*Honduras	122	D 3	43,277	2,495,000
Hong Kong	77	J 7	398	4,089,000
*Hungary	39	E 3	35,915	10,315,597
*Iceland	19	B 1	39,768	204,578
Idaho, U.S.A.	156		83,557	713,008
Illinois, U.S.A.	158		56,400	11,113,976
*India	70		1,261,483	546,955,945
Indiana, U.S.A.	163		36,291	5,193,669
*Indonesia	83		735,264	119,572,000
Iowa, U.S.A.	164		56,290	2,825,041
*Iran	68		636,293	28,448,000
*Iraq	68		167,924	9,431,000
*Ireland	15		27,136	3,109,000
Ireland, Northern, U.K.	15	G 2	5,452	1,537,200
Isle of Man, U.K.	11	C 3	227	62,000
*Israel	67		7,993	2,911,000
*Italy	32		116,303	54,504,000
*Ivory Coast	54	E10	127,520	6,673,013
*Jamaica	124	C 3	4,411	1,972,000
*Japan	75		143,622	104,665,171
*Jordan	67		37,297	2,300,000
Kansas, U.S.A.	168		82,264	2,249,071
Kentucky, U.S.A.	173		40,395	3,219,311
*Kenya	57	O11	224,960	13,300,000
Korea, North	74	D 3	46,540	13,300,000
Korea, South	74	E 5	38,452	31,683,000
*Kuwait	60	E 4	8,000	733,196
*Laos	81	E 3	91,428	3,500,000
*Lebanon	64	F 6	4,015	2,800,000
*Lesotho	57	M17	11,720	1,100,000
*Liberia	54	E10	43,000	1,600,000
*Libya	54	J 6	679,358	2,500,000
Liechtenstein	37	J 2	61	21,000
Louisiana, U.S.A.	175		48,523	3,643,180
*Luxembourg	25	J 9	999	339,000
Macao	77	H 7	6.2	292,000
*Madagascar	57	R16	226,657	7,700,000
Madeira, Portugal	30	A 2	307	268,700
Maine, U.S.A.	178		33,215	993,663
*Malawi	57	N14	45,747	5,100,000
Malaya, Malaysia	81	D 6	50,806	9,000,000
*Malaysia	81, 83		128,308	12,368,000
Maldives	58	L 9	115	110,770
*Mali	54	F 8	464,873	5,800,000
*Malta	32	E 7	122	321,000
Man, Isle of, U.K.	11	C 3	227	62,000
Manitoba, Canada	110		251,000	1,021,506
Martinique	125	G 4	425	332,000
Maryland, U.S.A.	181		10,577	3,922,399
Massachusetts, U.S.A.	184		8,257	5,689,170
*Mauritania	54	D 8	452,702	1,318,000
*Mauritius	57	S19	790	899,000
Mayotte	57	P14	144	40,000
*Mexico	119		761,601	48,313,438
Michigan, U.S.A.	186		58,216	8,875,083
Midway Islands	154	A 5	1.9	2,220
Minnesota, U.S.A.	190		84,068	3,805,069
Mississippi, U.S.A.	192		47,716	2,216,912
Missouri, U.S.A.	197		69,686	4,677,399
Monaco	26	G 6	368 Acres	23,035
*Mongolia	77	F 2	604,247	1,300,000
Montana, U.S.A.	198		147,138	694,409
Montserrat	125	G 3	40	12,300
*Morocco	54	E 5	241,224	18,000,000
*Mozambique	57	N16	308,641	9,300,000
Namibia (South-West Africa)	57	K16	317,827	883,000
Nauru	89	G 6	8.2	7,000
Nebraska, U.S.A.	201		77,227	1,483,791
*Nepal	70	E 3	54,362	10,845,000
*Netherlands	25		13,958	13,077,000
Netherlands Antilles	124	D 4,F 3	390	220,000
Nevada, U.S.A.	202		110,540	488,738
New Brunswick, Canada	102		28,354	677,250
New Caledonia and Dependencies	89	G 8	8,548	100,579
Newfoundland, Canada	99		156,185	557,725

* Members of the United Nations.

GAZETTEER-INDEX OF THE WORLD

Country	Page No.	Index Ref.	Area (Sq. Miles)	Population
New Hampshire, U.S.A.	204		9,304	737,681
New Hebrides	89	G 7	5,700	80,000
New Jersey, U.S.A.	209		7,836	7,168,164
New Mexico, U.S.A.	210		121,666	1,016,000
New York, U.S.A.	212		49,576	18,241,266
*New Zealand	87		103,736	2,815,000
*Nicaragua	122	D 4	45,698	1,984,000
*Niger	54	H 8	489,189	4,700,000
*Nigeria	54	H10	379,628	83,800,000
Niue	89	K 7	100	5,323
North America	94		9,363,000	314,000,000
North Carolina, U.S.A.	217		52,586	5,082,059
North Dakota, U.S.A.	218		70,665	617,761
Northern Ireland, U.K.	15	G 2	5,452	1,537,200
Northwest Territories, Canada	96	E 2	1,304,903	42,609
*Norway	16		125,181	3,893,000
Nova Scotia, Canada	100		21,425	828,571
Oceania	88-89		3,292,000	21,800,000
Ohio, U.S.A.	220		41,222	10,652,017
Oklahoma, U.S.A.	225		69,919	2,559,253
*Oman	60	G 6	82,000	565,000
Ontario, Canada	107-108		412,582	8,264,465
Oregon, U.S.A.	226		96,981	2,091,385
Pacific Islands, U.S. Trust Terr. of the	88-89	E, F 5	707	98,009
*Pakistan	70	B 3	310,403	60,000,000
*Panama	122	G 6	29,209	1,425,343
*Papua New Guinea	82;89	B 7;E 6	183,540	2,563,610
*Paraguay	93	J 8	157,047	2,314,000
Pennsylvania, U.S.A.	230		45,333	11,793,909
*Persia (Iran)	68		636,293	28,448,000
*Peru	90	E 5	496,222	13,586,300
*Philippines	83	H 4	115,707	43,751,000
Pitcairn Islands	89	O 8	18	74
*Poland	45		120,725	34,364,000
*Portugal	30		35,510	9,560,000
Prince Edward Island, Canada	100	E 2	2,184	118,229
Puerto Rico	124-125	G 1	3,435	2,712,033
*Qatar	60	F 4	8,500	100,000
Québec, Canada	105-106		594,860	6,234,445
Réunion	57	R20	969	475,700
Rhode Island, U.S.A.	184	H 5	1,214	949,723
Rhodesia (Zimbabwe)	57	M15	150,803	6,600,000
*Rumania	43	F 3	91,699	20,394,000
*Rwanda	57	N12	10,169	4,241,000
Sabah, Malaysia	83	F 4	28,460	633,000
St. Christopher-Nevis-Anguilla	124	F 3	155	71,500
St. Helena and Dependencies	5	H 8	162	6,400
St. Lucia	125	G 4	238	110,000
St-Pierre and Miquelon	99	B 4	93.5	6,000
St. Vincent	125	F 4	150	89,129
San Marino	32	D 3	23.4	19,000
*São Tomé e Príncipe	57	G11	372	80,000
Sarawak, Malaysia	83	E 5	48,050	950,000
Saskatchewan, Canada	113		251,700	921,323
*Saudi Arabia	60	D 4	920,000	7,200,000
Scotland, U.K.	13		30,414	5,261,000
*Senegal	54	D 9	75,954	5,085,388
*Seychelles	58	J10	145	60,000
*Siam (Thailand)	81	D 3	198,456	35,448,000
*Sierra Leone	54	C10	27,925	3,100,000
*Singapore	81	F 6	226	2,300,000
*Solomon Islands	89	G 6	11,500	161,525
*Somalia	55	R10	246,200	3,170,000
*South Africa	57	L18	458,179	24,400,000
South America	90		6,875,000	186,000,000
South Carolina, U.S.A.	232		31,055	2,590,516
South Dakota, U.S.A.	234		77,047	666,257
South-West Africa (Namibia)	57	K16	317,827	883,000
*Spain	31		194,896	33,290,000
*Sri Lanka	70	E 7	25,332	12,300,000
*Sudan	54	M 9	967,494	18,347,000
*Surinam	90	J 3	55,144	389,000
*Swaziland	57	N17	6,705	500,000
*Sweden	16		173,665	7,978,000
Switzerland	37		15,941	6,230,000
*Syria	64	G 5	71,498	5,866,000
*Tanzania	57	N13	363,708	15,506,000
Tennessee, U.S.A.	173		42,244	3,924,164
Texas, U.S.A.	238		267,339	11,196,730
*Thailand	81	D 3	198,455	42,700,000
*Togo	54	G10	21,622	2,300,000
Tokelau	89	J 6	3.95	2,000
Tonga	89	J 8	270	83,000
*Trinidad and Tobago	125	G 5	1,980	1,040,000
Tristan da Cunha	5	J 8	38	292
*Tunisia	54	H 5	63,170	5,776,000
*Turkey	64		301,381	34,375,000
Turks and Caicos Is.	124	D 2	166	6,000
Tuvalu	89	H 6	9.78	5,887
*Uganda	57	N11	91,076	11,400,000
*Ukrainian S.S.R., U.S.S.R.	50	C 5	232,046	47,126,517
*Union of Soviet Socialist Republics	46, 50		8,649,498	241,748,000
*United Arab Emirates	60	F 5	31,628	155,881
*United Kingdom	8		94,399	56,076,000
*United States of America	126-127	F 9	3,615,123	217,739,000
*Upper Volta	54		105,869	6,144,013
*Uruguay	93	J10	72,172	2,900,000
Utah, U.S.A.	240		84,916	1,059,273
Vatican City	32	B 6	109 Acres	1,000
*Venezuela	92		352,143	10,398,907
Vermont, U.S.A.	204		9,609	444,732
*Vietnam	81	E 3	128,405	46,600,000
Virginia, U.S.A.	243		40,817	4,648,494
Virgin Islands, British	125	H 1	59	10,484
Virgin Islands, U.S.A.	125	H 1	133	62,468
Wake Island, U.S.A.	89	G 4	2.5	1,647
Wales, U.K.	11	D 5	8,017	2,778,000
Washington, U.S.A.	246		68,192	3,409,169
West Indies	124-125		91,118	28,500,000
*Western Samoa	89	J 7	1,097	139,810
West Virginia, U.S.A.	248		24,181	1,744,237
*White Russian S.S.R. (Byelorussian S.S.R.), U.S.S.R.	50	C 4	80,154	9,002,338
Wisconsin, U.S.A.	253		56,154	4,417,933
World	5		57,970,000	4,124,000,000
Wyoming, U.S.A.	254		97,914	332,416
*Yemen Arab Republic	60	D 7	75,000	5,000,000
*Yemen, Peoples Dem. Rep. of	60	E 7	111,075	1,220,000
*Yugoslavia	43	C 3	98,766	20,586,000
Yukon Territory, Canada	96	C 3	207,076	21,836
*Zaire	57	L12	918,962	25,600,000
*Zambia	57	M14	290,586	4,936,000
Zimbabwe (Rhodesia)	57	M15	150,803	6,600,000

* Members of the United Nations.

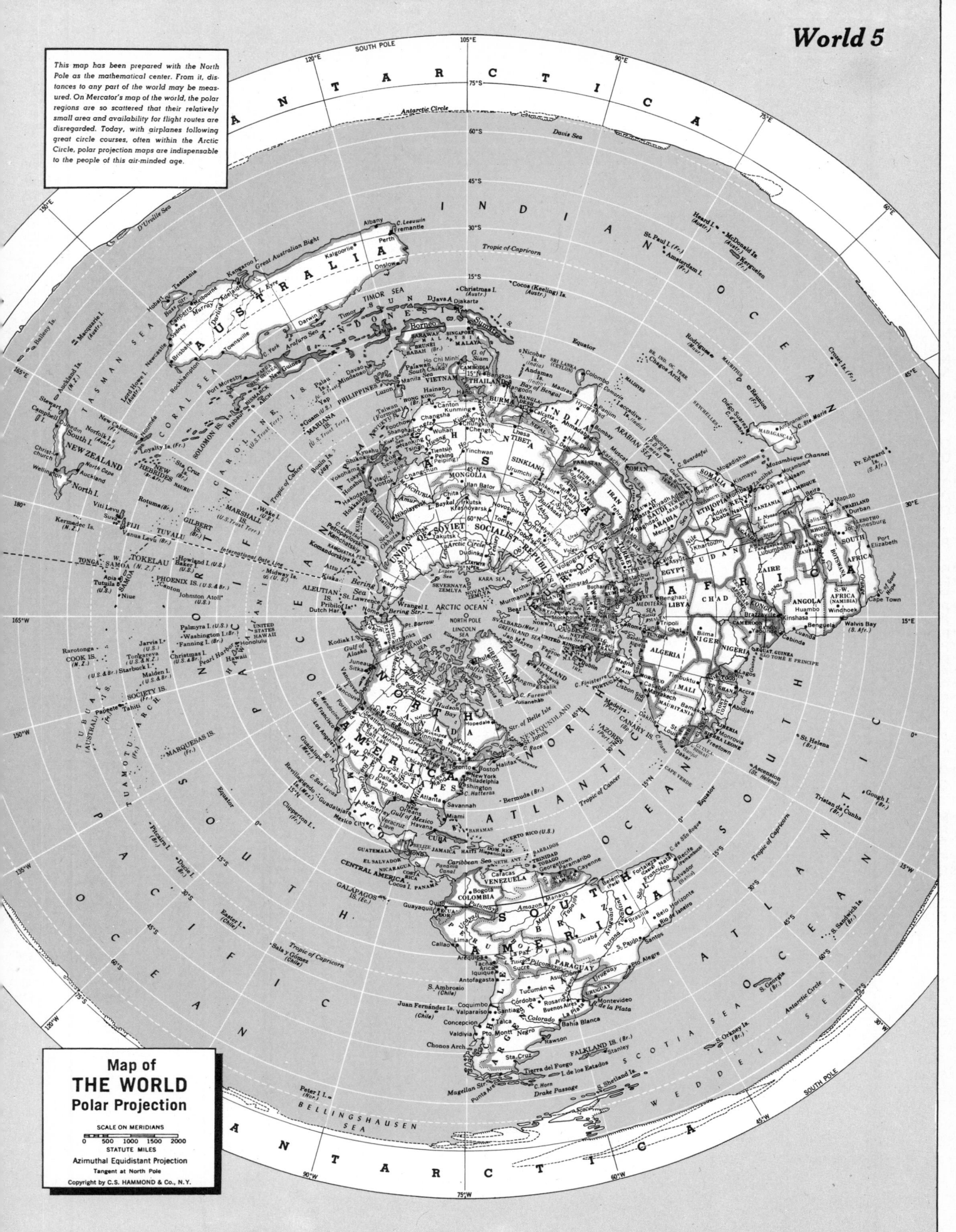

World 5

This map has been prepared with the North Pole as the mathematical center. From it, distances to any part of the world may be measured. On Mercator's map of the world, the polar regions are so scattered that their relatively small area and availability for flight routes are disregarded. Today, with airplanes following great circle courses, often within the Arctic Circle, polar projection maps are indispensable to the people of this air-minded age.

Map of
THE WORLD
Polar Projection

SCALE ON MERIDIANS

0   500   1000   1500   2000
STATUTE MILES

Azimuthal Equidistant Projection
Tangent at North Pole

Copyright by C.S. HAMMOND & Co., N.Y.

AREA 4,063,000 sq. mi.
POPULATION 652,000,000
LARGEST CITY London
HIGHEST POINT El'brus 18,481 ft.
LOWEST POINT Caspian Sea -92 ft.

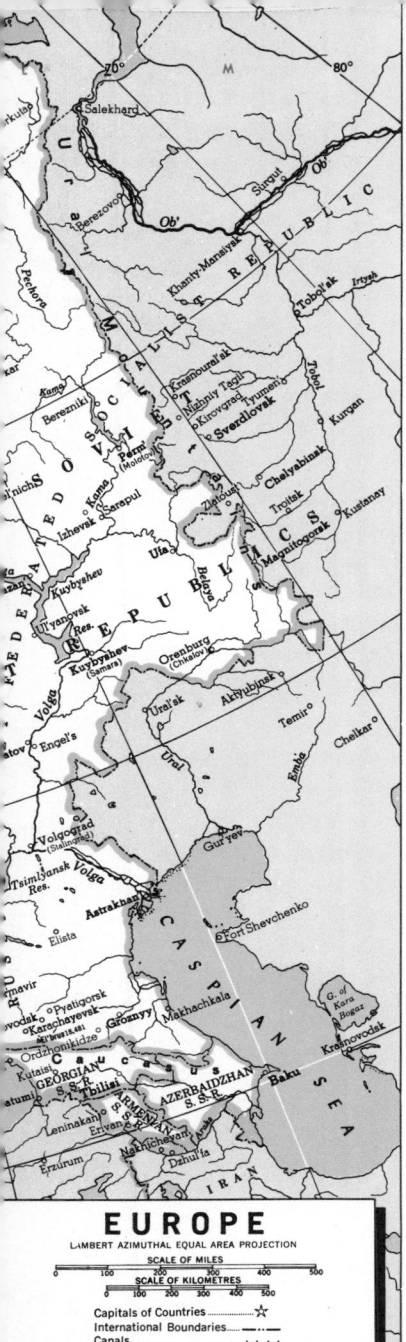

EUROPE
LAMBERT AZIMUTHAL EQUAL AREA PROJECTION

SCALE OF MILES
0 100 200 300 400 500

SCALE OF KILOMETRES
0 100 200 300 400 500

Capitals of Countries ....☆
International Boundaries..........
Canals.........................

Copyright by C.S. Hammond & Co., N.Y.

POPULATION DISTRIBUTION

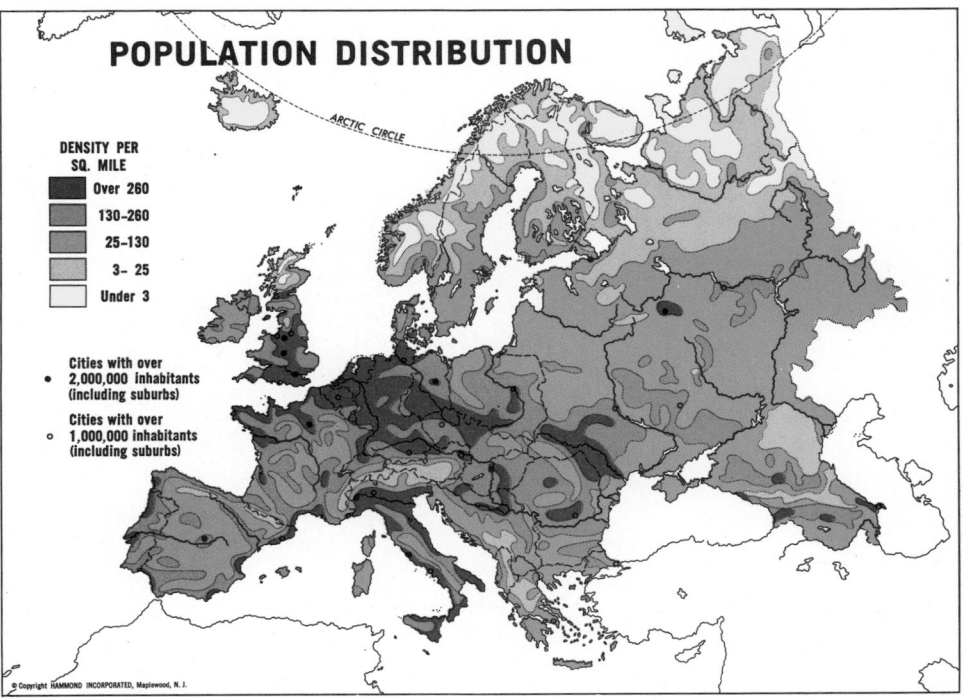

DENSITY PER SQ. MILE
- Over 260
- 130–260
- 25–130
- 3–25
- Under 3

• Cities with over 2,000,000 inhabitants (including suburbs)

○ Cities with over 1,000,000 inhabitants (including suburbs)

© Copyright HAMMOND INCORPORATED, Maplewood, N.J.

VEGETATION

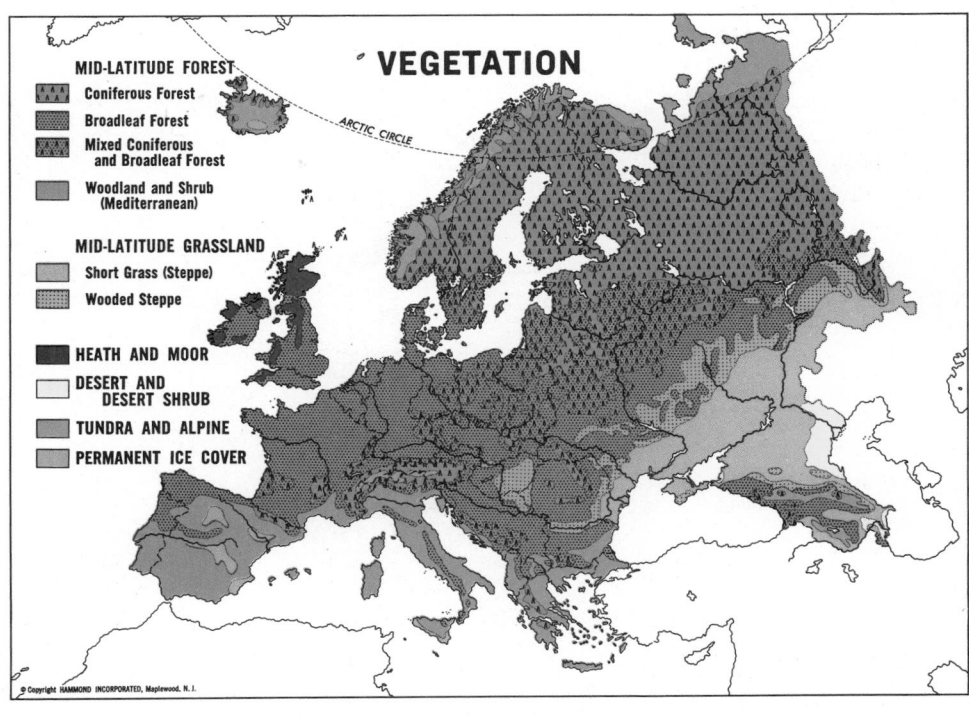

MID-LATITUDE FOREST
- Coniferous Forest
- Broadleaf Forest
- Mixed Coniferous and Broadleaf Forest
- Woodland and Shrub (Mediterranean)

MID-LATITUDE GRASSLAND
- Short Grass (Steppe)
- Wooded Steppe

- HEATH AND MOOR
- DESERT AND DESERT SHRUB
- TUNDRA AND ALPINE
- PERMANENT ICE COVER

© Copyright HAMMOND INCORPORATED, Maplewood, N.J.

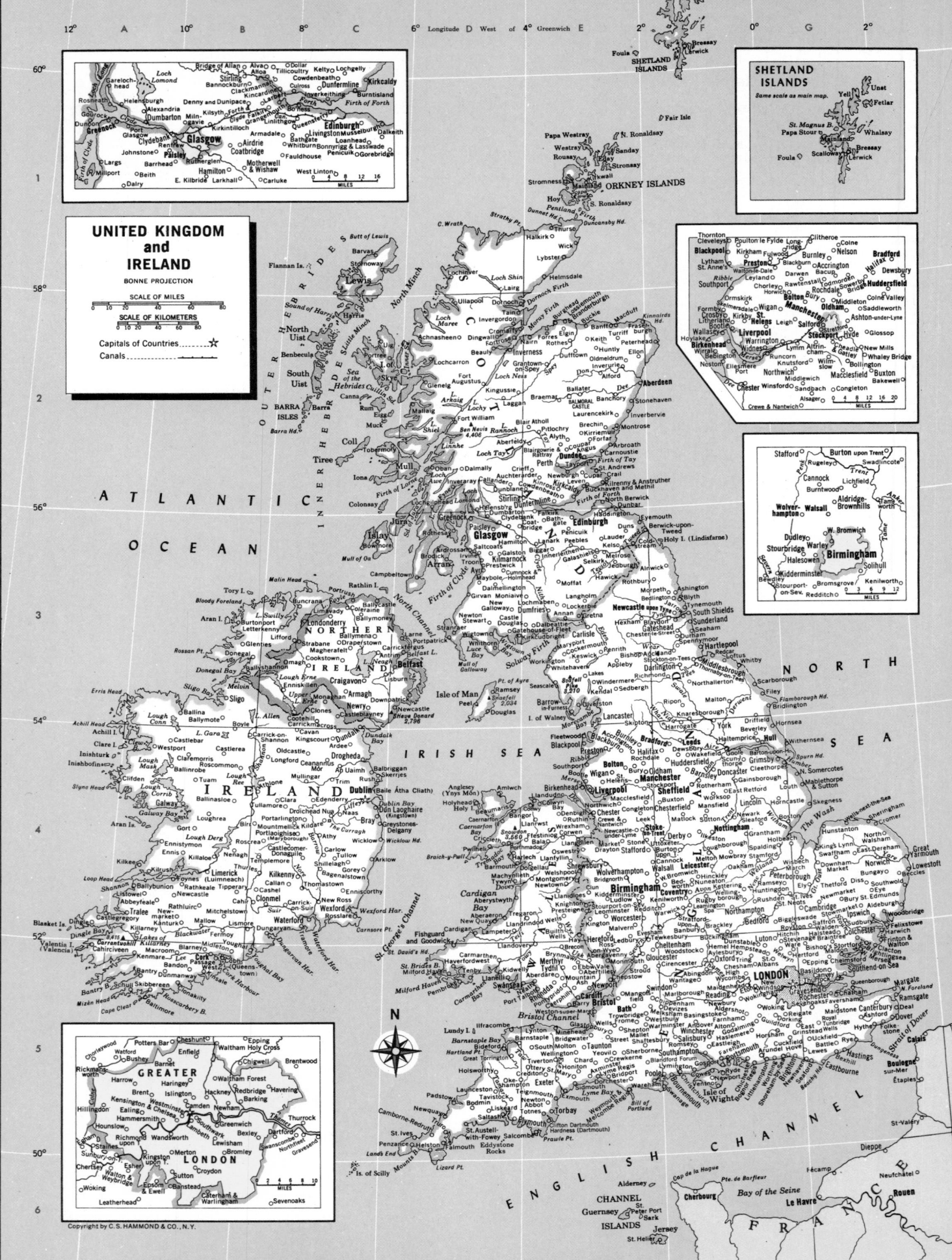

UNITED KINGDOM and IRELAND

BONNE PROJECTION

SCALE OF MILES

SCALE OF KILOMETERS

Capitals of Countries..........☆
Canals.................

SHETLAND ISLANDS

Same scale as main map.

GREATER LONDON

LONDON

UNITED KINGDOM

AREA 94,399 sq. mi.
POPULATION 56,076,000
CAPITAL London
LARGEST CITY London
HIGHEST POINT Ben Nevis 4,406 ft.
MONETARY UNIT pound sterling
MAJOR LANGUAGES English, Gaelic, Welsh
MAJOR RELIGIONS Protestantism, Roman Catholicism

IRELAND

AREA 27,136 sq. mi.
POPULATION 3,109,000
CAPITAL Dublin
LARGEST CITY Dublin
HIGHEST POINT Carrantuohill 3,415 ft.
MONETARY UNIT Irish pound
MAJOR LANGUAGES English, Gaelic (Irish)
MAJOR RELIGION Roman Catholicism

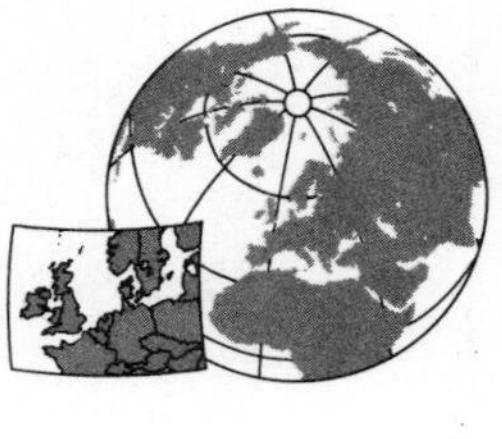

UNITED KINGDOM

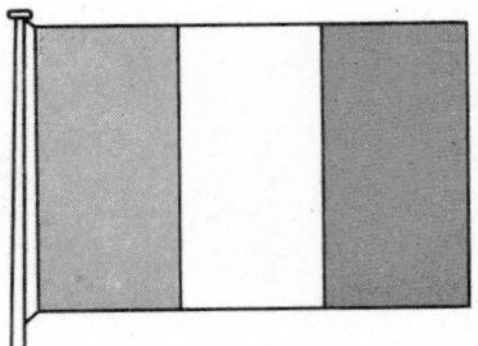

IRELAND

ENGLAND

COUNTIES

Avon, 920,200 . . . E 6
Bedfordshire, 491,700 . . . G 5
Berkshire, 659,000 . . . F 6
Buckinghamshire, 512,000 . . . G 6
Cambridgeshire, 563,000 . . . G 5
Cheshire, 916,400 . . . E 4
Cleveland, 567,900 . . . F 3
Cornwall, 405,200 . . . C 7
Cumbria, 473,600 . . . D 3
Derbyshire, 887,600 . . . F 5
Devon, 942,100 . . . D 7
Dorset, 575,800 . . . E 7
Durham, 610,400 . . . F 3
East Sussex, 655,600 . . . H 7
Essex, 1,426,200 . . . H 6
Gloucestershire, 491,500 . . . E 6
Greater London, 7,028,200 . . . H 8
Greater Manchester, 2,684,100 . . . H 2
Hampshire, 1,456,100 . . . F 6
Hereford and Worcester, 594,200 . . . E 5
Hertfordshire, 937,300 . . . G 6
Humberside, 848,600 . . . G 4
Isle of Wight, 111,300 . . . F 7
Isles of Scilly, 1,900 . . . A 7
Kent, 1,448,100 . . . H 6
Lancashire, 1,375,500 . . . E 4
Leicestershire, 837,900 . . . F 5
Lincolnshire, 524,500 . . . G 4
London, Greater, 7,028,200 . . . H 8
Manchester, Greater, 2,684,100 . . . H 2
Merseyside, 1,578,000 . . . G 2
Norfolk, 662,500 . . . H 5
Northamptonshire, 505,900 . . . G 5
Northumberland, 287,300 . . . E 2
North Yorkshire, 653,000 . . . F 3
Nottinghamshire, 977,500 . . . F 4
Oxfordshire, 541,800 . . . F 6
Salop, 359,000 . . . E 5
Somerset, 404,400 . . . E 6
South Yorkshire, 1,318,300 . . . F 4
Staffordshire, 997,600 . . . E 5
Suffolk, 577,600 . . . H 5
Surrey, 1,002,900 . . . G 6
Sussex, East, 655,600 . . . H 7
Sussex, West, 623,400 . . . G 7
Tyne and Wear, 1,182,900 . . . H 3
Warwickshire, 471,000 . . . F 5
West Midlands, 2,743,300 . . . F 5
West Sussex, 623,400 . . . G 7
West Yorkshire, 2,072,500 . . . J 1
Wiltshire, 512,800 . . . E 6
Yorkshire, North, 653,000 . . . F 3
Yorkshire, South, 1,318,300 . . . F 4
Yorkshire, West, 2,072,500 . . . J 1

CITIES and TOWNS

Abingdon, 20,130 . . . F 6
Accrington, 36,470 . . . H 1
Adwick le Street, 17,650 . . . K 2
Aldeburgh, 2,750 . . . J 5
Aldershot, 33,750 . . . G 8
Aldridge Brownhills, 89,370 . . . E 5
Alfreton, 21,560 . . . F 4
Alnwick, 7,300 . . . F 2
Altrincham, 40,800 . . . H 2
Amersham, ⊙17,254 . . . G 7
Andover, 27,620 . . . F 6
Appleby, 2,240 . . . E 3
Arnold, 35,090 . . . F 4
Arundel, 2,390 . . . G 7
Ashford, 36,380 . . . H 6
Ashington, 24,720 . . . F 2
Ashton-under-Lyne, 48,500 . . . H 2
Axminster, ⊙4,515 . . . D 7
Aycliffe, ⊙20,203 . . . F 3
Aylesbury, 41,420 . . . G 7
Bacup, 14,990 . . . H 1
Bakewell, 4,100 . . . J 2
Banbury, 31,060 . . . F 5
Banstead, 44,100 . . . H 8
Barking, 153,800 . . . H 8
Barnet, 305,200 . . . H 7
Barnsley, 74,730 . . . J 2
Barnstaple, 17,820 . . . D 6
Barrow-in-Furness, 73,400 . . . D 3
Barton-upon-Humber, 7,750 . . . G 4
Basildon, 135,720 . . . J 8
Basingstoke, 60,910 . . . F 6
Bath, 83,100 . . . E 6
Batley, 41,630 . . . J 1
Battle, ⊙4,987 . . . H 7
Bebington, 62,500 . . . G 2
Bedford, 74,390 . . . G 5
Bedlington, 27,200 . . . F 2
Bedworth, 41,600 . . . F 5
Beeston and Stapleford, 65,360 . . . F 5
Benfleet, 49,180 . . . J 8
Bentley with Arksey, 22,320 . . . F 4
Berkhamsted, 15,920 . . . G 7
Beverley, 16,920 . . . G 4
Bexhill, 34,680 . . . H 7
Bexley, 213,500 . . . H 8
Biddulph, 18,720 . . . H 2
Birkenhead, 135,750 . . . G 2
Birmingham, 1,058,800 . . . F 5
Bishop Auckland, 32,940 . . . E 3
Bishop's Stortford, 21,720 . . . H 6
Blackburn, 101,670 . . . H 1
Blackpool, 149,000 . . . G 1
Blaydon, 31,940 . . . H 3
Blyth, 35,390 . . . F 2
Bodmin, 10,430 . . . C 7
Bognor Regis, 34,620 . . . G 7
Boldon, 24,430 . . . J 3
Bolton, 154,480 . . . H 2
Bootle, 71,160 . . . G 2
Boston, 26,700 . . . G 5
Bournemouth, 144,100 . . . F 7
Bracknell, ⊙34,067 . . . G 8
Bradford, 458,900 . . . J 1
Braintree and Bocking, 26,300 . . . H 6
Brent, 256,500 . . . H 8
Brentwood, 58,690 . . . J 8
Bridgwater, 26,700 . . . E 6
Bridlington, 26,920 . . . G 3
Bridport, 6,660 . . . E 7
Brigg, 4,870 . . . G 4
Brighowe, 35,320 . . . J 1
Brightlingsea, 7,170 . . . J 6
Brighton, 156,500 . . . G 7
Bristol, 416,300 . . . E 6
Broadstairs and Saint Peter's, 21,670 . . . J 6
Bromley, 299,100 . . . H 8
Bromsgrove, 41,430 . . . E 5
Buckfastleigh, 2,870 . . . C 7
Buckingham, 5,290 . . . G 6
Bude-Stratton, 5,750 . . . C 7
Bungay, 4,120 . . . J 5
Burgess Hill, 20,030 . . . G 7
Burnham-on-Crouch, 4,920 . . . H 6
Burnley, 74,300 . . . H 1
Burntwood, ⊙23,088 . . . F 5
Burton upon Trent, 49,480 . . . F 5
Bury, 69,550 . . . H 2
Bury Saint Edmunds, 26,800 . . . H 5
Bushey, 24,500 . . . H 7
Buxton, 20,050 . . . J 2
Caister-on-Sea, ⊙6,287 . . . J 5
Camborne-Redruth, 43,970 . . . B 7
Cambridge, 106,400 . . . G 5
Camden, 185,800 . . . H 8
Cannock, 56,440 . . . E 5
Canterbury, 115,600 . . . H 6
Canvey Island, 29,550 . . . J 8
Carlisle, 99,600 . . . D 3
Carlton, 46,690 . . . F 5
Caterham and Warlingham, 35,840 . . . H 8
Chatham, 59,550 . . . J 8
Cheadle and Gatley, 62,460 . . . H 2
Chelmsford, 58,320 . . . J 7
Cheltenham, 75,910 . . . E 6
Chertsey, 45,070 . . . G 8
Chesham, 20,830 . . . G 7
Cheshunt, 45,750 . . . H 7
Chester, 117,200 . . . G 2
Chesterfield, 69,480 . . . J 2
Chester-le-Street, 20,720 . . . J 3
Chichester, 20,940 . . . G 7
Chigwell, 54,220 . . . H 8
Chippenham, 18,550 . . . E 6
Chorley, 31,800 . . . G 2
Christchurch, 31,610 . . . F 7
Cirencester, 14,500 . . . E 6
Clacton, 39,380 . . . J 6
Clay Cross, 9,630 . . . J 2
Cleator Moor, ⊙7,686 . . . D 3
Cleethorpes, 37,200 . . . H 4
Clevedon, 15,140 . . . D 6
Clun, ⊙1,261 . . . D 6
Coalville, 28,740 . . . F 5
Cockermouth, 6,480 . . . D 3
Colchester, 79,600 . . . H 6
Colne, 19,030 . . . H 1
Colne Valley, 21,190 . . . J 2
Congleton, 21,500 . . . H 2
Consett, 35,080 . . . H 3
Corby, 48,850 . . . G 5
Coventry, 336,800 . . . F 5
Cowes, 19,190 . . . F 7
Crawley, 72,600 . . . G 6
Crewe and Nantwich, 98,100 . . . E 4
Cromer, 5,720 . . . J 5
Crook and Willington, 21,120 . . . E 3
Crosby, 56,750 . . . G 2
Croydon, 330,600 . . . H 8
Cuckfield, 26,500 . . . G 6
Darlington, 85,120 . . . F 3
Dartford, 44,130 . . . J 8
Darton, 15,710 . . . J 2
Darwen, 29,290 . . . H 1
Deal, 26,840 . . . J 6
Dearne, 24,780 . . . K 2
Denton, 38,110 . . . H 2
Derby, 213,700 . . . F 5
Dewsbury, 50,560 . . . J 1
Didcot, ⊙14,277 . . . F 6
Doncaster, 81,530 . . . F 4
Dorking, 22,410 . . . G 8
Dover, 34,160 . . . J 6
Downham Market, 4,120 . . . H 5
Droitwich, 13,950 . . . E 5
Dronfield, 20,000 . . . J 2
Dudley, 187,110 . . . E 5
Dunstable, 32,090 . . . G 6
Durham, 88,800 . . . J 3
Ealing, 293,800 . . . H 8
Eastbourne, 73,200 . . . H 7
East Grinstead, 19,420 . . . G 6
Eastleigh, 46,340 . . . F 7
East Retford, 18,260 . . . G 4
Egham, 30,320 . . . G 8
Egremont, ⊙7,253 . . . D 3
Eling, ⊙20,006 . . . F 7
Ellesmere, ⊙2,630 . . . E 5
Ellesmere Port, 63,870 . . . G 2
Enfield, 260,900 . . . H 7
Epsom and Ewell, 70,700 . . . G 8
Esher, 63,970 . . . H 8
Eston, ⊙46,219 . . . F 3
Eton, 4,950 . . . G 8
Evesham, 14,090 . . . F 5
Exeter, 93,300 . . . D 7
Exminster, ⊙3,181 . . . D 7
Exmouth, 26,840 . . . D 7
Falmouth, 17,530 . . . B 7
Fareham, 86,300 . . . F 7
Farnborough, 43,520 . . . G 8
Farnham, 33,140 . . . G 8
Farnworth, 26,110 . . . H 2
Faversham, 15,010 . . . H 6
Felixstowe, 19,460 . . . J 6
Felling, 38,990 . . . J 3
Filey, 5,660 . . . G 3
Fleet, 22,930 . . . G 8
Fleetwood, 30,070 . . . D 4
Folkestone, 45,610 . . . J 6
Formby, 24,850 . . . G 2
Framlingham, ⊙2,258 . . . J 5
Frimley and Camberley, 47,390 . . . G 8
Fulwood, 22,910 . . . G 1
Gainsborough, 17,440 . . . G 4
Gateshead, 91,230 . . . J 3
Gillingham, Dorset, ⊙4,050 . . . E 6
Gillingham, Kent, 93,900 . . . J 8
Glastonbury, 6,580 . . . E 6
Glossop, 24,820 . . . J 2
Gloucester, 91,600 . . . E 6
Godalming, 18,840 . . . G 8
Golborne, 28,720 . . . G 2
Goole, 17,920 . . . G 4
Gosport, 82,300 . . . F 7
Grange, 3,520 . . . E 3
Grantham, 27,830 . . . G 5
Gravesend, 53,500 . . . J 8
Great Baddow, ⊙18,755 . . . J 7
Great Torrington, 3,430 . . . C 7
Great Yarmouth, 49,410 . . . J 5
Greenwich, 207,200 . . . H 8
Grimsby, 93,800 . . . G 4
Guildford, 58,470 . . . G 8
Guisborough, 14,860 . . . F 3
Hackney, 192,500 . . . H 8
Hale, 17,080 . . . H 2
Halesowen, 54,120 . . . E 5
Halifax, 88,580 . . . J 1
Haltemprice, 54,850 . . . G 4
Haltwhistle, ⊙3,511 . . . E 2
Hammersmith, 170,000 . . . H 8
Haringey, 228,200 . . . H 8
Harlow, 79,160 . . . H 7
Harrogate, 64,620 . . . J 1
Harrow, 200,200 . . . G 8
Hartlepool, 97,100 . . . F 3
Harwich, 15,280 . . . J 6
Haslingden, 15,140 . . . H 1
Hastings, 74,600 . . . H 7
Hatfield, ⊙25,359 . . . H 7
Havant and Waterloo, 112,430 . . . G 7
Haverhill, 14,550 . . . H 5
Havering, 239,200 . . . J 8
Hayle, ⊙5,378 . . . B 7
Hazel Grove and Bramhall, 40,400 . . . H 2
Heanor, 24,590 . . . F 4
Hebburn, 23,150 . . . J 3
Hedon, 3,010 . . . G 4
Hemel Hempstead, 71,150 . . . G 7
Hereford, 47,800 . . . E 5
Hertford, 20,760 . . . H 7
Hetton, 16,810 . . . J 3
Hexham, 9,820 . . . E 3
Heywood, 31,720 . . . H 2
High Wycombe, 61,190 . . . G 8
Hillingdon, 230,800 . . . G 8
Hinckley, 49,310 . . . F 5
Hinderwell, ⊙2,551 . . . G 3
Hitchin, 29,190 . . . G 6
Hoddesdon, 27,510 . . . H 7
Holmfirth, 19,790 . . . J 2
Horley, ⊙18,593 . . . H 8
Hornsea, 7,280 . . . G 4
Horsham, 26,770 . . . G 6
Horwich, 16,670 . . . G 2
Houghton-le-Spring, 33,150 . . . J 3
Hounslow, 199,100 . . . G 8
Hove, 72,000 . . . G 7
Hoylake, 32,000 . . . G 2
Hoyland Nether, 15,500 . . . J 2
Hucknall, 27,110 . . . F 4
Huddersfield, 130,060 . . . J 2
Hugh Town, ⊙1,958 . . . A 8
Hull, 276,600 . . . G 4
Hunstanton, 4,140 . . . H 5
Huntingdon and Godmanchester, 17,200 . . . G 5
Huyton-with-Roby, 65,950 . . . G 2
Hyde, 37,040 . . . H 2
Ilfracombe, 9,350 . . . C 6
Ilkeston, 33,690 . . . F 5
Immingham, ⊙10,259 . . . G 4
Ipswich, 121,500 . . . J 5
Islington, 171,600 . . . H 8
Jarrow, 28,510 . . . J 3
Kendal, 22,440 . . . E 3
Kenilworth, 19,730 . . . F 5
Kensington and Chelsea, 161,400 . . . G 8
Keswick, 4,790 . . . D 3
Kettering, 44,480 . . . G 5
Keynsham, 18,970 . . . E 6
Kidderminster, 49,960 . . . E 5
Kidsgrove, 22,690 . . . E 4
King's Lynn, 29,990 . . . H 5
Kingston upon Thames, 135,600 . . . H 8
Kingswood, 30,450 . . . E 6
Kirkburton, 20,320 . . . J 2
Kirkby, 59,100 . . . G 2
Kirkby Lonsdale, ⊙1,506 . . . E 3
Kirkby Stephen, ⊙1,539 . . . E 3
Knutsford, 14,840 . . . H 2
Lambeth, 290,300 . . . H 8
Lancaster, 126,300 . . . E 3
Leatherhead, 40,830 . . . G 8
Leeds, 744,500 . . . J 1
Leek, 19,460 . . . H 2
Leicester, 289,400 . . . F 5
Leigh, 46,390 . . . H 2
Leighton-Linslade, 22,590 . . . F 7
Letchworth, 31,520 . . . G 6
Lewes, 14,170 . . . H 7
Lewisham, 237,300 . . . H 8
Leyland, 23,690 . . . G 1
Lichfield, 23,690 . . . F 5
Lincoln, 73,700 . . . G 4
Liskeard, 5,360 . . . C 7
Litherland, 23,530 . . . G 2
Littlehampton, 20,320 . . . G 7

(continued on following page)

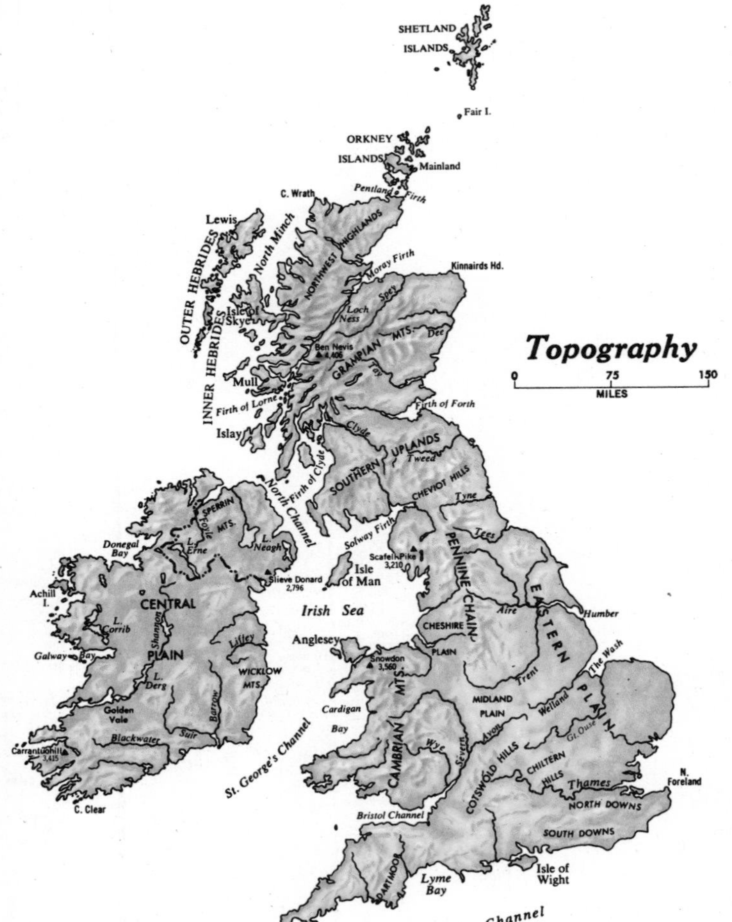
SHETLAND
ISLANDS
Fair I.
ORKNEY
ISLANDS
Mainland
C. Wrath
Pentland Firth
Lewis
OUTER HEBRIDES
North Minch
NORTHWEST HIGHLANDS
Moray Firth
Kinnairds Hd.
Isle of Skye
Loch Ness
Spey
INNER HEBRIDES
Ben Nevis
4,406
GRAMPIAN MTS.
Dee
Topography
0
75
150
MILES
Mull
Firth of Lorne
Firth of Forth
Islay
Clyde
Firth of Clyde
UPLANDS
SOUTHERN
Tweed
CHEVIOT HILLS
North Channel
Tyne
SPERRIN MTS.
L. Neagh
Donegal Bay
L. Erne
Solway Firth
Tees
Scafell Pike
3,210
PENNINE CHAIN
Isle of Man
Slieve Donard
2,796
Achill I.
CENTRAL
Irish Sea
Aire
Humber
L. Corrib
Shannon
PLAIN
Anglesey
CHESHIRE
PLAIN
EASTERN
Liffey
Galway Bay
L. Derg
WICKLOW MTS.
Snowdon
3,560
Trent
The Wash
Golden Vale
Barrow
Cardigan Bay
CAMBRIAN MTS.
MIDLAND PLAIN
Welland
PLAIN
Blackwater
Suir
Wye
Severn
Avon
Gt. Ouse
Carrantuohill
3,415
St. George's Channel
COTSWOLD HILLS
CHILTERN HILLS
Thames
N. Foreland
C. Clear
Bristol Channel
NORTH DOWNS
SOUTH DOWNS
DARTMOOR
Isle of Wight
Lyme Bay
IS. OF SCILLY
Land's End
English Channel
CHANNEL ISLANDS
5,000 m. 16,404 ft.
2,000 m. 6,562 ft.
1,000 m. 3,281 ft.
500 m. 1,640 ft.
200 m. 656 ft.
100 m. 328 ft.
Sea Level
Below

ENGLAND

AREA 50,516 sq.mi.
POPULATION 46,417,600
CAPITAL London
LARGEST CITY London
HIGHEST POINT Scafell Pike 3,210 ft.

WALES

AREA 8,017 sq. mi.
POPULATION 2,778,000
LARGEST CITY Cardiff
HIGHEST POINT Snowdon 3,560 ft.

SCOTLAND

AREA 30,414 sq. mi.
POPULATION 5,261,000
CAPITAL Edinburgh
LARGEST CITY Glasgow
HIGHEST POINT Ben Nevis 4,406 ft.

NORTHERN IRELAND

AREA 5,452 sq. mi.
POPULATION 1,537,200
CAPITAL Belfast
LARGEST CITY Belfast
HIGHEST POINT Slieve Donard 2,796 ft.

10 United Kingdom and Ireland

(continued)

Liverpool, 539,700 . . . G 2
Loftus, 7,850 . . . G 3
London (cap.), 7,028,200 . . . H 8
London, ★12,332,900 . . . H 8
Long Eaton, 33,560 . . . F 5
Longbenton, 50,120 . . . J 3
Looe, 4,060 . . . C 7
Loughborough, 49,010 . . . F 5
Lowestoft, 53,260 . . . J 5
Ludlow, ⊙7,466 . . . E 5
Luton, 164,500 . . . G 6
Lydd, 4,670 . . . H 7
Lyme Regis, 3,460 . . . E 7
Lymington, 36,780 . . . F 7
Lynton, 1,770 . . . D 6
Lytham Saint Anne's, 42,120 . . . G 1
Mablethorpe and Sutton, 6,750 . . . H 4
Macclesfield, 45,420 . . . H 2
Maidenhead, 48,210 . . . G 8
Maidstone, 72,110 . . . J 8
Maldon, 14,350 . . . H 6
Malmesbury, 2,550 . . . E 6
Malton, 4,010 . . . G 3
Malvern, 30,420 . . . E 5
Manchester, 490,000 . . . H 2
Mangotsfield, 23,000 . . . E 6
Mansfield, 58,450 . . . K 2
Mansfield Woodhouse, 25,400 . . . F 4
March, 14,560 . . . H 5
Margate, 50,290 . . . J 6
Market Harborough, 15,230 . . . G 5
Marlborough, 6,370 . . . F 6
Matlock, 20,300 . . . J 2
Melton Mowbray, 20,680 . . . G 5
Merton, 169,400 . . . H 8
Middlesbrough, 153,900 . . . F 3
Middleton, 53,340 . . . H 2
Middlewich, 7,600 . . . H 2
Mildenhall, ⊙9,269 . . . H 5
Millom, ⊙7,101 . . . D 3
Milton Keynes, 89,900 . . . F 5
Minehead, 8,230 . . . D 6
Moretonhampstead, ⊙1,440 . . . C 7
Morpeth, 14,450 . . . F 2
Mundesley, ⊙1,536 . . . J 5
Nelson, 31,220 . . . H 1
Neston, 18,210 . . . G 2
Newark, 24,760 . . . G 4
Newbury, 24,850 . . . F 6
Newcastle upon Tyne, 295,800 . . . H 3
Newcastle-under-Lyme, 75,940 . . . E 4
Newham, 228,900 . . . H 8
Newhaven, 9,970 . . . H 7
Newport, 22,430 . . . F 7
New Romney, 3,830 . . . J 7
Newton Abbot, 19,940 . . . D 7
Newton-le-Willows, 21,780 . . . H 2
New Windsor, 29,660 . . . G 8
Northallerton . . . F 3
Northam, 8,310 . . . C 6
Northampton, 128,290 . . . F 5
Northfleet, 27,150 . . . J 8
North Sunderland, ⊙1,725 . . . F 2
Northwich, 17,710 . . . H 2
Norton, 5,580 . . . G 3
Norton-Radstock, 15,900 . . . E 6
Norwich, 119,200 . . . J 5
Nottingham, 280,300 . . . F 5
Nuneaton, 69,210 . . . F 5
Oadby, 20,700 . . . F 5
Oakham, 7,280 . . . G 5
Okehampton, 4,000 . . . D 7
Oldham, 103,690 . . . H 2
Ormskirk, 28,860 . . . G 2
Oswaldtwistle, 14,270 . . . H 1
Oxford, 117,400 . . . F 6
Padstow, ⊙2,802 . . . B 7
Penryn, 5,660 . . . B 7
Penzance, 19,360 . . . B 7
Peterborough, 118,900 . . . G 5
Peterlee, ⊙21,846 . . . J 3
Plymouth, 259,100 . . . C 7
Polperro, ⊙1,491 . . . C 7
Poole, 110,600 . . . E 7
Porlock, ⊙1,290 . . . D 6
Portishead, 9,680 . . . E 6
Portland, 14,860 . . . E 7
Portslade-by-Sea, 18,040 . . . G 7
Portsmouth, 198,500 . . . F 7
Potters Bar, 24,670 . . . H 7
Poulton-le-Fylde, 16,340 . . . G 1
Preston, 94,760 . . . G 1
Prestwich, 32,850 . . . H 2
Queenborough, 31,550 . . . H 6
Radcliffe, 29,630 . . . H 2
Ramsbottom, 16,710 . . . H 2
Ramsgate, 40,090 . . . J 6
Rawtenstall, 20,950 . . . H 1
Rayleigh, 26,740 . . . J 8
Reading, 131,200 . . . G 8
Redbridge, 231,600 . . . H 8
Redcar, ⊙46,325 . . . F 3
Redditch, 44,750 . . . E 5
Reigate, 55,600 . . . H 8
Richmond upon Thames, 166,800 . H 8
Rickmansworth, 29,030 . . . G 8
Ripley, 18,060 . . . F 4
Rochdale, 93,780 . . . H 2
Rochester, 56,030 . . . J 8
Rothbury, ⊙1,818 . . . E 2
Rotherham, 84,770 . . . K 2
Royal Leamington Spa, 44,950 . . . F 5
Royal Tunbridge Wells, 44,800 . . . H 6
Rugby, 60,380 . . . F 5
Rugeley, 24,440 . . . E 5
Runcorn, 42,730 . . . G 2
Rushden, 21,840 . . . G 5
Ryde, 23,170 . . . F 7
Rye, 4,530 . . . H 7
Ryton, 15,170 . . . H 3
Saddleworth, 21,340 . . . J 2
Saint Agnes, ⊙4,747 . . . B 7
Saint Albans, 123,800 . . . H 7
Saint Austell-with-Fowey, 32,710 . . . C 7
Saint Columb Major, ⊙3,953 . . . B 7
Saint Helens, 104,890 . . . G 2
Saint Ives, Cornwall, 9,760 . . . B 7
Saint Neots, 17,940 . . . G 5
Salcombe, 2,370 . . . D 7
Sale, 59,060 . . . H 2
Salford, 261,100 . . . H 2
Salisbury, 35,460 . . . F 6
Saltburn and Marske-by-the-Sea, 21,170 . . . G 3
Sandbach, 14,280 . . . H 2
Sandown-Shanklin, 14,800 . . . F 7
Sandwich, 4,420 . . . J 6
Saxmundham, 1,820 . . . J 5
Scarborough, 43,300 . . . G 3
Scunthorpe, 68,100 . . . G 4
Seaford, 18,020 . . . H 7
Seaham, 22,470 . . . J 3
Seascale, ⊙2,106 . . . D 3
Seaton, 4,500 . . . D 7
Seaton Valley, 35,880 . . . J 3
Sedbergh, ⊙2,741 . . . E 3
Selsey, ⊙6,491 . . . G 7
Sevenoaks, 18,160 . . . J 8
Shaftesbury, 4,180 . . . E 7
Sheffield, 558,000 . . . J 2
Sherborne, 9,230 . . . E 7
Sheringham, 4,940 . . . J 5
Shildon, 15,360 . . . F 3
Shoreham-by-Sea, 19,620 . . . G 7
Shrewsbury, 56,120 . . . E 5
Silloth, ⊙2,662 . . . D 3
Sittingbourne and Milton, 32,830 . . . H 6
Skelmersdale, 35,850 . . . G 2
Skelton and Brotton, 15,930 . . . G 3
Sleaford, 8,050 . . . G 5
Slough, 89,060 . . . G 8
Solihull, 108,230 . . . F 5
Southampton, 213,700 . . . F 7
Southend-on-Sea, 159,300 . . . H 6
Southport, 86,030 . . . G 1
South Shields, 96,900 . . . J 3
Southwark, 224,900 . . . H 8
Southwold, 1,960 . . . J 5
Sowerby Bridge, 15,700 . . . H 1
Spalding, 17,040 . . . G 5
Spenborough, 41,460 . . . J 1
Spennymoor, 19,050 . . . F 3
Stafford, 54,860 . . . E 5
Staines, 56,380 . . . G 8
Stamford, 14,980 . . . G 5
Stanley, 42,280 . . . H 3
Staveley, 17,620 . . . K 2
Stevenage, 72,600 . . . G 6
Stockport, 138,350 . . . H 2
Stockton-on-Tees, 165,400 . . . F 3
Stoke-on-Trent, 256,200 . . . E 4
Stourbridge, 56,530 . . . E 5
Stourport-on-Severn, 19,430 . . . E 5
Stowmarket, 9,020 . . . J 5
Stratford-upon-Avon, 20,080 . . . F 5
Stretford, 52,450 . . . H 2
Stroud, 19,600 . . . E 6
Sudbury, 8,860 . . . H 5
Sunbury-on-Thames, 40,070 . . . G 8
Sunderland, 214,820 . . . J 3
Sutton, 166,700 . . . H 8
Sutton Bridge, ⊙3,113 . . . H 5
Sutton in Ashfield, 40,330 . . . K 2
Swadlincote, 21,060 . . . F 5
Swanage, 8,000 . . . E 7
Swindon, 90,680 . . . F 6
Tamworth, 46,960 . . . F 5
Taunton, 37,570 . . . D 6
Tavistock, ⊙7,620 . . . C 7
Telford, ⊙79,451 . . . E 5
Tenbury, ⊙2,151 . . . E 5
Tewkesbury, 9,210 . . . E 6
Thetford, 15,690 . . . H 5
Thirsk, ⊙2,884 . . . F 3
Thornaby-on-Tees, ⊙42,385 . . . F 3
Thorne, ⊙16,694 . . . F 4
Thornton Cleveleys, 27,090 . . . G 1
Thurrock, 127,700 . . . J 8
Tiverton, 16,190 . . . D 7
Todmorden, 14,540 . . . H 1
Tonbridge, 31,410 . . . H 8
Torbay, 109,900 . . . D 7
Torpoint, 6,840 . . . C 7
Tower Hamlets, 146,100 . . . H 8
Tow Law, 2,460 . . . H 4
Trowbridge, 20,120 . . . E 6
Truro, 15,690 . . . B 7
Turton, 22,800 . . . H 2
Tynemouth, 67,090 . . . J 3
Upton upon Severn, ⊙2,048 . . . E 5
Urmston, 44,130 . . . H 2
Uttoxeter, 9,100 . . . E 5
Ventnor, 6,980 . . . F 7
Wainfleet All Saints, ⊙1,116 . . . H 4
Wakefield, 306,500 . . . J 2
Wallasey, 94,520 . . . G 2
Wallsend, 45,490 . . . J 3
Walsall, 182,430 . . . E 5
Waltham Forest, 223,700 . . . H 8
Waltham Holy Cross, 14,810 . . . H 7
Walton and Weybridge, 51,270 . . . G 8
Walton-le-Dale, 27,660 . . . G 1
Wandsworth, 284,600 . . . H 8
Wantage, 8,490 . . . F 6
Ware, 14,900 . . . H 7
Wareham, 4,630 . . . E 7
Warley, 161,260 . . . E 5
Warminster, 14,440 . . . E 6
Warrington, 65,320 . . . G 2
Warwick, 17,870 . . . F 5
Washington, 27,720 . . . J 3
Watchet, 2,980 . . . D 6
Watford, 77,000 . . . H 7
Wellingborough, 39,570 . . . G 5
Wells, 8,960 . . . E 6
Wells-next-the-Sea, 2,450 . . . H 5
Welwyn, 39,900 . . . H 7
Wem, ⊙3,411 . . . E 5
West Bridgford, 28,340 . . . F 5
West Bromwich, 162,740 . . . F 5
West Mersea, 4,730 . . . H 6
Westminster, 216,100 . . . H 8
Weston-super-Mare, 51,960 . . . D 6
Weymouth and Melcombe Regis, 41,080 . . . E 7
Whickham, 29,710 . . . J 3
Whitchurch, ⊙7,142 . . . E 5
Whitehaven, 26,260 . . . D 3
Whitley Bay, 37,010 . . . J 3
Widnes, 58,330 . . . G 2
Wigan, 80,920 . . . G 2
Wigston, 31,650 . . . F 5
Wilmslow, 31,250 . . . H 2
Wilton, 4,090 . . . F 6
Winchester, 88,900 . . . F 6
Windermere, 7,860 . . . E 3
Winsford, 26,920 . . . G 2
Wirral, 27,510 . . . G 2
Wisbech, 16,990 . . . H 5
Witham, 19,730 . . . H 6
Withernsea, 6,300 . . . H 4
Wivenhoe, 5,630 . . . J 6
Woking, 79,300 . . . G 8
Wokingham, 22,390 . . . G 8
Wolverhampton, 266,400 . . . E 5
Wombwell, 17,850 . . . K 2
Woodhall Spa, 2,420 . . . G 4
Woodley and Sandford, ⊙24,581 . . G 8
Woodstock, 2,070 . . . F 6
Wooler, ⊙1,833 . . . F 2
Worcester, 73,900 . . . E 5
Workington, 28,260 . . . D 3
Worksop, 36,590 . . . F 4
Worsbrough, 15,180 . . . J 2
Worsley, 49,530 . . . H 2
Worthing, 89,100 . . . G 7
Wymondham, 9,390 . . . J 5
Yateley, ⊙16,505 . . . G 8
Yeovil, 26,180 . . . E 7
York, 101,900 . . . F 4

OTHER FEATURES

Aire (riv.) . . . F 4
Atlantic Ocean . . . A 7
Avon (riv.) . . . F 5
Avon (riv.) . . . F 7
Axe Edge (mt.) . . . H 2
Barnstaple (bay) . . . C 6
Beachy (head) . . . H 7
Bigbury (bay) . . . C 7
Blackwater (riv.) . . . H 6
Bristol (chan.) . . . C 6
Brown Willy (mt.) . . . C 7
Cheviot (hills) . . . E 2
Cheviot, The (mt.) . . . E 2
Chiltern (hills) . . . G 6
Cleveland (hills) . . . F 3
Colne (riv.) . . . G 8
Cornwall (cape) . . . B 7
Cotswold (hills) . . . E 6
Cross Fell (mt.) . . . E 3
Cumbrian (mts.) . . . D 3
Dart (riv.) . . . D 7
Dartmoor National Park . . . C 7
Dee (riv.) . . . D 4
Derwent (riv.) . . . G 3
Derwent (riv.) . . . H 3
Don (riv.) . . . F 4
Dorset Heights (hills) . . . E 7
Dove (riv.) . . . J 2
Dover (str.) . . . J 7
Dungeness (prom.) . . . J 7
Dunkery (hill) . . . D 6
Eddystone (rocks) . . . C 7
Eden (riv.) . . . E 3
English (chan.) . . . D 8
Esk (riv.) . . . D 2
Exe (riv.) . . . D 7
Exmoor National Park . . . D 6
Fens, The (reg.) . . . G 5
Flamborough (head) . . . G 3
Formby (head) . . . G 2
Foulness Island (pen.) . . . J 6
Gibraltar (pt.) . . . H 4
Great Ouse (riv.) . . . H 5
Hartland (pt.) . . . C 6
High Willhays (mt.) . . . C 7
Hodder (riv.) . . . H 1
Holderness (pen.), 43,900 . . . G 4
Holy (isl.), 189 . . . F 2
Humber (riv.) . . . G 4
Irish (sea) . . . B 4
Kennet (riv.) . . . F 6
Lake District National Park . . . D 3
Land's End (prom.) . . . B 7
Lea (riv.) . . . G 6
Lincoln Wolds (hills) . . . G 4
Lindisfarne (Holy) (isl.), 189 . . . F 2
Liverpool (bay) . . . D 4
Lizard, The (pen.), 7,371 . . . B 8
Lundy (isl.), 49 . . . C 6
Lune (riv.) . . . E 3
Lyme (bay) . . . D 7
Manacle (pt.) . . . C 7
Medway (riv.) . . . H 6
Mendip (hills) . . . E 6
Mersea (isl.), 4,423 . . . J 6
Mersey (riv.) . . . G 2
Morecambe (bay) . . . D 3
Mounts (bay) . . . B 7
Naze, The (prom.) . . . J 6
Nene (riv.) . . . H 5
New (for.) . . . F 6
North (sea) . . . J 4
North Downs (hills) . . . G 6
North Foreland (prom.) . . . J 6
Northumberland National Park . . . E 2
North York Moors National Park . . . G 3
Orford Ness (prom.) . . . J 5
Ouse (riv.) . . . G 4
Ouse (riv.) . . . G 6
Parrett (riv.) . . . E 6
Peak District National Park . . . F 4
Peak, The (mt.) . . . J 2
Peel Fell (mt.) . . . E 2
Pennine Chain (range) . . . E 3
Plymouth (sound) . . . C 7
Portland, Bill of (pt.) . . . E 7
Prawle (pt.) . . . D 7
Purbeck, Isle of (pen.), 39,500 . . . F 7
Ribble (riv.) . . . E 4
Saint Alban's (head) . . . F 7
Saint Bees (head) . . . D 3
Saint Martin's (isl.), 106 . . . A 8
Saint Mary's (isl.), 1,958 . . . A 8
Scafell Pike (mt.) . . . D 3
Scilly (isls.), 1,900 . . . A 7
Selsey Bill (prom.) . . . G 7
Severn (riv.) . . . E 6
Sheppey (isl.), 31,550 . . . J 6
Sherwood (for.) . . . F 4
Skiddaw (mt.) . . . D 3
Solent (chan.) . . . F 7
Solway (firth) . . . D 3
South Downs (hills) . . . G 7
Spithead (chan.) . . . F 7
Spurn (head) . . . H 4
Stonehenge (ruins) . . . F 6
Stour (riv.) . . . E 7
Stour (riv.) . . . H 6
Stour (riv.) . . . J 6
Swale (riv.) . . . F 3
Tamar (riv.) . . . C 7
Taw (riv.) . . . D 7
Tees (riv.) . . . F 3
Test (riv.) . . . F 6
Thames (riv.) . . . H 6
Tintagel (head) . . . C 7
Torridge (riv.) . . . C 7
Trent (riv.) . . . G 4
Tresco (isl.), 246 . . . A 8
Tweed (riv.) . . . E 2
Tyne (riv.) . . . F 3
Ure (riv.) . . . F 3
Ver (riv.) . . . H 7
Walney, Isle of (isl.), 11,241 . . . D 3
Wash, The (bay) . . . H 5
Weald, The (reg.) . . . H 6
Wear (riv.) . . . F 3
Weaver (riv.) . . . G 2
Welland (riv.) . . . G 5
Wey (riv.) . . . G 6
Wharfe (riv.) . . . E 3
Wirral (pen.), 432,900 . . . G 2
Witham (riv.) . . . G 4
Wolds, The (hills) . . . G 4
Wye (riv.) . . . D 5
Wyre (riv.) . . . G 1
Yare (riv.) . . . J 5
Yorkshire Dales National Park . . . E 3

CHANNEL ISLANDS

CITIES and TOWNS

Saint Anne . . . E 8
Saint Helier (cap.), Jersey, ⊙28,135 . . . E 8
Saint Peter Port (cap.), Guernsey, ⊙16,303 . . . E 8
Saint Sampson's, ⊙6,534 . . . E 8

OTHER FEATURES

Alderney (isl.), 1,686 . . . E 8
Guernsey (isl.), 51,351 . . . E 8
Herm (isl.), 96 . . . E 8
Jersey (isl.), 72,629 . . . E 8
Sark (isl.), 590 . . . E 8

ISLE of MAN

CITIES and TOWNS

Castletown, 2,820 . . . C 3
Douglas (cap.), 20,389 . . . C 3
Laxey, 1,170 . . . C 3
Michael, 408 . . . C 3
Onchan, 4,807 . . . C 3
Peel, 3,081 . . . C 3
Port Erin, 1,714 . . . C 3
Port Saint Mary, 1,508 . . . C 3
Ramsey, 5,048 . . . C 3

OTHER FEATURES

Ayre (pt.) . . . C 3
Calf of Man (isl.) . . . C 3
Langness (prom.) . . . C 3
Snaefell (mt.) . . . C 3
Spanish (head) . . . C 3

WALES

COUNTIES

Clwyd, 376,000 . . . D 4
Dyfed, 323,100 . . . C 6
Gwent, 439,600 . . . D 6
Gwynedd, 225,100 . . . C 4
Mid Glamorgan, 540,400 . . . D 6
Powys, 101,500 . . . D 5
South Glamorgan, 389,200 . . . A 7
West Glamorgan, 371,900 . . . D 6

CITIES and TOWNS

Aberaeron, 1,340 . . . C 5
Abercarn, 18,370 . . . B 6
Aberdare, 38,030 . . . A 6
Abertillery, 20,550 . . . B 6
Amlwch, 3,630 . . . C 4
Bala, 1,650 . . . D 5
Bangor, 16,030 . . . C 4
Barmouth, 2,070 . . . C 5
Barry, 42,780 . . . B 7
Beaumaris, 2,090 . . . C 4
Bedwellty, 25,460 . . . B 6
Bethesda, 4,180 . . . D 4
Betws-y-Coed, 720 . . . D 4
Brecknock (Brecon), 6,460 . . . D 6
Brecon, 6,460 . . . D 6
Bridgend, 14,690 . . . A 7
Brynmawr, 5,970 . . . B 6
Builth Wells, 1,480 . . . D 5
Burry Port, 5,990 . . . C 6
Caernarfon, 8,840 . . . C 4
Caerphilly, 42,190 . . . B 6
Cardiff, 281,500 . . . B 7
Cardigan, 3,830 . . . C 5
Chepstow, 8,260 . . . E 6
Chirk, ⊙3,564 . . . D 5
Colwyn Bay, 25,370 . . . D 4
Criccieth, 1,590 . . . C 5
Cwmamman, 3,950 . . . D 6
Cwmbran, 32,980 . . . B 6
Denbigh, 8,420 . . . D 4
Dolgellau, 2,430 . . . D 5
Ebbw Vale, 25,670 . . . B 6
Ffestiniog, 5,510 . . . D 5
Fishguard and Goodwick, 5,020 . . . B 5
Flint, 15,070 . . . G 2
Gelligaer, 33,820 . . . A 6
Harlech, ⊙332 . . . C 5
Haverfordwest, 8,930 . . . B 6
Hawarden, ⊙20,389 . . . G 2
Hay, 1,200 . . . D 5
Holywell, 8,570 . . . G 2
Kidwelly, 3,090 . . . C 6
Knighton, 2,190 . . . D 5
Llandeilo, 1,780 . . . C 6
Llandovery, 2,040 . . . D 5
Llandrindod Wells, 3,460 . . . D 5
Llandudno, 17,700 . . . D 4
Llanelli, 25,870 . . . C 6
Llanfairfechan, 3,800 . . . D 4
Llangefni, 4,070 . . . C 4
Llangollen, 3,050 . . . D 5
Llanguicke, ⊙15,029 . . . D 6
Llanidloes, 2,390 . . . D 5
Llantrisant, ⊙27,490 . . . A 7
Llanwrtyd Wells, 460 . . . D 5
Llwchwr, 27,530 . . . D 6
Machynlleth, 1,830 . . . D 5
Maesteg, 21,100 . . . D 6
Menai Bridge, 2,730 . . . C 4
Merthyr Tydfil, 61,500 . . . A 6
Milford Haven, 13,960 . . . B 6
Mold, 8,700 . . . G 2
Montgomery, 1,000 . . . D 5
Mountain Ash, 27,710 . . . A 6
Mynyddislwyn, 15,590 . . . B 6
Narberth, 970 . . . C 6
Neath, 27,280 . . . D 6
Nefyn, ⊙2,086 . . . C 5
Newcastle Emlyn, 690 . . . C 5
Newport, Dyfed, ⊙1,062 . . . C 5
Newport, Gwent, 110,090 . . . B 6
New Quay, 760 . . . C 5
Newtown, 6,400 . . . D 5
Neyland, 2,690 . . . B 6
Ogmore and Garw, 19,680 . . . A 6
Pembroke, 14,570 . . . C 6
Penarth, 24,180 . . . B 7
Penmaenmawr, 4,050 . . . C 4
Pontypool, 36,710 . . . B 6
Pontypridd, 34,180 . . . A 6
Porthcawl, 14,980 . . . D 6
Porthmadog, 3,900 . . . C 5
Port Talbot, 58,200 . . . D 6
Prestatyn, 15,480 . . . D 4
Presteigne, 1,330 . . . D 5
Pwllheli, 4,020 . . . C 5
Rhondda, 85,400 . . . A 6
Rhyl, 22,150 . . . D 4
Risca, 15,780 . . . B 6
Ruthin, 4,780 . . . D 4
Saint David's, ⊙1,638 . . . B 6
Swansea, 190,800 . . . C 6
Tenby, 4,930 . . . C 6
Tredegar, 17,450 . . . B 6
Tywyn, 3,850 . . . C 5
Welshpool, 7,370 . . . D 5
Wrexham, 39,530 . . . E 4

OTHER FEATURES

Anglesey (isl.), 64,500 . . . C 4
Aran Fawddwy (mt.) . . . C 5
Bardsey (isl.), 9 . . . C 5
Berwyn (mts.) . . . D 5
Black (mts.) . . . D 6
Braich-y-Pwll (prom.) . . . C 5
Brecon Beacons (mt.) . . . D 6
Brecon Beacons National Park . . . D 6
Caldy (isl.), 70 . . . C 6
Cambrian (mts.) . . . D 5
Cardigan (bay) . . . C 5
Carmarthen (bay) . . . C 6
Cemmaes (head) . . . C 5
Dee (riv.) . . . D 4
Dovey (riv.) . . . D 5
Ely (riv.) . . . B 7
Gower (pen.), 17,220 . . . C 6
Great Ormes (head) . . . C 4
Holy (isl.), 13,715 . . . C 4
Lleyn (pen.), 25,800 . . . C 5
Menai (str.) . . . C 4
Milford Haven (inlet) . . . B 6
Pembrokeshire Coast National Park . . . C 6
Plynlimon (mt.) . . . D 5
Preseli (mts.) . . . C 6
Radnor (for.) . . . D 5
Rhymney (riv.) . . . B 6
Saint Brides (bay) . . . B 6
Saint David's (head) . . . B 6
Saint George's (chan.) . . . B 5
Saint Gowans (head) . . . C 6
Severn (riv.) . . . E 5
Snowdon (mt.) . . . D 4
Snowdonia National Park . . . D 4
Taff (riv.) . . . B 7
Teifi (riv.) . . . C 5
Towy (riv.) . . . D 6
Tremadoc (bay) . . . C 5
Usk (riv.) . . . B 6
Wye (riv.) . . . D 5
Ynys Môn (Anglesey) (isl.), 64,500 . . . C 4

★Population of met. area.
⊙Population of parish.

SCOTLAND

REGIONS

Borders, 99,409 . . . E 5
Central, 269,281 . . . D 4
Dumfries and Galloway, 143,667 . . . E 5
Fife, 336,339 . . . E 4
Grampian, 448,772 . . . F 3
Highland, 182,044 . . . D 3
Lothian, 754,008 . . . E 5
Orkney (islands area), 17,675 . . . E 1
Shetland (islands area), 18,494 . . . F 2
Strathclyde, 2,504,909 . . . C 4
Tayside, 401,987 . . . E 4
Western Isles (islands area), 29,615 . . . A 3

CITIES and TOWNS

Aberchirder, 877 . . . F 3
Aberdeen, 210,362 . . . F 3
Aberdour, 1,576 . . . D 1
Aberfeldy, 1,552 . . . E 4
Aberfoyle, 793 . . . D 4
Aberlady, 737 . . . F 4
Aberlour, 842 . . . E 3
Abernethy, 776 . . . E 4
Aboyne, 1,040 . . . F 3
Acharacle, ⊙764 . . . C 4
Achiltibuie, ⊙1,564 . . . C 3
Achnasheen, ⊙1,078 . . . C 3
Ae, 239 . . . E 5
Airdrie, 38,491 . . . C 2
Alexandria, 9,758 . . . A 1
Alford, 764 . . . F 3
Alloa, 13,558 . . . C 1
Alness, 2,560 . . . D 3
Altnaharra, ⊙1,227 . . . D 2
Alva, 4,593 . . . C 1
Alyth, 1,738 . . . E 4
Ancrum, 266 . . . F 5
Annan, 6,250 . . . E 6
Annat, ⊙550 . . . C 3
Annbank Station, 2,530 . . . D 5
Applecross, ⊙550 . . . C 3
Arbroath, 22,706 . . . F 4
Ardavasar, ⊙449 . . . B 3
Ardersier, 942 . . . E 3
Ardgay, 193 . . . D 3
Ardrishaig, 946 . . . C 4
Ardrossan, 11,072 . . . D 5
Armadale, 7,200 . . . C 2
Arrochar, 543 . . . D 4
Ascog, 230 . . . A 2
Auchenblae, 339 . . . F 4
Auchencairn, 215 . . . E 6
Auchinleck, 4,883 . . . D 5
Auchterarder, 1,738 . . . E 4
Auchtermuchty, 1,426 . . . E 4
Auldearn, 405 . . . E 3
Aviemore, 1,224 . . . E 3
Avoch, 776 . . . D 3
Ayr, 47,990 . . . D 5
Ayton, 410 . . . F 5
Bailivanish, 347 . . . A 3
Baillieston, 7,671 . . . B 2
Balallan, 283 . . . B 2
Balerno, 3,576 . . . D 2
Balfron, 1,149 . . . B 1
Ballantrae, 262 . . . C 5
Ballater, 981 . . . F 3
Ballingry, 4,332 . . . D 1
Ballinluig, 188 . . . E 4
Balloch, Highland, 572 . . . D 3
Balloch, Strathclyde, 1,484 . . . B 1
Baltasound, 246 . . . G 2
Banchory, 2,435 . . . F 3
Banff, 3,832 . . . F 3
Bankfoot, 868 . . . E 4
Bankhead, 1,492 . . . F 3
Bannockburn, 5,889 . . . C 1
Barrhead, 18,736 . . . B 2
Barrhill, 236 . . . D 5
Barvas, 279 . . . B 2
Bathgate, 14,038 . . . C 2
Bayble, 543 . . . B 2
Bearsden, 25,128 . . . B 2
Beattock, 309 . . . E 5
Beauly, 1,141 . . . D 3
Beith, 5,859 . . . D 5
Bellsbank, 3,066 . . . D 5
Bellshill, 18,166 . . . C 2
Berriedale, ⊙1,927 . . . E 2
Bieldside, 1,137 . . . F 3
Biggar, 1,718 . . . E 5
Birnam, 659 . . . E 4
Bishopbriggs, 21,570 . . . B 2
Bishopton, 2,931 . . . B 2
Blackburn, 7,636 . . . C 2
Blackford, 529 . . . E 4
Blair Atholl, 437 . . . E 4
Blairgowrie and Rattray, 5,681 . . . E 4
Blanefield, 835 . . . B 1
Blantyre, 13,992 . . . B 2
Blyth Bridge, ⊙441 . . . E 5
Bo'ness, 12,959 . . . C 1
Boat of Garten, 406 . . . E 3
Boddam, 1,429 . . . G 3
Bonar Bridge, 519 . . . D 3
Bonhill, 4,385 . . . B 1
Bonnybridge, 5,701 . . . C 1
Bonnyrigg and Lasswade, 7,429 . . . D 2
Bowmore, 947 . . . B 5
Braemar, 394 . . . E 3
Breasclete, 234 . . . B 2
Brechin, 6,759 . . . F 4
Bridge of Allan, 4,638 . . . C 1
Bridge of Don, 4,086 . . . F 3
Bridge of Weir, 4,724 . . . A 2
Brightons, 3,106 . . . C 1
Broadford, 310 . . . B 3
Brodick, 630 . . . C 5
Brora, 1,436 . . . E 2
Broxburn, 7,776 . . . D 1
Buchlyvie, 412 . . . B 1
Buckhaven and Methil, 17,930 . . . F 4
Buckie, 8,145 . . . E 3
Bucksburn, 6,567 . . . F 3
Bunessan, ⊙585 . . . B 4
Burghead, 1,321 . . . E 3
Burnmouth, 300 . . . F 5
Burntisland, 5,626 . . . D 1
Cairndow, ⊙874 . . . D 4
Cairnryan, 199 . . . D 6
Callander, 1,805 . . . D 4
Cambuslang, 14,607 . . . B 2
Campbeltown, 6,428 . . . C 5
Cannich, 203 . . . D 3
Canonbie, 234 . . . F 5
Caol, 3,719 . . . C 4
Carbost, ⊙772 . . . B 3
Cardenden, 6,802 . . . D 1
Carloway, 178 . . . B 2
Carluke, 8,864 . . . E 5
Carnoustie, 6,838 . . . F 4
Carnwath, 1,246 . . . E 5
Carradale, 262 . . . C 5
Carrbridge, 416 . . . E 3
Carron, 2,626 . . . C 1
Carsphairn, 186 . . . D 5
Castlebay, 284 . . . A 4
Castle Douglas, 3,384 . . . E 6
Castle Kennedy, 307 . . . D 6
Castletown, 902 . . . E 2
Catrine, 2,681 . . . D 5
Cawdor, 111 . . . E 3
Chirnside, 888 . . . F 5
Chryston, 8,322 . . . C 2
Clackmannan, 3,248 . . . C 1
Clarkston, 8,404 . . . B 2
Closeburn, 225 . . . E 5
Clovulin, ⊙315 . . . C 4
Clydebank, 47,538 . . . B 2
Coalburn, 1,460 . . . E 5
Coatbridge, 50,806 . . . C 2
Cockburnspath, 233 . . . F 5
Cockenzie and Port Seton, 3,539 . . . D 1
Coldingham, 423 . . . F 5
Coldstream, 1,393 . . . F 5
Coll, 305 . . . B 2
Colmonell, 218 . . . D 5
Comrie, 1,119 . . . E 4
Connel, 300 . . . C 4
Cononbridge, 914 . . . D 3
Corpach, 1,296 . . . C 4
Coupar Angus, 2,010 . . . E 4
Cove and Kilcreggan, 1,402 . . . A 1
Cove Bay, 765 . . . F 3
Cowdenbeath, 10,215 . . . D 1
Cowie, 2,751 . . . C 1
Craigellachie, 382 . . . E 3
Craignure, ⊙544 . . . C 4
Crail, 1,033 . . . F 4
Crawford, 384 . . . E 5
Creetown, 769 . . . D 6
Crieff, 5,718 . . . E 4
Crimond, 313 . . . G 3
Crinan, ⊙462 . . . C 4
Cromarty, 492 . . . E 3
Crosshill, 535 . . . D 5
Crossmichael, 317 . . . D 6
Cruden Bay, 528 . . . G 3
Cullen, 1,199 . . . F 3
Culross, 504 . . . C 1
Cults, 3,336 . . . F 3
Cumbernauld, 41,200 . . . C 1
Cumnock and Holmhead, 6,298 . . . D 5
Cupar, 6,607 . . . E 4
Currie, 6,764 . . . D 2
Dailly, 1,258 . . . D 5
Dalbeattie, 3,659 . . . E 6
Daliburgh, 261 . . . A 3
Dalkeith, 9,713 . . . D 2
Dalmally, 283 . . . D 4
Dalmellington, 1,949 . . . D 5
Dalry, 5,833 . . . D 5
Dalrymple, 1,336 . . . D 5
Darvel, 3,177 . . . D 5
Daviot, ⊙513 . . . D 3
Denholm, 581 . . . F 5
Denny and Dunipace, 10,424 . . . C 1
Dervaig, ⊙1,081 . . . B 4
Dingwall, 4,275 . . . D 3
Dollar, 2,573 . . . E 4
Dornoch, 880 . . . D 3
Douglas, 1,843 . . . E 5
Doune, 859 . . . D 4
Drongan, 3,609 . . . D 5
Drumbeg, ⊙833 . . . C 2
Drummore, 336 . . . D 6
Drumnadrochit, 359 . . . D 3
Drymen, 659 . . . B 1
Dufftown, 1,481 . . . E 3
Dumbarton, 25,469 . . . B 1
Dumfries, 29,259 . . . E 5
Dunbar, 4,609 . . . F 4
Dunbeath, 161 . . . E 2
Dunbeg, 939 . . . C 4
Dunblane, 5,222 . . . E 4
Dundee, 194,732 . . . F 4
Dundonald, 2,256 . . . D 5
Dunfermline, 52,098 . . . D 1
Dunkeld, 273 . . . E 4
Dunning, 564 . . . E 4
Dunoon, 8,759 . . . A 2
Dunragit, 323 . . . D 6
Duns, 1,812 . . . F 5
Duntochter, 3,532 . . . B 2
Dunure, 452 . . . D 5
Dunvegan, 301 . . . B 3
Dyce, 2,733 . . . F 3
Eaglesfield, 581 . . . E 5
Eaglesham, 2,788 . . . D 5
Earlston, 1,415 . . . F 5
East Calder, 2,690 . . . D 2
East Kilbride, 71,200 . . . B 2
East Linton, 882 . . . F 5
Eastriggs, 1,455 . . . E 5
Ecclefechan, 844 . . . E 5
Edinburgh (cap.), 470,085 . . . D 1
Edzell, 658 . . . F 4
Elderslie, 5,204 . . . B 2
Elgin, 17,042 . . . E 3
Elie and Earlsferry, 807 . . . F 4
Ellon, 2,855 . . . F 3
Embo, 260 . . . E 3
Errol, 762 . . . E 4
Evanton, 562 . . . D 3
Eyemouth, 2,704 . . . F 5
Fairlie, 1,029 . . . D 5
Falkirk, 36,901 . . . C 1
Falkland, 998 . . . E 4
Fallin, 3,159 . . . C 1
Fauldhouse, 5,247 . . . C 2
Ferness, ⊙287 . . . E 3
Ferryden, 740 . . . F 4
Findhorn, 664 . . . E 3
Findochty, 1,229 . . . E 3
Fintry, 296 . . . B 1
Fochabers, 1,238 . . . E 3
Forfar, 11,179 . . . F 4
Forres, 5,317 . . . E 3
Fort Augustus, 670 . . . D 3
Forth, 2,929 . . . C 2
Fortrose, 1,150 . . . D 3
Fort William, 4,370 . . . C 4
Foyers, 276 . . . D 3
Fraserburgh, 10,930 . . . G 3
Friockheim, 807 . . . F 4
Furnace, 220 . . . C 4
Fyvie, 405 . . . F 3
Gairloch, 125 . . . C 3
Galashiels, 12,808 . . . F 5
Galston, 4,256 . . . D 5
Gardenstown, 892 . . . F 3
Garelochhead, 1,552 . . . A 1
Gargunnock, 457 . . . B 1
Garlieston, 385 . . . D 6
Garmouth, 352 . . . E 3
Garrabost, 307 . . . B 2
Gartmore, 253 . . . B 1
Gatehouse-of-Fleet, 835 . . . D 6
Giffnock, 10,987 . . . B 2
Gifford, 575 . . . F 5
Girvan, 7,597 . . . D 5
Glamis, 190 . . . F 4
Glasgow, 880,617 . . . B 2
Glasgow, ★1,674,789 . . . B 2
Glenbarr, ⊙691 . . . C 5
Glencaple, 275 . . . E 5
Glencoe, 195 . . . C 4
Glenelg, ⊙1,468 . . . C 3
Glenluce, 725 . . . D 6
Glenrothes, 31,400 . . . E 4
Golspie, 1,374 . . . E 3
Gordon, 320 . . . F 5
Gorebridge, 3,426 . . . D 2
Gourock, 11,192 . . . A 1
Grangemouth, 24,430 . . . C 1
Grantown-on-Spey, 1,578 . . . E 3
Greenlaw, 574 . . . F 5
Greenock, 67,275 . . . A 2
Gretna, 1,907 . . . E 5
Gullane, 1,701 . . . F 4
Haddington, 6,767 . . . F 5
Halkirk, 679 . . . E 2
Hamilton, 45,495 . . . C 2
Hamnavoe, 307 . . . G 2
Harthill, 4,712 . . . C 2
Hatton, 315 . . . G 3
Hawick, 16,484 . . . F 5
Heathhall, 1,365 . . . E 5
Helensburgh, 13,327 . . . A 1
Helmsdale, 727 . . . E 2
Hill of Fearn, 233 . . . D 3
Hillside, 692 . . . F 4
Hillswick, ⊙696 . . . G 2
Hopeman, 1,248 . . . E 3
Huntly, 4,078 . . . F 3
Hurlford, 4,294 . . . D 5
Inchnadamph, ⊙833 . . . D 2
Innellan, 922 . . . A 2
Innerleithen, 2,293 . . . E 5
Insch, 881 . . . F 3
Inveraray, 473 . . . C 4
Inverbervie, 853 . . . F 4
Invercassley, ⊙1,067 . . . D 3
Invergordon, 2,385 . . . D 3
Invergowrie, 1,389 . . . E 4
Inverie, ⊙1,468 . . . C 3
Inverkeithing, 6,102 . . . D 1
Inverness, 35,801 . . . D 3
Inverurie, 5,534 . . . F 3
Irvine, 48,500 . . . D 5
Isle of Whithorn, 222 . . . D 6
Jedburgh, 3,953 . . . F 5
John O'Groats, 195 . . . E 2
Johnshaven, 544 . . . F 4
Johnstone, 23,251 . . . B 2
Kames, 230 . . . C 5
Keiss, 344 . . . E 2
Keith, 4,192 . . . F 3
Kelso, 4,934 . . . F 5
Kelty, 6,573 . . . D 1
Kemnay, 1,042 . . . F 3
Kenmore, 211 . . . E 4
Kilbarchan, 2,669 . . . A 2
Kilbirnie, 8,259 . . . A 2
Kilchoan, ⊙764 . . . B 4
Kildonan, ⊙1,105 . . . E 2
Killearn, 1,086 . . . B 1
Killin, 600 . . . D 4
Kilmacolm, 3,348 . . . A 2
Kilmarnock, 50,175 . . . D 5
Kilmaurs, 2,518 . . . D 5
Kilninver, ⊙247 . . . C 4
Kilrenny and Anstruther, 2,951 . . . F 4
Kilsyth, 10,210 . . . B 1
Kilwinning, 8,460 . . . D 5
Kinbrace, ⊙1,105 . . . E 2
Kincardine, 3,278 . . . C 1
Kinghorn, 2,163 . . . D 1
Kingussie, 1,036 . . . D 3
Kinlochewe, ⊙1,794 . . . C 3
Kinlochleven, 1,243 . . . D 4
Kinloch Rannoch, 241 . . . D 4
Kinloss, 2,378 . . . E 3
Kinross, 2,829 . . . E 4
Kintore, 970 . . . F 3
Kippen, 529 . . . B 1
Kirkcaldy, 50,207 . . . D 1
Kirkcolm, 346 . . . C 6
Kirkconnel, 3,318 . . . E 5
Kirkcowan, 354 . . . D 6
Kirkcudbright, 2,690 . . . E 6
Kirkhill, 210 . . . D 3
Kirkintilloch, 26,664 . . . B 2
Kirkmuirhill, 2,575 . . . E 5
Kirkton of Glenisla, ⊙331 . . . E 4
Kirkwall, 4,777 . . . E 2
Kirriemuir, 4,295 . . . E 4
Kyleakin, 268 . . . C 3
Kyle of Lochalsh, 687 . . . C 3
Kylestrome, ⊙745 . . . D 2
Ladybank, 1,216 . . . E 4
Laggan, 393 . . . D 3
Lairg, 572 . . . D 2
Lamlash, 613 . . . C 5
Lanark, 8,842 . . . E 5
Langholm, 2,509 . . . E 5
Larbert, 4,922 . . . C 1
Largs, 9,461 . . . A 2
Larkhall, 15,926 . . . E 5
Lauder, 639 . . . F 5
Laurencekirk, 1,416 . . . F 4

(continued)

ENGLAND and WALES
CONIC PROJECTION

MILES
0   20   40   80

KILOMETERS
0   20   40   60   80

Capitals of Countries..........⊛
Administrative Centers..........●
Other Capitals..................●

International Boundaries.......
County Boundaries.............
Other Boundaries..............
Canals........................

The administrative centers
for MID GLAMORGAN,
NORTHUMBERLAND and SURREY
are Cardiff, Newcastle upon
Tyne and Kingston upon Thames,
respectively.

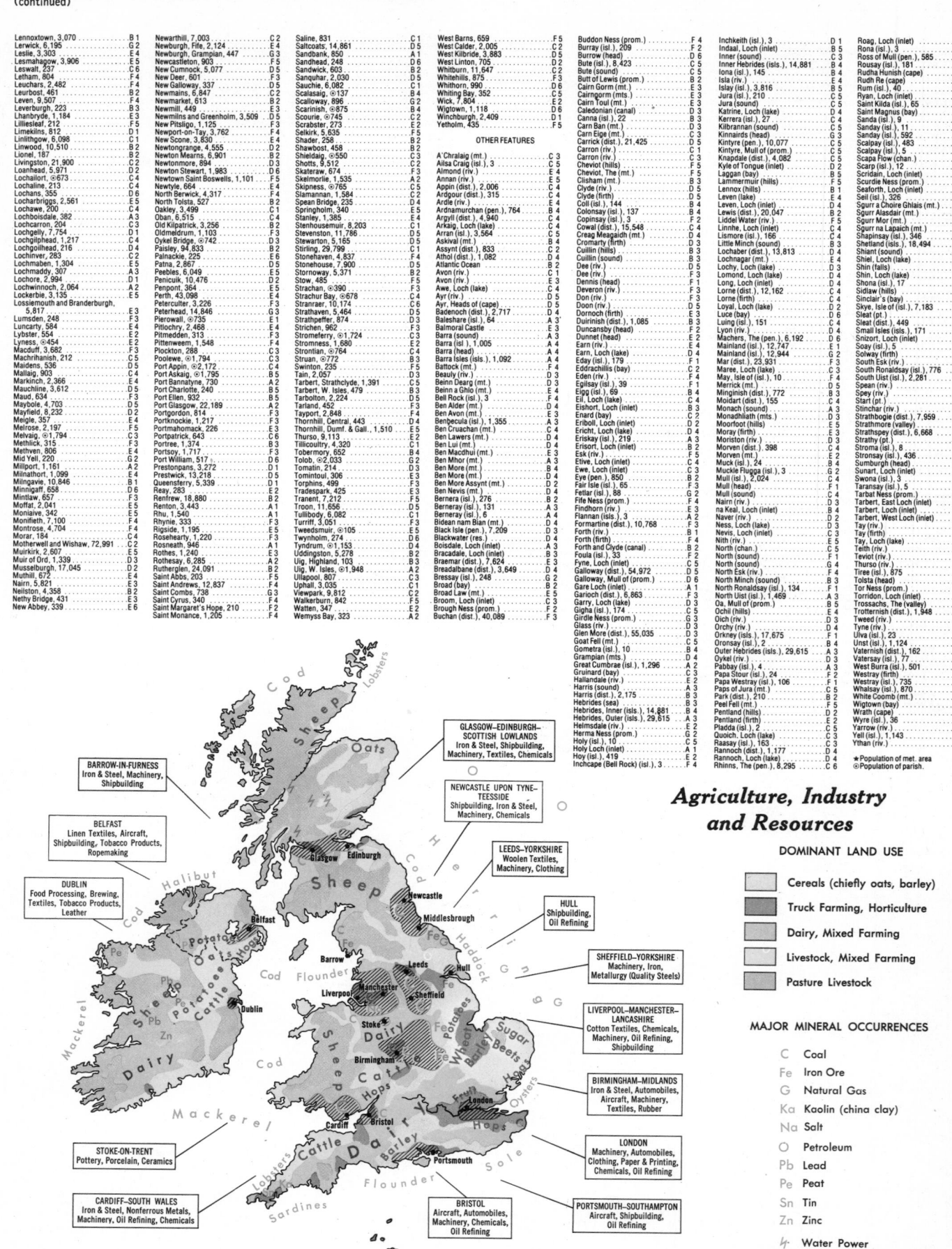

BARROW-IN-FURNESS — Iron & Steel, Machinery, Shipbuilding

BELFAST — Linen Textiles, Aircraft, Shipbuilding, Tobacco Products, Ropemaking

DUBLIN — Food Processing, Brewing, Textiles, Tobacco Products, Leather

GLASGOW–EDINBURGH–SCOTTISH LOWLANDS — Iron & Steel, Shipbuilding, Machinery, Textiles, Chemicals

NEWCASTLE UPON TYNE–TEESSIDE — Shipbuilding, Iron & Steel, Machinery, Chemicals

LEEDS–YORKSHIRE — Woolen Textiles, Machinery, Clothing

HULL — Shipbuilding, Oil Refining

SHEFFIELD–YORKSHIRE — Machinery, Iron, Metallurgy (Quality Steels)

LIVERPOOL–MANCHESTER–LANCASHIRE — Cotton Textiles, Chemicals, Machinery, Oil Refining, Shipbuilding

BIRMINGHAM–MIDLANDS — Iron & Steel, Automobiles, Aircraft, Machinery, Textiles, Rubber

LONDON — Machinery, Automobiles, Clothing, Paper & Printing, Chemicals, Oil Refining

STOKE-ON-TRENT — Pottery, Porcelain, Ceramics

CARDIFF–SOUTH WALES — Iron & Steel, Nonferrous Metals, Machinery, Oil Refining, Chemicals

BRISTOL — Aircraft, Automobiles, Machinery, Chemicals, Oil Refining

PORTSMOUTH–SOUTHAMPTON — Aircraft, Shipbuilding, Oil Refining

Agriculture, Industry and Resources

DOMINANT LAND USE

- Cereals (chiefly oats, barley)
- Truck Farming, Horticulture
- Dairy, Mixed Farming
- Livestock, Mixed Farming
- Pasture Livestock

MAJOR MINERAL OCCURRENCES

- C Coal
- Fe Iron Ore
- G Natural Gas
- Ka Kaolin (china clay)
- Na Salt
- O Petroleum
- Pb Lead
- Pe Peat
- Sn Tin
- Zn Zinc
- ⚡ Water Power
- ▨ Major Industrial Areas

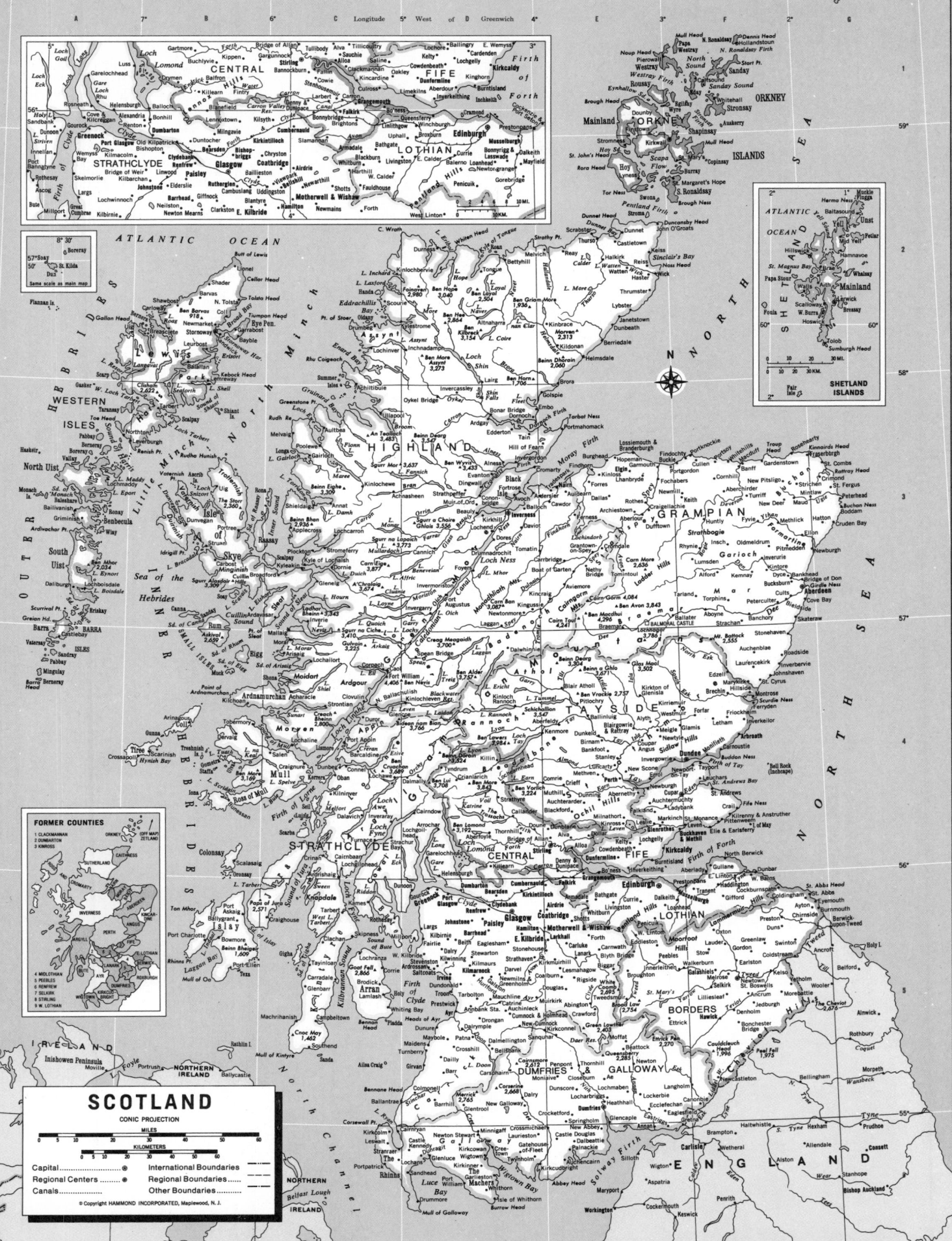

IRELAND

COUNTIES

Carlow, 34,237 H 6
Cavan, 52,618 G 4
Clare, 75,008 D 6
Cork, 352,883 D 7
Donegal, 108,344 K 2
Dublin, 852,219 J 5
Galway, 149,223 D 5
Kerry, 112,772 B 7
Kildare, 71,977 H 5
Kilkenny, 61,473 G 6
Laoighis, 45,259 G 6
Leitrim, 28,360 E 3
Leix (Laoighis), 45,259 G 6
Limerick, 140,459 D 7
Longford, 28,250 F 4
Louth, 74,951 J 4
Mayo, 109,525 C 4
Meath, 71,729 H 4
Monaghan, 46,242 H 3
Offaly, 51,829 F 5
Roscommon, 53,519 E 4
Sligo, 50,275 D 3
Tipperary, 123,565 F 6
Waterford, 77,315 F 7
Westmeath, 53,570 G 5
Wexford, 86,351 H 7
Wicklow, 66,295 J 5

CITIES and TOWNS

Abbeydorney, 188 B 7
Abbeyfeale, 1,337 C 7
Abbeylara, ‡290 F 4
Abbeyleix, 1,033 G 6
Achill Sound, ‡1,163 B 4
Aclare, ‡336 D 3
Adare, 545 D 6
Aghada-Farsid-Rostellan, 461 E 8
Aghadoe, ‡497 B 7
Aghagower, ‡693 C 4
Ahascragh, 221 E 5
Annagry, 201 E 1
Annascaul, 236 B 7
An Uaimh, 4,605 H 4
An Uaimh, *6,665 H 4
Ardagh, Limerick, 213 C 7
Ardagh, Longford, ‡974 F 4
Ardara, 683 E 2
Ardee, *3,183 H 4
Ardee, 3,096 H 4
Ardfert, 286 B 7
Ardfinnan, 510 F 7
Ardmore, 233 F 8
Ardrahan, ‡239 D 5
Arklow, 6,948 J 6
Arthurstown, 1,188 H 7
Arva, 370 F 4
Ashford, 341 J 5
Askeaton, 844 D 6
Athboy, 705 H 4
Athea, 328 C 7
Athenry, 1,240 D 5
Athleague, ‡955 E 4
Athlone, 9,825 F 5
Athlone, *11,611 F 5
Athy, 4,270 H 6
Athy, *4,654 H 6
Aughrim, 451 J 6
Avoca, ‡620 J 6
Bagenalstown (Muinebeag), 2,321 H 6
Baile Átha Cliath (Dublin) (cap.), 567,866 K 5
Bailieborough, 1,293 G 4
Balbriggan, 3,741 J 4
Balla, 293 C 4
Ballaghaderreen, 1,121 E 4
Ballina, Mayo, 6,063 C 3
Ballina, *6,369 C 3
Ballina, Tipperary, 336 E 6
Ballinagh, 459 G 4
Ballinakill, 300 G 6
Ballineen D 8
Ballinamore, 808 F 3
Ballinasloe, 5,969 E 5
Ballincollig-Carrigrohane, 2,110 D 8
Ballindine, 232 C 4
Ballingarry, Limerick, 422 D 7
Ballingarry, Tipperary, ‡574 F 6
Ballinlough, 242 D 4
Ballinrobe, 1,272 C 4
Ballintober, ‡867 E 4
Ballintra, 197 E 2
Ballisodare, 486 E 3
Ballivor, 287 H 4
Ballybay, 754 G 3
Ballybay, *1,159 G 3
Ballybofey-Stranorlar, 2,214 F 2
Ballybunion, 1,287 B 7
Ballycanew, ‡460 J 6
Ballycarney, ‡294 J 6
Ballycastle, ‡724 C 3
Ballyconnell, 421 F 3
Ballycotton, 389 F 8
Ballydehob, 253 C 8
Ballyduff, 406 B 7
Ballygar, 359 E 4
Ballygeary, 725 J 7
Ballyhaise, 274 G 3
Ballyhaunis, 1,093 D 4
Ballyheigue, 450 B 7
Ballyjamesduff, 673 G 4
Ballylanders, 266 E 7
Ballylongford, 504 B 6
Ballymahon, 707 F 4
Ballymakeery, 272 C 8
Ballymore, ‡447 F 5
Ballymore Eustace, 433 J 5
Ballymote, 952 D 3
Ballyporeen, ‡810 E 7
Ballyragget, 519 G 6
Ballyroan, ‡478 G 6
Ballyshannon, 2,325 E 3
Ballytore, ‡580 H 5
Baltimore, 200 C 9
Baltinglass, 909 H 6
Baltray, 236 J 4
Banagher, 1,052 F 5
Bandon, 2,257 D 8
Bandon, *4,071 D 8
Bannow, ‡798 H 7
Bansha, 184 E 7
Bantry, 2,579 C 8
Barna, ‡1,734 C 5
Belmullet, 744 B 3
Belturbet, 1,092 G 3
Bennettsbridge, 367 G 6
Birr, 3,319 F 5
Birr, *3,881 F 5
Blanchardstown, 3,279 H 5
Blarney, 1,128 D 8
Blessington, 637 J 5
Boherbue, 372 C 7
Borris, 430 H 6
Borris-in-Ossory, 276 F 6
Borrisokane, 769 E 6
Borrisoleigh, 471 E 6
Boyle, 1,727 E 4
Boyle, *1,939 E 4
Bray, 14,467 K 5
Bray, *15,841 K 5
Bri Chualann (Bray), 14,467 K 5
Broadford, 226 C 7
Brosna, 250 C 7
Bruff, 547 D 7
Bruree, 243 D 7
Bunbeg-Derrybeg, 878 E 1
Bunclody-Carrickduff, 929 H 6
Buncrana, 2,955 G 1
Buncrana, *3,334 G 1
Bundoran, 1,337 E 3
Burtonport, ‡1,288 E 2
Buttevant, 1,045 D 7
Cahir, 1,747 F 7
Cahirciveen, 1,547 A 8
Callan, 1,283 G 7
Camolin, 306 J 6
Campile, 231 H 7
Cappamore, 567 E 6
Cappawhite, 305 E 6
Cappoquin, 872 F 7
Carbury, ‡894 H 5
Carlingford, 559 J 3
Carlow, 9,588 H 6
Carlow, *10,399 H 6
Carndonagh, 1,146 G 1
Carnew, 570 H 6
Carrickmacross, 2,100 H 4
Carrickmacross, *2,475 H 4
Carrick-on-Shannon, 1,854 F 4
Carrick-on-Suir, 5,006 F 7
Carrigaholt, ‡493 B 6
Carrigaline, 951 E 8
Carrigallen, 230 F 4
Carrigart, ‡753 F 1
Carrigtwohill, 622 E 8
Carrowkeel, ‡326 G 1
Cashel, 2,692 F 7
Castlebar, 5,979 C 4
Castlebar, *6,476 C 4
Castlebellingham, 407 J 4
Castleblayney, 2,118 H 3
Castleblayney, *2,395 H 3
Castlecomer-Donaguile, 1,244 G 6
Castledermot, 583 H 6
Castlefin, 610 F 2
Castlegregory, 216 A 7
Castleisland, 1,929 B 7
Castlemartyr, 491 E 8
Castlepollard, 693 G 4
Castlerea, 1,752 D 4
Castletown, ‡504 F 6
Castletownbere, 812 B 8
Castletownroche, 399 D 7
Castletownshend, 170 C 9
Causeway, 215 B 7
Cavan, 3,273 G 3
Cavan, *4,312 G 3
Ceanannus Mór, 2,391 G 4
Ceanannus Mór, *2,653 G 4
Celbridge, 1,568 H 5
Charlestown-Bellahy, 677 D 4
Charleville (Rathluirc), 2,232 D 7
Clara, 2,156 F 5
Claregalway, ‡594 D 5
Claremorris, 1,718 C 4
Clashmore, ‡379 F 8
Clifden, 790 B 5
Cloghan, 404 F 5
Clogh-Chatsworth, 324 G 6
Clogheen, 530 F 7
Clogherhead, 649 J 4
Clonakilty, 2,430 D 8
Clonaslee, 285 F 5
Clondalkin, 7,009 J 5
Clonegal, 202 H 6
Clones, 2,164 G 3
Clonfert, ‡430 E 5
Clonmany, ‡936 G 1
Clonmel, 11,622 F 7
Clonmel, *12,291 F 7
Clonmellon, 328 H 4
Clonroche, 222 H 7
Clontuskert, 351 E 4
Cloone, ‡460 F 4
Cloughjordan, 480 E 6
Cloyne, 654 E 8
Coachford, 290 D 8
Cóbh, 6,076 E 8
Cóbh, *7,141 E 8
Coill Dubh, 920 H 5
Collon, 262 J 4
Collooney, 546 E 3
Cong, 233 C 4
Convoy, 654 F 2
Coolaney, ‡352 D 3
Coolgreany, ‡603 J 6
Cootehill, 1,415 G 3
Cootehill, *1,542 G 3
Cork, 128,645 E 8
Cork, *134,430 E 8
Corofin, 342 C 6
Courtmacsherry, 210 D 8
Courtown Harbour, 291 J 6
Creeslough, 269 F 1
Crookhaven, ‡400 B 9
Croom, 756 D 6
Crosshaven, 1,222 E 8
Crossmolina, 1,077 C 3
Crusheen, ‡405 D 6
Culdaff, ‡621 G 1
Daingean, 492 G 5
Delvin, 223 G 4
Dingle, 1,401 A 7
Doaghbeg, ‡701 F 1
Donabate, 426 J 5
Donegal, 1,725 F 2
Doneraile, 799 D 7
Dooagh-Keel, 649 A 4
Doon, 387 E 6
Douglas, ‡4,448 D 8
Drimoleague, 415 C 8
Drishane, ‡1,548 C 7
Drogheda, 19,762 J 4
Drogheda, *20,095 J 4
Droichead Nua, 5,053 H 5
Droichead Nua, *6,444 H 5
Dromahair, 177 E 3
Drumcar, ‡1,215 J 4
Drumconrath, ‡1,044 H 4
Drumkeerin, ‡467 E 3
Drumlish, 205 F 4
Drumshanbo, 576 E 3
Dublin (cap.), 567,866 K 5
Dublin, *679,748 K 5
Duleek, 658 J 4
Duncannon, 228 H 7
Dundalk, 21,672 H 3
Dundalk, *23,816 H 3
Dunfanaghy, 303 F 1
Dungarvan, 5,583 F 7
Dungloe, 940 E 2
Dunkineely, 288 E 2
Dún Laoghaire, 53,171 K 5
Dún Laoghaire, *98,379 K 5
Dunlavin, 423 H 5
Dunleer, 855 J 4
Dunmanway, 1,392 C 8
Dunmore, 522 D 4
Dunmore East, 656 G 7
Dunshaughlin, ‡283 H 5
Durrow, Laoighis, 596 G 6
Durrow, Offaly, ‡441 F 5
Easky, 184 D 3
Edenderry, 2,953 G 5
Edenderry, *3,116 G 5
Elphin, 489 E 4
Emyvale, 281 G 3
Ennis, 5,972 D 6
Ennis, *10,840 D 6
Enniscorthy, 5,704 J 7
Enniscorthy, *6,642 J 7
Enniskerry, 772 J 5
Ennistymon, 1,013 C 6
Eyrecourt, 314 E 5
Fahan, ‡1,023 G 1
Falcarragh, 506 E 1
Feakle, ‡398 D 6
Fenit, 360 B 7
Ferbane, 1,064 F 5
Fermoy, 3,237 E 7
Fermoy, *4,033 E 7
Ferns, 712 J 6
Fethard, Tipperary, 1,064 F 7
Fethard, Wexford, ‡637 H 7
Foxford, 868 C 4
Foynes, 624 C 6
Frankford (Kilcormac), 1,089 F 5
Frenchpark, ‡693 E 4
Freshford, 585 G 6
Galbally, 258 E 7
Galway, 27,726 C 5
Galway, *29,375 C 5
Geashill, ‡751 G 5
Glandore, ‡695 C 8
Glanmire-Riverstown, 1,113 E 8
Glanworth, 335 E 7
Glenamaddy, 315 D 4
Glenbeigh, 266 B 7
Glencolumbkille, ‡787 D 2
Glengarriff, 244 C 8
Glenties, 734 E 2
Glenville, ‡264 D 7
Glin, 623 C 6
Golden, ‡640 F 7
Gorey, 2,946 J 6
Gorey, *3,024 J 6
Gormanston, ‡1,384 J 4
Gort, 975 D 5
Gowran, 402 G 6
Graiguenamanagh-Tinnahinch, 1,303 H 6
Granard, 1,054 F 4
Greencastle, 322 H 1
Greenore, 882 J 4
Greystones-Delgany, 4,517 K 5
Gurteen, 165 D 3
Hacketstown, 574 H 6
Headford, 673 C 5
Holycross, ‡902 F 6
Hospital, 525 E 7
Inchigeelagh, ‡516 C 8
Inishannon, 190 D 8
Inistioge, 179 G 7
Inniscrone, 582 C 3
Johnstown, 303 G 6
Kanturk, 2,063 D 7
Keel-Dooagh, 649 A 4
Kells, ‡423 G 6
Kells (Ceanannus Mór), 2,391 G 4
Kenmare, 903 B 8
Kilbaha, ‡471 B 6
Kilbeggan, 635 G 5
Kilcar, 273 D 2
Kilcock, 827 H 5
Kilconnell, ‡629 E 5
Kilcoole, 679 K 5
Kilcormac, 1,089 F 5
Kilcullen, 880 H 5
Kildare, 3,137 H 5
Kildysart, 239 C 6
Kilfenora, ‡441 C 6
Kilfinane, 561 D 7
Kilgarvan, 228 B 8
Kilkee, 1,287 B 6
Kilkelly, 225 D 4
Kilkenny, 9,838 G 6
Kilkenny, *13,306 G 6
Killala, 368 C 3
Killaloe, 871 D 6
Killarney, 7,184 C 7
Killarney, *7,541 C 7
Killavullen, 221 D 7
Killenaule, 592 F 6
Killeshandra, 432 F 3
Killimor, 221 E 5
Killinaboy, ‡297 C 6
Killorglin, 1,150 B 7
Killucan-Rathwire, 290 G 4
Killybegs, 1,094 E 2
Kilmacrennan, 274 F 1
Kilmacthomas, 396 G 7
Kilmallock, 1,170 D 7
Kilmeadan, ‡262 G 7
Kilmihill, 284 C 6
Kilmoganny, 181 G 7
Kilmore Quay, 273 H 7
Kilmurry, ‡387 C 6
Kilnaleck, 273 G 4
Kilronan, 243 B 5
Kilrush, 2,671 C 6
Kilsheelan, ‡665 F 7
Kiltimagh, 978 C 4
Kilworth, 360 E 7
Kingscourt, 1,016 H 4
Kingstown (Dun Laoghaire), 53,171 K 5
Kinlough, 160 E 3
Kinnegad, 362 G 5
Kinnitty, ‡420 F 5
Kinsale, 1,622 D 8
Kinsale, *1,989 D 8
Kinvara, 293 D 5
Knightstown, 236 A 8
Knock, ‡1,202 D 4
Knocklong, 248 D 7
Knocknagashel, 168 C 7
Labasheeda, ‡468 C 6
Laghey, ‡625 E 2
Lahinch, 455 C 6
Lanesborough-Ballyleague, 906 E 4
Laracor, ‡404 H 4
Laytown-Bettystown-Mornington, 1,882 J 4
Leenane, ‡271 B 4
Leighlindridge, 379 H 6
Leitrim, ‡544 F 3
Leixlip, 2,402 H 5
Letterkenny, 4,930 F 2
Letterkenny, *5,207 F 2
Lifford, 1,121 F 2
Limerick, 57,161 D 6
Limerick, *63,002 D 6
Liscarroll, 231 D 7
Lisdoonvarna, 459 C 5
Lismore, 884 F 7
Lismore, *1,041 F 7
Listowel, 3,021 C 7
Littleton, 322 F 6
Longford, 3,876 F 4
Longford, *4,791 F 4
Lorrha, ‡685 E 5
Loughrea, 3,075 E 5
Louisburgh, 310 B 4
Louth, 208 J 4
Lucan-Doddsborough, 4,245 J 5
Luimneach (Limerick), 57,161 D 6
Lusk, 553 J 4
Macroom, 2,256 C 8
Malahide, 3,834 J 5
Malin, ‡552 G 1
Mallow, 5,901 D 7
Mallow, *6,506 D 7
Manorhamilton, 858 E 3
Manulla, ‡660 C 4
Maryborough (Portlaoighise), 3,902 G 5
Maynooth, 1,296 H 5
Meathas Truim, 546 G 4
Midleton, 3,075 E 8
Midleton, *4,666 E 8
Milford, 763 F 1
Millstreet, 1,319 D 7
Milltown, 260 A 7
Miltown-Malbay, 677 C 6
Minard, ‡397 A 7
Mitchelstown, 2,783 E 7
Moate, 1,378 F 5
Mohill, 868 F 4
Monaghan, 5,256 G 3
Monasterevan, 1,619 H 5
Moneygall, 282 F 6
Monivea, ‡405 D 5
Mooncoin, 413 G 7
Mount Bellew, 275 D 5
Mountcharles, 445 E 2
Mountmellick, 2,595 G 5
Mountmellick, *2,864 G 5
Mountrath, 1,098 F 5
Moville, 1,089 G 1
Moycullen, ‡498 C 5
Moynalty, ‡583 H 4
Muff, 240 G 1
Muinebeag, 2,321 H 6
Mullagh, 293 H 4
Mullaghmore, ‡629 D 3
Mullinahone, 262 F 7
Mullinavat, 343 G 7
Mullingar, 6,790 G 4
Mullinger, *9,245 G 4
Naas, 5,078 H 5
Navan (An Uaimh), 4,605 H 4
Nenagh, 5,085 E 6
Nenagh, *5,174 E 6
Newbliss, ‡547 G 3
Newbridge (Droichead Nua), 5,053 H 5
Newcastle, 2,549 D 7
Newcastle, *2,680 D 7
Newmarket, 886 C 7
Newmarket-on-Fergus, 1,052 D 6
New Pallas, ‡1,271 E 6
Newport, Mayo, 420 C 4
Newport, Tipperary, 582 E 6
New Ross, 4,775 H 7
New Ross, *5,153 H 7
Newtownforbes, ‡495 F 4
Newtownmountkennedy, 882 J 5
Newtownsandes, 268 C 6
O'Briensbridge-Montpelier, 237 D 6
Oldcastle, 759 G 4
Old Leighlin, ‡309 G 6
Oola, 348 E 6
Oranmore, 440 D 5
Oughterard, 628 C 5
Passage East, 408 G 7
Passage West, 2,709 E 8
Patrickswell, 415 D 6
Pettigo, 332 F 2
Piltown, 456 G 7
Portarlington, 3,117 G 5
Portlaoighise, 3,902 G 5
Portlaoighise, *6,470 G 5
Portlaw, 1,166 G 7
Portmarnock, 1,726 J 5
Portumna, 913 E 5
Queenstown (Cóbh), 6,076 E 8
Rahan, ‡531 F 5
Ramelton, 807 F 1
Raphoe, 945 F 2
Rathangan, 868 G 5
Rathcoole, 1,740 J 5
Rathcormac, 191 E 7
Rathdowney, 892 F 6
Rathdrum, 1,141 J 6
Rathgormuck, ‡231 F 7
Rathkeale, 1,543 D 7
Rathluirc, 2,232 D 7
Rathmore, 437 J 5
Rathmullen, 486 F 1
Rathnew-Merrymeeting, 954 J 6
Rathowen, ‡294 F 4
Rathvilly, 230 H 6
Ratoath, 300 J 5
Riverstown, 236 E 3
Rockcorry, 233 H 3
Rosapenna, ‡822 F 1
Roscommon, 1,556 E 4
Roscommon, *2,821 E 4
Roscrea, 3,855 F 6
Rosscarbery, 309 C 8
Rosses Point, 464 D 3
Rosslare, 588 J 7
Rosslare Harbour (Ballygeary), 725 J 7
Roundstone, 204 A 5
Roundwood, 260 J 5
Rush, 2,633 J 4
Saint Johnston, 463 F 2
Scarriff, 619 E 6
Schull, 457 B 8
Scotstown, 264 H 3
Shanagolden, 231 C 6
Shannon Airport, 3,657 D 6
Shannon Bridge, 188 F 5
Shercock, 313 G 4
Shillelagh, 246 J 6
Shinrone, 365 F 5
Shrule, 288 C 4
Sixmilebridge, 567 D 6
Skerries, 3,044 J 4
Skibbereen, 2,104 C 8
Slane, 483 H 4
Sligo, 14,080 E 3
Sligo, *14,456 E 3
Sneem, 285 B 8
Spiddal, ‡819 C 5
Stepaside, 748 J 5
Stradbally, Laoighis, 891 G 5
Stradbally, Waterford, 158 F 7
Strokestown, 563 E 4
Swanlinbar, 257 F 3
Swinford, 1,105 C 4
Swords, 4,133 J 5
Taghmon, 369 H 7
Tallaght, 6,174 J 5
Tallow, 883 F 7
Tarbert, 485 C 6
Teltown, ‡739 H 4
Templemore, 2,174 F 6
Templetuohy, 197 F 6
Termonfeckin, 328 J 4
Thomastown, 1,270 G 7
Thurles, 6,840 F 6
Thurles, *7,087 F 6
Timoleague, 257 D 8
Tinahely, 450 H 6
Tipperary, 4,631 E 7
Tipperary, *4,717 E 7
Toomevara, 272 E 6
Tralee, 12,287 B 7
Tralee, *13,263 B 7
Tramore, 3,792 G 7
Trim, 1,700 H 4
Trim, *2,255 H 4
Tuam, 3,808 D 4
Tuam, *4,952 D 4
Tubbercurry, 959 D 3
Tulla, 415 D 6
Tullamore, 6,809 G 5
Tullamore, *7,474 G 5
Tullaroan, ‡301 G 6
Tullow, 1,838 H 6
Tullow, *1,945 H 6
Tynagh, ‡452 E 5
Tyrrellspass, 289 G 5
Urlingford, 652 F 6
Virginia, 583 G 4
Waterford, 31,968 G 7
Waterford, *33,676 G 7
Waterville, 547 A 8
Westport, 3,023 C 4
Wexford, 11,849 H 7
Wexford, *13,293 H 7
Whitegate, 370 E 8
Wicklow, 3,786 K 6
Wicklow, *3,915 K 6
Woodenbridge, ‡620 J 6
Woodford, 198 E 5
Youghal, 5,445 F 8
Youghal, *5,626 F 8

OTHER FEATURES

Achill (isl.), 3,129 A 4
Allen (lake) E 3
Allen, Bog of (marsh) H 5
Aran (isl.), 773 D 2
Aran (isls.), 1,499 B 5
Arklow (bank) K 6
Arrow (lake) E 3
Awbeg (riv.) D 7
Ballinskelligs (bay) A 8
Ballycotton (bay) F 8
Ballyheige (bay) B 7
Ballyhoura (hills) E 7
Ballyteige (bay) H 7
Bandon (riv.) D 8
Bann (riv.) J 6
Bantry (bay) B 8
Barrow (riv.) H 7
Baurtregaum (mt.) A 7
Bear (isl.), 288 B 8
Blacksod (bay) A 3
Blackstairs (mt.) H 6
Blackwater (riv.) D 7
Blackwater (riv.) H 4
Blasket (isls.) A 7
Bloody Foreland (prom.) E 1
Blue Stack (mts.) E 2
Boderg (lake) E 4
Boggeragh (mts.) D 7
Boyne (riv.) J 4
Brandon (head) A 7
Bride (riv.) E 7
Broad Haven (harb.) B 3
Brosna (riv.) F 5
Bull, The (isl.), 5 A 8
Caha (mts.) B 8
Carlingford (inlet) J 3
Carnsore (pt.) J 7
Carrantuohill (mt.) B 7
Clare (riv.) D 5
Clare (isls.), 168 A 4
Clear (cape) B 9
Clear (isl.), 192 C 9
Clew (bay) B 4
Comeragh (mts.) F 7
Conn (lake) C 3
Connacht (prov.), 390,902 C 4
Connemara (dist.), 7,599 B 5
Cork (harb.) E 8
Corrib (lake) C 5
Courtmacsherry (bay) D 8
Curragh, The H 5
Dee (riv.) H 4
Deel (riv.) D 7
Deele (riv.) F 2
Derg (lake) E 6
Derravaragh (lake) G 4
Derryveagh (mts.) E 2
Dingle (bay) A 7
Donegal (bay) D 3
Drum (hills) F 7
Dublin (bay) J 5
Dundalk (bay) J 4
Dunmanus (bay) B 8
Dursey (isl.), 38 A 8
Ennell (lake) G 5
Erne (riv.) E 3
Errigal (mt.) E 1
Erris (head) A 3
Fanad (head) F 1
Fastnet Rock (isl.), 3 B 9
Feale (riv.) C 7
Fergus (riv.) D 6
Finn (riv.) F 2
Finn (riv.) G 3
Flesk (riv.) C 7
Foyle (inlet) G 1
Foyle (riv.) G 2
Galley (head) D 9
Galtee (mts.) E 7
Galtymore (mt.) E 7
Galway (bay) C 5
Gara (lake) D 4
Garadice (lake) F 3
Gill (lake) E 3
Glyde (riv.) H 4
Golden Vale (plain) E 7
Gorumna (isl.), 1,108 B 5
Gowna (lake) G 4
Grand (canal) G 5
Greenore (pt.) J 7
Gweebarra (bay) D 2
Hags (head) B 6
Helvick (head) G 7
Hook (head) H 7
Horn (head) E 1
Iar Connacht (dist.), 10,774 C 5
Inishbofin (isl.), 236 A 4
Inishbofin (isl.), 103 E 1
Inisheer (isl.), 313 B 5
Inishmaan (isl.), 319 C 5
Inishmore (isl.), 864 B 5
Inishowen (head) H 1
Inishowen (pen.), 24,109 G 1
Inishtrahull (isl.), 3 G 1
Inishturk (isls.), 83 A 4
Inny (riv.) A 8
Inny (riv.) F 4
Inver (bay) E 2
Ireland's Eye (isl.) K 5
Irish (sea) K 4
Joyce's Country (dist.), 2,021 B 4
Kenmare (riv.) A 8
Kerry (head) A 7
Key (lake) E 3
Kilkieran (bay) B 5
Killala (bay) C 3
Killary (harb.) A 4
Kinsale (harb.) E 8
Kippure (mt.) J 5
Knockboy (mt.) B 8
Knockmealdown (mts.) F 7
Lady's Island Lake (inlet) J 7
Lambay (isl.), 24 K 4
Laune (riv.) B 7
Leane (lake) B 7
Leane (lake) G 4
Lee (riv.) D 8
Leinster (mt.) H 6
Leinster (prov.), 1,498,140 G 5
Lettermullan (isl.), 221 B 5
Liffey (riv.) H 5
Liscannor (bay) B 6
Long Island (bay) B 9
Loop (head) A 6
Lugnaquillia (mt.) J 5
Macgillicuddy's Reeks (mts.) B 7
Macnean (lake) F 3
Maigue (riv.) D 6
Maine (riv.) C 7
Malin (head) F 1
Mask (lake) C 4
Maumturk (mts.) B 5
Melvin (lake) E 3
Mizen (head) B 9
Moher (cliffs) B 6
Monavullagh (mts.) F 7
Moy (riv.) C 3
Mulkear (riv.) E 6
Mullaghareirk (mts.) C 7
Mulroy (bay) F 1
Munster (prov.), 882,002 D 7
Mweelrea (mt.) B 4
Mweenish (isl.), 198 B 5
Nagles (mts.) E 7
Nenagh (riv.) E 6
Nephin (mt.) C 3
Nore (riv.) G 7
North (sound) B 5
Omey (isl.), 34 A 5
Oughter (lake) G 3
Ovoca (riv.) J 6
Owenmore (riv.) D 3
Owey (isl.), 51 D 1
Paps, The (mt.) C 7
Partry (mts.) C 4
Pollaphuca (res.) J 5
Punchestown H 5
Rathlin O'Birne (isl.), 3 C 2
Ree (lake) F 5
Roaringwater (bay) B 9
Rosses (bay) D 1
Rosskeeragh (pt.) D 3
Royal (canal) G 4
Saint Finan's (bay) A 8
Saint George's (chan.) K 7
Saint John s (pt.) D 2
Saltee (isls.) H 7
Seven (heads) D 8
Seven Hogs, The (isls.) A 7
Shannon (riv.) E 6
Sheeffry (hills) B 4
Sheelin (lake) G 4
Sheep Haven (harb.) F 1
Sheeps (head) B 8
Sherkin (isl.), 82 C 9
Silvermine (mts.) E 6
Slaney (riv.) H 7
Slieve Aughty (mts.) D 5
Slieve Bloom (mts.) F 5
Slieve Gamph (mts.) D 3
Slievenaman (mt.) F 7
Sligo (bay) D 3
Slyne (head) A 5
South (sound) C 5
Stacks (mts.) B 7
Suck (riv.) E 5
Suir (riv.) G 7
Swilly (inlet) F 1
Tara (hill) H 4
Tory (isl.), 273 E 1
Tory (sound) E 1
Tralee (bay) B 7
Trawbreaga (bay) F 1
Ulster (part) (prov.), 207,204 G 2
Valencia (Valentia) (isl.), 770 A 8
Valentia (isl.), 770 A 8
Waterford (harb.) G 7
Wexford (bay) J 7
Wicklow (head) K 6
Wicklow (mts.) J 6
Youghal (bay) F 8

NORTHERN IRELAND

COUNTIES

Antrim, 37,600 J 2
Ards, 52,100 K 2
Armagh, 47,500 H 3
Ballymena, 52,200 J 2
Ballymoney, 22,700 J 1
Bainbridge, 28,800 J 3
Belfast, 368,200 J 2
Carrickfergus, 27,500 K 2
Castlereagh, 63,600 K 2
Coleraine, 44,900 H 1
Cookstown, 27,500 H 2
Craigavon, 71,200 J 3
Down, 48,800 K 3
Dungannon, 43,000 H 3
Fermanagh, 50,900 F 3
Larne, 29,000 K 2
Limavady, 25,000 H 1
Lisburn, 80,800 J 2
Londonderry, 86,600 G 2
Magherafelt, 32,200 H 2
Mourne (Newry and Mourne), 75,300 J 3
Moyle, 13,400 J 1
Newtownabbey, 71,500 J 2
North Down, 59,600 K 2
Omagh, 41,800 G 2
Strabane, 35,500 G 2

CITIES and TOWNS

Ahoghill, ‡1,929 J 2
Annalong, 1,001 K 3
Antrim, 8,351 J 2
Ardglass, 1,052 K 3
Armagh, 13,606 H 3
Armoy, ‡1,051 J 1
Augher, ‡1,986 G 3
Aughnacloy, ‡1,885 H 3
Ballycastle, 2,899 J 1
Ballyclare, 5,155 J 2
Ballygawley, ‡2,165 G 3
Ballykelly, 1,116 G 1
Ballymena, 23,386 J 2
Ballymoney, 5,697 J 1
Ballynahinch, 3,485 J 3
Banbridge, 7,968 J 3
Bangor, 35,260 K 2
Belfast (cap.), 353,700 J 2
Belfast, *551,940 J 2
Bellaghy, ‡2,265 H 2
Belleek, ‡2,487 E 3
Beragh, ‡2,137 G 2
Bessbrook, 2,619 J 3
Brookeborough, ‡2,534 G 3
Broughshane, 1,288 J 2
Bushmills, 1,288 J 1
Caledon, ‡1,828 H 3
Carnlough, 1,416 J 2
Carrickfergus, 16,603 K 2
Carrowdore, 2,548 K 2
Castledawson, 1,162 H 2
Castlederg, 1,766 F 2
Castlewellan, 1,488 K 3
Claudy, ‡2,507 G 2
Clogher, ‡1,888 G 3
Coalisland, 3,614 H 2
Coleraine, 16,354 H 1
Comber, 5,575 K 2
Cookstown, 6,965 H 2
Craigavon, 12,740 J 3
Crossgar, 1,098 K 3
Crossmaglen, 1,085 H 3
Crumlin, 1,450 J 2
Cullybackey, 1,649 J 2
Derrygonnelly, ‡2,539 F 3
Dervock, ‡1,191 J 1
Donaghadee, 4,008 K 2
Downpatrick, 7,918 K 3
Draperstown, ‡2,247 H 2
Dromore, Bainbridge, 2,848 J 3
Dromore, Omagh, ‡2,224 G 3
Drumquin, ‡1,982 F 2
Dundrum, ‡2,245 K 3
Dungannon, 8,190 H 3
Dungiven, 1,536 H 2
Dunnamanagh, ‡2,242 G 2
Ederny and Kesh, ‡2,497 F 2
Enniskillen, 9,679 F 3
Feeny, ‡1,459 H 2
Fintona, 1,190 G 3
Fivemiletown, ‡1,649 G 3
Garvagh, ‡2,363 H 2
Gilford, 1,592 J 3
Glenarm, ‡1,728 J 2
Glenavy, ‡2,360 J 2
Glynn, ‡1,872 K 2
Gortin, ‡2,033 G 2
Greyabbey, ‡2,646 K 2
Hillsborough, 1,021 J 3
Holywood, 9,892 K 2
Irvinestown, 1,457 F 3
Keady, 2,145 H 3
Kells, ‡2,560 J 2
Kesh, ‡2,497 F 3
Kilkeel, 4,090 K 3
Killough, ‡3,295 K 3
Killyleagh, 2,359 K 3
Kilrea, 1,196 H 2
Kircubbin, 1,075 K 3
Larne, 18,482 K 2
Limavady, 6,004 H 1
Lisburn, 31,836 J 2
Lisnaskea, 1,443 G 3
Londonderry, 51,200 G 2
Loughbrickland, ‡2,056 J 3
Maghera, 2,085 H 2
Magherafelt, 4,704 H 2
Markethill, ‡2,352 H 3
Millisle, 1,172 K 2
Moneymore, 1,178 H 2
Moy, ‡2,349 H 3
Moygashel, 1,086 H 3
Newcastle, 4,647 J 3
Newry, 20,279 J 3
Newtownabbey, 58,114 K 2
Newtownards, 15,484 K 2
Newtownbutler, ‡2,663 G 3
Newtownhamilton, ‡1,936 H 3
Newtownstewart, 1,433 G 2
Omagh, 14,594 G 2
Pomeroy, ‡1,786 H 2
Portaferry, 1,730 K 3
Portavogie, 1,310 K 3
Portglenone, ‡2,061 H 2
Portrush, 5,376 H 1
Portstewart, 5,085 H 1
Randalstown, 2,799 J 2
Rathfriland, 1,886 J 3
Rostrevor, 1,617 J 3
Saintfield, ‡2,198 K 3
Sion Mills, 1,588 G 2
Sixmilecross, ‡1,980 G 2
Stewartstown, ‡1,759 H 2
Strabane, 9,413 G 2
Strangford, ‡1,987 K 3
Tandragee, 1,725 J 3
Tempo, ‡2,282 G 3
Trillick, ‡2,167 G 3
Warrenpoint, 4,291 J 3
Whitehead, 2,642 K 2

OTHER FEATURES

Bann (riv.) H 2
Belfast (inlet) K 2
Blackwater (riv.) H 3
Bush (riv.) H 1
Derg (riv.) F 2
Divis (mt.) J 2
Dundrum (bay) K 3
Erne (lake) F 3
Foyle (inlet) G 1
Foyle (riv.) G 2
Giant's Causeway H 1
Lagan (riv.) K 2
Larne (inlet) K 2
Magee, Island (pen.), 1,581 K 2
Magilligan (pt.) H 1
Main (riv.) J 2
Mourne (mts.) J 3
Mourne (riv.) G 2
Neagh (lake) J 2
North (chan.) K 1
Rathlin (isl.), 109 J 1
Red (bay) K 1
Roe (riv.) H 1
Saint John's (pt.) K 3
Slieve Donard (mt.) K 3
Sperrin (mts.) G 2
Strangford (inlet) K 3
Torr (head) K 1
Ulster (part) (prov.), 1,537,200 G 2
Upper Lough Erne (lake) F 3

*City and suburbs.
‡Population of district.

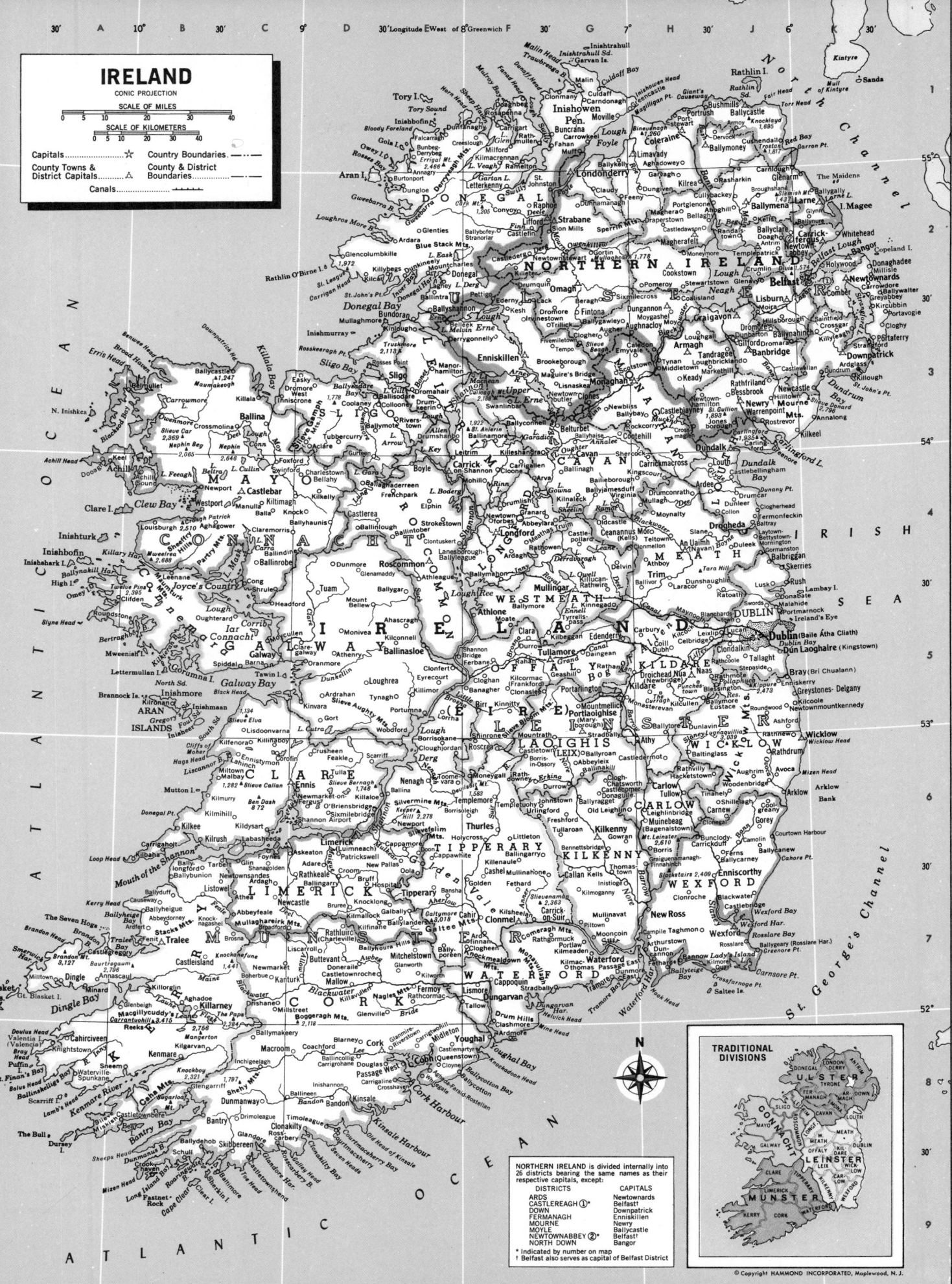

IRELAND

CONIC PROJECTION

SCALE OF MILES
0 5 10 20 30 40

SCALE OF KILOMETERS
0 5 10 20 30 40

Capitals .... ☆
County Towns & District Capitals .... △
County Boundaries .... – – –
County & District Boundaries ....
Canals ....

TRADITIONAL DIVISIONS

ULSTER
CONNACHT
LEINSTER
MUNSTER

NORTHERN IRELAND is divided internally into 26 districts bearing the same names as their respective capitals, except:

DISTRICTS	CAPITALS
ARDS	Newtownards
CASTLEREAGH ① *	Belfast
DOWN	Downpatrick
FERMANAGH	Enniskillen
MOURNE	Newry
MOYLE	Ballycastle
NEWTOWNABBEY ② *	Belfast†
NORTH DOWN	Bangor

* Indicated by number on map
† Belfast also serves as capital of Belfast District

© Copyright HAMMOND INCORPORATED, Maplewood, N.J.

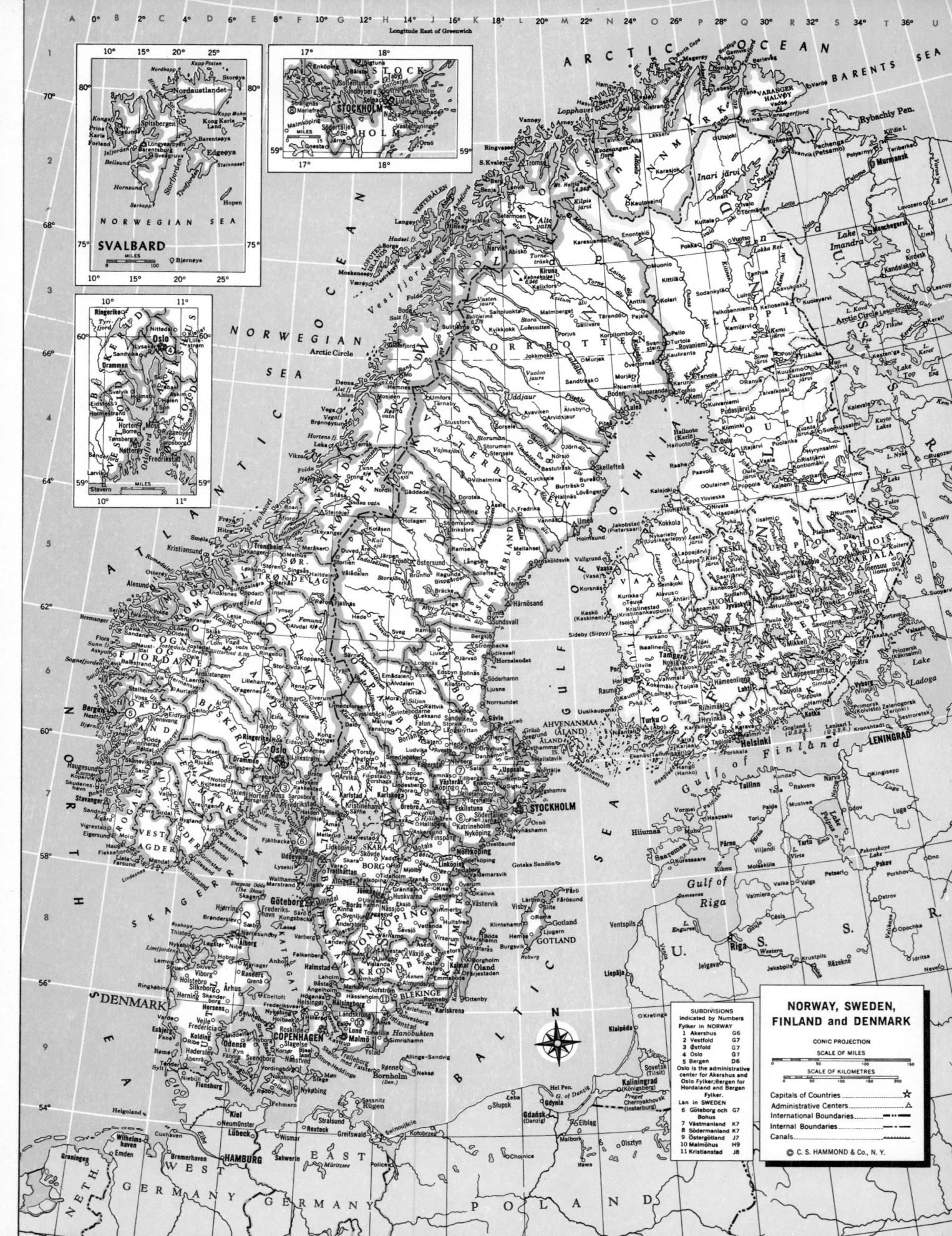

NORWAY, SWEDEN, FINLAND and DENMARK

CONIC PROJECTION

SCALE OF MILES

SCALE OF KILOMETRES

Capitals of Countries	☆
Administrative Centers	△
International Boundaries	
Internal Boundaries	
Canals	

© C. S. HAMMOND & Co., N. Y.

SUBDIVISIONS
indicated by Numbers
Fylker in NORWAY

1	Akershus	G6
2	Vestfold	G7
3	Østfold	G7
4	Oslo	G7
5	Bergen	D6

Oslo is the administrative
center for Akershus and
Oslo Fylker; Bergen for
Hordaland and Bergen
Fylker.

Län in SWEDEN

6	Göteborg och	G7
	Bohus	
7	Västmanland	K7
8	Södermanland	K7
9	Östergötland	J7
10	Malmöhus	H9
11	Kristianstad	J8

SVALBARD

STOCKHOLM

OSLO

NORWAY

AREA 125,181 sq. mi.
POPULATION 3,893,000
CAPITAL Oslo
LARGEST CITY Oslo
HIGHEST POINT Glittertind 8,110 ft.
MONETARY UNIT krone (crown)
MAJOR LANGUAGE Norwegian
MAJOR RELIGION Protestantism

SWEDEN

AREA 173,665 sq. mi.
POPULATION 7,978,000
CAPITAL Stockholm
LARGEST CITY Stockholm
HIGHEST POINT Kebnekaise 6,946 ft.
MONETARY UNIT krona (crown)
MAJOR LANGUAGE Swedish
MAJOR RELIGION Protestantism

FINLAND

AREA 130,128 sq. mi.
POPULATION 4,706,000
CAPITAL Helsinki
LARGEST CITY Helsinki
HIGHEST POINT Mt. Haltia 4,343 ft.
MONETARY UNIT Markka (Mark)
MAJOR LANGUAGES Finnish, Swedish
MAJOR RELIGION Protestantism

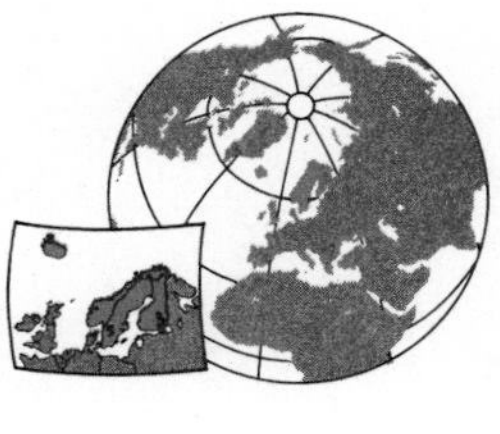

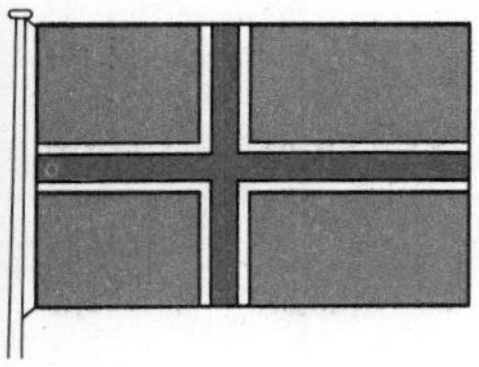

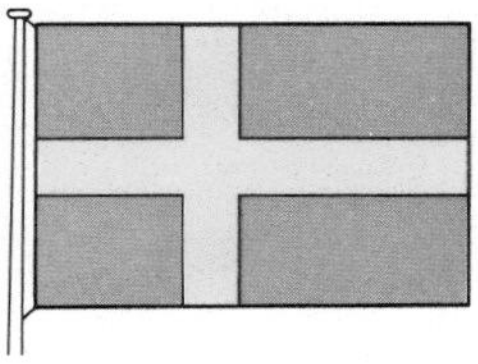

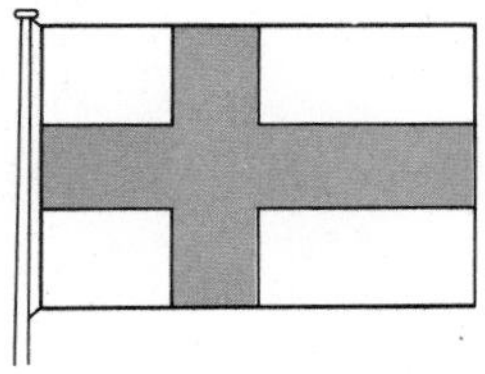

FINLAND

PROVINCES

Ahvenanmaa, 21,584 ....L 6
Häme, 623,756 ....O 6
Keski-Suomi, 248,599 ....O 5
Kuopio, 265,434 ....P 5
Kymi, 348,989 ....Q 6
Lappi, 220,755 ....P 3
Mikkeli, 225,685 ....P 6
Oulu, 422,828 ....P 4
Pohjois-Karjala, 193,199 ....Q 5
Turku-Pori, 680,713 ....N 6
Uusimaa, 999,053 ....O 6
Vaasa, 447,785 ....N 5

CITIES and TOWNS

Äänekoski, 10,977 ....O 5
Åbo (Turku), 155,000 ....N 6
Alavus (Alavo), †11,139 ....N 5
Björneborg (Pori), 71,972 ....M 6
Borgå (Porvoo), 15,738 ....O 6
Brahestad (Raahe), 7,637 ....O 4
Ekenäs (Tammisaari), 6,401 ....N 6
Espoo (Esbo), 88,086 ....O 6
Forssa, 15,260 ....N 6
Fredrikshamn (Hamina), 10,872 ....P 6
Gamlakarleby (Kokkola), 20,715 ....N 5
Haapajärvi, 8,943 ....O 5
Haapamäki, 2,200 ....O 5
Hämeenlinna (Tavastehus), 37,333 ....O 6
Hamina, 10,872 ....P 6
Hangö (Hanko), 9,668 ....N 7
Harjavalta, 8,191 ....N 6
Heinola, 13,696 ....P 6
Helsinki (Helsingfors) (cap.), 531,286 ....O 6
Helsinki, *700,000 ....O 6
Himanka, †3,260 ....N 5
Hyrynsalmi, †5,629 ....Q 4
Hyvinkää (Hyvinge), 33,062 ....O 6
Iisalmi, 7,551 ....P 5
Ilomantsi, †12,050 ....R 5
Imatra, 35,054 ....Q 6
Ivalo ....P 2
Jakobstad (Pietarsaari), 19,114 ....N 5
Joensuu, 35,385 ....R 5
Juuka, †9,925 ....Q 5
Jyväskylä, 56,824 ....O 5
Kajaani, 19,131 ....P 4
Kalajoki, †7,314 ....N 4
Karis (Karjaa), 7,940 ....N 6
Karkkila, 8,504 ....N 6
Kaskö (Kaskinen), 1,436 ....M 5
Kauttua ....M 6
Kemi, 30,199 ....O 4
Kemijärvi, 6,546 ....P 3
Kerava (Kervo), 13,322 ....O 6
Kittilä, †8,347 ....O 3
Kokemäki, †10,922 ....N 6
Kokkola (Gamlakarleby), 20,715 ....N 5
Kotka, 33,953 ....P 6
Kouvola, 25,275 ....P 6
Kristiinankaupunki (Kristinestad), 2,726 ....N 5
Kuhmo, †14,847 ....Q 4
Kuopio, 63,800 ....Q 5
Kurikka, 11,373 ....M 5
Kuusamo, †20,324 ....Q 4
Lahti, 87,237 ....O 6
Lappeenranta, 50,543 ....P 6
Lieksa, 4,703 ....R 5
Loimaa, 6,366 ....N 6
Lovisa (Loviisa), 6,695 ....P 6
Maarianhamina (Mariehamn), 8,512 ....M 7
Mänttä, 7,277 ....O 6
Mariehamn (Maarianhamina), 8,512 ....M 7
Mikkeli (Sankt Michel), 24,962 ....P 6
Muonio, †3,226 ....O 3
Naantali (Nådendal), 6,784 ....M 6
Nivala, †10,784 ....O 5
Nokia, 19,200 ....N 6
Nurmes, 2,329 ....Q 5
Nykarleby (Uusikaarlepyy), 1,289 ....N 5
Nyslott (Savonlinna), 17,618 ....Q 6
Nystad (Uusikaupunki), 6,845........M 6
Oulainen, 7,898 ....O 4
Oulu (Uleåborg), 85,094 ....O 4
Outokumpu, 10,862 ....Q 5
Parikkala, †7,052 ....Q 6
Parkano, †8,587 ....N 6
Pello, †7,139 ....O 3
Pieksämäki, 12,821 ....P 5
Pietarsaari (Jakobstad), 19,114 ....N 5
Pori (Björneborg), 71,972 ....M 6
Porvoo (Borgå), 15,738 ....O 6
Posio, †7,454 ....Q 3
Pudasjärvi, †15,622 ....P 4
Raahe (Brahestad), 7,637 ....O 4
Rauma (Raumo), 25,218 ....M 6
Riihimäki, 22,442 ....O 6
Rovaniemi, 28,680 ....O 3
Saarijärvi, †11,586 ....O 5
Salo, 16,715 ....N 6
Sankt Michel (Mikkeli), 24,962..P 6
Savonlinna, 17,618 ....Q 6
Savukoski, †2,392 ....Q 3
Seinäjoki, 19,836 ....N 5
Sodankylä, †11,745 ....P 3
Sotkamo, †14,127 ....Q 4
Suolahti, 5,563 ....O 5
Suomussalmi, †15,507 ....Q 4
Suonenjoki, 10,012 ....P 5
Tammerfors (Tampere), 156,100 ....N 6
Tammisaari (Ekenäs), 6,401 ....N 6
Tampere (Tammerfors), 156,000 ....N 6
Tapiola ....O 6
Tavastehus (Hämeenlinna), 37,333 ....O 6
Teuva, †8,280 ....N 5
Toijala, 7,505 ....N 6
Tornio (Torneå), 7,325 ....O 4
Turku (Åbo), 155,000 ....N 6
Uleåborg (Oulu), 85,094 ....O 4
Ulvila (Ulvsby), †7,800 ....N 6
Utsjoki, †1,436 ....P 2
Uusikaarlepyy (Nykarleby), 1,289 ....N 5
Uusikaupunki (Nystad), 6,845...M 6
Vaala, †6,675 ....P 4
Vaasa (Vasa), 49,109 ....M 5
Valkeakoski, 15,949 ....N 6
Vammala, 5,605 ....N 6
Varkaus, 24,619 ....Q 5
Vasa (Vaasa), 48,262 ....M 5

OTHER FEATURES

Ahvenanmaa (Åland) (isls.), 21,584 ....L 6
Finland (gulf) ....P 7
Haltia (mt.) ....M 2
Hangöudd (prom.) ....N 7
Hauki (lake) ....Q 5
Ii (river) ....O 4
Inari (lake) ....P 2
Juo (lake) ....Q 5
Kala (river) ....O 4
Kalla (lake) ....P 5
Keitele (lake) ....O 5
Kemi (lake) ....Q 3
Kemi (river) ....O 3
Kianta (lake) ....Q 4
Kilpis (lake) ....M 2
Kitinen (river) ....P 3
Kivi (lake) ....O 5
Koitere (lake) ....R 5
Kuusamo (lake) ....Q 4
Längelmä (lake) ....O 6
Lapland (reg.) ....O 2
Lapuan (river) ....N 5
Lesti (lake) ....O 5
Lokka (res.) ....P 3
Muo (lake) ....R 4
Muonio (river) ....M 2
Nasi (lake) ....O 6
Onkivesi (lake) ....P 5
Orihvesi (lake) ....Q 5
Oulu (river) ....O 4
Ounas (river) ....O 3
Päijänne (lake) ....O 6
Pasvik (river) ....Q 2
Pielinen (lake) ....Q 5
Puru (lake) ....Q 6
Puula (lake) ....P 5
Pyhä (lake) ....M 6
Pyhä (lake) ....O 5
Saimaa (lake) ....Q 6
Siika (river) ....O 4
Simo (lake) ....P 3
Simo (river) ....O 4
Tana (Teno) (river) ....P 2
Tornio (river) ....O 3
Vallgrund (isl.), 2,063 ....M 5
Ylikitka (lake) ....Q 3

NORWAY

COUNTIES

Akershus, 282,928 ....D 4
Aust-Agder, 78,184 ....E 7
Bergen, 117,465 ....D 6
Buskerud, 191,789 ....F 6
Finnmark, 75,553 ....O 2
Hedmark, 177,300 ....G 6
Hordaland, 243,545 ....E 6
Møre og Romsdal, 219,384 ....E 5
Nord-Trøndelag, 117,376 ....H 4
Nordland, 244,165 ....J 3
Oppland, 168,819 ....F 6
Oslo (city), 485,200 ....D 3
Østfold, 212,450 ....D 4
Rogaland, 256,501 ....E 7
Sogn og Fjordane, 100,711 ....E 6
Sør-Trøndelag, 224,654 ....G 5
Telemark, 155,834 ....F 7
Troms, 132,407 ....L 2
Vest-Agder, 117,226 ....E 7
Vestfold, 167,778 ....D 4

CITIES and TOWNS

Åfjord, †4,105 ....G 5
Ål, †4,377 ....F 6
Ålesund, 18,558 ....D 5
Åndalsnes, 2,202 ....F 5
Arendal, 11,579 ....F 7
Askim, †9,673 ....E 4
Bamble, †8,338 ....F 7
Barentsburg ....C 2
Bergen, 117,465 ....D 6
Bergen, *270,000 ....D 6
Bodø, 14,048 ....J 3
Borre, 6,636 ....D 4
Drammen, 47,261 ....C 4
Drammen, *48,700 ....C 4
Drøbak, 2,683 ....D 4
Eigersund, 9,730 ....D 7
Elverum, †13,604 ....G 6
Farsund, 7,697 ....E 7
Flekkefjord, 8,616 ....E 7
Flora, 7,836 ....D 6
Fredrikstad, 30,006 ....D 4
Gjøvik, 24,256 ....G 6
Grimstad, 2,610 ....F 7
Gulen, †3,212 ....D 6
Halden, 10,006 ....G 7
Hamar, 14,712 ....G 6
Hammerfest, 6,806 ....N 1
Harstad, 18,892 ....K 2
Haugesund, 27,569 ....D 7
Holmestrand, 6,857 ....C 4
Honningsvåg, 2,813 ....O 1
Horten, 13,387 ....D 4
Kirkenes, 4,433 ....Q 2
Kongsberg, 17,578 ....F 7
Kongsvinger, 13,080 ....H 6
Kragerø, †10,067 ....F 7
Kristiansand, 52,542 ....F 8
Kristiansand, *54,900 ....F 8
Kristiansund, 18,466 ....E 5
Kvinnherad, †9,848 ....E 6
Larvik, 10,728 ....C 4
Lenvik, †10,209 ....L 2
Lesja, †2,755 ....F 5
Lillehammer, 19,808 ....F 6
Lillesand, †4,975 ....F 7
Lillestrøm, 10,547 ....E 3
Løkken, †5,054 ....F 5
Longyearbyen ....D 2
Lysaker, 5,393 ....D 3
Mandal, 10,622 ....E 7
Mo, 8,348 ....J 3
Molde, 17,862 ....E 5
Moss, 23,198 ....D 4
Mysen, 2,500 ....G 7
Namsos, 10,998 ....G 4
Narvik, 13,543 ....K 2
Nesttun, 3,827 ....D 6
Notodden, 13,680 ....F 7
Odda, †10,444 ....E 6
Orkanger, 2,874 ....F 5
Oslo (cap.), 483,196 ....D 3
Oslo, *635,700 ....D 3
Porsgrunn, 28,167 ....G 7
Ringerike, 28,577 ....C 3
Risør, 6,110 ....F 7
Rjukan, 6,308 ....F 7
Røros, †5,259 ....G 5
Sandefjord, 6,085 ....C 4
Sandnes, 28,534 ....D 7
Sandvika, 3,751 ....C 3
Sarpsborg, 13,185 ....D 4
Ski, †12,337 ....D 4
Skien, 47,302 ....F 7
Skjåk, †2,692 ....F 6
Stavanger, 79,700 ....D 7
Stavanger, *80,800 ....D 7
Stavern, 2,148 ....D 4
Steinkjer, 19,874 ....G 4
Stor-Elvdal, †4,151 ....G 6
Sulitjelma, 2,129 ....K 3
Sunndalsøra, 2,376 ....F 5
Svolvaer, 3,812 ....J 2
Tana, †3,286 ....Q 1
Telemark ....C 4
Tønsberg, 11,566 ....D 4
Tromsø, 34,600 ....L 2
Trondheim, 118,703 ....F 5
Trondheim, *123,600 ....F 5
Ullensvang, †4,940 ....E 6
Vadsø, 5,320 ....Q 1
Vardø, 4,185 ....R 1
Volda, 2,647 ....E 5
Voss, †13,473 ....E 6

OTHER FEATURES

Alst (fjord) ....G 3
Alsten (isl.), 4,348 ....H 4
Alta (river) ....N 2
Alte (lake) ....L 2
Ands (fjord) ....K 2
Bardu (river) ....L 2
Barentsöya (isl.) ....D 2
Bellsund (bay) ....C 2
Bjørna (fjord) ....D 6
Bjørnøya (isl.) ....D 3
Bokn (fjord) ....D 7
Bremanger (isl.), 2,028 ....D 6
Dønna (isl.), 1,978 ....H 3
Dovrefjeld (mts.) ....F 5
Edgeøya (isl.) ....E 2
Femund (lake) ....G 5
Folda (fjord) ....G 4
Folda (fjord) ....J 3
Frohavet (bay) ....F 5
Frøya (isl.), 4,034 ....F 5
Glittertind (mt.) ....F 6
Glomma (river) ....G 6
Hadsel (fjord) ....J 2
Hardanger (fjord) ....D 7
Hardanger (mts.) ....E 6
Hinlopen (strait) ....C 1
Hinnøy (isl.), 27,599 ....K 2
Hitra (isl.), 3,134 ....F 5
Hopen (isl.) ....E 2
Hornsund (bay) ....C 2
Hortens (fjord) ....G 4
Is (fjord) ....B 2
Jostedals (glacier) ....E 6
Karmøy (isl.), 19,234 ....D 7
Kob (fjord) ....O 1
Kong Karls Land (isls.)........E 1
Kvaløy (isl.), 6,869 ....O 1
Lagen (river) ....G 6
Lakse (fjord) ....P 1
Langøy (isl.), 16,500 ....J 2
Lapland (reg.) ....K 2
Lindesnes (cape) ....E 8
Lista (pen.), 7,702 ....E 7
Lofoten (isls.), 28,980 ....H 2
Lopphavet (bay) ....M 1
Magerøy (isl.), 5,545 ....P 1
Mohn (cape) ....E 1
Moskenesøy (isl.), 2,318 ....H 3
Namsen (river) ....H 4
Nord (fjord) ....E 6
Nordaustlandet (isl.) ....D 1
Nordkyn (cape) ....Q 1
North (cape) ....P 1
Norwegian (sea) ....F 3
Ofot (fjord) ....K 2
Otter (river) ....E 7
Pasvik (river) ....Q 2
Platen (cape) ....D 1
Porsanger (fjord) ....O 1
Rana (river) ....J 3
Ran (fjord) ....H 3
Rauma (river) ....F 5
Reisa (river) ....M 2
Ringvassøy (isl.), 1,472 ....L 2
Romsdals (fjord) ....E 5
Salt (fjord) ....J 3
Seiland (isl.), 769 ....N 1
Senja (isl.), 10,541 ....K 2
Skagerrak (strait) ....E 8
Smøla (isl.), 2,840 ....E 5
Snåsa (lake) ....H 4
Sogne (fjord) ....D 6
Sørkapp (cape) ....C 2
Sørøy (isl.), 2,350 ....N 1
South Kvaløy (isl.), 3,444 ....K 2
Spitsbergen (isl.) ....C 2
Steinneset (cape) ....E 2
Stor (fjord) ....D 2
Sunn (fjord) ....D 6
Tana (river) ....P 1
Tjuv (fjord) ....D 2
Tunn (lake) ....H 4
Tyri (fjord) ....C 3
Vågå (lake) ....F 6
Vannøy (isl.), 1,112 ....L 1
Varanger (fjord) ....Q 1
Vega (isl.) ....G 4
Vest (fjord) ....H 3

(continued on following page)

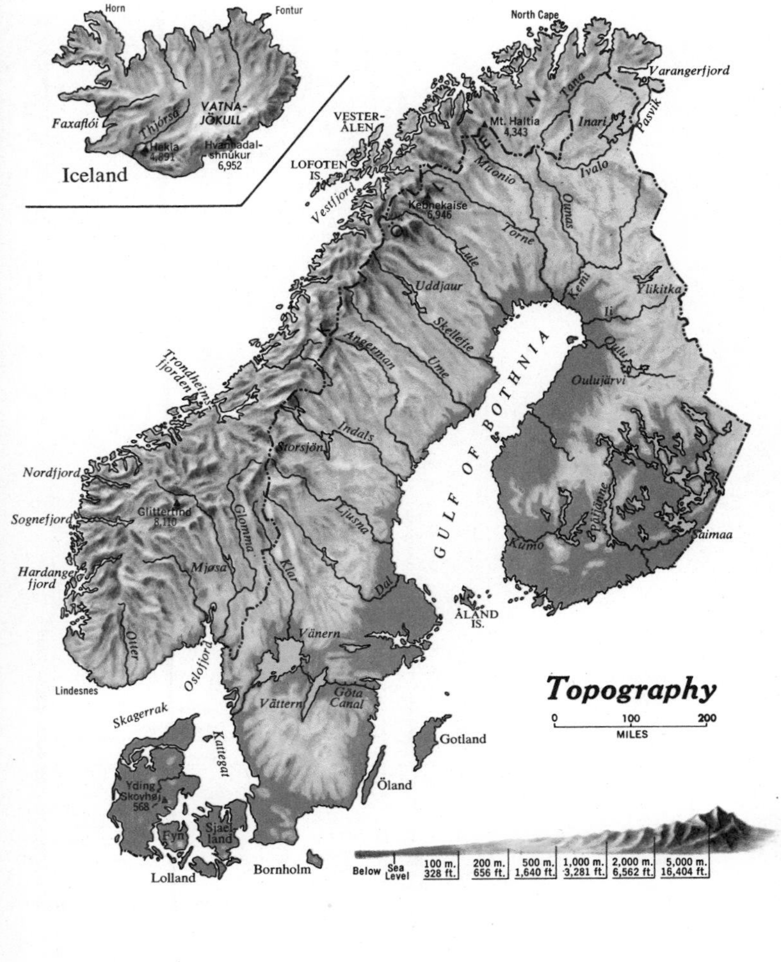

Horn
Fontur
Faxaflói
Thjórsá
VATNA-JÖKULL
Hekla 4,891
Hvannadalshnúkur 6,952
Iceland
North Cape
Varangerfjord
VESTER-ÅLEN
LOFOTEN IS.
Vestfjord
Mt. Haltia 4,343
Inari
Pasvik
Tana
Ivalo
Muonio
Ounas
Kebnekaise 6,946
Torne
Lule
Uddjaur
Kemi
Ylikitka
Ii
Skellefte
Ume
Ångerman
Oulu
Oulujärvi
GULF OF BOTHNIA
Trondheimsfjorden
Indals
Storsjön
Nordfjord
Sognefjord
Glittertind 8,110
Glomma
Ljusna
Päijänne
Saimaa
Kumo
Hardangerfjord
Mjøsa
Klar
Dal
ÅLAND IS.
Vänern
Oslofjord
Otter
Lindesnes
Topography
0 100 200 MILES
Vättern
Göta Canal
Skagerrak
Kattegat
Gotland
Öland
Yding Skovhøj 568
Fyn
Sjælland
Lolland
Bornholm
Below Sea Level
100 m. 328 ft.
200 m. 656 ft.
500 m. 1,640 ft.
1,000 m. 3,281 ft.
2,000 m. 6,562 ft.
5,000 m. 16,404 ft.

18 Norway, Sweden, Finland, Denmark and Iceland
(continued)

NORWAY (continued)

Vesterålen (isls.), 34,385 ... J 2
Vestvågøy (isl.), 11,749 ... H 3
Vikna (isl.), 3,411 ... G 4

SWEDEN

COUNTIES

Älvsborg, 391,851 ... H 7
Blekinge, 150,901 ... J 8
Gävleborg, 294,916 ... K 6
Göteborg och Bohus, 685,449 ... G 7
Gotland, 50,438 ... L 8
Halland, 185,810 ... H 8
Jämtland, 121,552 ... J 5
Jönköping, 292,303 ... H 8
Kalmar, 234,175 ... K 8
Kopparberg, 270,971 ... J 6
Kristianstad, 258,295 ... J 8
Kronoberg, 164,309 ... J 8
Malmöhus, 683,752 ... H 9
Norrbotten, 261,410 ... L 3
Örebro, 259,794 ... J 7
Östergötland, 369,374 ... J 7
Skaraborg, 248,970 ... H 7
Södermanland, 239,451 ... K 7
Stockholm, 1,406,580 ... L 7
Uppsala, 191,821 ... K 6
Värmland, 273,139 ... H 7
Västerbotten, 235,307 ... K 4
Västernorrland, 277,715 ... K 5
Västmanland, 255,142 ... K 7

CITIES and TOWNS

Åhus, 4,758 ... J 9
Alingsås, 19,810 ... H 7
Älmhult, 6,023 ... H 8
Alvesta, 8,957 ... J 8
Älvsbyn, 4,343 ... M 4
Åmål, 9,397 ... H 7
Anderstorp, 3,960 ... H 8
Ånge, 4,000 ... J 5
Ängelholm, 13,985 ... H 8
Arboga, 12,266 ... J 7
Årjäng, 2,893 ... H 7
Arvidsjaur, 7,767 ... L 4
Arvika, 15,901 ... H 7
Åseda, 3,629 ... J 8
Åsele, 4,727 ... K 4
Åtvidaberg, 9,010 ... K 7
Avesta, 29,232 ... J 6
Båstad, 2,202 ... H 8
Bengtsfors, 3,411 ... H 7
Boden, 24,912 ... M 4
Bollnäs, 17,123 ... K 6
Borås, 70,238 ... H 8
Borlänge, 29,097 ... J 6
Bräcke, 2,658 ... J 5
Brunflo, 2,700 ... J 5
Bureå, 4,583 ... M 4
Burträsk, 6,747 ... M 4
Charlottenberg, 3,112 ... H 6
Danderyd, 15,657 ... H 1
Djursholm, 7,681 ... H 1
Dorotea, 3,964 ... K 4
Edsbyn, 7,132 ... J 6
Eksjö, 9,897 ... J 8
Emmaboda, 3,697 ... J 8
Enköping, 17,684 ... G 1
Eskilstuna, 65,580 ... K 7
Eslöv, 14,737 ... H 9
Fagersta, 16,609 ... J 6
Falkenberg, 12,920 ... H 8
Falköping, 16,032 ... H 7
Falun, 33,840 ... J 6
Filipstad, 7,559 ... H 7
Finspång, 17,616 ... J 7
Flen, 9,112 ... K 7
Forshaga, 4,655 ... H 7
Frösö, 9,520 ... J 5
Frövi, 3,082 ... J 7
Gällivare, 9,718 ... M 3
Gamleby, 3,949 ... K 8
Gävle, 60,868 ... K 6
Gnesta, 3,275 ... G 2
Göteborg, 444,131 ... G 8
Göteborg, *647,122 ... G 8
Gränna, 3,195 ... J 8
Hagfors, 8,964 ... H 6
Hällefors, 12,011 ... J 7
Hallsberg, 12,121 ... J 7
Hallstahammar, 14,099 ... K 7
Halmstad, 46,655 ... H 8
Hälsingborg, 80,801 ... H 8
Haparanda, 9,429 ... N 4
Härnösand, 16,637 ... L 5
Hässleholm, 16,031 ... H 8
Hedemora, 17,744 ... K 6
Hjo, 4,783 ... J 7
Höganäs, 13,846 ... H 8
Holmsund, 5,778 ... M 5
Hudiksvall, 16,057 ... K 6
Hultsfred, 4,979 ... K 8
Huskvarna, 18,198 ... J 8
Järna, 4,591 ... G 2
Järpen, 2,962 ... H 5
Järvsö, 4,850 ... K 6
Jokkmokk, 4,869 ... L 3
Jönköping, 53,774 ... H 8
Jörn, 4,275 ... M 4
Kalmar, 37,938 ... K 8
Karlshamn, 12,351 ... J 8
Karlskoga, 38,284 ... J 7
Karlskrona, 37,358 ... K 8
Karlstad, 54,321 ... H 7
Katrineholm, 21,660 ... K 7
Kinna, 6,386 ... H 8
Kiruna, 29,210 ... L 3
Kisa, 4,353 ... J 8
Köping, 20,807 ... J 7
Kopparberg, 7,985 ... J 7
Kramfors, 11,729 ... K 5
Kristianstad, 27,527 ... J 9
Kristinehamn, 21,925 ... H 7
Kumla, 15,039 ... J 7
Kungälv, 11,213 ... G 8
Kungsbacka, 7,205 ... G 8
Laholm, 3,853 ... H 8
Landskrona, 32,079 ... H 9
Långsele, 4,640 ... K 5
Långshyttan, 3,124 ... K 6
Laxå, 9,498 ... J 7
Leksand, 8,608 ... J 6
Lidingö, 35,400 ... H 1
Lidköping, 19,700 ... H 7
Lindesberg, 6,863 ... J 7
Linköping, 77,881 ... K 7
Ljungby, 11,930 ... J 8
Ljusdal, 10,630 ... J 6
Ljusne, 4,808 ... K 6
Ludvika, 21,989 ... J 6
Luleå, 36,428 ... N 4
Lund, 50,494 ... H 9
Lycksele, 6,333 ... L 4
Lysekil, 8,000 ... G 7
Malmberget, 12,384 ... M 3
Malmköping, 3,450 ... F 1
Malmö, 256,064 ... H 9
Malmö, *428,338 ... H 9
Markaryd, 5,980 ... H 8
Mariefred, 2,502 ... G 1
Mariestad, 15,700 ... H 7
Mellerud, 4,317 ... H 7
Mjölby, 12,790 ... J 7
Mölndal, 31,072 ... H 8
Mönsterås, 6,687 ... K 8
Mora, 13,307 ... J 6
Motala, 27,907 ... J 7
Nacka, 25,798 ... H 1
Nässjö, 20,000 ... J 8
Nora, 9,215 ... J 7
Norberg, 6,160 ... K 6
Norrköping, 94,296 ... K 7
Norrsundet, 4,575 ... K 6
Norrtälje, 11,803 ... L 7
Norsjö, 5,171 ... L 4
Nybro, 10,956 ... J 8
Nyköping, 31,195 ... K 7
Nynäshamn, 10,676 ... L 7
Ockelbo, 5,819 ... K 6
Olofström, 16,218 ... J 8
Örbyhus, 2,266 ... K 6
Örebro, 86,977 ... J 7
Öregrund, 2,026 ... L 6
Örnsköldsvik, 16,539 ... L 5
Oskarshamn, 24,873 ... K 8
Östersund, 26,600 ... J 5
Östhammar, 8,858 ... L 6
Övertorneå, 3,589 ... N 3
Överum, 2,533 ... K 7
Oxelösund, 14,835 ... K 7
Pajala, 3,871 ... N 3
Piteå, 8,476 ... M 4
Ramnäs, 4,092 ... J 7
Ramsele, 4,547 ... K 5
Rättvik, 7,551 ... J 6
Rimbo, 3,426 ... L 7
Ronneby, 10,125 ... J 8
Ryd, 4,100 ... J 8
Säffle, 12,599 ... H 7
Sala, 11,800 ... K 7
Saltsjöbaden, 6,507 ... J 1
Sandviken, 25,476 ... K 6
Säter, 4,629 ... J 6
Sävsjö, 5,547 ... J 8
Sigtuna, 3,970 ... H 1
Simrishamn, 7,966 ... J 9
Skänninge, 4,482 ... J 7
Skara, 10,376 ... H 7
Skellefteå, 61,880 ... M 4
Skövde, 27,976 ... H 7
Smedjebacken, 10,504 ... J 6
Söderhamn, 13,778 ... K 6
Söderköping, 5,954 ... K 7
Södertälje, 52,601 ... G 1
Sollefteå, 9,715 ... K 5
Sollentuna, 35,038 ... H 1
Solna, 57,707 ... H 1
Sölvesborg, 6,782 ... J 9
Sorsele, 3,550 ... K 4
Stockholm (cap.), 756,697 ... G 1
Stockholm, *1,288,769 ... G 1
Storvik, 2,432 ... K 6
Strängnäs, 9,506 ... F 1
Strömstad, 9,817 ... G 7
Strömsund, 6,058 ... K 5
Sundbyberg, 28,773 ... G 1
Sundsvall, 62,222 ... K 5
Sunne, 11,018 ... H 7
Sveg, 4,975 ... J 5
Svenljunga, 2,925 ... H 8
Täby, 33,694 ... H 1
Tidaholm, 7,250 ... J 7
Tierp, 4,303 ... K 6
Tillberga, 270 ... K 7
Timrå, 12,800 ... K 5
Tomelilla, 6,349 ... J 9
Torsby, 6,796 ... H 6
Torshälla, 7,939 ... K 7
Tranås, 18,845 ... J 7
Trelleborg, 35,249 ... H 9
Trollhättan, 40,945 ... H 7
Uddevalla, 36,510 ... G 7
Ulricehamn, 8,504 ... H 8
Umeå, 51,955 ... M 5
Uppsala, 97,315 ... L 7
Vadstena, 6,893 ... J 7
Vaggeryd, 4,840 ... J 8
Valdemarsvik, 3,590 ... K 7
Vänersborg, 19,975 ... H 7
Vännäs, 4,045 ... L 5
Vansbro, 2,941 ... H 6
Vara, 11,056 ... H 7
Varberg, 18,451 ... G 8
Värnamo, 15,939 ... J 8
Västerås, 110,539 ... J 7
Västerhaninge, 9,814 ... H 1
Västervik, 23,014 ... K 8
Vaxholm, 4,322 ... J 1
Vaxjö, 32,760 ... J 8
Vetlanda, 10,780 ... J 8
Vilhelmina, 9,426 ... K 4
Vimmerby, 7,257 ... J 8
Virserum, 4,650 ... J 8
Visby, 18,338 ... L 8
Vislanda, 2,594 ... H 8
Wallhamn ... G 7
Ystad, 14,002 ... H 9

OTHER FEATURES

Angerman (river) ... K 5
Asnen (lake) ... J 8
Bothnia (gulf) ... M 5
Byske (river) ... L 4
Fårö (isl.), 790 ... L 8
Göta (river) ... H 7
Gotland (isl.), 50,438 ... L 8
Hornslandet (pen.) ... K 6
Kalix (river) ... N 3
Kalmarsund (sound) ... K 8
Kattegat (strait) ... G 8
Kebnekaise (mt.) ... L 3
Lainio (river) ... N 3
Lapland (dist.) ... K 2
Lule (river) ... M 3
Muonio (river) ... M 2
Öland (isl.), 20,416 ... K 8
Ornö (isl.), 224 ... J 1
Österdal (river) ... H 6
Pite (river) ... M 4
Skellefte (river) ... L 4
Stora Lulevatten (lake) ... L 3
Storuman (lake) ... K 4
Sulitjelma (mt.) ... K 3
Torne (river) ... M 3
Torneträsk (lake) ... L 2
Uddjaur (lake) ... L 4
Ume (river) ... L 4
Vänern (lake) ... H 7
Vättern (lake) ... J 7
Vesterdal (river) ... H 6
Vindel (river) ... L 4
Vojmsjön (lakes) ... J 4

*City and suburbs.
†Population of parish or commune.

DENMARK

INTERNAL DIVISIONS

Århus (county), 525,167 ... D 5
Bornholm (county), 47,405 ... F 9
Copenhagen (commune), 634,500 ... F 6
Færøe Islands, 38,000 ... B 2
Frederiksberg (commune), 102,751 ... F 6
Frederiksborg (county), 252,557 ... F 5
Fyn (county), 430,958 ... D 7
København (Copenhagen) (commune), 634,500 ... F 6
København (county), 609,469 ... F 6
Nordjylland (county), 455,062 ... D 4
Ribe (county), 196,894 ... B 6
Ringkøbing (county), 240,014 ... B 5
Roskilde (county), 147,434 ... E 6
Sønderjylland (county), 237,270 ... C 7
Storstrøm (county), 251,815 ... E 7
Vejle (county), 304,358 ... C 6
Vestsjælland (county), 256,997 ... E 6
Viborg (county), 220,214 ... B 4

CITIES and TOWNS

Åbenrå, 15,156 ... C 7
Åbybro, 6,309 ... C 3
Ærøskøbing, 1,228 ... D 8
Agerbæk, 804, ... B 6
Åkirkeby, 1,549 ... F 9
Ålborg, 82,346 ... D 4
Ålborg, *153,307 ... D 4
Ålestrup, 5,228 ... C 4
Allingåbro, 1,352 ... D 5
Allinge-Sandvig, 2,023 ... F 8
Ansager, 1,123 ... B 6
Arden, 1,353 ... C 4
Århus, 109,498 ... D 5
Århus, *232,173 ... D 5
Års, 5,075 ... C 4
Årup, †5,033 ... D 7
Aså, 1,348 ... D 3
Askov, 725 ... C 7
Asnæs, 2,493 ... E 6
Assens, Århus, 1,266 ... D 4
Assens, Fyn, †10,777 ... D 7
Augustenborg, 3,537 ... D 8
Auning, 1,367 ... D 5
Avlum, 3,694 ... B 5
Bælum, 1,922 ... D 4
Bagenkop, 774 ... D 8
Ballerup, †50,128 ... F 6
Bandholm, 1,248 ... E 8
Bested, 1,886 ... B 4
Birkerød, †20,835 ... F 6
Bjerringbro, 6,469 ... C 5
Bogense, †6,450 ... D 6
Bolderslev, 729 ... C 8
Børkop, †9,053 ... C 6
Borup, 2,344 ... E 7
Brabrand, 12,514 ... C 5
Brædstrup, 3,925 ... C 6
Bramminge, 5,937 ... B 7
Brande, 6,814 ... B 6
Bredebro, †3,747 ... B 7
Broager, †5,387 ... C 8
Brønderslev, 10,274 ... C 3
Brøns, 867 ... B 7
Brørup, 4,066 ... C 7
Brovst, †8,086 ... C 3
Christiansfeld, 958 ... C 7
Copenhagen (cap.), 634,500 ... F 6
Copenhagen, 1,346,720 ... F 6
Dronninglund, 9,179 ... D 3
Dybvad, 793 ... D 3
Ebeltoft, 3,168 ... D 5
Egernsund, 1,360 ... C 8
Egtved, 2,857 ... C 6
Ejby, 3,265 ... D 7
Esbjerg, 62,483 ... B 7
Fåborg, 5,630 ... D 7
Fakse, 7,268 ... F 7
Fakse Ladeplads, 1,639 ... F 7
Farsø, 4,126 ... C 4
Farum, †9,583 ... F 6
Fjerritslev, 2,686 ... C 3
Fredensborg, 3,977 ... F 6
Fredericia, 34,464 ... C 6
Frederiksberg, 102,751 ... F 6
Frederikshavn, 24,640 ... D 3
Frederikssund, 7,835 ... E 6
Frederiksværk, 4,385 ... E 6
Fuglebjerg, 5,082 ... E 7
Gedser, 1,195 ... F 8
Gedsted, 1,924 ... C 4
Gelsted, 2,461 ... C 7
Gentofte, †78,641 ... F 6
Gilleleje, 4,300 ... F 5
Give, 8,573 ... C 6
Gjerlev, 1,209 ... D 4
Glamsbjerg, †5,677 ... D 7
Glostrup, †28,169 ... F 6
Glumsø, 819 ... E 7
Glyngøre, 1,047 ... C 4
Gørding, 2,422 ... B 7
Gørlev, 2,437 ... E 6
Græsted, 2,899 ... F 5
Gram, 3,935 ... C 7
Gråsten, †6,336 ... C 8
Grenå, 13,277 ... D 5
Grindsted, 9,345 ... B 6
Gylling, 990 ... D 6
Haderslev, 20,291 ... C 7
Hadsten, 6,919 ... C 5
Hadsund, 6,862 ... D 4
Hals, 3,016 ... D 3
Hammel, 7,456 ... C 5
Hammerum, 2,415 ... C 5
Hanstholm, 3,358 ... B 3
Harboør, 2,224 ... A 4
Hårby, †4,671 ... D 7
Hårlev, 980 ... F 7
Hasle, 1,542 ... F 8
Haslev, 10,173 ... E 7
Havdrup, 5,163 ... F 6
Hedensted, 4,791 ... C 6
Hellebæk, 2,240 ... F 5
Helsinge, 4,707 ... F 6
Helsingør, 30,211 ... F 6
Herning, 32,512 ... B 5
Hillerød, 23,500 ... F 6
Hinnerup, †5,614 ... D 5
Hirtshals, 8,598 ... C 2
Hjallerup, 1,385 ... C 3
Hjerm, 1,421 ... B 5
Hjørring, 15,699 ... C 3
Hobro, 8,845 ... C 4
Højer, 1,407 ... B 8
Højslev, 2,863 ... C 4
Holbæk, 17,892 ... E 6
Holeby, 4,359 ... E 8
Holstebro, 24,009 ... B 5
Holsted, 2,773 ... B 6
Høng, †7,355 ... E 7
Hornslet, 3,371 ... D 5
Horsens, 35,621 ... C 6
Hørsholm, 18,060 ... F 6
Hørve, 2,829 ... E 6
Hov, 607 ... D 6
Humlum, 2,357 ... B 4
Hundested, †6,301 ... E 6
Hurup, 2,560 ... B 4
Hvidbjerg, 2,361 ... B 4
Hvide Sande, 1,775 ... A 6
Hviding, 750 ... B 7
Ikast, 11,110 ... C 5
Jelling, 4,780 ... C 6
Jerslev, 2,672 ... D 3
Juelsminde, 7,245 ... D 6
Jyderup, 3,246 ... E 6
Kalundborg, 11,762 ... D 6
Karby, 2,302 ... B 4
Karise, 1,733 ... F 7
Karup, 1,891 ... C 5
Kastrup ... F 6
Kerteminde, †10,296 ... D 7
Kibæk, 1,179 ... B 5
Kjellerup, 3,506 ... C 5
Klaksvík, Færøe Is., 3,894 ... B 2
København (Copenhagen), (cap.), 634,500 ... F 6
Køge, 17,360 ... F 7
Kolding, 39,609 ... C 7
Kolind, 2,590 ... D 5
Kørsør, 15,550 ... E 7
Kværndrup, 1,963 ... D 7
Langå, 2,801 ... C 5
Lem, 1,060 ... B 5
Lemvig, 6,766 ... B 4
Løgstør, 3,666 ... C 4
Løgumkloster, 2,089 ... B 7
Lohals, 634 ... D 7
Løjt Kirkeby, 2,724 ... C 7
Løkken, 1,388 ... C 3
Løsning, 2,418 ... C 6
Lundby, 2,392 ... E 7
Lunderskov, †4,402 ... C 7
Lyngby, †61,245 ... F 6
Malling, 4,332 ... D 5
Mariager, 3,733 ... D 4
Maribo, 5,235 ... E 8
Marstal, 4,095 ... D 8
Middelfart, 9,015 ... C 7
Møgeltønder, 1,181 ... B 8
Næstved, 24,831 ... E 7
Nakskov, 15,994 ... E 8
Neksø, 3,499 ... F 9
Nibe, 2,786 ... C 4
Nordborg, 3,016 ... C 7
Nordby, 2,353 ... B 7
Nørre Åby, †5,195 ... C 7
Nørre Alslev, 1,939 ... E 8
Nørre Broby, 858 ... D 7
Nørre Nebel, 867 ... B 6
Nørre Snede, 3,019 ... C 6
Nørresundby, 23,848 ... D 3
Nørre Vorupør, 632 ... B 4
Nyborg, 11,698 ... D 7
Nykøbing, Storstrøm, 17,364 ... E 8
Nykøbing, Vestsjælland, 4,905 ... E 6
Nykøbing, Viborg, 8,710 ... B 4
Nysted, 1,211 ... E 8
Odder, 8,144 ... D 6
Odense, 102,698 ... D 7
Odense, *163,593 ... D 7
Ølgod, 7,091 ... B 6
Ørsted, 1,925 ... D 5
Øster Vrå, 931 ... D 3
Otterup, †10,462 ... D 7
Ovtrup, 549 ... B 6
Pandrup, 1,383 ... C 3
Pedersborg, 1,560 ... E 7

Agriculture, Industry and Resources

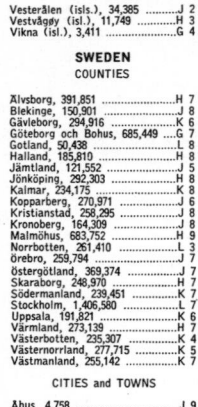

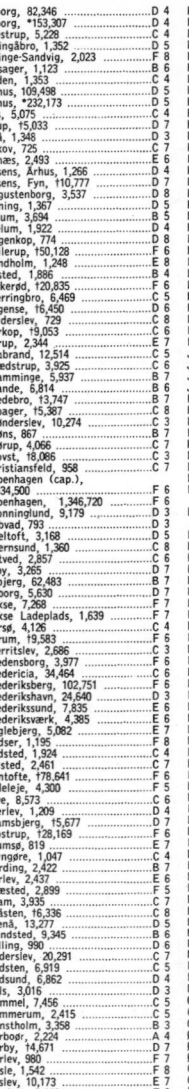

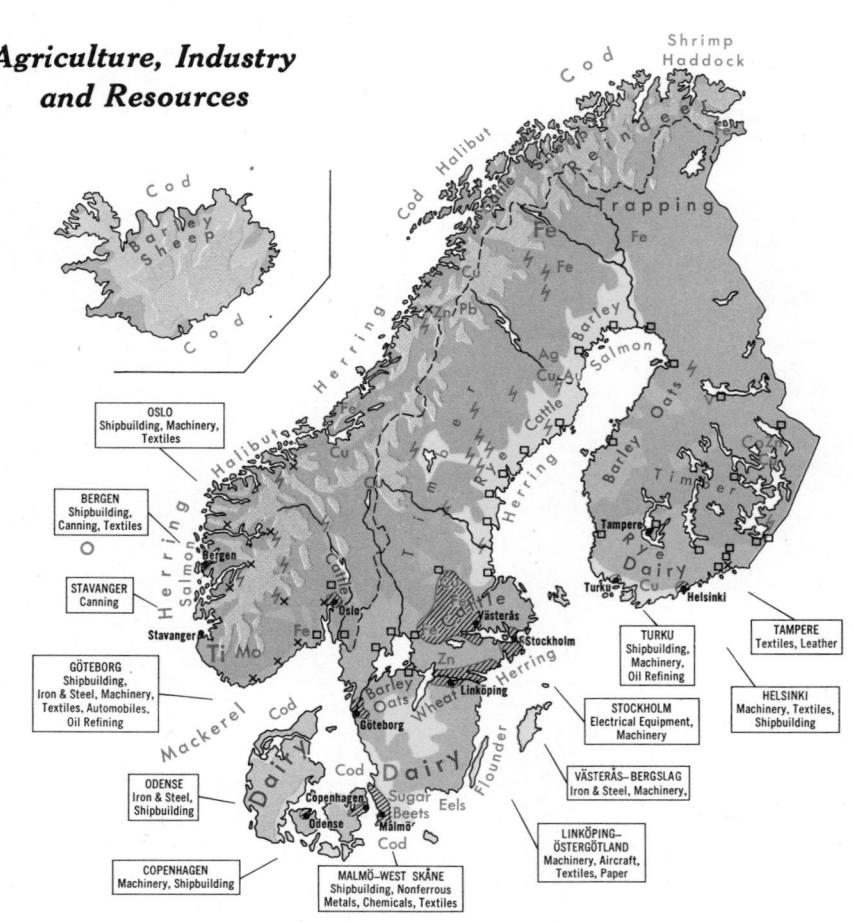

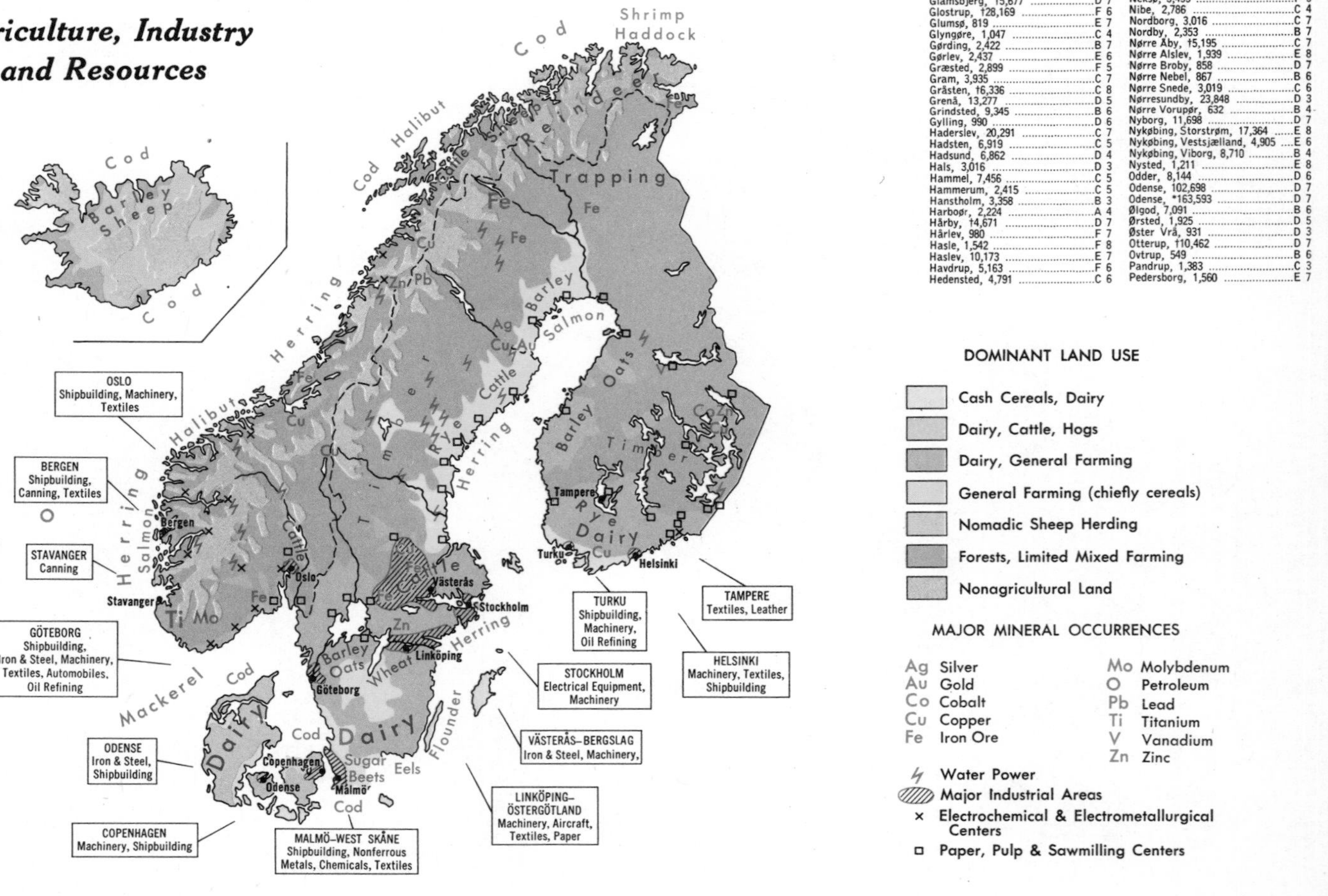

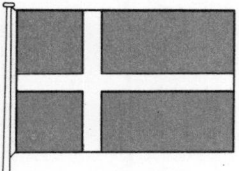

DENMARK

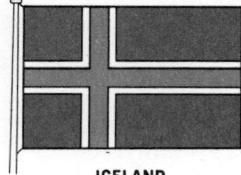

ICELAND

DENMARK
AREA 16,614 sq. mi.
POPULATION 4,912,865
CAPITAL Copenhagen
LARGEST CITY Copenhagen
HIGHEST POINT Yding Skovhøj 568 ft.
MONETARY UNIT krone (crown)
MAJOR LANGUAGE Danish
MAJOR RELIGION Protestantism

ICELAND
AREA 39,768 sq. mi.
POPULATION 204,578
CAPITAL Reykjavík
LARGEST CITY Reykjavík
HIGHEST POINT Hvannadalshnúkur 6,952 ft.
MONETARY UNIT króna (crown)
MAJOR LANGUAGE Icelandic
MAJOR RELIGION Protestantism

DENMARK and ICELAND

CONIC PROJECTION

SCALE OF MILES
0 10 20 30 40 50

SCALE OF KILOMETERS
0 10 20 30 40 50

Capitals of Countries _____ ☆
Capitals of Counties (amter) ___ ⌂
International Boundaries _____
Internal Boundaries _____

Denmark is divided into fourteen counties plus
Copenhagen and Frederiksberg communes.

© Copyright HAMMOND INCORPORATED, Maplewood, N.J.

FAERØE ISLANDS

BORNHOLM

Same scale as main map

GERMANY

CONIC PROJECTION

SCALE OF MILES

SCALE OF KILOMETERS

Capitals of Countries .... ✩
State and District Capitals .... ◉
International Boundaries ....
State and District Boundaries ....
Canals ....

East Germany is divided into districts bearing the same name as their respective capitals.

BERLIN inset

© Copyright by C.S. Hammond & Co., Maplewood, N.J.

WEST GERMANY

AREA 95,959 sq. mi.
POPULATION 61,194,600
CAPITAL Bonn
LARGEST CITY Berlin (West)
HIGHEST POINT Zugspitze 9,718 ft.
MONETARY UNIT West German Deutsch mark
MAJOR LANGUAGE German
MAJOR RELIGIONS Protestantism, Roman Catholicism

EAST GERMANY

AREA 41,814 sq. mi.
POPULATION 17,117,000
CAPITAL Berlin (East)
LARGEST CITY Berlin (East)
HIGHEST POINT Fichtelberg 3,983 ft.
MONETARY UNIT East German Deutsch mark
MAJOR LANGUAGE German
MAJOR RELIGIONS Protestantism, Roman Catholicism

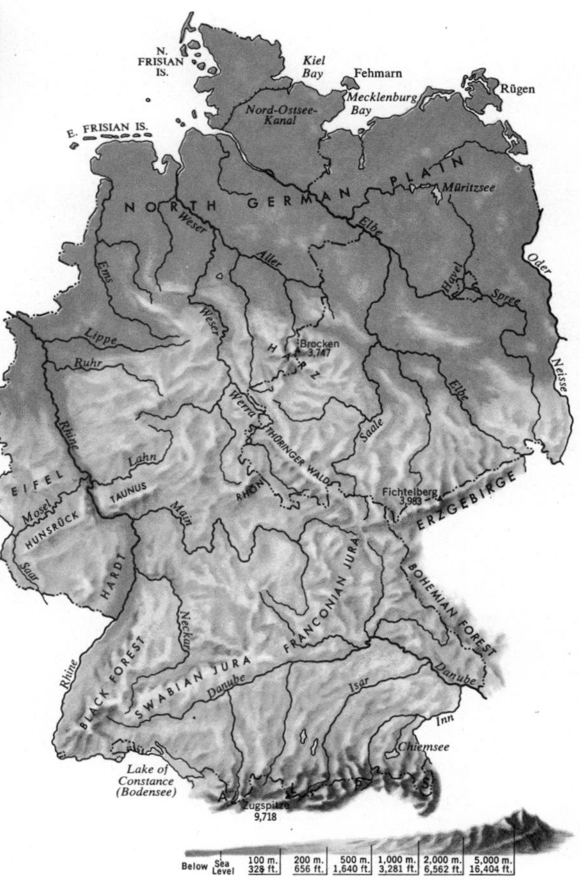
Topography
0
50
100
MILES
N. FRISIAN IS.
Kiel Bay
Fehmarn
Rügen
Mecklenburg Bay
Nord-Ostsee-Kanal
E. FRISIAN IS.
NORTH GERMAN PLAIN
Müritzsee
Weser
Elbe
Oder
Ems
Aller
Havel
Spree
Lippe
Brocken 3,747
HARZ
Ruhr
Werra
Neisse
Rhine
Lahn
THÜRINGER WALD
Saale
EIFEL
TAUNUS
RHÖN
Main
Mosel
HUNSRÜCK
Fichtelberg 3,983
ERZGEBIRGE
Saar
HARDT
FRANCONIAN JURA
BOHEMIAN FOREST
Neckar
SWABIAN JURA
BLACK FOREST
Danube
Isar
Inn
Chiemsee
Lake of Constance (Bodensee)
Zugspitze 9,718
Below
Sea Level
100 m. 328 ft.
200 m. 656 ft.
500 m. 1,640 ft.
1,000 m. 3,281 ft.
2,000 m. 6,562 ft.
5,000 m. 16,404 ft.

EAST GERMANY

DISTRICTS

Berlin (East), 1,084,000 F 4
Cottbus, 839,133 F 3
Dresden, 1,887,739 E 3
Erfurt, 1,249,540 D 3
Frankfurt, 660,666 F 2
Gera, 735,175 D 3
Halle, 1,932,733 E 3
Karl-Marx-Stadt, 2,082,927 E 3
Leipzig, 1,510,773 E 3
Magdeburg, 1,323,644 D 2
Neubrandenburg, 633,209 E 2
Potsdam, 1,127,498 E 2
Rostock, 842,743 D 1
Schwerin, 594,786 D 2
Suhl, 549,398 D 3

CITIES and TOWNS

Aken, 12,126 D 3
Altenburg, 47,462 E 3
Angermünde, 12,200 E 2
Anklam, 19,436 E 2
Annaberg-Buchholz, 28,663 E 3
Apolda, 29,735 D 3
Arnstadt, 27,674 D 3
Aschersleben, 36,777 D 3
Aue, 31,723 E 3
Auerbach, 19,673 E 3
Bad Doberan, 13,197 D 1
Bad Dürrenberg, 16,500 D 3
Bad Freienwalde, 11,845 F 2
Bad Langensalza, 16,952 D 3
Bad Salzungen, 12,722 C 3
Barth, 12,688 E 1
Bautzen, 44,041 F 3
Bergen, 10,979 E 1
Berlin (East) (capital), 1,084,000 F 4
Bernau, 14,078 E 2
Bernburg, 45,885 D 3
Bischofswerda, 11,345 F 3
Bitterfeld, 30,916 E 3
Blankenburg, 19,595 D 3
Boizenburg, 11,370 D 2
Borna, 20,669 E 3
Brandenburg, 90,753 E 2
Burg, 29,906 D 2
Calbe, 16,464 D 3
Chemnitz (Karl-Marx-Stadt), 295,443 D 3
Coswig, 18,600 E 3
Cottbus, 75,541 F 3
Crimmitschau, 30,752 E 3
Delitzsch, 23,480 E 3
Demmin, 16,755 E 2
Dessau, 95,682 E 3
Döbeln, 28,430 E 3
Dresden, 499,848 E 3
Ebersbach, 11,293 F 3
Eberswalde, 33,680 E 2
Eilenburg, 21,366 E 3
Eisenach, 50,234 D 3
Eisenberg, 13,858 D 3
Eisenhüttenstadt, 38,138 F 2
Eisleben, 32,402 D 3
Erfurt, 193,745 D 3
Falkensee, 29,884 E 3
Falkenstein, 15,269 E 3
Finsterwalde, 22,441 E 3
Forst, 29,823 F 3
Frankfurt-an-der-Oder, 58,866 F 2
Freiberg, 49,122 E 3
Freital, 42,675 E 3
Fürstenwalde, 30,527 F 2
Gardelegen, 13,218 D 2
Genthin, 15,619 E 2
Gera, 109,989 E 3
Glauchau, 33,103 E 3
Görlitz, 88,632 F 3
Gotha, 57,692 D 3
Greifswald, 47,402 E 1
Greiz, 39,313 E 3
Grevesmühlen, 10,914 D 2
Grimma, 16,509 E 3
Grimmen, 12,943 E 1
Grossenhain, 19,848 E 3
Grossräschen, 12,737 E 3
Guben (Wilhelm-Pieck-Stadt), 26,586 F 3
Güstrow, 38,185 E 2
Hagenow, 10,434 D 2
Halberstadt, 46,071 D 3
Haldensleben, 20,547 D 2
Halle, 263,928 D 3
Heidenau, 20,161 E 3
Heiligenstadt, 12,627 D 3
Hennigsdorf, 21,398 E 3
Hettstedt, 19,218 D 3
Hoyerswerda, 43,922 F 3
Ilmenau, 19,852 D 3
Jena, 85,032 D 3
Johanngeorgenstadt, 10,801 E 3
Jüterbog, 14,416 E 3
Kamenz, 16,236 F 3
Karl-Marx-Stadt, 295,443 E 3
Kleinmachnow, 13,919 E 4
Klingenthal, 14,748 E 3
Köpenick, 52,294 F 4
Köthen, 38,154 E 3
Kottbus (Cottbus), 75,541 F 3
Lauchhammer, 28,680 E 3
Leipzig, 590,291 E 3
Lichtenberg, 62,841 F 4
Limbach-Oberfrohna, 26,053 E 3
Löbau, 17,068 F 3
Lübben, 12,742 E 3
Lübbenau, 16,976 F 3
Luckenwalde, 29,282 E 2
Ludwigslust, 11,512 D 2
Magdeburg, 268,269 D 2
Markkleeberg, 21,854 E 3
Meerane, 24,262 E 3
Meiningen, 25,025 D 3
Meissen, 47,166 E 3
Merseburg, 55,562 D 3
Meuselwitz, 10,582 E 3
Mittweida, 20,440 E 3
Mücheln, 10,842 D 3
Mühlhausen, 46,155 D 3
Nauen, 12,017 E 2
Naumburg, 37,990 D 3
Neubrandenburg, 38,740 E 2
Neuenhagen, 13,116 F 4
Neugersdorf, 11,889 F 3
Neuruppin, 22,424 E 2
Neustadt, 10,085 D 3
Neustrelitz, 27,624 E 2
Nordhausen, 42,279 D 3
Oelsnitz, 15,954 E 3
Oelsnitz im Erzgebirge, 18,377 E 3
Olbernhau, 14.240 E 3
Oranienburg, 20,401 E 2
Oschatz, 15,582 E 3
Oschersleben, 18,078 D 2
Pankow. 68,785 F 3
Parchim, 19,226 D 2
Pasewalk, 14,086 F 2
Perleberg, 13,707 D 2
Pirna, 42,562 E 3
Plauen, 81,739 E 3
Pössneck, 19,468 D 3
Potsdam, 110,671 E 2
Prenzlau, 20,276 F 2
Quedlinburg, 30,840 D 3
Radeberg, 17,410 E 3
Radebeul, 41,437 E 3
Rathenow, 28,979 E 2
Reichenbach, 29,372 E 3
Ribnitz-Damgarten, 15,301 E 1
Riesa, 43,322 E 3
Rosslau, 16,256 E 3
Rosswein, 10,649 E 3
Rostock, 190,275 E 1
Rüdersdorf, 11,837 E 2
Rudolstadt, 30,433 D 3
Saalfeld, 32,145 D 3
Salzwedel, 19,534 D 2
Sangerhausen, 29,373 D 3
Sassnitz, 13,253 E 1
Schkeuditz, 17,131 E 3
Schmalkalden, 14,569 D 3
Schmölln, 13,992 E 3
Schneeberg, 21,225 E 3
Schönebeck, 44,551 D 2
Schöneiche, 10,101 E 2
Schwedt, 23,359 F 2
Schwerin, 92,356 D 2
Sebnitz, 14,655 F 3
Senftenberg, 24,532 F 3
Sömmerda, 16,061 D 3
Sondershausen, 22,456 D 3
Sonneberg, 29,804 D 3
Spremberg, 23,367 F 3
Stassfurt, 25,622 D 3
Stendal, 36,193 D 2
Stralsund, 68,925 E 1
Strausberg, 17,985 F 2
Suhl, 28,698 D 3
Tangermünde, 12,992 D 2
Teltow, 13,735 E 4
Templin, 11,203 E 2
Teterow, 11,039 E 2
Thale, 17,273 D 3
Torgau, 20,941 E 3
Torgelow, 13,584 F 2
Treptow, 22,302 F 4
Ueckermünde, 11,614 F 2
Zwickau, 127,688 E 3
Waltershausen, 14,250 D 3
Waren, 20,008 E 2
Weida, 11,950 D 3
Weimar, 64,300 D 3
Weissenfels, 47,704 D 3
Weissensee, 50,691 F 3
Weisswasser, 16,016 F 3
Werdau, 23,783 E 3
Wernigerode, 32,579 D 3
Wilhelm-Pieck-Stadt, 26,586 F 3
Wismar, 55,235 D 2
Wittenberg, 46,816 E 3
Wittenberge, 32,621 D 2
Wittstock, 10,358 E 2
Wolgast, 14,955 E 1
Wurzen, 24,349 E 3
Zehdenick, 12,306 E 2
Zeitz, 46,393 E 3
Zella-Mehlis, 17,121 D 3
Zerbst, 19,527 E 3
Zeulenroda, 18,534 D 3
Zittau, 43,259 F 3
Zwickau, 127,688 E 3

OTHER FEATURES

Altmark (reg.), 288,928 D 2
Arkona (cape) E 1
Baltic (sea) F 1
Black Elster (riv.) E 3
Brandenburg (region), 3,726,413 E 2
Brocken (mt.) D 3
Darsser Ort (point) E 1
Elbe (riv.) D 2
Elster (riv.) E 3
Erzgebirge (Ore) (mts.) E 3
Fichtelberg (mt.) E 3
Havel (riv.) E 2
Kummerowersee (lake) E 2
Lusatia (reg.) F 3
Malchinersee (lake) E 2
Mecklenburg (region), 1,226,685 E 2
Mecklenburg (bay) D 1
Mulde (riv.) E 3
Müritzee (lake) E 2
Neisse (riv.) F 3
Oder (riv.) F 2
Ore (Erzgebirge) (mts.) E 3
Penne (riv.) E 2
Plauersee (lake) E 2
Pomerania (region), 711,075 E 2
Pomeranian (bay) F 1
Rhön (mts.) D 3
Rügen (isl.), 92,348 E 1
Saale (riv.) D 3
Saxony (region), 5,318,661 E 3
Schaalsee (lake) D 2
Schwerinersee (lake) D 2
Spree (riv.) F 3
Spreewald (forest) F 3
Stettin (bay) F 2
Stubbenkammer (point) E 1
Thüringer Wald (forest) D 3
Thuringia (Thüringen) (reg.), 2,017,924 D 3
Tollensee (lake) E 2
Ücker (riv.) E 2
Unstrut (riv.) D 3
Usedom (isl.) F 1
Warnow (riv.) D 2
Werra (riv.) D 3
White Elster (riv.) E 3

WEST GERMANY

STATES

Baden-Württemberg, 8,909,700 C 4
Bavaria, 10,568,900 D 4
Berlin (West) (free city), 2,134,256 E 4
Bremen, 755,977 C 2
Hamburg, 1,817,122 D 2
Hesse, 5,422,600 C 3
Lower Saxony, 7,100,400 C 2
North Rhine-Westphalia, 17,129,800 B 3
Rhineland-Palatinate, 3,671,300 B 4
Saarland, 1,127,400 B 4
Schleswig-Holstein, 2,557,200 C 1

CITIES and TOWNS

Aachen, 177,642 B 3
Aalen, 35,102 D 4
Ahlen, 50,411 B 3
Ahrensburg, 25,829 D 2
Alfeld, 13,726 C 2
Alsdorf, 31,726 B 3
Altena, 31,164 B 3
Altona C 2
Alzey, 12,749 C 4
Amberg, 42,141 E 4
Andernach, 22,367 B 3
Ansbach, 30,083 D 4
Arnsberg, 22,577 C 3
Aschaffenburg, 56,236 C 4
Augsburg, 214,376 D 4
Aurich, 12,299 B 2
Backnang, 28,086 C 4
Bad Dürkheim, 15,792 C 4
Baden-Baden, 38,852 C 4
Bad Harzburg, 11,356 D 3
Bad Hersfeld, 23,494 C 3
Bad Homburg vor der Höhe, 41,236 C 3
Bad Honnef am Rhein, 20,649 B 3
Bad Kissingen, 12,672 D 3
Bad Kreuznach, 42,707 B 4
Bad Mergentheim, 12,552 D 4
Bad Nauheim, 15,222 C 3
Bad Oeynhausen, 14,127 C 2
Bad Oldesloe, 18,915 D 2
Bad Pyrmont, 16,527 C 2
Bad Reichenhall, 14,894 E 5
Bad Salzuflen, 49,030 C 2
Bad Schwartau, 16,909 D 2
Bad Segeberg, 12,494 D 2
Bad Tölz, 12,468 D 5
Bad Vilbel, 18,315 C 3
Bad Wildungen, 12,189 C 3
Balingen, 13,693 C 4
Bamberg, 68,713 D 4
Bayreuth, 63,387 D 4
Bendorf, 14,361 B 3
Bensheim, 27,495 C 4
Berchtesgaden, 4,074 E 5
Bergisch Gladbach, 50,095 B 3
Berlin (West), 2,134,256 E 4
Betzdorf, 10,388 B 3
Biberach an der Riss, 25,597 C 4
Bielefeld, 169,347 C 2
Bietigheim, 22,488 C 4
Bingen, 24,452 B 4
Böblingen, 36,644 C 4
Bocholt, 48,134 B 3
Bochum, 346,886 B 3
Bonn (cap.), 299,376 B 3
Borghorst, 17,072 B 2
Borken, 30,614 B 3
Bottrop, 108,161 B 3
Brackwede, 40,254 C 3
Brake, 19,388 C 2
Bramsche, 10,733 B 2
Braunschweig (Brunswick), 225,168 D 2
Bremen, 607,184 C 2
Bremerhaven, 148,793 C 2
Brilon, 15,301 C 3
Bruchsal, 27,103 C 4
Brühl, 41,782 B 3
Brunswick, 225,168 D 2
Bückeburg, 13,396 C 2
Burghausen, 16,630 E 4
Burgsteinfurt, 12,554 B 2
Buxtehude, 23,140 C 2
Celle, 56,335 D 2
Charlottenburg F 4
Clausthal-Zellerfeld, 15,744 D 3
Cloppenburg, 18,162 B 2
Coburg, 41,369 D 3
Coesfeld, 26,565 B 3
Cologne, 866,308 B 3
Crailsheim, 16,687 D 4
Cuxhaven, 45,218 C 2
Dachau, 33,093 D 4
Darmstadt, 141,075 C 4
Deggendorf, 18,601 E 4
Delmenhorst, 63,685 C 2
Detmold, 64,473 C 3
Diepholz, 11,639 C 2
Dillenburg, 10,236 C 3
Dillingen an der Donau, 11,606 D 4
Dingolfing, 10,747 E 4
Donaueschingen, 11,643 C 5
Donauwörth, 11,266 D 4
Dorsten, 39,393 B 3
Dortmund, 648,883 B 3
Duderstadt, 10,421 D 3
Dudweiler, 30,078 B 4
Duisburg, 457,891 B 3
Dülmen, 21,094 B 3
Düren, 54,867 B 3
Düsseldorf, 680,806 B 3
Eberbach, 14,369 C 4
Ebingen, 22,004 C 4
Eckernförde, 21,971 D 1
Ehingen, 12,957 C 4
Eichstätt, 10,040 D 4
Einbeck, 18,618 C 3
Eiserfeld, 22,490 B 1
Ellwangen, 13,128 D 4
Elmshorn, 41,353 C 2
Emden, 48,313 B 2
Emmendingen, 15,986 B 4
Emmerich, 24,512 B 3
Erkelenz, 12,275 B 3
Erlangen, 85,727 D 4
Eschwege, 22,219 D 3
Eschweiler, 39,622 B 3
Espelkamp, 12,309 C 2
Essen, 704,769 B 3
Esslingen am Neckar, 86,497 C 4
Ettlingen, 21,342 C 4
Euskirchen, 41,965 B 3
Eutin, 18,177 D 1
Fellbach, 29,343 C 4
Flensburg, 96,778 C 1
Forchheim, 21,582 D 4
Frankenthal, 40,505 C 4
Frankfurt am Main, 660,410 C 3
Frechen, 30,786 B 3
Freiburg im Breisgau, 165,960 B 5
Freising, 30,264 D 4
Freudenstadt, 14,356 C 4
Friedberg, 17,401 C 3
Friedrichshafen, 42,483 C 5
Fulda, 44,262 C 3
Fürstenfeldbruck, 22,495 D 4
Fürth, 94,310 D 4
Füssen, 10,891 D 5
Gaggenau, 14,773 C 4
Garmisch-Partenkirchen, 27,313 D 5
Geesthacht, 23,594 D 2
Geislingen an der Steige, 27,209 C 4
Geldern, 22,602 B 3
Gelsenkirchen, 348,620 B 3
Giessen, 74,731 C 3
Gifhorn, 23,001 D 2
Glückstadt, 16,199 C 2
Goch, 27,721 B 3
Göggingen, 15,840 D 4
Göppingen, 46,899 C 4
Goslar, 41,653 D 3
Göttingen, 115,227 D 3
Grevenbroich, 28,197 B 3
Griesheim, 16,392 C 4
Gronau, 26,596 B 2
Gummersbach, 45,026 B 3
Günzburg, 13,449 D 4
Gütersloh, 76,343 C 3
Haar, 12,388 D 4
Hagen, 203,048 B 3
Haltern, 15,264 B 3
Hamburg, 1,817,122 D 2
Hameln, 47,114 C 2
Hamm, 84,302 B 3
Hanau, 55,674 C 3
Hannover, 517,783 C 2
Harburg-Wilhelmsburg C 2
Hassloch, 17,852 C 4
Haunstetten, 22,205 D 4
Heide, 23,419 C 1
Heidelberg, 121,929 C 4
Heidenheim an der Brenz, 50,170 D 4
Heilbronn, 99,440 C 4
Helmstedt, 27,161 D 2
Hennef, 26,589 B 3
Herborn, 10,395 C 3
Herford, 67,267 C 2
Herne, 100,798 B 3
Hildesheim, 95,926 D 2
Hockenheim, 15,615 C 4
Hof, 54,805 D 3
Holzminden, 22,273 C 3
Homburg, 32,258 B 4
Höxter, 32,823 C 3
Hürth, 52,011 B 3
Husum, 25,037 C 1
Hüttental, 40,287 C 3
Ibbenbüren, 17,780 B 2
Idar-Oberstein, 32,590 B 4
Immenstadt, 10,775 D 5
Ingolstadt, 71,954 D 4
Iserlohn, 57,792 B 3
Itzehoe, 35,678 C 2
Jülich, 20,152 B 3
Kaiserslautern, 99,859 B 4
Karlsruhe, 257,144 C 4
Kassel, 213,494 C 3
Kaufbeuren, 39,940 D 5
Kehl, 15,958 B 4
Kelheim, 11,701 D 4
Kempten, 44,617 D 5
Kevelaer, 20,257 B 3
Kiel, 276,600 C 1
Kirchheim unter Teck, 28,878 C 4
Kitzingen, 18,308 D 4
Kleve, 44,150 B 3
Koblenz, 106,189 B 3
Köln (Cologne), 866,308 B 3
Konstanz, 61,617 C 5
Korbach, 17,324 C 3
Kornwestheim, 28,574 C 4
Krefeld, 228,726 B 3
Kulmbach, 22,768 D 3
Lage, 30,949 C 3
Lahr, 25,028 B 4
Lampertheim, 24,053 C 4
Landau in der Pfalz, 32,318 C 4
Landsberg am Lech, 14,378 D 4
Landshut, 51,393 E 4
Langen, 30,230 C 4
Langenhagen, 37,077 C 2
Lauenburg, 11,445 D 2
Lauf an der Pegnitz, 15,771 D 4
Leer, 29,919 B 2
Lehrte, 21,792 D 2
Lemgo, 38,526 C 2
Lengerich, 21,451 B 2
Leverkusen, 111,588 B 3
Lichtenfels, 11,218 D 3
Limburg an der Lahn, 14,889 C 3
Lindau, 26,260 C 5
Lingen, 25,810 B 2
Lippstadt, 42,299 C 3
Lohr am Main, 11,291 C 4
Lörrach, 32,939 B 5
Lübbecke, 11,433 C 2
Lübeck, 242,191 D 2
Lüdenscheid, 80,096 B 3
Ludwigsburg, 79,538 C 4
Ludwigshafen am Rhein, 174,698 C 4
Lüneburg, 59,944 D 2
Lünen, 72,195 B 3

(continued on following page)

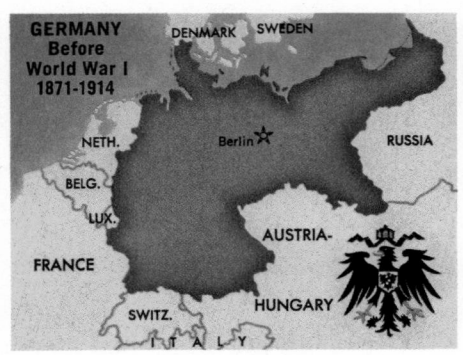

GERMANY Before World War I 1871-1914

DENMARK · SWEDEN · NETH. · Berlin ☆ · RUSSIA · BELG. · LUX. · FRANCE · AUSTRIA-HUNGARY · SWITZ. · ITALY

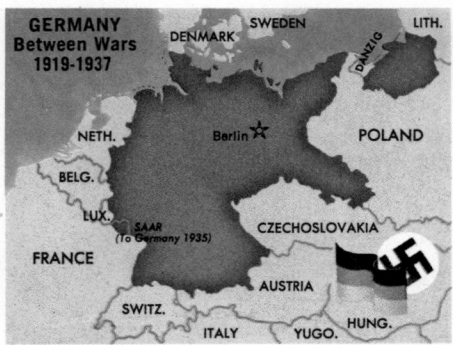

GERMANY Between Wars 1919-1937

DENMARK · SWEDEN · LITH. · DANZIG · NETH. · Berlin ☆ · POLAND · BELG. · LUX. · SAAR (To Germany 1935) · CZECHOSLOVAKIA · FRANCE · AUSTRIA · SWITZ. · ITALY · YUGO. · HUNG.

Occupied GERMANY 1945-1949

DENMARK · SWEDEN · U.S.S.R. · NETH. · BRITISH ZONE · BERLIN · RUSSIAN ZONE · POLAND · BELG. · LUX. · FRENCH ZONE · SAAR · AMERICAN ZONE · CZECHOSLOVAKIA · FRANCE · AUSTRIA · SWITZ. · ITALY · YUGO. · HUNG.

WEST GERMANY (continued)

Mainz, 176,720	C 4
Mannheim, 330,920	C 4
Marburg an der Lahn, 51,382	C 3
Marktredwitz, 15,605	E 3
Marl, 75,779	B 3
Mayen, 18,485	B 3
Memmingen, 35,454	D 5
Meppen, 17,892	B 2
Merzig, 12,443	B 4
Meschede, 16,222	C 3
Metzingen, 14,093	C 4
Minden, 51,527	C 2
Mittenwald, 10,026	D 5
Mölln, 15,307	D 2
Mönchengladbach, 152,172	B 3
Moosburg an der Isar, 11,730	D 4
Mosbach, 13,876	C 4
Mühldorf am Inn, 10,998	E 4
Mülheim an der Ruhr, 191,080	B 3
Münden, 19,111	C 3
Munich (München), 1,326,331	D 4
Münster, 204,571	B 3
Neckarsulm, 18,523	C 4
Neheim-Hüsten, 36,864	C 3
Neuburg an der Donau, 18,530	D 4
Neu-Isenburg, 36,014	C 3
Neumarkt in der Oberpfalz, 18,930	D 4
Neumünster, 84,636	C 1
Neunkirchen, 44,326	B 4
Neuss, 117,599	B 3
Neustadt an der Weinstrasse, 51,058	B 4
Neustadt bei Coburg, 12,496	D 3
Neustadt in Holstein, 16,222	D 1
Neu-Ulm, 27,710	D 4
Neuwied, 31,359	B 3

Nienburg, 22,467	C 2
Norden, 16,355	B 2
Nordenham, 27,368	C 2
Nordhorn, 42,895	B 2
Nördlingen, 14,238	D 4
Northeim, 19,150	C 3
Nuremberg (Nürnberg), 477,108	D 4
Nürtingen, 21,284	C 4
Oberammergau, 4,641	D 5
Oberhausen, 249,045	B 3
Oberlahnstein, 20,131	B 3
Oberursel, 24,933	C 3
Ochtrup, 15,823	B 2
Offenbach am Main, 118,754	C 3
Offenburg, 32,628	B 4
Oldenburg, 131,434	C 2
Opladen, 43,531	B 3
Osnabrück, 141,000	C 2
Osterholz-Scharmbeck, 15,211	C 2
Osterode am Harz, 16,757	D 3
Paderborn, 68,735	C 3
Papenburg, 16,714	B 2
Passau, 31,574	E 4
Peine, 30,882	D 2
Penzberg, 10,784	D 5
Pforzheim, 90,780	C 4
Pfullingen, 15,967	C 4
Pinneberg, 36,439	C 2
Pirmasens, 56,172	B 4
Plettenberg, 30,233	C 3
Plön, 11,142	D 1
Porz am-Rhein, 78,076	B 3
Preetz, 14,653	D 1
Radolfzell, 15,512	C 5
Rastatt, 29,102	C 4
Rastede, 16,851	C 2
Ratingen, 43,420	B 3
Ratzeburg, 12,335	D 2
Ravensburg, 31,819	C 5
Recklinghausen, 125,535	B 3
Regensburg, 128,083	E 4
Rehau, 10,565	D 3

Remscheid, 137,374	B 3
Rendsburg, 35,453	C 1
Reutlingen, 77,853	C 4
Rheine, 51,167	B 2
Rheinfelden, 16,547	B 5
Rheinhausen, 71,698	B 3
Rheydt, 100,633	B 3
Rosenheim, 36,376	D 5
Rotenburg, 16,664	C 2
Roth bei Nürnberg, 11,550	D 4
Rothenburg ob der Tauber, 12,002	D 4
Rottenburg am Neckar, 13,495	C 4
Rottweil, 19,881	C 4
Rüsselsheim, 57,308	C 4
Saarbrücken, 130,765	B 4
Saarlouis (Saarlautern), 36,251	B 4
Säckingen, 12,614	C 5
Salzgitter, 118,020	D 2
Sankt Ingbert, 28,774	B 4
Sankt Wendel, 10,138	B 4
Schleswig, 33,317	C 1
Schönberg, 14,551	D 2
Schönebeck	E 4
Schramberg, 19,050	C 4
Schwabach, 25,774	D 4
Schwäbisch Gmünd, 44,628	C 4
Schwäbisch Hall, 23,765	C 4
Schwandorf in Bayern, 15,995	E 4
Schweinfurt, 59,293	D 3
Schwelm, 34,199	B 3
Schwenningen am Neckar, 35,487	C 4
Schwetzingen, 16,613	C 4
Seesen, 13,027	D 3
Selb, 18,498	E 3
Sennestadt, 20,518	C 3
Siegburg, 34,586	B 3
Siegen, 57,996	C 3
Sindelfingen, 41,029	C 4
Singen, 39,719	C 5

Soest, 40,580	C 3
Solingen, 175,895	B 3
Soltau, 14,981	C 2
Sonthofen, 16,504	D 5
Spandau	C 2
Speyer, 42,323	C 4
Springe, 12,698	C 2
Stade, 31,637	C 2
Stadthagen, 16,876	C 2
Starnberg, 10,622	D 4
Stolberg, 39,589	B 3
Straubing, 36,943	E 4
Stuttgart, 628,412	C 4
Sulzbach-Rosenberg, 18,691	D 4
Tailfingen, 16,787	C 4
Tempelhof	F 4
Traunstein, 14,117	E 5
Trier, 103,412	B 4
Tübingen, 56,008	C 4
Tuttlingen, 26,587	C 5
Überlingen, 12,837	C 5
Uelzen, 23,775	D 2
Uetersen, 16,734	C 2
Ulm, 92,486	D 4
Varel, 12,759	C 2
Vechta, 16,326	C 2
Verden, 16,741	C 2
Viersen, 83,988	B 3
Villingen im Schwarzwald, 37,652	C 4
Völklingen, 39,763	B 4
Waldshut, 10,621	C 5
Walsrode, 13,904	C 2
Wangen im Allgäu, 14,159	C 5
Wanne-Eickel, 99,923	B 3
Warendorf, 18,969	C 3
Wedel, 31,134	C 2
Weiden in der Oberpfalz, 43,097	D 4
Weilheim in Oberbayern, 14,433	D 5
Weingarten, 18,420	C 5
Weinheim, 29,544	C 4
Weissenburg in Bayern, 13,718	D 4

Wertheim, 12,035	C 4
Wesel, 44,710	B 3
Westerstede, 16,387	B 2
Wetzlar, 37,230	B 3
Wiesbaden, 260,614	B 3
Wilhelmshaven, 103,150	B 2
Witten, 97,807	B 3
Wolfenbüttel, 41,225	D 2
Wolfsburg, 89,442	C 2
Worms, 78,004	C 4
Wunstorf, 17,589	C 2
Wuppertal, 414,722	B 3
Würzburg, 120,317	C 4
Zirndorf, 15,363	D 4
Zweibrücken, 32,883	B 4
Zwischenahn, 19,906	B 2

OTHER FEATURES

Aller (riv.)	C 2
Allgäu (reg.), 249,600	D 5
Alz (riv.)	E 4
Ammersee (lake)	D 4
Amrum (isl.), 2,155	C 1
Baltrum (isl.), 924	B 2
Bavarian (forest)	E 4
Bavarian Alps (mts.)	D 5
Black (forest)	C 4
Bodensee (Constance)	
Bohemian (forest)	E 4
Borkum (isl.), 5,348	B 2
Breisgau (reg.), 675,500	B 5
Chiemsee (lake)	E 5
Constance (lake)	C 5
Danube (Donau) (riv.)	C 4
Dümmer (lake)	C 2
East Friesland (region), 599,700	B 2
East Frisian (isls.), 20,962	C 2
Eder (res.)	C 3
Eider (riv.)	C 1

Eifel (mts.)	B 3
Elbe (riv.)	C 2
Ems (riv.)	B 2
Fehmarn (isl.), 12,586	D 1
Feldberg (mt.)	B 5
Fichtelgebirge (mts.)	D 3
Föhr (isl.), 8,585	C 1
Franconian Jura (mts.)	D 4
Frankenwald (forest)	D 3
Fulda (riv.)	C 3
Grosser Arber (mt.)	E 4
Halligen, The (isls.), 5,112	C 1
Hardt (mts.)	B 4
Harz (mts.)	D 3
Hegau (reg.)	C 5
Helgoland (isl.), 3,184	B 1
Hunsrück (mts.)	B 4
Iller (riv.)	D 4
Inn (riv.)	E 4
Isar (riv.)	D 4
Jade (bay)	C 2
Juist (isl.), 2,147	B 2
Kaiserstuhl (mt.)	B 4
Kiel (canal)	C 1
Königssee (lake)	E 5
Lahn (riv.)	C 3
Langeoog (isl.), 2,611	B 2
Lech (riv.)	D 4
Leine (riv.)	C 2
Lippe (riv.)	C 3
Lüneburger Heide (dist.)	C 2
Main (riv.)	C 4
Mecklenburg (bay)	D 1
Mosel (riv.)	B 4
Neckar (riv.)	C 4
Nord-Ostsee (Kiel) (canal)	C 1
Norderney (isl.), 8,983	B 2

Nordstrand (isl.), 3,079	C 1
North (sea)	A 1
North Friesland (reg.)	C 1
North Frisian (islands), 36,259	B 1
Oberpfälzer Wald (forest)	E 4
Odenwald (forest)	C 4
Pellworm (isl.), 2,033	C 1
Regen (riv.)	E 4
Regnitz (riv.)	D 4
Rhine (Rhein) (riv.)	B 3
Rhön (mts.)	D 3
Ruhr (riv.)	B 3
Saar (riv.)	B 4
Salzach (riv.)	E 5
Sauer (riv.)	B 4
Sauerland (reg.)	B 3
Schwarzwald (Black) (forest)	C 4
Spessart (range)	C 4
Spiekeroog (isl.), 823	B 2
Starnbergersee (lake)	D 5
Steigerwald (forest)	D 4
Steinhuder (lake)	C 2
Swabian Jura (mts.)	C 4
Sylt (isl.), 20,407	C 1
Tauber (riv.)	C 4
Taunus (range)	C 3
Tegernsee (lake)	D 5
Teutoburger Wald (forest)	C 2
Vechte (riv.)	B 2
Vogelsberg (mt.)	C 3
Walchensee (lake)	D 5
Wangerooge (isl.), 2,126	B 2
Wasserkuppe (mt.)	C 3
Watzmann (mt.)	E 5
Werra (riv.)	C 3
Weser (riv.)	C 2
Westerwald (forest)	C 3
Wurmsee (Starnbergersee) (lake)	D 5
Zugspitze (mt.)	D 5

Agriculture, Industry and Resources

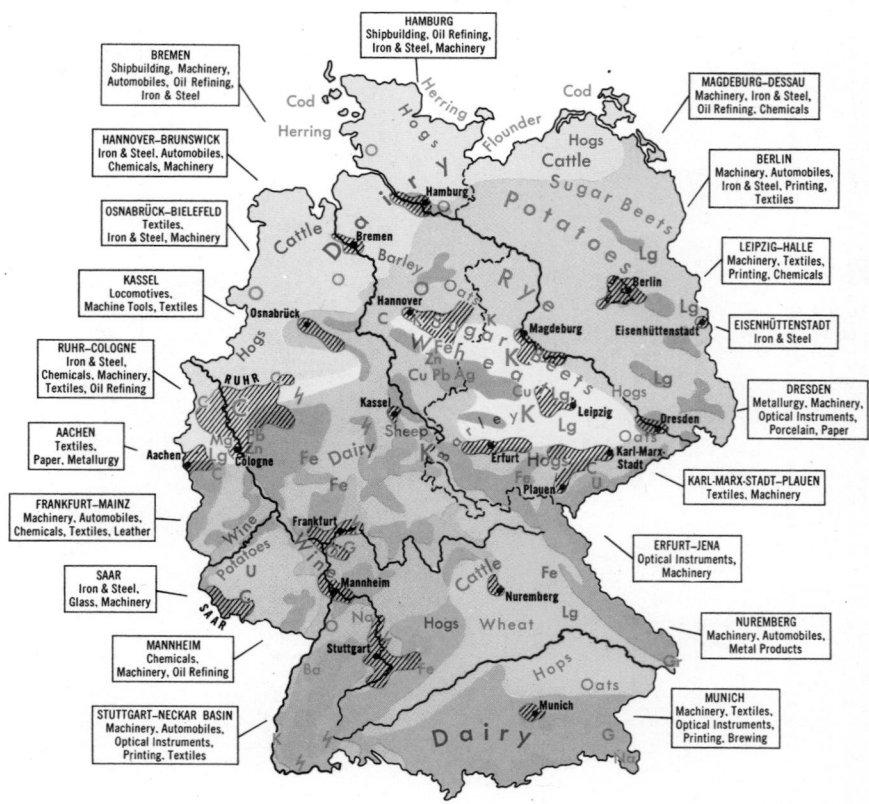

DOMINANT LAND USE

- Wheat, Sugar Beets
- Cereals (chiefly rye, oats, barley)
- Potatoes, Rye
- Dairy, Livestock
- Mixed Cereals, Dairy
- Truck Farming
- Grapes, Fruit
- Forests

MAJOR MINERAL OCCURRENCES

Ag	Silver	Lg	Lignite
Ba	Barite	Mg	Magnesium
C	Coal	Na	Salt
Cu	Copper	O	Petroleum
Fe	Iron Ore	Pb	Lead
G	Natural Gas	U	Uranium
Gr	Graphite	Zn	Zinc
K	Potash		

⚡ Water Power

🗠 Major Industrial Areas

HAMBURG — Shipbuilding, Oil Refining, Iron & Steel, Machinery

BREMEN — Shipbuilding, Machinery, Automobiles, Oil Refining, Iron & Steel

MAGDEBURG–DESSAU — Machinery, Iron & Steel, Oil Refining, Chemicals

HANNOVER–BRUNSWICK — Iron & Steel, Automobiles, Chemicals, Machinery

BERLIN — Machinery, Automobiles, Iron & Steel, Printing, Textiles

OSNABRÜCK–BIELEFELD — Textiles, Iron & Steel, Machinery

LEIPZIG–HALLE — Machinery, Textiles, Printing, Chemicals

KASSEL — Locomotives, Machine Tools, Textiles

EISENHÜTTENSTADT — Iron & Steel

RUHR–COLOGNE — Iron & Steel, Chemicals, Machinery, Textiles, Oil Refining

DRESDEN — Metallurgy, Machinery, Optical Instruments, Porcelain, Paper

AACHEN — Textiles, Paper, Metallurgy

KARL-MARX-STADT–PLAUEN — Textiles, Machinery

FRANKFURT–MAINZ — Machinery, Automobiles, Chemicals, Textiles, Leather

ERFURT–JENA — Optical Instruments, Machinery

SAAR — Iron & Steel, Glass, Machinery

NUREMBERG — Machinery, Automobiles, Metal Products

MANNHEIM — Chemicals, Machinery, Oil Refining

MUNICH — Machinery, Textiles, Optical Instruments, Printing, Brewing

STUTTGART–NECKAR BASIN — Machinery, Automobiles, Optical Instruments, Printing, Textiles

NETHERLANDS
AREA 13,958 sq. mi.
POPULATION 13,077,000
CAPITALS The Hague, Amsterdam
LARGEST CITY Amsterdam
HIGHEST POINT Vaalserberg, 1,056 ft.
MONETARY UNIT guilder
MAJOR LANGUAGE Dutch
MAJOR RELIGIONS Protestantism, Roman Catholicism

BELGIUM
AREA 11,779 sq. mi.
POPULATION 9,660,154
CAPITAL Brussels
LARGEST CITY Brussels (greater)
HIGHEST POINT Botrange 2,277 ft.
MONETARY UNIT Belgian franc
MAJOR LANGUAGES French (Walloon), Flemish
MAJOR RELIGION Roman Catholicism

LUXEMBOURG
AREA 999 sq. mi.
POPULATION 339,000
CAPITAL Luxembourg
LARGEST CITY Luxembourg
HIGHEST POINT Ardennes Plateau, 1,825 ft.
MONETARY UNIT Luxembourg franc
MAJOR LANGUAGES Luxembourgeois (German dialect), French, German
MAJOR RELIGION Roman Catholicism

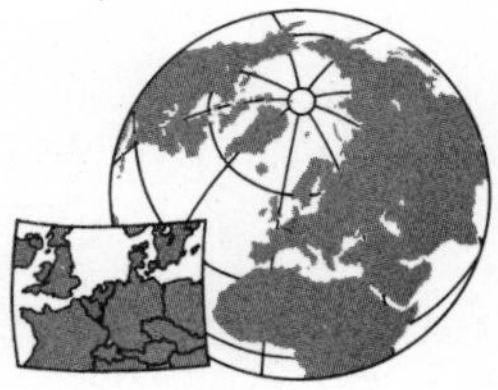

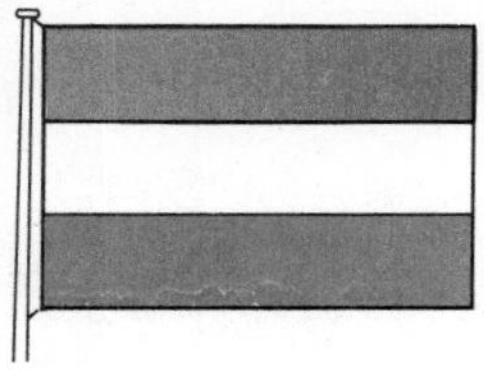

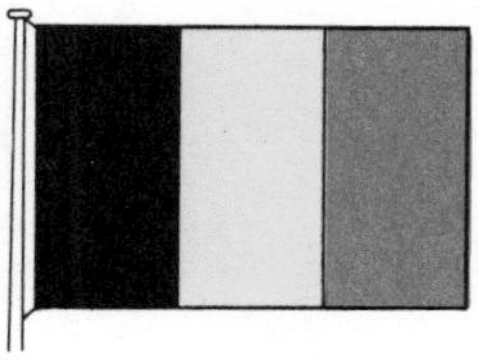

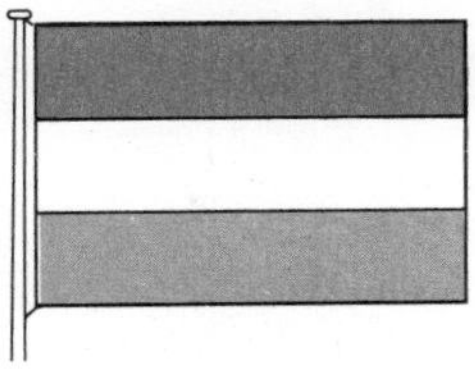

BELGIUM

PROVINCES

Antwerp, 1,529,826 ..... F 6
Brabant, 2,166,372 ..... F 7
East Flanders, 1,310,638 ..... D 7
Hainault, 1,331,810 ..... D 7
Liège, 1,016,131 ..... H 7
Limburg, 650,338 ..... G 7
Luxembourg, 219,369 ..... G 9
Namur, 383,618 ..... F 8
West Flanders, 1,052,052 ..... B 7

CITIES and TOWNS†

Aalst, 45,900 ..... D 7
Aalter, 8,569 ..... C 6
Aarlen (Arlon), 14,191 ..... H 9
Aarschot, 12,329 ..... F 7
Aat (Ath), 11,094 ..... D 7
Adinkerke, 2,713 ..... A 6
Alken, 8,054 ..... G 7
Alost (Aalst), 45,900 ..... D 7
Amay, 7,561 ..... G 7
Andenne, 8,068 ..... G 8
Anderlecht, 103,832 ..... B 9
Anderlues, 12,930 ..... E 8
Antoing, 3,435 ..... C 7
Antwerp (Antwerpen), 234,099 ..... E 6
Antwerp, *673,259 ..... E 6
Ardooie, 7,163 ..... C 7
Arendonk, 9,516 ..... G 6
Arlon, 14,191 ..... H 9
As, 4,087 ..... H 6
Asse, 12,631 ..... E 7
Assebroek, 15,195 ..... C 6
Assesse, 1,138 ..... G 8
Ath, 11,094 ..... D 7
Athus, 7,185 ..... H 9
Audenarde (Oudenaarde), 21,980 ..... D 7
Auderghem, 32,782 ..... C 9
Autelbas, 1,606 ..... H 9
Auvelais, 8,412 ..... F 8
Aywaille, 3,813 ..... H 8
Baerle-Duc, 2,171 ..... F 6
Balen, 14,719 ..... G 6
Barvaux, 1,727 ..... H 8
Basècles, 4,245 ..... D 7
Bastogne (Bastenaken), 6,476 ..... H 9
Beaumont, 1,762 ..... E 8
Beauraing, 2,703 ..... F 8
Berchem, 49,880 ..... F 6
Berchem-Sainte-Agathe, 17,689 ..... B 9
Bergen (Mons), 27,042 ..... E 8
Bertrix, 4,481 ..... G 9
Beveren, 15,350 ..... E 6
Bilzen, 7,000 ..... G 7
Binche, 10,340 ..... E 8
Blankenberge, 10,400 ..... C 6
Bocholt, 5,582 ..... H 6
Boom, 17,280 ..... E 6
Borgerhout, 50,226 ..... E 6
Borgloon, 3,543 ..... G 7
Borgworm (Waremme), 7,623 ..... G 7
Bouillon, 3,089 ..... G 9
Bourg-Leopold (Leopoldsburg), 9,621 ..... G 6
Boussu, 11,626 ..... D 8
Bovigny, 1,015 ..... H 8
Braine-l'Alleud, 16,028 ..... E 7
Braine-le-Comte, 11,343 ..... D 7
Bredene, 9,381 ..... B 6
Bree, 10,462 ..... H 6
Bruges (Brugge), 52,249 ..... C 6
Bruges, *112,611 ..... C 6
Brussels (Bruxelles) (cap.), *1,073,111 ..... C 9
Charleroi, 24,895 ..... E 8
Charleroi, *218,089 ..... E 8
Châtelet, 15,314 ..... F 8
Châtelineau, 20,293 ..... F 8
Chièvres, 3,154 ..... D 7
Chimay, 3,309 ..... E 8
Ciney, 7,431 ..... G 8
Comblain-au-Pont, 3,538 ..... G 8
Comines, 8,219 ..... B 7
Couillet, 15,055 ..... E 8
Courcelles, 17,157 ..... E 8
Courtrai, 45,310 ..... C 7
Couvin, 4,192 ..... F 8
Cul-des-Sarts, 993 ..... E 9
Deinze, 6,214 ..... D 7
Denderleeuw, 9,699 ..... E 7
Dendermonde, 9,663 ..... E 6
De Panne, 6,792 ..... A 6
Dessel, 7,170 ..... G 6
Deurne, 75,819 ..... F 6
Diegem, 4,760 ..... C 9
Diest, 9,587 ..... F 7
Diksmuide, 6,557 ..... B 6
Dilbeek, 13,620 ..... B 9
Dinant, 9,700 ..... G 8
Dison, 8,809 ..... H 7
Dixmude (Diksmuide), 6,557 ..... B 6
Doel, 1,395 ..... E 6
Doornik (Tournai), 33,309 ..... C 7
Dour, 10,407 ..... D 8
Drogenbos, 4,648 ..... B 9
Drongen, 8,312 ..... D 6
Dudzele, 2,112 ..... C 6
Duffel, 13,560 ..... F 6
Ecaussinnes d'Enghien, 6,696 ..... E 7
Edingen (Enghien), 4,279 ..... D 7
Eeklo, 19,007 ..... D 6
Eernegem, 5,865 ..... B 6
Eigenbrakel (Braine-l'Alleud), 16,028 ..... E 7
Ekeren, 24,535 ..... E 6
Ellezelles, 3,676 ..... D 7
Enghien, 4,279 ..... D 7
Ensival, 5,515 ..... H 7
Erquelinnes, 4,812 ..... E 8
Esneux, 5,923 ..... H 7
Essen, 10,515 ..... F 6
Étalle, 1,179 ..... H 9
Etterbeek, 52,299 ..... C 9
Eupen, 14,856 ..... J 7
Evere, 24,289 ..... C 9
Evergem, 12,329 ..... D 6
Flémalle-Haute, 7,800 ..... G 7
Fleurus, 8,475 ..... F 8
Florennes, 4,070 ..... F 8
Florenville, 2,526 ..... G 9
Forest, 55,799 ..... B 9
Fosses-la-Ville, 3,887 ..... F 8
Frameries, 11,624 ..... D 8
Frasnes-lez-Buissenal, 2,672 ..... D 7
Furnes (Veurne), 7,475 ..... B 6
Ganshoren, 19,154 ..... B 9
Gaurain-Ramecroix, 3,599 ..... D 7
Gedinne, 1,021 ..... F 9
Geel, 28,484 ..... F 6
Geldenaken (Jodoigne), 4,194 ..... F 7
Gembloux, 11,030 ..... F 7
Gemmenich, 2,608 ..... H 7
Genk, 55,596 ..... H 7
Gent (Ghent), 153,301 ..... D 6
Gentbrugge, 22,986 ..... D 6
Geraardsbergen, 9,201 ..... D 7
Ghent, 153,301 ..... D 6
Ghent, *229,687 ..... D 6
Gilly, 24,155 ..... E 8
Gosselies, 10,970 ..... E 8
Grammont (Geraardsbergen), 9,201 ..... D 7
Haacht, 4,372 ..... F 7
Hal (Halle), 20,071 ..... E 7
Halen, 5,321 ..... G 7
Halle, 20,071 ..... E 7
Hamme, 17,083 ..... E 6
Hamont, 6,626 ..... H 6
Hannut (Hannuit), 3,069 ..... G 7
Harelbeke, 17,981 ..... C 7
Hasselt, 38,773 ..... G 7
Havelange, 1,495 ..... G 8
Heer, 578 ..... F 8
Heist, 9,289 ..... C 6
Heist-op-den-Berg, 13,206 ..... F 6
Herbeumont, 590 ..... G 9
Herentals, 18,377 ..... F 6
Herselt, 7,318 ..... F 6
Herstal, 29,602 ..... H 7
Herve, 4,357 ..... H 7
Hoboken, 31,815 ..... E 6
Hoei (Huy), 13,398 ..... G 8
Hoeselt, 5,570 ..... H 7
Hoogstraten, 4,376 ..... F 6
Hornu, 10,905 ..... D 8
Houffalize, 1,297 ..... H 8
Huy, 13,398 ..... G 8
Ieper, 18,461 ..... B 7
Ingelmunster, 9,973 ..... C 7
Ixelles, 92,532 ..... C 9
Izegem, 22,729 ..... C 7
Jambes, 14,924 ..... F 8
Jemappes, 12,906 ..... D 8
Jemeppe, 12,232 ..... G 7
Jette, 37,354 ..... B 9
Jodoigne, 4,194 ..... F 7
Jumet, 28,811 ..... E 8
Kain, 4,900 ..... C 7
Kalmthout, 12,122 ..... F 6
Kapellen, 12,297 ..... F 6
Kessel-Lo, 21,351 ..... F 7
Knokke, 14,268 ..... C 6
Koekelare, 6,423 ..... B 6
Koekelberg, 17,348 ..... B 9
Koersel, 10,756 ..... G 6
Kontich, 13,193 ..... E 6
Kortemark, 5,839 ..... C 6
Kortrijk (Courtrai), 45,310 ..... C 7
Kraainem, 10,560 ..... C 9
La Louvière, 23,447 ..... E 8
La Louvière, *113,795 ..... E 8
La Roche-en-Ardenne, 1,894 ..... G 8
Lanaken, 8,216 ..... H 7
Landen, 5,247 ..... G 7
Langemark, 4,787 ..... B 7
Lede, 10,229 ..... D 7
Ledeberg, 11,056 ..... D 7
Lens, 1,790 ..... D 7
Leopoldsburg, 9,621 ..... G 6
Lessines (Lessen), 9,047 ..... D 7
Leuven (Louvain), 32,125 ..... F 7
Leuze, 7,128 ..... D 7
Libramont, 2,774 ..... G 9
Lichtervelde, 7,372 ..... C 6
Liedekerke, 10,273 ..... D 7
Liège, 150,127 ..... H 7
Liège, *446,990 ..... H 7
Lier (Lierre), 28,557 ..... F 6
Lierneux, 2,847 ..... H 8
Limbourg (Limburg), 3,973 ..... J 7
Linkebeek, 4,096 ..... C10
Lokeren, 26,654 ..... D 6
Lommel, 20,567 ..... G 6
Looz (Borgloon), 3,543 ..... G 7
Louvain, 32,125 ..... F 7
Luik (Liège), 150,127 ..... H 7
Maaseik, 8,383 ..... H 6
Machelen, 7,331 ..... C 9
Maldegem, 14,182 ..... C 6
Malines (Mechelen), 65,728 ..... F 6
Malmédy, 6,482 ..... J 8
Marche-en-Famenne, 4,423 ..... G 8
Marchin, 4,361 ..... G 8
Marcinelle, 25,992 ..... E 8
Mariembourg, 1,776 ..... E 8
Martelange, 1,594 ..... H 9
Mechelen, 65,728 ..... F 6
Meerhout, 8,359 ..... G 6
Meerle, 2,809 ..... F 6
Melsbroek, 2,034 ..... D 9
Menen (Menin), 22,458 ..... C 7
Merchtem, 8,772 ..... E 7
Merelbeke, 13,755 ..... D 7
Merksem, 39,011 ..... E 6
Merksplas, 4,950 ..... F 6
Messancy, 3,064 ..... H 9
Mettet, 3,366 ..... F 8
Meulebeke, 10,619 ..... C 7
Moeskron (Mouscron), 37,624 ..... C 7
Mol, 27,320 ..... G 6
Molenbeek-Saint-Jean, 67,271 ..... B 9
Mons, 27,042 ..... E 8
Montegnée, 11,882 ..... G 7
Montignies-sur-Sambre, 24,048 ..... F 8
Mortsel, 27,999 ..... E 6
Mouscron, 37,624 ..... C 7
Namur (Namen), 32,621 ..... F 8
Neerlinter, 1,431 ..... G 7
Neerpelt, 8,273 ..... G 6
Neufchâteau, 2,739 ..... G 9
Nieuwpoort (Nieuport), 7,165 ..... B 6
Ninove, 12,087 ..... D 7
Nivelles (Nijvel), 15,384 ..... E 7
Oostende (Ostend), 57,749 ..... B 6
Oostkamp, 8,560 ..... C 6
Ophoven, 2,487 ..... H 6
Opwijk, 9,622 ..... E 7
Ostend, 57,749 ..... B 6
Oud-Turnhout, 8,219 ..... F 6
Oudenaarde, 21,980 ..... D 7
Ougrée, 21,152 ..... H 7
Overijse, 14,119 ..... F 7
Overpelt, 10,002 ..... G 6
Peer, 5,882 ..... G 6
Péruwelz, 7,814 ..... D 8
Perwez (Perwijs), 2,858 ..... F 7
Philippeville, 1,822 ..... E 8
Poperinge, 12,619 ..... B 7
Poppel, 2,246 ..... G 6
Putte, 6,856 ..... F 6
Quaregnon, 18,289 ..... D 8
Quiévrain, 5,685 ..... D 8
Raeren, 3,490 ..... J 7
Rance, 1,443 ..... E 8
Rebecq-Rognon, 3,831 ..... E 7
Renaix (Ronse), 25,371 ..... D 7
Retie, 6,339 ..... G 6
Rièzes, 307 ..... E 9
Rochefort, 4,242 ..... G 8
Roeselare, 40,077 ..... C 7
Roeulx, 2,605 ..... E 8
Ronse, 25,371 ..... D 7
Roulers (Roeselare), 40,077 ..... C 7
Ruisbroek, 5,685 ..... B 9
's Gravenbrakel (Braine-le-Comte), 11,343 ..... D 7
Saint-Georges, 6,085 ..... G 7
Saint-Gérard, 1,626 ..... F 8
Saint-Gilles, 57,238 ..... B 9
Saint-Hubert, 3,104 ..... G 8
Saint-Josse-ten-Noode, 24,335 ..... C 9
Saint-Léger, 1,600 ..... H 9
Saint-Vith (Sankt-Vith), 2,935 ..... J 8
Schaerbeek, 120,650 ..... C 9
Schoten, 28,543 ..... F 6
Seraing, 40,937 ..... G 7
Sint-Amandsberg, 24,778 ..... D 6
Sint-Andries, 15,062 ..... C 6
Sint-Lenaarts, 4,464 ..... F 6
Sint-Niklaas, 48,851 ..... E 6
Sint-Pieters-Leeuw, 15,978 ..... B 9
Sint-Truiden (Saint-Trond), 21,131 ..... G 7
Sivry, 1,384 ..... E 8
Soignies, 11,320 ..... D 7
Spa, 9,683 ..... H 8
Staden, 5,581 ..... B 7
Stavelot, 4,661 ..... H 8
Steenokkerzeel, 3,877 ..... C 9
Stene, 9,304 ..... B 6
Stokkem, 3,380 ..... H 6
Strombeek-Bever, 10,027 ..... C 9
Tamines, 8,139 ..... F 8
Tamise (Temse), 14,559 ..... E 6
Templeuve, 3,737 ..... C 7
Temse, 14,559 ..... E 6
Termonde (Dendermonde), 9,663 ..... E 6
Tessenderlo, 10,665 ..... G 6
Theux, 5,491 ..... H 8
Thuin, 5,877 ..... E 8
Tielt, Brabant, 3,813 ..... F 7
Tielt, West Flanders, 13,887 ..... C 7
Tienen (Tirlemont), 22,660 ..... F 7
Tongeren (Tongres), 16,880 ..... G 7
Torhout, 14,301 ..... C 6
Tournai, 33,309 ..... C 7
Tronchiennes (Drongen), 8,312 ..... D 6
Tubize (Tubeke), 10,269 ..... E 7
Turnhout, 37,828 ..... F 6
Uccle (Ukkel), 76,579 ..... B 9
Verviers, 35,730 ..... H 7

(continued on following page)

Agriculture, Industry and Resources

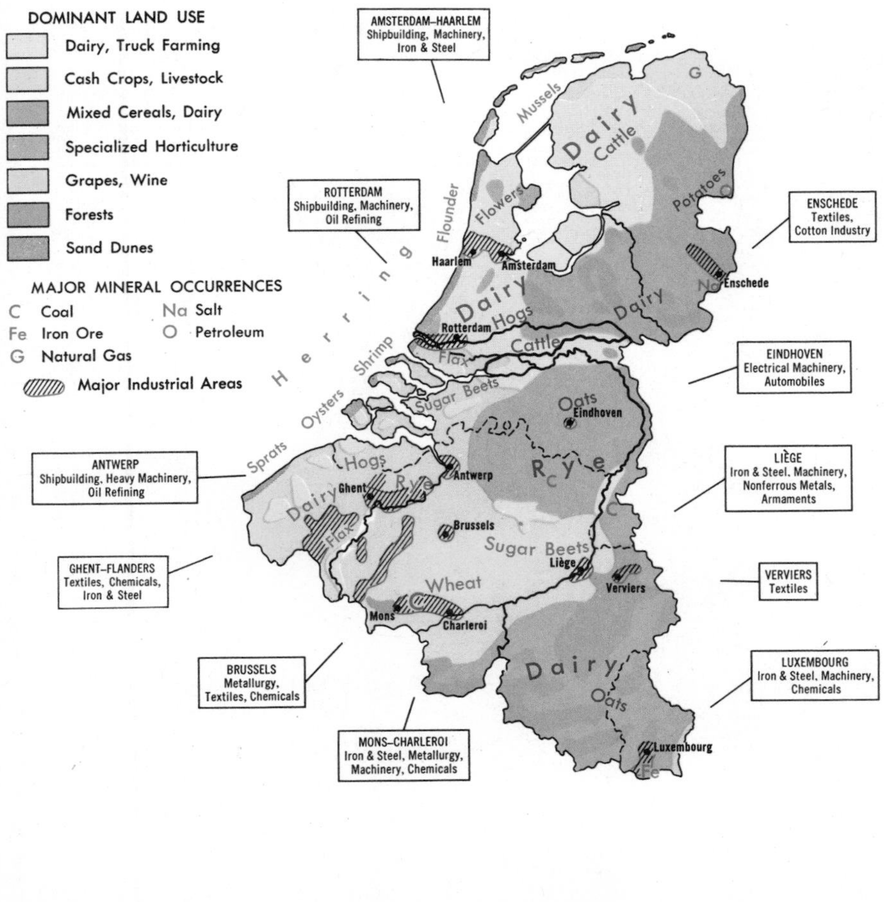
DOMINANT LAND USE
Dairy, Truck Farming
Cash Crops, Livestock
Mixed Cereals, Dairy
Specialized Horticulture
Grapes, Wine
Forests
Sand Dunes
MAJOR MINERAL OCCURRENCES
C Coal
Fe Iron Ore
G Natural Gas
Na Salt
O Petroleum
Major Industrial Areas
AMSTERDAM–HAARLEM
Shipbuilding, Machinery, Iron & Steel
ROTTERDAM
Shipbuilding, Machinery, Oil Refining
ENSCHEDE
Textiles, Cotton Industry
EINDHOVEN
Electrical Machinery, Automobiles
ANTWERP
Shipbuilding, Heavy Machinery, Oil Refining
LIÈGE
Iron & Steel, Machinery, Nonferrous Metals, Armaments
GHENT–FLANDERS
Textiles, Chemicals, Iron & Steel
VERVIERS
Textiles
BRUSSELS
Metallurgy, Textiles, Chemicals
LUXEMBOURG
Iron & Steel, Machinery, Chemicals
MONS–CHARLEROI
Iron & Steel, Metallurgy, Machinery, Chemicals
Mussels
Dairy
Cattle
Potatoes
Flowers
Flounder
Herring
Haarlem
Amsterdam
Enschede
Dairy
Hogs
Rotterdam
Cattle
Flax
Shrimp
Oysters
Sprats
Sugar Beets
Oats
Eindhoven
Rye
Hogs
Antwerp
Ghent
Dairy
Flax
Brussels
Sugar Beets
Liège
Verviers
Wheat
Mons
Charleroi
Dairy
Oats
Luxembourg

24 Netherlands, Belgium and Luxembourg
(continued)

BELGIUM (continued)

Veurne, 7,475 ....B 6
Vielsalm, 3,702 ....J 8
Villers-devant-Orval, 777 ....G 9
Vilvoorde (Vilvorde), 34,040 ....F 7
Virton, 3,956 ....H 9
Visé, 6,595 ....H 7
Vorst (Forest), 55,799 ....B 9
Waarschoot, 7,852 ....D 6
Waasten (Warneton), 3,215 ....B 7
Waha, 2,664 ....G 8
Waimes, 2,787 ....J 8
Walcourt, 2,077 ....F 8
Wandre, 6,833 ....H 7
Waregem, 16,928 ....C 7
Waremme, 7,623 ....G 7
Warneton, 3,215 ....B 7
Wasmes, 13,933 ....D 7
Waterloo, 14,615 ....E 7
Watermael-Boitsfort, 24,730 ....C 9
Watervliet, 1,812 ....D 6
Wavre (Waver), 11,007 ....F 7
Weismes (Waimes), 2,787 ....J 8
Wemmel, 11,404 ....B 9
Wenduine, 1,756 ....C 6
Wervik, 12,728 ....B 7
Westende, 2,746 ....B 6
Westerlo, 7,630 ....F 6
Wetteren, 20,775 ....D 7
Wezembeek-Oppem, 10,536 ....D 9
Wezet (Visé), 6,595 ....H 7
Willebroek, 15,650 ....E 6
Wilrijk, 42,109 ....E 6
Wingene, 7,178 ....C 6
Woluwe-Saint-Lambert, 44,102 ....C 9
Woluwe-Saint-Pierre, 37,314 ....C 9
Wolvertem, 5,326 ....E 7
Ypres (Ieper), 18,461 ....B 7
Yvoir, 2,837 ....F 8
Zaventem, 9,941 ....C 9
Zeebrugge ....C 6
Zele, 18,386 ....E 6
Zellik, 5,165 ....B 9
Zelzate, 11,751 ....D 6
Zinnik (Soignies), 11,320 ....D 7
Zonhoven, 12,910 ....G 6
Zottegem, 6,905 ....D 7

OTHER FEATURES

Albert (canal) ....F 6
Ardennes (plateau) ....F 9
Botrange (mt.) ....J 8
Dender (river) ....D 7
Dyle (river) ....F 7
Hohe Venn (plateau) ....H 8
Lesse (river) ....F 8
Mark (river) ....F 6
Meuse (river) ....F 8
Nethe (river) ....F 6
Ourthe (river) ....H 8
Rupel (river) ....F 7
Scheldt (Schelde) (river) ....C 7
Schnee Eifel (plateau) ....J 8
Semois (river) ....G 9
Senne (river) ....E 7
Vesdre (river) ....H 7
Weisserstein (mt.) ....J 8
Yser (river) ....B 7
Zitterwald (plateau) ....J 8

LUXEMBOURG

CITIES and TOWNS

Clervaux, 933 ....J 8
Diekirch, 4,899 ....J 9
Differdange, 9,808 ....H 9
Dudelange, 14,849 ....J10
Echternach, 3,472 ....J 9
Esch-sur-Alzette, 27,921 ....J 9
Esch-sur-Sauer, 265 ....H 9
Ettelbrück, 5,557 ....J 9
Grevenmacher, 2,850 ....J 9
Luxembourg (cap.), 77,458 ....J 9
Mersch, 1,682 ....J 9
Pétange, 6,251 ....H 9
Redange, 990 ....H 9
Remich, 1,958 ....J 9
Troisvierges, 928 ....J 8
Vianden, 1,381 ....J 9
Wasserbillig, 2,047 ....J 9
Wiltz, 1,538 ....H 9

OTHER FEATURES

Alzette (river) ....J 9
Clerf (river) ....J 8
Eisling (mts.) ....H 9
Mosel (river) ....J 9
Our (river) ....J 9
Sauer (river) ....J 9

NETHERLANDS

PROVINCES

Drenthe, 366,590 ....K 3
Friesland, 521,751 ....H 2
Gelderland, 1,505,760 ....H 4
Groningen, 517,305 ....K 2
Limburg, 998,570 ....H 6
North Brabant, 1,787,783 ....F 5
North Holland, 2,244,456 ....F 3
Overijssel, 920,882 ....J 4
South Holland, 2,968,670 ....E 5
Utrecht, 801,285 ....G 4
Zeeland, 305,754 ....D 6

CITIES and TOWNS

Aalsmeer, †18,166 ....F 4
Aalst, 4,423 ....G 6
Aalten, †16,295 ....K 5
Aardenburg, †3,853 ....C 6
Akkrum, 2,296 ....H 2
Alkmaar, †52,091 ....F 3
Almelo, †58,941 ....K 4
Amersfoort, †78,189 ....G 4
Amstelveen, †69,167 ....B 5
Amsterdam (cap.), 831,463 ....B 4
Amsterdam, *918,676 ....B 4
Andijk, †4,602 ....G 3
Anjum, 939 ....J 2
Apeldoorn, 123,628 ....H 4
Apeldoorn, *214,974 ....H 4
Appelscha, 1,622 ....J 3
Appingedam, †10,987 ....K 2
Arnhem, 132,531 ....H 4
Arnhem, *232,860 ....H 4
Assen, †38,956 ....K 3
Asten, †11,209 ....H 6
Axel, †8,904 ....D 6
Baarle-Nassau, †4,948 ....F 6
Baarn, †24,106 ....G 4
Badhoevedorp, 8,699 ....B 5
Balkbrug, 2,468 ....J 3
Barneveld, †30,046 ....H 4
Bath, 128 ....E 6
Beilen, †12,289 ....K 3
Bergeijk (Hof), †7,816 ....G 6
Bergen, †13,060 ....F 3
Bergen op Zoom, †39,051 ....E 5
Bergum, †4,252 ....H 2
Berkel, †5,936 ....F 5
Berkhout, †3,941 ....F 3
Beverwijk, †41,357 ....F 4
Blerick, 14,593 ....J 6
Bloemendaal, †19,253 ....E 4
Blokzijl, †1,375 ....H 3
Bodegraven, †14,083 ....F 4
Bolsward, †9,247 ....H 2
Borculo, †8,510 ....J 4
Borger, †10,972 ....K 3
Borne, †15,423 ....K 4
Boskoop, †11,600 ....F 4
Boxmeer, †10,850 ....H 5
Boxtel, †19,080 ....G 5
Breda, 121,209 ....F 5
Breda, *233,704 ....F 5
Breezand, 1,962 ....F 3
Breskens, †3,857 ....C 6
Brielle, †8,314 ....E 5
Broek, †2,260 ....C 4
Brouwershaven, †3,256 ....D 5
Brummen, †18,077 ....J 4
Buiksloot, 23,738 ....B 4
Bussum, †41,787 ....G 4
Callantsoog, †1,698 ....F 3
Coevorden, †12,481 ....K 3
Colijnsplaat, 1,477 ....D 5
Culemborg, 11,083 ....G 5
Cuyk, †12,144 ....H 5
Dalen, †4,630 ....K 3
De Bilt, †29,153 ....G 4
Dedemsvaart, 6,384 ....J 3
De Koog, 701 ....F 2
Delft, 83,698 ....E 4
Delfzijl, †21,990 ....K 2
Den Burg, 3,579 ....F 2
Den Helder, †60,612 ....F 3
Denekamp, †10,919 ....L 4
Deurne, †23,949 ....H 6
Deventer, †65,319 ....J 4
De Wijk, †4,120 ....J 3
Diemen, †9,558 ....C 5
Dieren, 8,612 ....J 4
Diever, †3,180 ....J 3
Dinxperlo, †6,248 ....K 5
Dirksland, †6,092 ....E 5
Doesburg, †9,451 ....J 4
Doetinchem, †31,097 ....J 5
Dokkum, †9,886 ....H 2
Domburg, †3,154 ....C 5
Dongen, †16,231 ....F 5
Doorn, †10,084 ....G 4
Doornspijk, †10,463 ....H 4
Dordrecht, †88,699 ....F 5
Dordrecht, *99,284 ....F 5
Drachten, 16,529 ....J 2
Driebergen, †15,828 ....G 4
Druten, †9,761 ....H 5
Duivendrecht, 2,656 ....C 5
Durgerdam, 640 ....C 4
Echt, †15,795 ....H 6
Edam, †18,184 ....G 4
Ede, †71,952 ....H 4
Eefde, 2,396 ....J 4
Egmond aan Zee, †5,554 ....E 3
Eindhoven, 188,631 ....G 6
Eindhoven, *301,049 ....G 6
Elburg, †5,135 ....H 4
Elst, †15,182 ....H 5
Emmeloord, 7,251 ....H 3
Emmen, †79,707 ....K 3
Enkhuizen, †11,502 ....G 3
Enschede, 139,245 ....K 4
Epe, †27,515 ....H 4
Erica, 3,026 ....K 3
Ermelo, †37,198 ....H 4
Etten, †19,698 ....F 5
Flushing, †40,197 ....C 6
Franeker, †9,575 ....H 2
Geertruidenberg, †5,575 ....F 5
Geldermalsen, †7,946 ....G 5
Geldrop, †26,909 ....H 6
Geleen, †36,121 ....H 7
Gemert, †14,329 ....H 5
Gendringen, †18,028 ....J 5
Genemuiden, †5,524 ....H 3
Gennep, †6,922 ....H 5
Giessendam, †13,588 ....F 5
Giethoorn, †2,486 ....J 3
Goes, †25,822 ....D 6
Goirle, †11,428 ....G 5
Goor, †9,702 ....K 4
Gorinchem, †26,380 ....G 5
Gorredijk, 3,006 ....J 2
Gouda, †45,990 ....F 4
Gouda, *84,695 ....F 4
Graauw, †1,277 ....E 6
Gramsbergen, †5,431 ....K 3
Grave, †7,405 ....H 5
Groenlo, †7,888 ....K 4
Groesbeek, †17,308 ....H 5
Groningen, 168,843 ....K 2
Groningen, *185,757 ....K 2
Grouw, 3,191 ....H 2
Haamstede, 1,179 ....D 5
Haarlem, 172,235 ....F 4
Haarlemmermeer (Hoofddorp), 4,949 ....F 4
Hague, The (cap.), 550,613 ....E 4
Hague, The, *702,296 ....E 4
Halfweg, 2,171 ....A 4
Hallum, 1,424 ....H 2
Hardenberg, †26,011 ....J 3
Harderwijk, 14,054 ....H 4
Hardinxveld, †13,588 ....G 5
Harlingen, †12,552 ....G 2
Hasselt, †5,005 ....J 3
Hattem, †9,034 ....H 4
Heemstede, †26,507 ....F 4
Heer, †12,217 ....H 7
Heerde, †15,341 ....H 4
Heerenveen, †31,434 ....H 3
Heerlen, †75,147 ....J 7
Heiloo, †17,736 ....F 3
Hellendoorn, †29,410 ....J 4
Hellevoetsluis, †9,653 ....E 5
Helmond, †57,889 ....H 6
Helmond, *79,164 ....H 6
Hengelo, Gelderland, †7,360 ....J 4
Hengelo, Overijssel, †69,618 ....K 4
Heusden, †4,587 ....G 5
Hillegom, †16,963 ....E 4
Hilvarenbeek, †7,358 ....G 6
Hilversum, 99,792 ....G 4
Hindeloopen, †881 ....G 3
Hippolytushoef, 3,035 ....G 3
Hoek, †2,817 ....D 6
Hoek van Holland (Hook of Holland), 5,114 ....D 5
Hoensbroek, †22,703 ....H 7
Hof, †7,816 ....G 6
Holijsloot, 344 ....C 4
Hollum, 890 ....H 2
Holwerd, 1,691 ....H 2
Hoofddorp, 4,949 ....F 4
Hoogeveen, †37,485 ....J 3
Hoogezand, †30,189 ....K 2
Hoogkarspel, †3,681 ....G 3
Hook of Holland, 5,114 ....D 5
Hoorn, †18,574 ....G 3
Horst, †15,310 ....H 6
Huissen, †9,101 ....J 5
Huizen, †20,554 ....G 4
Hulst, †6,699 ....E 6
IJlst, †1,932 ....H 2
IJmuiden, 3,587 ....E 4
IJsselstein, †9,633 ....F 4
IJzendijke, †2,492 ....D 6
Ilpendam, †2,955 ....C 4
Joure, 5,509 ....H 3
Kampen, †28,902 ....H 3
Katwijk aan Zee, †36,236 ....E 4
Kerkbuurt en Thij, †8,244 ....J 3
Kerkdriel, 3,122 ....G 5
Kerkrade, †48,150 ....J 7
Kesteren, †7,290 ....G 5
Kloosterveen, †7,296 ....K 3
Kollum, 2,543 ....J 2
Koog aan de Zaan, †6,114 ....A 4
Krimpen aan den IJssel, †17,801 ....F 5
Landsmeer, †6,511 ....C 4
Laren, †6,528 ....G 4
Leek, †11,628 ....J 2
Leerdam, †13,282 ....F 5
Leeuwarden, 100,006 ....H 2
Leiden, 101,221 ....E 4
Lelystad, 716 ....H 4
Lemmer, 4,399 ....H 3
Lent, 2,032 ....H 5
Lisse, †17,049 ....F 4
Lith, †4,698 ....G 5
Lochem, †9,452 ....J 4
Lonneker, 1,599 ....L 4
Loon op Zand, †16,437 ....G 5
Losser, 18,713 ....L 4
Maarssen, †14,734 ....F 4
Maasbree, †7,676 ....H 6
Maassluis, †25,878 ....E 5
Maastricht, †93,927 ....H 7
Makkum, 2,416 ....G 2
Margraten, †2,844 ....H 7
Medemblik, †5,192 ....G 3
Meerssen, †8,800 ....H 7
Meppel, †19,364 ....J 3
Middelburg, †30,211 ....C 6
Middelharnis, †12,488 ....E 5
Middenmeer, 1,775 ....F 3
Millingen aan den Rijn, †4,764 ....J 5
Moerdijk, 601 ....F 5
Monnikendam, †6,014 ....C 4
Montfoort, †2,392 ....G 4
Muiden, †5,724 ....G 4
Muntendam, †3,695 ....K 2
Naaldwijk, †22,306 ....E 4
Naarden, †17,447 ....G 4
Nagele, 766 ....H 3
Neede, †9,739 ....K 4
Nes, 894 ....H 2
Nieuw-Buinen, 3,966 ....K 3
Nieuw-Schoonebeek, 1,602 ....L 3

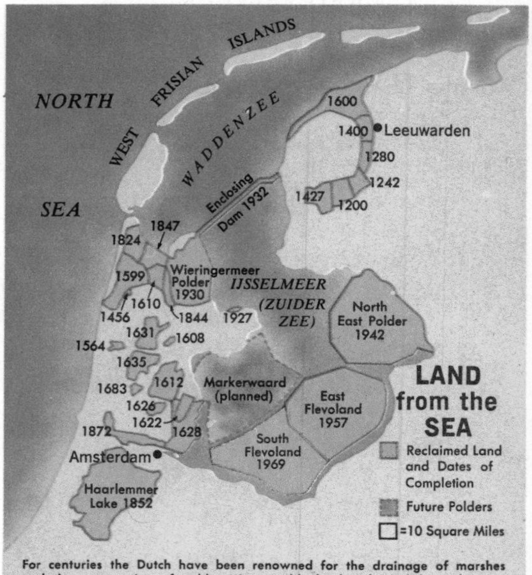

NORTH
SEA
WEST FRISIAN ISLANDS
WADDENZEE
1600
1400
Leeuwarden
1280
1242
1427
1200
Enclosing Dam 1932
1847
1824
Wieringermeer Polder 1930
IJSSELMEER (ZUIDER ZEE)
1599
1610
1844
1927
North East Polder 1942
1456
1631
1608
1564
1635
1683
1612
Markerwaard (planned)
East Flevoland 1957
1626
1622
1628
1872
South Flevoland 1969
Amsterdam
Haarlemmer Lake 1852
LAND from the SEA
Reclaimed Land and Dates of Completion
Future Polders
=10 Square Miles

For centuries the Dutch have been renowned for the drainage of marshes and the construction of polders, i.e., arable land reclaimed from the sea. Future projects will convert much of the present IJsselmeer to agricultural land.

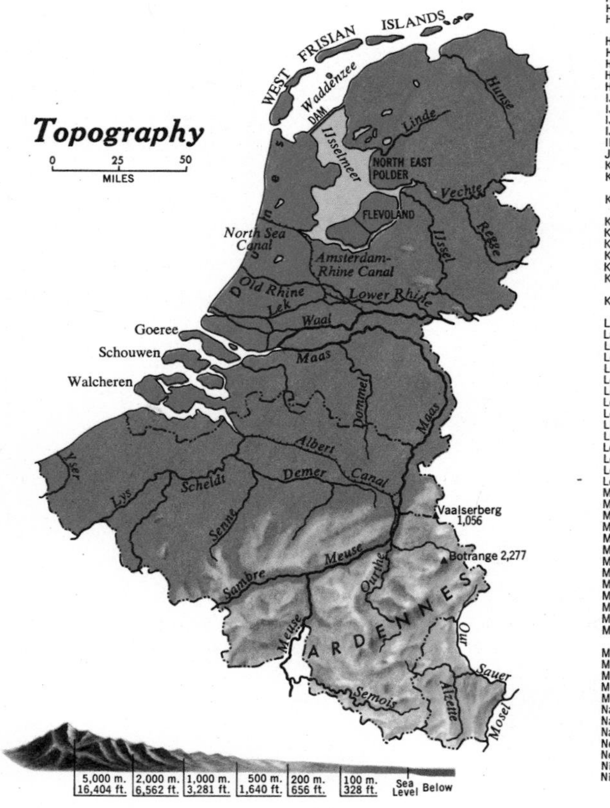

Topography
0 25 50
MILES
WEST FRISIAN ISLANDS
Waddenzee
DAM
IJsselmeer
NORTH EAST POLDER
Linde
Hunse
Vechte
FLEVOLAND
Regge
IJssel
North Sea Canal
Amsterdam-Rhine Canal
Old Rhine
Lek
Lower Rhine
Waal
Goeree
Schouwen
Walcheren
Maas
Dommel
Albert
Demer
Canal
Scheldt
Lys
Yser
Senne
Vaalserberg 1,056
Botrange 2,277
Meuse
Ourthe
Sambre
ARDENNES
Semois
Our
Sauer
Alzette
Mosel
5,000 m. 16,404 ft.
2,000 m. 6,562 ft.
1,000 m. 3,281 ft.
500 m. 1,640 ft.
200 m. 656 ft.
100 m. 328 ft.
Sea Level
Below

Nieuwe Pekela, †5,163 ....L 2
Nieuwendam, 15,679 ....C 4
Nieuweschans, †1,846 ....L 2
Nieuwkoop, †7,835 ....F 4
Nijkerk, †17,718 ....H 4
Nijmegen, 148,790 ....H 5
Nijmegen, *210,865 ....H 5
Nijverdal, 11,986 ....J 4
Noordwijk, †20,925 ....E 4
Norg, †5,386 ....J 2
Numansdorp, †5,169 ....E 5
Nunspeet, 7,103 ....H 4
Odoorn, †11,730 ....K 3
Oisterwijk, †13,797 ....G 5
Oldenzaal, †22,604 ....K 4
Olst, †8,325 ....J 4
Ommen, †14,712 ....J 3
Onstwedde, 1,867 ....K 2
Oostburg, †4,044 ....C 6
Oosterend, 118 ....G 2
Oosterhout, †31,826 ....F 5
Oostmahorn, 131 ....J 2
Oost-Vlieland, 695 ....F 2
Oostzaan, †4,869 ....C 4
Ootmarsum, †3,339 ....K 4
Oss, †40,085 ....H 5
Otterlo, 984 ....H 4
Oud-Beijerland, †10,114 ....E 5
Ouddorp, †4,226 ....D 5
Oude-Pekela, †8,085 ....K 2
Oude-Tonge, 2,459 ....E 5
Oudenbosch, †9,346 ....E 5
Oudeschild, 939 ....F 2
Oudewater, †4,466 ....F 4
Overloon, 1,007 ....H 5
Purmerend, †23,288 ....F 4
Putten, †15,726 ....H 4
Raalte, †19,885 ....J 4
Renkum, †33,619 ....H 5
Reusel, †6,144 ....G 6
Rheden, †48,713 ....J 4
Rhenen, †14,860 ....H 5
Ridderkerk, †41,899 ....F 5
Rijnsburg, †8,600 ....F 4
Rijssen, †17,360 ....J 4
Rijswijk, †50,172 ....E 4
Roden, †12,444 ....J 2
Roermond, †35,850 ....J 6
Roosendaal, †45,935 ....F 5
Rotterdam, 686,586 ....E 5
Rotterdam, *1,052,871 ....E 5
Rutten, 491 ....H 3
Ruurlo, †6,829 ....J 4
's Gravendeel, †5,830 ....E 5
's Gravenhage (The Hague) (cap.), 550,613 ....E 4
's Gravenhage, *702,296 ....E 4
's Gravenzande, †12,907 ....E 4
's Heerenberg, 5,196 ....J 5
's Hertogenbosch, †81,574 ....G 5
's Hertogenbosch, *193,356 ....G 5
Sappemeer, †30,189 ....K 2
Schagen, †6,772 ....F 3
Scheveningen, 80,015 ....E 4
Schiedam, †83,049 ....E 5
Schiermonnikoog, †814 ....J 1
Schijndel, †16,362 ....H 5
Schiphol, 3,368 ....B 5
Schoonebeek, †7,426 ....L 3
Schoonhoven, †7,565 ....F 5
Sint-Annaland, †2,826 ....E 5
Sint Jacobiparochie, 1,246 ....H 2
Sittard, †33,887 ....H 6
Sliedrecht, †19,868 ....F 5
Slochteren, †12,901 ....K 2
Sloten, Friesland, †751 ....H 3
Sloten, North Holland, 1,332 ....B 5
Sloterdijk, 1,215 ....B 4
Sluis, †2,810 ....C 6
Smilde (Kloosterveen), †7,296 ....K 3
Sneek, †26,244 ....H 2
Soest, †35,713 ....G 4
Soesterberg, 4,627 ....G 4
Stadskanaal, †32,829 ....L 3
Staphorst, †10,498 ....J 3
Staveren, †934 ....G 3
Steenbergen, †12,512 ....E 5
Steenwijk, †12,226 ....J 3
Steenwijkerwold (Kerkbuurt en Thij), †8,244 ....J 3
Stiens, 2,008 ....H 2
Tegelen, †18,168 ....J 6
Ter Apel, 2,508 ....L 3
Termunten, †4,721 ....K 2
Terneuzen, †22,014 ....D 6
Tholen, †3,798 ....E 5
Tiel, †21,789 ....G 5
Tilburg, 152,589 ....G 5
Tilburg, *268,395 ....G 5
Twello, 5,929 ....J 4
Uden, †23,311 ....H 5
Uitgeest, †7,151 ....F 3
Uithoorn, †17,492 ....F 4
Uithuizen, †4,939 ....K 2
Ulrum, †3,631 ....J 2
Urk, 8,027 ....H 3
Utrecht, 278,966 ....G 4
Utrecht, *401,981 ....G 4
Vaals, †10,338 ....H 7
Valkenswaard, †23,238 ....H 6
Van Ewijcksluis, 231 ....F 3
Veendam, †23,709 ....K 2
Veenendaal, †29,637 ....G 4
Veenhuizen, †4,097 ....J 2
Veere, †3,822 ....D 5
Veghel, †18,374 ....H 5
Velp, †9,488 ....J 5
Velsen, †67,580 ....F 4
Venlo, †62,694 ....J 6
Venlo, *95,516 ....J 6
Venraij, †26,056 ....H 6
Vianen, †8,173 ....G 5
Vlaardingen, †79,085 ....E 5
Vlagtwedde, †16,622 ....L 3
Vlijmen, †12,314 ....G 5
Vlissingen (Flushing), †40,197 ....C 6
Volendam, 10,123 ....G 4
Voorburg, †45,011 ....E 4
Voorst, †21,379 ....J 4
Vorden, †6,893 ....J 4
Vreeswijk, †5,393 ....G 4
Vrieseveen, †14,658 ....K 4
Vught, †22,633 ....G 5
Waalwijk, †23,304 ....F 5
Wageningen, †26,572 ....H 5
Wamel, †8,217 ....H 5
Weert, †35,190 ....H 6
Weesp, †17,261 ....C 5
West-Terschelling, †4,294 ....G 2
Westkapelle, †2,478 ....C 5
Westzaan, †4,502 ....A 4
Wierden, †17,653 ....K 4
Wierum, 628 ....H 2
Wijhe, †6,225 ....J 4
Wijk aan Zee, 2,414 ....E 4
Wijk bij Duurstede, †5,342 ....G 5
Wijk en Aalburg, †3,583 ....G 5
Wildervank, 5,280 ....K 2
Willemstad, †2,306 ....F 5
Winkel, †2,450 ....F 3
Winschoten, †18,043 ....L 2
Winsum, †3,631 ....K 2
Winterswijk, †26,230 ....K 5
Woensdrecht, †7,892 ....E 6
Woerden, †18,448 ....F 4
Wolvega, 6,620 ....J 3
Workum, †4,019 ....G 3
Wormerveer, †14,804 ....F 4
Yerseke, 4,799 ....E 6
Zaandam, †63,535 ....B 4
Zaandijk, †5,696 ....B 4
Zaltbommel, †7,004 ....G 5
Zandvoort, †15,451 ....E 4
Zeist, †55,619 ....G 4
Zevenbergen, †10,270 ....E 5
Zierikzee, †7,842 ....D 5
Zoutkamp, 1,083 ....J 2
Zundert, †12,124 ....F 6
Zutphen, †27,610 ....J 4
Zwanenburg, 6,999 ....B 4
Zwartsluis, †4,091 ....H 3
Zwijndrecht, †31,761 ....F 5
Zwolle, †76,167 ....J 3

OTHER FEATURES

Alkmaardermeer (lake) ....F 3
Ameland (isl.), †2,899 ....H 2
Bergumeer (lake) ....J 2
Beulaker Wijde (lake) ....H 3
Borndiep (channel) ....H 2
De Fluessen (lake) ....G 3
De Honte (bay) ....D 6
De Peel (region), 69,356 ....H 6
De Twente (reg.), 491,403 ....K 4
De Zaan (river) ....B 4
Dollart (bay) ....L 2
Dommel (river) ....H 6
Duiveland (isl.), 13,317 ....D 5
Eastern Scheldt (estuary) ....D 5
Eijerlandsche Gat (strait) ....F 2
Flevoland Polder, 15,788 ....G 4
Friesche Gat (channel) ....J 2
Galgenberg (hill) ....H 4
Goeree (isl.) ....D 5
Grevelingen (strait) ....E 5
Griend (isl.) ....G 2
Groninger Wad (sound) ....J 2
Groote IJ Polder, 20 ....B 4
Haarlemmermeer Polder, 58,966 ....B 5
Haringvliet (strait) ....E 5
Het IJ (estuary) ....C 4
Hoek van Holland (cape) ....D 5
Hondsrug (hills) ....K 3
Houtrak Polder, 339 ....A 4
Hunse (river) ....K 3
IJmeer (bay) ....C 4
IJssel (river) ....J 4
IJsselmeer (lake) ....G 3
Lauwers (channel) ....J 1
Lauwers Zee (bay) ....J 2
Lek (river) ....F 5
Lemelerberg (hill) ....J 4
Linde (river) ....J 3
Lower Rhine (river) ....H 5
Maas (river) ....G 5
Mark (river) ....F 6
Marken (isl.), 1,865 ....G 4
Markerwaard Polder ....G 3
Marsdiep (channel) ....F 3
Noordergat (channel) ....F 2
North (sea) ....E 3
North Beveland (isl.), 6,777 ....D 5
North East Polder, 31,929 ....H 3
North Holland (canal) ....C 4
North Sea (canal) ....F 4
Old Rhine (river) ....E 4
Ooster Eems (channel) ....K 1
Oostzaan Polder, 4,869 ....B 4
Orange (canal) ....K 3
Overflakkee (isl.), 27,814 ....E 5
Pinkegat (channel) ....H 2
Regge (river) ....K 4
Roer (river) ....J 6
Rottumeroog (isl.), 3 ....J 1
Schiermonnikoog (isl.), 814 ....J 1
Schouwen (isl.), 9,731 ....D 5
Simonszand (isl.) ....J 1
Slotermeer (lake) ....H 3
Sneekermeer (lake) ....H 2
South Beveland (isl.), 61,968 ....D 6
Terschelling (isl.), 4,294 ....G 2
Texel (isl.), 11,394 ....F 2
Tjeukemeer (lake) ....H 3
Vaalserberg (mt.) ....J 7
Vecht (river) ....J 4
Vechte (river) ....J 3
Veeregat (channel) ....D 5
Veluwe (region), 457,834 ....H 4
Vlie Stroom (strait) ....G 2
Vlieland (isl.), 933 ....F 2
Voorne (isl.), 22,742 ....D 5
Waal (river) ....G 5
Waddenzee (sound) ....G 2
Walcheren (isl.), 89,793 ....C 5
West Frisian (isls.), 18,336 ....F 2
Wester Eems (channel) ....K 1
Western Scheldt (De Honte) (bay) ....D 6
Westgat (channel) ....F 3
Wieringermeer Polder, 16,562 ....G 3
Wilhelmina (canal) ....G 6
Willems (canal) ....G 5

*City and suburbs.
†Populations of communes.

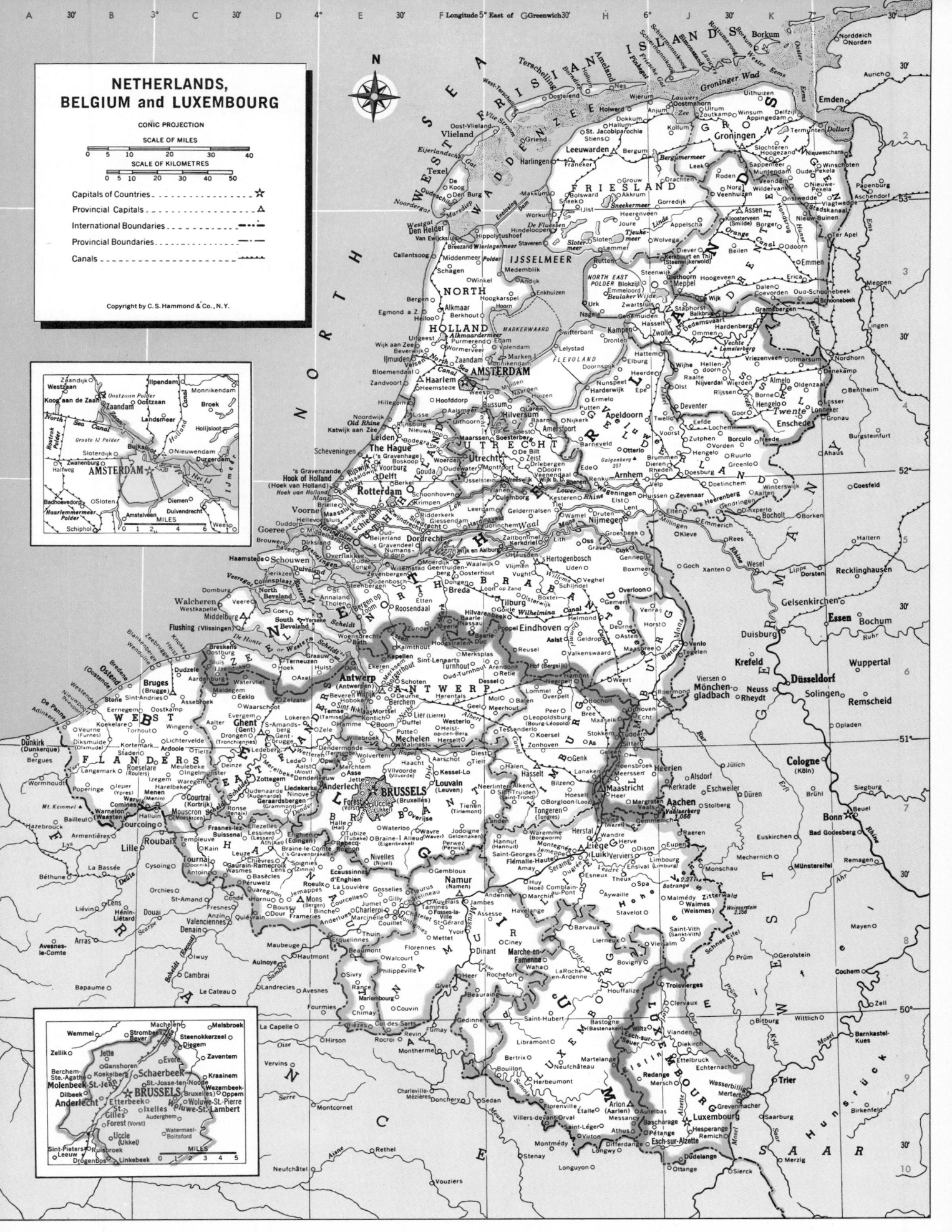

FRANCE

CONIC PROJECTION

SCALE OF MILES

SCALE OF KILOMETRES

Capitals of Countries .... ☆
Capitals of Departments .... △
International Boundaries ....
Department Boundaries ....
Canals ....

© C.S. Hammond & Co., N.Y.

PARIS and ENVIRONS

CORSICA

Same Scale as Main Map

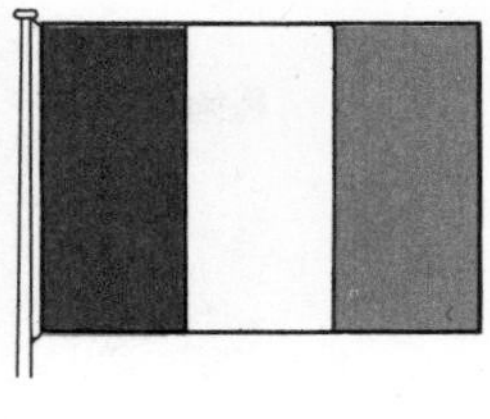

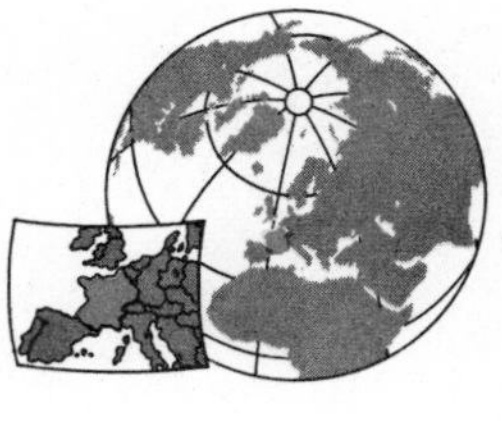

AREA 212,841 sq. mi.
POPULATION 50,770,000
CAPITAL Paris
LARGEST CITY Paris
HIGHEST POINT Mont Blanc 15,771 ft.
MONETARY UNIT franc
MAJOR LANGUAGE French
MAJOR RELIGION Roman Catholicism

Topography

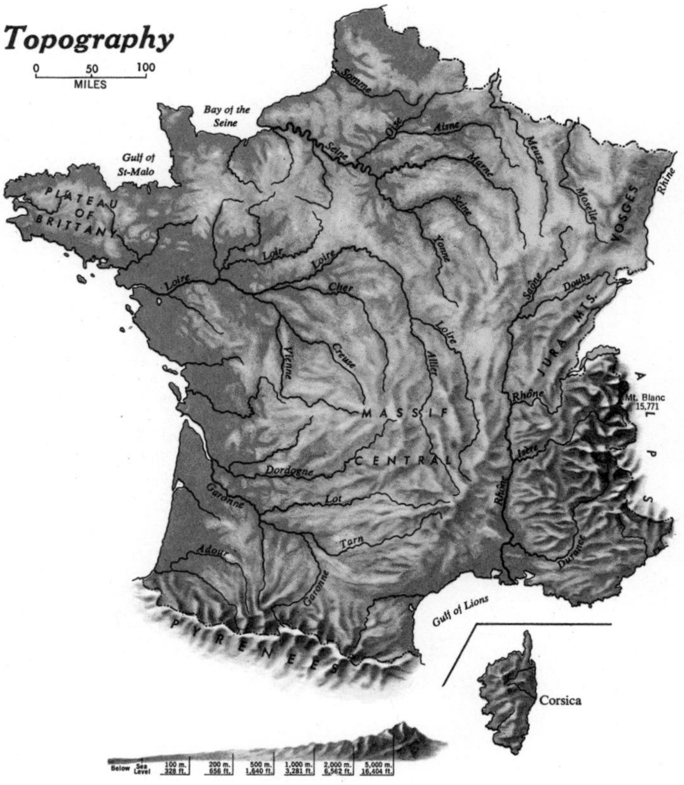

DEPARTMENTS

Ain, 339,262 ....F 4
Aisne, 526,346 ....E 3
Allier, 386,533 ....E 4
Alpes-de-Haute-Provence, 104,813 ....G 5
Alpes-Maritimes, 722,070 ....G 6
Ardèche, 256,927 ....F 5
Ardennes, 309,380 ....F 3
Ariège, 138,478 ....D 6
Aube, 270,325 ....E 3
Aude, 278,323 ....E 6
Aveyron, 281,568 ....E 5
Bas-Rhin, 827,367 ....G 3
Belfort (terr.), 118,450 ....G 4
Bouches-du-Rhône, 1,470,271 ....F 6
Calvados, 519,695 ....C 3
Cantal, 169,330 ....E 5
Charente, 331,016 ....D 5
Charente-Maritime, 483,622 ....C 5
Cher, 304,601 ....E 4
Corrèze, 237,858 ....D 5
Corsica (Corse), 269,831 ....B 6
Côte-d'Or, 421,192 ....F 4
Côtes-du-Nord, 506,102 ....B 3
Creuse, 156,876 ....D 4
Deux-Sèvres, 326,462 ....C 4
Dordogne, 374,073 ....D 5
Doubs, 426,363 ....G 4
Drôme, 342,891 ....F 5
Essonne, 674,157 ....E 3
Eure, 383,385 ....D 3
Eure-et-Loir, 302,207 ....D 3
Finistère, 768,929 ....A 3
Gard, 478,544 ....F 6
Gers, 181,577 ....D 6
Gironde, 1,009,390 ....C 5
Haut-Rhin, 585,018 ....G 4
Haute-Garonne, 690,712 ....D 6
Haute-Loire, 208,337 ....E 5
Haute-Marne, 214,336 ....F 3
Haute-Saône, 214,176 ....G 4
Haute-Savoie, 378,550 ....G 5
Haute-Vienne, 341,589 ....D 5
Hautes-Alpes, 91,790 ....G 5
Hautes-Pyrénées, 225.730 ....D 6
Hauts-de-Seine, 1,461,619 ....A 2
Hérault, 591,397 ....E 6
Ille-et-Vilaine, 652,722 ....C 3
Indre, 247,178 ....D 4
Indre-et-Loire, 437,870 ....D 4
Isère, 768,450 ....F 5
Jura, 233,547 ....F 4
Landes, 277,381 ....C 5
Loir-et-Cher, 267,896 ....D 4
Loire, 722,383 ....F 5
Loire-Atlantique, 861,452 ....C 4
Loiret, 430,629 ....E 4
Lot, 151,198 ....D 5
Lot-et-Garonne, 290,592 ....D 5
Lozère, 77,258 ....E 5
Maine-et-Loire, 584,709 ....C 4
Manche, 451,939 ....C 3
Marne, 485,388 ....F 3
Mayenne, 252,762 ....C 3
Meurthe-et-Moselle, 705,413 ....G 3
Meuse, 209,513 ....F 3
Morbihan, 540,474 ....B 4
Moselle, 971,314 ....G 3
Nièvre, 247,702 ....E 4
Nord, 2,417,899 ....E 2
Oise, 540,988 ....E 3
Orne, 288,524 ....C 3
Paris, 2,590,771 ....B 2
Pas-de-Calais, 1,397,159 ....E 2
Puy-de-Dôme, 547,743 ....E 5
Pyrénées-Atlantiques, 508,734 ....C 6
Pyrénées-Orientales, 281,976 ....E 6
Rhône, 1,325,611 ....F 5
Saône-et-Loire, 550,362 ....F 4
Sarthe, 461,839 ....D 3
Savoie, 288,921 ....G 5
Seine-et-Marne, 604,340 ....E 3
Seine-Maritime, 1,113,977 ....D 3
Seine-Saint-Denis, 1,251,792 ....B 1
Somme, 512,113 ....E 3
Tarn, 332,011 ....E 6
Tarn-et-Garonne, 183,572 ....D 5
Val-de-Marne, 1,121,340 ....B 2
Val-d'Oise, 693,269 ....E 3
Var, 555,926 ....G 6
Vaucluse, 353,966 ....F 6
Vendée, 421,250 ....C 4
Vienne, 340,256 ....D 4
Vosges, 388,201 ....G 3
Yonne, 283,376 ....E 4
Yvelines, 853,386 ....D 3

CITIES and TOWNS

Abbeville, 23,770 ....D 2
Agde, 8,812 ....E 6
Agen, 34,592 ....D 5
Aix-en-Provence, 74,948 ....F 6
Aix-les-Bains, 20,594 ....G 5
Ajaccio, 38,776 ....B 7
Albert, 10,937 ....E 2
Albertville, 15,422 ....G 5
Albi, 38,867 ....E 6
Alençon, 30,368 ....D 3
Aléria, 1,000 ....B 6
Alès, 31,948 ....E 5
Ambérieu-en-Bugey, 8,570 ....F 5
Amboise, 8,408 ....D 4
Amiens, 116,107 ....D 3
Angers, 127,415 ....C 4
Angoulême, 46,584 ....D 5
Annecy, 53,361 ....G 5
Annonay, 19,591 ....F 5
Antibes, 47,393 ....G 6
Antony, 56,556 ....B 2
Apt, 8,502 ....F 6
Arcachon, 14,852 ....C 5
Argentan, 14,418 ....D 3
Argenteuil, 87,106 ....A 1
Arles, 33,575 ....F 6
Armentières, 24,460 ....E 2
Arras, 48,494 ....E 2
Asnières, 79,942 ....A 1
Aubagne, 17,055 ....F 6
Aubenas, 10,480 ....F 5
Aubervilliers, 73,559 ....B 1
Aubusson, 5,641 ....E 4
Auch, 18,072 ....D 6
Audincourt, 13,487 ....G 4
Aulnay-sous-Bois, 61,384 ....B 1
Auray, 8,180 ....B 4
Aurignac, 783 ....D 6
Aurillac, 26,776 ....E 5
Autun, 17,194 ....F 4
Auxerre, 33,700 ....E 4
Avallon, 6,615 ....E 4
Avesnes-sur-Helpe, 6,253 ....F 2
Avignon, 78,871 ....F 6
Avion, 22,390 ....E 2
Avranches, 9,751 ....C 3
Bagnères-de-Bigorre, 9,139 ....D 6
Bagnères-de-Luchon, 4,079 ....D 6
Bagnolet, 33,607 ....B 2
Bagnols-sur-Cèze, 15,336 ....F 5
Bar-le-Duc, 18,874 ....F 3
Bar-sur-Seine, 2,642 ....F 3
Barfleur, 825 ....C 3
Bastia, 48,800 ....B 6
Bayeux, 11,190 ....C 3
Bayonne, 39.761 ....C 6
Beaucaire, 8,820 ....F 6
Beaune, 16,441 ....F 4
Beauvais, 46,284 ....E 3
Bédarieux, 6,929 ....E 6
Belfort, 53,001 ....G 4
Belley, 5,958 ....F 5
Berck, 13,658 ....D 2
Bergerac, 24,184 ....D 5
Bernay, 9,298 ....D 3
Besançon, 107,939 ....G 4
Bessèges, 5,421 ....F 5
Béthune, 26,144 ....E 2
Béziers, 74,517 ....E 6
Biarritz, 26,628 ....C 6
Blois, 39,279 ....D 4
Bobigny, 39,321 ....B 1
Bolbec, 12,517 ....D 3
Bondy, 51,555 ....B 1
Bordeaux, 263,808 ....C 5
Bordeaux, †648,000 ....C 5
Boulogne-Billancourt, 108,846....A 2
Boulogne-sur-Mer, 49,064 ....D 2
Bourg-en-Bresse, 35,064 ....F 4
Bourges, 67,137 ....E 4
Bressuire, 8,010 ....C 4
Brest, 150,696 ....A 3
Briançon, 7,551 ....G 5
Briare, 4,725 ....E 4
Brignoles, 8,010 ....G 6
Brive-la-Gaillarde, 45,314 ....D 5
Bruay-en-Artois, 38,608 ....E 2
Caen, 106,790 ....C 3
Cahors, 17,775 ....D 5
Calais, 70,153 ....D 2
Caluire-et-Cuire, 37,541 ....F 5
Calvi, 2,523 ....B 6
Cambrai, 37,290 ....E 2
Cannes, 66,590 ....G 6
Carcassonne, 40,580 ....D 6
Carentan, 5,207 ....C 3
Carmaux, 13,423 ....E 5
Carpentras, 18,092 ....F 5
Castelnaudary, 8,550 ....E 6
Castelsarrasin, 7,912 ....D 6
Castres, 35,975 ....E 6
Cavaillon, 14,815 ....F 6
Cayeux-sur-Mer, 2,489 ....D 2
Chalon-sur-Saône, 47,004 ....F 4
Châlons-sur-Marne, 48,558 ....F 3
Chambéry, 49,858 ....F 5
Chambord, 200 ....D 4
Chamonix-Mont Blanc, 5,907 ....G 5
Champigny-sur-Marne, 70,353 ....C 2
Chantilly, 10,156 ....E 3
Charenton-le-Pont, 22,220 ....B 2
Charleville-Mézières, 55,230 ....F 3
Chartres, 34,128 ....D 3
Château-du-Loir, 5,239 ....D 4
Château-Gontier, 7,881 ....C 4
Château-Renault, 5,082 ....D 4
Château-Thierry, 10,858 ....E 3
Châteaubriant, 11,196 ....C 4
Châteaudun, 13,715 ....D 3
Châteauneuf-sur-Loire, 4,603 ....E 4
Châteauroux, 48,867 ....D 4
Châtellerault, 33,491 ....D 4
Châtillon, 24,468 ....B 2
Châtillon-sur-Seine, 6,128 ....F 4
Chatou, 22,495 ....A 1
Chaumont, 25,602 ....F 3
Chauny, 13,714 ....E 3
Chelles, 22,111 ....C 1
Cherbourg, 37,933 ....C 3
Chinon, 5,435 ....D 4
Choisy-le-Roi, 41,080 ....B 2
Cholet, 40,224 ....C 4
Clamart, 54,866 ....A 2
Clermont, 7,119 ....E 3
Clermont-Ferrand, 145,856 ....E 5
Clichy, 52,398 ....B 1
Cluny, 3,552 ....F 4
Cluses, 12,391 ....G 4
Cognac, 21,137 ....C 5
Colmar, 58,623 ....G 3
Colombes, 80,224 ....A 1
Commentry, 8,129 ....E 4
Commercy, 7,043 ....F 3
Compiègne, 28,881 ....E 3
Concarneau, 16,458 ....A 4
Cosne-sur-Loire, 8,931 ....E 4
Coudekerque-Branche, 22,972 ....E 2
Coulommiers. 11.182 ....E 3
Courbevoie, 57,998 ....A 1
Coutances, 8,599 ....C 3
Coutras, 4,251 ....C 5
Creil, 31,792 ....E 3
Crépy-en-Valois, 8,506 ....E 3
Créteil, 48,757 ....B 2
Cusset, 12,286 ....E 4
Dax, 18,185 ....C 6
Deauville, 5,103 ....C 3
Decazeville, 9,581 ....E 5
Denain, 27,840 ....E 2
Dieppe, 29,829 ....D 3
Digne, 11,973 ....G 5
Digoin, 9,585 ....F 4
Dijon, 143,120 ....F 4
Dinan, 12,999 ....B 3
Dinard, 9,042 ....B 3
Dôle, 25,620 ....F 4
Domrémy-la-Pucelle, 184 ....F 3
Douai, 47,347 ....E 2
Douarnenez, 18,442 ....A 3
Draguignan, 16,139 ....G 6
Drancy, 69,226 ....B 1
Dreux, 28,156 ....D 3
Dunkirk (Dunkerque), 26,038 ....E 2
Elbeuf, 19,110 ....D 3
Embrun, 3,986 ....G 5
Épernay, 26,094 ....E 3
Épinal, 36,219 ....G 3
Épinay-sur-Seine, 41,538....B 1
Étampes, 15,542 ....E 3
Étaples, 9,092 ....D 2
Eu, 7,866 ....D 3
Évreux, 41,004 ....D 3
Évry, 7,047 ....E 3
Falaise, 6,977 ....C 3
Fécamp, 21,098 ....D 3
Figeac, 8,462 ....D 5
Firminy, 24,545 ....F 5
Flers, 16,677 ....C 3
Foix, 9,061 ....D 6
Fontainebleau, 17,565 ....E 3
Fontenay-le-Comte, 10,884 ....C 4
Fontenay-sous-Bois, 38,737 ....C 2
Forbach, 23,062 ....G 3
Fougères, 25,745 ....C 3
Fourmies, 14,895 ....F 2
Fréjus, 22,567 ....G 6
Gagny, 35,745 ....C 1
Gap, 22,027 ....G 5
Gardanne, 12,601 ....F 6
Gennevilliers, 45,925 ....B 1
Gentilly, 18,638 ....B 2
Gex, 3,078 ....G 4
Gien, 11,655 ....E 4
Gisors, 7,024 ....D 3
Givet, 7,697 ....F 2
Givors, 17,545 ....F 5
Granville, 12,315 ....C 3
Grasse, 24,398 ....G 6
Graulhet, 10,318 ....E 6
Gray, 7,782 ....F 4
Grenoble, 161,230 ....F 5
Guebwiller, 10,684 ....G 4
Guéret, 12,441 ....D 4
Guingamp, 9,091 ....B 3
Guise, 6,732 ....E 3
Haguenau, 22,335 ....G 3
Ham, 5,565 ....E 3
Harfleur, 15,503 ....D 3
Hautmont, 17,818 ....F 2
Hayange, 10,218 ....F 3
Hazebrouck, 16,768 ....E 2
Hendaye, 7,536 ....C 6
Hénin-Liétard, 25,067 ....E 2
Hennebont, 7,605 ....B 4
Héricourt, 7,376 ....G 4
Hirson, 11,764 ....F 3
Honfleur, 9,017 ....D 3
Hyères, 27,600 ....G 6
Issoire, 11,745 ....E 5
Issoudun, 14,559 ....D 4
Issy-les-Moulineaux, 50,260 ....A 2
Istres, 8,713 ....F 6
Ivry-sur-Seine, 60,342 ....B 2
Joigny, 9,609 ....E 3
La Baule-Escoublac, 11,962 ....B 4
La Ciotat, 19,485 ....F 6
La Courneuve, 42,812 ....B 1
La Flèche, 9,536 ....C 4
La Grand-Combe, 8,608 ....E 5
La Roche-sur-Yon, 32,279 ....C 4
La Rochelle, 72,075 ....C 4
La Seyne-sur-Mer, 42,958 ....F 6
La Tour-du-Pin, 5,649 ....F 5
L'Aigle, 7,478 ....D 3
Landerneau, 12,356 ....B 3
Langeac, 4,584 ....E 5
Langres, 8,945 ....F 4
Lannion, 10,066 ....B 3
Laon, 25,623 ....E 3
Laval, 45,051 ....C 3
Lavelanet, 8,512 ....E 6
Le Blanc-Mesnil, 48,212 ....B 1
Le Bourget, 9,625 ....B 1
Le Cateau, 8,922 ....E 2
Le Chesnay, 13,586 ....A 2
Le Creusot, 33,581 ....F 4
Le Croisic, 4,092 ....B 4
Le Havre, 198,021 ....C 3
Le Mans, 140,520 ....C 3
Le Puy, 24,816 ....F 5
Le Teil, 7,872 ....F 5
Le Touquet-Paris-Plage, 4,403....D 2
Le Tréport, 6,194 ....D 2
Lens, 41,800 ....E 2
Les Andelys, 6,292 ....D 3
Les Sables-d'Olonne, 17,856 ....B 4
Levallois-Perret, 58,890 ....B 1
Lézignan-Corbières, 7,101 ....E 6
Libourne, 19,981 ....C 5
Liévin, 35,733 ....E 2
Lille, 189,697 ....E 2
Lille, †1,042,000 ....E 2
Limoges, 127,605 ....D 5
Limoux, 9,150 ....E 6
Lisieux, 23,337 ....D 3
Livry-Gargan, 32,015 ....C 1
Lodève, 6,899 ....E 6
Longwy, 21,052 ....F 3
Lons-le-Saunier, 18,649 ....F 4
Lorient, 66,023 ....B 4
Loudun, 6,118 ....D 4
Lourdes, 17,627 ....C 6
Louviers, 15,159 ....D 3
Lunel, 10,178 ....E 6
Lunéville, 22,961 ....G 3
Luxeuil-les-Bains, 9,203 ....G 4
Lyon, 524,500 ....F 5
Lyon, †1,305,000 ....F 5
Mâcon, 33,266 ....F 4
Maisons-Alfort, 53,118 ....B 2
Maisons-Laffitte, 24,041 ....A 1
Malakoff, 36,198 ....B 2
Manosque, 13,352 ....G 6
Mantes-la-Jolie, 25,842 ....D 3
Marmande, 12,145 ....C 5
Marseille, 880,527 ....F 6
Marseille, †1,015,000 ....F 6
Martigues, 17,771 ....F 6
Maubeuge, 31,992 ....F 2
Mayenne, 10,010 ....C 3
Mazamet, 14,650 ....E 6
Meaux, 29,966 ....E 3
Melun, 33,345 ....E 3
Mende, 9,424 ....E 5
Menton, 23,401 ....G 6
Metz, 105,533 ....G 3
Meudon, 30,735 ....A 2
Millau, 21,420 ....E 5
Moissac, 7,694 ....D 5
Mont-de-Marsan, 22,771 ....C 6
Mont-Dore, 2,045 ....E 5
Mont-Saint-Michel, 72 ....C 3
Montargis, 18,087 ....E 3
Montauban, 33,945 ....D 5
Montbéliard, 23,402 ....G 4
Montbrison, 8,733 ....E 5
Montceau-les-Mines, 18,621 ....F 4
Montdidier, 5,785 ....E 3
Montélimar, 23,831 ....F 5
Montfort, 2,563 ....C 3
Montigny-les-Metz, 24,417 ....G 3
Montluçon, 57,638 ....E 4
Montpellier, 152,105 ....E 6
Montreuil, 95,420 ....B 2
Montrouge, 44,788 ....B 2
Morlaix, 16,750 ....B 3
Moulins, 25,778 ....E 4
Moûtiers, 4,066 ....G 5
Moyeuvre-Grande, 14,559 ....G 3
Mulhouse, 115,632 ....G 4
Muret, 10,515 ....D 6
Nancy, 121,910 ....G 3
Nanterre, 90,124 ....A 1
Nantes, 253,105 ....C 4
Narbonne, 35,236 ....E 6
Nemours, 8,081 ....E 3
Neufchâteau, 7,656 ....F 3
Neufchâtel-en-Bray, 5,734 ....D 3
Neuilly-sur-Seine, 70,787 ....B 1
Nevers, 42,092 ....E 4
Nice, 301,400 ....G 6
Nîmes, 115,561 ....F 6
Niort, 46,749 ....C 4
Nogent-le-Rotrou, 11,040 ....D 3
Nogent-sur-Seine, 4,271 ....E 3
Noisy-le-Sec, 34,058 ....B 1
Noyon, 11,567 ....E 3
Nyons, 4,311 ....F 5
Oloron-Sainte-Marie, 12,597 ....C 6
Orange, 17,582 ....F 5
Orléans, 94,382 ....D 3
Orly, 30,151 ....B 2
Orthez, 8,778 ....C 6
Oullins, 26,520 ....F 5
Oyonnax, 19,571 ....F 4
Pamiers, 13,183 ....D 6
Pantin, 47,580 ....B 1
Paray-le-Monial, 10,324 ....F 4
Paris (cap.), 2,580,010 ....B 2
Paris, *7,953,065 ....B 2
Paris, †9,283,000 ....B 2
Parthenay, 11,177 ....C 4
Pau, 71,865 ....C 6
Périgueux, 36,991 ....D 5
Perpignan, 100,086 ....E 6
Pessac, 35,343 ....C 5
Ploërmel, 3,720 ....B 4
Poitiers, 68,082 ....D 4
Pont-à-Mousson, 13,283 ....G 3
Pont-l'Abbé, 6,227 ....A 4
Pont-l'Évêque, 2,823 ....D 3
Pontarlier, 16,250 ....G 4
Pontivy, 9,674 ....B 3
Pontoise, 16,633 ....E 3
Port-de-Bouc, 13,447 ....F 6
Port-Louis, 3,921 ....B 4

(continued on following page)

HISTORIC PROVINCES

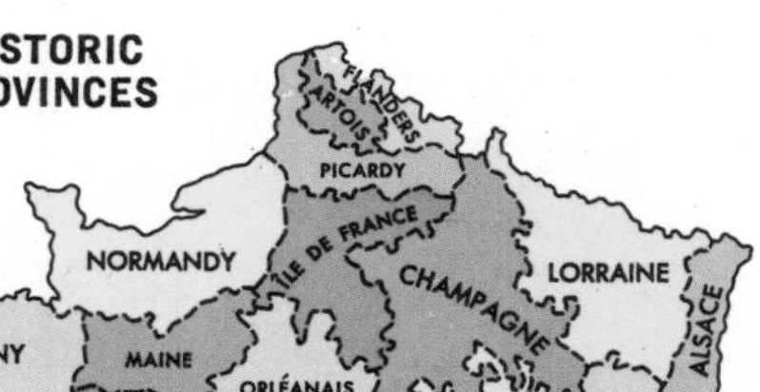

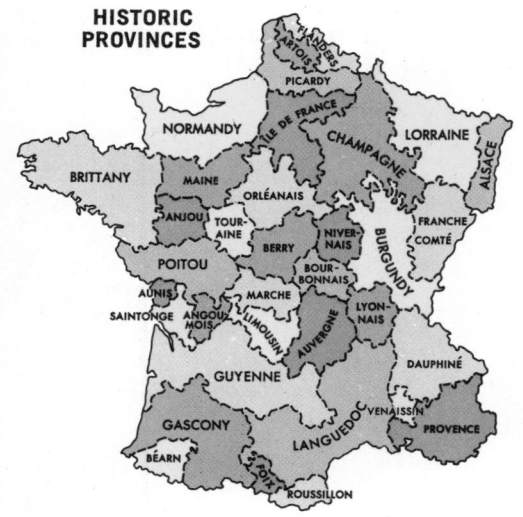

A resident of the city of Caen thinks of himself as a Norman rather than as a citizen of the modern department of Calvados. In spite of the passing of nearly two centuries, the historic provinces which existed before 1790 command the local patriotism of most Frenchmen.

28 France
(continued)

Port-St-Louis-du-Rhône, 7,194 ....F 6
Port-Vendres, 5,358 ....E 6
Porto-Vecchio, 3,324 ....B 7
Privas, 8,113 ....F 5
Provins, 11,205 ....E 3
Puteaux, 37,801 ....A 2
Quiberon, 4,305 ....B 4
Quimper, 47,811 ....A 4
Quimperlé, 9,701 ....B 4
Rambouillet, 14,043 ....D 3
Redon, 8,767 ....C 4
Reims, 151,988 ....E 3
Remiremont, 9,018 ....G 3
Rennes, 176,024 ....C 3
Rethel, 7,737 ....F 3
Révin, 11,978 ....F 3
Rezé, 31,113 ....C 4
Rive-de-Gier, 15,483 ....F 5
Roanne, 53,178 ....E 4
Rochefort, 28,223 ....C 4
Rodez, 23,041 ....E 5
Romans-sur-Isère, 29,430 ....F 5
Romilly-sur-Seine, 16,867 ....F 3
Romorantin-Lanthenay, 13,516 ...D 4
Roubaix, 114,239 ....E 2
Rouen, 118,323 ....D 3
Royan, 17,187 ....C 5
Rueil-Malmaison, 60,130 ....A 2
Sablé-sur-Sarthe, 8,194 ....C 4
Saint-Affrique, 6,443 ....E 6
Saint-Amand-Mont-Rond, 11,035..E 4
Saint-Brieuc, 49,305 ....B 3
Saint-Céré, 3,682 ....D 5
Saint-Chamond, 35,362 ....F 5
Saint-Claude, 12,344 ....F 4
Saint-Cloud, 28,016 ....A 2
Saint-Denis, 99,027 ....B 1
Saint-Dié, 24,652 ....G 3
Saint-Dizier, 35,742 ....F 3
Saint-Étienne, 212,843 ....F 5
Saint-Florent-sur-Cher, 6,261....E 4
Saint-Flour, 5,582 ....E 5
Saint-Gaudens, 9,776 ....D 6
Saint-Germain-en-Laye, 36,251....D 3
Saint-Girons, 7,462 ....D 6
Saint-Jean-d'Angély, 8,883 ....C 4
Saint-Jean-de-Luz, 10,206 ....C 6
Saint-Jean-de-Maurienne, 8,407...G 5
Saint-Jean-Pied-de-Port, 1,677 ...C 6
Saint-Junien, 8,624 ....D 5
Saint-Lô, 17,347 ....C 3
Saint-Malo, 40,252 ....B 3
Saint-Mandé, 22,998 ....B 2
Saint-Maur-des-Fossés, 77,122 ....B 2
Saint-Mihiel, 5,262 ....F 3
Saint-Nazaire, 60,696 ....B 4
Saint-Omer, 17,647 ....E 2
Saint-Ouen, 48,304 ....B 1
Saint-Quentin, 63,932 ....E 3
Saint-Raphaël, 16,117 ....G 6
Saint-Tropez, 5,138 ....G 6
Saint-Vallier, 4,863 ....F 5
Saint-Yrieix-la-Perche 4,655 ....D 5
Sainte-Mère-Église, 889 ....C 3
Sainte-Savine, 11,616 ....E 3
Saintes, 24,594 ....C 4
Salins-les-Bains, 4,084 ....F 4
Salon-de-Provence, 24,803 ....F 6
Sarrebourg, 11,104 ....G 3
Sarreguemines, 23,074 ....G 3
Sartène, 4,117 ....B 7
Sartrouville, 39,722 ....A 1
Saumur, 21,354 ....D 4
Saverne, 9,432 ....G 3
Sceaux, 19,837 ....A 2
Sedan, 22,998 ....F 3
Sélestat, 14,558 ....G 3
Senlis, 10,111 ....E 3
Sens, 22,658 ....E 3
Sète, 40,220 ....E 6
Sèvres, 20,025 ....A 2
Soissons, 25,409 ....E 3
Sotteville-lès-Rouen, 33,503 ....D 3
Stiring-Wendel, 13,757 ....G 3
Strasbourg, 247,526 ....H 3
Suresnes, 40,393 ....A 2
Tarare, 12,116 ....F 5
Tarascon, 8,848 ....F 6
Tarbes, 55,200 ....D 6
Thann, 8,108 ....G 4
Thiers, 14,430 ....E 5
Thionville, 35,747 ....G 3
Thonon-les-Bains, 20,095 ....G 4
Thouars, 11,526 ....C 4
Tonnerre, 5,562 ....E 4
Toulon, 169,593 ....F 6
Toulouse, 331,751 ....D 6
Tourcoing, 93,675 ....E 2
Tours, 126,414 ....D 4
Trouville-sur-Mer, 5,718 ....C 3
Troyes, 74,409 ....F 3
Tulle, 17,640 ....D 5
Uckange, 10,326....G 3
Uzès, 6,201 ....F 5
Valence, 60,662 ....F 5
Valenciennes, 46,237 ....E 2
Valognes, 5,218 ....C 3
Vannes, 36,380 ....B 4
Vence, 6,450 ....G 6
Vendôme, 15,854 ....D 4
Vénissieux, 47,460 ....F 5
Verdun-sur-Meuse, 21,308 ....F 3
Vernon, 16,983 ....D 3
Versailles, 89,035 ....A 2
Vesoul, 16,079 ....F 4
Vichy, 33,458 ....E 4
Vienne, 26,512 ....F 5
Vierzon, 32,429 ....D 4
Villefranche, 6,619 ....G 6
Villefranche-de-Rouergue, 9,382...E 5
Villefranche-sur-Saône, 25,995....F 4
Villejuif, 48,737 ....B 2
Villemomble, 28,731 ....C 1
Villeneuve-St-Georges, 30,229 ....E 3
Villeneuve-sur-Lot, 18,612 ....D 5
Villeurbanne, 119,420 ....F 5
Vincennes, 49,116 ....B 2
Vire, 10,819 ....C 3
Vitré, 10,125 ....C 3
Vitry-le-Francois, 16,409 ....F 3
Vitry-sur-Seine, 77,616 ....B 2
Vittel, 6,343 ....F 3
Voiron, 15,693 ....F 5
Wissembourg, 5,341 ....G 3
Yvetot, 9,208 ....D 3

OTHER FEATURES

Adour (river) ....C 6
Ain (river) ....F 4
Aisne (river) ....E 3
Ajaccio (gulf) ....B 7
Allier (river) ....E 5
Aube (river) ....F 3
Auvergne (mts.) ....E 5
Belle-Île (isl.), 4,442 ....B 4
Biscay (bay) ....B 5
Blanc (mt.) ....G 5
Bonifacio (strait) ....B 7
Calais (strait) ....D 2
Causses (region) ....E 5
Cévennes (mts.) ....E 5
Charente (river) ....C 5
Cher (river) ....D 4
Corse (cape) ....B 6
Corsica (isl.), 269,831 ....B 6
Côte-d'Or (mts.) ....F 4
Cotentin (pen.) ....C 3
Cottian Alps (range) ....G 5
Creuse (river) ....D 4
Dordogne (river) ....D 5
Dore (mts.) ....E 5
Doubs (river) ....G 4
Drôme (river) ....F 5
Dronne (river) ....D 5
Durance (river) ....F 6
English (channel) ....B 3
Eure (river) ....D 3
Forez (mts.) ....E 5
Fréjus (pass) ....G 5
Gard (river) ....F 5
Gave de Pau (river) ....C 6
Garonne (river) ....C 5
Geneva (lake) ....G 4
Gers (river) ....D 6
Gironde (river) ....C 5
Graian Alps (range) ....G 5
Gris-Nez (cape) ....D 2
Groix (isl.), 3,161 ....B 4
Hague (cape) ....C 3
Hérault (river) ....E 6
Hyères (isls.) ....G 6
Indre (river) ....D 4
Isère (river) ....F 5
Isle (river) ....D 5
Jura (mts.) ....F 4
Langres (plateau) ....F 4
Limousin (region) ....D 5
Lions (gulf) ....F 6
Little Saint Bernard (pass) ....G 5
Loir (river) ....D 4
Loire (river) ....C 4
Lot (river) ....D 5
Manche, La (English) (chan.)....B 3
Maritime Alps (range) ....G 5
Marne (river) ....C 2
Mayenne (river) ....C 4
Mediterranean (sea) ....E 7
Médoc (reg.) ....C 5
Meuse (river) ....F 3
Mont Cenis (tunnel) ....G 5
Morvan (plateau) ....E 4
Moselle (river) ....G 3
Noirmoutier (isl.), 8,091 ....B 4
North (sea) ....E 1
Oise (river) ....E 3
Oléron, d' (isl.), 16,355 ....C 5
Omaha (beach) ....C 3
Orb (river) ....E 6
Orne (river) ....C 3
Ouessant (isl.), 1,817 ....A 3
Penmarch (point) ....A 4
Perche (reg.) ....D 3
Puy-de-Dôme (mt.) ....E 5
Pyrenees (range) ....C 6
Ré (isl.), 9,967 ....C 4
Rhine (river) ....G 3
Rhône (river) ....F 5
Risle (river) ....D 3
Riviera (region) ....G 6
Saint-Florent (gulf) ....B 6
Saint-Malo (gulf) ....B 3
Saône (river) ....F 4
Sarthe (river) ....D 4
Sein (isl.), 835 ....A 3
Seine (bay) ....C 3
Seine (river) ....D 3
Sologne (reg.) ....E 4
Somme (river) ....D 2
Tarn (river) ....E 6
Ushant (Ouessant) (isl.), 1,817..A 3
Utah (beach) ....C 3
Vaccarès (lagoon) ....F 6
Vienne (river) ....D 4
Vilaine (river) ....C 4
Vosges (mts.) ....G 3
Yeu, d' (isl.), 4,786 ....B 4
Yonne (river) ....E 3

*City and suburbs.
†Population of metropolitan area.

MONACO

CITIES and TOWNS

Monte Carlo, 9,948 ....G 6

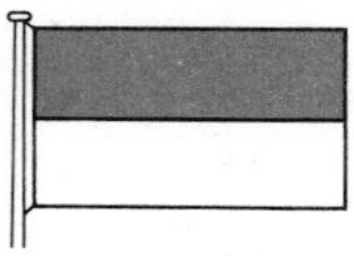

MONACO
AREA 368 acres
POPULATION 23,035

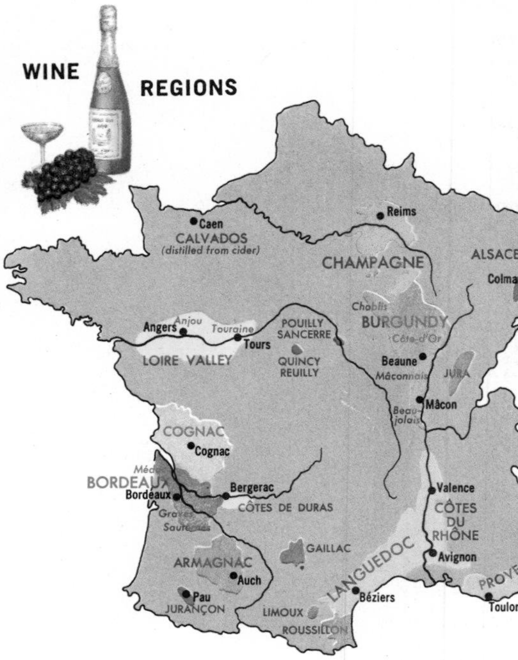

WINE
REGIONS
Caen
CALVADOS
(distilled from cider)
Reims
CHAMPAGNE
ALSACE
Colmar
Chablis
BURGUNDY
Côte d'Or
Angers
Anjou
Touraine
Tours
POUILLY
SANCERRE
LOIRE VALLEY
QUINCY
REUILLY
Beaune
Mâconnais
JURA
Mâcon
Beaujolais
COGNAC
Cognac
Médoc
BORDEAUX
Bordeaux
Bergerac
Graves
Sauternes
CÔTES DE DURAS
Valence
CÔTES
DU
RHÔNE
GAILLAC
ARMAGNAC
Auch
LANGUEDOC
Avignon
PROVENCE
Pau
JURANÇON
Béziers
LIMOUX
ROUSSILLON
Toulon

Climate, soil and variety of grape planted determine the quality of wine. Long, hot and fairly dry summers with cool, humid nights constitute an ideal climate. The nature of the soil is such a determining influence that identical grapes planted in Bordeaux, Burgundy and Champagne, will yield wines of widely different types.

Agriculture, Industry and Resources

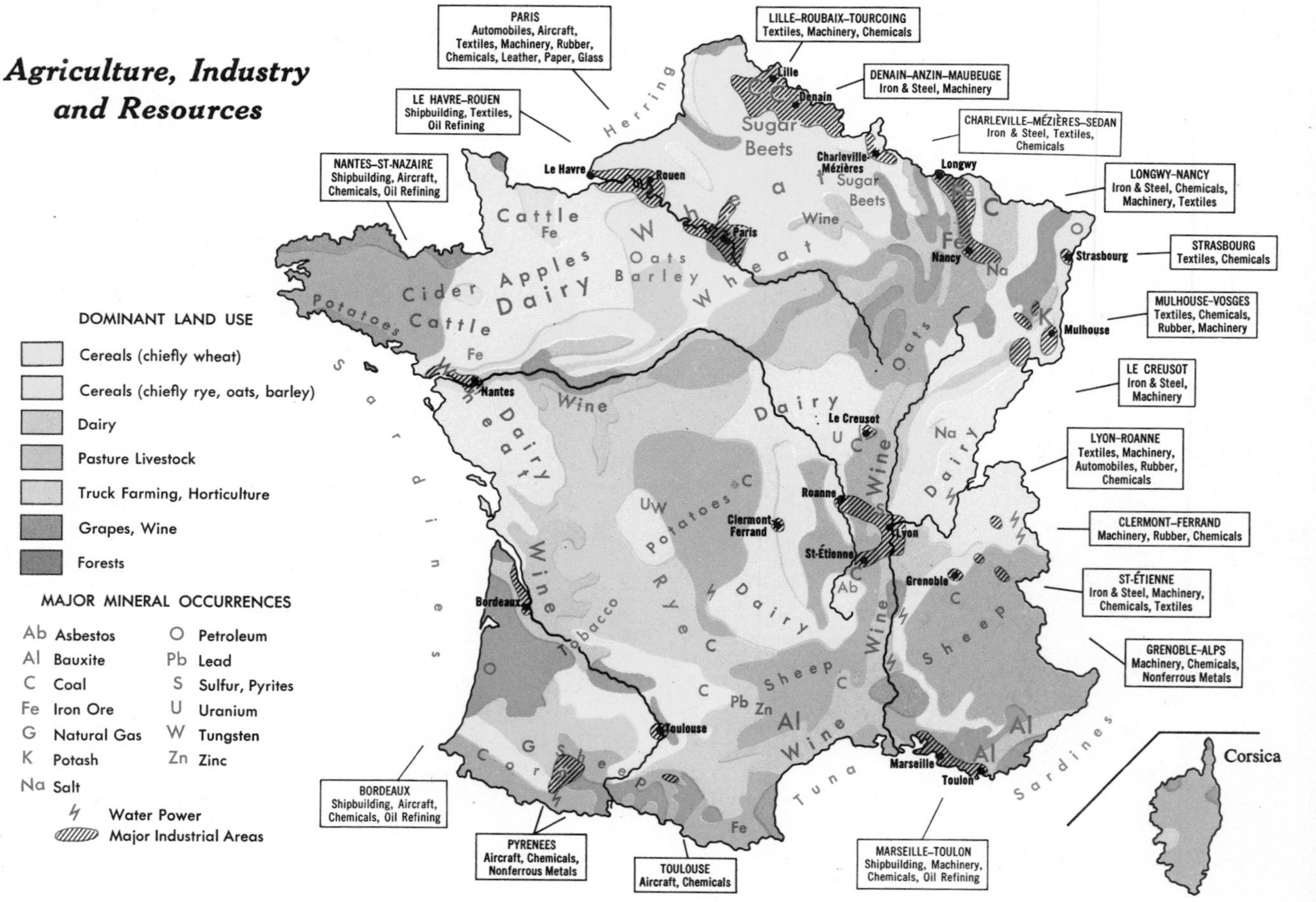

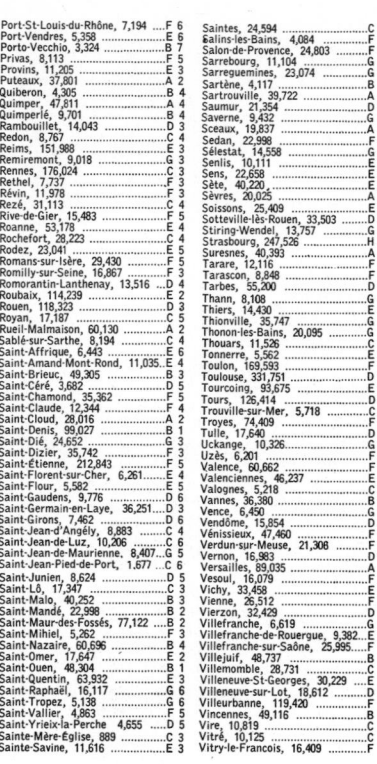

DOMINANT LAND USE
Cereals (chiefly wheat)
Cereals (chiefly rye, oats, barley)
Dairy
Pasture Livestock
Truck Farming, Horticulture
Grapes, Wine
Forests
MAJOR MINERAL OCCURRENCES
Ab Asbestos
Al Bauxite
C Coal
Fe Iron Ore
G Natural Gas
K Potash
Na Salt
O Petroleum
Pb Lead
S Sulfur, Pyrites
U Uranium
W Tungsten
Zn Zinc
Water Power
Major Industrial Areas
PARIS
Automobiles, Aircraft, Textiles, Machinery, Rubber, Chemicals, Leather, Paper, Glass
LILLE–ROUBAIX–TOURCOING
Textiles, Machinery, Chemicals
DENAIN–ANZIN–MAUBEUGE
Iron & Steel, Machinery
LE HAVRE–ROUEN
Shipbuilding, Textiles, Oil Refining
CHARLEVILLE–MÉZIÈRES–SEDAN
Iron & Steel, Textiles, Chemicals
NANTES–ST-NAZAIRE
Shipbuilding, Aircraft, Chemicals, Oil Refining
LONGWY–NANCY
Iron & Steel, Chemicals, Machinery, Textiles
STRASBOURG
Textiles, Chemicals
MULHOUSE–VOSGES
Textiles, Chemicals, Rubber, Machinery
LE CREUSOT
Iron & Steel, Machinery
LYON–ROANNE
Textiles, Machinery, Automobiles, Rubber, Chemicals
CLERMONT–FERRAND
Machinery, Rubber, Chemicals
ST-ÉTIENNE
Iron & Steel, Machinery, Chemicals, Textiles
GRENOBLE–ALPS
Machinery, Chemicals, Nonferrous Metals
BORDEAUX
Shipbuilding, Aircraft, Chemicals, Oil Refining
PYRENEES
Aircraft, Chemicals, Nonferrous Metals
TOULOUSE
Aircraft, Chemicals
MARSEILLE–TOULON
Shipbuilding, Machinery, Chemicals, Oil Refining
Herring
Sardines
Tuna
Sugar Beets
Cattle
Cider Apples
Dairy
Potatoes
Wheat
Oats
Barley
Wine
Tobacco
Rye
Sheep
Corsica
Lille
Denain
Le Havre
Rouen
Charleville-Mézières
Longwy
Paris
Nancy
Strasbourg
Mulhouse
Nantes
Le Creusot
Roanne
Clermont-Ferrand
Lyon
St-Étienne
Grenoble
Bordeaux
Toulouse
Marseille
Toulon

ANDORRA

CITIES and TOWNS

Andorra la Vella (cap.), 2,250....G 1

GIBRALTAR

PHYSICAL FEATURES

Europa (point) ....D 4

PORTUGAL

PROVINCES

Algarve, 315,300 ....B 4
Alto Alentejo, 410,200 ....C 3
Baixo Alentejo, 275,000 ....B 3
Beira Alta, 761,500 ....C 2
Beira Baixa, 321,100 ....C 3
Beira Litoral, 1,448,800 ....B 2
Douro Litoral, 1,352,600 ....B 2
Estremadura, 1,998,600 ....B 3
Madeira, 268,700 ....A 2
Minho, 944,800 ....B 2
Ribatejo, 479,400 ....B 3
Trás-os-Montes e Alto Douro,
586,500 ....C 2

CITIES and TOWNS

Águeda, 8,345 ....B 2
Alcácer do Sal, 14,733 ....B 3
Alcântara, 30,625 ....A 1
Alcobaça, 5,166 ....B 3
Aldeia Nova, 7,678 ....C 4
Algés, 14,517 ....A 1
Alhos Vedros, 19,606 ....B 3
Aljezur, 5,333 ....B 4
Aljustrel, 9,913 ....B 4
Almada, 30,688 ....A 1
Almeirim, 8,902 ....B 3
Alpiarça, 7,856 ....B 3
Amadora, 36,331 ....A 1
Amareleja, 4,816 ....C 3
Aveiro, 16,011 ....B 2
Baixa da Banheira, 12,525..........B 3
Barcelos, 5,420 ....B 2
Batalha, 7,053 ....B 3
Beja, 15,702 ....C 3
Belas, 7,509 ....A 1
Belém, 20,416 ....A 1
Benfica, 23,161 ....A 1
Braga, 40,977 ....B 2
Bragança; 8,075 ....C 2
Caldas da Rainha, 10,635 ....B 3
Calheta, 5,404 ....A 2
Campo Maior, 8,807 ....C 3
Cantanhede, 6,630 ....B 2
Caparica, 10,363 ....A 1
Carnaxide, 28,301 ....A 1
Cartaxo, 6,665 ....B 3
Cascais, 10,861 ....B 3
Castelo Branco, 14,838 ....C 3
Castro Marim, 5,347 ....C 4
Chaves, 13,156 ....C 2
Coimbra, 46,313 ....B 2
Cova da Piedade, 15,720 ....A 1
Covilhã, 23,091 ....C 2
Elvas, 11,742 ....C 3
Espinho, 13,503 ....B 2
Estoril, 11,193 ....B 3
Estremoz, 10,122 ....C 3
Évora, 24,144 ....C 3
Fafe, 7,126 ....B 2
Faro, 18,909 ....B 4
Fátima, 5,852 ....B 3
Ferreira do Alentejo, 8,108............B 3
Figueira da Foz, 10,855 ....B 2
Funchal, 43,301 ....A 2
Gondomar, 11,182 ....B 2
Guarda, 9,094 ....C 2
Guimarães, 23,229 ....B 2
Ilhavo, 12,646 ....B 2
Lagos, 10,008 ....B 4
Lamego, 10,236 ....C 2
Lavos, 5,744 ....B 2
Leiria, 7,477 ....B 3
Lisbon (Lisboa) (cap.), 828,000..A 1
Loulé, 16,152 ....B 4
Louriçal, 5,608 ....B 3
Lourinhã, 8,677 ....B 3
Lousã, 8,191 ....B 2
Machico, 11,608 ....A 2
Marinha Grande, 15,699 ....B 3
Matosinhos, 37,694 ....B 2
Mértola, 5,682 ....C 4
Miranda do Corvo, 5,103 ....B 2
Montargil, 6,357 ....B 3
Montemor-o-Novo, 13,115 ....B 3
Montijo, 17,751 ....B 3
Moscavide, 22,065 ....A 1
Mourão, 12,126 ....C 3
Muge, 5,546 ....B 3
Nazaré, 9,189 ....B 3
Nisa, 5,262 ....C 3
Óbidos, 4,599 ....B 3
Odivelas, 27,423 ....A 1
Oeiras, 6,857 ....B 3
Olhão, 16,017 ....C 4
Olivais, 11,896 ....A 1
Oporto, 324,400 ....B 2
Ovar, 14,128 ....B 2
Peniche, 11,357 ....B 3
Pombal, 9,973 ....B 3
Ponta do Sol, 7,426 ....A 2
Ponte de Sor, 13,010 ....B 3
Portalegre, 11,017 ....C 3
Portimão, 12,129 ....B 4
Porto (Oporto), 324,400 ....B 2
Povoa de Varzim, 17,696 ....B 2
Proença-a-Nova, 6,060 ....B 3
Queluz, 14,703 ....A 1
Ribeira Brava, 8,726 ....A 2
Sacavém, 10,624 ....A 1
Santa Cruz, 9,858 ....A 2
Santarém, 16,449 ....B 3
Santiago do Cacém, 6,939 ....B 3
São Brás de Alportel, 9,058........................C 4
São João da Madeira,
11,921 ....B 2
São Teotónio, 8,183 ....B 4
Serpa, 10,967 ....C 4
Sertã, 6,909 ....B 3
Sesimbra, 16,837 ....B 3
Setúbal, 44,435 ....B 3
Sines, 8,866 ....B 4
Sintra, 19,930 ....B 3
Soure, 9,655 ....B 2
Tavira, 12,046 ....C 4
Tomar, 12,974 ....B 3
Tôrres Novas, 11,974 ....B 3
Tôrres Vedras, 13,091 ....B 3
Vagos, 8,281 ....B 2
Vendas Novas, 9,675 ....B 3
Viana do Castelo, 14,371 ....B 2
Vila do Conde, 12,771 ....B 2
Vila Franca de Xira, 13,404...........................B 3
Vila Nova de Gaia, 45,739..............................B 2
Vila Real, 10,263 ....C 2
Vila Real de Sto. António,
11,096 ....C 4
Viseu, 16,961 ....C 2

OTHER FEATURES

Carvoeiro (cape) ....B 3
Desertas (isls.) ....A 2
Douro (river) ....C 2
Estrela, Serra da (mts.) ....C 2
Foia (mt.) ....B 4
Guadiana (river) ....C 4
Lima (river) ....B 2
Madeira (isl.), 265,432 ....A 2
Minho (river) ....B 2
Mira (river) ....B 4
Monchique (mts.) ....B 4
Mondego (cape) ....B 3
Mondego (river) ....C 2
Monsanto (hill) ....A 1
Ossa (mts.) ....C 3
Palha, Mar da (bay) ....A 1
Roca (cape) ....B 3
Sado (river) ....B 3
Saint Vincent (cape) ....B 4
Santa María (cape) ....C 4
Setúbal (bay) ....B 3
Tagus (river) ....B 3
Tâmega (river) ....C 2
Tejo (Tagus) (river) ....B 3
Xarrama (river) ....B 3

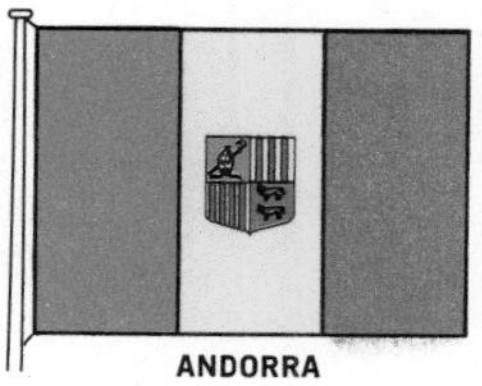

ANDORRA

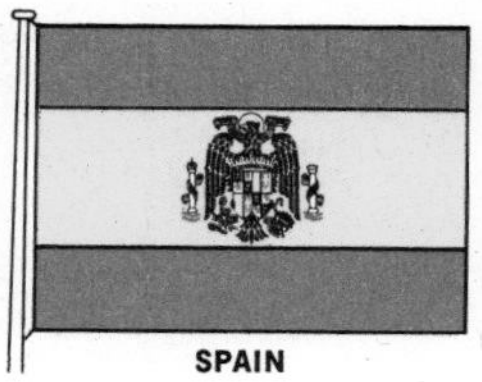

SPAIN

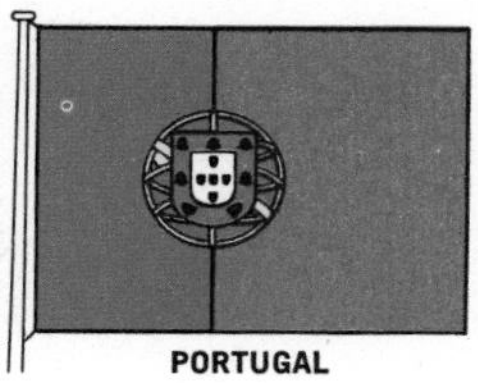

PORTUGAL

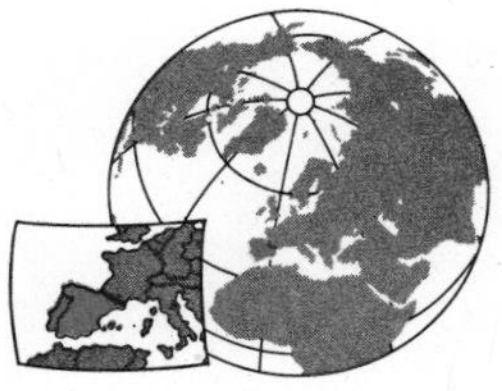

SPAIN

AREA 194,896 sq. mi.
POPULATION 33,290,000
CAPITAL Madrid
LARGEST CITY Madrid
HIGHEST POINT Pico de Teide 12,172 ft. (Canary Is.); Mulhacén 11,411 ft. (mainland)
MONETARY UNIT peseta
MAJOR LANGUAGES Spanish, Catalan, Basque
MAJOR RELIGION Roman Catholicism

ANDORRA

AREA 175 sq. mi.
POPULATION 19,000
CAPITAL Andorra la Vella
MONETARY UNIT French franc, Spanish peseta
MAJOR LANGUAGE Catalan
MAJOR RELIGION Roman Catholicism

PORTUGAL

AREA 35,510 sq. mi.
POPULATION 9,560,000
CAPITAL Lisbon
LARGEST CITY Lisbon
HIGHEST POINT Malhão da Estrêla 6,532 ft.
MONETARY UNIT escudo
MAJOR LANGUAGE Portuguese
MAJOR RELIGION Roman Catholicism

GIBRALTAR

AREA 2 sq. mi.
POPULATION 27,000
CAPITAL Gibraltar
MONETARY UNIT pound sterling
MAJOR LANGUAGES English, Spanish
MAJOR RELIGION Roman Catholicism

SPAIN

PROVINCES

Álava, 148,899 ....E 1
Albacete, 358,290 ....E 3
Alicante, 746,917 ....F 3
Almería, 360,798 ....E 4
Ávila, 231,916 ....D 2
Badajoz, 839,363 ....C 3
Baleares (Balearic Is.), 451,343..H 3
Barcelona, 3,213,212 ....G 2
Burgos, 372,138 ....E 1
Cáceres, 540,060 ....C 3
Cádiz, 874,837 ....D 4
Castellón, 344,350 ....G 2
Ciudad Real, 589,262 ....D 3
Córdoba, 802,633 ....D 3
Cuenca, 305,432 ....E 2
Gerona, 361,250 ....H 1
Granada, 760,210 ....E 4
Guadalajara, 174,572 ....E 2
Guipúzcoa, 532,095 ....E 1
Huelva, 413,459 ....C 4
Huesca, 231,376 ....F 1
Jaén, 720,559 ....E 4
La Coruña, 1,004,149 ....B 1
Las Palmas, 492,466 ....C 4
León, 600,935 ....C 1
Lérida, 336,818 ....G 2
Logroño, 228,922 ....E 1
Lugo, 464,922 ....C 1
Madrid, 2,973,619 ....E 2
Málaga, 783,436 ....D 4
Murcia, 817,545 ....F 4
Navarra, 409,239 ....F 1
Orense, 442,420 ....C 1
Oviedo, 1,034,244 ....C 1
Palencia, 230,426 ....D 1
Pontevedra, 681,295 ....B 1
Salamanca, 401,276 ....C 2
Santa Cruz de Tenerife,
525,095 ....B 5
Santander, 443,113 ....D 1
Saragossa, 670,357 ....F 2
Segovia, 192,229 ....D 2
Seville, 1,295,094 ....D 4
Soria, 140,517 ....E 2
Tarragona, 363,830 ....G 2
Teruel, 205,565 ....F 2
Toledo, 516,870 ....D 3
Valencia, 1,462,005 ....F 3
Valladolid, 368,685 ....D 2
Vizcaya, 852,768 ....E 1
Zamora, 293,489 ....D 2

CITIES and TOWNS

Adra, 10,211 ....E 4
Aguilar, 13,760 ....D 4
Aguilas, 11,970 ....F 4
Alagón, 5,270 ....F 2
Alayor, 4,988 ....J 3
Albacete, 61,635 ....F 3
Albox, 4,036 ....E 4
Alburqerque, 9,540 ....C 3
Alcalá de Chivert, 4,049 ....G 2
Alcalá de Guadaira. 27,378 ....D 4
Alcalá de Henares, 20,572 ....G 4
Alcalá de los Gazules, 7,015 ....D 4
Alcalá la Real, 8,351 ....E 4
Alcanar, 6,332 ....G 2
Alcañiz, 9,489 ....F 2
Alcántara, 3,564 ....C 3
Alcantarilla, 15,748 ....F 4
Alcaudete, 9,280 ....E 4
Alcázar de San Juan, 23,788...............E 3
Alcira, 22,417 ....F 3
Alcoy, 48,712 ....F 3
Alfaro, 8,570 ....F 1
Algeciras, 51,096 ....D 4
Algemesí, 16,683 ....F 3
Alhama de Granada, 6,989 ....E 4
Alhama de Murcia, 7,175 ....F 4
Alicante, 103,289 ....F 3
Almadén, 13,206 ....D 3
Almagro, 9,232 ....E 3
Almansa, 15,391 ....F 3
Almendralejo, 20,867 ....C 3
Almería, 76,643 ....E 4
Almodóvar del Campo, 8,115................D 3
Almonte, 9,444 ....C 4
Almuñécar, 5,644 ....E 4
Álora, 6,459 ....D 4
Amposta, 11,026 ....G 2
Andújar, 23,897 ....D 3
Antequera, 28,400 ....D 4
Aracena, 5,605 ....C 4
Aranda de Duero, 12,623 ....E 2
Aranjuez, 25,988 ....E 2
Archena, 5,802 ....F 3
Archidona. 7.262 ....D 4
Arcos de la Frontera, 13,536 ......D 4
Arenas de San Pedro, 5,585........D 2
Arenys de Mar, 6,665 ....H 2
Argamasilla de Alba, 6,411 ....E 3
Arganda, 5,253 ....G 4
Arnedo, 7,958 ....E 1
Aroche, 5,319 ....C 4
Arrecife, 12,748 ....C 4
Arroyo de la Luz, 9,781 ....C 3
Arta, 5,173 ....H 3
Arucas, 10,917 ....B 5
Aspe, 9,742 ....F 3
Astorga, 10,101 ....C 1
Ávila de los Caballeros,
26,738 ....D 2
Avilés, 19,992 ....C 1
Ayamonte, 9,608 ....C 4
Ayora, 5,635 ....F 3
Azpeitia, 8,219 ....E 1
Azuaga, 15,477 ....D 3
Badajoz, 23,715 ....C 3
Badalona, 90,655 ....H 2
Baena, 17,612 ....D 4
Baeza, 13,329 ....E 4
Bailén, 11,144 ....E 3
Balaguer, 8,342 ....G 2
Bañolas, 7,531 ....H 1
Barajas, 9,058 ....F 4
Barbastro, 9,730 ....F 1
Barcarrota, 7,443 ....C 3
Barcelona, 1,555,564 ....H 2
Barruelo de Santullán, 3,761..........D 1
Baza, 13,323 ....E 4
Beas de Segura, 8,194 ....E 3
Béjar, 14,225 ....D 2
Bélmez, 6,907 ....D 3
Benavente, 11,061 ....D 1
Benicarló, 10,627 ....G 2
Berga, 8,923 ....G 1
Berja, 7,989 ....E 4
Bermeo, 12,398 ....E 1
Betanzos, 6,999 ....B 1
Bilbao, 293,939 ....E 1
Blanes, 9,256 ....H 2
Borja, 4,335 ....F 2
Borjas Blancas, 5,086 ....G 2
Brozas, 5,634 ....C 3
Bujalance, 10,465 ....D 4
Bullas, 7,326 ....F 4
Burgos, 79,810 ....E 1
Burriana, 15,670 ....G 3
Cabeza del Buey, 10,734 ....D 3
Cabra, 15,688 ....D 4
Cáceres, 42,903 ....C 3
Cádiz, 117,871 ....C 4
Calahorra, 14,400 ....E 1
Calasparra, 7,543 ....F 3
Calatayud, 15,777 ....F 2
Calella, 7,947 ....H 2
Callosa de Ensarria, 4,617 ....G 3
Calzada de Calatrava, 7,536...............E 3
Campanario, 8,910 ....D 3
Campillos, 8,791 ....D 4
Campo de Criptana, 13,616.................E 3
Candeleda, 6,507 ....D 2
Cangas, 4,059 ....B 1
Caniles, 5,026 ....E 4
Caravaca, 10,016 ....E 3
Carcagente, 15,791 ....F 3
Carmona, 26,368 ....D 4
Cartagena, 42,424 ....F 4
Casar de Cáceres, 4,560 ....C 3
Caspe, 8,251 ....G 2
Castellón de la Plana, 52,868..............G 3
Castro del Río, 11,200 ....D 4
Castro-Urdiales, 7,128 ....E 1
Castuera, 9,905 ....D 3
Caudete, 7,481 ....F 3
Cazalla de la Sierra, 9,414...................D 4
Cazorla, 7,932 ....E 4
Cebreros, 3,898 ....D 2
Ceclavín, 4,778 ....C 3
Cehegín, 10,467 ....F 3
Cervera, 5,215 ....G 2
Cervera del Río Alhama, 3,648............E 1
Ceuta, 88,000 ....D 5
Chiclana de la Frontera, 19,155..........C 4
Chinchón, 4,432 ....G 5
Chiva, 3,978 ....F 3
Ciempozuelos, 9,042 ....F 5
Cieza, 20,620 ....F 3
Ciudadela, 10,872 ....H 2
Ciudad Real, 35,015 ....D 3
Cocentaina, 7,405 ....F 3
Coín, 11,441 ....D 4
Colmenar de Oreja, 5,119 ....G 5
Colmenar Viejo, 8,133 ....F 4
Constantina, 12,015 ....D 4
Consuegra, 10,572 ....E 3
Córdoba, 167,808 ....D 4
Corella, 5,591 ....F 1
Coria del Río, 13,781 ....C 4
Corral de Almaguer, 8,621 ....E 3
Crevillente, 12,025 ....F 3
Cuéllar, 5,703 ....D 2
Cuenca, 26,663 ....E 2
Cúllar de Baza, 3,769 ....E 4
Cullera, 13,040 ....F 3
Daimiel, 19,485 ....E 3
Denia, 8,281 ....G 3
Don Benito, 22,642 ....C 3
Dos Hermanas, 21,517 ....D 4
Durango, 11,882 ....E 1
Écija, 29,262 ....D 4
Eibar, 31,371 ....E 1
Ejea de los Caballeros, 9,000..................F 1
El Arahal, 15,107 ....D 4
El Bonillo, 5,215 ....E 3
Elche, 50,989 ....F 3
Elda, 24,182 ....F 3
El Ferrol del Caudillo, 62,010.................B 1
El Puerto de Santa María,
31,848 ....C 4
Énguera, 4,606 ....F 3
Espejo, 8,006 ....D 4
Estella, 8,142 ....E 1
Estepa, 8,628 ....D 4
Estepona, 11,309 ....D 4
Felanitx, 7,860 ....H 3
Fermoselle, 3,885 ....C 2
Figueras, 16,460 ....H 1
Fraga, 8,264 ....G 2

Agriculture, Industry and Resources

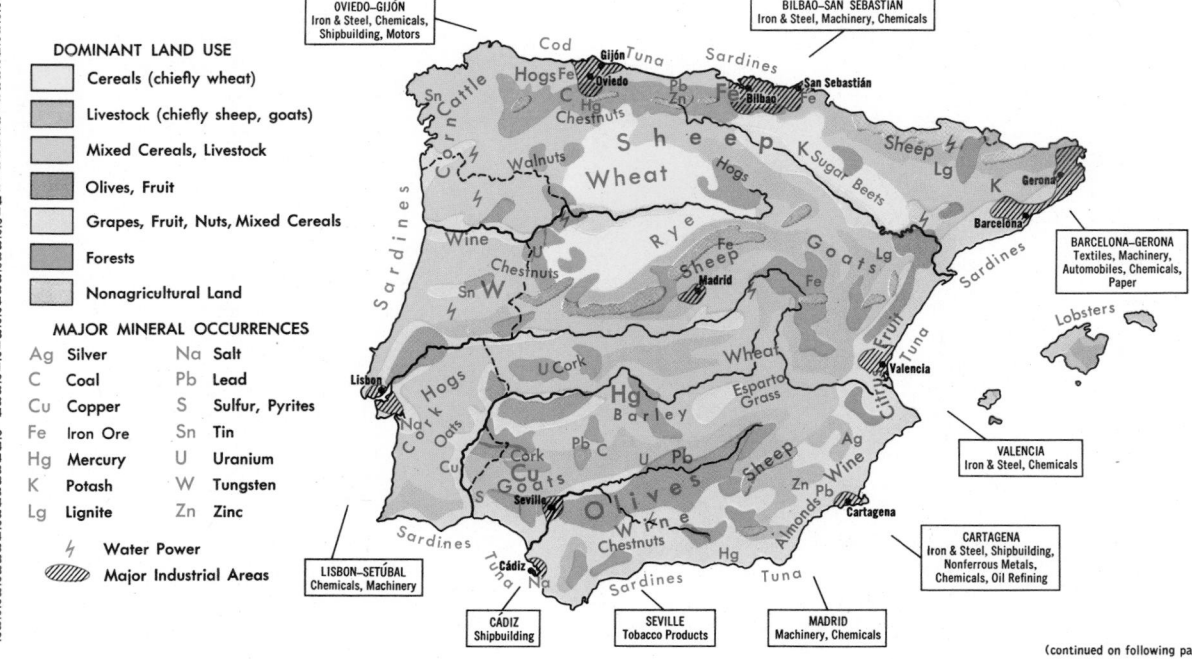

DOMINANT LAND USE

- Cereals (chiefly wheat)
- Livestock (chiefly sheep, goats)
- Mixed Cereals, Livestock
- Olives, Fruit
- Grapes, Fruit, Nuts, Mixed Cereals
- Forests
- Nonagricultural Land

MAJOR MINERAL OCCURRENCES

Ag	Silver	Na	Salt
C	Coal	Pb	Lead
Cu	Copper	S	Sulfur, Pyrites
Fe	Iron Ore	Sn	Tin
Hg	Mercury	U	Uranium
K	Potash	W	Tungsten
Lg	Lignite	Zn	Zinc

Water Power

Major Industrial Areas

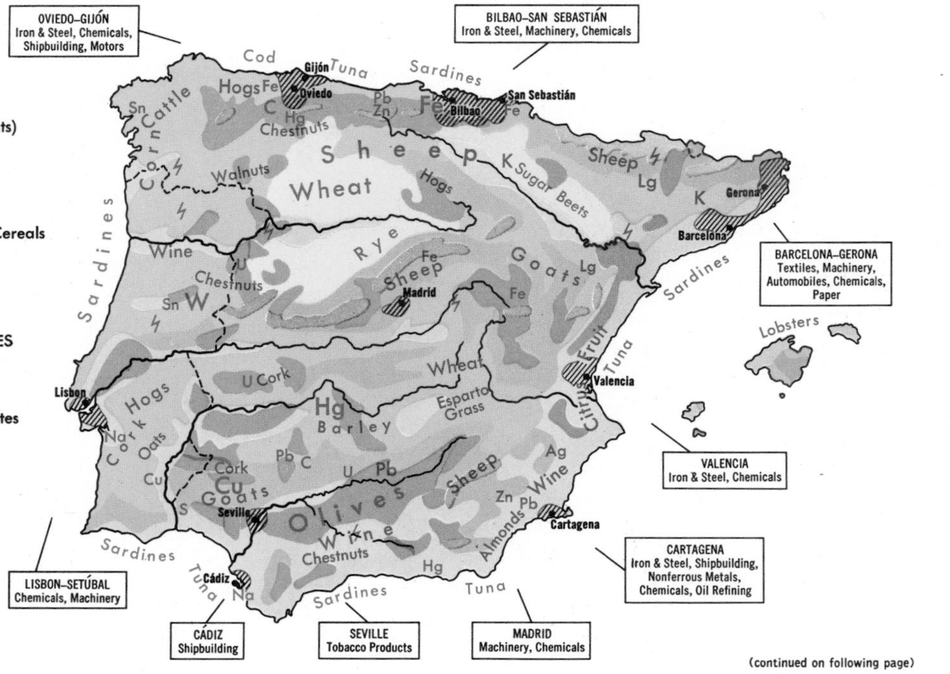

(continued on following page)

30 Spain and Portugal
(continued)

SPAIN (continued)

Fregenal de la Sierra, 9,506......C 3
Fuengirola, 5,622 ....D 4
Fuensalida, 4,697 ....D 3
Fuente de Cantos, 8,484 ....C 3
Fuentes de Andalucía, 8,357......D 4
Gálvez, 3,828 ....D 3
Gándara, 400 ....C 1
Gandía, 15,940 ....F 3
Garrovillas, 5,665 ....C 2
Gerona, 28,134 ....H 1
Getafe, 21,066 ....F 4
Gijón, 92,020 ....D 1
Granada, 150,186 ....E 4
Granollers, 18,810 ....H 2
Guadalajara, 20,135 ....E 2
Guadalcanal, 5,483 ....D 3
Guadix, 15,897 ....E 4
Guareña, 8,438 ....C 3
Guernica y Luno, 4,855 ....E 1
Haro, 8,375 ....E 1
Hellín, 17,071 ....F 3
Herencia, 8,606 ....E 3
Herrera del Duque, 5,404.......D 3
Hinojosa del Duque, 14,074.....D 3
Hortaleza, 8,552 ....E 2
Hospitalet, 122,813 ....H 2
Huelma, 5,468 ....E 4
Huelva, 96,548 ....C 4
Huércal-Overa, 4,406 ....F 4
Huesca, 24,338 ....F 1
Huéscar, 5,097 ....E 4
Ibiza, 11,259 ....G 3
Igualada, 19,866 ....G 2
Illora, 5,589 ....D 4
Inca, 13,816 ....H 3
Iniesta, 4,292 ....F 3
Irún, 20,212 ....F 1
Isla Cristina, 9,616 ....B 4
Jaca, 9,871 ....F 1
Jaén, 59,699 ....E 4
Jaraíz, 8,130 ....D 2

Jativa, 19,195 ....F 3
Jávea, 4,929 ....G 3
Jerez de la Frontera, 96,209 .....C 4
Jerez de los Caballeros, 12,349 ..C 3
Jijona, 5,147 ....F 3
Jimena de la Frontera, 3,620.....D 4
Jódar, 14,289 ....E 4
Jumilla, 15,703 ....F 3
La Bañeza, 7,869 ....D 1
La Bisbal, 5,194 ....H 1
La Carolina, 10,915 ....E 3
La Coruña, 161,260 ....B 1
La Gineta, 3,237 ....E 3
La Línea, 58,169 ....D 4
La Orotava, 8,019 ....B 4
La Palma del Condado, 8,526......C 4
La Puebla, 9,931 ....H 3
La Puebla de Montalbán, 7,286...D 3
La Rambla, 8,057 ....D 4
La Roda, 11,739 ....E 3
La Solana, 14,948 ....E 3
Las Palmas, 166,236 ....B 4
Las Pedroñeras, 6,418 ....E 3
La Unión, 9,357 ....F 4
Lavaderos, 9,708 ....B 1
Lebrija, 13,663 ....C 4
Ledesma, 2,527 ....C 2
Leganés, 8,064 ....F 4
Lena, Pola de, 3,966 ....D 1
León, 73,483 ....D 1
Lérida, 50,047 ....G 2
Linares, 50,527 ....E 3
Liria, 9,723 ....F 3
Llerena, 7,854 ....D 3
Lluchmayor, 9,827 ....H 3
Logroño, 58,545 ....E 1
Logrosán, 6,595 ....D 3
Loja, 11,441 ....D 4
Lora del Río, 15,086 ....D 4
Lorca, 19,854 ....F 4
Los Navalmorales, 4,686 ....D 3
Los Navalucillos, 4,823 ....D 3
Los Santos de Maimona, 8,910....C 3

Los Yébenes, 6,596 ....E 3
Luarca, 4,070 ....C 1
Lucena, 19,975 ....D 4
Lugo, 45,497 ....C 1
Madrid (cap.), 2,850,631 ....F 4
Madridejos, 9,795 ....E 3
Madroñera, 5,256 ....D 2
Mahón, 14,836 ....J 3
Málaga, 259,245 ....D 4
Malagón, 9,246 ....E 3
Malpartida de Cáceres, 5,751.....C 2
Malpartida de Plasencia, 6,757...C 2
Manacor, 17,544 ....H 3
Mancha Real, 7,587 ....E 4
Manlleu, 8,489 ....H 1
Manresa, 46,105 ....G 2
Manzanares, 16,639 ....E 3
Marbella, 7,302 ....D 4
Marchena, 15,879 ....D 4
Marín, 8,838 ....B 1
Martos, 16,442 ....E 4
Mataró, 29,937 ....H 2
Mazarrón, 3,379 ....F 4
Medina del Campo, 13,640 ....D 2
Medina de Ríoseco, 4,897 ....D 2
Medina-Sidonia, 6,869 ....C 4
Menasalbas, 4,407 ....D 3
Mérida, 28,791 ....C 3
Miajadas, 8,632 ....D 3
Mieres, 19,308 ....D 1
Miranda de Ebro, 22,836 ....E 1
Moguer, 6,776 ....C 4
Monasterio, 7,559 ....D 3
Monforte, 13,737 ....C 1
Monóvar, 7,972 ....F 3
Montánchez, 4,190 ....C 3
Montefrío, 4,317 ....D 4
Montehermoso, 6,006 ....C 2
Montellano, 8,694 ....D 4
Montijo, 12,519 ....C 3
Montilla, 19,830 ....D 4
Montoro, 11,243 ....D 3
Monzón, 9,020 ....G 2
Mora, 10,613 ....E 3

Moratalla, 5,675 ....E 3
Morón de la Frontera, 29,096.....D 4
Mota del Cuervo, 5,403 ....E 3
Motril, 18,624 ....E 4
Mula, 9,912 ....F 4
Munera, 5,931 ....E 3
Murcia, 83,190 ....F 4
Nava del Rey, 3,815 ....D 2
Navalcarnero, 4,681 ....F 4
Navalmoral de la Mata, 8,978.....D 3
Navalucillos, Los, 4,823 ....D 3
Nerja, 5,767 ....E 4
Nerva, 11,974 ....C 4
Novelda, 11,003 ....F 3
Nules, 7,626 ....F 3
Ocaña, 6,592 ....E 3
Oliva, 13,342 ....F 3
Oliva de la Frontera, 11,141.....C 3
Olivenza, 8,304 ....C 3
Olot, 13,099 ....H 1
Olvera, 9,088 ....D 4
Onda, 10,666 ....F 3
Onteniente, 18,787 ....F 3
Orellana la Vieja, 6,925 ....D 3
Orense, 42,371 ....C 1
Orihuela, 15,873 ....F 3
Osuna, 17,671 ....D 4
Oviedo, 91,550 ....D 1
Padul, 6,868 ....E 4
Palafrugell, 7,476 ....H 2
Palamós, 5,531 ....H 2
Palencia, 48,144 ....D 2
Palma, 136,431 ....H 3
Palma del Río, 14,053 ....D 4
Pamplona, 59,227 ....F 1
Paredes de Nava, 4,065 ....D 2
Pego, 8,291 ....F 3
Peñafiel, 5,333 ....D 2
Peñaranda de Bracamonte, 5,943..D 2
Peñarroya-Pueblonuevo, 17,449...D 3
Piedrabuena, 5,453 ....D 3
Pinos-Puente, 8,311 ....E 4
Plasencia, 21,297 ....C 2
Pollensa, 7,370 ....H 3

Ponferrada, 17,042 ....C 1
Pontevedra, 19,739 ....B 1
Porcuna, 9,671 ....D 4
Portugalete, 20,514 ....E 1
Posadas, 8,440 ....D 4
Pozoblanco, 14,728 ....D 3
Priego de Córdoba, 13,469 ....D 4
Puebla de Don Fadrique, 3,771....E 4
Puebla de Montalbán, La, 7,286..D 3
Puente-Genil, 24,836 ....D 4
Puertollano, 48,528 ....D 3
Puerto Real, 12,717 ....C 4
Quesada, 6,503 ....E 4
Quintana de la Serena, 7,160.....D 3
Quintanar de la Orden, 9,483.....E 3
Reinosa, 10,004 ....D 1
Requena, 8,278 ....F 3
Reus, 32,037 ....G 2
Ripoll, 7,821 ....H 1
Ronda, 17,703 ....D 4
Rota, 14,236 ....C 4
Rute, 8,945 ....D 4
Sabadell, 98,049 ....H 2
Sagunto, 15,210 ....F 3
Salamanca, 90,388 ....D 2

Sallent, 7,462 ....H 2
Sama, 7,149 ....D 1
San Carlos de la Rápita, 6,844...G 2
San Clemente, 6,411 ....E 3
San Feliú de Guixols, 9,077......H 2
San Fernando, 54,121 ....C 4
San Lorenzo de El Escorial, 7,455.E 2
Sanlúcar de Barrameda, 32,580...C 4
Sanlúcar la Mayor, 6,094 ....C 4
San Sebastián, 98,603 ....F 1
Santa Cruz de la Palma, 9,928...B 4
Santa Cruz de la Mudela, 8,724..E 3
Santa Cruz de la Zarza, 5,588....E 3
Santa Cruz de Tenerife, 82,520...B 4
Santa Eugenia, 5,336 ....B 1
Santafe, 8,212 ....D 4
Santander, 98,784 ....E 1
Santiago, 37,916 ....B 1
Santoña, 7,535 ....E 1
San Vicente de Alcántara, 8,059..C 3
Saragossa, 295,080 ....F 2
Segorbe, 7,136 ....F 3
Segovia, 33,360 ....D 2
Sestao, 24,992 ....E 1
Seville (Sevilla), 423,762.......D 4

Sitges, 6,796 ....G 2
Socuéllamos, 14,742 ....E 3
Sóller, 6,011 ....H 3
Sonseca, 5,994 ....D 3
Soria, 18,872 ....E 2
Sueca, 19,005 ....F 3
Tabernes de Valldigna, 12,890....F 3
Tafalla, 7,320 ....F 1
Talavera de la Reina, 28,107.....D 3
Tarancón, 7,678 ....E 3
Tarazona de Aragón, 11,004.......F 1
Tarazona de la Mancha, 6,850....E 3
Tarifa, 9,147 ....D 4
Tarragona, 35,689 ....G 2
Tárrasa, 89,128 ....G 2
Tárrega, 7,317 ....G 2
Tauste, 6,544 ....F 1
Telde, 11,761 ....B 5
Teruel, 18,304 ....F 2
Tobarra, 7,029 ....F 3
Toledo, 29,367 ....D 3
Tolosa, 10,980 ....E 1
Tomelloso, 27,715 ....E 3
Toro, 9,123 ....D 2
Torredonjimeno, 12,848 ....D 4

Topography

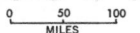

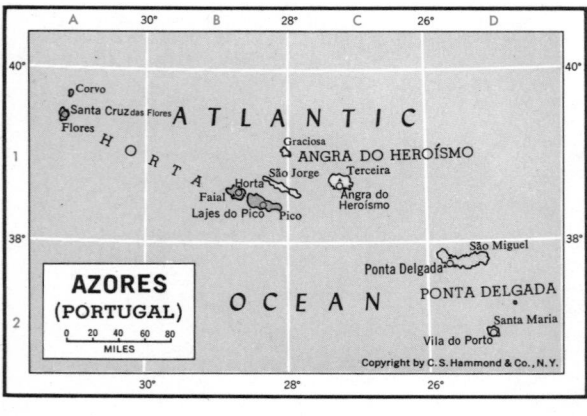

AZORES
DISTRICTS

Angra do Heroísmo, 103,800.......C 1
Horta, 44,900 ....A 1
Ponta Delgada, 185,600 ....D 2

CITIES and TOWNS

Angra do Heroísmo, 13,502 ....C 1
Horta, 7,109 ....B 1
Lajes do Pico, 2,508 ....B 1
Ponta Delgada, 22,316 ....D 2
Santa Cruz das Flores, 1,898 .....A 1
Vila do Porto, 5,373 ....D 2

OTHER FEATURES

Corvo (isl.), 681 ....A 1
Faial (isl.), 20,281 ....B 1
Flores (isl.), 6,583 ....A 1
Graciosa (isl.), 8,669 ....C 1
Pico (isl.), 21,831 ....B 1
Santa Maria (isl.), 13,233 ....D 2
São Jorge (isl.), 15,895 ....B 1
São Miguel (isl.), 168,691 ....C 1
Terceira (isl.), 71,610 ....C 1

Copyright by C. S. Hammond & Co., N.Y.

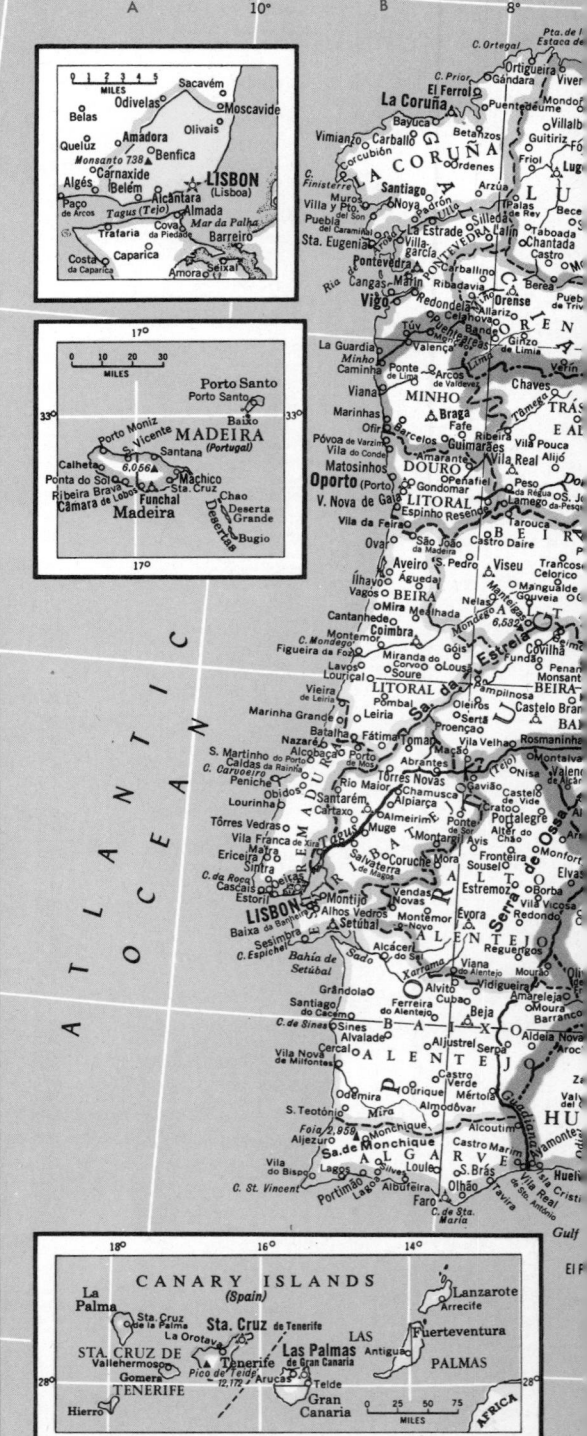

SPAIN and PORTUGAL

CONIC PROJECTION

SCALE OF MILES

SCALE OF KILOMETRES

Capitals of Countries .... ☆
Provincial Capitals .... ▲
International Boundaries .... ▬▬▬▬
Provincial Boundaries .... ▬ ▬ ▬ ▬

© Copyright by C.S. HAMMOND & Co., Maplewood, N.J.

ITALY

CONIC PROJECTION

SCALE OF MILES

0 20 40 60 80 100

SCALE OF KILOMETERS

0 20 40 60 80 100

Capitals of Countries _____ ☆
Regional Capitals _____ ⊕
Provincial Capitals _____ △
International Boundaries ___ . ___
Regional Boundaries ___ . . ___

ITALY is divided for administrative purposes into
20 regions, shown on the map in separate colors.
The regions are subdivided into provinces bearing
the same names as their respective capitals, except:

PROVINCE	CAPITAL
MASSA-CARRARA	Massa
PESARO-URBINO	Pesaro

Copyright by C.S. HAMMOND & Co., N.Y.

VATICAN CITY

SCALE

ROME and ENVIRONS

MILES
0   5   10   15

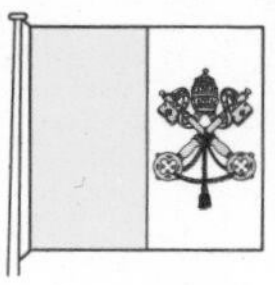

VATICAN CITY
AREA 109 acres
POPULATION 1,000

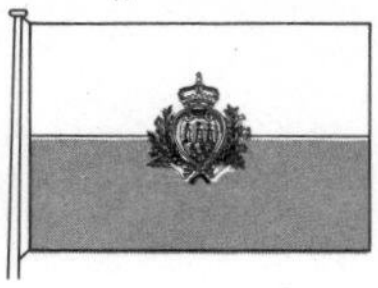

SAN MARINO
AREA 23.4 sq. mi.
POPULATION 19,000

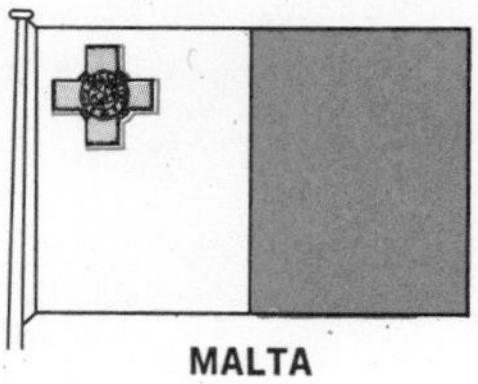

MALTA
AREA 122 sq. mi.
POPULATION 321,000
CAPITAL Valletta
LARGEST CITY Sliema
HIGHEST POINT 787 ft.
MONETARY UNIT Maltese pound
MAJOR LANGUAGES Maltese, English
MAJOR RELIGION Roman Catholicism

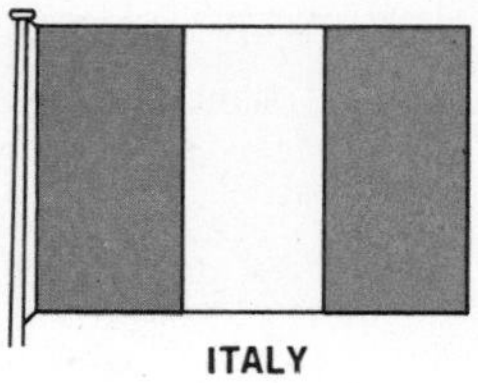

ITALY
AREA 116,303 sq. mi.
POPULATION 54,504,000
CAPITAL Rome
LARGEST CITY Rome
HIGHEST POINT Dufourspitze (Mte. Rosa) 15,203 ft.
MONETARY UNIT lira
MAJOR LANGUAGE Italian
MAJOR RELIGION Roman Catholicism

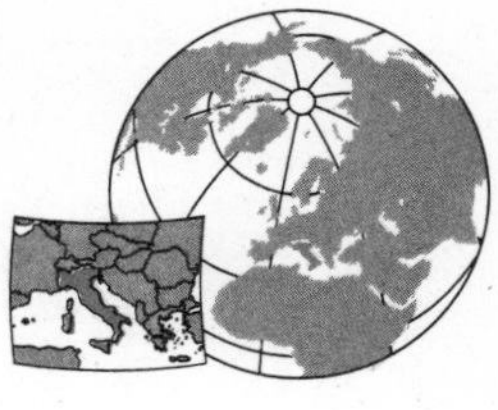

ITALY
REGIONS

Abruzzi, 1,206,266 ....D 3
Aosta, 100,959 ....A 2
Apulia, 3,421,217 ....F 4
Basilicata, 644,297 ....F 4
Calabria, 2,045,047 ....F 5
Campania, 4,760,759 ....E 4
Emilia-Romagna, 3,666,680 ....C 2
Friuli-Venezia Giulia, 1,204,298...D 1
Latium, 3,958,957 ....D 4
Liguria, 1,735,349 ....B 2
Lombardy, 7,406,152 ....B 2
Marche, 1,347,489 ....D 3
Molise, 358,052 ....E 4
Piedmont, 3,914,250 ....A 2
Puglia (Apulia), 3,421,217 ....F 4
Sardinia, 1,419,362 ....B 4
Sicily, 4,721,001 ....E 6
Trentino-Alto Adige, 785,967 ....C 1
Tuscany, 3,286,160 ....C 3
Umbria, 794,745 ....D 3
Venetia, 3,846,562 ....C 2

PROVINCES

Agrigento, 472,945 ....D 6
Alessandria, 478,613 ....B 2
Ancona, 405,709 ....D 3
Aosta, 100,959 ....A 2
Arezzo, 308,964 ....C 3
Ascoli Piceno, 335,627 ....D 3
Asti, 214,604 ....B 2
Avellino, 464,904 ....E 4
Bari, 1,263,245 ....F 4
Belluno, 234,921 ....D 1
Benevento, 313,020 ....E 4
Bergamo, 744,670 ....B 2
Bologna, 841,474 ....C 2
Bolzano, 373,863 ....C 1
Brescia, 882,949 ....C 2
Brindisi, 345,635 ....G 4
Cagliari, 754,965 ....B 5
Caltanissetta, 302,513 ....D 6
Campobasso, 358,052 ....E 4
Caserta, 649,327 ....E 4
Catania, 893,542 ....E 6
Catanzaro, 741,509 ....F 5
Chieti, 373,632 ....E 3
Como, 622,132 ....B 2
Cosenza, 694,398 ....F 5
Cremona, 351,160 ....B 2
Cuneo, 536,356 ....A 2
Enna, 229,126 ....E 6
Ferrara, 403,218 ....C 2
Florence, 1,012,703 ....C 3
Foggia, 665,286 ....E 4
Forlì, 521,128 ....D 2
Frosinone, 438,254 ....D 4
Genoa, 1,031,091 ....B 2
Gorizia, 137,745 ....D 2
Grosseto, 220.305 ....C 3
Imperia, 202,160 ....B 3
L'Aquila, 328,989 ....D 3
La Spezia, 239,256 ....B 2
Latina, 319,056 ....D 4
Lecce, 678,338 ....G 4
Leghorn, 310,210 ....C 3
Lucca, 365,540 ....C 3
Macerata, 291,412 ....D 3
Mantua, 387,255 ....C 2
Massa-Carrara, 202,981 ....C 2
Matera, 200,131 ....F 4
Messina, 685,260 ....E 5
Milan, 3,156,815 ....B 2
Modena, 511,355 ....C 2
Naples, 2,421,243 ....E 4
Novara, 460,190 ....B 2
Nuoro, 283,206 ....B 4
Padua, 694,017 ....C 2
Palermo, 1,111,397 ....D 5
Parma, 389,199 ....C 2
Pavia, 518,193 ....B 2
Perugia, 570,149 ....D 3
Pesaro e Urbino, 314,741 ....D 3
Pescara, 242,958 ....E 3
Piacenza, 291,059 ....B 2
Pisa, 362,396 ....C 3
Pistoia, 232,999 ....C 2
Pordenone, 241,724 ....D 2
Potenza, 444,166 ....E 4
Ragusa, 252,769 ....E 6
Ravenna, 329,559 ....D 2
Reggio di Calabria, 609,140....E 5
Reggio nell'Emilia, 379,688 ....C 2
Rieti, 162,405 ....D 3
Rome, 2,775,380 ....F 6
Rovigo, 277,811 ....C 2
Salerno, 912,265 ....E 4
Sassari, 381,191 ....B 4
Savona, 262,842 ....B 2
Siena, 270,062 ....C 3
Sondrio, 161,450 ....B 1
Syracuse, 345,777 ....E 6
Taranto, 468,713 ....F 4
Teramo, 260,687 ....D 3
Terni, 224,596 ....D 3
Trapani, 427,672 ....D 5
Trento, 412,104 ....C 1
Treviso, 607,616 ....D 2
Trieste, 298,645 ....E 2
Turin, 1,824,254 ....A 2
Udine, 526,184 ....D 1
Varese, 581,528 ....B 2
Venice, 749,173 ....D 2
Vercelli, 400,233 ....B 2
Verona, 667,517 ....C 2
Vicenza, 615,507 ....C 2
Viterbo, 263,862 ....C 3

CITIES and TOWNS

Acireale, 26,744 ....E 6
Acqui Terme, 14,070 ....B 2
Acri, 7,660 ....F 5
Adrano, 31,411 ....E 6
Adria, 11,456 ....D 2
Agira, 13,157 ....E 6
Agrigento, 46,947 ....D 6
Agropoli, 7,200 ....E 4
Alassio, 10,492 ....A 2
Alatri, 5,311 ....D 4
Alba, 16,396 ....B 2
Albano Laziale, 13,007 ....F 7
Albenga, 9,429 ....B 3
Albino, 6,875 ....B 2
Alcamo, 42,974 ....D 6
Alessandria, 65,908 ....B 2
Alghero, 22,139 ....B 4
Altamura, 41,528 ....F 4
Amalfi, 5,183 ....E 4
Amantea, 5,910 ....E 5
Ancona, 77,748 ....D 3
Andria, 69,499 ....F 4
Anzio, 12,102 ....D 4
Aosta, 28,637 ....A 2
Aprilia, 8,784 ....D 4
Aragona, 12,119 ....D 6
Arezzo, 43,868 ....C 3
Ariano Irpino, 11,302 ....E 4
Ascoli Piceno, 33,825 ....D 3
Assisi, 5,302 ....D 3
Asti, 44,455 ....B 2
Augusta, 25,774 ....E 6
Avellino, 31,744 ....E 4
Aversa, 40,245 ....E 4
Avezzano, 24,120 ....D 3
Avigliano, 5,119 ....E 4
Avola, 27,197 ....E 6
Bagheria, 31,435 ....D 5
Barcellona Pozzo di Gotto, 32,147 ....D 5
Bari, 293,963 ....F 4
Barletta, 67,419 ....F 4
Bassano del Grappa, 24,077....C 2
Belluno, 15,400 ....D 1
Benevento, 41,467 ....E 4
Bergamo, 110,666 ....B 2
Biancavilla, 19,858 ....E 6
Biella, 42,994 ....B 2
Bisceglie, 40,520 ....F 4
Bitonto, 34,160 ....F 4
Bitti, 5,623 ....B 4
Bologna, 443,178 ....C 2
Bolzano, 84,685 ....C 1
Bondeno, 6,413 ....C 2
Bonorva, 6,192 ....B 4
Bordighera, 9,045 ....A 3
Borgomanero, 11,843 ....B 2
Borgo San Lorenzo, 6,135 ....C 2
Bosa, 7,890 ....B 4
Bra, 14,472 ....A 2
Bracciano, 6,460 ....C 3
Brescia, 140,518 ....C 2
Bressanone, 10,095 ....C 1
Brindisi, 63,480 ....G 4
Bronte, 19,418 ....E 6
Busto Arsizio, 58,483 ....B 2
Cagliari, 172,925 ....B 5
Caltagirone, 37,634 ....E 6
Caltanissetta, 51,699 ....D 6
Camaiore, 7,130 ....C 3
Campobasso, 27,568 ....E 4
Campo Tures, 1,162 ....C 1
Canicatti, 29,613 ....E 6
Canosa di Puglia, 32,908 ....E 4
Cantù, 17,298 ....B 2
Capua, 13,334 ....E 4
Caravaggio, 9,938 ....B 2
Carbonia, 26,227 ....B 5
Carini, 15,486 ....D 5
Carloforte, 7,153 ....B 5
Carmagnola, 6,583 ....A 2
Carpi, 27,647 ....C 2
Carrara, 37,386 ....C 2
Casale Monferrato, 31,226 ....B 2
Casalmaggiore, 5,995 ....C 2
Cascina-Navacchio, 23,739 ....C 3
Caserta, 36,337 ....E 4
Cassano allo Ionio, 9,250 ....F 5
Cassino, 11,369 ....E 4
Castelfranco Veneto, 9,978 ....D 2
Castel Gandolfo, 2,861 ....F 7
Castellammare del Golfo, 16,581 ....D 5
Castellammare di Stabia, 49,064 ....E 4
Castel San Pietro Terme, 4,824..C 2
Castelvetrano, 30,009 ....D 6
Castrovillari, 13,063 ....F 5
Catania, 358,700 ....E 6
Catanzaro, 44,198 ....F 5
Cava de'Tirreni, 19,883 ....E 4
Cavarzere, 6,109 ....D 2
Cecina, 13,749 ....C 3
Cefalù, 10,360 ....E 5
Ceglie Messapico, 17,891 ....F 4
Celano, 9,743 ....D 3
Cerignola, 43,345 ....E 4
Cernobbio, 6,857 ....B 2
Cesena, 31,153 ....D 2
Cesenatico, 7,684 ....D 2
Chiari, 9,552 ....C 2
Chiavari, 22,835 ....B 2
Chieri, 15,358 ....A 2
Chieti, 31,374 ....E 3
Chioggia, 25,058 ....D 2
Chivasso, 11,806 ....A 2
Ciampino, 10,012 ....F 7
Cittadella, 5,698 ....C 2
Città di Castello, 15,564 ....D 3
Cittanova, 11,567 ....F 5
Cividale del Friuli, 7,698 ....D 1
Civitavecchia, 34,996 ....C 3
Clusone, 5,729 ....C 2
Codriopo, 5,064 ....D 2
Colle di Val d'Elsa, 7,329 ....C 3
Comacchio, 9,743 ....D 2
Comiso, 24,016 ....E 6
Como, 64,301 ....B 2
Conegliano, 16,910 ....D 2
Conversano, 15,543 ....F 4
Corato, 38,774 ....F 4
Cori, 6,930 ....F 7
Corigliano Calabro, 13,526 ....F 5
Corleone, 14,185 ....D 6
Correggio, 8,146 ....C 2
Cortina d'Ampezzo, 4,291 ....D 1
Cosenza, 70,201 ....F 5
Courmayeur, 1,013 ....A 2
Crema, 20,679 ....B 2
Cremona, 64,775 ....B 2
Crotone, 36,516 ....F 5
Cuneo, 32,978 ....A 2
Desenzano del Garda, 8,017 ....C 2
Domodossola, 15,097 ....B 1
Dorgali, 6,976 ....B 4
Eboli, 19,550 ....E 4
Empoli, 22,484 ....C 3
Enna, 26,206 ....E 6
Este, 11,007 ....C 2
Fabriano, 15,127 ....D 3
Faenza, 40,425 ....D 2
Fano, 24,591 ....D 3
Fasano, 17,990 ....F 4
Favara, 27,523 ....D 6
Feltre, 9,446 ....C 1
Fermo, 14,453 ....D 3
Ferrandina, 8,381 ....F 4
Ferrara, 90,419 ....C 2
Fidenza, 13,567 ....B 2
Finale Emilia, 6,711 ....C 2
Finale Ligure, 9,789 ....B 2
Firenze (Florence), 413,455....C 3
Fiumicino, 9,489 ....F 7
Florence, 413,455 ....C 3
Floridia, 16,104 ....E 6
Foggia, 108,682 ....E 4
Foligno, 23.094 ....D 3
Fondi, 14,991 ....D 4
Forlì, 65,376 ....D 2
Formia, 15,048 ....D 4
Fossano, 12,563 ....A 2
Francavilla Fontana, 27,629....F 4
Frascati, 12,602 ....F 6
Frosinone, 20,998 ....D 4
Gaeta, 20,436 ....D 4
Galatina, 19,654 ....G 4
Galatone, 13,487 ....F 4
Gallarate, 34,870 ....B 2
Gallipoli, 15,958 ....F 4
Gela, 54,526 ....E 6
Gemona, 7,698 ....D 1
Genoa (Genova), 747,794....B 2
Genzano di Roma, 11,666 ....F 7
Giarre, 11,859 ....E 6
Gioia del Colle, 23,734 ....F 4
Giovinazzo, 14,189 ....F 4
Giulianova, 11,220 ....E 3
Gorizia, 35,307 ....D 2
Gravina in Puglia, 30,615 ....F 4
Grosseto, 36,558 ....C 3
Grottaferrata, 5,356 ....F 7
Grottaglie, 22,218 ....F 4
Guastalla, 7.511 ....C 2
Gubbio, 9,730 ....D 3
Iesi, 26,018 ....D 3
Iglesias, 20,518 ....B 5
Imola, 32,148 ....C 2
Imperia, 30,522 ....B 3
Isernia, 9,689 ....E 4
Ivrea, 19,344 ....B 2
La Maddalena, 10,414 ....B 4
Lanciano, 15,182 ....E 3
Lanusei, 5,208 ....B 5
L'Aquila, 29,462 ....D 3
La Spezia, 111,768 ....B 2
Latina, 26,171 ....D 4
Lavello, 12,857 ....E 4
Lecce, 68,385 ....G 4
Lecco, 47,468 ....B 2
Leghorn, 152,517 ....C 3
Legnago, 10,126 ....C 2
Lendinara, 6,475 ....C 2
Lentini, 31,788 ....E 6
Leonforte, 17,690 ....E 6
Licata, 38,222 ....D 6
Lido di Ostia, 25,662 ....F 7
Lido di Venezia, 16,581 ....D 2
Lipari, 3,852 ....E 5
Livorno (Leghorn), 152,517....C 3
Lodi, 34,281 ....B 2
Lonigo, 5,774 ....C 2
Lucca, 45,398 ....C 3
Lucera, 24,399 ....E 4
Lugo, 16,550 ....D 2
Macerata, 27,054 ....D 3
Macomer, 7,782 ....B 4
Maglie, 12,205 ....G 4
Manduria, 23,971 ....F 4
Manfredonia, 34,583 ....F 4
Mantua, 55,806 ....C 2
Marino, 9,798 ....F 7
Marsala, 34,294 ....D 6
Martina Franca, 27,588 ....F 4
Massa, 46,992 ....C 2
Massafra, 18.884 ....F 4
Massa Marittima, 6,804 ....C 3
Matera, 36,727 ....F 4
Mazara del Vallo, 35,356 ....D 6
Mazzarino, 17,195 ....E 6
Melfi, 15,122 ....E 4
Menfi, 12,335 ....D 6
Merano, 29,196 ....C 1
Mesagne, 25,042 ....G 4
Messina, 202,095 ....E 5
Mestre, 138,822 ....D 2
Milan, 1,573,009 ....B 2
Milazzo, 14,034 ....E 5
Mirandola, 9,272 ....C 2
Mira Taglio, 8,380 ....D 2
Mistretta, 9.979 ....E 6
Modena, 107,814 ....C 2
Modica, 28,998 ....E 6
Mola di Bari, 22,397 ....F 4
Molfetta, 61,226 ....F 4
Moncalieri, 14,339 ....A 2
Mondovì Breo, 9,893 ....A 2
Monfalcone, 26,708 ....D 2
Monopoli, 25,161 ....F 4
Monreale, 18,881 ....D 5
Monselice, 7,766 ....C 2
Montebelluna, 6,088 ....D 2
Montefiascone, 6,428 ....D 3
Monterotondo, 9,616 ....F 6
Monte Sant'Angelo, 20,512 ....F 4
Montevarchi, 12,413 ....C 3
Monza, 79,715 ....B 2
Mortara, 12,243 ....B 2
Naples, 1,119,392 ....E 4
Nardo, 23,006 ....F 4
Narni, 5,551 ....D 3
Naro, 14,295 ....D 6
Nettuno, 16,187 ....D 4
Nicastro, 21,240 ....F 5
Nicosia, 16,624 ....E 6
Niscemi, 24,468 ....E 6
Nizza Monferrato, 6,229 ....B 2
Nocera Inferiore, 38,690 ....E 4
Noto, 21,586 ....E 6
Novara, 79,188 ....B 2
Novi Ligure, 23,349 ....B 2
Nuoro, 22,559 ....B 4
Olbia, 13,795 ....B 4
Oliena, 6,974 ....B 4
Orbetello, 6,800 ....C 3
Oristano, 16,305 ....B 5
Ortona, 11,315 ....E 3
Orvieto, 9,617 ....D 3
Osimo, 9,406 ....D 3
Ostuni, 25,190 ....F 4
Otranto, 3,510 ....G 4
Ozieri, 10,194 ....B 4
Pachino, 20,645 ....E 6
Padua, 169,298 ....C 2
Palazzolo Acreide, 10,802 ....E 6
Palermo, 531,306 ....D 5
Palestrina, 7,897 ....F 7
Palma di Montechiaro, 20,425....D 6
Palmi, 14,576 ....E 5
Pantelleria, 3,100 ....C 6
Paola, 9,701 ....E 5
Parma, 118,602 ....C 2
Partanna, 12,931 ....D 6
Partinico, 25,924 ....D 6
Paterno, 39,912 ....E 6
Patti, 6,748 ....E 5
Pavia, 69,581 ....B 2
Penne, 5,709 ....D 3
Pergine Valsugana, 4,877 ....C 1
Perugia, 52,534 ....D 3
Pesaro, 47,185 ....D 3
Pescara, 81,697 ....E 3
Pescia, 8,737 ....C 3
Piacenza, 78,905 ....B 2
Piazza Armerina, 23,915 ....E 6
Pietrasanta, 6,785 ....B 3
Pinerolo, 25,262 ....A 2
Piombino, 30,843 ....C 3
Piove di Sacco, 6,230 ....C 2
Pisa, 76,846 ....C 3
Pisticci, 11,469 ....F 4
Pistoia, 41,058 ....C 2
Poggibonsi, 12,932 ....C 3
Pont-Canavese, 4,071 ....A 2
Pontecorvo, 5,845 ....D 4
Pontremoli, 4,839 ....C 2
Popoli, 6,749 ....E 3
Pordenone, 29,461 ....D 2
Porto Civitanova, 18,288 ....D 3
Porto Empedocle, 16,110 ....D 6
Portoferraio, 6,318 ....C 3
Portofino, 735 ....B 2
Portogruaro, 8,913 ....D 2
Portomaggiore, 5,532 ....C 2
Porto Recanati, 4,986 ....D 3
Porto Torres, 10,108 ....B 4
Potenza, 34,216 ....F 4
Pozzallo, 11,862 ....E 6
Pozzuoli, 44,038 ....D 4
Prato, 75,402 ....C 3
Prima Porta, 9,978 ....F 6
Priverno, 9,154 ....D 4
Putignano, 15,976 ....F 4
Quartu Sant'Elena, 22,271 ....B 5
Ragusa, 50,718 ....E 6
Rapallo, 16,628 ....B 2
Ravenna, 56,815 ....D 2
Recanati, 7,242 ....D 3
Reggio di Calabria, 93,964....E 5
Reggio nell'Emilia, 83,073 ....C 2
Rho, 27,586 ....B 2
Riesi, 17,899 ....E 6
Rieti, 21,278 ....D 3
Rimini, 72,720 ....D 2
Rionero in Vulture, 13,567 ....E 4
Riva, 7,626 ....C 2
Rome (cap.), 2,043,055 ....F 6
Rome, *2,656,104 ....F 6
Ronciglione, 5,772 ....C 3
Rossano, 13,323 ....F 5
Rovereto, 20,505 ....C 2
Rovigo, 22,804 ....C 2
Ruvo di Puglia, 23,216 ....F 4
Sala Consilina, 6,742 ....E 4
Salemi, 12,237 ....D 6
Salerno, 103,778 ....E 4
Salsomaggiore Terme, 10,376 ....B 2
Saluzzo, 11,991 ....A 2
Sambiase, 11,551 ....F 5
San Bartolomeo in Galdo, 8,745..E 4
San Benedetto del Tronto, 28,053 ....E 3
San Cataldo, 21,778 ....D 6
San Giovanni in Fiore, 16,528 ....F 5
San Giovanni in Persiceto, 8,692 ....C 2
San Marco in Lamis, 17,933 ....E 4
Sannicandro Garganico, 17,238 ....E 4
San Remo, 40,068 ....A 3
Sansepolcro, 10,063 ....D 3
San Severino Marche, 5,582 ....D 3
San Severo, 47,897 ....E 4
Santa Maria Capua Vetere, 29,925 ....E 4
Santeramo in Colle, 19,587....F 4
San Vito al Tagliamento, 5,278 D 2

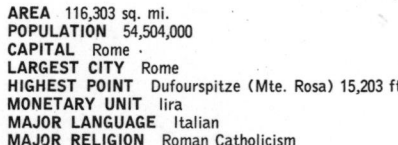

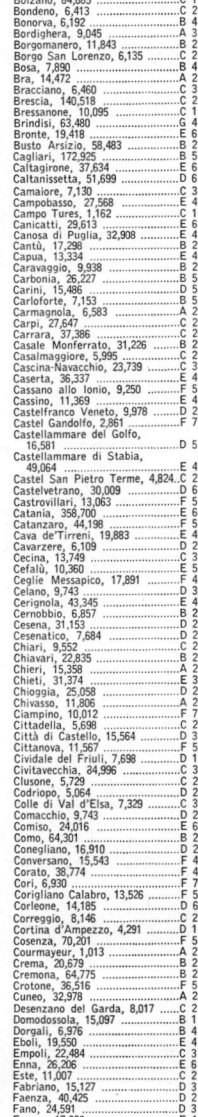

(continued on following page)

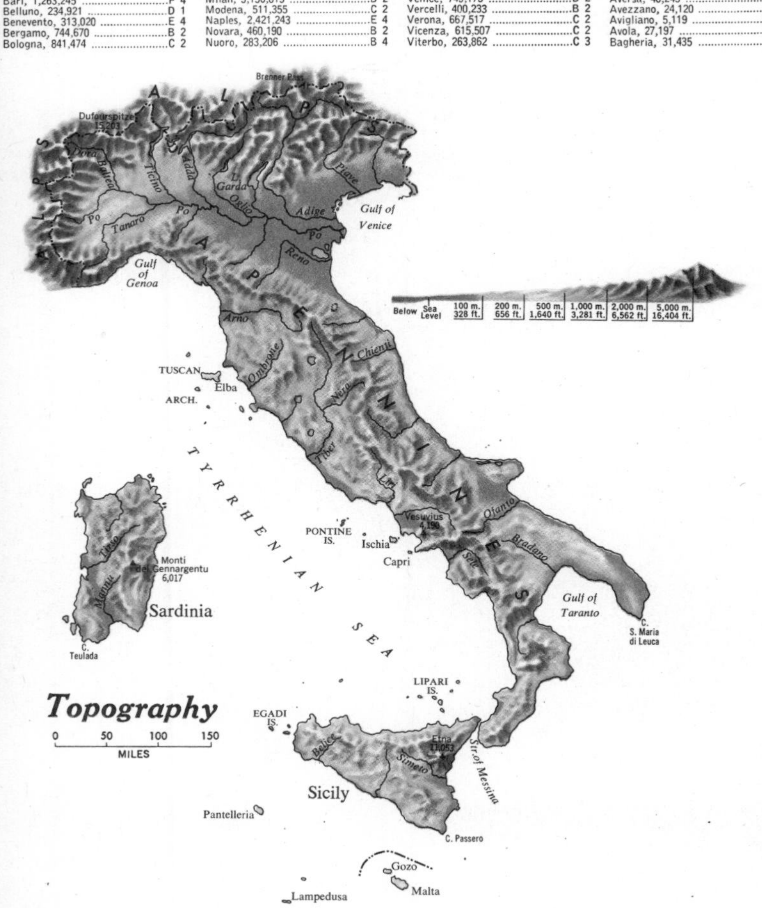
Brenner Pass
Dufourspitze 15,203
A L P S
Dora Baltea
Ticino
Adda
L. Garda
Oglio
Adige
Piave
Po
Tanaro
Gulf of Venice
Gulf of Genoa
Reno
A P E N N I N E S
Arno
Ombrone
Tiber
Nera
Chienti
Liri
TUSCAN ARCH.
Elba
T Y R R H E N I A N   S E A
Vesuvius 4,190
Ofanto
Sele
Bradano
PONTINE IS.
Ischia
Capri
Monti del Gennargentu 6,017
Tirso
Mannu
Sardinia
C. Teulada
Gulf of Taranto
C. S. Maria di Leuca
LIPARI IS.
EGADI IS.
Etna 11,053
Belice
Simeto
Str. of Messina
Sicily
Pantelleria
C. Passero
Gozo
Malta
Lampedusa
Below Sea Level
100 m. 328 ft.
200 m. 656 ft.
500 m. 1,640 ft.
1,000 m. 3,281 ft.
2,000 m. 6,562 ft.
5,000 m. 16,404 ft.
Topography
0 50 100 150
MILES

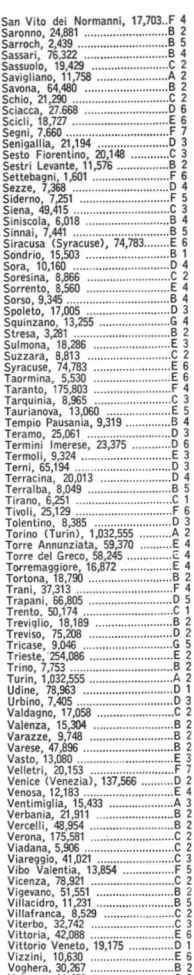

San Vito dei Normanni, 17,703..F 4
Saronno, 24,881 ....B 2
Sarroch, 2,439 ....B 5
Sassari, 76,322 ....B 4
Sassuolo, 19,429 ....C 2
Savigliano, 11,758 ....A 2
Savona, 64,480 ....B 2
Schio, 21,290 ....C 1
Sciacca, 27,668 ....D 6
Scicli, 18,727 ....E 6
Segni, 7,660 ....F 7
Senigallia, 21,194 ....D 3
Sesto Fiorentino, 20,148 ....C 2
Sestri Levante, 11,576 ....B 2
Settebagni, 1,601 ....F 6
Sezze, 7,368 ....D 4
Siderno, 7,251 ....F 5
Siena, 49,415 ....C 3
Siniscola, 6,018 ....B 4
Sinnai, 7,441 ....B 5
Siracusa (Syracuse), 74,783....E 6
Sondrio, 15,503 ....B 1
Sora, 10,160 ....D 4
Soresina, 8,866 ....B 2
Sorrento, 8,560 ....E 4
Sorso, 9,345 ....B 4
Spoleto, 17,005 ....D 3
Squinzano, 13,255 ....G 4
Stresa, 3,281 ....B 2
Sulmona, 18,286 ....E 3
Suzzara, 8,813 ....C 2
Syracuse, 74,783 ....E 6
Taormina, 5,530 ....E 6
Taranto, 175,803 ....F 4
Tarquinia, 8,965 ....C 3
Taurianova, 13,060 ....E 5
Tempio Pausania, 9,319 ....B 4
Teramo, 25,061 ....D 3
Termini Imerese, 23,375 ....D 6
Termoli, 9,324 ....E 3
Terni, 65,194 ....D 3
Terracina, 20,013 ....D 4
Terralba, 8,049 ....B 5
Tirano, 6,251 ....C 1
Tivoli, 25,129 ....F 6
Tolentino, 6,385 ....D 3
Torino (Turin), 1,032,555 ....A 2
Torre Annunziata, 59,370 ....E 4
Torre del Greco, 58,245 ....E 4
Torremaggiore, 16,872 ....E 3
Tortona, 18,790 ....B 2
Trani, 37,313 ....F 4
Trapani, 66,805 ....D 5
Trento, 50,174 ....C 1
Treviglio, 18,189 ....B 2
Treviso, 75,208 ....D 2
Tricase, 9,046 ....G 5
Trieste, 254,086 ....E 2
Trino, 9,753 ....B 2
Turin, 1,032,555 ....A 2
Udine, 78,963 ....D 1
Urbino, 7,405 ....D 3
Valdagno, 17,058 ....C 2
Valenza, 15,304 ....B 2
Varazze, 9,748 ....B 2
Varese, 47,896 ....B 2
Vasto, 13,080 ....E 3
Velletri, 20,153 ....F 7
Venice (Venezia), 137,566 ......D 2
Venosa, 12,183 ....E 4
Ventimiglia, 15,433 ....A 2
Verbania, 21,911 ....B 2
Vercelli, 48,954 ....B 2
Verona, 175,581 ....C 2
Viadana, 5,906 ....C 2
Viareggio, 41,021 ....C 2
Vibo Valentia, 13,854 ....F 5
Vicenza, 78,921 ....C 2
Vigevano, 51,551 ....B 2
Vilacidro, 11,231 ....B 5
Villafranca, 8,529 ....C 2
Viterbo, 32,742 ....C 3
Vittoria, 42,088 ....E 6
Vittorio Veneto, 19,175 ....D 1
Vizzini, 10,630 ....D 6
Voghera, 30,267 ....B 2
Volterra, 11,460 ....C 3

OTHER FEATURES

Adda (river) ....B 2
Adige (river) ....C 2
Adriatic (sea) ....E 3
Albano (lake) ....F 7
Alicudi (isl.), 230 ....E 5
Aniene (river) ....F 6
Apennines (range) ....D 3
Apennines, Central (range) .....D 3
Apennines, Northern (range) ...B 2
Apennines, Southern (range) ...E 4
Arno (river) ....C 2
Asinara (isl.), 709 ....B 4
Bernina (mt.) ....B 1
Bernina (pass) ....C 1
Blanc (mt.) ....A 2
Bolsena (lake) ....C 3
Bonifacio (strait) ....B 4
Bracciano (lake) ....D 3
Brenner (pass) ....D 1
Cagliari (gulf) ....B 5
Capraia (isl.), 467 ....B 3
Capri (isl.), 10,845 ....E 4
Carbonara (cape) ....B 5
Carnic Alps (range) ....D 1
Castellammare (gulf) ....D 5
Chienti (river) ....D 3
Cimone (mt.) ....C 2
Circeo (cape) ....D 4
Coghinas (river) ....B 4
Como (lake) ....B 1
Cottian Alps (range) ....A 2
Crati (river) ....F 5
Dolomite Alps (range) ....C 1
Dora Baltea (river) ....A 2
Dora Riparia (river) ....A 2
Egadi (isls.), 6,133 ....C 6
Elba (isl.), 27,577 ....C 3
Etna (volcano) ....E 6
Favignana (isl.), 4,726 ....D 6
Filicudi (isl.), 447 ....E 5
Gaeta (gulf) ....D 4
Garda (lake) ....C 2
Gennargentu (mts.) ....B 5
Genoa (gulf) ....B 2
Giannutri (isl.), 3 ....C 3
Giglio (isl.), 2,256 ....C 3
Gorgona (isl.), 292 ....B 3
Graian Alps (range) ....A 2
Gran Paradiso (mt.) ....A 2
Great Saint Bernard (pass)....A 2
Ionian (sea) ....F 6
Ischia (isl.), 34,213 ....D 4
Iseo (lake) ....B 1
Julian Alps (range) ....D 1
Lampedusa (isl.), 4,387 ....D 7
Lepontine Alps (range) ....B 1
Levanzo (isl.), 307 ....D 5
Ligurian (sea) ....B 2
Linosa (isl.), 424 ....D 7
Lipari (isl.), 8,844 ....E 5
Lipari (isls.), 13,774 ....E 5
Liri (river) ....D 4

Maggiore (lake) ....B 1
Malta (channel) ....E 6
Manfredonia (gulf) ....F 4
Mannu (river) ....B 5
Marettimo (isl.), 1,100 ....C 6
Maritime Alps (range) ....A 2
Marmolada (mt.) ....C 1
Mediterranean (sea) ....E 6
Messina (strait) ....E 6
Metauro (river) ....D 3
Mincio (river) ....C 2
Mont Cenis (tunnel) ....A 2
Montecristo (isl.), 8 ....C 3
Nera (river) ....D 3
Ofanto (river) ....E 4
Ombrone (river) ....C 3
Oristano (gulf) ....B 5
Orosei (gulf) ....C 4
Ortles (range) ....C 1
Otranto (strait) ....G 5
Ötztal Alps (range) ....C 1
Palmarola (isl.) ....D 4
Panarea (isl.), 272 ....E 5
Panaro (river) ....C 2
Pantelleria (isl.), 9,601 ....D 6
Parma (river) ....C 2
Pelagie (isls.), 4,811 ....D 7
Pennine Alps (range) ....A 2
Pescara (river) ....D 3
Pianosa (isl.), 878 ....C 3
Piave (river) ....D 2
Po (river) ....C 2
Policastro (gulf) ....E 4
Pompeii (ruins) ....E 4
Pontine (isls.), 5,732 ....D 4
Ponza (isl.), 4,660 ....C 4
Rosa (mt.) ....A 1
Salerno (gulf) ....E 4
Salina (isl.), 2,737 ....E 5
Salso (river) ....D 6
Sangro (river) ....E 3
San Pietro (isl.), 7,275 ....B 5
Santa Maria di Leuca (cape)...G 5
Sant'Antioco (isl.), 10,993 ....B 5
Sant'Eufemia (gulf) ....F 5
San Vito (cape) ....D 5
Sardinia (island), 1,400,103 ..B 4
Sele (river) ....E 4
Sicily (island), 4,683,076 ......D 6
Sicily (strait) ....C 6
Simeto (river) ....E 6
Spartivento (cape) ....F 6
Spartivento (cape) ....B 5
Squillace (gulf) ....F 5
Stromboli (isl.), 469 ....E 5
Stura (river) ....A 2
Tagliamento (river) ....D 1
Tanaro (river) ....B 2
Taranto (gulf) ....F 4
Testa del Gargano (cape) ......F 4
Teulada (cape) ....B 5
Tiber (river) ....D 3
Trasimeno (lake) ....D 3
Trebbia (river) ....B 2
Tremiti (isls.), 349 ....E 3
Trieste (gulf) ....E 2
Tuscan (arch.), 31,481 ....B 3
Tyrrhenian (sea) ....C 4
Ustica (isl.), 1,262 ....D 5
Varano (lake) ....F 3
Vaticano (cape) ....E 4
Venice (gulf) ....D 2
Ventotene (isl.), 811 ....D 4
Vesuvius (volcano) ....E 4
Volturno (river) ....E 4
Vulcano (isl.), 356 ....E 5

MALTA

CITIES and TOWNS

Sliema, 21,000 ....E 7
Valletta (cap.), 15,432 ....E 7
Victoria, 5,456 ....E 6

OTHER FEATURES

Gozo and Comino (isls.), 29,975..E 6
Malta (isl.), 288,200 ....E 7

SAN MARINO

CITIES and TOWNS

San Marino (cap.), 2,621 ....D 3
San Marino *3,817 ....D 3

VATICAN CITY

Vatican City, 1,000 ....B 6

*City and suburbs.

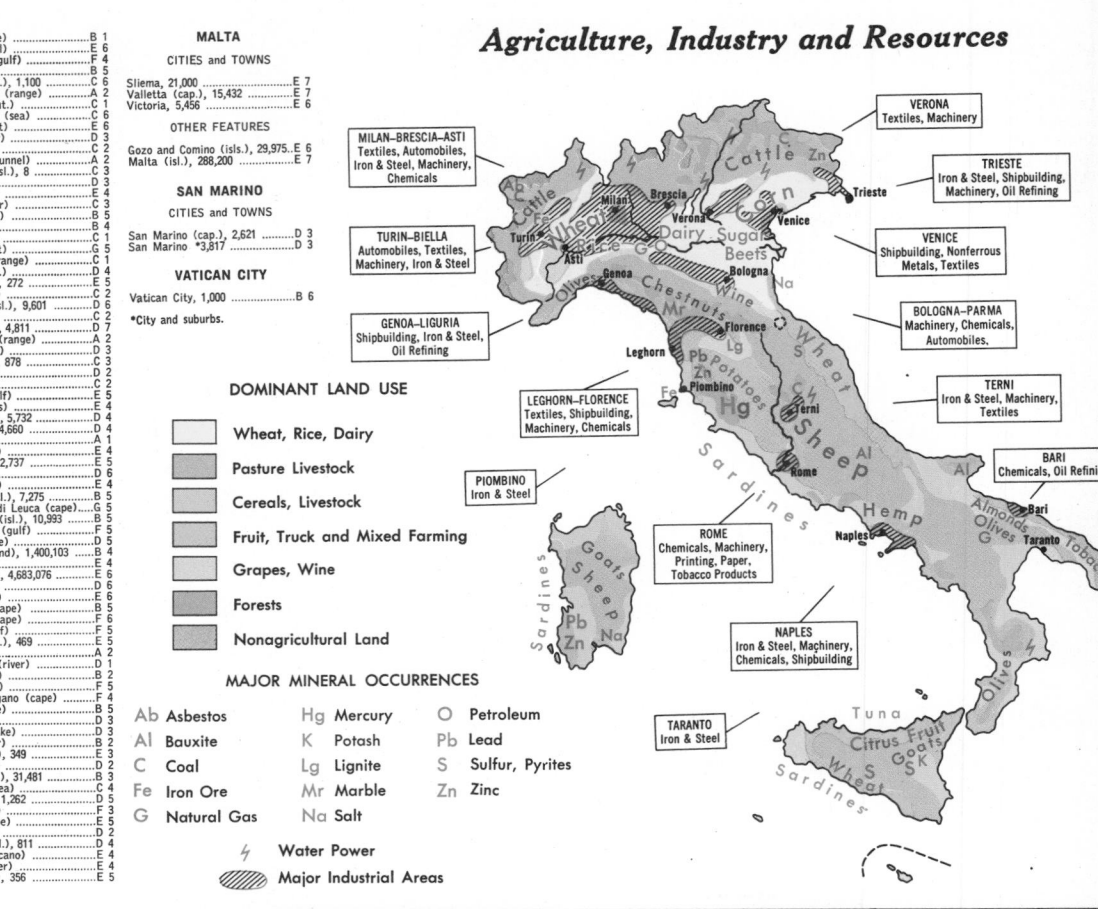

Agriculture, Industry and Resources

VERONA
Textiles, Machinery

TRIESTE
Iron & Steel, Shipbuilding, Machinery, Oil Refining

VENICE
Shipbuilding, Nonferrous Metals, Textiles

BOLOGNA–PARMA
Machinery, Chemicals, Automobiles.

TERNI
Iron & Steel, Machinery, Textiles

BARI
Chemicals, Oil Refining

MILAN–BRESCIA–ASTI
Textiles, Automobiles, Iron & Steel, Machinery, Chemicals

TURIN–BIELLA
Automobiles, Textiles, Machinery, Iron & Steel

GENOA–LIGURIA
Shipbuilding, Iron & Steel, Oil Refining

LEGHORN–FLORENCE
Textiles, Shipbuilding, Machinery, Chemicals

PIOMBINO
Iron & Steel

ROME
Chemicals, Machinery, Printing, Paper, Tobacco Products

NAPLES
Iron & Steel, Machinery, Chemicals, Shipbuilding

TARANTO
Iron & Steel

DOMINANT LAND USE

Wheat, Rice, Dairy

Pasture Livestock

Cereals, Livestock

Fruit, Truck and Mixed Farming

Grapes, Wine

Forests

Nonagricultural Land

MAJOR MINERAL OCCURRENCES

Ab Asbestos
Al Bauxite
C Coal
Fe Iron Ore
G Natural Gas

Hg Mercury
K Potash
Lg Lignite
Mr Marble
Na Salt

O Petroleum
Pb Lead
S Sulfur, Pyrites
Zn Zinc

Water Power

Major Industrial Areas

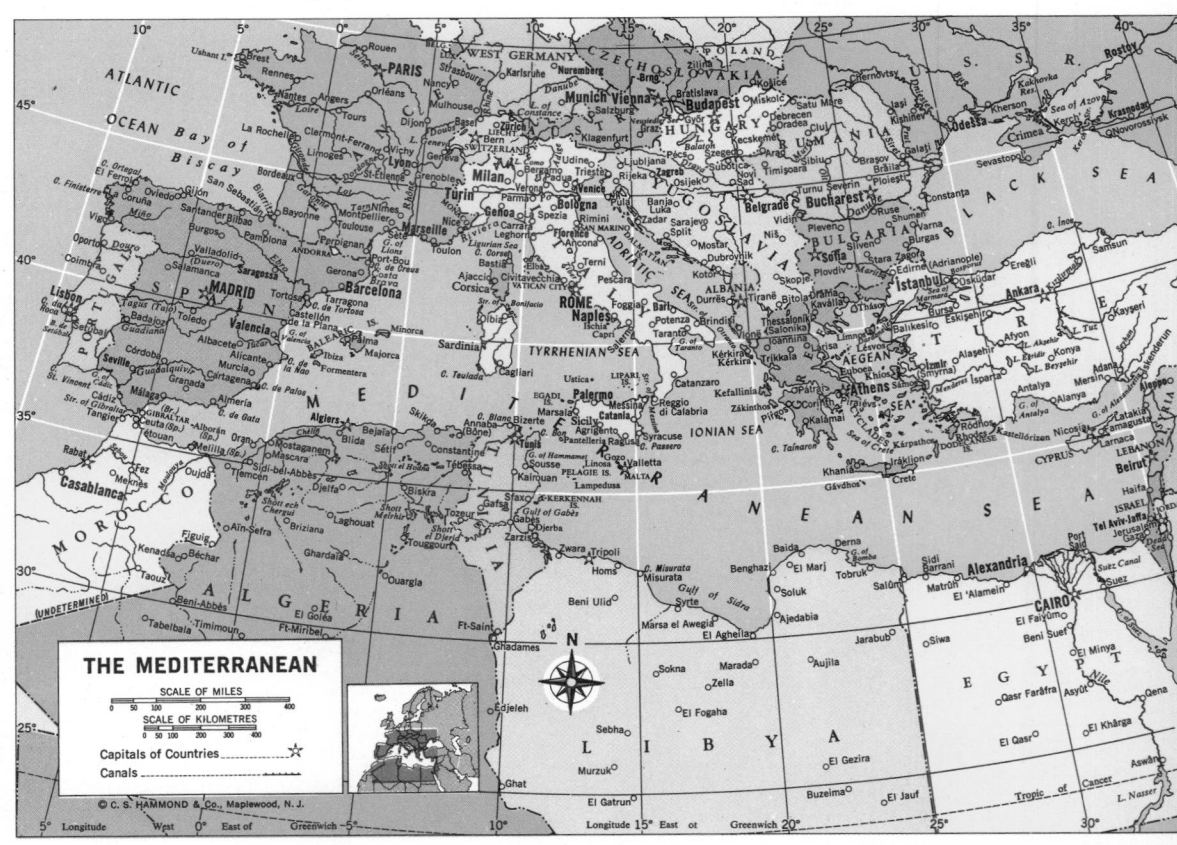

THE MEDITERRANEAN

SCALE OF MILES
0 50 100   200   300   400

SCALE OF KILOMETRES
0 50 100   200   300   400

Capitals of Countries ....☆
Canals _____

© C. S. HAMMOND & Co., Maplewood, N. J.

SWITZERLAND
AREA 15,941 sq. mi.
POPULATION 6,230,000
CAPITAL Bern
LARGEST CITY Zürich
HIGHEST POINT Dufourspitze (Mte. Rosa) 15,203 ft.
MONETARY UNIT Swiss franc
MAJOR LANGUAGES German, French, Italian, Romansch
MAJOR RELIGIONS Protestantism, Roman Catholicism

LIECHTENSTEIN
AREA 61 sq. mi.
POPULATION 21,000
CAPITAL Vaduz
LARGEST CITY Vaduz
HIGHEST POINT Naafkopf 8,445 ft.
MONETARY UNIT Swiss franc
MAJOR LANGUAGE German
MAJOR RELIGION Roman Catholicism

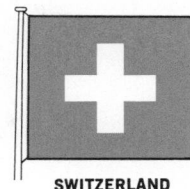

SWITZERLAND

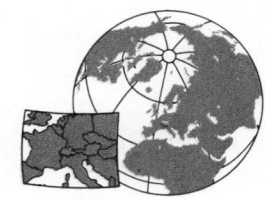

LIECHTENSTEIN

LANGUAGES

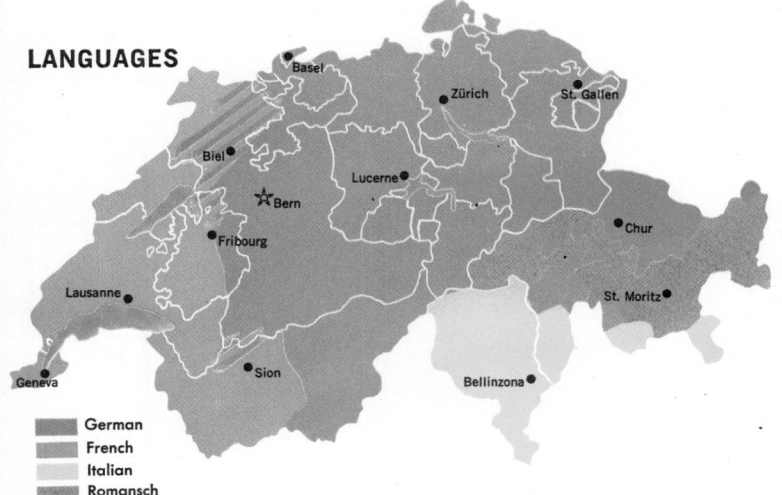

German
French
Italian
Romansch

Switzerland is a multilingual nation with four official languages. 70% of the people speak German, 19% French, 10% Italian and 1% Romansch.

SWITZERLAND

CANTONS

Aargau, 397,000	F 2
Appenzell, Ausser-Rhoden, 50,000	H 2
Appenzell, Inner-Rhoden, 13,500	H 2
Baselland, 177,900	E 2
Baselstadt, 237,300	E 1
Bern, 958,000	D 2
Fribourg, 163,000	D 3
Geneva, 304,400	B 4
Glarus, 42,000	H 3
Graubünden (Grisons), 155,000	J 3
Luzern (Lucerne), 274,000	F 2
Neuchâtel, 161,000	C 3
Nidwalden, 25,000	F 3
Obwalden, 25,000	F 3
Sankt Gallen, 363,000	H 2
Schaffhausen, 72,000	G 1
Schwyz, 84,800	G 2
Solothurn (Soleure), 220,000	E 2
Thurgau, 183,000	H 1
Ticino, 220,000	G 4
Uri, 33,000	G 3
Valais, 191,000	E 4
Vaud, 486,000	C 3
Zug, 61,000	G 2
Zürich, 1,048,000	G 2

CITIES and TOWNS

Aadorf, 2,258	G 2
Aarau, 17,400	F 2
Aarau, *47,800	F 2
Aarberg, 2,355	D 2
Aarburg, 5,302	E 2
Adelboden, 2,881	E 3
Aeschi bei Spiez, 1,319	E 3
Affoltern am Albis, 4,904	F 2
Affoltern im Emmental, 1,206	E 2
Aigle, 4,381	C 4
Airolo, 2,023	G 3
Alle, 1,471	C 2
Allschwil, 15,500	D 1
Alpnach, 3,211	F 3
Altdorf, 7,477	G 3
Altstätten, 8,751	J 2
Amriswil, 6,752	H 1
Andermatt, 1,523	G 3
Appenzell, 5,082	H 2
Arbedo-Castione, 1,467	G 4
Arbon, 13,100	H 1
Ardon, 1,432	D 4
Arlesheim, 5,219	E 2
Arosa, 2,600	J 3
Arth, 6,321	F 2
Ascona, 3,053	G 4
Attalens, 1,023	C 3
Aubonne, 1,766	B 4
Avenches, 1,776	D 3
Baar, 9,114	G 2
Baden, 14,900	F 2
Baden, *54,500	F 2
Bad Ragaz, 2,699	H 2
Balerna, 3,040	G 4
Balsthal, 5,735	E 2
Bäretswil, 2,577	G 2
Basel, 213,000	E 1
Basel, *364,800	E 1
Bassecourt, 2,284	C 2
Bättenkinden, 1,916	E 2
Bauma, 3,214	G 2
Beatenberg, 1,303	E 3
Beckenried, 2,042	G 3

Beinwil am See, 2,346	F 2
Bellinzona, 14,900	H 4
Bellinzona, *25,700	H 4
Belp, 4,922	D 3
Bergün-Bravuogn, 551	J 3
Bern (cap.), 166,800	D 3
Bern, *258,000	D 3
Beromünster, 1,443	F 2
Bex, 4,667	D 4
Biasca, 3,349	H 4
Biberist, 7,188	D 2
Biel (Bienne), 67,800	D 2
Biel, *87,000	D 2
Bière, 1,166	B 3
Binningen, 13,800	D 1
Bischofszell, 3,811	H 1
Blumenstein, 1,121	E 3
Bodio, 1,276	G 4
Bolligen, 19,400	E 3
Boltigen, 1,691	D 3
Boncourt, 1,493	C 2
Bönigen, 1,883	E 3
Boswil, 1,663	F 2
Boudry, 3,086	C 3
Bourg-Saint-Pierre, 524	D 5
Breil-Brigels, 1,272	H 3
Breitenbach, 1,851	E 2
Bremgarten, 4,555	F 2
Brienz, 2,864	E 3
Brig, 4,647	E 4
Brissago, 1,845	G 4
Brittnau, 3,070	F 2
Brugg, 6,683	F 2
Brusio, 1,445	K 4
Bubendorf, 1,690	E 2
Bubikon, 2,612	G 2
Buchs, 6,345	H 2
Bülach, 8,188	G 1
Bulle, 5,983	D 3
Buochs, 2,733	F 3
Büren an der Aare, 2,432	D 2
Burgdorf, 15,600	E 2
Bürglen, 3,175	G 3
Bürglen, 1,899	H 1
Bussigny-près-Lausanne, 2,381	B 3
Bütschwil, 3,414	H 2
Carouge, 15,600	B 4
Castagnola, 3,775	G 4
Cazis, 1,553	H 3
Cernier, 1,545	C 2
Chalais, 1,597	E 4
Cham, 6,483	G 2
Chamoson, 2,088	D 4
Charmey, 1,144	D 3
Château-d'Oex, 3,378	D 4
Châtel-Saint-Denis, 2,666	C 3
Chavornay, 1,414	C 3
Chexbres, 1,449	C 3
Chiasso, 7,377	G 5
Chur, 29,100	H 3
Churwalden, 877	J 3
Coire (Chur), 29,100	H 3
Conthey, 3,563	D 4
Coppet, 774	B 4
Corcelles-près-Payerne, 1,253	C 3
Corgémont, 1,414	D 2
Cossonay, 1,284	C 3
Courgenay, 1,666	C 2
Courroux, 1,667	D 2
Court, 1,493	D 2
Courtelary, 1,330	C 2
Courtételle, 1,618	C 2
Couvet, 3,450	C 3
Cully, 1,375	C 4
Därstetten, 900	D 3
Davos (Dorf and Platz), 9,588	J 3
Degersheim, 3,221	H 2
Delémont, 9,542	D 2
Derendingen, 4,463	E 2
Diemtigen, 1,934	D 3
Diessenhofen, 2,222	G 1
Dietikon, 20,600	F 2
Disentis-Mustér, 2,376	G 3
Dombresson, 1,040	C 2
Dornach, 4,260	E 2
Dübendorf, 17,100	G 2
Düdingen, 4,248	D 3
Dürnten, 4,271	G 2
Dürrenroth, 1,221	E 2
Ebnat-Kappel, 4,979	H 2
Echallens, 1,428	C 3
Egg, 3,018	G 2
Eggiwil, 2,591	E 3
Eglisau, 1,911	G 1
Egnach, 3,483	H 1
Einsiedeln, 8,792	G 2
Elgg, 2,643	G 2
Emmen, 21,400	F 2
Engelberg, 2,646	F 3
Engi, 1,064	H 3
Ennenda, 3,076	H 2
Entlebuch, 3,318	F 3
Erlenbach im Simmental, 1,471	E 3
Ermatingen, 1,857	H 1
Erstfeld, 4,126	G 3
Eschenbach, 2,866	G 2
Escholzmatt, 3,257	F 3
Estavayer-le-Lac, 2,583	C 3
Evolène, 1,786	D 4
Faido, 1,441	G 4

(continued on following page)

Agriculture, Industry and Resources

DOMINANT LAND USE
Cereals, Dairy
Pasture Livestock
General Farming, Livestock
Fruit, Truck, Mixed Farming
Forests
Nonagricultural Land

Water Power
Major Industrial Areas

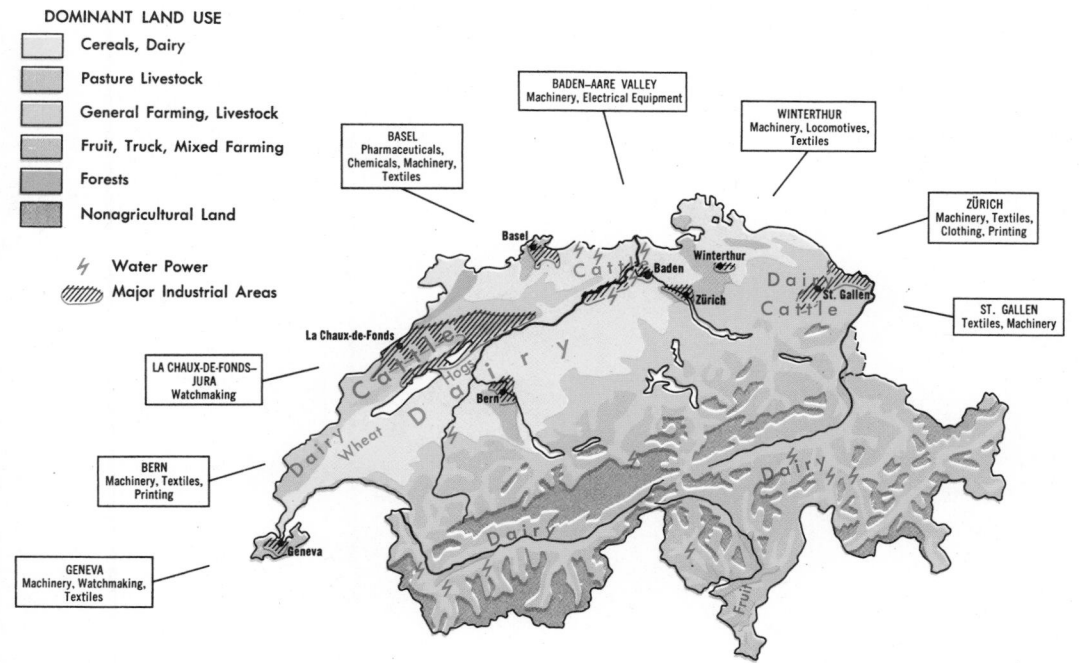

BADEN–AARE VALLEY
Machinery, Electrical Equipment

WINTERTHUR
Machinery, Locomotives, Textiles

BASEL
Pharmaceuticals, Chemicals, Machinery, Textiles

ZÜRICH
Machinery, Textiles, Clothing, Printing

ST. GALLEN
Textiles, Machinery

LA CHAUX-DE-FONDS–JURA
Watchmaking

BERN
Machinery, Textiles, Printing

GENEVA
Machinery, Watchmaking, Textiles

(continued)

Topography

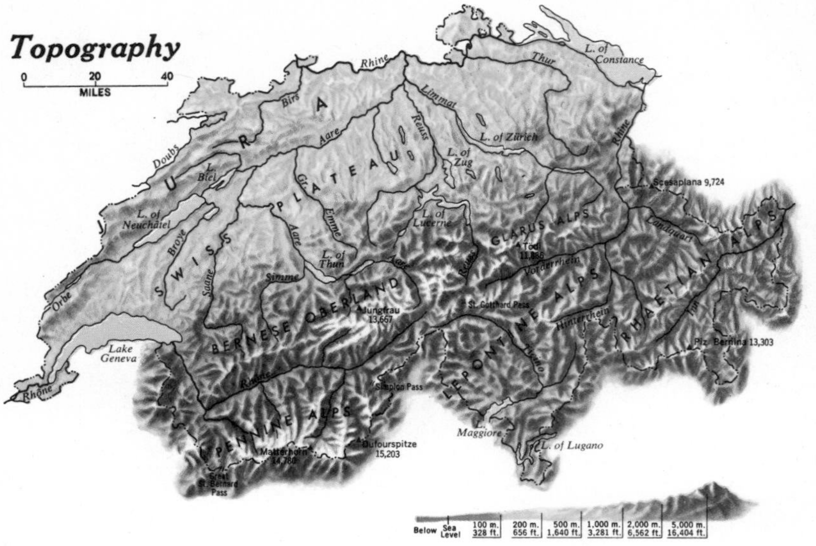

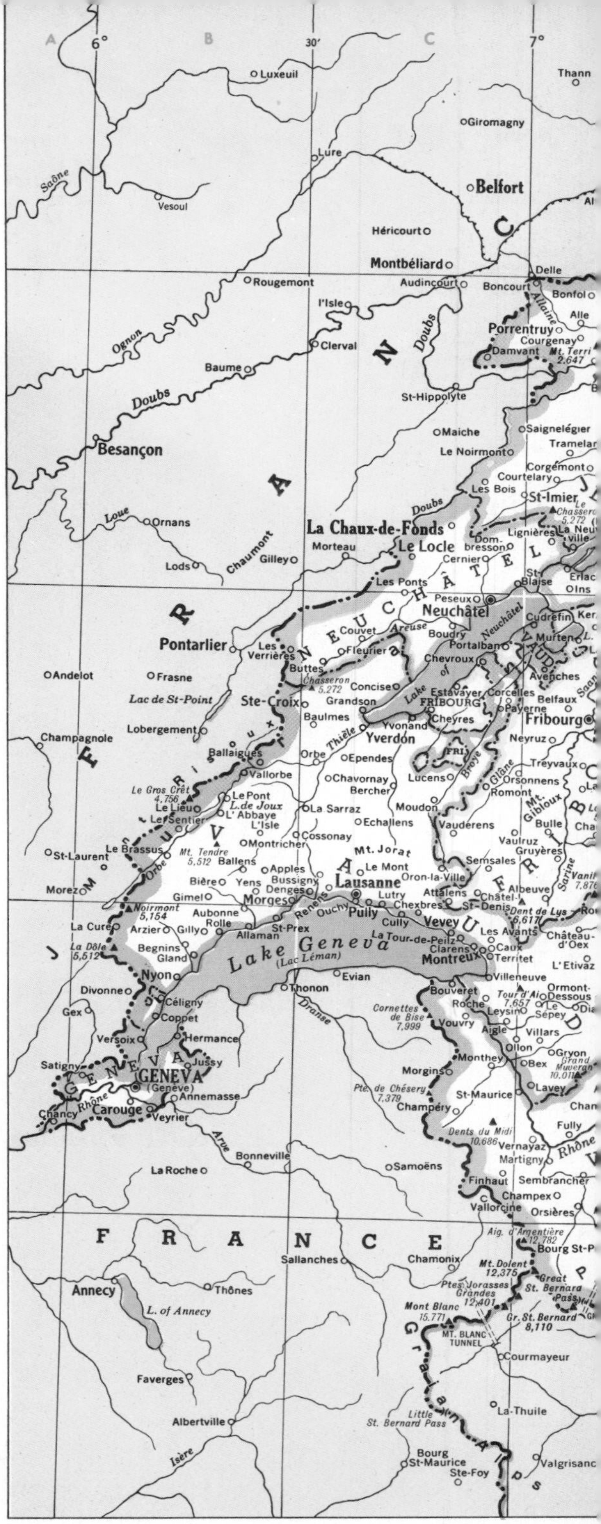

SWITZERLAND (continued)

Flawil, 7,256 ....H 2
Fleurier, 3,814 ....C 3
Flims, 1,444 ....H 3
Flüelen, 1,717 ....G 3
Flums, 4,462 ....H 2
Frauenfeld, 16,800 ....G 1
Fribourg, 38,500 ....D 3
Fribourg, *47,300 ....D 3
Frick, 2,123 ....E 1
Frutigen, 5,565 ....E 3
Fully, 3,419 ....D 4
Gais, 2,488 ....H 2
Gelterkinden, 3,870 ....E 2
Geneva (Genève), 169,500 ....B 4
Geneva, *307,500 ....B 4
Gersau, 1,754 ....G 2
Gimel, 1,091 ....B 3
Giornico, 1,063 ....G 4
Giswil, 2,656 ....F 3
Giubiasco, 4,281 ....H 4
Gland, 1,545 ....B 4
Glarus, 5,852 ....H 2
Glattfelden, 2,426 ....F 1
Gordola, 1,794 ....G 4
Göschenen, 1,284 ....G 3
Gossau, 9,731 ....H 2
Grabs, 4,218 ....H 2
Grandson, 2,091 ....C 3
Gränichen, 4,411 ....F 2
Grenchen, 19,800 ....D 2
Grenchen, *23,400 ....D 2
Grindelwald, 3,244 ....E 3
Grossandelfingen, 1,102 ....G 1
Grosswangen, 2,373 ....F 2
Gruyères, 1,349 ....D 3
Gsteig, 937 ....D 4
Guggisberg, 2,021 ....D 3
Gurtnellen, 1,048 ....G 3
Hallau, 1,966 ....F 1
Heiden, 3,158 ....H 2
Heimberg, 2,125 ....E 3
Hemberg, 1,011 ....H 2
Henau (Uzwil), 7,828 ....H 2
Hérémence, 1,868 ....D 4
Herisau, 15,500 ....H 2
Hermance, 512 ....B 4
Herzogenbuchsee, 4,641 ....E 2
Hinwil, 4,811 ....G 2
Hochdorf, 4,452 ....F 2
Horgen, 15,300 ....G 2
Hospental, 289 ....F 3
Huttwil, 4,664 ....E 2
Igis, 3,902 ....J 3
Ilanz, 1,843 ....H 3
Illnau, 6,160 ....G 2
Ingenbohl, 5,046 ....G 2
Innertkirchen, 1,230 ....F 3
Ins, 2,486 ....D 2
Interlaken, 4,738 ....E 3
Jegenstorf, 1,397 ....D 2
Jenaz, 1,143 ....J 3
Jona, 5,686 ....G 2
Jungfraujoch ....E 3
Kaltbrunn, 2,527 ....H 2
Kandersteg, 937 ....E 4
Kerns, 3,553 ....F 3
Kerzers, 2,228 ....D 3
Kilchberg, 6,784 ....F 2
Kirchberg, 3,304 ....E 2
Kirchberg, 5,554 ....G 2
Kleinlützel, 1,269 ....D 2
Klingnau, 2,192 ....F 1
Klosters, 3,181 ....J 3
Kloten, 8,446 ....G 2
Koblenz, 1,114 ....F 1
Kölliken, 3,007 ....F 2
Köniz, 30,600 ....D 3
Kreuzlingen, 14,900 ....H 1
Kriens, 17,200 ....F 2
Küsnacht, 12,800 ....G 2
Küssnacht, 12,400 ....F 2
Küttigen, 3,457 ....F 2
L'Abbaye, 1,124 ....B 3
La Chaux-de-Fonds, 42,800 ....C 2
Lachen, 3,913 ....G 2
La Neuveville, 3,216 ....D 2
Langenthal, 12,400 ....E 2
Langnau, 9,201 ....E 3
Langnau am Albis, 2,850 ....G 2
La Roche, 1,043 ....D 3
La Sarraz, 1,026 ....C 3
La Tour-de-Peilz, 6,820 ....C 4
Läufelfingen, 1,176 ....E 2
Laufen, 3,955 ....D 2
Laufenburg, 1,850 ....F 1
Laupen, 1,607 ....D 3
Lauperswil, 2,652 ....E 3
Lausanne, 138,300 ....C 3
Lausanne, *214,900 ....C 3
Lauterbrunnen, 3,216 ....E 3
Le Brassus (Le Chenit), 5,242....B 3
Le Châble, 4,237 ....D 4
Le Lieu, 970 ....B 3
Le Locle, 15,100 ....C 2
Le Mont, 1,719 ....C 3
Lengnau, 3,524 ....D 2
Lenk, 1,900 ....D 4
Le Noirmont, 1,559 ....C 2
Lens, 1,743 ....D 4
Lenzburg, 6,378 ....F 2
Les Bois, 1,098 ....C 2
Les Ponts-de-Martel, 1,429 ....C 2
Les Verrières, 1,084 ....B 3
Leuk, 2,546 ....E 4
Leukerbad, 619 ....E 4
Leysin, 2,241 ....C 4
Liestal, 11,300 ....E 2
Linthal, 2,645 ....H 3
Littau, 8,715 ....F 2
Locarno, 12,200 ....G 4
Locarno, *21,000 ....G 4
Lucens, 1,620 ....C 3
Lucerne, 73,000 ....F 2
Lucerne, *148,500 ....F 2
Lugano, 21,100 ....G 4
Lugano, *50,000 ....G 4
Lungern, 1,794 ....F 3
Luthern, 1,801 ....E 2
Lutry, 3,481 ....C 3
Lützelflüh, 3,960 ....E 3
Luzein, 1,013 ....J 3
Luzern (Lucerne), 73,000 ....F 2
Lyss, 5,616 ....D 2
Maienfeld, 1,488 ....J 2
Malans, 1,358 ....J 3
Malters, 4,579 ....F 2
Malvaglia, 1,120 ....H 4
Männedorf, 6,182 ....G 2
Marbach, 1,347 ....E 3
Martigny, 7,593 ....C 4
Meilen, 8,203 ....G 2
Meiringen, 3,749 ....F 3
Melchnau, 1,511 ....E 2
Melide, 1,046 ....G 5
Mellingen, 1,941 ....F 2
Mels, 5,254 ....H 2
Mendrisio, 5,100 ....G 5
Menzingen, 3,340 ....G 2
Menznau, 2,275 ....E 2
Mesocco, 1,324 ....H 4
Minusio, 3,663 ....G 4
Möhlin, 4,681 ....E 1
Mollis, 2,303 ....H 2
Montana-Vermala, 1,543 ....E 4
Monthey, 6,834 ....C 4
Montreux-Le Châtelard, 20,100 ..C 4
Morges, 8,420 ....B 3
Moudon, 2,806 ....C 3
Moutier, 7,472 ....D 2
Müllheim, 1,475 ....G 1
Mümliswil-Ramiswil, 2,714 ....E 2
Münchenbuchsee, 3,652 ....E 2
Münsingen, 6,051 ....E 3
Muotathal, 2,592 ....G 3
Muri, 3,957 ....F 2
Muri bei Bern, 7,855 ....E 3
Murten, 3,330 ....D 3
Müstair, 717 ....K 3
Muttenz, 14,000 ....E 1
Näfels, 3,617 ....H 2
Naters, 3,797 ....E 4
Nebikon, 1,206 ....F 2
Nesslau, 2,002 ....H 2
Netstal, 2,925 ....H 2
Neuchâtel, 36,300 ....C 3
Neuchâtel, *52,600 ....C 3
Neuenegg, 2,921 ....D 3
Neuhausen am Rheinfall, 11,800..G 1
Neunkirch, 1,208 ....F 1
Niederbipp, 3,141 ....E 2
Niederurnen, 3,347 ....G 2
Niederweningen, 1,027 ....F 1
Nunningen, 1,372 ....E 2
Nyon, 7,643 ....B 4
Oberägeri, 2,656 ....G 2
Oberburg, 3,030 ....E 2
Oberdiessbach, 1,927 ....E 3
Oberdorf, 1,132 ....E 2
Oberriet, 5,498 ....J 2
Obersaxen, 710 ....H 3
Oberuzwil, 4,394 ....H 2
Oensingen, 2,907 ....E 2
Ollon, 4,126 ....D 4
Olten, 21,900 ....E 2
Olten, *47,100 ....E 2
Orbe, 3,824 ....C 3
Ormont-Dessous, 996 ....D 4
Orsières, 2,281 ....D 4
Payerne, 6,024 ....C 3
Peseux, 4,933 ....C 3
Pfäffikon, 5,735 ....G 2
Pfaffnau, 2,575 ....E 2
Pieterlen, 2,978 ....D 2
Pontresina, 1,067 ....J 3
Porrentruy, 7,095 ....C 2
Poschiavo, 3,743 ....J 4
Pratteln, 9,492 ....E 1
Pully, 15,900 ....C 4
Quinto, 1,365 ....G 3
Rafz, 1,925 ....G 1
Ramsen, 1,181 ....G 1
Rapperswil, 7,585 ....G 2
Raron, 1,077 ....E 4
Rechthalten, 1,015 ....D 3
Regensdorf, 4,997 ....F 2
Reichenbach, 2,829 ....E 3
Reiden, 2,795 ....F 2
Reigoldswil, 1,192 ....E 2
Reinach, 5,174 ....F 2
Renens, 15,200 ....C 3
Rheinau, 2,363 ....G 1
Rheineck, 3,047 ....J 2
Rheinfelden, 5,197 ....E 1
Richterswil, 5,842 ....G 2
Riehen, 20,100 ....E 1
Riggisberg, 1,949 ....E 3
Riva San Vitale, 1,358 ....G 5
Rivera, 950 ....G 4
Roggwil, 3,420 ....E 2
Rohrbach, 1,534 ....E 2
Rolle, 2,942 ....B 4
Romanshorn, 7,755 ....H 1
Romont, 2,982 ....C 3
Rorschach, 13,400 ....H 2
Rorschach, *24,500 ....H 2
Rosenlaui ....F 3
Rothrist, 5,048 ....E 2
Rougemont, 860 ....D 4
Roveredo, 1,878 ....H 4
Rüeggisberg, 2,035 ....E 3
Rüschegg, 1,628 ....D 3
Ruswil, 4,657 ....F 2
Rüthi, 1,521 ....J 2
Rüti, Glarus, 738 ....H 3
Rüti, Zürich, 8,282 ....G 2
Saanen, 5,649 ....D 4
Saas-Fee, 739 ....E 4
Sachseln, 2,721 ....F 3
Saignelégier, 1,636 ....D 2
Saint-Blaise, 2,412 ....D 2
Sainte-Croix, 6,925 ....B 3
Saint-Imier, 6,704 ....D 2
Saint-Martin, 1,155 ....E 4
Saint-Maurice, 3,196 ....C 4
Saint Moritz, 3,751 ....J 3
Saint Niklaus, 2,071 ....E 4
Saint-Prex, 1,897 ....B 4
Saint-Stephan, 1,227 ....D 3
Saint-Ursanne, 1,304 ....D 2
Samedan, 2,106 ....J 3
Sankt Gallen, 78,900 ....H 2
Sargans, 2,571 ....H 2
Sarnen, 6,554 ....F 3
Satigny, 1,594 ....A 4
Savièse, 3,203 ....D 4
Savognin, 632 ....J 3
Saxon, 2,305 ....D 4
Schaffhausen, 37,400 ....G 1
Schaffhausen, *56,900 ....G 1
Schangnau, 1,031 ....E 3
Schänis, 2,328 ....H 2
Schiers, 2,363 ....J 3
Schinznach-Dorf, 1,081 ....F 2
Schlarigna-Celerina, 868....J 3
Schleitheim, 1,494 ....G 1
Schlieren, 11,600 ....F 2
Schönenwerd, 4,561 ....E 2
Schüpfheim, 3,771 ....F 3
Schwanden, 3,020 ....H 2
Schwyz, 12,200 ....G 2
Scuol-Schuls, 1,429 ....K 3
Sedrun, 1,855 ....G 3
Seewis, 969 ....J 3
Sembrancher, 710 ....D 4
Sempach, 1,345 ....F 2
Semsales, 762 ....C 3
Seon, 3,006 ....F 2
Sevelen, 2,370 ....H 2
Sierre, 8,690 ....D 4
Siggenthal, 7,376 ....F 1
Signau, 2,555 ....E 3
Sigriswil, 3,739 ....E 3
Silenen, 2,261 ....G 3
Sils im Domleschg, 737 ....H 3
Silvaplana, 346 ....J 4
Sins, 2,195 ....F 2
Sion, 18,900 ....D 4
Sirnach, 3,075 ....G 2
Sissach, 4,574 ....E 2
Solothurn (Soleure), 18,900 ....E 2
Solothurn, *36,400 ....E 2
Sonvico, 1,005 ....G 4
Spiez, 8,168 ....E 3
Stäfa, 6,947 ....G 2
Stalden, 1,007 ....E 4
Stammheim, 1,460 ....G 1
Stans, 4,337 ....F 3
Steckborn, 3,514 ....G 1
Steffisburg, 12,100 ....E 3
Stein, 1,060 ....E 1
Stein am Rhein, 2,588 ....G 1
Sulgen, 1,252 ....H 1
Sulz, 1,022 ....F 1
Sumiswald, 5,525 ....E 2
Sursee, 5,324 ....F 2
Tafers, 1,621 ....D 3
Täuffelen, 1,500 ....D 2
Tavannes, 3,939 ....D 2
Thalwil, 13,200 ....G 2
Thayngen, 3,013 ....G 1
Therwil, 1,946 ....E 1
Thun, 33,700 ....E 3
Thun, *56,700 ....E 3
Thusis, 1,998 ....H 3
Trachselwald, 1,269 ....E 2
Tramelan, 5,567 ....D 2
Trogen, 2,101 ....H 2
Trub, 1,981 ....E 3
Trun, 1,583 ....G 3
Turbenthal, 2,685 ....G 2
Turgi, 1,860 ....F 1
Ueberstorf, 1,536 ....D 3
Uetendorf, 2,810 ....E 3
Unterägeri, 3,832 ....G 2
Unterkulm, 2,149 ....F 2
Unterseen, 3,783 ....E 3
Untervaz, 1,142 ....H 3
Urnäsch, 2,330 ....H 2
Uster, 20,800 ....G 2
Utzenstorf, 2,821 ....E 2
Uznach, 3,173 ....H 2
Uzwil, 7,828 ....H 2
Vallorbe, 3,990 ....B 3
Vals, 968 ....H 3
Vaz-Obervaz, 1,568 ....J 3
Vechigen, 3,153 ....E 3
Vernayaz, 1,188 ....D 4
Versoix, 3,426 ....B 4
Vevey, 18,000 ....C 4
Vevey, *29,600 ....C 4
Veyrier, 2,705 ....B 4
Villeneuve, 2,366 ....C 4
Visp, 3,658 ....E 4
Vouvry, 1,368 ....C 4
Wädenswil, 14,300 ....G 2
Wahlern, 4,723 ....D 3
Wald, 7,778 ....G 2
Waldenburg, 1,284 ....E 2
Waldkirch, 2,487 ....H 2
Wallenstadt, 3,296 ....H 2
Walzenhausen, 2,345 ....J 2
Wangen an der Aare, 1,936....E 2
Wängi, 1,681 ....H 1
Wartau, 3,284 ....H 2
Wattwil, 7,480 ....H 2
Weesen, 1,280 ....H 2
Weggis, 2,243 ....F 2
Weinfelden, 6,954 ....H 1
Wettingen, 19,700 ....F 2
Wetzikon, 12,600 ....G 2
Wil, 12,900 ....H 2
Wilchingen, 1,061 ....F 1
Wilderswil, 1,701 ....E 3
Wildhaus, 1,179 ....H 2
Willisau, 2,508 ....F 2
Wimmis, 1,756 ....E 3
Windisch, 5,377 ....F 1
Winterthur, 92,500 ....G 1
Winterthur, *104,600 ....G 1
Wohlen, 8,636 ....F 2
Wohlen bei Bern, 2,985 ....D 3
Wolfenschiessen, 1,647 ....F 3
Wolhusen, 3,446 ....F 2
Wollerau, 2,415 ....G 2
Worb, 5,885 ....E 3
Wynigen, 2,221 ....E 2
Yverdon, 19,200 ....C 3
Yvonand, 1,290 ....C 3
Zäziwil, 1,265 ....E 3
Zell, Luzern, 1,582 ....E 2
Zell, Zürich, 3,347 ....G 2
Zermatt, 2,731 ....E 4
Zizers, 1,290 ....J 3
Zofingen, 1,290 ....F 2
Zollikofen, 6,237 ....E 3
Zollikon, 12,100 ....G 2
Zug, 22,300 ....G 2
Zuoz, 1,001 ....J 3
Zürich, 432,400 ....F 2
Zürich, *671,500 ....F 2
Zurzach, 2,694 ....F 1
Zweisimmen, 2,676 ....D 3

OTHER FEATURES

Aa (river) ....F 3
Aare (river) ....E 3
Ägerisee (lake) ....G 2
Albristhorn (mt.) ....D 4
Aletschhorn (mt.) ....F 4
Allaine (river) ....D 2
Areuse (river) ....C 3
Ault (peak) ....H 3
Baldeggersee (lake) ....F 2
Balmhorn (mt.) ....E 4
Bärenhorn (mt.) ....H 3
Basodino (mt.) ....G 4
Bernese Oberland (region)....E 3
Bernina, Piz (mt.) ....J 4
Bernina (pass) ....K 4
Bernina (river) ....J 4
Beverin (mt.) ....H 3
Biel (lake) ....D 2
Birs (river) ....D 2
Blindenhorn (mt.) ....F 4
Blümlisalp (mt.) ....E 3
Bodensee (Constance) (lake)....H 1
Borgne (river) ....D 4
Breithorn (mt.) ....E 5
Breithorn (mt.) ....E 4
Brienz (lake) ....F 3
Brienzer Rothorn (mt.) ....F 3
Broye (river) ....C 3
Brulé (mt.) ....D 4
Buchegg (mts.) ....D 2
Bürkelkopf (mt.) ....K 3
Bütschelegg (mt.) ....D 3
Calancasca (river) ....H 4
Campo Tencia (peak) ....G 4
Ceneri (mt.) ....G 4
Cheville (pass) ....D 4
Churfirsten (mt.) ....H 2
Claridenstock (mt.) ....G 3
Collon (mt.) ....D 5
Constance (lake) ....H 1
Dammastock (mt.) ....F 3
Davos (valley) ....J 3
Dent Blanche (mt.) ....E 4
Dent de Lys (mt.) ....D 4
Dent de Ruth (mt.) ....D 3
Dent d'Hérens (mt.) ....E 5
Dents du Midi (mt.) ....C 4
Diablerets (mt.) ....D 4
Doldenhorn (mt.) ....E 4
Dolent (mt.) ....C 5
Dom (mt.) ....E 4
Doubs (river) ....C 2
Drance (river) ....D 4
Dufourspitze (mt.) ....E 5
Emmental (valley) ....E 3
Engadine (valley) ....J-K 3-4
Err (mt.) ....J 3
Finsteraarhorn (mt.) ....F 3
Finstermünz (pass) ....K 3
Fletschhorn (mt.) ....F 4
Flüela (pass) ....J 3
Fluhberg (mt.) ....G 2
Fort (mt.) ....D 4
Furka (pass) ....F 3
Generoso (mt.) ....H 5
Geneva (lake) ....C 4
Giacomo (pass) ....G 4
Gibloux (mt.) ....D 3
Glâne (river) ....C 3
Glärnisch (mt.) ....H 2

AUSTRIA

PROVINCES

Burgenland, 271,001 ....D 3
Carinthia, 495,226 ....B 3
Lower Austria, 1,374,012 ....C 2
Salzburg, 347,292 ....B 3
Styria, 1,137,865 ....C 3
Tirol, 462,899 ....A 3
Upper Austria 1,131,623 ....B 2
Vienna (city), 1,631,423 ....D 2
Vorarlberg, 226,323 ....A 3

CITIES and TOWNS

Admont, 3,057 ....C 3
Aigen, 1,941 ....B 2
Alt Aussee, 2,026 ....B 3
Altheim, 4,271 ....B 2
Althofen, 3,221 ....C 3
Amstetten, 12,086 ....C 2
Andau, 3,011 ....D 3
Arnoldstein, 6,229 ....B 3
Aspang, 2,359 ....D 3
Attnang-Puchheim, 7,525 ....B 2
Bad Aussee, 5,144 ....B 3
Bad Goisern, 6,028 ....B 3
Bad Hofgastein, 4,700 ....B 3
Bad Ischl, 12,703 ....B 3
Bad Sankt Leonhard, 1,939 ....C 3
Baden, 22,484 ....D 2
Badgastein, 5,742 ....B 3
Berndorf, 8,992 ....C 3
Bischofshofen, 8,287 ....B 3
Bludenz, 11,127 ....A 3
Bramberg, 2,620 ....B 3
Braunau, 14,449 ....B 2
Bregenz, 21,428 ....A 3
Bruck an der Leitha, 6,791 ....D 2
Bruck an der Mur, 16,087 ....C 3
Deutsch Feistritz, 3,427 ....C 3
Deutsch Landsberg, 5,227 ....C 3
Deutsch Wagram, 4,207 ....D 2
Deutschkreutz, 3,901 ....D 3
Dornbirn, 28,075 ....A 3
Ebenfurth, 2,342 ....D 3
Ebensee, 9,602 ....B 3
Eferding, 3,151 ....B 2
Eggenburg, 3,338 ....C 2
Eisenerz, 12,435 ....C 3
Horn, 4,705 ....C 2
Hüttenberg, 2,257 ....C 3
Imst, 5,057 ....A 3
Innsbruck, 113,468 ....A 3
Jenbach, 5,479 ....A 3
Judenburg, 9,869 ....C 3
Kapfenberg, 23,859 ....C 3
Kappl, 1,970 ....A 3
Kaprun, 2,164 ....B 3
Kindberg, 5,766 ....C 3
Kirchdorf an der Krems, 2,964 ..C 3
Kitzbühel, 7,744 ....B 3
Klagenfurt, 69,218 ....C 3
Klosterneuburg, 22,787 ....D 2
Knittelfeld, 14,259 ....C 3
Köflach, 12,367 ....C 3
Königswiesen, 2,707 ....C 2
Korneuburg, 8,276 ....D 2
Kössen, 2,361 ....B 3
Kötschach-Mauthen, 2,763 ....B 3
Krems, 21,046 ....C 2
Kufstein, 11,215 ....B 3
Kundl, 2,508 ....A 3
Laa an der Thaya, 4,925 ....D 2
Laakirchen, 6,722 ....B 3
Lambach, 3,019 ....C 2
Landeck, 6,514 ....A 3
Landskron, 9,058 ....B 3
Längenfeld, 2,314 ....A 3
Langenlois, 4,655 ....C 2
Langenwang, 3,734 ....C 3
Lavamünd, 2,506 ....C 3
Leibnitz, 6,356 ....C 3
Lenzing, 5,372 ....B 3
Leoben, 36,257 ....C 3
Leonfelden, 2,546 ....C 2
Lienz, 11,132 ....B 3
Liezen, 5,444 ....C 3
Lilienfeld, 3,307 ....C 3
Linz, 205,762 ....C 2
Lustenau, 12,582 ....A 3
Mannersdorf, 3,909 ....D 3
Marchegg, 2,159 ....D 2
Mariazell, 2,191 ....C 3
Matrei, 3,430 ....B 3
Mattersburg, 4,270 ....D 3
Mattighofen, 3,919 ....B 2
Mauerkirchen, 2,175 ....B 2
Mautern, 2,365 ....C 3
Mauthausen, 3,836 ....C 2
Mauthen-Kötschach, 2,763 ....B 3
Mayrhofen, 2,523 ....A 3
Schärding, 5,710 ....B 2
Scheibbs, 3,231 ....C 2
Schladming, 3,249 ....B 3
Schrems, 3,080 ....C 2
Schruns, 3,304 ....A 3
Schwarzach, 3,186 ....B 3
Schwaz, 9,455 ....A 3
Schwertberg, 3,369 ....C 2
Sierning, 7,527 ....C 2
Sillian, 1,948 ....B 3
Solbad Hall, 10,750 ....A 3
Spital, 2,421 ....C 3
Spittal, 10,045 ....B 3
Steinach, 2,155 ....A 3
Steyr, 38,306 ....C 2
Stockerau, 11,853 ....D 2
Strassburg, 2,972 ....C 3
Tamweg, 4,431 ....B 3
Telfs, 5,438 ....A 3
Ternitz, 9,032 ....D 3
Traiskirchen, 7,026 ....D 2
Traun, 16,026 ....C 2
Trieben, 4,023 ....C 3
Trofaiach, 6,909 ....C 3
Tulln, 6,306 ....D 2
Velden, 2,039 ....C 3
Vienna (capital), 1,642,072 ....D 2
Villach, 32,971 ....B 3
Vöcklabruck, 9,353 ....B 2
Voitsberg, 6,353 ....C 3
Völkermarkt, 3,678 ....C 3
Vordernberg, 2,896 ....C 3
Waidhofen an der Thaya,
 3,748 ....C 2
Waidhofen an der Ybbs,
 5,586 ....C 3
Weitensfeld, 2,998 ....B 3
Weiz, 8,146 ....C 3
Wels, 41,060 ....C 2
Weyer, 2,367 ....C 3
Wiener Neustadt, 33,845 ....D 3
Wildon, 2,020 ....C 3
Wilhelmsburg, 6,196 ....C 2
Wolfsberg, 9,470 ....C 3
Wörgl, 6.828 ....A 3
Ybbs, 5,324 ....C 2
Zams, 2,782 ....A 3
Zell am See, 6,455 ....B 3
Zeltweg, 7,340 ....C 3
Zirl, 3,165 ....A 3
Zistersdorf, 3,011 ....D 2
Zwettl, 3,836 ....C 2

OTHER FEATURES

Allgäu Alps (mts.) ....A 3
Atter (lake) ....B 3
Bavarian Alps (mts.) ....A 3
Bodensee (Constance) (lake) ....A 3
Brenner (pass) ....A 3
Carnic Alps (mts.) ....B 3
Coglians (Hohe Warte) (peak)...B 3
Constance (lake) ....A 3
Danube (river) ....C 2
Donau (Danube) (river) ....D 2
Drau (river) ....C 3
Enns (river) ....C 3
Fertő tó (Neusiedler) (lake).....D 3
Greiner (forest) ....C 2
Grossglockner (mt.) ....B 3
Gross Höllkogel (mt.) ....B 3
Gross Peilstein (mt.) ....C 2
Hochgolling (mt.) ....B 3
Hohe Tauern (range) ....B 3
Hohe Warte (peak) ....B 3
Inn (river) ....B 2
Kamp (river) ....C 2
Karawanken (mts.) ....C 3
Laufnitz (river) ....D 3
March (river) ....D 2
Mühlviertel (region),
 196,037 ....C 2
Mur (river) ....C 3
Mürz (river) ....C 3
Neusiedler (lake) ....D 3
Niedere Tauern (range) ....B 3
Olsa (river) ....C 3
Ötztal Alps (mts.) ....A 3
Parseierspitze (mt.) ....A 3
Raab (river) ....C 3
Rhine (river) ....A 3
Salzach (river) ....B 2
Salzkammergut (region) ....B 3
Semmering (pass) ....C 3
Thaya (river) ....C 2
Traun (lake) ....B 3
Traun (river) ....C 2
Wildspitze (mt.) ....A 3
Zugspitze (mt.) ....A 3

CZECHOSLOVAKIA

REPUBLICS

Czech Soc. Rep., 9,778,000 ....B 1
Slovak Soc. Rep., 4,421,000 ....E 2

REGIONS

Jihočeský, 659,000 ....C 2
Jihomoravský, 1,941,000 ....D 2
Prague (city), 1,025,000 ....C 1
Severočeský, 1,122,000 ....C 1
Severomoravský, 1,695,000 ....C 1
Středočeský, 1,271,000 ....C 2
Středoslovenský, 1,379,000 ....E 2
Východočeský, 1,213,000 ....C 1
Východoslovenský, 1,199,000 ....F 2
Západočeský, 852,000 ....B 2
Západoslovenský, 1,843.000 ....D 2

CITIES and TOWNS

As, 10,000 ....B 1
Austerlitz (Slavkov), 4,869 ....D 2
Bánovce, 3,563 ....E 2
Banská Bystrica, 29,000 ....E 2
Banská Štiavnica, 10,381 ....E 2
Bardejov, 11,000 ....F 2
Bechyně, 2,398 ....C 2
Benešov, 10,000 ....C 2
Beroun, 17,000 ....B 2
Bílina, 12,000 ....B 1
Blansko, 11,000 ....D 2
Blatná, 3,596 ....B 2
Blovice, 2,629 ....B 2
Bojkovice, 2,902 ....D 2
Bor, 2,257 ....B 2
Boskovice, 6,396 ....D 2
Brandýs nad Labem-Stará
 Boleslav, 13,161 ....C 1
Bratislava, 278,835 ....D 2
Břeclav, 13,000 ....D 2
Březnice, 2,634 ....B 2
Brezno, 11,000 ....E 2
Brno, 333,831 ....D 2
Broumov, 6,370 ....D 1
Brtnice, 2,176 ....C 2
Bruntál, 9,000 ....D 2
Bučovice, 3,381 ....D 2
Budišov, 3,677 ....D 2
Bystřice nad Pernštejnem,
 2,653 ....D 2
Bystřice pod Hostýnem, 4,973 ....D 2
Bytča, 4,528 ....E 2
Čadca, 13,000 ....E 2
Čalovo, 4,536 ....D 3
Čáslav, 10,000 ....C 2
Česká Kamenice, 6,084 ....C 1
Česká Lípa, 15,000 ....C 1
Česká Třebová, 14,000 ....D 2
České Budějovice, 70,000 ....C 2
Český Brod, 5,754 ....C 1
Český Krumlov, 10,000 ....C 2
Český Těšín, 16,000 ....E 2
Cheb, 24,000 ....B 1
Chlumec, 4,345 ....C 1
Choceň, 6,789 ....D 1
Chodov, 5,383 ....B 1
Chomutov, 37,000 ....B 1
Chotěboř, 4,846 ....C 2
Chrastava, 3,618 ....C 1
Chrudim, 17,000 ....C 2
Čierny Balog, 5,978 ....E 2
Cukmantl, 2,362 ....D 1
Dačice, 2,810 ....C 2
Děčín, 42,000 ....C 1
Detva, 7,786 ....E 2
Dobřany, 4,905 ....B 2
Dobříš, 4,390 ....C 2
Dobruška, 4,093 ....D 1
Dobšiná, 3,957 ....F 2
Doksy, 3,061 ....C 1
Dolný Kubín, 5,000 ....E 2
Domažlice, 8,000 ....B 2
Dubnica nad Váhom, 11,250 ......E 2
Duchcov, 8,229 ....B 1
Dunajská Streda, 9,000 ....D 3
Dvory, 5,475 ....E 3
Dvůr Králové nad Labem. 16,000..C 1
Falknov (Sokolov), 20,000 ....B 1
Fiľakovo, 5,950 ....E 2
Františkovy Lázně, 5,212 ....B 1
Frýdek-Místek, 32,000 ....E 2
Frýdlant nad Ostravicí, 4,178 .....E 2
Frýdlant v čechách, 5,460 ....C 1
Fulnek, 2,765 ....D 2
Galanta, 8,000 ....D 2
Gelnica, 3,240 ....F 2
Golčův Jeníkov, 1,920 ....C 2
Gottwaldov, 63,000 ....D 2
Handlová, 16,000 ....E 2
Havířov, 72,000 ....E 2
Havlíčkův, Brod, 16,000 ....C 2
Hlinsko, 5,189 ....D 2
Hlohovec, 14,000 ....D 2
Hlučín, 11,000 ....E 2
Hodonín, 19,000 ....D 2

(continued)

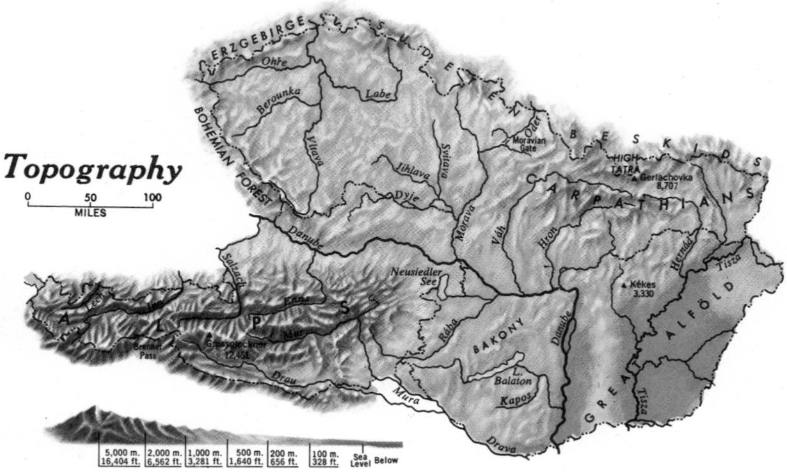
Topography
0
50
100
MILES
ERZGEBIRGE
Ohře
Berounka
Labe
BOHEMIAN FOREST
Vltava
Jihlava
Svitava
Dyje
Odra
Moravian Gate
HIGH TATRA
Gerlachovka 8,707
CARPATHIANS
Morava
Váh
Hron
Hernád
Tisza
Danube
Neusiedler See
Kékes 3,330
BAKONY
Balaton
Kapos
Rába
Mura
Drava
GREAT ALFÖLD
Salzach
Enns
Mur
Drau
5,000 m. 16,404 ft.
2,000 m. 6,562 ft.
1,000 m. 3,281 ft.
500 m. 1,640 ft.
200 m. 656 ft.
100 m. 328 ft.
Sea Level
Below

Eisenstadt, 7,167 ....D 3
Enns, 8,919 ....C 2
Feldbach, 3,687 ....C 3
Feldkirch, 17,343 ....A 3
Feldkirchen in Kärnten, 3,181 ....B 3
Ferlach, 5,672 ....C 3
Fieberbrunn, 3,010 ....B 3
Fohnsdorf, 11,571 ....C 3
Frankenmarkt, 2,565 ....B 3
Frauenkirchen, 2,812 ....D 3
Friesach, 3,388 ....C 3
Freistadt, 5,375 ....C 2
Frohnleiten, 4,969 ....C 3
Fulpmes, 2,282 ....A 3
Fürstenfeld, 6,415 ....C 3
Gaming, 4,218 ....C 3
Gänserndorf, 3,378 ....D 2
Gleisdorf, 4,385 ....C 3
Gloggnitz, 7,228 ....D 3
Gmünd, Carinthia, 2,195 ....B 3
Gmünd, Lower Austria, 6,522 ....C 2
Gmunden, 12,518 ....B 3
Golling an der Salzach,
 2,845 ....B 3
Götzis, 7,034 ....A 3
Gratwein, 2,515 ....C 3
Graz, 253,000 ....C 3
Grein, 2,518 ....C 2
Grieskirchen, 4,137 ....B 2
Gross Sieghart s, 2,599 ....C 2
Grünburg, 3,609 ....C 3
Güssing, 2,715 ....D 3
Haag, 4,671 ....C 2
Hainburg, 6,437 ....D 2
Hainfeld, 3,883 ....C 2
Hallein, 13,329 ....B 3
Hallstatt, 1,373 ....B 3
Hartberg, 3,629 ....C 3
Haslach an der Mühl, 2,565 ....C 2
Heidenreichstein, 3,653 ....C 2
Heiligenblut, 1,195 ....B 3
Hermagor, 2,778 ....B 3
Herzogenburg, 5,166 ....C 2
Hieflau, 2,003 ....C 3
Hohenau an der March, 3,907 ....D 2
Hohenberg, 2,093 ....C 3
Hohenems, 9,188 ....A 3
Hollabrunn, 5,832 ....D 2
Hopfgarten in Nordtirol, 4,163....B 3
Melk, 3,534 ....C 2
Mistelbach an der Zaya, 5,434....D 2
Mittersill, 3,502 ....B 3
Mödling, 17,274 ....D 2
Mondsee, 2,050 ....B 3
Murau, 2,755 ....C 3
Mürzzuschlag, 11,586 ....C 3
Nassereith, 1,744 ....A 3
Neuberg an der Mürz, 2,411 .....C 3
Neumarkt, Styria, 1,880 ....C 3
Neumarkt am Wallersee, 2,877...B 3
Neunkirchen, 10,027 ....C 3
Neusiedl am See, 3,826 ....D 3
Neustift im Stubaital, 2,195 ......A 3
Ober Grafendorf, 3,825 ....C 2
Oberndorf bei Salzburg, 3,084....B 3
Obervellach, 2,371 ....B 3
Oberwart, 4,740 ....D 3
Paternion, 5,581 ....B 3
Perg, 4,106 ....C 2
Peuerbach, 2,105 ....B 2
Pinkafeld, 3,826 ....C 3
Pöchlarn, 2,921 ....C 2
Pörtschach, 2,449 ....C 3
Poysdorf, 2,738 ....D 2
Pregarten, 2,818 ....C 2
Radenthein, 5,651 ....B 3
Radstadt, 3,311 ....B 3
Rankweil, 6,451 ....A 3
Rechnitz, 3,374 ....D 3
Reichenau an der Rax, 4,441 .....C 3
Retz, 2,941 ....D 2
Reutte, 4,285 ....A 3
Ried im Innkreis, 9,471 ....B 2
Rottenmann, 4,139 ....C 3
Saalfelden, 8,901 ....B 3
Salzburg, 120,204 ....B 3
Sankt Aegyd am Neuwalde,
 3,206 ....C 3
Sankt Anton am Arlberg, 1,741....A 3
Sankt Johann, 4,713 ....B 3
Sankt Michael, 3,433 ....C 3
Sankt Michael im Lungau,
 2,422 ....B 3
Sankt Paul, 1,808 ....C 3
Sankt Pölten, 40,112 ....C 2
Sankt Valentin, 7,750 ....C 2
Sankt Veit an der Glan, 10,950 ...C 3
Sankt Wolfgang, 2,234 ....B 3

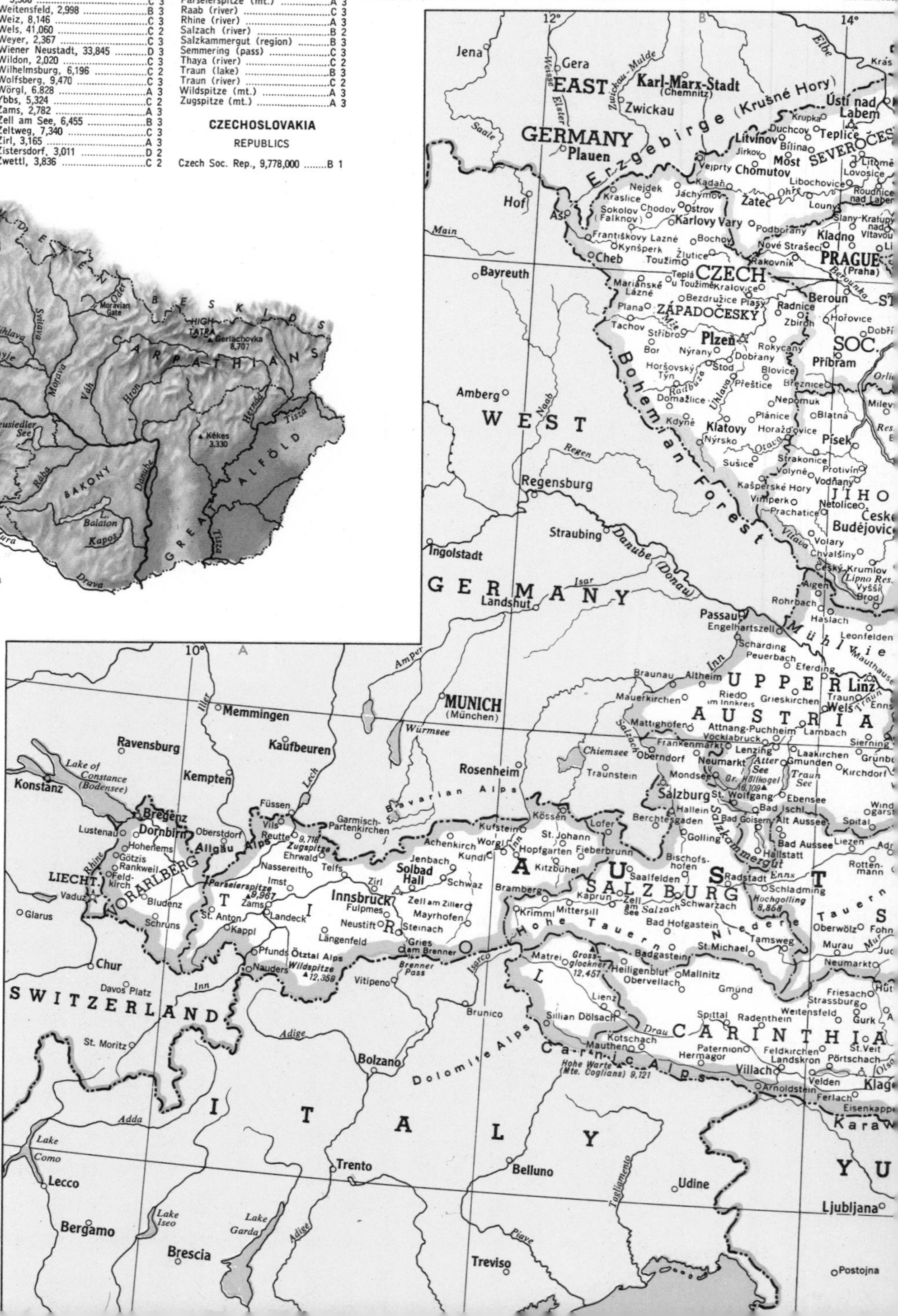
12°
14°
10°
B
A
Jena
Gera
EAST
GERMANY
Karl-Marx-Stadt
(Chemnitz)
Zwickau
Plauen
Erzgebirge (Krušné Hory)
Elbe
Ústí nad Labem
Teplice
Most
Chomutov
Karlovy Vary
Žatec
Kladno
PRAGUE
(Praha)
CZECH
SOC.
Cheb
Hof
Main
Bayreuth
Plzeň
ZÁPADOČESKÝ
Příbram
Beroun
Domažlice
Klatovy
Písek
Strakonice
Bohemian Forest
WEST
GERMANY
Amberg
Regensburg
Straubing
Danube (Donau)
Ingolstadt
Landshut
Isar
Passau
České Budějovice
Český Krumlov
Vltava
Mühlviertel
UPPER AUSTRIA
Linz
Wels
Braunau
MUNICH
(München)
Memmingen
Kaufbeuren
Ravensburg
Kempten
Lake of Constance (Bodensee)
Konstanz
Bregenz
Dornbirn
Feldkirch
Bludenz
VORARLBERG
LIECHT.
Vaduz
Rhine
Glarus
Chur
Davos Platz
St. Moritz
Allgäu Alps
Reutte
Zugspitze 9,718
Garmisch-Partenkirchen
Bavarian Alps
Rosenheim
Chiemsee
Traunstein
Kufstein
Wörgl
Kitzbühel
Innsbruck
Solbad Hall
Schwaz
Zell am Ziller
Mayrhofen
Landeck
Imst
Telfs
Parseierspitze 9,967
Ötztal Alps
Wildspitze 12,359
Brenner Pass
TIROL
SALZBURG
Salzburg
Hallein
Bad Ischl
Gmunden
Vöcklabruck
Hohe Tauern
Gross-Glockner 12,457
Heiligenblut
Lienz
Mittersill
Zell am See
Kaprun
Bad Hofgastein
Badgastein
Radstadt
Schladming
Hochgolling 9,386
Tamsweg
CARINTHIA
Spittal
Villach
Hermagor
Karawanken
Carnic Alps
Hohe Warte (Mte. Coglians) 9,121
SWITZERLAND
ITALY
Bolzano
Brunico
Dolomite Alps
Trento
Belluno
Udine
Lecco
Bergamo
Brescia
Treviso
Lake Como
Lake Iseo
Lake Garda
Adige
Adda
Piave
Tagliamento
Ljubljana
Postojna
YU

AUSTRIA
AREA 32,374 sq. mi.
POPULATION 7,419,341
CAPITAL Vienna
LARGEST CITY Vienna
HIGHEST POINT Grossglockner 12,457 ft.
MONETARY UNIT schilling
MAJOR LANGUAGE German
MAJOR RELIGION Roman Catholicism

CZECHOSLOVAKIA
AREA 49,370 sq. mi.
POPULATION 14,497,000
CAPITAL Prague
LARGEST CITY Prague
HIGHEST POINT Gerlachovka 8,707 ft.
MONETARY UNIT koruna (crown)
MAJOR LANGUAGES Czech, Slovak
MAJOR RELIGIONS Roman Catholicism, Protestantism

HUNGARY
AREA 35,915 sq. mi.
POPULATION 10,315,597
CAPITAL Budapest
LARGEST CITY Budapest
HIGHEST POINT Kékes 3,330 ft.
MONETARY UNIT forint
MAJOR LANGUAGE Hungarian
MAJOR RELIGIONS Roman Catholicism, Protestantism

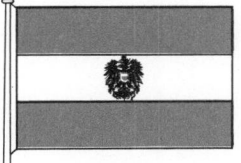

AUSTRIA

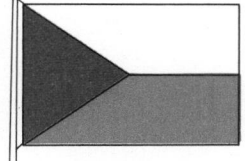

CZECHOSLOVAKIA

HUNGARY

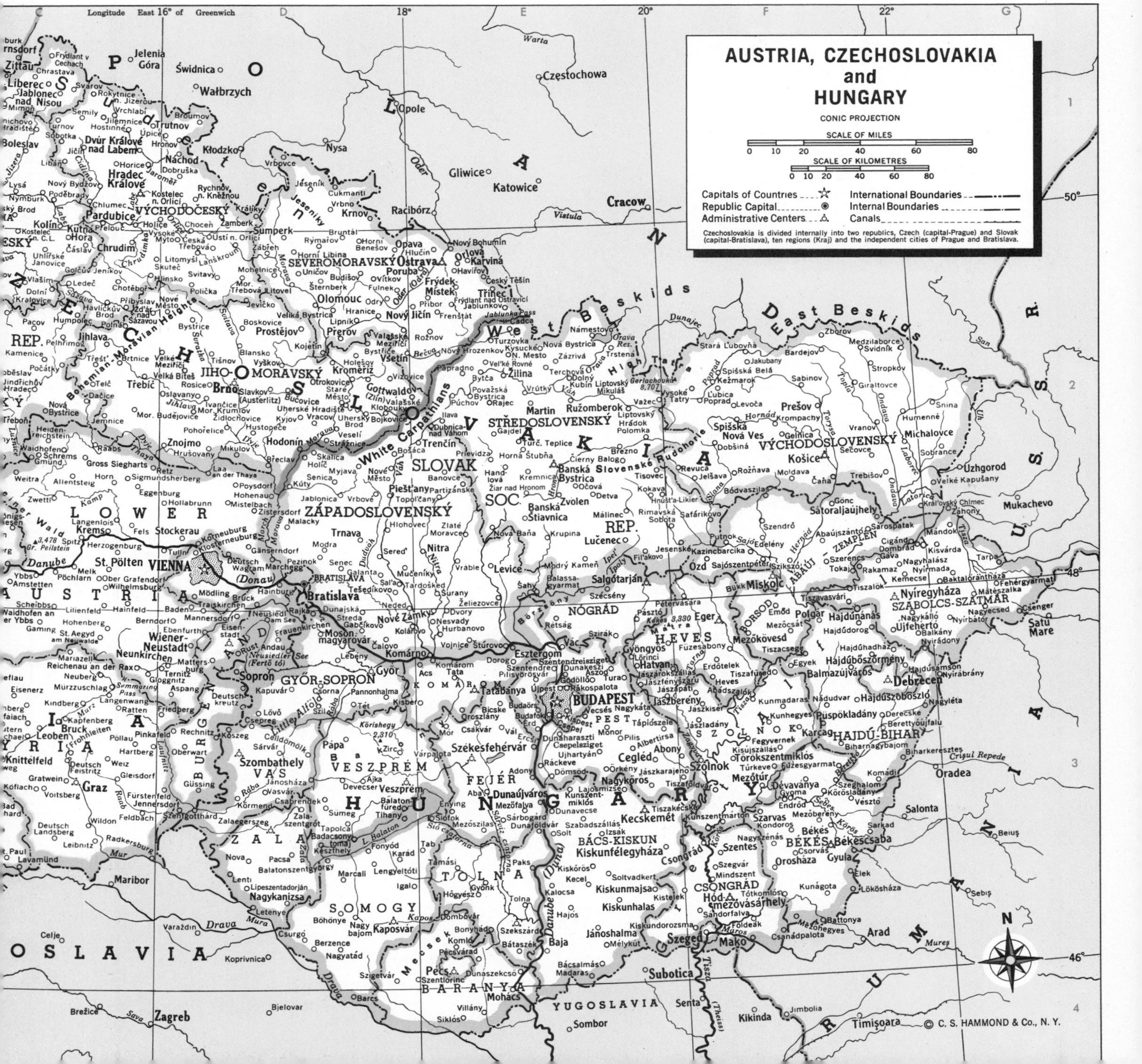

AUSTRIA, CZECHOSLOVAKIA and HUNGARY
CONIC PROJECTION

SCALE OF MILES
0 10 20 40 60 80

SCALE OF KILOMETRES
0 10 20 40 60 80

Capitals of Countries ☆
Republic Capital ◉
Administrative Centers △
International Boundaries
Internal Boundaries
Canals

Czechoslovakia is divided internally into two republics, Czech (capital-Prague) and Slovak (capital-Bratislava), ten regions (Kraj) and the independent cities of Prague and Bratislava.

© C. S. HAMMOND & Co., N.Y.

CZECHOSLOVAKIA (continued)

Holešov, 6,599 .... D 2
Holíč, 5,881 .... D 2
Holice, 5,695 .... D 1
Horažďovice, 3,098 .... B 2
Hořice, 7,133 .... D 1
Horní Benešov, 3,181 .... D 2
Horní Lideč, 4,583 .... D 2
Hořovice, 4,697 .... B 2
Horšovský Týn, 3,475 .... B 2
Hostinné, 4,412 .... C 1
Hradec Králové, 62,000 .... C 1
Hranice, 12,000 .... D 2
Hronov, 11,000 .... D 1
Hrušovany, 3,128 .... D 2
Humenné, 14,000 .... G 2
Humpolec, 5,083 .... C 2
Hurbanovo, 3,578 .... E 3
Hustopeče, 2,698 .... D 2
Ilava, 2,043 .... E 2
Ivančice, 4,742 .... D 2
Jablonec nad Nisou, 33,000 .... C 1
Jablunkov, 4,467 .... E 2
Jáchymov, 6,806 .... B 1
Jaroměř, 12,000 .... C 1
Jelšava, 2,456 .... F 2
Jemnice, 3,383 .... C 2
Jeseník, 5,873 .... D 1
Jesenské, 1,567 .... F 2
Jevíčko, 2,881 .... D 2
Jičín, 13,000 .... C 1
Jihlava, 37,000 .... C 2
Jilemnice, 3,367 .... C 1
Jindřichův Hradec, 12,000 .... C 2
Jirkov, 12,000 .... B 1
Kadaň, 5,062 .... B 1
Kamenice, 2,692 .... C 2
Kaplice, 1,931 .... C 2
Karlovy Vary, 45,000 .... B 1
Karviná, 70,000 .... E 2
Kašperské Hory, 2,814 .... B 2
Kdyně, 2,609 .... B 2
Kežmarok, 7,372 .... F 2
Kladno, 55,000 .... B 1
Klatovy, 16,000 .... B 2
Kojetín, 5,292 .... D 2
Kokava, 5,398 .... F 2
Kolárovo, 11,000 .... D 3
Kolín, 25,000 .... C 1

Mělník, 15,000 .... C 1
Michalovce, 18,000 .... G 2
Mikulov, 5,220 .... D 2
Milevsko, 3,754 .... C 2
Mimoň, 5,348 .... C 1
Mladá Boleslav, 27,000 .... C 1
Mladá Vožice, 1,732 .... C 2
Mnichovo Hradiště, 4,647 .... C 1
Modra, 6,239 .... D 2
Modrý Kameň, 1,836 .... E 2
Mohelnice, 4,949 .... D 2
Moldava, 2,241 .... F 2
Moravská Třebová, 5,844 .... D 2
Moravské Budějovice, 4,348 .... D 2
Moravský Krumlov, 2,897 .... D 2
Most, 56,000 .... B 1
Mučeníky, 5,207 .... D 2
Myjava, 9,935 .... D 2
Náchod, 18,000 .... D 1
Neded, 4,553 .... D 2
Nejdek, 5,748 .... B 1
Nepomuk, 1,860 .... B 2
Nesvady, 5,070 .... E 3
Netolice, 2,503 .... C 2
Nitra, 39,000 .... E 2
Nová Baňa, 5,113 .... E 2
Nová Bystřice, 2,418 .... C 2
Nové Město na Moravě, 3,250 .... D 2
Nové Město nad Váhom, 14,000 .... D 2
Nové Strašecí, 3,288 .... B 1
Nové Zámky, 24,000 .... D 3
Nový Bohumín, 12,000 .... E 2
Nový Bor, 5,994 .... C 1
Nový Bydžov, 6,120 .... C 1
Nový Hrozenkov, 5,302 .... E 2
Nový Jičín, 17,000 .... E 2
Nymburk, 13,000 .... C 1
Nýřany, 4,420 .... B 2
Nýrsko, 4,124 .... B 2
Odry, 5,340 .... D 2
Olomouc, 77,000 .... D 2
Opava, 66,000 .... E 2
Orlová, 22,000 .... E 2
Oslavany, 3,606 .... D 2
Ostrava, 271,905 .... E 2
Ostrov, 19,000 .... B 1
Otrokovice-Kvítkovice, 11,000 .... D 2
Pacov, 2,775 .... C 2
Pardubice, 65,000 .... C 1

Rýmařov, 4,328 .... D 2
Sabinov, 3,909 .... F 2
Šafaříkovo, 3,180 .... F 2
Šahy, 4,019 .... E 2
Šaľa, 4,397 .... D 2
Sečovce, 3,354 .... G 2
Sedlčany, 2,083 .... C 2
Semily, 6,549 .... C 1
Senec, 6,184 .... D 2
Senica, 8,000 .... D 2
Sered', 6,208 .... D 2
Skalica, 5,440 .... D 2
Skuteč, 3,348 .... D 2
Slaný, 12,000 .... C 1
Slavkov, 4,869 .... D 2
Snina, 5,600 .... G 2
Soběslav, 4,643 .... C 2
Sobotka, 2,147 .... C 1
Sokolov, 20,000 .... B 1
Spišská Belá, 3,072 .... F 2
Spišská Nová Ves, 20,000 .... F 2
Stará Ľubovňa, 1,989 .... F 2
Staré Město, 6,350 .... D 2
Šternberk, 12,000 .... D 2
Stod, 2,502 .... B 2
Strakonice, 16,000 .... B 2
Strážnice, 5,147 .... D 2
Stříbro, 4,659 .... B 2
Stropkov, 2,506 .... F 2
Štúrovo, 4,082 .... D 2
Šumperk, 22,000 .... D 1
Šurany, 5,381 .... D 2
Sušice, 6,793 .... B 2
Svárov, 3,381 .... C 1
Svitavy, 14,000 .... D 2
Tábor, 21,000 .... C 2
Tachov, 8,000 .... B 1
Tardošked, 6,689 .... E 2
Telč, 4,381 .... C 2
Teplá u Toužimě, 2,500 .... B 1
Teplice, 52,000 .... B 1
Terchová, 4,400 .... E 2
Tišnov, 4,885 .... D 2
Tisovec, 3,988 .... F 2
Topoľčany, 12,000 .... E 2
Trebišov, 10,000 .... G 2
Třeboň, 4,663 .... C 2
Trenčín, 26,000 .... D 2
Třešť, 4,200 .... C 2

Zbiroh, 1,718 .... B 2
Zborov, 1,551 .... F 2
Žd'ár nad Sázavou, 12,000 .... C 2
Železnice, 3,748 .... C 1
Žiar nad Hronom, 11,000 .... E 2
Zidlochovice, 2,696 .... D 2
Žilina, 38,000 .... E 2
Zlaté Moravce, 4,003 .... E 2
Zlín (Gottwaldov), 63,000 .... D 2
Žluvice, 2,114 .... B 1
Znojmo, 25,000 .... D 2
Zvolen, 23,000 .... E 2

OTHER FEATURES

Berounka (river) .... C 2
Beskids, East (mts.) .... F 1
Beskids, West (mts.) .... E 2
Bohemia (region), 6,142,000 .... C 2
Bohemian (forest) .... B 2
Bohemian-Moravian Heights .... C 2
Dudváh (river) .... D 2
Dunajec (river) .... F 2
Dyje (river) .... D 2
Erzgebirge (mts.) .... A 1
Gerlachovka (mt.) .... F 2
Hornád (river) .... F 2
Hron (river) .... E 2
Ipeľ (river) .... E 2
Jablunka (pass) .... E 2
Jeseníky (mts.) .... D 1
Jihlava (river) .... C 2
Kamýcká (res.) .... C 2
Krušné Hory (Erzgebirge) (mts.) .... B 1
Labe (river) .... C 1
Laborec (river) .... G 2
Lipno (res.) .... C 2
Lužnice (river) .... C 2
Moldau (Vltava) (river) .... C 2
Morava (river) .... D 2
Moravia (region), 3,636,000 .... D 2
Nitra (river) .... E 2
Oder (Odra) (river) .... D 2
Ohře (river) .... B 1
Orava (river) .... E 2
Orava (res.) .... E 2
Orlice (river) .... C 1
Orlická (res.) .... C 1
Otava (river) .... B 2

Abádszalók, 7,257 .... F 3
Abaújszántó, 4,586 .... F 2
Abony, 16,048 .... E 3
Ács, 8,507 .... D 3
Adony, 4,211 .... E 3
Ajka, 21,000 .... D 3
Albertirsa, 11,490 .... E 3
Aszód, 5,361 .... E 3
Bácsalmás, 9,514 .... E 4
Baja, 34,000 .... E 3
Balassagyarmat, 13,000 .... E 2
Balatonfüred, 7,561 .... D 3
Balkány, 8,224 .... F 3
Balmazújváros, 18,645 .... F 3
Barcs, 7,245 .... D 4
Bátaszék, 7,378 .... E 3
Battonya, 11,019 .... F 3
Békés, 21,296 .... F 3
Békéscsaba, 53,000 .... F 3
Berettyóújfalu, 11,577 .... F 3
Bercence, 3,651 .... D 3
Bicske, 9,106 .... E 3
Biharkeresztes, 4,844 .... F 3
Biharnagybajom, 4,762 .... F 3
Bőhönye, 3,809 .... D 3
Bonyhád, 9,354 .... E 3
Budafok, 39,870 .... E 3
Budaörs, 12,682 .... E 3
Budapest (capital), 1,990,000 .... E 3
Cegléd, 37,000 .... E 3
Celldömölk, 9,762 .... D 3
Cigánd, 5,220 .... F 2
Csákvár, 5,135 .... E 3
Csanádpalota, 5,264 .... F 3
Csenger, 4,835 .... G 3
Csepel, 86,287 .... E 3
Csepreg, 4,348 .... D 3
Csongrád, 20,000 .... E 3
Csorna, 9,192 .... D 3
Csorvás, 7,622 .... F 3
Csurgó, 5,400 .... D 3
Debrecen, 160,000 .... F 3
Derecske, 9,980 .... F 3
Devaványa, 12,137 .... F 3
Devecser, 5,741 .... D 3
Dombóvár, 15,605 .... E 3
Dombrád, 6,868 .... F 2
Dömsöd, 6,532 .... E 3
Dorog, 9,994 .... E 3
Dunaföldvár, 11,039 .... E 3

Jászkarajenő, 4,955 .... E 3
Jászkisér, 7,280 .... F 3
Jászladány, 8,841 .... F 3
Kalocsa, 15,000 .... E 3
Kaposvár, 52,000 .... D 3
Kapuvár, 10,748 .... D 3
Karád, 3,438 .... D 3
Karcag, 24,000 .... F 3
Kazincbarcika, 29,000 .... F 2
Kecel, 10,193 .... E 3
Kecskemét, 76,000 .... E 3
Kemecse, 4,681 .... F 2
Keszthely, 17,000 .... D 3
Kisbér, 4,567 .... D 3
Kiskőrös, 12,954 .... E 3
Kiskundorozsma, 8,679 .... E 3
Kiskunfélegyháza, 33,000 .... E 3
Kiskunhalas, 28,000 .... E 3
Kiskunmajsa, 12,311 .... E 3
Kispest, 66,547 .... E 3
Kistelek, 8,925 .... E 3
Kisújszállás, 13,000 .... F 3
Kisvárda, 13,050 .... G 2
Komádi, 9,850 .... F 3
Komárom, 11,000 .... D 3
Komló, 28,000 .... E 3
Kondoros, 7,462 .... F 3
Körmend, 7,548 .... D 3
Kőrösladány, 7,302 .... F 3
Kőszeg, 10,000 .... D 3
Kunágota, 5,547 .... F 3
Kunhegyes, 10,792 .... F 3
Kunmadaras, 8,463 .... F 3
Kunszentmárton, 13,383 .... F 3
Kunszentmiklós, 8,198 .... E 3
Lajosmizse, 12,617 .... E 3
Lébény, 3,588 .... D 3
Lengyeltóti, 3,392 .... D 3
Letenye, 4,507 .... D 3
Lőkösháza, 2,511 .... F 3
Lőrinci, 11,142 .... E 3
Madaras, 5,177 .... E 3
Makó, 29,000 .... F 3
Mándok, 4,828 .... G 2
Marcali, 7,877 .... D 3
Mátészalka, 11,496 .... G 3
Mélykút, 8,168 .... E 3
Mezőberény, 12,830 .... F 3
Mezőcsát, 6,583 .... F 3
Mezőhegyes, 9,137 .... F 3

Sándorfalva, 5,815 .... E 3
Sárbogárd, 6,853 .... E 3
Sarkad, 12,169 .... F 3
Sárospatak, 12,799 .... F 2
Sárvár, 11,247 .... D 3
Sátoraljaújhely, 17,000 .... F 2
Siklós, 5,897 .... E 4
Siófok, 10,322 .... D 3
Solt, 7,198 .... E 3
Soltvadkert, 8,244 .... E 3
Sopron, 45,000 .... D 3
Sümeg, 5,925 .... D 3
Szabadszállás, 8,799 .... E 3
Szarvas, 19,000 .... F 3
Szécsény, 4,410 .... E 2
Szeged, 120,000 .... E 3
Szeghalom, 10,093 .... F 3
Szegvár, 6,970 .... F 3
Székesfehérvár, 71,000 .... E 3
Szekszárd, 23,000 .... E 3
Szendrő, 3,713 .... F 2
Szentendre, 12,000 .... E 3
Szentes, 32,000 .... F 3
Szentgotthárd, 5,421 .... D 3
Szerencs, 7,789 .... F 2
Szigetvár, 10,000 .... D 3
Szikszó, 6,110 .... F 2
Szolnok, 50,000 .... F 3
Szombathely, 62,000 .... D 3
Tab, 4,265 .... D 3
Tamási, 7,689 .... E 3
Tápiószele, 5,632 .... E 3
Tapolca, 10,000 .... D 3
Tarpa, 3,966 .... G 2
Tata, 19,000 .... E 3
Tatabánya, 64,000 .... E 3
Tét, 4,861 .... D 3
Tiszacsege, 7,002 .... F 3
Tiszaföldvár, 12,377 .... F 3
Tiszafüred, 11,214 .... F 3
Tiszakécske, 12,834 .... E 3
Tiszalök, 6,125 .... F 2
Tiszavasvári, 12,201 .... F 2
Tokaj, 5,031 .... F 2
Tolna, 8,741 .... E 3
Törökszentmiklós, 24,000 .... F 3
Tótkomlós, 9,368 .... F 3
Tura, 8,169 .... E 3
Túrkeve, 11,000 .... F 3
Újfehértó, 14,386 .... F 3

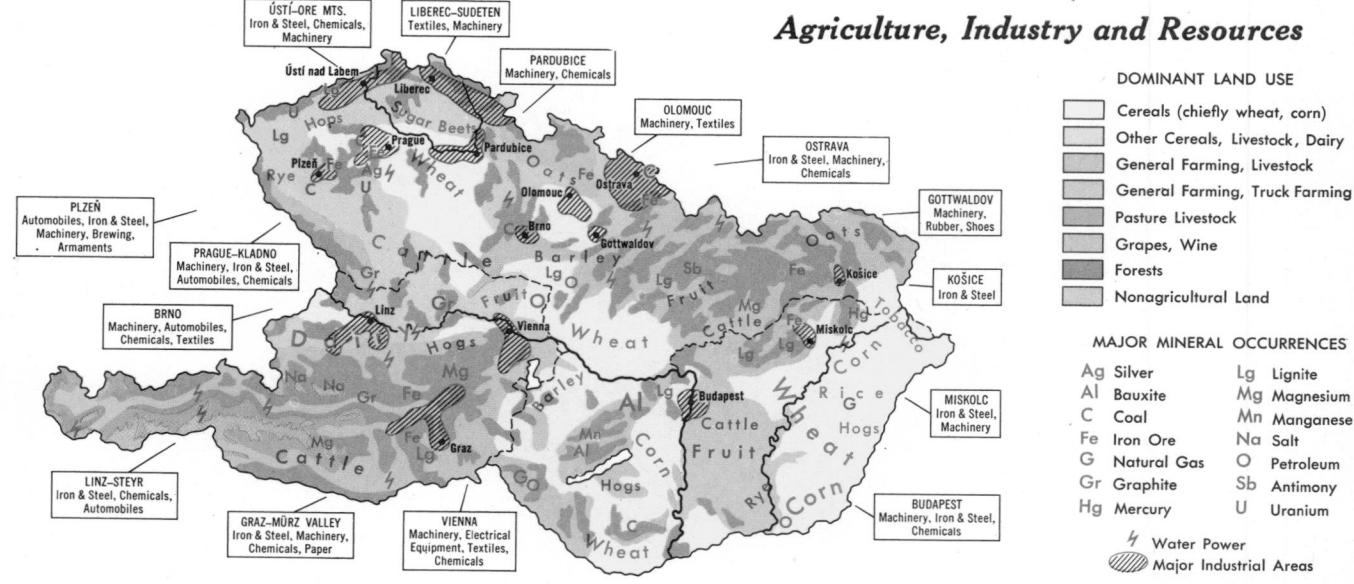

Agriculture, Industry and Resources

ÚSTÍ-ORE MTS.
Iron & Steel, Chemicals, Machinery

LIBEREC–SUDETEN
Textiles, Machinery

PARDUBICE
Machinery, Chemicals

OLOMOUC
Machinery, Textiles

OSTRAVA
Iron & Steel, Machinery, Chemicals

GOTTWALDOV
Machinery, Rubber, Shoes

KOŠICE
Iron & Steel

PLZEŇ
Automobiles, Iron & Steel, Machinery, Brewing, Armaments

PRAGUE–KLADNO
Machinery, Iron & Steel, Automobiles, Chemicals

BRNO
Machinery, Automobiles, Chemicals, Textiles

MISKOLC
Iron & Steel, Machinery

LINZ–STEYR
Iron & Steel, Chemicals, Automobiles

GRAZ–MÜRZ VALLEY
Iron & Steel, Machinery, Chemicals, Paper

VIENNA
Machinery, Electrical Equipment, Textiles, Chemicals

BUDAPEST
Machinery, Iron & Steel, Chemicals

DOMINANT LAND USE

Cereals (chiefly wheat, corn)
Other Cereals, Livestock, Dairy
General Farming, Livestock
General Farming, Truck Farming
Pasture Livestock
Grapes, Wine
Forests
Nonagricultural Land

MAJOR MINERAL OCCURRENCES

Ag	Silver	Lg	Lignite
Al	Bauxite	Mg	Magnesium
C	Coal	Mn	Manganese
Fe	Iron Ore	Na	Salt
G	Natural Gas	O	Petroleum
Gr	Graphite	Sb	Antimony
Hg	Mercury	U	Uranium

Water Power
Major Industrial Areas

Komárno, 26,000 .... D 3
Košice, 115,332 .... F 2
Kostelec nad Černými, Lesy, 3,616 .... C 2
Kostelec nad Orlicí, 5,539 .... C 1
Králíky, 3,895 .... D 1
Kralovice, 2,258 .... B 2
Kráľovský Chlmec, 3,410 .... G 2
Kralupy nad Vltavou, 14,000 .... C 1
Kraslice, 6,294 .... B 1
Krásná Lípa, 5,041 .... C 1
Kremnica, 4,979 .... E 2
Krnov, 22,000 .... D 2
Kroměříž, 22,000 .... D 2
Krompachy, 3,340 .... F 2
Krupina, 5,418 .... E 2
Krupka, 10,000 .... B 1
Kutná Hora, 17,000 .... C 1
Kúty, 3,348 .... D 2
Kyjov, 5,620 .... D 2
Kynšperk, 5,388 .... B 1
Kysucké Nové Mesto, 2,318 .... E 2
Lanškroun, 6,558 .... D 2
Ledeč, 2,625 .... C 2
Levice, 15,000 .... E 2
Levoča, 7,584 .... F 2
Libáň, 2,261 .... C 1
Liberec, 71,000 .... C 1
Libochovice, 2,879 .... B 1
Lidice, 478 .... B 1
Lipník, 6,887 .... D 2
Liptovský Mikuláš, 14,000 .... E 2
Lišov, 2,691 .... C 2
Litoměřice, 18,000 .... C 1
Litomyšl, 6,384 .... D 2
Litovel, 4,496 .... D 2
Litvínov, 22,000 .... B 1
Lomnice, 2,228 .... C 2
Louny, 13,000 .... B 1
Lovosice, 4,962 .... C 1
Ľubica, 3,335 .... F 2
Lučenec, 18,000 .... F 2
Lysá, 6,500 .... C 1
Malacky, 11,000 .... D 2
Mariánské Lázně, 13,000 .... B 1
Martin, 29,000 .... E 2

Partizánske, 3,171 .... E 2
Pelhřimov, 8,000 .... C 2
Pezinok, 12,000 .... D 2
Piešťany, 21,000 .... D 2
Písek, 22,000 .... C 2
Planá, 5,216 .... B 2
Plánice, 1,718 .... B 2
Plasy, 1,472 .... B 2
Plzeň, 143,945 .... B 2
Počátky, 2,141 .... C 2
Podbořany, 3,893 .... B 1
Poděbrady, 13,000 .... C 1
Pohořelice, 3,068 .... D 2
Polička, 5,600 .... D 2
Polná, 4,005 .... C 2
Poprad, 18,000 .... F 2
Poruba, 21,179 .... E 2
Považská Bystrica, 13,000 .... E 2
Prachatice, 6,000 .... B 2
Prague (Praha) (capital), 1,031,870 .... C 1
Přelouč, 4,228 .... C 1
Přerov, 35,000 .... D 2
Prešov, 39,000 .... F 2
Přeštice, 4,616 .... B 2
Příbor, 5,491 .... E 2
Příbram, 29,000 .... C 2
Přibyslav, 2,594 .... C 2
Prievidza, 24,000 .... E 2
Prostějov, 35,000 .... D 2
Protivín, 3,217 .... C 2
Púchov, 4,316 .... E 2
Radnice, 2,342 .... B 2
Rajec, 2,753 .... E 2
Rakovník, 12,000 .... B 1
Ričany, 6,376 .... C 1
Rimavská Sobota, 12,000 .... F 2
Rokycany, 13,000 .... B 2
Rokytnice nad Jizerou, 3,893 .... C 1
Rosice, 4,900 .... D 2
Roudnice nad Labem, 11,000 .... C 1
Rožňov, 3,989 .... E 2
Rumburk, 6,759 .... C 1
Ružomberok, 20,000 .... E 2
Rychnov nad Kněžnou, 6,000 .... D 1

Trhové Sviny, 2,953 .... C 2
Třinec, 27,000 .... E 2
Trnava, 35,000 .... D 2
Trstená, 2,468 .... E 2
Trutnov, 24,000 .... D 1
Turnov, 12,000 .... C 1
Turzovka, 9,823 .... E 2
Týn, 4,135 .... C 2
Uherské Hradiště, 15,000 .... D 2
Uherský Brod, 6,457 .... D 2
Uhlířské Janovice, 1,979 .... C 1
Uničov, 3,325 .... D 2
Úpice, 5,900 .... D 1
Ústí nad Labem, 72,000 .... C 1
Ústí nad Orlicí, 11,000 .... D 2
Valašské Klobouky, 2,525 .... D 2
Valašské Meziříčí, 15,000 .... D 2
Varnsdorf, 14,000 .... C 1
Važec, 2,747 .... E 2
Vejprty, 5,476 .... B 1
Velká Bíteš, 1,714 .... D 2
Velká Bystřice, 4,459 .... D 2
Veľké Kapušany, 2,371 .... G 2
Velké Meziříčí, 6,217 .... D 2
Veselí nad Lužnicí, 4,382 .... C 2
Veselí nad Moravou, 4,636 .... D 2
Vítkov, 2,685 .... D 2
Vizovice, 3,583 .... D 2
Vlašim, 5,066 .... C 2
Vodňany, 5,034 .... C 2
Volary, 5,034 .... B 2
Volyně, 3,019 .... B 2
Votice, 2,191 .... C 2
Vráble, 3,148 .... E 2
Vracov, 4,171 .... D 2
Vranov, 3,964 .... F 2
Vrchlabí, 11,000 .... C 1
Vrútky, 5,927 .... E 2
Vsetín, 20,000 .... D 2
Vyškov, 13,000 .... D 2
Vysoké Mýto, 7,983 .... D 2
Vysoké Tatry, 18,445 .... F 2
Vyšší Brod, 1,905 .... C 2
Zábřeh, 5,847 .... D 2
Žamberk, 4,278 .... D 1
Žatec, 16,000 .... B 1

Poprad (river) .... F 2
Slaná (river) .... F 2
Slapská (res.) .... C 2
Slovakia (region), 4,421,000 .... E 2
Slovenske Rudohorie (mts.) .... E 2
Štěchovická (res.) .... C 2
Sudeten (mts.) .... C 1
Tatra, High (mts.) .... E 2
Uh (river) .... G 2
Váh (river) .... D 2
Vltava (river) .... C 2
White Carpathians (mts.) .... E 2

HUNGARY

COUNTIES

Bács-Kiskun, 560,000 .... E 3
Baranya, 280,000 .... E 4
Békés, 440,000 .... F 3
Borsod-Abaúj-Zemplén, 600,000 .... F 2
Budapest (city), 1,990,000 .... E 3
Csongrád, 320,000 .... E 3
Fejér, 390,000 .... E 3
Győr-Sopron, 400,000 .... D 3
Hajdú-Bihar, 360,000 .... F 3
Heves, 340,000 .... E 3
Komárom, 300,000 .... E 3
Nógrád, 240,000 .... E 2
Pest, 870,000 .... E 3
Somogy, 360,000 .... D 3
Szabolcs-Szatmár, 540,000 .... G 3
Szolnok, 440,000 .... F 3
Tolna, 260,000 .... E 3
Vas, 280,000 .... D 3
Veszprém, 420,000 .... D 3
Zala, 260,000 .... D 3

CITIES and TOWNS

Aba, 4,369 .... E 3

Dunaharaszti, 13,655 .... E 3
Dunakeszi, 15,636 .... E 3
Dunaújváros, 45,000 .... E 3
Dunavecse, 4,908 .... E 3
Edelény, 6,851 .... F 2
Eger, 45,000 .... E 3
Egyek, 8,678 .... F 3
Elek, 6,325 .... F 3
Emőd, 5,233 .... F 3
Endrőd, 9,263 .... F 3
Enying, 6,406 .... E 3
Ercsi, 7,850 .... E 3
Érd, 25,900 .... E 3
Erdőtelek, 4,634 .... F 3
Esztergom, 26,000 .... E 3
Fegyvernek, 7,835 .... F 3
Fehérgyarmat, 6,024 .... G 3
Földeák, 4,275 .... F 3
Füzesabony, 7,125 .... F 3
Füzesgyarmat, 7,807 .... F 3
Gödöllő, 22,000 .... E 3
Gönc, 3,093 .... F 2
Gyoma, 10,921 .... F 3
Gyöngyös, 32,000 .... E 3
Gyón, 2,684 .... E 3
Győr, 81,000 .... D 3
Gyula, 25,000 .... F 3
Hajdúböszörmény, 30,000 .... F 3
Hajdúdorog, 10,559 .... F 3
Hajdúhadház, 13,030 .... F 3
Hajdúnánás, 17,000 .... F 3
Hajdúsámson, 7,764 .... F 3
Hajdúszoboszló, 22,000 .... F 3
Hajós, 5,584 .... E 3
Hatvan, 24,000 .... E 3
Hercegfalva, 4,951 .... E 3
Heves, 11,349 .... F 3
Hogyesz, 3,501 .... E 3
Hódmezővásárhely, 53,000 .... F 3
Izsák, 8,670 .... E 3
Jánoshalma, 12,897 .... E 3
Jánossomorja, 3,481 .... D 3
Jászapáti, 10,495 .... F 3
Jászárokszállás, 10,745 .... E 3
Jászberény, 30,000 .... E 3
Jászfényszaru, 7,542 .... E 3

Mezőkövesd, 18,160 .... F 3
Mezőszilas, 3,434 .... E 3
Mezőtúr, 22,000 .... F 3
Mindszent, 9,179 .... F 3
Miskolc, 180,000 .... F 2
Mohács, 18,000 .... E 4
Monor, 15,360 .... E 3
Mór, 11,622 .... E 3
Mosonmagyaróvár, 25,000 .... D 3
Nádudvar, 10,006 .... F 3
Nagyatád, 8,791 .... D 3
Nagybajom, 4,972 .... D 3
Nagyecsed, 8,348 .... G 3
Nagyhalász, 6,650 .... F 2
Nagykálló, 11,329 .... F 3
Nagykanizsa, 38,000 .... D 3
Nagykáta, 11,924 .... E 3
Nagykőrös, 26,000 .... E 3
Nagyléta, 6,902 .... F 3
Nagyszénás, 7,439 .... F 3
Nyírábrány, 7,325 .... G 3
Nyírbátor, 10,167 .... G 3
Nyíregyháza, 65,000 .... F 3
Nyírmada, 4,826 .... F 2
Örkény, 5,001 .... E 3
Oroszlány, 23,000 .... E 3
Orosziány, 20,000 .... E 3
Ózd, 40,000 .... F 2
Paks, 19,119 .... E 3
Pannonhalma, 3,529 .... D 3
Pápa, 27,000 .... D 3
Pásztó, 6,091 .... E 3
Pécs, 140,000 .... E 4
Pécsvárad, 3,199 .... E 3
Pétervására, 2,727 .... E 3
Pilis, 8,407 .... E 3
Pilisvörösvár, 9,627 .... E 3
Polgár, 9,353 .... F 3
Püspökladány, 15,488 .... F 3
Putnok, 6,440 .... F 2
Ráckeve, 7,456 .... E 3
Rakamaz, 5,381 .... F 2
Rákospalota, 63,344 .... E 3
Sajószentpéter, 12,846 .... F 2
Salgótarján, 37,000 .... E 2

Újpest, 79,961 .... E 3
Vác, 29,000 .... E 3
Várpalota, 27,000 .... E 3
Vasvár, 4,293 .... D 3
Vecsés, 16,411 .... E 3
Veszprém, 33,000 .... D 3
Vésztő, 10,463 .... F 3
Villány, 2,769 .... E 4
Zahony, 2,117 .... G 2
Zalaegerszeg, 33,000 .... D 3
Zalaszentgrót, 4,470 .... D 3
Zirc, 5,427 .... D 3

OTHER FEATURES

Bakony (mts.) .... D 3
Balaton (lake) .... D 3
Berettyó (river) .... F 3
Börsöny (mts.) .... E 3
Bükk (mts.) .... F 2
Cserehát (mts.) .... F 2
Csepelsziget (isl.) .... E 3
Danube (river) .... E 3
Dráva (river) .... D 4
Duna (Danube) (river) .... E 3
Fertő tó (Neusiedler) (lake) .... D 3
Great Alföld (plain) .... F 3
Hernád (river) .... F 2
Ipoly (river) .... E 2
Kapos (river) .... D 3
Kékes (mt.) .... E 2
Kőrishegy (mt.) .... D 3
Körös (river) .... F 3
Little Alföld (plain) .... D 3
Maros (river) .... F 3
Matra (mts.) .... E 2
Mecsek (mts.) .... E 4
Neusiedler (lake) .... D 3
Rába (river) .... D 3
Sajo (river) .... F 2
Sebes Körös (river) .... F 3
Sió (canal) .... E 3
Szentendreiszíget (isl.) .... E 3
Tarna (river) .... E 2
Tisza (river) .... F 3
Zala (river) .... D 3

YUGOSLAVIA

AREA 98,766 sq. mi.
POPULATION 20,586,000
CAPITAL Belgrade
LARGEST CITY Belgrade
HIGHEST POINT Triglav 9,393 ft.
MONETARY UNIT Yugoslav dinar
MAJOR LANGUAGES Serbo-Croatian, Slovenian, Macedonian, Albanian
MAJOR RELIGIONS Eastern Orthodoxy, Roman Catholicism, Islam

ALBANIA

AREA 11,100 sq. mi.
POPULATION 2,126,000
CAPITAL Tiranë
LARGEST CITY Tiranë
HIGHEST POINT Korab 9,026 ft.
MONETARY UNIT lek
MAJOR LANGUAGE Albanian
MAJOR RELIGIONS Islam, Eastern Orthodoxy, Roman Catholicism

RUMANIA

AREA 91,699 sq. mi.
POPULATION 20,394,000
CAPITAL Bucharest
LARGEST CITY Bucharest
HIGHEST POINT Moldoveanul 8,343 ft.
MONETARY UNIT leu
MAJOR LANGUAGES Rumanian, Hungarian
MAJOR RELIGION Eastern Orthodoxy

BULGARIA

AREA 42,829 sq. mi.
POPULATION 8,501,000
CAPITAL Sofia
LARGEST CITY Sofia
HIGHEST POINT Musala 9,597 ft.
MONETARY UNIT lev
MAJOR LANGUAGE Bulgarian
MAJOR RELIGION Eastern Orthodoxy

GREECE

AREA 50,548 sq. mi.
POPULATION 8,838,000
CAPITAL Athens
LARGEST CITY Athens
HIGHEST POINT Olympus 9,570 ft.
MONETARY UNIT drachma
MAJOR LANGUAGE Greek
MAJOR RELIGION Eastern (Greek) Orthodoxy

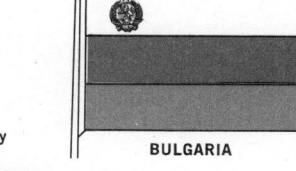

BULGARIA

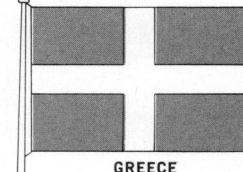

GREECE

YUGOSLAVIA

ALBANIA

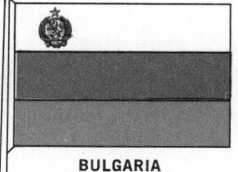

RUMANIA

DOMINANT LAND USE

- ☐ Cereals (chiefly wheat, corn)
- ▦ Mixed Farming, Horticulture
- ▨ Pasture Livestock
- ▩ Tobacco, Cotton
- ▧ Grapes, Wine
- ▤ Forests
- ☐ Nonagricultural Land

Agriculture, Industry and Resources

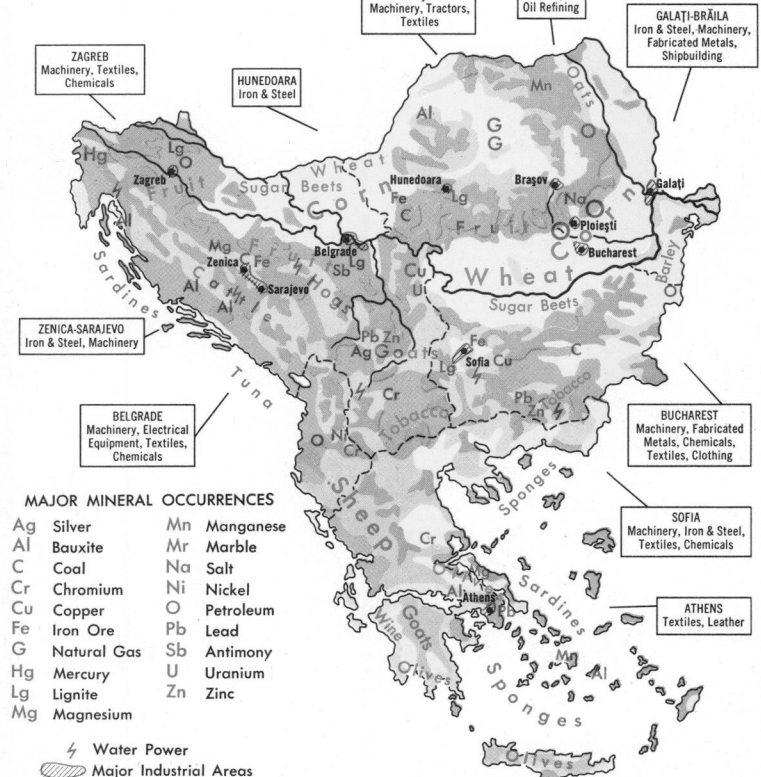

ZAGREB
Machinery, Textiles, Chemicals

HUNEDOARA
Iron & Steel

ZENICA-SARAJEVO
Iron & Steel, Machinery

BELGRADE
Machinery, Electrical Equipment, Textiles, Chemicals

BRAŞOV
Machinery, Tractors, Textiles

PLOIEŞTI
Oil Refining

GALAŢI-BRĂILA
Iron & Steel, Machinery, Fabricated Metals, Shipbuilding

BUCHAREST
Machinery, Fabricated Metals, Chemicals, Textiles, Clothing

SOFIA
Machinery, Iron & Steel, Textiles, Chemicals

ATHENS
Textiles, Leather

MAJOR MINERAL OCCURRENCES

Ag	Silver	Mn	Manganese
Al	Bauxite	Mr	Marble
C	Coal	Na	Salt
Cr	Chromium	Ni	Nickel
Cu	Copper	O	Petroleum
Fe	Iron Ore	Pb	Lead
G	Natural Gas	Sb	Antimony
Hg	Mercury	U	Uranium
Lg	Lignite	Zn	Zinc
Mg	Magnesium		

⚡ Water Power
▨ Major Industrial Areas

ALBANIA

CITIES and TOWNS

Berat, 22,000	D 5
Bajram Cur, 1,795	D 4
Burrel, 3,150	D 5
Çorovodë, 1,790	D 5
Delvinë, 5,700	D 6
Durrës, 47,900	D 5
Elbasan, 35,300	E 5
Ersekë, 2,150	E 5
Fier, 17,900	D 5
Gjirokastër, 15,000	D 5
Kavajë, 17,700	D 5
Korcë, 43,700	E 5
Kruë, 6,700	D 5
Kucovë (Stalin), 12,300	D 5
Kukës, 3,900	E 4
Leskovik, 1,625	E 5
Lezh, 3,000	D 5
Lushnje, 16,000	D 5
Peqin, 3,800	D 5
Përmet, 4,000	E 5
Peshkopi, 5,500	E 5
Pogradec, 8,900	E 5
Pukë, 1,700	E 4
Sarandë, 7,700	E 6
Shijak, 5,100	D 5
Shkodër, 47,000	D 5
Stalin, 12,300	D 5
Tepelenë, 2,500	D 5
Tiranë (Tirana) (cap.), 170,000	E 5
Vlorë, 46,900	D 5

OTHER FEATURES

Adriatic (sea)	B 4
Drin (riv.)	E 4
Korab (mt.)	E 4
Ohrid (lake)	E 5
Otranto (str.)	D 5
Prespa (lake)	E 5
Sazan (isl.)	D 5
Scutari (lake)	D 4
Tomor (mt.)	E 5
Vijosë (riv.)	D 5

BULGARIA

CITIES and TOWNS

Alfatar, 3,650	H 4
Akhtopol, 1,058	H 4
Alfatar, 4,042	H 4
Ardino, 2,558	G 5
Asenovgrad, 37,411	G 5
Aytos, 17,769	H 4
Balchik, 8,714	H 4
Bansko, 7,851	F 5
Belogradchik, 5,174	F 4
Berkovitsa, 11,553	F 4
Blagoevgrad, 32,744	F 5
Botevgrad, 12,051	F 4
Bregovo, 4,725	F 3
Breznik, 4,093	F 4
Burgas, 122,212	H 4
Byala, 9,347	G 4
Byala Slatina, 14,942	F 4
Chirpan, 17,857	G 4
Devin, 4,475	G 5
Dimitrovgrad, 41,787	G 4
Dobrich (Tolbukhin), 55,111	H 4
Dryanovo, 8,187	G 4
Elena, 4,071	G 4
Elin Pelin, 8,074	F 4
Ekhovo, 11,315	H 4
Gabrovo, 57,758	G 4
General Toshevo, 8,251	H 4
Godech, 4,074	F 4
Gorna Dzhumaya (Blagoevgrad), 32,744	F 5
Gorna Oryakhovitsa, 26,290	G 4
Gotse Delchev, 14,457	F 5
Grudovo, 9,177	H 4
Ikhtiman, 10,325	F 4
Isperikh, 8,445	H 4
Ivaylovgrad, 2,907	H 5
Karapelit, 2,033	H 4
Karlovo (Levskigrad), 20,287	G 4
Karnobat (Polyanovgrad), 18,727	H 4
Kavarna, 8,291	J 4
Kazanlúk, 44,418	G 4
Kharmanlii, 15,478	H 5
Khaskovo, 57,682	G 5
Kolarovgrad (Shumen), 59,362	H 4

Kotel, 7,209	H 4
Krumovgrad, 2,230	G 5
Kubrat, 7,531	H 4
Kula, 6,474	F 4
Kŭrdzhali, 33,319	G 5
Kyustendil, 38,199	F 4
Levskigrad, 20,287	G 4
Lom, 28,189	F 4
Lovech, 30,843	G 4
Lukovit, 9,716	G 4
Mallco Tŭrnovo, 3,744	H 4
Maritsa, 8,532	H 4
Mezhurin, 2,783	H 4
Mikhaylovgrad, 27,240	F 4
Momchilgrad, 6,084	G 5
Nesebŭr, 2,333	H 4
Nikopol, 5,763	G 4
Nova Zagora, 19,257	H 4
Novi Pazar, 12,476	H 4
Omurtag, 8,148	H 4
Oryakhovo, 7,498	F 4
Panagyurishte, 18,298	F 4
Pazardzhik, 55,410	G 4
Pernik, 75,844	F 4
Peshtera, 14,606	G 4
Petrich, 20,653	F 5
Pirdop, 8,252	G 4
Pleven, 79,234	G 4
Plovdiv, 234,547	G 4
Polyanovgrad, 18,727	H 4
Pomorie, 9,567	H 4
Popina, 2,699	H 3
Popovo, 15,609	H 4
Provadiya, 13,837	H 4
Radomir, 8,458	F 4
Razgrad, 26,297	H 4
Razlog, 10,425	F 5
Rositsa, 1,505	H 4
Ruse, 142,894	H 4
Samokov, 21,585	F 4
Sandanski, 14,590	F 5
Sevlievo, 20,396	G 4
Shabla, 3,788	J 4
Shumen, 59,362	H 4
Silistra, 32,996	H 3
Simeonovgrad (Maritsa), 8,532	H 4
Sliven, 68,331	H 4
Smolyan, 17,479	G 5
Smyadovo, 5,349	H 4
Sofia (cap.), 840,113	F 4
Sofia, *923,400	F 4
Sozopol, 3,257	H 4
Stanke Dimitrov, 35,813	F 4
Stara Zagora, 100,565	G 4
Sveti Vrach (Sandanski), 14,590	F 5
Svilengrad, 12,438	G 5
Svishtov, 21,522	G 4
Teteven, 9,807	G 4
Tolbukhin, 55,111	H 4
Topolovgrad, 6,633	H 4
Troyan, 18,982	G 4
Trŭn, 2,922	F 4
Tŭrgovishte, 25,528	H 4
Tutrakan, 9,909	H 4
Varna, 200,827	J 4
Veliko Tŭrnovo, 37,269	G 4
Vidin, 36,820	F 4
Vratsa, 39,052	F 4
Yambol, 58,405	H 4
Zlatograd, 6,508	G 5

OTHER FEATURES

Balkan (mts.)	G 4
Black (sea)	J 4
Danube (Dunav) (riv.)	H 4
Emine (cape)	H 4
Iskŭr (riv.)	G 4
Kaliakra (cape)	J 4
Lom (riv.)	F 4
Maritsa (riv.)	G 4
Mesta (riv.)	F 5
Musala (mt.)	F 4
Osŭm (riv.)	G 4
Rhodope (mts.)	F 4
Ruen (mt.)	F 4
Struma (riv.)	F 5
Timok (riv.)	F 3
Tundzha (riv.)	G 4
Vit (riv.)	G 4

GREECE

REGIONS

Aegean Islands, 477,476	G 6
Ayion Óros (aut. dist.), 2,687	G 5
Central Greece and Euboea, 2,823,658	F 6
Crete, 483,258	G 8
Epirus, 352,604	E 6
Greater Athens, 1,852,709	F 7
Ionian Islands, 212,573	D 6
Macedonia, 1,890,654	F 5
Peloponnísos, 1,096,390	F 7
Thessalía, 695,385	F 6
Thrace, 356,555	G 5

CITIES and TOWNS

Agrínion, 24,763	E 6
Aíyina, 4,989	F 7
Aíyion, 17,782	F 6
Alexandroúpolis, 18,712	H 5
Alivérion, 3,523	G 6
Almirós, 6,010	F 6
Amaliás, 15,468	E 7
Amfilokhía, 5,408	E 6
Ámfissa, 6,076	F 6
Ándissa, 2,530	H 6
Andravídha, 3,155	E 6
Ándros, 2,032	G 7
Áno Viánnos, 1,820	G 8
Anóyia, 2,461	G 8
Ardhéa, 3,222	F 5
Argalastí, 1,864	G 6
Árgos, 16,712	F 7
Argostólion, 7,322	E 6
Arkhángelos, 2,918	J 7
Arnaía, 2,612	F 5
Árta, 16,899	E 6
Astipálaia, 1,205	H 7
Atalándi, 4,552	F 6
Athens (cap.), 627,564	F 7
Athens, *2,347,000	F 7
Áyios Matthaíos, 1,892	D 6
Áyios Nikólaos, 3,709	G 8
Candia (Iráklion), 63,458	G 8
Canea (Khaniá), 38,467	G 8
Chalcis (Khalkís), 24,745	F 6
Corinth, 15,892	F 7
Delviniákion, 1,076	E 6
Dhidhimótikhon, 7,287	H 5
Dhíkaia, 1,181	H 5
Dhimitsána, 1,300	F 7
Dhomokós, 2,017	F 6
Dráma, 32,195	F 5
Édhessa, 15,534	F 5
Elassón, 6,501	F 6
Eleutheroúpolis, 5,448	G 5
Ermoúpolis, 14,402	G 7
Fársala, 6,356	F 6
Filiátes, 3,065	E 6
Filiatrá, 6,753	E 7
Flórina, 11,933	E 5
Gargaliánoi, 6,637	E 7
Grevená, 6,892	E 5
Ídhra, 2,546	F 7
Ierápetra, 6,488	G 8
Igoumenítsa, 3,235	E 6
Ioánnina, 34,997	E 6
Iráklion, 63,458	G 8
Istiaía, 3,882	F 6
Itháki, 2,632	E 6
Kalámai, 39,211	F 7
Kalampáka, 4,640	F 6
Kalávrita, 2,039	F 6
Kálimnos, 10,211	H 7
Kardhítsa, 23,708	F 6
Kariá, 1,739	E 6
Kariaí, 429	G 5
Káristos, 3,335	G 6
Karpeníson, 3,523	F 6
Kastéllion, 2,271	F 8
Kastéllion, 1,351	G 8
Kastoria, 10,162	E 5
Kateríni, 28,046	F 5
Kaválla, 44,517	G 5
Kéa, 1,788	G 7
Kérkira, 26,991	D 6
Khalkís, 24,745	F 6
Khaniá, 38,467	G 8
Khíos, 24,053	H 6
Kiáton, 6,069	F 6
Kilkís, 10,963	F 5
Kími, 3,252	G 6
Kiparissía, 4,602	E 7
Kíthira, 469	F 7
Komotiní, 28,355	G 5
Kónitsa, 3,485	E 6
Koropí, 7,862	G 7
Kos, 8,138	H 7

(continued on following page)

(continued)

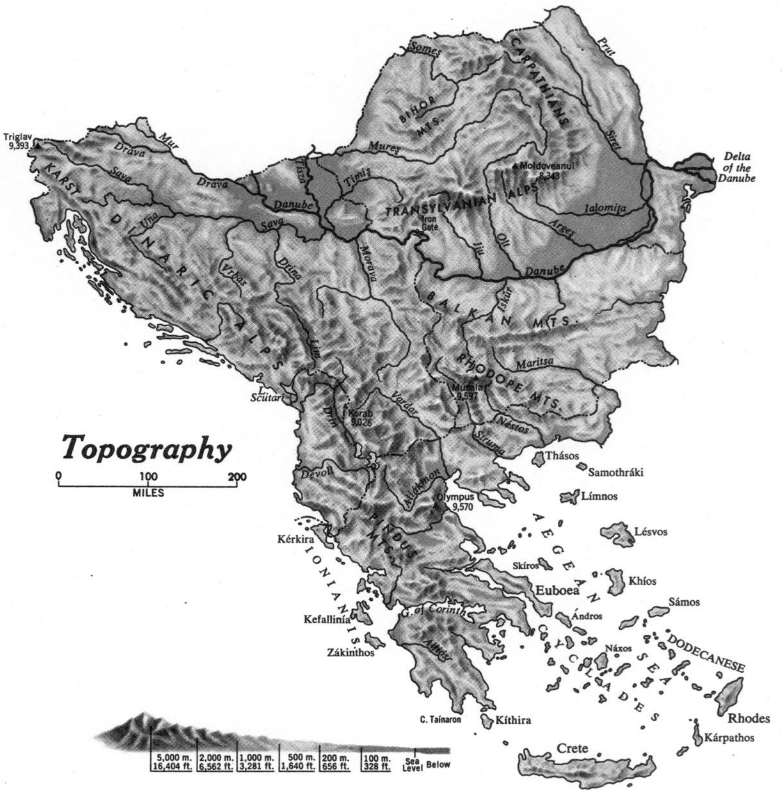

GREECE (continued)

Kozáni, 21,537 F 5
Kranídhion, 3,942 F 7
Lamía, 21,509 F 6
Langadhás, 6,739 F 5
Lárisa, 55,391 F 6
Lávrion, 6,553 G 7
Leonídhion, 3,297 F 7
Levádhia, 12,609 F 6
Levkás, 6,552 E 6
Limenária, 1,999 G 5
Limín Vathéos, 5,469 H 7
Límni, 2,394 F 6
Litókhoron, 5,032 F 5
Lixoúrion, 3,977 E 6
Loutrá Aidhipsoú, 1,859 F 6
Marathón, 2,167 G 6
Megalópolis, 2,235 E 7
Mégara, 15,450 F 6
Meligalá, 1,960 F 7
Mesolóngion, 11,266 E 6
Messíni, 8,249 E 7
Métsovon, 2,976 E 6
Mikínai, 361 F 7
Mílos, 944 G 7
Mírina, 3,460 G 6
Missolonghi (Mesolóngion), 11,266 E 6
Míthimna, 1,828 G 6
Mitilíni, 25,758 H 6
Moláoi, 2,526 F 7
Monólithos, 496 H 7
Moúdhros, 1,236 G 6
Náousa, 15,492 F 5
Návpaktos, 7,080 F 6
Návplion, 8,918 F 7
Náxos, 2,458 G 7
Néa Filippiás, 3,001 E 6
Neápolis, 2,464 F 7
Neméa, 4,720 F 7
Néon Karlóvasi, 5,308 H 7
Nigríta, 9,979 F 5
Olimbía, 771 E 7
Orestiás, 10,281 H 5
Paramithiá, 2,827 E 6
Pátrai, 95,364 E 6
Péta, 2,522 E 6
Pigádhia, 1,281 H 8
Pílos, 2,434 E 7
Piraiévs (Piraeus), 183,877 F 7
Pírgos, 20,558 E 7
Piryí, 1,914 G 6
Píthion, 1,535 H 5
Plomárion, 5,172 H 6
Políkastron, 3,821 F 5
Políkhnitos, 5,131 G 6
Políyiros, 3,541 F 5
Póros, 4,392 F 7
Préveza, 11,172 E 6
Psakhná, 4,433 F 6
Ptolemaïs, 12,747 E 5
Réthimnon, 14,999 G 8
Ródhos (Rhodes), 27,393 J 7
Salamís, 11,161 F 6
Salonika (Thessaloníki), 448,000 F 5
Sámi, 1,065 E 6
Samothráki, 1,555 G 5
Sápai, 2,589 G 5
Sérrai, 40,063 F 5
Sérvia, 4,132 F 5
Siátista, 4,737 E 5
Sidhirókastron, 8,177 F 5
Sími, 2,982 H 7
Sitía, 5,327 H 8
Skíros, 2,411 G 6
Skópelos, 2,955 F 6
Souflíon, 6,693 H 5
Sparta, 10,412 F 7
Spétsai, 3,314 F 7
Stilís, 4,673 F 6
Thebes (Thívai), 15,779 F 6
Thessaloníki, 448,000 F 5
Thásos, 1,875 G 5
Thíra, 1,481 G 7
Thívai, 15,779 F 6
Timbákion, 2,816 G 8
Tínos, 2,888 G 7
Tírnavos, 10,805 F 6
Tríkkala, 27,876 E 6
Trípolis, 18,500 F 7
Vartholomión, 3,244 E 7
Vathí, 3,161 H 7
Velvendós, 4,158 F 5
Vérroia, 25,765 F 5
Vólos, 49,221 F 6
Vólos, *67,424 F 6
Vónitsa, 2,996 E 6
Vrondádhes, 4,685 G 6
Xánthi, 26,377 G 5
Yiannitsá, 19,693 F 5
Yíthion, 4,992 F 7
Zákinthos, 9,506 E 7
Zante (Zúkinthos), 9,506 E 7

OTHER FEATURES

Aegean (sea) G 6
Akrítas (cape) E 7
Aktí (pen.) G 5
Amorgós (isl.), 2,396 G 7
Anáfi (isl.), 471 G 7
Andikíthira (isl.), 178 F 8
Ándros (isl.), 12,928 G 7
Arda (riv.) G 5
Argolís (gulf) F 7
Astipálaia (isl.), 1,539 H 7
Áthos (mt.) G 5
Áyios Evstrátios (isl.), 1,061 G 6
Áyios Yeóryios (cape) G 5
Cephalonia (Kefallinía) (isl.), 39,793 E 6
Chios (Khíos) (isl.), 60,061 G 6
Corfu (Kérkira) (isl.), 99,092 D 6
Corinth (gulf) F 6
Crete (isl.), 483,075 G 8
Crete (sea) G 7
Cyclades (isls.), 99,959 G 7
Dhrépanon (cape) G 6
Dodecanese (isls.), 123,021 H 8
Euboea (isl.), 163,215 G 6
Évros (riv.) H 5
Gávdhos (isl.), 172 F 8
Ikaría (isl.), 9,577 G 7
Ionian (sea) D 7
Íos (isl.), 1,343 G 7
Itháki (Ithaca) (isl.), 5,210 E 6
Kálimnos (isl.), 10,211 H 7
Kafirévs (cape) G 6
6,689 H 8
Kárpathos (isl.), 6,689 H 8
Kásos (isl.), 1,422 H 8
Kassándra (pen.) F 6
Kéa (isl.), 2,361 G 7
Kefallinía (isl.), 39,793 E 6
Kérkira (isl.), 99,092 D 6
Khálki (isl.), 501 H 7
Khani, (gulf) G 8
Khíos (isl.), 60,061 G 6
Kiparissía (gulf) E 7
Kíthira (isl.), 5,340 F 7
Kíthnos (isl.), 2,064 G 7
Kos (isl.), 18,187 H 7
Kriós (cape) F 8
Lakonía (gulf) F 7
Léros (isl.), 6,611 H 7
Lésvos (isl.), 117,371 G 6
Levítha (isl.), 7 H 7
Levkás (isl.), 2,697 E 6
Límnos (isl.), 21,808 G 6
Maléa (cape) F 7
Matapan (Taínaron) (cape) F 7
Merabéllou (gulf) H 8
Mesará (gulf) G 8
Messíni (gulf) E 7
Míkonos (isl.), 3,633 G 7
Mílos (isl.), 4,910 G 7
Mirtóön (sea) F 7
Náxos (isl.), 16,703 G 7
Néstos (riv.) G 5
Nísiros (isl.), 1,788 H 7
Northern Sporades (isls.), 9,810 F 6
Olympus (mt.) F 5
Óssa (mt.) F 6
Parnassus (mt.) F 6
Páros (isl.), 7,830 G 7
Pátmos (isl.), 2,564 H 7
Paxoí (isl.), 2,678 D 6
Pindus (mts.) E 6
Piniós (riv.) E 6
Prespa (lake) E 5
Psará (isl.), 576 G 6
Rhodes (isl.), 63,951 H 7
Rhodope (mts.) G 5
Salonika (Thermaic) (gulf) F 6
Sámos (isl.), 41,124 H 7
Samothráki (isl.), 3,830 G 5
Saría (isl.), 18 H 8
Saronic (gulf) F 7
Sérifos (isl.), 1,878 G 7
Sídheros (cape) H 8
Sífnos (isl.), 2,258 G 7
Sími (isl.), 3,123 H 7
Síros (isl.), 19,570 G 7
Sithoniá (pen.) F 5
Skíros (isl.), 2,882 G 6
Spátha (cape) F 8
Strimón (gulf) G 5
Strofádhes (isls.), 10 E 7
Taínaron (cape) F 7
Thásos (isl.), 15,916 G 5
Thermaic (gulf) F 6
Thíra (isl.), 7,751 G 7
Tílos (isl.), 789 H 7
Tínos (isl.), 9,273 G 7
Toronaic (gulf) F 5
Vardar (riv.) E 5
Voïviïs (lake) F 6
Vólvi (lake) F 5
Voúxa (cape) F 8
Zákinthos (Zante) (isl.), 35,499 E 7

RUMANIA

CITIES and TOWNS

Aiud, 11,886 F 2
Alba Iulia, 22,225 F 2
Alexandria, 21,907 G 3
Anina, 11,837 E 3
Arad, 132,757 E 2
Arad, *137,444 E 2
Babadag, 5,549 J 3
Bacău, 73,481 H 2
Bacău, *87,465 H 2
Baia Mare, 62,769 F 2
Baia Mare, *108,709 F 2
Băileşti, 15,932 F 3
Balş, 6,956 G 3
Beiuş, 6,467 F 2
Bîrlad, 41,061 H 2
Bîrlad, *52,497 H 2
Bistriţa, 25,534 G 2
Blaj, 8,731 F 2
Botoşani, 35,185 H 2
Botoşani, *50,204 H 2
Brad, 9,963 F 2
Brăila, 147,495 H 3
Braşov, 175,264 G 3
Braşov, *264,537 G 3
Bucharest (Bucureşti) (cap.), 1,431,993 G 3
Bucharest, *1,518,725 G 3
Buhuş, 12,382 H 2
Buzău, 56,380 H 3
Buzău, *82,454 H 3
Buziaş, 5,140 E 3
Călafat, 8,069 F 3
Călăraşi, 35,698 H 3
Caracal, 22,715 G 3
Caransebeş, 15,195 F 3
Carei, 16,780 F 2
Cernavodă, 8,802 J 3
Cîmpia Turzii, 11,514 F 2
Cîmpina, 22,862 H 3
Cîmpulung, 24,891 G 3
Cîmpulung Moldovenesc, 13,627 G 2
Cisnădie, 12,246 F 3
Cluj, 193,375 F 2
Cluj, *223,519 F 2
Comaneşti, 12,392 H 2
Constanţa, 165,245 J 3
Constanţa, *202,024 J 3
Corabia, 11,502 G 4
Craiova, 166,249 F 3
Craiova, *174,669 F 3
Curtea de Argeş, 10,764 G 3
Dej, 26,968 F 2
Deva, 26,952 F 3
Deva, *45,836 F 3
Dorohoi, 14,771 H 2
Drăgăşani, 9,963 F 3
Făgăraş, 22,941 G 3
Fălticeni, 13,305 H 2
Feteşti, 21,425 H 3
Focşani, 35,075 H 3
Focşani, *40,701 H 3
Găeşti, 7,179 G 3
Galaţi, 160,097 H 3
Gheorgheni, 11,969 G 2
Gherla, 7,617 G 2
Giurgiu, 39,225 G 3
Giurgiu, *55,471 G 3
Haţeg, 3,853 F 3
Hîrşova, 4,761 J 3
Hunedoara, 68,303 F 3
Hunedoara, *100,953 F 3
Huşi, 20,703 J 2
Iaşi, 173,569 H 2
Iaşi, *196,167 H 2
Isaccea, 5,203 J 3
Jimbolia, 11,281 E 3
Lipova, 10,064 E 2
Lugoj, 35,388 F 3
Lupeni, 29,377 F 3
Mangalia, 4,792 J 4
Medgidia, 27,989 J 3
Mediaş, 46,396 G 2
Miercurea Ciuc, 11,996 G 2
Mizil, 7,460 H 3
Moineşti, 12,934 H 2
Moldova Nouă, 3,582 E 3
Moreni, 11,687 G 3
Năsăud, 5,725 G 2
Ocna Mureş, 10,701 G 2
Odobeşti, 4,977 H 3
Odorhei, 14,162 G 2
Olteniţa, 14,111 H 3
Oradea, 132,266 E 2
Oradea, *136,375 E 2
Orăstie, 10,488 F 3
Oraşul Gheorghe Georghiu-Dej, 35,689 H 2
Oraviţa, 8,175 E 3
Orşova, 6,527 F 3
Panciu, 7,679 H 3
Paşcani, 15,008 H 2
Petrila, 24,804 F 3
Petroşeni, 35,237 F 3
Petroşeni, *130,111 F 3
Piatra Neamţ, 45,925 G 2
Piatra Neamţ, *58,397 G 2
Piteşti, 60,094 G 3
Piteşti, *78,784 G 3
Ploieşti, 156,382 H 3
Ploieşti, *191,663 H 3
Pucioasa, 9,259 G 3
Rădăuti, 15,949 G 2
Reghin, 23,317 G 2
Reşiţa, 58,683 E 3
Reşiţa, *121,458 E 3
Rîmnicu Sărat, 22,325 H 3
Rîmnicu Vîlcea, 23,880 F 3
Roman, 38,990 H 2
Roman, *49,496 H 2
Roşiori de Vede, 21,707 G 3
Săcele, 22,822 G 3
Salonta, 16,276 E 3
Satu Mare, 68,257 F 2
Sebeş, 11,628 F 3
Sfîntu Gheorge, 20,759 G 3
Sibiu, 117,020 G 3
Sighetul-Marmaţiei, 29,768 F 2
Sighişoara, 25,100 G 2
Şimleu Silvaniei, 8,560 F 2
Sinaia, 9,006 G 3
Sînnicolau Mare, 9,956 E 2
Siret, 5,664 G 1
Slănic, 6,842 G 3
Slatina, 13,381 G 3
Slobozia, 9,632 H 3
Solca, 2,384 G 2
Strehaia, 8,545 F 3
Suceava, 37,715 G 2
Suceava, *76,327 G 2
Sulina, 3,622 J 3
Techirghiol, 2,705 J 3
Tecuci, 28,458 H 3
Timişoara, 184,797 E 3
Timişoara, *194,159 E 3
Tîrgovişte, 29,754 G 3
Tîrgovişte, *48,005 G 3
Tîrgu Jiu, 30,837 F 3
Tîrgu Jiu, *33,019 F 3
Tîrgu Mureş, 86,458 G 2
Tîrgu Mureş, *104,922 G 2
Tîrgu Neamţ, 10,373 G 2
Tîrgu Ocna, 11,227 H 2
Tîrgu Secuiesc, 7,500 H 2
Tîrnăveni, 20,354 F 2
Topliţa, 8,944 G 2
Tulcea, 35,552 J 3
Turda, 42,318 G 2
Turda, *69,768 G 2
Turnu Măgurele, 26,409 G 4
Turnu Severin, 45,394 F 3
Turnu Severin, *52,497 F 3
Urlaţi, 8,658 H 3
Urziceni, 6,061 H 3
Vasile Roaită, 3,286 J 3
Vaslui, 14,850 H 2
Vatra Dornei, 10,822 G 2
Vişeu de Sus, 13,956 F 2
Zalău, 13,378 F 2
Zărneşti, 6,673 G 3
Zimnicea, 12,445 G 4

OTHER FEATURES

Argeş (riv.) G 3
Buzău (riv.) H 3
Carpathian (mts.) G 2
Crişul Alb (riv.) F 2
Crişul Repede (riv.) F 2
Danube (river) H 4
Ialomiţa (marshes) J 3
Jiu (riv.) F 3
Moldoveanul (mt.) G 3
Mureş (riv.) E 2
Negoiul (mt.) G 3
Olt (riv.) G 3
Pietrosul (mt.) G 2
Prut (riv.) J 2
Siret (riv.) H 2
Someş (riv.) F 2
Timiş (riv.) E 3
Transylvanian Alps (mts.) G 3

YUGOSLAVIA

INTERNAL DIVISIONS

Bosnia and Hercegovina (rep.), 3,594,000 C 3
Croatia (rep.), 4,281,000 C 3
Kosovo-Mitohiyan (aut. prov.), 1,089,000 E 4
Macedonia (rep.), 1,506,000 E 5
Montenegro (rep.), 471,894 D 4
Serbia (rep.), 7,637,800 E 3
Slovenia (rep.), 1,624,900 B 2
Voyvodina (aut. prov.), 1,880,000 D 3

CITIES and TOWNS

Aleksinac, 8,828 E 4
Apatin, 17,000 D 3
Bačka Topola, 14,000 D 3
Bakar B 3
Banja Luka, 55,000 C 3
Bar, 2,184 D 4
Bečej, 22,000 E 3
Bela Crkva, 11,000 E 3
Belgrade (Beograd) (cap.), 745,000 E 3
Belgrade, *1,050,000 E 3
Bihać, 17,000 B 3
Bijeljina, 19,000 D 3
Bijelo Polje, 5,856 D 4
Bileća, 2,491 D 4
Biograd, 2,418 B 4
Bitola (Bitolj), 52,000 E 5
Bjelovar, 16,000 C 3
Bled, 4,156 A 2
Bor, 19,000 E 3
Bosanska Dubica, 6,259 C 3
Bosanska Gradiška, 6,363 C 3
Bosaska Kostajnica, 2,034 B 3
Bosanska Krupa, 6,191 C 3
Bosanski Brod, 7,350 D 3
Bosanski Novi, 7,023 C 3
Bosanski Petrovac, 3,473 C 3
Bosanski Šamac, 3,654 D 3
Brčko, 20,000 D 3
Brežice, 2,641 B 3
Brod, 30,000 D 3
Bugojno, 5,453 C 3
Buje, 1,955 A 3
Čačak, 30,000 F 4
Čapljina, 3,275 C 4
Caribrod (Dimitrovgrad), 3,665 F 4
Celje, 28,000 B 2
Cetinje, 9,359 D 4
Ćuprija, 12,000 E 4
Debar, 6,323 E 5
Derventa, 9,843 C 3
Dimitrovgrad, 3,665 F 4
Djakovica, 22,000 E 4
Djakovo, 13,000 D 3
Donji Vakuf, 3,764 C 3
Drvar, 3,646 C 3
Dubrovnik, 24,000 C 4
Fiume (Rijeka), 108,000 B 3
Foča, 6,763 D 4
Fojnica, 1,549 C 4
Gacko, 1,368 D 4
Gevgelija, 7,332 F 5
Glamoč, 1,626 C 3
Gnjilane, 14,000 E 4
Gornji Vafuf, 1,860 C 4
Gospić, 6,767 B 3
Gostivar, 14,000 E 5
Gračac, 2,183 B 3
Gračanica, 7,656 D 3
Gradačac, 5,878 D 3
Grubišno Polje, 2,655 C 3
Gusinje, 2,756 D 4
Hercegnovi, 3,797 D 4
Ivangrad, 6,969 E 4
Jajce, 6,853 C 3
Jesenice, 16,000 A 2
Kamnik, 5,062 B 2
Kanjiža, 10,000 D 2
Kardeljevo, 3,267 C 4
Karlovac, 35,000 B 3
Kavadarci, 13,000 E 5
Kičevo, 11,000 E 5
Kikinda, 32,000 E 3
Kladanj, 2,825 D 3
Ključ, 2,320 C 3
Knin, 5,116 C 3
Knjaževac, 7,448 F 4
Kočevje, 5,819 B 3
Konjic, 5,927 D 4
Koper, 12,000 A 3
Koprivnica, 12,000 C 2
Korčula, 2,458 C 4
Kosovska Mitrovica, 29,000 E 4
Kostajnica, 2,080 C 3
Kotor, 4,764 D 4
Kragujevac, 56,000 E 3
Kraljevo (Rankovičevo), 26,000 E 4
Kranj, 23,000 B 2
Križevci, 6,642 C 2
Krk, 1,280 B 3
Krško, 3,518 B 3
Kruševac, 31,000 E 4
Kumanovo, 33,000 E 4
Leskovac, 37,000 E 4
Livno, 5,181 C 4
Ljubljana, 183,000 B 3
Ljubuški, 2,168 C 4
Loznica, 12,000 D 3
Maglaj, 4,556 D 3
Makarska, 3,634 C 4
Maribor, 89,000 B 2
Mladenovac, 12,000 E 4
Modriča, 5,053 D 3
Mostar, 53,000 D 4
Našice, 4,187 C 3
Negotin, 8,635 F 3
Nevesinje, 2,349 D 4
Nikšić, 25,000 D 4
Niš, 92,000 F 4
Nova Gradiška, 9,229 C 3
Novi, 2,075 B 3
Novi Pazar, 23,000 E 4
Novi Sad, 119,000 D 3
Novo Mesto, 6,885 B 3
Novska, 3,844 C 3
Ogulin, 3,522 B 3
Ohrid, 18,000 E 5
Omiš, 2,171 C 4
Opatija, 7,974 A 3
Osijek, 78,000 D 3
Pag, 2,431 B 3
Pančevo, 49,000 E 3
Paraćin, 17,000 E 4
Peć, 30,000 E 4
Petrinja, 7,366 B 3
Piran, 5,474 A 3
Pirot, 20,000 F 4
Plav, 2,535 D 4
Pljevlja, 12,000 D 4
Podgorica (Titograd), 37,000 D 4
Pola (Pula), 40,000 A 3
Poreč, 3,006 A 3
Postojna, 4,857 B 3
Požarevac, 23,000 E 3
Požega, 14,000 C 3
Preševo, 5,680 E 4
Priboj, 5,490 D 4
Prijedor, 13,000 C 3
Prijepolje, 4,566 D 4
Prilep, 40,000 E 5
Priština, 43,000 E 4
Prizren, 29,000 E 4
Prokuplje, 15,000 E 4
Prozor, 1,052 C 4
Ptuj, 7,392 C 2
Pula, 40,000 A 3
Rab, 1,548 B 3
Rača, 1,351 E 3
Radeče, 1,500 B 2
Radoviš, 6,246 F 5
Ragusa (Dubrovnik), 24,000 C 4
Rankovićevo, 26,000 E 4
Raška, 2,278 E 4
Rijeka, 108,000 B 3
Rogatica, 3,040 D 4
Rovinj, 7,155 A 3
Ruma, 21,000 D 3
Šabac, 30,000 D 3
Sanski Most, 5,096 C 3
Sarajevo, 223,000 D 4
Senj, 3,903 B 3
Senta, 22,000 D 3
Šibenik, 27,000 C 4
Sinj, 4,134 C 4
Sisak, 29,000 C 3
Škofja Loka, 3,429 A 2
Skopje, 230,000 E 5
Skradin, 1,118 C 4
Smederevo, 29,000 E 3
Sombor, 31,000 D 3
Split, 106,000 C 4
Srebrenica, 1,859 D 3
Sremska Mitrovica, 22,000 D 3
Sremski Karlovci, 6,390 D 3
Stari Majdan, 1,445 C 3
Štip, 22,000 F 5
Stolac, 2,970 D 4
Struga, 6,857 E 5
Strumica, 17,000 F 5
Subotica, 76,000 D 2
Surdulica, 5,007 F 4
Svetozarevo, 22,000 E 4
Svilajnac, 5,895 E 3
Tešanj, 3,148 C 3
Tetovo, 27,000 E 5
Titograd, 37,000 D 4
Titovo Užice, 26,000 D 4
Titov Veles, 29,000 E 5
Travnik, 12,000 C 3
Trbovlje, 16,000 B 2
Trebinje, 4,073 D 4
Trogir, 5,003 C 4
Tržič, 4,881 B 2
Tuzla, 55,000 D 3
Ulcinj, 5,705 D 5
Valjevo, 27,000 D 3
Varaždin, 28,000 B 2
Vareš, 7,647 D 3
Veliki Bečkerek (Zrenjanin), 56,000 E 3
Vinkovci, 24,000 D 3
Virovitica, 10,000 C 3
Višegrad, 3,309 D 4
Vranje, 18,000 F 4
Vrbas, 19,000 D 3
Vršac, 32,000 E 3
Vukovar, 25,000 D 3
Žabari, 1,984 E 3
Zadar, 28,000 B 3
Zagreb, 503,000 C 3
Zaječar, 18,000 E 4
Zara (Zadar), 28,000 B 3
Zenica, 50,000 C 3
Žepče, 2,709 D 3
Zrenjanin, 56,000 E 3
Zvornik, 5,444 D 3

OTHER FEATURES

Adriatic (sea) B 4
Bobotov Kuk (mt.) D 4
Bosna (riv.) D 3
Brač (isl.), 14,227 C 4
Čazma (riv.) C 3
Cres (isl.), 4,949 B 3
Danube (riv.) E 3
Dinaric Alps (mts.) B 3
Drava (riv.) C 3
Drina (riv.) D 3
Dugi Otok (isl.), 4,873 B 3
Hvar (isl.), 12,147 C 4
Ibar (riv.) E 4
Kamenjak (cape) A 3
Korab (mt.) E 5
Korčula (isl.), 10,245 C 4
Kornat (isl.), 6 B 4
Krk (isl.), 14,548 B 3
Kvarner (gulf) B 3
Lastovo (Lagosta) (isl.), 1,449 C 4
Lim (riv.) D 4
Lošinj (isl.), 5,068 B 3
Mljet (isl.), 1,963 C 4
Morava (riv.) E 3
Mur (riv.) B 2
Neretva (riv.) D 4
Ohrid (lake) E 5
Pag (isl.), 8,017 B 3
Pelagruž (Pelagosa) (isl.) C 4
Prespa (lake) E 5
Rab (isl.), 8,400 B 3
Ruen (mt.) F 4
Sava (riv.) D 3
Scutari (lake) D 4
Solta (isl.), 2,735 C 4
Tara (riv.) D 4
Timok (riv.) F 3
Tisza (riv.) E 4
Triglav (mt.) A 2
Una (riv.) C 3
Vardar (riv.) E 5
Vis (isl.), 7,004 C 4
Vrbas (riv.) C 3
Žirje (isl.), 506 B 4

*City and suburbs.

THE BALKAN STATES

CONIC PROJECTION

SCALE OF MILES

0 25 50 75 100 125 150 175

SCALE OF KILOMETRES

0 25 50 75 100 125 150 175

Capitals of Countries ———————— ☆
Administrative Centers ———————— △
International Boundaries —— — —— — ——
Major Internal Boundaries —— — — — —
Minor Internal Boundaries ················
Canals ————————

BULGARIA and GREECE are divided into counties and departments, respectively. Because of the scale no attempt has been made to delimit and name these subdivisions; their administrative centers have, however, been designated.

The larger divisions named in Greece are well-known geographical regions, without administrative function.

RUMANIA consists of thirty-nine counties and three cities of regional status, Bucharest, Constanța and Petroșeni. Scale does not permit delimiting these counties.

ALBANIA is divided into twenty-seven districts. Scale does not permit the delimitation of these divisions.

YUGOSLAVIA is a federation of six republics. The Serbian republic includes an autonomous province (Voyvodina), and an autonomous region (Kosovo-Mitohiyan).

© C. S. HAMMOND & Co., N.Y.

Topography

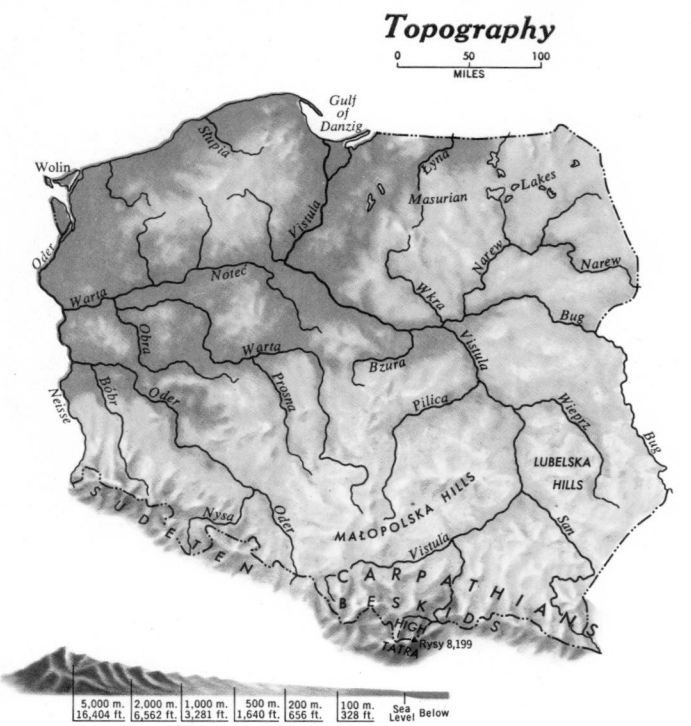

5,000 m. | 2,000 m. | 1,000 m. | 500 m. | 200 m. | 100 m. | Sea Level | Below
16,404 ft. | 6,562 ft. | 3,281 ft. | 1,640 ft. | 656 ft. | 328 ft.

PROVINCES			
Biała Podlaska, 283,200	F 3	Nowy Sącz, 600,300	E 4
Białystok, 613,800	F 2	Olsztyn, 654,400	E 2
Bielsko, 765,500	D 4	Opole, 961,600	C 3
Bydgoszcz, 982,100	C 2	Piła, 414,000	C 2
Chełm, 221,000	F 3	Piotrków, 581,900	D 3
Ciechanów, 398,500	E 2	Płock, 479,700	D 2
Cracow, 1,097,600	E 4	Poznań, 1,156,500	C 2
Cracow (city), 651,300	E 4	Radom, 674,400	E 3
Częstochowa, 723,200	D 3	Przemyśl, 373,100	F 4
Elbląg, 419,800	D 1	Rzeszów, 602,200	F 4
Gdańsk, 1,220,500	D 1	Siedlce, 662,100	F 2
Gorzów, 428,700	B 2	Sieradz, 388,000	D 3
Jelenia Góra, 483,400	B 3	Skierniewice, 388,300	E 3
Kalisz, 640,300	C 3	Słupsk, 352,900	C 1
Katowice, 3,439,700	D 3	Suwałki, 412,700	F 1
Kielce, 1,030,400	E 3	Szczecin, 841,400	B 2
Konin, 423,700	D 2	Tarnobrzeg, 532,200	E 3
Koszalin, 428,500	C 1	Tarnów, 573,900	E 4
Krosno, 418,000	E 4	Toruń, 580,500	D 2
Legnica, 405,600	C 3	Wałbrzych, 709,600	C 3
Leszno, 340,600	C 3	Warsaw, 2,117,700	E 2
Łódź, 1,063,700	D 3	Warsaw (city), 1,377,100	E 2
Łódź (city), 777,800	D 3	Włocławek, 402,000	D 2
Łomża, 320,600	F 2	Wrocław, 1,014,600	C 3
Lublin, 875,300	F 3	Zamość, 472,300	F 3
		Zielona Góra, 575,000	B 3

CITIES and TOWNS	
Aleksandrów Łódzki, 14,800	D 3
Andrespol, 12,500	D
Andrychów, 14,300	E
Augustów, 20,200	F
Bartoszyce, 15,700	E
Będzin, 42,500	B
Bełchatów, 9,230	D
Bełżyce, 5,333	B
Biała Podlaska, 26,700	F
Białogard, 20,800	C
Białystok, 182,300	F
Bielawa, 31,300	C
Bielsk Podlaski, 14,600	F
Bielsko-Biała, 114,200	D
Biłgoraj, 13,600	F
Bochnia, 15,000	E
Bogatynia, 12,300	B
Boguszów-Gorce, 11,900	B
Bolesławiec, 31,400	B
Braniewo, 12,400	D
Brodnica, 17,700	D
Brzeg, 31,500	C
Brzeg Dolny, 10,900	C
Brzesko, 10,800	E

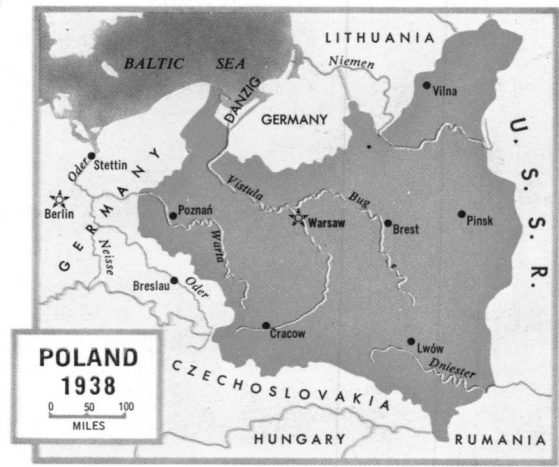

POLAND 1938
0 50 100 MILES

POLAND 1945
0 50 100 MILES

Agriculture, Industry and Resources

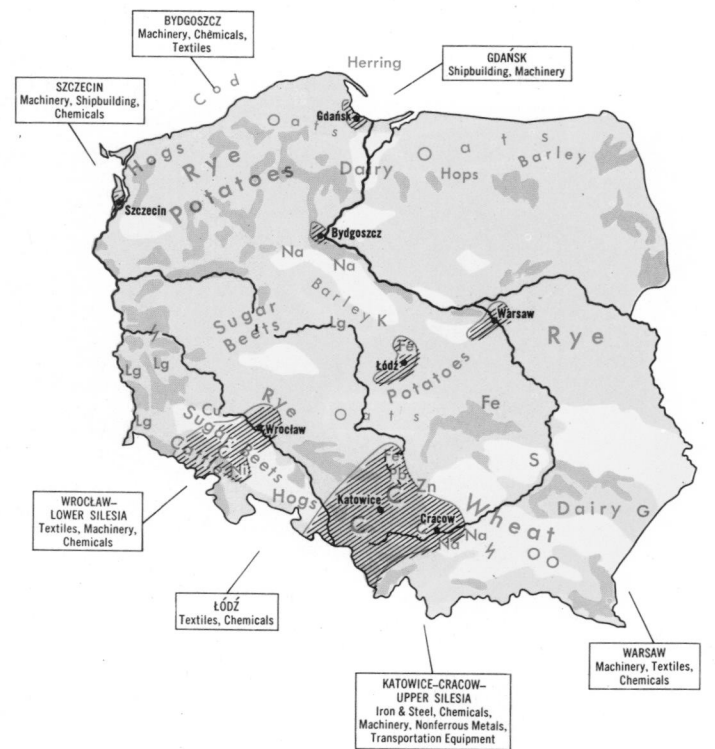

BYDGOSZCZ
Machinery, Chemicals, Textiles

GDAŃSK
Shipbuilding, Machinery

SZCZECIN
Machinery, Shipbuilding, Chemicals

WROCŁAW—
LOWER SILESIA
Textiles, Machinery, Chemicals

ŁÓDŹ
Textiles, Chemicals

KATOWICE—CRACOW—
UPPER SILESIA
Iron & Steel, Chemicals, Machinery, Nonferrous Metals, Transportation Equipment

WARSAW
Machinery, Textiles, Chemicals

DOMINANT LAND USE

- Cereals (chiefly wheat)
- Rye, Oats, Barley, Potatoes
- General Farming, Livestock
- Forests

MAJOR MINERAL OCCURRENCES

C	Coal	Na	Salt
Cu	Copper	Ni	Nickel
Fe	Iron Ore	O	Petroleum
G	Natural Gas	Pb	Lead
K	Potash	S	Sulfur
Lg	Lignite	Zn	Zinc

⚡ Water Power

▨ Major Industrial Areas

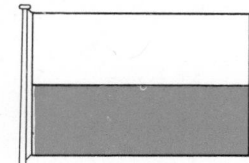

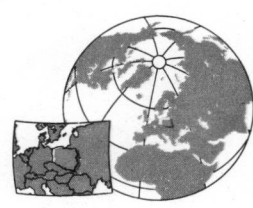

AREA 120,725 sq. mi.
POPULATION 34,364,000
CAPITAL Warsaw
LARGEST CITY Warsaw
HIGHEST POINT Rysy 8,199 ft.
MONETARY UNIT zloty
MAJOR LANGUAGE Polish
MAJOR RELIGION Roman Catholicism

Brzozów, 8,591	F 4	Jaworzno, 64,500 .... B 4
Busko-Zdrój, 11,400	E 3	Jędrzejów, 13,700 .... E 3
Bydgoszcz, 305,500	C 2	Jelenia Góra, 56,200 .... B 3
Bytom, 192,000	B 4	Kalisz, 82,400 .... D 3
Bytów, 10,900	C 1	Kamienna Góra, 21,200 .... B 3
Chełm, 40,000	F 3	Kamień Pomorski, 8,725 .... B 2
Chełmno, 18,100	D 2	Kartuzy, 10,800 .... C 1
Chełmża, 14,500	D 2	Katowice, 317,700 .... B 4
Chodzież, 14,300	C 2	Kazimierza Wielka, 8,571 .... E 3
Chojnice, 24,000	C 2	Kędzierzyn, 34,200 .... C 3
Chojnów, 11,100	B 3	Kępno, 12,000 .... D 3
Chorzów, 154,300	B 4	Kętrzyn, 19,600 .... E 1
Choszczno, 10,200	B 2	Kęty, 12,000 .... D 4
Chrzanów, 29,300	D 4	Kielce, 138,700 .... E 3
Ciechanów, 23,500	E 2	Kłobuck, 12,500 .... D 3
Cieplice Śląskie-Zdrój, 15,600	B 3	Kłodzko, 26,300 .... C 3
Cieszyn, 25,600	D 4	Kluczbork, 18,200 .... D 3
Cracow (Kraków), 651,300	E 4	Knurów, 30,600 .... A 4
Czechowice-Dziedzice, 25,700	D 4	Kolno, 7,980 .... F 2
Czeladź, 32,700	B 4	Koło, 13,400 .... D 2
Czerwionka, 10,600	A 4	Kołobrzeg, 26,600 .... B 1
Częstochowa, 193,400	D 3	Konin, 42,800 .... D 2
Dąbrowa Górnicza, 62,400	B 3	Końskie, 13,700 .... E 3
Dąbrowa Tarnowska, 9,703	E 4	Konstantynów Łódzki, 13,000 .... D 3
Darłowo, 11,500	C 1	Kościan, 19,000 .... C 2
Dębica, 23,600	E 3	Kościerzyna, 15,500 .... C 1
Dęblin, 14,900	E 3	Kostrzyn, 11,700 .... B 2
Dębno, 11,000	B 2	Koszalin, 66,800 .... C 1
Działdowo, 10,500	E 2	Kowary, 11,400 .... B 3
Dzierżoniów, 33,400	C 3	Koźle, 13,300 .... C 3
Elbląg, 91,400	D 1	Krapkowice, 14,200 .... D 3
Ełk, 27,900	F 2	Kraśnik, 14,700 .... F 3
Gdańsk, 394,000	D 1	Kraśnik Fabryczny, 13,800 .... F 3
Gdynia, 207,600	D 1	Krasnystaw, 12,700 .... F 3
Giżycko, 18,500	E 1	Krosno, 27,200 .... E 4
Gliwice, 178,300	B 4	Krotoszyn, 22,200 .... C 3
Głogów, 22,700	C 3	Krynica, 10,400 .... E 4
Głowno, 13,200	D 2	Kutno, 30,600 .... D 2
Głubczyce, 11,500	C 3	Kwidzyn, 23,400 .... D 2
Głuchołazy, 13,400	C 3	Łańcut, 12,300 .... F 3
Gniezno, 57,300	C 2	Łaziska Górne, 10,900 .... A 4
Goldap, 8,886	F 1	Łebork, 25,300 .... C 1
Goleniów, 15,000	B 2	Łęczyca, 13,900 .... D 2
Góra, 9,905	C 3	Lędziny, 12,800 .... B 4
Gorlice, 16,000	E 4	Legionowo, 21,000 .... E 2
Gorzów Wielkopolski, 76,200	C 3	Legnica, 76,800 .... C 3
Gostyń, 13,300	C 3	Leszczyna, 12,100 .... A 4
Gostynin, 12,200	D 2	Leszno, 34,600 .... C 3
Grajewo, 11,400	F 2	Leżajsk, 9,647 .... F 3
Grodziec, 10,200	A 4	Libiąż, 10,700 .... D 4
Grodzisk Mazowiecki, 21,000	E 2	Lidzbark Warmiński, 13,200 .... E 1
Grójec, 10,400	E 2	Lipno, 11,100 .... D 2
Grudziądz, 76,600	D 2	Łódź, 777,800 .... D 3
Gryfice, 13,600	B 2	Łomża, 26,400 .... F 2
Gryfino, 7,446	B 2	Łosice, 4,197 .... F 2
Gubin, 15,000	B 3	Łowicz, 21,100 .... D 2
Hajnówka, 14,600	F 2	Lubaczów, 8,298 .... F 3
Hrubieszów, 15,500	F 3	Lubań, 17,500 .... B 3
Iława, 17,100	D 2	Lubartów, 10,300 .... F 2
Iłża, 4,419	E 3	Lubin, 254,700 .... F 3
Inowrocław, 55,900	D 2	Lubliniec, 20,100 .... D 3
Janów Lubelski, 5,944	F 3	Luboń, 17,000 .... C 2
Jarocin, 18,300	C 3	Lubsko, 13,000 .... B 3
Jarosław, 29,500	F 4	Łuków, 16,100 .... F 2
Jasło, 17,600	E 4	Malbork, 31,500 .... D 1
Jastrzębie-Zdrój, 34,400	D 3	Maków Mazowiecki, 7,694 .... E 2
Jawor, 15,700	C 3	

Międzyrzec Podlaski, 13,800 ....F 3	Piekary Śląskie, 36,600 ....B 3	Słupca, 8,634 ....D 2	Tuchola, 9,439 ....D 2	Żyrardów, 33,300 ....E 2
Międzyrzecz, 15,200 ....B 2	Piła, 44,500 ....C 2	Słupsk, 69,900 ....C 1	Turek, 18,700 ....D 2	Żywiec, 22,900 ....D 4
Mielec, 27,700 ....E 3	Pińczów, 7,080 ....E 3	Sochaczew, 21,000 ....D 2	Tychy, 72,800 ....B 4	
Mikołów, 21,800 ....B 4	Pionki, 14,000 ....E 3	Sokółka, 10,300 ....F 2	Ursus, 30,900 ....E 2	**OTHER FEATURES**
Mława, 20,600 ....E 2	Piotrków Trybunalski, 60,800 ....D 3	Sokołów Podlaski, 9,569 ....F 2	Wabrzeźno, 11,900 ....D 2	
Mońki, 9,560 ....F 2	Pisz, 11,400 ....F 2	Solec Kujawski, 10,800 ....C 2	Wadowice, 12,000 ....D 4	Baltic (sea) ....B 1
Morąg, 9,681 ....E 2	Pleszew, 13,700 ....C 3	Sopot, 48,500 ....D 1	Wągrowiec, 16,000 ....C 2	Beskids (mts.) ....D 4
Morzów, 13,700 ....E 2	Płock, 74,100 ....D 2	Sosnowiec, 148,300 ....B 4	Wałbrzych, 127,400 ....C 3	Brda (river) ....C 2
Mrągowo, 13,700 ....E 2	Płońsk, 11,900 ....E 2	Śrem, 16,400 ....C 2	Wałcz, 19,200 ....C 2	Brynica (river) ....B 3
Myślenice, 12,40u ....E 4	Police, 13,200 ....B 2	Środa Wielkopolska, 15,000 ....C 2	Warsaw (Warszawa) (cap.),	Bug (river) ....D 1
Mysłowice, 45,100 ....B 4	Polkowice, 10,600 ....C 3	Stalowa Wola, 31,100 ....F 3	1,377,100 ....E 2	Danzig (gulf) ....D 1
Myszków, 18,300 ....D 3	Poznań, 495,200 ....C 2	Starachowice, 43,700 ....E 3	Węgorzewo, 8,522 ....E 1	Dunajec (river) ....E 4
Nakło nad Notecią, 17,000 ....C 2	Prudnik, 20,400 ....C 3	Stargard Szczeciński, 45,600 ....B 2	Wejherowo, 34,600 ....C 1	Gwda (river) ....C 2
Namysłów, 11,200 ....C 3	Pruszcz Gdański, 13,100 ....D 1	Starogard Gdański, 34,200 ....D 1	Wieliczka, 14,000 ....E 4	Hel (pen.) ....D 1
Nidzica, 10,000 ....E 2	Pruszków, 43,500 ....E 2	Staszów, 8,449 ....E 3	Wieluń, 14,900 ....D 3	High Tatra (mts.) ....E 4
Nisko, 10,200 ....F 3	Przasnysz, 11,400 ....E 2	Strzegom, 14,400 ....C 3	Wieruszów, 3,650 ....D 3	Kłodnica (river) ....A 4
Nowa Ruda, 18,300 ....C 3	Przemyśl, 53,400 ....F 4	Strzelce Opolskie, 15,000 ....D 3	Włocławek, 79,900 ....D 2	Łyna (river) ....E 1
Nowa Sól, 34,000 ....B 3	Pszczyna, 11,900 ....B 4	Strzemieszyce Wielkie, 11,500 ....B 3	Władawa, 7,354 ....F 3	Mamry (lake) ....E 1
Nowy Dwór Gdański, 7,146 ....D 1	Pułtusk, 12,800 ....E 2	Sulechów, 10,500 ....B 2	Wodzisław Śląski, 27,500 ....D 4	Masurian (lakes) ....E 2
Nowy Dwór Mazowiecki, 17,200 ....E 2	Pyskowice, 23,300 ....A 3	Suwałki, 26,500 ....F 1	Wołomin, 24,100 ....E 2	Narew (river) ....E 2
Nowy Sącz, 42,100 ....E 4	Rabka, 10,800 ....D 4	Swarzędz, 12,200 ....C 2	Wołów, 10,600 ....C 3	Neisse (river) ....B 3
Nowy Targ, 22,600 ....E 4	Raciborz, 40,600 ....C 3	Świdnica, 48,200 ....C 3	Wrocław, 557,200 ....C 3	Noteć (river) ....C 2
Nysa, 33,100 ....C 3	Radom, 166,000 ....E 3	Świdnik, 29,100 ....F 3	Września, 18,400 ....C 2	Nysa Kłodzka (river) ....C 3
Obornik, 10,200 ....C 2	Radomsko, 31,600 ....D 3	Świdwin, 12,600 ....B 2	Wschowa, 10,100 ....C 3	Nysa Łużycka (Neisse) (riv.) ....B 3
Oława, 18,500 ....C 3	Radziejów, 4,165 ....D 2	Świebodzice, 18,900 ....C 3	Wysokie Mazowieckie, 5,296 ....F 2	Oder (Odra) (river) ....D 4
Olecko, 9,120 ....F 1	Radzionków, 28,200 ....A 3	Świebodzin, 15,200 ....B 3	Wyszków, 12,200 ....E 2	Orava (res.) ....D 4
Oleśnica, 28,100 ....C 3	Rawicz, 14,300 ....C 3	Świecie, 18,300 ....D 2	Żabki, 16,200 ....E 2	Pilica (river) ....D 3
Olkusz, 16,500 ....D 4	Ruda Śląska, 146,200 ....A 4	Strzelce Śląskie, 14,400 ....C 3	Zabrze, 200,700 ....A 4	Pomeranian (bay) ....B 1
Olsztyn, 104,300 ....E 2	Rumia, 23,800 ....D 1	Świnoujście, 28,800 ....A 2	Żagań, 21,700 ....B 3	Prosna (river) ....D 3
Opatów, 9,784 ....E 3	Rybnik, 44,600 ....D 4	Szamotuły, 14,800 ....C 2	Zagórze, 13,000 ....B 4	Przemsza (river) ....B 4
Opoczno, 12,400 ....E 3	Rydułtowy, 19,500 ....D 3	Szczecin, 355,600 ....B 2	Zakopane, 25,500 ....E 4	Rysy (mt.) ....F 3
Opole, 87,800 ....C 3	Rypin, 10,200 ....D 2	Szczecinek, 29,500 ....C 2	Zamość, 17,900 ....F 2	San (river) ....E 3
Orneta, 8,500 ....E 1	Rzeszów, 83,900 ....F 4	Szczytno, 17,500 ....E 2	Zawiercie, 14,500 ....D 2	Słupia (river) ....C 1
Ostróda, 21,600 ....E 2	Sandomierz, 17,300 ....E 3	Szprotawa, 11,500 ....B 3	Zamość, 35,600 ....F 3	Śniardwy (lake) ....E 1
Ostrołęka, 23,000 ....E 2	Sanok, 22,100 ....F 4	Szydłowiec, 12,400 ....E 3	Żary, 28,500 ....B 3	Sudeten (mts.) ....B 3
Ostrów Mazowiecka, 15,800 ....E 2	Siedlce, 39,600 ....F 2	Tarnobrzeg, 21,300 ....E 3	Zduńska Wola, 29,500 ....D 3	Uznam (Usedom) (isl.) ....B 1
Ostrów Wielkopolski, 50,300 ....C 3	Siemianowice Śląskie, 67,800 ....A 4	Tarnów, 87,200 ....E 4	Zgierz, 44,100 ....D 2	Vistula (river) ....D 1
Ostrowiec Świętokrzyski, 51,400 ....E 3	Sieradz, 19,000 ....D 3	Tarnowskie Góry, 35,000 ....A 3	Zgorzelec, 28,800 ....B 3	Warmia (river) ....E 1
Otwock, 40,200 ....E 2	Sierpc, 12,900 ....D 2	Tczew, 42,100 ....D 1	Zielona Góra, 75,000 ....B 3	Warta (river) ....B 1
Ozorków, 18,600 ....D 3	Skarzysko-Kamienna, 39,700 ....E 3	Tomaszów Lubelski, 12,800 ....F 3	Złocieniec, 10,400 ....C 2	Wieprz (river) ....F 3
Pabianice, 63,500 ....D 3	Skawina, 16,300 ....D 4	Tomaszów Mazowiecki, 55,600 ....E 3	Złotoryja, 12,400 ....C 3	Wisła (Vistula) (river) ....E 2
Parczew, 6,952 ....F 2	Skierniewice, 25,800 ....E 3	Toruń, 139,000 ....D 2	Złotów, 12,100 ....C 2	Wkra (river) ....E 2
Pasłęk, 8,030 ....D 1	Sławno, 10,900 ....C 1	Trzcianka, 11,200 ....C 2	Zwoleń, 5,216 ....E 3	Wolin (isl.) ....B 2
Piaseczno, 20,500 ....E 2	Słubice, 12,200 ....B 2	Trzebinia-Siersza, 19,600 ....C 4		

UNION REPUBLICS

Armenian S.S.R., 2,491,900 ....E 6
Azerbaidzhan S.S.R.,
  5,117,100 ....E 5
Estonian S.S.R., 1,356,100 ....C 4
Georgian S.S.R., 4,686,000 ....E 5
Kazakh S.S.R., 12,849,000 ....G 5
Kirgiz S.S.R., 2,932,800 ....H 5
Latvian S.S.R., 2,364,100 ....C 4
Lithuanian S.S.R.,
  3,128,000 ....C 4
Moldavian S.S.R., 3,568,900 ....C 5
Russian S.F.S.R.,
  130,079,210 ....D 4
Tadzhik S.S.R., 2,900,000 ....H 6
Turkmen S.S.R., 2,158,880 ....F 6
Ukrainian S.S.R.,
  47,126,517 ....C 5
Uzbek S.S.R., 11,960,000 ....G 5
White Russian S.S.R.,
  9,002,338 ....C 4

INTERNAL DIVISIONS

Abkhaz A.S.S.R., 487,000 ....E 5
Adygey Aut. Oblast,
  385,000 ....D 5
Adzhar A.S.S.R. 310,000 ....E 5
Aginsk-Buryat Nat'l Okrug,
  66,000 ....M 4
Bashkir A.S.S.R., 3,818,000 ....F 4
Buryat A.S.S.R., 812,000 ....M 4
Chechen-Ingush A.S.S.R.,
  1,065,000 ....E 5

Chukchi Nat'l Okrug,
  101,000 ....R 3
Chuvash A.S.S.R.,
  1,224,000 ....E 4
Dagestan A.S.S.R.,
  1,429,000 ....E 5
Evenki Nat'l Okrug,
  13,000 ....K 3
Gorno-Altay Aut. Oblast,
  168,000 ....J 4
Gorno-Badakhshan Aut. Oblast,
  98,000 ....H 6
Jewish Aut. Oblast,
  172,000 ....O 5
Kabardin-Balkar A.S.S.R.,
  588,000 ....E 5
Kalmuck A.S.S.R.,
  268,000 ....E 5
Karachay-Cherkess Aut. Oblast,
  345,000 ....E 5
Karakalpak A.S.S.R.,
  702,000 ....G 5
Karelian A.S.S.R.,
  713,000 ....D 3
Khakass Aut. Oblast,
  446,000 ....J 4
Khanty-Mansi Nat'l Okrug,
  271,000 ....F 3
Komi A.S.S.R., 965,000 ....F 3
Komi-Permyak Nat'l Okrug,
  212,000 ....F 4
Koryak Nat'l Okrug,
  31,000 ....R 3
Mari A.S.S.R., 685,000 ....E 4
Mordvinian A.S.S.R.,
  1,029,000 ....E 4

Nagorno-Karabakh Aut. Oblast,
  150,000 ....E 5
Nakhichevan' A.S.S.R.,
  202,000 ....E 6
Nenets Nat'l Okrug, 39,000 ....F 3
North Ossetian A.S.S.R.,
  552,000 ....E 5
South Ossetian Aut. Oblast,
  99,000 ....E 5
Tatar A.S.S.R., 3,131,000 ....F 4
Taymyr Nat'l Okrug, 38,000 ....K 3
Tuvinian A.S.S.R., 231,000 ....K 4
Udmurt A.S.S.R., 1,418,000 ....F 4
Ust'-Ordynsk-Buryat Nat'l Okrug,
  146,000 ....L 4
Yakut A.S.S.R., 664,000 ....N 3
Yamal-Nenets Nat'l Okrug,
  80,000 ....H 3

CITIES and TOWNS

Abakan, 90,000 ....K 4
Achinsk, 97,000 ....J 4
Adimi ....O 5
Aginskoye, 9,000 ....M 4
Akmolinsk (Tselinograd),
  180,000 ....G 4
Aktyubinsk, 150,000 ....F 4
Aldan, 19,000 ....N 4
Aleksandrovsk-Sakhalinskiy,
  22,000 ....P 5
Aleysk, 32,000 ....J 4
Alga, 17,000 ....F 5
Allakh-Yun' ....O 3
Alma-Ata, 730,000 ....H 5

Ambarchik ....R 3
Amderma ....F 3
Amursk, 15,000 ....O 4
Anadyr', 8,000 ....T 3
Andizhan, 188,000 ....H 5
Angarsk, 203,000 ....L 4
Anzhero-Sudzhensk,
  106,000 ....J 4
Aral'sk, 26,000 ....G 5
Archangel, 343,000 ....E 3
Arkalyk, 15,000 ....G 4
Armavir, 145,000 ....E 5
Artem, 61,000 ....O 5
Artemovskiy ....M 4
Arzamas, 67,000 ....E 4
Ashkhabad, 253,000 ....F 6
Ashkhabad *256,000 ....F 6
Asino, 30,000 ....J 4
Astrakhan', 410,000 ....E 5
Atbasar, 41,000 ....G 4
Atka ....Q 3
Ayaguz, 40,000 ....H 5
Aykhal ....M 3
Baghdarin ....M 4
Baku, 852,000 ....F 5
Baku, *1,266,000 ....F 5
Balashov, 83,000 ....E 4
Balkhash, 76,000 ....H 5
Balturino, 10,000 ....K 4
Barabinsk, 40,000 ....H 4
Baranovichi, 101,000 ....C 4
Barnaul, 439,000 ....J 4
Batumi, 101,000 ....E 5
Baykit ....K 3
Baykonur ....G 5

Bayram-Ali, 33,000 ....G 6
Belgorod, 151,000 ....D 4
Belogorsk, 57,000 ....O 4
Belomorsk, 18,000 ....D 3
Beloretsk, 67,000 ....F 4
Belovo, 108,000 ....J 4
Berdichev, 71,000 ....C 5
Berdsk, 53,000 ....J 4
Berezniki, 146,000 ....F 4
Berezovo, 6,000 ....G 3
Beringovskiy ....T 3
Bilibino, 13,000 ....R 3
Birobidzhan, 56,000 ....O 5
Biysk, 186,000 ....J 4
Blagoveshchensk,
  128,000 ....N 4
Bobruysk, 138,000 ....C 4
Bodaybo, 19,000 ....M 4
Borisoglebsk, 64,000 ....E 4
Borzya, 28,000 ....M 4
Boshchakul' ....H 4
Bratsk, 155,000 ....L 4
Brest, 122,000 ....C 4
Bryansk, 318,000 ....D 4
Bugul'ma, 72,000 ....F 4
Bukhara, 112,000 ....G 5
Bulun ....N 2
Buzuluk, 67,000 ....F 4
Chagda ....O 4
Chapayevo ....F 4
Chapayevsk, 86,000 ....F 4
Chardzhou, 96,000 ....G 6
Cheboksary, 216,000 ....E 4
Chelkar, 25,000 ....F 5
Chelyabinsk,
  875,000 ....G 4

Cheremkhovo, 99,000 ....L 4
Cherepovets, 188,000 ....D 4
Cherkessk, 67,000 ....E 5
Chernigov, 159,000 ....D 4
Chernovtsy, 187,000 ....C 5
Chernyshevsk, 10,000 ....M 4
Chernyshevskiy,
  10,000 ....M 3
Cherskiy ....R 3
Chimbay, 20,000 ....F 5
Chimkent, 247,000 ....G 5
Chirchik, 107,000 ....H 5
Chita, 241,000 ....M 4
Chokurdakh ....Q 2
Chu'man ....N 4
Chumikan ....O 4
Dalnegorsk, 33,500 ....O 5
Dalnerechensk, 30,000 ....O 5
Daugavpils, 100,400 ....C 4
Dikson ....J 2
Dimitrovgrad, 81,000 ....F 4
Dnepropetrovsk,
  862,000 ....D 5
Dolinsk, 18,000 ....P 5
Donetsk, 879,000 ....D 5
Drogobych, 56,000 ....C 5
Druzhina ....P 3
Dudinka, 22,000 ....J 3
Dushanbe, 376,000 ....G 6
Dzerzhinsk, 221,000 ....E 4
Dzhalal-Abad, 44,000 ....H 5
Dzhalinda ....N 4
Dzhambul, 187,000 ....H 5
Dzhetygara, 39,000 ....G 4
Dzhezkazgan, 62,000 ....G 5
Ekibastuz, 46,000 ....H 4

Ekimchan ....O 4
El'dikan ....P 3
Elista, 50,000 ....E 5
Engel's, 130,000 ....E 4
Erivan, 767,000 ....E 6
Evensk ....R 3
Fergana, 111,000 ....H 5
Fort-Shevchenko,
  12,000 ....F 5
Frolovo, 30,000 ....E 4
Frunze, 430,600 ....H 5
Gasan-Kuli ....F 6
Gol'chikha ....J 2
Gomel', 272,000 ....D 4
Gor'kiy, 1,170,000 ....E 4
Gorno-Altaysk,
  34,000 ....J 4
Grodno, 132,000 ....C 4
Groznyy, 341,000 ....E 5
Gubakha, 40,000 ....F 4
Gulistan, 31,000 ....G 5
Gur'yev, 114,000 ....F 5
Gusinoozersk, 10,000 ....L 4
Gydy ....H 2
Igarka, 22,000 ....J 3
Ilanskiy, 24,000 ....K 4
Iliysk, 17,000 ....H 5
Indiga ....E 3
Inta, 50,000 ....F 3
Iolotan', 10,000 ....G 6
Irkutsk, 451,000 ....L 4
Ishim, 56,000 ....G 4
Ishimbay, 54,000 ....F 4
Isil'-Kul', 26,000 ....H 4
Ivano-Frankovsk, 105,000 ....C 5

UNION OF SOVIET SOCIALIST REPUBLICS
CONIC PROJECTION
SCALE OF MILES
0 100 200 300 400 500 600
SCALE OF KILOMETERS
0 100 200 300 400 500 600

Capitals
★ National
☆ Union Republic
◉ A.S.S.R.
○ Autonomous Oblast
○ National Okrug

Boundaries

ADMINISTRATIVE DIVISIONS NOT NAMED ON MAP			
Division	Ref.	Division	Ref.
1. Abkhaz A.S.S.R.	E5	13. Khakass Aut. Oblast	J4
2. Adygey Aut. Oblast	D5	14. Komi-Permyak Nat'l Okrug	F4
3. Adzhar A.S.S.R.	E5	15. Mari A.S.S.R.	E4
4. Aginsk-Buryat Nat'l Okrug	M4	16. Mordvinian A.S.S.R.	E4
5. Chechen-Ingush A.S.S.R.	E5	17. Nagorno-Karabakh Aut. Oblast.	E5
6. Chuvash A.S.S.R.	E4	18. Nakhichevan' A.S.S.R.	E6
7. Gorno-Altay Aut. Oblast	J4	19. North Ossetian A.S.S.R.	E5
8. Gorno-Badakhshan Aut. Oblast.	H6	20. South Ossetian Aut. Oblast.	E5
9. Jewish Aut. Oblast	O5	21. Tatar A.S.S.R.	F4
10. Kabardin-Balkar A.S.S.R.	E5	22. Tuvinian A.S.S.R.	K4
11. Karachay-Cherkess Aut. Oblast.	E5	23. Udmurt A.S.S.R.	F4
12. Karakalpak A.S.S.R.	G5	24. Ust'-Ordynsk-Buryat Nat'l Okrug	L4

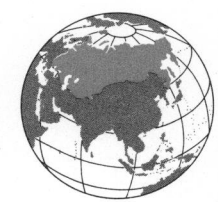

AREA 8,649,498 sq. mi.
POPULATION 241,748,000
CAPITAL Moscow
LARGEST CITY Moscow
HIGHEST POINT Communism Peak 24,590 ft.
MONETARY UNIT ruble
MAJOR LANGUAGES Russian, Ukrainian, White Russian, Uzbek, Azerbaidzhani, Tatar, Georgian, Lithuanian, Armenian, Yiddish, Latvian, Mordvinian, Kirghiz, Tadzhik, Estonian, Kazakh, Moldavian, German, Chuvash, Turkmenian, Bashkir
MAJOR RELIGIONS Eastern (Russian) Orthodoxy, Islam, Judaism, Protestantism (Baltic States)

UNION REPUBLICS

	AREA (sq. mi.)	POPULATION	CAPITAL and LARGEST CITY
RUSSIAN S.F.S.R.	6,592,819	130,079,210	Moscow 6,942,000
KAZAKH S.S.R.	1,048,301	12,849,000	Alma-Ata 730,000
UKRAINIAN S.S.R.	232,046	47,126,517	Kiev 1,632,000
TURKMEN S.S.R.	188,456	2,158,880	Ashkhabad 253,000
UZBEK S.S.R.	173,591	11,960,000	Tashkent 1,385,000
WHITE RUSSIAN S.S.R.	80,154	9,002,338	Minsk 907,000
KIRGIZ S.S.R.	76,641	2,932,800	Frunze 430,600
TADZHIK S.S.R.	55,251	2,900,000	Dushanbe 376,000
AZERBAIDZHAN S.S.R.	33,436	5,117,100	Baku 852,000
GEORGIAN S.S.R.	26,911	4,686,000	Tbilisi 889,000
LITHUANIAN S.S.R.	25,174	3,128,000	Vilna 371,700
LATVIAN S.S.R.	24,595	2,364,100	Riga 731,800
ESTONIAN S.S.R.	17,413	1,356,100	Tallinn 362,706
MOLDAVIAN S.S.R.	13,012	3,568,900	Kishinev 356,900
ARMENIAN S.S.R.	11,500	2,491,900	Erivan 767,000

Ivanovo, 420,000	E 4	Karazhal, 18,000	H 5	
Izhevsk, 422,000	F 4	Karkaralinsk, 9,000	H 5	
Izmail, 70,000	C 5	Karshi, 71,000	G 6	
Kachug	L 4	Kaunas, 306,200	C 4	
Kalachinsk, 24,000	H 4	Kazach'ye	O 2	
Kalakan	L 4	Kazalinsk, 22,000	G 5	
Kalinin, 345,000	D 4	Kazan', 869,000	F 4	
Kaliningrad, 297,000	B 4	Kazandzhik	D 6	
Kalmykovo	F 5	Kem, 23,000	D 3	
Kaluga, 211,000	D 4	Kemerovo, 385,000	J 4	
Kamenskoye	R 3	Kentau, 55,000	G 5	
Kamensk-Ural'skiy, 169,000	G 4	Kerki, 23,000	G 6	
Kamyshin, 97,000	E 4	Kezhma	K 4	
Kamyshlov, 34,000	G 4	Khabarovsk, 436,000	O 5	
Kansk, 95,000	K 4	Khandyga	O 3	
Karabekaul	G 6	Khanty-Mansiysk, 25,000	H 3	
Karaganda, 523,000	H 5	Khar'kov, 1,223,000	D 4	
Karasuk, 26,000	H 4	Kharovsk, 10,000	D 3	

Khatanga	L 2	Kovel', 35,000	C 4	Labytnangi	G 3	Markovo	S 3	Nagornyy	N 4
Kherson, 261,000	C 5	Kovrov, 123,000	E 4	Leninabad, 103,200	G 5	Mary, 62,000	G 6	Nakhichevan',	E 6
Khilok, 17,000	M 4	Kozhevnikovo	L 2	Leninakan, 165,000	E 5	Maykop, 110,000	D 5	33,200	E 6
Khiva, 25,000	F 5	Krasino	F 2	Leningrad, 3,513,000	D 4	Mednogorsk, 41,000	F 4	Nakhodka, 104,000	O 5
Khodzheyli, 36,000	F 5	Krasnodar, 464,000	E 5	Leningrad, *3,950,000	D 4	Medvezh'yegorsk, 18,000	D 3	Nal'chik, 146,000	E 5
Kholmsk, 42,000	P 5	Krasnokamsk, 55,000	F 4	Leninogorsk, 72,000	J 5	Megion	H 3	Namangan, 175,000	H 5
Khorog, 12,300	H 6	Krasnotur'insk, 59,000	G 3	Leninsk-Kuznetskiy, 128,000	J 4	Mezen'	E 3	Naminga, 5,000	M 4
Kiev, 1,632,000	C 4	Krasnoural'sk, 42,000	F 3	Leninskoye	O 5	Miass, 131,000	G 4	Napas	J 4
Kirensk, 10,000	L 4	Krasnovishersk, 16,000	F 3	Lenkoran', 35,500	E 6	Michurinsk, 94,000	E 4	Nar'yan-Mar, 15,000	F 3
Kirov, 333,000	E 4	Krasnovodsk, 49,000	F 5	Lensk, 21,000	M 3	Millerovo, 38,000	E 5	Naryn, 21,000	H 5
Kirovabad, 189,800	E 5	Krasnoyarsk, 648,000	K 4	Lesozavodsk, 37,000	O 5	Minsk, 907,000	C 4	Navoi, 61,000	G 6
Kirovograd, 189,000	D 5	Kremenchug, 148,000	D 5	Liepāja, 92,800	B 4	Minsk, *917,000	C 4	Nebit-Dag, 56,000	F 6
Kiselevsk, 127,000	J 4	Krivoy Rog, 573,000	D 5	Lipetsk, 289,000	E 4	Minusinsk, 47,000	K 4	Nel'kan	O 4
Kishinev, 356,900	C 5	Kudymkar, 20,000	F 4	Luga, 30,000	D 4	Mirnyy, 24,000	M 3	Nepa	L 4
Kizel, 49,000	F 4	Kul'sary, 14,000	F 5	Lutsk, 94,000	C 4	Mogilev, 202,000	D 4	Nerchinsk, 10,000	M 4
Kizyl-Arvat, 24,000	F 6	Kungur, 74,000	F 4	Luza, 10,000	E 3	Mogocha, 10,000	N 4	Nikolayev, 331,000	D 5
Klaipeda, 139,900	B 4	Kupino, 24,000	H 4	L'vov, 553,000	C 4	Molodechno, 50,000	C 4	Nikolayevsk, 34,000	P 4
Kokand, 133,000	H 5	Kurgan, 244,000	G 4	Lys'va, 73,000	F 4	Monchegorsk, 49,000	C 3	Nikol'skoye	R 4
Kokchetav, 81,000	H 4	Kurgan-Tyube, 34,600	G 6	Magadan, 92,000	P 4	Moscow (capital), 6,942,000	D 4	Nimnyrskiy	N 4
Kolomna, 135,900	D 4	Kuril'sk, 2,000	P 5	Magdagachi, 10,000	N 4	Moscow, *7,061,000	D 4	Nizhne-Angarsk	M 4
Kolpashevo, 27,000	J 4	Kursk, 284,000	D 4	Magnitogorsk, 364,000	G 4	Motygino, 10,000	K 4	Nizhneudinsk, 39,000	K 4
Komsomol'sk, 218,000	O 4	Kushka	G 6	Makhachkala, 186,000	E 5	Mozyr', 49,000	D 4	Nizhniy Tagil, 378,000	G 4
Kondopoga, 25,000	D 3	Kustanay, 124,000	G 4	Makinsk, 28,000	H 4	Murgab	H 6	Nordvik	L 2
Kopeysk, 156,000	G 4	Kutaisi, 161,000	E 5	Maklakovo, 20,000	K 4	Murmansk, 309,000	D 3	Noril'sk, 135,000	J 3
Korf	R 3	Kuybyshev, 1,045,000	F 4	Mama	M 4	Muvnak, 12,000	F 5	Novaya Kazanka	F 5
Korsakov, 35,000	P 5	Kyakhta	L 4			Nadym	H 3	Novgorod, 128,000	D 4
Koslan	N 2	Kyusyur	N 2					Novokuznetsk, 499,000	J 4
Kostroma, 223,000	E 4	Kyzyl, 52,000	K 4					Novomoskovsk, 134,000	E 4
Kotlas, 56,000	E 3	Kyzyl-Orda, 122,000	G 5						

Topography

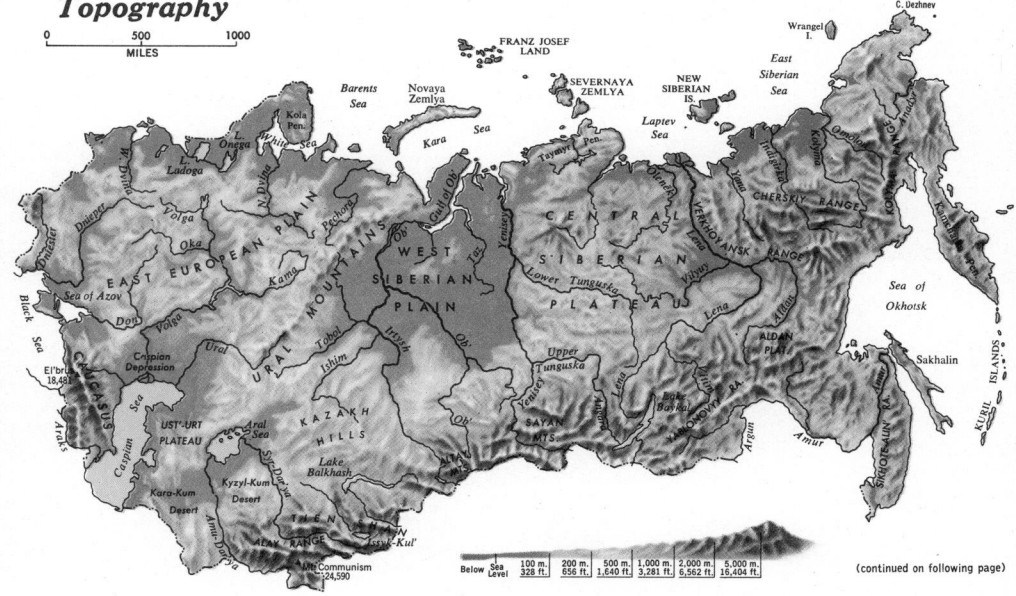

0   500   1000
MILES

Below Sea Level | 100 m. 328 ft. | 200 m. 656 ft. | 500 m. 1,640 ft. | 1,000 m. 3,281 ft. | 2,000 m. 6,562 ft. | 5,000 m. 16,404 ft.

(continued on following page)

U.S.S.R. (continued)

Agriculture, Industry and Resources

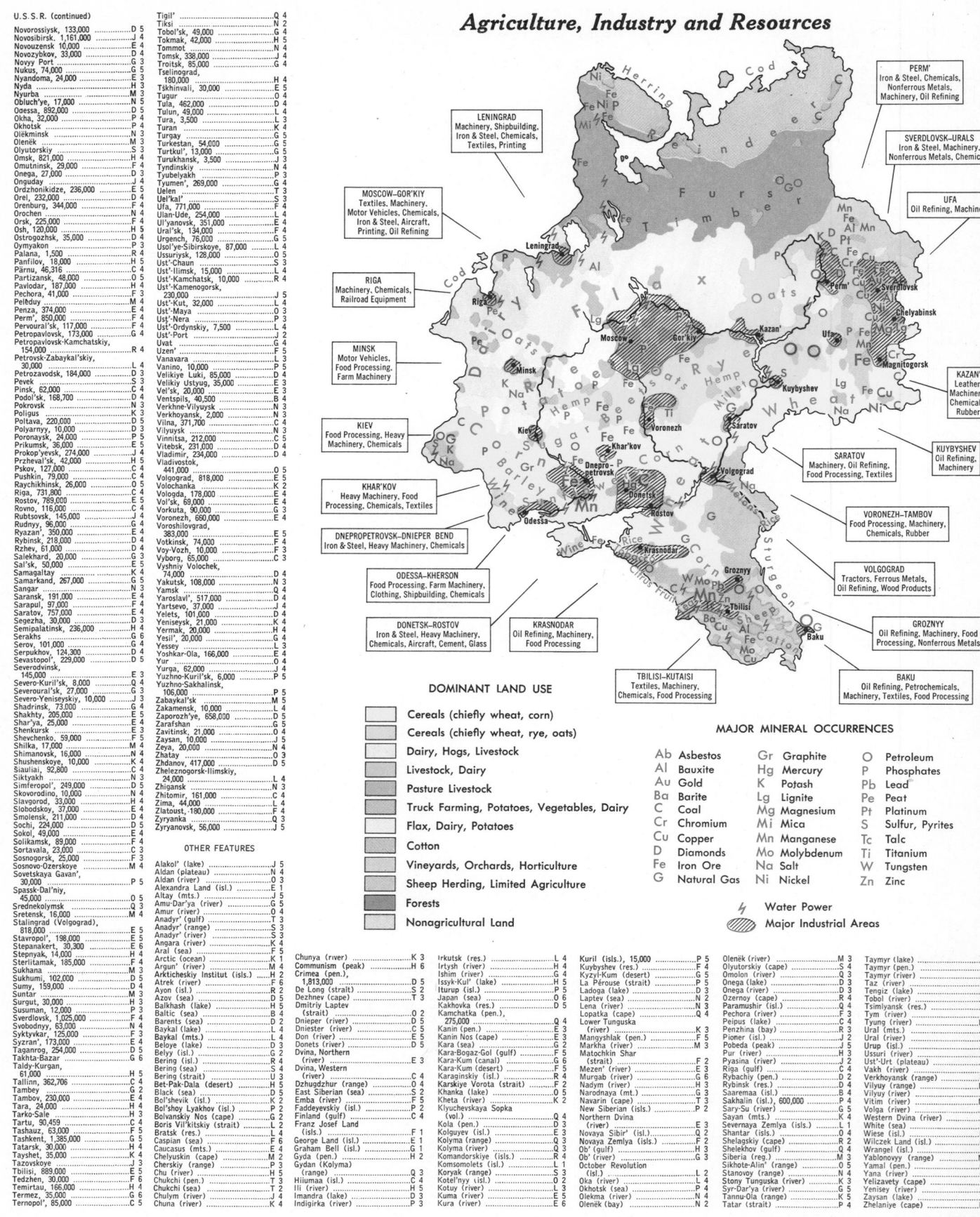

PERM'
Iron & Steel, Chemicals, Nonferrous Metals, Machinery, Oil Refining

SVERDLOVSK–URALS
Iron & Steel, Machinery, Nonferrous Metals, Chemicals

UFA
Oil Refining, Machinery

LENINGRAD
Machinery, Shipbuilding, Iron & Steel, Chemicals, Textiles, Printing

MOSCOW–GOR'KIY
Textiles, Machinery, Motor Vehicles, Chemicals, Iron & Steel, Aircraft, Printing, Oil Refining

RIGA
Machinery, Chemicals, Railroad Equipment

MINSK
Motor Vehicles, Food Processing, Farm Machinery

KIEV
Food Processing, Heavy Machinery, Chemicals

KHAR'KOV
Heavy Machinery, Food Processing, Chemicals, Textiles

DNEPROPETROVSK–DNIEPER BEND
Iron & Steel, Heavy Machinery, Chemicals

ODESSA–KHERSON
Food Processing, Farm Machinery, Clothing, Shipbuilding, Chemicals

DONETSK–ROSTOV
Iron & Steel, Heavy Machinery, Chemicals, Aircraft, Cement, Glass

KRASNODAR
Oil Refining, Machinery, Food Processing

KAZAN'
Leather, Machinery, Chemicals, Rubber

KUYBYSHEV
Oil Refining, Machinery

SARATOV
Machinery, Oil Refining, Food Processing, Textiles

VORONEZH–TAMBOV
Food Processing, Machinery, Chemicals, Rubber

VOLGOGRAD
Tractors, Ferrous Metals, Oil Refining, Wood Products

GROZNYY
Oil Refining, Machinery, Food Processing, Nonferrous Metals

TBILISI–KUTAISI
Textiles, Machinery, Chemicals, Food Processing

BAKU
Oil Refining, Petrochemicals, Machinery, Textiles, Food Processing

DOMINANT LAND USE

- Cereals (chiefly wheat, corn)
- Cereals (chiefly wheat, rye, oats)
- Dairy, Hogs, Livestock
- Livestock, Dairy
- Pasture Livestock
- Truck Farming, Potatoes, Vegetables, Dairy
- Flax, Dairy, Potatoes
- Cotton
- Vineyards, Orchards, Horticulture
- Sheep Herding, Limited Agriculture
- Forests
- Nonagricultural Land

MAJOR MINERAL OCCURRENCES

Ab	Asbestos	Gr	Graphite	O	Petroleum
Al	Bauxite	Hg	Mercury	P	Phosphates
Au	Gold	K	Potash	Pb	Lead
Ba	Barite	Lg	Lignite	Pe	Peat
C	Coal	Mg	Magnesium	Pt	Platinum
Cr	Chromium	Mi	Mica	S	Sulfur, Pyrites
Cu	Copper	Mn	Manganese	Tc	Talc
D	Diamonds	Mo	Molybdenum	Ti	Titanium
Fe	Iron Ore	Na	Salt	W	Tungsten
G	Natural Gas	Ni	Nickel	Zn	Zinc

⚡ Water Power

▨ Major Industrial Areas

Agriculture, Industry and Resources

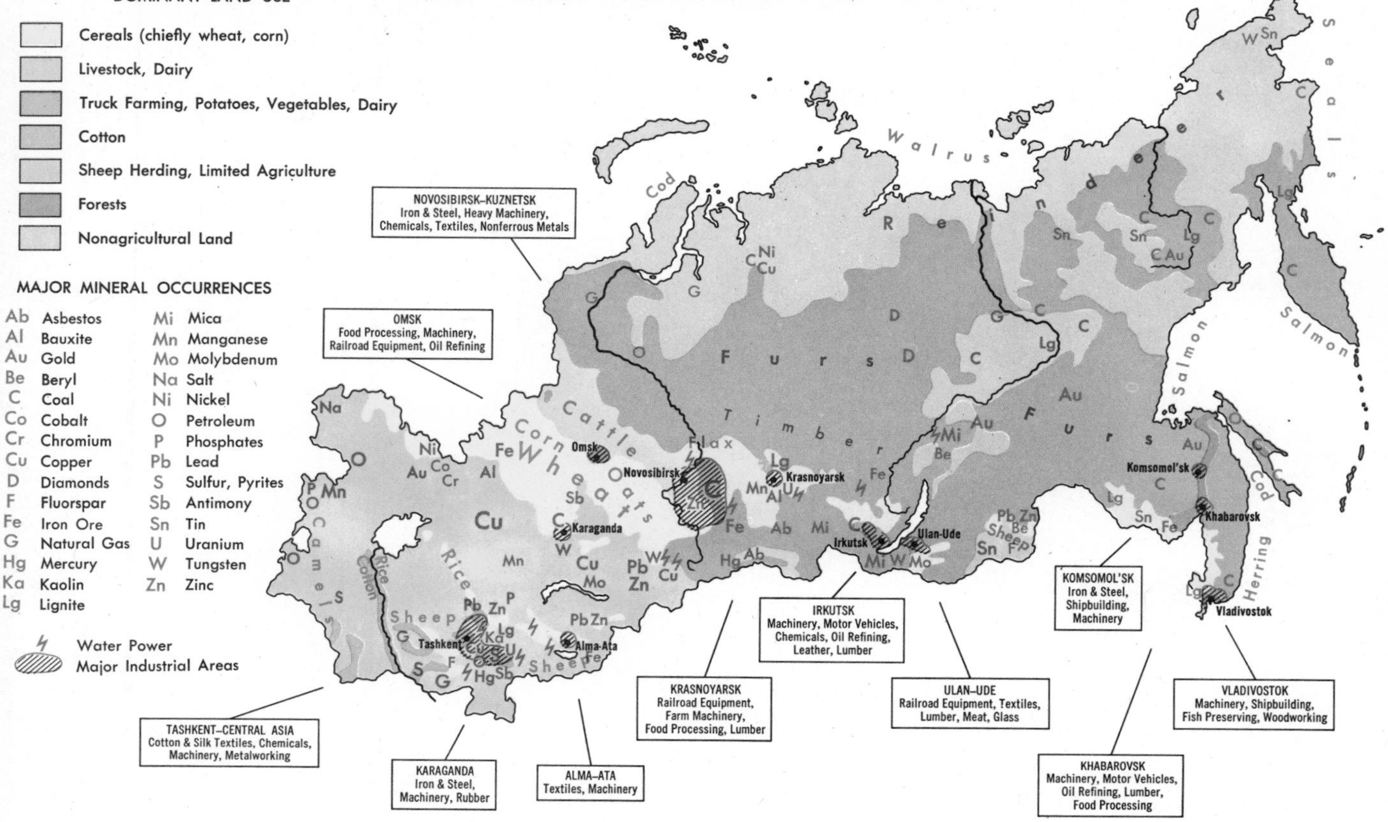
DOMINANT LAND USE
Cereals (chiefly wheat, corn)
Livestock, Dairy
Truck Farming, Potatoes, Vegetables, Dairy
Cotton
Sheep Herding, Limited Agriculture
Forests
Nonagricultural Land
MAJOR MINERAL OCCURRENCES
Ab Asbestos
Al Bauxite
Au Gold
Be Beryl
C Coal
Co Cobalt
Cr Chromium
Cu Copper
D Diamonds
F Fluorspar
Fe Iron Ore
G Natural Gas
Hg Mercury
Ka Kaolin
Lg Lignite
Mi Mica
Mn Manganese
Mo Molybdenum
Na Salt
Ni Nickel
O Petroleum
P Phosphates
Pb Lead
S Sulfur, Pyrites
Sb Antimony
Sn Tin
U Uranium
W Tungsten
Zn Zinc
Water Power
Major Industrial Areas
NOVOSIBIRSK–KUZNETSK
Iron & Steel, Heavy Machinery, Chemicals, Textiles, Nonferrous Metals
OMSK
Food Processing, Machinery, Railroad Equipment, Oil Refining
TASHKENT–CENTRAL ASIA
Cotton & Silk Textiles, Chemicals, Machinery, Metalworking
KARAGANDA
Iron & Steel, Machinery, Rubber
ALMA-ATA
Textiles, Machinery
KRASNOYARSK
Railroad Equipment, Farm Machinery, Food Processing, Lumber
IRKUTSK
Machinery, Motor Vehicles, Chemicals, Oil Refining, Leather, Lumber
ULAN-UDE
Railroad Equipment, Textiles, Lumber, Meat, Glass
KOMSOMOL'SK
Iron & Steel, Shipbuilding, Machinery
KHABAROVSK
Machinery, Motor Vehicles, Oil Refining, Lumber, Food Processing
VLADIVOSTOK
Machinery, Shipbuilding, Fish Preserving, Woodworking
Omsk
Novosibirsk
Karaganda
Tashkent
Alma-Ata
Krasnoyarsk
Irkutsk
Ulan-Ude
Komsomol'sk
Khabarovsk
Vladivostok
Walrus
Seals
Salmon
Cod
Herring
Reindeer
Furs
Timber
Flax
Cattle
Corn
Oats
Wheat
Rice
Cotton
Sheep
Camels

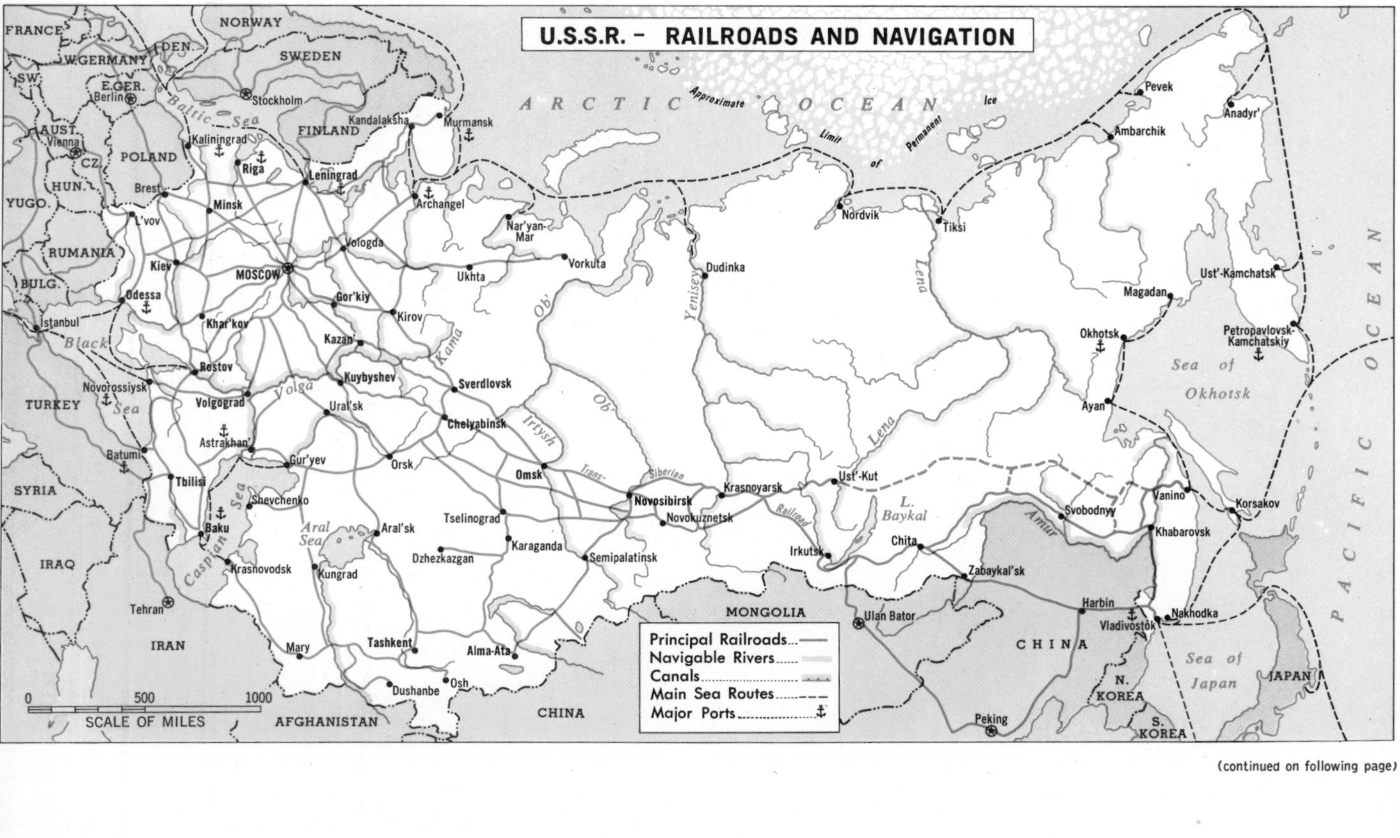
U.S.S.R. - RAILROADS AND NAVIGATION
ARCTIC OCEAN
Approximate Limit of Permanent Ice
PACIFIC OCEAN
Sea of Okhotsk
Sea of Japan
Baltic Sea
Black Sea
Caspian Sea
Aral Sea
L. Baykal
FRANCE
W.GERMANY
DEN.
NORWAY
SWEDEN
FINLAND
E.GER.
SW.
AUST.
CZ.
POLAND
HUN.
YUGO.
RUMANIA
BULG.
TURKEY
SYRIA
IRAQ
IRAN
AFGHANISTAN
MONGOLIA
CHINA
N. KOREA
S. KOREA
JAPAN
Berlin
Vienna
Stockholm
Kaliningrad
Riga
Leningrad
Murmansk
Kandalaksha
Archangel
Brest
Minsk
L'vov
Kiev
Odessa
Istanbul
Khar'kov
Rostov
Novorossiysk
Volgograd
Astrakhan'
Batumi
Tbilisi
Baku
Tehran
Shevchenko
Krasnovodsk
Kungrad
Mary
Tashkent
Dushanbe
Osh
Alma-Ata
Aral'sk
Dzhezkazgan
Karaganda
Tselinograd
Semipalatinsk
Gur'yev
Orsk
Ural'sk
Kuybyshev
Kazan'
Gor'kiy
Kirov
MOSCOW
Vologda
Ukhta
Nar'yan-Mar
Vorkuta
Sverdlovsk
Chelyabinsk
Omsk
Novosibirsk
Novokuznetsk
Krasnoyarsk
Irkutsk
Ust'-Kut
Chita
Zabaykal'sk
Ulan Bator
Harbin
Peking
Svobodnyy
Khabarovsk
Vanino
Vladivostok
Nakhodka
Korsakov
Ayan
Okhotsk
Magadan
Petropavlovsk-Kamchatskiy
Ust'-Kamchatsk
Anadyr'
Pevek
Ambarchik
Tiksi
Nordvik
Dudinka
Ob'
Irtysh
Volga
Kama
Yenisey
Lena
Amur
Trans-Siberian Railroad
Principal Railroads
Navigable Rivers
Canals
Main Sea Routes
Major Ports
0 500 1000
SCALE OF MILES

(continued on following page)

UNION OF SOVIET SOCIALIST REPUBLICS
European Part

CONIC PROJECTION

SCALE OF MILES
0 50 100   200   300

SCALE OF KILOMETRES
0 50 100 200   300

National Capitals	☆
Capitals of Union Republics	⊞
Administrative Centers	△
International boundaries	
Union Republic boundaries	
A.S.S.R., Oblast, Kray boundaries	
Autonomous Oblast boundaries	
National Okrug boundaries	
Canals	

The government of the United States has not recognized the
incorporation of Estonia, Latvia and Lithuania into the Soviet
Union, nor does it recognize as final the de facto western limit
of Polish administration in Germany (the Oder-Neisse line).

Administrative Divisions bear same
names as their respective Capitals
or Centers, except:

Abkhaz A.S.S.R.	Sukhumi	F6
Adygey Aut. Oblast	Maykop	F6
Adzhar A.S.S.R.	Batumi	F6
Bashkir A.S.S.R.	Ufa	J4
Chechen-Ingush A.S.S.R.	Groznyy	G6
Chuvash A.S.S.R.	Cheboksary	G3
Crimean A.S.S.R.	Simferopol'	D6
Dagestan A.S.S.R.	Makhachkala	G6
Kabardin-Balkar A.S.S.R.	Nal'chik	F6
Kalmuck A.S.S.R.	Elista	F5
Karachay-Cherkess Aut. Obl.	Cherkessk	F6
Karelian A.S.S.R.	Petrozavodsk	D2
Komi A.S.S.R.	Syktyvkar	H2
Komi-Permyak Nat'l Okrug	Kudymkar	H3
Mari A.S.S.R.	Yoshkar-Ola	G3
Mordvinian A.S.S.R.	Saransk	G4
Nagorno-Karabakh Aut. Obl.	Stepanakert	G7
Nenets Nat'l Okrug	Nar'yan-Mar	H1
North Ossetian A.S.S.R.	Ordzhonikidze	F6
South Ossetian Aut. Obl.	Tskhinvali	F6
Tatar A.S.S.R.	Kazan'	G3
Trans-Carpathian Oblast	Uzhgorod	B5
Udmurt A.S.S.R.	Izhevsk	H3
Volyn Oblast	Lutsk	C4

Copyright by C.S. HAMMOND & CO., N.Y.

U.S.S.R. - EUROPEAN

UNION REPUBLICS

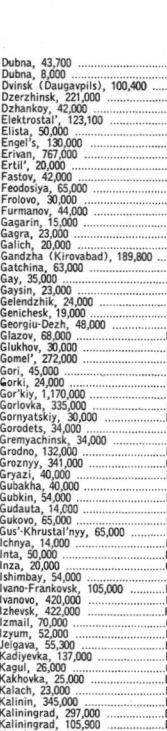

Armenian S.S.R., 2,491,900 ....F 6
Azerbaidzhan S.S.R., 5,117,100 ..G 6
Estonian S.S.R., 1,356,100 ....C 3
Georgian S.S.R., 4,686,000 ....F 6
Latvian S.S.R., 2,364,100 ....B 3
Lithuanian S.S.R., 3,128,000 .....B 3
Moldavian S.S.R., 3,568,900 ......C 5
Russian S.F.S.R., 130,079,210 ....F 3
Ukrainian S.S.R., 47,126,517 .....D 5
White Russian S.S.R., 9,002,338..C 4

INTERNAL DIVISIONS

Abkhaz A.S.S.R., 487,000 ....F 6
Adygey Aut. Oblast, 385,000 ......F 6
Adzhar A.S.S.R., 310,000 ....F 6
Bashkir A.S.S.R., 3,818,000 ... ...J 4
Chechen-Ingush A.S.S.R., 1,065,000 ....G 6
Chuvash A.S.S.R., 1,224,000 ......G 3
Crimean Oblast, 1,813,000 ....D 6
Dagestan A.S.S.R., 1,429,000 ....G 6
Kabardin-Balkar A.S.S.R., 588,000 ....F 6
Kalmuck A.S.S.R., 268,000 ....F 5
Karachay-Cherkess Aut. Oblast, 345,000 ....F 6
Karelian A.S.S.R., 713,000 ....D 2
Komi A.S.S.R., 965,000 ....H 2
Komi-Permyak Nat'l Okrug, 212,000 ....H 3
Mari A.S.S.R., 685,000 ....G 3
Mordvinian A.S.S.R., 1,029,000 ..G 4
Nagorno-Karabakh Aut. Oblast, 150,000 ....G 7
Nakhichevan' A.S.S.R., 202,000..F 7
Nenets Nat'l Okrug, 39,000 ....H 1
North Ossetian A.S.S.R., 552,000 F 6
South Ossetian Aut. Oblast, 99,000 ....F 6
Tatar A.S.S.R., 3,131,000 ....G 3
Trans-Carpathian Oblast, 1,057,000 ....B 5
Udmurt A.S.S.R., 1,418,000 ......H 3
Volyn Oblast, 974,000 ....C 4

CITIES and TOWNS

Abdulino, 27,000 ....H 4
Agdam, 21,300 ....G 6
Agryz, 21,000 ....H 3
Akhaltsikhe, 20,000 ....F 6
Akhtubinsk, 33,000 ....G 5
Akhtyrka, 42,000 ....E 4
Alagir, 18,000 ....F 6
Alatyr', 47,000 ....G 4
Aleksandriya, 69,000 ....D 5
Alekseyevka, 24,000 ....E 4
Aleksin, 61,000 ....E 4
Ali-Bayramly, 33,900 ....G 7
Al'met'yevsk, 87,000 ....H 3
Alushta, 21,000 ....D 6
Anapa, 25,000 ....E 6
Apatity, 40,000 ....D 1
Apsheronsk, 36,000 ....F 6
Archangel (Arkhangel'sk), 343,000 ....F 2
Armavir, 145,000 ....F 5
Arzamas, 67,000 ....F 3
Astrakhan', 410,000 ....G 5
Atkarsk, 30,000 ....G 4
Azov, 59,000 ....E 5
Bakhchisaray, 12,000 ....D 6
Bakhmach, 14,000 ....D 4
Baku, 852,000 ....H 6
Baku, *1,266,000 ....H 6
Balakhna, 36,000 ....F 3
Balaklava, 5,000 ....D 6
Balakovo, 103,000 ....G 4
Balashoy, 83,000 ....F 4
Baltiysk, 18,000 ....A 4
Baranovichi, 101,000 ....C 4
Barysh, 21,000 ....G 4
Bataysk, 85,000 ....E 5
Batumi, 101,000 ....F 6
Belaya Tserkov', 109,000 ....C 5
Belebey, 35,000 ....H 4
Belev, 18,000 ....E 4
Belgorod, 151,000 ....E 4
Belgorod-Dnestrovskiy, 30,000 ....D 5
Belomorsk, 18,000 ....D 2
Beloretsk, 67,000 ....J 4
Bel'tsy, 101,800 ....C 5
Bendery, 72,300 ....C 5
Berdichev, 71,000 ....C 5
Berdyansk, 100,000 ....E 5
Beregovo, 30,000 ....B 5
Berezniki, 146,000 ....J 3
Beslan, 28,000 ....F 6
Bezhetsk, 31,000 ....E 3
Birsk, 36,000 ....J 3
Blagoveshchensk, 15,000 ....J 4
Bobruysk, 138,000 ....C 4
Bologoye, 32,000 ....D 3
Bor, 55,000 ....F 3
Borislav, 36,000 ....B 5
Borisoglebsk, 64,000 ....F 4
Borisov, 84,000 ....C 4
Borovichi, 55,000 ....D 3
Borzhomi, 17,000 ....F 6
Brest, 122,000 ....B 4
Bryansk, 318,000 ....D 4
Bugul'ma, 72,000 ....H 4
Buguruslan, 49,000 ....H 4
Buy, 25,000 ....F 3
Buynaksk, 41,000 ....G 6
Buzuluk, 67,000 ....H 4
Bykhov, 16,000 ....C 4
Cēsis, 17,700 ....C 3
Chadyr-Lunga, 20,200 ....C 5
Chapayevsk, 86,000 ....G 4
Chaykovskiy, 48,000 ....H 3
Cheboksary, 216,000 ....G 3
Cherepovets, 188,000 ....E 3
Cherkassy, 158,000 ....D 5
Cherkessk, 67,000 ....F 6
Chernigov, 159,000 ....D 4
Chernovtsy, 187,000 ....C 5
Chervonograd, 41,000 ....B 4
Chiatura, 30,000 ....F 6
Chistopol', 60,000 ....H 3
Chkalov (Orenburg), 344,000 ......J 4
Chortkov, 21,000 ....B 5
Chusovoy, 58,000 ....J 3
Danilov, 17,000 ....E 3
Daugavpils, 100,400 ....C 3
Davlekanovo, 22,000 ....H 4
Derbent, 57,000 ....G 6
Dimitrovgrad, 81,000 ....G 4
Dneprodzerzhinsk, 227,000 ....D 5
Dnepropetrovsk, 862,000 ....D 5
Dobrush, 17,000 ....D 4
Donetsk, 879,000 ....E 5
Drogobych, 56,000 ....B 5
Dubna, 43,700 ....E 3
Dubna, 8,000 ....E 4
Dvinsk (Daugavpils), 100,400 .....C 3
Dzerzhinsk, 221,000 ....F 3
Dzhankoy, 42,000 ....D 5
Elektrostal', 123,100 ....E 3
Elista, 50,000 ....F 5
Engel's, 130,000 ....G 4
Erivan, 767,000 ....F 6
Ertil', 20,000 ....F 4
Fastov, 42,000 ....C 4
Feodosiya, 65,000 ....D 5
Frolovo, 30,000 ....F 5
Furmanov, 44,000 ....F 3
Gagarin, 15,000 ....D 3
Gagra, 23,000 ....E 6
Galich, 20,000 ....F 3
Gandzha (Kirovabad), 189,800 ...G 6
Gatchina, 63,000 ....D 3
Gay, 35,000 ....J 4
Gaysin, 23,000 ....C 5
Gelendzhik, 24,000 ....E 6
Genichesk, 19,000 ....E 5
Georgiu-Dezh, 48,000 ....E 4
Glazov, 68,000 ....H 3
Glukhov, 30,000 ....D 4
Gomel', 272,000 ....D 4
Gori, 45,000 ....F 6
Gorki, 24,000 ....D 4
Gor'kiy, 1,170,000 ....F 3
Gorlovka, 335,000 ....E 5
Gornyatskiy, 30,000 ....K 1
Gorodets, 34,000 ....F 3
Gremyachinsk, 34,000 ....J 3
Grodno, 132,000 ....B 4
Groznyy, 341,000 ....G 6
Gryazi, 40,000 ....F 4
Gubakha, 40,000 ....J 3
Gubkin, 54,000 ....E 4
Gudauta, 14,000 ....F 6
Gukovo, 65,000 ....F 5
Gus'-Khrustal'nyy, 65,000 ....F 3
Ichnya, 14,000 ....D 4
Inta, 50,000 ....K 1
Inza, 20,000 ....G 4
Ishimbay, 54,000 ....J 4
Ivano-Frankovsk, 105,000 ....B 5
Ivanovo, 420,000 ....E 3
Izhevsk, 422,000 ....H 3
Izmail, 70,000 ....C 5
Izyum, 52,000 ....E 5
Jelgava, 55,300 ....B 3
Kadiyevka, 137,000 ....E 5
Kagul, 26,000 ....C 5
Kakhovka, 25,000 ....D 5
Kalach, 23,000 ....F 5
Kalinin, 345,000 ....E 3
Kaliningrad, 297,000 ....B 4
Kaliningrad, 105,900 ....E 3
Kalinkovichi, 22,000 ....C 4
Kaluga, 211,000 ....E 4
Kamenets-Podol'skiy, 57,000 ......C 5
Kamenka, 30,000 ....F 4
Kamensk-Shakhtinskiy, 68,000 ....F 5
Kamyshin, 97,000 ....F 4
Kanash, 45,000 ....G 3
Kandalaksha, 42,000 ....D 1
Kapsukas, 28,700 ....B 4
Kashin, 19,000 ....E 3
Kasimov, 37,000 ....F 4
Kaspiysk, 39,000 ....G 6
Kaunas, 306,200 ....B 4
Kazan', 869,000 ....G 3
Kazatin, 28,000 ....C 5
Kem', 21,000 ....D 2
Kerch', 128,000 ....E 5
Khachmas, 22,300 ....G 6
Khar'kov, 1,223,000 ....E 5
Khasavyurt, 54,000 ....G 6
Kherson, 261,000 ....D 5
Khmel'nitskiy, 113,000 ....C 5
Khorol, 13,000 ....D 5
Khvalynsk, 19,000 ....G 4
Kiev, 1,632,000 ....D 4
Kiliya, 26,000 ....C 5
Kimovsk, 44,000 ....E 4
Kimry, 53,000 ....E 3
Kinel', 38,000 ....H 4
Kineshma, 96,000 ....F 3
Kirov, 30,000 ....D 4
Kirov, 333,000 ....G 3
Kirovabad, 189,800 ....G 6
Kirovakan, 107,000 ....G 6
Kirovo-Chepetsk, 51,000 ....H 3
Kirovograd, 189,000 ....D 5
Kirovsk, 48,000 ....D 1
Kirsanov, 24,000 ....F 4
Kishinev, 356,900 ....C 5
Kislovodsk, 90,000 ....F 6
Kizel, 49,000 ....J 3
Kizlyar, 30,000 ....G 6
Klaipėda, 139,900 ....B 3
Klimovichi, 13,000 ....D 4
Klintsy, 58,000 ....D 4
Kobrin, 25,000 ....B 4
Kobuleti, 18,000 ....F 6
Kohtla-Järve, 68,318 ....C 3
Kolomna, 135,900 ....E 4
Kolpino, 70,000 ....D 3
Kommunarsk, 123,000 ....E 5
Komrat, 21,400 ....C 5
Kondopoga, 25,000 ....D 2
Königsberg (Kaliningrad), 297,000 ....B 4
Konotop, 68,000 ....D 4
Konstantinovka, 105,000 ....E 5
Korosten', 56,000 ....C 4
Kostroma, 223,000 ....F 3
Kotel'nich, 30,000 ....G 3
Kotel'nikovo, 21,000 ....F 5
Kotlas, 56,000 ....G 2
Kotovo, 20,000 ....G 4
Kotovsk, 38,000 ....C 5
Kotovsk, 32,000 ....F 4
Kovel', 35,000 ....C 4
Kovrov, 123,000 ....F 3
Kramatorsk, 150,000 ....E 5
Krasnoarmeysk, 21,000 ....G 4
Krasnodar, 464,000 ....E 6
Krasnograd, 18,000 ....E 5
Krasnokamsk, 55,000 ....H 3
Krasnovishersk, 16,000 ....J 2
Krasnyy Kut, 17,000 ....G 4
Krasnyy Luch, 103,000 ....E 5
Kremenchug, 148,000 ....D 5
Krichev, 26,000 ....D 4
Krivoy Rog, 573,000 ....D 5
Krolevets, 18,000 ....D 4
Kropotkin, 68,000 ....F 5
Krymsk, 44,000 ....E 6
Kuba, 18,900 ....G 6
Kudymkar, 20,000 ....H 3
Kulebaki, 48,000 ....F 3
Kumertau, 42,000 ....J 4
Kungur, 74,000 ....J 3
Kupyansk, 28,000 ....E 5
Kursk, 284,000 ....E 4
Kutaisi, 161,000 ....F 6

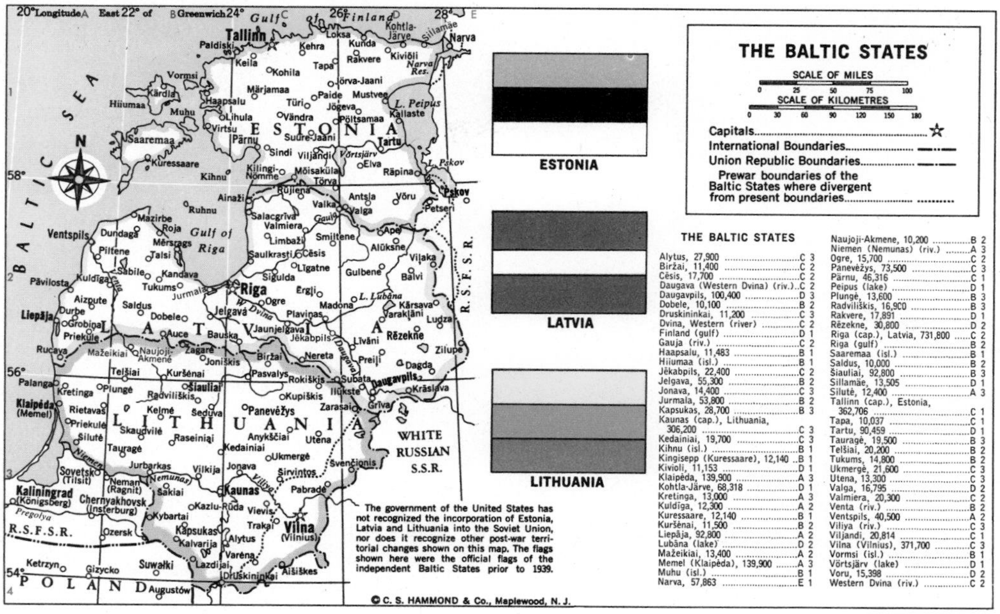

The government of the United States has not recognized the incorporation of Estonia, Latvia and Lithuania into the Soviet Union, nor does it recognize other post-war territorial changes shown on this map. The flags shown here were the official flags of the independent Baltic States prior to 1939.

© C. S. HAMMOND & Co., Maplewood, N. J.

THE BALTIC STATES

Alytus, 27,900 ....C 3
Biržai, 11,400 ....C 2
Cēsis, 17,700 ....C 2
Daugava (Western Dvina) (riv.)..C 2
Daugavpils, 100,400 ....D 3
Dobele, 10,100 ....B 2
Druskininkai, 11,200 ....C 3
Dvina, Western (river) ....C 2
Finland (gulf) ....D 1
Gauja (riv.) ....C 2
Haapsalu, 11,483 ....B 1
Hiiumaa (isl.) ....B 1
Jēkabpils, 22,400 ....C 2
Jelgava, 55,300 ....B 2
Jonava, 14,400 ....C 3
Jurmala, 53,800 ....B 2
Kapsukas, 28,700 ....B 3
Kaunas (cap.), Lithuania, 306,200 ....C 3
Kedainiai, 19,700 ....C 3
Kihnu (isl.) ....B 1
Kingisepp (Kuressaare), 12,140 ..B 1
Kivioli, 11,153 ....D 1
Klaipėda, 139,900 ....A 3
Kohtla-Järve, 68,318 ....D 1
Kretinga, 13,000 ....A 3
Kuldīga, 12,300 ....A 2
Kuressaare, 12,140 ....B 1
Kuršėnai, 11,500 ....B 2
Liepāja, 92,800 ....A 2
Lubāna (lake) ....D 2
Mažeikiai, 13,400 ....A 2
Memel (Klaipėda), 139,900 ....A 3
Muhu (isl.) ....B 1
Narva, 57,863 ....E 1
Naujoji-Akmene, 10,200 ....B 2
Niemen (Nemunas) (riv.) ....A 3
Ogre, 15,700 ....C 2
Panevėžys, 73,500 ....C 3
Pärnu, 46,316 ....C 1
Peipus (lake) ....D 1
Plungė, 13,600 ....B 3
Radviliškis, 16,900 ....B 3
Rakvere, 17,891 ....D 1
Rēzekne, 30,800 ....D 2
Riga (cap.), Latvia, 731,800 ......C 2
Riga (gulf) ....B 2
Saaremaa (isl.) ....B 1
Saldus, 10,000 ....B 2
Šiauliai, 92,800 ....B 3
Sillamäe, 13,505 ....D 1
Silutė, 12,400 ....A 3
Tallinn (cap.), Estonia, 362,706 ....C 1
Tapa, 10,037 ....C 1
Tartu, 90,459 ....D 1
Tauragė, 19,500 ....B 3
Telšiai, 20,200 ....B 2
Tukums, 14,800 ....B 2
Ukmergė, 21,600 ....C 3
Utena, 13,300 ....C 3
Valga, 16,795 ....D 2
Valmiera, 20,300 ....C 2
Venta (riv.) ....B 2
Ventspils, 40,500 ....A 2
Viliya (riv.) ....C 3
Viljandi, 20,814 ....C 1
Vilna (Vilnius), 371,700 ....C 3
Vormsi (isl.) ....B 1
Võrtsjärv (lake) ....D 1
Voru, 15,398 ....D 2
Western Dvina (riv.) ....C 2

Kuvandyk, 24,000 ....J 4
Kuybyshev, 1,045,000 ....H 4
Kuznetsk, 84,000 ....G 4
Labinsk, 50,000 ....F 6
Lebedin, 29,000 ....D 4
Leninakan, 165,000 ....F 6
Leningrad, 3,513,000 ....C 3
Leningrad, *3,950,000 ....C 3
Leninogorsk, 45,000 ....H 4
Lenkoran', 35,500 ....G 7
L'gov, 28,000 ....E 4
Lida, 48,000 ....C 4
Liepāja, 92,800 ....B 3
Lipetsk, 289,000 ....E 4
Lisichansk, 118,000 ....E 5
Livny, 37,000 ....E 4
Lodeynoye Pole, 20,000 ....D 2
Lozovaya, 34,000 ....E 5
Lubny, 39,000 ....D 4
Luga, 30,000 ....C 3
Lutsk, 94,000 ....B 4
L'vov (Lwów), 553,000 ....B 5
Lys'va, 73,000 ....J 3
Lyubertsy, 139,400 ....E 3
Lyubotin, 38,000 ....E 4
Lyudinovo, 33,000 ....D 4
Makeyevka, 392,000 ....E 5
Makhachkala, 186,000 ....G 6
Makharadze, 24,000 ....F 6
Manturovo, 21,000 ....F 3
Marganets, 47,000 ....E 5
Mariupol' (Zhdanov), 417,000 ....E 5
Marks, 18,000 ....G 4
Maykop, 110,000 ....F 6
Mednogorsk, 41,000 ....J 4
Medvezh'yegorsk, 18,000 ....D 2
Melenki, 19,000 ....F 3
Meleuz, 28,000 ....J 4
Melitopol', 137,000 ....D 5
Memel (Klaipėda), 139,900 ....B 3
Merefa, 32,000 ....E 5
Michurinsk, 94,000 ....F 4
Mikhaylovka, 50,000 ....F 4
Millerovo, 38,000 ....F 5
Mineralnye Vody, 55,000 ....F 6
Mingechaur, 43,100 ....G 6
Minsk, 907,000 ....C 4
Minsk, *917,000 ....C 4
Mirgorod, 28,000 ....D 5
Mogilev, 202,000 ....C 4
Mogilev-Podol'skiy, 27,000 ....C 5
Molodechno, 50,000 ....C 4
Molotov (Perm'), 850,000 ....J 3
Monchegorsk, 49,000 ....D 1
Morshansk, 45,000 ....F 4
Moscow (Moskva) (cap.), 6,942,000 ....E 3
Moscow, *7,061,000 ....E 3
Mozhaysk, 20,300 ....E 3
Mozhga, 34,000 ....H 3
Mozyr', 49,000 ....C 4
Mtsensk, 24,000 ....E 4
Mukachevo, 57,000 ....B 5
Murmansk, 309,000 ....D 1
Murom, 99,000 ....F 3
Mytishchi, 118,700 ....E 3
Naberezhnye Chelny, 38,000 ......H 3
Nakhichevan', 33,200 ....F 7
Nal'chik, 146,000 ....F 6
Narva, 57,863 ....C 3
Nar'yan-Mar, 15,000 ....H 1
Neftekamsk, 35,000 ....J 3
Nelidovo, 30,000 ....D 3
Nerekhta, 28,000 ....F 3
Nevinnomyssk, 85,000 ....F 6
Nezhin, 56,000 ....D 4
Nikel', 17,000 ....C 1
Nikolayev, 331,000 ....D 5
Nikopol', 125,000 ....D 5
Nizhnekamsk, 49,000 ....H 3
Nizhniy Lomov, 19,000 ....F 4
Nosovka, 23,000 ....D 4
Novaya Kakhovka, 40,000 ....D 5
Novgorod, 128,000 ....D 3
Novoanninskiy, 21,000 ....F 4
Novocherkassk, 162,000 ....F 5
Novograd-Volynskiy, 36,000 ....C 4
Novogrudok, 20,000 ....C 4
Novokuybyshevsk, 104,000 ....G 4
Novomoskovsk, 134,000 ....E 4
Novopolotsk, 40,000 ....C 3
Novorossiysk, 133,000 ....E 6
Novoshakhtinsk, 102,000 ....E 5
Novotroitsk, 83,000 ....J 4
Novoukrainka, 22,000 ....D 5
Novovolynsk, 40,000 ....B 4
Novozybkov, 33,000 ....D 4
Nyandoma, 24,000 ....F 2
Obninsk, 49,000 ....E 3
Ochamchire, 20,000 ....F 6
Odessa, 892,000 ....D 5
Oktyabr'sk, 36,000 ....G 4
Oktyabr'skiy, 77,000 ....H 4
Olenegorsk, 21,000 ....D 1
Omutninsk, 29,000 ....H 3
Onega, 27,000 ....E 2
Ordzhonikidze, 236,000 ....F 6
Orel, 232,000 ....E 4
Orenburg, 344,000 ....J 4
Orgeyev, 25,800 ....C 5
Orsha, 101,000 ....C 4
Orsk, 225,000 ....J 4
Osipenko (Berdyansk), 100,000....E 5
Osipovichi, 19,000 ....C 4
Ostashkov, 22,000 ....D 3
Ostrogozhsk, 35,000 ....E 4
Ostrov, 19,000 ....C 3
Otradnyy, 46,000 ....H 4
Panevėžys, 73,500 ....B 3
Pärnu, 46,316 ....C 3
Pavlovo, 63,000 ....F 3
Pechora, 41,000 ....J 1
Penza, 374,000 ....F 4
Perm', 850,000 ....J 3
Pervomaysk, 59,000 ....D 5
Pervomayskiy, 18,000 ....F 2
Petrovsk, 32,000 ....G 4
Petrozavodsk, 184,000 ....D 2
Pinsk, 62,000 ....C 4
Piryatin, 18,000 ....D 4
Pochep, 16,000 ....D 4
Podol'sk, 168,700 ....E 3
Polonnoye, 23,000 ....C 4
Polotsk, 64,000 ....C 3
Poltava, 220,000 ....D 5
Postavy, 13,000 ....C 3
Poti, 48,000 ....F 6
Povorino, 22,000 ....F 4
Prikumsk, 36,000 ....F 6
Priluki, 57,000 ....D 4
Primorsko-Akhtarsk, 30,000 ....E 5
Priyutovo, 20,000 ....H 4
Promyshlennyy, 22,000 ....K 1
Pskov, 127,000 ....C 3
Pugachev, 38,000 ....G 4
Pushkin, 79,000 ....C 3
Pyatigorsk, 93,000 ....F 6
Pyatikhatki, 20,000 ....D 5
Radomyshl', 12,000 ....C 4
Rakhov, 11,000 ....B 5
Rakvere, 17,891 ....C 3
Rasskazovo, 40,000 ....F 4
Rechitsa, 48,000 ....C 4
Revel (Tallinn), 362,706 ....B 3
Rēzekne, 30,800 ....C 3
Riga, 731,800 ....B 3
Rogachev, 12,000 ....D 4
Romny, 48,000 ....D 4
Roslavl', 48,000 ....D 4
Rossosh', 36,000 ....E 4
Rostov, 32,000 ....E 3
Rostov, 789,000 ....F 5
Rovno, 116,000 ....C 4
Rtishchevo, 40,000 ....F 4
Rubezhnoye, 58,000 ....E 5
Rustavi, 98,000 ....G 6
Ruzayevka, 38,000 ....F 4
Ryazan', 350,000 ....E 4
Rybinsk, 218,000 ....E 3
Rybnitsa, 32,400 ....C 5
Rzhev, 61,000 ....D 3
Safonovo, 44,000 ....D 3
Saki, 23,000 ....D 5
Salavat, 114,000 ....H 4
Sal'sk, 50,000 ....F 5
Sal'yany, 24,200 ....G 7
Samara (Kuybyshev), 1,045,000..H 4
Saransk, 191,000 ....G 4
Sarapul, 97,000 ....H 3
Saratov, 757,000 ....G 4
Sarny, 10,000 ....C 4
Sasovo, 28,000 ....F 4
Segezha, 30,000 ....D 2
Semenov, 25,000 ....F 3
Serdobel (Sortavala), 23,000 ....D 2
Serdobsk, 33,000 ....F 4
Serpukhov, 124,300 ....E 4
Sevastopol', 229,000 ....D 6
Severodonetsk, 90,000 ....E 5
Severodvinsk, 145,000 ....E 2
Severomorsk, 45,000 ....D 1
Shakhty, 205,000 ....F 5
Shakhun'ya, 22,000 ....G 3
Shar'ya, 25,000 ....G 3
Shchekino, 61,000 ....E 4
Shcherbakov (Rybinsk), 218,000..E 3
Sheki, 43,200 ....G 6
Shemakha, 17,900 ....G 6
Shepetovka, 39,000 ....C 4
Shostka, 64,000 ....D 4
Shumerlya, 33,000 ....G 3
Shuya, 69,000 ....F 3
Šiauliai, 92,800 ....B 3
Sibay, 42,000 ....J 4
Simferopol', 249,000 ....D 6
Skopin, 23,000 ....F 4
Slantsy, 40,000 ....C 3
Slavuta, 24,000 ....C 4
Slavyansk, 124,000 ....E 5
Slavyansk-na-Kubani, 52,000 ......E 5
Slobodskoy, 37,000 ....H 3
Slonim, 30,000 ....B 4
Slutsk, 36,000 ....C 4
Smela, 55,000 ....D 5
Smolensk, 211,000 ....D 4
Sochi, 224,000 ....E 6
Sokol, 49,000 ....F 3
Solikamsk, 89,000 ....J 3
Sol'-Iletsk, 25,000 ....J 4
Sorochinsk, 25,000 ....H 4
Soroki, 21,700 ....C 5
Sortavala, 23,000 ....D 2
Sosnogorsk, 25,000 ....H 2
Sovetsk, 38,000 ....B 4
Sovetsk, 19,000 ....G 3
Stalingrad (Volgograd), 818,000 ....F 5
Staraya Russa, 34,000 ....D 3
Staryy Oskol, 52,000 ....E 4
Stavropol', 198,000 ....F 5
Stepanakert, 30,300 ....G 7
Stepnoy (Elista), 50,000 ....G 5
Sterlitamak, 185,000 ....J 4
Stupino, 59,300 ....E 4
Sukhumi, 102,000 ....F 6
Sumgait, 124,400 ....G 6
Sumy, 159,000 ....E 4
Svetlogorsk, 40,000 ....C 4
Svetlograd, 30,000 ....F 5
Syktyvkar, 125,000 ....H 2
Syzran', 173,000 ....G 4
Taganrog, 254,000 ....E 5
Tallinn, 362,706 ....B 3
Tambov, 230,000 ....F 4
Tartu, 90,459 ....C 3
Tauragė, 19,500 ....B 3
Tbilisi, 889,000 ....F 6
Telavi, 23,000 ....G 6
Telšiai, 20,200 ....B 3
Temryuk, 28,000 ....E 5
Ternopol', 85,000 ....C 5
Teykovo, 34,000 ....E 3
Tiflis (Tbilisi), 889,000 ....F 6
Tighina (Bendery), 72,300 ....C 5
Tikhoretsk, 60,000 ....F 5
Tikhvin, 29,000 ....D 3
Timashevsk, 35,000 ....E 5
Tiraspol', 105,700 ....D 5
Togliatti, 251,000 ....G 4
Tokmak, 39,000 ....E 5
Torzhok, 47,000 ....D 3
Tskhinvali, 30,000 ....F 6
Tuapse, 51,000 ....E 6
Tula, 462,000 ....E 4
Tul'chin, 14,000 ....C 5
Tuymazy, 35,000 ....H 4
Tyrnyauz, 19,000 ....F 6
Uchaly, 18,000 ....J 4
Ufa, 771,000 ....J 4
Uglich, 36,000 ....E 3
Ukhta, 63,000 ....H 2
Ukmergė, 21,600 ....C 3
Ul'yanovsk, 351,000 ....G 4
Uman', 63,000 ....D 5
Uryupinsk, 37,000 ....F 4
Usman', 19,000 ....E 4
Uzhgorod, 65,000 ....B 5
Uzlovaya, 62,000 ....E 4
Valga, 16,795 ....C 3
Valmiera, 20,300 ....C 3
Valuyki, 29,000 ....E 4
Vasil'kov, 27,000 ....D 4
Velikiye Luki, 85,000 ....D 3
Velikiy Ustyug, 35,000 ....F 2
Vel'sk, 20,000 ....F 2
Ventspils, 40,500 ....B 3
Vichuga, 53,000 ....F 3
Viipuri (Vyborg), 65,000 ....C 2
Vilna (Vilnius), 371,700 ....C 4
Vinnitsa, 212,000 ....C 5
Vitebsk, 231,000 ....C 3
Vladimir, 234,000 ....F 3
Volgodonsk, 25,000 ....F 5
Volgograd, 818,000 ....F 5
Volkhov, 46,000 ....D 3
Volkovysk, 22,000 ....B 4
Vologda, 178,000 ....F 3
Vol'sk, 69,000 ....G 4
Volzhsk, 44,000 ....G 3
Volzhskiy, 142,000 ....G 5
Vorkuta, 90,000 ....K 1
Voronezh, 660,000 ....E 4
Voroshilovgrad, 383,000 ....F 5
Voskresensk, 66,900 ....E 3
Votkinsk, 74,000 ....H 3
Voznesensk, 36,000 ....D 5
Vyatskiye Polyany, 33,000 ....H 3
Vyaz'ma, 42,000 ....D 3
Vyborg, 65,000 ....C 2
Vyksa, 46,000 ....F 3
Vyshniy Volochek, 74,000 ....D 3
Yalta, 62,000 ....D 6
Yanaul, 18,000 ....J 3
Yaroslavl', 517,000 ....E 3
Yartsevo, 37,000 ....D 3
Yefremov, 47,000 ....E 4
Yelabuga, 36,000 ....H 3
Yelets, 101,000 ....E 4
Yenakiyevo, 92,000 ....E 5
Yershov, 20,000 ....G 4
Yessentuki, 65,000 ....F 6
Yevpatoria, 79,000 ....D 5
Yeysk, 64,000 ....E 5
Yoshkar-Ola, 166,000 ....G 3
Yur'yevets, 23,000 ....F 3
Zagorsk, 92,400 ....E 3
Zaporozh'ye, 658,000 ....E 5
Zelenodol'sk, 77,000 ....G 3
Zhdanov, 417,000 ....E 5
Zherdevka, 20,000 ....F 4
Zhigulevsk, 52,000 ....G 4
Zhitomir, 161,000 ....C 4
Zhlobin, 25,000 ....D 4
Zhmerinka, 34,000 ....C 5
Zhodino, 17,000 ....C 4
Znamenka, 30,000 ....D 5
Zolotonosha, 27,000 ....D 5
Zugdidi, 39,000 ....F 6
Zvenigorodka, 21,000 ....D 5

OTHER FEATURES

Apsheron (pen.) ....H 6
Araks (river) ....G 7
Azov (sea) ....E 5
Baltic (sea) ....B 3
Barents (sea) ....E 1
Belaya (river) ....H 3
Beloye (lake) ....E 2
Berezina (river) ....C 4
Black (sea) ....D 6
Bug (river) ....B 4
Bug (river) ....D 5
Caspian (sea) ....G 6
Caucasus (mts.) ....F 6
Central Ural (mts.) ....J 2
Chir (river) ....F 5
Crimea (pen.), 1,813,000 ....D 5
Dagö (Hiiumaa) (isl.) ....B 3
Denezhkin Kamen' (mt.) ....K 2
Desna (river) ....D 4
Dnieper (river) ....D 5
Dniester (river) ....C 5
Don (river) ....F 5
Donets (river) ....E 5
Dvina (bay) ....E 2
Dvina, Northern (river) ....F 2
Dvina, Western (river) ....C 3
Dykh-Tau (mt.) ....F 6
El'brus (mt.) ....F 6
Finland (gulf) ....C 3
Goryn' (river) ....C 4
Hiiumaa (isl.) ....B 3
Ilek (river) ....J 4
Il'men (lake) ....D 3
Izhma (river) ....H 2
Kakhovka (res.) ....D 5
Kama (river) ....H 3
Kandalaksha (gulf) ....D 1
Kanin (pen.) ....G 1
Kapydzhik (mt.) ....G 7
Kara (sea) ....K 1
Kazbek (mt.) ....F 6
Khoper (river) ....F 4
Kil'din (isl.) ....D 1
Kinel' (river) ....H 4
Kola (pen.) ....E 1
Kolguyev (isl.) ....G 1
Kolva (river) ....J 1
Kuban' (river) ....E 5
Kubeno (lake) ....E 3
Kura (river) ....G 6
Kuyto (lake) ....D 2
Ladoga (lake) ....D 2
Lapland (reg.) ....C 1
Lovat' (river) ....D 3
Mansel'ka (mts.) ....C 1
Manych-Gudilo (lake) ....F 5
Matveyev (isl.) ....J 1
Medveditsa (river) ....F 4
Mezen' (river) ....G 1
Mezhdusharskiy (isl.) ....G 1
Moksha (river) ....F 4
Moskva (river) ....E 3
Msta (river) ....D 3
Niemen (river) ....B 4
North Ural (mts.) ....K 1
Northern Dvina (river) ....F 2
Novaya Zemlya (isls.) ....H 1
Oka (river) ....F 4
Onega (bay) ....E 2
Onega (lake) ....E 2
Ösel (Saaremaa) (isl.) ....B 3
Pay-Yer (mt.) ....K 1
Pechora (river) ....H 1
Pechora (sea) ....H 1
Peipus (lake) ....C 3
Pinega (river) ....G 2
Ponoy (river) ....E 1
Pripet (marsh) ....C 4
Pripyat' (river) ....C 4
Prut (river) ....C 5
Psel (river) ....D 4
Riga (gulf) ....B 3
Russkiy Zavorot (cape) ....H 1
Rybachiy (pen.) ....D 1
Saaremaa (isl.) ....B 3
Samara (river) ....H 4
Seg (lake) ....D 2
Sevan (lake) ....G 6
Seym (river) ....D 4
Solovetskiye (isls.) ....E 1
South Ural (mts.) ....J 4
Suda (river) ....E 3
Sukhona (river) ....F 2
Sura (river) ....G 4
Svir' (river) ....D 2
Sysola (river) ....H 2
Tel'pos-Iz (mt.) ....K 2
Timan Ridge (mts.) ....H 1
Top (lake) ....D 1
Tuloma (river) ....D 1
Ufa (river) ....J 3
Undzha (river) ....F 3
Ural (mts.) ....J 2
Ural (river) ....J 4
Usa (river) ....K 1
Vaga (river) ....F 2
Valday (hills) ....D 3
Vaygach (isl.) ....K 1
Velikaya (river) ....C 3
Vetluga (river) ....G 3
Vodl (lake) ....E 2
Volga (river) ....G 5
Volga-Don (canal) ....F 5
Volkhov (river) ....D 3
Vorona (river) ....F 4
Vorskla (river) ....E 4
Vozhe (lake) ....F 2
Vyatka (river) ....H 3
Vychegda (river) ....G 2
Vyg (lake) ....E 2
Vym' (river) ....H 2
Western Dvina (river) ....C 3
White (sea) ....E 1
Yamantau (mt.) ....J 4
Yug (river) ....G 2
Yugorskiy (pen.) ....K 1

*City and suburbs.

ALGERIA
AREA 919,591 sq. mi.
POPULATION 16,776,000
CAPITAL Algiers
LARGEST CITY Algiers
HIGHEST POINT Tahat 9,850 ft.
MONETARY UNIT Algerian dinar
MAJOR LANGUAGES Arabic, Berber, French
MAJOR RELIGION Islam

ANGOLA
AREA 481,351 sq. mi.
POPULATION 6,761,000
CAPITAL Luanda
LARGEST CITY Luanda
HIGHEST POINT Mt. Moco 8,593 ft.
MONETARY UNIT kwanza
MAJOR LANGUAGES Mbundu, Kongo, Lunda, Portuguese
MAJOR RELIGIONS Tribal religions, Roman Catholicism

BENIN
AREA 43,483 sq. mi.
POPULATION 3,200,000
CAPITAL Porto-Novo
LARGEST CITY Cotonou
HIGHEST POINT Atakora Mts. 2,083 ft.
MONETARY UNIT CFA franc
MAJOR LANGUAGES Fon, Somba, Yoruba, Bariba, French, Mina, Dendi
MAJOR RELIGIONS Tribal religions, Islam, Roman Catholicism

BOTSWANA
AREA 224,764 sq. mi.
POPULATION 700,000
CAPITAL Gaborone
LARGEST CITIES Selebi-Pikwe
HIGHEST POINT Tsodilo Hill 5,922 ft.
MONETARY UNIT pula
MAJOR LANGUAGES Setswana, Shona, Bushman, English, Afrikaans
MAJOR RELIGIONS Tribal religions, Protestantism

BURUNDI
AREA 10,747 sq. mi.
POPULATION 4,100,000
CAPITAL Bujumbura
LARGEST CITY Bujumbura
HIGHEST POINT 8,858 ft.
MONETARY UNIT Burundi franc
MAJOR LANGUAGES Kirundi, French, Swahili
MAJOR RELIGIONS Tribal religions, Roman Catholicism, Islam

CAMEROON
AREA 183,568 sq. mi.
POPULATION 6,600,000
CAPITAL Yaoundé
LARGEST CITY Douala
HIGHEST POINT Cameroon 13,350 ft.
MONETARY UNIT CFA franc
MAJOR LANGUAGES Fang, Bamileke, Fulani, Duala, French, English
MAJOR RELIGIONS Tribal religions, Christianity, Islam

CAPE VERDE
AREA 1,557 sq. mi.
POPULATION 302,000
CAPITAL Praia
LARGEST CITY Praia
HIGHEST POINT 9,281 ft.
MONETARY UNIT Cape Verde escudo
MAJOR LANGUAGE Portuguese
MAJOR RELIGION Roman Catholicism

CENTRAL AFRICAN EMPIRE
AREA 236,293 sq. mi.
POPULATION 1,800,000
CAPITAL Bangui
LARGEST CITY Bangui
HIGHEST POINT Gao 4,659 ft.
MONETARY UNIT CFA franc
MAJOR LANGUAGES Banda, Gbaya, Sangho, French
MAJOR RELIGIONS Tribal religions, Christianity, Islam

CHAD
AREA 495,752 sq. mi.
POPULATION 4,178,000
CAPITAL N'Djamena
LARGEST CITY N'Djamena
HIGHEST POINT Emi Koussi 11,204 ft.
MONETARY UNIT CFA franc
MAJOR LANGUAGES Arabic, Bagirmi, French, Sara, Massa, Moudang
MAJOR RELIGIONS Islam, Tribal religions

COMOROS
AREA 719 sq. mi.
POPULATION 266,000
CAPITAL Moroni
LARGEST CITY Moroni
HIGHEST POINT Karthala 8,399 ft.
MONETARY UNIT CFA franc
MAJOR LANGUAGES Arabic, French, Swahili
MAJOR RELIGION Islam

CONGO
AREA 132,046 sq. mi.
POPULATION 1,400,000
CAPITAL Brazzaville
LARGEST CITY Brazzaville
HIGHEST POINT Leketi Mts. 3,412 ft.
MONETARY UNIT CFA franc
MAJOR LANGUAGES Kikongo, Bateke, Lingala, French
MAJOR RELIGIONS Christianity, Tribal religions, Islam

DJIBOUTI
AREA 8,880 sq. mi.
POPULATION 250,000
CAPITAL Djibouti
LARGEST CITY Djibouti
HIGHEST POINT Moussa Ali 6,768 ft.
MONETARY UNIT Djibouti franc
MAJOR LANGUAGES Arabic, Somali, Afar, French
MAJOR RELIGIONS Islam, Roman Catholicism

EGYPT
AREA 386,659 sq. mi.
POPULATION 37,900,000
CAPITAL Cairo
LARGEST CITY Cairo
HIGHEST POINT Jeb. Katherina 8,651 ft.
MONETARY UNIT Egyptian pound
MAJOR LANGUAGE Arabic
MAJOR RELIGIONS Islam, Coptic Christianity

EQUATORIAL GUINEA
AREA 10,831 sq. mi.
POPULATION 320,000
CAPITAL Malabo
LARGEST CITY Malabo
HIGHEST POINT 9,868 ft.
MONETARY UNIT ekuele
MAJOR LANGUAGES Fang, Bubi, Spanish, English, Ibo
MAJOR RELIGIONS Tribal religions, Christianity

ETHIOPIA
AREA 471,776 sq. mi.
POPULATION 27,946,000
CAPITAL Addis Ababa
LARGEST CITY Addis Ababa
HIGHEST POINT Ras Dashan 15,157 ft.
MONETARY UNIT Ethiopian dollar
MAJOR LANGUAGES Amharic, Gallinya, Tigrinya, Somali, Sidamo, Arabic, Ge'ez, Italian
MAJOR RELIGIONS Coptic Christianity, Islam

GABON
AREA 103,346 sq. mi.
POPULATION 526,000
CAPITAL Libreville
LARGEST CITY Libreville
HIGHEST POINT Ibounzi 5,165 ft.
MONETARY UNIT CFA franc
MAJOR LANGUAGES Fang and other Bantu languages, French
MAJOR RELIGIONS Tribal religions, Christianity, Islam

GAMBIA
AREA 4,127 sq. mi.
POPULATION 524,000
CAPITAL Bathurst
LARGEST CITY Bathurst
HIGHEST POINT 100 ft.
MONETARY UNIT dalasi
MAJOR LANGUAGES Mandingo, Fulani, Wolof, English, Malinke
MAJOR RELIGIONS Islam, Tribal religions, Christianity

GHANA
AREA 92,099 sq. mi.
POPULATION 9,900,000
CAPITAL Accra
LARGEST CITY Accra
HIGHEST POINT Togo Hills 2,900 ft.
MONETARY UNIT new cedi
MAJOR LANGUAGES Twi, Fante, Dagbani, Ewe, Ga, English, Hausa, Akan
MAJOR RELIGIONS Tribal religions, Christianity, Islam

GUINEA
AREA 94,925 sq. mi.
POPULATION 4,500,000
CAPITAL Conakry
LARGEST CITY Conakry
HIGHEST POINT Nimba Mts. 6,070 ft.
MONETARY UNIT syli
MAJOR LANGUAGES Fulani, Mandingo, Susu, French
MAJOR RELIGIONS Islam, Tribal religions

GUINEA-BISSAU
AREA 13,948 sq. mi.
POPULATION 517,000
CAPITAL Bissau
LARGEST CITY Bissau
HIGHEST POINT 689 ft.
MONETARY UNIT Guinea-Bissau peso
MAJOR LANGUAGES Balante, Fulani, Crioulo, Mandingo, Portuguese
MAJOR RELIGIONS Islam, Tribal religions, Roman Catholicism

IVORY COAST
AREA 127,520 sq. mi.
POPULATION 6,673,013
CAPITAL Abidjan
LARGEST CITY Abidjan
HIGHEST POINT Nimba Mts. 5,745 ft.
MONETARY UNIT CFA franc
MAJOR LANGUAGES Bale, Bete, Senufu, French, Dioula
MAJOR RELIGIONS Tribal religions, Islam

KENYA
AREA 224,960 sq. mi.
POPULATION 13,300,000
CAPITAL Nairobi
LARGEST CITY Nairobi
HIGHEST POINT Kenya 17,058 ft.
MONETARY UNIT Kenya shilling
MAJOR LANGUAGES Kikuyu, Luo, Kavirondo, Kamba, Swahili, English
MAJOR RELIGIONS Tribal religions, Christianity, Hinduism, Islam

LESOTHO
AREA 11,720 sq. mi.
POPULATION 1,100,000
CAPITAL Maseru
LARGEST CITY Maseru
HIGHEST POINT 11,425 ft.
MONETARY UNIT South African rand
MAJOR LANGUAGES Sesotho, English
MAJOR RELIGIONS Tribal religions, Christianity

LIBERIA
AREA 43,000 sq. mi.
POPULATION 1,600,000
CAPITAL Monrovia
LARGEST CITY Monrovia
HIGHEST POINT Wutivi 5,584 ft.
MONETARY UNIT Liberian dollar
MAJOR LANGUAGES Kru, Kpelle, Bassa, Vai, English
MAJOR RELIGIONS Christianity, Tribal religions, Islam

LIBYA
AREA 679,358 sq. mi.
POPULATION 2,500,000
CAPITAL Tripoli
LARGEST CITY Tripoli
HIGHEST POINT Bette Pk. 7,500 ft.
MONETARY UNIT Libyan dinar
MAJOR LANGUAGES Arabic, Berber, Italian
MAJOR RELIGION Islam

MADAGASCAR
AREA 226,657 sq. mi.
POPULATION 7,700,000
CAPITAL Antananarivo
LARGEST CITY Antananarivo
HIGHEST POINT Maromokotro 9,436 ft.
MONETARY UNIT Malagasy franc
MAJOR LANGUAGES Malagasy, French
MAJOR RELIGIONS Tribal religions, Roman Catholicism, Protestantism

MALAWI
AREA 45,747 sq. mi.
POPULATION 5,100,000
CAPITAL Lilongwe
LARGEST CITY Blantyre
HIGHEST POINT Mlanje 9,843 ft.
MONETARY UNIT Malawi kwacha
MAJOR LANGUAGES Chichewa, Yao, English, Nyanja, Tumbuka, Tonga, Ngoni
MAJOR RELIGIONS Tribal religions, Islam, Christianity

MALI
AREA 464,873 sq. mi.
POPULATION 5,800,000
CAPITAL Bamako
LARGEST CITY Bamako
HIGHEST POINT Hombori Mts. 3,789 ft.
MONETARY UNIT Mali franc
MAJOR LANGUAGES Bambara, Senufu, Fulani, Soninke, French
MAJOR RELIGIONS Islam, Tribal religions

MAURITANIA
AREA 452,702 sq. mi.
POPULATION 1,318,000
CAPITAL Nouakchott
LARGEST CITY Nouakchott
HIGHEST POINT 2,972 ft.
MONETARY UNIT ouguiya
MAJOR LANGUAGES Arabic, French,
Wolof, Tukolor
MAJOR RELIGION Islam

MAURITIUS
AREA 790 sq. mi.
POPULATION 899,000
CAPITAL Port Louis
LARGEST CITY Port Louis
HIGHEST POINT 2,711 ft.
MONETARY UNIT Mauritian rupee
MAJOR LANGUAGES English, French,
French Creole, Hindi, Urdu
MAJOR RELIGIONS Hinduism,
Christianity, Islam

AFRICA
AREA 11,682,000 sq. mi.
POPULATION 345,000,000
LARGEST CITY Cairo
HIGHEST POINT Kilimanjaro 19,304 ft.
LOWEST POINT Qattara Depression -436 ft.

MOROCCO
AREA 241,224 sq. mi.
POPULATION 18,000,000
CAPITAL Rabat
LARGEST CITY Casablanca
HIGHEST POINT Jeb. Toubkal 13,665 ft.
MONETARY UNIT dirham
MAJOR LANGUAGES Arabic, Berber, French
MAJOR RELIGIONS Islam, Judaism,
Christianity

MOZAMBIQUE
AREA 308,641 sq. mi.
POPULATION 9,300,000
CAPITAL Maputo
LARGEST CITY Maputo
HIGHEST POINT Mt. Binga 7,992 ft.
MONETARY UNIT Mozambique escudo
MAJOR LANGUAGES Makua, Thonga,
Shona, Portuguese
MAJOR RELIGIONS Tribal religions,
Roman Catholicism, Islam

NIGER
AREA 489,189 sq. mi.
POPULATION 4,700,000
CAPITAL Niamey
LARGEST CITY Niamey
HIGHEST POINT Banguezane 6,234 ft.
MONETARY UNIT CFA franc
MAJOR LANGUAGES Hausa, Songhai, Fulani,
French, Tamashek, Djerma
MAJOR RELIGIONS Islam, Tribal religions

NIGERIA
AREA 379,628 sq.mi.
POPULATION 83,800,000
CAPITAL Lagos
LARGEST CITY Lagos
HIGHEST POINT Vogel 6,700 ft.
MONETARY UNIT naira
MAJOR LANGUAGES Hausa, Yoruba, Ibo, Ijaw,
Fulani, Tiv, Kanuri, Ibibio, English, Edo
MAJOR RELIGIONS Islam, Christianity,
Tribal religions

RHODESIA (ZIMBABWE)
AREA 150,803 sq. mi.
POPULATION 6,600,000
CAPITAL Salisbury
LARGEST CITY Salisbury
HIGHEST POINT Mt. Inyangani 8,517 ft.
MONETARY UNIT Rhodesian dollar
MAJOR LANGUAGES English, Shona,
Ndebele
MAJOR RELIGIONS Tribal religions,
Protestantism

RWANDA
AREA 10,169 sq. mi.
POPULATION 4,241,000
CAPITAL Kigali
LARGEST CITY Kigali
HIGHEST POINT Karisimbi 14,780 ft.
MONETARY UNIT Rwanda franc
MAJOR LANGUAGES Kinyarwanda, French,
Swahili
MAJOR RELIGIONS Tribal religions, Roman
Catholicism, Islam

SÃO TOMÉ E PRÍNCIPE
AREA 372 sq. mi.
POPULATION 80,000
CAPITAL São Tomé
LARGEST CITY São Tomé
HIGHEST POINT Pico 6,640 ft.
MONETARY UNIT São Tomean escudo
MAJOR LANGUAGES Bantu
languages, Portuguese
MAJOR RELIGIONS Tribal
religions, Roman Catholicism

SENEGAL
AREA 75,954 sq. mi.
POPULATION 5,085,388
CAPITAL Dakar
LARGEST CITY Dakar
HIGHEST POINT Futa Jallon 1,640 ft.
MONETARY UNIT CFA franc
MAJOR LANGUAGES Wolof, Peul (Fulani),
French, Mende, Mandingo, Dida
MAJOR RELIGIONS Islam, Tribal religions,
Roman Catholicism

SEYCHELLES
AREA 145 sq. mi.
POPULATION 60,000
CAPITAL Victoria
LARGEST CITY Victoria
HIGHEST POINT Morne Seychellois 2,970 ft.
MONETARY UNIT Seychellois rupee
MAJOR LANGUAGES English, French, Creole
MAJOR RELIGION Roman Catholicism

SIERRA LEONE
AREA 27,925 sq. mi.
POPULATION 3,100,000
CAPITAL Freetown
LARGEST CITY Freetown
HIGHEST POINT Loma Mts. 6,390 ft.
MONETARY UNIT leone
MAJOR LANGUAGES Mende, Temne,
Vai, English, Krio (pidgin)
MAJOR RELIGIONS Tribal religions,
Islam, Christianity

SOMALIA
AREA 246,200 sq. mi.
POPULATION 3,170,000
CAPITAL Mogadishu
LARGEST CITY Mogadishu
HIGHEST POINT Surud Ad 7,900 ft.
MONETARY UNIT Somali shilling
MAJOR LANGUAGES Somali, Arabic,
Italian, English
MAJOR RELIGIONS Islam

SOUTH AFRICA
AREA 458,179 sq. mi.
POPULATION 24,400,000
CAPITALS Cape Town, Pretoria
LARGEST CITY Johannesburg
HIGHEST POINT Injasuti 11,182 ft.
MONETARY UNIT rand
MAJOR LANGUAGES Afrikaans,
English, Xhosa, Zulu, Sesotho
MAJOR RELIGIONS Protestantism,
Roman Catholicism, Islam, Hinduism

SOUTH-WEST AFRICA (NAMIBIA)
AREA 317,827 sq. mi.
POPULATION 883,000
CAPITAL Windhoek
LARGEST CITY Windhoek
HIGHEST POINT Brandberg 8,550 ft.
MONETARY UNIT S. African rand
MAJOR LANGUAGES Ovambo,
Hottentot, Herero, Afrikaans, English
MAJOR RELIGIONS Tribal religions,
Protestantism

SUDAN
AREA 967,494 sq. mi.
POPULATION 18,347,000
CAPITAL Khartoum
LARGEST CITY Khartoum
HIGHEST POINT Jeb. Marra 10,073 ft.
MONETARY UNIT Sudanese pound
MAJOR LANGUAGES Arabic, Dinka, Nubian,
Beja, Nuer, English
MAJOR RELIGIONS Islam, Tribal religions

SWAZILAND
AREA 6,705 sq. mi.
POPULATION 500,000
CAPITAL Mbabane
LARGEST CITY Mbabane
HIGHEST POINT Emlembe 6,109 ft.
MONETARY UNIT lilangeni
MAJOR LANGUAGES siSwati, English
MAJOR RELIGIONS Tribal religions,
Christianity

TANZANIA
AREA 363,708 sq. mi.
POPULATION 15,506,000
CAPITAL Dar es Salaam
LARGEST CITY Dar es Salaam
HIGHEST POINT Kilimanjaro 19,340 ft.
MONETARY UNIT Tanzanian shilling
MAJOR LANGUAGES Nyamwezi-Sukuma,
Swahili, English
MAJOR RELIGIONS Tribal religions,
Christianity, Islam

TOGO
AREA 21,622 sq. mi.
POPULATION 2,300,000
CAPITAL Lomé
LARGEST CITY Lomé
HIGHEST POINT Agou 3,445 ft.
MONETARY UNIT CFA franc
MAJOR LANGUAGES Ewe, French, Twi, Hausa
MAJOR RELIGIONS Tribal religions, Roman
Catholicism, Islam

TUNISIA
AREA 63,170 sq. mi.
POPULATION 5,776,000
CAPITAL Tunis
LARGEST CITY Tunis
HIGHEST POINT Jeb. Chambi 5,066 ft.
MONETARY UNIT Tunisian dinar
MAJOR LANGUAGES Arabic, French
MAJOR RELIGION Islam

UGANDA
AREA 91,076 sq. mi.
POPULATION 11,400,000
CAPITAL Kampala
LARGEST CITY Kampala
HIGHEST POINT Margherita 16,795 ft.
MONETARY UNIT Ugandan shilling
MAJOR LANGUAGES Luganda, Acholi, Teso,
Nyoro, Soga, Nkole, English, Swahili
MAJOR RELIGIONS Tribal religions, Christianity,
Islam

UPPER VOLTA
AREA 105,869 sq. mi.
POPULATION 6,144,013
CAPITAL Ouagadougou
LARGEST CITY Ouagadougou
HIGHEST POINT 2,352 ft.
MONETARY UNIT CFA franc
MAJOR LANGUAGES Mossi, Lobi, French,
Samo, Gourounsi
MAJOR RELIGIONS Islam, Tribal religions,
Roman Catholicism

ZAIRE
AREA 918,962 sq. mi.
POPULATION 25,600,000
CAPITAL Kinshasa
LARGEST CITY Kinshasa
HIGHEST POINT Margherita 16,795 ft.
MONETARY UNIT zaire
MAJOR LANGUAGES Tshiluba, Mongo, Kikongo,
Kingwana, Zande, Lingala, Swahili, French
MAJOR RELIGIONS Tribal religions, Christianity

ZAMBIA
AREA 290,586 sq. mi.
POPULATION 4,936,000
CAPITAL Lusaka
LARGEST CITY Lusaka
HIGHEST POINT Sunzu 6,782 ft.
MONETARY UNIT Zambian kwacha
MAJOR LANGUAGES Bemba, Tonga,
Lozi, Luvale, Nyanja, English, Afrikaans
MAJOR RELIGIONS Tribal religions

MAYOTTE
AREA 144 sq. mi.
POPULATION 40,000
CAPITAL Mamoutzou

RÉUNION
AREA 969 sq. mi.
POPULATION 475,700
CAPITAL St-Denis

ALGERIA
CITIES and TOWNS

Adrar, 13,332	G 6
Aïn-Sefra, 16,818	G 5
Algiers (cap.), 943,142	G 4
Algiers, *1,800,000	G 4
Annaba, 152,006	H 4
Annaba, *223,000	H 4
Aoulef, 11,285	G 6
Béchar, 46,505	F 5
Béjaïa, 64,876	H 4
Biskra, 59,275	H 5
Blida, 99,238	G 4
Bône (Annaba), 152,006	H 4
Bou-Saâda, 26,262	G 5
Constantine, 243,558	H 4
Djelfa, 30,304	G 5
Djidjelli, 35,371	H 4
El Asnam, 69,745	G 4
El Djezair (Algiers) (cap.), 943,142	G 4
El Goléa, 16,679	G 5
El Oued, 43,547	H 5
Ghardaïa, 46,609	G 5
In Salah, 12,645	G 6
Laghouat, 38,166	G 5
Mascara, 43,108	G 4
Méchéria, 12,151	F 5
Mostaganem, 75,332	F 4
Oran, 327,493	F 4
Oran, *393,000	F 4
Ouargla, 48,323	H 5
Philippeville (Skikda), 72,742	H 4
Reggan, 11,075	G 6
Saïda, 38,348	F 4
Sétif, 98,337	H 4
Sidi-bel-Abbès, 91,527	F 4
Skikda, 72,742	H 4

(continued on following page)

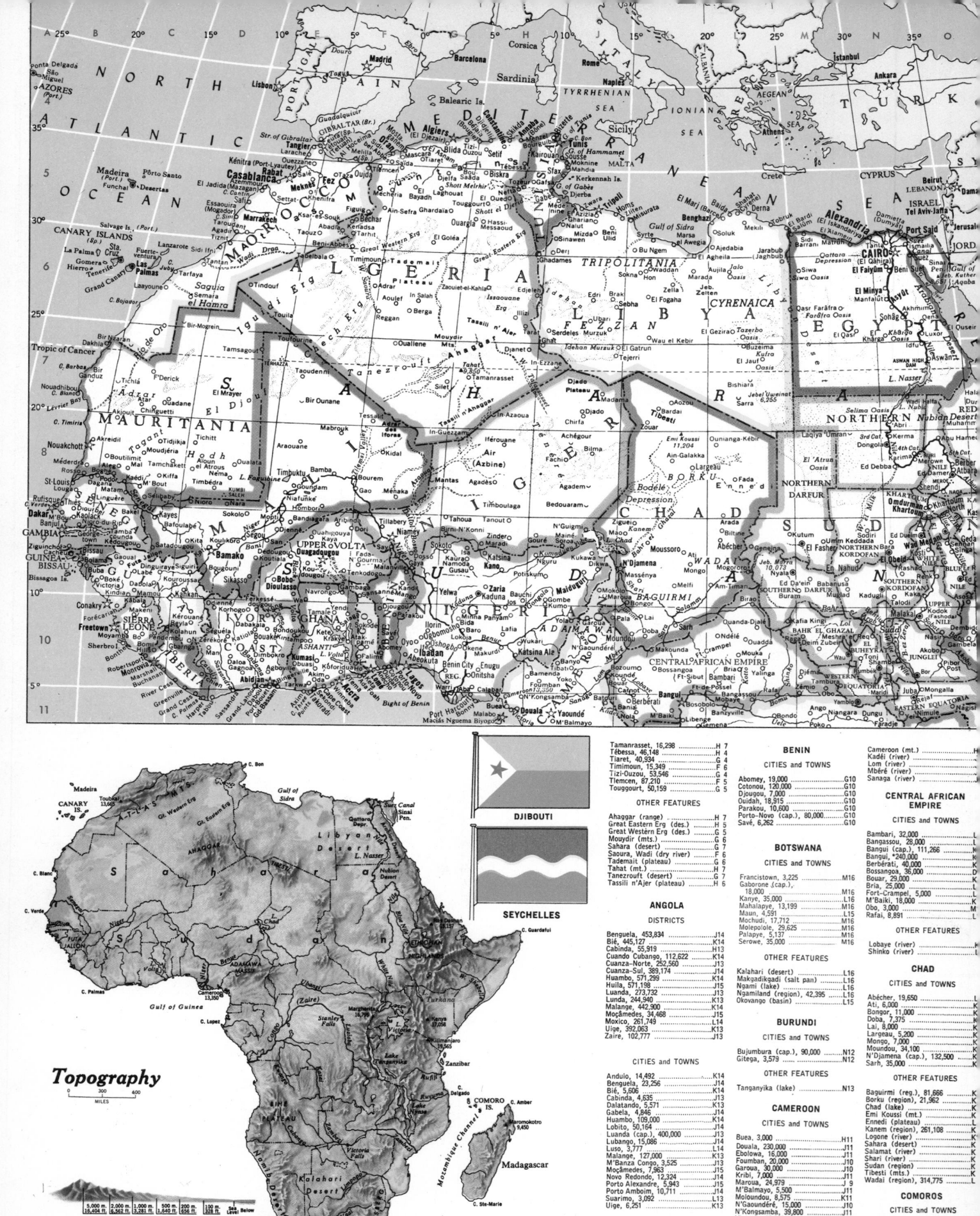

Topography

MILES
0 300 400

5,000 m. | 2,000 m. | 1,000 m. | 500 m. | 200 m. | 100 m. | Sea Level | Below
16,404 ft. | 6,562 ft. | 3,281 ft. | 1,640 ft. | 656 ft. | 328 ft.

DJIBOUTI

SEYCHELLES

Tamanrasset, 16,298 .... H 7
Tébessa, 46,148 .... H 4
Tiaret, 40,934 .... G 4
Timimoun, 15,349 .... G 4
Tizi-Ouzou, 53,546 .... G 4
Tlemcen, 87,210 .... F 5
Touggourt, 50,159 .... G 5

OTHER FEATURES

Ahaggar (range) .... H 7
Great Eastern Erg (des.) .... G 5
Great Western Erg (des.) .... G 5
Mouydir (mts.) .... G 6
Sahara (desert) .... G 6
Saoura, Wadi (dry river) .... F 6
Tademait (plateau) .... G 6
Tahat (mt.) .... G 7
Tanezrouft (desert) .... G 7
Tassili n'Ajer (plateau) .... H 6

ANGOLA

DISTRICTS

Benguela, 453,834 .... J14
Bié, 445,127 .... K14
Cabinda, 55,919 .... K13
Cuando Cubango, 112,622 .... K14
Cuanza-Norte, 252,560 .... J14
Cuanza-Sul, 389,174 .... J14
Huambo, 571,299 .... K14
Huíla, 571,198 .... J15
Luanda, 273,732 .... J13
Lunda, 244,940 .... K13
Malange, 442,900 .... K14
Moçâmedes, 34,468 .... J15
Moxico, 261,749 .... L14
Uíge, 392,063 .... J13
Zaire, 102,777 .... J13

CITIES and TOWNS

Anduío, 14,492 .... K14
Benguela, 23,256 .... J14
Bié, 5,606 .... K14
Cabinda, 4,635 .... J13
Dalatando, 5,571 .... K13
Gabela, 4,846 .... J14
Huambo, 109,000 .... K14
Lobito, 50,164 .... J14
Luanda (cap.), 400,000 .... J13
Lubango, 15,086 .... J15
Luso, 3,777 .... L14
Malange, 127,000 .... K13
M'Banza Congo, 3,525 .... J13
Moçâmedes, 7,963 .... J15
Novo Redondo, 12,324 .... J14
Porto Alexandre, 5,943 .... J15
Porto Amboim, 10,711 .... J14
Suarimo, 3,092 .... L13
Uíge, 6,251 .... K13

OTHER FEATURES

Cuanza (river) K13
Cunene (river) J15

BENIN

CITIES and TOWNS

Abomey, 19,000 .... G10
Cotonou, 120,000 .... G10
Djougou, 7,000 .... G10
Ouidah, 18,915 .... G10
Parakou, 10,600 .... G10
Porto-Novo (cap.), 80,000 .... G10
Savé, 6,262 .... G10

BOTSWANA

CITIES and TOWNS

Francistown, 3,225 .... M16
Gaborone (cap.), 18,000 .... M16
Kanye, 35,000 .... L16
Mahalapye, 13,199 .... M16
Maun, 4,591 .... L15
Mochudi, 17,712 .... M16
Molepolole, 29,625 .... M16
Palapye, 5,137 .... M16
Serowe, 35,000 .... M16

OTHER FEATURES

Kalahari (desert) L16
Makgadikgadi (salt pan) L16
Ngami (lake) L16
Ngamiland (region), 42,395 .... L16
Okovango (basin) L15

BURUNDI

CITIES and TOWNS

Bujumbura (cap.), 90,000 .... N12
Gitega, 3,579 .... N12

OTHER FEATURES

Tanganyika (lake) N13

CAMEROON

CITIES and TOWNS

Buea, 3,000 .... H11
Douala, 230,000 .... H11
Ebolowa, 16,000 .... J11
Foumban, 20,000 .... J10
Garoua, 30,000 .... J10
Kribi, 7,000 .... J11
Maroua, 24,979 .... J9
M'Balmayo, 5,000 .... J11
Moloundou, 8,575 .... J11
N'Gaoundéré, 15,000 .... J10
N'Kongsamba, 39,800 .... J11
Victoria, 15,000 .... H11
Yaoundé (cap.), 130,000 .... J11

OTHER FEATURES

Biafra (bight) H11

Cameroon (mt.) .... H
Kadéi (river) .... J
Lom (river) .... J
Mbéré (river) .... J
Sanaga (river) .... J

CENTRAL AFRICAN EMPIRE

CITIES and TOWNS

Bambari, 32,000 L
Bangassou, 28,000 L
Bangui (cap.), 111,266 .... K
Bangui, *240,000 .... K
Berbérati, 40,000 .... K
Bossangoa, 36,000 .... K
Bouar, 29,000 .... K
Bria, 25,000 L
Fort-Crampel, 5,000 .... K
M'Baïki, 18,000 .... K
Obo, 3,000 .... M
Rafai, 8,891 L

OTHER FEATURES

Lobaye (river) .... K
Shinko (river) L

CHAD

CITIES and TOWNS

Abécher, 19,650 .... K
Ati, 6,000 .... K
Bongor, 11,000 .... K
Doba, 7,375 .... K
Lai, 8,000 .... K
Largeau, 5,200 .... K
Mongo, 7,000 .... K
Moundou, 34,100 .... K
N'Djamena (cap.), 132,500 .... K
Sarh, 35,000 .... K

OTHER FEATURES

Baguirmi (reg.), 81,666 .... K
Borku (region), 21,962 .... K
Chad (lake) .... K
Emi Koussi (mt.) .... K
Ennedi (region), 261,108 .... K
Kanem (region), 261,108 .... K
Logone (river) .... K
Sahara (desert) .... K
Salamat (river) .... K
Shari (river) .... K
Sudan (region) .... K
Tibesti (mts.) .... K
Wadai (region), 314,775 .... K

COMOROS

CITIES and TOWNS

Moroni (cap.), 11,515 .... P

OTHER FEATURES

Anjouan (island), 83,486 .... P

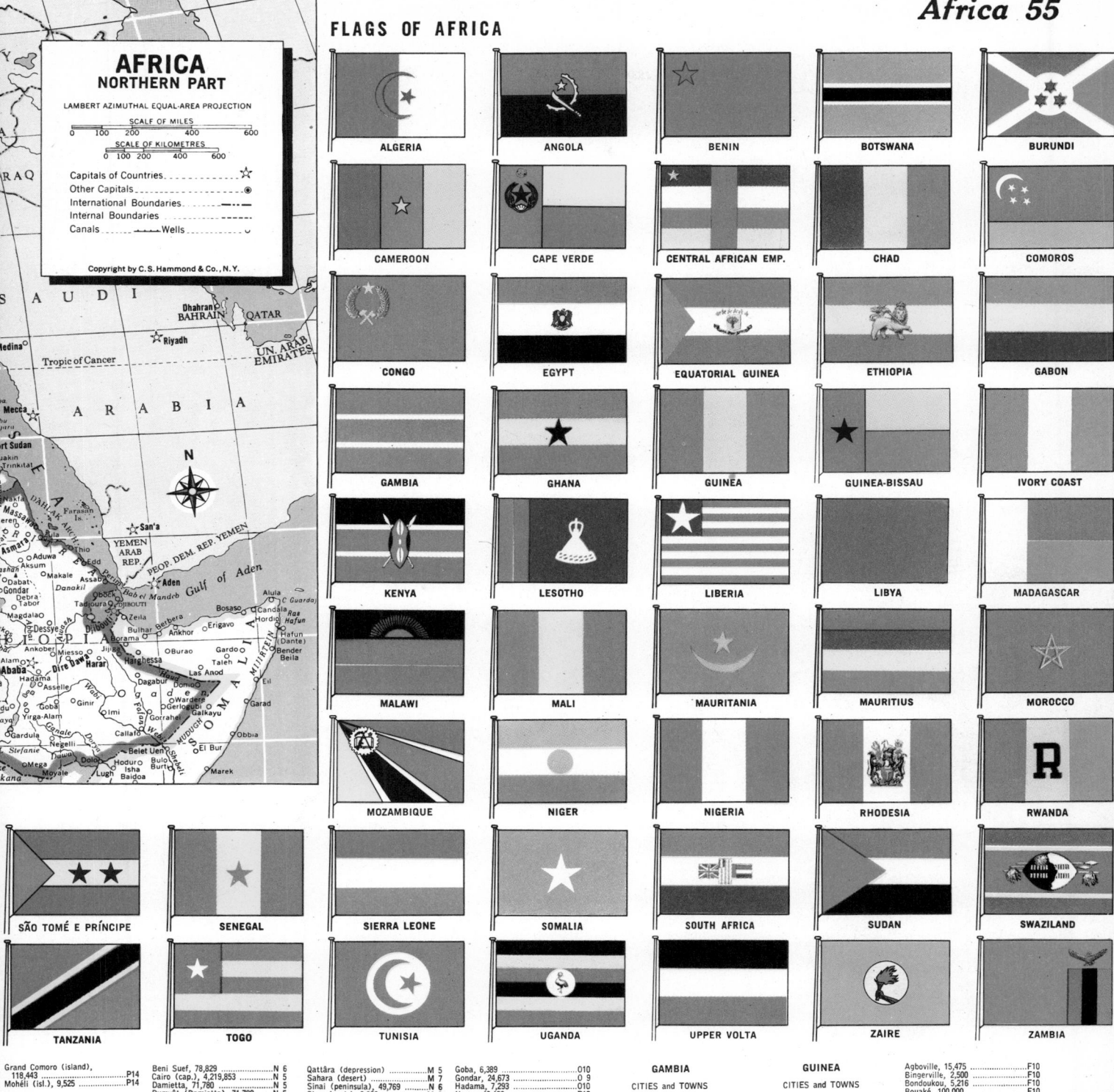

AFRICA
NORTHERN PART
LAMBERT AZIMUTHAL EQUAL-AREA PROJECTION

SCALE OF MILES
0 100 200 300 400 500 600

SCALE OF KILOMETRES
0 100 200 300 400 500 600

Capitals of Countries .... ☆
Other Capitals .... ◉
International Boundaries .... —·—·—
Internal Boundaries .... ———
Canals .... Wells .... ○

Copyright by C.S. Hammond & Co., N.Y.

FLAGS OF AFRICA

ALGERIA | ANGOLA | BENIN | BOTSWANA | BURUNDI

CAMEROON | CAPE VERDE | CENTRAL AFRICAN EMP. | CHAD | COMOROS

CONGO | EGYPT | EQUATORIAL GUINEA | ETHIOPIA | GABON

GAMBIA | GHANA | GUINEA | GUINEA-BISSAU | IVORY COAST

KENYA | LESOTHO | LIBERIA | LIBYA | MADAGASCAR

MALAWI | MALI | MAURITANIA | MAURITIUS | MOROCCO

MOZAMBIQUE | NIGER | NIGERIA | RHODESIA | RWANDA

SÃO TOMÉ E PRÍNCIPE | SENEGAL | SIERRA LEONE | SOMALIA | SOUTH AFRICA | SUDAN | SWAZILAND

TANZANIA | TOGO | TUNISIA | UGANDA | UPPER VOLTA | ZAIRE | ZAMBIA

Grand Comoro (island),
  118,443 .... P14
Mohéli (isl.), 9,525 .... P14

CONGO
CITIES and TOWNS
Brazzaville (cap.), 94,000 .... J12
Brazzaville, *200,000 .... J12
Dolisie, 20,000 .... J12
Fort-Rousset, 5,082 .... K12
Ouesso, 4,464 .... K11
Pointe-Noire, 100,000 .... J12

OTHER FEATURES
Congo (river) K12
Ubangi (river) K11

DJIBOUTI
CITIES and TOWNS
Djibouti (cap.), 41,200 .... P 9
Djibouti, *61,500 .... P 9
Tadjoura, 2,000 .... P 9

EGYPT
CITIES and TOWNS
Akhmim, 41,580 .... N 6
Alexandria, 1,803,900 .... M 5
Aswân, 127,700 .... N 7
Asyût, 154,100 .... N 6

Beni Suef, 78,829 .... N 6
Cairo (cap.), 4,219,853 ...... N 5
Damietta, 71,780 .... N 5
Dumyât (Damietta), 71,780 ... N 5
El 'Alamein, 593 .... M 5
El Faiyûm, 133,800 .... M 6
El Iskandariya (Alexandria),
  1,803,900 .... M 5
El Khârga, 9,277 .... N 6
El Minya, 112,800 .... M 6
El Qâhira (Cairo) (cap.),
  4,219,853 .... N 5
El Qasr, 1,789 .... N 6
El Quseir, 4,336 .... O 6
Idfu, 25,105 .... N 7
Ismailia, 156,500 .... N 5
Luxor, 35,074 .... N 6
Manfalût, 28,540 .... M 6
Matrûh, 9,254 .... M 5
Port Said, 283,400 .... N 5
Qena, 57,417 .... N 6
Salûm, 7,348 .... M 5
Sidi Barrani, 1,583 .... M 5
Sohâg, 61,944 .... N 6
Suez, 264,500 .... N 6
Tanta, 230,400 .... N 5

Qattâra (depression) .... M 5
Sahara (desert) .... M 7
Sinai (peninsula), 49,769 .... N 6
Siwa (oasis), 3,839 .... M 6
Suez (canal) .... N 5
Suez (gulf) .... N 6

EQUATORIAL GUINEA
CITIES and TOWNS
Bata, 27,024 .... H11
Malabo (cap.), 37,237 .... H11

OTHER FEATURES
Pagalu (isl.), 1,415 .... G12
Corisco (isl.) H11
Elobey (isls.) H11
Macías Nguema Biyogo
  (isl.), 78,000 .... H11
Río Muni (terr.), 203,000 .... H11

ETHIOPIA
CITIES and TOWNS
Addis Ababa (cap.), 644,120 ... O10
Addis Alam, 7,789 .... O10
Aksum, 11,596 .... O 9
Ankober, 12,871 .... O10
Asmara, 190,500 .... O10
Asselle, 9,523 .... O10
Debra Markos, 20,096 .... O 9
Dessye, 40,000 .... O 9
Dire Dawa, 40,000 .... P10
Gambela, 9,955 .... N10

Goba, 6,389 .... O10
Gondar, 24,673 .... O 9
Harar, 7,293 .... O10
Harar, 40,499 .... P10
Jimma, 39,559 .... O10
Hadama, 7,000 .... O10
Makale, 16,873 .... O 9
Massawa, 25,000 .... O 8
Miesso, 32,960 .... O10
Soddu, 5,595 .... O10

OTHER FEATURES
Abaya (lake) O10
Abbai (river) .... O 9
Bab el Mandeb (str.) .... R 9
Dahlak (archipelago) .... P 8
Danakil (region) .... P 9
Dashan, Ras (mt.) .... O 9
Eritrea (region), 1,757,912 .. O 8
Ogaden (region) P10
Tana (lake) .... O 9

GABON
CITIES and TOWNS
Bitam, 2,080 .... J11
Franceville, 2,000 .... J12
Koula-Moutou, 3,170 .... J12
Lambaréné, 7,000 .... H12
Lastoursville, 2,000 .... J12
Libreville (cap.), *57,000 ... H11
Oyem, 3,050 .... J11
Port-Gentil, 30,000 .... H12
Tchibanga, 2,080 .... J12

OTHER FEATURES
Lopez (cape) H12
Ogooué (river) J12

GAMBIA
CITIES and TOWNS
Banjul (cap.), 31,800 .... C 9
Banjul, *48,333 .... C 9
Georgetown, 1,582 .... C 9

GHANA
CITIES and TOWNS
Accra (cap.), 337,828 .... G11
Accra, *848,825 .... G11
Akim Oda, 19,666 .... F10
Axim, 5,619 .... F11
Cape Coast, 41,230 .... F11
Ho, 14,519 .... G10
Keta, 16,719 .... G10
Koforidua, 34,856 .... F10
Kumasi, 281,600 .... F10
Kumasi, *340,200 .... F10
Obuasi, 22,818 .... F11
Sekondi, 34,513 .... F11
Sekondi-Takoradi, *209,400 ... F11
Takoradi, 40,937 .... F11
Tamale, 40,443 .... F10
Tarkwa, 13,545 .... F11
Tema, 14,937 .... G11
Wa, 14,342 .... F 9
Winneba, 25,376 .... F11
Yendi, 16,096 .... F11

OTHER FEATURES
Ashanti (region), 1,109,133 .. F10
Volta (lake) F10
Volta (river) F10

GUINEA
CITIES and TOWNS
Beyla, 6,035 .... E10
Boké, 6,000 .... D 9
Conakry (cap.), 43,000 .... D10
Conakry, *197,267 .... D10
Kankan, 50,000 .... E 9
Kindia, 25,000 .... D10
Kouroussa, 6,100 .... E 9
Labé, 11,609 .... D 9
Mamou, 9,000 .... D 9
N'Zérékoré, 11,000 .... E10
Siguiri, 12,000 .... E 9

OTHER FEATURES
Futa Jallon (mts.) .... D 9
Niger (river) .... E 9

GUINEA-BISSAU
CITIES and TOWNS
Bissau (cap.), 20,000 .... D 9
Bolama, *4,642 .... D 9

OTHER FEATURES
Bijagós (isls.), 9,332 .... C 9

IVORY COAST
CITIES and TOWNS
Abidjan (cap.), 180,000 ...... E10
Abidjan, *425,000 .... E10

Agboville, 15,475 .... F10
Bingerville, 2,500 .... F10
Bondoukou, 5,216 .... F10
Bouaké, 100,000 .... E10
Dabou, 4,500 .... F11
Daloa, 20,000 .... E10
Dimbokro, 10,260 .... F10
Ferkessédougou, 9,110 .... E10
Gagnoa, 18,000 .... E10
Grand-Basam, 12,330 .... F11
Grand-Lahou, 4,040 .... E10
Katiola, 7,778 .... E10
Kong, 4,073 .... E10
Korhogo, 25,000 .... E10
Man, 24,000 .... E10
Odienné, 6,000 .... E10
Sassandra, 5,300 .... E11
Séguéla, 7,598 .... E10
Tabou, 3,030 .... E11

OTHER FEATURES
Cavally (river) E10
Sassandra (river) E10

KENYA
CITIES and TOWNS
Eldoret, 16,900 .... L11
Fort Hall, 5,389 .... O12
Kisumu, 30,700 .... N12
Kitale, 11,500 .... O11
Lamu, 5,828 .... P12
Malindi, 5,818 .... P12
Mombasa, 234,400 .... P12
Nairobi (cap.), 477,600 ...... O12
Nakuru, 47,800 .... O11
Nanyuki, 11,200 .... O11
Nyeri, 9,900 .... O12
(continued on following page)

Agriculture, Industry and Resources

DOMINANT LAND USE

- Cereals, Horticulture, Livestock
- Cash Crops, Mixed Cereals
- Cotton, Cereals
- Diversified Tropical Crops
- Plantation Agriculture
- Oases
- Pasture Livestock
- Nomadic Livestock Herding
- Forests
- Nonagricultural Land

MAJOR MINERAL OCCURRENCES

Ab	Asbestos	Mi	Mica
Ag	Silver	Mn	Manganese
Al	Bauxite	Na	Salt
Au	Gold	O	Petroleum
Be	Beryl	P	Phosphates
C	Coal	Pb	Lead
Co	Cobalt	Pt	Platinum
Cr	Chromium	Sb	Antimony
Cu	Copper	Sn	Tin
D	Diamonds	So	Soda Ash
Fe	Iron Ore	Ti	Titanium
G	Natural Gas	U	Uranium
Gp	Gypsum	V	Vanadium
Gr	Graphite	W	Tungsten
K	Potash	Zn	Zinc

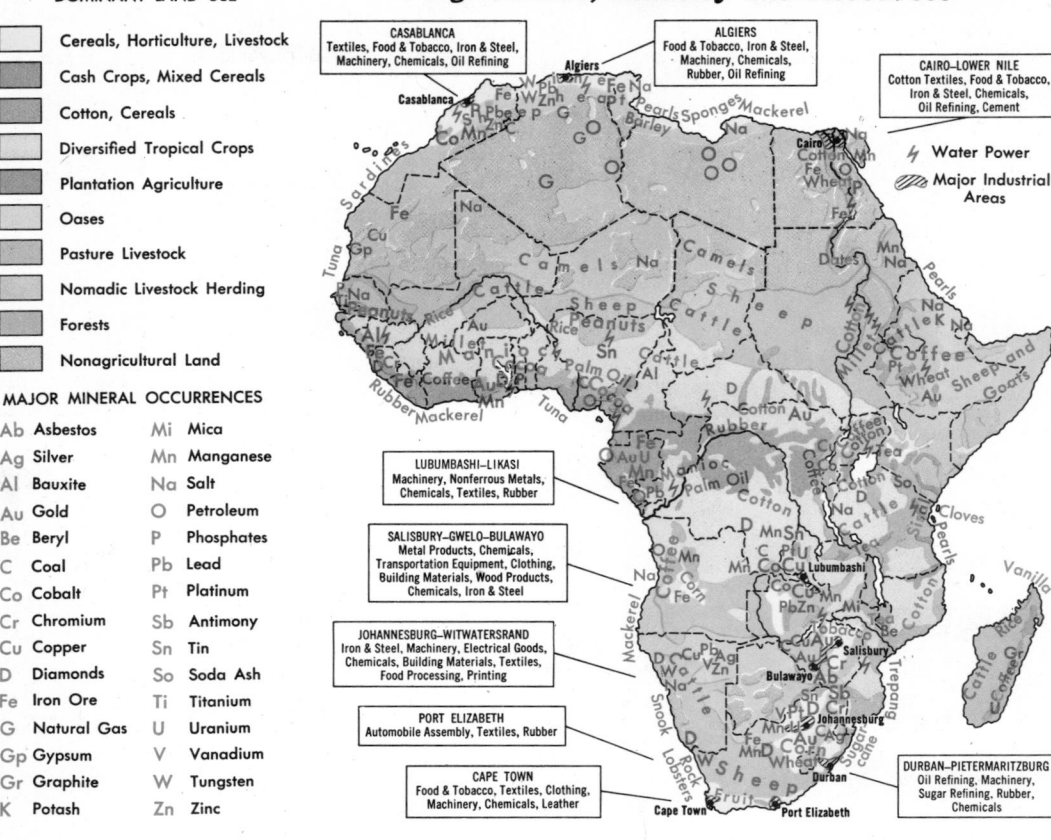

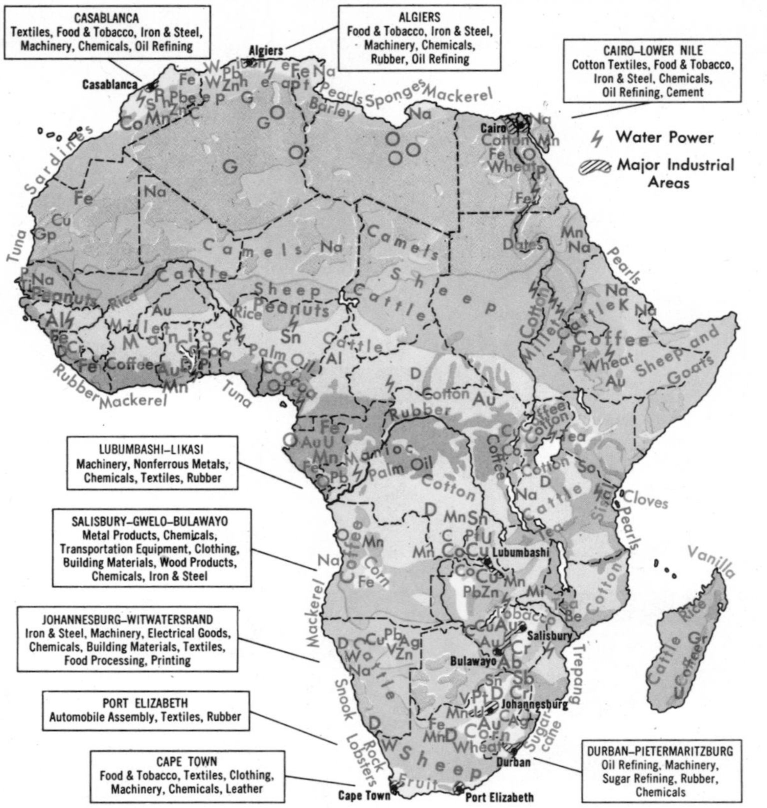
CASABLANCA
Textiles, Food & Tobacco, Iron & Steel, Machinery, Chemicals, Oil Refining
ALGIERS
Food & Tobacco, Iron & Steel, Machinery, Chemicals, Rubber, Oil Refining
CAIRO–LOWER NILE
Cotton Textiles, Food & Tobacco, Iron & Steel, Chemicals, Oil Refining, Cement
Water Power
Major Industrial Areas
LUBUMBASHI–LIKASI
Machinery, Nonferrous Metals, Chemicals, Textiles, Rubber
SALISBURY–GWELO–BULAWAYO
Metal Products, Chemicals, Transportation Equipment, Clothing, Building Materials, Wood Products, Chemicals, Iron & Steel
JOHANNESBURG–WITWATERSRAND
Iron & Steel, Machinery, Electrical Goods, Chemicals, Building Materials, Textiles, Food Processing, Printing
PORT ELIZABETH
Automobile Assembly, Textiles, Rubber
CAPE TOWN
Food & Tobacco, Textiles, Clothing, Machinery, Chemicals, Leather
DURBAN–PIETERMARITZBURG
Oil Refining, Machinery, Sugar Refining, Rubber, Chemicals
Algiers
Casablanca
Cairo
Lubumbashi
Salisbury
Bulawayo
Johannesburg
Durban
Cape Town
Port Elizabeth

OTHER FEATURES

Elgon (mt.) N11
Kenya (mt.) O12
Turkana (lake) O11
Victoria (lake) N12

LESOTHO

CITIES and TOWNS

Maseru (cap.), 18,797 .... M17

LIBERIA

CITIES and TOWNS

Bomi Hills, 2,441 .... D10
Buchanan, 11,909 .... D10
Greenville, 3,962 .... E11
Harper, 6,095 .... E11
Monrovia (cap.), 85,000 .... D10
Monrovia, *100,000 .... D10
Robertsport, 2,417 .... D10

OTHER FEATURES

Palmas (cape) E11

LIBYA

CITIES and TOWNS

Ajedabia, ‡15,430 .... L 5
Baida, 12,799 .... L 5
Barce (El Marj), 10,645 .... L 5
Benghazi, 137,295 .... K 5
Brak, ‡7,042 .... J 6
Cyrene (Shahat), ‡6,266 .... L 5
Derna, 21,432 .... L 5
El Azizia, ‡18,753 .... J 5
El Bardi, ‡3,755 .... M 5
El Jauf, ‡4,330 .... L 7
El Marj, 10,645 .... L 5
Ghadames, ‡2,636 .... J 6
Gharian, ‡10,807 .... J 5
Ghat, ‡1,639 .... J 6
Homs, ‡13,864 .... J 5
Hon, ‡3,435 .... K 6
Jarabub, ‡1,101 .... L 5
Misurata, ‡36,850 .... K 5
Murzuk, ‡3,863 .... J 6
Nalut, ‡9,010 .... J 5
Sebha, ‡9,804 .... K 6
Shahat, ‡6,266 .... L 5
Sokna, ‡1,873 .... K 6
Soluk, ‡12,395 .... L 5
Syrte, 7,093 .... K 5
Tobruk, 15,867 .... L 5
Tripoli (cap.), 247,365 .... J 5
Waddan, ‡3,519 .... K 6
Zliten, ‡17,950 .... K 5
Zwara, ‡14,578 .... J 5

OTHER FEATURES

Cyrenaica (reg.), 450,954 .... L 6
Fezzan (reg.), 79,326 .... J 6
Libyan (desert) .... M 6
Jalo (oasis), 3,910 .... L 6
Kufra (oasis), 5,509 .... L 7
Sahara (desert) .... L 7
Sidra (gulf) .... K 5
Tazerbo (oasis), ‡1,307 .... L 6
Tripolitania (reg.), 1,034,089 .... J 5

MADAGASCAR

CITIES and TOWNS

Ambalavao, 6,045 .... R16
Ambanja, 5,198 .... R14
Ambatondrazaka, 14,297 .... R15
Ambilobe, 7,877 .... R14
Ambositra, 15,131 .... R16
Antalaha, 18,083 .... S14
Antananarivo (cap.), 332,885 .... R15
Antsirabe, 29,914 .... R16
Arivonimamo, 7,011 .... R15
Belo-sur-Tsiribihina, 4,391 .... P15
Betroka, 4,071 .... R16
Diégo-Suarez, 40,237 .... R14
Farafangana, 10,753 .... R16
Fénérive, 7,080 .... S15
Fianarantsoa, 45,790 .... R16
Fort-Dauphin, 12,677 .... R16
Hell-Ville, 9,481 .... R14
Ihosy, 6,578 .... R16
Maevatanana, 5,147 .... R15
Maintirano, 4,594 .... P15
Majunga, 47,654 .... R15
Manakara, 17,567 .... R16
Mananjary, 13,019 .... R16
Maroantsetra, 7,184 .... S15
Marovoay, 18,074 .... R15
Moramanga, 10,706 .... R15
Morombe, 6,684 .... P16
Morondava, 15,032 .... P16
Sambava, 6,198 .... S14
Tamatave, 53,173 .... S15
Tuléar, 33,842 .... P16
Vangaindrano, 2,665 .... R16
Vohémar, 3,622 .... S14

OTHER FEATURES

Amber (cape) S14
Madagascar (island) R16
Mangoky (river) P16
Mozambique (channel) O16
Nossi-Bé (isl.), 26,462 .... R14
Sainte-Marie (isl.), 9,090 .... S15
Tsiafajavona (mt.) R15
Tsiribihina (river) R15

MALAWI

CITIES and TOWNS

Blantyre, 109,461 .... N15
Fort Johnston, 1,467 .... N14
Karonga, 1,128 .... N13
Lilongwe (cap.), 19,425 .... N14
Mzimba, 4,156 .... N14
Nsanje, 1,373 .... O15
Zomba, 19,666 .... N15

OTHER FEATURES

Mlanje (mt.) O15
Nyasa (lake) N14
Shire (river) N15

MALI

CITIES and TOWNS

Bamako (cap.), 88,500 .... E 9
Bamako, *182,000 .... E 9
Bandiagara, 6,700 .... F 9
Bougouni, 5,500 .... E 9
Djenné, 8,200 .... F 9
Gao, 15,400 .... G 8
Goundam, 10,000 .... F 8
Kati, 5,900 .... E 9
Kayes, 23,600 .... D 9
Kita, 8,600 .... E 9
Koulikoro, 10,000 .... E 9
Koutiala, 11,300 .... F 9
Mopti, 32,000 .... F 9
Niafunké, 5,100 .... F 8
Nioro, 11,000 .... E 8
San, 14,900 .... F 9
Ségou, 27,200 .... E 9
Sikasso, 21,800 .... E 9
Sokolo, 3,457 .... E 9
Timbuktu, 14,900 .... F 8

OTHER FEATURES

Niger (river) .... E 9
Sahara (desert) .... F 7
Terhazza (ruins) .... F 7

MAURITANIA

CITIES and TOWNS

Aïoun el Atrous, 3,054 .... E 8
Akjoujt, 2,500 .... D 7
Atar, 7,120 .... D 7
Boghé, 2,316 .... D 8
Boutilimit, 3,000 .... D 8
Dakhla, 4,000 .... C 7
Kaédi, 11,000 .... D 8
Kiffa, 2,600 .... D 8
Néma, 2,946 .... E 8
Nouadhibou, 11,250 .... C 7
Nouakchott (cap.), 14,500 .... C 8
Rosso, 3,923 .... C 8
Sélibaby, 2,600 .... D 8
Tidjikja, 5,900 .... D 8

OTHER FEATURES

Adrar (region), 50,920 .... D 7
Barbas (cape) .... C 7
Blanc (cape) .... C 7
Hodh (region), 183,945 .... E 8
Kumbi Saleh (ruins) .... E 8
Lévrier (bay) .... C 7
Sahara (desert) .... E 7
Senegal (river) .... D 8
Tagant (region), 52,703 .... D 8

MAURITIUS

CITIES and TOWNS

Curepipe, 49,000 .... S19
Mahébourg, 13,005 .... T19
Port Louis (cap.), 131,000 .... S19
Quatre Bornes, 28,389 .... S19

OTHER FEATURES

Black River (mt.) S19
Mascarene (isls.), 1,259,000 .... R20

MAYOTTE

CITIES and TOWNS

Mamoutzou (cap.), 1,090 .... R14

MOROCCO

CITIES and TOWNS

Agadir, 16,695 .... D 5
Al Hoceima, 11,262 .... F 4
Azemmour, 12,449 .... E 5
Casablanca, 1,320,000 .... E 5
El Jadida, 40,302 .... E 5
Essaouira, 26,392 .... D 5
Fez, 280,000 .... F 5
Figuig, 12,108 .... F 5
Kénitra, 125,000 .... E 5
Khenifra, 18,503 .... F 5
Laayoune, 10,000 .... D 6
Larache, 30,763 .... E 4
Marrakech, 295,000 .... E 5
Meknès, 235,000 .... E 5
Ouezzane, 26,203 .... E 5
Oujda, 150,000 .... F 5
Port-Lyautey (Kénitra), 125,000 .. E 5
Rabat (cap.), 227,445 .... E 5
Rabat, *435,000 .... E 5
Safi, 125,000 .... E 5
Salé, 75,799 .... E 5
Settat, 29,617 .... E 5
Sidi Ifni, 12,751 .... D 6
Tangier, 160,000 .... E 4
Taroudant, 17,141 .... E 5
Taza, 31,667 .... F 5
Tétouan, 120,000 .... F 4

OTHER FEATURES

Atlas (mts.) .... E 5
Bojador (cape) .... C 6
Draa, Wadi (dry river) .... E 6
Juby (cape) .... D 6
Saguia el Hamra (reg.) .... D 6

MOZAMBIQUE

DISTRICTS

Cabo Delgado, 542,165 .... O14
Gaza, 675,150 .... N16
Inhambane, 583,772 .... N16
Manica, 367,337 .... N15
Maputo, 436,897 .... N17
Nampula, 1,444,555 .... O14
Niassa, 276,810 .... O14
Sofala, 712,381 .... N15
Tete, 470,100 .... N15
Zambézia, 1,363,619 .... O15

CITIES and TOWNS

Angoche, ‡33,245 .... P15
Beira, ‡58,235 .... O15
Caniçado, ‡30,647 .... N16
Chemba, ‡28,317 .... N15
Chibuto, ‡122,989 .... N16
Chimoio, ‡36,406 .... N15
Chinde, ‡25,617 .... O15
Homoíne, ‡57,959 .... O16
Ibo, ‡4,394 .... P14
Inhambane, ‡22,016 .... O16
Inharrime, ‡40,721 .... O16
Lichinga, ‡28,701 .... O14
Lourenço Marques (Maputo) (cap.), 65,716 .... N17
Magude, ‡44,183 .... N16
Maputo (cap.), 65,716 .... N17
Marromeu, ‡33,096 .... O15
Massinga, ‡80,526 .... O16
Meconta, ‡28,187 .... O14
Moçambique, ‡12,166 .... P15
Mocímboa da Praia, ‡28,335 .... P14
Mocuba, ‡43,484 .... O15
Nacala, ‡43,439 .... P14
Nampula, ‡104,648 .... P15
Nova Sofala, ‡16,468 .... O16
Pebane, ‡18,826 .... O15
Pemba, ‡21,005 .... P14
Quelimane, ‡62,717 .... O15
Tete, ‡38,196 .... N15
Vila de Manica, ‡14,151 .... N15
Vila de Sena, ‡46,616 .... N15
Vila Fontes, ‡29,434 .... N15
Xai-Xai, ‡48,959 .... O17
Zumbo, ‡9,978 .... N15

OTHER FEATURES

Delagoa (bay) N17
Delgado (cape) P14
Mozambique (channel) O16
Namuli (mt.) O15
Nyasa (lake) N14
Ruvuma (river) O14
Save (river) N16
Zambezi (river) N15

NIGER

CITIES and TOWNS

Agadès, 7,100 .... H 8
Birni-N'Konni, 7,900 .... H 9
Dosso, 3,500 .... G 9
Gaya, 4,200 .... G 9
Maradi, 22,400 .... H 9
N'Guigmi, 4,000 .... J 9
Niamey (cap.), 42,000 .... G 9
Niamey, *122,672 .... G 9
Say, 2,700 .... G 9
Tahoua, 18,100 .... H 9
Zinder, 24,000 .... H 9

OTHER FEATURES

Air (mt.) .... H 8
Djado (plateau) .... J 7
Niger (river) .... G 9
Sahara (desert) .... J 7
Ténéré (desert) .... J 8

NIGERIA

CITIES and TOWNS

Aba, 151,923 .... H10
Abeokuta, 217,201 .... G10
Bauchi .... H 9
Benin City, 116,774 .... H10
Calabar, 46,705 .... H10
Enugu, 160,567 .... H10
Gusau, 40,202 .... H 9
Ibadan, 727,565 .... G10
Ife, 150,818 .... G10
Ilorin, 241,849 .... G10
Jos, 38,527 .... H 9
Kaduna, 173,849 .... H 9
Kano, 342,610 .... H 9
Katsina, 52,672 .... H 9
Lagos (cap.), 841,749 .... G10
Lokoja, 13,103 .... H10
Maiduguri, 162,316 .... J 9
Nguru, 23,084 .... J 9
Ogbomosho, 370,963 .... H10
Okene, 32,602 .... H10
Onitsha, 189,067 .... H10
Oshogbo, 242,336 .... H10
Oyo, 130,290 .... G10
Port Harcourt, 208,237 .... H11
Sokoto, 47,643 .... H 9
Warri, 19,526 .... H10
Zaria, 192,706 .... H 9

OTHER FEATURES

Adamawa (region) J10
Benin (bight) G11
Benue (river) H10
Gongola (river) .... J 9
Guinea (gulf) F11
Kaduna (river) .... H 9
Niger (river) .... G 9
Sudan (region) .... H 9

RÉUNION

CITIES and TOWNS

Le Port, 13,281 .... P20
Saint-Benoït, 4,095 .... R20
Saint-Denis (cap.), 37,047 .... P19
Saint-Denis, *65,614 .... P19
Saint-Joseph, 5,969 .... P20
Saint-Louis, 7,753 .... P20
Saint-Paul, 5,624 .... P20
Saint-Pierre, 8,752 .... P20

OTHER FEATURES

Bassas da India (isls.) O16
Europa (isl.) P16
Glorioso (isls.) R14
Juan de Nova (isl.) P15
Mascarene (isls.), 1,259,000 .... R20
Piton des Neiges (mt.) P20

RHODESIA (ZIMBABWE)

CITIES and TOWNS

Bulawayo, †270,000 .... M16
Fort Victoria, †12,000 .... N15
Gatooma, †23,000 .... M15
Gwanda, 5,880 .... M16
Gwelo, †50,000 .... M15
Hartley, 7,170 .... M15
Kariba, 5,950 .... M15
Matopos, ‡9,390 .... M16
Rusape, 3,960 .... N15
Salisbury (cap.), 385,530 .... N15
Salisbury, ‡423,000 .... N15
Selukwe, 3,030 .... M15
Sinoia, ‡14,000 .... M15
Umtali, ‡50,000 .... N15
Wankie, ‡21,000 .... M15

OTHER FEATURES

Kariba (lake) M15
Limpopo (river) N16
Lundi (river) N16
Sabi (river) N16
Victoria (falls) M15
Zimbabwe (ruins) N16

RWANDA

CITIES and TOWNS

Kigali (cap.), 24,000 .... N12

SÃO TOMÉ E PRÍNCIPE

CITIES and TOWNS

Santo António, ‡4,605 .... H11
São Tomé (cap.), 7,364 .... H11

OTHER FEATURES

Príncipe (isl.), 4,605 .... H11
São Tomé (island), 58,880 .... H11

SENEGAL

CITIES and TOWNS

Bakel, 2,500 .... D 9
Dagana, 4,000 .... D 8
Dakar (cap.), 550,000 .... C 9
Dakar, *661,000 .... C 9
Diourbel, 30,000 .... C 9
Kaolack, 70,000 .... C 9
Louga, 15,000 .... C 8
Matam, 5,000 .... D 8
M'Bour, 15,000 .... C 9
Nioro-du-Rip, 2,788 .... D 9
Podor, 5,000 .... D 8
Rufisque, 50,000 .... C 9
Saint-Louis, 50,000 .... C 8
Tambacounda, 10,027 .... D 9
Thiès, 70,000 .... C 9
Ziguinchor, 30,000 .... C 9

OTHER FEATURES

Senegal (river) .... D 8
Verde (cape) .... C 9

SEYCHELLES

PHYSICAL FEATURES

Aldabra (isls.), 100 .... P13
Assumption (island), 31 .... R14
Astove (isl.), 50 .... R14
Cerf (isl.), 34 .... S13
Cosmoledo (islands), 57 .... R13
Farquhar (isls.), 172 .... S14
Providence (isl.), 70 .... S13
Saint Pierre (island), 45 .... S13

SIERRA LEONE

CITIES and TOWNS

Bo, 26,613 .... D10
Bonthe, 6,230 .... D10
Freetown (cap.), 170,600 .... D10
Kabala, 4,610 .... D10
Makeni, 12,304 .... D10
Moyamba, 4,564 .... D10
Pendembu, 2,696 .... D10

OTHER FEATURES

Sherbro (isl.), 6,894 .... D10

SOMALIA

CITIES and TOWNS

Afmadu, ⊛2,580 .... P1
Alula, ⊛6,063 .... S
Baidoa, ⊛14,962 .... P1
Barawa (Brava), ⊛6,168 .... P1
Bardera, ⊛7,874 .... P1
Belet Uen, ⊛11,426 .... P1
Bender Beila, ⊛6,084 .... S1
Berbera, ⊛12,219 .... R
Bosaso, ⊛7,560 .... R
Brava, ⊛6,168 .... P1
Bur Acaba, ⊛10,924 .... P1
Burao, ⊛12,617 .... R1
Eil, ⊛2,234 .... S1
El Bur, ⊛3,224 .... R1
Erigavo, ⊛4,279 .... R
Galkayu, ⊛9,477 .... R1
Gardo, ⊛4,076 .... R1
Harghessa, ⊛40,254 .... P1
Hodur, ⊛3,137 .... P1
Jamama, ⊛22,030 .... P
Johar, ⊛13,156 .... R1
Kismayu, ⊛17,872 .... P1
Las Anod, ⊛2,441 .... R1
Lugh, ⊛3,768 .... P1
Merka, ⊛56,385 .... R1
Mogadishu (cap.), 172,677 .... R1
Obbia, ⊛2,106 .... R1
Zeila, ⊛1,226 .... P

OTHER FEATURES

Benadir (region), 392,189 .... P1
Chiamboni (cape) P1
Guardafui (cape) .... S
Hafun (cape) .... S
Juba (river) P1
Mijirtein (region), 82,710 .... R1
Mudugh (region), 141,197 .... R1
Webi Shebeli (river) R1

SOUTH AFRICA

PROVINCES

Bophuthatswana, 903,883 .... L17
Cape of Good Hope, 3,936,226 .... M18
Natal, 2,979,920 .... N17
Orange Free State, 1,386,547 .... M17
Transkei, 1,439,195 .... M18
Transvaal, 6,273,477 .... M16

CITIES and TOWNS

Alexander Bay, 2,073 .... J17
Aliwal North, 10,700 .... M18
Barkly East, 3,650 .... M18
Beaufort West, 16,300 .... L18
Bellville, 42,500 .... G19
Benoni, 126,700 .... M17
Bethlehem, 31,400 .... M17
Bloemfontein, †147,000 .... L17
Caledon, 4,300 .... H20
Calvinia, 6,700 .... K18
Cape Town (cap.), 625,000 .... F19
Cape Town, †817,000 .... F19
Carnarvon, 4,800 .... L18
Ceres, 6,200 .... H18
Cradock, 21,300 .... M18
De Aar, 16,600 .... L18
Durban, †690,000 .... N18
Durbanville, 3,057 .... G19
East London, 134,100 .... M18
George, 19,600 .... L18
Germiston, †222,000 .... M17
Goodwood, 82,600 .... G19
Graaff-Reinet, 17,700 .... M18
Grabouw, 5,200 .... H20
Grahamstown, 37,600 .... M18
Griquatown, 2,526 .... L17
Hermanus, 5,200 .... H20
Hopetown, 2,631 .... L17
Johannesburg, †1,305,000 .... M17
Kimberley, 95,200 .... L17
King William's Town, 15,000 .... M18
Knysna, 13,900 .... L1
Kraaifontein, 4,800 .... G1
Kroonstad, 50,700 .... M1
Ladysmith, 27,900 .... N1
Louis Trichardt, 14,800 .... M1
Lydenburg, 8,000 .... N1
Maclear, 3,550 .... M1
Malmesbury, 8,800 .... G1
Messina, 12,500 .... M1
Middelburg, Cape of Good Hope, 11,700 .... M1
Middelburg, Transvaal, 25,100 .... N1
Mmabatho L1
Moorreesburg, 4,000 .... K1
Mossel Bay, 15,600 .... L1
Muizenberg, 10,000 .... G2
Newcastle, 16,900 .... N1
Oudtshoorn, 25,800 .... L1
Paarl, 48,800 .... H1
Parow, 48,100 .... G1
Pietermaritzburg, †128,598 .... N1
Pietersburg, 35,700 .... N1
Pinelands, 14,100 .... G1
Port Elizabeth, †448,000 .... M1
Port Nolloth, 2,624 .... K1
Port Shepstone, 4,200 .... N1
Potchefstroom, 51,800 .... M1
Potgietersrus, 12,700 .... M1
Pretoria (cap.), 479,700 .... M1
Prieska, 7,600 .... L1
Prince Albert, 4,500 .... L1
Queenstown, 42,200 .... M1
Riversdale, 5,100 .... L1
Saldanha, 2,243 .... K1
Simonstown, 8,900 .... F2
Somerset West, 9,500 .... G2
Springbok, 4,100 .... K1
Stellenbosch, 29,000 .... G1
Strand, 21,200 .... G2
Swellendam, 4,900 .... L1
Uitenhage, 63,400 .... M1
Umtata, 17,200 .... M1
Upington, 28,000 .... L1
Victoria West, 4,100 .... L1
Vishoek, 7,500 .... F2
Vryburg, 17,100 .... L1
Walvis Bay, 12,234 .... J1
Warrenton, 8,600 .... M1
Wellington, 13,200 .... H1
Willowmore, 4,200 .... L1
Worcester, 37,000 .... J1

OTHER FEATURES

Agulhas (cape) K1
Algoa (bay) .... M
Bot (river) H2
Breede (river) H1
Cape (peninsula) F2
Cape (point) .... F
Diep (river) .... G
False (bay) .... G
Good Hope (cape) .... F
Great Berg (river) .... H

Hangklip (cape)	G20
Hex River (mts.)	J18
Hooks (river)	H19
Kasteel (mts.)	G18
Limpopo (river)	N16
Maclear (cape)	F20
Orange (river)	K17
Robben (isl.)	F19
Saint Helena (bay)	K18
Sandown (bay)	G20
Seal (isl.)	G20
Slangkop (point)	H20
Sneeuwkop (mt.)	F19
Table (bay)	F19
Table (mt.)	F19
Vaal (river)	M17
Walker (bay)	H20
Zonderend (mts.)	J19
Zonderend (river)	H20
Zululand (district), 570,160	N17

SOUTH-WEST AFRICA (NAMIBIA)

CITIES and TOWNS

Bethanie, 1,142	K17
Gobabis, 4,326	K16
Grootfontein, 1,919	K15
Karasburg, 2,234	K17
Karibib, 1,398	K16
Keetmanshoop, 8,064	K16
Lüderitz, 3,633	J17
Maltahöhe, 1,048	K16
Mariental, 3,498	K16
Okahandja, 2,977	K16
Omaruru, 2,698	K16
Oranjemund, 3,125	J17
Otavi, 1,303	K15
Otjiwarongo, 6,368	K16
Outjo, 2,963	K15
Rehoboth, 2,973	K16
Swakopmund, 4,701	J16
Tsumeb, 7,823	K15
Usakos, 4,278	K16
Windhoek (cap.), 36,050	K16

OTHER FEATURES

Caprivi Strip (reg.), 15,871	L15
Cunene (river)	J15
Damaraland (reg.)	K16
Etosha (salt pan)	K15
Fish (river)	K17
Fria (cape)	J16
Great Namaland (reg.)	K17
Kaokoveld (mts.)	J15
Namib (desert)	J15
Okavango (river)	K17
Ovamboland (reg.), 203,862	K15

SUDAN

PROVINCES

Bahr el Ghazal, 813,000	M10
Blue Nile, 216,000	N 9
Eastern Equatoria, 507,000	N11
El Buheyrat, 574,000	M10
El Gezira, 1,775,000	N 9
Jonglei, 202,000	N10
Kassala, 1,113,000	O 8
Khartoum, 1,160,000	N 8
Nile, 552,000	N 8
Northern, 416,000	M 7
Northern Darfur, 1,013,000	L 8
Northern Kordofan, 1,266,000	M 8
Red Sea, 446,000	O 7
Southern Darfur, 1,160,000	L 9
Southern Kordofan, 951,000	M 9
Upper Nile, 621,000	N 9
Western Equatoria, 251,000	M10
White Nile, 1,122,000	N 9

CITIES and TOWNS

Atbara, 36,000	N 8
Berber, 10,977	N 8
Bor, 5,000	N10
Dongola, 3,350	M 8
Ed Damazin, 12,000	N 9
Ed Damer, 5,458	N 8
Ed Dueim, 12,319	N 9
El Fasher, 26,161	L 9
El Obeid, 53,000	N 9
En Nahud, 16,499	M 9
Er Roseires, 3,927	O 9
Fashoda (Kodok), 9,100	N10
Gedaref, 17,537	O 9
Gemeina, 11,817	L 9
Juba, 10,660	N10
Kadugli, 4,716	M 9
Karima, 5,989	N 8
Kassala, 40,000	O 8
Khartoum (cap.), 194,000	N 8
Khartoum North, 40,000	N 8
Kodok, 9,100	N10
Kosti, 22,688	N 9
Malakal, 9,680	N10
Nyala, 12,278	L 9
Omdurman, 206,000	N 8
Port Sudan, 110,000	O 7
Rumbek, 17,000	M10
Sennar, 8,093	N 9
Shendi, 11,031	N 8
Singa, 9,436	N 9
Suakin, 4,228	O 8
Tokar, 16,802	O 8
Wadi Halfa, 11,006	N 7
Wad Medani, 48,000	N 9

OTHER FEATURES

Abu Shagara, Ras (cape)	O 7
Atbara (river)	O 8
Bahr el 'Arab (river)	M10
Blue Nile (river)	N 9
Cataract, 3rd (rapids)	N 8
Cataract, 4th (rapids)	N 8
Cataract, 5th (rapids)	N 8
Cataract, 6th (rapids)	N 8
Geziza, El (region)	N 9
Lol (dry river)	M10
Meroe (ruins)	N 8
Naqa (ruins)	N 7
Nile (river)	N 8
Nubia (lake)	N 8
Nuri (ruins)	N 8
Sahara (desert)	M 7
Sobat (river)	N10
Sudan (region)	M 9
Sudd (swamp)	N10
White Nile (river)	N10
Yei (river)	N10

SWAZILAND

CITIES and TOWNS

Mbabane (cap.), 13,803	N17

TANZANIA

CITIES and TOWNS

Arusha, 32,452	O12
Bagamoyo, 5,112	O13
Bukoba, 8,141	N12
Chake Chake, 4,862	O13
Chunya, 2,398	N13
Dar es Salaam (cap.), 272,821	P13
Dodoma, 23,559	O13
Geita, 3,066	N12
Iringa, 21,746	O13
Kasanga, †10,462	N13
Kigoma-Ujiji, 21,369	N12
Kilosa, 4,458	O13
Kilwa Kivinje, 2,790	P13
Kondoa, 4,514	O12
Lindi, 13,352	O13
Liwale, †22,205	O13
Mahenge, †32,047	O13
Manyoni, 14,362	N13
Mbeya, 12,479	N13
Morogoro, 25,262	O13
Moshi, 26,864	O12
Mtwara-Mikindani, 20,413	P14
Musoma, 15,412	N12
Mwadui, 7,383	N12
Mwanza, 34,861	N12
Nachingwea, 3,751	O13
Pangani, 2,955	O13
Shinyanga, 5,135	N12
Singida, 9,478	N13
Songea, 5,430	O14
Tabora, 21,012	N13
Tanga, 61,058	O12
Zanzibar, 68,490	P13
Zanzibar, *95,047	P13

OTHER FEATURES

Eyasi (lake)	O12
Great Ruaha (river)	O13
Juani (island), 696	P13
Kilimanjaro (mt.)	O12
Mafia (island), 15,459	P13
Natron (lake)	O12
Nyasa (lake)	N14
Pangani (river)	O13
Pemba (island), 164,321	P13
Rufiji (river)	O13
Rukwa (lake)	N13
Ruvuma (river)	N14
Tanganyika (lake)	N12
Victoria (lake)	N12
Zanzibar (island), 190,494	P13

TOGO

CITIES and TOWNS

Anécho, †11,040	G10
Atakpamé, †18,008	G10
Lomé (cap.), 90,600	G10
Lomé, †149,879	G10
Palimé, †20,331	G10
Sansanné-Mango	G 9
Sokodé, †30,271	G10

TUNISIA

CITIES and TOWNS

Bizerte, 51,700	J 4
Gabès, 32,300	H 5
Gafsa, 32,400	H 5
Kairouan, 46,200	H 4
Mahdia, 10,000	J 4
Médenine, 8,000	J 5
Menzel Bourguiba, 36,700	J 4
Moknine, 14,500	J 4
Nefta, 15,000	H 5
Sfax, 65,000	J 4
Sousse, 48,200	J 4
Tozeur, 11,820	H 5
Tunis (cap.), 662,000	J 4
Tunis, *800,000	J 4

OTHER FEATURES

Bon (cape)	J 4
Djerba (isl.), 62,445	J 5
Gabès (gulf)	J 5
Hammamet (gulf)	J 4
Kerkennah (islands), 13,704	J 5
Tunis (gulf)	J 4

UGANDA

CITIES and TOWNS

Arua, 4,645	N11
Butiaba, 1,216	N11
Entebbe, 10,941	N12
Fort Portal, 8,317	N11
Jinja, 29,741	N11
Kabale, 10,919	N12
Kampala (cap.), 330,000	N11
Masindi, 1,571	N11
Mbarara, 3,844	N12
Soroti, 6,645	N11

OTHER FEATURES

Kioga (lake)	N11
Ruwenzori (mt.)	N11
Victoria (lake)	N12

UPPER VOLTA

CITIES and TOWNS

Bobo-Dioulasso, 56,100	F 9
Dédougou, 3,680	F 9
Dori, 3,500	G 9
Fada-N'Gourma, 4,867	G 9
Gaoua, 5,907	F 9
Kaya, 10,304	F 9
Koudougou, 7,940	F 9
Ouagadougou (cap.), 77,500	F 9
Ouagadougou, *100,000	F 9
Ouahigouya, 12,960	F 9
Tenkodogo, 6,561	G 9

OTHER FEATURES

Black Volta (river)	F 9
Red Volta (river)	F 9
Sudan (region)	F 9
White Volta (river)	F 9

ZAIRE

CITIES and TOWNS

Aketi, 15,339	L11
Banana	J13
Bandundu, 74,467	K12
Banzyville, 6,608	L11
Basankusu, 5,613	L12
Bikoro, 6,491	L12
Boma, 33,143	J13
Bukavu, 134,861	M12
Bumba, 5,182	L11
Bunia, 12,410	M11
Buta, 10,845	L11
Butembo, 9,980	M11
Elisabethville (Lubumbashi), 318,000	M14
Gemena, 8,135	L11
Goma, 14,115	M12
Ingende, 6,730	K12
Isiro, 17,430	M11
Kalemie, 29,934	M11
Kambove (with Shinkolobwe), 14,517	M14
Kamina, 20,915	L13
Kikwit, 111,960	K13
Kindu-Port Empain, 19,385	L12
Kinshasa (cap.), 1,323,039	K12
Kipushi, 22,602	M14
Kisangani, 229,596	M11
Kolwezi, 45,192	L14
Kongolo, 10,434	M12
Léopoldville (Kinshasa) (cap.), 1,323,039	K12
Likasi, 80,075	M14
Lodja, 7,227	L12
Lubumbashi, 318,000	M14
Luluabourg, 428,960	L13
Lusambo, 9,395	L12
Manono, 12,234	M13
Matadi, 110,436	J13
Mbandaka, 107,910	K11
Mbuji-Mayi, 256,154	L13
Mushie, 12,118	K12
Paulis (Isiro), 17,430	M11
Shinkolobwe (with Kambove), 14,517	M14
Thysville, 16,369	K13
Watsa, 6,077	M11
Yangambi, 18,849	L11

OTHER FEATURES

Albert (lake)	M11
Bomu (river)	M11
Congo (river)	K12
Edward (lake)	M12
Kasai (region), 4,306,092	L12
Kasai (river)	K12
Katanga (region), 2,753,714	M13
Kivu (lake)	M12
Kivu (region), 3,361,883	M12
Leopold II (lake)	K12
Lomami (river)	L12
Lualaba (river)	M13
Luapula (river)	M14
Mweru (lake)	M13
Ruwenzori (mt.)	N11
Stanley (falls)	M11
Stanley (pool)	K12
Tanganyika (lake)	N13
Ubangi (river)	K11
Uele (river)	L11
Zaire (Congo) (river)	K12

ZAMBIA

CITIES and TOWNS

Chipata, †13,300	N14
Choma, †11,300	M15
Kabwe, †67,200	M14
Kalomo, 2,560	M15
Kasama, 18,900	N13
Livingstone, †43,000	L15
Lusaka (cap.) †238,200	M15
Mankoya, 1,600	L14
Mansa, 15,700	M14
Mazabuka, †9,400	M15
Mbala, 15,000	N13
Mongu, †10,700	L14
Monze, †4,300	M15
Ndola, †150,800	M14
Nkana, 54,500	M14
Serenje, 1,650	M14
Solwezi, 1,930	M14

OTHER FEATURES

Bangweulu (lake)	N14
Barotseland (region), 417,000	L15
Kafue (river)	M15
Kariba (lake)	M15
Mweru (lake)	M13
Tanganyika (lake)	N13
Victoria (falls)	L15
Zambezi (river)	M15

*City and suburbs.
†Population of urban area.
‡Population of sub-division.
⊙Population of municipality.

AFRICA
SOUTHERN PART
LAMBERT AZIMUTHAL EQUAL-AREA PROJECTION

SCALE OF MILES
0 100 200 300 400 500 600

SCALE OF KILOMETRES
0 100 200 300 400 500 600

Capitals of Countries .... ☆
Other Capitals .... ◉
International Boundaries .... ———
Internal Boundaries .... ——

MAURITIUS

RÉUNION (Fr.)

Copyright by C.S. HAMMOND & CO., N.Y.

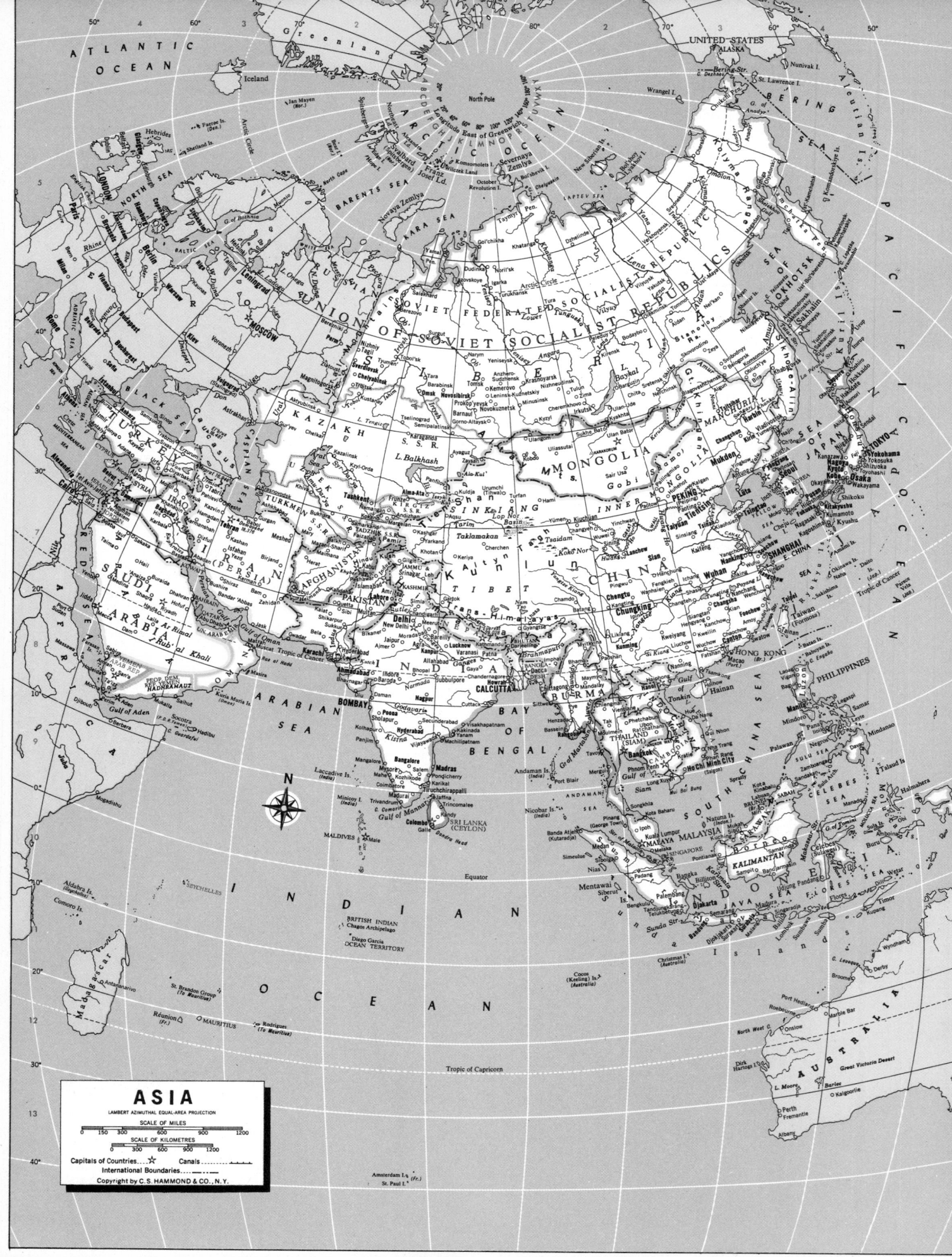

ASIA

LAMBERT AZIMUTHAL EQUAL-AREA PROJECTION

SCALE OF MILES

0 150 300 600 900 1200

SCALE OF KILOMETRES

0 300 600 900 1200

Capitals of Countries... ☆   Canals ....

International Boundaries.........

Copyright by C.S. HAMMOND & CO., N.Y.

POPULATION DISTRIBUTION

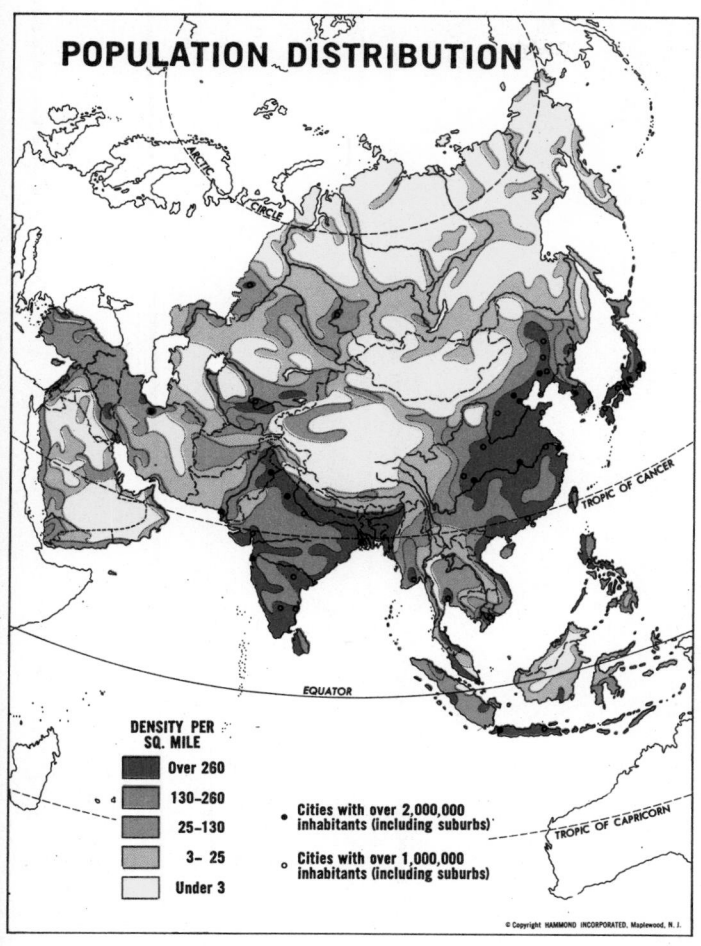

DENSITY PER SQ. MILE

- Over 260
- 130–260
- 25–130
- 3– 25
- Under 3

• Cities with over 2,000,000 inhabitants (including suburbs)

○ Cities with over 1,000,000 inhabitants (including suburbs)

© Copyright HAMMOND INCORPORATED, Maplewood, N. J.

AREA 17,032,000 sq. mi.
POPULATION 2,043,997,000
LARGEST CITY Tokyo
HIGHEST POINT Mt. Everest 29,028 ft.
LOWEST POINT Dead Sea -1,290 ft.

VEGETATION

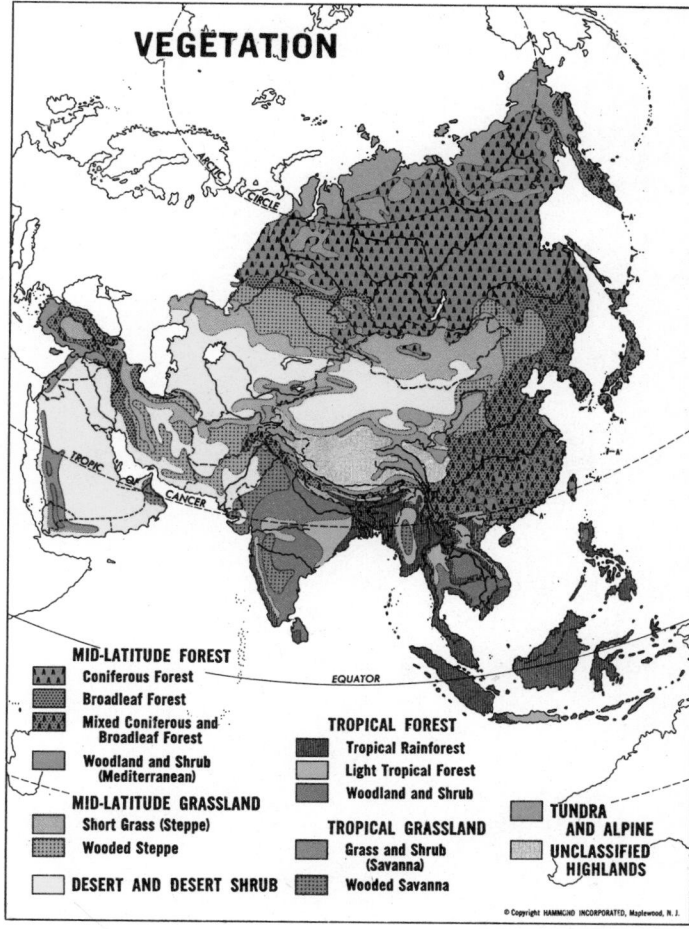

MID-LATITUDE FOREST
- Coniferous Forest
- Broadleaf Forest
- Mixed Coniferous and Broadleaf Forest
- Woodland and Shrub (Mediterranean)

MID-LATITUDE GRASSLAND
- Short Grass (Steppe)
- Wooded Steppe

DESERT AND DESERT SHRUB

TROPICAL FOREST
- Tropical Rainforest
- Light Tropical Forest
- Woodland and Shrub

TROPICAL GRASSLAND
- Grass and Shrub (Savanna)
- Wooded Savanna

TUNDRA AND ALPINE

UNCLASSIFIED HIGHLANDS

© Copyright HAMMOND INCORPORATED, Maplewood, N. J.

60 Near and Middle East

SAUDI ARABIA | KUWAIT | YEMEN ARAB REPUBLIC | BAHRAIN | QATAR | OMAN | PEOPLES DEM. REP. OF YEMEN

AFGHANISTAN

CITIES and TOWNS

Andkhui, 30,000 .... J 2
Baghlan, 92,000 .... J 3
Bala Murghab, 10,000 .... H 2
Balkh, 15,000 .... J 3
Bamian, 25,000 .... J 3
Chahar Burjak. 500 .... H 3

Charikar, 83,700 .... J 3
Daulatabad, 15,000 .... H 3
Daulat Yar, 2,000 .... J 2
Doshi, 5,000 .... J 2
Faizabad, 57,000 .... K 2
Farah, 26,400 .... H 3
Gardez, 33,000 .... J 3
Ghazni, 39,900 .... J 3
Ghurian, 10,000 .... H 3
Girishk, 10,000 .... H 3

Haibak, 35,200 .... J 3
Herat, 71,563 .... H 3
Jalalabad, 48,919 .... K 3
Jurm, 10,000 .... K 2
Kabul (capital), 472,313
Kabul, *600,000 .... J 3
Kala Bist, 26,100 .... H 3
Kalat-i-Ghilzai, 40,500 .... J 3

Kandahar, 127,036 .... J 3
Kandahar, *142,000 .... J 3
Khanabad, 30,000 .... K 2
Kushk, 10,000 .... H 2
Landi Muhammad Amin Khan, 1,000 .... K 3
Maimana, 48,750 .... J 2
Matun, 15,000 .... J 3
Mazar-i-Sharif, 43,197 .... J 2
Mukur, 10,000 .... J 3

Obeh, 5,000 .... H 3
Panjao, 3,000 .... J 3
Qala Panja, 1,000 .... K 2
Qaleh-i-Kang, 15,600 .... H 3
Rudbar, 1,000 .... H 3
Rustak, 10,000 .... K 2
Sabzawar, 5,000 .... H 3
Sar-i-Pul, 5,000 .... J 2
Shahjui, 5,000 .... J 3
Shibarghan, 50,440 .... H 2

Shindand (Sabzawar), 5,000 .... H 3
Taiwara, 5,000 .... H 3
Tashkurghan, 30,000 .... J 2
Zebak, 3,000 .... K 2

OTHER FEATURES

Chagai (hills) .... H 4
Farah Rud (river) .... H 3

Gaud-i-Zirreh (marsh) .... H 4
Hari Rud (river) .... H 3
Helmand (river) .... H 3
Hindu Kush (mts.) .... J 2
Jam (mt.) .... J 3
Kabul (river) .... K 3
Kunar (river) .... K 2
Kunduz (river) .... J 3
Lora (river) .... J 3
Margo, Dasht-i (desert) .... H 3

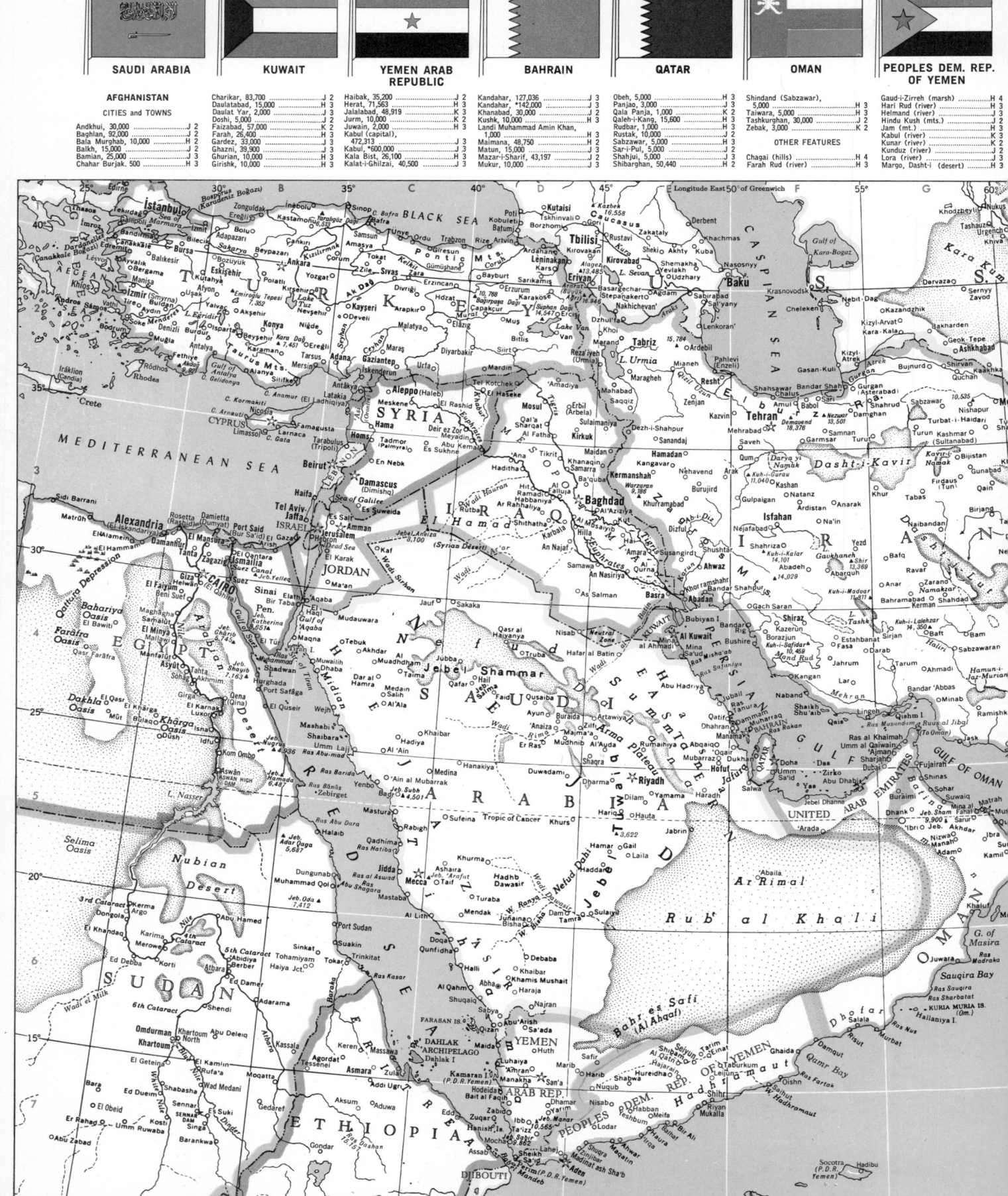

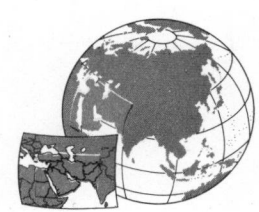

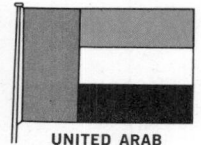

UNITED ARAB EMIRATES

Murghab (river) ....H 2
Namaksar (salt lake) ....H 3
Paropamisus (range) ....H 3
Pyandzh (river) ....K 2
Registan (desert) ....H 3

BAHRAIN
CITIES and TOWNS

Manama (capital),
79,098 ....F 4
Muharraq, 34,430 ....F 4

IRAN
CITIES and TOWNS

Abadan, 272,962 ....E 3
Abadeh, 16,000 ....F 3

Abarquh, 8,000 ....F 3	Borazjun, 20,000 ....F 4
Ahwaz, 206,375 ....E 3	Bujnurd, 31,248 ....G 2
Amul, 40,076 ....F 2	Burujird, 71,476 ....E 3
Anarak, 2,038 ....F 3	Bushire, 26,032 ....F 4
Arak, 71,925 ....E 3	Chalus, 15,000 ....F 2
Ardebil, 83,596 ....E 3	Damghan, 13,000 ....F 2
Ardistan, 6,645 ....F 3	Darab, 13,000 ....G 4
Asterabad (Gurgan),	Dizful, 84,499 ....E 3
51,181 ....F 2	Duzdab (Zahidan),
Babol, 49,973 ....F 2	40,000 ....H 4
Bafq, 5,000 ....G 3	
Baft, 6,000 ....G 4	
Bahramabad, 21,000 ....G 4	
Bam, 22,000 ....G 4	
Bandar 'Abbas, 34,627 ....G 4	
Bandar Shah, 13,000 ....F 2	
Bandar Shahpur, 6,000 ....E 3	
Barfrush (Babol),	
49,973 ....F 2	
Birjand, 25,854 ....G 3	

(continued on following page)

SAUDI ARABIA
AREA 920,000 sq. mi.
POPULATION 7,200,000
CAPITALS Riyadh, Mecca
MONETARY UNIT riyal
MAJOR LANGUAGE Arabic
MAJOR RELIGION Islam

YEMEN ARAB REPUBLIC
AREA 75,000 sq. mi.
POPULATION 5,000,000
CAPITAL San'a
MONETARY UNIT bakcha
MAJOR LANGUAGE Arabic
MAJOR RELIGION Islam

BAHRAIN
AREA 231 sq. mi.
POPULATION 207,000
CAPITAL Manama
MONETARY UNIT Bahrain dinar
MAJOR LANGUAGE Arabic
MAJOR RELIGION Islam

UNITED ARAB EMIRATES
AREA 31,628 sq. mi.
POPULATION 155,881
CAPITAL Abu Dhabi
MONETARY UNIT rupee, Bahrain dinar, Qatar-Dubai riyal
MAJOR LANGUAGE Arabic
MAJOR RELIGION Islam

KUWAIT
AREA 8,000 sq. mi.
POPULATION 733,196
CAPITAL Al Kuwait
MONETARY UNIT Kuwaiti dinar
MAJOR LANGUAGE Arabic
MAJOR RELIGION Islam

PEOPLES DEMOCRATIC REPUBLIC OF YEMEN
AREA 111,075 sq. mi.
POPULATION 1,220,000
CAPITAL Aden
MONETARY UNIT East African shilling
MAJOR LANGUAGE Arabic
MAJOR RELIGION Islam

QATAR
AREA 8,500 sq. mi.
POPULATION 100,000
CAPITAL Doha
MONETARY UNIT Qatar-Dubai riyal
MAJOR LANGUAGE Arabic
MAJOR RELIGION Islam

OMAN
AREA 82,000 sq. mi.
POPULATION 565,000
CAPITAL Muscat
MONETARY UNIT rial saidi
MAJOR LANGUAGE Arabic
MAJOR RELIGION Islam

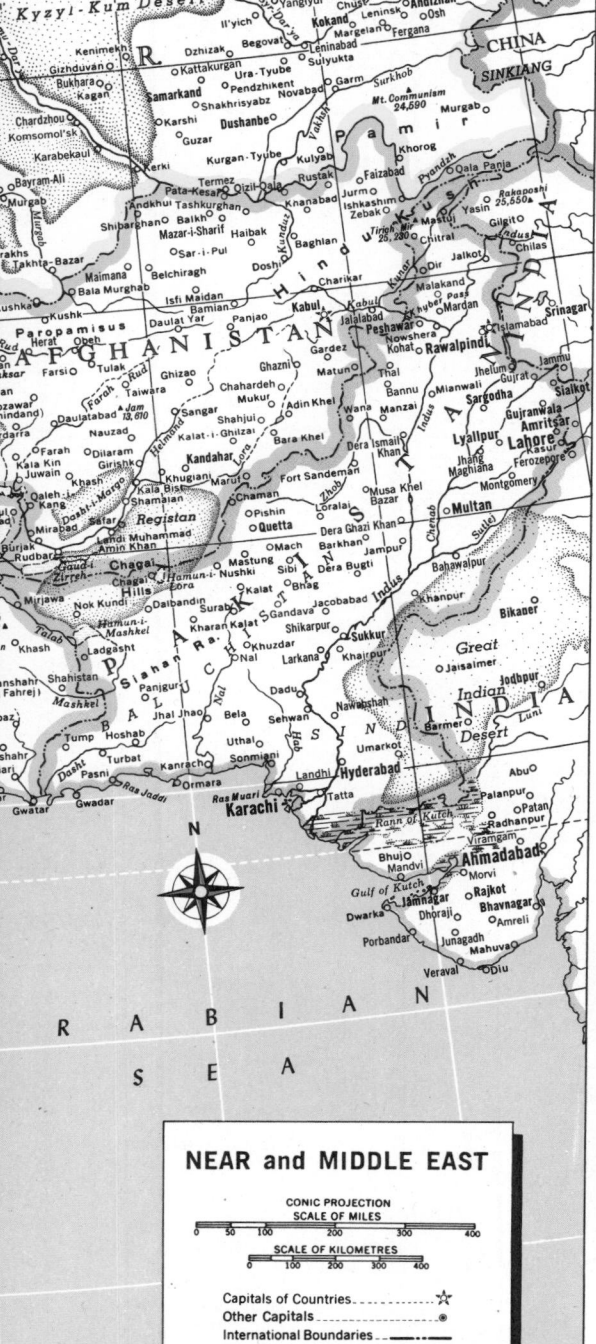

NEAR and MIDDLE EAST

CONIC PROJECTION
SCALE OF MILES

SCALE OF KILOMETRES

Capitals of Countries ....☆
Other Capitals ....◉
International Boundaries ....

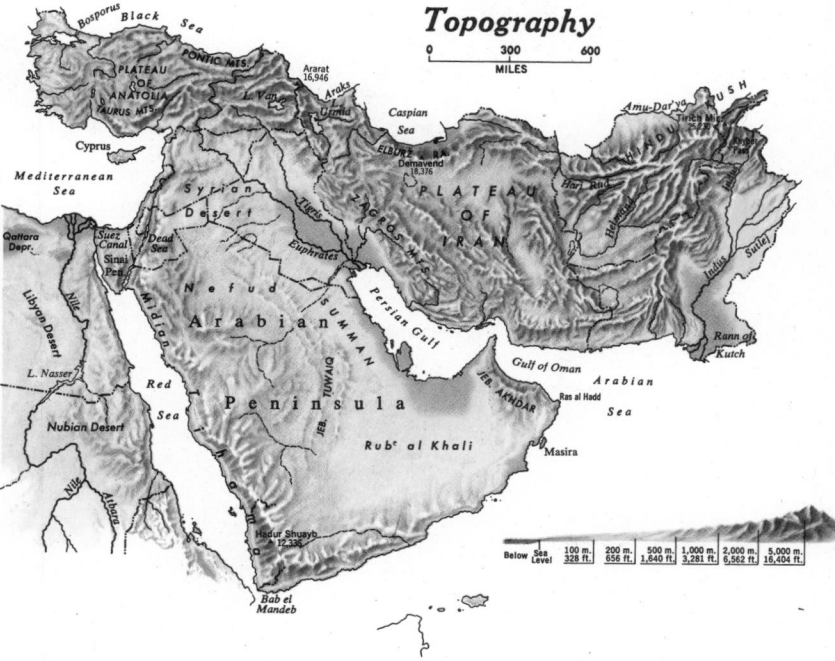

Topography

62 Near and Middle East

(continued)

IRAN (continued)

Enzeli (Pahlevi), 41,785 ....E 2
Estahbanat, 18,187 ....F 4
Fahrej (Iranshahr), 5,000 ....H 4
Fasa, 19,000 ....F 4
Firdaus, 11,000 ....G 3
Gach Saran ....F 3
Garmsar, 4,723 ....F 2
Gulpaigan, 20,515 ....F 3
Gunabad, 8,000 ....G 3
Gurgan, 51,181 ....F 2
Hamadan, 124,167 ....E 3
Iranshahr, 5,000 ....H 4
Isfahan, 424,045 ....F 3
Jahrum, 38,236 ....F 4
Juimand (Gunabad), 8,000 ....G 3
Kangavar, 9,414 ....E 3
Kashan, 58,468 ....F 3
Kashmar, 17,000 ....G 2
Kazerun, 39,758 ....F 4
Kazvin, 88,106 ....E 2
Kerman, 85,404 ....G 3
Kermanshah, 187,930 ....E 3
Khaf, 5,000 ....H 3
Khoi, 47,648 ....E 2
Khorramshahr, 88,536 ....E 3
Khur, 2,912 ....G 3
Khurramabad, 59,578 ....E 3
Lar, 22,000 ....F 4
Mahabad, 28,610 ....E 2
Maragheh, 54,106 ....E 2
Marand, 24,000 ....E 2
Meshed, 409,616 ....H 2
Mianeh, 28,447 ....E 2
Mirjawa, 11,000 ....H 4
Na'in, 5,925 ....F 3
Naishapur (Nishapur), 33,482 ....G 2
Nasratabad (Zabul), 20,000 ....H 3
Natanz, 4,370 ....F 3
Nehavend, 24,000 ....E 3
Nejafabad, 43,384 ....F 3
Nishapur, 33,482 ....G 2
Pahlevi, 41,785 ....E 2
Qain, 6,000 ....G 3
Quchan, 29,133 ....G 2
Qum, 134,292 ....F 3
Ravar, 7,000 ....G 3
Resht, 143,557 ....E 2
Reza'iyeh, 110,749 ....D 2
Sabzawar, 42,415 ....G 2
Sabzawaran, 7,000 ....G 4
Samnan, 31,058 ....F 2
Sanandaj, 54,578 ....E 2
Saqqiz, 17,000 ....E 2
Sari, 44,547 ....F 2
Saveh, 17,565 ....F 2
Shahr-i-Tajan (Sari), 44,547 ....F 2
Shahriza, 34,220 ....F 3
Shahrud, 30,767 ....G 2
Shahsawar, 12,000 ....F 2
Shiraz, 269,865 ....F 4
Shirvan, 11,000 ....G 2
Shushtar, 24,000 ....E 3
Sirjan, 12,160 ....G 4
Sultanabad (Arak), 71,925 ....E 3
Sultanabad (Kashmar), 17,000 ....G 2
Susangird, 21,000 ....E 3
Tabas (Tabas-Masina), 10,000 ....H 3
Tabriz, 403,413 ....E 2
Tehran (capital), 2,719,730 ....F 2
Tun (Firdaus), 11,000 ....G 3
Turbat-i-Haidari, 30,106 ....G 2
Turbat-i-Shaikh Jam, 13,000 ....H 2
Turshiz (Kashmar), 17,000 ....G 2
Turun ....G 2
Urmia (Reza'iyeh), 110,749 ....D 2
Yezd, 93,241 ....F 3
Zabul, 20,000 ....H 3
Zahidan, 39,732 ....H 4
Zarand, 5,000 ....G 3
Zenjan, 58,714 ....E 2

OTHER FEATURES

Araks (river) ....E 2
Atrek (river) ....G 2
Bazman, Kuh-i-(mt.) ....H 4
Demavend (mt.) ....F 2
Diz, Ab-i- (river) ....E 3
Elburz (mts.) ....F 2
Galvkhaneh (lake) ....F 3
Gurgan (river) ....F 2
Haliri (river) ....G 4
Jaz Murian, Hamun-i- (marsh) ....G 4
Karun (river) ....E 3
Kavir, Dasht-i- (salt desert) ....G 3
Kavir-i-Namak (salt desert) ....G 3
Lut, Dasht-i- (desert) ....G 3
Maidani, Ras (cape) ....G 4
Mand Rud (river) ....F 4
Mashkel (river) ....H 4
Mehran (river) ....F 4
Namak, Darya-i- (salt lake) ....F 3
Namaksar (salt lake) ....H 3
Namakzar (marsh) ....G 3
Nezwar (mt.) ....F 2
Oman (gulf) ....G 5
Persian (gulf) ....F 4
Qais (isl.) ....F 4
Qishm (isl.) ....G 4
Qizil Uzun (river) ....E 2
Safidar, Kuh-i- (mt.) ....F 4
Shaikh Shu'aib (isl.) ....F 4
Shir (mt.) ....F 3
Taftan (mt.) ....H 4
Talab (river) ....H 4
Tashk (lake) ....F 4
Urmia (lake) ....E 2
Zagros (mts.) ....E 3

IRAQ

CITIES and TOWNS

Al 'Aziziya, 7,450 ....E 3
Al Falluja, 38,072 ....D 3
Al Musaiyib, 15,955 ....D 3
Al Qurna, 5,638 ....E 3
'Amadiya, 2,578 ....D 2
'Amara, 64,847 ....E 3
An Najaf, 128,096 ....D 3
An Nasiriya, 60,405 ....E 3
'Ana, 6,884 ....D 3
Ar Rahhaliya ....D 3
Arbela (Erbil), 90,320 ....D 2
As Salman, 1,789 ....E 3
Baghdad (capital), 502,503 ....E 3
Baghdad, *1,745,328 ....E 3
Ba'quba, 34,575 ....D 3
Basra, 313,327 ....E 3
Erbil, 90,320 ....D 2
Habbaniya, 14,405 ....D 3
Haditha, 6,870 ....D 3
Hai, 16,988 ....E 3
Hilla, 84,717 ....D 3
Hit, 9,131 ....D 3
Karbala', 83,301 ....D 3
Khanaqin, 23,522 ....D 3
Kirkuk, 167,413 ....D 2
Kut, 42,116 ....E 3
Maidan, 354 ....E 3
Mosul, 315,157 ....D 2
Qal'a Sharqat, 2,434 ....D 2
Ramadi, 28,723 ....D 3
Rutba, 5,091 ....D 3
Samarra, 24,746 ....D 3
Samawa, 33,473 ....D 3
Shithatha, 2,326 ....D 3
Sulaimaniya, 86,822 ....E 2
Tikrit, 9,921 ....D 3

OTHER FEATURES

Al Batin, Wadi (river) ....E 4
'Aneiza, Jebel (mt.) ....C 3
'Ar'ar, Wadi (dry river) ....D 3
El Hamad (desert) ....D 3
Euphrates (river) ....E 3
Hauran, Wadi (dry river) ....D 3
Mesopotamia (reg.) ....D 3
Tigris (river) ....E 3

KUWAIT

CITIES and TOWNS

Al Kuwait (capital), 80,008 ....E 4
Al Kuwait, *217,364 ....E 4
Mina al-Ahmadi ....E 4

OTHER FEATURES

Bubiyan (isl.) ....E 4
Persian (gulf) ....F 4

OMAN

CITIES and TOWNS

Adam ....G 5
Buraimi ....G 5
Dhank ....G 5
Ibra ....G 5
'Ibri ....G 5
Juwara ....G 6
Kamil ....G 5
Khaluf ....G 5
Khasab ....G 4
Manah ....G 5
Matrah, 15,000 ....G 5
Mina al Fahal ....G 5
Murbat ....G 6
Muscat (capital), 7,500 ....G 5
Nizwa ....G 5
Quryat ....G 5
Risut ....F 6
Salala, 4,000 ....F 6
Sarur ....G 5
Shinas ....G 5
Sohar ....G 5
Sur ....G 5
Suwaiq ....G 5

OTHER FEATURES

Akhdar, Jebel (range) ....G 5
Arabian (sea) ....H 5
Batina (reg.) ....G 5
Dhofar (reg.), 120,000 ....F 6
Hadd, Ras al (cape) ....G 5
Hallaniya (isl.), 78 ....G 6
Jibsh, Ras (cape) ....G 5
Kuria Muria (isls.), 78 ....G 6
Madraka, Ras (cape) ....G 6
Masira (gulf) ....G 6
Masira (isl.) ....G 5
Musandam, Ras (cape) ....G 4
Nus, Ras (cape) ....G 6
Oman (gulf) ....G 5
Oman (reg.) ....G 5
Ruus al Jibal (dist.) ....G 4
Sauqira (bay) ....G 6
Sauqira, Ras (cape) ....G 6
Sham, Jebel (mt.) ....G 5
Sharbatat, Ras (cape) ....G 6

QATAR

CITIES and TOWNS

Doha (capital), 45,000 ....F 4
Dukhan, 2,500 ....F 4
Umm Sa'id, 3,500 ....F 5

OTHER FEATURES

Persian (gulf) ....F 4
Rakan, Ras (cape) ....F 4

SAUDI ARABIA

PROVINCES

'Asir, 900,000 ....D 6
Eastern, 2,250,000 ....E 4
Hejaz, 1,250,000 ....C 4
Nejd, 1,500,000 ....D 4

CITIES and TOWNS

Abha ....D 6
Abqaiq ....E 4
Abu 'Arish ....D 6
Abu Hadriya ....E 4
'Ain al Mubarrak ....C 5
Al 'Ain ....C 4
Al 'Ala ....C 4
Al 'Auda ....E 4
Al Lith ....C 5
Al Muadhdham ....C 4
Al Qahm ....D 6
'Anaiza ....D 4
Artawiya ....E 4
Badr ....C 5
Buraida ....D 4
Buraimi ....G 5
Dam ....D 5
Dammam, 3,000 ....F 4
Dar al Hamra ....C 4
Dhaba ....C 4
Dhahran, 12,500 ....E 4
Dharma ....E 5
Dilam ....E 5
Doqa ....D 6
Duwadami ....D 5
Er Ras ....D 4
Faid ....D 4
Haddar ....E 5
Hadiya ....C 4
Hafar al Batin ....E 4
Hail, 20,000 ....D 4
Halli ....D 6
Hamar ....E 5
Hanakiya ....D 5
Haql ....C 4
Haradh ....E 5
Haraja ....D 6
Hariq ....E 5
Hauta ....E 5
Hofuf, 83,000 ....E 4
Jabrin ....E 5
Jauf, 5,000 ....C 4
Jidda, 194,000 ....C 5
Jubail ....F 4
Jubba ....D 4
Junaina ....D 5
Kaf ....C 3
Khaibar ....D 6
Khamis Mushait ....D 6
Khurma ....D 5
Khurs ....D 5
Laila ....E 5
Majma'a ....D 4
Maqna ....C 4
Mastaba ....C 5
Mastura ....C 5
Mecca (capital), 185,000 ....C 5
Medain Salih ....C 4
Medina, 72,000 ....D 5
Mendak ....D 5
Mina Sa'ud ....E 4
Mubarraz ....E 4
Mudhnib ....D 4
Muwailih ....C 4
Najran ....D 6
Nisab ....D 4
Oqair ....E 4
Qadhima ....C 5
Qafar ....D 4
Qasr al Haiyanya ....D 4
Qatif ....E 4
Qizan ....D 6
Qunfidha ....D 6
Qusaiba ....D 4
Rabigh ....C 5
Ras Tanura ....F 4
Riyadh (capital), 225,000 ....E 5
Rumaihiya ....E 4
Sabya ....D 6
Sakaka ....D 4
Salwa ....F 5
Shaqra ....D 4
Shuqaiq ....D 6
Sufeina ....D 5
Sulaiyil ....E 5
Taif, 54,000 ....D 5
Taima ....C 4
Tamra ....D 5
Tebuk ....C 4
Truba ....D 4
Turaba ....D 5
Umm Lajj ....C 4
Wejh ....C 4
Yamama ....E 5
Yenbo ....C 5
Zilfi ....E 4

OTHER FEATURES

Abu-mad (cape) ....C 5
'Ar'ar, Wadi (dry river) ....D 3
Al Ahqaf (Bahr es Safi) (desert) ....E 6
'Aneiza, Jebel (mt.) ....C 3
'Aqaba (gulf) ....C 4
Arafat, Jebel (mt.) ....D 5
Ar'ar, Wadi (dry river) ....D 3
Arma (plateau) ....E 4
Aswad, Ras al (cape) ....C 5
Bahr es Safi (desert) ....E 6
Barida, Ras (cape) ....C 5
Bisha, Wadi (dry river) ....D 5
Dahana (desert) ....E 4
Dawasir, Wadi (dry river) ....E 5
Dawasir, Hadb (range) ....D 5
Farasan (isls.) ....D 6
Hasa (reg.) ....E 4
Hatiba, Ras (cape) ....C 5
Jafura (desert) ....F 5
Mashabi (isl.) ....C 4
Midian (district) ....C 4
Misha'ab, Ras (cape) ....E 4
Nefud (desert) ....D 4
Nefud Dahi (desert) ....D 5
Persian (gulf) ....F 4
Ranya, Wadi (dry river) ....D 5
Red (Nefud) (desert) ....D 4
Red (sea) ....C 5
Rima, Wadi (river) ....D 4
Rimal, Ar (desert) ....F 5
Rub' al Khali (desert) ....F 5
Safaniya, Ras (cape) ....E 4
Salma, Jebel (mts.) ....D 4
Shaibara (isl.) ....C 4
Shammar, Jebel (plateau) ....D 4
Sirhan, Wadi (dry river) ....C 3
Subh, Jebel (mt.) ....C 5
Summan (plateau) ....E 4
Tihama (reg.) ....C 5
Tiran (isl.) ....B 4
Tiran (str.) ....B 4
Tuwaiq, Jebel (range) ....E 5

UNITED ARAB EMIRATES

CITIES and TOWNS

Abu Dhabi (capital), 22,000 ....F 5
Abu Dhabi, *35,000 ....F 5
'Ajman, 3,725 ....G 4
'Arada ....F 5
Buraimi ....G 5
Dubai, 13,092 ....F 4
Dubai, *57,400 ....F 4
Fujairah, 761 ....G 4
Jebel Dhauna ....F 5
Ras al Khaimah, 5,244 ....F 4
Sharjah, 19,198 ....F 4
Sharjah, *20,621 ....F 4
Umm al Qaiwain, 2,928 ....F 4

OTHER FEATURES

Das (isl.) ....F 4
Persian (gulf) ....F 4
Yas (isl.) ....F 5
Zirko (isl.) ....F 5

YEMEN ARAB REP.

CITIES and TOWNS

'Amran ....D 6
Bait al Faqih ....D 7
Dhamar ....D 7
Harib ....E 6
Hodeida, 40,000 ....D 7
Huth ....D 6
Ibb ....D 7
Luhaiya (Loheia) ....D 6
Maida, 2,500 ....D 6
Manakha ....D 6
Marib ....D 6
Mocha ....D 7
Sa'ada ....D 6
Safir ....E 6
San'a (capital), 100,000 ....D 6
Sheikh Sa'id ....D 7
Ta'izz, 80,000 ....D 7
Yarim, 5,000 ....D 7
Zabid, 8,000 ....D 7

OTHER FEATURES

Hanish (isls.) ....D 7
Manar, Jebel (mt.) ....D 7
Red (sea) ....C 5
Sabir, Jebel (mt.) ....D 7
Tihama (reg.) ....C 5
Zuqar (isl.) ....D 7

YEMEN, PEOPLES DEM. REPUBLIC OF

CITIES and TOWNS

Aden (capital), 150,000 ....E 7
Aden, *225,000 ....E 7
Ahwar ....E 7
Al Qatn ....E 6
Balhaf ....E 7
Bir 'Ali ....E 7
Damqut ....F 6
'Einat ....E 6
Ghaida ....F 6
Hadibu ....F 7
Hajarain ....E 6
Haura ....E 7
Hureidha ....E 6
'Irqa ....E 7
Lahej ....E 7
Leijun ....E 6
Lodar ....E 7
Madinat ash Sha'b, 29,897 ....E 7
Maqatin ....E 7
Meifa ....E 7
Mukalla, 30,000 ....E 7
Nisab ....E 7
Nuqub ....E 6
Qishn ....F 6
Riyan ....E 7
Saihut, 10,000 ....F 6
Seiyun ....E 6
Shabwa ....E 6
Shibam, 6,000 ....E 6
Shihr ....E 7
Shuqra ....E 7
Taburkum ....E 6
Tarim ....E 6
Yeshbum ....E 7
Zinjibar ....E 7

OTHER FEATURES

Fartak, Ras (cape) ....F 6
Hadhramaut (dist.), 350,000 ....E 7
Hadhramaut, Wadi (dry river) ....F 7
Kamaran (island), 2,200 ....D 6
Mandeb, Bab el (strait) ....D 7
Perim (isl.), 381 ....D 7
Socotra (island), 14,000 ....F 7

*City and suburbs.

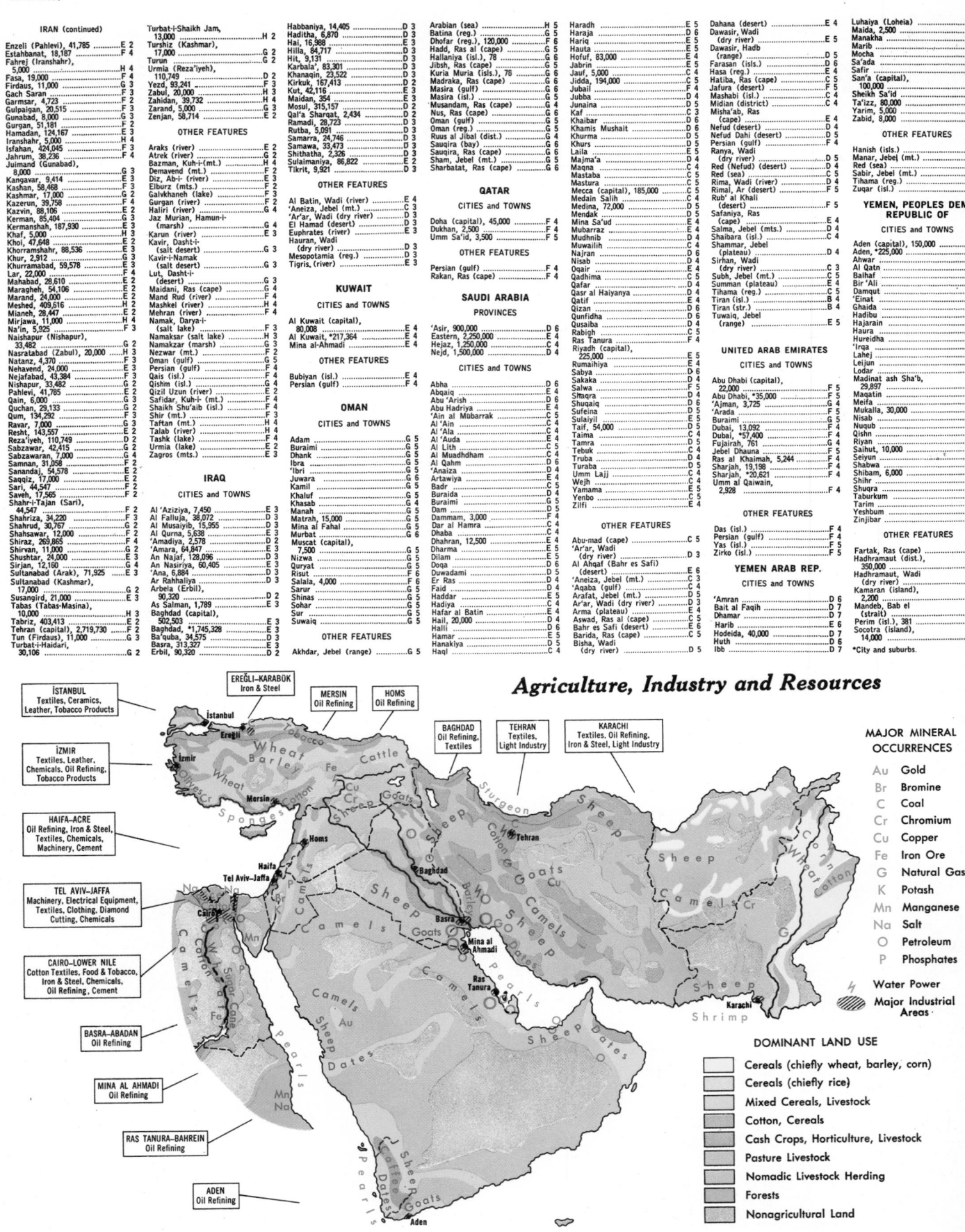

Agriculture, Industry and Resources

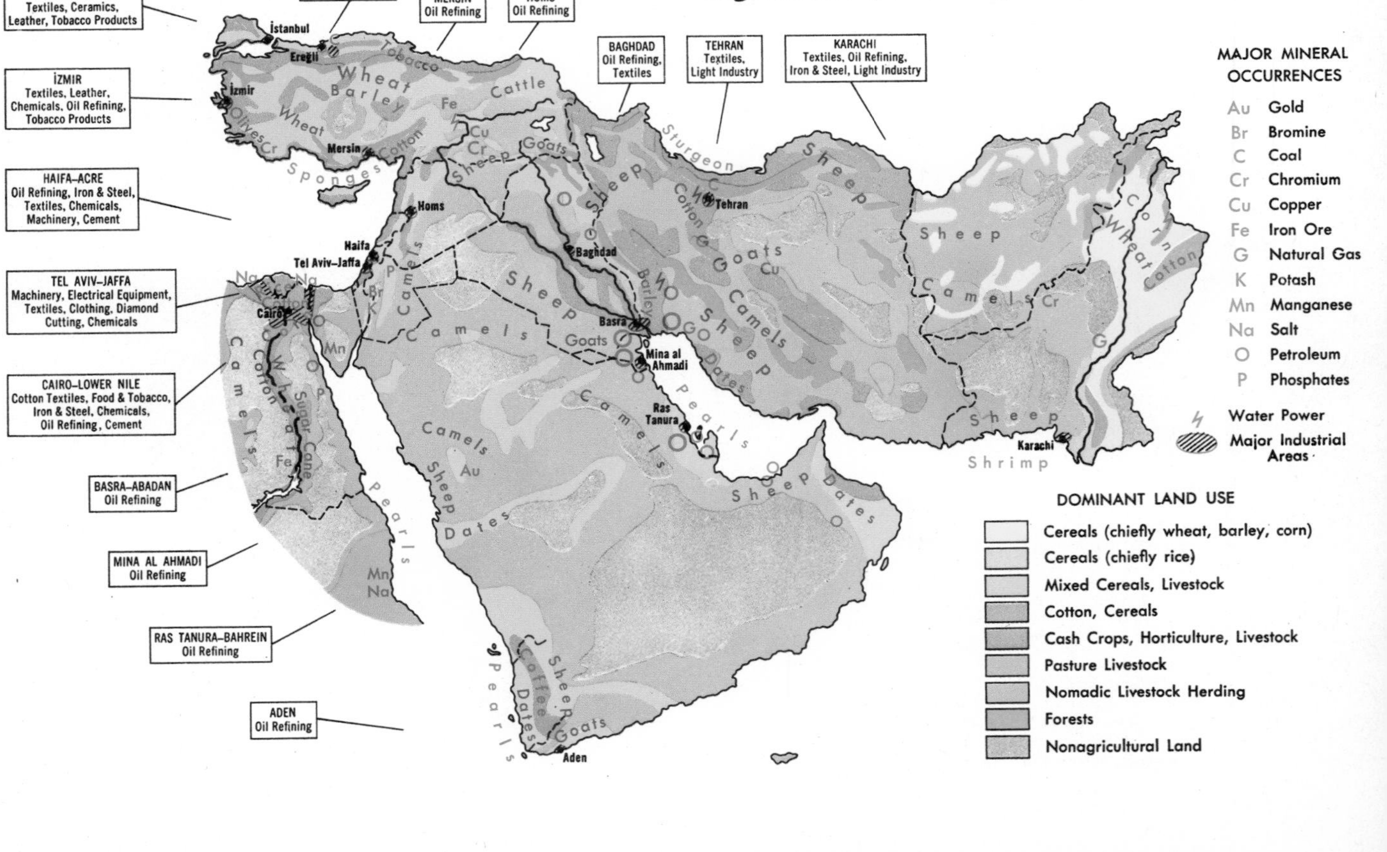
İSTANBUL
Textiles, Ceramics, Leather, Tobacco Products
EREĞLI–KARABÜK
Iron & Steel
MERSIN
Oil Refining
HOMS
Oil Refining
BAGHDAD
Oil Refining, Textiles
TEHRAN
Textiles, Light Industry
KARACHI
Textiles, Oil Refining, Iron & Steel, Light Industry
İZMIR
Textiles, Leather, Chemicals, Oil Refining, Tobacco Products
HAIFA–ACRE
Oil Refining, Iron & Steel, Textiles, Chemicals, Machinery, Cement
TEL AVIV–JAFFA
Machinery, Electrical Equipment, Textiles, Clothing, Diamond Cutting, Chemicals
CAIRO–LOWER NILE
Cotton Textiles, Food & Tobacco, Iron & Steel, Chemicals, Oil Refining, Cement
BASRA–ABADAN
Oil Refining
MINA AL AHMADI
Oil Refining
RAS TANURA–BAHREIN
Oil Refining
ADEN
Oil Refining
İstanbul
Ereğli
İzmir
Mersin
Homs
Haifa
Tel Aviv–Jaffa
Cairo
Baghdad
Tehran
Basra
Mina al Ahmadi
Ras Tanura
Karachi
Aden
Tobacco
Wheat
Barley
Cattle
Olives
Cotton
Sponges
Sheep
Goats
Camels
Sturgeon
Pearls
Dates
Sugar Cane
Coffee
Corn
Shrimp
MAJOR MINERAL OCCURRENCES
Au Gold
Br Bromine
C Coal
Cr Chromium
Cu Copper
Fe Iron Ore
G Natural Gas
K Potash
Mn Manganese
Na Salt
O Petroleum
P Phosphates
Water Power
Major Industrial Areas
DOMINANT LAND USE
Cereals (chiefly wheat, barley, corn)
Cereals (chiefly rice)
Mixed Cereals, Livestock
Cotton, Cereals
Cash Crops, Horticulture, Livestock
Pasture Livestock
Nomadic Livestock Herding
Forests
Nonagricultural Land

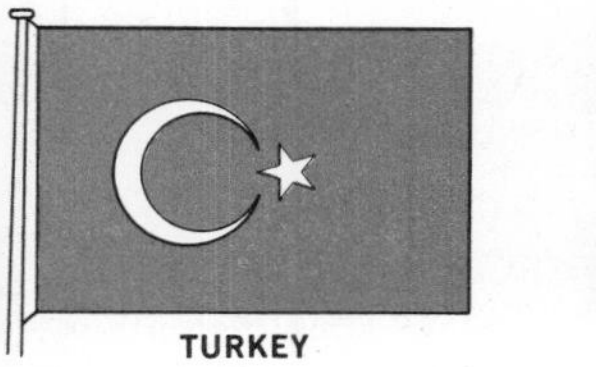
TURKEY

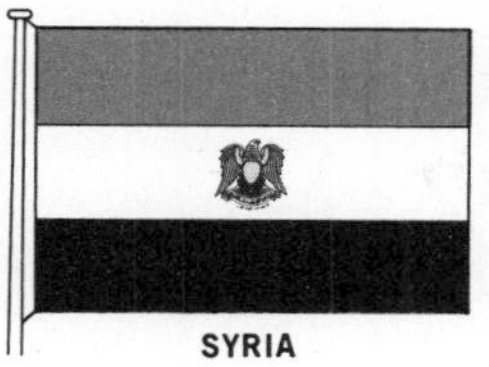
SYRIA

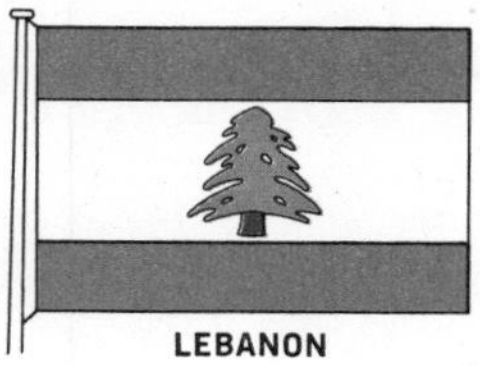
LEBANON

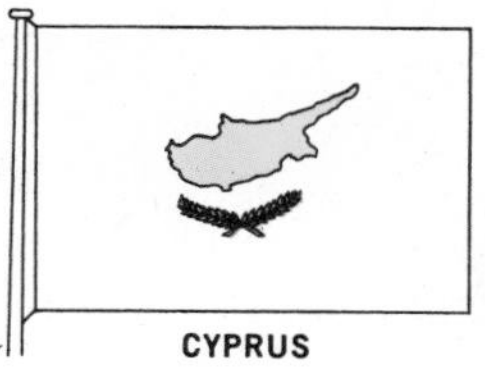
CYPRUS

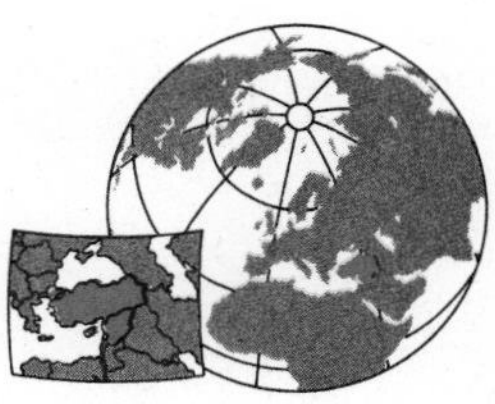

TURKEY

AREA 301,381 sq. mi.
POPULATION 34,375,000
CAPITAL Ankara
LARGEST CITY Istanbul (greater)
HIGHEST POINT Ararat 16,914 ft.
MONETARY UNIT Turkish pound (lira)
MAJOR LANGUAGE Turkish
MAJOR RELIGION Islam

SYRIA

AREA 71,498 sq. mi.
POPULATION 5,866,000
CAPITAL Damascus
LARGEST CITY Damascus
HIGHEST POINT Hermon 9,232 ft.
MONETARY UNIT Syrian pound
MAJOR LANGUAGES Arabic, Kurdish, Armenian
MAJOR RELIGIONS Islam, Christianity

LEBANON

AREA 4,015 sq. mi.
POPULATION 2,800,000
CAPITAL Beirut
LARGEST CITY Beirut
HIGHEST POINT Qurnet es Sauda 10,131 ft.
MONETARY UNIT Lebanese pound
MAJOR LANGUAGE Arabic
MAJOR RELIGIONS Christianity, Islam

CYPRUS

AREA 3,473 sq. mi.
POPULATION 649,000
CAPITAL Nicosia
LARGEST CITY Nicosia
HIGHEST POINT Troodos 6,406 ft.
MONETARY UNIT Cypriot pound
MAJOR LANGUAGES Greek, Turkish
MAJOR RELIGIONS Eastern (Greek) Orthodoxy, Islam

CYPRUS

CITIES and TOWNS

Famagusta, 38,000 .... F 5
Famagusta, *41,000 .... F 5
Kyrenia, 3,500 .... E 5
Kyrenia, *4,500 .... E 5
Larnaca, 20,000 .... E 5
Larnaca, *21,000 .... E 5
Lefka, 3,673 .... E 5
Lefkara, 2,075 .... E 5
Limassol, 46,500 .... E 5
Limassol, *50,000 .... E 5
Morphou, 6,642 .... E 5
Nicosia (capital), 47,000 .... E 5
Nicosia, *112,000 .... E 5
Paphos, 10,000 .... E 5
Paphos, *11,500 .... E 5
Yialousa, 2,541 .... F 5

OTHER FEATURES

Andreas (cape) .... F 5
Arnauti (cape) .... E 5
Famagusta (bay) .... F 5
Gata (cape) .... E 5
Greco (cape) .... F 5
Klides (isls.) .... F 5
Kormakiti (cape) .... E 5
Larnaca (bay) .... E 5
Morphou (bay) .... E 5
Sovereign Base Area, 3,602 .... E 5
Troodos (mt.) .... E 5

LEBANON

CITIES and TOWNS

'Aleih, 18,630 .... F 6
Amyun, 7,926 .... F 5
Ba'albek, 15,560 .... G 5
Batrun, 5,976 .... F 5
Beirut (capital), 700,000 .... F 6
Beirut, *840,000 .... F 6
En Naqura, 967 .... F 6
Hermil, 2,652 .... G 5
Merj 'Uyun, 9,318 .... F 6
Rasheiya, 6,731 .... F 6
Rayak, 1,480 .... G 6
Saida, 32,200 .... F 6
Sidon (Saida), 32,200 .... F 6
Sur, 16,483 .... F 6
Tarabulus (Tripoli), 127,611 .... F 5
Tyre (Sur), 16,483 .... F 6
Zahle, 53,121 .... F 6
Zegharta, 18,210 .... G 5

OTHER FEATURES

Hermon (mt.) .... F 6
Lebanon (range) .... F 6
Litani (Leontes) (river) .... F 6
Sauda, Qurnet es (mt.) .... G 5

SYRIA

GOVERNORATES

Aleppo, 1,131,854 .... G 4
Damascus, 1,060,484 .... G 6
Damascus (municipality), 630,063 .... G 6
Deir es Zor, 286,010 .... H 5
Der'a, 221,275 .... G 6
El Quneitra, 6,396 .... F 6
Es Suweida, 151,500 .... G 6
Hama, 390,084 .... G 5
Haseke, 309,279 .... J 4
Homs, 504,098 .... G 5
Idlib, 374,751 .... G 5
Latakia, 625,473 .... G 5
Rashid, 124,876 .... H 5

CITIES and TOWNS

Abu Kemal, 6,907 .... J 5
Aleppo, 566,770 .... G 4
A'zaz, 13,923 .... G 4
Baniyas, 8,537 .... F 5
Damascus (cap.), 789,840 .... G 6
Deir ez Zor, 60,335 .... H 5
Der'a, 20,465 .... G 6
Dimishq (Damascus) (capital), 789,840 .... G 6
Duma, 30,050 .... G 6
El Bab, 27,366 .... G 4
El Haseke, 23,074 .... J 4
El Ladhiqiya (Latakia), 72,378 .... F 5
El Quneitra, 206 .... F 6
El Rashid, 11,998 .... H 5
En Nebk, 16,334 .... G 5
Es Suweida, 17,592 .... G 6
Haleb (Aleppo), 566,770 .... G 4
Hama, 196,224 .... G 5
Harim, 6,837 .... G 4
Homs, 231,877 .... G 5
Idlib, 37,501 .... G 5
Jeble, 15,715 .... F 5
Jerablus, 8,610 .... G 4
Jisr esh Shughur, 13,131 .... G 5
Latakia, 72,378 .... F 5
Masyaf, 7,058 .... G 5
Membij, 13,796 .... G 4
Meyadin, 12,515 .... J 5
Palmyra (Tadmor), 10,670 .... H 5
Qamishliye, 31,448 .... J 4
Quteife, 4,993 .... G 6
Raqqa (El Rashid), 11,998 .... H 5
Safita, 9,650 .... G 5
Selemiya, 25,728 .... G 5
Tadmor, 10,670 .... H 5
Tartus, 19,137 .... F 5
Zebdani, 10,010 .... G 6

OTHER FEATURES

'Abdul 'Aziz, Jebel (mts.) .... J 4
Abu Rujmein, Jebel (mts.) .... H 5
'Asi (river) .... G 5
Druz, Jebel ed (mts.) .... G 6
Euphrates (El Furat) (river) .... J 5
Furat, El (river) .... H 4
Hermon (mt.) .... F 6
Khabur (river) .... J 5
Orontes ('Asi) (river) .... G 5
Ruad (island) .... F 5
Sharqi, Jebel esh (range) .... G 5
Tigris (river) .... K 4

TURKEY

PROVINCES

Adana, 902,712 .... F 4
Adıyaman, 267,288 .... H 4
Afyon-Karahisar, 502,248 .... D 3
Ağrı, 246,961 .... K 3
Amasya, 285,729 .... G 2
Ankara, 1,644,302 .... E 3
Antalya, 486,910 .... D 4
Artvin, 210,065 .... J 2
Aydın, 524,918 .... B 4
Balıkesir, 708,342 .... B 3
Bilecik, 139,041 .... D 2
Bingöl, 150,521 .... J 3
Bitlis, 154,069 .... J 3
Bolu, 383,939 .... D 2
Burdur, 194,950 .... D 4
Bursa, 755,504 .... C 2
Çanakkale, 350,317 .... B 2
Çankırı, 250,706 .... E 2
Çorum, 485,567 .... F 2
Denizli, 463,369 .... C 4
Diyarbakır, 475,916 .... H 4
Edirne, 303,234 .... B 2
Elâzığ, 322,727 .... H 3
Erzincan, 258,586 .... H 3
Erzurum, 628,001 .... J 3
Eskişehir, 415,101 .... D 3
Gaziantep, 511,026 .... G 4
Giresun, 428,015 .... H 2
Gümüşhane, 262,731 .... H 2
Hakkâri, 83,937 .... K 4
Hatay, 506,154 .... G 4
Içel, 511,273 .... F 4
Isparta, 266,240 .... D 4
Istanbul, 2,293,823 .... C 2
Izmir, 1,234,667 .... B 3
Kars, 606,313 .... K 2
Kastamonu, 441,638 .... E 2
Kayseri, 536,206 .... F 3
Kırklareli, 258,386 .... B 2
Kırsehir, 196,836 .... F 3
Kocaeli, 335,518 .... D 2
Konya, 1,122,622 .... E 4
Kütahya, 398,081 .... C 3
Malatya, 452,624 .... H 3
Manisa, 748,545 .... B 3
Maraş, 438,423 .... G 4
Mardin, 397,880 .... J 4
Muğla, 334,973 .... C 4
Muş, 198,716 .... J 3
Nevşehir, 203,316 .... F 3
Niğde, 362,044 .... F 4
Ordu, 543,863 .... G 2
Rize, 281,099 .... J 2
Sakarya, 404,078 .... D 2
Samsun, 755,946 .... F 2
Siirt, 264,832 .... J 4
Sinop, 266,069 .... F 2
Sivas, 705,186 .... G 3
Tekirdağ, 287,381 .... B 2
Tokat, 495,352 .... G 2
Trabzon, 595,782 .... H 2
Tunceli, 154,175 .... H 3
Urfa, 450,798 .... H 4
Uşak, 190,536 .... C 3
Van, 266,840 .... K 3
Yozgat, 437,883 .... F 3
Zonguldak, 650,191 .... D 2

CITIES and TOWNS

Abana, 2,455 .... F 1
Acıgol, 3,265 .... F 3
Acıpayam, 4,118 .... C 4
Adalia (Antalya), 71,833 .... D 4
Adana, 289,919 .... F 4
Adapazarı, 86,124 .... D 2
Adilcevaz, 6,148 .... K 3
Adıyaman, 22,153 .... H 4
Afşin, 8,069 .... G 3
Afyon, 44,026 .... D 3
Ağlasun, 3,730 .... D 4
Ağlı, 3,425 .... E 2
Ağrı (Karaköse), 24,168 .... K 3
Ahlat, 5,879 .... K 3
Akçaabat, 7,600 .... H 2
Akçadağ, 5,995 .... G 3
Akçakale, 4,526 .... H 4
Akçakoca, 7,179 .... D 2
Akdağmadeni, 4,321 .... F 3
Akhisar, 46,167 .... B 3
Aksaray, 24,414 .... F 3
Akşehir, 25,269 .... D 3
Akseki, 2,505 .... D 4
Akviran, 3,786 .... E 4
Akyazi, 9,090 .... D 2
Alaca, 8,288 .... F 2
Alaçam, 7,833 .... F 2
Alanya, 12,436 .... D 4
Alaşehir, 16,012 .... C 3
Alexandretta (Iskenderun), 69,382 .... G 4
Aliağa, 3,087 .... B 3
Alibeyköyü, 15,199 .... D 6
Almus, 4,110 .... G 2
Alpu, 2,709 .... D 3
Altindağ, 89,838 .... E 2
Altınova, 6,368 .... B 3
Altıntaş, 2,361 .... C 3
Amasya, 34,168 .... G 2
Anadoluhisari, 13,959 .... D 6
Anamur, 11,246 .... E 4
Andırın, 3,695 .... G 4
Ankara (capital), 905,660 .... E 3
Antâkya, 57,855 .... G 4
Antalya, 71,833 .... D 4
Araç, 2,820 .... E 2
Aralık, 2,879 .... L 3
Arapkir, 7,056 .... H 3
Ardahan, 9,117 .... K 2
Ardeşen, 5,488 .... J 2
Arhavi, 4,510 .... J 2
Arnavutköy, 22,468 .... D 6
Arsin, 4,028 .... H 2
Artova, 2,863 .... G 2
Artvin, 9,847 .... J 2
Aşkale, 6,943 .... J 3
Aslanköy, 3,656 .... F 4
Avanos, 5,675 .... F 3
Ayancık, 5,320 .... F 2
Ayas, 3,873 .... E 2
Aybastı, 7,450 .... G 2
Aydın, 43,483 .... B 4
Ayvacık, 2,277 .... B 3
Ayvalık, 16,283 .... B 3
Babadağ, 5,511 .... C 4
Babaeski, 13,879 .... B 2
Bafra, 26,239 .... F 2
Bahçe, 2,264 .... G 4
Bakırköy, 65,285 .... D 6
Baklan, 2,680 .... C 4
Balâ, 3,646 .... E 3
Balıkesir, 69,341 .... B 3
Banaz, 3,495 .... C 3
Bandırma, 33,116 .... B 2
Barak, 3,117 .... G 4
Bartın, 14,259 .... E 2
Başkale, 4,007 .... K 3
Başmakçı, 5,093 .... D 4
Batman, 24,990 .... J 4
Bayburt, 15,184 .... H 2
Bayındır, 11,273 .... B 3
Bayramiç, 4,607 .... B 3
Bergama, 24,121 .... B 3
Beşiktaş, 58,814 .... D 6
Besni, 11,625 .... G 4
Beykoz, 37,730 .... D 5
Beylerbeyi, 21,741 .... D 6
Beyoğlu, 39,984 .... D 6
Beypazarı, 9,860 .... D 2
Beyşehir, 7,456 .... D 4
Biga, 12,063 .... B 2
Bigadiç, 4,820 .... C 3
Bilecik, 9,722 .... D 2
Bingöl (Çapakçur), 11,727 .... J 3
Birecik, 15,317 .... H 4
Bismil, 4,444 .... J 4
Bitlis, 18,725 .... J 3
Bodrum, 5,136 .... B 4
Boğazlıyan, 7,925 .... F 3
Bolu, 21,700 .... D 2
Bolvadin, 20,139 .... D 3
Bor, 14,309 .... F 4
Borçka, 3,763 .... J 2
Bornova, 30,445 .... B 3
Boyabat, 9,418 .... F 2
Bozdoğan, 6,739 .... C 4
Bozkır, 3,112 .... E 4
Bozkurt, 2,954 .... F 2
Bozova, 3,425 .... H 4
Bozüyük, 10,842 .... D 3
Bucak, 10,094 .... D 4
Bulancak, 9,343 .... G 2
Bulanık, 6,186 .... K 3
Buldan, 9,813 .... C 3
Bünyan, 8,467 .... G 3
Burdur, 29,268 .... D 4
Burhaniye, 12,597 .... B 3

(continued on following page)

Agriculture, Industry and Resources

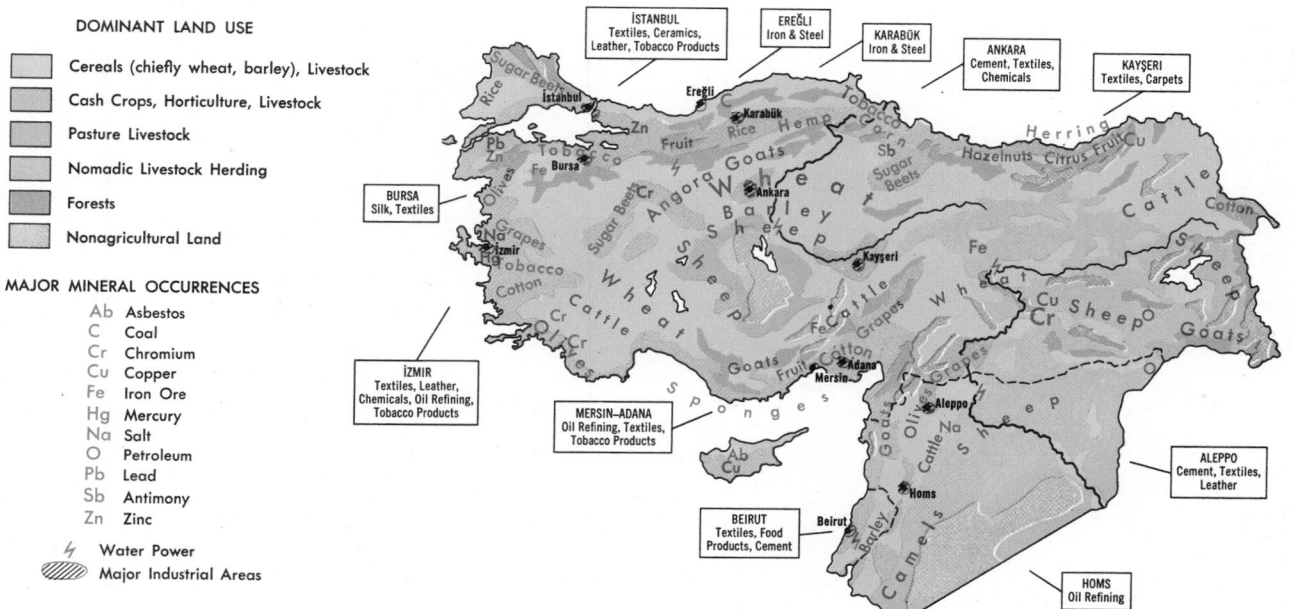

DOMINANT LAND USE

- Cereals (chiefly wheat, barley), Livestock
- Cash Crops, Horticulture, Livestock
- Pasture Livestock
- Nomadic Livestock Herding
- Forests
- Nonagricultural Land

MAJOR MINERAL OCCURRENCES

- Ab Asbestos
- C Coal
- Cr Chromium
- Cu Copper
- Fe Iron Ore
- Hg Mercury
- Na Salt
- O Petroleum
- Pb Lead
- Sb Antimony
- Zn Zinc

Water Power
Major Industrial Areas

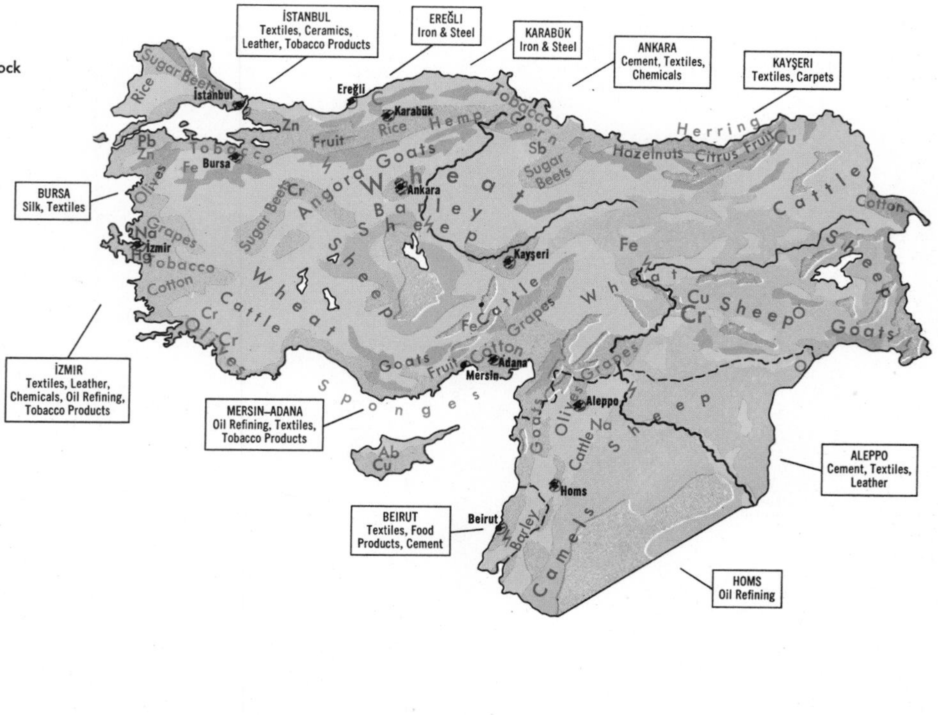
İSTANBUL
Textiles, Ceramics, Leather, Tobacco Products
EREĞLI
Iron & Steel
KARABÜK
Iron & Steel
ANKARA
Cement, Textiles, Chemicals
KAYŞERI
Textiles, Carpets
BURSA
Silk, Textiles
İZMIR
Textiles, Leather, Chemicals, Oil Refining, Tobacco Products
MERSIN–ADANA
Oil Refining, Textiles, Tobacco Products
ALEPPO
Cement, Textiles, Leather
BEIRUT
Textiles, Food Products, Cement
HOMS
Oil Refining
İstanbul
Ereğli
Karabük
Bursa
Ankara
Kayseri
İzmir
Mersin
Adana
Aleppo
Homs
Beirut
Sugar Beets
Rice
Tobacco
Fruit
Hemp
Goats
Angora Goats
Wheat
Barley
Sheep
Herring
Hazelnuts
Citrus Fruit
Cattle
Cotton
Olives
Grapes
Sponges
Camels

64 Turkey, Syria, Lebanon and Cyprus

(continued)

TURKEY (continued)

Bursa, 211,644 .... C 2
Büyükada, 5,261 .... D 6
Büyükdere .... D 5
Çal, 2,925 .... C 3
Çalköy, 2,232 .... C 3
Çamlıdere, 3,132 .... E 2
Çan, 5,826 .... B 2
Çanakkale, 22,789 .... B 6
Çandır, 4,619 .... F 3
Çankaya, 161,804 .... E 3
Çankırı, 21,450 .... E 2
Çapakçur, 11,727 .... J 3
Çardak, 2,410 .... C 6
Çarşamba, 18,003 .... G 2
Çatalca, 5,811 .... C 2
Çay, 9,761 .... D 3
Çayeli, 11,496 .... J 2
Çayırıralan, 4,357 .... F 3
Cebeci, 204,592 .... E 3
Çekerek, 3,286 .... F 2
Çelikhan, 3,305 .... H 4
Çemişkezek, 2,235 .... H 3
Çerkeş, 2,865 .... E 2
Çerkezköy, 5,355 .... C 2
Çermik, 5,420 .... H 3
Çeşme, 4,068 .... B 3
Çetinkaya, 2,525 .... G 3
Cevizli, 2,580 .... D 4
Ceyhan, 41,124 .... F 4
Ceylanpınar, 12,508 .... H 4
Cide, 2,130 .... E 2
Çifteler, 5,901 .... D 3
Cihanbeyli, 6,739 .... E 3
Çıldır, 2,040 .... K 2
Cimin, 4,405 .... H 3
Çine, 8,271 .... B 4
Çivril, 5,780 .... C 3
Cizre, 8,662 .... K 4
Çölemerik, 6,129 .... K 4
Çorlu, 27,187 .... B 2
Çorum, 41,574 .... F 2
Çubuk, 8,857 .... E 2
Çukur, 4,045 .... F 3
Çumra, 10,299 .... E 4
Darende, 7,643 .... G 3
Demirci, 10,050 .... C 3
Demirkent, 3,855 .... E 4
Demirköy, 3,309 .... C 2
Denizli, 64,331 .... C 4
Derik, 6,684 .... J 4
Derinkuyu, 4,056 .... F 3
Develi, 13,411 .... F 3
Devrek, 5,058 .... D 2
Dicle, 3,577 .... J 3
Dikili, 5,805 .... B 3
Dinar, 11,298 .... D 3
Dirmil, 2,736 .... C 4
Divriği, 9,160 .... H 3
Diyadin, 2,934 .... K 3
Diyarbakır, 102,653 .... H 4
Doğanbey, 3,058 .... D 4
Doğanhisar, 5,966 .... D 3
Doğanşehir, 4,944 .... G 3
Döger, 2,913 .... D 3
Doğubeyazıt, 8,523 .... K 3
Dörtyol, 11,595 .... F 4
Dumlu, 3,416 .... J 2
Dursunbey, 6,533 .... C 3
Düzce, 22,274 .... D 2
Eceabat, 2,842 .... B 6
Edirne, 46,091 .... B 2
Edremit, 25,003 .... B 3
Eğridir, 8,912 .... D 4
Elâzığ, 78,605 .... H 3
Elbistan, 13,492 .... G 3
Eldivan, 3,344 .... E 2
Eleşkirt, 6,019 .... K 3
Elmalı, 8,482 .... C 4
Emet, 4,815 .... C 3
Emirdağ, 10,914 .... D 3
Emirgazi, 3,509 .... E 4
Enez, 1,808 .... B 2
Erbaa, 13,168 .... G 2
Erciş, 14,072 .... K 3
Erdek, 7,813 .... B 2
Erdemli, 10,304 .... F 4
Ereğli, 38,362 .... F 4
Ereğli, 18,978 .... D 2
Erenköy, 35,980 .... D 6
Ergani, 10,528 .... H 3
Erkilet, 3,223 .... F 3
Ermenak, 8,017 .... E 4
Eruh, 3,298 .... K 4
Erzin, 10,257 .... G 4
Erzincan, 45,197 .... H 3
Erzurum, 105,317 .... J 3
Eskimalatya, 4,244 .... H 3
Eskişehir, 173,882 .... D 3
Eşme, 5,035 .... C 3
Espiye, 5,318 .... H 2
Eynesil, 5,210 .... H 2
Eyüp, 58,244 .... D 6
Ezbider, 3,185 .... H 2
Ezine, 7,819 .... B 3
Fakılı, 3,377 .... F 3
Fatih, 71,965 .... D 6
Fatsa, 9,738 .... G 2
Feke, 3,030 .... F 4
Fethiye, 8,386 .... C 4
Fevzipaşa, 3,917 .... G 4
Fındıklı, 3,928 .... J 2
Finike, 4,352 .... D 4
Foça, 2,953 .... B 3
Gallipoli, 12,945 .... C 6
Gaziantep, 160,152 .... G 4
Gazipaşa, 3,524 .... E 4
Gebze, 9,269 .... C 2
Gediz, 7,486 .... C 3
Gelibolu (Gallipoli), 12,945 .... C 6
Gemerek, 4,660 .... G 3
Gemlik, 15,716 .... C 2
Genç, 3,114 .... J 3
Genezin, 4,691 .... F 3
Gercüş, 2,593 .... J 4
Gerede, 6,677 .... E 2
Germencik, 7,344 .... B 4
Gerze, 5,387 .... E 2
Gevaş, 4,019 .... K 3
Geyve, 5,001 .... D 2
Giresun, 25,331 .... H 2
Göksun, 4,511 .... G 3
Gölbaşı, 5,044 .... G 4
Gölcük, 21,544 .... C 2
Göle, 3,826 .... K 2
Gölhisar, 5,562 .... C 4
Gölköy, 5,852 .... G 2
Gölmarmara, 8,301 .... C 3
Gölpazarı, 3,960 .... D 2
Gönen, 11,666 .... B 2
Gördes, 5,665 .... C 3
Görele, 5,687 .... H 2
Göynük, 2,084 .... D 2
Güdül, 4,385 .... E 2
Gülnar, 4,983 .... E 4
Gülşehir, 3,549 .... F 3
Gümüş, 2,949 .... F 2
Gümüşhacıköy, 10,199 .... F 2
Gümüşhane, 8,092 .... H 2
Güney, 7,416 .... C 3
Gürün, 6,374 .... G 3
Hacıbektaş, 3,739 .... F 3
Hacılar, 10,149 .... F 3
Hadım, 7,176 .... E 4
Hafik, 2,634 .... G 3
Hakkâri (Çölemerik), 6,129 .... K 4
Halfeti, 2,622 .... H 4
Hani, 4,802 .... J 3
Harput, 2,205 .... H 3
Haruniye, 5,198 .... G 4
Hatay (Antâkya), 57,855 .... G 4
Havran, 7,205 .... B 3
Havza, 10,338 .... F 2
Haymana, 5,396 .... E 3
Hayrabolu, 9,444 .... B 2
Hazro, 3,483 .... J 3
Hekimhan, 4,288 .... H 3
Helete, 3,636 .... G 4
Hendek, 10,788 .... D 2
Hilvan, 3,390 .... H 4
Hınıs, 5,263 .... J 3
Hisarönü, 3,730 .... E 2
Hopa, 5,703 .... J 2
Horasan, 5,236 .... K 2
Hozat, 4,540 .... H 3
Içel (Mersin), 86,692 .... F 4
Içme, 2,680 .... J 3
Idil, 2,109 .... J 4
Iğdır, 15,701 .... K 3
Ilgaz, 2,924 .... E 2
Ilgın, 10,196 .... D 3

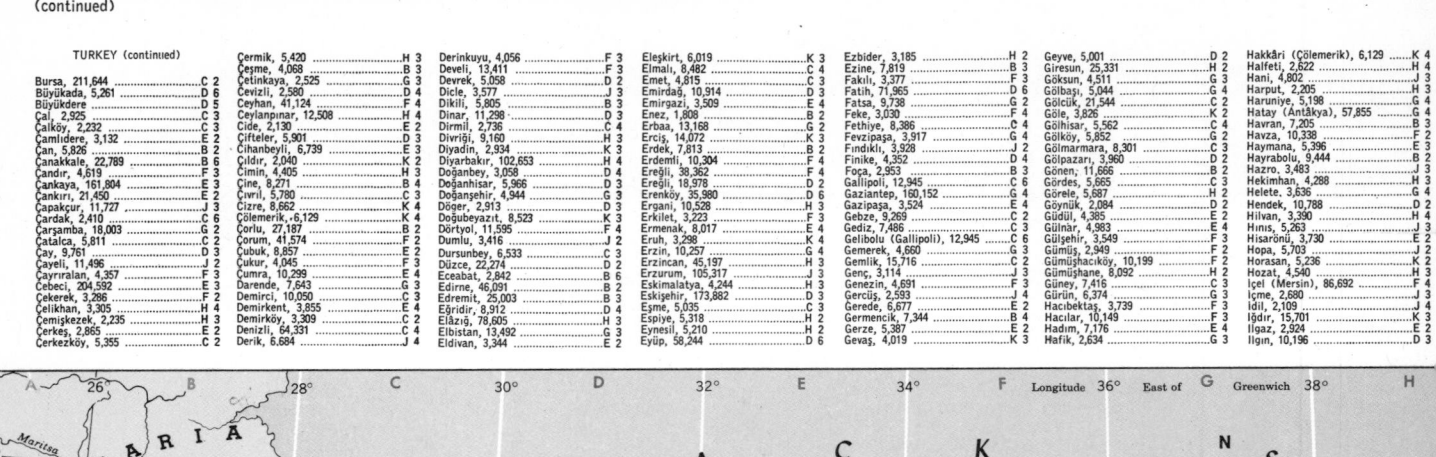

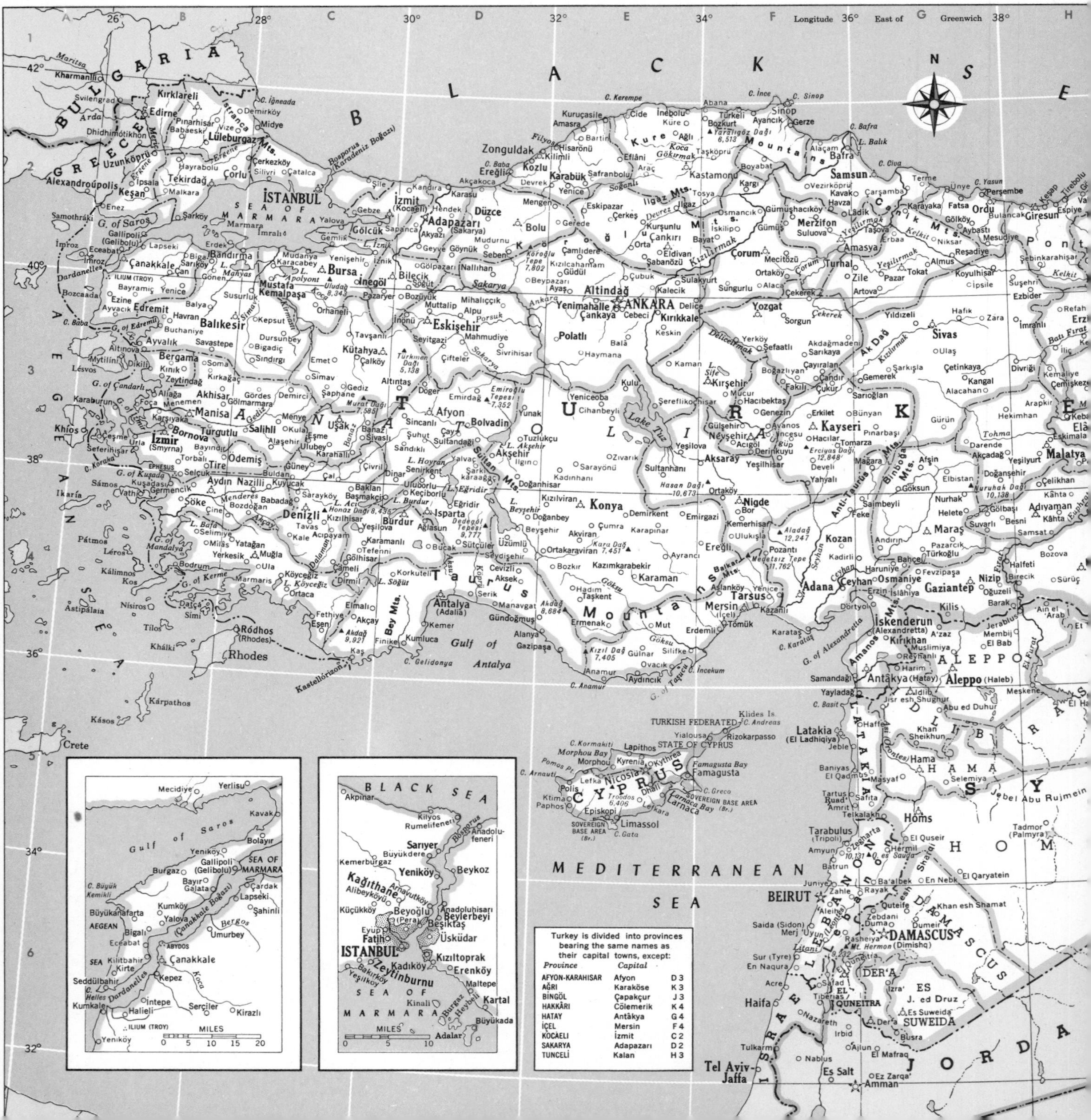

İlica, 7,612 ...J 3
İmranlı, 3,176 ...H 3
İmroz, 2,721 ...F 3
İncesu, 5,775 ...E 2
İnebolu, 5,935 ...E 2
İnegöl, 27,777 ...C 2
İnönü, 4,246 ...D 3
İpsala, 6,544 ...B 2
İpsile, 2,246 ...C 2
İskenderun, 69,382 ...G 4
İskilip, 12,400 ...F 2
İslâhiye, 13,775 ...G 4
Isparta, 42,901 ...C 4
İstanbul, 2,294 ...J 2
İstanbul, 1,742,978 ...D 6
İstanbul, *2,043,447 ...D 6
İzmir, 263,521 ...B 3
İzmir, *411,626 ...B 3
İzmit, 89,547 ...C 2
İznik, 8,213 ...C 2
Kadıköy, 81,945 ...D 6
Kadınhanı, 8,398 ...E 3
Kadirli, 15,926 ...F 4
Kağıthane, 56,157 ...D 6
Kağızman, 9,417 ...K 2
Kâhta, 6,685 ...H 4

Kalan, 5,825 ...H 3
Kale, 3,166 ...C 4
Kalecik, 4,022 ...E 2
Kaman, 10,067 ...E 3
Kandıra, 5,992 ...D 2
Kangal, 4,412 ...G 3
Karabük, 46,169 ...E 2
Karacabey, 18,368 ...C 3
Karahallı, 4,987 ...C 3
Karakoçan, 2,965 ...J 3
Karaköse, 24,168 ...K 3
Karaman, 26,051 ...E 4
Karamanlı, 4,694 ...C 4
Karapınar, 12,889 ...J 2
Karasu, 7,060 ...D 2
Karataş, 3,686 ...F 4
Karayaka, 3,631 ...G 2
Kargı, 3,954 ...F 2
Kars, 41,376 ...K 2
Karşıyaka, 82,574 ...B 3
Kartal, 20,139 ...D 6
Kastamonu, 23,485 ...E 2
Kavak, 2,135 ...F 2
Kavak, 2,473 ...C 2
Kayseri, 126,653 ...F 3
Kazanlı, 3,360 ...F 4

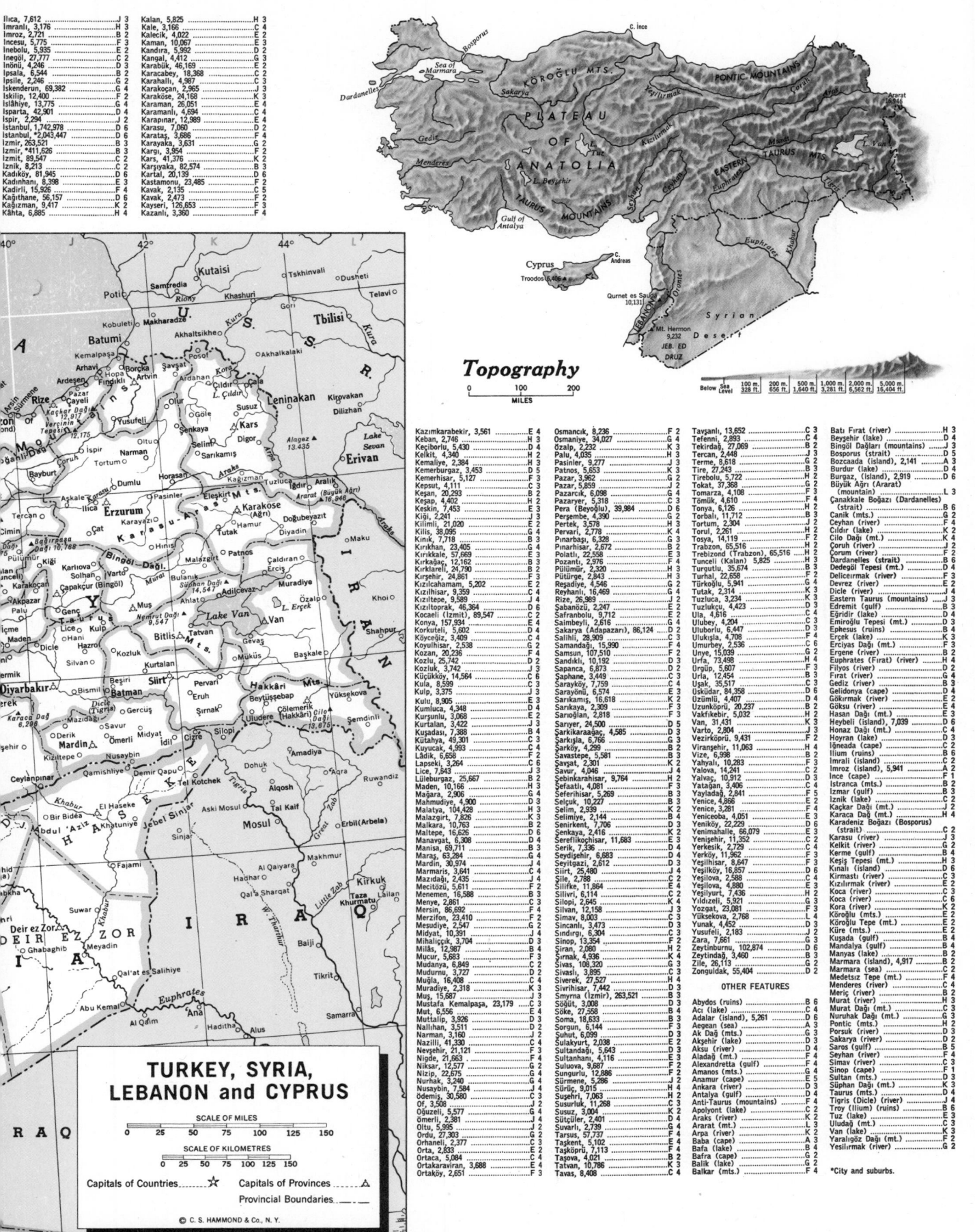

Topography

0 ─ 100 ─ 200
MILES

Below Sea Level | 100 m. 328 ft. | 200 m. 656 ft. | 500 m. 1,640 ft. | 1,000 m. 3,281 ft. | 2,000 m. 6,562 ft. | 5,000 m. 16,404 ft.

Kazımkarabekir, 3,561 ...E 4
Keban, 3,962 ...H 3
Keçiborlu, 5,430 ...D 4
Kelkit, 4,340 ...H 2
Kemaliye, 2,384 ...H 3
Kemerburgaz, 3,453 ...D 5
Kemerhisar, 5,127 ...F 3
Kepsut, 4,111 ...C 3
Keşan, 20,293 ...B 2
Keşap, 4,402 ...H 2
Keskin, 7,453 ...E 3
Kiği, 2,241 ...J 3
Kilimli, 21,020 ...J 2
Kilis, 38,095 ...G 4
Kınık, 7,718 ...B 3
Kırıkhan, 23,405 ...G 4
Kırıkkale, 57,669 ...E 3
Kırkağaç, 12,162 ...B 3
Kırklareli, 24,790 ...B 2
Kırşehir, 24,861 ...F 3
Kızılcahamam, 5,202 ...E 2
Kızılhisar, 9,359 ...C 4
Kızıltepe, 9,589 ...J 4
Kızıltoprak, 46,364 ...D 6
Kocaeli (İzmit), 89,547 ...C 2
Konya, 157,934 ...E 4
Korkuteli, 5,602 ...D 4
Köprübaşı, 3,409 ...C 3
Koyulhisar, 2,538 ...G 2
Kozan, 20,236 ...F 4
Kozlu, 25,742 ...D 2
Kozluk, 3,742 ...J 3
Küçükkuyu, 14,564 ...J 4
Kula, 8,599 ...C 3
Kulp, 3,375 ...J 3
Kulu, 8,905 ...E 3
Kumluca, 4,348 ...D 4
Kurşunlu, 3,068 ...E 2
Kurtalan, 3,422 ...J 3
Kuşadası, 7,388 ...B 4
Kütahya, 49,301 ...C 3
Kuyucak, 4,993 ...C 4
Lâdik, 6,658 ...F 2
Lapseki, 3,264 ...B 2
Lice, 7,643 ...J 3
Lüleburgaz, 25,667 ...B 2
Maden, 10,166 ...H 3
Mağara, 2,906 ...F 3
Mahmudiye, 4,900 ...D 3
Malatya, 104,428 ...H 3
Malazgirt, 7,826 ...K 3
Malkara, 10,763 ...B 2
Maltepe, 16,626 ...D 6
Manavgat, 6,308 ...D 4
Manisa, 69,711 ...B 3
Maraş, 63,284 ...G 4
Mardin, 30,974 ...J 4
Marmaris, 3,641 ...C 4
Mazıdağı, 2,435 ...J 4
Mecitözü, 5,611 ...F 2
Menemen, 16,588 ...B 3
Menye, 2,861 ...C 3
Mersin, 86,692 ...F 4
Merzifon, 23,410 ...F 2
Mesudiye, 2,847 ...G 2
Midyat, 10,391 ...J 4
Mihalıçcık, 3,704 ...D 3
Milâs, 12,987 ...B 4
Mucur, 5,683 ...F 3
Mudanya, 6,849 ...C 2
Mudurnu, 3,727 ...D 2
Muğla, 16,408 ...C 4
Muradiye, 2,318 ...K 3
Muş, 15,687 ...J 3
Mustafa Kemalpaşa, 23,179 ...C 3
Mut, 6,556 ...E 4
Mutalip, 3,926 ...D 3
Nallıhan, 3,511 ...D 2
Narman, 3,160 ...J 2
Nazilli, 41,330 ...C 4
Nevşehir, 21,121 ...F 3
Niğde, 21,663 ...F 3
Niksar, 12,577 ...G 2
Nizip, 22,675 ...G 4
Nurhak, 3,240 ...G 4
Nusaybin, 12,886 ...J 4
Ödemiş, 30,580 ...C 3
Of, 3,508 ...H 2
Oğuzeli, 5,577 ...G 4
Ömerli, 2,381 ...J 4
Oltu, 5,995 ...J 2
Ordu, 27,303 ...G 2
Orhaneli, 2,377 ...C 3
Orta, 2,833 ...E 2
Ortaca, 5,084 ...C 4
Ortakaraviran, 3,688 ...E 4
Ortaköy, 2,651 ...F 3

Osmancık, 8,236 ...F 2
Osmaniye, 34,027 ...G 4
Özalp, 2,232 ...K 3
Palu, 4,035 ...J 3
Pasinler, 9,277 ...J 2
Patnos, 5,653 ...K 3
Pazar, 3,962 ...H 2
Pazar, 5,859 ...J 2
Pazarcık, 6,098 ...G 4
Pazaryer, 5,318 ...C 3
Pera (Beyoğlu), 39,984 ...D 6
Perşembe, 4,390 ...G 2
Pertek, 3,578 ...H 3
Pervari, 2,579 ...K 4
Pınarbaşı, 6,328 ...G 3
Pınarhisar, 2,672 ...B 2
Polatlı, 22,250 ...E 3
Pozantı, 2,976 ...F 4
Pülümür, 2,320 ...H 3
Pütürge, 2,843 ...H 3
Reşadiye, 4,546 ...G 2
Reyhanlı, 16,469 ...G 4
Rize, 26,989 ...J 2
Şabanözü, 2,247 ...E 2
Safranbolu, 9,712 ...E 2
Saimbeyli, 2,616 ...G 4
Sakarya (Adapazarı), 86,124 ...D 2
Salihli, 28,909 ...C 3
Samandağı, 15,990 ...F 4
Samsun, 107,510 ...F 2
Sandıklı, 10,192 ...D 3
Sapanca, 6,873 ...D 2
Şaphane, 3,449 ...C 3
Sarayköy, 7,759 ...C 4
Sarayönü, 6,574 ...E 3
Sarıkamış, 16,618 ...K 2
Sarıkaya, 2,309 ...F 3
Sarıoğlan, 2,818 ...F 3
Sarıyer, 24,500 ...D 5
Şarkikaraağaç, 4,585 ...D 3
Şarkışla, 6,766 ...G 3
Şarköy, 4,299 ...B 2
Savaştepe, 5,581 ...B 3
Şavşat, 2,301 ...K 2
Savur, 4,046 ...J 4
Şebinkarahisar, 9,764 ...H 2
Şefaatli, 4,081 ...F 3
Seferihisar, 5,269 ...B 3
Selçuk, 10,227 ...B 3
Selim, 2,959 ...K 2
Selimiye, 2,144 ...B 4
Senirkent, 7,706 ...D 3
Şenkaya, 2,416 ...K 2
Şereflikoçhisar, 11,683 ...E 3
Serik, 7,336 ...D 4
Seydişehir, 6,683 ...D 4
Seyitgazi, 2,612 ...D 3
Siirt, 25,480 ...J 4
Şile, 2,788 ...C 2
Silifke, 11,864 ...E 4
Silivri, 6,114 ...C 2
Silopi, 2,645 ...K 4
Silvan, 12,158 ...J 3
Simav, 8,003 ...C 3
Sincanlı, 3,473 ...D 3
Sındırgı, 6,304 ...C 3
Sinop, 13,354 ...F 2
Şiran, 2,080 ...H 2
Şırnak, 4,936 ...K 4
Sivas, 108,320 ...G 3
Sivaslı, 3,895 ...C 3
Siverek, 27,527 ...H 4
Sivrihisar, 7,442 ...D 3
Smyrna (İzmir), 263,521 ...B 3
Söğüt, 3,008 ...D 3
Söke, 27,558 ...B 4
Soma, 18,633 ...B 3
Sorgun, 6,144 ...F 3
Şuhut, 6,099 ...D 3
Sulakyurt, 2,038 ...E 2
Sultandağı, 5,643 ...D 3
Sultanhanı, 4,116 ...E 3
Suluova, 9,687 ...F 2
Sungurlu, 12,886 ...F 2
Sürmene, 5,286 ...J 2
Sürüç, 9,015 ...H 4
Suşehri, 7,063 ...H 2
Susurluk, 11,268 ...C 3
Susuz, 3,004 ...K 2
Sütçüler, 2,401 ...D 4
Suvarlı, 2,739 ...G 4
Tarsus, 57,737 ...F 4
Taşkent, 5,102 ...E 4
Taşköprü, 7,113 ...F 2
Taşova, 4,021 ...G 2
Tatvan, 10,786 ...K 3
Tavas, 8,408 ...C 4

Tavşanlı, 13,652 ...C 3
Tefenni, 2,893 ...C 4
Tekirdağ, 27,069 ...B 2
Tercan, 2,448 ...J 3
Terme, 8,618 ...G 2
Tire, 27,243 ...B 3
Tirebolu, 5,722 ...H 2
Tokat, 37,368 ...G 2
Tomarza, 4,108 ...F 3
Tömük, 4,610 ...F 4
Tonya, 6,126 ...H 2
Torbalı, 11,712 ...B 3
Tortum, 2,304 ...J 2
Tosya, 14,119 ...F 2
Trabzon, 65,516 ...H 2
Trebizond (Trabzon), 65,516 ...H 2
Tunceli (Kalan), 5,825 ...H 3
Turgutlu, 35,674 ...B 3
Turhal, 22,658 ...G 2
Türkoğlu, 5,941 ...G 4
Tutak, 2,314 ...K 3
Tuzluca, 3,234 ...K 2
Tuzlukçu, 4,423 ...D 3
Ula, 4,616 ...C 4
Ulubey, 4,204 ...C 3
Uluborlu, 5,607 ...D 3
Ulukışla, 4,708 ...F 4
Umurbey, 2,536 ...C 6
Ünye, 15,039 ...G 2
Urfa, 73,498 ...H 4
Urla, 12,454 ...B 3
Uşak, 35,517 ...C 3
Üsküdar, 84,358 ...D 6
Üzümlü, 4,407 ...C 3
Uzunköprü, 20,237 ...B 2
Vakfıkebir, 5,032 ...H 2
Van, 31,431 ...K 3
Varto, 2,804 ...J 3
Vezirköprü, 9,431 ...F 2
Viranşehir, 11,063 ...H 4
Vize, 6,998 ...B 2
Yahyalı, 10,283 ...F 3
Yalova, 14,491 ...C 2
Yalvaç, 10,912 ...D 3
Yatağan, 3,406 ...C 4
Yayladağ, 2,841 ...F 5
Yenice, 4,866 ...B 2
Yenice, 3,281 ...F 4
Yeniceoba, 4,051 ...E 3
Yeniköy, 22,229 ...E 3
Yenişehir, 11,352 ...C 2
Yerkesik, 2,729 ...C 4
Yerköy, 11,952 ...F 3
Yeşilköy, 16,857 ...D 6
Yeşilova, 2,588 ...C 4
Yeşilova, 4,880 ...H 2
Yeşilyurt, 7,436 ...H 2
Yıldızeli, 5,921 ...G 3
Yozgat, 23,081 ...F 3
Yüksekova, 2,768 ...L 4
Yunak, 4,452 ...D 3
Yusufeli, 2,183 ...J 2
Zara, 7,661 ...G 3
Zeytinburnu, 102,874 ...D 6
Zeytindağ, 3,460 ...B 3
Zile, 26,113 ...G 2
Zonguldak, 58,000 ...D 2

OTHER FEATURES

Abydos (ruins) ...B 6
Acı (lake) ...B 4
Adalar (island), 5,261 ...D 6
Aegean (sea) ...A 3
Ak Dağ (mts.) ...D 3
Akşehir (lake) ...D 3
Aksu (river) ...D 4
Aladağ (mt.) ...F 3
Alexandretta (gulf) ...F 4
Amanos (mts.) ...G 4
Anamur (cape) ...E 5
Ankara (river) ...E 3
Antalya (gulf) ...D 4
Anti-Taurus (mountains) ...F 4
Apolyont (lake) ...C 3
Araks (river) ...K 2
Ararat (mt.) ...L 3
Arpa (river) ...K 2
Baba (cape) ...A 3
Bafa (lake) ...B 4
Bafra (cape) ...F 2
Balık (lake) ...E 2
Balkar (mts.) ...F 4

Batı Fırat (river) ...H 3
Beyşehir (lake) ...D 4
Bingöl Dağları (mountains) ...J 3
Bosporus (strait) ...D 5
Bozcaada (island), 2,141 ...A 3
Burdur (lake) ...D 4
Burgaz (island) ...A 3
Burgaz, (island), 2,919 ...D 6
Büyük Ağrı (Ararat) (mountain) ...L 3
Çanakkale Boğazı (Dardanelles) (strait) ...B 6
Canik (mts.) ...G 2
Ceyhan (river) ...K 2
Çıldır (lake) ...K 2
Cilo Dağı (mt.) ...K 3
Çoruh (river) ...J 2
Çorum (river) ...F 2
Dardanelles (strait) ...B 6
Dedeğöl Tepesi (mt.) ...D 4
Delicermak (river) ...F 3
Devrez (river) ...E 2
Dicle (river) ...J 4
Eastern Taurus (mountains) ...J 3
Edremit (gulf) ...A 3
Eğridir (lake) ...D 4
Emiroğlu Tepesi (mt.) ...D 3
Ephesus (ruins) ...B 3
Ergek (lake) ...K 3
Erciyas Dağı (mt.) ...F 3
Ergene (river) ...B 2
Euphrates (Fırat) (river) ...H 4
Filyos (river) ...D 2
Fırat (river) ...H 4
Gediz (river) ...B 3
Gelidonya (cape) ...D 4
Gökırmak (river) ...E 2
Göksu (river) ...E 4
Hasan Dağı (mt.) ...E 3
Heybeli Dalanı (mt.), 7,039 ...D 6
Honaz Dağı (mt.) ...C 4
Hoyran (lake) ...D 3
İğneada (cape) ...C 1
İmralı (island) ...B 6
İmroz (island), 5,941 ...F 1
İnce (cape) ...F 1
İstranca (mts.) ...B 2
İzmir (gulf) ...B 3
İznik (lake) ...C 2
Kaçkar Dağı (mt.) ...J 2
Karaca Dağ (mt.) ...H 4
Karadeniz Boğazı (Bosporus) (strait) ...C 2
Karasu (river) ...D 2
Kelkit (river) ...G 2
Kerme (gulf) ...B 4
Keşiş Tepesi (mt.) ...H 3
Kınalı (island) ...
Kirmasti (river) ...C 2
Kızılırmak (river) ...E 2
Koca (river) ...K 2
Koca (river) ...C 2
Köroğlu (mts.) ...D 2
Köroğlu Tepe (mt.) ...E 2
Küre (mts.) ...E 2
Kuşada (gulf) ...B 4
Mandalya (gulf) ...B 4
Manyas (lake) ...B 2
Marmara (island), 4,917 ...B 2
Marmara (sea) ...C 2
Medetsiz Tepe (mt.) ...F 4
Menderes (river) ...C 4
Meriç (river) ...B 2
Murat (river) ...J 3
Murat Dağı (mt.) ...C 3
Nuruhak Dağı (mt.) ...G 3
Pontic (mts.) ...G 2
Porsuk (river) ...D 3
Sakarya (river) ...D 2
Saros (gulf) ...B 2
Seyhan (river) ...F 4
Simav (river) ...C 3
Sinop (cape) ...F 1
Sultan (cape) ...C 4
Süphan Dağı (mt.) ...K 3
Taurus (mts.) ...E 4
Tigris (Dicle) (river) ...J 4
Troy (Ilium) (ruins) ...B 3
Tuz (lake) ...E 3
Uludağ (mt.) ...C 2
Van (lake) ...K 3
Yaralıgöz Dağı (mt.) ...F 2
Yeşilırmak (river) ...G 2

*City and suburbs.

TURKEY, SYRIA, LEBANON and CYPRUS

SCALE OF MILES
0 25 50 75 100 125 150

SCALE OF KILOMETRES
0 25 50 75 100 125 150

Capitals of Countries ......☆   Capitals of Provinces ......△
Provincial Boundaries _____

© C. S. HAMMOND & Co., N.Y.

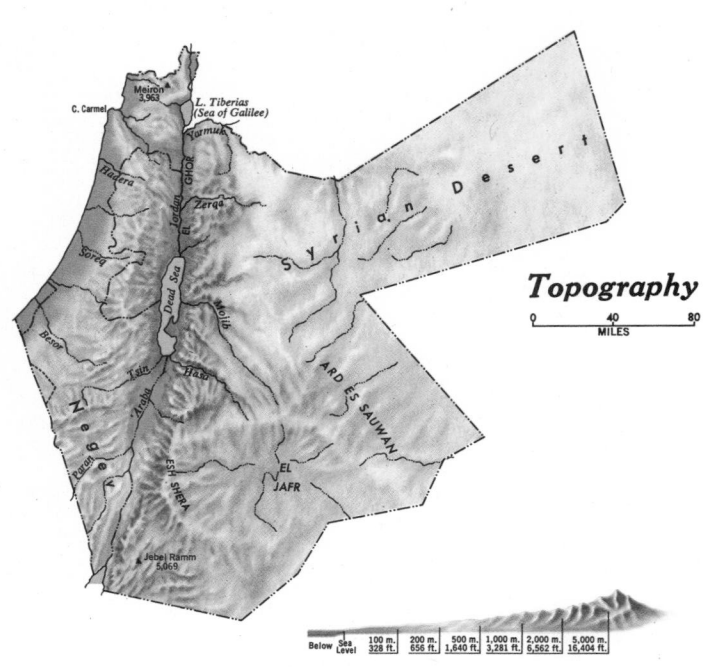

Topography

0 40 80
MILES

Below Sea Level | 100 m. 328 ft. | 200 m. 656 ft. | 500 m. 1,640 ft. | 1,000 m. 3,281 ft. | 2,000 m. 6,562 ft. | 5,000 m. 16,404 ft.

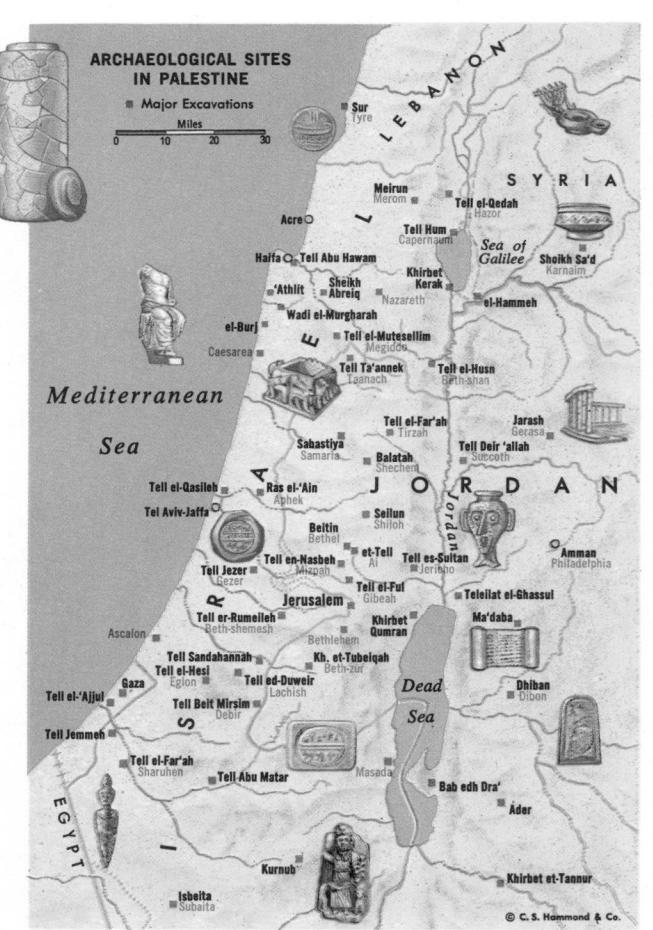

ARCHAEOLOGICAL SITES IN PALESTINE

■ Major Excavations

Miles
0 10 20 30

© C. S. Hammond & Co.

ISRAEL

DISTRICTS

Central, 426,454 ....B 3
Haifa, 391,380 ....C 2
Jerusalem, 201,749 ....B 4
Northern, 363,159 ....C 2
Southern, 213,283 ....B, D 5
Tel Aviv, 735,776 ....B 3

CITIES and TOWNS

Acre, 28,100 ....C 2
Afiqim, 1,243 ....D 2
Afula, 15,000 ....C 2
Ahuzzam, 407 ....B 4
Akko (Acre), 28,100 ....C 2
Arad ....C 5
'Arrabe, 3,636 ....C 2
Ashdod, 11,700 ....B 4
Ashdot Ya'aqov,
  1,197 ....D 2
Ashqelon, 28,400 ....A 4
Atlit, 1,516 ....B 2
Avihayil, 1,580 ....B 3
Azor, 3,687 ....B 3
Bat Shelomo, 218 ....B 2
Bat Yam, 39,100 ....B 3
Beer Ora ....D 5
Be'er Tuveya, 602 ....B 4
Be'eri, 390 ....A 5
Beersheba, 51,600 ....D 4
Bene Beraq, 51,700 ....B 3
Bet Dagan, 2,932 ....B 4
Bet Hagaddi, 566 ....B 4
Bet Qama, 228 ....B 5
Bet She'an, 10,900 ....D 3
Bet Shemesh, 8,200 ....B 4
Binyamina, 2,950 ....B 2
Carmiel ....C 2
Dafna, 577 ....D 1
Dalyat al-Karmel,
  4,124 ....B 2
Dan, 498 ....D 1
Dimona, 12,100 ....C 5
Dor, 195 ....B 2
'Ein Harod, 1,372 ....C 2
El 'Auja ....D 5
Elath (Elat), 7,000 ....D 6
Elyakim, 568 ....C 2
Elyashiv, 435 ....B 3
Even Yehuda, 3,464 ....B 3
Gal'on, 356 ....B 4
Gan Yavne, 2,668 ....B 4
Gat, 430 ....B 4
Gedera, 4,561 ....B 4
Gesher, 360 ....D 2
Gesher Haziv, 238 ....C 1
Gevar'am, 283 ....B 4
Gilat, 561 ....B 5
Ginnosar, 473 ....C 2
Giv'atayim, 30,932 ....B 3
Giv'at Brenner, 1,505 ....B 4
Giv'at Hayyim, 1,360 ....B 2
Gosh Halav (Jish), 1,498 ...C 1
Habonim, 189 ....B 2
Hadera, 27,200 ....B 2
Hadera, 212,200 ....B 3
Haifa, *447,800 ....B 2
Hazerim, 127 ....B 5
Helez, 466 ....B 4
Herzeliyya, 30,000 ....B 3

Hod Hasharon ....B 3
Hodiyya, 400 ....B 4
Holon, 55,200 ....B 3
Iksal, 2,156 ....C 2
Jerusalem (capital),
  275,000 ....C 4
Jish, 1,498 ....C 1
Kafar Kanna, 3,549 ....C 2
Kafar Yasif, 2,975 ....C 1
Karkur, 2,856 ....C 3
Kefar Atta, 16,300 ....C 2
Kefar Blum, 565 ....D 1
Kefar Gil'adi, 701 ....D 1
Kefar Ruppin, 306 ....D 3
Kefar Sava, 19,000 ....B 3
Kefar Vitkin, 808 ....B 2
Kefar Yona, 2,372 ....B 3
Kefar Zekharlya, 420 ....B 4
Kinneret, 909 ....C 2
Kurnub ....C 5
Lod (Lydda), 21,000 ....B 4
Lydda, 21,000 ....B 4
Magen, 149 ....A 5
Malkiya ....D 1
Mash' Abbe Sade, 238 ....B 6
Mavq'lm, 177 ....B 4
Megiddo ....C 2
Me'ona, 317 ....C 1
Metula, 261 ....D 1
Migdal, 688 ....C 2
Mikhmoret, 608 ....B 2
Mishmar Hanegev, 336 ......B 5
Mishmar Hayarden ....D 1
Mivtahim, 398 ....A 5
Mizpe Ramon, 331 ....D 5
Qedma, 157 ....C 4
Moza Illit, 219 ....C 4
Mughar, 4,010 ....B 4
Muqeible, 459 ....C 2
Nahariyya, 15,900 ....C 1
Nazareth, 26,400 ....C 2
Negba, 453 ....B 4
Nes Ziyyona, 11,200 ....B 4
Nesher, 8,450 ....C 2
Netanya, 46,200 ....B 3
Nevatim, 436 ....B 5
Newe Yam, 211 ....B 2
Nir Am, 210 ....B 4
Nir Yitzhaq, 209 ....A 5
Nizzanim, 479 ....B 4
'Omer ....B 5
Oron ....C 6
Pardes Hanna, 8,200 ....C 2
Peduyim, 361 ....B 5
Petah Tiqwa, 58,700 ....B 3
Qadima, 2,937 ....B 3
Qedma, 157 ....C 4
Qiryat Bialik, 10,400 ....C 2
Qiryat Gat, 10,111 ....B 4
Qiryat Haayin, 9,256 ....C 2
Qiryat Motzkin, 10,300 ......C 2
Qiryat Shemona, 13,900 ....C 1
Qiryat Tiv'on, 9,650 ....C 2
Qiryat Yam, 11,600 ....C 2
Ra'anana, 10,000 ....B 3
Ramat Gan, 109,400 ....B 3
Ramat Hasharon, 11,100 ...B 3
Rame, 2,986 ....C 2
Ramla, 23,900 ....B 4
Rehovot, 30,400 ....B 4
Re'im, 155 ....A 5
Revadim, 175 ....B 4
Revivim, 258 ....D 5
Rishon Le Ziyyon, 30,000 ...B 4

Rosh Pinna, 700 ....D 2
Ruhama, 497 ....B 4
Sa'ad, 418 ....B 4
Safad (Zefat), 11,500 ....C 2
Sakhnin, 5,500 ....C 2
Sede Boqer ....D 5
Sedom ....C 5
Sedot Yam, 511 ....B 2
Shave Ziyyon, 269 ....C 1
Shefar'am, 7,650 ....C 2
Shefayim, 614 ....B 3
Shoval, 393 ....B 5
Tayibe, 8,100 ....C 3
Tel Aviv-Jaffa, 384,700 ......B 3
Tel Aviv-Jaffa, *838,000 ....B 3
Tiberias, 22,300 ....C 2
Tirat Hakarmel, 11,300 ......B 2
Tirat Zevi, 353 ....D 3
Tur'an, 2,304 ....C 2
Umm el Fahm, 8,100 ....C 2
Urim, 203 ....A 5
Uzza, 487 ....B 4
Yad Mordekhai, 416 ....A 4
Yagur, 1,266 ....C 2
Yavne, 6,200 ....B 4
Yavne'el, 1,580 ....C 2
Yehud, 7,000 ....B 3
Yeroham, 1,574 ....C 5
Yesodot, 293 ....B 4
Yesud Hama'ala, 428 ....D 2
Yiftah ....C 2
Yirka, 2,715 ....C 1
Yoqne'am, 2,884 ....C 2
Yotvata ....D 6
Zavdi'el, 396 ....B 4
Ze'elim, 148 ....B 5
Zefat, 11,500 ....C 2
Zikhron Ya'aqov, 4,393 ......B 2
Zippori, 241 ....C 2

OTHER FEATURES

'Araba, Wadi
  (dry river) ....D 5
Beer Efe (well) ....C 5
Beer Sheva', Wadi
  (dry river) ....B 5
Besor (river) ....B 5
Borot Kidod (well) ....C 5
Carmel (cape) ....B 2
Carmel (mt.) ....C 2
Dead (sea) ....C 4
Dimona (mt.) ....C 5
'Ein Gedi (well) ....C 4
'Ein Netafim (well) ....D 6
Galilee (region) ....D 2
Galilee, Sea of (sea) ....D 2
Gerar, Wadi (dry river) ....B 4
Hadera (river) ....B 2
Haifa (bay) ....C 2
Hatira (mt.) ....C 5
Hemar, Wadi
  (dry river) ....C 5
Judaea (region) ....C 4
Lakhish, Wadi
  (dry river) ....B 4
Meiron (mt.) ....C 1
Negev (region) ....C 5
Paran, Wadi
  (dry river) ....D 5
Qarn (river) ....C 1
Qishon (river) ....C 2
Ramon (mt.) ....D 5

Agriculture, Industry and Resources

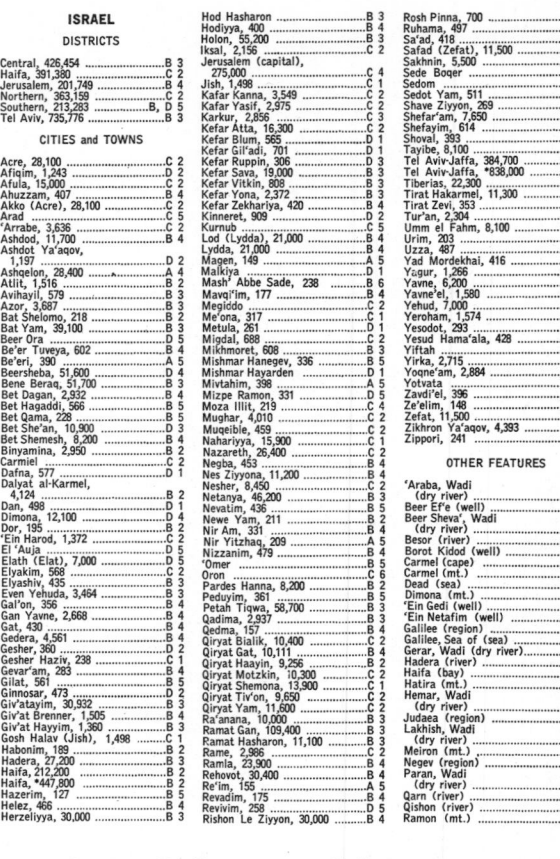

ACRE
Iron & Steel, Chemicals, Textiles

HAIFA
Oil Refining, Textiles, Cement, Machinery

NETANYA
Diamond Cutting

TEL AVIV-JAFFA
Machinery, Electrical Equipment, Textiles, Clothing, Diamond Cutting, Chemicals

JERUSALEM
Ceramics, Textiles, Leather

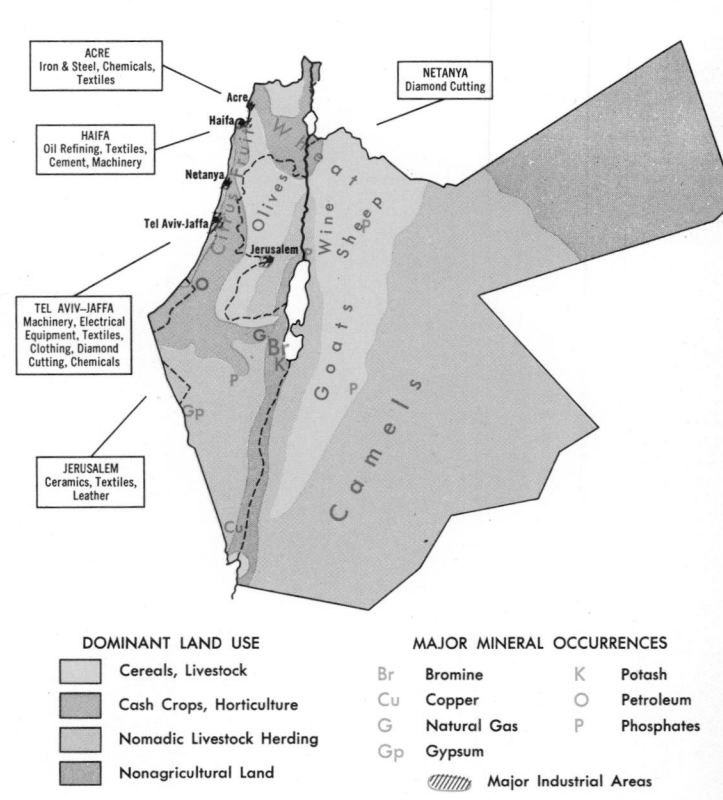

DOMINANT LAND USE

Cereals, Livestock
Cash Crops, Horticulture
Nomadic Livestock Herding
Nonagricultural Land

MAJOR MINERAL OCCURRENCES

Br Bromine
Cu Copper
G   Natural Gas
Gp Gypsum
K   Potash
O   Petroleum
P   Phosphates

///// Major Industrial Areas

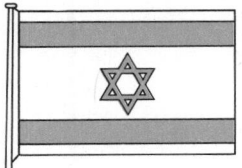

ISRAEL

JORDAN

ISRAEL	
AREA	7,993 sq. mi.
POPULATION	2,911,000
CAPITAL	Jerusalem
LARGEST CITY	Tel Aviv-Jaffa
HIGHEST POINT	Meiron 3,963 ft.
MONETARY UNIT	Israeli pound
MAJOR LANGUAGES	Hebrew, Arabic
MAJOR RELIGIONS	Judaism, Islam, Christianity

JORDAN	
AREA	37,297 sq. mi.
POPULATION	2,300,000
CAPITAL	Amman
LARGEST CITY	Amman
HIGHEST POINT	Jeb. Ramm 5,069 ft.
MONETARY UNIT	Jordanian dinar
MAJOR LANGUAGE	Arabic
MAJOR RELIGION	Islam

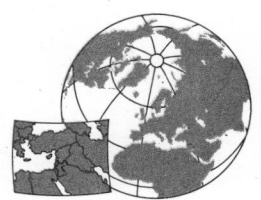

Rubin, Wadi
(dry river) .... B 4
Shiqma (river) .... B 4
Tabor (mt.) .... C 2
Tiberias (Galilee) (sea) ... D 2
Tseelim, Wadi
(dry river) .... C 5
Tsin, Wadi
(dry river) .... D 5
Yarmuk (river) .... D 2
Yarqon (river) .... B 3

JORDAN

GOVERNORATES

El Asima, 526,000 .... D 4
El Balqa, 95,000 .... D 4
El Karak, 81,000 .... E 5
Hebron, 145,000 .... C 4
Irbid, 334,000 .... D 3
Jerusalem, 418,000 .... C 4
Ma'an, 58,000 .... D 5
Nablus, 414,000 .... C 3

CITIES and TOWNS

'Ajja, 1,322 .... C 3
'Ajlun, 5,390 .... D 3
Amman (capital),
330,220 .... D 4
'Anabta, 4,018 .... C 3
Anin, 914 .... C 2
'Anjara, 3,163 .... D 3
'Anza, 807 .... C 3
'Aqaba, 8,908 .... D 6
'Aqraba, 2,501 .... C 3
Ariha (Jericho), 5,312 ...... C 4
'Arraba, 4,231 .... C 3
'Arura, 849 .... C 3
'Attil, 3,808 .... C 3
Bal'ama, 769 .... C 3
Baqura, 3,042 .... D 2
Beit Fajjar, 2,474 .... C 4
Beit Hanina, 3,067 .... C 4
Beit Jala, 6,041 .... C 4
Beit Lahm (Bethlehem),
14,439 .... C 4
Beit Nuba, 1,350 .... B 4
Beit Sahur, 5,380 .... C 4
Bethlehem, 14,439 .... C 4
Biddu, 1,259 .... C 4
Bir Zeit, 2,311 .... C 4
Birqin, 2,036 .... C 3
Burqa, 2,477 .... C 3
Damiya, 483 .... C 3
Dana, 844 .... D 5
Deir Abu Sa'id, 1,927 ...... D 3
Deir Ballut, 1,058 .... C 3
Deir Sharaf, 973 .... C 3
Dhahiriya, 4,875 .... B 5
Dhira', 214 .... C 5
Duma, 524 .... C 3
Dura, 4,954 .... C 4
El 'Al, 492 .... D 4
El Bira, 9,674 .... C 4
El Husn, 3,728 .... D 3
El Karak, 7,422 .... E 4
El Khalil (Hebron),
38,309 .... C 4
El Kitta, 987 .... D 3
El Madwar, 164 .... E 3
El Mafraq, 9,499 .... E 3
El Majdal, 259 .... D 3
El Quweira, 268 .... D 5
El Yaduda, 251 .... D 4
Er Ramtha, 10,791 .... E 2
Er Rihiya, 555 .... C 4
Er Rumman, 293 .... D 3
Er Ruseifa, 6,200 .... D 4
Es Sahab, 2,580 .... E 4
Es Salt, 16,176 .... D 3
Es Sukhna, 649 .... E 4
Esh Shaubak .... D 5
Et Tafila, 4,506 .... D 5
Et Taiyiba, 2,606 .... E 2
Ez Zababida, 1,474 .... C 3
Ez Zarqa', 121,303 .... D 4
Falama, 162 .... C 3
Halhul, 6,041 .... C 4
Harima, 635 .... D 2
Haris, 641 .... C 3
Hawara, 2,342 .... C 3
Hebron, 38,309 .... C 4
Hisban, 718 .... D 4
'Ibbin, 1,364 .... D 3
Idna, 3,713 .... C 4
'Imwas, 1,955 .... C 4
Irbid, 44,685 .... D 3
Jaba', 2,817 .... C 3
Jabir, 135 .... E 2
Jalama, 784 .... C 3
Jalbun, 914 .... C 3
Jalud, 221 .... C 3
Jarash, 3,796 .... D 3
Jenin, 8,346 .... C 3
Jericho, 5,312 .... C 4
Jerusalem (old city),
60,488 .... C 4
Jifna, 655 .... C 4

Kharas, 1,364 .... C 3
Kitim, 1,026 .... D 3
Kuraiyima .... D 3
Ma'ad, 125 .... D 2
Ma'an, 6,643 .... E 5
Ma'daba, 11,224 .... D 4
Ma'in, 1,271 .... D 4
Manja, 353 .... D 4
Mazra', 1,194 .... C 5
Nablus (Nablus). 41,709 . C 3
Nahhalin, 1,109 .... C 4
Na'ur, 2,382 .... D 4
Ni'lin, 1,227 .... C 4
Nitil, 348 .... D 4
Qabalan, 1,970 .... C 3
Qabatiya, 6,005 .... C 3
Qaffin, 2,480 .... C 3
Qalqiliya, 8,926 .... C 3
Qibya, 926 .... C 4
Qumeim, 955 .... D 2
Rafidiya, 1,123 .... C 3
Ramallah, 12,134 .... C 4
Rammun, 1,198 .... C 4
Rantis, 897 .... C 3
Ra's en Naqb, 225 .... E 5
Safi, 3,468 .... C 5
Safut, 421 .... D 3
Salfit, 3,201 .... C 3
Samar, 716 .... D 2
Samu, 3,784 .... C 5
Sarih, 3,390 .... D 2
Shu'fat, 2,732 .... C 4
Shunat Nimrin, 109 .... D 4
Shuweika, 2,332 .... C 3
Silat Dhahr, 3,566 .... C 3
Sinjil, 1,823 .... C 3
Siris, 1,285 .... C 3
Subeihi, 514 .... D 3
Suf, 3,259 .... D 3
Suweileh, 3,457 .... D 3
Tammun, 315 .... C 3
Tammun, 2,952 .... C 4
Tarqumiya, 2,412 .... C 4
Tubas, 5,262 .... C 3
Tulkarm, 10,255 .... C 3
Tur, 4,289 .... C 4
Um Jauza, 582 .... D 3
Wadi es Sir, 4,455 .... D 4
Wadi Musa, 654 .... E 5
Waqqas, 2,321 .... C 3
Ya'bad, 4,857 .... C 3
Yabrud, 277 .... C 3
Yamun, 4,173 .... C 3
Yatta, 7,281 .... C 4
Zububa, 633 .... C 2
Zuweiza, 126 .... D 4

OTHER FEATURES

'Ajlun (range) .... D 3
Anabta (mt.) .... D 3
'Aqaba (gulf) .... D 6
'Araba, Wadi
(dry river) .... D 5
Dead (sea) .... C 5
Hebron (riv.) .... D 3
Jordan (river) .... C 4
Judaea (region) .... C 4
Khirbet Qumran
(site) .... D 4
Kufrinja, Wadi
(dry river) .... D 3
Mashash, Wadi
(dry river) .... C 4
Nebo (mt.) .... D 4
Petra (ruins) .... D 5
Samaria (region) .... C 3
Shallala, Wadi
(dry river) .... D 2
Shu'eib, Wadi
(dry river) .... D 3
Tell 'Asur (mt.) .... C 4
Tur (mt.) .... C 4
Yabis, Wadi
(dry river) .... D 3
Yamun (mt.) .... D 3
Zarqa' (river) .... D 3

GAZA STRIP

Total Population, 480,000

CITIES and TOWNS

'Abasan, 1,481 .... A 5
Bani Suheila, 7,561 ...... A 5
Beit Hanun, 4,756 .... A 5
Deir el Balah, 10,854 .... A 5
Gaza, 87,793 .... A 4
Gaza, *118,272 .... A 4
Jabaliya, 10,508 .... A 4
Khan Yunis, 29,522 ...... A 5
Rafah, 10,812 .... A 5

*City and suburbs.

ISRAEL and JORDAN

CYLINDRICAL PROJECTION

SCALE OF MILES
0   5   10   15   20   25   30

SCALE OF KILOMETRES
0 5 10 15 20 25 30

Capitals of Countries .... ☆
Other Capitals .... ◉
International Boundaries .... — — —
Internal Boundaries .... — · — · —
Demilitarized Zone Boundaries .... — ·· — ·· —
Neutral Zone Boundaries .... ——————

Copyright by C. S. Hammond & Co., N.Y.

IRAN

INTERNAL DIVISIONS

Bakhtiari (governorate),
298,448 .... F 4
Boyer Ahmedi and Kahkiluye
(governorate) .... G 5
Central (province), 4,979,081 ... G 3
East Azerbaijan (province),
2,596,439 .... E 1
Fars (province), 1,429,804 ...... H 6
Gilan (province), 1,752,504 ..... F 2
Hamadan (governorate)
889,888 .... E 3
Ilam (governorate)
1,703,701 .... H 4
Isfahan (province),
1,703,701 .... H 4
Kerman (province), 761,851 ...... K 6
Kermanshah (prov.), 924,717 ..... E 3
Khurasan (prov.), 2,497,381 ..... K 5
Khuzistan (province), 1,578,079 . F 5
Kurdistan (province), 619,573 ... E 3
Luristan (governorate)
686,307 .... H 4
Mazanderan (province),
1,841,637 .... H 2
Ports and Islands (province),
346,410 .... H 7
Samnan (governorate),
207,786 .... J 3
Seistan and Baluchistan (prov.),
454,996 .... M 6
Southern Coast (province),
251,921 .... G 6
West Azerbaijan (province),
1,087,182 .... D 1
Yezd (governorate) .... J 5
Zenjan (governorate) .... F 2

CITIES and TOWNS

Abadan, 272,962 .... F 5
Abadeh, 16,000 .... H 5
Abarquh, 8,000 .... H 5
Ahar, 11,000 .... F 2
Ahar, 24,000 .... E 1
Ahwaz, 206,375 .... F 5
Anarak, 2,038 .... H 4
Andimeshk, 16,000 .... F 4
Aradan, 18,978 .... H 3
Arak, 71,925 .... F 3
Ardebil, 83,596 .... F 1
Ardistan, 6,645 .... H 4
Asadabad, 7,000 .... F 3
Asterabad (Gurgan),
51,181 .... J 2
Azarshahr, 6,000 .... D 2
Azna, 5,000 .... F 3
Babol, 49,973 .... H 2
Babulsar, 12,000 .... H 2
Bafq, 5,000 .... J 5
Baft, 6,000 .... K 6
Bahramabad, 21,000 .... K 5
Bam, 22,000 .... L 6
Bandar Abbas, 34,627 .... J 7
Bandar Ma'shur,
17,000 .... F 5
Bandar Shah, 13,000 .... H 2
Bandar Shahpur, 6,000 .... F 5
Behbehan, 39,874 .... G 5
Behshahr, 26,032 .... H 2
Bijar, 12,000 .... E 3
Birjand, 25,854 .... L 4
Borazjun, 20,000 .... G 6
Bujnurd, 31,248 .... K 2
Bukan, 9,000 .... D 2
Burujird, 71,476 .... F 4

Bushire, 26,032 .... G 6
Chalus, 15,000 .... G 2
Dalijan, 6,000 .... G 4
Damghan, 13,000 .... J 3
Darab, 13,000 .... J 6
Daran, 4,609 .... G 4
Darreh Gaz, 11,000 .... L 2
Daulatabad (Malayer), 28,434 ..... F 3
Deh Haqq, 4,115 .... H 3
Demavend, 5,391 .... H 3
Dizful, 84,499 .... F 4
Duzdab (Zahidan), 40,000 .... M 6
Enzeli (Pahlevi), 41,785 .... F 2
Estahbanat, 18,187 .... H 6
Fahrej (Iranshahr), 5,000 .... M 7
Fariman, 8,000 .... L 3
Farrashband, 3,532 .... H 6
Fasa, 19,000 .... H 6
Firdaus, 11,000 .... K 3
Firuzabad, 8,718 .... H 6
Firuzkuh, 4,684 .... H 3
Fumen, 9,000 .... F 2
Gach Saran .... G 5
Ganaveh, 9,000 .... G 6
Garmsar, 4,723 .... H 3
Golshan (Tabas), 10,000 .... K 4
Gulpaigan, 20,515 .... G 4
Gumishan, 6,000 .... J 2
Gunabad, 8,000 .... L 3
Gunbad-i-Qabus, 40,667 .... J 2
Gurgan, 51,181 .... J 2
Haft Kel, 10,000 .... F 5
Hamadan, 124,167 .... F 3
Hashtpar, 5,000 .... F 2
Homayunshahr, 46,836 .... G 4
Ilam, 15,000 .... E 4
Iranshahr, 5,000 .... M 7
Isfahan, 424,045 .... G 4
Jahrum, 38,236 .... H 6

Kangavar, 9,414 .... F 3
Karaj, 44,243 .... G 3
Kashan, 58,468 .... G 3
Kazerun, 17,000 .... G 6
Kazerun, 39,758 .... G 6
Kazvin, 88,106 .... F 3
Kerman, 85,404 .... K 5
Kermanshah, 187,930 .... E 3
Khaf, 5,000 .... M 3
Khomeyn .... G 4
Khoi, 47,648 .... D 1
Khorramshahr, 88,536 .... F 5
Khunsar, 10,947 .... G 4
Khur, 2,912 .... J 4
Khurramabad, 59,578 .... F 4
Lahijan, 25,725 .... F 2
Lar, 22,000 .... J 7
Mahabad, 28,610 .... D 2
Mahallat, 12,000 .... G 4
Mahan, 8,000 .... K 5
Maku, 7,000 .... D 1
Malayer, 28,434 .... F 3
Maragheh, 54,106 .... E 2
Marand, 24,000 .... D 1
Mashad, 25,498 .... L 2
Masjid-i-Sulaiman, 64,488 .... F 5
Meshed, 409,616 .... L 2
Meshed-i-Sar (Babulsar),
12,000 .... H 2
Meshkinshahr, 9,000 .... F 1
Mianeh, 28,447 .... E 2
Mirjawa, 11,000 .... M 6
Miyanduab, 15,000 .... E 2
Naft-i-Shah, 3,043 .... E 4
Na'in, 5,925 .... H 4
Nasratabad (Zabul), 20,000 .... M 5
Natanz, 4,370 .... H 4
Naushahr, 8,000 .... G 2
Nehavend, 24,000 .... F 3

Nejafabad, 43,384 .... G 4
Niriz, 16,114 .... J 6
Nishapur, 33,482 .... L 2
Pahlevi (Enzeli), 41,785 .... F 2
Qain, 6,000 .... L 3
Qasr-i-Shirin, 15,904 .... E 3
Quchan, 29,133 .... L 2
Qum, 134,292 .... G 3
Rafsenjan (Bahramabad),
21,000 .... K 5
Rai, 102,825 .... H 3
Ram Hormuz, 9,000 .... F 5
Ramsar, 12,000 .... G 2
Ravar, 7,000 .... K 5
Resht, 143,557 .... F 2
Reza'iyeh, 110,749 .... D 1
Sabzawar, 42,415 .... L 2
Sabzawaran, 7,000 .... K 6
Saidabad (Sirjan), 20,000 .... J 6
Saman, 31,058 .... F 1
Sanandaj, 54,578 .... E 3
Sang-i-Sar, 9,000 .... H 3
Saqqiz, 17,000 .... E 2
Sarab, 16,000 .... E 2
Sardasht, 6,000 .... D 2
Sari, 46,547 .... H 2
Savanat (Estahbanat),
18,187 .... H 6
Saveh, 17,565 .... G 3
Shahabad, 12,000 .... E 3
Shahdegan, 6,000 .... F 5
Shahi, 38,898 .... H 2
Shahpur, 22,000 .... D 1
Shahr-i-Kurd, 24,000 .... G 4
Shahriza, 34,220 .... G 4
Shahrud, 30,767 .... J 2
Shahsawar, 12,000 .... G 2
Shiraz, 269,865 .... H 6
Shirvan, 11,000 .... K 2

Shushtar, 24,000 .... F 4
Sinneh (Sanandaj), 54,578 .... E 3
Sirjan, 20,000 .... J 6
Sultanabad (Kashmar),
17,000 .... L 3
Sunqur, 10,433 .... E 3
Susangird, 21,000 .... F 5
Tabas, 10,000 .... K 4
Tabriz, 403,413 .... D 2
Taft, 7,000 .... J 5
Tajrish, 157,486 .... H 3
Takistan, 13,485 .... F 2
Tehran (capital), 2,719,730 ...... G 3
Tuiserkan, 12,000 .... F 3
Tun (Firdaus), 11,000 .... K 3
Turbat-i-Haidari, 30,106 .... L 3
Turbat-i-Shaikh Jam, 13,000 ...... M 3
Urmia (Reza'iyeh), 110,749 .... D 1
Ushnuiyeh, 5,000 .... D 2
Veramin, 11,183 .... H 3
Yezd, 93,241 .... J 5
Zabul, 20,000 .... M 5
Zahedan, 39,732 .... M 6
Zarand, 5,000 .... K 5
Zarghan, 7,000 .... H 6
Zenjan, 58,714 .... F 2

OTHER FEATURES

Ab-i-Diz (river) .... F 4
Aji Chai (river) .... E 2
Arabi (isl.) .... G 7
Aras (Araks) (river) .... D 1
Atrek (river) .... K 2
Bakhtegan (lake) .... H 6
Baluchistan (region) .... M 7
Bampur (river) .... M 7
Behistun (ruins) .... E 3
Caspian (sea) .... F 1

Darya-yi-Namak (salt lake) .... H 3
Dasht-i-Kavir (salt desert) ...... J 3
Dasht-i-Lut (desert) .... K 5
Demavend (mt.) .... H 3
Dez (Ab-i-Diz) (river) .... G 3
Elburz (range) .... G 2
Farsi (isl.) .... G 7
Gurgan (river) .... J 2
Hamun-i-Helmand (marsh) .... M 5
Hamun-i-Jaz-Murian
(marsh) .... L 7
Hamun-i-Sabari (lake) .... M 5
Hanjan (isl.) .... J 7
Hari Rud (river) .... M 3
Hashtadan (reg.) .... M 3
Hormuz (strait) .... J 7
Kalar, Kuh-i- (mt.) .... F 3
Karkheh (river) .... E 4
Kashaf Rud (river) .... L 2
Kharg (isl.), 647 .... G 6
Kuh, Ras el (cape) .... K 8
Kuh-i-Aladagh (mts.) .... K 2
Kuh-i-Bagraband (mts.) .... M 8
Kuh-i-Bazqush (mts.) .... E 2
Kuh-i-Dinar (mts.) .... G 5
Kuh-i-Gugird (mts.) .... H 3
Kuh-i-Jagatai (mts.) .... L 2
Kuh-i-Shah Jehan (mts.) .... K 2
Kur Rud (river) .... H 6
Kurang (river) .... F 4
Laristan (region) .... J 7
Maidani (cape) .... J 7
Makran (region) .... L 8
Mand Rud (river) .... G 6
Mashkel (river) .... M 7
Mehran (river) .... J 7
Mura, Qal'eh-i- (river) .... M 4
Namaksar (salt) .... M 4

IRAN and IRAQ

CONIC PROJECTION

SCALE OF MILES
0 25 50 100 150 200

SCALE OF KILOMETRES
0 25 50 100 150 200

Capitals of Countries .... ☆
Capitals of Provinces .... △
Capitals of Governorates .... ◉
International Boundaries ....
Provincial Boundaries ....
Governorate Boundaries ....

Iran consists of fifteen provinces
called ostans. Attached to seven of
these provinces are eight governorates.

Namakzar (dry lake)	L 4	
Nezwar (mt.)	H 3	
Nihing (river)	N 7	
Oman (gulf)	M 8	
Pasargadae (ruins)	H 5	
Persepolis (ruins)	F 6	
Persian (gulf)	E 6	
Pusht-i-Kuh (mts.)	E 4	
Qais (isl.)	J 7	
Qarajeh Dagh (mts.)	E 1	
Qara Su (river)	E 1	
Qara Su (river)	E 2	
Qaranqu (river)	E 2	
Qishm (isl.)	J 7	
Qizil Uzun (river)	F 2	
Sefid Rud (river)	F 2	
Shaikh Shu'aib (island)	J 7	
Shelagh (river)	M 5	
Shirvan (river)	E 3	
Shur (river)	J 7	
Siah Kuh (mts.)	L 5	
Silop (river)	M 8	
Susa (ruins)	F 4	
Talab (river)	N 6	
Tashk (lake)	H 5	
Urmia (lake)	D 2	
Yezd (region)	J 5	
Zagros (mts.)	E 4	
Zaindeh Rud (river)	H 4	
Zarineh (river)	E 2	
Zilbir Chai (river)	D 1	
Zuhreh Rud (river)	F 5	

IRAQ

PROVINCES

Anbar	B 4
An Najaf	C 5

CITIES and TOWNS

Ad Diwaniya, 60,553	D 5
'Afaq, 5,390	D 4
Al 'Azair, 2,255	E 5
Al 'Aziziya, 7,450	D 4
Al Falluja, 38,072	C 4
Al Kufa, 30,862	D 4
Al Kumait, 2,225	E 4
Al Musaiyib, 15,955	D 4
Al Qa'im, 3,372	B 3
Al Qaiyara, 3,060	C 2
Al Qosh, 3,863	C 2
Al Qurna, 5,638	E 5
'Ali Gharbi, 5,735	E 4
Ali Sharqi, 1,980	E 4
'Amadiya, 2,578	D 2
'Amara, 64,847	E 5
An Najaf, 128,096	D 5
An Nasiriya, 60,405	D 5
'Ana, 6,884	B 3
'Aqra, 8,659	D 2

Ar Rahhaliya	C 4
Arbela (Erbil), 90,320	D 2
As Salman, 1,789	D 5
Az Zubair, 41,408	E 5
Badra, 3,564	D 4
Baghdad (capital), 502,503	D 4
Baghdad, *1,745,328	D 4
Baiji, 6,785	C 3
Ba'quba, 34,575	D 4
Basra, 313,327	E 5
Dohuk, 16,998	C 2
Erbil, 90,320	D 2
Fao, 15,399	F 6
Habbaniya, 14,405	C 4
Hadhar, 1,019	C 3
Haditha, 6,870	C 3
Hai, 16,988	E 4
Halabja, 11,206	D 4
Hilla, 84,717	D 4
Hindiya, 16,436	D 4
Hit, 9,131	C 4
Karbala', 83,301	C 4
Khanaqin, 23,522	D 3
Kifri, 8,500	D 3
Kirkuk, 167,413	D 3
Kut, 42,116	D 4
Lailan, 1,526	D 3
Maidan, 354	D 3
Makhmur, 2,556	C 3
Mandali, 3,872	D 4
Mosul, 315,157	C 2
Muqdadiyah, 12,181	D 4
Na'maniya, 11,943	D 4
Qal'a Sharqat, 2,434	C 3
Qal'at Diza, 6,250	D 2
Ramadi, 28,723	C 4
Rania, 4,090	D 2
Refa'i, 7,681	D 5
Rumaitha, 10,222	D 5
Rutba, 5,091	B 4
Ruwandiz, 5,807	D 2
Sa'diya, 5,285	D 3
Samarra, 24,746	C 3
Samawa, 33,473	D 5
Shaikh Sa'ad, 2,958	E 4
Shaqlawa, 6,814	D 2
Shatra, 18,822	E 5
Shithatha, 2,326	C 4
Sinjar, 7,942	B 2
Sulaimaniya, 86,822	D 2
Tal Kaif, 7,482	C 2
Tauq, 845	D 3
Taza Khurmatu, 2,681	D 3
Tikrit, 9,921	C 3
Tuz Khurmatu, 13,860	D 3
Zakho, 14,790	C 2
Zorbatiya, 1,602	D 4

OTHER FEATURES

Adhaim (river)	D 3
Al Hajara (plain)	D 5
'Aneiza, Jebel (mt.)	A 4
'Arab, Shatt al- (river)	F 5
'Ar'ar, Wadi (dry river)	B 5
Babylon (ruins)	D 4
Bahr al Milh (lake)	C 4
Batin, Wadi al (dry river)	E 6
Ctesiphon (ruins)	D 4
Darbandikhan (dam)	D 3
Euphrates (river)	D 4
Great Zab (river)	C 2
Hajara, Al (plain)	D 5
Haji Ibrahim (mt.)	D 2
Hammar, Hor al (lake)	E 5
Hauran, Wadi (dry river)	B 4
Ibrahim, Haji (mt.)	D 2
Little Zab (river)	C 3
Mesopotamia (region)	B 3
Nineveh (ruins)	C 2
Sa'diya, Hor (lake)	E 4
Saniya, Hor (lake)	E 5
Sha'ib Hisb, Wadi (dry river)	C 5
Shatt-al-'Arab (river)	F 5
Sinjar, Jebel (mts.)	B 2
Siyah Kuh (mt.)	A 4
Syrian (desert)	B 4
Tigris (river)	D 4
Ubaiyidh, Wadi (dry river)	B 5
Ur (ruins)	D 5

*City and suburbs.
†Population of sub-district.

Babil ... D 4
Baghdad ... D 4
Basra ... E 5
Dhi Qar ... E 5
Diyala ... D 4
Dohuk ... C 2
Erbil ... C 2
Karbala' ... B 4
Maysan ... E 5
Muthanna ... D 5
Ninawa ... B 3
Qadisiya ... C 3
Salahuddin ... C 3
Sulaimaniya ... D 3
Tamim ... C 3
Wasit ... D 4

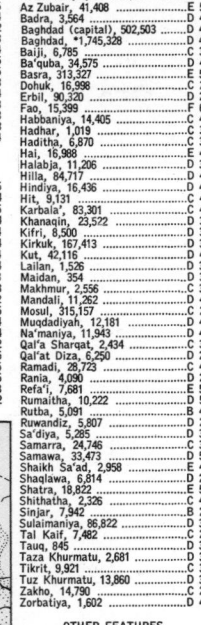
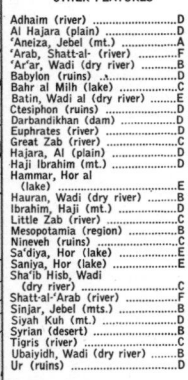
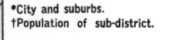

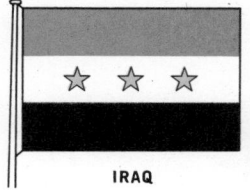

IRAN   IRAQ

IRAN
AREA 636,293 sq. mi.
POPULATION 28,448,000
CAPITAL Tehran
LARGEST CITY Tehran
HIGHEST POINT Demavend 18,376 ft.
MONETARY UNIT rial
MAJOR LANGUAGES Persian, Azerbaijani, Kurdish
MAJOR RELIGIONS Islam, Zoroastrianism

IRAQ
AREA 167,924 sq. mi. .
POPULATION 9,431,000
CAPITAL Baghdad
LARGEST CITY Baghdad
HIGHEST POINT Haji Ibrahim 11,811 ft.
MONETARY UNIT Iraqi dinar
MAJOR LANGUAGES Arabic, Kurdish
MAJOR RELIGION Islam

Topography

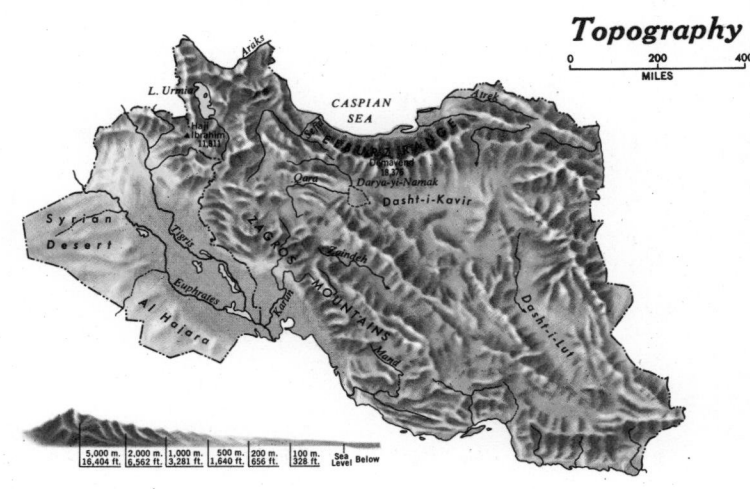

0 200 400
MILES

Agriculture, Industry and Resources

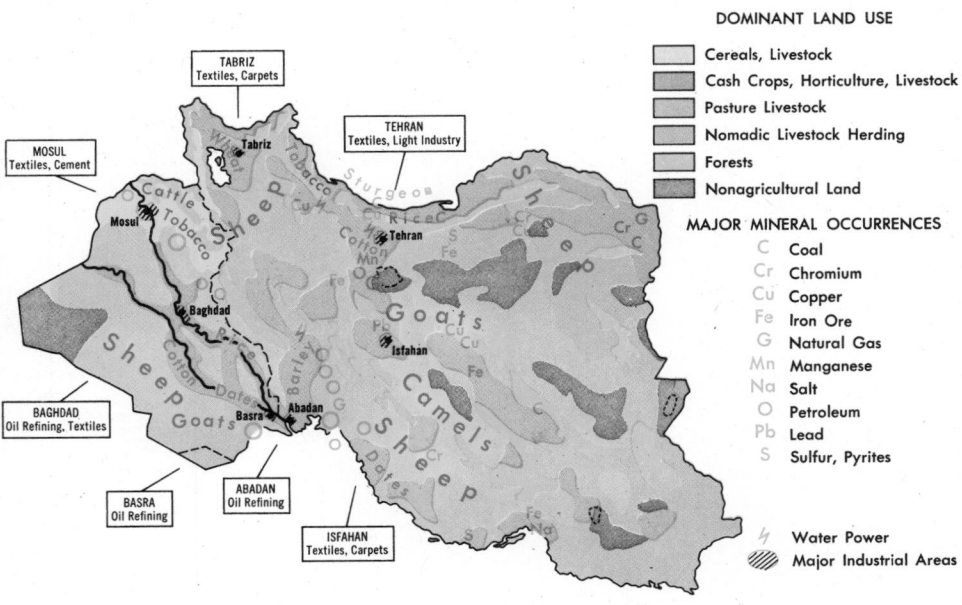

DOMINANT LAND USE

- Cereals, Livestock
- Cash Crops, Horticulture, Livestock
- Pasture Livestock
- Nomadic Livestock Herding
- Forests
- Nonagricultural Land

MAJOR MINERAL OCCURRENCES

- C Coal
- Cr Chromium
- Cu Copper
- Fe Iron Ore
- G Natural Gas
- Mn Manganese
- Na Salt
- O Petroleum
- Pb Lead
- S Sulfur, Pyrites

⚡ Water Power
▨ Major Industrial Areas

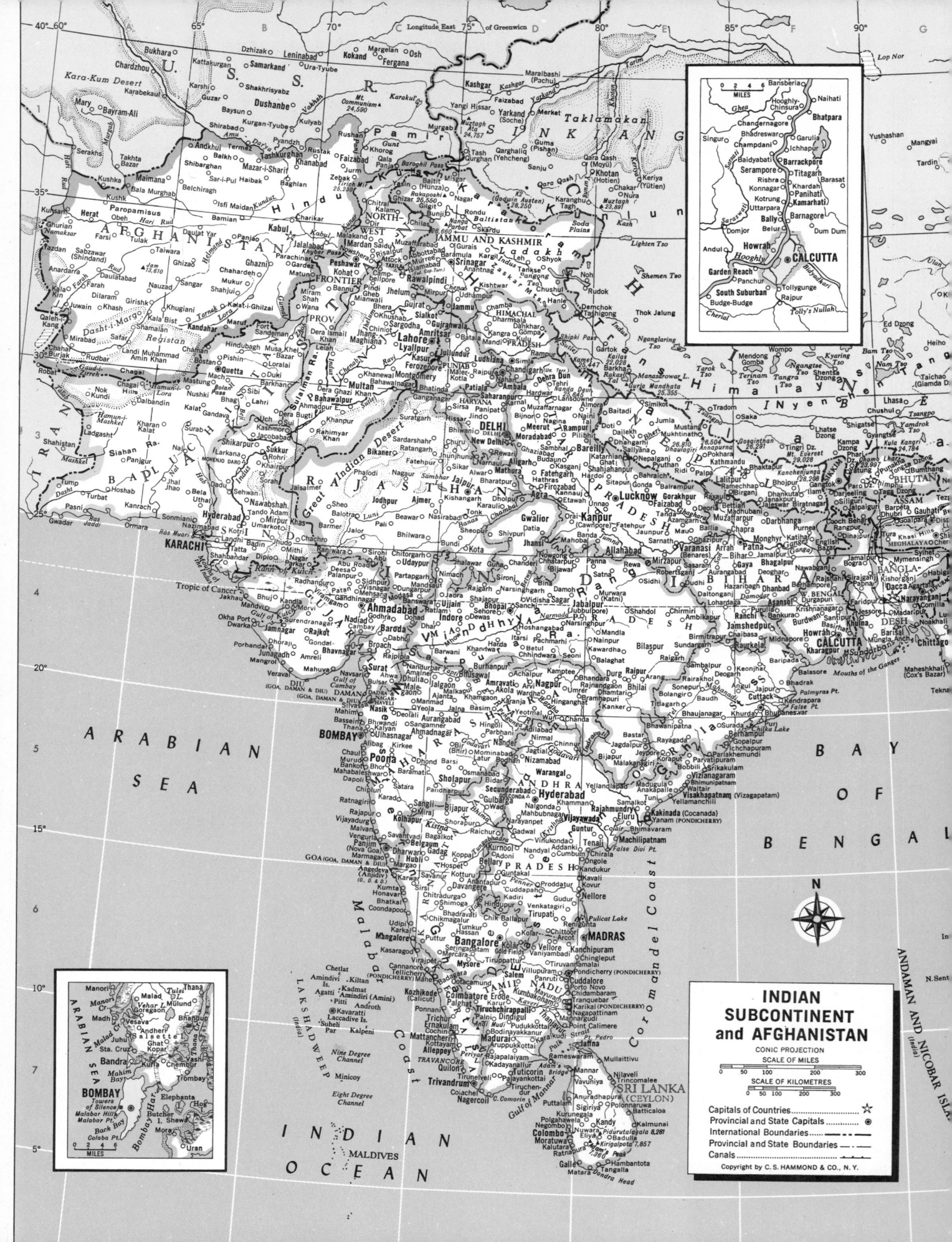

INDIAN SUBCONTINENT and AFGHANISTAN

CONIC PROJECTION

SCALE OF MILES

SCALE OF KILOMETRES

Capitals of Countries .... ☆
Provincial and State Capitals .... ◉
International Boundaries _____
Provincial and State Boundaries __ _ __
Canals ....

Copyright by C. S. HAMMOND & CO., N.Y.

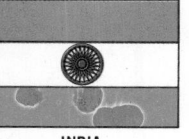
INDIA

PAKISTAN

SRI LANKA (CEYLON)

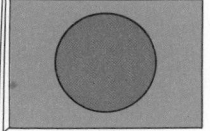
AFGHANISTAN

BANGLADESH

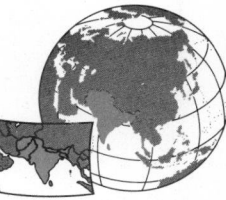

INDIA

AREA 1,261,483 sq. mi.
POPULATION 546,955,945
CAPITAL New Delhi
LARGEST CITY Calcutta (greater)
HIGHEST POINT K2 (Godwin Austen) 28,250 ft.
MONETARY UNIT Indian rupee
MAJOR LANGUAGES Hindi, English, Bihari, Telugu, Marathi, Bengali, Tamil, Gujarati, Rajasthani, Kanarese, Malayalam, Oriya, Punjabi, Assamese, Kashmiri
MAJOR RELIGIONS Hinduism, Islam, Christianity, Sikhism, Buddhism, Jainism, Zoroastrianism, Animism

AFGHANISTAN

AREA 250,000 sq. mi.
POPULATION 17,078,263
CAPITAL Kabul
LARGEST CITY Kabul
HIGHEST POINT Hindu Kush 24,556 ft.
MONETARY UNIT afghani
MAJOR LANGUAGES Pushtu, Dari, Uzbek
MAJOR RELIGION Islam

MALDIVES

AREA 115 sq. mi.
POPULATION 110,770
CAPITAL Male
LARGEST CITY Male
HIGHEST POINT 20 ft.
MONETARY UNIT Indian & Ceylonese rupee
MAJOR LANGUAGE Divehi
MAJOR RELIGION Islam

BHUTAN

MALDIVES

PAKISTAN

AREA 310,403 sq. mi.
POPULATION 60,000,000
CAPITAL Islamabad
LARGEST CITY Karachi
HIGHEST POINT Tirich Mir 25,230 ft.
MONETARY UNIT Pakistani rupee
MAJOR LANGUAGES Urdu, English, Punjabi, Pushtu, Sindhi, Baluchi
MAJOR RELIGIONS Islam, Hinduism, Sikhism, Christianity

SRI LANKA (CEYLON)

AREA 25,332 sq. mi.
POPULATION 12,300,000
CAPITAL Colombo
LARGEST CITY Colombo
HIGHEST POINT Pidurutalagala 8,281 ft.
MONETARY UNIT Ceylonese rupee
MAJOR LANGUAGES Singhalese, Tamil, English
MAJOR RELIGIONS Buddhism, Hinduism, Christianity

BANGLADESH

AREA 55,126 sq. mi.
POPULATION 70,000,000
CAPITAL Dacca
LARGEST CITY Dacca
HIGHEST POINT Mowdok Mual 3,292 ft.
MONETARY UNIT taka
MAJOR LANGUAGES Bengali, English
MAJOR RELIGIONS Islam, Hinduism, Christianity

NEPAL

NEPAL

AREA 54,362 sq. mi.
POPULATION 10,845,000
CAPITAL Kathmandu
LARGEST CITY Kathmandu
HIGHEST POINT Mt. Everest 29,028 ft.
MONETARY UNIT Nepalese rupee
MAJOR LANGUAGES Nepali, Maithili, Tamang, Newari, Tharu
MAJOR RELIGIONS Hinduism, Buddhism

BHUTAN

AREA 18,000 sq. mi.
POPULATION 1,034,774
CAPITAL Thimphu
LARGEST CITY Thimphu
HIGHEST POINT Chomo Lhari 23,997 ft.
MONETARY UNIT Indian rupee
MAJOR LANGUAGES Tibetan dialects, Nepali
MAJOR RELIGIONS Buddhism, Hinduism

AFGHANISTAN
CITIES and TOWNS

Andkhui, 30,000 .... B 1
Baghlan, 92,000 .... B 1
Balkh, 15,000 .... B 1
Bamian, 25,000 .... B 2
Charikar, 83,700 .... B 1
Faizabad, 57,000 .... C 1
Farah, 26,400 .... A 2
Gardez, 33,000 .... B 2
Ghazni, 39,900 .... B 2
Haibak, 35,200 .... B 1
Herat, 71,563 .... A 2
Jalalabad, 48,919 .... B 2
Kabul (cap.), 472,313 .... B 2
Kala Bist, 26,100 .... A 2
Kalat-i-Ghilzai, 40,500 .... B 2
Kandahar, 127,036 .... B 2
Kandahar, *142,000 .... B 2
Khanabad, 30,000 .... B 1
Maimana, 48,750 .... A 1
Mazar-i-Sharif, 43,197 .... B 1
Shibarghan, 50,440 .... B 1
Tashkurghan, 30,000 .... B 1

OTHER FEATURES

Hari Rud (river) .... A 1
Helmand (river) .... B 2
Hindu Kush (mts.) .... B 1
Kabul (river) .... C 1
Kunar (river) .... C 1
Kunduz (river) .... B 1
Paropamisus (range) .... A 2
Registan (desert) .... B 2

BANGLADESH
CITIES and TOWNS

Barisal, 69,936 .... G 4
Bogra, 33,784 .... F 4
Chittagong, 364,205 .... G 4
Chittagong, *437,000 .... G 4
Comilla, 54,504 .... G 4
Dacca (cap.), 556,712 .... G 4
Dacca, *829,000 .... G 4
Dinajpur, 37,711 .... F 3
Faridpur, 28,333 .... F 4
Jessore, 46,366 .... F 4
Khulna, 127,970 .... F 4
Khulna, *320,000 .... F 4
Mymensingh, 53,256 .... G 4
Narayanganj, 162,054 .... G 4
Narayanganj, *327,000 .... G 4
Noakhali, 19,874 .... G 4
Pabna, 40,792 .... F 4
Rajshahi, 56,885 .... F 4
Rangamati, 6,416 .... G 4
Rangpur, 40,634 .... F 3
Sylhet, 37,740 .... G 4

OTHER FEATURES

Bengal (bay) .... F 5
Brahamputra (riv.) .... F 3
Ganges (river) .... F 3
Sundarbans (swamp) .... F 4

BHUTAN
CITIES and TOWNS

Bumthang, 10,000 .... G 3
Paro Dzong, 35,000 .... F 3
Punakha, 12,000 .... G 3
Taga Dzong, 18,000 .... G 3
Thimphu (cap.), 50,000 .... G 3
Tongsa Dzong .... G 3

OTHER FEATURES

Chomo Lhari (mt.) .... F 3
Kula Kangri (mt.) .... G 3

INDIA
INTERNAL DIVISIONS

Andaman and Nicobar Islands (terr.), 115,092 .... G 6
Andhra Pradesh (state), 43,394,951 .... D 5
Arunachal Pradesh (terr.), 381,000 .... G 3
Assam (state), 14,630,422 .... G 3
Bihar (state), 56,387,296 .... F 4
Chandigarh (terr.), 150,000 ...... D 2
Dadra and Nagar Haveli (terr.), 69,000 .... C 4
Delhi (terr.), 4,044,281 .... D 2
Goa, Daman and Diu (terr.), 675,000 .... C 4
Gujarat (state), 25,189,000 ...... C 4
Haryana (state), 9,914,145 .... D 3
Himachal Pradesh (state), 3,432,000 .... D 2
Jammu and Kashmir (state), 4,615,025 .... D 2
Karnataka (state), 27,985,000 .... D 6
Kerala (state), 20,296,000 .... C 6
Lakshadweep (terr.), 27,000 ...... C 6
Madhya Pradesh (state), 41,449,729 .... C 4
Maharashtra (state), 50,295,081 .. C 5
Manipur (state), 1,035,000 .... G 4
Meghalaya (state), 983,336 .... G 3
Mizoram (terr.), 321,686 .... G 4
Nagaland (state), 515,551 .... G 3
Orissa (state), 20,674,000 .... E 5
Pondicherry (terr.), 430,000 ..... E 6
Punjab (state), 13,935,000 .... D 2
Rajasthan (state), 25,724,595 .... C 3
Sikkim (state), 191,000 .... F 3
Tamil Nadu (state), 33,686,953 .... D 6
Tripura (state), 1,424,000 .... G 4
Uttar Pradesh (state), 88,299,453 .... D 3
West Bengal (state), 44,440,095 .. F 4

CITIES and TOWNS

Achalpur, 36,538 .... D 4
Achalpur, *54,028 .... D 4
Adoni, 69,951 .... D 5
Agartala, 54,878 .... G 4
Agra, 610,328 .... D 3
Agra, *658,781 .... D 3
Ahmadabad, 1,507,921 .... C 4
Ahmadabad, *1,746,111 .... C 4
Ahmadnagar, 131,973 .... C 5
Aizwal, 31,436 .... G 4
Ajmer, 265,156 .... C 3
Akola, 143,919 .... D 4
Aligarh, 232,278 .... D 3
Allahabad, 521,568 .... E 3
Allahabad, *537,047 .... E 3
Alleppey, 161,279 .... D 7
Alwar, 72,707 .... D 3
Amalner, 46,963 .... D 4
Ambala, 87,750 .... D 2
Ambala, *200,576 .... D 2
Amravati, 177,066 .... D 4
Amreli, 34,699 .... C 4
Amritsar, 424,961 .... C 2
Amritsar, *459,179 .... C 2
Anakapalle, 46,402 .... E 5
Anantapur, 52,280 .... D 6
Andheri, 122,401 .... B 7
Arcot, 25,029 .... D 6
Arrah, 76,766 .... E 3
Aruppukkottai, 50,200 .... D 7
Aruppukkottai, *55,977 .... D 7
Asansol, 134,056 .... F 4
Asansol, *278,350 .... F 4
Aurangabad, Bihar, 14,154 .... E 4
Aurangabad, Maharashtra, 87,579 .... D 5
Aurangabad, *97,701 .... D 5
Azamgarh, 32,391 .... E 3
Badagara, 43,908 .... D 6
Bagalkot, 39,934 .... D 5
Bahraich, 56,033 .... E 3
Baidyabati, 44,312 .... F 1

Topography

0   200   400
MILES

5,000 m.   2,000 m.   1,000 m.   500 m.   200 m.   100 m.   Sea
16,404 ft. 6,562 ft. 3,281 ft. 1,640 ft. 656 ft. 328 ft. Level   Below

Balasore, 33,931 .... F 4
Ballia, 38,216 .... E 3
Bally, 247,844 .... F 1
Balrampur, 31,776 .... E 3
Banda, 37,744 .... D 3
Bandra, 38,099 .... B 7
Bangalore, 1,027,327 .... D 6
Bangalore, *1,648,232 .... D 6
Bankura, 62,833 .... F 4
Bansberia, 45,463 .... F 1
Barasat, 29,281 .... F 2
Barasat, *61,621 .... F 1
Bareilly, 325,560 .... D 3

Bareilly, *343,559 .... D 3
Baripada, 20,301 .... F 4
Barmer, 27,600 .... B 3
Barnagore, 143,621 .... F 1
Baroda, 400,725 .... C 4
Barrackpore, 63,778 .... F 1
Barrackpore, *158,244 .... F 1
Barsi, 50,389 .... D 5
Basirhat, 53,943 .... F 4
Bassein, 22,598 .... C 5
Bassein, *28,238 .... C 5
Batala, 51,300 .... D 2
Beawar, 53,931 .... C 3

Belgaum, 156,105 .... C 5
Belgaum, *176,857 .... C 5
Belgaum, 85,673 .... C 5
Belur, 29,737 .... F 1
Benares (Varanasi), 619,822 ...... E 3
Berhampore, 62,317 .... F 4
Berhampur, 76,931 .... F 5
Bettiah, 39,990 .... E 3
Bhadrak, 25,285 .... F 4
Bhadreswar, 35,489 .... F 1
Bhagalpur, 174,538 .... F 4
Bhandara, 27,710 .... E 4
Bhandup, 33,020 .... B 7

Bharatpur, 49,776 .... D 3
Bhatinda, 52,253 .... C 2
Bhatpara, 159,219 .... F 1
Bhavnagar, 217,533 .... C 4
Bhilai, 86,116 .... E 4
Bhilwara, 43,499 .... C 3
Bhimavaram, 43,281 .... E 5
Bhir (Bir), 33,066 .... D 5
Bhiwandi, 47,630 .... C 5
Bhiwani, 58,194 .... D 3
Bhopal, 310,733 .... D 4
Bhopal, *441,939 .... D 4
Bhubaneswar, 38,211 .... F 4

(continued on following page)

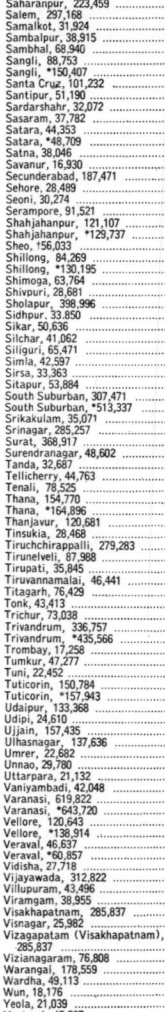
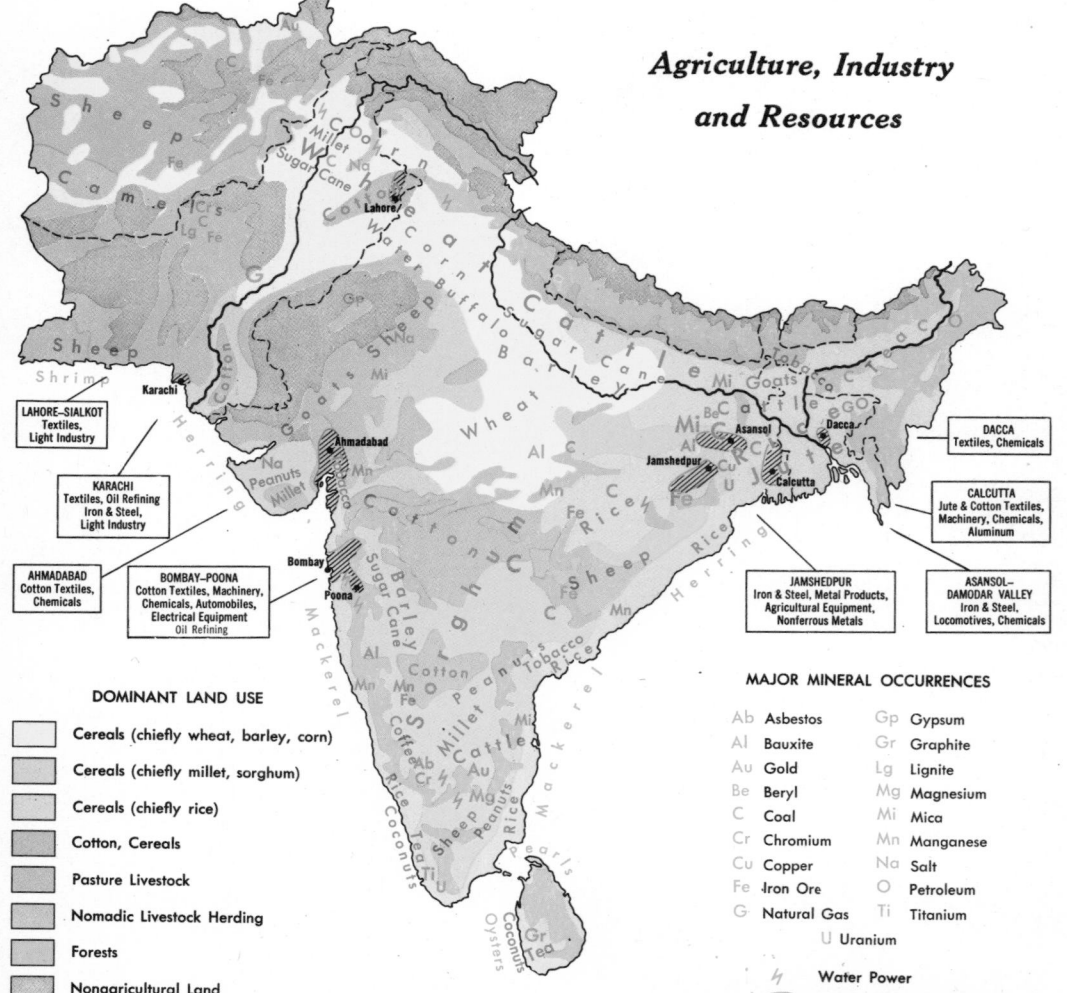

Agriculture, Industry and Resources

LAHORE–SIALKOT Textiles, Light Industry

KARACHI Textiles, Oil Refining, Iron & Steel, Light Industry

AHMADABAD Cotton Textiles, Chemicals

BOMBAY–POONA Cotton Textiles, Machinery, Chemicals, Automobiles, Electrical Equipment, Oil Refining

DACCA Textiles, Chemicals

CALCUTTA Jute & Cotton Textiles, Machinery, Chemicals, Aluminum

JAMSHEDPUR Iron & Steel, Metal Products, Agricultural Equipment, Nonferrous Metals

ASANSOL–DAMODAR VALLEY Iron & Steel, Locomotives, Chemicals

DOMINANT LAND USE

- Cereals (chiefly wheat, barley, corn)
- Cereals (chiefly millet, sorghum)
- Cereals (chiefly rice)
- Cotton, Cereals
- Pasture Livestock
- Nomadic Livestock Herding
- Forests
- Nonagricultural Land

MAJOR MINERAL OCCURRENCES

Ab	Asbestos	Gp	Gypsum
Al	Bauxite	Gr	Graphite
Au	Gold	Lg	Lignite
Be	Beryl	Mg	Magnesium
C	Coal	Mi	Mica
Cr	Chromium	Mn	Manganese
Cu	Copper	Na	Salt
Fe	Iron Ore	O	Petroleum
G	Natural Gas	Ti	Titanium
		U	Uranium

Water Power

Major Industrial Areas

JAPAN

AREA 143,622 sq. mi.
POPULATION 104,665,171
CAPITAL Tokyo
LARGEST CITY Tokyo
HIGHEST POINT Fuji 12,389 ft.
MONETARY UNIT yen
MAJOR LANGUAGE Japanese
MAJOR RELIGIONS Buddhism, Shintoism

NORTH KOREA

AREA 46,540 sq. mi.
POPULATION 13,300,000
CAPITAL P'yŏngyang
LARGEST CITY P'yŏngyang
HIGHEST POINT Paektu 9,003 ft.
MONETARY UNIT won
MAJOR LANGUAGE Korean
MAJOR RELIGIONS Confucianism, Buddhism, Christianity

SOUTH KOREA

AREA 38,452 sq. mi.
POPULATION 31,683,000
CAPITAL Seoul
LARGEST CITY Seoul
HIGHEST POINT Halla 6,398 ft.
MONETARY UNIT won
MAJOR LANGUAGE Korean
MAJOR RELIGIONS Confucianism, Buddhism, Chondogyo, Christianity

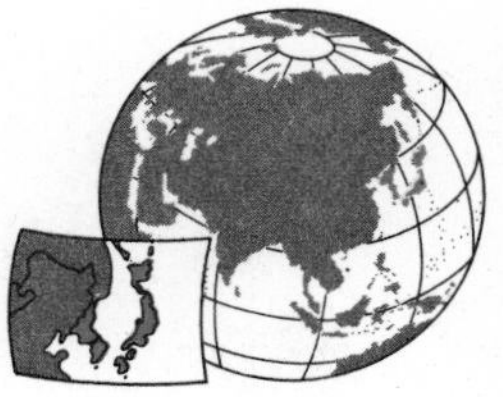

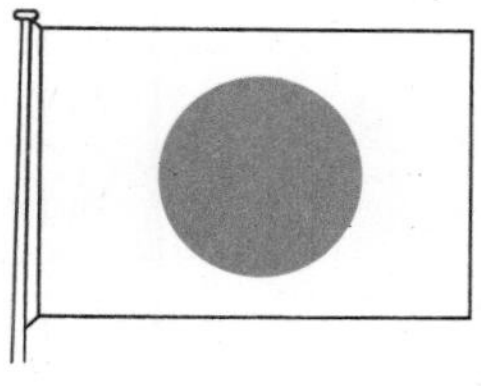

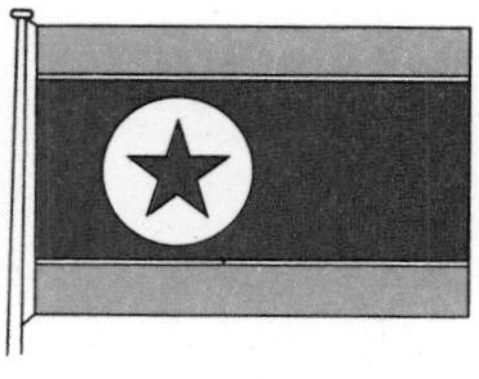

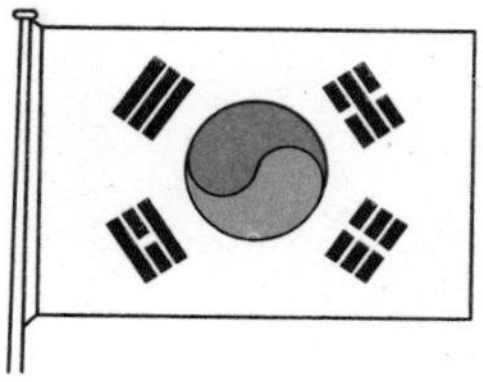

JAPAN

PREFECTURES

Aichi, 4,798,653	H 6
Akita, 1,279,835	J 4
Aomori, 1,416,591	K 3
Chiba, 2,701,770	P 2
Ehime, 1,446,384	F 7
Fukui, 750,557	G 5
Fukuoka, 3,964,611	D 7
Fukushima, 1,983,754	K 5
Gifu, 1,700,365	H 6
Gumma, 1,605,584	J 5
Hiroshima, 2,281,146	E 6
Hokkaido, 5,171,800	K 2
Hyogo, 4,309,944	H 7
Ibaraki, 2,056,154	K 5
Ishikawa, 980,499	H 5
Iwate, 1,411,118	K 4
Kagawa, 900,845	G 6
Kagoshima, 1,853,541	E 8
Kanagawa, 4,430,743	O 2
Kochi, 812,714	F 7
Kumamoto, 1,770,736	E 7
Kyoto, 2,102,808	J 7
Mie, 1,514,467	H 6
Miyagi, 1,753,126	F 4
Miyazaki, 1,080,692	E 8
Nagano, 1,958,007	J 5
Nagasaki, 1,641,245	D 7
Nara, 825,965	J 8
Niigata, 2,398,931	J 5
Oita, 1,187,480	E 7
Okayama, 1,645,135	F 6
Okinawa, 1,108,271	N 6
Osaka, 6,657,189	J 8
Saga, 871,885	E 7
Saitama, 3,014,983	O 2
Shiga, 853,385	J 7
Shimane, 821,620	F 6
Shizuoka, 2,912,521	H 6
Tochigi, 1,521,656	K 5
Tokushima, 815,115	G 7
Tokyo, 10,869,244	O 2
Tottori, 579,853	G 6
Toyama, 1,025,465	H 5
Wakayama, 1,026,975	G 6
Yamagata, 1,263,103	K 4
Yamaguchi, 1,543,573	E 6
Yamanashi, 763,194	J 6

CITIES and TOWNS

Abashiri, 44,195	M 1
Ageo, 54,776	O 2
Aizuwakamatsu, 104,000	J 5
Ajigasawa, 20,504	J 3
Akabira, 46,646	K 2
Akashi, 187,000	H 8
Aki, 26,605	F 7
Akita, 233,000	J 4
Akkeshi, 19,039	M 2
Akune, 36,026	E 7
Amagasaki, 532,000	H 8
Amagi, 44,060	E 7
Amaha, 18,062	O 3
Anan, 59,105	G 7
Aomori, 252,000	K 3
Asahi, 31,063	K 6
Asahikawa, 293,000	L 2
Ashibetsu, 52,123	L 2
Ashikaga, 153,000	J 5
Ashiya, 63,195	H 8
Atami, 54,540	J 6
Atsugi, 61,383	O 2
Awaji, 9,972	H 8
Ayabe, 48,339	G 6
Beppu, 144,000	E 7
Bibai, 63,051	L 2
Biratori, 12,930	L 2
Chiba, 407,000	P 2
Chichibu, 60,330	J 6
Chigasaki, 119,000	O 3
Chitose, 51,243	K 2
Chofu, 145,000	O 2
Choshi, 91,492	K 6
Daito, 57,107	J 8
Ebetsu, 44,510	K 2
Esashi, Hokkaido, 15,380	J 3
Esashi, Hokkaido, 11,401	L 1
Esashi, Iwate, 42,666	K 4
Fuchu, Hiroshima, 45,341	F 6
Fuchu, Tokyo, 148,000	O 2
Fuji, 173,000	J 6
Fujieda, 70,789	J 6
Fujisawa, 211,000	O 3
Fukuchiyama, 58,223	G 6
Fukue, 36,876	D 7
Fukui, 193,000	G 5
Fukuoka, 812,000	D 7
Fukushima, 225,000	K 5
Fukuyama, 233,000	F 6
Funabashi, 281,000	P 2
Furukawa, 52,853	K 4
Futtsu, 16,445	O 3
Gifu, 398,000	H 6
Gobo, 30,040	G 7
Gose, 35,788	J 8
Gosen, 38,113	J 5
Goshogawara, 47,433	K 3
Gotsu, 30,209	F 6
Habikino, 50,333	J 8
Haboro, 30,266	K 1
Hachinohe, 209,000	K 3
Hachioji, 229,000	O 2
Hagi, 53,905	E 6
Hakodate, 249,000	K 3
Hakui, 29,090	H 5
Hamada, 44,439	E 6
Hamamatsu, 420,000	H 6
Hanamaki, 62,710	K 4
Hanawa, 20,507	K 3
Hanno, 47,825	O 2
Haramachi, 40,643	K 5
Hayama, 17,617	O 3
Higashiosaka, 454,000	J 8
Hikone, 62,740	H 6
Himeji, 403,000	G 6
Himi, 62,452	H 5
Hirakata, 164,000	J 7
Hirara, 32,591	L 7
Hirata, 33,128	F 6
Hiratsuka, 151,000	O 3
Hiroo, 13,598	L 2
Hirosaki, 162,000	K 3
Hiroshima, 542,000	E 6
Hitachi, 184,000	K 5
Hitachiota, 36,974	K 5
Hitoyoshi, 44,831	E 7
Hofu, 94,342	E 6
Hondo, 39,790	E 7
Honjo, 38,361	J 4
Hyuga, 43,678	E 7
Ibaraki, 143,000	J 7
Ibusuki, 32,386	E 8
Ichihara, 134,000	P 2
Ichikawa, 236,000	P 2
Ichinohe, 25,165	K 3
Ichinomiya, 210,000	H 6
Ichinoseki, 57,238	K 4
Ide, 8,199	J 7
Iida, 79,145	H 6
Iizuka, 82,033	E 7
Ikeda, Hokkaido, 15,529	L 2
Ikeda, Osaka, 82,478	H 7
Ikuno, 9,466	G 6
Imabari, 109,000	F 6
Imari, 67,316	D 7
Imazu, 11,245	G 6
Ina, 51,944	H 6
Isahaya, 63,886	D 7
Ise, 104,000	H 6
Ishigaki, 41,315	L 7
Ishige, 18,481	P 2
Ishinomaki, 106,000	K 4
Ishioka, 36,789	K 5
Itami, 141,000	H 7
Ito, 59,404	J 6
Itoigawa, 39,332	H 5
Itoman, 34,065	N 6
Iwaizumi, 24,846	K 4
Iwaki, 337,000	K 5
Iwakuni, 106,000	E 6
Iwami, 18,004	G 6
Iwamisawa, 65,508	L 2
Iwanai, 25,405	K 2
Iwasaki, 5,432	J 3
Iwata, 58,940	H 6
Iwatsuki, 41,946	O 2
Iyo, 28,611	F 7
Izuhara, 21,989	D 6
Izumi, 84,771	J 8
Izumiotsu, 53,312	J 8
Izumisano, 66,521	G 6
Izumo, 68,765	F 6
Joyo, 20,038	J 7
Kadoma, 121,000	J 7
Kaga, 54,860	H 5
Kagoshima, 406,000	E 8
Kaizuka, 69,365	H 8
Kakogawa, 115,000	G 6
Kamaishi, 82,104	L 4
Kamakura, 136,000	O 3
Kameoka, 43,335	J 7
Kaminoyama, 38,679	J 4
Kamiyaku, 12,458	E 8
Kamo, 9,034	J 7
Kanazawa, 344,000	H 5
Kanonji, 44,200	F 6
Kanoya, 70,519	E 8
Kanuma, 77,240	J 5
Karatsu, 73,999	D 7
Kaseda, 28,565	D 8
Kashihara, 57,065	J 8
Kashiwa, 133,000	P 2
Kashiwazaki, 71,465	J 5
Kasugai, 141,000	H 6
Kasukabe, 42,460	O 2
Katsuta, 52,625	K 5
Katsuura, 29,133	K 6
Kawachi, 91,853	J 8
Kawachinagano, 40,109	J 8
Kawagoe, 148,000	O 2
Kawaguchi, 284,000	O 2
Kawanishi, 61,282	H 7
Kawasaki, 910,000	J 6
Kazusa, 12,787	P 3
Kembuchi, 8,013	L 1
Kesennuma, 59,884	K 4
Kikonai, 11,353	K 3
Kiryu, 132,000	J 5
Kisarazu, 54,928	P 3
Kishiwada, 156,000	J 8
Kitaibaraki, 55,334	K 5
Kitakata, 40,424	J 5
Kitakyushu, 1,042,319	E 6
Kitami, 74,841	L 2
Kizu, 10,814	J 7
Kobayashi, 41,922	E 8
Kobe, 1,288,754	H 7
Kochi, 242,000	F 7
Kodaira, 125,000	O 2
Kofu, 185,000	J 6
Kokubu, 31,249	E 8
Komagane, 28,327	H 6
Komatsu, 91,163	H 5
Koriyama, 240,000	K 5
Koshigaya, 112,000	P 2
Koza, 55,923	N 6
Kuji, 38,374	K 3
Kuki, 26,773	O 2
Kumagaya, 119,000	J 5
Kumamoto, 432,000	E 7
Kumano, 30,041	H 7
Kumiyama, 7,231	J 7
Kurashiki, 332,000	F 6
Kurayoshi, 50,114	F 6
Kure, 237,000	F 6
Kurume, 188,000	E 7
Kushikino, 31,781	E 8
Kushima, 36,425	E 8
Kushimoto, 20,252	G 7
Kushiro, 195,000	M 2
Kutchan, 19,738	K 2
Kyonan, 13,980	O 3
Kyoto, 1,418,933	J 7
Machida, 154,000	O 2
Maebashi, 225,000	J 5
Maibara, 13,415	G 6
Maizuru, 96,641	G 6
Mashike, 13,063	K 2
Masuda, 52,729	E 6
Matsubara, 71,406	H 8
Matsudo, 206,000	P 2
Matsue, 115,000	F 6
Matsumae, 19,111	J 3
Matsumoto, 159,000	H 5
Matsunaga, 34,610	F 6
Matsusaka, 104,000	H 6
Matsuto, 29,649	H 5
Matsuyama, 310,000	F 7
Mihara, 82,175	F 6
Miki, 38,542	H 7
Mikuni, 22,135	G 5
Minamata, 45,577	E 7
Minobu, 12,250	J 6
Minoo, 43,851	J 7
Misawa, 36,326	K 3
Mishima, 43,479	J 7
Mitaka, 146,000	O 2
Mito, 167,000	K 5
Mitsukaido, 36,584	P 2
Miura, 42,601	O 3
Miyako, 56,575	L 4
Miyakonojo, 121,000	E 8
Miyazaki, 212,000	E 8
Miyazu, 33,285	G 6
Miyoshi, 37,871	F 6
Mizusawa, 45,985	K 4
Mobara, 42,486	K 6
Mombetsu, 40,389	L 1
Mooka, 38,117	K 5
Mori, 18,330	K 2
Moriguchi, 164,000	J 7
Morioka, 191,000	K 4
Motobu, 15,068	N 6
Muko, 20,730	J 7
Murakami, 32,651	J 4
Muroran, 181,000	K 2
Muroto, 28,746	G 7
Musashino, 135,000	O 2
Mutsu, 39,282	K 3
Nachikatsuura, 24,889	H 7
Nagahama, Ehime, 16,193	F 7
Nagahama, Shiga, 49,871	H 6
Nagano, 280,000	J 5
Nagaoka, 27,522	J 7
Nagaoka, 159,000	J 5
Nagasaki, 422,000	D 7
Nagato, 29,246	E 6
Nago, 19,601	N 6
Nagoya, 2,036,022	H 6
Naha, 284,000	N 6
Nakaminato, 33,620	K 5
Nakamura, 35,717	F 7
Nakasato, 15,898	K 3
Nakatsu, 58,371	E 7
Nakoso, 46,731	K 5
Nanao, 48,715	H 5
Nankoku, 41,237	F 7
Naoetsu, 45,650	H 5
Nara, 191,000	J 8
Narashino, 64,897	P 2
Nayoro, 36,106	L 1
Naze, 44,111	O 5
Nemuro, 45,149	M 2
Neyagawa, 174,000	J 7
Nichinan, 57,612	E 8
Niigata, 379,000	J 5
Niihama, 130,000	F 6
Niimi, 34,063	F 6
Niitsu, 56,594	J 5
Nikko, 32,031	J 5
Nishinomiya, 357,000	H 8
Nishinoomote, 30,490	E 8
Nobeoka, 134,000	E 7
Noboribetsu, 39,101	K 2
Noda, 59,799	P 2
Nogata, 57,839	E 7
Nose, 9,906	J 7
Noshiro, 61,921	J 3
Noto, 17,719	H 5
Numata, 44,347	J 5
Numazu, 186,000	J 6
Obama, 35,160	G 6
Obihiro, 129,000	L 2
Oda, 42,322	F 6
Odate, 59,662	K 3
Odawara, 151,000	J 6
Ofunato, 38,347	K 4
Oga, 43,333	J 4
Ogaki, 134,000	H 6

(continued on following page)

Agriculture, Industry and Resources

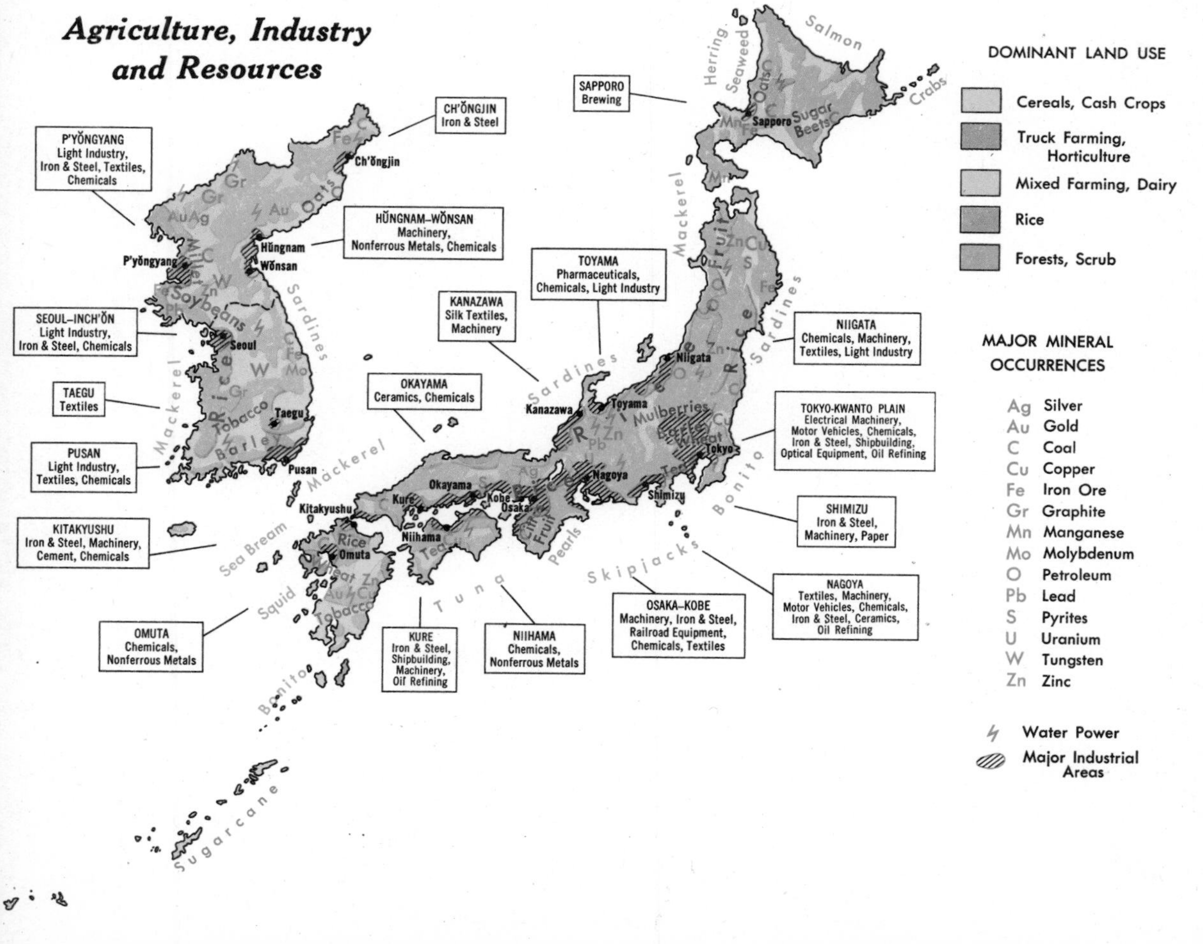
P'YŎNGYANG
Light Industry, Iron & Steel, Textiles, Chemicals
CH'ŎNGJIN
Iron & Steel
HŬNGNAM–WŎNSAN
Machinery, Nonferrous Metals, Chemicals
SEOUL–INCH'ŎN
Light Industry, Iron & Steel, Chemicals
TAEGU
Textiles
PUSAN
Light Industry, Textiles, Chemicals
KITAKYUSHU
Iron & Steel, Machinery, Cement, Chemicals
OMUTA
Chemicals, Nonferrous Metals
KURE
Iron & Steel, Shipbuilding, Machinery, Oil Refining
NIIHAMA
Chemicals, Nonferrous Metals
OSAKA–KOBE
Machinery, Iron & Steel, Railroad Equipment, Chemicals, Textiles
NAGOYA
Textiles, Machinery, Motor Vehicles, Chemicals, Iron & Steel, Ceramics, Oil Refining
SHIMIZU
Iron & Steel, Machinery, Paper
TOKYO-KWANTO PLAIN
Electrical Machinery, Motor Vehicles, Chemicals, Iron & Steel, Shipbuilding, Optical Equipment, Oil Refining
NIIGATA
Chemicals, Machinery, Textiles, Light Industry
OKAYAMA
Ceramics, Chemicals
KANAZAWA
Silk Textiles, Machinery
TOYAMA
Pharmaceuticals, Chemicals, Light Industry
SAPPORO
Brewing
Ch'ŏngjin
Hŭngnam
Wŏnsan
P'yŏngyang
Seoul
Taegu
Pusan
Kitakyushu
Omuta
Niihama
Kure
Okayama
Kobe
Osaka
Nagoya
Shimizu
Tokyo
Toyama
Kanazawa
Niigata
Sapporo
Herring
Seaweed
Salmon
Crabs
Sugar Beets
Oats
Mackerel
Sardines
Soybeans
Rice
Tobacco
Barley
Wheat
Fruit
Mulberries
Tea
Pearls
Bonito
Skipjacks
Tuna
Squid
Sea Bream
Sugarcane
DOMINANT LAND USE
Cereals, Cash Crops
Truck Farming, Horticulture
Mixed Farming, Dairy
Rice
Forests, Scrub
MAJOR MINERAL OCCURRENCES
Ag Silver
Au Gold
C Coal
Cu Copper
Fe Iron Ore
Gr Graphite
Mn Manganese
Mo Molybdenum
O Petroleum
Pb Lead
S Pyrites
U Uranium
W Tungsten
Zn Zinc
Water Power
Major Industrial Areas

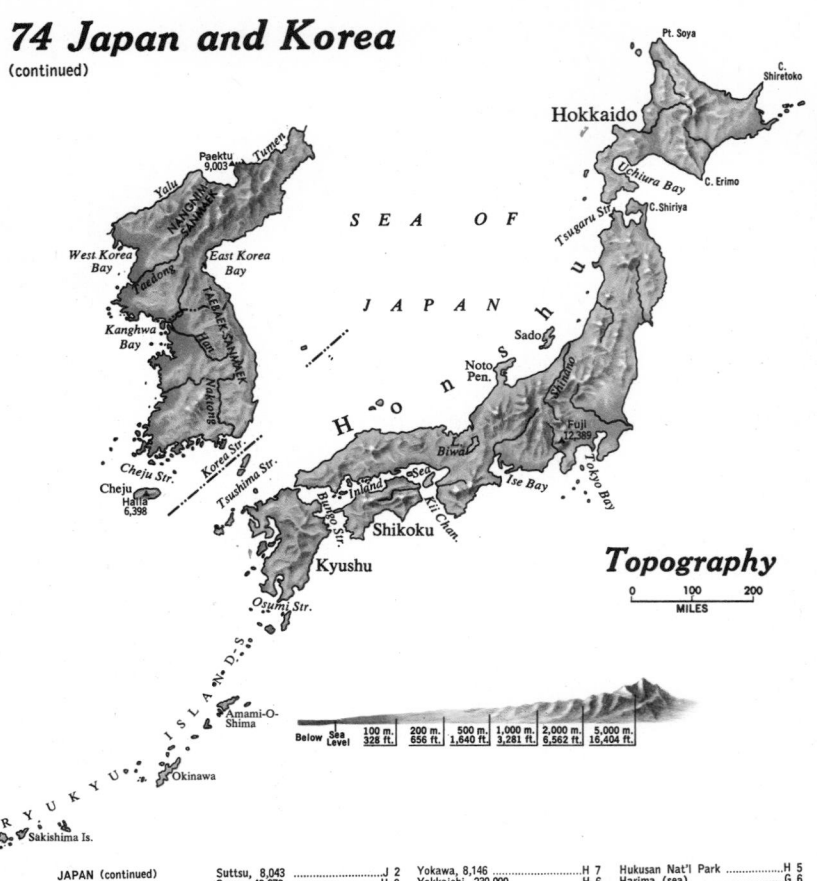

Topography

0 100 200 MILES

Below Sea Level | 100 m. 328 ft. | 200 m. 656 ft. | 500 m. 1,640 ft. | 1,000 m. 3,281 ft. | 2,000 m. 6,562 ft. | 5,000 m. 16,404 ft.

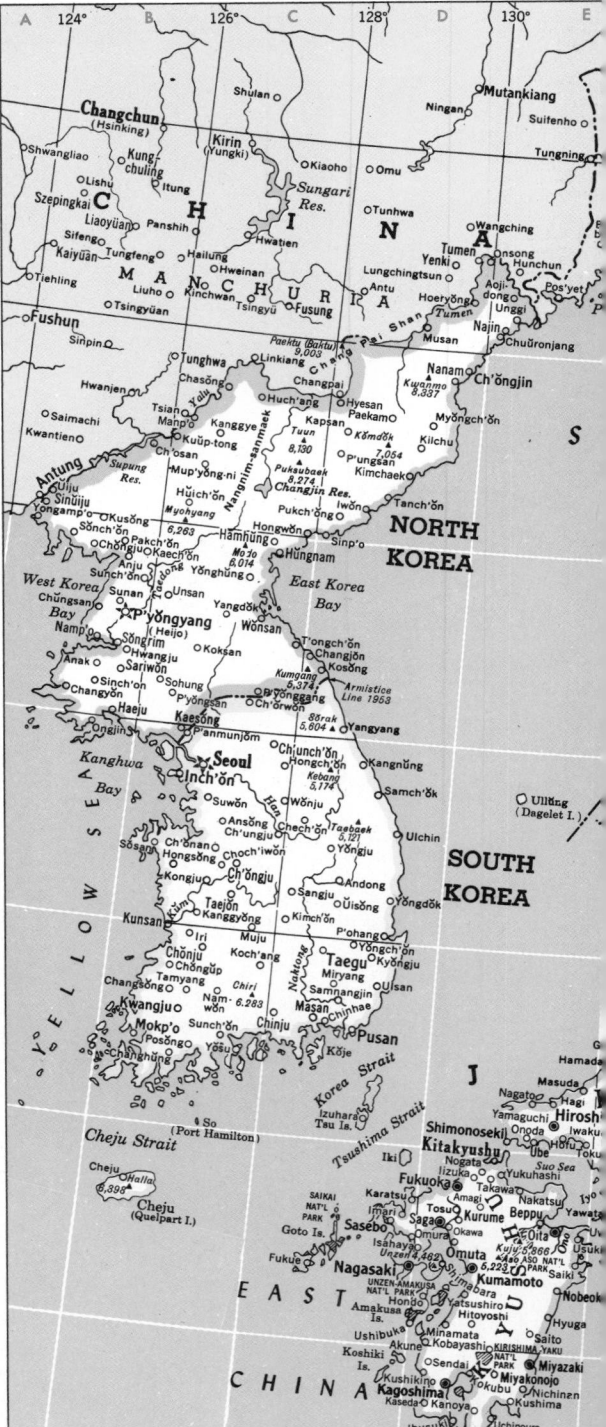

Otakine (mt.)	K 5	Shiretoko (cape)	M 1	Toyama (bay)	H 5
Rebun (isl.), 8,374	K 1	Shiriya (cape)	K 3	Tsu (isls.), 65,304	D 6
Rikuchu-Kaigan Nat'l Park	L 1	Soya (point)	L 1	Tsugaru (strait)	K 3
Rishiri (isl.), 17,663	K 1	Suo (sea)	E 7	Tsurugi (mt.)	G 7
Ryukyu (isls.), 1,108,271	J 4	Suruga (bay)	J 6	Tsushima (isls.), 65,304	D 6
Sado (isl.), 102,925	J 4	Suwanose (isl.)	O 4	Tsushima (strait)	D 6
Sagami (bay)	O 3	Suzu (point)	H 5	Unzen (mt.)	D 7
Sagami (river)	O 3	Takeshima (isls.)	F 5	Unzen-Amakusa Nat'l Park	D 7
Sagami (sea)	J 6	Tama (river)	O 3	Volcano (isls.)	M 4
Saikai Nat'l Park	D 7	Tanega (isl.), 60,130	E 8	Wakasa (bay)	G 6
Sakishima (isls.), 121,837	K 7	Tarama (isl.), 2,603	K 7	Yaeyama (isls.), 52,012	K 7
San'in Kaigan Nat'l Park	G 6	Tazawa (lake)	K 3	Yaku (isl.), 22,242	E 8
Sata (cape)	E 8	Teshio (mt.)	L 1	Yonaguni (isl.), 3,671	K 8
Setonaikai Nat'l Park	H 7	Teshio (river)	L 1	Yoron (isl.), 7,181	N 6
Shikoku (isl.), 3,975,058	F 7	Tobi (bay)	J 4	Yoshino (river)	G 6
Shikotan (isl.)	N 2	Tokachi (mt.)	L 2	Yoshino-Kumano Nat'l Park	H 7
Shikotsu (lake)	K 2	Tokachi (river)	M 2	Zao (mt.)	K 5
Shikotsu-Toya Nat'l Park	K 2	Tokara (arch.), 2,722	O 5		
Shimane (pen.)	F 6	Tokuno (isl.), 18,920	O 5	**KOREA (NORTH)**	
Shimokita (pen.)	L 2	Tokyo (bay)	O 3	CITIES and TOWNS	
Shinano (river)	H 5	Tone (river)	J 5		
Shiragami (cape)	J 3	Tosa (bay)	F 7	Anju	B 4
Shirane (mt.)	J 6	Towada (lake)	K 3		
Shirane (mt.)	H 6	Towada-Hachimantai Nat'l Park	K 2		
		Toya (lake)	K 2		

JAPAN (continued)

Ogi, 5,500	J 5	Suttsu, 8,043	J 2	Yokawa, 8,146	H 7
Ohata, 13,015	K 3	Suwa, 46,276	H 6	Yokkaichi, 230,000	H 6
Oita, 243,000	E 7	Suzu, 32,122	H 5	Yokohama, 2,237,513	O 3
Ojiya, 47,376	J 5	Suzuka, 115,000	O 2	Yokosuka, 340,000	O 3
Okawa, 51,197	E 7	Tachikawa, 115,000	O 2	Yokote, 44,331	K 4
Okaya, 56,986	J 5	Tajimi, 60,175	H 6	Yonago, 108,000	F 6
Okayama, 322,000	F 6	Takada, 73,668	J 5	Yonezawa, 94,435	K 5
Okazaki, 200,000	H 6	Takaishi, 45,679	H 7	Yono, 51,746	O 2
Omagari, 39,900	K 4	Takamatsu, 271,000	G 6	Yotsukura, 20,226	K 5
Omiya, 248,000	O 2	Takaoka, 158,000	H 5	Yubari, 85,141	L 2
Omu, 9,484	L 1	Takarazuka, 109,000	H 7	Yubetsu, 9,720	L 1
Omura, Bonin Islands, 203	M 3	Takasaki, 184,000	J 5	Yukuhashi, 47,495	E 7
Omura, Nagasaki, 56,425	E 7	Takatsuki, 178,000	L 1	Yuzawa, 39,879	K 4
Omuta, 206,000	E 7	Takawa, 74,063	E 7	Zushi, 43,211	O 3
Onagawa, 18,080	K 4	Takayama, 53,399	H 5		
Ono, 43,747		Takefu, 62,588	G 6	**OTHER FEATURES**	
Onoda, 43,584	E 6	Tanabe, Kyoto, 17,333	J 7		
Onomichi, 90,740	F 6	Tanabe, Wakayama, 62,276	G 7	Abashiri (river)	M 1
Osaka, 2,980,409	J 8	Tateyama, 55,866	J 4	Abukuma (river)	K 4
Ota, 87,898	J 5	Tendo, 43,903	K 4	Agano (river)	J 5
Otaru, 205,000	K 2	Tenri, 54,169	J 8	Akan Nat'l Park	M 2
Otawara, 41,026	K 5	Teshio, 9,493	K 1	Amakusa (isls.), 233,465	D 7
Otsu, 164,000	H 6	Toba, 115,000	K 2	Amami (isls.), 186,193	N 5
Owase, 34,019	H 6	Tobetsu, 19,406	K 2	Amami-O-Shima (isl.), 94,348	N 5
Oyabe, 35,646	H 5	Togane, 31,922	P 2	Ara (river)	O 2
Oyama, 90,632	J 5	Tojo, 16,866	F 6	Asahi (mt.)	J 4
Ozu, 40,165	F 7	Tokushima, 225,000	G 7	Asama (mt.)	J 5
Raasu, 8,931	M 1	Tokuyama, 100,000	F 6	Ashizuri (cape)	F 7
Rikuzentakata, 31,040	K 4	Tokyo (capital), 8,832,647	O 2	Aso (mt.)	E 7
Rumoi, 40,231	K 2	Tokyo, *11,350,000	O 2	Aso Nat'l Park	E 7
Ryotsu, 26,494	J 4	Tomakomai, 81,812	K 2	Atsumi (bay)	H 6
Ryugasaki, 34,917	P 2	Tomiyama, 7,863	O 3	Awa (isl.), 771	J 4
Sabae, 50,114	H 5	Tondabayashi, 47,985	J 8	Awaji (isl.), 185,473	H 8
Saga, 153,000	E 7	Tosa, 30,772	F 7	Bandai (mt.)	K 5
Sagamihara, 224,000	O 2	Tosashimizu, 26,725	F 7	Bandai-Asahi Nat'l Park	J 4
Saijo, 16,569	F 7	Tosu, 44,419	E 7	Biwa (lake)	H 6
Saiki, 51,145	E 7	Tottori, 117,000	G 6	Bonin (isls.), 203	M 3
Saito, 42,543	E 7	Towada, 46,713	K 3	Boso (pen.)	K 6
Sakado, 24,854	O 2	Toyama, 264,000	H 5	Bungo (strait)	F 7
Sakai, Ibaraki, 21,689	P 1	Toyohashi, 253,000	H 6	Chichi (isl.), 203	M 3
Sakai, Osaka, 544,000	J 8	Toyonaka, 334,000	J 7	Chichibu-Tama Nat'l Park	J 6
Sakaide, 61,284	G 6	Toyooka, 43,259	G 6	Chokai (mt.)	J 4
Sakaiminato, 32,846	F 6	Toyota, 161,000	H 6	Chubu Sangaku Nat'l Park	H 5
Sakata, 95,582	J 4	Tsu, 123,000	H 6	Dai (mt.)	F 6
Saku, 55,149	J 5	Tsubame, 40,134	J 5	Daimanji (mt.)	F 5
Sakurai, 49,939	J 8	Tsuchiura, 78,971	J 5	Daio (cape)	H 6
Sanda, 32,265	H 7	Tsuruga, 54,508	J 4	Daisen-Oki National Park	F 6
Sanjo, 74,080	J 5	Tsuruoka, 95,615	J 4	Daisetsu (mt.)	L 2
Sapporo, 1,010,122	K 2	Tsuyama, 76,007	F 6	Daisetsu-Zan Nat'l Park	L 2
Sarufutsu, 7,450	L 1	Ube, 149,000	E 6	Dogo (isl.), 23,669	F 5
Sasebo, 268,000	D 7	Uchinoura, 10,036	E 8	Dozen (isls.), 12,516	F 5
Satte, 25,169	O 1	Ueda, 73,940	J 5	East China (sea)	C 8
Sawara, 47,561	K 6	Ugo, 25,661	K 4	Edo (river)	P 2
Sayama, 40,183	O 2	Uji, 68,934	J 7	Erabu (isl.), 22,049	N 5
Sendai, Kagoshima, 67,142	E 8	Uozu, 46,854	H 5	Erimo (cape)	L 3
Sendai, Miyagi, 515,000	K 4	Urakawa, 21,552	L 2	Esan (point)	K 3
Seta, 20,327	M 2	Urawa, 250,000	O 2	Fuji (mt.)	J 6
Shari, 18,015	M 1	Ushibuka, 30,995	D 7	Fuji (river)	J 6
Shibata, 73,992	J 5	Usuki, 42,731	E 7	Fuji-Hakone-Izu Nat'l Park	H 6
Shibetsu, 36,502	M 2	Utsunomiya, 283,000	K 5	Gassan (mt.)	J 4
Shimabara, 44,175	E 7	Wajima, 66,484	H 5	Goto (isls.), 159,190	D 7
Shimizu, 230,000	H 6	Wajima, 35,484	H 5	Habomai (isls.)	N 2
Shimoda, 20,645	H 6	Wakasa, 8,455	G 8	Hachiro (lagoon)	J 3
Shimonoseki, 276,000	E 6	Wakayama, 353,000	J 8	Haha (isl.), 203	M 3
Shingu, 40,051	H 7	Wakkanai, 51,539	K 1	Hakken (mt.)	H 5
Shinjo, 43,037	K 4	Warabi, 69,715	O 2	Haku (mt.)	H 5
Shiogama, 58,363	K 4	Yaizu, 77,008	J 6	Hukusan Nat'l Park	H 5
Shiroishi, 26,533	K 4	Yakumo, 22,487	J 2	Harima (sea)	G 6
Shizunai, 21,021	L 2	Yamagata, 201,000	K 4	Hida (river)	H 5
Shizuoka, 392,000	H 6	Yamaguchi, 103,000	E 6	Hodaka (mt.)	H 5
Shobara, 26,515	F 6	Yamato, 64,991	O 2	Hokkaido (isl.), 5,171,800	L 2
Soka, 102,000	O 2	Yamatokoriyama, 45,765	J 8	Honshu (isl.), 76,757,913	H 5
Soma, 38,430	K 5	Yamatotakada, 47,371	J 8	Ie (isl.), 7,059	N 6
Sonobe, 15,241	J 7	Yao, 197,000	J 8	Iheya (isl.), 3,083	N 6
Suita, 239,000	J 7	Yatabe, 20,093	P 2	Iki (isl.), 45,654	D 7
Sukagawa, 46,999	K 5	Yatsushiro, 105,000	E 7	Ina (river)	O 2
Sukumo, 25,992	E 7	Yawata, 19,204	M 3	Inawashiro (lake)	K 5
Sumoto, 46,313	G 6	Yawatahama, 50,005	F 7	Inubo (cape)	K 6
Sunagawa, 30,205	K 2	Yoichi, 26,154	K 2	Iriomote (isl.), 7,026	K 7
Susaki, 32,020	F 7			Iro (cape)	J 6
				Ise (bay)	H 6
				Ise-Shima Nat'l Park	H 6
				Ishigaki (isl.), 41,315	L 7
				Ishikari (bay)	K 2
				Ishikari (river)	L 2
				Ishizuchi (mt.)	F 7
				Iwaki (mt.)	K 3
				Iwate (mt.)	K 3
				Iwo (isl.)	M 4
				Iyo (sea)	E 7
				Izu (isls.), 35,592	O 4
				Izu (pen.)	J 6
				Japan (sea)	G 4
				Joshinetsu-Kogen Nat'l Park	J 5
				Kagoshima (bay)	E 8
				Kamui (cape)	J 2
				Kariba (mt.)	J 2
				Kasumiga (lagoon)	K 5
				Kazan-Retto (Volcano) (isls.)	M 4
				Kerama (isls.), 2,467	N 6
				Kii (channel)	G 7
				Kikai (isl.), 14,231	O 5
				Kino (river)	G 6
				Kirishima-Yaku Nat'l Park	E 8
				Kita Iwo (isl.)	M 4
				Kitakami (river)	K 4
				Koma (mt.)	K 2
				Koshiki (isls.), 16,301	D 8
				Kuchino (isl.)	O 4
				Kuju (mt.)	E 7
				Kume (isl.), 5,922	M 6
				Kutcharo (lake)	L 1
				Kyushu (isl.), 12,370,190	E 7
				Meakan (mt.)	M 2
				Minami Iwo (isl.)	L 5
				Miura (pen.)	O 3
				Miyake (isl.), 47,150	L 7
				Miyako (isl.), 69,825	K 7
				Mogami (river)	K 4
				Motsuta (cape)	J 2
				Muko (river)	H 7
				Muroto (point)	G 7
				Mutsu (bay)	K 3
				Naka (river)	K 5
				Nampo-Shoto (isls.), 203	M 3
				Nii (isl.), 3,913	J 6
				Nikko Nat'l Park	J 5
				Nojima (cape)	H 2
				Noshappu (point)	N 2
				Noto (pen.)	H 5
				Nyudo (cape)	J 3
				Oani (river)	P 3
				Obitsu (river)	P 2
				Oga (pen.)	J 4
				Ogasawara-Gunto (Bonin) (isls.), 203	M 3
				Okhotsk (sea)	N 1
				Oki (isls.), 36,185	F 5
				Okinawa (isl.), 782,267	N 6
				Okinawa (isls.), 812,339	N 6
				Okushiri (isl.), 7,142	J 2
				Oma (cape)	K 3
				Omono (river)	K 4
				Ono (river)	E 7
				Ontake (mt.)	H 6
				Osaka (bay)	J 8
				Oshima (isl.), 11,840	J 6
				Osumi (isls.), 82,372	E 8
				Osumi (pen.)	E 8
				Osumi (str.)	E 8

Changjon	D 4	Pak'chŏn	B 4	East Korea (bay)	D 4	Chinju, 107,126	D 6	P'anmunjŏm	C 5
Chasong	C 3	P'anmunjŏm	B 4	Kömdŏk (mt.)	D 4	Choch'iwon, 25,423	C 5	P'ohang, 66,190	D 5
Ch'ŏngjin, 1250,000	E 3	Puch'ŏn	C 4	Kumgang (mt.)	C 4	Ch'ŏnan, 71,315	C 5	Posŏng, 22,247	C 7
Chŏngju	B 4	P'yŏnggang	C 4	Nangnim-sanmaek (range)	C 3	Ch'ŏngju, 123,736	C 5	Pusan, 1,425,703	D 6
Chŭngsan	B 4	P'yŏngyang (cap.), †800,000	C 4	Paektu (Baktu) (mt.)	C 3	Chŏngŭp, 47,036	C 6	Samch'ŏk, 35,117	D 5
Haeju, 1140,000	B 4	P'yŏngyang, *1,221,300	C 4	Puksubaek (mt.)	C 3	Chŏnju, 220,654	C 6	Samnangjin, 21,936	D 6
Hamhŭng-Hŭngnam, 1,200,000	D 4	Sariwŏn	B 4	Sŏ-Chosŏn-man		Ch'unch'ŏn, 100,043	D 5	Sangju, 47,558	D 6
Hoeryŏng	D 2	Sinp'o	D 3	Supong (res.)		Hongch'ŏn, 23,473	C 5	Sŏul (cap.), 4,100,000	C 5
Hongwŏn	D 3	Sinŭiju, 1300,000	B 3	Taedong (river)	C 4	Hongsŏng, 21,912	C 5	Sŏsan, 30,416	C 5
Hŭngnam-Hamhŭng, 1,200,000	C 4	Sŏnch'ŏn	B 3	Tumen (river)		Inch'ŏn, 525,072	C 5	Sunch'ŏn, 79,313	C 7
Hyesan	C 3	Tanch'ŏn	D 3	Tuun (river)		Iri, 78,448	C 6	Suwŏn, 127,752	C 5
Iwŏn	D 3	Ŭiju	B 3	West Korea (bay)	B 4	Kanggyŏng, 26,430	C 5	Taegu, 845,073	D 6
Kaesŏng, 1175,000	C 4	Unggi	E 2	Yalu (river)	C 3	Kangnŭng, 65,422	D 5	Taejŏn, 315,094	C 5
Kanggye	C 3	Unsan	C 3			Kimch'ŏn, 56,981	D 5	Tamyang, 14,856	C 6
Kapsan	C 3	Wŏnsan, 1275,000	C 4			Koch'ang, 34,707	C 6	Ŭisŏng, 21,306	D 5
Kilchu	D 3	Yangdŏk	C 4			Kongju, 30,320	C 5	Ulchin, 27,579	D 5
Kimchaek, 1,100,000	D 3	Yongamp'o	B 4			Kŏje, 102,343	C 6	Ulsan, 112,858	D 6
Kosŏng	D 4					Kwangju, 403,737	C 6	Wŏnju, 103,852	D 5
Kusŏng	B 3					Kyŏngju, 85,895	D 6	Yangyang, 10,832	D 5
Manp'o	C 3					Masan, 154,856	D 6	Yŏngch'ŏn, 44,305	D 6
Musan	D 2					Miryang, 40,288	D 6	Yŏngdŏk, 19,220	D 5
Najin	E 2					Mokp'o, 162,322	C 6	Yŏngju, 46,338	D 5
Namp'o, 1140,000	B 4					Muju, 18,174	C 6	Yŏsu, 102,011	C 6
Nanam						Namwŏn, 44,193	C 6		
Ongjin	B 5								

East Korea (bay) ... D 4

KOREA (SOUTH)

CITIES and TOWNS

Andong, 63,816	D 5		
Ansŏng, 23,698	C 5		
Changhŭng, 30,166	C 6		
Changsŏng, 26,816	C 6		
Chech'ŏn, 49,883	D 5		
Chinhae, 80,804	D 6		

OTHER FEATURES

Baktu (mt.)	C 3
Chang Pai Shan (range)	C 2
Changjin (res.)	C 3

Cheju (isl.), 336,694	C 7
Cheju (strait)	C 7
Dagelet (Ullŭng) (isl.), 27,032	E 5
Halla (mt.)	C 7
Han (river)	C 5
Kŏje (isl.), 117,906	D 6
Korea (strait)	D 6
Kŭm (river)	C 5
Naktong (river)	D 6
Port Hamilton (So) (isl.)	C 7
Quelpart (Cheju) (isl.), 336,694	C 7
So (isl.)	E 5
Taebaek (mt.)	D 5
Ullŭng (isl.), 22,032	E 5

*City and suburbs.

†Populations courtesy of Kingsley Davis, Office of Int'l Pop. & Urban Research, Inst. of Int'l Studies, Univ. of California.

OTHER FEATURES

JAPAN is divided into prefectures bearing the same names as their capitals except:

Prefecture	Capital	Ref.
AICHI	NAGOYA	H 6
EHIME	MATSUYAMA	F 7
GUMMA	MAEBASHI	J 5
HOKKAIDO	SAPPORO	K 2
HYOGO	KOBE	H 7
IBARAKI	MITO	K 5
ISHIKAWA	KANAZAWA	H 5
IWATE	MORIOKA	K 4
KAGAWA	TAKAMATSU	G 6
KANAGAWA	YOKOHAMA	O 3
MIE	TSU	H 6
MIYAGI	SENDAI	K 4
OKINAWA	NAHA	N 6
SAITAMA	URAWA	O 2
SHIGA	OTSU	F 6
SHIMANE	MATSUE	F 6
TOCHIGI	UTSUNOMIYA	K 5
YAMANASHI	KOFU	J 6

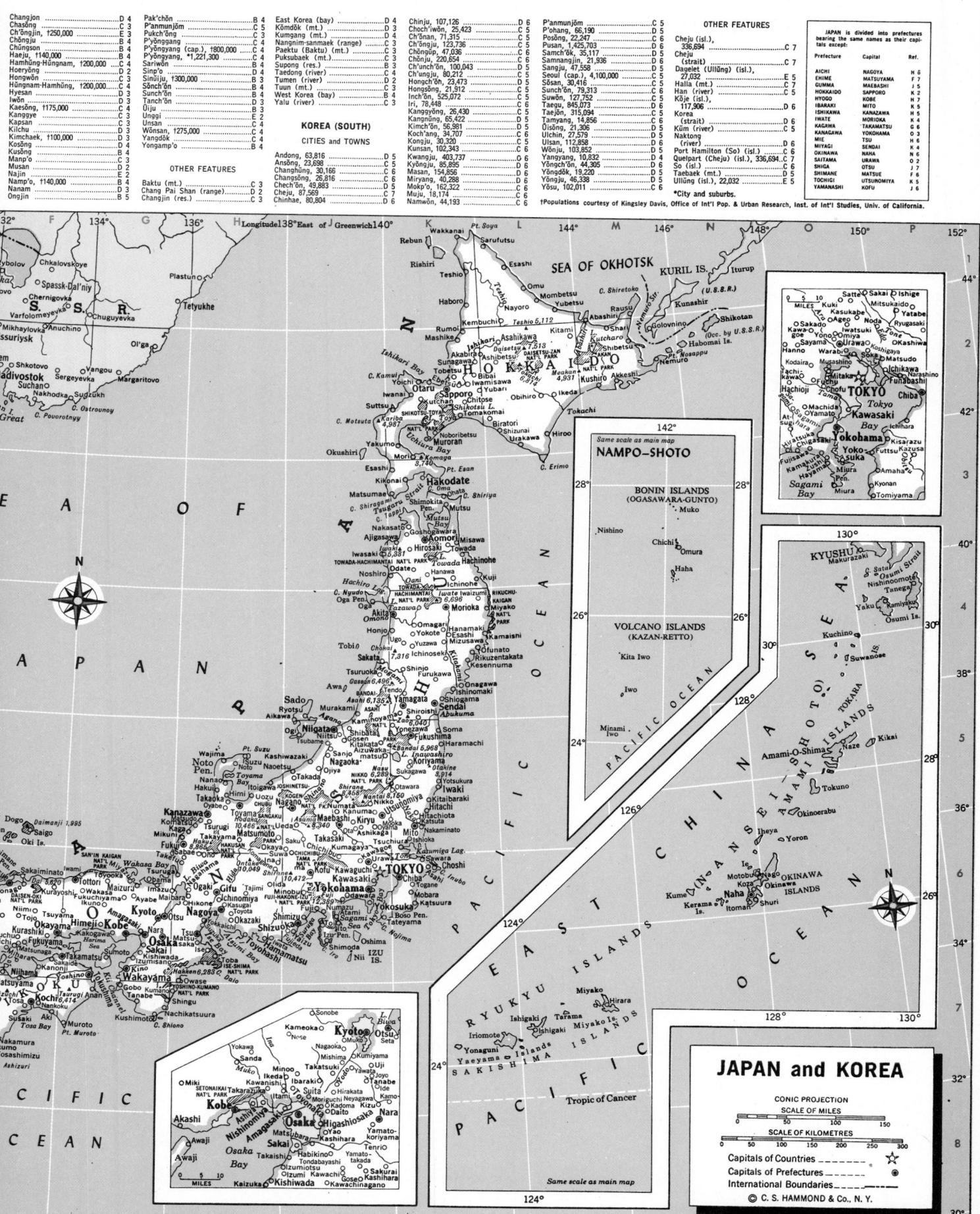

JAPAN and KOREA

CONIC PROJECTION

SCALE OF MILES

SCALE OF KILOMETRES

Capitals of Countries ☆
Capitals of Prefectures ◉
International Boundaries

© C. S. HAMMOND & Co., N. Y.

76 China and Mongolia

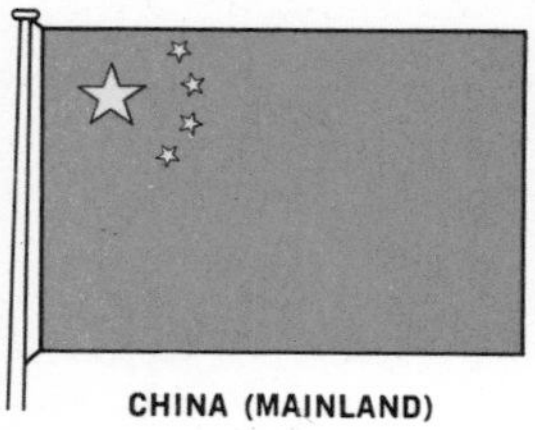

CHINA (MAINLAND)

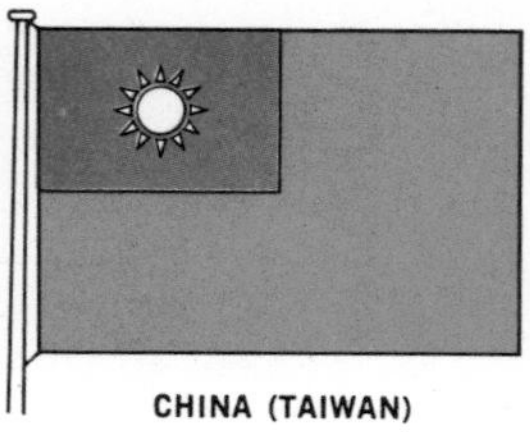

CHINA (TAIWAN)

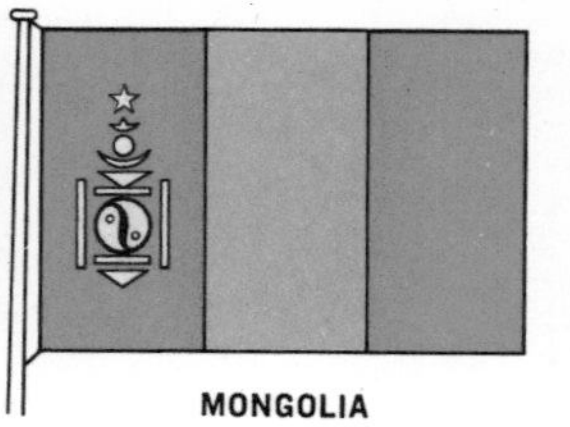

MONGOLIA

CHINA (MAINLAND)

AREA 3,691,506 sq. mi.
POPULATION 740,000,000
CAPITAL Peking
LARGEST CITY Shanghai
HIGHEST POINT Mt. Everest 29,028 ft.
MONETARY UNIT yüan
MAJOR LANGUAGES Chinese, Chuang, Uigur, Yi, Tibetan, Miao, Mongol
MAJOR RELIGIONS Confucianism, Buddhism, Taoism, Islam

Topography

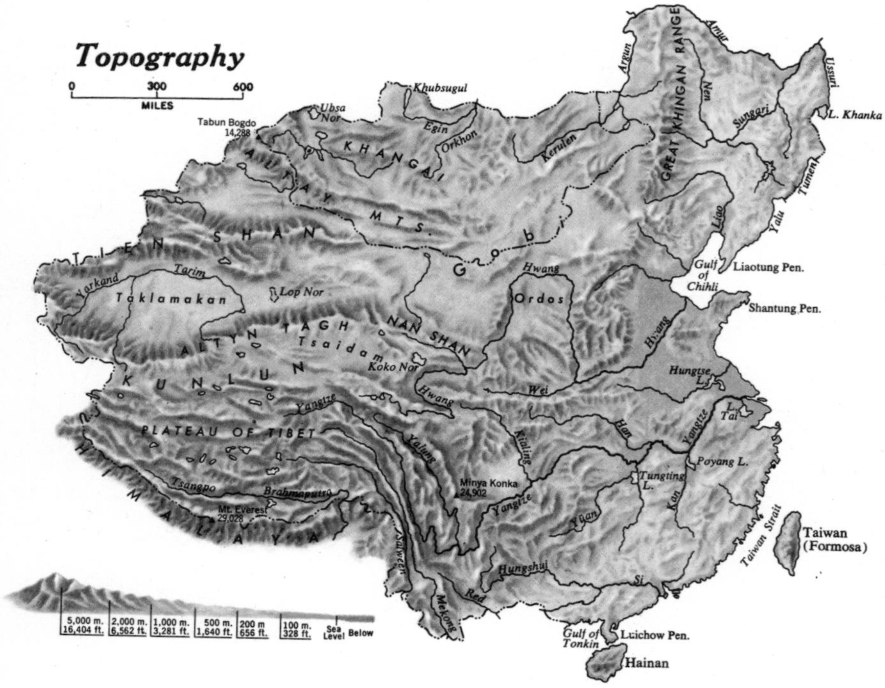
0
300
600
MILES
Tabun Bogdo
14,288
Ubsa Nor
Khubsugul
Egin
Orkhon
KHANGAI
Kerulen
Argun
Amur
GREAT KHINGAN RANGE
Nen
Sungari
Ussuri
L. Khanka
ALTAY MTS.
Gobi
Liao
Yalu
Tumen
TIEN SHAN
Tarim
Yarkand
Taklamakan
Lop Nor
Hwang
Ordos
Gulf of Chihli
Liaotung Pen.
Shantung Pen.
ALTYN TAGH
NAN SHAN
Tsaidam
Koko Nor
KUNLUN
Hungtse L.
Wei
Hwang
Han
Yangtze
Tai L.
PLATEAU OF TIBET
Yalung
Kialing
Minya Konka
24,902
Tungting L.
Poyang L.
Tsangpo
Brahmaputra
Mt. Everest
29,028
HIMALAYA
Salween
Mekong
Yüan
Kan
Taiwan Strait
Taiwan (Formosa)
Hungshui
Red
Si
Gulf of Tonkin
Luichow Pen.
Hainan
5,000 m. 16,404 ft.
2,000 m. 6,562 ft.
1,000 m. 3,281 ft.
500 m. 1,640 ft.
200 m. 656 ft.
100 m. 328 ft.
Sea Level
Below

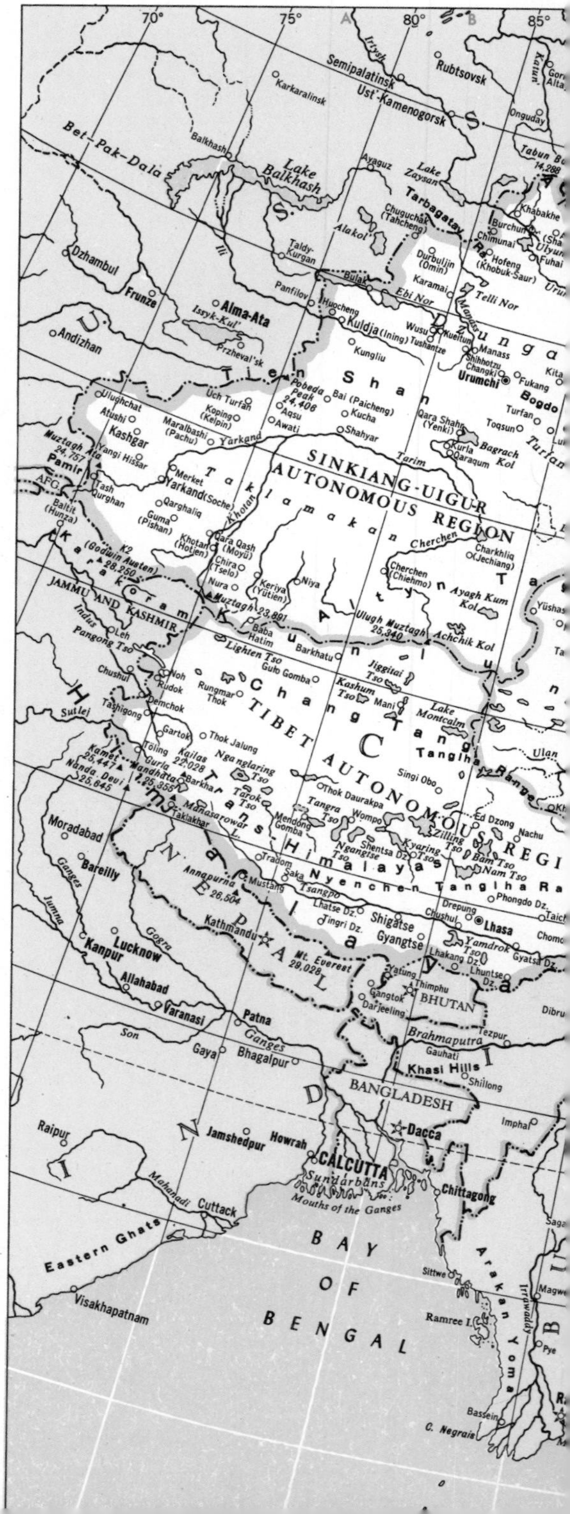
70°
75°
80°
85°
Semipalatinsk
Rubtsovsk
Karkaralinsk
Ust'-Kamenogorsk
Bet-Pak-Dala
Balkhash
Lake Balkhash
Ayaguz
Lake Zaysan
Tabun Bogdo 14,288
Tarbagatay Ra.
Chuguchak (Tacheng)
Alakol'
Dzhambul
Taldy-Kurgan
Durbuljin (Omin)
Karamai
Hofeng (Khobuk-Saur)
Ebi Nor
Telli Nor
Frunze
Alma-Ata
Issyk-Kul'
Kuldja (Ining)
Wusu
Manass
Andizhan
Przheval'sk
Kungliu
Tien Shan
Urumchi
Bogdo
Pobeda Peak 24,406
Uch Turfan
Koping (Kelpin)
Bai (Paicheng)
Kucha
Aqsu
Awati
Shahyar
Turfan
Toqsun
Qara Shahr (Yenki)
Kurla
Bagrach Kol
Tarim
Ulughchat
Atushi
Maralbashi (Pachu)
Kashgar
Yangi Hissar
Yarkand
Muztagh Ata 24,757
Pamir
SINKIANG-UIGUR AUTONOMOUS REGION
Taklamakan
Merket
Yarkand (Soche)
Qarghaliq
Guma (Pishan)
Khotan (Hotien)
Qara Qash (Moyü)
Chira (Tselo)
Nura
Keriya (Yütien)
Niya
Cherchen
Charkhliq (Jechiang)
Cherchen (Chiehmo)
Ayagh Kum Kol
Ulugh Muztagh 25,340
Achchik Kol
K2 (Godwin Austen) 28,250
Karakoram
Muztagh 23,891
JAMMU AND KASHMIR
Indus
Leh
Pangong Tso
Baba Hatim
Barkhatu
Lighten Tso
Kunlun
Chushul
Noh
Rudok
Rungmar Thok
Gufo Gomba
Jiggitai Tso
Kashum Tso
Mani
Lake Montcalm
Chang Tang
Tanglha Range
TIBET AUTONOMOUS REGION
Sutlej
Tashigong
Demchok
Gartok
Thok Jalung
Nganglaring Tso
Singi Obo
Kamet 25,447
Nanda Devi 25,645
Toling
Gurla Mandhata 25,355
Barkha
Tarok Tso
Thok Daurakpa
Tangra Tso
Wompo
Mendong Gomba
Manasarowar L.
Taklakhar
Trans Himalaya
Shentsa Dz.
Ngangtse Tso
Zilling Tso
Nam Tso
Ed Dzong
Nachu
Moradabad
Bareilly
Ganges
Jumna
Tradom
Saka
Annapurna 26,504
Nyenchen Tangiha Ra.
Mustang
Tsangpo
Lhatse Dz.
Tingri Dz.
Shigatse
Gyangtse
Lhasa
Drepung
Chushul
Yamdrok Tso
Lhakang Dz.
Lhuntse Dz.
Kathmandu
Mt. Everest 29,028
NEPAL
Lucknow
Kanpur
Gogra
Allahabad
Varanasi
Patna
Thimphu
Gangtok
Darjeeling
BHUTAN
Brahmaputra
Tezpur
Gauhati
Khasi Hills
Shillong
Dibrugarh
Son
Gaya
Bhagalpur
Ganges
BANGLADESH
Dacca
Imphal
Raipur
Jamshedpur
Howrah
CALCUTTA
Sundarbans
Mouths of the Ganges
Chittagong
Mahanadi
Cuttack
Eastern Ghats
BAY OF BENGAL
Visakhapatnam
Sittwe
Arakan Yoma
Ramree I.
Irrawaddy
Bassein
C. Negrais
Pye
INDIA

CHINA

PROVINCES

Anhwei, 33,560,000 ... J 5
Chekiang, 25,280,000 ... J 6
Fukien, 14,650,000 ... J 6
Heilungkiang, 14,860,000 ... L 2
Honan, 48,670,000 ... H 5
Hopei, 44,720,000 ... J 4
Hunan, 36,220,000 ... H 6
Hupei, 30,790,000 ... H 5
Inner Mongolian Autonomous Region, 9,200,000 ... G 3
Kansu, 12,800,000 ... F 4
Kiangsi, 18,610,000 ... J 6
Kiangsu, 45,230,000 ... K 5
Kirin, 12,550,000 ... L 3
Kwangsi Chuang Autonomous Region, 19,390,000 ... G 7
Kwangtung, 37,960,000 ... H 7
Kweichow, 16,890,000 ... G 6
Liaoning, 24,090,000 ... K 3
Ningsia Hui Autonomous Region, 1,810,000 ... G 4
Shansi, 15,960,000 ... H 4
Shantung, 54,030,000 ... J 4
Shensi, 18,130,000 ... G 5
Sinkiang-Uigur Autonomous Region, 5,640,000 ... B 3
Szechwan, 72,160,000 ... F 5
Taiwan, 14,577,000 ... K 7
Tibet Autonomous Region, 1,270,000 ... C 5
Tsinghai, 2,050,000 ... E 4
Yünnan, 19,100,000 ... F 7

CITIES and TOWNS†

Ahpa ... F 5
Aicheng ... G 8
Aigun ... L 1
Aihui (Aigun) ... L 1
Aliho ... K 1
Altai ... C 2
Amoy, 400,000 ... J 7
Ankang ... G 5
Anking, 160,000 ... J 5
Anshan, 1,500,000 ... K 3
Anshun, 40,000 ... G 6
Ansi ... E 3
Antung (Tantung), 450,000 ... K 3
Anyang, 225,000 ... H 4
Aqsu ... B 3
Atushi, 5,000 ... A 4
Awati ... B 3
Baba Hatim ... B 4
Bai ... B 3
Barkha ... B 5
Barkhatu ... B 4
Barkol ... D 3
Batang ... E 6
Bayinhot ... F 4
Canton, 2,300,000 ... H 7
Chalainor ... J 2
Chamdo ... E 5
Changchih, 300,000 ... H 4
Changchow, 400,000 ... J 5
Changchow, 81,200 ... J 7
Changchun, 1,500,000 ... K 3
Changsha, 850,000 ... H 6
Changteh, 225,000 ... H 6
Changyeh, 45,000 ... E 4
Chankiang, 220,000 ... H 7
Chaoan (Chaochow), 101,000 ... J 7
Chaochow, 101,000 ... J 7
Chaotung, 50,000 ... F 6
Chaoyang, 30,000 ... J 3
Charkhliq ... C 4
Chefoo, 180,000 ... K 4
Chengchow, 1,500,000 ... H 5
Chengteh, 200,000 ... J 3
Chengtu, 2,000,000 ... F 5
Chenpa ... G 5
Cherchen ... C 4
Chiai, 221,817 ... K 7
Chiehmo (Cherchen) ... C 4
Chihfeng, 49,000 ... J 3
Chinchow, 750,000 ... J 3
Chinkiang, 250,000 ... K 5
Chinsi, 45,000 ... K 3
Chinwangtao, 400,000 ... K 4
Chomo Dzong ... D 6
Chüanchow, 130,000 ... J 7
Chuchow, 350,000 ... H 6
Chuguchak ... B 2
Chumatien, 45,000 ... H 5
Chungking, 3,500,000 ... G 6
Chungning ... G 4
Chungshan, 135,000 ... H 7
Chushul ... D 6
Dairen (in Lüta) ... K 4
Denchin ... E 5
Drepung ... D 6
Durbuljin ... B 2
Ed Dzong ... D 5
Fatshan, 120,000 ... H 7
Fengfeng, 45,000 ... H 4
Fenyang, 25,000 ... H 4
Foochow, 900,000 ... J 6
Fowyang, 75,000 ... J 5
Fuchin ... M 2
Fuhai ... C 2
Fushun, 1,700,000 ... K 3
Fusin, 350,000 ... K 3
Fusingchen, 20,000 ... F 7
Fuyü, 62,969 ... L 2
Gartok ... B 5
Giamda Dzong (Taichao) ... D 5
Guma ... A 4
Gyangtse ... C 6
Gyatsa Dzong ... D 6
Haikow (Hoihow), 500,000 ... H 7
Hailar, 60,000 ... J 2
Hailun ... L 2
Hailung, 20,000 ... L 3
Hami ... D 3
Hanchung, 120,000 ... G 5
Hangchow, 1,100,000 ... J 5
Hankow (in Wuhan) ... H 5
Hantan, 500,000 ... H 4
Hanyang (in Wuhan) ... H 5
Harbin, 2,750,000 ... L 2
Hengshui ... J 4
Hengyang, 310,000 ... H 6
Hochwan, 75,000 ... G 5
Hofei, 400,000 ... J 5
Hofeng ... C 2
Hoihow, 500,000 ... H 7
Hokang, 350,000 ... M 2
Hoppo, 80,000 ... G 7
Hotien (Khotan) ... A 4
Hsüchang, 58,000 ... H 5
Huhehot, 700,000 ... H 3
Huma ... L 1
Hunchun, 13,246 ... M 3
Hwainan, 350,000 ... J 5
Hwaiteh, 60,000 ... K 3
Hwangchung ... F 4
Hwangling ... G 4
Hwangshih, 200,000 ... J 5
Hwangyüan ... F 4
Hwohsien ... H 4
Ichang, 150,000 ... H 5
Ichun, 200,000 ... L 2
Ierhsieh ... J 2
Ining (Kuldja), 160,000 ... B 3
Ipin, 275,000 ... F 6
Ishan ... G 7
Jechiang (Charkhliq) ... C 4
Jyekundo ... E 5
Kaifeng, 330,000 ... J 5
Kalgan, 1,000,000 ... J 3
Kanchow, 135,000 ... H 6
Kangting ... F 6
Kaohsiung, 719,899 ... J 7
Karamai, 43,000 ... B 2
Kashgar, 175,000 ... A 4
Kashing, 132,000 ... K 5
Keelung, 304,740 ... K 6
Kelpin (Koping) ... A 3
Keriya ... B 4
Khabakhe ... C 2
Khetinsiring ... D 5
Khobuk-Saur (Hofeng) ... C 2
Khotan ... A 4
Kiamusze, 275,000 ... L 2
Kian, 100,000 ... J 6
Kiayükwan ... E 4
Kienow ... J 6
Kienyang, 50,000 ... H 6
Kinghung ... E 7
Kingku ... F 7
Kingtehchen, 300,000 ... J 6
Kinhwa, 46,200 ... J 6
Kirin, 1,200,000 ... L 3
Kisi, 350,000 ... M 2
Kitai ... C 3
Kiuchüan, 50,000 ... E 4
Kiukiang, 120,000 ... J 6
Kokiu, 250,000 ... F 7
Kongmoon, 150,000 ... H 7
Koping ... A 3
Kucha ... B 3
Kulang ... F 4
Kuldja, 160,000 ... B 3
Kungju ... B 3
Kunming, 1,700,000 ... F 6
Kwanghwa ... H 5
Kweilin, 225,000 ... G 6
Kweisui (Huhehot), 700,000 ... H 3
Kweiyang, 1,500,000 ... G 6
Lanchow, 1,500,000 ... F 4
Lantsang ... E 7
Lhakang Dzong ... D 6
Lhasa, 175,000 ... D 6
Lhatse Dzong ... C 6
Lhuntse Dzong ... D 6
Liaoyang, 250,000 ... K 3
Liaoyüan, 300,000 ... L 3
Lienyünkang, 300,000 ... J 5
Likiang ... F 6
Linchwan, 45,000 ... J 6
Linsia, 75,000 ... F 4
Lintsing, 45,000 ... J 4
Liuchow, 250,000 ... G 7
Loho, 55,000 ... H 5
Loshan, 250,000 ... F 6
Loyang, 750,000 ... H 5
Luchow, 225,000 ... F 6
Lungchen, 14,000 ... L 2
Lüshun (Port Arthur) (in Lüta) ... K 4
Lüta, ‡4,000,000 ... K 4
Mahai ... D 4
Manass ... C 3
Manchouli, 30,000 ... J 2
Mani ... C 5
Manning (Wanning) ... H 8
Maralbashi ... A 4
Markham Dzong ... E 6
Mato ... E 4
Mendong Gomba ... C 5
Merket ... A 4
Minhsien ... F 5
Mowming, 15,000 ... H 7
Moyü (Qara Qash) ... B 4
Mukden, 3,750,000 ... K 3
Muli ... F 6
Mutankiang, 400,000 ... M 3
Nachü ... D 5
Nanchang, 900,000 ... H 6
Nancheng, 50,000 ... J 6
Nanchung, 275,000 ... G 5
Nanking, 2,000,000 ... J 5
Nanning, 375,000 ... G 7
Nanping, 53,445 ... J 6
Nanyang, 75,000 ... H 5
Neikiang, 240,000 ... F 6
Ningpo, 350,000 ... K 6
Ningsia (Yinchwan), 175,000 ... F 4
Omin (Durbuljin) ... B 2
Pachen ... D 5
Pachu (Maralbashi) ... A 4
Paicheng, 75,000 ... K 2
Paiyin, 50,000 ... F 4
Paiyü ... E 5
Pakhoi, 175,000 ... G 7
Paoki, 275,000 ... G 5
Paoting, 350,000 ... J 4
Paotow, 800,000 ... G 3
Pehan, 130,000 ... L 2
Peihai (Pakhoi), 175,000 ... G 7

(continued on following page)

CHINA (TAIWAN)
AREA 13,948 sq. mi.
POPULATION 14,577,000
CAPITAL Taipei
LARGEST CITY Taipei
HIGHEST POINT Hsinkao Shan 12,959 ft.
MONETARY UNIT new Taiwan dollar
MAJOR LANGUAGES Chinese, Formosan
MAJOR RELIGIONS Confucianism, Buddhism,
Taoism, Christianity, Tribal religions

MONGOLIA
AREA 604,247 sq. mi.
POPULATION 1,300,000
CAPITAL Ulan Bator
LARGEST CITY Ulan Bator
HIGHEST POINT Tabun Bogdo 15,266 ft.
MONETARY UNIT tugrik
MAJOR LANGUAGES Mongolian, Kazakh
MAJOR RELIGION Buddhism

HONG KONG
AREA 398 sq. mi.
POPULATION 4,089,000
CAPITAL Victoria
MONETARY UNIT Hong Kong dollar
MAJOR LANGUAGES Chinese, English
MAJOR RELIGIONS Confucianism, Buddhism,
Christianity

MACAO
AREA 6.2 sq. mi.
POPULATION 292,000
CAPITAL Macao
MONETARY UNIT pataca
MAJOR LANGUAGES Chinese, Portuguese
MAJOR RELIGIONS Confucianism, Buddhism,
Taoism, Christianity

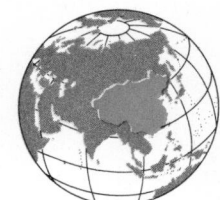

*Wuhan municipality consists of
Hankow, Hanyang and Wuchang.*

CHINA and MONGOLIA

CONIC PROJECTION

SCALE OF MILES
0   100   200   300   400   500

SCALE OF KILOMETRES
0   100   200   300   400   500

Capitals of Countries....☆   International Boundaries _____
Provincial Capitals.......◉   Provincial Boundaries _____
Canals _____   Walls _____

© Copyright by C.S. HAMMOND & CO., N.Y.

(continued)

Agriculture, Industry and Resources

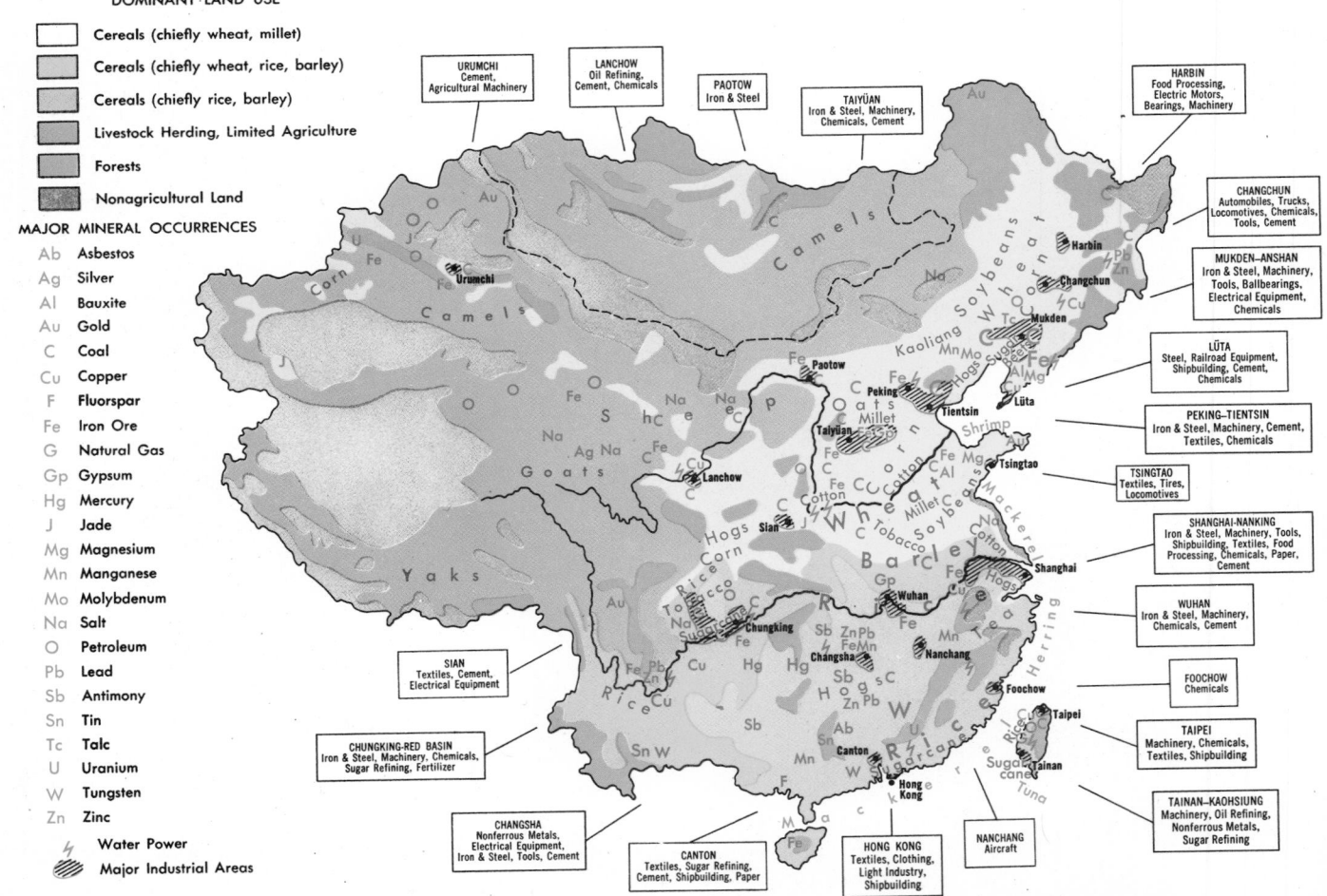

DOMINANT LAND USE

- Cereals (chiefly wheat, millet)
- Cereals (chiefly wheat, rice, barley)
- Cereals (chiefly rice, barley)
- Livestock Herding, Limited Agriculture
- Forests
- Nonagricultural Land

MAJOR MINERAL OCCURRENCES

Ab Asbestos
Ag Silver
Al Bauxite
Au Gold
C Coal
Cu Copper
F Fluorspar
Fe Iron Ore
G Natural Gas
Gp Gypsum
Hg Mercury
J Jade
Mg Magnesium
Mn Manganese
Mo Molybdenum
Na Salt
O Petroleum
Pb Lead
Sb Antimony
Sn Tin
Tc Talc
U Uranium
W Tungsten
Zn Zinc

Water Power
Major Industrial Areas

URUMCHI
Cement, Agricultural Machinery

LANCHOW
Oil Refining, Cement, Chemicals

PAOTOW
Iron & Steel

TAIYÜAN
Iron & Steel, Machinery, Chemicals, Cement

HARBIN
Food Processing, Electric Motors, Bearings, Machinery

CHANGCHUN
Automobiles, Trucks, Locomotives, Chemicals, Tools, Cement

MUKDEN–ANSHAN
Iron & Steel, Machinery, Tools, Ballbearings, Electrical Equipment, Chemicals

LÜTA
Steel, Railroad Equipment, Shipbuilding, Cement, Chemicals

PEKING–TIENTSIN
Iron & Steel, Machinery, Cement, Textiles, Chemicals

TSINGTAO
Textiles, Tires, Locomotives

SHANGHAI–NANKING
Iron & Steel, Machinery, Tools, Shipbuilding, Textiles, Food Processing, Chemicals, Paper, Cement

WUHAN
Iron & Steel, Machinery, Chemicals, Cement

FOOCHOW
Chemicals

TAIPEI
Machinery, Chemicals, Textiles, Shipbuilding

TAINAN–KAOHSIUNG
Machinery, Oil Refining, Nonferrous Metals, Sugar Refining

SIAN
Textiles, Cement, Electrical Equipment

CHUNGKING–RED BASIN
Iron & Steel, Machinery, Chemicals, Sugar Refining, Fertilizer

CHANGSHA
Nonferrous Metals, Electrical Equipment, Iron & Steel, Tools, Cement

CANTON
Textiles, Sugar Refining, Cement, Shipbuilding, Paper

HONG KONG
Textiles, Clothing, Light Industry, Shipbuilding

NANCHANG
Aircraft

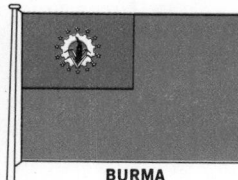

BURMA

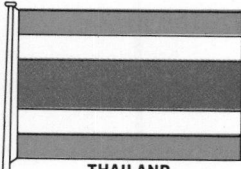

THAILAND

LAOS

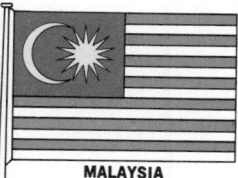

CAMBODIA

VIETNAM

MALAYSIA

SINGAPORE

BURMA
AREA   261,789 sq. mi.
POPULATION   31,240,000
CAPITAL   Rangoon
LARGEST CITY   Rangoon
HIGHEST POINT   Hkakabo Razi 19,296 ft.
MONETARY UNIT   kyat
MAJOR LANGUAGES   Burmese, Karen, Shan,
    Kachin, Chin, Kayah, English
MAJOR RELIGIONS   Buddhism, Tribal religions

THAILAND
AREA   198,455 sq. mi.
POPULATION   42,700,000
CAPITAL   Bangkok
LARGEST CITY   Bangkok
HIGHEST POINT   Doi Inthanon 8,452 ft.
MONETARY UNIT   baht
MAJOR LANGUAGES   Thai, Lao, Chinese,
    Khmer, Malay
MAJOR RELIGIONS   Buddhism, Tribal religions

LAOS
AREA   91,428 sq. mi.
POPULATION   3,500,000
CAPITAL   Vientiane
LARGEST CITY   Vientiane
HIGHEST POINT   Phu Bia 9,252 ft.
MONETARY UNIT   kip
MAJOR LANGUAGES   Lao, French
MAJOR RELIGIONS   Buddhism, Tribal religions

CAMBODIA
AREA   69,898 sq. mi.
POPULATION   8,110,000
CAPITAL   Phnom Penh
LARGEST CITY   Phnom Penh
HIGHEST POINT   5,948 ft.
MONETARY UNIT   riel
MAJOR LANGUAGES   Khmer (Cambodian),
    French
MAJOR RELIGION   Buddhism

VIETNAM
AREA   128,405 sq. mi.
POPULATION   46,600,000
CAPITAL   Hanoi
LARGEST CITY   Ho Chi Minh City (Saigon)
HIGHEST POINT   Fan Si Pan 10,308 ft.
MONETARY UNIT   dong
MAJOR LANGUAGES   Vietnamese, Thai, Muong,
    Meo, Yao, Khmer, French, Chinese, Cham
MAJOR RELIGIONS   Buddhism, Taoism,
    Confucianism, Roman Catholicsm, Cao-Dai

MALAYSIA
AREA   128,308 sq. mi.
POPULATION   12,368,000
CAPITAL   Kuala Lumpur
LARGEST CITY   Kuala Lumpur
HIGHEST POINT   Mt. Kinabalu 13,455 ft.
MONETARY UNIT   Malaysian dollar
MAJOR LANGUAGES   Malay, Chinese,
    English, Tamil, Dayak, Kadazan
MAJOR RELIGIONS   Islam, Confucianism,
    Buddhism, Tribal religions, Hinduism,
    Taoism, Christianity, Sikhism

SINGAPORE
AREA   226 sq. mi.
POPULATION   2,300,000
CAPITAL   Singapore
LARGEST CITY   Singapore
HIGHEST POINT   Bukit Timah 581 ft.
MONETARY UNIT   Singapore dollar
MAJOR LANGUAGES   Chinese, Malay,
    Tamil, English, Hindi
MAJOR RELIGIONS   Confucianism, Buddhism,
    Taoism, Hinduism, Islam, Christianity

Topography

0   200   400
MILES

5,000 m. | 2,000 m. | 1,000 m. | 500 m. | 200 m. | 100 m. | Sea
16,404 ft. | 6,562 ft. | 3,281 ft. | 1,640 ft. | 656 ft. | 328 ft. | Level / Below

BURMA

INTERNAL DIVISIONS

Arakan (div.) ....B 3
Chin Hills (special div.) ......B 2
Irrawaddy (div.) ....B 3
Kachin (state) ....C 1
Kawthoolei (state) ....C 1
Kayah (state) ....C 3
Magwe (div.) ....B 2
Mandalay (div.) ....B 2
Pegu (div.) ....B 3
Sagaing (div.) ....B 1
Shan (state) ....C 2
Tenasserim (div.) ....C 4

CITIES and TOWNS

Allanmyo, 15,580 ....B 3
Amarapura, 11,268 ....B 2
Amherst, 6,000 ....C 3
Athok, 4,819 ....B 3
Bassein, ±105,000 ....B 3
Bhamo, 9,821 ....C 1
Bilin, 5,248 ....C 3
Chauk, 24,464 ....B 2
Danubyu, 9,833 ....B 3
Falam ....B 3
Fort Hertz (Putao) ....C 1
Gangaw, 3,800 ....B 2
Gyobingauk, 9,922 ....C 3
Henzada, ±100,000 ....B 3
Insein, 27,030 ....C 3
Kalemyo, 3,158 ....B 2
Kalewa, 2,230 ....B 2
Kama, 3,523 ....B 3
Kamayut, 23,032 ....C 3
Kanbalu, 3,281 ....B 2
Kani, 2,600 ....B 1
Katha, 7,648 ....C 1
Kawlin, 3,735 ....B 2
Kyaikto, 13,154 ....C 3
Kyangin, 6,073 ....B 3
Kyaukpadaung, 5,480 ....B 2
Kyaukpyu, 7,335 ....B 3
Kyaukse, 8,659 ....C 2
Kywebwe, 3,150 ....C 3
Labutta, 12,982 ....B 3
Lashio ....C 2
Letpadan, 15,896 ....C 3
Loi-kaw ....C 3
Madauk, 4,618 ....C 3
Magwe, 13,270 ....B 2
Mahlaing, 6,543 ....B 2
Mandalay, ±300,000 ....B 2
Martaban, 5,661 ....C 3
Ma-ubin, 23,362 ....B 3
Maungdaw, 3,772 ....B 2
Mawlaik, 2,993 ....B 2
Maymyo, 22,287 ....B 2
Meiktila, 19,474 ....B 2
Mergui, 33,697 ....C 4
Minbu, 9,096 ....B 2
Minbya, 5,783 ....B 3
Minhla, 6,470 ....B 3
Mogaung, 2,920 ....C 1
Mogok, 8,334 ....C 2
Monywa, 26,297 ....B 2
Moulmein, ±175,000 ....C 3
Mudon, 20,136 ....C 3
Myanaung, 11,155 ....B 3
Myaungmya, 24,532 ....B 3
Myebon, 3,499 ....B 3
Myingyan, 36,439 ....B 2
Myitkyina, 12,382 ....C 1
Myitnge, 3,888 ....C 2
Myohaung, 6,534 ....B 2
Nyaunglebin, 12,155 ....C 3
Pa-an, 4,139 ....C 3
Pagan, 2,824 ....B 2
Pakokku, 30,943 ....B 2
Palaw, 5,596 ....C 4
Papun ....C 3
Paungde, 17,286 ....B 3
Pegu, 47,378 ....C 3

Putao ....C 1
Pyapon, 19,174 ....B 3
Pye, 36,997 ....A 3
Pyinmana, 22,025 ....C 3
Pyu, 10,443 ....C 3
Rangoon (capital), *1,700,000..C 3
Rathedaung, 2,969 ....B 2
Sagaing, 15,382 ....B 2
Sandoway, 5,172 ....B 3
Shwebo, 17,827 ....B 2
Shwegyin, 5,439 ....C 3
Shwenyaung ....C 2
Singkaling Hkamti ....B 1
Singu, 4,027 ....C 2
Sittwe, 42,329 ....A 3
Syriam, 15,296 ....C 3
Taungdwingyi, 16,233 ....C 2
Taunggyi ....C 2
Taungup, 4,065 ....B 3
Tavoy, 40,312 ....C 4
Tenasserim, 1,086 ....C 5
Tharrawaddy, 8,977 ....C 3
Thaton, 38,047 ....C 3
Thayetmyo, 11,649 ....B 3
Thazi, 7,531 ....C 2
Thongwa, 10,829 ....C 3
Thonze, 14,443 ....C 3
Toungoo, 31,589 ....C 3
Victoria Point, 1,520 ....C 5
Wakema, 20,716 ....B 3
Yamethin, 11,167 ....C 2
Yandoon, 15,245 ....B 3
Ye, 12,852 ....C 4
Yenangyaung, 24,416 ....B 2
Yesagyo, 7,880 ....B 2
Ye-u, 5,307 ....B 2

OTHER FEATURES

Amya (pass) ....C 4
Andaman (sea) ....C 4
Arakan Yoma (mts.) ....B 3
Bengal (bay) ....B 3
Bilauktaung (range) ....C 4
Chauken (pass) ....C 1
Cheduba (isl.), 2,621 ....B 3
Chin (hills) ....B 2
Chindwin (river) ....B 2
Coco (chan.) ....B 4
Combermere (bay) ....B 3
Dawna (range) ....C 3
Great Coco (isl.) ....B 4
Great Tenasserim (river) ....C 4
Hkakabo Razi (mt.) ....C 1
Indawgyi (lake) ....C 2
Inle (lake) ....C 2
Irrawaddy (river) ....B 2
Irrawaddy, Mouths of the
   (delta) ....B 4
Kaladan (river) ....B 2
Khao Luang (mt.) ....C 5
Loi Leng (mt.) ....C 2
Manipur (river) ....B 2
Martaban (gulf) ....C 4
Mekong (river) ....D 2
Mergui (arch.) ....C 5
Mon (river) ....B 2
Mu (river) ....B 2
Nam Hka (river) ....C 2
Nam Pawn (river) ....C 2
Nam Teng (river) ....C 2
Negrais (cape) ....B 3
Pakchan (river) ....C 5
Pangsau (pass) ....B 1
Pegu Yoma (mts.) ....B 3
Preparis (isl.) ....B 4
Ramree (isl.), 11,133 ....B 3
Salween (river) ....C 3
Shan (plateau) ....C 2
Sittang (river) ....C 3
Taungthonton (mt.) ....B 1
Tavoy (point) ....C 4
Tenasserim (isl.) ....C 4
Three Pagodas (pass) ....C 4
Victoria (mt.) ....B 2

(continued on following page)

(continued)

CAMBODIA

CITIES and TOWNS

Banam, †87,048 .... E 5
Battambang, 38,846 .... D 4
Cheom Ksan .... E 4
Chhlong, †46,108 .... E 4
Chong Kal, †16,918 .... D 4
Kampot, 12,558 .... E 5
Kep, 7,565 .... E 5
Khemarak Phouinville .... D 5
Kohnieh .... E 4
Kompong Cham, 28,534 .... E 4
Kompong Chhnang, 12,847 .... D 4
Kompong Kleang .... E 4
Kompong Som, 6,578 .... D 5
Kompong Speu, 7,453 .... E 5
Kompong Thom, 9,682 .... E 4
Kompong Trabek, †108,227 .... E 5
Koulen .... E 4
Kratie, 11,908 .... E 4
Krauchmar, †63,262 .... E 4
Moung, †88,321 .... D 4
Pailin, †15,536 .... D 4
Phnom Penh (capital), *500,000 .... E 5
Phsar Babau .... D 4
Phsar Oudong, †50,456 .... E 5
Phum Rovieng, †21,151 .... E 4
Phum Troun .... E 4
Poipet .... D 4
Prek Po .... E 5
Prey Veng, 8,792 .... E 5
Pursat, 14,329 .... D 4
Ream .... D 5
Sambor, †11,213 .... E 4
Siem Pang, †8,959 .... E 4
Siem Reap, 10,230 .... D 4
Sisophon, †29,581 .... D 4
Sre Khtum .... E 4
Stung Treng, 3,369 .... E 4
Suong .... E 5
Svay Rieng, 11,184 .... E 5
Takeo, 11,312 .... E 5
Virachei, †16,912 .... E 4

OTHER FEATURES

Angkor Wat (ruins) .... E 4
Dang Raek, Phanom (mts.) .... D 4
Joncs (plain) .... E 5
Kas Kong (isl.) .... D 5
Kas Tang (isl.) .... D 5
Kong, Kas (isl.) .... D 5
Mekong (river) .... E 4
Phanom Dang Raek (mts.) .... D 4
Preapatang (rapids) .... E 4
Rong, Koh (isl.) .... D 5
Samit (point) .... D 5
Se Khong (river) .... E 4
Se San (river) .... E 4
Siam (gulf) .... D 5
Srepok (river) .... E 4
Stung Sen (river) .... E 4
Tang, Kas (isl.) .... D 5
Tonle Sap (lake) .... D 4

LAOS

CITIES and TOWNS

Attopeu, 2,750 .... E 4
Ban Bung Sai .... E 4
Borikhane .... D 3
Botene .... D 3
Boun Neua, 2,500 .... D 2
Boun Tai, †1,681 .... D 2
Champassak, 3,500 .... E 4
Houei Sai, 1,500 .... D 2
Hua Muong .... D 2
Keng Kok, 2,000 .... E 3
Kham Keut, †31,206 .... E 3
Khone .... E 4
Khong, 1,750 .... E 4
Khong Sédone, 2,000 .... E 4
Luang Prabang, 7,596 .... D 3
Mahaxay, 2,000 .... E 3
Muong Beng, †2,305 .... D 2
Muong Bo .... D 3
Muong Hai, †476 .... D 2
Muong Hôm .... D 3
Muong Lan, †836 .... D 3
Muong May .... E 4
Muong Phalane .... E 3
Muong Phine .... E 3
Muong Phong .... D 3
Muong Sai, 2,000 .... D 2
Muong Sing, 1,091 .... D 2
Muong Son .... D 2
Muong Song Khone, 2,000 .... E 3
Muong Wapi .... E 4
Muong Yo .... D 2
Nam Tha, 1,459 .... D 2
Napé .... E 3
Nong Het .... D 3
Ou Neua, †4,300 .... D 2
Pak Beng, †2,964 .... D 3
Pak Hin Boun, 1,750 .... E 3
Pak Sane, 2,500 .... D 3
Paklay, 2,000 .... D 3
Pakse, 8,000 .... E 4
Phiafay, †17,216 .... E 4
Phon Tiou .... E 3
Phong Saly, 2,500 .... D 2
Sam Neua, 3,000 .... E 2
Saravane, 2,350 .... E 4
Savannakhet, 8,500 .... E 3
Sayaboury, 2,500 .... D 3
Tchepone, 1,250 .... E 3
Tha-deua .... D 3
Thakhek, 5,500 .... E 3
Tourakom .... D 3
Vang Vieng, 1,250 .... D 3
Vien Phou Kha .... D 2
Vientiane (capital), 132,253 .... D 3
Vientiane, *162,297 .... D 3
Xieng Khouang, 3,500 .... D 3

OTHER FEATURES

Bolovens (plateau) .... E 4
Hou, Nam (river) .... D 2
Jars (plain) .... D 3
Mekong (river) .... D 3
Nam Hou (river) .... D 2
Nam Tha (river) .... D 2
Phu Bia (mt.) .... D 3
Phu Co Pi (mt.) .... E 3
Phu Loi (mt.) .... D 2
Rao Co (mt.) .... E 3
Se Khong (river) .... E 4
Tha, Nam (river) .... D 2
Tran Ninh (plateau) .... D 3

MALAYSIA★

STATES

Federal Territory .... D 7
Johor, 1,236,412 .... D 7
Kedah, 885,775 .... D 6
Kelantan, 645,200 .... D 6
Melaka, 391,003 .... D 7
Negeri Sembilan, 488,318 .... D 7
Pahang, 405,156 .... D 7
Perak, 1,568,024 .... D 6
Perlis, 113,350 .... D 6
Pinang, 724,169 .... D 6
Selangor, 1,339,142 .... D 7
Terengganu, 360,388 .... D 6

CITIES and TOWNS

Alor Gajah, 2,135 .... D 7
Alor Setar, 52,915 .... D 6
Baling, 4,121 .... D 6
Bandar Maharani, 39,046 .... D 7
Bandar Penggaram, 39,294 .... D 7
Batu Gajah, 10,143 .... D 6
Bentong, 18,845 .... D 7
Butterworth, 42,504 .... D 6
Cameron Highlands .... D 6
Chukai, 10,803 .... D 6
Gemas, 4,873 .... D 7
George Town (Pinang), 234,903 .... C 6
Ipoh, 125,770 .... D 6
Johor Baharu, 74,909 .... F 5
Kampar, 24,602 .... D 6
Kangar, 6,064 .... D 6
Kelang, 75,649 .... D 7
Keluang, 31,181 .... D 7
Kota Baharu, 38,103 .... D 6
Kota Tinggi, 7,475 .... F 5
Kuala Dungun, 12,515 .... D 6
Kuala Lipis, 8,753 .... D 6
Kuala Lumpur (cap.), 325,000 .... D 7
Kuala Pilah, 12,024 .... D 7
Kuala Selangor, 2,285 .... D 7
Kuala Terengganu, 29,446 .... D 6
Kuantan, 23,034 .... D 7
Kulai, 7,759 .... F 5
Lumut, 2,947 .... D 6
Melaka (Malacca), 69,848 .... D 7
Mersing, 7,228 .... E 7
Pekan, 2,070 .... D 7
Pekan Nanas, 7,129 .... E 5
Pinang, 234,903 .... C 6
Pontian Kechil, 8,459 .... E 5
Port Dickson, 4,416 .... D 7
Port Swettenham, 16,925 .... D 7
Port Weld, 2,260 .... D 6
Raub, 15,363 .... D 7
Segamat, 18,445 .... D 7
Seremban, 52,091 .... D 7
Shah Alam .... D 7
Sungei Petani, 22,916 .... C 6
Taiping, 48,206 .... D 6
Tanah Merah, 775 .... D 6
Telok Anson, 37,042 .... D 6
Tumpat, 8,946 .... D 6

OTHER FEATURES

Aur, Pulau (isl.), 415 .... E 7
Belumut, Gunong (mt.) .... D 7
Gelang, Tanjong (point) .... D 6
Johor (river) .... F 5
Johore (str.) .... E 6
Kelantan (river) .... D 6
Langkawi, Palau (isl.), 16,535 .... C 6
Ledang, Gunong (mt.) .... D 7
Lima, Pulau (isl.) .... F 6
Malacca (str.) .... D 7
Malaya (region), 9,000,000 .... E 6
Pahang (river) .... D 7
Pangkor, Pulau (isl.), 2,580 .... D 6
Perak, Gunong (mt.) .... D 6
Perhentian (isls.), 447 .... D 6
Pulai (river) .... E 5
Pinang, Pulau (isl.), 338,898 .... C 6
Ramunia, Tanjong (point) .... F 6
Redang, Pulau (isl.), 470 .... D 6
Sedili Kechil, Tanjong (point) .... F 5
Tahan, Gunong (mt.) .... D 6
Temiang, Bukit (mt.) .... D 6
Tenggol, Pulau (isl.), 2,386 .... D 6
Tinggi, Pulau (isl.), 440 .... E 7

SINGAPORE

CITIES and TOWNS

Jurong .... E 6
Nee Soon, 6,043 .... F 6
Paya Lebar, 45,440 .... F 6
Serangoon, 3,798 .... F 6
Singapore (cap.), *1,987,900 .... F 6
Woodlands, 737 .... F 6

OTHER FEATURES

Johore (str.) .... E 6
Keppel (harb.) .... F 6
Main (str.) .... F 6
Singapore (str.) .... F 6
Tekong Besar, Pulau (isl.), 4,074 .... F 6

THAILAND (SIAM)

CITIES and TOWNS

Amnat, 11,335 .... E 4
Ang Thong, 6,458 .... C 4
Ayutthaya, 24,597 .... D 4
Ban Aranyaprathet, 11,112 .... D 4
Ban Kantang, 5,076 .... C 6
Ban Khlong Yai, 3,815 .... D 5
Ban Pak Phanang, 11,963 .... D 5
Ban Pua, 12,317 .... D 3
Ban Sattahip, 22,942 .... D 4
Ban Tha Uthen, 7,297 .... D 3
Bang Lamung, 9,087 .... D 4
Bang Saphan, 6,959 .... C 5
Bangkok (capital), 1,299,528 .... D 4
Bangkok, *2,000,000 .... D 4
Banphot Phisai, 6,036 .... C 3
Buriram, 12,579 .... D 4
Chachoengsao, 19,809 .... G 4
Chai Badan, 6,158 .... D 4
Chai Buri, †31,135 .... D 3
Chainat, 4,652 .... D 4
Chaiya, 3,607 .... C 5
Chaiyaphum, 9,633 .... D 4
Chang Khoeng, 6,037 .... C 3
Chanthaburi, 10,780 .... D 4
Chiang Dao, 8,017 .... C 3
Chiang Khan, 5,810 .... D 3
Chiang Rai, 11,663 .... C 3
Chiang Saen, 5,443 .... C 2
Chiengmai, 65,600 .... C 3
Chon Buri, 32,496 .... D 4
Chumphon, 9,342 .... C 5
Dan Sai, 6,710 .... D 3
Den Chai, 12,732 .... C 3
Hat Yai, 35,504 .... C 6
Hua Hin, 17,078 .... D 4
Kabin Buri, 3,703 .... D 4
Kalasin, 11,043 .... D 3
Kamphaeng Phet, 7,171 .... C 3
Kanchanaburi, 12,957 .... C 4
Khemmarat, 5,426 .... E 4
Khon Kaen, 19,591 .... D 3
Khorat (Nakhon Ratchasima), 41,037 .... D 4
Khu Khan, †122,206 .... E 4
Kra Buri, 3,717 .... C 5
Krung Thep (Bangkok) (cap.), 1,299,528 .... D 4
Kumphawapi, 20,759 .... D 3
Lae, 5,743 .... D 3
Lampang, 36,488 .... C 3
Lamphun, 10,602 .... C 3
Lang Suan, 4,108 .... C 5
Loei, 7,301 .... D 3
Lom Sak, 8,386 .... D 3
Lop Buri, 21,244 .... D 4
Maha Sarakham, 15,680 .... D 3
Mukdahan, 17,738 .... E 3
Nakhon Nayok, 8,048 .... D 4
Nakhon Pathom, 28,426 .... C 4
Nakhon Phanom, 14,799 .... D 3
Nakhon Ratchasima, 41,037 .... D 4
Nakhon Sawan, 34,947 .... D 4
Nakhon Si Thammarat, 25,919 .... D 5
Nan, 13,843 .... D 3
Nang Rong, 15,623 .... D 4
Narathiwat, 17,508 .... D 6
Ngao, †32,643 .... D 3
Nong Khai, 21,120 .... D 3
Pattani, 16,804 .... D 6
Phanat Nikhom, 9,307 .... D 4
Phangnga, 4,782 .... C 5
Phatthalung, 10,420 .... D 6
Phayao, 17,959 .... C 3
Phet Buri, 24,654 .... C 4
Phetchabun, 5,947 .... D 3
Phichai, 5,258 .... D 3
Phichit, 9,258 .... D 3
Phitsanulok, 30,364 .... D 3
Phon Phisai, 6,745 .... D 3
Phrae, 16,005 .... D 3
Phuket, 28,163 .... C 6
Phutthaisong, 9,315 .... D 4
Prachin Buri, 13,420 .... D 4
Prachuap Khiri Khan, 6,303 .... D 5
Pran Buri, 7,795 .... D 4
Rahaeng (Tak), 13,274 .... C 3
Ranong, 5,993 .... C 5
Rat Buri, 20,383 .... C 4
Rayong, 9,680 .... D 4
Roi Et, 12,930 .... D 4
Rong Kwang, †39,375 .... D 3
Sakon Nakhon, 16,457 .... E 3
Samut Prakan, 21,769 .... D 4
Samut Sakhon, 27,802 .... D 4
Samut Songkhram, 12,801 .... C 4
Sara Buri, 17,572 .... D 4
Satun, 4,369 .... C 6
Sawankhalok, 7,880 .... C 3
Selaphum, 10,395 .... E 3
Sing Buri, 8,384 .... D 4
Singora (Songkhla), 31,014 .... D 6
Sisaket, 9,519 .... E 4
Songkhla, 31,014 .... D 6
Sukhothai, 8,627 .... D 3
Suphan Buri, 13,859 .... C 4
Surat Thani, 19,738 .... C 5
Surin, 13,860 .... D 4
Suwannaphum, 15,731 .... D 4
Tak, 13,274 .... C 3
Takua Pa, 6,308 .... C 5
Thoen, 17,283 .... C 3
Thonburi, 403,818 .... D 4
Thonburi, *460,000 .... D 4
Trang, 17,158 .... C 6
Trat, 3,813 .... D 4
Ubon, 27,092 .... E 4
Udon Thani, 29,965 .... D 3
Uthai Thani, 10,729 .... C 4
Uttaradit, 9,120 .... D 3
Warin Chamrap, 7,067 .... E 4
Yala, 18,083 .... D 6
Yasothon, 9,717 .... D 4

OTHER FEATURES

Amya (pass) .... C 4
Bilauktaung (range) .... C 4
Chao Phraya, Mae Nam (river) .... D 4
Chi, Mae Nam (river) .... D 3
Chong Pak Phra (cape) .... C 5
Dang Raek, Phanom (mts.) .... D 4
Doi Inthanon (mt.) .... C 3
Doi Pha Hom Pok (mt.) .... C 2
Doi Pia Fai (mt.) .... D 4
Kao Prawa (mt.) .... C 3
Khao Luang (mt.) .... C 5
Khwae Noi, Mae Nam (river) .... C 4
Ko Chang (isl.) .... D 4
Ko Kut (isl.) .... D 5
Ko Lanta (isl.), 9,486 .... C 6
Ko Phangan (isl.) .... D 5
Ko Phuket (isl.), 75,652 .... C 5
Ko Samui (isl.), 30,818 .... D 5
Ko Tao (isl.) .... C 5
Ko Terutao (isl.) .... C 6
Ko Thalu (isls.) .... C 5
Kra (isthmus) .... C 5
Laem Pho (cape) .... D 6
Laem Talumphuk (cape) .... D 5
Luang (mt.) .... C 5
Mae Klong, Mae Nam (river) .... C 4
Mekong (river) .... E 3
Mulayit Taung (mt.) .... C 3
Mun, Mae Nam (river) .... D 4
Nan, Mae Nam (river) .... D 3
Nong Lahan (lake) .... D 3
Pa Sak, Mae Nam (river) .... D 4
Pakchan (river) .... C 5
Phanom Dang Raek (mts.) .... D 4
Ping, Mae Nam (river) .... C 3
Samui (str.) .... D 5
Siam (gulf) .... D 5
Tapi, Mae Nam (river) .... C 5
Tha Chin, Mae Nam (river) .... C 4
Thale Luang (lagoon) .... D 6
Three Pagodas (pass) .... C 4
Wang, Mae Nam (river) .... C 3

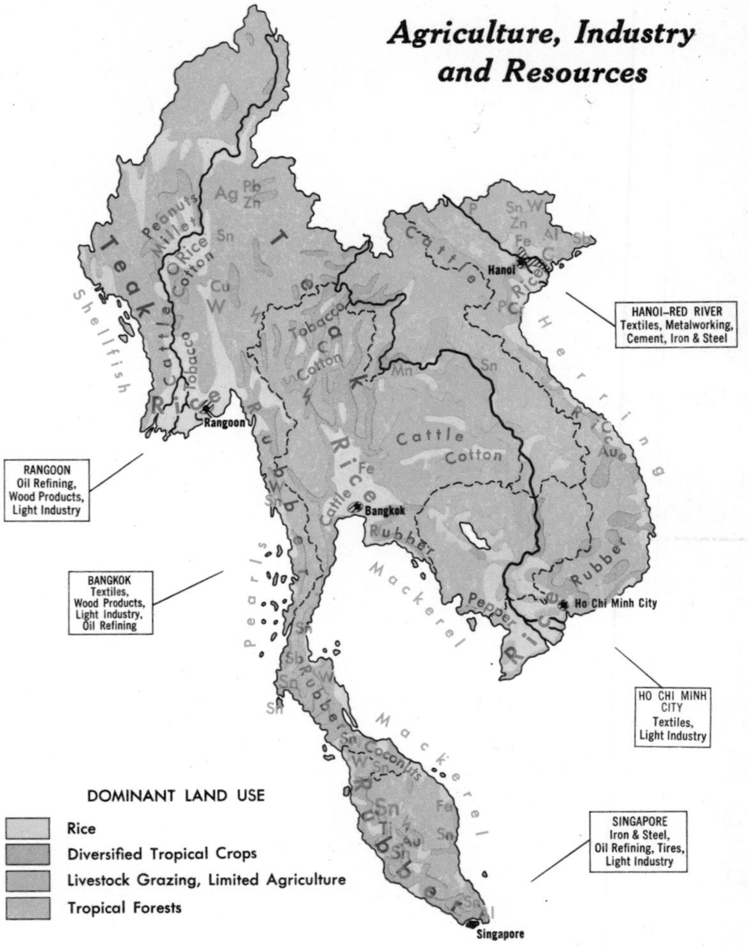
Agriculture, Industry and Resources
HANOI–RED RIVER
Textiles, Metalworking, Cement, Iron & Steel
RANGOON
Oil Refining, Wood Products, Light Industry
BANGKOK
Textiles, Wood Products, Light Industry, Oil Refining
HO CHI MINH CITY
Textiles, Light Industry
SINGAPORE
Iron & Steel, Oil Refining, Tires, Light Industry
Hanoi
Rangoon
Bangkok
Ho Chi Minh City
Singapore
Teak
Rice
Rubber
Cattle
Cotton
Tobacco
Peanuts
Millet
Pepper
Coconuts
Shellfish
Herring
Mackerel
Pearls

DOMINANT LAND USE

Rice
Diversified Tropical Crops
Livestock Grazing, Limited Agriculture
Tropical Forests

MAJOR MINERAL OCCURRENCES

Ag Silver
Al Bauxite
Au Gold
C Coal
Cr Chromium
Cu Copper
Fe Iron Ore
Mn Manganese
O Petroleum
P Phosphates
Pb Lead
Sb Antimony
Sn Tin
Ti Titanium
W Tungsten
Zn Zinc

Water Power
Major Industrial Areas

VIETNAM

CITIES and TOWNS

An Khe .... F 4
An Loc, 15,276 .... E 5
Bac Can .... E 2
Bac Lieu (Vinh Loi), 53,841 .... E 5
Bac Ninh, 22,560 .... E 2
Ba Don .... E 3
Bai Thuong .... E 3
Ban Me Thuot, 68,771 .... F 4
Bao Ha .... D 2
Bao Lac .... E 2
Bien Hoa, 87,135 .... E 5
Binh Dinh .... F 4
Binh Son .... F 4
Bong Son .... F 4
Bu Dop .... E 4
Cam Ranh, 84,281 .... F 5
Can Tho, 92,132 .... E 5
Cao Bang .... E 2
Cao Lanh, 16,482 .... E 5
Cap Saint-Jacques (Vung Tau), 79,270 .... E 5
Chau Phu, 37,175 .... E 5
Cheo Reo .... E 4
Chu Lai .... F 4
Co Lieu .... E 3
Con Cuong .... E 3
Cua Rao .... E 3
Dak Bla .... E 4
Da Lat, 83,992 .... F 5
Dam Doi .... E 5
Da Nang, 363,343 .... E 3
Dien Bien Phu .... D 2
Di Linh .... F 5
Dong Hoi .... E 3
Duong Dong .... D 5
Go Cong, 33,191 .... E 5
Go Quao .... E 5
Ha Giang .... E 2
Haiphong, 182,496 .... E 2
Haiphong, ‡*600,000 .... E 2
Ham Tan, 19,323 .... E 5
Hanoi (capital), 414,620 .... E 2
Hanoi, ‡*1,400,000 .... E 2
Ha Tien .... E 5
Ha Tinh .... E 3
Hoa Binh .... E 2
Hoa Da .... F 5
Ho Chi Minh City, 1,706,869 .... E 5
Hoi An, 45,059 .... F 4
Hoi Xuan .... E 2
Hon Chong .... E 5
Hon Gay, ‡100,000 .... E 2
Hue, 170,884 .... E 3
Huong Khe .... E 3
Ke Bao .... E 2
Khanh Hoa .... F 4
Khanh Hung, 59,015 .... E 5
Kontum, 33,554 .... E 4
Lai Chau .... D 2
Lang Mo .... E 3
Lang Son, 15,071 .... E 2
Lao Cai .... E 2
Loc Chou .... E 3
Loc Ninh .... E 5
Long Xuyen, 72,658 .... E 5
Luc An Chau .... E 2
Moc Hoa, 3,191 .... E 5
Mo Duc .... F 4
Mon Cay .... E 2
Muong Khuong .... E 2
My Tho, 109,967 .... E 5
Nam Dinh, ‡125,000 .... E 2
Nghia Lo .... D 2
Nha Trang, 103,184 .... F 4
Ninh Binh .... E 2
Phan Rang, 33,377 .... F 5
Phan Ri .... F 5
Phan Thiet, 80,122 .... F 5
Phoc Tuy, 16,419 .... E 5
Phuc Loi .... E 3
Phu Cuong, 28,267 .... E 5
Phu Dien .... E 3
Phu Lang Thuong .... E 2
Phu Loc .... E 5
Phuly .... E 2
Phu My .... F 4
Phu Qui .... E 3
Phu Rieng .... E 5
Phu Tho, 10,888 .... E 2
Phu Vinh (Tra Vinh), 48,485 .... E 5
Pleiku, 23,720 .... E 4
Pleime .... E 4
Quang Nam .... E 4
Quang Khe .... E 3
Quang Ngai, 14,119 .... F 4
Quang Tri, 15,874 .... E 3
Quang Yen .... E 2
Quan Long, 59,331 .... E 5
Qui Nhon, 116,821 .... F 4
Rach Gia, 66,745 .... E 5
Ron .... E 3
Sa Dec, 51,867 .... E 5
Saigon (Ho Chi Minh City), 1,706,869 .... E 5
Song Cau .... F 4
Son Ha .... F 4
Son La .... D 2
Son Tay, 19,213 .... E 2
Tam Ky, 38,532 .... F 4
Tam Quan .... F 4
Tan An, 38,082 .... E 5
Tay Ninh, 22,957 .... E 5
Thai Binh, 14,739 .... E 2
Thai Nguyen, ‡110,000 .... E 2
Thanh Hoa, 31,211 .... E 3
That Khe .... E 2
Tien Yen .... E 2
Tra Vinh, 48,485 .... E 5
Truc Giang, 68,629 .... E 5
Trung Khanh Phu .... E 2
Tuyen Quang .... E 2
Tuy Hoa, 63,552 .... F 4
Van Gia .... F 4
Van Hoa .... E 2
Van Yen .... E 2
Vinh, 43,954 .... E 3
Vinh Loi, 53,841 .... E 5
Vinh Long, 30,667 .... E 5
Vinh Yen .... E 2
Vo Dat .... E 5
Vu Liet .... E 3
Vung Tau, 79,270 .... E 5
Yen Bai .... E 2
Yen Minh .... E 2

OTHER FEATURES

Bach Long Vi, Dao (isl.) .... F 2
Batangan (cape) .... F 4
Bên Gôi (bay) .... F 4
Black (river) .... D 2
Ca Mau (Mui Bai Bung) (pt.) .... E 5
Cam Ranh (bay) .... F 5
Cat Ba, Dao (isl.) .... E 2
Chon May (bay) .... F 3
Chu Yang Sin (mt.) .... F 4
Con Son (isls.), 3,147 .... E
Cu Lao Hon (isls.) .... F
Dama, Poulo (isls.) .... D
Dao Bach Long Vi (isl.) .... F
Dao Phu Quoc (isl.) .... D
Darlac (plateau) .... F
Dent du Tigre (mt.) .... E
Deux Frères, Les (isls.) .... E
Fan Si Pan (mt.) .... D
Hon Khoai (isl.) .... E
Hon Panjang (isl.) .... D
Ia Drang (riv.) .... E
Joncs (plain) .... E
Ke Ga (point) .... F
Kontum (plateau) .... E
Lang Bian (mts.) .... E
Lay (cape) .... E
Mekong, Mouths of the (delta) .... E
Mui Bai Bung (pt.) .... E
Mui Dinh (cape) .... F
Mui Duong (cape) .... E
Nam Tram (cape) .... F
Nightingale (Bach Long Vi) (isl.) .... F
Nui Ba Den (mt.) .... E
Phu Quoc, Dao (isl.) .... D
Poulo Dama (isls.) .... D
Poulo Way (isls.) .... D
Rao Co (mt.) .... E
Red (river) .... E
Se San (river) .... E
Siam (gulf) .... D
Sip Song Chau Thai (mts.) .... D
Song Ba (river) .... F
Song Bo (Black) (river) .... D
Song Ca (river) .... E
Song Cai (river) .... E
Song Coi (Red) (river) .... E
South China (sea) .... F
Tigre (isl.) .... E
Tonkin (gulf) .... E
Varella (cape) .... F
Way, Poulo (isls.) .... D

★See page 84 for other Malaysian entries.
*City and suburbs.
†Population of district.

‡City populations courtesy of Kingsley Davis, Office of Int'l Pop. & Urban Research, Inst. of Int'l Studies, Univ. of California.

BURMA, THAILAND, INDOCHINA and MALAYA

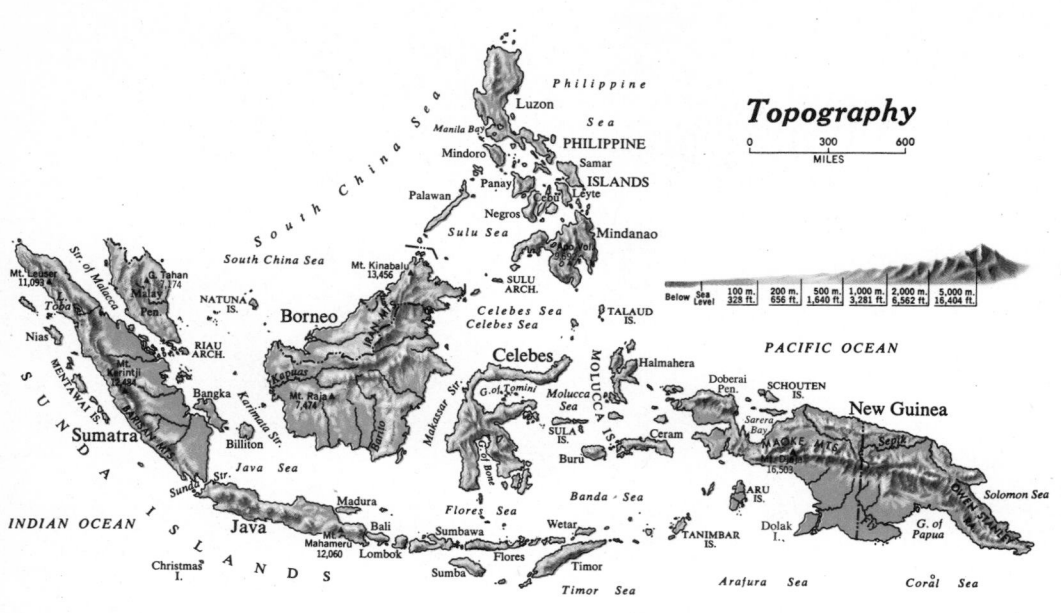

Topography

0 300 600
MILES

Below Sea Level | 100 m. 328 ft. | 200 m. 656 ft. | 500 m. 1,640 ft. | 1,000 m. 3,281 ft. | 2,000 m. 6,562 ft. | 5,000 m. 16,404 ft.

PHILIPPINES

AREA 115,707 sq. mi.
POPULATION 43,751,000
CAPITAL Manila
LARGEST CITY Manila
HIGHEST POINT Apo 9,692 ft.
MONETARY UNIT piso
MAJOR LANGUAGES Pilipino (Tagalog), Engl Spanish, Bisayan, Ilocano, Bikol
MAJOR RELIGIONS Roman Catholicism, Islam, Protestantism, Tribal religions

BRUNEI

CITIES and TOWNS

Bandar Seri Begawan (cap.), 37,000 ....E 4

INDONESIA

CITIES and TOWNS

Agats, 300 ....K 7
Amahai, 18,017 ....H 6
Amboina, 70,000 ....H 6
Ambon (Amboina), 70,000 ....H 6
Balikpapan, 113,000 ....F 6
Banda Atjeh, 49,000 ....A 4
Bandanaira, 13,686 ....H 6
Bandjarmasin, 264,000 ....E 6
Bandung, 1,006,000 ....J 2
Bangil, 34,112 ....K 2
Bangkalan, 129,536 ....K 2
Banjuwangi, 53,576 ....L 2
Bantul, 30,572 ....J 2
Barabai, 9,366 ....F 6
Barus, †35,716 ....B 5
Batang, 57,561 ....J 2
Batavia (Djakarta) (cap.), 3,429,000 ....H 1
Baturadja, 126,706 ....C 6
Batusangkar, 10,437 ....C 6
Bekasi, 32,012 ....H 2
Bengkajang, 117,029 ....E 5
Bengkalis, †36,433 ....C 5
Bengkulu, 31,000 ....C 6
Benteng, 7,035 ....G 7
Bindjai, 56,000 ....B 5
Bitung, 15,249 ....H 5
Blitar, 78,000 ....K 2

Blora, 49,296 ....K 2
Bodjonegoro, 161,749 ....J 2
Bogor, 172,000 ....H 2
Bondowoso, 144,215 ....L 2
Brebes, †72,971 ....J 2
Bukittinggi, 62,000 ....B 6
Bula, 3,116 ....J 6
Bulukumba, 14,137 ....G 7
Bumiaju, †52,790 ....J 2
Buntok, 3,884 ....F 6
Demak, †42,915 ....J 2
Denpasar, †52,000 ....E 7
Djailolo, 110,170 ....H 5
Djajapura, 14,462 ....K 6
Kutaradja (Banda Atjeh), 49,000 ....A 4
Djakarta (cap.), 3,429,000 ....H 1
Djakarta, *5,692,000 ....H 1
Djambi (Telanaipura) 139,000 ....C 6
Djeneponto, 10,350 ....F 7
Djepara, †54,025 ....J 2
Djokjakarta, 385,000 ....J 2
Djombang, †57,370 ....K 2
Dompu, 8,886 ....F 7
Fakfak, 2,430 ....J 6
Galela, 17,384 ....H 5
Garut, 167,542 ....H 2
Gorontalo, 88,000 ....G 5
Gresik, 36,790 ....K 2
Gunungsitoli, 144,712 ....A 5
Hollandia (Djajapura), 14,462 ....K 6
Indramaju, 156,117 ....H 2
Isimu, 4,304 ....G 5
Kaimana, 1,128 ....J 6
Kajuagung, 15,000 ....D 6
Kalianda, †31,073 ....C 6
Kampung Baru (Tolitoli), 8,333 ....G 5
Karangasem, 16,022 ....F 7
Kau, 17,497 ....H 5
Kebumen, 164,874 ....J 2

Kediri, 196,000 ....K 2
Kendal, 23,129 ....J 2
Kendari, 191,065 ....G 6
Kendawangan, 6,845 ....D 6
Klaten, 33,400 ....J 2
Kolaka, 118,671 ....G 6
Kotaagung, 125,314 ....C 7
Kragan, 23,786 ....K 7
Krawang, 49,867 ....H 2
Kualakurun, 111,489 ....E 6
Kudus, 62,130 ....J 2
Kumai, 15,000 ....E 6
Kuningan, †77,181 ....H 2
Kupang, 7,171 ....H 8
Kutaradja (Banda Atjeh), 49,000 ....A 4
Kutoardjo, 44,962 ....J 2
Labuan, †22,259 ....G 2
Lahat, †25,781 ....C 6
Lamongan, 134,825 ....K 2
Langsa, †47,044 ....B 5
Lawang, 140,239 ....K 2
Longiram, 7,776 ....F 5
Longnawan, †16,234 ....F 5
Lubuklinggau, 14,890 ....C 6
Lubuksikaping, 11,778 ....B 5
Lumadjang, 55,700 ....K 2
Madiun, 152,000 ....K 2
Madjalengka, 147,055 ....H 2
Madjene, 17,727 ....F 6
Magelang, 119,000 ....J 2
Magetan, 154,159 ....K 2
Makassar (Udjung Pandang), 473,000 ....F 7
Malang, 419,000 ....K 2
Malili, 5,735 ....G 6
Malinau, 9,677 ....F 5
Mamudju, 147,309 ....F 6
Manado, 160,000 ....G 5
Manokwari, 10,461 ....J 6

Marabahan, 8,893 ....E 6
Martapura, †53,216 ....F 6
Masamba, †15,152 ....G 6
Medan, 590,000 ....B 5
Menggala, 20,343 ....D 6
Meulaboh, 6,544 ....B 5
Merak, 136,293 ....G 1
Merauke, 5,989 ....K 7
Mindiptana, 1,577 ....L 7
Modjokerto, 64,000 ....K 2
Muarabungo, 10,706 ....C 6
Muarateweh, 6,135 ....F 6
Muntok, †25,883 ....D 6
Namlea, 16,018 ....H 6
Nangapinoh, †24,836 ....E 6
Nangatajap, 18,285 ....E 6
Negara, 10,161 ....D 7
Ngabang, 124,516 ....D 5
Ngawi, 29,220 ....J 2
Padang, 178,000 ....B 6
Padangpandjang, 32,000 ....B 6
Padangsidimpuan, 171,704 ....B 5
Painan, 12,060 ....C 6
Pajakumbuh, 174,393 ....C 6
Pakanbaru, 87,000 ....C 5
Palangkaraja, 9,000 ....E 6
Paleleh, 5,466 ....G 5
Palembang, 585,000 ....D 6
Pamekasan, 116,234 ....L 2
Pamekasan, 142,650 ....L 2
Pameungpeuk, †24,662 ....H 2
Panarukan, 6,846 ....L 2
Pandeglang, 124,823 ....G 1
Pangkalanberandan, †23,806 ....B 5
Pangkalpinang, 74,000 ....D 6
Parc, †65,528 ....K 2
Parepare, 84,000 ....F 6
Pariaman, †45,812 ....B 6
Pasuruan, 78,000 ....K 2
Pati, †56,749 ....J 2

Patjitan, 44,383 ....J 2
Pekalongan, 125,000 ....J 2
Pemalang, 193,608 ....J 2
Pematangsiantar, 142,000 ....B 5
Perahbumulih, 41,951 ....C 6
Pinrang, 23,818 ....F 6
Piru, 123,633 ....H 6
Ponorogo, 49,993 ....J 2
Pontianak, 185,000 ....D 6
Poso, 141,292 ....G 6
Praja, 26,729 ....F 7
Prapat, 5,552 ....B 5
Probolinggo, 85,000 ....K 2
Purbolinggo, 31,719 ....J 2
Purwakarta, †88,680 ....H 2
Purwodadi, †54,648 ....J 2
Purwokerto, 22,623 ....J 2
Purworedjo, 23,209 ....J 2
Putussibau, 18,357 ....E 5
Rangkasbitung, 151,176 ....G 2
Rantauprapat, 25,707 ....C 5
Rembang, 39,939 ....K 2
Rengat, †22,982 ....C 6
Ruteng, 15,814 ....F 7
Sabang, 6,747 ....B 4
Salatiga, 72,000 ....J 2
Samarinda, 87,000 ....F 6
Sambas, †53,290 ....D 5
Sampang, 47,596 ....L 2
Sanana, 23,388 ....H 6
Sanggau, †28,039 ....E 5
Sangkulirang, 6,108 ....F 5
Saparua, 53,390 ....H 6
Saumlaki, 122,732 ....J 7
Sawahlunto, 15,000 ....C 6
Semarang, 619,000 ....J 2
Semitau, 19,255 ....E 5
Sengkang, †17,948 ....F 6
Serang, †43,661 ....G 1
Serui, 2,743 ....K 6

(continued on following page)

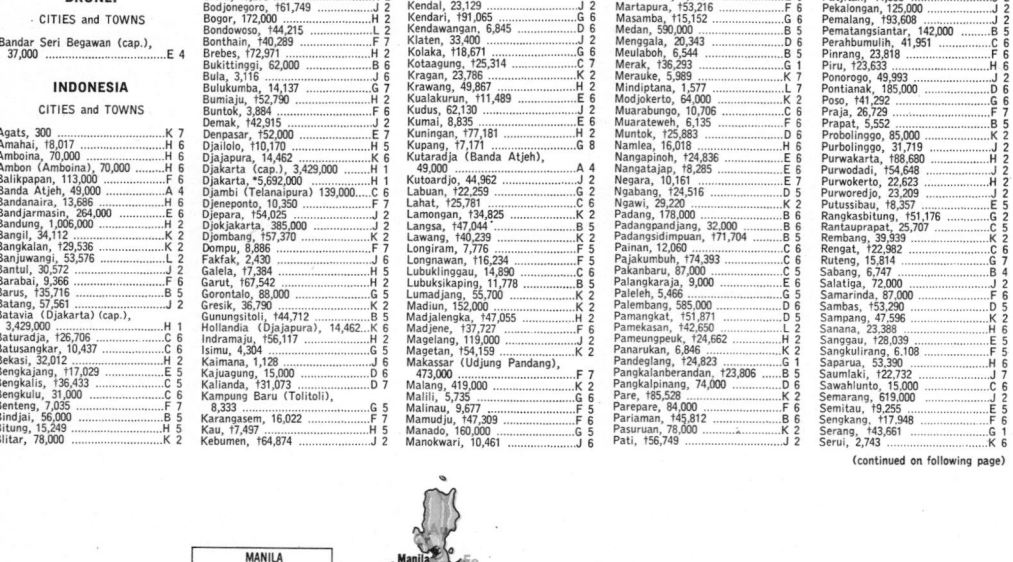

MANILA
Light Industry, Automobile Assembly, Tobacco Products, Textiles

ILIGAN
Iron & Steel, Fertilizers, Cement

SINGAPORE
Iron & Steel, Oil Refining, Tires, Light Industry

DJAKARTA
Textiles, Light Industry

Agriculture, Industry and Resources

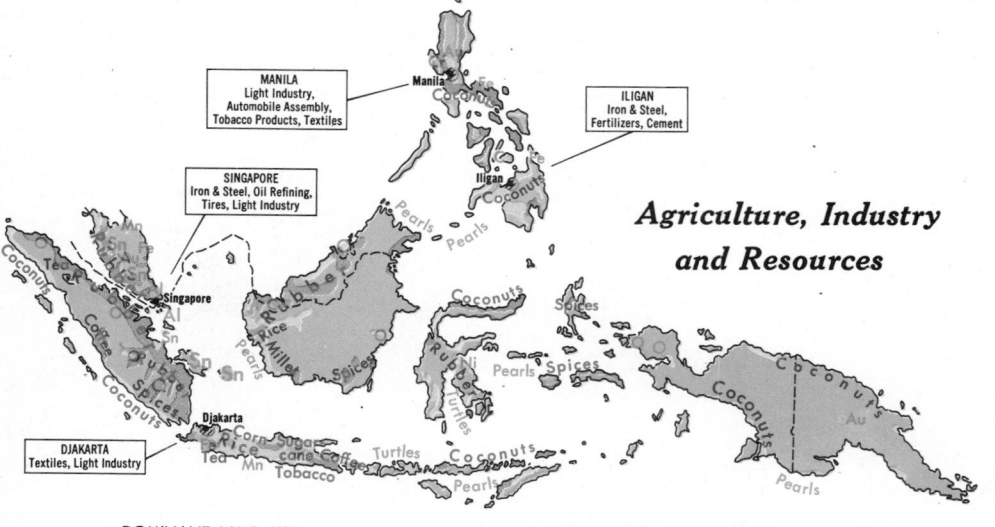

DOMINANT LAND USE

Cereals (chiefly rice, corn)
Diversified Tropical Crops
Forests

MAJOR MINERAL OCCURRENCES

Al Bauxite
Au Gold
C Coal
Cr Chromium
Fe Iron Ore
Mn Manganese
Ni Nickel
O Petroleum
Sn Tin
Major Industrial Areas

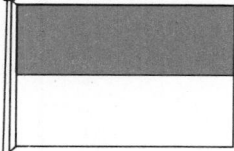

INDONESIA

AREA 735,264 sq. mi.
POPULATION 119,572,000
CAPITAL Djakarta
LARGEST CITY Djakarta
HIGHEST POINT Mt. Djaja 16,400 ft.
MONETARY UNIT rupiah
MAJOR LANGUAGES Bahasa Indonesian, local
  Indonesian languages, Papuan languages
MAJOR RELIGIONS Islam, Tribal religions,
  Christianity, Hinduism

PAPUA NEW GUINEA

AREA 183,540 sq. mi.
POPULATION 2,563,610
CAPITAL Port Moresby
LARGEST CITY Port Moresby
HIGHEST POINT Mt. Wilhelm 15,400 ft.
MONETARY UNIT kina
MAJOR LANGUAGES Pidgin English,
  Motuan, English
MAJOR RELIGIONS Tribal religions,
  Christianity

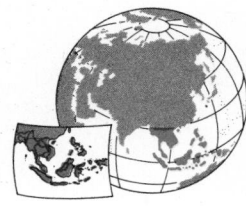

BRUNEI
AREA 2,226 sq. mi.
POPULATION 130,000
CAPITAL Bandar Seri Begawan

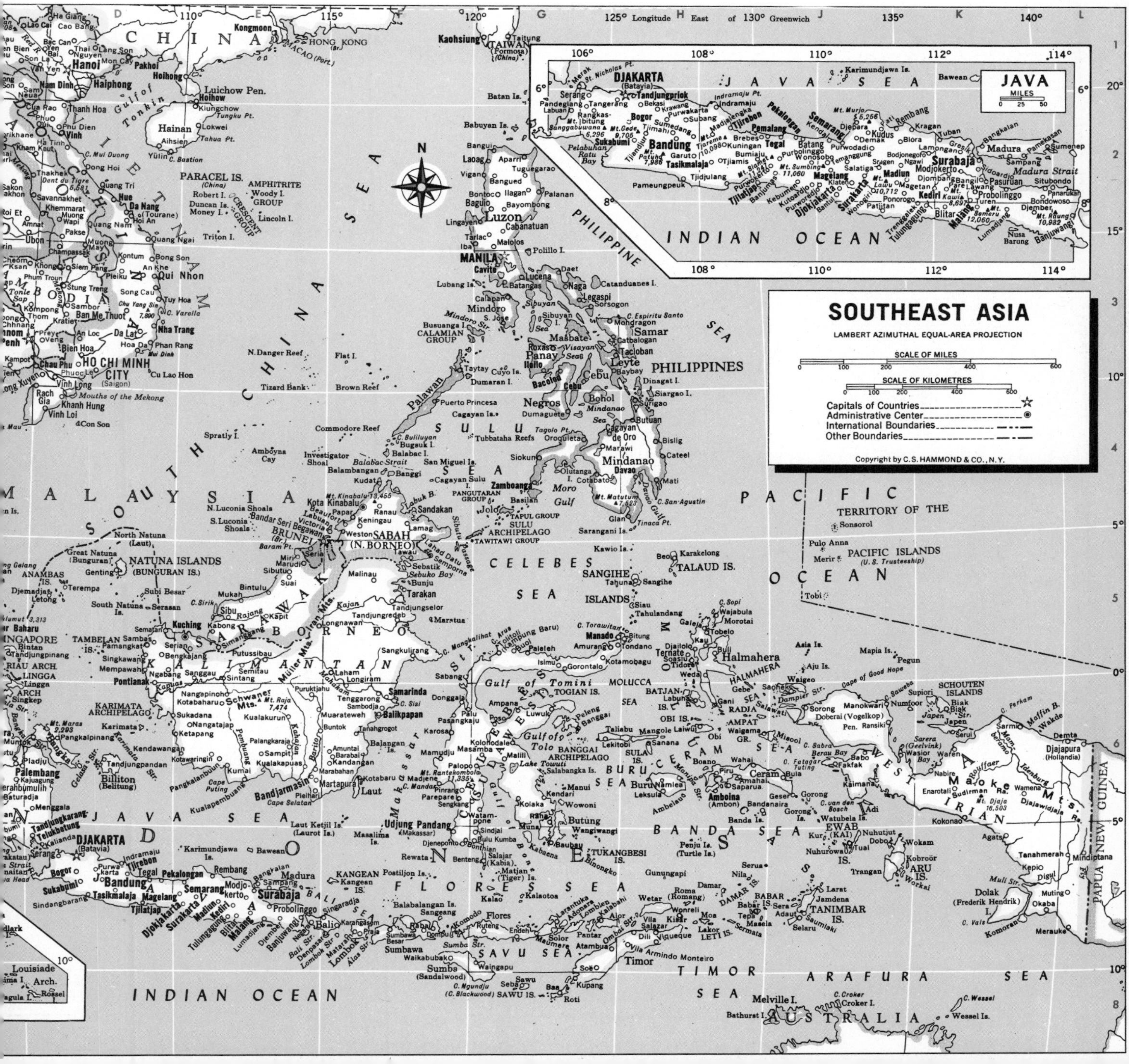

JAVA
MILES
0 25 50

SOUTHEAST ASIA
LAMBERT AZIMUTHAL EQUAL-AREA PROJECTION

SCALE OF MILES
0   100   200   300   400   500   600

SCALE OF KILOMETRES
0   100   200   300   400   500   600

Capitals of Countries ⭐
Administrative Center ◉
International Boundaries _____
Other Boundaries _____

Copyright by C.S. HAMMOND & CO., N.Y.

Sibolga, 48,000 ....B 5	Banjak (isls.), 1,696 ....B 5	Lingga (arch.), 39,307 ....D 5	Sunda (str.) ....C 7	Ambunti, ‡697 ....B 6	Bangued, 7,602 ....G 2
Sidoardjo, 140,591 ....K 2	Barisan (mts.) ....C 6	Lingga (isl.), 14,309 ....D 6	Tahulandang (isl.), 13,584 ..H 5	Angoram, 1,822 ....B 6	Bangui, 1,674 ....G 2
Sigli, 4,050 ....B 4	Barito (river) ....E 6	Lombok (isl.), 1,602,000 .....F 7	Talaud (isls.), 26,738 ....H 5	Baniara, ‡1,110 ....B 7	Batangas, ‡102,100 ....G 3
Sindjai, 18,390 ....G 7	Batjan (isls.), 21,861 ....H 6	Madura (isl.), 2,650,000 .....K 2	Taliabu (isl.), 7,391 ....G 6	Bogia, 639 ....B 6	Baybay, 10,021 ....H 4
Singaradja ....F 7	Batu (isls.), 60,806 ....B 6	Mahakam (river) ....E 6	Tambelan (isls.), 3,551 ....D 5	Bulolo, 2,724 ....B 7	Bayombong, 8,312 ....G 2
Singkawang, 125,067 ....D 5	Bawean (isl.) 47,589 ....K 1	Makassar (str.) ....F 6	Tanimbar (isls.), 41,233 ....J 7	Buna, 307 ....B 7	Bislig, 1,968 ....H 4
Sintang, 125,067 ....D 5	Belitung (Billiton) (isl.),	Malacca (str.) ....C 5	Tidore (isl.), 24,064 ....H 5	Daru, 3,663 ....B 7	Bontoc, 5,472 ....G 2
Situbondo, 30,000 ....L 2	126,000 ....D 6	Mamberamo (river) ....K 6	Timor (sea) ....G 8	Finschhafen, 436 ....C 7	Butuan, ‡110,100 ....H 4
Sorong, 9,151 ....J 6	Bengalen (passage) ....A 4	Maoke (mts.) ....K 6	Timor, Indonesian (reg.),	Goroka, 4,826 ....B 7	Cabanatuan, ▲80,000 ....G 3
Sragen, 32,310 ....J 2	Berau (bay) ....J 6	Mapia (isls.) ....K 5	866,000 ....H 7	Ioma, ‡3,552 ....C 7	Cagayan de Oro,
Subang, 122,825 ....H 2	Biak (isl.), 31,139 ....K 6	Mentawai (isls.), 23,649 .....B 6	Toba (lake) ....B 5	Kairuku, ‡4,582 ....C 7	▲78,000 ....H 4
Sukabumi, 90,000 ....H 2	Billiton (isl.), 126,000 ....D 6	Misool (isl.), 3,022 ....J 6	Tolo (gulf) ....G 6	Kerema, 820 ....B 7	Calapan, 4,180 ....G 3
Sukadana, 6,999 ....E 6	Binongko (isl.), 10,580 ....G 7	Molucca (sea) ....H 6	Tomini (gulf) ....G 6	Kiunga, ‡918 ....B 7	Catbalogan, 14,274 ....H 4
Sumbawa Besar, ‡22,308 ......F 7	Bintan (isl.), 65,301 ....C 5	Moluccas (isls.), 973,000 ....H 6	Tukangbesi (isls.), 59,775 ...G 7	Kokoda, ‡1,615 ....C 7	Cateel, 2,626 ....H 4
Sumedang, 174,062 ....H 2	Bone (gulf) ....F 6	Morotai (isl.), 19,523 ....H 5	Vals (cape) ....K 7	Kungu, 12,392 ....B 7	Cebu, ▲332,100 ....G 3
Sumenep, 328,000 ....L 2	Borneo (isl.) ....E 5	Muli (str.) ....K 7	Vogelkop (Deberai) (pen.) ...J 6	Madang, 6,601 ....B 7	Cotabato, ‡43,000 ....H 4
Surabaja, 1,241,000 ....K 2	Borneo (Kalimantan) (reg.),	Müller (mts.) ....E 6	Waigeo (isl.), 9,011 ....J 5	Mendi, 1,687 ....B 7	Daet, 19,726 ....G 3
Surakarta, 453,000 ....J 2	4,243,000 ....E 5	Muna (isl.), 139,000 ....G 7	Wangiwangi (isl.), 19,719 ....G 7	Morobe, 12,132 ....C 7	Davao, ▲337,000 ....H 4
Tandjungbalai, 36,000 ....C 5	Bosch, van den (cape) ....J 6	Musi (river) ....C 6	Weh (isl.) ....B 4	Popondetta, 2,139 ....C 7	Dumaguete, ▲40,000 ....G 4
Tandjungkarang-Telukbetung,	Bunguran (Natuna) (isls.),	Natuna (isls.), 15,261 ....D 5	West Irian (reg.), 933,000 ...K 6	Port Moresby (cap.), 56,206 ..B 7	Glan, 2,112 ....H 4
164,000 ....D 7	15,261 ....D 5	Ngundju (cape) ....F 8	Wetar (isl.), 11,383 ....H 7	Rigo, 1,184 ....C 7	Iba, 4,241 ....F 2
Tandjungpandan, 139,253 .....D 6	Buru (isl.), 16,018 ....H 6	Nias (isl.), 388,000 ....B 5		Saidor ....B 7	Ilagan, 6,375 ....G 2
Tandjungpriok, ‡140,573 ......H 1	Butung (isl.), 311,000 ....G 6	Obi (isls.), 6,358 ....H 6	**MALAYSIA★**	Samarai, 2,201 ....C 8	Iloilo, ▲201,000 ....G 3
Tandjungpura, ‡20,726 ....B 5	Celebes (isl.), 7,665,000 .....G 6	Ombai (str.) ....H 7	**STATES**	Telefomin, ‡395 ....B 7	Laoag, ▲50,198 ....G 2
Tangerang, ‡81,042 ....G 1	Celebes (sea) ....G 5	Perkam (cape) ....J 6		Tufi, ‡462 ....C 7	Legaspi, ‡69,000 ....G 3
Tapaktuan, 9,650 ....B 5	Ceram (isl.), 73,453 ....H 6	Puting (cape),Borneo ....E 6	Sabah, 633,000 ....F 4	Vanimo, 512 ....A 6	Lingayen, 8,221 ....F 2
Tarakan, 24,807 ....F 5	Damar (isl.) ....H 7	Puting (cape), Sumatra ....C 6	Sarawak, 950,000 ....E 5	Wau, 1,072 ....B 7	Lucena, ▲56,000 ....G 3
Tarutung, ‡41,041 ....B 5	Dampier (point) ....B 4	Radja Ampat Group (isls.),		Wewak, 5,090 ....B 6	Malolos, 2,240 ....G 3
Tasikmalaja, ‡101,466 ....H 2	Diamond (point) ....B 4	17,158 ....H 6	**CITIES and TOWNS**		Manila (cap.), ‡1,499,000 ....G 3
Tebingtinggi, 32,000 ....B 5	Digul (river) ....K 7	Raja (mt.) ....E 6		**OTHER FEATURES**	Manila, ▲2,369,000 ....G 3
Tegal, 110,000 ....J 2	Djaja (mt.) ....K 6	Rakata (isl.) ....C 7	Beaufort, ‡25,408 ....F 4		Marawi, ▲31,000 ....G 4
Telanaipura, 139,000 ....C 6	Djajawidjaja (range) ....K 6	Rantekombola (mt.) ....F 6	Bintulu, 5,307 ....E 5	Dampier (str.) ....C 7	Mati, 7,870 ....H 4
Temanggung, 8,107 ....J 2	Djemadja (isl.), 3,874 ....D 5	Riau (arch.), 342,000 ....C 5	Keningau, 114,645 ....F 4	D'Entrecasteaux (isls.), 32,288...C 7	Mondragon, 3,746 ....H 3
Tenggarong, 115,516 ....F 6	Doberai (pen.) ....J 6	Rokan (river) ....C 5	Kota Kinabalu, 21,704 ....F 4	Fly (river) ....A 7	Naga, ▲63,000 ....G 3
Ternate, 23,500 ....H 5	Dolak (isl.) ....K 7	Roti (isl.), 68,330 ....G 8	Kuching, 56,000 ....E 5	Huon (gulf) ....C 7	Oroquieta, 5,331 ....G 4
Tjiamis, ‡80,018 ....H 2	Enggano (isl.), 686 ....C 7	Rouffaer (river) ....K 6	Kudat, 3,660 ....F 4	Karkar (isl.), 14,966 ....B 6	Palanan, 5,599 ....G 2
Tjiandjur, ‡77,927 ....H 2	Ewab (isls.), 76,606 ....J 7	Salajar (isl.), 107,000 ....G 7	Lahad Datu, 119,534 ....F 4	Kirikwina (isl.), 8,990 ....C 7	Puerto Princesa,
Tjidulang, ‡32,475 ....H 2	Flores (isl.), 1,108,000 ....G 7	Salawati (isl.), 5,125 ....J 6	Marudi, 2,663 ....E 5	Long (isl.), 7,044 ....B 7	7,551 ....F 4
Tjilatjap, 78,619 ....H 2	Flores (sea) ....F 7	Sandalwood (Sumba) (isl.),	Miri, 20,000 ....E 5	Louisiade (arch.), 11,451 .....D 8	Roxas, ▲57,000 ....G 3
Tjimahi, 190,718 ....H 2	Frederik Hendrik (Dolak) (isl.)...K 7	311,000 ....F 7	Papar, 128,210 ....F 4	Milne (bay) ....C 8	San Jose, 4,247 ....G 3
Tjirebon, 176,000 ....H 2	Gebe (isl.), 5,410 ....H 6	Sangihe (isl.), 83,585 ....H 5	Ranau, ‡17,033 ....F 4	Misima (isl.), 5,247 ....C 8	Siokun, 1,660 ....H 4
Tjurup, 14,480 ....C 6	Geelvink (Sarera) (bay) ......J 6	Sangihe (isls.), 126,931 ......H 5	Sandakan, 28,805 ....F 4	New Britain (isl.), 138,689 ....C 7	Sorsogon, 13,983 ....H 3
Tobelo, ‡14,430 ....H 5	Good Hope (cape) ....J 5	Sarera (bay) ....K 6	Sematan ....D 5	Papua (gulf) ....B 7	Surigao, 15,561 ....H 3
Tolitoli, 8,333 ....G 5	Gorong (isls.), 33,241 ....J 6	Sawu (isls.), 78,785 ....G 8	Semporna, ‡16,895 ....F 4	Ramu (river) ....B 7	Tacloban, ‡61,000 ....H 3
Tondano, 129,584 ....H 5	Halmahera (isl.), 97,133 ......H 5	Sawu (sea) ....G 8	Sibu, 29,630 ....E 5	Rossel (isl.), 1,933 ....D 8	Tarlac, ‡121,400 ....G 3
Trenggalek, 137,762 ....K 2	Idenburg (river) ....K 6	Schouten (isls.), 41,647 ......K 6	Simanggang, 5,648 ....E 5	Schouten (isls.), 6,633 ....B 6	Taytay, 811 ....F 3
Tuban, 48,123 ....K 2	Japen (isl.), 23,701 ....K 6	Schwaner (mts.) ....E 6	Tawau, 10,276 ....F 5	Sepik (river) ....B 6	Tuguegarao, 10,497 ....G 2
Tulungagung, 43,115 ....K 2	Java (head) ....C 7	Seaflower (channel) ....B 5	Victoria, 3,213 ....E 4	Solomon (sea) ....C 8	Vigan, 10,498 ....G 2
Turen, 157,711 ....K 2	Java (isl.), 69,323,000 ....J 2	Sebuko (bay) ....E 6		Tagula (isl.), 1,654 ....C 8	Zamboanga, ▲176,800 ....G 4
Udjung Pandang, 473,000 .....F 7	Java (sea) ....D 6	Selatan (cape) ....E 6	**OTHER FEATURES**	Torres (str.) ....A 7	
Wahai, ‡8,781 ....H 6	Kabaena (isl.), 14,380 ....G 7	Semeru (mt.) ....K 2		Trobriand (isls.), 10,199 .....C 7	**OTHER FEATURES**
Wonogiri, 145,704 ....J 2	Kabia (Salajar) (isl.), 107,000...G 7	Siau (isl.), 29,762 ....H 5	Balambangan (isl.) ....F 4	Woodlark (isl.), 1,848 ....C 7	
Wonosobo, 33,917 ....J 2	Kai (Ewab) (isls.), 76,606 ....J 7	Siberut (str.) ....B 6	Banggi (isl.) ....F 4		Babuyan (isls.), 5,388 ....G 2
	Kalao (isl.), 670 ....G 7	Simeulue (isl.), 25,951 ....A 5	Iran (mts.) ....E 5	**PHILIPPINES**	Balabac (isl.), 2,870 ....F 4
OTHER FEATURES	Kalaotoa (isl.), 2,031 ....G 7	Singkep (isl.), 17,712 ....D 6	Kinabalu (mt.) ....F 4		Balabac (str.) ....F 4
	Kalimantan (reg.), 4,243,000...E 5	Sipora (isl.), 5,671 ....B 6	Labuan (isl.), 14,904 ....E 4	**CITIES and TOWNS**	Basilan (isl.), 134,435 ....G 4
Alas (str.) ....F 7	Kangean (isls.), 52,893 ....F 7	Slamet (mt.) ....H 2	Labuk (bay) ....F 4		Batan (isls.), 10,309 ....G 1
Anambas (isls.), 15,700 ......D 5	Kapuas (river) ....D 6	Sorik Merapi (mt.) ....B 5	Rajang (river) ....E 5	Aparri, 13,167 ....G 2	Bohol (isl.), 531,707 ....G 4
Arafura (sea) ....K 7	Karakelong (isl.), 15,276 .....H 5	South Natuna (isls.), 3,318 ..D 5	Sirik (cape) ....E 5	Bacolod, ‡156,900 ....G 3	Bugsuk (isl.), 482 ....F 4
Aru (isls.), 27,006 ....K 7	Karimata (arch.), 1,623 ....D 5	Sudirman (range) ....K 6		Baguio, ▲58,000 ....G 2	Buliluyan (cape) ....F 4
Asahan (river) ....B 5	Karimundjawa (isls.), 1,611 ...J 1	Sula (isls.), 30,779 ....H 6			Busuanga (isl.), 13,190 ......F 3
Babar (isls.), 14,133 ....H 7	Kerintji (mt.) ....C 6	Sulawesi (Celebes) (isl.),	**PAPUA NEW GUINEA**		Cagayan (isls.), 3,880 ....F 4
Bali, 2,196,000 ....F 7	Kisar (isl.), 16,569 ....H 7	7,665,000 ....G 6	**CITIES and TOWNS**		Cagayan Sulu (isl.), 10,789 ..F 4
Bali (sea) ....F 7	Komodo (isl.) ....F 7	Sumatra (isl.), 17,345,000 ...B 5			Calamian Group (isls.), 21,975...F 3
Banda (sea) ....H 7	Krakatau (Rakata) (isl.) ....C 7	Sumba (isl.), 311,000 ....F 7	Abau, ‡3,024 ....C 7		Catanduanes (isl.), 154,698 ..G 3
Banggai (arch.), 144,747 .....G 6	Laut (isl.), 42,099 ....F 6	Sumba (str.) ....F 7	Aitape, 540 ....B 6		
Bangka (isl.), 384,000 ....D 6	Leuser (mt.) ....B 5	Sumbawa (isl.), 625,000 .....F 7			Catanduanes (isl.),
					154,698 ....G 3
					Cebu (isl.), 1,163,756 ....G 3
					Celebes (sea) ....G 5
					Cuyo (isls.), 24,728 ....G 3
					Davao (gulf) ....H 4
					Dimagat (isl.), 19,543 ....H 3
					Dumaran (isl.), 4,453 ....G 4
					Espiritu Santo (cape) ....H 4
					Leyte (isl.), 1,053,782 ....H 3
					Lubang (isls.),
					16,748 ....F 3
					Luzon (isl.), 12,702,731 ......G 2
					Masbate (isl.), 264,273 ....G 3
					Matutum (mt.) ....H 4
					Mindanao (isl.), 4,699,475 ...H 4
					Mindanao (sea) ....G 3
					Mindoro (isl.), 290,394 ....G 3
					Mindoro (str.) ....F 3
					Moro (gulf) ....G 4
					Negros (isl.), 1,862,115 ......G 4
					Olutanga (isl.), 16,616 ....G 4
					Palawan (isl.), 100,664 ....F 4
					Panay (isl.), 1,659,832 ....G 3
					Pangutaran Group (isls.),
					10,235 ....F 4
					Philippine (sea) ....G 2
					Polillo (isl.), 18,766 ....G 3
					Samar (isl.), 733,809 ....H 3
					San Agustin (cape) ....H 4
					Sarangani (isls.),
					4,701 ....H 4
					Siargao (isl.), 38,388 ....H 4
					Sibutu (passage) ....F 5
					Sibuyan (isl.), 25,161 ....G 3
					Sibuyan (sea) ....G 3
					South China (sea) ....F 2
					Sulu (arch.), 315,573 ....G 4
					Sulu (sea) ....F 4
					Tagolo (point) ....G 4
					Tapul Group (isls.),
					57,856 ....G 4
					Tawitawi Group (isls.),
					56,645 ....G 4
					Tinaca (point) ....H 4
					Tubbataha (reefs) ....G 3
					Visayan (sea) ....G 3

*City and suburbs.
†Population of district.
‡Population of sub-district.
▲Population of municipality.
★See page 80 for other Malaysian entries.

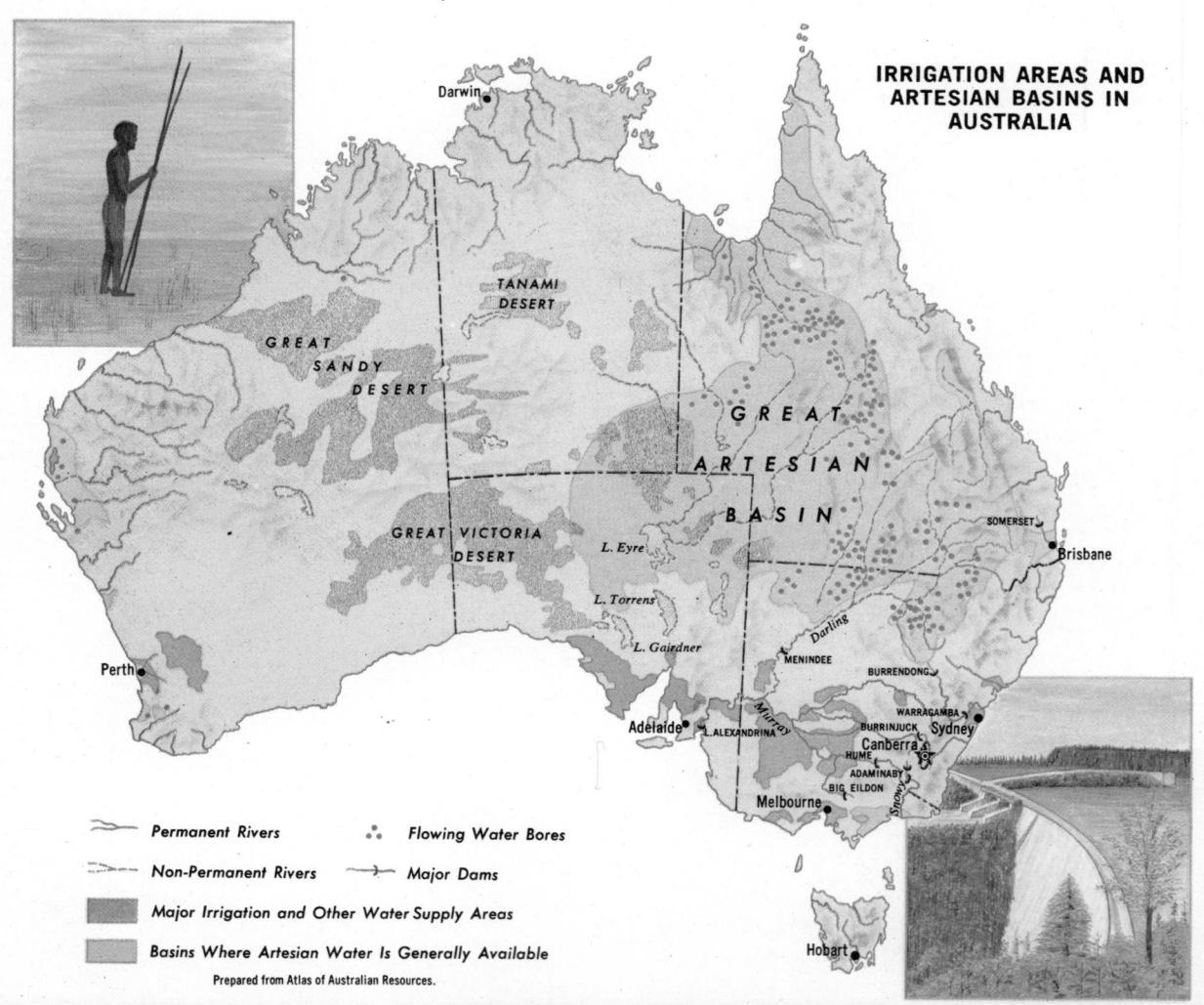

IRRIGATION AREAS AND ARTESIAN BASINS IN AUSTRALIA

➤➤ Permanent Rivers   ∴∴ Flowing Water Bores

➤➤ Non-Permanent Rivers   → Major Dams

Major Irrigation and Other Water Supply Areas

Basins Where Artesian Water Is Generally Available

Prepared from Atlas of Australian Resources.

AUSTRALIA
AREA 2,967,741 sq. mi.
POPULATION 12,630,000
CAPITAL Canberra
LARGEST CITY Sydney (greater)
HIGHEST POINT Mt. Kosciusko 7,316 ft.
LOWEST POINT Lake Eyre -39 ft.
MONETARY UNIT Australian dollar
MAJOR LANGUAGE English
MAJOR RELIGIONS Protestantism, Roman Cath.

NEW ZEALAND
AREA 103,736 sq. mi.
POPULATION 2,815,000
CAPITAL Wellington
LARGEST CITY Auckland
HIGHEST POINT Mt. Cook 12,349 ft.
MONETARY UNIT New Zealand dollar
MAJOR LANGUAGES English, Maori
MAJOR RELIGION Protestantism

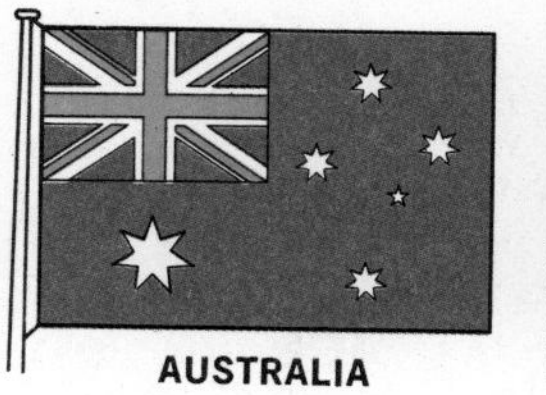
AUSTRALIA

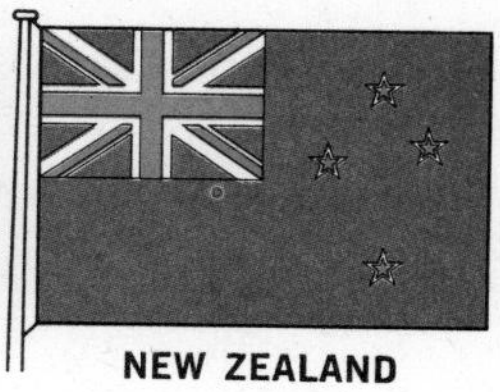
NEW ZEALAND

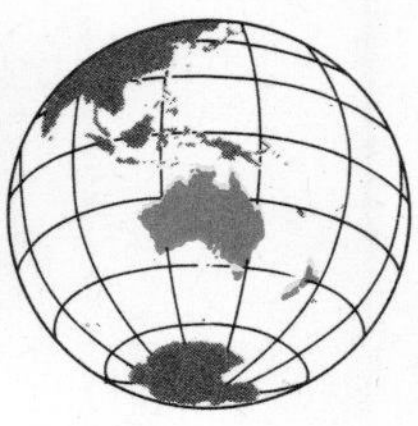

AUSTRALIA

STATES and TERRITORIES

Australian Capital Terr., 136,300 ..... J 7
Coral Sea Islands Terr., 3 ..... J 3
New South Wales, 4,595,400 ..... H 6
Northern Territory, 73,000 ..... E 3
Queensland, 1,810,000 ..... G 4
South Australia, 1,169,600 ..... F 6
Tasmania, 393,700 ..... H 8
Victoria, 3,461,400 ..... G 7
Western Australia, 991,300 ..... C 5

CITIES and TOWNS

Adelaide (capital), S.A., †727,916 ..... D 7
Adelaide River, N.T., ‡300 ..... E 2
Albany, W.A., 11,419 ..... B 6
Albury, N.S.W., 25,112 ..... H 7
Alice Springs, N.T., 6,037 ..... E 4
Aramac, Q. ..... H 4
Ararat, V., 8,233 ..... G 7
Armadale, W.A., 3,463 ..... B 2
Armidale, N.S.W., 14,984 ..... J 6
Augathella, Q. ..... H 5
Ayr, Q., 8,674 ..... H 3
Bacchus Marsh, V., 3,707 ..... K 1
Bairnsdale, V., 7,785 ..... H 7
Balhannah, S.A. ..... E 8
Ballarat, V., *56,290 ..... G 7
Ballina, N.S.W., 4,931 ..... J 5
Balranald, N.S.W., 1,490 ..... G 6
Bankstown, N.S.W., 159,981 ..... L 3
Barcaldine, Q., 1,779 ..... G 4
Bargo, N.S.W. ..... K 4
Barraba, N.S.W., 1,425 ..... J 6
Bathurst, N.S.W., 17,222 ..... H 6
Beachport, S.A., ‡1,903 ..... F 7
Bega, N.S.W., 3,925 ..... J 7
Bendigo, V., *42,208 ..... G 7
Beverley, W.A., ‡1,773 ..... B 2
Bingara, N.S.W., 1,504 ..... H 5
Blackall, Q., 2,004 ..... G 4
Blacktown, N.S.W., 111,488 ..... K 3
Blair Athol, Q. ..... H 4
Blue Mts., N.S.W., 30,731 ..... H 6
Bombala, N.S.W., 1,495 ..... H 7
Bordertown, S.A., 1,758 ..... G 7
Botany, N.S.W., 31,871 ..... L 3
Boulder, W.A., 5,234 ..... C 6
Bourke, N.S.W., 3,262 ..... H 6
Bowen, Q., 5,144 ..... H 3
Brewarrina, N.S.W., 1,255 ..... H 5
Bridgetown, W.A., 1,569 ..... B 6
Bright, V., 747 ..... H 7
Brighton, V., 40,617 ..... L 2
Brisbane (capital), Q., †718,822 ..... J 5
Broken Hill, N.S.W., 30,014 ..... G 6
Brookton, W.A., ‡1,341 ..... B 2
Broome, W.A., 1,570 ..... C 3
Bullfinch, W.A. ..... B 6
Bulli, N.S.W. ..... L 4
Bunbury, W.A., 15,459 ..... A 6
Bundaberg, Q., 25,402 ..... J 5
Burnie, T., 15,806 ..... H 8
Busselton, W.A., 4,278 ..... A 6
Cairns, Q., 29,326 ..... H 3
Camberwell, V., 99,908 ..... L 2
Camden, N.S.W., 3,427 ..... K 4
Camooweal, Q. ..... F 4
Campbelltown, N.S.W., 25,695 ..... L 3
Canberra, A.C.T. (cap.), Australia, *136,300 ..... H 7
Cardwell, Q. ..... H 3
Carnarvon, W.A., 2,956 ..... A 4
Casino, N.S.W., 8,502 ..... J 5
Casterton, V., 2,492 ..... G 7
Caulfield, V., 76,119 ..... L 2
Ceduna, S.A., 1,406 ..... E 6
Cessnock, N.S.W., *34,515 ..... J 6
Charleville, Q., 4,871 ..... H 5
Charters Towers, Q., 7,602 ..... G 4
Chelsea, V., 24,789 ..... L 2
Clermont, Q., 1,649 ..... H 4
Cloncurry, Q., 2,149 ..... G 4
Cobar, N.S.W., 2,348 ..... H 6
Coburg, V., 68,568 ..... L 1
Coffs Harbour, N.S.W., 7,667 ..... J 6
Coleraine, V., 1,518 ..... G 7
Collie, W.A., 7,628 ..... B 6
Collinsville, Q., 1,887 ..... H 4
Condobolin, N.S.W., 3,571 ..... H 6
Coober Pedy, S.A. ..... E 5
Cooktown, Q. ..... H 3
Coolgardie, W.A., ‡762 ..... C 6
Cooma, N.S.W., 9,103 ..... H 7
Coonamble, N.S.W., 3,396 ..... H 6
Cootamundra, N.S.W., 6,219 ..... H 6
Corio, V. ..... K 2
Corrigin, W.A., ‡2,099 ..... B 5
Corrimal, N.S.W. ..... L 4
Cowra, N.S.W., 7,076 ..... H 6
Cudgewa, V. ..... H 7
Cue, W.A., ‡430 ..... B 5
Culcairn, N.S.W., 1,019 ..... H 7
Cunnamulla, Q., 1,980 ..... H 5
Cygnet, T. ..... H 8
Dalby, Q., 8,860 ..... J 5
Daly Waters, N.T., ‡265 ..... E 3
Dandenong, V., 31,698 ..... L 2
Darwin (capital), N.T., 18,042 ..... E 2
Daylesford, V., 2,664 ..... G 7
Deloraine, T., 1,793 ..... H 8
Deniliquin, N.S.W., 6,239 ..... H 7
Derby, W.A., 1,424 ..... C 3
Devonport, T., 14,874 ..... H 8
Dirranbandi, Q. ..... H 5
Dubbo, N.S.W., 15,561 ..... H 6
Echuca, V., 7,043 ..... G 7
Echunga, S.A. ..... E 7
Eidsvold, Q. ..... J 5
Elizabeth, S.A., 32,949 ..... D 7
Emerald, Q., 2,193 ..... H 4
Esperance, W.A., 2,677 ..... C 6
Essendon, V., 58,258 ..... K 2
Footscray, V., 58,823 ..... K 2
Forbes, N.S.W., 7,369 ..... H 6
Frankston, V., 38,718 ..... L 2
Fremantle, W.A., 25,284 ..... B 2
Gawler, S.A., 5,703 ..... D 7
Geelong, V., *105,059 ..... K 2
Geraldton, W.A., 12,125 ..... A 5
Gingin, W.A., ‡1,021 ..... B 1
Gladstone, Q., 12,426 ..... J 4
Glen Innes, N.S.W., 5,737 ..... J 5
Glenmorgan, Q. ..... H 5
Gold Coast, Q., 49,481 ..... J 5
Goomalling, W.A., ‡1,567 ..... B 1
Goondiwindi, Q., 3,529 ..... H 5
Goulburn, N.S.W., 20,871 ..... J 7
Grafton, N.S.W., 15,951 ..... J 5
Griffith, N.S.W., 9,537 ..... H 6
Gunnedah, N.S.W., 7,507 ..... H 6
Gympie, Q., 11,279 ..... J 5
Halls Creek, W.A., ‡577 ..... D 3
Hamilton, V., 10,054 ..... G 7
Hay, N.S.W., 2,952 ..... H 6
Heidelberg, V. 63,929 ..... L 1
Helensburgh, N.S.W., 2,334 ..... L 4
Henley and Grange, S.A., 14,146 ..... D 7
Hillston, N.S.W., 1,034 ..... G 6
Hindmarsh, S.A., 11,352 ..... D 7
Hobart (capital), T., †119,469 ..... H 8
Home Hill, Q., 3,507 ..... H 3
Horsham, V., 10,562 ..... G 7
Hughenden, Q., 2,033 ..... G 4
Hurstbridge, V. ..... L 1
Hurstville, N.S.W., 64,851 ..... L 3
Ingham, Q., 5,354 ..... H 3
Injune, Q. ..... H 5
Innisfail, Q., 7,432 ..... H 3
Inverell, N.S.W., 8,413 ..... J 5
Ipswich, Q., 54,531 ..... J 5
Iron Knob, S.A. ..... F 6
Ivanhoe, N.S.W. ..... G 6
Jamestown, S.A. 1,282 ..... F 6
Jandowae, Q. ..... J 5
Jericho, Q. ..... H 4
Junee, N.S.W., 3,904 ..... H 6
Kadina, S.A., 1,865 ..... F 6
Kalgoorlie, W.A., *19,908 ..... C 6
Katanning, W.A., 3,506 ..... B 6
Katherine, N.T., 1,302 ..... E 2
Kelmscott, W.A., 914 ..... B 2
Kempsey, N.S.W., 8,181 ..... J 6
Kensington and Norwood, S.A., 11,928 ..... D 8
Kerang, V., 4,164 ..... G 7
Kew, V., 32,816 ..... L 1
Kingaroy, Q., 5,080 ..... J 5
Kingscote, S.A., 1,071 ..... F 7
Kingston, S.A., 1,065 ..... F 7
Kogarah, N.S.W., 47,654 ..... L 3
Kwinana, W.A., 1,272 ..... B 2
Lake Cargelligo, N.S.W., 1,128 ..... H 6
Larrimah, N.T., ‡88 ..... E 3
Launceston, T., 37,217 ..... H 8
Laverton, W.A., ‡206 ..... C 5
Leigh Creek, S.A., 1,014 ..... F 6
Leonora, W.A., 623 ..... C 5
Lismore, N.S.W., 19,734 ..... J 5
Lithgow, N.S.W., 13,165 ..... J 6
Liverpool, N.S.W., 68,959 ..... K 3
Longford, T., 1,688 ..... H 8
Longreach, Q., 3,871 ..... G 4
Loxton, S.A., 2,418 ..... G 6
Mackay, Q., 24,578 ..... H 4
Maitland, N.S.W., 28,428 ..... J 6
Mandurah, W.A., 2,730 ..... B 2
Manilla, N.S.W., 1,761 ..... J 6
Manly, N.S.W., 38,141 ..... L 3
Maralinga and Woomera, S.A., 4,745 ..... E 5
Marble Bar, W.A., ‡567 ..... C 4
Mareeba, Q., 4,799 ..... H 3
Marion, S.A., 66,950 ..... D 8
Maryborough, Q., 20,393 ..... J 5
Maryborough, V., 7,707 ..... G 7
Mataranka, N.T., ‡114 ..... E 2
Meekatharra, W.A., ‡1,011 ..... B 5
Melbourne (cap.), V., †2,110,168 ..... L 1
Merredin, W.A., 3,599 ..... B 6
Midland, W.A., 9,335 ..... B 2
Mildura, V., 12,931 ..... G 6
Miles, Q., 1,485 ..... H 5
Mingenew, W.A., ‡978 ..... B 5
Mitchell, Q., 1,704 ..... H 5
Moonta, S.A., 1,122 ..... F 6
Moora, W.A., 1,185 ..... B 6
Morawa, W.A., ‡1,718 ..... B 5
Mordialloc, V., 28,076 ..... L 2
Moree, N.S.W., 8,031 ..... H 5
Mornington, V., 7,349 ..... L 2
Mossman, Q., 1,614 ..... G 3
Mount Barker, S.A., 1,934 ..... E 8
Mount Gambier, S.A., 17,251 ..... F 7
Mount Garnet, Q. ..... G 3
Mount Isa, Q., 16,877 ..... F 4
Mount Lofty, S.A. ..... D 8
Mount Magnet, W.A. ..... B 5
Mount Morgan, Q., 4,055 ..... H 4
Mount Pleasant, S.A., ‡1,433 ..... E 7
Mount Torrens, S.A. ..... E 7
Mudgee, N.S.W., 5,372 ..... J 6
Mullewa, W.A., ‡1,825 ..... B 5
Murray Bridge, S.A., 5,957 ..... F 7
Murwillumbah, N.S.W., 7,311 ..... J 5
Muswellbrook, N.S.W., 6,312 ..... J 6
Nanango, Q., 1,300 ..... J 5
Nannup, W.A., ‡1,272 ..... B 6
Naracoorte, S.A., 4,378 ..... F 7
Narembeen, W.A., ‡1,590 ..... B 6
Narrabri, N.S.W., 5,953 ..... H 6
Narrandera, N.S.W., 4,905 ..... H 6
Narrogin, W.A., 4,861 ..... B 6
Narromine, N.S.W., 2,465 ..... H 6
Nedlands, W.A., 23,320 ..... B 2
New Norfolk, T., 5,770 ..... H 8
Newcastle, N.S.W., *233,936 ..... J 6
Normanton, Q. ..... G 3
Norseman, W.A., 1,863 ..... C 6
Northam, W.A., 7,400 ..... B 2
Northampton, W.A., ‡2,021 ..... A 5
Nowra, N.S.W., 9,633 ..... J 6
Nyngan, N.S.W., 2,584 ..... H 6
Orange, N.S.W., 22,196 ..... H 6
Orbost, V., 2,797 ..... H 7
Parkes, N.S.W., 8,438 ..... H 6
Parramatta, N.S.W., 106,996 ..... K 3
Penrith, N.S.W., 46,357 ..... K 3
Perth (capital), W.A., †499,969 ..... B 2
Peterborough, S.A., 3,117 ..... F 6
Picton, N.S.W., 1,327 ..... K 4
Pine Creek, N.T., ‡577 ..... E 2
Pingelly, W.A., ‡1,453 ..... B 2
Pinnaroo, S.A., ‡1,717 ..... G 7
Port Adelaide, S.A., 39,823 ..... D 7
Port Albert, V. ..... H 7
Portarlington, V., 1,224 ..... K 2
Port Augusta, S.A., 10,103 ..... F 6
Port Fairy, V., 2,579 ..... G 7
Port Hedland, W.A., 1,778 ..... B 3
Port Kembla, N.S.W. ..... J 6
Portland, V., 6,690 ..... G 7
Port Lincoln, S.A., 8,888 ..... E 6
Port Macquarie, N.S.W., 7,063 ..... J 6
Port Melbourne, V., 12,591 ..... K 2
Port Pirie, S.A., 15,566 ..... F 6
Port Wakefield, S.A., ‡1,020 ..... F 6
Proserpine, Q., 2,951 ..... H 4
Queenstown, T., 4,295 ..... G 8
Quirindi, N.S.W., 2,730 ..... H 6
Quorn, S.A., 588 ..... F 6
Radium Hill, S.A. ..... G 6
Randwick, N.S.W., 113,634 ..... L 3
Ravensthorpe, W.A., ‡782 ..... C 6
Renmark, S.A., 6,275 ..... G 6
Reynella-Port Noarlunga, 11,818 ..... D 8
Richmond, V., 32,530 ..... L 2
Ringwood, V., 29,141 ..... L 1
Rockdale, N.S.W., 81,463 ..... L 3
Rockhampton, Q., 46,083 ..... J 4
Rockingham, W.A., 3,767 ..... B 2
Roebourne, W.A., ‡1,782 ..... B 4
Roma, Q., 5,996 ..... H 5
Ryde, N.S.W., 81,291 ..... L 3
Saint Arnaud, V., 3,004 ..... G 7
Saint George, Q., 2,233 ..... H 5
Saint Kilda, V., 58,129 ..... L 2
Sale, V., 8,640 ..... H 7
Salisbury, S.A., 35,762 ..... D 7
Sandgate, Q., 22,621 ..... J 5
Sandringham, V., 36,671 ..... L 2
Sarina, Q., 2,422 ..... H 4
Scone, N.S.W., 2,915 ..... J 6
Singleton, N.S.W., 6,188 ..... J 6
Spalding, S.A., ‡705 ..... F 6
Stanthorpe, Q., 3,641 ..... J 5
Stawell, V., 5,909 ..... G 7
Strathalbyn, S.A., 1,449 ..... D 8
Strathfield, N.S.W., 26,704 ..... L 3
Streaky Bay, S.A., ‡2,134 ..... E 6
Subiaco, W.A., 16,621 ..... B 2
Sunbury, V., 3,526 ..... K 1
Swan Hill, V., 7,381 ..... G 7
Sydney (cap.), N.S.W., †2,446,345 ..... L 3
Tamworth, N.S.W., 21,680 ..... J 6
Taree, N.S.W., 10,560 ..... J 6
Temora, N.S.W., 4,536 ..... H 6
Tennant Creek, N.T., 1,001 ..... E 3
Tenterfield, N.S.W., 3,270 ..... J 5
Theodore, Q. ..... H 4
Thursday Island, Q., 2,551 ..... G 2
Toowoomba, Q., 55,799 ..... J 5
Townsville, Q., 58,847 ..... H 3
Truro, S.A., ‡588 ..... F 6
Tully, Q., 2,860 ..... H 3
Tumbarumba, N.S.W., 1,443 ..... H 7
Tumut, N.S.W., 4,277 ..... H 7
Ulverstone, T., 6,842 ..... H 8
Unley, S.A., 39,727 ..... D 8
Victor Harbor, S.A., 2,160 ..... F 7
Wagga Wagga, N.S.W., 25,819 ..... H 7
Wagin, W.A., 1,750 ..... B 6
Walcha, N.S.W., 1,544 ..... J 6
Walgett, N.S.W., 1,985 ..... H 6
Wallaroo, S.A., 2,094 ..... F 6
Wandoan, Q. ..... H 5
Wangaratta, V., 15,175 ..... H 7
Waroona, W.A., 1,013 ..... B 2

(continued on following page)

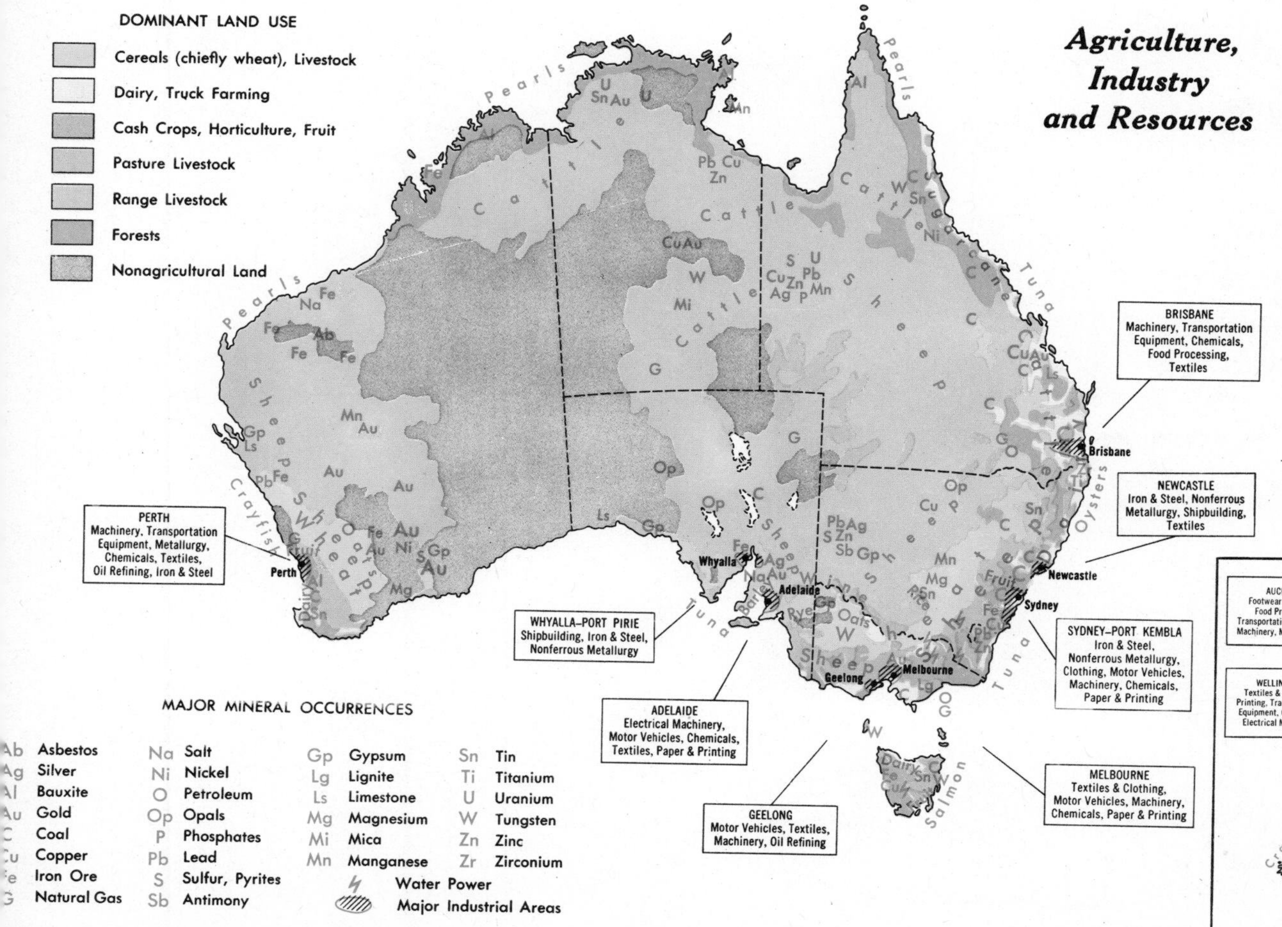

DOMINANT LAND USE
Cereals (chiefly wheat), Livestock
Dairy, Truck Farming
Cash Crops, Horticulture, Fruit
Pasture Livestock
Range Livestock
Forests
Nonagricultural Land
Agriculture, Industry and Resources
PERTH
Machinery, Transportation Equipment, Metallurgy, Chemicals, Textiles, Oil Refining, Iron & Steel
WHYALLA–PORT PIRIE
Shipbuilding, Iron & Steel, Nonferrous Metallurgy
ADELAIDE
Electrical Machinery, Motor Vehicles, Chemicals, Textiles, Paper & Printing
GEELONG
Motor Vehicles, Textiles, Machinery, Oil Refining
MELBOURNE
Textiles & Clothing, Motor Vehicles, Machinery, Chemicals, Paper & Printing
SYDNEY–PORT KEMBLA
Iron & Steel, Nonferrous Metallurgy, Clothing, Motor Vehicles, Machinery, Chemicals, Paper & Printing
NEWCASTLE
Iron & Steel, Nonferrous Metallurgy, Shipbuilding, Textiles
BRISBANE
Machinery, Transportation Equipment, Chemicals, Food Processing, Textiles
Perth
Whyalla
Adelaide
Geelong
Melbourne
Sydney
Newcastle
Brisbane
MAJOR MINERAL OCCURRENCES
Asbestos
Silver
Bauxite
Gold
Coal
Copper
Iron Ore
Natural Gas
Na Salt
Ni Nickel
O Petroleum
Op Opals
P Phosphates
Pb Lead
S Sulfur, Pyrites
Sb Antimony
Gp Gypsum
Lg Lignite
Ls Limestone
Mg Magnesium
Mi Mica
Mn Manganese
Sn Tin
Ti Titanium
U Uranium
W Tungsten
Zn Zinc
Zr Zirconium
Water Power
Major Industrial Areas

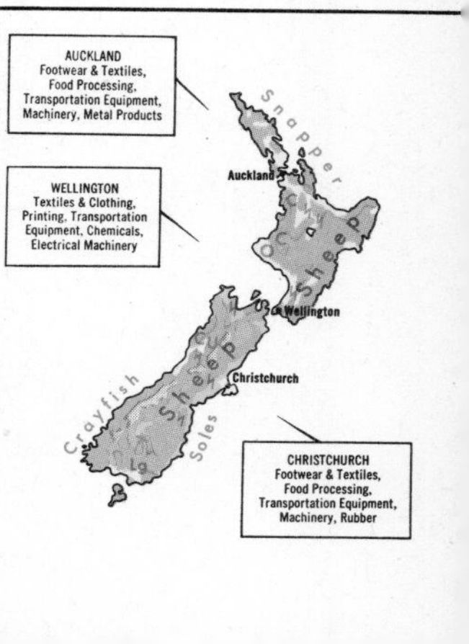

AUCKLAND
Footwear & Textiles, Food Processing, Transportation Equipment, Machinery, Metal Products
WELLINGTON
Textiles & Clothing, Printing, Transportation Equipment, Chemicals, Electrical Machinery
CHRISTCHURCH
Footwear & Textiles, Food Processing, Transportation Equipment, Machinery, Rubber
Auckland
Wellington
Christchurch
Snapper
Sheep
Crayfish
Soles

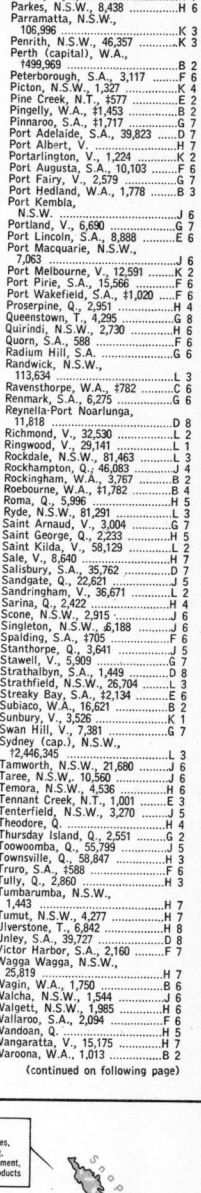

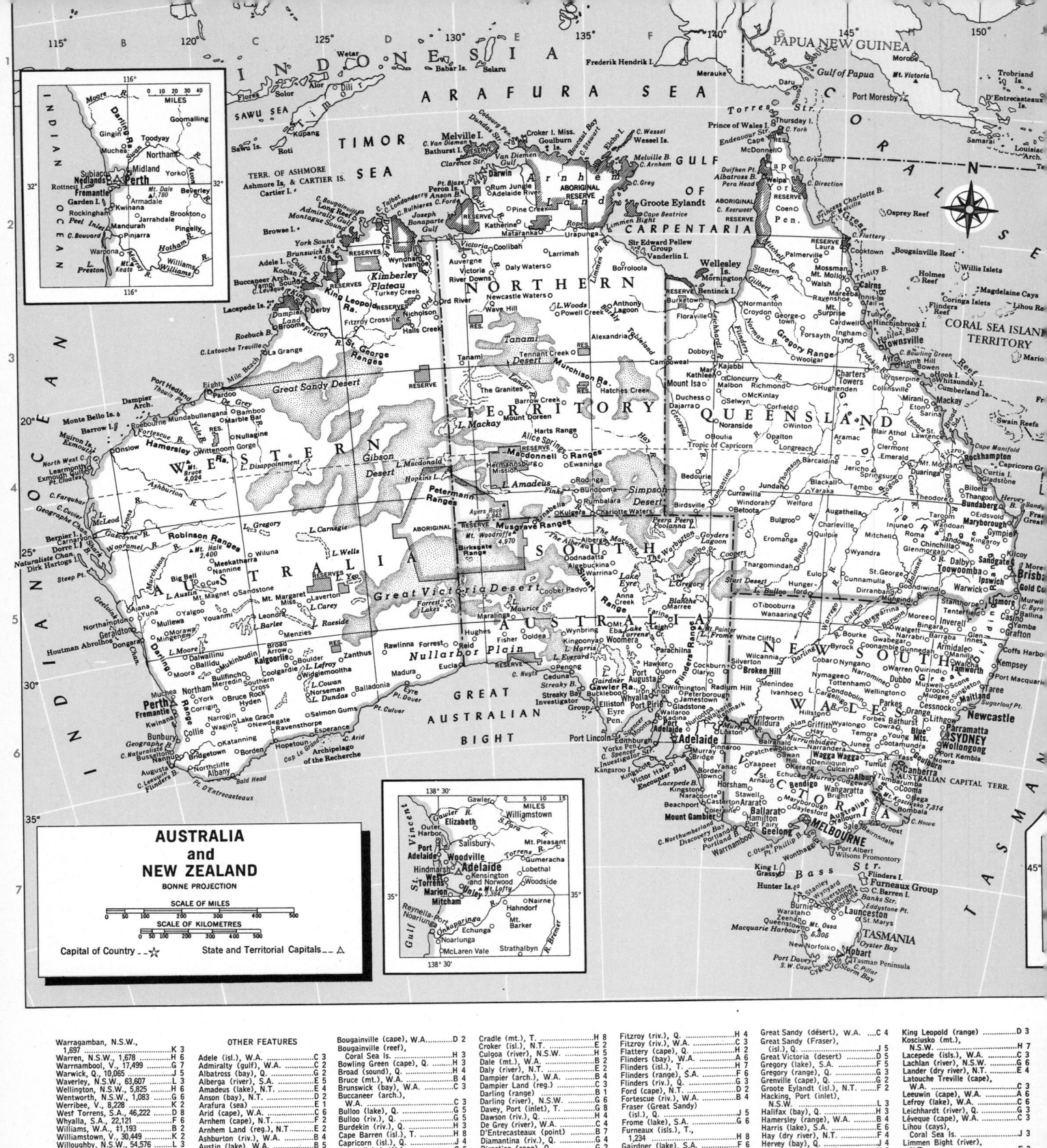

AUSTRALIA and NEW ZEALAND

BONNE PROJECTION

SCALE OF MILES

SCALE OF KILOMETRES

Capital of Country ⭐   State and Territorial Capitals △

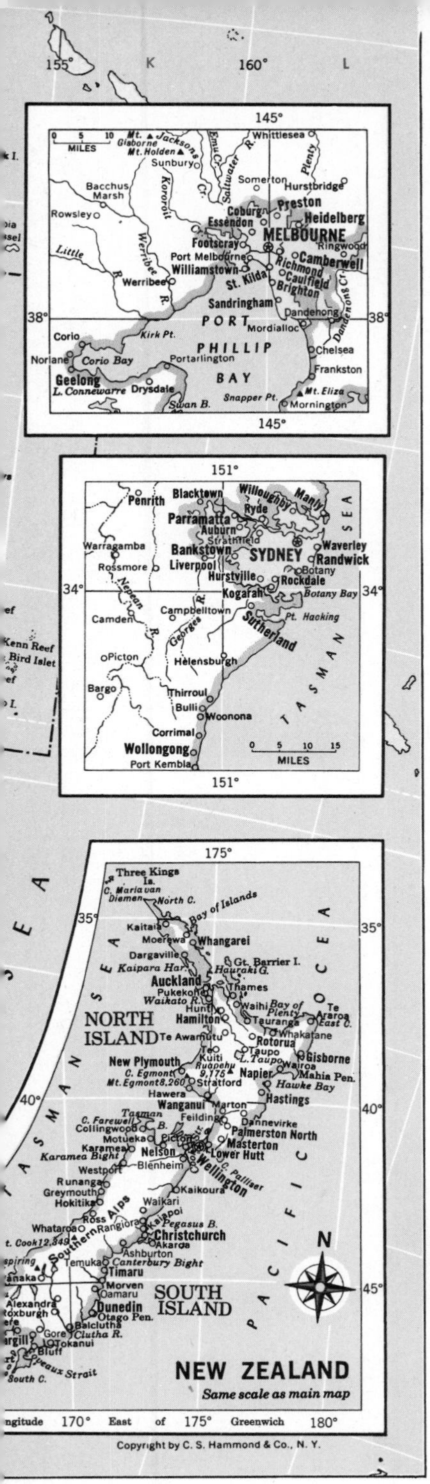

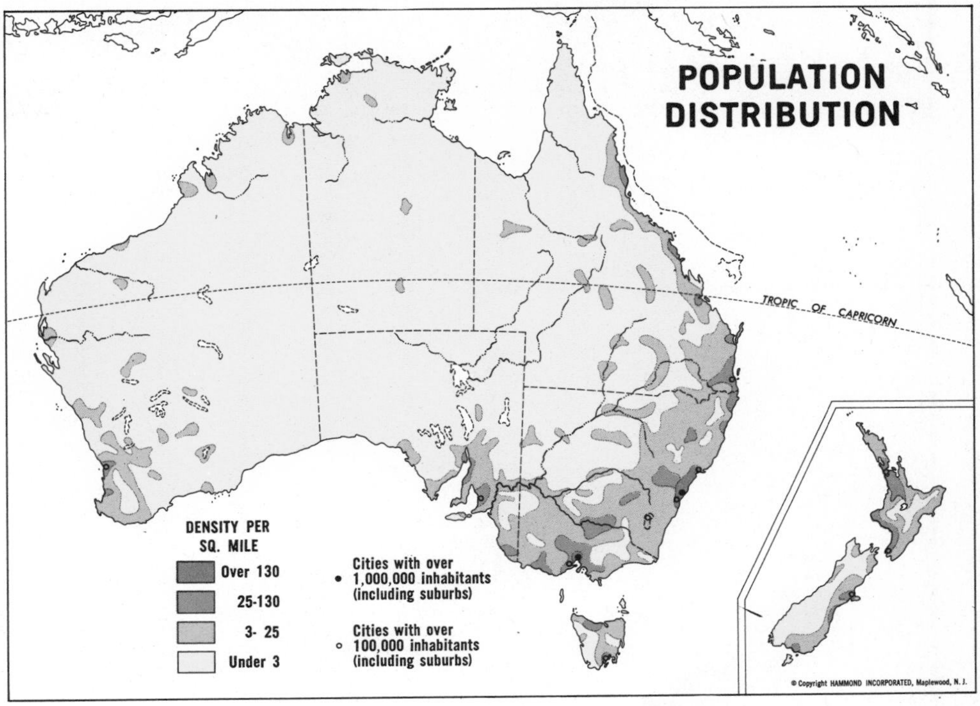

POPULATION DISTRIBUTION

DENSITY PER SQ. MILE

- Over 130
- 25-130
- 3- 25
- Under 3

● Cities with over 1,000,000 inhabitants (including suburbs)

○ Cities with over 100,000 inhabitants (including suburbs)

© Copyright HAMMOND INCORPORATED, Maplewood, N.J.

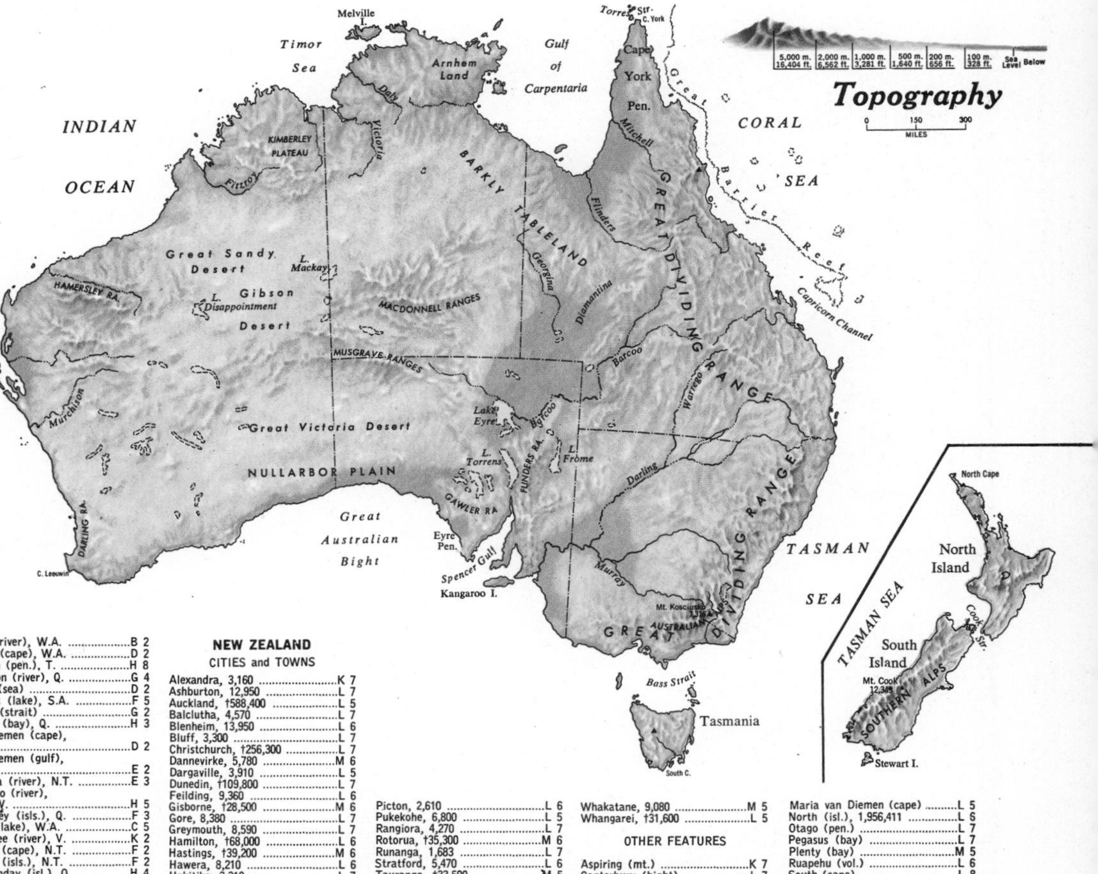

Topography

| 5,000 m. 16,404 ft. | 2,000 m. 6,562 ft. | 1,000 m. 3,281 ft. | 500 m. 1,640 ft. | 200 m. 656 ft. | 100 m. 328 ft. | Sea Level | Below |

NEW ZEALAND

Same scale as main map

Copyright by C. S. Hammond & Co., N.Y.

...ontague (sound), W.A.	C 2	
...onte Bello (isls.), W.A.	A 4	
...oore (lake), W.A.	B 5	
...oore (river), W.A.	B 1	
...oreton (isl.), Q.	J 5	
...ornington (isl.), Q.	G 3	
...urchison (range)	E 4	
...urchison (river), W.A.	B 5	
...urray (river), V.	G 6	
...urray (river), W.A.	B 2	
...urrumbidgee (river), N.S.W.	G 6	
...aturaliste (range)	E 5	
...aturaliste (cape), W.A.	A 6	
...aturaliste (channel), W.A.	A 5	
...epean (river), N.S.W.	K 3	
...orman (river), Q.	G 3	
...orth West (cape), W.A.	A 4	
...orthumberland (cape), S.A.	F 7	
...ullarbor (plain)	D 6	
...nkaparinga (river), S.A.	D 8	
...ord (river), W.A.	D 3	
...yster (bay), T.	H 8	
...roo (river), N.S.W.	G 5	
...el (inlet), T.	B 2	
...era Peera Poolanna (lake),	F 5	
...ron (head), S.A.	F 7	
...eron (islands), N.T.	D 2	
...illar (cape), T.	H 8	

Plenty (river), V.	L 1	
Port Philip (bay), V.	K 2	
Portland (bay), V.	G 7	
Preston (lake), W.A.	B 2	
Prince of Wales (isl.), Q.	G 2	
Princess Charlotte (bay), Q.	G 2	
Recherche (arch.), W.A.	C 6	
Roebuck (bay), W.A.	C 3	
Roper (river), N.T.	E 2	
Rottnest (isl.), W.A.	A 2	
Rulhieres (cape), W.A.	D 2	
Saint George (ranges), W.A.	D 3	
Saint Vincent (gulf), S.A.	D 7	
Saltwater (river), V.	K 1	
Sandy (cape), Q.	J 4	
Shark (bay), W.A.	A 4	
Simpson (desert), N.T.	F 5	
Sir Edward Pellew (isls.), N.T.	F 3	
South Para (river), S.A.	E 7	
South West (cape), T.	G 8	
Spencer (cape), S.A.	A 5	
Spencer (gulf), S.A.	F 6	
Steep (point), W.A.	A 5	
Stewart (cape), N.T.	F 2	
Storm (bay), T.	H 8	
Stuart (range), S.A.	E 6	
Sturt (desert)	G 5	
Swain (reefs), Q.	J 4	
Swan (bay), V.	K 2	

Swan (river), W.A.	B 2	
Talbot (cape), W.A.	D 2	
Tasman (pen.), T.	H 8	
Thomson (river), Q.	G 4	
Timor (sea)	D 2	
Torrens (lake), S.A.	F 5	
Torres (strait)	G 2	
Trinity (bay), Q.	H 3	
Van Diemen (cape), N.T.	D 2	
Van Diemen (gulf), N.T.	E 2	
Victoria (river), N.T.	E 3	
Warrego (river), N.S.W.	H 5	
Wellesley (isls.), Q.	F 3	
Wells (lake), W.A.	C 5	
Werribee (river), V.	J 1	
Wessel (cape), N.T.	F 2	
Wessel (isls.), N.T.	F 2	
Whitsunday (isl.), Q.	H 4	
Wilberforce (cape), N.T.	F 2	
Williams (river), W.A.	B 3	
Willis (islets), Coral Sea Is., 3	J 3	
Wilsons (promontory), V.	H 7	
Wooramel (river), W.A.	A 5	
York (cape), Q.	G 2	
York (sound), W.A.	C 2	
Yorke (pen.), S.A.	F 7	
Yule (river), W.A.	B 4	

NEW ZEALAND

CITIES and TOWNS

Alexandra, 3,160	K 7	
Ashburton, 12,950	L 7	
Auckland, †588,400	L 5	
Balclutha, 4,570	L 7	
Blenheim, 13,950	L 7	
Bluff, 3,300	L 7	
Christchurch, †256,300	L 7	
Dannevirke, 5,780	M 6	
Dargaville, 3,910	L 5	
Dunedin, †109,800	L 7	
Feilding, 9,360	L 6	
Gisborne, †28,500	M 6	
Gore, 8,380	L 7	
Greymouth, 8,590	L 7	
Hamilton, 168,000	L 6	
Hastings, †39,200	M 6	
Hawera, 8,210	L 6	
Hokitika, 3,310	L 7	
Invercargill, †47,800	K 7	
Kaiapoi, 3,610	L 7	
Kaitaia, 3,110	L 5	
Lower Hutt, 58,700	L 6	
Marton, 4,780	L 6	
Masterton, 17,950	M 6	
Motueka, 3,840	L 6	
Napier, †39,900	M 6	
Nelson, 128,400	L 6	
New Plymouth, 135,800	L 6	
Oamaru, 13,350	L 7	
Palmerston North, †50,900	M 6	
Picton, 2,610	L 6	
Pukekohe, 6,800	L 5	
Rangiora, 4,270	L 7	
Rotorua, †35,300	M 6	
Runanga, 1,683	L 7	
Stratford, 5,470	L 6	
Tauranga, †33,500	M 5	
Te Awamutu, 6,780	L 6	
Te Kuiti, 4,930	L 6	
Temuka, 3,190	L 7	
Timaru, †28,400	L 7	
Tuatapere, 954	K 7	
Waihi, 3,170	L 5	
Wairoa, 5,190	M 6	
Wanganui, †38,500	L 6	
Wellington (capital), †175,500	L 6	
Westport, 5,230	L 6	
Whakatane, 9,080	M 5	
Whangarei, 131,600	L 5	

OTHER FEATURES

Aspiring (mt.)	K 7	
Canterbury (bight)	L 7	
Cook (mt.)	K 7	
Cook (strait)	L 6	
East (cape)	M 5	
Egmont (cape)	L 6	
Egmont (mt.)	L 6	
Farewell (cape)	L 6	
Foveaux (strait)	K 7	
Great Barrier (isl.), 272	L 5	
Hauraki (gulf)	L 5	
Hawke (bay)	M 6	
Islands (bay)	L 5	
Karamea (bight)	K 6	

Maria van Diemen (cape)	L 5	
North (isl.), 1,956,411	L 6	
Otago (pen.)	L 7	
Pegasus (bay)	L 7	
Plenty (bay)	M 5	
Ruapehu (vol.)	L 6	
South (cape)	L 8	
South (isl.), 798,681	L 7	
Southern Alps (mts.)	L 7	
Stewart (isl.), 332	K 8	
Tasman (isl.)		
Tasman (sea)	K 6	
Taupo (lake)	M 6	
Te Anau (lake)	K 7	
Waikato (river)	L 6	

*City and suburbs.
†Population of metropolitan area.
‡Population of district or sub-division.

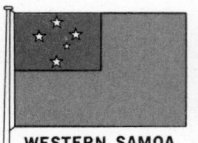

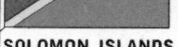
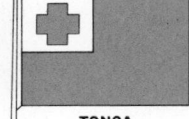

WESTERN SAMOA   **SOLOMON ISLANDS**   **TONGA**   **FIJI**

WESTERN SAMOA

AREA 1,133 sq. mi.
POPULATION 159,000
CAPITAL Apia
LARGEST CITY Apia
HIGHEST POINT Mt. Silisili 6,094 ft.
MONETARY UNIT tala
MAJOR LANGUAGES Samoan, English
MAJOR RELIGIONS Protestantism,
  Roman Catholicism

TONGA

AREA 270 sq. mi.
POPULATION 102,000
CAPITAL Nuku'alofa
LARGEST CITY Nuku'alofa
HIGHEST POINT 3,389 ft.
MONETARY UNIT pa'anga
MAJOR LANGUAGES Tongan, English
MAJOR RELIGION Protestantism

NAURU

AREA 7.7 sq. mi.
POPULATION 8,000
CAPITAL Yaren (district)
MONETARY UNIT Australian dollar
MAJOR LANGUAGES Nauruan, English
MAJOR RELIGION Protestantism

SOLOMON ISLANDS

AREA 11,500 sq. mi.
POPULATION 196,708
CAPITAL Honiara
HIGHEST POINT Mount Popomanatseu 7,647
MONETARY UNIT Solomon Islands dollar
MAJOR LANGUAGES English, Pidgin English,
  Melanesian dialects
MAJOR RELIGIONS Tribal religions, Protestantism,
  Roman Catholicism

FIJI

AREA 7,055 sq. mi.
POPULATION 569,468
CAPITAL Suva
LARGEST CITY Suva
HIGHEST POINT Tomaniivi 4,341 ft.
MONETARY UNIT Fijian dollar
MAJOR LANGUAGES Fijian, Hindi, English
MAJOR RELIGIONS Protestantism, Hinduism

TUVALU

AREA 9.78 sq. mi.
POPULATION 5,887
CAPITAL Fongafale
MONETARY UNIT Australian dollar
MAJOR LANGUAGES English, Tuvaluan
MAJOR RELIGION Protestantism

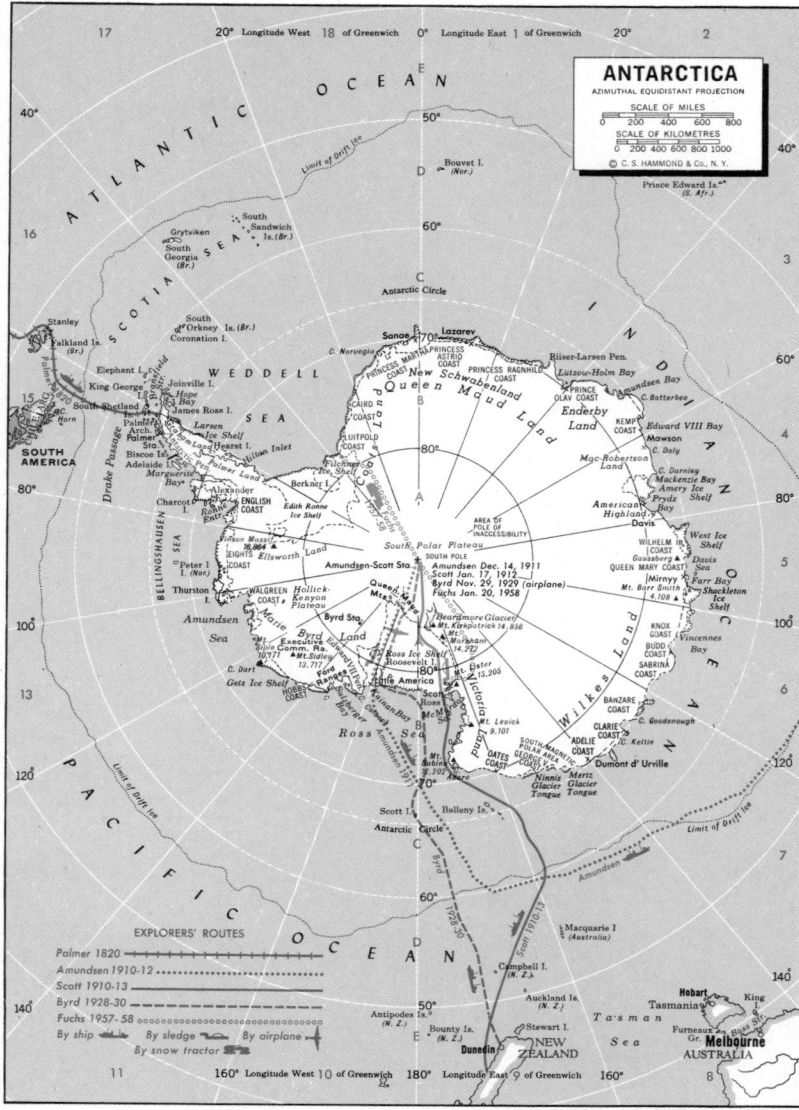

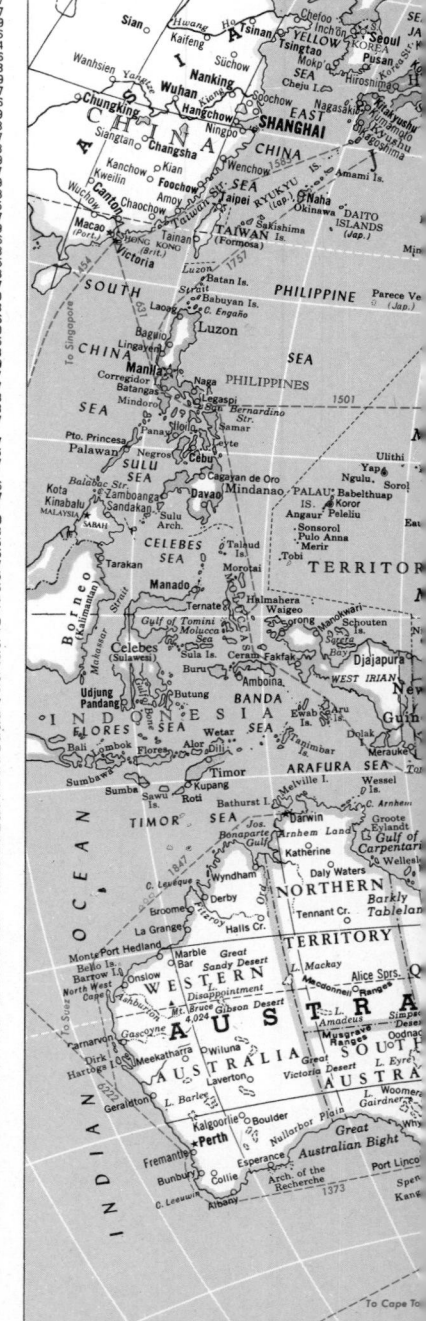

Pacific Ocean and Antarctica 89

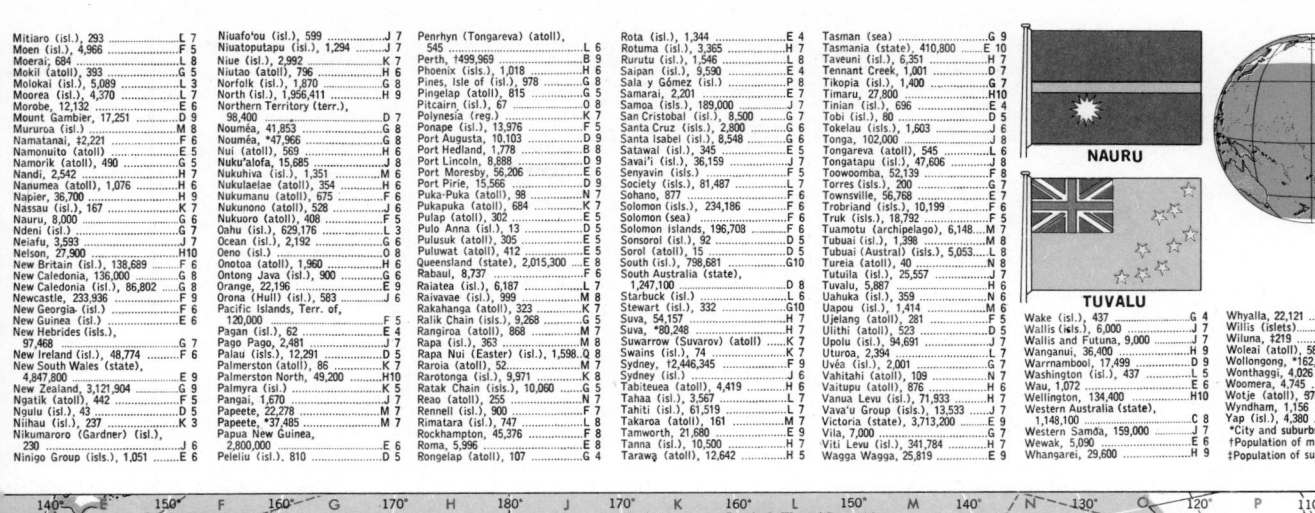

Mitiaro (isl.), 293	L 7	
Moen (isl.), 4,966	F 5	
Moerai, 684	L 8	
Mokil (atoll), 393	G 5	
Molokai (isl.), 5,089	L 3	
Moorea (isl.), 4,370	L 7	
Morobe, 12,132	E 6	
Mount Gambier, 17,251	D 10	
Mururoa (isl.)	M 8	
Namatanai, *2,221	F 6	
Namonuito (atoll)	E 5	
Namorik (atoll), 490	G 5	
Nandi, 2,542	H 7	
Nanumea (atoll), 1,076	H 6	
Napier, 36,700	G 9	
Nassau (isl.), 167	K 7	
Nauru, 8,000	G 6	
Ndeni (isl.)	G 7	
Neiafu, 3,593	H 10	
Nelson, 27,900	H 10	
New Britain, 138,689	F 6	
New Caledonia, 136,000	G 8	
New Caledonia (isl.), 86,802	G 8	
Newcastle, 233,936	F 9	
New Georgia (isls.)	E 6	
New Guinea (isl.)		
New Hebrides (isls.), 97,468		
New Ireland (isl.), 48,774	F 6	
New South Wales (state), 4,847,800		
New Zealand, 3,121,904	E 9	
Ngatik (atoll), 442	G 5	
Ngulu (isl.), 43	D 5	
Niihau (isl.), 237	K 3	
Nikumaroro (Gardner) (isl.), 230		
Ninigo Group (isls.), 1,051	E 6	

Niuafo'ou (isl.), 599	J 7	
Niuatoputapu (isl.), 1,294	J 7	
Niue (isl.), 2,992	K 7	
Niutao (atoll), 796	H 6	
Norfolk (isl.), 1,870	G 8	
North (isl.), 1,956,411	H 9	
Northern Territory (terr.), 98,400		
Nouméa, 41,853	G 8	
Nouméa, *47,966	G 8	
Nui (atoll), 569	H 6	
Nuku'alofa, 15,685	J 8	
Nukuhiva (isl.), 1,351	M 6	
Nukulaelae (atoll), 354	H 6	
Nukumanu (atoll), 675	F 6	
Nukunono (atoll), 528	J 6	
Nukuoro (atoll), 408	F 5	
Oahu (isl.), 629,176	L 3	
Ocean (isl.), 2,192	G 6	
Oeno (isl.)	N 8	
Onotoa (atoll), 1,960	H 6	
Ontong Java (isl.), 900	F 6	
Orange, 22,196	E 9	
Orona (Hull) (atoll), 583	J 6	
Pacific Islands, Terr. of, 120,000	F 5	
Pagan (isl.), 62	F 5	
Pago Pago, 2,481	J 7	
Palau (isls.), 12,291	D 5	
Palmerston (atoll), 86	K 7	
Palmerston North, 49,200	H 10	
Palmyra (isl.)	K 5	
Pangai, 1,670	J 7	
Papeete, 22,278	M 7	
Papeete, *37,485	M 7	
Papua New Guinea, 2,800,000	E 6	
Peleliu (isl.), 810	D 5	

Penrhyn (Tongareva) (atoll), 545	L 6	
Phoenix (isls.), 1,018	H 6	
Pines, Isle of (isl.), 978	G 8	
Pingelap (atoll), 815	G 5	
Pitcairn (isl.), 67	O 8	
Polynesia (reg.)	K 7	
Ponape (isl.), 13,976	F 5	
Port Augusta, 10,103	D 9	
Port Hedland, 1,778	B 8	
Port Lincoln, 8,888	D 9	
Port Moresby, 56,206	E 6	
Port Pirie, 15,566	D 9	
Puka-Puka (atoll), 98	N 7	
Pukapuka (atoll), 684	K 7	
Pulap (atoll), 302	E 5	
Pulo Anna (isl.), 13	D 5	
Pulusuk (atoll), 305	E 5	
Puluwat (atoll), 412	E 5	
Queensland (state), 2,015,300	E 8	
Rabaul, 8,737	F 6	
Rakahanga (atoll), 323	K 7	
Ralik Chain (isls.), 9,268	G 5	
Rangiroa (atoll), 868	M 7	
Rapa (isl.), 363	M 8	
Rapa Nui (Easter) (isl.), 1,598	Q 8	
Raroia (atoll), 52	N 7	
Rarotonga (isl.), 9,971	K 8	
Ratak Chain (isls.), 10,060	G 5	
Reao (atoll), 255	N 7	
Rennell (isl.), 900	F 7	
Rimatara (isl.), 747	L 8	
Raivavae (isl.), 1,399	M 8	
Takaroa (atoll), 161	M 7	
Rockhampton, 45,376	F 8	
Roma, 5,996	E 8	
Rongelap (atoll), 107	G 4	

Rota (isl.), 1,344	E 4	
Rotuma (isl.), 3,365	H 7	
Rurutu (isl.), 1,546	L 8	
Saipan (isl.), 9,590	E 4	
Sala y Gómez (isl.)	P 8	
Samarai, 2,201	E 7	
Samoa (isls.), 189,000	J 7	
San Cristobal (isl.), 8,500	G 7	
Santa Cruz (isls.), 2,800	G 6	
Santa Isabel (isl.), 8,548	G 6	
Satawal (isl.), 345	E 5	
Savai'i (isl.), 36,159	J 7	
Senyavin (isls.)	F 5	
Society (isls.), 81,487	L 7	
Sohano, 877	F 6	
Solomon (isls.), 234,186	F 6	
Solomon (sea)	F 6	
Solomon Islands, 196,708	F 6	
Sonsorol (isl.), 92	D 5	
Sorol (atoll), 15	D 5	
South (isl.), 798,681	G 10	
South Australia (state), 1,247,100	D 8	
Starbuck (isl.)	L 6	
Stewart (isl.), 332	G 10	
Suva, 54,157	H 7	
Suva, *80,248	H 7	
Swains (isl.), 74	K 7	
Sydney, 2,446,345	F 9	
Sydney (isl.)	J 6	
Tabiteuea (atoll), 4,419	H 6	
Tahaa (isl.), 3,567	L 7	
Tahiti (isl.), 61,519	L 7	
Tamworth, 21,680	F 9	
Tanna (isl.), 10,500	H 7	
Tarawa (atoll), 12,642	H 5	

Tasman (sea)	G 8	
Tasmania (state) 410,800	E 10	
Taveuni (isl.), 6,351	H 7	
Tennant Creek, 1,001	C 7	
Tikopia (isl.), 1,400	G 7	
Timaru, 27,800	H 10	
Tinian (isl.), 696	E 4	
Tobi (isl.), 80	D 5	
Tokelau (isls.), 1,603	J 6	
Tonga, 102,000	J 8	
Tongareva (atoll), 545	L 6	
Tongatapu (isl.), 47,606	J 8	
Toowoomba, 52,139	F 8	
Torres (isls.), 200	G 7	
Townsville, 56,768	E 7	
Trobriand (isls.), 10,199	F 6	
Truk (isls.), 18,792	F 5	
Tuamotu (archipelago), 6,148	M 7	
Tubuai (isl.), 1,398	M 8	
Tubuai (Austral) (isls.), 5,053	L 8	
Tureia (atoll), 40	N 8	
Tutuila (isl.), 25,557	J 7	
Tuvalu, 5,887	H 6	
Uahuka (isl.), 359	M 6	
Uapou (isl.), 1,414	M 6	
Ujelang (atoll), 281	F 5	
Ulithi (atoll), 523	D 5	
Upolu (isl.), 94,691	J 7	
Uturoa, 2,394	L 7	
Uvéa (isl.), 2,001	G 7	
Vahitahi (atoll), 109	N 7	
Vaitupu (atoll), 876	H 6	
Vanua Levu (isl.), 71,933	H 7	
Vava'u Group (isls.), 13,533	J 7	
Victoria (state), 3,713,200	E 9	
Vila, 7,000	G 7	
Viti Levu (isl.), 341,784	H 7	
Wagga Wagga, 25,819	E 9	

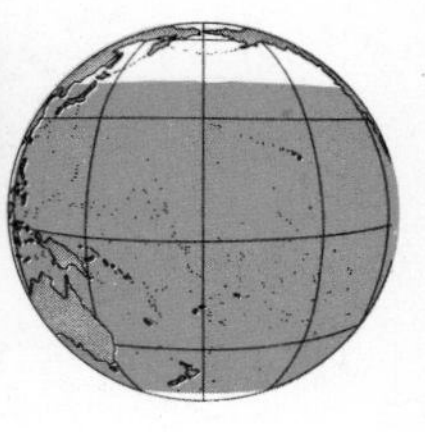

Wake (isl.), 437	G 4	
Wallis (isls.), 6,000	J 7	
Wallis and Futuna, 9,000	J 7	
Wanganui, 36,400	H 9	
Warrnambool, 17,499	D 9	
Washington (isl.), 437	L 5	
Wau, 1,072	E 6	
Wellington, 134,400	H 10	
Western Australia (state), 1,148,100		
Western Samoa, 159,000	J 7	
Wewak, 5,090	E 6	
Whangarei, 29,600	H 9	

Whyalla, 22,121	D 9	
Willis (islets)	F 7	
Wiluna, 1219	C 8	
Woleai (atoll), 586	E 5	
Wollongong, *162,153	F 9	
Wonthaggi, 4,026	E 9	
Woomera, 4,745	D 9	
Wotje (atoll), 576	H 5	
Wyndham, 1,156	C 7	
Yap (isl.), 4,380	D 5	

*City and suburbs.
†Population of metropolitan area.
‡Population of sub-district.

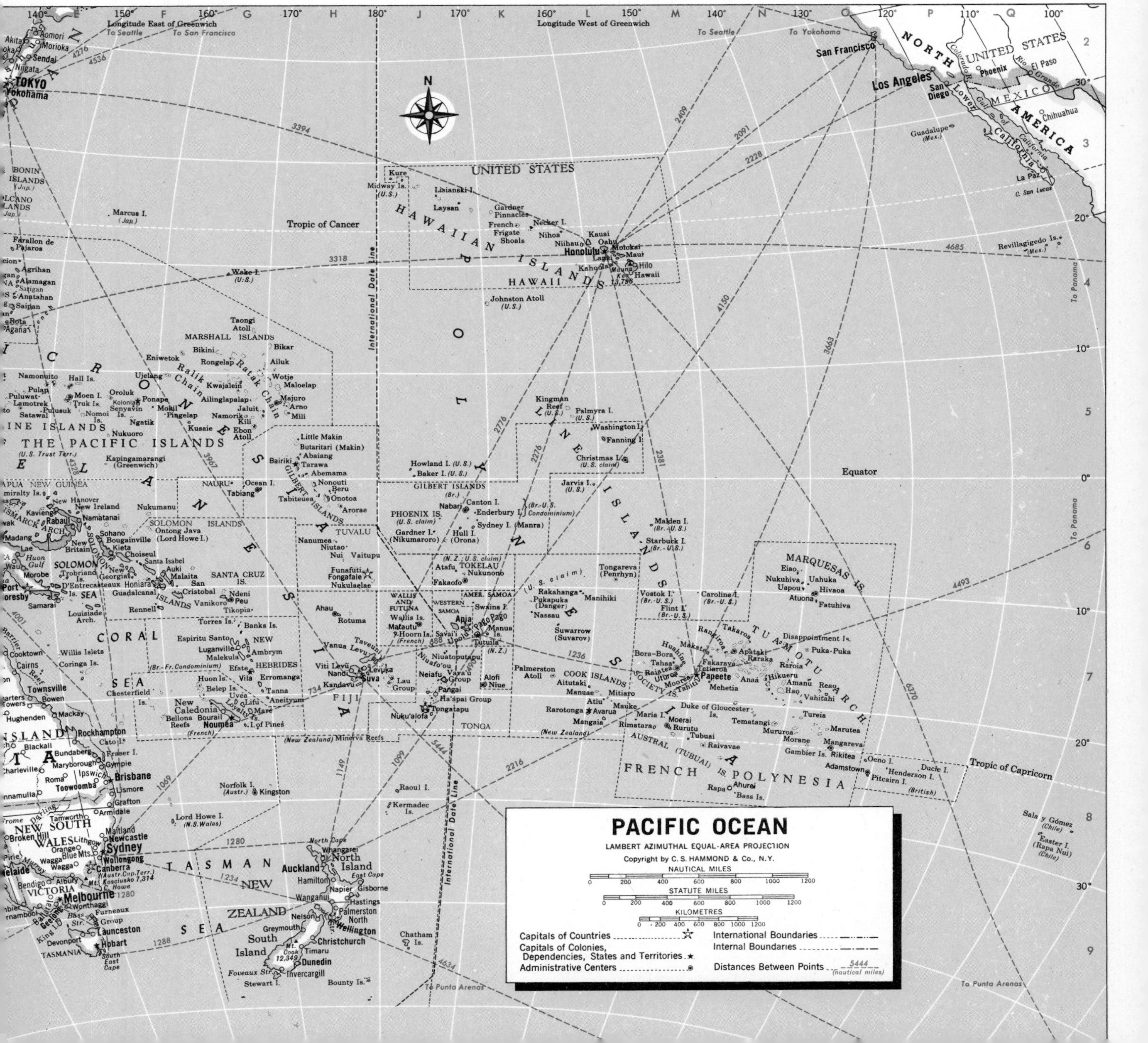

PACIFIC OCEAN
LAMBERT AZIMUTHAL EQUAL-AREA PROJECTION
Copyright by C. S. HAMMOND & Co., N.Y.

NAUTICAL MILES
STATUTE MILES
KILOMETRES

Capitals of Countries .... ☆
Capitals of Colonies, Dependencies, States and Territories. ★
Administrative Centers ....

International Boundaries ....
Internal Boundaries ....
Distances Between Points ___5444___ (nautical miles)

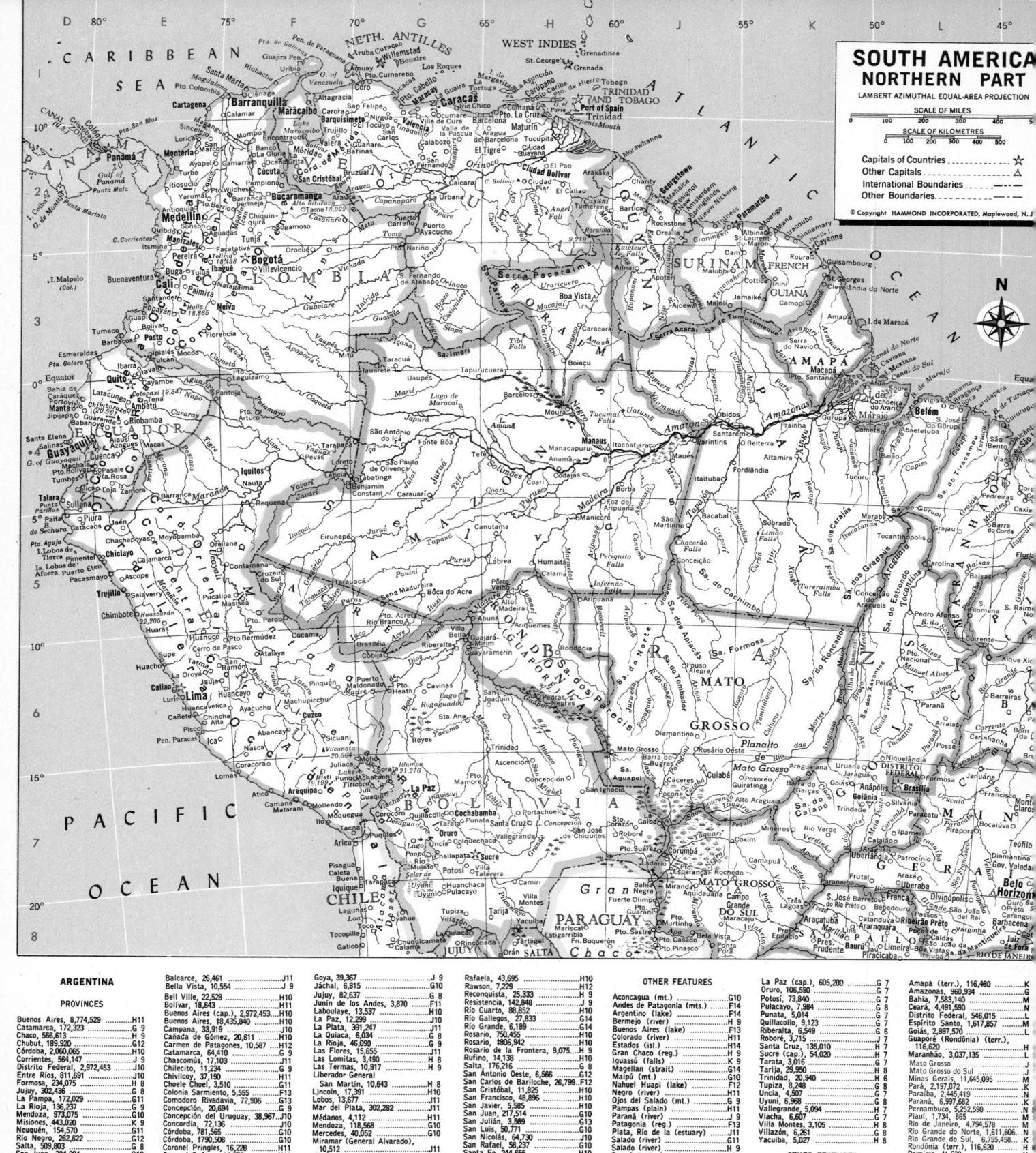

SOUTH AMERICA NORTHERN PART
LAMBERT AZIMUTHAL EQUAL-AREA PROJECTION

SCALE OF MILES
0 100 200 300 400 5

SCALE OF KILOMETRES
0 100 200 300 400 500

Capitals of Countries .... ☆
Other Capitals .... △
International Boundaries .... —·—·—
Other Boundaries .... ----------

© Copyright HAMMOND INCORPORATED, Maplewood, N.J.

ARGENTINA

PROVINCES

Buenos Aires, 8,774,529	H11
Catamarca, 172,323	G 9
Chaco, 566,613	J 9
Chubut, 189,920	G12
Córdoba, 2,060,065	H10
Corrientes, 564,147	J 9
Distrito Federal, 2,972,453	J10
Entre Ríos, 811,691	J10
Formosa, 234,075	H 8
Jujuy, 302,436	G 8
La Pampa, 172,029	G11
La Rioja, 136,237	G 9
Mendoza, 973,075	G10
Misiones, 154,570	K 9
Neuquén, 154,570	F11
Río Negro, 262,622	G12
Salta, 509,803	G 8
San Juan, 384,284	G10
San Luis, 183,460	G10
Santa Fe, 2,135,583	J10
Santiago del Estero, 495,419	H 9
Tierra del Fuego, Antártida e Islas del Atlántico Sur (terr.), 15,658	G14
Tucumán, 765,962	H 9

CITIES and TOWNS

Alta Gracia, 24,371	H10
Añatuya, 11,918	H 9
Andalgalá, 5,687	G 9
Ayacucho, 12,046	J11
Azul, 36,023	J11
Bahía Blanca, 182,158	H11

Balcarce, 26,461	J11
Bella Vista, 10,554	J 9
Bell Ville, 22,528	H10
Bolívar, 18,643	H11
Buenos Aires (cap.), 2,972,453	J10
Buenos Aires, ‡8,435,840	J10
Campana, 33,919	J10
Cañada de Gómez, 20,611	H10
Carmen de Patagones, 10,587	H12
Catamarca, 64,410	G 9
Chacomús, 17,103	J10
Chilecito, 11,234	G 9
Chivilcoy, 37,190	H10
Choele Choel, 3,510	G11
Colonia Sarmiento, 5,555	F13
Comodoro Rivadavia, 72,906	G13
Concepción, 20,694	J 9
Concepción del Uruguay, 38,967	J10
Concordia, 72,136	J10
Córdoba, 781,565	H10
Córdoba, ‡790,508	H10
Coronel Pringles, 16,228	H11
Coronel Suárez, 14,570	H11
Corrientes, 136,924	J 9
Curuzú Cuatiá, 20,636	J 9
Deán Funes, 15,592	H10
Dolores, 17,414	J11
Embarcación, 7,207	H 8
Empedrado, 4,269	J 9
Esperanza, 17,636	H10
Esquel, 13,771	F12
Formosa, 61,071	J 9
General Acha, 6,270	G11
General Alvarado, 10,512	J11
General Alvear, 17,277	G10
General Juan Madariaga, 10,280	J11
General Pico, 21,897	H11
General Roca, 29,320	G11
Godoy Cruz, 112,481	G10

Goya, 39,367	J 9
Jáchal, 6,815	G10
Jujuy, 82,637	G 8
Junín de los Andes, 3,870	F11
Labouaye, 13,537	H10
La Plata, 391,247	J10
La Quiaca, 6,034	G 8
La Rioja, 46,090	G 9
Las Flores, 15,655	J11
Las Lomitas, 3,490	H 8
Las Termas, 10,917	H 9
Libertador General San Martín, 10,643	H 8
Lincoln, 17,391	H10
Lobos, 13,677	J10
Mar del Plata, 302,282	J11
Médanos, 4,112	H11
Mendoza, 118,568	G10
Mercedes, 40,052	G10
Miramar (General Alvarado), 10,512	J11
Monte Caseros, 14,306	J10
Necochea, 39,868	J11
Neuquén, 43,070	G11
Olavarría, 52,453	H11
Orán, 20,212	H 8
Paraná, 127,635	J10
Paso de los Libres, 17,341	J 9
Pehuajó, 21,078	H10
Pergamino, 56,078	H10
Perico, 7,096	G 8
Plaza Huincul, 4,714	G11
Posadas, 97,514	J 9
Presidencia Roque Sáenz Peña, 38,620	H 9
Puerto Deseado, 3,735	H13
Puerto Madryn, 6,467	H12
Punta Alta, 38,805	H11
Quequén, 9,299	J11
Quimilí, 4,076	H 9

Rafaela, 43,695	H10
Rawson, 7,229	H12
Reconquista, 25,333	H 9
Resistencia, 142,848	J 9
Río Cuarto, 88,852	H10
Río Grande, 6,189	G14
Rosario, 750,455	H10
Rosario, ‡806,942	H10
Rosario de la Frontera, 9,075	H 9
Rufino, 14,138	H10
Salta, 176,216	G 8
San Antonio Oeste, 6,566	G11
San Carlos de Bariloche, 26,799	F12
San Cristóbal, 11,825	H10
San Francisco, 48,896	H10
San Javier, 5,885	H10
San Juan, 217,514	G10
San Julián, 3,589	G13
San Luis, 50,771	G10
San Nicolás, 64,730	H10
San Rafael, 58,237	G10
Santa Fe, 244,655	H10
Santa Rosa, 33,649	G11
Santiago del Estero, 105,127	H 9
Tandil, 65,876	J11
Tartagal, 23,696	H 8
Tinogasta, 6,313	G 9
Trelew, 24,214	G12
Trenque Lauquen, 18,169	H11
Tres Arroyos, 37,991	H11
Tucumán, 365,351	H 9
Tunuyán, 10,813	G10
Ushuaia, 5,677	G14
Venado Tuerto, 35,677	H10
Victoria, 17,046	H10
Victorica, 3,184	G11
Viedma, 12,888	H12
Villa Ángela, 17,283	H 9
Villa Dolores, 19,010	G10
Villa María, 56,087	H10
Zapala, 11,385	F11

OTHER FEATURES

Aconcagua (mt.)	G10
Andes de Patagonia (mts.)	F14
Argentino (lake)	F14
Bermejo (river)	H 9
Buenos Aires (lake)	F13
Colorado (river)	G11
Estados (isl.)	H14
Gran Chaco (reg.)	H 9
Iguassú (falls)	K 9
Magellan (strait)	G14
Maipú (mt.)	G10
Nahuel Huapi (lake)	F12
Negro (river)	G11
Ojos del Salado (mt.)	G 9
Pampas (plain)	H11
Paraná (river)	J 9
Patagonia (reg.)	F13
Plata, Río de la (estuary)	J11
Salado (river)	J11
Salado (river)	H10
San Antonio (cape)	J11
San Martín (lake)	F13
San Matías (gulf)	H12
Staten (Estados) (isl.)	H14
Tierra del Fuego (isl.), 13,431	G14
Tres Puntas (cape)	H13
Uruguay (river)	J 9
Valdés (pen.)	H12

BOLIVIA

CITIES and TOWNS

Achacachi, 3,621	G 7
Camiri, 4,969	G 7
Challapata, 2,529	G 7
Cobija, 3,010	F 6
Cochabamba, 169,930	G 7
Corocoro, 4,431	G 7

La Paz (cap.), 605,200	G 7
Oruro, 106,590	G 7
Potosí, 73,840	G 7
Pulacayo, 7,984	G 7
Punata, 5,014	G 7
Quillacollo, 9,123	G 7
Riberalta, 6,549	G 6
Roboré, 3,715	H 7
Santa Cruz, 135,010	H 7
Sucre (cap.), 54,020	G 7
Tarata, 3,016	G 7
Tarija, 29,950	H 8
Trinidad, 20,940	H 6
Tupiza, 8,180	G 8
Uncía, 4,507	G 7
Uyuni, 6,368	G 8
Vallegrande, 5,094	H 7
Viacha, 6,607	G 7
Villa Montes, 3,105	H 8
Villazón, 6,261	G 8
Yacuiba, 5,027	H 8

OTHER FEATURES

Abuná (river)	G 6
Altiplano (plateau)	G 7
Beni (river)	G 6
Desaguadero (river)	G 7
Grande (river)	H 7
Guaporé (river)	H 6
Illampu (mt.)	G 7
Mamoré (river)	H 6
Poopó (lake)	G 7
Real, Cordillera (mts.)	G 7
Titicaca (lake)	G 7

BRAZIL

STATES

Acre, 218,006	F 5
Alagoas, 1,606,174	N 5

Amapá (terr.), 116,480	K
Amazonas, 960,934	H
Bahía, 7,583,140	M
Ceará, 4,491,590	N
Distrito Federal, 546,015	L
Espírito Santo, 1,617,857	M
Goiás, 2,997,570	K
Guaporé (Rondônia) (terr.), 116,620	G
Maranhão, 3,037,135	M
Mato Grosso	J
Mato Grosso do Sul	J
Minas Gerais, 11,645,095	M
Pará, 2,197,072	K
Paraíba, 2,445,419	N
Paraná, 6,997,682	K
Pernambuco, 5,252,590	N
Piauí, 1,734, 865	M
Rio de Janeiro, 4,794,578	M
Rio Grande do Norte, 1,611,606	N
Rio Grande do Sul, 6,755,458	K
Rondônia (terr.), 116,620	G
Roraima, 41,638	H
Santa Catarina, 3,930,411	L
São Paulo, 17,958,693	L
Sergipe, 911,251	N

CITIES and TOWNS

Abaetetuba, 19,197	L
Alagoinhas, 53,891	N
Alegrete, 45,522	J
Anápolis, 89,405	L
Aquidauana, 16,534	J
Aracaju, 179,512	N
Aracati, 14,509	N
Araçatuba, 85,660	L
Araçuaí, 9,190	M
Araguari, 48,702	L
Arapiraca, 43,875	N
Araranguá, 12,261	L
Araraquara, 82,607	L

AREA 6,875,000 sq. mi.
POPULATION 186,000,000
LARGEST CITY Buenos Aires (greater)
HIGHEST POINT Cerro Aconcagua 22,831 ft.
LOWEST POINT Salina Grande -131 ft.

Topography

0   300   600
MILES

ARGENTINA

BOLIVIA

BRAZIL

CHILE

COLOMBIA

ECUADOR

FRENCH GUIANA

GUYANA

PARAGUAY

PERU

SURINAM

URUGUAY

VENEZUELA

ARGENTINA
AREA 1,072,070
POPULATION 23,983,000
CAPITAL Buenos Aires
LARGEST CITY Buenos Aires
HIGHEST POINT Cerro Aconcagua 22,831 ft.
MONETARY UNIT Argentine peso
MAJOR LANGUAGE Spanish
MAJOR RELIGION Roman Catholicism

BOLIVIA
AREA 424, 163 sq. mi.
POPULATION 4,804,000
CAPITALS La Paz, Sucre
LARGEST CITY La Paz
HIGHEST POINT Nevada Ancohuma 21,489 ft.
MONETARY UNIT Bolivian peso
MAJOR LANGUAGES Spanish, Quechua, Aymara
MAJOR RELIGION Roman Catholicism

BRAZIL
AREA 3,284,426 sq. mi.
POPULATION 90,840,000
CAPITAL Brasília
LARGEST CITY São Paulo (greater)
HIGHEST POINT Pico da Neblina 9,889 ft.
MONETARY UNIT cruzeiro
MAJOR LANGUAGE Portuguese
MAJOR RELIGION Roman Catholicism

CHILE
AREA 292,257 sq. mi.
POPULATION 8,834,820
CAPITAL Santiago
LARGEST CITY Santiago
HIGHEST POINT Ojos del Salado 22,572 ft.
MONETARY UNIT Chilean escudo
MAJOR LANGUAGE Spanish
MAJOR RELIGION Roman Catholicism

COLOMBIA
AREA 439,513 sq. mi.
POPULATION 21,117,000
CAPITAL Bogotá
LARGEST CITY Bogotá
HIGHEST POINT Pico Cristóbal Colón 19,029 ft.
MONETARY UNIT Colombian peso
MAJOR LANGUAGE Spanish
MAJOR RELIGION Roman Catholicism

ECUADOR
REA 109,483 sq. mi.
OPULATION 6,144,000
APITAL Quito
ARGEST CITY Guayaquil
IGHEST POINT Chimborazo
MONETARY UNIT sucre
MAJOR LANGUAGES Spanish
MAJOR RELIGION Roman Cat

FRENCH GUIANA
AREA 35,135 sq. mi.
POPULATION 48,000
CAPITAL Cayenne
LARGEST CITY Cayenne
HIGHEST POINT 2,723 ft.
MONETARY UNIT French franc
MAJOR LANGUAGE French
MAJOR RELIGIONS Roman Catholicism,
Protestantism

GUYANA
AREA 83,000 sq. mi.
POPULATION 763,000
CAPITAL Georgetown
LARGEST CITY Georgetown
HIGHEST POINT Mt. Roraima 9,094 ft.
MONETARY UNIT Guyana dollar
MAJOR LANGUAGES English, Hindi
MAJOR RELIGIONS Christianity, Hinduism, Islam

PARAGUAY
AREA 157,047 sq. mi.
POPULATION 2,314,000
CAPITAL Asunción
LARGEST CITY Asunción
HIGHEST POINT Amambay Range 2,264 ft.
MONETARY UNIT guaraní
MAJOR LANGUAGES Spanish, Guaraní
MAJOR RELIGION Roman Catholicism

PERU
REA 496,222 sq. mi.
OPULATION 13,586,300
APITAL Lima
ARGEST CITY Lima
GHEST POINT Huascarán 22,205 ft.
ONETARY UNIT sol
AJOR LANGUAGES Spanish, Quechua,
Aymara
AJOR RELIGION Roman Catholicism

SURINAM
AREA 55,144 sq. mi.
POPULATION 389,000
CAPITAL Paramaribo
LARGEST CITY Paramaribo
HIGHEST POINT Julianatop 4,200 ft.
MONETARY UNIT Surinam guilder
MAJOR LANGUAGES Dutch, Hindi, Indonesian
MAJOR RELIGIONS Christianity, Islam, Hinduism

URUGUAY
AREA 72,172 sq. mi.
POPULATION 2,900,000
CAPITAL Montevideo
LARGEST CITY Montevideo
HIGHEST POINT Mirador Nacional 1,644 ft.
MONETARY UNIT Uruguayan peso
MAJOR LANGUAGE Spanish
MAJOR RELIGION Roman Catholicism

VENEZUELA
AREA 352,143 sq. mi.
POPULATION 10,398,907
CAPITAL Caracas
LARGEST CITY Caracas
HIGHEST POINT Pico Bolívar 16,427 ft.
MONETARY UNIT bolívar
MAJOR LANGUAGE Spanish
MAJOR RELIGION Roman Catholicism

Araripina, 8,397 ......M 5
Araxá, 31,498 ......L 7
Areia Branca, 10,778 ......N 4
Bacabal, 29,251 ......J 5
Bagé, 57,036 ......K10
Bahia (Salvador), 998,258 ......N 6
Balsas, 7,017 ......L 5
Barbacena, 57,766 ......M 8
Barra, 8,774 ......M 6
Barra do Corda, 9,528 ......L 5
Barra do Garças, 6,902 ......K 7
Barreiras, 9,855 ......M 6
Barretos, 53,050 ......L 8
Baturité, 8,799 ......N 4
Bauru, 120,178 ......L 8
Bebedouro, 28,824 ......L 8
Bela Vista, 10,563 ......J 8
Belém, 565,097 ......L 4
Belmonte, 7,072 ......N 7
Belo Horizonte, 1,106,722 ......M 7
Belo Horizonte, ‡1,235,001 ......M 7
Blumenau, 85,942 ......L 9
Boa Vista, 16,720 ......H 3
Bocaiúva, 9,417 ......M 7
Bom Jesus da Lapa, 12,313 ......M 6
Botucatu, 42,252 ......L 8
Bragança, 16,642 ......L 4
Brasília (cap.), 272,002 ......G 6
Brasília, ‡538,351 ......G 6
Brumado, 15,416 ......M 6
Cáceres, 16,102 ......J 7
Cachoeira do Sul, 50,001 ......K10
Cachoeiro de Itapemirim, 58,968 ......N 8

Caetité, 6,667 ......M 6
Caicó, 24,594 ......N 5
Cajàzeiras, 24,079 ......N 5
Cametá, 7,965 ......M 4
Camocim, 12,068 ......M 4
Campina Grande, 163,206 ......N 5
Campinas, 328,629 ......L 8
Campo Grande, 130,792 ......K 8
Campos, 153,310 ......M 8
Canavieiras, 11,680 ......N 7
Capanema, 15,616 ......M 4
Carangola, 14,924 ......M 8
Caratinga, 28,119 ......M 7
Carolina, 8,653 ......L 5
Caruaru, 101,006 ......N 5
Cascavel, 5,216 ......J 8
Castro, 11,887 ......L 8
Cataguases, 32,515 ......M 8
Catalão, 15,223 ......L 7
Catanduva, 48,446 ......L 8
Caxias, 31,069 ......M 4
Caxias do Sul, 107,487 ......K 9
Ceará (Fortaleza), 520,175 ......N 4
Coari, 8,880 ......H 4
Codó, 19,564 ......M 4
Colatina, 46,012 ......N 7
Coroatá, 11,926 ......M 4
Corumbá, 48,607 ......J 7
Crateús, 25,022 ......M 5
Crato, 36,836 ......N 5
Cruz Alta, 43,568 ......K 9
Cruzeiro do Sul, 8,426 ......F 5
Cuiabá, 83,621 ......J 7
Curitiba, 483,038 ......J 9

Cururupu, 8,544 ......M 4
Diamantina, 17,551 ......M 7
Divinópolis, 69,872 ......L 8
Erechim, 22,426 ......K 9
Estância, 20,265 ......N 6
Feira de Santana, 127,105 ......N 6
Floriano, 26,791 ......M 5
Florianópolis, 115,665 ......L 9
Formosa, 12,255 ......L 7
Foz do Iguaçú, 18,605 ......J 8
Franca, 86,852 ......L 8
Frutal, 16,937 ......L 7
Garanhuns, 49,579 ......N 5
Goiânia, 362,152 ......L 7
Goiás, 10,316 ......K 7
Governador Valadares, 125,174 ......M 7
Granja, 8,457 ......M 4
Guajará-Mirim, 10,823 ......G 6
Guarapuava, 14,419 ......K 9
Guiratinga, 5,768 ......K 7
Ibicaraí, 15,067 ......N 6
Iguape, 8,895 ......L 9
Iguatu, 27,851 ......N 5
Ilhéus, 58,529 ......N 6
Ipameri, 11,572 ......L 7
Ipiaú, 18,383 ......N 6
Ipu, 8,989 ......N 4
Itabuna, 89,928 ......N 6
Itacoatiara, 15,881 ......J 4
Itajaí, 54,315 ......L 9
Itajubá, 42,485 ......L 8
Itapetinga, 30,578 ......N 7
Itapipoca, 11,902 ......N 4

Itaqui, 17,262 ......J 9
Jacarèzinho, 19,161 ......K 8
Jacobina, 18,892 ......N 6
Jaguarão, 16,541 ......K 10
Jaguariaíva, 7,213 ......K 8
Januária, 13,605 ......M 7
Jaraguá, 8,551 ......K 7
Jaú, 40,989 ......L 8
Jequié, 62,341 ......N 6
João Pessoa, 197,398 ......O 5
Joinville, 77,760 ......L 9
Juàzeiro, 36,273 ......N 5
Juàzeiro do Norte, 79,796 ......N 5
Juiz de Fora, 218,832 ......M 8
Ladário, 18,892 ......J 7
Laguna, 16,916 ......L 9
Lajes, 82,325 ......K 9
Limeira, 77,243 ......L 8
Lins, 38,080 ......L 8
Londrina, 156,670 ......K 8
Macaé, 29,348 ......M 8
Macapá, 51,563 ......K 3
Macau, 18,853 ......N 4
Maceió, 242,867 ......N 5
Manacapuru, 5,113 ......H 4
Manaus, 294,118 ......H 4
Marabá, 14,913 ......L 5
Maranguape, 12,746 ......N 4
Marília, 73,161 ......K 8
Maués, 6,011 ......J 4
Miguel Calmon, 5,672 ......N 6
Mineiros, 9,836 ......K 7
Montes Claros, 81,572 ......M 7

Mossoró, 77,251 ......N 5
Natal, 250,787 ......O 5
Nazaré, 16,285 ......N 6
Niterói, 291,970 ......M 8
Óbidos, 8,657 ......J 4
Olinda, 187,553 ......O 5
Ouro Prêto, 24,050 ......M 8
Paracatú, 17,453 ......L 7
Paraíba (João Pessoa), 197,398 ......O 5
Paranaguá, 51,510 ......K 9
Paranaíba, 8,410 ......K 7
Parintins, 16,721 ......J 4
Parnaíba, 57,010 ......M 4
Passo Fundo, 69,135 ......K 9
Passos, 39,184 ......L 8
Patrocínio, 19,820 ......L 7
Pedra Azul, 11,083 ......M 7
Pedreiras, 19,539 ......L 4
Pelotas, 150,278 ......K10
Penedo, 23,411 ......N 6
Pernambuco (Recife), 1,046,454 ......O 5
Pesqueira, 24,421 ......N 5
Petrolina, 37,801 ......M 5
Petrópolis, 116,080 ......M 8
Picos, 18,092 ......M 5
Piracicaba, 125,490 ......L 8
Pirapora, 18,990 ......L 7
Piripiri, 18,487 ......M 4
Poconé, 7,755 ......J 7
Poços de Caldas, 51,844 ......L 8
Ponta Grossa, 92,344 ......K 9
Ponta Porã, 12,684 ......J 8
Pôrto Alegre, 869,795 ......K10
Pôrto Nacional, 9,027 ......L 6

Pôrto Velho, 41,146 ......H 5
Presidente Epitácio, 17,410 ......K 8
Presidente Prudente, 91,186 ......K 8
Propriá, 18,386 ......N 5
Puerto Guaíra, 10,737 ......K 8
Recife, 1,046,454 ......O 5
Recife, ‡1,060,752 ......O 5
Remanso, 6,910 ......M 5
Ribeirão Prêto, 190,897 ......L 8
Rio Branco, 34,531 ......G 5
Rio de Janeiro, 4,252,009 ......M 8
Rio de Janeiro, ‡5,618,001 ......M 8
Rio Grande, 96,863 ......K10
Rio Largo, 21,968 ......N 5
Rio Pardo, 16,857 ......K 9
Rio Tinto, 13,432 ......O 5
Rio Verde, 22,337 ......K 7
Tefé, 7,076 ......H 4
Rosário, 8,518 ......M 4
Salgueiro, 18,951 ......N 5
Salvador, 998,258 ......N 6
Salvador, ‡1,007,744 ......N 6
Santa Maria, 120,667 ......K 9
Santana do Livramento, 48,448 ......K10
Santarém, 51,123 ......J 4
Santa Vitória do Palmar, 10,879 ......K10
Santo Amaro, 20,767 ......N 6
Santo Ângelo, 36,020 ......J 9
Santos, 341,317 ......L 8
São Bento, 7,351 ......M 4
São Bernardo do Campo, 187,368 ......L 8
São Borja, 28,875 ......J 9
São Francisco, 6,445 ......M 7

São Francisco do Sul, 12,868 ......L 9
São João da Bôa Vista, 33,061 ......L 8
São João del Rei, 45,019 ......M 8
São José do Rio Prêto, 108,319 ......K 8
São Leopoldo, 62,861 ......K 9
São Luís, 167,529 ......M 4
São Mateus, 10,680 ......N 7
São Paulo, 5,186,752 ......L 8
São Paulo, ‡5,921,796 ......L 8
São Raimundo Nonato, 5,264 ......M 5
Senhor do Bonfim, 25,863 ......N 6
Serrinha, 16,754 ......N 6
Sobral, 51,064 ......M 4
Sorocaba, 165,990 ......L 8
Soure, 8,958 ......L 4
Taubaté, 98,933 ......L 8
Teresina, 181,071 ......M 5
Três Lagoas, 40,157 ......K 8
Trindade, 13,786 ......L 7
Tubarão, 51,121 ......L 9
Tucuruí, 5,549 ......L 4
Uberaba, 108,576 ......L 7
Uberlândia, 110,463 ......L 7
União da Vitória, 14,445 ......J 9
Uruana, 5,194 ......L 7
Uruguaiana, 60,667 ......J 9
Valença, 21,531 ......N 6
Varginha, 36,447 ......L 8
Veranópolis, 5,457 ......K 9
Viana, 5,986 ......M 4
Vigia, 10,231 ......L 4
Vitória, 121,978 ......N 8
Vitória da Conquista, 82,477 ......M 7
Volta Redonda, 120,645 ......M 8
Xique-Xique, 9,998 ......M 6

OTHER FEATURES

Acre (river) ......G 5
Amazon (Amazonas) (river) ......J 4
Araguaia (river) ......L 6
Aripuanã (river) ......H 5
Bandeira, Pico da (mt.) ......M 8
Branco (river) ......H 3
Caatingas (forest) ......M 5
Campos (plain) ......M 7
Frio (cape) ......M 8
Grande, Rio (river) ......L 7
Iguassú (falls) ......J 9
Itapecuru (river) ......M 4
Japurá (river) ......G 4
Javari (river) ......F 5
Jequitinhonha (river) ......N 7
Juruá (river) ......G 5
Madeira (river) ......H 5
Mantiqueira, Serra da (mts.) ......L 8
Mar, Serra do (mts.) ......L 8
Marajó (isl.), 147,895 ......L 4
Mato Grosso, Planalto de (plateau) ......K 7
Negro (river) ......H 4
Pacaraima, Serra (mts.) ......H 3
Paraguai (river) ......J 7
Parecis, Serra dos (mts.) ......H 6
Parnaíba (river) ......M 4
Patos, Lagôa dos (lagoon) K10
Roosevelt (river) ......H 5
Santa Catarina (isl.), 138,556 ......L 9
São Francisco (river) ......N 6
São Roque (cape) ......O 4
São Sebastião (isl.), 5,724 ......L 8
São Tomé (cape) ......N 8
Selvas (forest) ......H 5
Sertão (reg.) ......M 5
Solimões (river) ......G 4
Tapajós (river) ......J 5
Tocantins (river) ......L 5
Todos-os-Santos (bay) ......N 6
Tumucumaque, Serra de (mts.) ......J 3
Uruguai (river) ......J 9
Xingu (river) ......K 5

CHILE

CITIES and TOWNS

Ancud, 11,900 ......F
Antofagasta, 137,968 ......F
Arauco, 5,400 ......F
Arica, 87,700 ......F
Calama, 45,900 ......G
Calbuco, *21,673 ......F
Caldera, *3,268 ......F
Cañete, 7,900 ......F
Castro, 11,200 ......F
Cauquenes, 20,200 ......F
Chañaral, *36,349 ......F
Chillán, 87,600 ......F
Chuquicamata, 22,100 ......G
Concepción, 196,317 ......F
Constitución, 11,500 ......F
Copiapó, 45,200 ......F
Coquimbo, 52,100 ......F
Corral, *5,533 ......F
Curacautín, 9,800 ......F
Illapel, 12,200 ......F
Iquique, 64,500 ......F
La Serena, 61,900 ......F
La Unión, 15,200 ......F
Lebu, 12,500 ......F
Linares, 37,900 ......F
Los Ángeles, 49,500 ......F
Los Vilos, *10,453 ......F
Lota, 48,100 ......F
Mejillones, *3,333 ......F
Mulchén, 13,700 ......F
Nueva Imperial, 8,000 ......F
Osorno, 68,800 ......F
Ovalle, 31,700 ......F
Parral, 17,000 ......F
Potrerillos, 5,800 ......G
Pueblo Hundido, 6,200 ......F
Puerto Aisén, 7,100 ......F
Puerto Montt, 62,700 ......F
Puerto Natales, 11,500 ......F
Puerto Varas, 10,900 ......F
Punta Arenas, 61,800 ......F
Quirihue, *11,178 ......F
Rancagua, 86,500 ......F
San Fernando, 27,600 ......F
Santiago (cap.), 2,661,920 ......F
Santiago (cap.), ‡3,236,900 ......F
Talca, 94,400 ......F
Talcahuano, 115,568 ......F
Taltal, 6,400 ......G
Temuco, 104,372 ......F
Tocopilla, 22,000 ......F
Traiguén, 11,400 ......F
Valdivia, 82,300 ......F
Vallenar, 26,800 ......F
Valparaíso, 292,847 ......F
Villarrica, 13,000 ......F
Viña del Mar, 153,085 ......F

OTHER FEATURES

Andes (mts.) ......F
Atacama (desert) ......G
Chiloé (isl.), 45,809 ......E
Chonos (arch.) ......F
Corcovado (gulf) ......F
Coronados (gulf) ......F
Horn (cape) ......G
Llullaillaco (volcano) ......G
Loa (river) ......G
Magellan (strait) ......F
Navarino (isl.), 436 ......G

Agriculture, Industry and Resources

AMUAY–PUNTA CARDÓN
Oil Refining

MEDELLÍN
Textiles, Clothing, Leather Goods

BOGOTÁ
Textiles, Leather Goods, Cement, Electrical Equipment

CARACAS
Textiles, Chemicals, Automobiles

CIUDAD GUAYANA
Iron & Steel, Aluminum

MAJOR MINERAL OCCURRENCES

Al Bauxite
Ag Silver
Au Gold
Be Beryl
C Coal
Cr Chromium
Cu Copper
D Diamonds
Em Emeralds
Fe Iron Ore
G Natural Gas
Hg Mercury
Id Iodine
Mi Mica
Mn Manganese
Mo Molybdenum
N Nitrates
Na Salt
Ni Nickel
O Petroleum
P Phosphates
Pb Lead
Pt Platinum
Q Quartz Crystal
S Sulfur
Sb Antimony
Sn Tin
U Uranium
V Vanadium
W Tungsten
Zn Zinc

⚡ Water Power
▨ Major Industrial Areas

LIMA–CALLAO
Textiles, Chemicals, Leather Goods

CÓRDOBA
Automobiles, Aircraft, Food Processing, Chemicals, Cement

SANTIAGO–VALPARAÍSO
Textiles, Chemicals, Food Processing, Metal Products, Oil Refining, Leather Goods

CONCEPCIÓN
Iron & Steel, Food Processing, Textiles, Oil Refining

BELO HORIZONTE
Iron & Steel, Textiles, Cement, Metal Products

RIO DE JANEIRO
Iron & Steel, Chemicals, Food Processing, Textiles, Glass Products, Cement, Oil Refining

SÃO PAULO–SANTOS
Food Processing, Textiles, Chemicals, Iron & Steel, Machinery, Motor Vehicles, Oil Refining

BUENOS AIRES–ROSARIO
Food Processing, Textiles, Machinery, Shipbuilding, Oil Refining, Chemicals

DOMINANT LAND USE

Wheat, Livestock
Wheat, Corn, Livestock
Cereals, Livestock
Diversified Tropical Crops (chiefly plantation agriculture)
Truck Farming, Horticulture, Special Crops
Upland Cultivated Areas
Intensive Livestock Ranching
Upland Livestock Grazing, Limited Agriculture
Extensive Livestock-Ranching
Forests
Nonagricultural Land

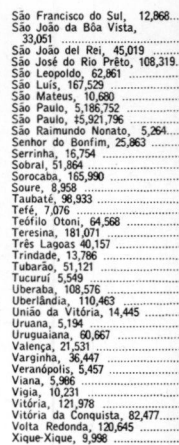
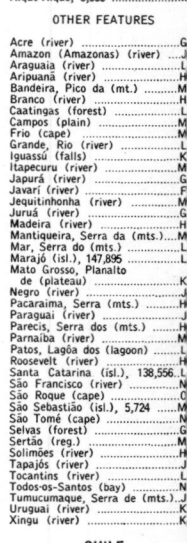

COLOMBIA (left column, continued)

'Higgins (lake) F13
ios del Salado (mt.) .....G 9
enas (pt.) E13
aitao (pen.) E13
erra del Fuego (isl.), 7,086.....G14

COLOMBIA
CITIES and TOWNS
guadas, 9,449 .....E 2
ntioquia, 7,072 .....E 2
auca, 4,280 .....E 2
rapel, 4,892 .....E 2
arbacoas, 4,653 .....E 3
acaramanga, 82,171 .....F 2
enaventura, 115,770 .....E 3
gua, 71,016 .....E 3
lamar, 5,923 .....E 1
i, 898,253 .....E 1
artagena, 289,649 .....E 1
iquinquirá, 37,504 .....F 2
icoa, 2,571 .....E 3
ompós, 14,120 .....E 2
onteria, 89,552 .....E 2
agatagima, 7,867 .....E 3
eiva, 105,595 .....E 3
amplona, 28,911 .....F 2
ereira, 174,902 .....E 3
erto Berrío, 19,258 .....E 2
erto Colombia, 9,479 .....E 1
erto Leguízamo, 3,014 .....E 4
erto Wilches, 5,088 .....E 2
sibdó, 27,318 .....E 2
pchacha, 19,469 .....F 1
an Marcos, 10,890 .....E 2
anta Marta, 126,719 .....E 1
antander, 13,625 .....E 3
orocejo, 73,465 .....E 2
ogamoso, 48,891 .....F 2
msón, 15,206 .....E 2
nja, 51,301 .....E 2
rbo, 13,424 .....F 1
bia, 10,072 .....F 1
llavicencio, 60,211 .....F 3
urumal, 18,849 .....E 2

OTHER FEATURES
o Ritacuva (mt.) .....F 2
aporis (river) .....F 4
quetá (river) .....F 4
asanare (river) .....F 2
uca (river) .....E 2
ntral, Cordillera (mts.) .....E 2
uainía (river) .....G 3
ajira (pen.) .....F 1
aviare (river) .....F 3
uila (mt.) .....E 3
rida (river) .....E 3
agdalena (river) .....E 2
eta (river) .....F 2
ccidental, Cordillera (mts.) .....E 2
iental, Cordillera (mts.) .....F 2
inoco, Llanos del (plain) .....F 2
lima (mt.) .....E 3
utumayo (river) .....E 4
chada (river) .....F 3

ECUADOR
CITIES and TOWNS
ausí, 7,155 .....E 4
abato, 77,052 .....E 4
ogues, 10,939 .....E 4
banoyo, 28,345 .....D 4
ría de Caráquez, 11,327 .....D 4
ica, 3,091 .....D 4
meraldas, 30,612 .....E 4
randa, 11,387 .....E 4
ayaquil, 814,064 .....D 4
rra, 41,057 .....E 4
ijapa, 19,719 .....D 4
tacunga, 22,106 .....E 4
chala, 47,268 .....D 4
chala, 68,379 .....D 4
avalo, 20,822 .....E 4
rtoviejo, 59,404 .....D 4
to (cap.), 597,133 .....E 4
ambo, 58,029 .....E 4
omas, 12,243 .....D 4
nta Elena, 7,762 .....D 4
nta Rosa, 18,846 .....D 4
cán, 24,443 .....E 4
acao, 2,700 .....D 4

OTHER FEATURES
imborazo (mt.) .....E 4
topaxi (mt.) .....E 4
ayaquil (gulf) .....D 4
rona (river) .....D 4
ccidental, Cordillera (mts.) .....E 4
staza (river) .....E 4
al, Cordillera (mts.) .....E 4
ntiago (river) .....E 4

FALKLAND ISLANDS
CITIES and TOWNS
tanley (cap.), 1,079 .....J14

OTHER FEATURES
st Falkland (isl.), 1,577 .....J14
kland (sound) H14
kland (isl.), 380 .....H14

FRENCH GUIANA
CITIES and TOWNS
Cayenne (cap.), 19,668 .....K 2
Saint-Laurent-du-Maroni, 3,486..K 2
Sinnamary, 1,355 .....J 2

OTHER FEATURES
Devils (isl.) .....K 2
Maroni (river) .....K 3
Oyapock (river) .....K 3

GUYANA
CITIES and TOWNS
Bartica, 2,352 .....J 2
Georgetown (cap.), ‡195,250 .....J 2
Mackenzie, 130,000 .....J 2
Mahaica, 8,646 .....J 2
New Amsterdam, 20,000 .....J 2
Rosignol, 1,204 .....J 2

OTHER FEATURES
Courantyne (river) .....J 3
Cuyuni (river) .....H 2
Essequibo (river) .....J 2
Kaieteur (falls) .....J 2
Mazaruni (river) .....J 2
Roraima (mt.) .....H 2
Rupununi (river) .....J 3

PARAGUAY
CITIES and TOWNS
Asunción (cap.), 392,753 .....J 9
Asunción, ‡563,681 .....J 9
Caacupú, 1,400 .....J 9
Caazapá, 3,117 .....J 9
Carapeguá, 3,416 .....J 9
Concepción, 19,200 .....J 8
Encarnación, 23,343 .....J 9
Fuerte Olimpo, 3,061 .....J 8
General Artigas, 3,547 .....J 9

(next column)
Horqueta, 4,240 .....J 8
Luque, 13,932 .....J 9
Mariscal Estigarribia, 1,508 .....H 8
Paraguarí, 5,036 .....J 9
Pilar, 12,440 .....J 9
San Pedro, 3,158 .....J 9
Tacuarupucú, 2,881 .....J 9
Villarrica, 17,448 .....J 9

OTHER FEATURES
Gran Chaco (reg.) .....H 8
Paraguay (river) .....J 9
Paraná (river) .....K 9
Pilcomayo (river) .....H 8

PERU
CITIES and TOWNS
Abancay, 12,172 .....F 6
Arequipa, 304,653 .....F 7
Ascope, 4,763 .....E 5
Atico, 3,053 .....F 7
Ayacucho, 34,593 .....F 6
Cajamarca, 37,608 .....E 5
Callao, ‡296,220 .....E 6
Camaná, 10,121 .....F 7
Cañete, 19,155 .....D 5
Catacaos, 19,155 .....D 5
Cerro de Pasco, 47,178 .....E 6
Chachapoyas, 10,418 .....E 5
Chiclayo, 189,685 .....E 5
Chimbote, 159,045 .....E 5
Chincha Alta, 26,785 .....E 6
Contamaná, 5,088 .....F 5
Coracora, 4,506 .....F 6
Cuzco, 120,881 .....F 6
Huacho, 36,203 .....E 6
Huancavelica, 15,916 .....E 6
Huancayo, 115,693 .....E 6
Huánuco, 41,123 .....E 6
Huarás, 29,719 .....E 5
Ica, 73,883 .....E 6
Ilo, 21,551 .....F 7
Iquitos, 111,327 .....F 4
Jaén, 13,912 .....E 5
Jauja, 13,936 .....E 6
Juli, 5,398 .....G 7

(next column)
Juliaca, 38,475 .....F 6
La Oroya, 25,906 .....E 6
Lima (cap.), 2,836,374 .....E 6
Lima, ‡3,317,648 .....E 6
Lurín, 2,921 .....E 6
Mollendo, 15,373 .....F 7
Moquegua, 16,959 .....F 7
Moyobamba, 10,004 .....E 5
Nasca, 21,025 .....F 6
Nauta, 3,768 .....F 4
Pacasmayo, 15,381 .....D 5
Paita, 14,875 .....D 5
Pimentel, 7,742 .....D 5
Pisco, 41,429 .....E 6
Piura, 126,702 .....D 5
Pucallpa, 57,525 .....E 5
Puerto Etén, 2,521 .....E 5
Puerto Maldonado, 6,419 .....G 6
Puno, 41,166 .....F 7
Requena, 7,300 .....F 5
Salaverry, 5,316 .....E 5
San Ramón, 1,956 .....E 6
Sicuani, 12,956 .....F 6
Sullana, 60,112 .....D 4
Supe, 15,623 .....E 6
Tacna, 55,752 .....F 7
Talara, 29,864 .....D 4
Tarma, 26,100 .....E 6
Trujillo, 241,882 .....D 5
Tumbes, 32,972 .....D 4

OTHER FEATURES
Aguja (point) .....D 5
Altiplano (plateau) .....F 7
Apurímac (river) .....F 6
Central, Cordillera (mts.) .....E 5
Huascarán (mt.) .....E 5
Madre de Dios (river) .....G 6
Marañón (river) .....E 4
Misti, El (mt.) .....F 7
Montaña, La (reg.) .....F 5
Napo (river) .....E 4
Occidental, Cordillera (mts.) .....E 5
Oriental, Cordillera (mts.) .....E 5
Paracas (pen.), 1,213 .....E 6
Putumayo (river) .....F 4
Real, Cordillera (mts.) .....F 6
Sechura (bay) .....D 5

(next column)
Titicaca (lake) .....F 7
Ucayali (river) .....F 5
Urubamba (river) .....F 6
Vilcanota (mt.) .....F 6

SURINAM
CITIES and TOWNS
Albina, 1,000 .....K 3
Moengo, 2,100 .....K 3
Nieuw-Nickerie, 7,400 .....K 2
Paramaribo (cap.), 135,000 .....K 2
Totness, 1,300 .....J 2

OTHER FEATURES
Coeroeni (river) .....J 3
Tapanahoni (river) .....J 3

URUGUAY
CITIES and TOWNS
Artigas, 23,781 .....J10
Bella Unión, 4,955 .....J10
Canelones, 14,180 .....J10
Carmelo, 12,707 .....J10
Colonia, 12,839 .....J10
Dolores, 12,466 .....J10
Durazno, 22,495 .....J10
Florida, 20,923 .....J10
Fray Bentos, 20,755 .....J10
Juan L. Lacaze, 11,022 .....J10
Maldonado, 15,361 .....K10
Melo, 33,378 .....K10
Mercedes, 31,352 .....J10
Minas, 31,386 .....K10
Montevideo (cap.), ‡1,500,000 .....J11
Paso de los Toros 11,008 .....J10
Paysandú, 52,472 .....J10
Rivera, 41,263 .....J10
Rocha, 19,063 .....K10
Salto, 57,956 .....J10
San José, 27,478 .....J10

(next column)
Tacuarembó, 29,056 .....J10
Treinta y Tres, 22,422 .....K10
Trinidad, 15,460 .....J10

OTHER FEATURES
Mirim (lagoon) K10
Negro (river) J10
Plata, Río de la (estuary) J11
Uruguay (river) .....J 9

VENEZUELA
CITIES and TOWNS
Altagracia, 21,084 .....F 1
Aragua de Barcelona, 9,614 .....H 2
Barcelona, 76,410 .....H 2
Barinas, 56,329 .....G 2
Barquisimeto, 334,333 .....G 1
Caicara, 10,804 .....G 2
Calabozo, 37,262 .....G 2
Caracas (cap.), 1,035,499 .....G 1
Caracas, ‡2,183,935 .....G 1
Carora, 36,115 .....F 1
Carúpano, 50,935 .....H 1
Ciudad Bolívar, 103,728 .....H 2
Ciudad Guayana, 143,240 .....H 2
Coro, 68,701 .....G 1
Cumaná, 119,751 .....H 1
El Callao, 6,113 .....H 2
El Tigre, 49,801 .....H 2
El Tocuyo, 24,065 .....G 2
Encontrados, 12,502 .....F 2
Guanare, 37,715 .....G 2
La Asunción, 6,334 .....H 1
La Grita, 23,371 .....F 2
La Guaira, 20,344 .....G 1
La Urbana, 2,538 .....G 2
Maracaibo, 650,002 .....F 1
Maracaibo, ‡677,122 .....F 1
Maracay, 255,134 .....G 1
Maturín, 121,662 .....H 2
Mérida, 74,214 .....F 2
Nirgua, 21,009 .....G 1
Ocumare, 24,229 .....G 1

(next column)
Puerto Ayacucho, 10,417 .....G 3
Puerto Cabello, 73,360 .....G 1
Puerto Cumarebo, 13,339 .....G 1
Puerto La Cruz, 63,276 .....H 1
Río Caribe, 21,387 .....H 1
Río Chico, 8,356 .....G 1
San Carlos, 21,029 .....G 2
San Cristóbal, 152,239 .....F 2
San Felipe, 43,801 .....G 1
San Fernando, 38,960 .....G 2
San Fernando de Atabapo, ...G 3
Tinaquillo, 18,552 .....G 2
Trujillo, 25,921 .....F 2
Tucacas, 7,738 .....G 1
Tucupita, 21,417 .....H 2
Valencia, 367,154 .....G 1
Valle de la Pascua, 36,809 .....G 2
Villa de Cura, 27,632 .....G 2

OTHER FEATURES
Angel (fall) .....H 2
Apure (river) .....G 2
Apure (river) .....G 2
Bolívar (mt.) .....F 2
Caroní (river) .....H 2
Casiquiare, Brazo (river) .....G 3
Cojedes (river) .....G 2
Guayana Guayana (plain) .....F 2
Margarita (isl.), 113,967 .....H 1
Mérida, Cordillera de (mts.) .....F 2
Orinoco (river) .....H 2
Orinoco, Llanos del (plain) .....G 2
Paraguaná (pen.), 134,401 .....F 1
Paria (gulf) .....H 1
Roques, Los (isls.), 438 .....G 1
Serpents Mouth (strait) .....H 2
Tortuga, La (isl.), 25 .....H 1
Venezuela (gulf) .....F 1

*Population of commune.
‡City and suburbs.
†Population of municipality.

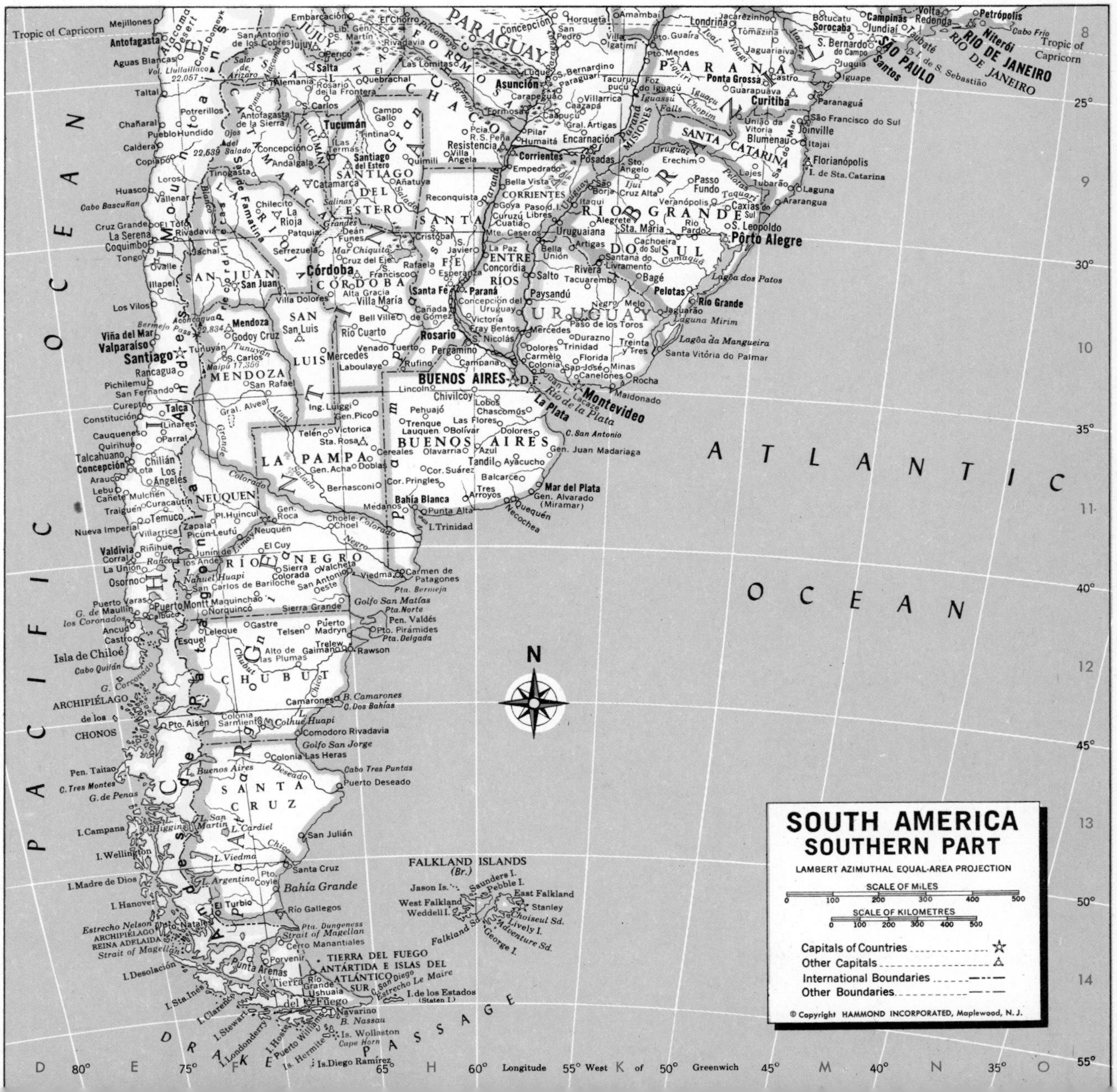

SOUTH AMERICA SOUTHERN PART
LAMBERT AZIMUTHAL EQUAL-AREA PROJECTION

SCALE OF MILES
0 100 200 300 400 500

SCALE OF KILOMETRES
0 100 200 300 400 500

Capitals of Countries .... ☆
Other Capitals .... △
International Boundaries .... _____
Other Boundaries .... _____

© Copyright HAMMOND INCORPORATED, Maplewood, N.J.

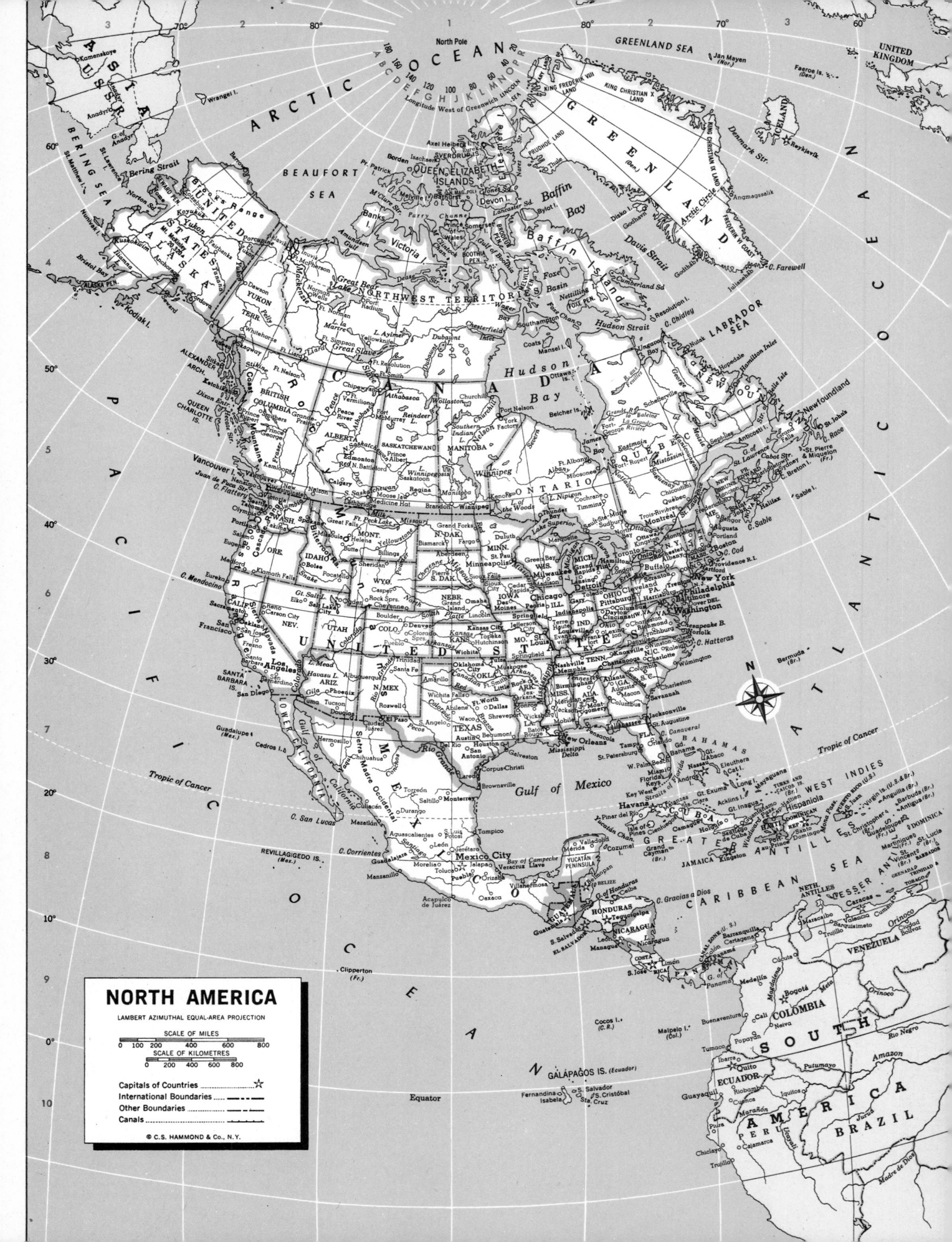

POPULATION DISTRIBUTION

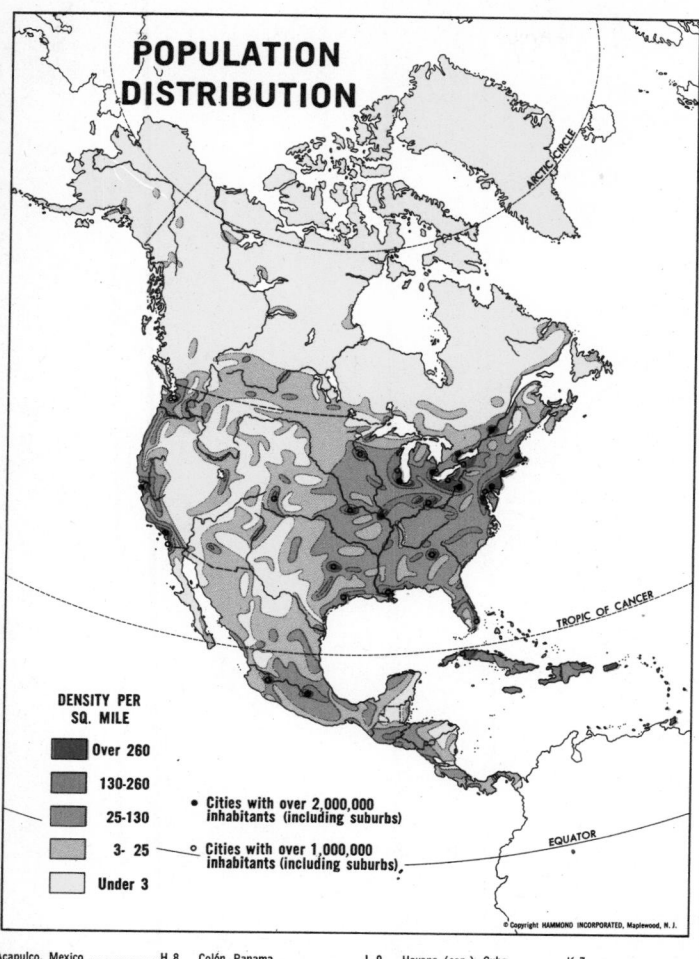

AREA 9,363,000 sq. mi.
POPULATION 314,000,000
LARGEST CITY New York
HIGHEST POINT Mt. McKinley 20,320 ft.
LOWEST POINT Death Valley 282 ft.

DENSITY PER SQ. MILE

- Over 260
- 130-260
- 25-130
- 3- 25
- Under 3

● Cities with over 2,000,000 inhabitants (including suburbs)
○ Cities with over 1,000,000 inhabitants (including suburbs)

VEGETATION

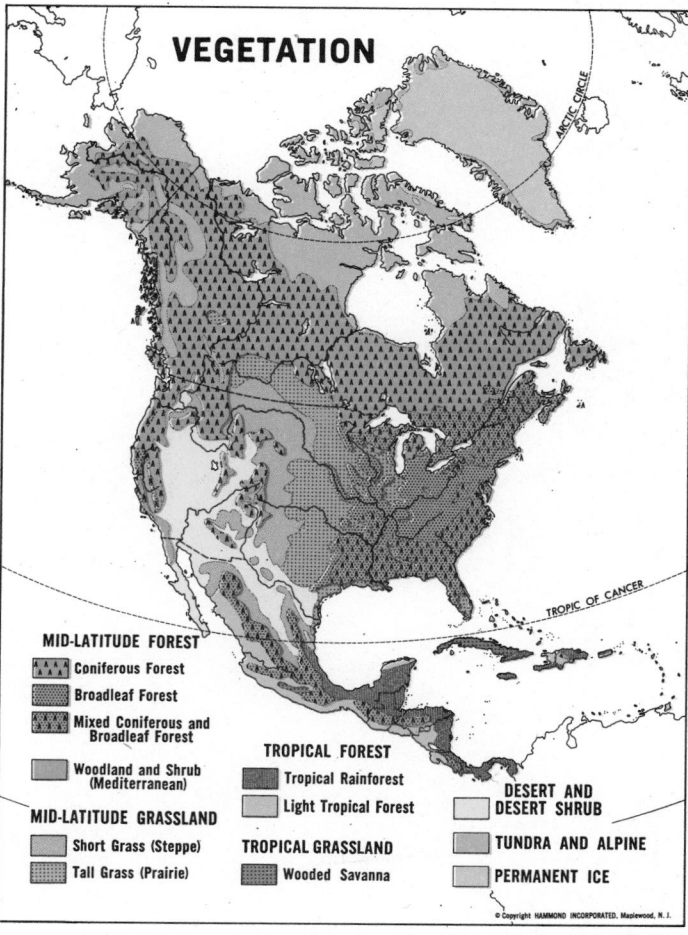

MID-LATITUDE FOREST
- Coniferous Forest
- Broadleaf Forest
- Mixed Coniferous and Broadleaf Forest
- Woodland and Shrub (Mediterranean)

MID-LATITUDE GRASSLAND
- Short Grass (Steppe)
- Tall Grass (Prairie)

TROPICAL FOREST
- Tropical Rainforest
- Light Tropical Forest

TROPICAL GRASSLAND
- Wooded Savanna

DESERT AND DESERT SHRUB

TUNDRA AND ALPINE

PERMANENT ICE

CANADA

SCALE

0 50 100 200 300 400 500MI.

0 50 100 200 300 400 500 KM.

Capitals of Countries.................★
Provincial & Territorial Capitals....△
International Boundaries............—·—·—
Provincial Boundaries..............—··—··—
Canals

© C.S. HAMMOND & Co., N.Y.

Abitibi (lake), Ont. ....H 6	Cape Breton (isl.), N.S., 162,989 ....K 6	Ellesmere (isl.), N.W.T. ....N 3	Hamilton, Ont., †498,523 .....H 7
Aklavik, N.W.T., 677 ....C 2	Englehart, Ont., 1,721 ....H 6	Hanna, Alta., 2,545 ....E 5
Albany (river), Ont. ....H 5	Carberry (res.), Que. ....H 6	Eskimo Point, N.W.T., 598 ....G 3	Harbour Grace, Newf., 2,771 ..L 6
Alberta (prov.), 1,838,037 .....E 5	Carman, Man., 2,030 ....G 6	Estevan, Sask., 9,150 ....F 6	Havre-Saint-Pierre, Que., 2,998..K 5
Amherst, N.S., 9,966 ....K 6	Chandler, Que., 3,843 ....K 6	Eston, Sask., 1,418 ....E 5	Hay River, N.W.T., 2,406 .....D 3
Amos, Que., 6,984 ....J 6	Channel-Port aux Basques, Newf., 5,942 ....L 6	Fernie, B.C., 4,422 ....E 6	Hearst, Ont., 3,501 ....H 6
Anticosti (isl.), Que., 419 .....K 5	Chapleau, Ont., 3,389 ....H 6	Finlay (river), B.C. ....D 4	High River, Alta., 2,676 ......E 5
Athabasca, Alta., 1,765 ....E 5	Charlottetown (cap.), P.E.I., 19,133 ....K 6	Flin Flon, Man.-Sask., 9,344 ..F 4	Hope, B.C., 3,153 ....D 6
Athabasca (lake) ....F 4	Chatham, N.B., 7,833 ....K 6	Fogo (isl.), Newf., 4,094 ......L 6	Hull, Que., 63,580 ....J 6
Athabasca (river), Alta. ....E 4	Chibougamau, Que., 9,701 ....J 2	Fort-Chimo, Que., 693 ....K 4
Atikokan, Ont., 6,087 ....G 6	Chicoutimi, Que., 33,893 .....J 6	Fort Frances, Ont., 9,947 .....G 6	Humboldt, Sask., 3,881 ....F 5
Axel Heiberg (isl.), N.W.T. ....N 3	Chicoutimi-Jonquière, 1133,703	Fort-George, Que., 1,280 .....J 5	Indian Head, Sask., 1,810 ....F 5
Baffin (bay) ....J 1	Chidley (cape) ....K 3	Fort Macleod, Alta., 2,715 ....E 6	Inuvik, N.W.T., 2,669 ....F 2
Baffin (isl.), N.W.T. ....J 2	Chilliwack, B.C., 9,135 ....D 6	Fort McMurray, Alta., 6,847 ..E 4	Inverness, N.S., 1,846 ....K 6
Banff, Alta., 3,219 ....E 5	Churchill, Man., 973 ....G 4	Fort McPherson, N.W.T., 679 ..C 2	Iroquois Falls, Ont., 7,271 ....H 6
Banff National Park, Alta., 3,532 ....E 5	Churchill (falls), Newf. ....K 5	Fort Nelson, B.C., 2,289 ......D 4	Jasper, Alta., 2,932 ....E 5
Banks (isl.), N.W.T. ....E 1	Coast (mts.) ....C 4	Fort Providence, N.W.T., 587 ..E 3	Jasper Nat'l Park, Alta., 3,064..E 5
Baskatong (res.), Que. ....J 6	Cobalt, Ont., 2,197 ....H 6	Fort Resolution, N.W.T., 623 ..E 3	Jonquière, Que., 28,430 ....J 6
Bathurst, N.B., 16,674 ....K 6	Cochrane, Ont., 4,965 ....H 6	Fort Saskatchewan, Alta., 5,726..E 5	Juan de Fuca (strait), B.C. ....D 6
Battleford, Sask., 1,803 ....E 5	Coleman, Alta., 1,534 ....E 6	Fort Simpson, N.W.T., 747 ....D 3	Kamloops, B.C., 26,168 ....D 5
Belle Isle (strait), Newf. ......L 5	Columbia (river), B.C. ....D 5	Fort Smith, N.W.T., 2,364 ....E 3	Kamsack, Sask., 2,783 ....F 5
Biggar, Sask., 2,607 ....E 5	Coppermine, N.W.T., 637 .....E 2	Foxe (basin), N.W.T. ....J 2	Kane (basin), N.W.T. ....M 1
Blind River, Ont., 3,450 ....H 6	Corner Brook, Newf., 26,309 ..L 6	Franklin (dist.), N.W.T., 7,747..H 1	Kapuskasing, Ont., 12,834 ....H 6
Boissevain, Man., 1,506 ....G 6	Cornwall, Ont., 47,116 ....J 6	Fraser (river), B.C. ....D 5	Keewatin (dist.), N.W.T., 3,403..G 3
Bonavista, Newf., 4,215 ....L 6	Courtenay, B.C., 7,152 ....D 6	Fredericton (cap.), N.B., 24,254..K 6	Kelowna, B.C., 19,412 ....D 6
Boothia (pen.), N.W.T. ....G 1	Cranbrook, B.C., 12,000 ......E 6	Frobisher Bay, N.W.T., 2,014 ..K 3	Kenora, Ont., 10,952 ....G 6
Bow (river), Alta. ....E 5	Cree (lake), Sask. ....F 4	Fundy (bay) ....K 7	Killarney, Man., 2,074 ....G 6
Brandon, Man., 31,150 ....F 6	Dartmouth, N.S., 64,770 ......K 6	Gagnon, Que., 3,787 ....K 5	Kindersley, Sask., 3,451 ......E 5
Bridgewater, N.S., 5,231 ......K 7	Dauphin, Man., 8,891 ....F 5	Gander, Newf., 7,748 ....L 6	Kingston, Ont., 59,047 ....J 7
British Columbia (prov.), 2,466,608 ....D 4	Davis (strait), N.W.T. ....K 1	Geraldton, Ont., 3,178 ....H 6	Kirkland Lake, Ont., 13,599 ...H 6
Burns Lake, B.C., 1,259 ....D 4	Dawson, Yukon, 762 ....C 2	Glace Bay, N.S., 22,440 ......L 6	Kitimat, B.C., 11,824 ....C 5
Cabot (strait) ....L 6	Devon (isl.), N.W.T. ....M 3	Goose Bay, Newf., 496 ....L 5	Kluane (lake), Yukon ....C 3
Calgary, Alta., †403,319 .....E 5	Didsbury, Alta., 1,821 ....E 5	Gouin (res.), Que. ....J 6	Kootenay (lake), B.C. ....E 6
Callander, Ont., 1,190 ....H 6	Drumheller, Alta., 5,446 ......E 5	Grand Falls, Newf., 7,677 .....L 6	Labrador (reg.), Newf., 28,166..K 4
Cambridge Bay, N.W.T., 716 ..F 2	Edmonton (cap.), Alta., †495,702	Grande Prairie, Alta., 13,079 ..E 4	Labrador (sea) ....L 4
Campbellton, N.B., 10,335 ....K 6	Edmundston, N.B., 12,365 ....K 6	Great Bear (lake), N.W.T. .....D 2	Lac La Biche, Alta., 1,791 .....E 5
Camrose, Alta., 8,673 ....E 5	Edson, Alta., 3,818 ....E 5	Great Slave (lake), N.W.T. ....E 3	Lacombe, Alta., 3,436 ....E 5
Cap-Chat, Que., 3,868 ....J 6		Guelph, Ont., 60,087 ....H 7	Lake Louise, Alta., 165 ....E 5
		Halifax (cap.), N.S., 1,222,637..K 7	Lancaster (sound), N.W.T. .....H 1
			La Sarre, Que., 5,185 ....J 6
			La Tuque, Que., 13,099 ....J 6

Leduc, Alta., 4,000 ....E 5	Nelson (river), Man. ....G 4	Prince Edward Island (prov.), 118,229 ....K 6
Lesser Slave (lake), Alta. ......E 4	Newcastle, N.B., 6,460 ....K 6	Prince George, B.C., 33,101 ...D 5
Lethbridge, Alta., 41,217 ......E 6	New Brunswick (prov.), 677,250..K 6	Prince Patrick (isl.), N.W.T. ...E 1
Liard (river) ....D 3	Newfoundland (prov.), 557,725..L 5	Prince Rupert, B.C., 15,747 ...C 5
Lloydminster, Alta.-Sask., 8,691..E 5	Newfoundland (isl.), 493,938 ..L 6	Québec (prov.), 6,234,445 .....J 5
Lilloooet, B.C., 1,514 ....D 5	New Liskeard, Ont., 5,488 ....H 6	Québec (cap.), Que., 1480,502..J 6
Logan (mt.), Yukon ....B 3	New Westminster, B.C., 42,835..D 6	Queen Charlotte (isls.), B.C., 2,390 ....C 5
London, Ont., †286,011 ....H 7	Niagara Falls, Ont., 67,163 ...J 7
Lunenburg, N.S., 3,215 ....K 7	Nipigon, Ont., 2,141 ....H 6	Queen Elizabeth (isls.), N.W.T..M 3
Mackenzie (river), N.W.T. .....D 2	Noranda, Que., 10,741 ....J 6	Quesnel, B.C., 6,252 ....D 5
Mackenzie (dist.) N.W.T. ......D 2	North Battleford, Sask., 12,698..F 5	Race (cape), Newf. ....L 6
Magdalen (isls.), Que., 13,303..K 6	North Bay, Ont., 49,187 ......J 6	Radville, Sask., 1,024 ....F 6
Manicouagan (riv.), Que. ......K 5	North Magnetic Pole ....F 1	Rae-Edzo, N.W.T., 1,081 .....D 3
Manitoba (prov.), 1,021,506 ...G 5	North Saskatchewan (river) ...E 5	Rainy (lake), Ont. ....G 6
Manitoba (lake), Man. ....G 5	North Vancouver, B.C., 31,847..D 6	Rainy River, Ont., 1,196 ......G 6
Manitoulin (isl.), Ont. ....H 6	Northwest Territories, 42,609 ..E 2	Ray (cape), Newf. ....L 6
Maple Creek, Sask., 2,268 ....F 6	Nottawasaga (riv.), Ont. ......J 5	Raymond, Alta., 2,156 ....E 6
Marathon, Ont., 2,456 ....H 6	Nova Scotia (prov.), 828,571 ..K 7	Red Deer, Alta., 27,674 ......E 5
Mattawa, Ont., 2,881 ....J 6	Okanagan (lake), B.C. ....D 6	Regina (cap.), Sask., 1140,734..F 5
Mayo, Yukon, 381 ....C 2	Ontario (prov.), 8,264,465 .....H 5	Reindeer (lake) ....F 4
1Clintock (chan.), N.W.T. .....F 1	Ottawa (cap.), Canada, 302,341..J 6	Renfrew, Ont., 9,173 ....J 6
Medicine Hat, Alta., 26,518 ...E 5	Ottawa (river) ....J 6	Revelstoke, B.C., 4,867 ....E 5
Melfort, Sask., 4,725 ....F 5	Ottawa (river)	Riding Mtn. Nat'l Park, Man., 158 ....F 5
Melville, Sask., 5,375 ....F 5	Owen Sound, Ont., 18,469 ....H 7
Melville (isl.), N.W.T. ....E 1	Parry (chan.), N.W.T. ....E-H 1	Rimouski, Que., 26,887 ....K 6
Merritt, B.C., 5,289 ....D 5	Parry Sound, Ont., 5,842 .....J 6	Rivière-du-Loup, Que., 12,760..K 6
Minto (lake), Que. ....J 5	Peace (river) ....E 4	Roberval, Que., 8,330 ....J 6
Mistassini (river), Que. ....J 5	Peace River, Alta., 5,039 .....E 4	Robson (mt.), B.C. ....D 5
Mistassini (lake), Que. ....J 5	Peel (river) ....C 2	Rocky (mts.) ....D 4
Moncton, N.B., 47,891 ....K 6	Pelly (river), Yukon ....C 3	Rocky Mtn. House, Alta., 2,968..E 5
Mont-Joli, Que., 6,698 ....K 6	Pembroke, Ont., 16,544 ......J 6	Rosetown, Sask., 2,614 ....E 5
Mont-Laurier, Que., 8,240 ....J 6	Péribonca (river), Que. ....J 5	Rossland, B.C., 3,896 ....E 6
Montréal, Que., 12,743,208 ...J 6	Peterborough, Ont., 58,111 ...J 7	Rosthern, Sask., 1,431 ....F 5
Moose Jaw, Sask., 31,854 ....F 5	Pincher Creek, Alta., 3,227 ...E 6	Rouyn, Que., 17,821 ....J 6
Moosomin, Sask., 2,407 ......F 5	Portage la Prairie, Man., 12,950..G 5
Moosonee, Ont., 1,793 ....H 5	Port-Cartier, Que., 3,730 .....K 5	Sable (cape), N.S. ....K 7
Morden, Man., 3,266 ....G 6	Poste-de-la-Baleine, Que., 987..J 4	Sable (isl.), N.S., 147 ....L 7
Nanaimo, B.C., 14,948 ....D 6	Povungnituk, Que., 676 ....J 3	Saint Elias (mt.), Yukon ......B 3
Nares (strait), N.W.T. ....M 1	Prince Albert, Sask., 28,464 ..F 5	Saint John, N.B., 1106,744 ...K 6
Nelson, B.C., 9,400 ....E 6	Prince Albert Nat'l Park, Sask., 182 ....F 5	Saint John's (cap.), Newf., †131,814 ....L 6

AREA 3,851,809 sq. mi.
POPULATION 23,388,100
CAPITAL Ottawa
LARGEST CITY Montréal
HIGHEST POINT Mt. Logan 19,850 ft.
MONETARY UNIT Canadian dollar
MAJOR LANGUAGES English, French
MAJOR RELIGIONS Protestantism, Roman Catholicism

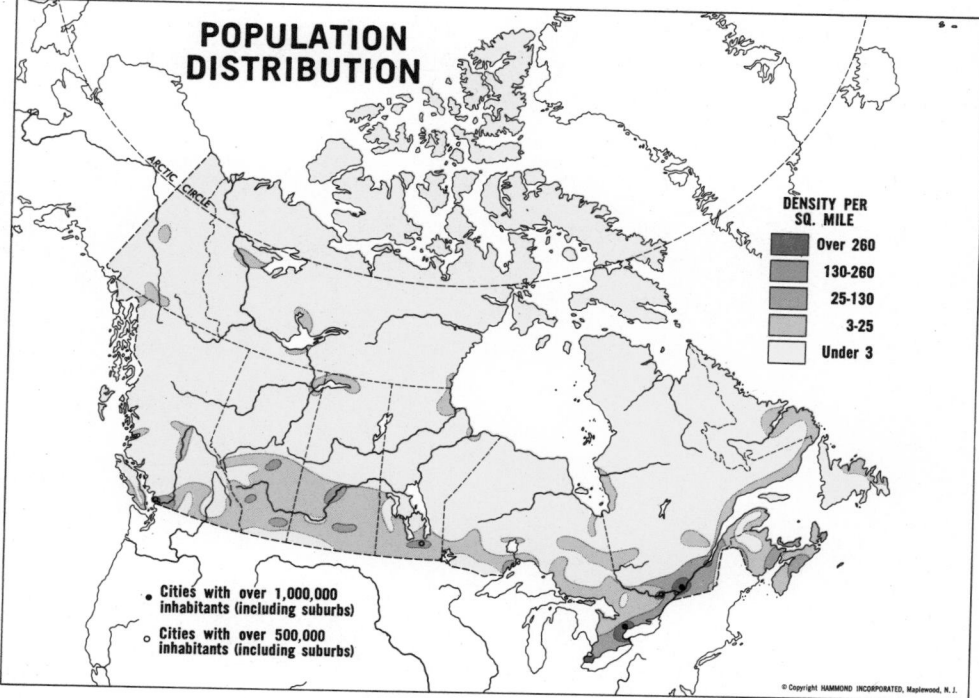

POPULATION DISTRIBUTION

DENSITY PER SQ. MILE

Over 260
130-260
25-130
3-25
Under 3

● Cities with over 1,000,000 inhabitants (including suburbs)
○ Cities with over 500,000 inhabitants (including suburbs)

© Copyright HAMMOND INCORPORATED, Maplewood, N.J.

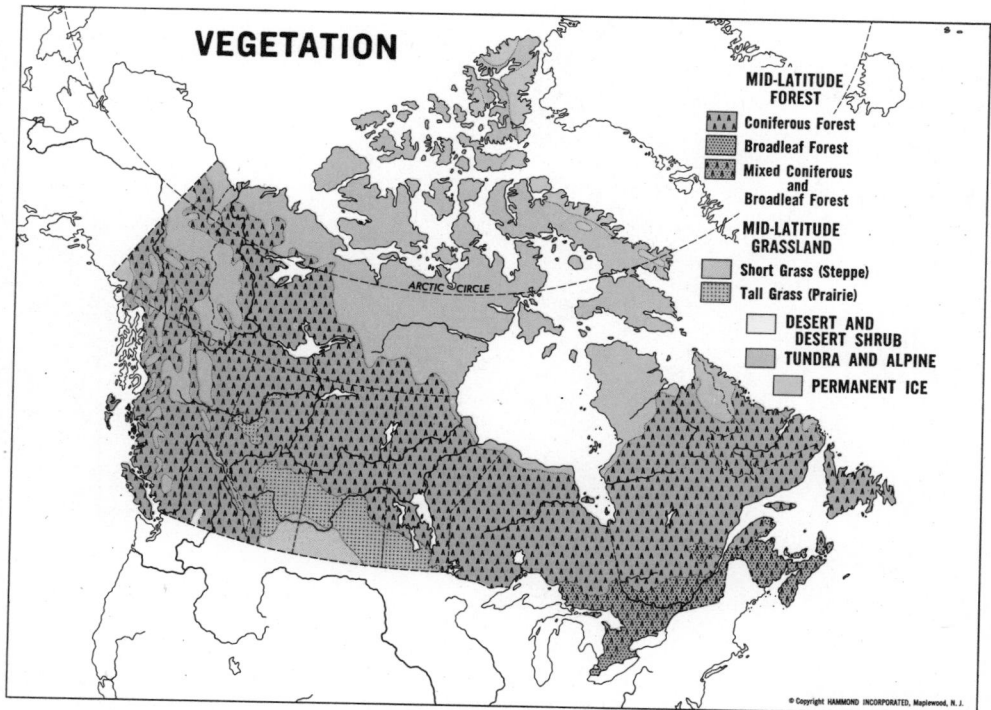

VEGETATION

MID-LATITUDE FOREST

Coniferous Forest
Broadleaf Forest
Mixed Coniferous and Broadleaf Forest

MID-LATITUDE GRASSLAND

Short Grass (Steppe)
Tall Grass (Prairie)

DESERT AND DESERT SHRUB
TUNDRA AND ALPINE
PERMANENT ICE

© Copyright HAMMOND INCORPORATED, Maplewood, N.J.

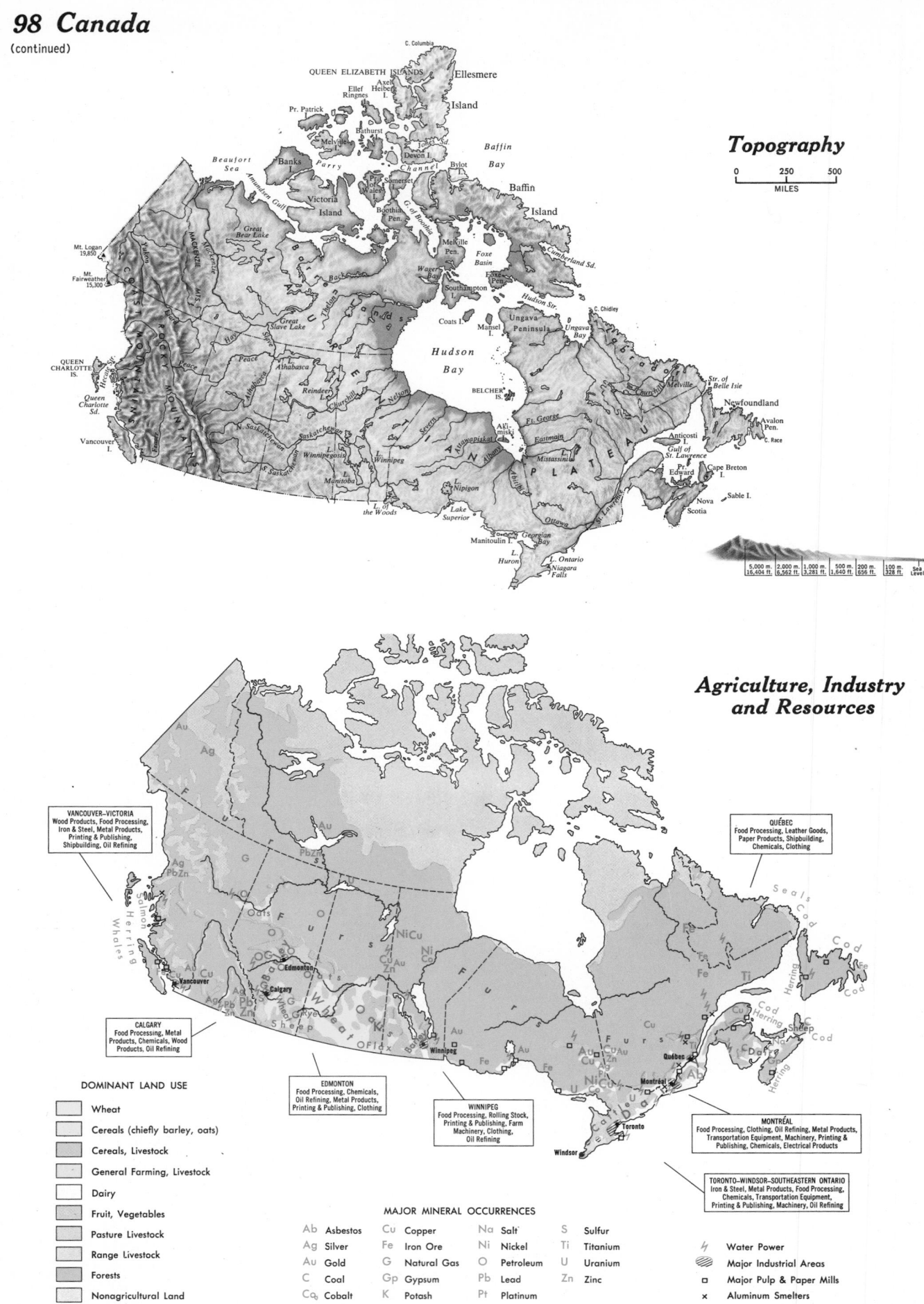

Topography

0   250   500
MILES

5,000 m.   2,000 m.   1,000 m.   500 m.   200 m.   100 m.   Sea   Below
16,404 ft. 6,562 ft. 3,281 ft. 1,640 ft. 656 ft. 328 ft. Level

Agriculture, Industry and Resources

VANCOUVER–VICTORIA
Wood Products, Food Processing,
Iron & Steel, Metal Products,
Printing & Publishing,
Shipbuilding, Oil Refining

CALGARY
Food Processing, Metal
Products, Chemicals, Wood
Products, Oil Refining

EDMONTON
Food Processing, Chemicals,
Oil Refining, Metal Products,
Printing & Publishing, Clothing

WINNIPEG
Food Processing, Rolling Stock,
Printing & Publishing, Farm
Machinery, Clothing,
Oil Refining

QUÉBEC
Food Processing, Leather Goods,
Paper Products, Shipbuilding,
Chemicals, Clothing

MONTRÉAL
Food Processing, Clothing, Oil Refining, Metal Products,
Transportation Equipment, Machinery, Printing &
Publishing, Chemicals, Electrical Products

TORONTO–WINDSOR–SOUTHEASTERN ONTARIO
Iron & Steel, Metal Products, Food Processing,
Chemicals, Transportation Equipment,
Printing & Publishing, Machinery, Oil Refining

DOMINANT LAND USE

- Wheat
- Cereals (chiefly barley, oats)
- Cereals, Livestock
- General Farming, Livestock
- Dairy
- Fruit, Vegetables
- Pasture Livestock
- Range Livestock
- Forests
- Nonagricultural Land

MAJOR MINERAL OCCURRENCES

Ab	Asbestos	Cu	Copper	Na	Salt	S	Sulfur
Ag	Silver	Fe	Iron Ore	Ni	Nickel	Ti	Titanium
Au	Gold	G	Natural Gas	O	Petroleum	U	Uranium
C	Coal	Gp	Gypsum	Pb	Lead	Zn	Zinc
Co	Cobalt	K	Potash	Pt	Platinum		

- ⚡ Water Power
- ▨ Major Industrial Areas
- ▫ Major Pulp & Paper Mills
- ✕ Aluminum Smelters

Newfoundland 99

AREA 156,185 sq. mi.
POPULATION 557,725
CAPITAL St. John's
LARGEST CITY St. John's
HIGHEST POINT Cirque Mtn. 5,160 ft.
SETTLED IN 1610
ADMITTED TO CONFEDERATION 1949
PROVINCIAL FLOWER Pitcher Plant

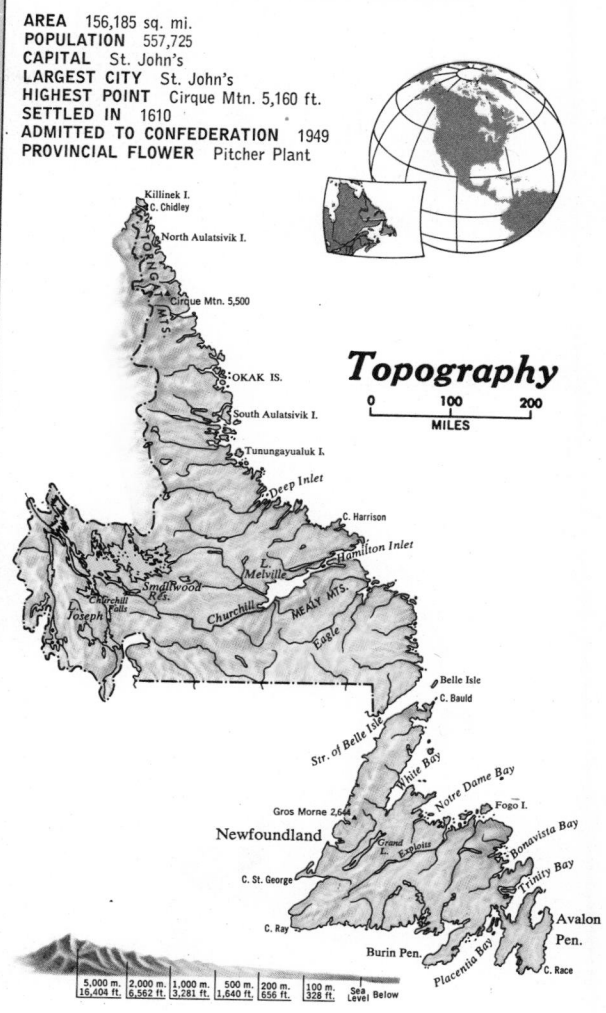

Topography

0 100 200
MILES

5,000 m. / 16,404 ft. | 2,000 m. / 6,562 ft. | 1,000 m. / 3,281 ft. | 500 m. / 1,640 ft. | 200 m. / 656 ft. | 100 m. / 328 ft. | Sea Level | Below

NEWFOUNDLAND
SCALE
0 10 20 40 60 80 100MI.
0 1020 40 60 80 100KM.
Provincial Capital...................⊛
Provincial Boundaries.........

© C.S. HAMMOND & Co., Maplewood, N.J.

Longitude   West of   Greenwich

LABRADOR
(PART OF NEWFOUNDLAND)
0   50   100   150 mi.

Agriculture, Industry and Resources

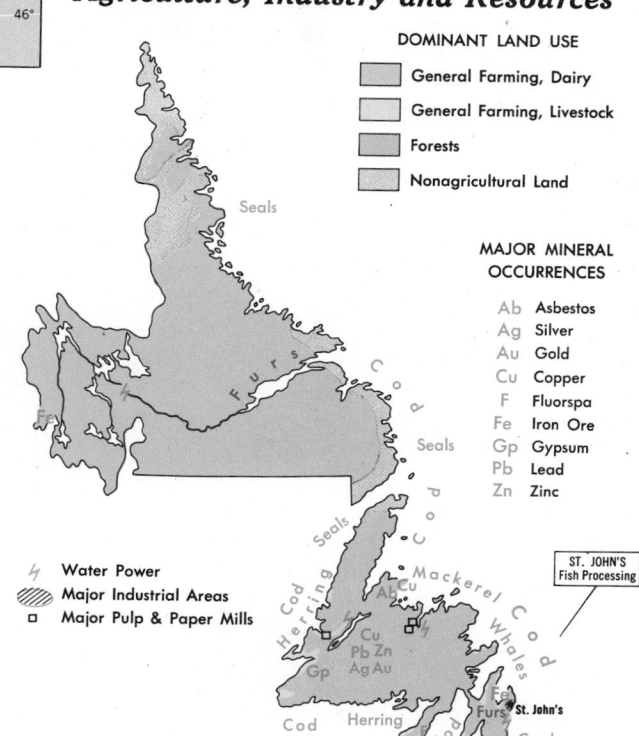

DOMINANT LAND USE
- General Farming, Dairy
- General Farming, Livestock
- Forests
- Nonagricultural Land

MAJOR MINERAL OCCURRENCES

Ab Asbestos
Ag Silver
Au Gold
Cu Copper
F   Fluorspa
Fe Iron Ore
Gp Gypsum
Pb Lead
Zn Zinc

ST. JOHN'S Fish Processing

⚡ Water Power
▨ Major Industrial Areas
□ Major Pulp & Paper Mills

CITIES and TOWNS

...adger, 1,187 ....B 3
...aie Verte, 2,397 ....B 1
...attle Harbour, 75 ....D 1
...ay Bulls, 1,011 ....D 4
...y de Verde, 826 ....D 3
...ay Roberts, 3,702 ....D 4
...elleoram, 530 ....C 4
...onavista, 4,215 ....D 3
...twood, 4,115 ....C 3
...anch, 516 ....D 4
...uchans, 1,907 ....B 3
...rgeo, 2,226 ....B 4
...urin, 2,586 ....C 4
...pe Broyle, 677 ....D 4
...rbonear, 4,732 ....D 4
...rmanville, 839 ....C 4
...rtwright, 752 ....B 1
...talina, 1,131 ....D 3
...342 ....A 4
...arenville, 2,193 ....C 3
...ok's Harbour, 325 ....B 2
...rner Brook, 26,309 ....A 3
...w Head, 501 ....A 3
...k's Cove, 797 ....B 3
...niel's Harbour, 415 ....A 2
...inlet, 193 ....D 1
...glee, 1,050 ....A 2
...er Lake, 4,421 ....B 3
...ryland, 716 ....D 4
...ur de Lys, 672 ....C 2
...wers Cove, 372 ....A 2
...go, 1,155 ....C 3
...teau, 312 ....B 2
...e Harbour, 214 ....C 1
...ncois, 220 ....A 4
...7,748 ....C 4
...nish, 618 ....C 4
...se Bay, 496 ....D 2
...nd Bank, 3,476 ....B 4
...nd Falls, 7,677 ....C 3
...at Harbour Deep, 329 .....D 2
...enspond, 449 ....D 3
...guet, 825 ....C 4
...npden, 739 ....B 2
...bour Breton, 2,196 ....C 4
...pulation of metropolitan area.

Harbour Deep, 334 ....B 2
Harbour Grace, 2,771 ....D 4
Hare Bay, 1,485 ....C 3
Heatherton, 329 ....A 3
Henley Harbour, 35 ....B 1
Holyrood, 1,282 ....D 4
Hopedale, 375 ....D 1
Howley, 409 ....B 3
Jackson's Arm, 491 ....B 3
Joe Batt's Arm, 886 ....D 3
King's Point, 651 ....B 3
Labrador City, 7,622 ....C 2
Lamaline, 553 ....C 4
L'Anse-au-Loup, 448 ....B 2
Lark Harbour, 590 ....A 3
La Scie, 1,255 ....C 3
Lewisporte, 3,175 ....C 3
Lourdes, 903 ....A 3
Lumsden, 630 ....D 3
Makkovik, 292 ....E 1
Mary's Harbour, 134 ....D 1
Marystown, 4,960 ....C 4
Milltown, 712 ....C 4
Mount Carmel, 435 ....D 4
Nain, 708 ....D 1
Nippers Harbour, 275 ......B 3
Norris Arm, 1,191 ....C 3
Norris Point, 986 ....A 3
North West River, 931 .....D 2
Placentia, 2,211 ....D 4
Port au Choix, 861 ....B 2
Port Blandford, 779 ....C 3
Port Hope Simpson, 232 ...D 1
Pouch Cove, 1,483 ....D 4
Ramea, 1,208 ....B 4
Red Bay, 296 ....B 1
Roddickton, 1,239 ....B 2
Rose Blanche, 703 ....A 4
Robert's Arm, 1,044 ....C 3
Saint Anthony, 2,593 ......C 2
Saint George's, 2,082 .....A 3
Saint John's (cap.),
   88,102 ....D 4
Saint John's, 1131,814 .....D 4
Saint Lawrence, 2,173 .....C 4
Saint Mary's, 375 ....D 4
Saint Vincent's, 593 ......D 4

Seal Cove, 698 ....B 2
Separation Point, 3 ....B 1
Shoal Cove, 236 ....B 2
Springdale, 3,224 ....B 3
Square Islands, 95 ....C 1
Stephenville, 7,770 ....A 3
Stephenville Crossing .....A 3
Sunnyside, 716 ....C 3
Terrenceville, 700 ....C 4
Torbay, 2,090 ....D 4
Trepassey, 1,443 ....D 4
Trinity, 288 ....D 3
Trout River, 689 ....A 3
Twillingate, 1,437 ....C 3
Victoria, 1,601 ....D 4
Wabana, 5,421 ....D 4
Wesleyville, 1,142 ....D 3
West Saint Modeste, 294 ..B 2
Windsor, 6,644 ....C 3

OTHER FEATURES

Ashuanipi (lake) ....C 2
Atikonak (lake) ....C 2
Avalon (peninsula) ....D 4
Bell (isl.) ....C 2
Bell (isl.), 6,079 ....D 4
Belle (isle) ....C 1
Belle Isle (strait) ....B 2
Bonavista (bay) ....D 3
Bonne (bay) ....A 3
Burin (peninsula) ....C 4
Cabot (strait) ....A 4
Chidley (cape) ....D 1
Churchill (falls) ....C 2
Churchill (river) ....D 2
Conception (bay) ....D 4
Exploits (river) ....B 3
Fogo (isl.), 4,094 ....C 3
Fortune (bay) ....C 4
Gander (river) ....C 3
Grand (lake) ....B 3
Grey (isls.) ....C 2
Groais (isl.) ....C 2
Gros Morne (mt.) ....A 3
Hamilton (inlet) ....B 1
Hamilton (sound) ....C 3
Hare (bay) ....C 2
Harrison (cape) ....E 1

Hermitage (bay) ....B 4
Humber (river) ....B 3
Ingornachoix (bay) ......B 2
Islands (bay) ....A 3
Killinek (isl.) ....C 1
Labrador (region), 28,166 ..C 2
Labrador (sea) ....E 1
La Poile (bay) ....A 4
Little (river) ....B 4
Long Range (mts.) ......B 3
Main Topsail (mt.) ......B 3
Mealy (mts.) ....A 1
Meelpaeg (lake) ....B 3
Melville (lake) ....A 1
Menihek (lakes) ....C 2
Newfoundland (isl.),
   493,938 ....B 3
New World (isl.), 4,563 ...C 3
North (river) ....B 1
North Aulatsivik (isl.) ....D 1
Notre Dame (bay) ....C 3
Paradise (river) ....B 1
Pine (cape) ....D 4
Pistolet (bay) ....C 2
Placentia (bay) ....C 4
Ponds (isl.), 164 ....C 1
Port au Port (pen.) .....A 3
Race (cape) ....D 4
Random (isl.), 1,353 ....D 3
Ray (cape) ....A 4
Red Indian (lake) ......B 3
Saint George's (bay) ...A 3
Saint John (cape) ......C 2
Saint John (river) .....A 2
Saint Lawrence (gulf) ..C 4
Saint Lewis (river) .....B 1
Saint Mary's (bay) .....D 4
Sandy (lake) ....B 3
Serpentine Prov. Park ..A 3
Sir R. A. Squires
   Memorial Park ....B 3
Smallwood (res.) ......C 2
South Aulatsivik (isl.) ..D 1
Sylvester (mt.) ....B 3
Terra Nova Nat'l Park ..D 3
Torngat (mts.) ....D 1
Trinity (bay) ....D 3
Victoria (lake) ....B 3
White (bay) ....B 2

100 Nova Scotia and Prince Edward Island

NOVA SCOTIA

Yarmouth, 24,682 ....C 5

COUNTIES

Annapolis, 21,841 ....C 4	
Antigonish, 16,814 ....F 3	
Cape Breton, 129,075 ....H 2	
Colchester, 37,735 ....E 3	
Cumberland, 35,160 ....D 3	
Digby, 20,349 ....C 4	
Guysborough, 12,864 ....F 3	
Halifax, 261,461 ....E 4	
Hants, 28,935 ....D 3	
Inverness, 20,375 ....G 2	
Kings, 44,975 ....D 4	
Lunenburg, 38,422 ....D 4	
Pictou, 46,104 ....F 3	
Queens, 12,950 ....D 4	
Richmond, 12,734 ....H 3	
Shelburne, 16,661 ....C 5	
Victoria, 7,823 ....H 2	

CITIES and TOWNS

Abercrombie, 532 ....F 3	
Alder Point, 844 ....H 2	
Aldershot, 1,729 ....D 3	
Amherst⊙, 9,966 ....D 3	
Annapolis Royal⊙, 758 ....C 4	
Antigonish⊙, 5,489 ....F 3	
Arcadia, 425 ....B 5	
Arichat⊙, 829 ....H 3	
Auburn, 519 ....D 3	
Aylesford, 680 ....D 3	
Baddeck⊙, 831 ....H 2	
Barrington Passage, 551 ....C 5	
Bear River, 733 ....C 4	
Beaverbank, 958 ....E 4	
Belliveau Cove, 486 ....B 4	
Belmont, 663 ....E 3	
Berwick, 1,412 ....D 4	

Bible Hill, 3,505 ....E 3	
Block House, 418 ....D 4	
Blue Rock, 394 ....D 4	
Bras d'Or, 655 ....H 2	
Bridgetown, 1,039 ....C 4	
Bridgewater, 5,231 ....D 4	
Brookfield, 658 ....E 3	
Brooklyn, 1,253 ....D 4	
Caledonia, 459 ....C 4	
Cambridge Station, 699 ....D 3	
Canning, 809 ....D 3	
Canso, 1,209 ....H 3	
Cape North, 118 ....H 2	
Centreville, 552 ....D 4	
Chester, 1,031 ....D 4	
Chester Basin, 588 ....D 4	
Chéticamp, 1,016 ....G 2	
Church Point, 258 ....B 4	
Clark's Harbour, 1,082 ....C 5	
Clementsport, 479 ....C 4	
Comeauville, 365 ....B 4	
Concession, 404 ....B 4	
Conquerall Bank, 480 ....D 4	

Conway, 363 ....C 4	
Dartmouth, 64,770 ....E 4	
Debert, 703 ....E 3	
Deep Brook, 494 ....C 4	
Digby⊙, 2,363 ....C 4	
Dominion, 2,879 ....J 2	
Donkin, 910 ....J 2	
East Chester, 485 ....D 4	
East Chezzetcook, 617 ....E 4	
Ellershouse, 424 ....E 4	
Elmsdale, 758 ....E 3	
Enfield, 1,056 ....E 4	
Fall River, 969 ....E 4	
Falmouth, 759 ....D 3	
Florence, 1,958 ....H 2	
Freeport, 475 ....B 4	
Glace Bay, 22,440 ....J 2	
Gold River, 448 ....D 4	
Granville Ferry, 445 ....C 4	
Great Village, 494 ....E 3	
Grosses Coques, 360 ....B 4	
Guysborough⊙, 494 ....G 3	
Halifax (cap.)⊙, 122,035 ....E 4	

Halifax, ‡222,637 ....E 4	
Hantsport, 1,447 ....D 3	
Havre Boucher, 385 ....G 3	
Head of Jeddore, 445 ....E 4	
Head of Saint Margarets Bay, 644 ....E 4	
Heatherton, 368 ....G 3	
Hebron, 463 ....B 5	
Herring Cove, 1,487 ....E 4	
Hilden, 803 ....E 3	
Hopewell, 439 ....F 3	
Hubbards, 427 ....D 4	
Ingonish, 338 ....H 2	
Ingonish Beach, 640 ....H 2	
Inverness, 1,846 ....G 2	
Joggins, 777 ....D 3	
Judique, 409 ....G 3	
Kentville⊙, 5,198 ....D 3	
Kingston, 1,429 ....D 3	
Lakeside, 1,687 ....E 4	
Lantz, 661 ....E 4	
L'Ardoise West, 432 ....H 3	
Lawrencetown, 512 ....C 4	

Lequille, 526 ....C 4	
Little Dover, 585 ....G 3	
Liverpool⊙, 3,654 ....D 4	
Lockeport, 1,208 ....C 5	
Louisbourg, 1,582 ....J 3	
Louisdale, 1,036 ....G 3	
Lower Wedgeport, 561 ....C 5	
Lower West Pubnico, 743 ....C 5	
Lower Woods Harbour, 589 ....C 5	
Lunenburg⊙, 3,215 ....D 4	
Lyons Brook, 441 ....F 3	
Mabou, 421 ....G 2	
Maccan, 492 ....D 3	
Mahone Bay, 1,333 ....D 4	
Main-à-Dieu, 394 ....J 2	
Meaghers Grant, 388 ....E 4	
Melvern Square, 427 ....C 3	
Meteghan, 909 ....B 4	
Meteghan Centre, 368 ....B 4	
Meteghan River, 414 ....B 4	
Middle Musquodoboit, 638 ....E 4	

Middleton, 1,870 ....C 4	
Middlewood, 395 ....D 4	
Milford Station, 650 ....E 4	
Milton, 1,854 ....D 4	
Mira Road, 1,503 ....H 2	
Monastery, 418 ....G 3	
Mount Uniacke, 813 ....E 4	
Mulgrave, 1,196 ....G 3	
Musquodoboit Harbour, 768 ....E 4	
New Germany, 584 ....D 4	
New Glasgow, 10,849 ....F 3	
New Minas, 1,503 ....D 3	
New Road, 1,333 ....H 2	
Newport, 471 ....D 3	
New Victoria, 1,377 ....H 2	
New Waterford, 9,579 ....J 2	
Nictaux, 578 ....C 4	
North Sydney, 8,604 ....H 2	
Oxford, 1,473 ....E 3	
Parkers Cove, 395 ....C 4	
Parrsboro, 1,807 ....D 3	
Petit-de-Grat, 1,032 ....H 3	

NOVA SCOTIA AND PRINCE EDWARD ISLAND

SCALE
0 10 20 30 40 50 MI.
0 10 20 30 40 50 KM.

Provincial Capitals ....⊛ Provincial Boundaries ___ ___
County Seats ....⊙ County Boundaries ___ ___

Copyright by C. S. HAMMOND & CO., N.Y.

Petit-Étang, 438	G 2	
Pictou⊙, 4,250	F 3	
Pictou Landing, 435	F 3	
Pomquet, 387	G 3	
Porters Lake, 840	E 4	
Port Hastings, 565	G 3	
Port Hawkesbury, 3,372	G 3	
Port Hood⊙, 523	G 2	
Port Maitland, 419	B 5	
Port Morien, 470	H 3	
Port Williams, 638	D 3	
Pugwash, 644	E 3	
Reserve Mines, 2,529	H 2	
River Bourgeois, 445	H 3	
River Hébert, 862	D 3	
River John, 468	E 3	
Riverport, 371	D 4	
Sackville, 5,701	E 4	
Saint Croix, 375	E 4	
Saint Peters, 663	H 3	
Sambro, 556	E 4	
Saulnierville, 481	B 4	
Sheet Harbour, 1,062	F 4	
Shelburne⊙, 2,689	C 5	
Shubenacadie, 633	E 3	
Somerset, 371	D 3	
Springhill, 5,262	E 3	
Stellarton, 5,357	F 3	
Stewiacke, 1,040	E 3	
Sydney⊙, 33,230	H 2	
Sydney Mines, 8,991	H 2	
Sydney River, 2,009	H 2	
Tatamagouche, 568	E 3	
Terence Bay, 1,134	F 4	
Thorburn, 1,019	F 3	
Three Mile Plains, 1,163	D 4	
Timberlea, 1,770	F 4	
Trenton, 3,331	F 3	
Troy, 441	G 3	
Truro⊙, 13,047	E 3	
Tusket, 423	B 5	
Upper Musquodoboit, 362	F 3	
Waterville, 552	D 3	
Waverley, 1,419	E 4	
Wedgeport, 840	C 5	
Wellington, 411	E 4	

PRINCE EDWARD ISLAND

AREA 2,184 sq. mi.
POPULATION 118,229
CAPITAL Charlottetown
LARGEST CITY Charlottetown
HIGHEST POINT 465 ft.
SETTLED IN 1720
ADMITTED TO CONFEDERATION 1873
PROVINCIAL FLOWER Lady's Slipper

NOVA SCOTIA

AREA 21,425 sq. mi.
POPULATION 828,571
CAPITAL Halifax
LARGEST CITY Halifax
HIGHEST POINT Cape Breton Highlands 1,747 ft.
SETTLED IN 1605
ADMITTED TO CONFEDERATION 1867
PROVINCIAL FLOWER Trailing Arbutus or Mayflower

West Arichat, 549	G 3	
West Dover, 362	E 4	
Western Shore, 774	D 4	
Westmount, 1,790	H 2	
Westport, 380	B 4	
Westville, 3,898	F 3	
Weymouth, 604	C 4	
Whites Lake, 432	E 4	
Wilmot Station, 597	D 4	
Windsor⊙, 3,775	D 3	
Wolfville, 2,861	D 3	
Yarmouth⊙, 8,516	B 5	

OTHER FEATURES

Ainslie (lake)	G 2	
Annapolis (basin)	C 4	
Annapolis (riv.)	C 4	
Aspy (bay)	H 1	
Avon (riv.)	D 4	
Barachois (pt.)	G 3	
Bedford (basin)	E 4	
Boularderie (isl.), 1,902	H 2	
Bras d'Or (lake)	H 3	
Breton (cape)	J 3	
Brier (isl.), 380	B 4	
Canso (cape)	H 3	
Canso (str.)	G 3	
Cape Breton (isl.), 162,989	J 2	
Cape Breton Highlands Nat'l Park	H 2	
Cape Sable (isl.), 3,151	C 5	
Caribou (isl.), 35	F 3	
Carleton (riv.)	C 4	
Chebogue (point)	B 5	
Chedabucto (bay)	G 3	
Chéticamp (isl.), 63	G 2	
Chignecto (bay)	D 3	
Chignecto (isth.)	D 3	
Cobequid (bay)	E 3	
Country (isl.)	G 3	
Craignish (hills)	G 3	
Cumberland (basin)	D 3	
Digby Gut (chan.)	C 4	
Digby Neck (pen.)	C 4	
Egmont (cape)	H 2	
Fourchu (cape)	B 5	
Fundy (bay)	C 3	
Gabarus (bay)	H 3	
Gaspereau (lake)	D 4	
George (cape)	G 3	
Georges (bay)	G 3	
Gold (riv.)	D 4	
Great Bras d'Or (chan.)	H 2	
Greville (bay)	D 3	
Guysborough (riv.)	G 3	
Halifax (harb.)	E 4	
Hébert (riv.)	D 3	
Ingonish North (bay)	H 2	
Janvrin (isl.), 162	G 3	
Jeddore (harb.)	F 4	
John (cape)	E 3	
Joli (pt.)	D 5	
Jordan (riv.)	C 5	
Kejimkujik Nat'l Park	C 4	
Kennetcook (riv.)	E 3	
La Have (isl.), 7	D 4	
La Have (riv.)	D 4	
Liscomb (isl.), 12	G 4	
Lomond, Loch (lake)	H 3	
Long (isl.), 846	B 4	
Louisbourg Nat'l Hist. Park	J 3	
Mabou Highlands (hills)	G 2	
Madame (isl.), 3,767	G 3	
Mahone (bay)	D 4	
Malagash (pt.)	E 3	
McNutt (isl.), 20	C 5	
Medway (riv.)	C 4	
Merigomish (harb.)	F 3	
Mersey (riv.)	C 4	
Minas (basin)	D 3	
Minas (chan.)	D 3	
Mira (bay)	J 2	
Musquodoboit (riv.)	F 4	
Necum Teuch (harb.)	F 4	
Negro (cape)	C 5	
North (cape)	H 1	
North (mt.)	C 4	
North Bay Ingonish (bay)	H 2	
North East Margaree (riv.)	H 2	
Northumberland (str.)	E 2	
Nuttby (mt.)	E 3	
Ohio (riv.)	D 4	
Panuke (lake)	D 4	
Pennant (pt.)	E 4	
Percé (cape)	J 2	
Petit-de-Grat (isl.), 1,032	H 3	
Petpeswick (head)	E 4	
Pictou (harb.)	F 3	
Pictou (isl.), 69	F 3	
Ponhook (lake)	D 4	
Port Hood (isl.), 39	G 2	
Port Joli (harb.)	D 5	
Prim (pt.)	C 4	

Roseway (riv.)	C 4	
Rossignol (lake)	C 4	
Sable (cape)	C 5	
Sable (isl.), 12	J 5	
Saint Andrews (chan.)	H 2	
Saint Ann's (bay)	H 2	
Saint Lawrence (bay)	H 1	
Saint Lawrence (cape)	H 1	
Saint Margarets (bay)	E 4	
Saint Mary's (bay)	B 4	
Saint Mary's (riv.)	F 3	
Saint Paul (isl.), 10	H 1	
Saint Peters (bay)	H 3	
Salmon (riv.)	E 3	
Scatarie (isl.), 8	J 2	
Scots (bay)	D 3	
Seal (isl.), 10	B 5	
Sheet (harb.)	F 4	
Sherbrooke (lake)	D 4	
Shubenacadie (lake)	E 4	
Shubenacadie (riv.)	E 3	
Sissiboo (riv.)	C 4	
Sober (isl.), 113	F 4	
Split (cape)	D 3	
Stewiacke (riv.)	E 3	

Sydney (harb.)	H 2	
Tor (bay)	G 3	
Tusket (riv.)	C 4	
Verte (bay)	D 2	
West (riv.)	F 3	
West Liscomb (riv.)	F 3	
Whitehaven (bay)	G 3	
Yarmouth (sound)	B 5	

PRINCE EDWARD ISLAND

COUNTIES

Kings, 18,424	F 2	
Prince, 42,082	D 2	
Queens, 51,135	E 2	

CITIES and TOWNS

Alberton, 973	E 2	

Borden, 624	E 2	
Bunbury, 527	F 2	
Charlottetown (cap.)⊙, 19,133	E 2	
Cornwall, 557	E 2	
Elmsdale, 403	D 2	
Georgetown⊙, 767	F 2	
Hunter River, 362	E 2	
Kensington, 1,086	E 2	
Miminegash, 417	D 2	
Miscouche, 750	D 2	
Montague, 1,608	F 2	
Morell, 387	F 2	
Mount Stewart, 413	F 2	
Murray Harbour, 367	F 2	
Murray River, 478	F 2	
North Rustico, 767	E 2	
O'Leary, 795	D 2	
Parkdale, 2,313	E 2	
Saint Edward, 537	D 2	
Saint Eleanors, 1,621	E 2	
Saint Peters, 370	F 2	
Sherwood, 3,807	E 2	
Souris, 1,393	F 2	
Stanhope, 203	E 2	

Summerside⊙, 9,439	E 2	
Tignish, 1,060	D 2	
Victoria, 171	E 2	
Wilmot, 737	E 2	

OTHER FEATURES

Bedeque (bay)	E 2	
Cardigan (bay)	F 2	
Cascumpeque (bay)	E 2	
East (pt.)	G 2	
Egmont (bay)	D 2	
Hillsborough (bay)	E 2	
Malpeque (bay)	E 1	
North (pt.)	D 1	
Panmure (isl.), 45	F 2	
Prince Edward Island Nat'l Park	E 2	
Saint Lawrence (gulf)	E 2	
Tracadie (bay)	F 2	

⊙ County seat.

‡ Population of metropolitan area.

Topography

0 30 60
MILES

Below Sea Level · 100 m. 328 ft. · 200 m. 656 ft. · 500 m. 1,640 ft. · 1,000 m. 3,281 ft. · 2,000 m. 6,562 ft. · 5,000 m. 16,404 ft.

Agriculture, Industry and Resources

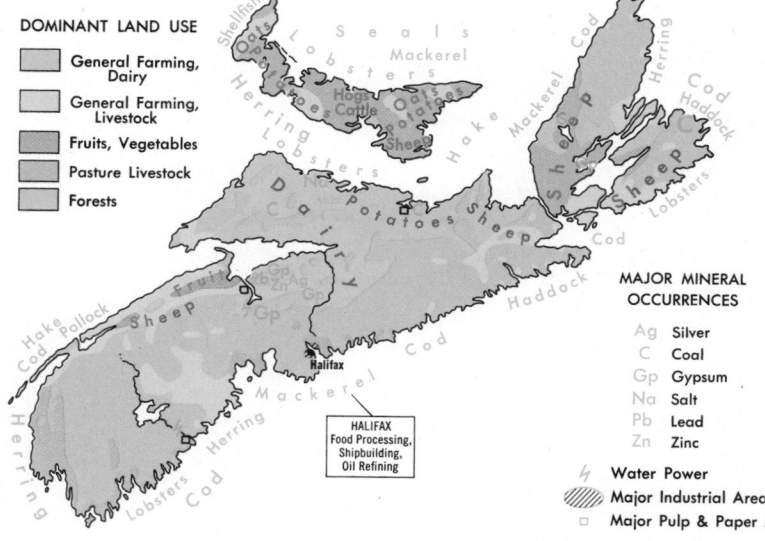

DOMINANT LAND USE

- General Farming, Dairy
- General Farming, Livestock
- Fruits, Vegetables
- Pasture Livestock
- Forests

MAJOR MINERAL OCCURRENCES

- Ag Silver
- C Coal
- Gp Gypsum
- Na Salt
- Pb Lead
- Zn Zinc

⚡ Water Power
▨ Major Industrial Areas
▫ Major Pulp & Paper Mills

HALIFAX
Food Processing, Shipbuilding, Oil Refining

102 New Brunswick

COUNTIES

Albert, 16,307..............F 3
Carleton, 24,428............C 2
Charlotte, 24,551...........C 3
Gloucester, 74,752.........E 1
Kent, 24,901...............E 2
King's, 33,285.............E 3
Madawaska, 34,976..........B 1
Northumberland, 51,561.....D 2
Queen's 12,486.............D 2
Restigouche, 41,289........C 1
Saint John, 92,162.........D 3
Sunbury, 21,268............D 3
Victoria, 19,796...........C 2
Westmorland, 98,669........F 2
York, 64,126...............C 3

CITIES and TOWNS

Acadie Siding, 112.........E 2
Acadieville, 144...........E 2
Adamsville, 119............E 2
Albert Mines, 130..........F 3
Alcida, 222................E 1
Aldouane, 83...............E 2
Allardville, 712...........E 1

Alma, 425..................F 3
Anagance, 109..............E 3
Apohaqui, 352..............E 3
Argyle, 63.................E 2
Armstrong Brook, 321.......E 1
Aroostook, 550.............C 2
Arthurette, 299............C 2
Astle, 194.................D 2
Atholville, 2,108..........D 1
Aulac, 128.................F 3
Back Bay, 567..............D 3
Baie-Sainte-Anne, 735......F 1
Baie-Verte, 177............F 2
Bailey, 143................C 3
Bairdsville, 171...........C 2
Baker Brook, 561...........B 1
Balmoral, 896..............D 1
Barker's Point, 1,882......D 3
Barnaby River, 87..........E 2
Barnettville, 182..........D 2
Bartibog Bridge, 163.......E 1
Bas-Caraquet, 1,685........F 1
Bass River, 129............E 2
Bath, 920..................C 2
Bathurst⊙, 16,674..........E 1
Bathurst Mines, 45.........E 1
Bayfield, 178..............G 2
Bayside, 207...............C 3
Beaver Brook Station, 276..E 1
Beaver Harbour, 355........D 3

Beechwood, 349.............C 2
Beersville, 85.............E 2
Belledune, 784.............E 1
Bellefleur, 145............C 1
Belleford, 294.............E 1
Belleisle Creek, 179.......E 3
Benjamin, 65...............D 1
Benton, 149................C 3
Beresford, 2,325...........E 1
Berry Mills, 349...........E 2
Bertrand, 1,094............E 1
Berwick, 130...............E 3
Black Point, 130...........D 1
Black River, 91............E 3
Black River Bridge, 335....E 2
Blacks Harbour, 1,771......D 3
Blackville, 185............D 2
Blissfield, 130............D 2
Bloomfield Ridge, 218......D 2
Blue Cove, 519.............E 1
Bocabec, 59................C 3
Boiestown, 332.............D 2
Bonny River, 134...........D 3
Bossé, 134.................B 1
Bourgeois, 306.............F 2
Brantville, 1,072..........F 1
Breau-Village, 249.........F 2
Brest, 117.................E 1
Bridgedale, 416............F 2
Briggs Corner, 138.........E 2

Bristol, 771...............C 2
Brockway, 68...............C 3
Browns Flats, 262..........D 3
Buctouche, 1,964...........F 2
Burnsville, 179............E 1
Burton⊙, 357...............D 3
Burtts Corner, 487.........C 2
Caissie-Village, 34........F 2
Cambridge-Narrows, 416.....E 3
Campbellton, 10,335........D 1
Canaan Road, 130...........E 2
Canaan Station, 102........E 2
Canterbury, 528............C 3
Cap-Bateau, 466............F 1
Cape Tormentine, 261.......G 2
Cap Lumière, 305...........F 2
Cap-Pelé, 2,081............F 2
Caraquet, 3,441............E 1
Caron Brook, 191...........B 1
Carrolls Crossing, 188.....D 2
Castalia, 199..............C 4
Central Blissville (Bailey),
143........................D 3
Centre-Acadie, 151.........E 2
Centre-Saint-Simon, 517....E 1
Centreville, 566...........C 2
Chance Harbour, 181........D 3
Charlo, 1,621..............D 1
Chartersville, 320.........F 2
Chatham, 7,833.............E 1

Chatham Head, 1,440........E 2
Chipman, 1,977.............E 2
Clair, 704.................B 1
Clarendon, 105.............C 3
Cliffordvale, 110..........C 2
Clifton, 231...............E 1
Cloverdale, 133............C 2
Coal Branch, 89............E 2
Coal Creek, 71.............E 2
Cocagne, 234...............F 2
Cocagne Cape, 258..........F 2
Codys, 67..................E 3
Coldstream, 160............C 2
Coles Island, 121..........E 2
College Bridge, 545........F 2
Collette, 178..............E 2
Connell, 107...............C 2
Connors, 231...............B 1
Cork Station, 170..........C 3
Cornhill, 83...............E 3
Cross Creek, 241...........D 2
Cumberland Bay, 246........E 2
Dalhousie⊙, 6,255.........D 1
Dalhousie Junction, 275....D 1
Darlington, 585............D 1
Daulnay, 539...............E 1
Dawsonville, 208...........C 1
Debec, 222.................C 2
Dieppe, 4,277..............F 2
Dipper Harbour, 109........D 3

Doaktown, 938..............D 2
Dorchester⊙, 1,199........F 3
Dorchester Crossing, 574...F 2
Douglas Harbour, 46........D 3
Douglastown, 637...........E 1
Drummond, 637..............C 1
Duguayville, 372...........E 1
Dumbarton, 59..............C 3
Dumfries, 257..............C 3
Dupuis Corner, 218.........F 2
Durham Bridge, 182.........D 2
East Shediac, 585..........F 2
Edmundston⊙, 12,365.......B 1
Eel River Bridge, 487......D 1
Eel River Crossing, 1,075..C 1
Elgin, 283.................E 3
Elmwood, 78................C 2
Enniskillen, 77............D 3
Evandale, 33...............D 3
Evangeline, 298............F 1
Fairhaven, 118.............C 4
Fairisle, 444..............E 1
Fairvale, 2,050............E 3
Ferry Road, 520............E 1
Fielding, 215..............C 2
Five Fingers, 148..........C 1
Flatlands, 280.............D 1
Florenceville, 584.........C 2
Fontaine, 318..............F 1
Forest City, 55............C 3

Fosterville, 71............C 3
Four Falls Corner, 97......C 2
Fox Creek, 488.............F 2
Fredericton (cap.)⊙,
24,254.....................D 3
Fredericton Junction, 615..D 3
Gagetown⊙, 609............D 3
Gardner Creek, 47..........E 3
Geary, 1,023...............D 3
Germantown, 71.............F 3
Gillespie, 88..............C 2
Glassville, 174............C 2
Glencoe, 143...............D 1
Glenlivet, 231.............D 1
Gloucester Junction, 167...E 1
Gondola Point, 850.........E 3
Grafton, 359...............C 2
Grand Bay, 1,066...........D 3
Grande-Anse, 545...........E 1
Grand Falls, 4,516.........C 1
Grand Falls Hill, 559......C 2
Grand Harbour, 556.........C 4
Gray Rapids, 307...........E 2
Gunningville, 1,669........F 2
Hammondvale, 127...........E 3
Hampstead, 118.............D 3
Hampton⊙, 1,748...........E 3
Harcourt, 163..............E 2
Hardwicke, 93..............E 1
Hardwood Ridge, 222........D 2

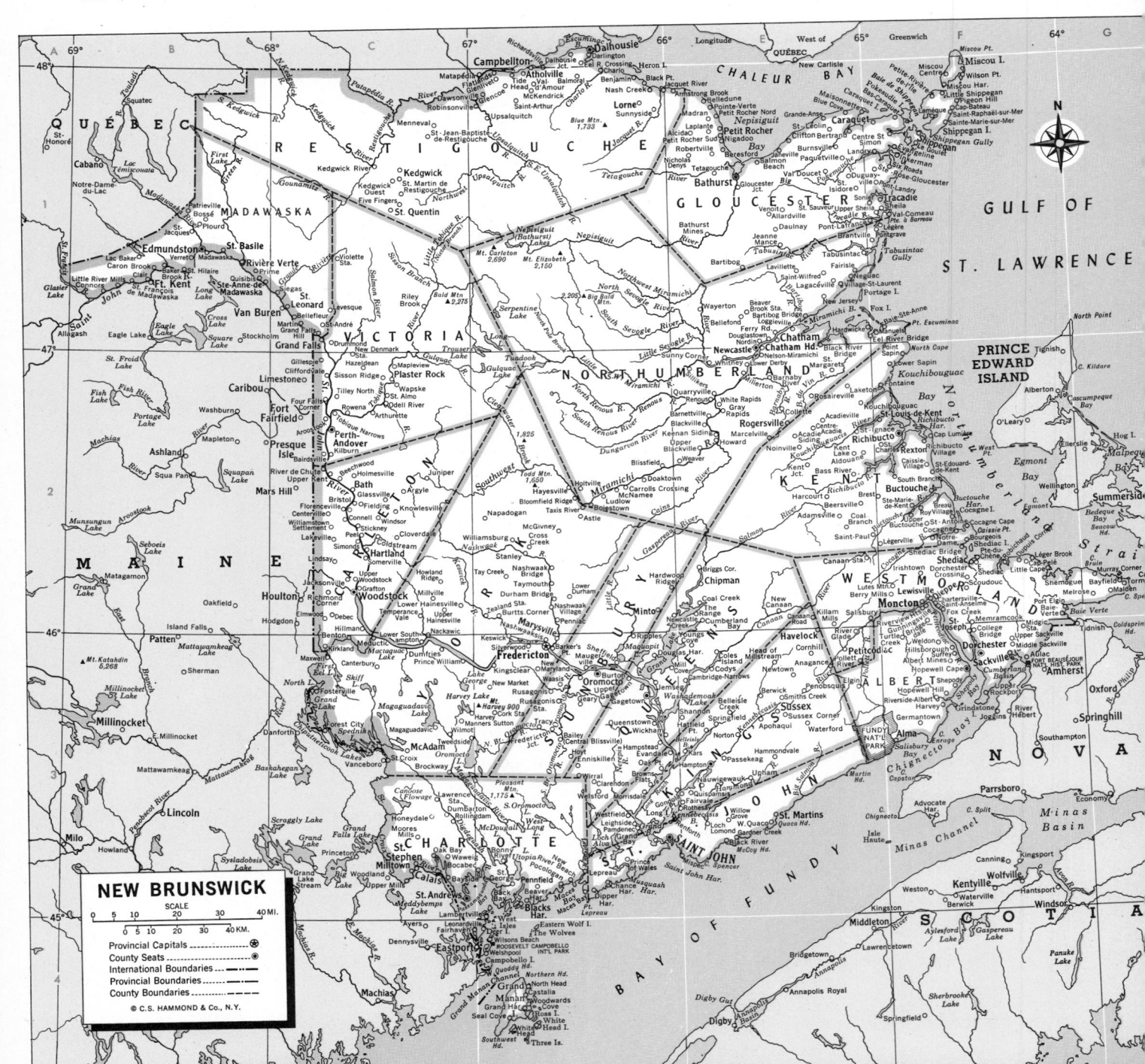

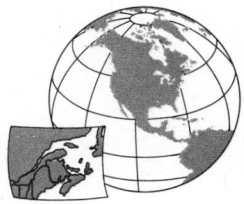

Topography

AREA 28,354 sq. mi.
POPULATION 677,250
CAPITAL Fredericton
LARGEST CITY Saint John
HIGHEST POINT Mt. Carleton 2,690 ft.
SETTLED IN 1611
ADMITTED TO CONFEDERATION 1867
PROVINCIAL FLOWER Purple Violet

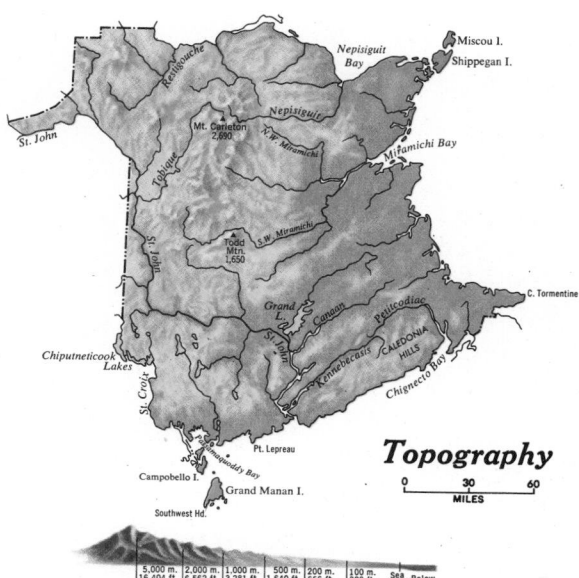

MILES
0   30   60

5,000 m.	2,000 m.	1,000 m.	500 m.	200 m.	100 m.	Sea Level	Below
16,404 ft.	6,562 ft.	3,281 ft.	1,640 ft.	656 ft.	328 ft.		

Agriculture, Industry and Resources

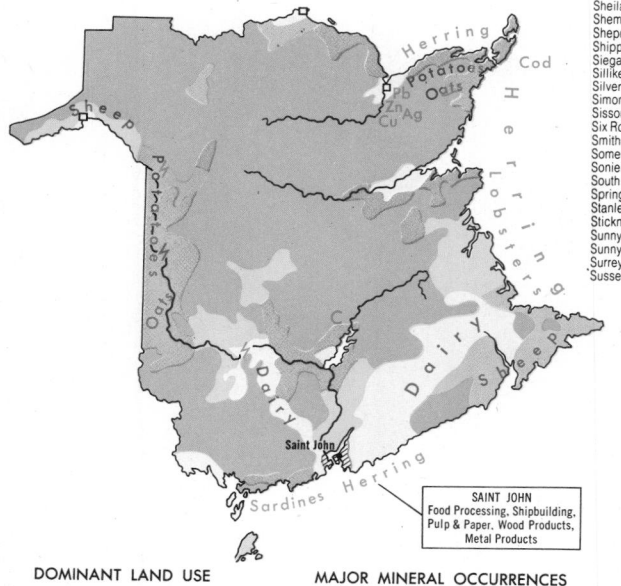

SAINT JOHN
Food Processing, Shipbuilding, Pulp & Paper, Wood Products, Metal Products

DOMINANT LAND USE

- Cereals, Livestock
- Dairy
- Potatoes
- General Farming, Livestock
- Pasture Livestock
- Forests

MAJOR MINERAL OCCURRENCES

Ag Silver
C Coal
Cu Copper
Pb Lead
Zn Zinc

⚡ Water Power
▨ Major Industrial Areas
▫ Major Pulp & Paper Mills

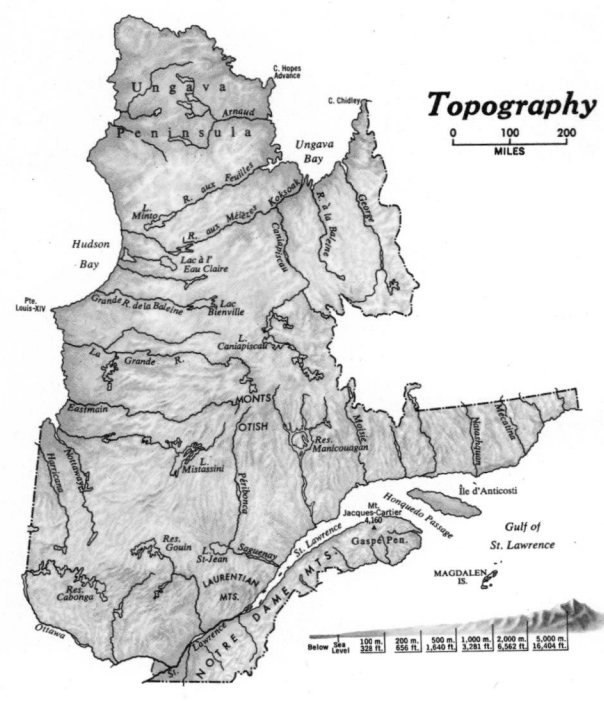

Topography

0   100   200
MILES

Ungava Peninsula

C. Hopes Advance

C. Chidley

Ungava Bay

Hudson Bay

Lac à l'Eau Claire

Pte.-Louis-XIV

Grande R. de la Baleine

La Grande R.

Eastmain

Caniapiscau

MONTS OTISH

Rés. Manicouagan

Rés. Gouin

Rés. Cabonga

St-Jean

Lac Mistassini

Saguenay

LAURENTIAN MTS.

Ottawa

St. Lawrence

NOTRE DAME MTS.

Gaspé Pen.

Honguedo Passage

Mt. Jacques-Cartier 4,160

Île d'Anticosti

Gulf of St. Lawrence

MAGDALEN IS.

| Below Sea Level | 100 m. 328 ft. | 200 m. 656 ft. | 500 m. 1,640 ft. | 1,000 m. 3,281 ft. | 2,000 m. 6,562 ft. | 5,000 m. 16,404 ft. |

QUÉBEC
COUNTIES

Argenteuil, 31,319......C 4
Arthabaska, 41,524......E 4
Bagot, 23,591......E 4
Beauce, 63,960......G 3
Beauharnois, 52,137......C 4
Bellechasse, 23,517......G 3
Berthier, 27,288......C 3
Bonaventure, 41,701......C 2
Brome, 15,311......E 4
Chambly, 231,590......J 4
Champlain, 113,150......F 2
Charlevoix-Est, 16,780......G 2
Charlevoix-Ouest, 13,650......G 2
Châteauguay, 53,737......D 4
Chicoutimi, 163,348......G 1
Compton, 21,367......F 4
Deux-Montagnes, 52,369......C 4
Dorchester, 32,473......G 3
Drummond, 64,144......E 4
Frontenac, 27,293......G 4
Gaspé-Est, 41,727......D 1
Gaspé-Ouest, 18,754......C 1
Gatineau, 55,729......B 3
Hull, 109,946......B 4
Huntingdon, 15,358......C 4
Iberville, 20,400......D 4
Île-de-Montréal, 1,959,143......H 4
Île-Jésus, 228,010......H 4
Joliette, 52,088......C 3
Kamouraska, 26,264......H 2
Labelle, 30,582......B 3
Lac-Saint-Jean-Est, 45,220......F 1
Lac-Saint-Jean-Ouest, 57,074......E 1
Laprairie, 61,691......H 4
L'Assomption, 62,198......D 4
Lévis, 62,776......J 3
L'Islet, 23,187......G 2
Lotbinière, 27,373......F 3

CITIES and TOWNS

Saint-Hyacinthe, 50,494......D 4
Saint-Jean, 45,892......D 4
Saint-Maurice, 108,366......D 3
Shefford, 62,361......E 4
Sherbrooke, 101,470......E 4
Soulanges, 11,449......C 4
Stanstead, 36,266......F 4
Témiscouata, 23,189......J 2
Terrebonne, 139,945......H 4
Vaudreuil, 36,593......C 4
Verchères, 35,273......J 4
Wolfe, 16,197......F 4
Yamaska, 15,206......E 3

Acton Vale, 4,564......E 4
Albanel, 788......E 1
Alma⊙, 22,622......F 1
Amqui⊙, 3,797......B 2
Ancienne-Lorette, 8,304......H 3
Angers, 881......B 4
Anjou, 33,886......H 4
Armagh, 987......G 3
Arthabaska⊙, 4,479......F 3
Arvida, 18,448......F 1
Asbestos, 9,749......F 4
Ayer's Cliff⊙, 873......E 4
Bagotville, 6,041......G 1
Baie-Comeau, 12,109......A 1
Baie-de-Shawinigan, 847......E 3
Baie-des-Sables, 638......A 1
Baie-d'Urfé, 3,881......G 4
Baie-Saint-Paul⊙, 4,163......G 2
Baie-Trinité, 734......B 1
Beaconsfield, 19,389......H 4
Beauceville, 2,098......G 3
Beauceville-Est⊙, 2,192......G 3
Beauharnois⊙, 8,121......D 4
Beaulieu, 659......J 4
Beaumont, 630......F 3
Beauport, 14,681......J 3
Beaupré, 2,862......G 2
Bécancour⊙, 8,182......E 3
Bedford⊙, 2,786......E 4
Beebe Plain, 1,236......E 4
Bélair, 4,505......H 3
Beloeil, 12,274......D 4
Bernierville, 2,415......F 3
Berthierville⊙, 4,080......D 3
Bic, 1,157......J 1
Black Lake, 4,123......F 3
Blainville, 9,630......H 4
Bois-des-Filion, 4,061......H 4
Bolduc, 1,496......G 4
Bonaventure, 1,079......C 2
Boucherville, 19,997......J 4
Breakeyville, 800......J 3
Bromont, 1,089......E 4
Bromptonville, 2,771......F 4
Brossard, 23,452......H 4
Brownsburg, 3,481......C 4
Buckingham, 7,304......B 4
Cabano, 3,063......J 2
Calumet, 764......C 4
Candiac, 5,185......J 4
Cap-à-l'Aigle, 679......G 2
Cap-Chat, 3,868......B 1
Cap-de-la-Madeleine, 31,463......E 3
Caplan, 693......C 2
Cap-Rouge, 1,750......H 3
Cap-Saint-Ignace, 1,338......G 2
Cap-Santé⊙, 610......F 3

Carignan, 3,340......J 4
Carleton, 899......C 2
Caughnawaga, 3,982......H 4
Causapscal, 2,965......B 2
Chambly, 11,469......J 4
Chambord, 1,106......E 1
Champlain, 632......E 3
Chandler, 3,843......D 2
Charlemagne, 4,111......H 4
Charlesbourg, 33,443......J 3
Charny, 5,175......J 3
Châteauguay, 15,797......H 4
Châteauguay-Centre, 17,942......H 4
Château-Richer⊙, 3,111......F 3
Chénéville, 718......B 4
Chicoutimi⊙, 33,893......G 1
Chicoutimi-Jonquière, ‡133,703......G 1
Chicoutimi-Nord, 14,086......G 1
Chute-aux-Outardes, 1,930......A 1
Clermont, 3,386......G 2
Coaticook, 6,569......F 4
Coleraine, 1,474......F 3
Contrecoeur, 2,694......D 4
Cookshire⊙, 1,484......F 4
Coteau-du-Lac, 838......C 4
Coteau-Landing⊙, 846......C 4
Côte-Saint-Luc, 24,375......H 4
Courcelles, 679......G 4
Courville, 6,222......J 3
Cowansville, 11,920......E 4
Crabtree, 1,706......D 3
Danville, 2,566......E 4
Daveluyville, 998......E 3
Deauville, 761......E 4
Dégelis, 3,046......J 2
Delson, 2,941......H 4
Desbiens, 1,813......E 1
Deschaillons-sur-Saint-Laurent, 1,176......E 3
Deschambault, 995......E 3
Deschênes, 1,806......B 4
Deux-Montagnes, 8,631......H 4
Didyme, 720......E 1
Disraëli, 3,341......F 3
Dolbeau, 7,633......E 1
Dollard-des-Ormeaux, 25,217......H 4
Donnacona, 5,940......F 3
Dorion, 6,209......H 4
Dorval, 20,469......H 4
Douville, 3,267......D 4
Drummondville⊙, 31,813......E 4
Drummondville-Sud, 8,989......E 4
East Angus, 4,715......F 4
East Broughton, 1,380......F 3
East Broughton Station, 1,127......F 3
Escoumints, 1,968......H 1
Farnham, 6,496......E 4
Ferme-Neuve, 1,990......B 3
Forestville, 1,606......H 1
Frampton, 711......G 3
Francoeur, 1,186......F 3
Gaspé, 17,211......D 1
Gatineau, 22,321......B 4
Giffard, 13,135......J 3
Girardville, 933......E 1
Glenwood Domaine, 3,997......B 4
Godbout, 653......B 1
Gracefield, 1,049......A 3
Granby, 34,385......D 4
Grande-Rivière, 1,330......D 2
Grande-Vallée, 779......D 1
Grand-Mère, 17,137......E 3
Greenfield Park, 15,348......J 4
Grenville, 1,495......C 4
Hampstead, 7,033......H 4
Ham-Sud⊙, 64......F 4
Hauterive, 13,181......A 1
Hébertville-Station, 1,163......F 1
Hemmingford, 810......D 4
Henryville, 666......D 4
Hudson, 4,345......C 4
Huntingdon⊙, 3,087......C 4
Iberville⊙, 9,331......D 4
Île-Bizard, 2,950......H 4
Île-Perrot, 4,021......G 4
Inverness⊙, 362......F 3
Joliette⊙, 20,127......D 3
Jonquière, 28,430......F 1
Kénogami, 10,970......F 1
Kirkland, 2,917......H 4
Labelle, 1,492......C 3
Lac-au-Saumon, 1,314......B 2
Lac-aux-Sables, 844......E 3
Lac-Beauport, 42......F 3
Lac-Bouchette, 954......E 1
Lac-Brome, 4,063......E 4
Lac-Carré, 660......C 3
Lac-Etchemin, 2,789......G 3
Lachine, 44,423......H 4
Lachute⊙, 11,813......C 4
Lac-Mégantic, 6,770......G 4
Lacolle, 1,254......D 4
Lac-Saint-Charles, 1,693......H 3
Lafontaine, 2,980......C 4
La Guadeloupe, 1,934......F 4
Lambton, 767......F 4
L'Ange-Gardien, 1,605......F 3
L'Annonciation, 2,162......C 3
Lanoraie, 1,151......D 3
La Pérade, 1,123......E 3
La Pocatière, 4,256......H 2
La Prairie, 8,309......H 4
La Providence, 4,709......E 4
La Salle, 72,912......H 4
La Station-du-Coteau, 885......C 4

La Tuque, 13,099......E 2
Laurentides, 1,746......D 4
Laurier-Station, 946......F 3
Laurierville, 922......F 3
Lauzon, 12,809......J 3
Laval, 228,010......H 4
Lavaltrie, 1,261......D 4
Le Moyne, 8,194......J 4
Lennoxville, 3,859......F 4
L'Épiphanie, 2,752......D 4
Léry, 2,247......H 4
Les Méchins, 792......B 1
Lévis, 16,597......J 3
Linière, 1,220......G 3
L'Islet, 1,195......G 2
L'Isle-sur-Mer, 772......G 2
L'Isle-Verte, 1,360......H 2
Longueuil⊙, 97,590......J 4
Loretteville, 11,644......H 3
Lorraine, 3,145......H 4
Louiseville⊙, 4,042......E 3
Luceville, 1,411......J 1
Lyster, 879......F 3
Magog, 13,281......E 4
Maniwaki⊙, 6,689......B 3
Manouane, 751......C 2
Manseau, 756......E 3
Maple Grove, 1,708......H 4
Maria, 1,157......C 2
Marieville⊙, 4,563......D 4
Mascouche, 8,812......H 4
Maskinongé, 996......E 3
Masson, 2,336......B 4
Massueville, 632......E 4
Matane⊙, 11,841......B 1
Melocheville, 1,601......C 4
Mercier, 4,011......H 4
Mistassini, 3,601......E 1
Mont-Carmel, 800......H 2
Montebello, 1,285......B 4
Mont-Joli, 6,698......J 1
Mont-Laurier⊙, 8,240......B 3
Mont-Louis, 815......C 1
Montmagny⊙, 12,432......G 3
Montmorency, 4,949......J 3
Montréal⊙, 1,214,352......H 4
Montréal, ‡2,743,208......H 4
Montréal-Est, 5,076......J 4
Montréal-Nord, 89,139......H 4
Mont-Rolland, 1,503......C 4
Mont-Royal, 21,561......H 4
Mont-Saint-Hilaire, 5,758......D 4
Morin Heights, 710......C 4
Murdochville, 2,891......C 1
Napierville⊙, 1,987......D 4
Neuville, 798......F 3
New Carlisle⊙, 1,384......C 2
New Richmond, 3,957......C 2
Nicolet, 4,714......E 3
Nitro, 1,827......F 4
Nominingue, 699......B 3
Normandin, 1,823......E 1
North Hatley, 728......F 4
Notre-Dame-de-la-Doré, 1,127......E 1
Notre-Dame-des-Anges, 790......E 3

Agriculture, Industry and Resources

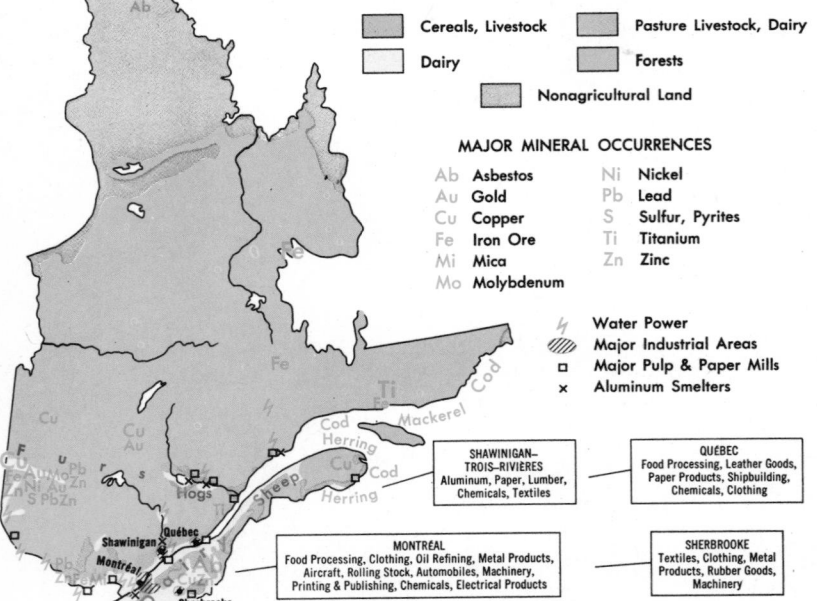

DOMINANT LAND USE

▨ Cereals, Livestock	▨ Pasture Livestock, Dairy
☐ Dairy	▨ Forests
▨ Nonagricultural Land	

MAJOR MINERAL OCCURRENCES

Ab	Asbestos	Ni	Nickel
Au	Gold	Pb	Lead
Cu	Copper	S	Sulfur, Pyrites
Fe	Iron Ore	Ti	Titanium
Mi	Mica	Zn	Zinc
Mo	Molybdenum		

⚡ Water Power
▨ Major Industrial Areas
☐ Major Pulp & Paper Mills
× Aluminum Smelters

SHAWINIGAN–TROIS-RIVIÈRES
Aluminum, Paper, Lumber, Chemicals, Textiles

QUÉBEC
Food Processing, Leather Goods, Paper Products, Shipbuilding, Chemicals, Clothing

MONTRÉAL
Food Processing, Clothing, Oil Refining, Metal Products, Aircraft, Rolling Stock, Automobiles, Machinery, Printing & Publishing, Chemicals, Electrical Products

SHERBROOKE
Textiles, Clothing, Metal Products, Rubber Goods, Machinery

QUÉBEC
SOUTHERN PART

SCALE					
0 5 10	20	30	40 MI.		
0 5 10	20	30	40 KM.		

National Capital ......⊛
Provincial Capital ......★
County Seats ......⊙
International Boundaries _____
Provincial & State Boundaries _____
County Boundaries _____

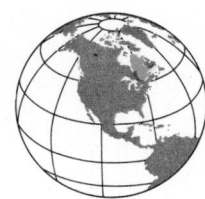

Index

Notre-Dame-des-
  Laurentides, 5,080 ....H 3
Notre-Dame-des-Prairies,
  3,541 ....D 3
Notre-Dame-
  d'Hébertville, 1,506 ......F 1
Notre-Dame-du-Bon-
  Conseil, 1,048 ....E 4
Notre-Dame-du-Lac⊙,
  2,107 ....J 2
Nouvelle, 722 ....C 2
Omerville, 1,102 ....E 4
Ormstown, 1,517 ....D 4
Orsainville, 12,520 ....H 3
Otterburn Park, 3,512 ......D 4
Ouiatchouan, 1,217 ....F 1
Outremont, 28,552 ....H 4
Pabos-Mills, 668 ....D 2
Papineauville, 1,384 ......C 2
Paspébiac, 1,317 ....D 2
Percé, 5,617 ....D 1
Petite-Matane, 668 ....B 1
Petit-Saguenay (Saint-
  François-d'Assise),
  691 ....G 1
Pierrefonds, 33,010 ....H 4
Pierreville, 1,455 ....E 3
Pincourt, 5,899 ....H 4
Pintendre, 796 ....J 3
Plaisance, 651 ....B 4
Plessisville, 7,204 ......F 3
Pointe-à-la-Croix, 753 ....C 2
Pointe-au-Pic, 1,231 ......G 2
Pointe-aux-Outardes, 836 ..A 1

Pointe-aux-Trembles,
  35,567 ....J 4
Pointe-Calumet, 2,214 .....G 4
Pointe-Claire, 27,303 .....H 4
Pointe-du-Lac, 1,314 ......E 3
Pointe-Gatineau, 15,640 ...B 4
Pointe-Lebel, 756 ....A 1
Pont-Rouge, 3,272 ....F 3
Port-Alfred, 9,228 ....G 1
Portneuf, 1,347 ....F 3
Price, 2,740 ....A 1
Princeville, 3,829 ....F 3
Québec (cap.), 186,088 ....H 3
Quyon, 879 ....A 4
Rawdon, 2,740 ....D 3
Repentigny, 19,520 ....J 4
Restigouche, 1,155 ....C 2
Richelieu, 1,777 ....D 4
Richmond⊙, 4,317 ....E 4
Rigaud, 2,138 ....C 4
Rimouski⊙, 26,887 ....J 1
Rimouski-Est, 2,069 ....J 1
Rivière-à-Pierre, 691 .....E 3
Rivière-du-Loup⊙, 12,760 .H 2
Rivière-du-Moulin, 4,393 ..L 4
Rivière-Portneuf, 987 .....H 1
Robertsonville, 1,294 .....F 3
Roberval⊙, 8,330 ....E 1
Rock Forest, 793 ....F 4
Rock Island, 1,341 ....E 4
Rosemère, 6,710 ....H 4
Rougemont, 853 ....D 4
Roxboro, 7,633 ....H 4

Roxton Falls, 1,139 ....E 4
Sacré-Coeur-de-Jésus,
  1,252 ....H 1
Saint-Adelphe, 708 ....E 3
Saint-Agapville, 1,493 ....F 3
Saint-Alban, 770 ....E 3
Saint-Alexandre-de-
  Kamouraska, 927 ....H 2
Saint-Alexis-des-Monts,
  1,905 ....D 3
Saint-Amable, 1,051 ....J 4
Saint-Ambroise, 1,928 .....L 4
Saint-Anaclet, 955 ....J 1
Saint-André-Avellin, 1,088 .B 4
Saint-André-Est, 1,201 ....C 4
Saint-Anselme, 1,400 ......F 3
Saint-Antoine, 5,831 ......H 4
Saint-Antonin, 748 ....H 2
Saint-Aubert, 952 ....G 2
Saint-Augustin-de-
  Québec, 4,402 ....H 3
Saint-Basile-le-Grand,
  4,402 ....D 4
Saint-Basile-Sud, 1,731 ...F 3
Saint-Bernard-sur-Mer,
  667 ....G 2
Saint-Boniface-de-
  Shawinigan, 2,581 ....D 3
Saint-Bruno, 1,276 ....F 1
Saint-Bruno-de-
  Montarville, 15,780 .....J 4
Saint-Camille-de-
  Bellechasse, 774 ....G 3
Saint-Casimir, 1,239 ......E 3

Saint-Césaire, 2,279 ......D 4
Saint-Charles, 969 ....G 3
Saint-Charles-de-
  Drummond, 2,266 ....E 4
Saint-Charles-de-
  Mandeville, 900 ....D 3
Saint-Chrysostome, 1,077 ..D 4
Saint-Coeur-de-Marie,
  1,218 ....F 1
Sainte-Côme, 914 ....D 3
Saint-Constant, 4,139 .....H 4
Saint-Cyprien ....J 2
Saint-Cyrille, 1,125 ......E 4
Saint-Damien-de-
  Buckland, 1,799 ....G 3
Saint-David-de-
  Falardeau, 770 ....F 1
Saint-Denis-de-
  l'Auberivière, 3,818 ....J 3
Saint-Denis, 899 ....D 4
Saint-Dominique, 1,722 ....E 4
Saint-Donat-de-
  Montcalm, 1,536 ....C 3
Sainte-Adélaïde-de-
  Pabos, 853 ....D 2
Sainte-Adèle, 2,581 ......C 4
Sainte-Agathe, 646 ....C 4
Sainte-Agathe-des-
  Monts, 5,532 ....C 3
Sainte-Angèle-de-Mérici,
  688 ....H 1
Sainte-Anne-de-Beaupré,
  1,797 ....F 2

Sainte-Anne-de-Bellevue,
  4,976 ....H 4
Sainte-Anne-des-Monts⊙,
  5,546 ....C 1
Sainte-Anne-des-Plaines,
  2,093 ....H 4
Sainte-Blandine, 941 .....J 1
Sainte-Catherine, 913 ....F 3
Sainte-Claire-de-Joliette,
  1,490 ....G 3
Sainte-Croix⊙, 1,545 ....F 3
Sainte-Famille-
  d'Orléans⊙, 295 ....G 3
Sainte-Félicité, 816 .....B 1
Sainte-Foy, 68,385 ....H 3
Sainte-Geneviève, 2,847 ..H 4
Sainte-Geneviève-de-
  Batiscan⊙, 556 ....E 3

Sainte-Hedwidge-de-
  Roberval, 641 ....E 1
Sainte-Hélène-de-
  Kamouraska, 656 ....H 2
Sainte-Hénédine⊙, 533 ..F 3
Sainte-Jeanne-d'Arc, 936 .E 1
Sainte-Julie-de-
  Verchères, 1,214 ....J 4
Sainte-Julienne⊙, 839 ..D 4
Sainte-Justine, 980 ......G 3
Saint-Éleuthère, 1,083 ...H 2
Sainte-Marie,
  4,307 ....G 3
Sainte-Martine⊙, 1,931 .D 4
Saint-Émile, 2,645 ....H 3
Sainte-Geneviève, 697 ....F 1
Sainte-Perpétue-de-
  L'Islet, 1,048 ....H 2

Saint-Éphrem-de-Tring, 954 G 1
Sainte-Pudentienne, 799 ...E 4
Sainte-Scholastique⊙,
  14,787 ....C 4
Saint-Esprit, 937 ....D 4
Sainte-Thècle, 1,725 .....E 3
Sainte-Thérèse, 17,175 ...H 4
Sainte-Thérèse-Ouest,
  7,278 ....H 4
Saint-Étienne-des-Grès,
  870 ....E 3
Saint-Eugène, 656 ....G 2
Saint-Eustache, 9,479 ....H 4
Saint-Eustache-Est, 4,993 .H 4
Saint-Fabien, 1,537 ......J 1
Saint-Félicien, 4,952 ....E 1
Saint-Félix-de-Valois,
  1,455 ....D 3

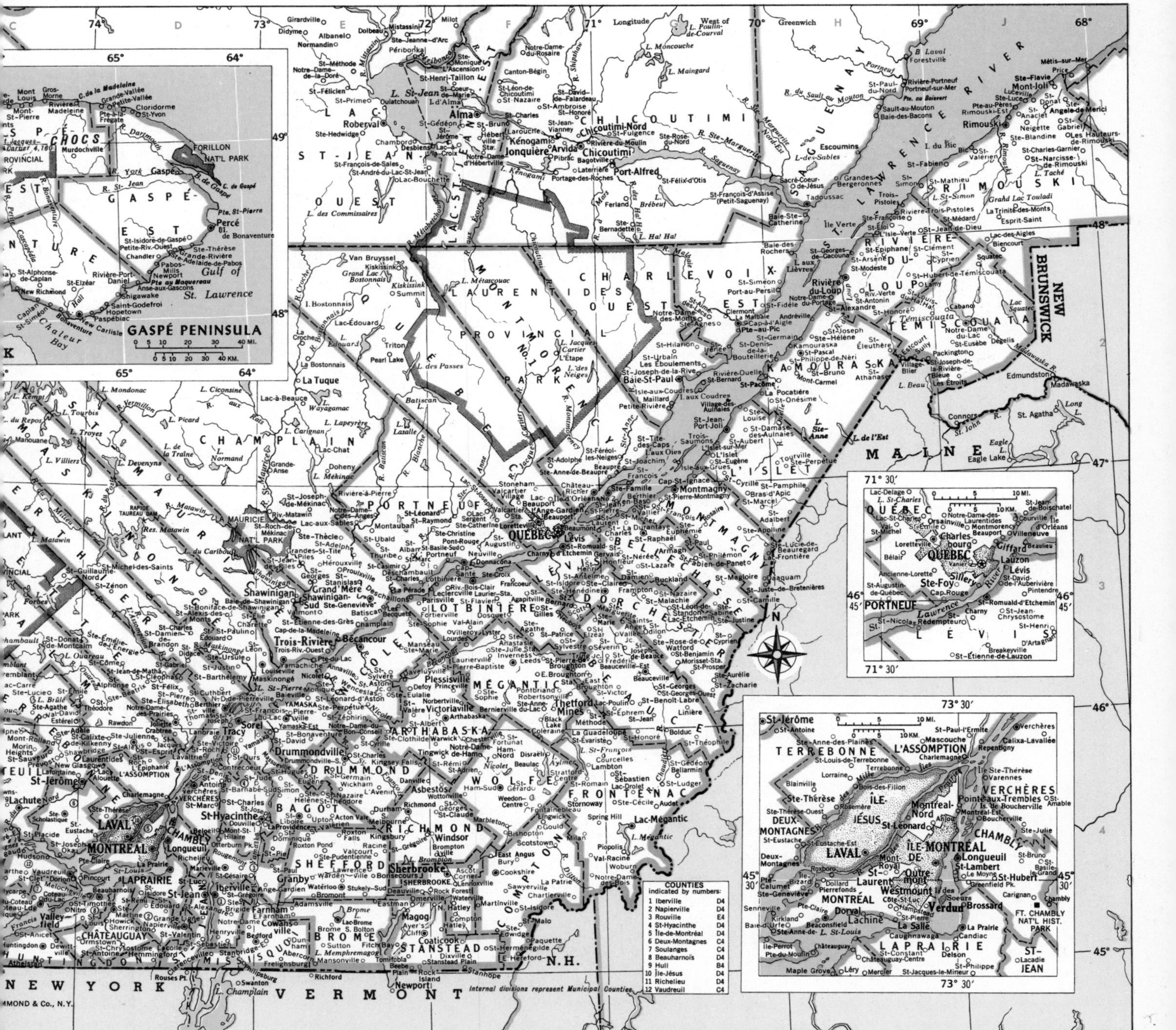

Facts

AREA 594,860 sq. mi.
POPULATION 6,234,445
CAPITAL Québec
LARGEST CITY Montréal
HIGHEST POINT Mt. Jacques Cartier 4,160 ft.
SETTLED IN 1608
ADMITTED TO CONFEDERATION 1867
PROVINCIAL FLOWER White Garden Lily

Saint-Féréol-les-Neiges, 692 ....G 2
Saint-Flavien, 645 ....F 3
Saint-François-d'Assise, 691 ....G 1
Saint-François-du-Lac©, 1,001 ....E 3
Saint-Fulgence, 999 ....G 1
Saint-Gabriel, 3,383 ....D 3
Saint-Gédéon, Frontenac, 1,174 ....G 4
Saint-Gédéon, Lac-St-Jean-E., 885 ....F 1
Saint-Georges, Beauce, 7,554 ....G 3
Saint-Georges, Champlain, 2,061 ....E 3
Saint-Georges-de-Cacouna, 1,001 ....H 2
Saint-Georges-Ouest, 6,000 ....G 3
Saint-Germain-de-Grantham, 1,104 ....E 4
Saint-Gilles, 694 ....F 3
Saint-Grégoire, 655 ....D 4
Saint-Grégoire-de-Greenlay, 694 ....E 4
Saint-Henri, 1,160 ....J 3
Saint-Honoré, Beauce, 1,045 ....G 4
Saint-Honoré, Chicoutimi, 1,055 ....F 1
Saint-Hubert, 85,634 ....J 4
Saint-Hubert-de-Témiscouata, 832 ....J 2
Saint-Hyacinthe©, 24,562 ....D 4
Saint-Isidore, 736 ....F 3
Saint-Isidore-de-Laprairie, 749 ....D 4
Saint-Jacques, 1,975 ....D 4
Saint-Jean©, 32,863 ....D 4
Saint-Jean-Chrysostome, 1,905 ....J 3
Saint-Jean-de-Boischatel, 1,685 ....J 3
Saint-Jean-de-Dieu, 1,148 ....J 1
Saint-Jean-de-Matha, 943 ....D 3
Saint-Jean-Port-Joli©, 1,795 ....G 2
Saint-Jérôme, Lac-St-Jean-E., 1,910 ....F 1
Saint-Jérôme, Terrebonne©, 26,524 ....H 4
Saint-Joachim, 920 ....G 2
Saint-Joachim-de-Tourelle, 1,021 ....C 1

Saint-Joseph, 4,945 ....E 3
Saint-Joseph-de-Beauce, 2,893 ....G 3
Saint-Joseph-de-la-Rivière-Bleue, 1,429 ....J 2
Saint-Joseph-de-Sorel, 3,290 ....D 3
Saint-Jovite, 3,132 ....C 3
Saint-Lambert, 18,616 ....J 4
Saint-Laurent, 62,955 ....H 4
Saint-Léonard, 52,040 ....H 4
Saint-Léonard-d'Aston, 995 ....E 3
Saint-Léon-de-Standon, 830 ....G 3
Saint-Léon-le-Grand, 695 ....B 2
Saint-Liboire©, 667 ....E 4
Saint-Louis-de-Terrebonne, 1,113 ....H 4
Saint-Louis-du-Ha! Ha!, 733 ....H 1
Saint-Luc, 4,850 ....D 4
Saint-Marc-des-Carrières, 2,650 ....E 3
Saint-Méthode-de-Frontenac, 793 ....F 3
Saint-Michel-de-Bellechasse, 967 ....G 3
Saint-Michel-des-Saints, 1,647 ....D 3
Saint-Nazaire-de-Chicoutimi, 884 ....F 1
Saint-Nicolas, 1,975 ....H 3
Saint-Noël, 910 ....B 1
Saint-Odilon, 704 ....G 3
Saint-Ours, 838 ....D 3
Saint-Pacôme, 1,180 ....G 2
Saint-Pamphile, 3,542 ....H 3
Saint-Pascal©, 2,513 ....H 2
Saint-Paul-de-Montminy, 746 ....G 2
Saint-Paulin©, 809 ....D 3
Saint-Paul-l'Ermite, 3,165 ....J 4
Saint-Philippe-de-Néri, 701 ....H 2
Saint-Pie, 1,709 ....E 4
Saint-Pierre, 6,801 ....H 4
Saint-Prime, 2,350 ....E 1
Saint-Prosper-de-Dorchester, 1,696 ....G 3
Saint-Raphaël©, 1,216 ....G 3
Saint-Raymond, 4,036 ....F 3
Saint-Rédempteur, 1,652 ....J 3
Saint-Régis, 727 ....C 4
Saint-Rémi, 2,282 ....D 4
Saint-Roch-de-l'Achigan, 962 ....D 4

Saint-Roch-de-Richelieu, 721 ....D 4
Saint-Romuald-d'Etchemin©, 8,394 ....J 3
Saint-Sauveur-des-Monts, 1,846 ....C 4
Saint-Siméon, 1,186 ....G 2
Saint-Thomas-de-Joliette, 728 ....D 3
Saint-Timothée, 1,613 ....D 4
Saint-Tite, 3,130 ....E 3
Saint-Ubald, 809 ....E 3
Saint-Ulric, 936 ....B 1
Saint-Urbain-de-Charlevoix, 1,172 ....G 2
Saint-Victor, 1,017 ....G 3
Saint-Zacharie, 1,390 ....G 3
Saint-Zotique, 1,243 ....C 4
Sault-au-Mouton, 951 ....H 1
Sawyerville, 864 ....F 4
Sayabec, 1,789 ....B 2
Scotstown, 917 ....F 4
Senneville, 1,412 ....H 4
Shawbridge, 969 ....C 4
Shawinigan, 27,792 ....E 3
Shawinigan-Sud, 11,470 ....E 3
Sherbrooke©, 80,711 ....E 4
Sillery, 13,932 ....J 3
Sorel©, 19,347 ....D 3
Squatec, 950 ....J 2
Stanstead Plain, 1,192 ....E 4
Sully, 776 ....H 2
Sutton, 1,684 ....E 4
Tadoussac©, 1,010 ....H 1
Templeton, 3,684 ....B 3
Terrebonne, 9,212 ....H 4
Thetford Mines, 22,003 ....F 3
Thurso, 3,219 ....B 3
Touraine, 6,978 ....B 4
Tourville, 678 ....H 2
Tracy, 11,842 ....D 3
Tring-Jonction, 1,283 ....G 3
Trois-Pistoles, 4,678 ....H 1
Trois-Rivières, 55,869 ....E 3
Trois-Rivières-Ouest, 8,057 ....E 3
Upton, 818 ....E 4
Val-Brillant, 690 ....B 2
Valcourt, 2,411 ....E 4
Val-David, 1,627 ....C 4
Vallée-Jonction, 1,295 ....G 3
Valleyfield, 30,173 ....C 4
Val-Saint-Michel, 2,050 ....H 3
Vanier, 9,717 ....J 3
Varennes, 2,382 ....J 4
Vaudreuil©, 3,843 ....C 4

Verchères©, 1,840 ....J 4
Verdun, 74,718 ....H 4
Victoriaville, 22,047 ....F 3
Villeneuve, 4,062 ....J 3
Warwick, 2,847 ....F 3
Waterloo©, 4,936 ....E 4
Waterville, 1,476 ....F 4
Weedon-Centre, 1,429 ....F 4
Westmount, 23,606 ....H 4
Windsor, 6,023 ....F 4
Wottonville, 683 ....F 4
Yamachiche©, 1,147 ....E 3

OTHER FEATURES

Alma (isl.) ....F 1
Aylmer (lake) ....A 4
Baskatong (res.) ....B 3
Batiscan (riv.) ....E 3
Bécancour (riv.) ....F 3
Bonaventure (isl.) ....D 1
Bonaventure (riv.) ....C 1
Brome (lake) ....E 4
Brompton (lake) ....E 4
Cascapédia (riv.) ....C 1
Chaleur (bay) ....C 1
Champlain (lake) ....D 4
Chaudière (riv.) ....G 4
Chic-Chocs (mts.) ....C 1
Chicoutimi (riv.) ....F 1
Coudres (isl.), 1,522 ....G 2
Deschênes (lake) ....A 4
Deux Montagnes (lake) ....H 4
Ditton (riv.) ....F 4
Forillon Nat'l Park ....D 1
Fort Chambly Nat'l Hist. Park ....J 4
Gaspé (bay) ....D 1
Gaspé (cape) ....D 1
Gaspé (pen.) ....B 1
Gaspésie Prov. Park ....C 1
Gatineau (riv.) ....B 3
Îles (lake) ....B 3
Jacques-Cartier (mt.) ....G 2
Jacques-Cartier (riv.) ....F 2
Kénogami (lake) ....F 1
Kiamika (riv.) ....C 3
La Maurice Nat'l Park ....E 3
Laurentides Prov. Park ....F 2
La Vérendrye Prov. Park ....A 2
Lièvre (riv.) ....B 3
Lièvres (isl.) ....H 1
Maskinongé (riv.) ....D 3
Matane (riv.) ....B 1
Matane Prov. Park ....B 1
Matapédia (riv.) ....B 2
Matawin (res.) ....D 3

Mégantic (lake) ....G 4
Memphrémagog (lake) ....E 4
Mercier (dam) ....A 3
Métabetchouane (riv.) ....F 1
Mille Îles (riv.) ....H 4
Montmorency (riv.) ....F 2
Mont-Tremblant Prov. Park ....C 3
Nicolet (riv.) ....E 3
Nominingue (lake) ....C 3
Nord (riv.) ....C 4
Orléans (isl.), 5,435 ....F 2
Ottawa (riv.) ....B 4
Ouareau (riv.) ....D 3
Patapédia (riv.) ....B 2
Péribonca (riv.) ....F 1
Petite Nation (riv.) ....B 3
Prairies (riv.) ....H 4
Rimouski (riv.) ....J 1
Ristigouche (riv.) ....B 2
Saguenay (riv.) ....G 1
Sainte-Anne (riv.) ....F 3
Sainte-Anne (riv.) ....E 3
Saint-François (lake) ....F 4
Saint-François (riv.) ....E 4
Saint-Jean (lake) ....E 1
Saint Lawrence (gulf) ....D 2
Saint Lawrence (riv.) ....H 3
Saint-Louis (lake) ....H 4
Saint-Maurice (riv.) ....E 3
Saint-Pierre (lake) ....E 3
Shawinigan (riv.) ....E 3
Shipshaw (riv.) ....F 1
Soeurs (riv.) ....H 4
Témiscouata (lake) ....J 2
Tremblant (lake) ....C 3
Trente et un Milles (lake) ....B 3
Verte (isl.), 175 ....H 1
Yamaska (riv.) ....E 4
York (riv.) ....D 1

© County seat.
‡ Population of metropolitan area.

QUÉBEC, NORTHERN

INTERNAL DIVISIONS

Abitibi (co.), 112,244 ....B 2
Abitibi (terr.), 21,308 ....B 3
Chicoutimi (county), 163,348 ....C 2
Lac-Saint-Jean-Ouest (county), 57,074 ....C 2
Mistassini (terr.), 2,702 ....B 2
Nouveau-Québec (terr.), 10,002 ....E 1

Pontiac (co.), 19,570 ....B 3
Saguenay (co.), 111,272 ....D 2
Témiscamingue (county), 54,656 ....B 3

CITIES and TOWNS

Aguanish, 442 ....E 2
Amos©, 6,984 ....B 3
Angliers, 404 ....B 3
Baie-du-Poste, 1,598 ....C 2
Barraute, 1,288 ....B 3
Belleterre, 614 ....B 3
Betsiamites, 1,574 ....D 3
Cadillac, 1,102 ....B 3
Chapais, 2,914 ....C 3
Chibougamau, 9,701 ....C 3
Clarke City, 750 ....D 2
Dolbeau, 7,633 ....C 2
Duparquet, 786 ....B 3
Dupuy, 439 ....B 3
Évain, 605 ....B 3
Forestville, 1,606 ....D 3
Fort-Chimo, 693 ....F 2
Fort-George, 1,280 ....B 2
Gagnon, 3,787 ....D 2
Godbout, 653 ....D 3
Hauterive, 13,181 ....D 3
Havre-St-Pierre, 2,999 ....E 2
Inoucdjouac, 525 ....E 1
La Reine, 450 ....B 3
La Sarre, 5,185 ....B 3
La Tabatière, 475 ....F 2
Lebel-sur-Quévillon, 2,936 ....B 3
Lorrainville, 906 ....B 3
Macamic, 1,705 ....B 3
Malartic, 5,347 ....B 3
Manicouagan, 500 ....D 2
Matagami, 2,411 ....B 3
Micoua, 851 ....D 3
Moisie, 570 ....D 2
Noranda, 10,741 ....B 3
Normétal, 1,851 ....B 3
Nouveau-Comptoir, 514 ....B 2
Obedjiwan, 712 ....C 3
Parent, 452 ....C 3
Port-Cartier, 3,730 ....D 2
Port-Cartier-Ouest, 500 ....D 3
Port-Menier, 394 ....D 2
Poste-de-la-Baleine, 987 ....B 1
Povungnituk, 676 ....E 1
Rivière-au-Tonnerre, 520 ....D 2
Rouyn, 17,821 ....B 3
Rupert House, 757 ....B 2

OTHER FEATURES

Anticosti (isl.), 419 ....E 2
Baleine, Grande Rivière de la (riv.) ....C 3
Betsiamites (riv.) ....C 3
Bienville (lake) ....C 3
Cabonga (res.) ....B 3
Caniapiscau (riv.) ....C 3
Daniel-Johnson (dam) ....D 3
Dozois (res.) ....B 3
Eastmain (riv.) ....B 3
George (riv.) ....F 2
Gouin (res.) ....C 3
Grande Rivière, La (riv.) ....B 2
Guillaume-Delisle (lake) ....B 2
Harricana (riv.) ....B 3
Honguedo (passg.) ....C 1
Hudson (bay) ....A 2
Hudson (str.) ....E 1
Jacques-Cartier (passg.) ....D 2
James (bay) ....A 2
Koksoak (riv.) ....E 1
La Vérendrye Prov. Park ....B 3
Louis-XIV (pt.) ....A 2
Manicouagan (res.) ....D 3
Mistassibi (riv.) ....C 2
Mistassini (lake) ....C 2
Moisie (riv.) ....D 2
Natashquan (riv.) ....E 2
Nottaway (riv.) ....B 2
Nouveau-Québec (crater) ....F 1
Otish (mts.) ....C 2
Ottawa (riv.) ....B 3
Reed (mt.) ....D 2
Romaine (riv.) ....E 2
Saguenay (riv.) ....D 2
Saguenay Prov. Park ....D 2
Saint Lawrence (gulf) ....E 2
Saint Lawrence (riv.) ....D 2
Ungava (bay) ....F 1
Ungava (pen.) ....E 1
Wolstenholme (cape) ....E 1
Wright (mt.) ....D 2

Sagluoc, 402 ....E 1
Saint-Augustin, 916 ....F 2
Schefferville, 3,271 ....D 2
Senneterre, 4,303 ....B 3
Sept-Îles, 24,320 ....D 2
Témiscaming, 2,428 ....B 3
Val-d'Or, 17,421 ....B 3
Ville-Marie©, 1,995 ....B 3

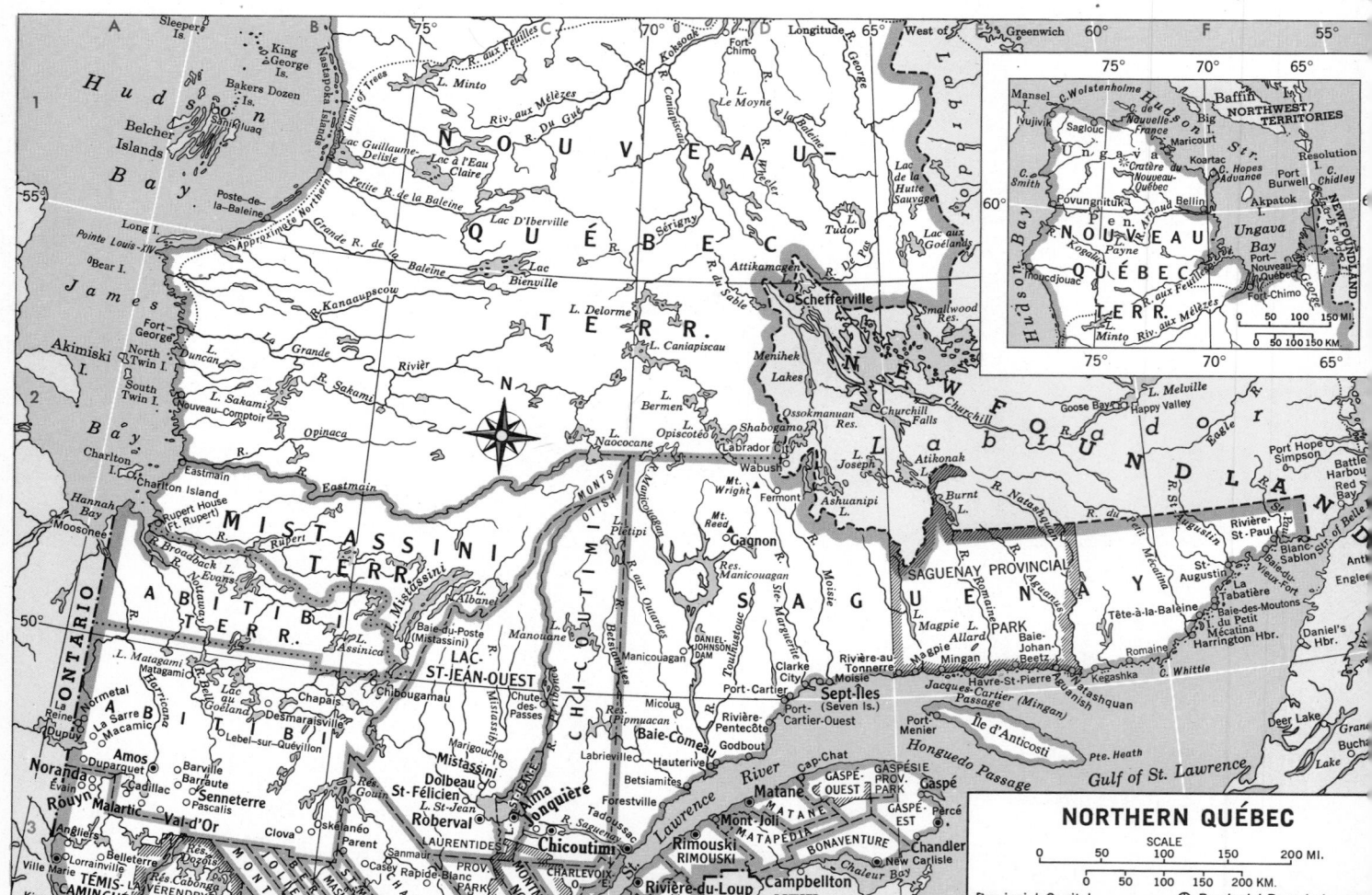

NORTHERN QUÉBEC

SCALE
0 ... 50 ... 100 ... 150 ... 200 MI.
0 ... 50 ... 100 ... 150 ... 200 KM.

Provincial Capital ....⊛   Provincial Boundaries ____
County Seats ....◎   County Boundaries ____
International Boundaries ___   Territorial Boundaries ___

© C.S. HAMMOND & Co., N.Y.

ONTARIO, NORTHERN

INTERNAL DIVISIONS

Algoma (terr. dist.),
121,937 ....D 3
Cochrane (terr. dist.),
95,836 ....D 2
Kenora (terr. dist.), 53,230 C 2
Manitoulin (terr. dist.),
10,931 ....D 3
Nipissing (terr. dist.),
78,867 ....E 3
Parry Sound (terr. dist.),
30,244 ....E 3
Rainy River (terr. dist.),
25,750 ....B 3
Renfrew (county), 90,875 .E 3
Sudbury (reg. munic.),
168,224 ....D 3
Sudbury (terr. dist.),
198,079 ....D 3
Thunder Bay (terr. dist.),
145,390 ....C 3
Timiskaming (terr. dist.),
46,485 ....D 3

CITIES and TOWNS

Atikokan, 6,007 ....B 3
Blind River, 3,450 ....D 3
Capreol, 3,994 ....D 3
Chalk River, 1,094 ....E 3
Chapleau, 3,365 ....D 3
Cochrane ⊙, 4,965 ....D 2
Deep River, 5,671 ....E 3
Dryden, 6,939 ....B 3
Elliot Lake, 8,727 ....D 3
Espanola, 6,045 ....D 3
Fort Albany, 25 ....D 2
Fort Frances ⊙, 9,947 ....B 3
Geraldton, 3,178 ....C 3
Haileybury ⊙, 5,280 ....D 3
Hearst, 5,354 ....C 3
Huntsville, 9,784 ....E 3
Iroquois Falls, 7,055 ....D 3
Kapuskasing, 12,834 ....C 3
Kenora ⊙, 10,952 ....B 3
Kirkland Lake, 13,599 ....D 3
Manitouwadge, 3,258 ....C 3
Mattawa, 2,881 ....E 3
Moose Factory, 849 ....D 2
Moosonee, 1,793 ....D 2

New Liskeard, 5,488 ....E 3
Nickel Centre, 13,037 ....D 3
North Bay ⊙, 49,187 ....E 3
Onaping Falls, 7,511 ....D 3
Parry Sound ⊙, 5,842 ....D 3
Pembroke ⊙, 16,544 ....E 3
Renfrew, 9,173 ....E 3
Sault Sainte Marie ⊙,
80,332 ....D 3
Sturgeon Falls, 6,662 ....E 3
Sudbury, 99,512 ....D 3
Sudbury, ‡155,424 ....D 3
Thunder Bay ⊙, 108,411 ..C 3
Thunder Bay, ‡112,093 ..C 3
Timmins, 43,182 ....D 3
Valley East, 17,937 ....D 3
Walden, 10,788 ....D 3
Wawa, 4,375 ....C 3

OTHER FEATURES

Abitibi (lake) ....E 3
Abitibi (riv.) ....D 2
Albany (riv.) ....C 2
Algonquin Prov. Park, 337 E 3
Attawapiskat (riv.) ....C 2
Big Trout (lake) ....B 2
Caribou (isl.), 3 ....C 2
Eabamet (lake) ....C 2
Ekwan (riv.) ....C 2
English (riv.) ....B 2
Groundhog (riv.) ....D 3
Hannah (bay) ....D 2
Henrietta Maria (cape) ..D 1
Hudson (bay) ....D 1
James (bay) ....D 2
Kapuskasing (riv.) ....D 3
Kenogami (riv.) ....D 3
Lake of the Woods (lake) ..B 3
Lake Superior Prov. Park ..D 3
Manitoulin (isl.), 10,064 ..D 3
Mattagami (riv.) ....D 3
Michipicoten (isl.), 4 ....C 3
Mille Lacs (lake) ....B 3
Missinaibi (riv.) ....C 2
Nipigon (lake) ....C 3
North Caribou (lake) ....B 2
Ogidaki (mt.) ....D 3
Ogoki (riv.) ....C 2
Ottawa (riv.) ....E 3
Pipestone (riv.) ....B 2
Polar Bear Prov. Park ....D 2
Quetico Prov. Park ....B 3
Rainy (lake) ....B 3

Red (lake) ....B 2
Sachigo (riv.) ....B 2
Saint Joseph (lake) ....B 2
Sandy (lake) ....B 2
Seine (riv.) ....B 3
Seul (lake) ....B 2
Severn (riv.) ....B 2
Sibley Prov. Park, 2 ....C 3
Slate (isls.), 4 ....C 3
Superior (lake) ....C 3
Sutton (riv.) ....D 2
Thunder (bay) ....C 3
Timagami (lake) ....D 3
Timiskaming (lake) ....E 3
Winisk (riv.) ....C 2
Winnipeg (riv.) ....A 2
Woods (lake) ....B 3

ONTARIO

INTERNAL DIVISIONS

Algoma (terr. dist.),
121,937 ....J 5
Brant (county), 96,767 ..C 4
Bruce (county), 47,385 ..C 3
Cochrane (terr. dist.),
95,836 ....J 4
Dufferin (county), 21,200 .D 3
Dundas (county), 17,457 .J 2
Durham (reg. munic.),
221,503 ....J 4
Elgin (county), 66,608 ..C 5
Essex (county), 306,399 .B 5
Frontenac (county),
101,692 ....H 3
Glengarry (county), 18,480 K 2
Grenville (county), 24,316 .J 3
Grey (county), 66,403 ..D 3
Haldimand-Norfolk (reg.
munic.), 86,772 ....D 5
Haliburton (county), 9,081 F 2
Hamilton-Wentworth (reg.
munic.), 401,883 ....D 4
Halton (reg. munic.),
190,469 ....E 4
Hastings (county), 99,393 G 3
Huron (county), 52,951 ..C 4
Kenora (terr. dist.), 53,230 B 2
Kent (county), 101,118 ..B 5
Lambton (county),
114,314 ....B 5
Lanark (county), 42,259 .H 3

Leeds (county), 50,093 ..H 3
Lennox and Addington
(county), 28,359 ....G 3
Manitoulin (terr. dist.),
10,931 ....B 2
Middlesex (county),
282,014 ....C 4
Muskoka (dist. munic.)
31,938 ....E 3
Niagara (reg. munic.),
347,328 ....E 4
Nipissing (terr. dist.),
78,867 ....F 2
Northumberland (county),
60,102 ....G 3
Ottawa-Carleton (reg. munic.),
471,931 ....J 2
Oxford (county), 80,349 .D 4
Parry Sound (terr. dist.),
30,244 ....D 2
Peel (reg. munic.),
259,402 ....E 4
Perth (county), 62,973 ..C 4
Peterborough (county),
92,417 ....F 3
Prescott (county),
27,832 ....K 2
Prince Edward (county),
20,640 ....G 3
Rainy River (terr. dist.),
25,750 ....G 5
Renfrew (county),
90,875 ....G 2
Russell (county), 16,287 .J 2
Simcoe (county),
175,604 ....E 3
Stormont (county),
61,302 ....K 2
Sudbury (reg. munic.),
168,224 ....K 6
Sudbury (terr. dist.),
198,079 ....J 5
Thunder Bay (terr. dist.),
145,390 ....H 5
Timiskaming (terr. dist.),
46,485 ....K 5
Toronto (metro. munic.),
2,086,017 ....K 4
Victoria (county),
36,641 ....F 3
Waterloo (reg. munic.),
254,037 ....D 4
Wellington (county),
108,581 ....D 4
York (reg. munic.),
166,060 ....E 4

CITIES and TOWNS

Ailsa Craig, 608 ....C 4
Ajax, 15,052 ....E 4
Alban, 420 ....D 1
Alcona Beach, 659 ....E 3
Alexandria, 3,240 ....K 2
Alfred, 1,230 ....K 2
Alliston, 3,176 ....E 3
Almonte, 3,696 ....H 2
Alvinston, 702 ....B 5
Amherstburg, 5,169 ....A 5
Amherst View, 3,121 ....H 3
Ancaster, 15,326 ....D 4
Angus, 3,174 ....E 3
Apple Hill, 318 ....K 2
Arkona, 469 ....C 4
Armstrong, 574 ....H 4
Arnprior, 6,016 ....H 2
Arthur, 1,414 ....D 4
Athens, 1,071 ....J 3
Atherley, 392 ....E 3
Atikokan, 6,007 ....G 5
Atwood, 690 ....D 4
Aurora, 13,614 ....J 3
Avonmore, 287 ....K 2
Aylmer, 4,755 ....C 5
Ayr, 1,272 ....D 4
Ayton, 423 ....D 4
Baden, 959 ....D 4
Bala, 462 ....E 2
Bancroft, 2,276 ....G 2
Barrie ⊙, 27,676 ....E 3
Barry's Bay, 1,432 ....G 2
Batawa, 667 ....G 3
Batchawana Bay, 586 ....J 5
Bath, 810 ....H 3
Bayfield, 503 ....C 4

Bayside, 1,732 ....G 3
Baysville, 283 ....E 2
Beachburg, 549 ....H 2
Beachville, 995 ....D 4
Beardmore, 754 ....H 5
Beaverton, 1,485 ....E 3
Beeton, 1,061 ....E 3
Belle River, 2,877 ....B 5
Belleville ⊙, 35,128 ....G 3
Belmont, 798 ....C 5
Bethany, 325 ....F 3
Bewdley, 446 ....F 3
Bicroft, 576 ....F 2
Blackburn, 3,841 ....J 2
Blenheim, 3,840 ....C 5
Blind River, 3,450 ....J 5
Bloomfield, 730 ....G 4
Blyth, 814 ....C 4
Bobcaygeon, 1,518 ....F 3
Bonfield, 694 ....E 1
Bothwell, 810 ....C 5
Bourget, 855 ....J 2
Bracebridge ⊙, 6,903 ....E 2
Bradford, 3,401 ....E 3
Braeside, 522 ....H 2
Brampton ⊙, 73,570 ....J 4
Brantford ⊙, 64,421 ....D 4
Bridgenorth, 1,380 ....F 3
Brigden, 582 ....B 5
Brighton, 2,956 ....G 3
Brights Grove, 730 ....B 4
Britt, 500 ....D 2
Brockville ⊙, 19,765 ....J 3
Bruce Mines, 505 ....J 5
Brussels, 908 ....C 4
Burford, 1,291 ....D 4
Burgessville, 329 ....D 4
Burk's Falls, 891 ....E 2

Burlington, 87,023 ....E 4
Cache Bay, 727 ....D 1
Caesarea, 352 ....F 3
Calabogie, 299 ....H 2
Caledon, 13,480 ....E 4
Callander, 1,190 ....E 1
Cambridge, 64,114 ....D 4
Campbellford, 3,522 ....G 3
Cannington, 1,083 ....E 3
Cape Croker, 681 ....D 3
Capreol, 3,994 ....K 5
Caramat, 520 ....H 5
Cardinal, 1,865 ....J 3
Carleton Place, 5,020 ....H 2
Carlisle, 488 ....D 4
Carp, 516 ....H 2
Cartier, 740 ....J 5
Casselman, 1,337 ....J 2
Castleton, 289 ....F 3
Cedar Springs, 302 ....B 5
Chalk River, 1,094 ....G 1
Chapleau, 3,365 ....J 5
Charing Cross, 436 ....B 5
Chatham ⊙, 35,317 ....B 5
Chatsworth, 399 ....D 3
Chesley, 1,693 ....C 3
Chesterville, 1,252 ....J 2
Chute-a-Blondeau, 420 ....K 2
City View, 4,500 ....J 2
Clarence Creek, 411 ....J 2
Clarksburg, 389 ....D 3
Clifford, 555 ....D 4
Clinton, 3,154 ....C 4
Cobalt, 2,197 ....K 5
Cobden, 926 ....H 2
Coboconk, 477 ....F 3
Cobourg ⊙, 11,282 ....F 4
Cochrane ⊙, 4,965 ....K 5
Colborne, 1,588 ....G 4
Colchester, 752 ....B 6
Coldwater, 759 ....E 3
Collingwood, 9,775 ....D 3
Collins Bay, 2,089 ....H 3
Comber, 642 ....B 5
Consecon, 332 ....G 3
Cookstown, 847 ....E 3
Cornwall ⊙, 47,116 ....K 2
Corunna, 3,052 ....B 5
Cottam, 530 ....B 5
Courtland, 574 ....D 5
Courtright, 590 ....B 5
Coverdale, 670 ....F 4
Crediton, 409 ....C 4
Creemore, 978 ....D 3
Crysler, 481 ....J 2
Cumberland, 581 ....J 2
Cumberland Beach, 477 ....E 3
Dashwood, 434 ....C 4
Deep River, 5,671 ....G 1
Delaware, 627 ....C 5
Delhi, 3,894 ....D 5
Delta, 465 ....H 3
Deseronto, 1,863 ....G 3
Dorchester, 1,796 ....C 5
Douglas, 307 ....H 2
Drayton, 752 ....D 4
Dresden, 2,369 ....B 5
Drumbo, 460 ....D 4
Dryden, 6,939 ....G 4
Dublin, 314 ....C 4
Dubreuilville, 654 ....J 5
Dundalk, 1,022 ....D 3
Dundas, 17,208 ....D 4
Dunnville, 11,422 ....E 5
Durham, 2,448 ....D 3
Dutton, 878 ....C 5
East York, 104,784 ....J 4
Echo Bay, 493 ....J 5
Eganville, 1,395 ....G 2
Egmondville, 492 ....C 4
Elgin, 322 ....H 3
Elk Lake, 627 ....K 5
Elliot Lake, 8,727 ....B 1
Elmira, 4,730 ....D 4
Elmvale, 1,103 ....E 3
Elmwood, 345 ....C 3
Elora, 1,904 ....D 4
Embro, 703 ....C 4
Embrun, 1,452 ....J 2
Emeryville, 1,719 ....B 5
Emo, 768 ....F 5
Englehart, 1,721 ....K 5
Erieau, 509 ....C 5
Erin, 1,446 ....D 4
Espanola, 6,045 ....J 5
Essex, 4,002 ....B 5
Etobicoke, 282,686 ....J 4
Everett, 405 ....E 3
Exeter, 3,354 ....C 4
Fauquier, 643 ....J 5
Fenelon Falls, 1,616 ....F 3
Fergus, 5,433 ....D 4
Field, 655 ....E 1
Finch, 397 ....J 2
Fingal, 322 ....C 5
Fitzroy Harbour, 317 ....H 2
Flesherton, 524 ....D 3
Foleyet, 637 ....J 5
Fordwich, 325 ....C 4

(continued on following page)

AREA, POPULATION, etc.

AREA 412,582 sq. mi.
POPULATION 7,707,000
CAPITAL Toronto
LARGEST CITY Toronto
HIGHEST POINT Ogidaki Mtn. 2,183 ft.
SETTLED IN 1749
ADMITTED TO CONFEDERATION 1867
PROVINCIAL FLOWER White Trillium

NORTHERN ONTARIO

SCALE
0 25 50 100 150 200 MI.
0 25 50 100 150 200 KM.

Provincial Capital ....⊛ Provincial and
County Seats ....⊙ State Boundaries ......─ ─ ─
International Boundaries ─ ─ Country Boundaries ..─ ─ ─

© C.S. HAMMOND & Co., N.Y.

Forest, 2,355 . . . . C 4
Formosa, 370 . . . . C 3
Fort Erie, 23,113 . . . . . . E 5
Fort Frances ⊙, 9,947 . . F 5
Foxboro, 590 . . . . G 3
Frankford, 1,862 . . . . . . G 3
Fraserdale, 337 . . . . . . J 5
Gananoque, 5,212 . . . . . H 3
Geraldton, 3,178 . . . . . H 5
Glencoe, 1,387 . . . . . . C 5
Glen Miller, 736 . . . . . . G 3
Glen Robertson, 345 . . . K 2
Glen Walter, 656 . . . . . K 2
Goderich ⊙, 6,813 . . . . C 4
Gogama, 578 . . . . J 5
Goodwood, 356 . . . . . . E 3
Gore Bay ⊙, 770 . . . . . B 2
Gorrie, 380 . . . . C 4
Grafton, 395 . . . . G 4
Grand Bend, 696 . . . . . C 4
Grand Valley, 904 . . . . . D 4
Granton, 350 . . . . C 4
Gravenhurst, 7,133 . . . . E 3
Green Valley, 363 . . . . . K 2
Grimsby, 15,770 . . . . . . E 4
Guelph ⊙, 60,087 . . . . . D 4
Hagar, 290 . . . . D 1
Haileybury ⊙, 5,280 . . . K 5
Haldimand, 15,839 . . . . E 5
Haliburton, 899 . . . . . . F 2
Halton Hills, 31,500 . . . . E 4
Hamilton ⊙, 309,173 . . . E 4
Hamilton, ‡498,523 . . . . E 4
Hanover, 5,063 . . . . C 3
Harriston, 1,785 . . . . . . D 4
Harrow, 1,971 . . . . B 5

Harrowsmith, 550 . . . . . H 3
Hastings, 938 . . . . G 3
Havelock, 1,225 . . . . . . G 3
Hawkesbury, 9,276 . . . . K 2
Hawkestone, 283 . . . . . E 3
Hawk Junction, 396 . . . . J 5
Hearst, 5,354 . . . . J 5
Hensall, 970 . . . . C 4
Hepworth, 372 . . . . C 3
Highgate, 424 . . . . C 5
Hillsburgh, 674 . . . . . . D 4
Hillsdale, 308 . . . . E 3
Holland Landing, 896 . . . E 3
Hornepayne, 1,826 . . . . J 5
Hudson, 543 . . . . G 4
Huntsville, 9,784 . . . . . . E 2
Huron Park, 1,217 . . . . . C 4
Ignace, 334 . . . . G 5
Ilderton, 297 . . . . C 4
Ingersoll, 7,783 . . . . . . D 4
Ingleside, 899 . . . . K 2
Innerkip, 584 . . . . D 4
Iron Bridge, 874 . . . . . . A 1
Iroquois, 1,224 . . . . J 2
Iroquois Falls, 7,055 . . . J 5
Johnstown, 414 . . . . . . J 2
Kakabeka Falls, 325 . . . G 5
Kaladar, 289 . . . . H 3
Kanata, 4,635 . . . . J 2
Kapuskasing, 12,834 . . . J 5
Kearney, 308 . . . . E 2
Keene, 334 . . . . F 3
Keewatin, 2,112 . . . . . . F 5
Kemptville, 2,413 . . . . . J 2
Kenora ⊙, 10,952 . . . . . F 4
Keswick, 1,031 . . . . E 3

Killaloe Station, 810 . . . G 2
Killarney, 475 . . . . C 2
Kincardine, 3,239 . . . . . C 3
King City, 2,091 . . . . . . J 3
Kingston ⊙, 59,047 . . . . H 3
Kingsville, 4,076 . . . . . . B 6
Kinmount, 371 . . . . F 3
Kiosk, 332 . . . . F 1
Kirkfield, 288 . . . . E 3
Kirkland Lake, 15,205 . . K 5
Kitchener ⊙, 116,096 . . . D 4
Kitchener, ‡226,846 . . . . D 4
Komoka, 698 . . . . C 5
Lakefield, 2,245 . . . . . . F 3
Lambeth, 3,023 . . . . . . C 5
Lanark, 861 . . . . H 2
Lancaster, 617 . . . . K 2
Langton, 478 . . . . D 5
Lansdowne, 520 . . . . . . H 3
Latchford, 535 . . . . K 5
Leamington, 10,435 . . . . B 5
Lefroy, 629 . . . . E 3
Limoges, 355 . . . . J 2
Lincoln, 14,247 . . . . E 4
Lindsay ⊙, 12,746 . . . . . F 3
Linwood, 482 . . . . D 4
Lion's Head, 467 . . . . . . C 2
Listowel, 4,677 . . . . D 4
Little Britain, 337 . . . . . F 3
Little Current, 1,565 . . . . B 2
London ⊙, 223,222 . . . . C 5
London, ‡286,011 . . . . . C 5
Longlac, 1,400 . . . . H 5
Long Sault, 965 . . . . . . K 2
L'Orignal, 1,405 . . . . . . K 2
Lucan, 1,178 . . . . C 4

Lucknow, 1,047 . . . . . . C 4
Lyn, 556 . . . . J 3
MacGregor's Bay, 312 . . G 2
MacTier, 794 . . . . E 2
Madawaska, 371 . . . . . . F 2
Madoc, 1,353 . . . . G 3
Maitland, 270 . . . . J 3
Mallorytown, 347 . . . . . J 3
Manitouwadge, 3,258 . . . H 5
Manitowaning, 437 . . . . C 2
Manotick, 476 . . . . J 2
Marathon, 2,409 . . . . . . H 5
Markdale, 1,236 . . . . . . D 3
Markham, 36,684 . . . . . K 4
Markstay, 491 . . . . D 1
Marmora, 1,350 . . . . . . G 3
Martintown, 394 . . . . . . K 2
Massey, 1,278 . . . . C 1
Matachewan, 533 . . . . . J 5
Matheson, 721 . . . . K 5
Mattawa, 2,881 . . . . . . F 1
Mattice, 860 . . . . J 5
Maxville, 846 . . . . K 2
Maynooth, 328 . . . . G 2
McGregor, 665 . . . . B 5
Meaford, 4,045 . . . . D 3
Melbourne, 305 . . . . . . C 5
Merlin, 757 . . . . B 5
Merrickville, 930 . . . . . . J 2
Metcalfe, 473 . . . . J 2
Midhurst, 342 . . . . E 3
Midland, 10,992 . . . . . . D 3
Mildmay, 963 . . . . D 4
Millbrook, 960 . . . . F 3
Milton ⊙, 10,463 . . . . . . E 4
Milverton, 1,193 . . . . . . D 4

Minaki, 299 . . . . F 4
Mindemoya, 458 . . . . . . B 2
Minden ⊙, 777 . . . . F 3
Mitchell, 2,545 . . . . C 4
Monkton, 550 . . . . C 4
Moonbeam, 920 . . . . . . J 5
Moorefield, 311 . . . . . . D 4
Moose Creek, 391 . . . . . K 2
Morrisburg, 2,055 . . . . . J 3
Mount Albert, 705 . . . . . E 3
Mount Brydges, 1,484 . . C 5
Mount Forest, 3,037 . . . . D 4
Mount Hope, 565 . . . . . E 4
Mount Pleasant, 574 . . . D 4
Nairn, 461 . . . . C 1
Nakina, 673 . . . . H 4
Nanticoke, 20,453 . . . . . D 5
Napanee ⊙, 4,638 . . . . . G 3
Neustadt, 579 . . . . D 3
Newboro, 296 . . . . H 3
Newburgh, 650 . . . . H 3
Newbury, 338 . . . . C 5
Newcastle, 27,198 . . . . . F 4
New Hamburg, 3,008 . . . D 4
New Liskeard, 5,488 . . . K 5
Newmarket ⊙, 18,941 . . E 3
Niagara Falls, 67,163 . . . E 4
Niagara-on-the-Lake,
12,552 . . . . E 4
Nickel Centre, 13,037 . . . D 1
Nipigon, 2,141 . . . . H 5
Nobel, 484 . . . . D 2
Nobleton, 1,356 . . . . . . J 3
Noelville, 856 . . . . D 1
North Bay ⊙, 49,187 . . . E 1

North Gower, 363 . . . . . J 2
North York, 504,150 . . . . J 4
Norwich, 1,806 . . . . D 5
Norwood, 1,183 . . . . . . F 3
Nottawa, 401 . . . . D 3
Novar, 294 . . . . E 2
Oakville, 61,483 . . . . . . E 4
Oakwood, 310 . . . . F 3
Odessa, 1,020 . . . . H 3
Oil Springs, 570 . . . . . . B 5
Omemee, 777 . . . . F 3
Onaping Falls, 7,511 . . . J 5
Orangeville ⊙, 8,074 . . . D 4
Orillia, 24,040 . . . . E 3
Orleans, 2,810 . . . . J 2
Osgoode, 823 . . . . J 2
Oshawa ⊙, 94,994 . . . . F 4
Ottawa (cap.), Canada ⊙,
302,341 . . . . J 2
Ottawa-Hull, ‡602,510 . . J 2
Otterville, 754 . . . . D 5
Owen Sound ⊙, 18,469 . D 3
Paincourt, 324 . . . . B 5
Painswick, 727 . . . . E 3
Paisley, 793 . . . . C 3
Pakenham, 371 . . . . . . J 2
Palmerston, 1,855 . . . . . D 4
Paris, 6,483 . . . . D 4
Parkhill, 1,167 . . . . C 4
Parry Sound ⊙, 5,842 . . E 2
Pefferlaw, 432 . . . . E 3
Pelham, 9,997 . . . . E 4
Pembroke ⊙, 16,544 . . . G 2
Penetanguishene, 5,497 . D 3
Perkinsfield, 368 . . . . . . D 3
Perth ⊙, 5,537 . . . . H 3

Petawawa, 5,784 . . . . . G 2
Peterborough ⊙, 58,111 . F 3
Petrolia, 4,044 . . . . B 5
Pickering, 31,734 . . . . . K 4
Picton ⊙, 4,875 . . . . . . G 3
Plantagenet, 909 . . . . . K 2
Plattsville, 526 . . . . D 4
Point Anne, 373 . . . . . . G 3
Point Edward, 2,773 . . . B 4
Pontypool, 288 . . . . F 3
Port Burwell, 700 . . . . . D 5
Port Carling, 617 . . . . . . E 2
Port Colborne, 21,420 . . E 5
Port Elgin, 2,855 . . . . . . C 3
Port Hope, 8,872 . . . . . . F 4
Port Lambton, 714 . . . . . B 5
Port Loring, 331 . . . . . . E 2
Port McNicoll, 1,450 . . . . E 3
Port Perry, 2,977 . . . . . . F 3
Port Rowan, 856 . . . . . . D 5
Port Stanley, 1,725 . . . . C 5
Pottageville, 381 . . . . . . J 3
Powassan, 1,163 . . . . . . E 1
Prescott, 5,165 . . . . J 3
Princeton, 456 . . . . D 4
Rainy River, 1,196 . . . . . F 5
Rayside-Balfour, 15,445 . K 5
Red Rock, 1,407 . . . . . . H 5
Renfrew, 9,173 . . . . H 2
Richards Landing, 318 . . J 5
Richmond, 2,122 . . . . . . J 2
Richmond Hill, 32,384 . . . J 4
Ridgetown, 2,836 . . . . . C 5
Ripley, 448 . . . . C 3
Rockcliffe Park, 2,138 . . C 4
Rockland, 3,649 . . . . . . J 2

Copyright by C. S. HAMMOND & CO., N.Y.

Rockwood, 996 . . . . D 4
Rodney, 1,016 . . . . C 5
Rolphton, 418 . . . . G 1
Russell, 583 . . . . J 2
Ruthven, 461 . . . . B 6
Saint Catharines ⊙,
 109,722 . . . . E 4
Saint Catharines-Niagara,
 ‡303,429 . . . . E 4
Saint Charles, 468 . . . . D 1
Saint Clair Beach, 1,987 . B 5
Saint-Eugène, 512 . . . . K 2
Saint George, 949 . . . . D 4
Saint Isidore de Prescott,
 615 . . . . K 2
Saint Jacobs, 787 . . . . D 4
Saint Mary's, 4,650 . . . . C 4
Saint Thomas ⊙, 25,545 . C 5
Saint Williams, 437 . . . . D 5
Salem, 348 . . . . D 4
Sarnia ⊙, 57,644 . . . . B 5
Sauble Beach, 338 . . . . C 3
Sault Sainte Marie ⊙,
 80,332 . . . . J 5
Scarborough, 334,310 . . K 4
Schomberg, 677 . . . . J 3
Schreiber, 2,072 . . . . H 5
Scotland, 542 . . . . D 4
Seaforth, 2,134 . . . . C 4
Searchmont, 375 . . . . J 5
Sebringville, 571 . . . . C 4
Seeleys Bay, 406 . . . . H 3
Shallow Lake, 385 . . . . C 3
Shanty Bay, 316 . . . . E 3
Sharbot Lake, 461 . . . . H 3
Shedden, 277 . . . . C 5

Shelburne, 1,790 . . . . D 3
Simcoe ⊙, 10,793 . . . . D 5
Sioux Lookout, 2,530 . . G 4
Smithfield, 319 . . . . G 3
Smiths Falls, 9,585 . . . . H 3
Smithville, 1,418 . . . . E 4
Smooth Rock Falls, 1,239 . J 5
Sombra, 685 . . . . B 5
Southampton, 2,036 . . . . C 3
South River, 1,052 . . . . E 2
Spanish, 1,257 . . . . J 5
Spencerville, 386 . . . . J 3
Springfield, 522 . . . . C 5
Springford, 296 . . . . D 5
Stayner, 1,937 . . . . E 3
Stirling, 1,500 . . . . G 3
Stittsville, 1,994 . . . . J 2
Stoney Creek, 27,373 . . E 4
Stoney Point, 749 . . . . B 5
Straffordville, 717 . . . . D 5
Stratford ⊙, 24,508 . . . . C 4
Strathroy, 6,592 . . . . C 5
Stroud, 548 . . . . E 3
Sturgeon Falls, 6,662 . . E 1
Sudbury ⊙, 99,512 . . . . K 5
Sudbury, ‡155,424 . . . . K 5
Sultan, 343 . . . . J 5
Sunderland, 807 . . . . E 3
Sundridge, 723 . . . . E 2
Sutton, 2,500 . . . . E 3
Sydenham, 556 . . . . H 3
Tamworth, 375 . . . . H 3
Tara, 643 . . . . C 3
Tavistock, 1,490 . . . . D 4
Tecumseh, 5,165 . . . . B 5
Teeswater, 983 . . . . C 3

Terrace Bay, 1,819 . . . . H 5
Thamesford, 1,185 . . . . C 4
Thamesville, 1,028 . . . . C 5
Thedford, 719 . . . . C 4
Thessalon, 1,879 . . . . J 5
Thornbury, 1,220 . . . . D 3
Thorndale, 463 . . . . C 4
Thornton, 313 . . . . E 3
Thorold, 15,065 . . . . E 4
Thunder Bay ⊙, 108,411 . H 5
Thunder Bay, ‡112,093 . H 5
Tilbury, 3,580 . . . . B 5
Tillsonburg, 6,608 . . . . D 5
Timagami, 693 . . . . K 5
Timmins, 43,182 . . . . J 5
Tiverton, 567 . . . . C 3
Tobermory, 315 . . . . C 2
Toronto (cap.) ⊙, 712,786 K 4
Toronto (Metro.),
 2,086,017 . . . . K 4
Toronto, ‡2,628,043 . . . . K 4
Tottenham, 1,616 . . . . E 3
Trenton, 14,589 . . . . G 3
Trout Creek, 586 . . . . E 2
Turkey Point, 373 . . . . D 5
Tweed, 1,738 . . . . G 3
Uxbridge, 3,077 . . . . E 3
Vanier, 22,477 . . . . J 2
Vankleek Hill, 1,691 . . . . K 2
Vars, 395 . . . . J 2
Vaughan, 15,873 . . . . J 4
Vermilion Bay, 637 . . . . G 4
Verner, 1,011 . . . . D 1
Verona, 689 . . . . H 3
Victoria Harbour, 1,243 . E 3
Vienna, 390 . . . . D 5
Vittoria, 455 . . . . D 5
Wabigoon, 312 . . . . G 5
Walden, 10,788 . . . . J 5
Walkerton ⊙, 4,479 . . . . C 3
Wallaceburg, 10,550 . . B 5
Wardsville, 388 . . . . C 5
Warkworth, 562 . . . . G 3
Warren, 613 . . . . D 1
Wasaga Beach, 1,923 . . D 3
Washago, 423 . . . . E 3
Waterdown, 2,146 . . . . D 4
Waterloo, 37,893 . . . . D 4
Watford, 1,400 . . . . C 5
Waubaushene, 718 . . . . E 3
Wawa, 4,375 . . . . J 5
Webbwood, 585 . . . . C 1
Welland, 44,397 . . . . E 5
Wellesley, 816 . . . . D 4
Wellington, 988 . . . . G 4
Wendover, 313 . . . . J 2
West Lorne, 1,094 . . . . C 5
Westport, 601 . . . . H 3
Wheatley, 1,657 . . . . B 5
Whitby ⊙, 25,324 . . . . F 4
Whitchurch-Stouffville,
 11,262 . . . . J 4
White River, 945 . . . . J 5
Whitney, 826 . . . . F 2
Wiarton, 2,222 . . . . C 3
Wikwemikong, 895 . . . . C 2
Williamsburg, 398 . . . . J 3
Williamstown, 312 . . . . K 2
Winchester, 1,575 . . . . J 2

Wingham, 2,913 . . . . C 4
Wolfe Island, 335 . . . . H 3
Woodstock ⊙, 26,173 . . D 4
Woodville, 473 . . . . F 3
Wroxeter, 291 . . . . C 4
Wyoming, 1,279 . . . . B 5
Yarker, 335 . . . . H 3
York, 147,301 . . . . J 4
Zephyr, 337 . . . . E 3
Zurich, 767 . . . . C 4

OTHER FEATURES

Abitibi (riv.) . . . . J 5
Algonquin Prov. Park, 337 F 2
Amherst (isl.), 367 . . . . H 3
Balsam (lake) . . . . F 3
Barrie (isl.), 109 . . . . B 1
Bays (lake) . . . . F 2

Big Rideau (lake) . . . . H 3
Black (riv.) . . . . E 3
Bruce (pen.) . . . . C 2
Buckhorn (lake) . . . . F 3
Cabot (head) . . . . C 2
Charleston (lake) . . . . J 3
Christian (isl.), 506 . . . . D 3
Clear (lake) . . . . F 3
Cockburn (isl.) . . . . A 2
Couchiching (lake) . . . . E 3
Croker (cape) . . . . C 3
Don (riv.) . . . . J 4
Dore (lake) . . . . G 2
Douglas (pt.) . . . . C 3
Erie (lake) . . . . E 5
Flowerpot (isl.) . . . . C 2
French (riv.) . . . . D 1
Georgian (bay) . . . . D 2
Georgian Bay Is. Nat'l Park D 3

Georgina (isl.), 181 . . . . E 3
Grand (riv.) . . . . D 4
Humber (riv.) . . . . J 3
Hurd (cape) . . . . C 2
Huron (lake) . . . . C 3
Ipperwash Prov. Park, 32 C 4
Joseph (lake) . . . . D 2
Killbear Point Prov. Park . D 2
Lake of the Woods (lake) . F 5
Lake Superior Prov. Park . J 5
Lonely (isl.), 3 . . . . C 2
Long (pt.) . . . . D 5
Long Point (bay) . . . . D 5
Madawaska (riv.) . . . . G 2
Magnetawan (riv.) . . . . D 2
Main (chan.) . . . . C 2
Manitou (lake) . . . . C 2
Manitoulin (isl.), 10,064 . B 2
Mattagami (riv.) . . . . J 5
Michipicoten (isl.), 4 . . . H 5
Missinaibi (riv.) . . . . J 5
Mississagi (riv.) . . . . A 1
Mississippi (lake) . . . . H 2
Muskoka (lake) . . . . E 2
Niagara (riv.) . . . . E 4
Nipigon (lake) . . . . H 5
Nipissing (lake) . . . . E 2
North (chan.) . . . . A 1
Nottawasaga (bay) . . . . D 3
Ogidaki (mt.) . . . . J 5
Ontario (lake) . . . . G 4
Opeongo (lake) . . . . F 2
Ottawa (riv.) . . . . J 2
Owen (sound) . . . . D 3
Panache (lake) . . . . C 1
Parry (isl.), 318 . . . . D 2
Parry (sound) . . . . D 2
Pelee (pt.) . . . . B 6

Petre (pt.) . . . . G 4
Point Pelee Nat'l Park, 202B 6
Presqu'île Prov. Park, 67 G 4
Quetico Prov. Park . . . . G 5
Rainy (lake) . . . . G 5
Rice (lake) . . . . F 3
Rideau (lake) . . . . H 3
Rondeau Prov. Park, 103 C 5
Rosseau (lake) . . . . E 2
Saint Clair (lake) . . . . B 5
Saint Clair (riv.) . . . . B 5
Saint Lawrence (lake) . . K 3
Saint Lawrence (riv.) . . . J 3
Saint Lawrence Is. Nat'l
 Park . . . . J 3
Saugeen (riv.) . . . . C 3
Scugog (lake) . . . . F 3
Seul (lake) . . . . G 4
Severn (riv.) . . . . J 5
Sibley Prov. Park, 2 . . . . H 5
Simcoe (lake) . . . . E 3
South (bay) . . . . C 2
Spanish (riv.) . . . . C 1
Stony (lake) . . . . G 3
Superior (lake) . . . . H 5
Sydenham (riv.) . . . . B 5
Thames (riv.) . . . . B 5
Theano (pt.) . . . . J 5
Thousand (isls.), 1,447 . H 3
Timagami (lake) . . . . K 5
Trout (lake) . . . . E 1
Vernon (lake) . . . . E 2
Walpole (isl.), 1,420 . . . . B 5
Welland (canal) . . . . E 5
Woods (lake) . . . . F 5

⊙ County seat.
‡ Population of metropolitan
 area.

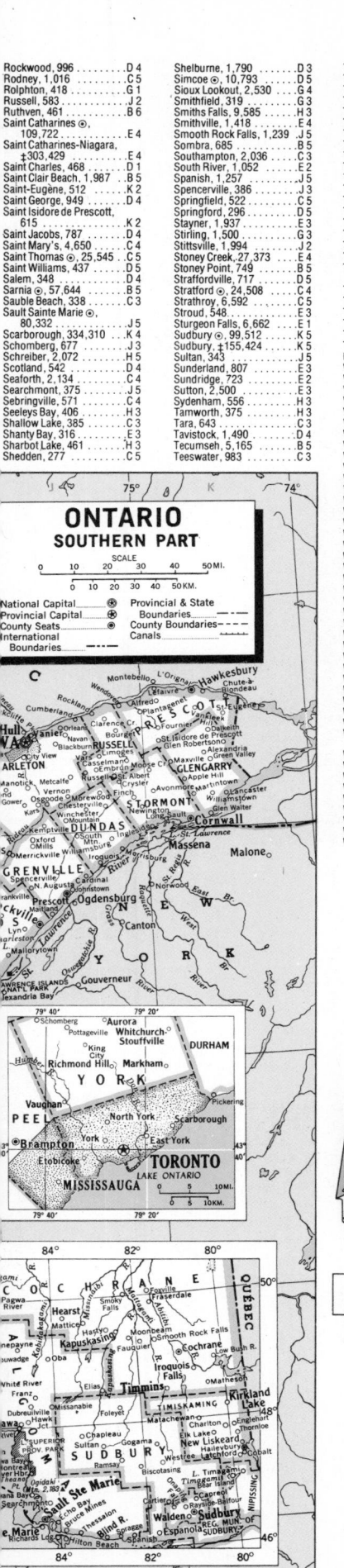

ONTARIO
SOUTHERN PART
SCALE
0 10 20 30 40 50 MI.
0 10 20 30 40 50 KM.

National Capital . . . . ⊛
Provincial Capital . . . . ⊛
County Seats . . . . ⊚
International
 Boundaries

Provincial & State
 Boundaries
County Boundaries . . . . .
Canals

Topography

0 100 200
MILES

Below Sea Level | 100 m. 328 ft. | 200 m. 656 ft. | 500 m. 1,640 ft. | 1,000 m. 3,281 ft. | 2,000 m. 6,562 ft. | 5,000 m. 16,404 ft.

Agriculture, Industry
and Resources

DOMINANT LAND USE

Cereals, Cash
 Crops, Livestock

Dairy

General Farming,
 Livestock

Fruits, Vegetables

Pasture Livestock

Forests

Nonagricultural
 Land

MAJOR MINERAL OCCURRENCES

Ab	Asbestos	Mg	Magnesium
Ag	Silver	Mr	Marble
Au	Gold	Na	Salt
Co	Cobalt	Ni	Nickel
Cu	Copper	Pb	Lead
Fe	Iron Ore	Pt	Platinum
G	Natural Gas	U	Uranium
Gr	Graphite	Zn	Zinc

⚡ Water Power
▨ Major Industrial Areas
▫ Major Pulp & Paper Mills

OTTAWA
Food Processing,
Printing & Publishing,
Wood Products, Machinery

THUNDER BAY
Pulp & Paper, Lumber,
Machinery, Shipbuilding

SAULT STE. MARIE
Iron & Steel, Pulp & Paper,
Lumber, Metal Products,
Chemicals

SARNIA
Chemicals, Oil Refining,
Rubber Products

WINDSOR
Motor Vehicles, Food
Processing, Metal Products,
Chemicals, Machinery

TORONTO-HAMILTON-NIAGARA
Iron & Steel, Metal Products, Food Processing, Electrical
Products, Chemicals, Printing & Publishing, Machinery,
Automobiles, Aircraft, Oil Refining

LONDON
Food Processing, Metal
Products, Printing & Publishing,
Locomotives, Chemicals,
Machinery, Leather Goods

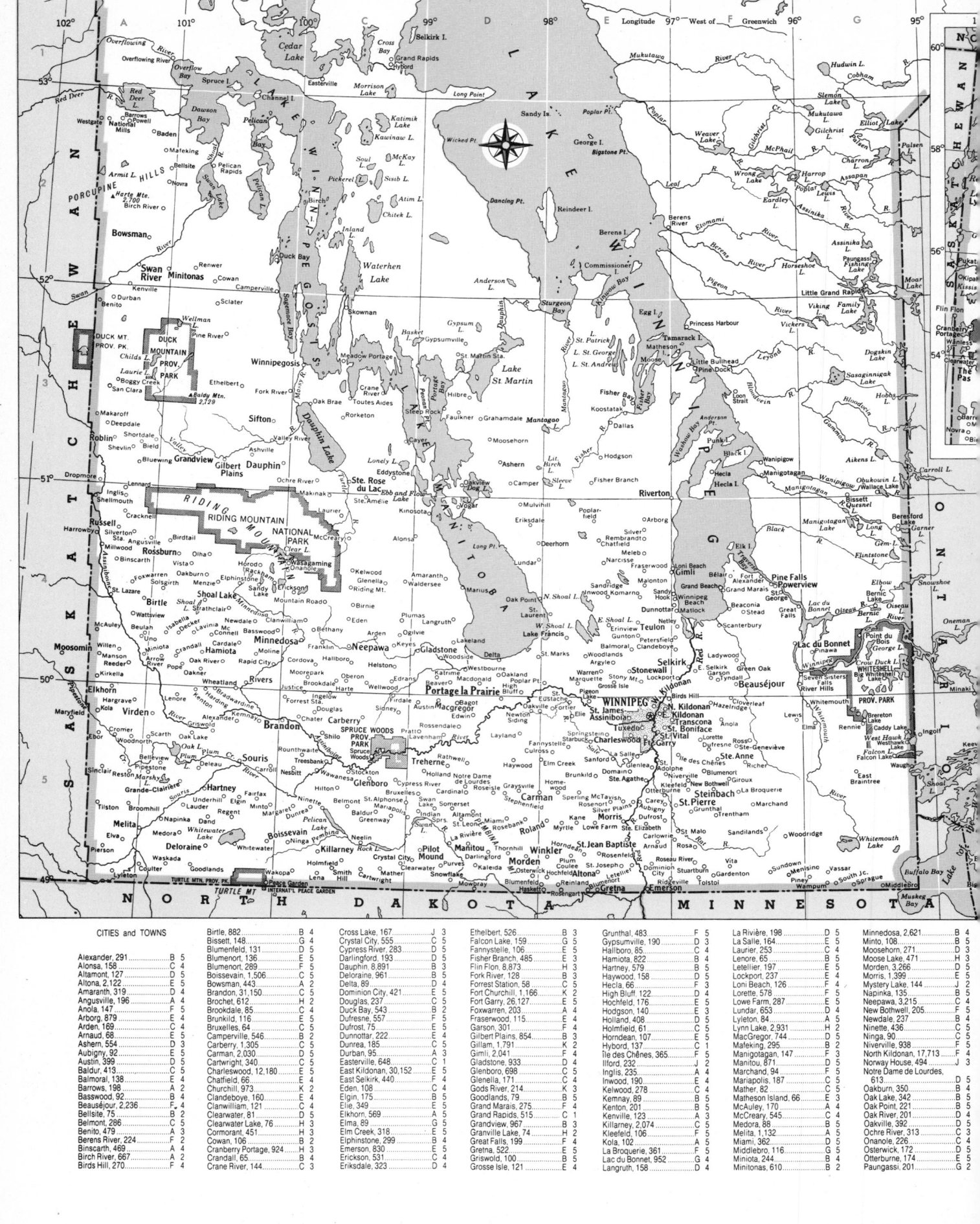

CITIES and TOWNS

Alexander, 291	B 4	Birtle, 882	B 4	Cross Lake, 167	J 3	Ethelbert, 526	B 3	
Alonsa, 158	C 4	Bissett, 148	G 4	Crystal City, 555	C 5	Falcon Lake, 159	G 5	
Altamont, 127	D 5	Blumenfeld, 131	D 5	Cypress River, 283	D 5	Fannystelle, 106	E 5	
Altona, 2,122	E 5	Blumenort, 136	E 5	Darlingford, 193	D 5	Fisher Branch, 485	E 3	
Amaranth, 319	D 4	Blumenort, 289	F 5	Dauphin, 8,891	B 3	Flin Flon, 8,873	H 1	
Angusville, 196	A 4	Boissevain, 1,506	C 5	Deloraine, 961	B 5	Fork River, 128	B 3	
Anola, 147	F 5	Bowsman, 443	A 2	Delta, 89	D 4	Forrest Station, 58	C 5	
Arborg, 879	E 4	Brandon, 31,150	C 5	Dominion City, 421	E 5	Fort Churchill, 1,166	K 2	
Arden, 169	C 4	Brochet, 612	H 2	Douglas, 237	C 5	Fort Garry, 26,127	E 4	
Arnaud, 68	E 5	Brookdale, 85	C 4	Duck Bay, 543	B 2	Foxwarren, 203	A 4	
Ashern, 554	D 3	Brunkild, 116	E 5	Dufresne, 557	F 5	Fraserwood, 115	E 4	
Aubigny, 92	E 5	Bruxelles, 64	C 5	Dufrost, 75	E 5	Garson, 301	F 4	
Austin, 399	D 5	Camperville, 546	B 2	Dunnottar, 222	E 4	Gilbert Plains, 854	B 3	
Baldur, 413	C 5	Carberry, 1,305	C 5	Dunrea, 185	C 5	Gillam, 1,791	K 2	
Balmoral, 138	E 4	Carman, 2,030	D 5	Durban, 95	A 3	Gimli, 2,041	F 4	
Barrows, 198	A 2	Cartwright, 340	C 5	Easterville, 648	C 1	Gladstone, 933	D 4	
Basswood, 92	B 4	Charleswood, 12,180	E 4	East Kildonan, 30,152	E 4	Glenboro, 698	C 5	
Beauséjour, 2,236	F 4	Chatfield, 66	E 4	East Selkirk, 440	F 4	Glenella, 171	C 4	
Bellsite, 75	B 2	Churchill, 973	K 2	Eden, 108	C 4	Gods River, 214	K 3	
Belmont, 286	C 5	Clandeboye, 160	E 4	Elgin, 175	C 5	Goodlands, 79	B 5	
Benito, 479	A 3	Clanwilliam, 121	C 4	Elie, 349	E 5	Grand Marais, 275	F 4	
Berens River, 224	F 2	Clearwater, 81	D 5	Elkhorn, 569	A 5	Grand Rapids, 515	C 1	
Binscarth, 469	A 4	Clearwater Lake, 76	H 3	Elma, 89	F 5	Grandview, 967	B 3	
Birch River, 667	B 2	Cormorant, 451	H 3	Elm Creek, 318	E 5	Granville Lake, 74	H 2	
Birds Hill, 270	F 4	Crandall, 65	B 4	Elphinstone, 299	C 4	Great Falls, 199	F 4	
		Crane River, 144	C 3	Emerson, 830	E 5	Gretna, 522	E 5	
				Erickson, 531	C 4	Griswold, 100	B 5	
				Eriksdale, 323	D 4	Grosse Isle, 121	E 4	

Grunthal, 483	F 5	La Rivière, 198	D 5	Minnedosa, 2,621	B 4
Gypsumville, 190	D 3	La Salle, 164	E 5	Minto, 108	B 5
Hallboro, 85	C 4	Laurier, 253	C 4	Moosehorn, 271	D 3
Hamiota, 822	B 4	Lenore, 65	B 5	Moose Lake, 471	H 3
Hartney, 579	B 5	Letellier, 197	E 5	Morden, 3,266	D 5
Haywood, 158	D 5	Lockport, 237	E 4	Morris, 1,399	E 5
Hecla, 66	F 3	Loni Beach, 126	F 4	Mystery Lake, 144	J 2
High Bluff, 122	D 4	Lorette, 578	E 4	Napinka, 135	B 5
Hochfeld, 176	E 5	Lowe Farm, 287	E 5	Neepawa, 3,215	C 4
Hodgson, 140	E 3	Lundar, 653	D 4	New Bothwell, 205	F 5
Holland, 408	D 5	Lyleton, 84	A 5	Newdale, 237	C 4
Holmfield, 61	C 5	Lynn Lake, 2,931	H 2	Ninette, 436	C 5
Horndean, 107	E 5	MacGregor, 744	D 5	Ninga, 90	C 5
Hybord, 137	C 1	Mafeking, 295	B 2	Niverville, 938	F 5
Île des Chênes, 365	F 5	Manigotagan, 147	F 4	North Kildonan, 17,713	E 4
Ilford, 232	J 2	Manitou, 871	D 5	Norway House, 494	J 3
Inglis, 235	A 4	Marchand, 94	F 5	Notre Dame de Lourdes, 613	D 5
Inwood, 190	E 4	Mariapolis, 187	D 5	Oakburn, 350	B 4
Kelwood, 278	C 4	Mather, 82	C 5	Oak Lake, 342	B 5
Kemnay, 89	B 5	Matheson Island, 66	E 3	Oak Point, 221	B 5
Kenton, 201	A 4	McAuley, 170	A 4	Oak River, 201	D 4
Kenville, 123	A 3	McCreary, 545	C 4	Oakville, 392	D 5
Killarney, 2,074	C 5	Medora, 88	B 5	Ochre River, 313	C 3
Kleefeld, 106	F 5	Melita, 1,132	A 5	Onanole, 226	C 4
Kola, 64	A 5	Miami, 362	D 5	Osterwick, 172	D 5
La Broquerie, 361	F 5	Middlebro, 116	G 5	Otterburne, 174	E 5
Lac du Bonnet, 952	D 4	Miniota, 244	B 4	Paungassi, 201	G 2
Langruth, 158	D 4	Minitonas, 610	B 2		

MANITOBA
NORTHERN PART

MANITOBA
SOUTHERN PART

SCALE

0 5 10 20   40   60 MI.

0 5 10 20   40   60 KM.

Provincial Capital .... ⊕
International Boundaries _ . _ . _
Provincial Boundaries _ . . _ . . _

© C.S. HAMMOND & Co., N.Y.

AREA 251,000 sq. mi.
POPULATION 1,021,506
CAPITAL Winnipeg
LARGEST CITY Winnipeg
HIGHEST POINT Baldy Mtn. 2,729 ft.
SETTLED IN 1812
ADMITTED TO CONFEDERATION 1870
PROVINCIAL FLOWER Prairie Crocus

Pelican Rapids, 217	B 2
Petersfield, 146	E 4
Pierson, 228	A 5
Pikwitonei, 255	J 3
Pilot Mound, 763	D 5
Pinawa, 2,174	G 4
Pine Dock, 98	F 3
Pine Falls, 1,122	F 4
Pine River, 392	B 3
Piney, 145	F 5
Pipestone, 145	B 5
Plumas, 303	D 4
Plum Coulee, 480	E 5
Point du Bois, 261	G 4
Poplarfield, 97	E 4
Poplar Point, 218	D 4
Portage la Prairie, 12,950	D 4
Powerview, 667	F 4
Rapid City, 374	B 4
Rathwell, 125	D 5
Red Sucker Lake, 233	K 3
Reinland, 177	E 5
Rennie, 12C	G 5
Reston, 551	A 5
Richer, 380	F 5
Riding Mountain, 215	C 4
River Hills, 126	G 4
Rivers, 1,175	B 4
Riverton, 797	E 3
Roblin, 1,753	A 3
Roland, 298	D 5
Rorketon, 238	C 3
Rosenfeld, 285	E 5
Rosengart, 81	E 5
Rosenort, 155	E 5
Ross, 70	J 2
Rossburn, 638	B 4
Russell, 1,526	A 4
Saint Adolphe, 460	E 5
Saint Boniface, 46,714	E 5
Saint Claude, 679	D 5
Sainte Agathe, 259	E 5
Sainte Anne, 1,062	F 5
Sainte-Geneviève, 71	F 5
Sainte Rose du Lac, 818	C 3
Saint Eustache, 392	E 5
Saint George, 418	F 4
Saint James-Assiniboia, 71,431	E 5
Saint Jean Baptiste, 533	E 5
Saint Joseph, 58	E 5
Saint Laurent, 281	D 4
Saint Lazare, 431	A 4
Saint Leon, 92	D 5
Saint Malo, 585	F 5
Saint Pierre, 846	E 5
Saint Vital, 32,963	E 5
San Clara, 163	A 3
Sandilands, 100	F 5
Sandy Hook, 100	E 4
Sandy Lake, 332	B 4
Sanford, 250	E 5
Selkirk, 9,331	F 4
Séven Sisters Falls, 243	G 4
Sherridon, 177	H 3
Shoal Lake, 833	B 4
Sidney, 147	C 5
Sifton, 196	B 3
Snow Lake, 1,011	H 3
Somerset, 646	D 5
Souris, 1,674	B 5
South Indian Lake, 590	H 2
South Junction, 143	G 5
Sperling, 117	E 5
Split Lake, 100	J 2
Sprague, 195	G 5
Springstein, 117	E 5
Spruce Woods, 183	C 5

Starbuck, 263	E 5
Steep Rock, 146	D 3
Steinbach, 5,197	F 5
Stockton, 58	C 5
Stonewall, 1,583	E 4
Stony Mountain, 1,268	E 4
Strathclair, 404	B 4
Sundown, 296	F 5
Swan Lake, 300	D 5
Swan River, 3,522	A 3
Teulon, 828	E 4
The Pas, 19,001	H 3
Thicket Portage, 318	J 3
Thompson, 6,062	J 2
Tilston, 72	A 5
Tolstoi, 88	F 5
Transcona, 22,490	F 5
Treherne, 628	D 5
Tuxedo, 3,258	E 5
Tyndall, 400	F 4
Vassar, 240	G 5
Virden, 2,823	A 5
Vista, 71	B 4
Vita, 349	F 5
Vogar, 126	D 4
Wabowden, 809	J 3
Wanless, 123	H 3
Warren, 267	E 4
Wasagaming, 122	C 4
Waskada, 247	B 5
Wawanesa, 478	C 5
Wellwood, 79	C 4
Westbourne, 113	D 4
West Kildonan, 23,959	E 4
Wheatland, 67	B 4
Whitemouth, 366	G 5
Winkler, 2,983	E 5
Winnipeg (cap.), 246,246	E 5
Winnipeg, ‡540,262	E 5
Winnipeg Beach, 687	F 4
Winnipegosis, 887	B 3
Woodlands, 123	E 4
Woodridge, 228	G 5

OTHER FEATURES

Assiniboine (riv.)	C 5
Assinika (riv.)	G 2
Baldy (mt.)	B 3
Berens (riv.)	F 2
Bernic (lake)	G 4
Birch (isl.)	C 2
Black (isl.)	F 3
Bloodvein (riv.)	F 3
Bonnet (lake)	G 4
Burntwood (riv.)	J 2
Cedar (lake)	B 1
Charron (lake)	G 2

Childs (lake)	A 3
Chitek (lake)	C 2
Churchill (cape)	K 2
Churchill (riv.)	J 2
Clear (lake)	C 4
Clearwater Prov. Park	H 3
Cormorant (lake)	H 3
Cross (lake)	J 3
Crow Duck (lake)	G 4
Dauphin (lake)	C 3
Dauphin (riv.)	D 3
Dawson (bay)	A 2
Dog (lake)	D 3
Duck Mountain Prov. Park	B 3
East Shoal (lake)	E 4
Ebb and Flow (lake)	C 3
Elk (isl.)	F 4
Falcon (lake)	G 5
Family (lake)	G 3
Fisher (bay)	E 3
Fishing (lake)	G 2
Fox (riv.)	K 2
Garner (lake)	G 4
George (lake)	G 4
Gods (lake)	K 3
Gods (riv.)	K 3
Granville (lake)	H 2
Grass (riv.)	J 3
Grass River Prov. Park	H 3
Harte (mt.)	A 2
Hayes (riv.)	K 3
Hecla (isl.)	F 3
Hudson (bay)	K 2
International Peace Garden	B 5
Island (lake)	K 3
Kawinaw (lake)	C 3
Kississing (lake)	H 2
Lake of the Woods (lake)	H 5
Lonely (lake)	C 3
Long (pt.)	D 1
Manigotagan (riv.)	G 3
Manitoba (lake)	D 4
Mantagao (riv.)	E 3
Minnedosa (riv.)	B 4
Moose (isl.)	E 3
Mossy (riv.)	C 3
Mukutawa (riv.)	D 3
Nejanilini (lake)	J 1
Nelson (riv.)	J 2
Northern Indian (lake)	J 2
North Shoal (lake)	E 4
Nueltin (lake)	H 1
Oak (lake)	B 5
Oiseau (riv.)	G 4
Overflowing (riv.)	A 1
Oxford (lake)	J 3
Paint (lake)	J 2
Pelican (bay)	B 2
Pelican (lake)	B 2

Pelican (lake)	C 5
Pembina (mt.)	D 5
Pembina (riv.)	C 5
Peonan (pt.)	D 3
Pigeon (riv.)	F 2
Pipestone (creek)	A 5
Plum (creek)	B 5
Poplar (riv.)	E 2
Porcupine (hills)	A 2
Portage (bay)	D 3
Rat (riv.)	F 5
Red (riv.)	E 4
Red Deer (lake)	A 2
Reindeer (isl.)	E 3
Reindeer (lake)	H 2
Riding (mt.)	B 4
Riding Mountain Nat'l Park, 158	B 4
Rock (lake)	C 5
Ross (isl.)	J 3
Sagemace (bay)	B 3
Saint George (lake)	C 3
Saint Martin (lake)	D 3
Sale (riv.)	E 5
Sasaginnigak (lake)	G 3
Seal (riv.)	J 2
Setting (lake)	H 3
Shoal (lake)	B 2
Sipiwesk (lake)	J 3
Souris (riv.)	B 5
Southern Indian (lake)	H 2
South Knife (riv.)	J 2
Split (lake)	J 2
Spruce Woods Prov. Park	C 5
Sturgeon (bay)	E 3
Swan (lake)	D 5
Swan (lake)	A 3
Swan (riv.)	A 3
Tadoule (lake)	J 1
Tatnan (cape)	K 2
Traverse (bay)	F 4
Turtle (riv.)	C 3
Turtle Mountain Prov. Park	B 5
Valley (riv.)	B 3
Wanipigow (riv.)	G 3
Washow (bay)	F 3
Waterhen (lake)	C 2
Weaver (lake)	F 2
West Hawk (lake)	G 5
West Shoal (lake)	E 4
Whitemouth (lake)	G 5
Whitemouth (riv.)	G 5
Whiteshell Prov. Park	G 4
Whitewater (lake)	B 5
Winnipeg (lake)	E 3
Winnipeg (riv.)	G 4
Winnipegosis (lake)	C 2
Woods (lake)	H 5
‡ Population of metropolitan area.	

Agriculture, Industry and Resources

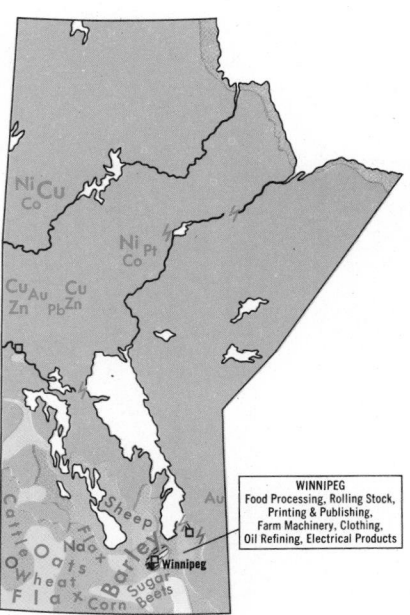

DOMINANT LAND USE

Cereals (chiefly barley, oats)
Cereals, Livestock
Dairy
Livestock
Forests
Nonagricultural Land

MAJOR MINERAL OCCURRENCES

Au Gold
Co Cobalt
Cu Copper
Na Salt
Ni Nickel
O Petroleum
Pb Lead
Pt Platinum
Zn Zinc

⚡ Water Power
▨ Major Industrial Areas
▫ Major Pulp & Paper Mills

WINNIPEG
Food Processing, Rolling Stock,
Printing & Publishing,
Farm Machinery, Clothing,
Oil Refining, Electrical Products

Topography

0   75   150
MILES

Below Sea Level	100 m. 328 ft.	200 m. 656 ft.	500 m. 1,640 ft.	1,000 m. 3,281 ft.	2,000 m. 6,562 ft.	5,000 m. 16,404 ft.

Topography

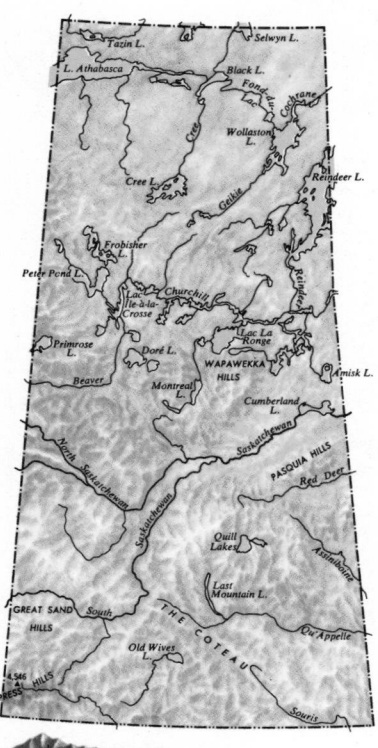

0   60   120
MILES

5,000 m. 15,404 ft.	2,000 m. 6,562 ft.	1,000 m. 3,281 ft.	500 m. 1,640 ft.	200 m. 656 ft.	100 m. 328 ft.	Sea Level Below

CITIES and TOWNS

Abbey, 246 ....C 5
Aberdeen, 288 ....E 3
Abernethy, 253 ....H 5
Air Ronge, 239 ....M 3
Alameda, 370 ....J 6
Alida, 230 ....K 6
Allan, 712 ....E 4
Alsask, 819 ....B 4
Alvena, 143 ....E 3
Aneroid, 163 ....C 6
Annaheim, 182 ....G 3
Antler, 125 ....K 6
Arborfield, 418 ....H 2
Archerwill, 302 ....H 3
Arcola, 539 ....J 6
Arran, 120 ....K 4
Asquith, 355 ....D 3
Assiniboia, 2,675 ....E 6
Avonlea, 391 ....F 5
Aylesbury, 88 ....F 5
Aylsham, 170 ....H 2
Balcarres, 678 ....H 5
Balgonie, 518 ....G 5
Batoche, 27 ....E 3
Battleford, 1,803 ....C 3
Beatty, 97 ....G 3
Beauval, 436 ....L 3
Beechy, 342 ....D 5
Bellevue, 122 ....F 3
Bengough, 650 ....F 6
Bethune, 291 ....F 5
Bienfait, 823 ....J 6
Biggar, 2,607 ....C 3
Big River, 836 ....D 2
Birch Hills, 696 ....F 3
Birsay, 123 ....D 4
Bjorkdale, 223 ....H 3
Black Lake, 471 ....M 2
Bladworth, 125 ....E 4
Blaine Lake, 671 ....D 3
Borden, 187 ....D 3
Bradwell, 100 ....E 4
Bredenbury, 472 ....K 5
Briercrest, 301 ....F 5
Broadview, 959 ....J 5
Brock, 205 ....C 4
Broderick, 115 ....E 4
Brownlee, 121 ....F 5
Bruno, 728 ....F 3
Buchanan, 442 ....J 4
Buffalo Narrows, 794 ...L 3
Bulyea, 109 ....F 5
Burstall, 507 ....B 5
Cabri, 737 ....C 5
Cadillac, 217 ....D 6
Calder, 186 ....K 4
Camsell Portage, 87 .....L 1

Cando, 193 ....C 3
Canoe Lake, 138 ....L 4
Canora, 2,603 ....J 4
Canwood, 325 ....E 2
Carievale, 229 ....K 6
Carlyle, 1,101 ....J 6
Carmel, 90 ....F 3
Carnduff, 1,075 ....K 6
Caron, 96 ....F 5
Carragana, 137 ....J 3
Carrot River, 953 ....H 2
Central Butte, 522 ....E 5
Ceylon, 279 ....G 6
Chamberlain, 161 ....F 5
Chaplin, 368 ....E 5
Chelan, 81 ....H 3
Chitek Lake, 131 ....D 2
Choiceland, 456 ....G 2
Christopher Lake, 143 ...F 2
Churchbridge, 973 ....J 5
Clair, 86 ....G 3
Climax, 341 ....C 6
Cochin, 163 ....C 2
Coderre, 161 ....E 5
Codette, 175 ....H 2
Coleville, 482 ....B 4
Colonsay, 526 ....F 4
Conquest, 261 ....D 4
Consul, 205 ....B 6
Coronach, 379 ....F 6
Craik, 503 ....F 4
Crane Valley, 84 ....F 6
Craven, 126 ....G 5
Creelman, 197 ....H 6
Creighton, 1,857 ....N 4
Crooked River, 106 ......H 3
Cudworth, 799 ....F 3
Cupar, 573 ....G 5
Cutbank, 217 ....E 4
Cut Knife, 560 ....B 3
Dalmeny, 417 ....E 3
Davidson, 1,043 ....E 4
Debden, 340 ....E 2
Delisle, 653 ....D 4
Delmas, 161 ....C 3
Denare Beach, 235 ......M 4
Denzil, 287 ....B 3
Deschambault Lake, 127 ..M 3
Dilke, 130 ....F 5
Dinsmore, 421 ....D 4
Dodsland, 404 ....C 4
Dollard, 92 ....C 6
Domremy, 208 ....F 3
Dorintosh, 87 ....L 2
Drake, 238 ....F 4
Drinkwater, 118 ....F 5
Dubuc, 93 ....J 5
Duck Lake, 584 ....E 3
Duff, 90 ....H 5
Dundurn, 354 ....E 4

Duval, 133 ....G 4
Dysart, 243 ....H 5
Earl Grey, 243 ....G 5
Eastend, 784 ....C 6
Eatonia, 610 ....B 4
Ebenezer, 140 ....J 4
Edam, 334 ....C 2
Edenwold, 129 ....G 5
Elbow, 361 ....E 4
Eldorado, 289 ....L 2
Elfros, 253 ....H 4
Elrose, 573 ....D 4
Elstow, 150 ....E 4
Endeavour, 193 ....J 3
Englefeld, 218 ....G 3
Ernfold, 100 ....D 5
Erwood, 94 ....J 3
Estérhazy, 2,896 ....K 5
Estevan, 9,150 ....J 6
Eston, 1,418 ....C 4
Eyebrow, 181 ....E 5
Fairlight, 127 ....K 6
Fenwood, 112 ....H 4
Ferland, 109 ....D 6
Fillmore, 396 ....H 6
Findlater, 96 ....F 5
Fiske, 85 ....C 4
Flaxcombe, 99 ....B 4
Fleming, 183 ....K 5
Flin Flon, 471 ....N 4
Foam Lake, 1,331 ....H 4
Fond du Lac, 328 ....L 1
Forget, 118 ....J 6
Fort Qu'Appelle, 1,606 ..H 5
Fosston, 119 ....H 3
Fox Valley, 489 ....B 5
Francis, 159 ....H 5
Frenchman Butte, 86 ...B 2
Frobisher, 245 ....J 6
Frontier, 249 ....C 6
Gainsborough, 375 ......K 6
Garrick, 120 ....G 2
Gerald, 174 ....K 5
Girvin, 86 ....F 4
Gladmar, 131 ....G 6
Glaslyn, 357 ....C 2
Glenavon, 340 ....J 5
Glen Ewen, 223 ....K 6
Glenside, 94 ....E 4
Glentworth, 126 ....E 6
Goodeve, 169 ....H 4
Goodsoil, 219 ....L 4
Gorlitz, 94 ....J 4
Govan, 354 ....G 4
Grand Coulee, 131 ......G 5
Gravelbourg, 1,428 ......E 6
Grayson, 260 ....J 5
Green Lake, 450 ....L 4
Grenfell, 1,350 ....J 5
Griffin, 90 ....H 6
Gronlid, 138 ....G 2
Guernsey, 142 ....F 4
Gull Lake, 1,156 ....C 5
Hafford, 580 ....D 3
Hague, 431 ....E 3
Halbrite, 166 ....H 6
Hanley, 390 ....E 4
Harris, 254 ....D 4
Hawarden, 190 ....E 4
Hazel Dell, 105 ....H 4
Hazenmore, 127 ....D 6
Hazlet, 198 ....C 5
Hepburn, 305 ....E 3
Herbert, 1,024 ....D 5
Herschel, 89 ....C 4
Hitchcock, 91 ....J 6
Hodgeville, 399 ....E 5
Hoey, 95 ....F 3

Holdfast, 399 ....F 5
Hubbard, 119 ....H 4
Hudson Bay, 1,971 ......J 3
Humboldt, 3,881 ....G 3
Hyas, 215 ....J 4
Île-à-la-Crosse, 908 .....L 3
Imperial, 486 ....F 4
Indian Head, 1,810 ......H 5
Invermay, 412 ....H 4
Ituna, 960 ....H 4
Jansen, 241 ....G 4
Kamsack, 2,783 ....K 4
Kayville, 84 ....F 6
Kelliher, 460 ....H 4
Kelvington, 1,053 ....H 3
Kenaston, 402 ....E 4
Kendal, 90 ....H 5
Kennedy, 264 ....J 5
Kenosee Park, 103 ......J 6
Kerrobert, 1,180 ....C 4
Khedive, 91 ....G 6
Killaly, 139 ....J 5
Kincaid, 306 ....D 6
Kindersley, 3,451 ....B 4
Kinistino, 767 ....G 3
Kinoosao, 95 ....N 3
Kipling, 927 ....J 5
Kisbey, 260 ....J 6
Krydor, 136 ....D 3
Kuroki, 167 ....H 4
Kyle, 509 ....D 4
Lacadena, 84 ....D 5
Lac Vert, 111 ....G 3
Lafleche, 715 ....E 6
Laird, 218 ....E 3
Lake Alma, 173 ....G 6
Lake Lenore, 392 ....G 3
La Loche, 1,136 ....L 3
Lampman, 830 ....J 6
Lancer, 199 ....C 5
Landis, 297 ....C 3
Lang, 183 ....G 5
Langenburg, 1,236 ......K 5
Langham, 535 ....E 3
Lanigan, 1,430 ....F 4
La Ronge, 906 ....L 3
Lashburn, 494 ....B 2
Leader, 1,105 ....B 5
Leask, 439 ....E 2
Lebret, 278 ....H 5
Leipzig, 87 ....C 3
Lemberg, 409 ....H 5
Leoville, 399 ....D 2
Leross, 147 ....H 4
Leroy, 435 ....G 4
Leslie, 87 ....H 4
Lestock, 452 ....G 4
Liberty, 141 ....F 4
Limerick, 178 ....E 6
Lintlaw, 212 ....H 4
Lipton, 401 ....H 5
Livelong, 126 ....C 2
Lloydminster, 3,953 .....A 2
Lone Rock, 120 ....A 2
Loon Lake, 348 ....B 1
Loreburn, 252 ....E 4
Love, 133 ....G 2
Lucky Lake, 378 ....D 5
Lumsden, 900 ....G 5
Luseland, 728 ....B 3
Macdowall, 173 ....E 2
Macklin, 829 ....A 3
Macoun, 172 ....H 6
Macrorie, 120 ....E 4
Maidstone, 691 ....B 2
Major, 164 ....B 4
Makwa, 115 ....B 2
Manitou Beach, 118 .....F 4

Mankota, 424 ....D 6
Manor, 409 ....K 6
Maple Creek, 2,268 .....B 6
Marcelin, 306 ....E 3
Marchwell, 129 ....K 5
Marengo, 133 ....B 4
Margo, 225 ....H 4
Marquis, 131 ....F 5
Marsden, 241 ....B 3
Marshall, 195 ....B 2
Martensville, 870 ....E 3
Maryfield, 408 ....K 6
Mayfair, 134 ....D 2
Maymont, 167 ....D 3
McKague, 91 ....G 3
McLean, 178 ....G 5
Meacham, 148 ....F 4
Meadow Lake, 3,435 ...C 1
Meath Park, 251 ....F 2
Medstead, 172 ....C 2
Melfort, 4,725 ....G 3
Mendham, 163 ....B 5
Meota, 233 ....C 2
Mervin, 198 ....C 2
Meyronne, 142 ....E 6
Midale, 647 ....H 6
Middle Lake, 292 ....F 3
Mikado, 90 ....J 4
Milden, 239 ....D 4
Milestone, 483 ....G 5
Minton, 215 ....G 6
Mistatim, 165 ....H 3
Molanosa, 213 ....M 4
Montmartre, 510 ....H 5
Moose Jaw, 31,854 .....F 5
Moosomin, 2,407 ....K 5
Morse, 455 ....D 5
Mortlach, 310 ....E 5
Mossbank, 460 ....E 6
Mozart, 93 ....G 4
Muenster, 280 ....G 3
Naicam, 711 ....G 3
Neilburg, 298 ....B 3
Neuanlage, 107 ....E 3
Neudorf, 469 ....H 5
Neville, 154 ....D 6
Nipawin, 4,057 ....H 2
Nokomis, 513 ....G 4
Norquay, 513 ....J 3
North Battleford, 12,698 ..C 3
North Portal, 189 ....J 6
Odessa, 224 ....H 5
Ogema, 457 ....G 6
Ormiston, 173 ....F 6
Osler, 182 ....E 3
Outlook, 1,767 ....E 4
Oxbow, 1,380 ....J 6
Paddockwood, 230 ......F 2
Pambrun, 91 ....D 6
Pangman, 242 ....G 6
Paradise Hill, 344 ....B 2
Parkside, 112 ....E 2
Paynton, 204 ....B 2
Pelican Narrows, 265 ...N 3
Pelly, 426 ....K 4
Pennant, 215 ....C 5
Pense, 411 ....G 5
Perdue, 411 ....D 3
Piapot, 140 ....B 6
Pierceland, 271 ....K 4
Pilger, 109 ....F 3
Pilot Butte, 403 ....G 5
Pine House, 427 ....M 3
Pleasantdale, 153 ....G 3
Plenty, 208 ....C 4
Plunkett, 152 ....F 4
Ponteix, 786 ....D 6
Porcupine Plain, 830 ...H 3

Preeceville, 1,118 ....J 4
Prelate, 407 ....B 5
Prince Albert, 28,464 ...F 2
Prud'homme, 260 ....F 3
Punnichy, 451 ....G 4
Qu'Appelle, 451 ....H 5
Quill Lake, 566 ....G 3
Quinton, 195 ....G 4
Rabbit Lake, 206 ....D 2
Radisson, 416 ....D 3
Radville, 1,024 ....G 6
Rama, 188 ....H 4
Raymore, 523 ....G 4
Redvers, 846 ....K 6
Regina (cap.), 139,469 ..G 5
Regina, ‡140,734 ....G 5
Regina Beach, 334 ......F 5
Regway, 19 ....G 6
Reserve, 153 ....J 3
Rhein, 295 ....J 4
Rhineland, 84 ....D 5
Riceton, 112 ....G 5
Richmound, 208 ....B 5
Ridgedale, 169 ....H 2
Riverhurst, 264 ....E 5
Rocanville, 891 ....K 5
Roche Percée, 167 ....J 6
Rockglen, 550 ....F 6
Rosetown, 2,614 ....D 4
Rose Valley, 591 ....H 3
Rosthern, 1,431 ....E 3
Rouleau, 395 ....G 5

Rush Lake, 162 ....D 5
Saint Benedict, 193 .....F 3
Saint Brieux, 367 ....G 3
Saint Front, 94 ....G 3
Saint Gregor, 125 ....G 3
Saint Louis, 387 ....E 3
Saint Victor, 85 ....E 6
Saint Walburg, 656 ......B 2
Saltcoats, 509 ....J 4
Sandy Bay, 494 ....N 3
Saskatoon, 126,449 .....E 3
Saskatoon, ‡126,449 ...E 3
Sceptre, 234 ....B 5
Scott, 254 ....C 3
Sedley, 268 ....G 5
Semans, 331 ....G 4
Senlac, 94 ....B 3
Shamrock, 105 ....E 5
Shaunavon, 2,244 ....C 6
Sheho, 320 ....H 4
Shellbrook, 1,048 ....E 2
Shell Lake, 255 ....D 2
Simmie, 100 ....C 6
Simpson, 239 ....F 4
Sintaluta, 272 ....H 5
Smeaton, 315 ....G 2
Smiley, 124 ....B 4
Snowden, 87 ....G 2
Sonningdale, 106 ....D 3
Southey, 548 ....G 5
Sovereign, 91 ....D 4
Spalding, 329 ....G 3

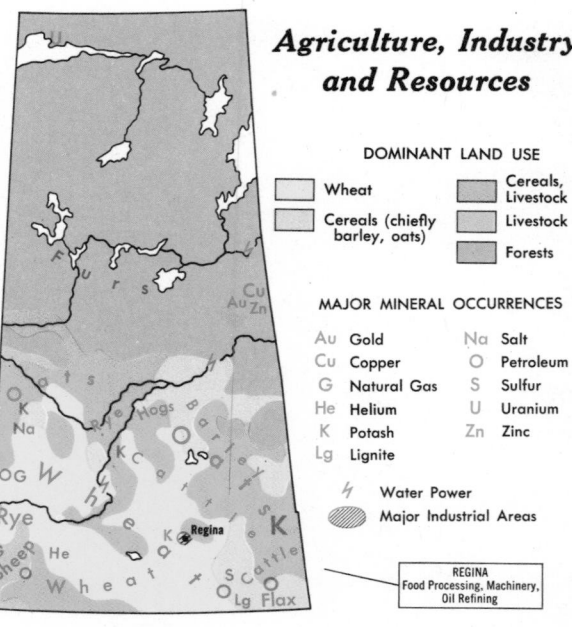

Agriculture, Industry and Resources

DOMINANT LAND USE

Wheat	Cereals, Livestock
Cereals (chiefly barley, oats)	Livestock
	Forests

MAJOR MINERAL OCCURRENCES

Au Gold Na Salt
Cu Copper O Petroleum
G Natural Gas S Sulfur
He Helium U Uranium
K Potash Zn Zinc
Lg Lignite

⚡ Water Power
▨ Major Industrial Areas

REGINA
Food Processing, Machinery,
Oil Refining

Speers, 117	D 3	
Spiritwood, 719	D 2	
Springside, 350	J 4	
Springwater, 99	C 4	
Spruce Lake, 106	B 2	
Spy Hill, 384	K 5	
Star City, 543	G 3	
Stenen, 225	J 4	
Stewart Valley, 138	D 5	
Stockholm, 357	J 5	
Stony Rapids, 147	M 2	
Storthoaks, 177	K 6	
Stoughton, 751	J 6	
Strasbourg, 759	G 4	
Strongfield, 110	E 4	
Sturgis, 617	J 4	
Success, 101	D 5	
Swift Current, 15,415	D 5	
Sylvania, 125	H 3	
Tantallon, 174	K 5	
Theodore, 434	J 4	
Tisdale, 2,798	H 3	
Togo, 227	K 4	
Tompkins, 353	C 5	
Torquay, 377	H 6	
Tramping Lake, 241	B 3	
Tribune, 136	H 6	
Tugaske, 196	E 5	
Turnor Lake, 276	L 3	
Turtleford, 419	B 2	
Tuxford, 153	F 5	
Tyvan, 86	H 5	

Unity, 2,294	B 3	
Uranium City, 1,867	L 2	
Val Marie, 307	D 6	
Vanguard, 315	D 6	
Vanscoy, 244	D 4	
Vawn, 119	C 2	
Veregin, 197	K 4	
Vibank, 275	H 5	
Viceroy, 152	F 6	
Viscount, 395	F 4	
Vonda, 258	F 3	
Wadena, 1,382	H 4	
Wakaw, 1,009	F 3	
Waldeck, 242	D 5	
Waldheim, 606	E 3	
Wapella, 518	K 5	
Warman, 781	E 3	
Waseca, 115	B 2	
Waskesiu Lake, 154	E 2	
Watrous, 1,541	F 4	
Watson, 840	G 3	
Wawota, 536	J 6	
Webb, 105	C 5	
Weekes, 183	J 3	
Weirdale, 108	F 2	
Weldon, 254	F 2	
Welwyn, 231	K 5	
Weyburn, 8,815	H 6	
White City, 129	H 5	
White Fox, 354	H 2	
Whitewood, 1,098	J 5	
Wilcox, 189	G 5	

Wilkie, 1,642	C 3	
Willow Bunch, 482	F 6	
Windthorst, 188	J 5	
Wiseton, 181	D 4	
Wishart, 269	H 4	
Wollaston Lake, 115	M 2	
Wolseley, 975	J 5	
Wood Mountain, 86	E 6	
Wroxton, 92	K 4	
Wymark, 199	D 5	
Wynyard, 1,932	G 4	
Yarbo, 160	K 5	
Yellow Creek, 163	F 3	
Yellow Grass, 500	H 6	
Yorkton, 13,430	J 4	
Young, 496	F 4	
Zealandia, 155	D 4	
Zenon Park, 346	H 2	

OTHER FEATURES

Allan (hills)	E 4	
Amisk (lake)	M 4	
Assiniboine (riv.)	J 3	
Athabasca (lake)	L 2	
Battle (creek)	B 6	
Battle (riv.)	B 2	
Bear (lake)	L 2	
Beaver (hills)	H 4	
Beaver (riv.)	D 1	

Beaverlodge (lake)	L 2	
Brightsand (lake)	B 2	
Candle (lake)	F 2	
Carrot (riv.)	J 2	
Churchill (riv.)	M 3	
Coteau, The (hills)	D 4	
Cowan (lake)	D 2	
Cree (lake)	L 3	
Cumberland (lake)	J 1	
Cypress (hills)	B 6	
Cypress Hills Prov. Park	B 6	
Delaronde (lake)	E 1	
Diefenbaker (lake)	E 5	
Doré (lake)	L 3	
Duck Mountain Prov. Park	K 4	
Eagle (hills)	C 3	
Eaglehill (creek)	C 3	
Fond du Lac (riv.)	M 2	
Fort Walsh Nat'l Hist. Park	A 6	
Frenchman (riv.)	C 6	
Frobisher (lake)	L 3	
Gardiner (dam)	E 4	
Good Spirit (lake)	J 4	
Goodspirit Prov. Park	J 4	
Great Sand (hills)	B 5	
Greenwater Lake Prov. Park, 13	H 3	
Île-à-la-Crosse (lake)	L 3	
Jackfish (lake)	C 2	
Lac La Ronge Prov. Park	M 3	
La Ronge (lake)	M 3	
Last Mountain (lake)	F 4	

Lenore (lake)	G 3	
Makwa (riv.)	B 1	
Manito (lake)	B 3	
Meadow Lake Prov. Park	G 1	
Meeting (lake)	D 2	
Missouri Coteau (hills)	F 6	
Montreal (lake)	F 1	
Moose Jaw (riv.)	G 5	
Moose Mountain Prov. Park	J 6	
Nipawin Prov. Park	G 1	
North Saskatchewan (riv.)	D 3	
Old Wives (lake)	E 5	
Pasquia (hills)	J 2	
Peter Pond (lake)	L 3	

Pheasant (hills)	J 5	
Prince Albert Nat'l Park, 182	E 1	
Qu'Appelle (riv.)	J 5	
Quill (lakes)	G 4	
Redberry (lake)	D 3	
Red Deer (riv.)	K 3	
Reindeer (lake)	N 3	
Rivers (lake)	F 6	
Saskatchewan (riv.)	H 2	
Souris (riv.)	J 6	
South Saskatchewan (riv.)	C 5	
Sturgeon (riv.)	E 2	
Swift Current (creek)	D 5	
Tazin (lake)	L 2	

Thickwood (hills)	D 2	
Tobin (lake)	H 2	
Torch (riv.)	H 2	
Touchwood (hills)	G 4	
Turtle (lake)	C 2	
Wapawekka (hills)	M 4	
Waskesiu (lake)	E 2	
Willow Bunch (lake)	F 6	
Witchekan (lake)	D 2	
Wollaston (lake)	N 2	
Wood (mt.)	E 6	
Wood (mts.)	E 6	

‡ Population of metropolitan area.

AREA 251,700 sq. mi.
POPULATION 921,323
CAPITAL Regina
LARGEST CITY Regina
HIGHEST POINT Cypress Hills 4,546 ft.
SETTLED IN 1774
ADMITTED TO CONFEDERATION 1905
PROVINCIAL FLOWER Prairie Lily

SASKATCHEWAN
SOUTHERN PART

SCALE

0 5 10 20 40 60 MI.

0 5 10 20 40 60 KM.

Provincial Capital ⊛
International Boundaries
Provincial Boundaries

© C.S. Hammond & Co., N.Y.

SASKATCHEWAN
NORTHERN PART

0 20 40 60 80 100 MI.

0 20 40 60 80 100 KM.

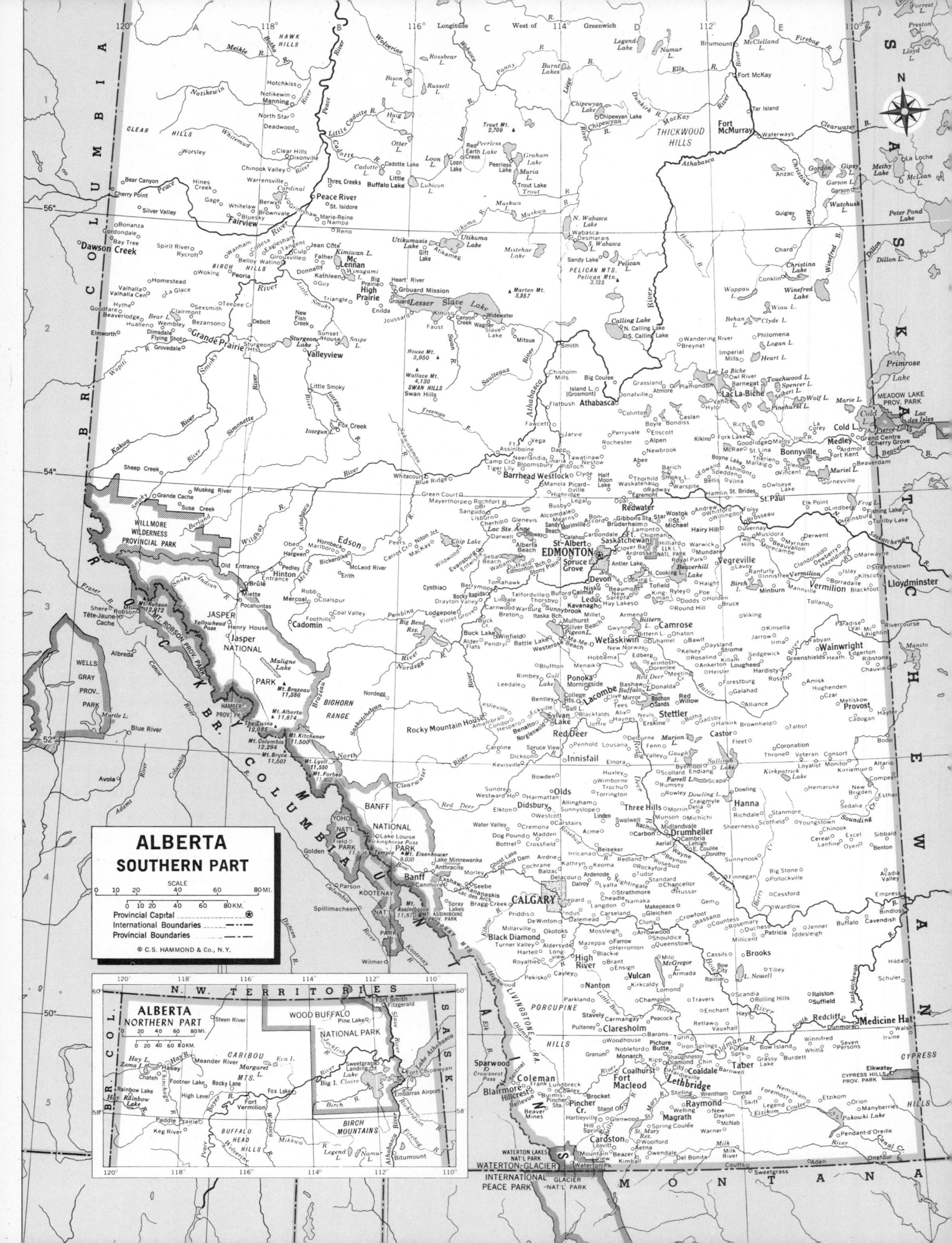

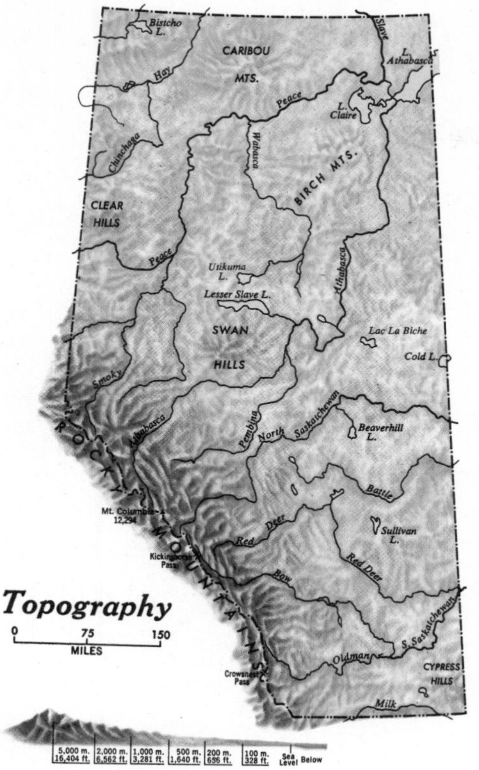
Bistcho L.
CARIBOU MTS.
Slave
L. Athabasca
Hay
Peace
L. Claire
Chinchaga
Wabasca
BIRCH MTS.
CLEAR HILLS
Peace
Utikuma L.
Athabasca
Lesser Slave L.
SWAN HILLS
Lac La Biche
Cold L.
Smoky
Athabasca
Pembina
North Saskatchewan
Beaverhill L.
Battle
Mt. Columbia 12,294
Red Deer
Sullivan L.
Kicking Horse Pass
Bow
Red Deer
S. Saskatchewan
Oldman
CYPRESS HILLS
Crowsnest Pass
Milk
ROCKY MOUNTAINS
5,000 m. 16,404 ft.
2,000 m. 6,562 ft.
1,000 m. 3,281 ft.
500 m. 1,640 ft.
200 m. 656 ft.
100 m. 328 ft.
Sea Level
Below

Topography

0 75 150 MILES

AREA 255,285 sq. mi.
POPULATION 1,838,037
CAPITAL Edmonton
LARGEST CITY Edmonton
HIGHEST POINT Mt. Columbia 12,294 ft.
SETTLED IN 1861
ADMITTED TO CONFEDERATION 1905
PROVINCIAL FLOWER Wild Rose

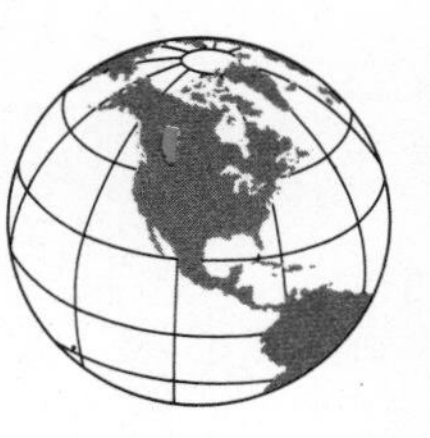

CITIES and TOWNS

Acadia Valley, 166	E 4
Acme, 300	D 4
Aerial, 151	D 4
Airdrie, 1,089	C 4
Alberta Beach, 320	C 3
Alder Flats, 133	C 3
Alix, 565	D 3
Alliance, 230	E 3
Amisk, 134	E 3
Andrew, 466	D 3
Anzac, 114	E 1
Ardmore, 230	E 2
Ardrossan, 137	D 3
Arrowwood, 166	D 4
Ashmont, 150	E 2
Athabasca, 1,765	D 2
Atikameg, 117	C 2
Banff, 3,219	C 4
Barnwell, 341	D 5
Barons, 237	D 4
Barrhead, 2,803	C 2
Bashaw, 757	D 3
Bassano, 861	D 4
Bawlf, 182	D 3
Beaumont, 337	D 3
Beaverlodge, 1,157	A 2
Beiseker, 414	D 4
Bellevue, 1,242	C 5
Bentley, 621	C 3
Berwyn, 474	B 1
Big Valley, 306	D 3
Black Diamond, 945	C 4
Blackfalds, 904	D 3
Blackfoot, 175	E 3
Blackie, 168	D 4
Blairmore, 2,037	C 5
Blue Ridge, 239	C 2
Bluesky, 124	A 1
Bon Accord, 332	D 3
Bonnyville, 2,587	E 2
Bowden, 560	C 4
Bow Island, 1,159	E 5
Boyle, 460	D 2
Bragg Creek, 203	C 4
Breton, 352	C 3
Brooks, 3,986	E 4
Brownvale, 161	B 1
Bruce, 110	E 3
Bruderheim, 350	D 3
Brûlé, 104	B 3
Buck Lake, 159	C 3
Burdett, 206	E 5
Cadomin, 109	B 3
Cadotte Lake, 192	B 1
Calgary, 403,319	C 4
Calgary, ‡403,319	C 4
Calmar, 799	D 3
Camrose, 8,673	D 3
Canmore, 1,538	C 4
Canyon Creek, 205	C 2
Carbon, 343	D 4
Carbondale, 115	D 3
Cardston, 2,685	D 5
Carmangay, 230	D 4
Caroline, 339	C 3
Carseland, 105	D 4
Carstairs, 884	D 4
Caslan, 117	D 2
Castor, 1,166	D 3
Cayley, 122	D 4
Cereal, 220	E 4
Champion, 335	D 4
Chateh, 400	A 5
Chauvin, 349	E 3
Chipewyan Lake, 118	D 1
Chipman, 181	D 3
Clairmont, 309	A 2
Clandonald, 119	E 3
Claresholm, 2,935	D 4
Clive, 247	D 3
Clyde, 233	D 2
Coaldale, 2,798	D 5
Coalhurst, 426	D 5
Cochrane, 1,046	C 4
Cold Lake, 1,309	E 2
Coleman, 1,534	C 5
Colinton, 125	D 2
College Heights, 331	D 3
Conklin, 119	E 2
Consort, 659	E 3
Cooking Lake, 196	D 3
Coronation, 877	E 3
Coutts, 407	D 5
Cowley, 201	D 5
Cremona, 186	C 4
Crossfield, 638	C 4
Czar, 196	E 3
Daysland, 593	D 3
Delburne, 383	D 3
Delia, 241	D 4
Derwent, 203	E 3
Desmarais, 258	D 2
Devon, 1,468	D 3
Dewberry, 160	E 3
Didsbury, 1,821	C 4
Dixonville, 113	B 1
Donalda, 232	D 3
Donnelly, 274	B 2
Drayton Valley, 3,900	C 3
Drumheller, 5,446	D 4
Duchess, 228	E 4
Eaglesham, 218	B 2
East Coulée, 312	D 4
Eckville, 660	C 3
Edberg, 145	D 3
Edgerton, 296	E 3
Edmonton (cap.), 438,152	D 3
Edmonton, ‡495,702	D 3
Edmonton Beach, 148	C 3
Edson, 3,818	B 3
Elk Point, 729	E 3
Elnora, 213	D 3
Empress, 266	E 4
Enilda, 201	B 2
Entwistle, 353	C 3
Erskine, 233	D 3
Evansburg, 528	C 3
Exshaw, 548	C 4
Fairview, 2,109	A 1
Falher, 918	B 2
Faust, 353	C 2
Fawcett, 141	C 2
Ferintosh, 127	D 3
Foremost, 568	E 5
Forestburg, 669	E 3
Fort Assiniboine, 173	C 2
Fort Chipewyan, 1,122	C 5
Fort Kent, 113	E 2
Fort Macleod, 2,715	D 5
Fort McKay, 200	E 1
Fort McMurray, 6,847	E 1
Fort Saskatchewan, 5,726	D 3
Fort Vermilion, 740	B 5
Fox Creek, 1,281	B 2
Frank, 224	C 5
Galahad, 179	E 3
Garden River, 134	B 5
Gibbons, 551	D 3
Gift Lake, 379	C 2
Girouxville, 347	B 2
Gleichen, 367	D 4
Glendon, 354	E 2
Glenwood, 200	D 5
Grand Centre, 2,088	E 2
Grande Cache, 2,525	A 3
Grande Prairie, 13,079	A 2
Granum, 324	D 5
Grassy Lake, 196	E 5
Grimshaw, 1,714	B 1
Grouard Mission, 277	C 2
Halkirk, 136	D 3
Hanna, 2,545	E 4
Hardieville, 473	D 5
Hardisty, 594	E 3
Hay Lakes, 211	D 3
Heisler, 199	D 3
High Level, 1,614	A 5
High Prairie, 2,354	B 2
High River, 2,676	D 4
Hillcrest, 613	C 5
Hill Spring, 213	D 5
Hines Creek, 438	A 1
Hinton, 4,911	B 3
Holden, 448	D 3
Hughenden, 267	E 3
Hussar, 170	D 4
Hythe, 487	A 2
Imperial Mills, 118	E 2
Innisfail, 2,474	D 3
Innisfree, 252	E 3
Irma, 423	E 3
Irricana, 139	D 4
Irvine, 194	E 5
Jarvie, 104	D 2
Jasper, 2,932	B 3
Joussard, 269	B 2
Kikino, 202	D 2
Killam, 851	E 3
Kinuso, 267	C 2
Kitscoty, 320	E 3
Lac La Biche, 1,791	E 2
Lacombe, 3,436	D 3
Lake Louise, 165	B 4
Lamont, 899	D 3
Langdon, 109	D 4
Lavoy, 114	E 3
Leduc, 4,000	D 3
Legal, 563	D 3
Leslieville, 159	C 3
Lethbridge, 41,217	D 5
Linden, 226	D 4
Little Buffalo Lake, 165	B 1
Lloydminster, 4,738	E 3
Lodgepole, 144	C 3
Lomond, 165	D 4
Longview, 189	C 4
Loon Lake, 135	C 1
Lougheed, 217	E 3
Lundbreck, 113	C 5
Magrath, 1,215	D 5
Mallaig, 190	E 2
Manning, 1,071	B 1
Mannville, 646	E 3
Marlboro, 156	B 3
Marwayne, 351	E 3
Mayerthorpe, 1,036	C 3
McLennan, 1,090	B 2
Meander River, 233	A 5
Medicine Hat, 26,518	E 4
Midlandvale, 392	D 4
Milk River, 775	D 5
Millet, 456	D 3
Milo, 117	D 4
Minburn, 106	E 3
Mirror, 365	D 3
Monarch, 102	D 5
Morinville, 1,475	D 3
Morrin, 197	D 4
Mulhurst, 139	D 3
Mundare, 511	D 3
Myrnam, 403	E 3
Nacmine, 350	D 4
Nampa, 283	B 1
Nanton, 991	D 4
Newbrook, 154	D 2
New Norway, 200	D 3
New Sarepta, 202	D 3
Nobleford, 401	D 5
North Calling Lake, 103	D 2
Okotoks, 1,247	C 4
Olds, 3,376	D 4
Onoway, 496	C 3
Oyen, 929	E 4
Paradise Valley, 144	E 3
Peace River, 5,039	B 1
Peerless Lake, 134	C 1
Peers, 129	B 3
Penhold, 452	D 3
Pibroch, 112	D 2
Picardville, 130	D 2
Picture Butte, 1,008	D 5
Pincher Creek, 3,227	D 5
Plamondon, 189	D 2
Pollockville, 29	E 4
Ponoka, 4,414	D 3
Provost, 1,489	E 3
Radway, 170	D 2
Rainbow Lake, 355	A 5
Ralston, 475	E 4
Ranfurly, 110	E 3
Raymond, 2,156	D 5
Redcliff, 2,255	E 4
Red Deer, 27,674	D 3
Redwater, 1,287	D 3
Rimbey, 1,450	C 3
Robb, 256	B 3
Rochester, 111	D 2
Rockyford, 286	D 4
Rocky Mountain House, 2,968	C 3
Rolling Hills, 127	E 4
Rosalind, 203	D 3
Rosemary, 208	E 4
Rycroft, 461	A 2
Ryley, 428	D 3
Saint Albert, 11,800	D 3
Saint Paul, 4,161	E 3
Sangudo, 360	C 3
Seba Beach, 165	C 3
Sedgewick, 730	E 3
Seebe, 108	C 4
Sexsmith, 559	A 2
Shaughnessy, 323	D 5
Sherwood Park, 14,282	D 3
Slave Lake, 2,052	C 2
Smith, 445	D 2
Smoky Lake, 881	D 2
Spirit River, 1,091	A 2
Spruce Grove, 3,029	D 3
Spruce View, 104	C 3
Standard, 267	D 4
Stavely, 351	D 4
Stettler, 4,168	D 3
Stirling, 436	D 5
Stony Plain, 1,770	C 3
Strathmore, 1,148	D 4
Strome, 226	E 3
Sundre, 933	C 4
Swan Hills, 1,376	C 2
Sylvan Lake, 1,597	C 3
Taber, 4,765	E 5
Thorhild, 509	D 2
Thorsby, 595	C 3
Three Hills, 1,354	D 4
Tilley, 270	E 4
Tofield, 924	D 3
Torrington, 118	D 4
Trochu, 739	D 4
Trout Lake, 162	C 1
Turin, 102	D 5
Turner Valley, 766	C 4
Two Hills, 979	E 3
Valleyview, 1,708	B 2
Vauxhall, 1,016	D 4
Vegreville, 3,691	E 3
Vermilion, 2,915	E 3
Veteran, 267	E 3
Viking, 1,178	E 3
Vilna, 303	E 2
Vulcan, 1,384	D 4
Wabamun, 336	C 3
Wabasca, 172	D 2
Wainwright, 3,872	E 3
Wanham, 268	A 2
Warburg, 464	C 3
Warner, 408	D 5
Warspite, 110	D 2
Waskatenau, 233	D 2
Waterton Park, 236	D 5
Wembley, 348	A 2
Westlock, 3,246	C 2
Westward Ho, 104	C 4
Wetaskiwin, 6,267	D 3
Whitecourt, 3,202	C 2
Whitelaw, 192	A 1
Widewater, 126	C 2
Wildwood, 386	C 3
Willingdon, 325	E 3
Winfield, 209	C 3
Youngstown, 305	E 4

OTHER FEATURES

Alberta (mt.)	B 3
Assiniboine (mt.)	C 4
Athabasca (lake)	C 5
Athabasca (riv.)	D 1
Banff Nat'l Park, 3,532	B 4
Battle (riv.)	D 3
Beaverhill (lake)	D 3
Belly (riv.)	D 5
Berry (creek)	E 4
Biche (lake)	E 2
Big Bend (res.)	C 3
Bighorn (range)	B 3
Birch (hills)	A 2
Birch (lake)	E 3
Birch (mts.)	B 5
Bow (riv.)	D 4
Boyer (riv.)	A 5
Brazeau (mt.)	B 3
Brazeau (riv.)	B 3
Buffalo (lake)	D 3
Buffalo Head (hills)	B 5
Cadotte (riv.)	B 1
Calling (lake)	D 2
Caribou (mts.)	B 5
Chinchaga (riv.)	A 5
Chip (lake)	C 3
Chipewyan (riv.)	D 1
Christina (riv.)	E 1
Claire (lake)	B 5
Clear (hills)	A 1
Clearwater (riv.)	C 4
Clearwater (riv.)	E 1
Cold (lake)	E 2
Columbia (mt.)	B 3
Crowsnest (pass)	C 5
Cypress (hills)	E 5
Cypress Hills Prov. Park	E 5
Eisenhower (mt.)	C 4
Elbow (riv.)	C 4
Elk Island Nat'l Park, 46	D 3
Etzikom Coulee (riv.)	E 5
Firebag (riv.)	E 1
Forbes (mt.)	B 4
Frog (lake)	E 3
Gordon (lake)	E 1
Gough (lake)	D 3
Graham (lake)	C 1
Gull (lake)	C 3
Hawk (hills)	B 1
Hay (riv.)	A 5
Highwood (riv.)	C 4
Iosegun (lake)	B 2
Jasper Nat'l Park, 3,064	A 3
Kickinghorse (pass)	B 4
Kimiwan (lake)	B 2
Kitchener (mt.)	B 3
Lesser Slave (lake)	C 2
Little Bow (riv.)	D 4
Little Smoky (riv.)	B 2
Livingstone (range)	C 4
Lyell (mt.)	B 4
Maligne (lake)	B 3
McGregor (lake)	D 4
McLeod (riv.)	B 3
Milk (riv.)	D 5
Muriel (lake)	E 2
Muskwa (riv.)	C 1
North Saskatchewan (riv.)	E 3
North Wabasca (lake)	D 1
Notikewin (riv.)	A 1
Oldman (riv.)	D 5
Pakowki (lake)	E 5
Peace (riv.)	B 1
Peerless (lake)	C 1
Pelican (mts.)	D 2
Pembina (riv.)	C 3
Pigeon (lake)	D 3
Porcupine (hills)	C 4
Red Deer (riv.)	D 4
Rocky (mts.)	C 4
Rosebud (riv.)	D 4
Sainte Anne (lake)	C 3
Saint Mary (riv.)	D 5
Saulteaux (riv.)	C 2
Slave (riv.)	C 5
Smoky (riv.)	A 2
Sounding (creek)	E 4
South Saskatchewan (riv.)	E 4
South Wabasca (lake)	D 2
Spray (mts.)	C 4
Sullivan (lake)	D 3
Swan (hills)	C 2
Temple (mt.)	B 4
The Twins (mt.)	B 3
Thickwood (hills)	D 1
Utikuma (lake)	C 2
Vermilion (riv.)	E 3
Wabasca (riv.)	C 1
Waterton-Glacier Int'l Peace Park, 259	C 5
Waterton Lakes Nat'l Park, 259	C 5
Whitemud (riv.)	A 1
Willmore Wilderness Prov. Park	A 3
Winagami (lake)	B 2
Winefred (lake)	E 2
Wood Buffalo Nat'l Park, 186	B 5
Yellowhead (pass)	A 3

‡ Population of metropolitan area.

Agriculture, Industry and Resources

DOMINANT LAND USE

- Wheat
- Cereals (chiefly barley, oats)
- Cereals, Livestock
- Dairy
- Pasture Livestock
- Range Livestock
- Forests
- Nonagricultural Land

MAJOR MINERAL OCCURRENCES

- C Coal
- G Natural Gas
- Na Salt
- O Petroleum
- S Sulfur

Water Power
Major Industrial Areas

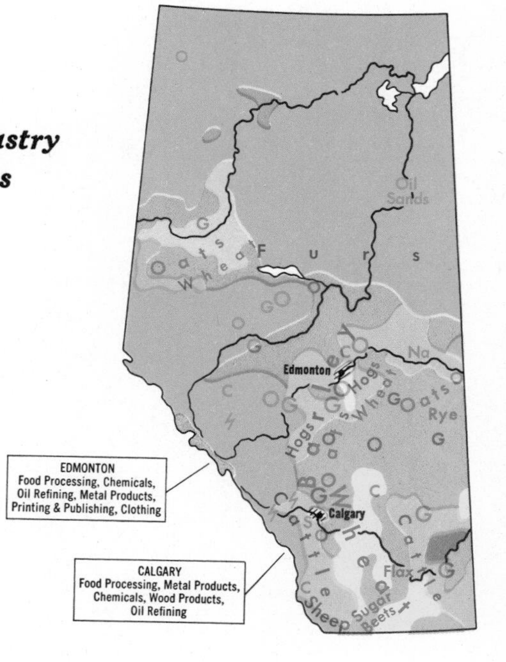
Oil Sands
Furs
Oats
Wheat
Edmonton
Hogs
Wheat
Oats
Rye
Calgary
Cattle
Wheat
Flax
Sheep
Sugar Beets
EDMONTON
Food Processing, Chemicals, Oil Refining, Metal Products, Printing & Publishing, Clothing
CALGARY
Food Processing, Metal Products, Chemicals, Wood Products, Oil Refining

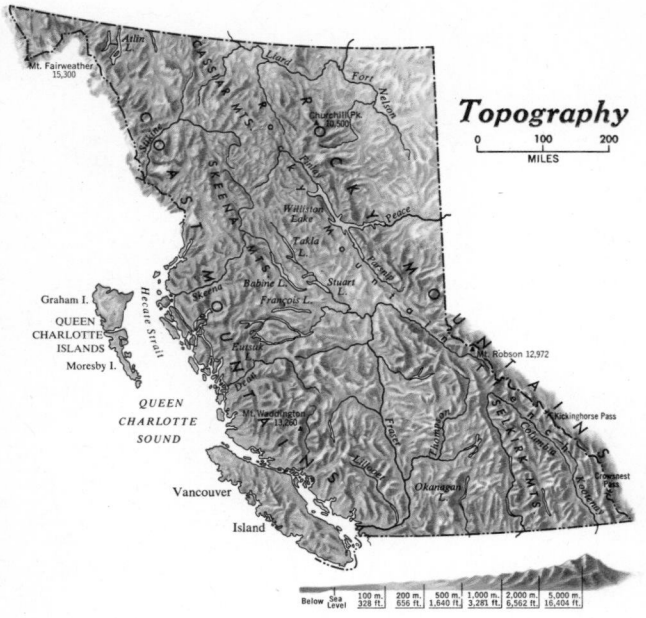

Topography

0   100   200
MILES

Mt. Fairweather 15,300

Graham I.
QUEEN CHARLOTTE ISLANDS
Moresby I.

QUEEN CHARLOTTE SOUND

Vancouver
Island

Mt. Robson 12,972

Mt. Waddington 13,260

Kickinghorse Pass
Yellowhead Pass
Crowsnest Pass

| Below Sea Level | 100 m. 328 ft. | 200 m. 656 ft. | 500 m. 1,640 ft. | 1,000 m. 3,281 ft. | 2,000 m. 6,562 ft. | 5,000 m. 16,404 ft. |

Agriculture, Industry and Resources

KITIMAT Aluminum

Kitimat

DOMINANT LAND USE

- Cereals, Livestock
- Dairy
- Fruits, Vegetables
- Pasture Livestock
- Forests
- Nonagricultural Land

MAJOR MINERAL OCCURRENCES

Ab	Asbestos	Gp	Gypsum
Ag	Silver	Mo	Molybdenum
Au	Gold	Ni	Nickel
C	Coal	O	Petroleum
Cu	Copper	Pb	Lead
Fe	Iron Ore	S	Sulfur
G	Natural Gas	Sn	Tin
		Zn	Zinc

⚡ Water Power
▨ Major Industrial Areas
▢ Major Pulp & Paper Mills

VANCOUVER–VICTORIA
Wood Products, Food Processing, Iron & Steel, Metal Products, Printing & Publishing, Shipbuilding, Oil Refining

CITIES and TOWNS

Abbotsford, 706..........L 3
Albert Head, 330..........J 4
Alert Bay, 760..........D 5
Alexandria, 168..........F 4
Armstrong, 1,648..........H 5
Ashcroft, 1,916..........G 5
Ashton Creek, 318..........H 5
Athalmer, 255..........K 5
Atlin, 258..........J 1
Avola, 265..........H 4
Balfour, 195..........J 5
Barrière, 829..........H 4
Bear Lake, 302..........F 3
Beaverdell, 241..........H 5
Bella Coola, 273..........D 4
Big Eddy, 654..........H 5
Birch Island, 219..........H 4
Blue River, 475..........H 4
Boston Bar, 548..........G 5
Bowen Island, 351..........K 3
Bowser, 169..........H 2

Brackendale, 692..........F 5
Bralorne, 379..........F 5
Britannia Beach, 738..........K 2
Brouse, 446..........J 5
Burnaby, ●125,660..........K 3
Burns Lake, 1,259..........D 3
Cache Creek, 1,013..........G 5
Campbell River, ●10,000..........E 5
Campbell River, 9,770..........E 5
Canal Flats, 902..........K 5
Cassiar, 1,073..........K 2
Castlegar, 3,072..........J 5
Cawston, 642..........H 5
Caycuse, 297..........J 3
Cedarside, 218..........H 4
Celista, 178..........H 5
Central Saanich, ●5,136..........K 3
Charlie Lake, 214..........G 2
Chase, 1,212..........H 5
Chase River, 728..........J 3
Chemainus, 2,129..........J 3
Cherry Creek, 449..........G 5
Cherryville, 284..........H 5
Chetwynd, 1,260..........G 2

Chilliwack, 9,135..........M 3
Chilliwhack, ●23,739..........M 3
Clearbrook, 3,653..........L 3
Clearwater, 513..........G 4
Clinton, 905..........G 4
Coal Harbour, 334..........D 5
Cobble Hill, 280..........K 3
Coldstream, ●3,602..........H 2
Comox, 3,980..........J 2
Coquitlam, ●53,073..........K 3
Courtenay, 7,152..........E 5
Cranbrook, 12,000..........K 5
Crawford Bay, 244..........J 5
Creston, 3,204..........J 5
Crofton, 972..........J 3
Cultus Lake, 554..........M 3
Cumberland, 1,718..........E 5
Dawson Creek, 11,885..........G 2
Delta, ●45,860..........K 3
Departure Bay, 3,744..........J 3
Donald, 235..........J 4
Duncan, 4,388..........J 3
East Kelowna, 826..........H 5
Eddontenajon, 180..........K 2

Edgewater, 346..........J 5
Elko, 196..........K 5
Endako, 242..........E 3
Enderby, 1,158..........H 5
Errington, 464..........J 3
Esquimalt, ●12,922..........K 4
Extension, 181..........J 3
Falkland, 375..........H 5
Fernie, 4,422..........K 5
Field, 358..........J 4
Flood, 295..........M 3
Forest Grove, 238..........G 4
Fort Fraser, 385..........E 3
Fort Langley, 1,342..........L 3
Fort Nelson, 2,289..........M 2
Fort Saint James, 1,483..........E 2
Fort Saint John, 8,264..........G 2
Franklin River, 187..........J 3
Fraser Lake, 1,292..........E 3
Fraser Mills, ●157..........K 3
Fruitvale, 1,379..........J 5
Gabriola Island, 655..........J 3
Galiano Island, 412..........K 3
Ganges, 333..........K 3
Gibsons, 1,934..........K 3
Gillies Bay, 543..........H 2
Giscome, 416..........F 3
Golden, 3,012..........J 4
Gold River, 1,896..........D 5
Grand Forks, 3,173..........H 6
Granisle, 451..........D 3
Granthams Landing, 404..........J 3
Greenwood, 868..........H 5
Grindrod, 283..........H 5
Hagensborg, 315..........D 4
Haney, 3,221..........L 3
Hatzic, 547..........L 3
Hazelton, 351..........D 2
Hedley, 385..........G 5
Heffley Creek, 503..........G 5
Hendrix Lake, 341..........G 4
Heriot Bay, 187..........E 5
Hixon, 385..........F 3
Holberg, 333..........C 5
Honeymoon Bay, 546..........J 3
Hope, 3,153..........M 3
Houston, ●2,232..........D 3
Houston, 3,003..........D 3
Hudson Hope, 1,116..........F 2
Hudson's Hope, ●1,741..........F 2
Huntingdon, 202..........L 3
Invermere, 1,065..........J 5
Ioco, 308..........K 3
Jaffray, 193..........K 5
Kaleden, 640..........H 5
Kamloops, 26,168..........G 5
Kaslo, 755..........J 5
Kelly Lake, 231..........G 4
Kelowna, 19,412..........H 5
Kemano, 346..........D 3
Kent, ●2,966..........M 3
Keremeos, 605..........G 5
Kimberley, 7,641..........K 5
Kinnaird, 2,846..........J 5
Kitimat, 11,824..........C 3
Kitsault, 343..........C 2
Kitwanga, 217..........D 2
Kokish, 222..........D 5
Lac La Hache, 417..........G 4
Ladysmith, 3,664..........J 3
Lake Cowichan, 2,364..........J 3

Lang Bay, 285..........E 5
Langley, ●21,936..........L 3
Langley, 4,684..........L 3
Lantzville, 565..........J 3
Lillooet, 1,514..........G 5
Lion's Bay, 396..........K 3
Lone Butte, 206..........G 4
Louis Creek, 289..........H 4
Lower Nicola, 361..........G 5
Lower Post, 206..........K 1
Lumby, 940..........H 5
Lytton, 494..........G 5
Mackenzie, ●2,332..........F 2
Mackenzie, 1,976..........F 2
Madeira Park, 351..........J 2
Maple Bay, 509..........K 3
Maple Ridge, ●24,476..........L 3
Masset, 975..........B 3
Matsqui, ●23,554..........L 3
Mayne Island, 293..........K 3
McBride, 658..........G 3
McConnell Creek, 233..........D 2
McLure, 193..........H 4
Merritt, 5,289..........G 5
Merville, 227..........E 5
Mesachie Lake, 266..........J 3
Metchosin, 540..........K 3
Mica Creek, 772..........H 4
Midway, 502..........H 6
Mill Bay, 347..........C 2
Milnes Landing, 254..........J 3
Mission, ●10,220..........L 3
Mission City, 3,649..........L 3
Moberly, 175..........J 4
Monte Lake, 176..........G 5
Montrose, 1,137..........J 5
Nakusp, 1,163..........J 5
Nanaimo, 14,948..........J 3
Naramata, 461..........H 5
Nelson, 9,400..........J 5
New Denver, 644..........J 5
New Hazelton, 475..........D 2
New Westminster, 42,835..........K 3
Nicholson, 619..........J 4
Nicomen Island, 527..........L 3
Nootka, 2..........D 5
North Bend, 424..........G 5
North Cowichan, ●12,170..........J 3
North Pender Island, 407..........K 3
North Saanich, ●3,601..........K 3
North Vancouver, 57,861..........K 3
North Vancouver, 31,847..........K 3
Nukko Lake, 182..........F 3
Oak Bay, ●18,426..........K 4
Ocean Falls, 1,085..........D 4
Okanagan Centre, 266..........H 5
Okanagan Falls, 621..........H 5
Okanagan Landing, 656..........H 5
Okanagan Mission, 857..........H 5
Old Barkerville, 3..........G 3
Oliver, 1,615..........H 5
One Hundred Mile House, 1,120..........G 4
Osoyoos, 1,285..........H 5
Oyama, 326..........H 5
Parksville, 2,169..........J 3
Parson, 306..........J 4
Peachland, ●1,446..........G 5
Penticton, 18,146..........H 5
Pine Valley, 264..........F 2
Pitt Meadows, ●2,771..........L 3
Popkum, 286..........M 3
Port Alberni, 20,063..........J 3
Port Alice, 1,507..........D 5
Port Clements, 406..........B 3
Port Coquitlam, 19,560..........L 3
Port Edward, 1,019..........B 3
Port Hammond, 1,556..........L 3
Port Hardy, 1,761..........D 5
Port McNeill, 934..........D 5
Port Moody, 10,778..........L 3
Port Renfrew, 362..........J 3
Pouce-Coupé, 595..........G 2
Powell River, ●13,726..........E 5
Prince George, 33,101..........F 3
Prince Rupert, 15,747..........B 3
Princeton, 2,601..........G 5
Procter, 183..........J 5
Qualicum Beach, 1,245..........J 3
Queen Charlotte, 665..........A 3
Quesnel, 6,252..........F 4
Radium Hot Springs, 393..........J 5
Rayleigh, 652..........G 5
Revelstoke, 4,867..........J 5
Richmond, ●62,121..........K 3
Riondel, 572..........J 5
Robson, 1,046..........J 5
Rossland, 3,896..........H 6
Royston, 532..........E 5
Rutland, 3,279..........H 5
Saanich, ●65,040..........K 3
Salmo, 872..........J 5
Salmon Arm, ●7,793..........H 5
Salmon Arm, 1,981..........H 5
Saltair, 1,008..........J 3
Sandspit, 459..........B 3
Sardis, 1,194..........M 3
Saseenos, 574..........J 3
Saturna Island, 174..........K 3
Savona, 670..........G 5
Sayward, 465..........D 5
Sechelt, 590..........J 3
Seventy Mile House, 225..........G 4
Shawnigan Lake, 213..........J 3
Shoreacres, 345..........J 5
Sicamous, 814..........H 5
Sidney, 4,866..........K 3
Silverton, 246..........J 5
Slocan, 345..........J 5
Slocan Park, 360..........J 5
Smithers, 3,864..........D 3
Sointula, 575..........D 5
Sooke, 836..........J 4
Sorrento, 269..........H 5
South Fort George, 1,282..........F 3
South Hazelton, 483..........D 2
South Slocan, 278..........J 5

South Wellington, 460..........J 3
Sparwood, ●2,990..........K 5
Sparwood, 2,154..........K 5
Spences Bridge, 199..........G 5
Sproat Lake, 321..........H 3
Squamish, ●6,121..........F 5
Squamish, 1,597..........F 5
Stewart, 1,357..........C 2
Stoner, 182..........F 3
Summerland, ●5,551..........H 5
Surrey, ●98,601..........K 3
Tahsis, 1,351..........D 5
Tasu, 331..........A 4
Taylor, 605..........G 2
Telkwa, 712..........D 3
Terrace, ●9,991..........C 3
Terrace, 7,820..........C 3
Thrums, 365..........J 5
Tofino, 461..........E 5
Trail, 11,149..........J 5
Ucluelet, 1,018..........E 6
Union Bay, 407..........H 2
Upper Fraser, 339..........G 3
Valemount, 693..........H 4
Valleyview, 3,787..........G 5
Vananda, 497..........E 5
Vancouver, 426,256..........K 3
Vancouver, ‡1,082,352..........K 3
Vancouver (Greater),
●1,028,334..........K 3
Vanderhoof, 1,653..........E 3
Vavenby, 331..........H 4
Vernon, 13,283..........H 5

Victoria (cap.), 61,761..........K 4
Victoria, ‡195,800..........K 4
Warfield, 2,132..........J 5
Wasa, 355..........K 5
Wells, 409..........G 3
Westbank, 747..........H 5
West Vancouver, ●36,440..........K 3
Westwold, 434..........G 5
White Rock, 10,349..........K 3
Williams Lake, 4,072..........F 4
Willow River, 422..........F 3
Wilmer, 200..........J 5
Wilson Creek, 408..........J 3
Windermere, 421..........K 5
Winfield, 875..........H 5
Winlaw, 383..........J 5
Woodfibre, 408..........K 3
Woss Lake, 394..........D 5
Wynndel, 579..........J 5
Yahk, 192..........K 5
Yale, 224..........M 2
Yarrow, 1,039..........M 3
Ymir, 292..........J 5
Youbou, 1,109..........J 3
Zeballos, 186..........D 5

OTHER FEATURES

Adams (riv.)..........H 4
Alberni (inlet)..........H 3
Alsek (riv.)..........H 1

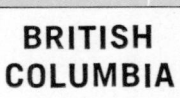

BRITISH COLUMBIA

SCALE
0 15 30   60   90   120 MI.
0 15 30   60   90   120 KM.

Provincial Capital.............⊛
State Capital................⊚
International Boundaries......——
Provincial Boundaries.........——

© C.S. HAMMOND & Co., N.Y.

AREA 366,255 sq. mi.
POPULATION 2,466,608
CAPITAL Victoria
LARGEST CITY Vancouver
HIGHEST POINT Mt. Fairweather 15,300 ft.
SETTLED IN 1806
ADMITTED TO CONFEDERATION 1871
PROVINCIAL FLOWER Dogwood

Aristazabal (isl.)	C 4
Assiniboine (mt.)	K 5
Atlin (lake)	J 1
Babine (lake)	D 2
Banks (isl.)	B 3
Barkley (sound)	E 6
Bennett, W.A.C. (dam)	F 2
Bowron Lake Prov. Park	G 3
Bryce (mt.)	J 4
Burke (chan.)	D 4
Burnaby (isl.)	B 4
Bute (inlet)	E 5
Caamaño (sound)	C 4
Calvert (isl.)	C 4
Canoe (riv.)	H 4
Cariboo (mts.)	G 3
Cassiar (mts.)	K 2
Chatham (sound)	B 3
Chilcotin (riv.)	E 4
Chilko (riv.)	E 4
Chilkoot (pass)	J 1
Churchill (peak)	L 2
Clayoquot (sound)	D 6
Clearwater (riv.)	G 4
Coast (mts.)	E 4
Columbia (lake)	K 5
Columbia (mt.)	J 4
Columbia (riv.)	H 4
Cowichan (lake)	E 6
Crowsnest (pass)	K 5
Dean (chan.)	D 4
Dease (lake)	K 2
Dixon Entrance (chan.)	A 3
Douglas (chan.)	C 3
Duncan (riv.)	J 5
Dundas (isl.)	B 3
Elk (riv.)	K 5
Eutsuk (lake)	D 3
Fairweather (mt.)	H 1
Finlay (riv.)	E 1
Flores (isl.)	D 6
Fort Nelson (riv.)	M 2
François (lake)	D 3
Fraser (riv.)	F 4
Galiano (isl.)	K 3
Gardner (canal)	C 3
Garibaldi Prov. Park	F 5
Georgia (str.)	J 3
Glacier Nat'l Park	J 4
Golden Ears Prov. Park	L 2
Graham (isl.)	A 3
Grenville (chan.)	C 3
Hamber Prov. Park	H 4
Harrison (lake)	M 2
Hazelton (mts.)	D 2
Hecate (str.)	B 3
Howe (sound)	H 5
Hunter (isl.)	C 4
Iskut (riv.)	B 2
Jervis (inlet)	D 5
Johnstone (str.)	D 5
Juan de Fuca (str.)	J 4
Kates Needle (mt.)	A 1
Kechika (riv.)	K 2
Kenney (dam)	E 3
Kettle (riv.)	H 5
Kickinghorse (pass)	J 4
King (isl.)	D 4
Klinaklini (riv.)	E 4
Knight (inlet)	E 5
Knox (cape)	A 3
Kokanee Glacier Prov. Park	J 5
Koocanusa (lake)	K 6
Kootenay (lake)	J 5
Kootenay (riv.)	K 5
Kootenay Nat'l Park	J 4
Kunghit (isl.)	B 4
Kyuquot (sound)	D 5
Langara (isl.)	A 3
Liard (riv.)	J 2
Lillooet (riv.)	F 5
Lower Arrow (lake)	H 5
Malaspina (str.)	J 2
Manning Prov. Park, 23	G 5
Masset (inlet)	A 3
Milbanke (sound)	C 4
Monashee (mts.)	H 4
Moresby (isl.)	B 4
Morice (riv.)	D 3
Mount Assiniboine Prov. Park	K 5
Mount Edziza Prov. Park and Rec. Area	B 1
Mount Revelstoke Nat'l Park	H 4
Mount Robson Prov. Park	H 3
Muncho Lake Prov. Park	L 2
Muskwa (riv.)	M 2
Nanika (dam)	D 3
Nass (riv.)	C 2
Nechako (riv.)	E 3
Nootka (isl.)	D 5
Nootka (sound)	D 5
North Thompson (riv.)	G 4
Observatory (inlet)	C 2
Okanagan (lake)	H 5
Okanogan (riv.)	H 6
Omineca (mts.)	D 2
Ootsa (lake)	D 3
Pacific Rim Nat'l Park	F 6
Parsnip (riv.)	F 2
Peace (riv.)	G 2
Pine (riv.)	F 2
Pitt (isl.)	C 3
Pitt (lake)	L 2
Porcher (isl.)	B 3
Portland (canal)	C 2
Portland (inlet)	C 3
Princess Royal (isl.)	C 3
Principe (chan.)	B 3
Prophet (riv.)	M 2
Purcell (mts.)	J 5
Quatsino (sound)	C 5
Queen Charlotte (isls.), 2,390	B 4
Queen Charlotte (sound)	C 4
Queen Charlotte (str.)	D 5
Quesnel (lake)	G 4
Rivers (inlet)	D 4
Robson (mt.)	H 3
Rocky (mts.)	F 2
Rose (pt.)	B 3
Saint James (cape)	B 4
Salmon (riv.)	F 3
Scott (cape)	C 5
Seechelt (inlet)	J 2
Seechelt (pen.)	J 2
Selkirk (mts.)	J 4
Seymour (inlet)	D 4
Shuswap (lake)	H 4
Sikanni Chief (riv.)	F 2
Sir Sandford (mt.)	H 4
Skeena (riv.)	C 2
Skidegate (inlet)	B 3
Slocan (lake)	J 5
Smith (sound)	C 4
Stave (lake)	L 2
Stikine (riv.)	B 2
Stone Mountain Prov. Park	L 2
Strathcona Prov. Park	E 3
Stuart (lake)	E 3
Tagish (lake)	J 1
Tahtsa (lake)	D 3
Takla (lake)	D 2
Taku (riv.)	J 2
Teslin (lake)	K 1
Tetachuck (lake)	D 3
Texada (isl.)	J 3
Thompson (riv.)	G 5
Tiedemann (mt.)	E 4
Tweedsmuir Prov. Park	D 3
Upper Arrow (lake)	H 5
Valdes (isl.)	D 5
Vancouver (isl.), 381,297	D 5
Waddington (mt.)	E 4
Wells Gray Prov. Park	H 4
Whitesail (lake)	D 3
Williston (lake)	F 2
Work (chan.)	C 3
Yellowhead (pass)	H 4
Yoho Nat'l Park	J 4

‡ Population of metropolitan area.
• Population of municipality.

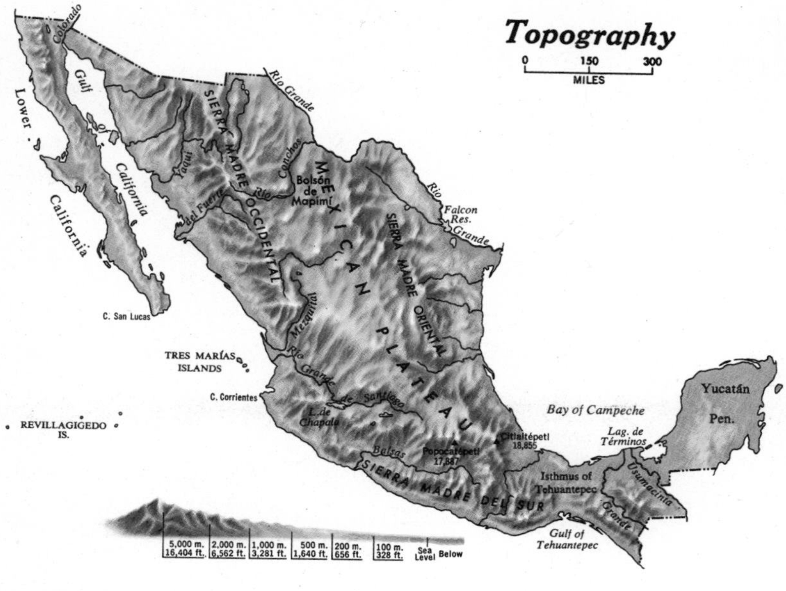
Topography
0 150 300
MILES
Colorado
Gulf
Lower
California
California
Rio Grande
SIERRA MADRE OCCIDENTAL
MEXICAN PLATEAU
Bolsón de Mapimí
SIERRA MADRE ORIENTAL
Falcon Res.
Grande
C. San Lucas
TRES MARÍAS ISLANDS
C. Corrientes
REVILLAGIGEDO IS.
L. de Chapala
Balsas
Popocatépetl 17,887
Citlaltépetl 18,855
SIERRA MADRE DEL SUR
Isthmus of Tehuantepec
Bay of Campeche
Lag. de Términos
Yucatán Pen.
Gulf of Tehuantepec
5,000 m. 16,404 ft.
2,000 m. 6,562 ft.
1,000 m. 3,281 ft.
500 m. 1,640 ft.
200 m. 656 ft.
100 m. 328 ft.
Sea Level
Below

STATES and TERRITORIES

Aguascalientes, 334,936 ....H 6
Baja California Norte, 856,773 ....B 1
Baja California Sur, 123,786 ....C 3
Campeche, 250,391 ....O 7
Chiapas, 1,578,180 ....N 8
Chihuahua, 1,730,012 ....F 2
Coahuila, 1,140,989 ....H 3
Colima, 240,235 ....G 7
Distrito Federal, 7,005,855 ....L 1
Durango, 919,381 ....G 4
Guanajuato, 2,285,249 ....J 6
Guerrero, 1,573,098 ....J 8
Hidalgo, 1,156,177 ....K 6
Jalisco, 3,322,750 ....H 6
México, 3,797,861 ....K 7
Michoacán, 2,341,556 ....H 7
Morelos, 620,392 ....K 7
Nayarit, 547,992 ....G 6
Nuevo León, 1,653,808 ....K 4
Oaxaca, 2,011,946 ....L 8
Puebla, 2,483,770 ....L 7
Querétaro, 464,226 ....J 6
Quintana Roo, 91,044 ....P 7
San Luis Potosí, 1,257,028 ....J 5
Sinaloa, 1,273,228 ....F 4
Sonora, 1,092,458 ....D 2
Tabasco, 766,346 ....N 7
Tamaulipas, 1,438,350 ....K 4
Tlaxcala, 418,334 ....N 1
Veracruz, 3,813,613 ....L 7
Yucatán, 774,011 ....P 6
Zacatecas, 949,663 ....H 5

CITIES and TOWNS

Acámbaro, 80,259 ....J 7
Acaponeta, 29,829 ....G 5
Acapulco de Juárez, 234,866 ....J 8
Acatlán, 22,507 ....K 7
Acatzingo, 14,809 ....N 2
Acayucan, 36,352 ....M 8
Aconchi, 2,313 ....D 2
Actopan, 26,608 ....Q 1
Agualeguas, 5,536 ....J 3
Agua Prieta, 21,627 ....E 1
Aguascalientes, 222,105 ....H 6
Aguililla, 20,752 ....H 7
Ahuacatlán, 14,180 ....G 6
Ajalpan, 20,413 ....L 7
Alamos, 24,123 ....E 3
Aldama, Chihuahua, 14,117 ....G 2
Aldama, Tamaulipas, 15,336 ....L 5
Aljojuca, 5,520 ....O 1
Allende, Chihuahua, 11,039 ....G 3
Allende, Coahuila, 12,736 ....J 2
Allende, Nuevo León, 14,263 ....J 4
Almoloya del Río, 3,692 ....K 1
Altamira, 28,667 ....K 5
Altar, 3,811 ....D 1
Altotonga, 31,231 ....P 1
Alvarado, 33,152 ....M 7
Amatlán de los Reyes, 21,011 ....P 2
Amealco, 26,222 ....K 6
Ameca, 42,016 ....H 6
Amecameca de Juárez, 21,753 ....L 1
Amozoc de Mota, 13,381....N 2
Angostura, 29,709 ....E 4
Apan, 21,550 ....M 1
Apatzingán de la Constitución, 67,384 ....J 7
Apizaco, 20,998 ....N 1
Aquiles Serdán, 5,159 ....G 2
Aramberri, 16,051 ....J 5
Arandas, 41,958 ....H 6
Arcelia, 25,631 ....J 7
Arizpe, 4,415 ....D 1
Armería, 16,334 ....G 7
Arriaga, 23,582 ....N 8
Arteaga, 17,455 ....H 7
Ascensión, 8,810 ....E 1
Atlixco, 72,256 ....M 2
Atotonilco, 35,297 ....H 6
Autlán de Navarro, 30,853 ....G 7
Ayutla de los Libres, 23,668 ....K 8
Azcapotzalco, 545,513 ....L 1
Azoyú, 23,554 ....K 8
Bacadéhuachi, 1,470 ....D 2
Bacerac, 2,306 ....E 1
Bácum, 17,598 ....D 3
Badiraguato, 28,995 ....F 4
Balancán, 27,241 ....O 8
Balleza, 15,122 ....F 3
Batopilas, 8,780 ....F 3
Baviácora, 4,202 ....E 2
Bavispe, 2,048 ....E 1
Benjamín Hill, 5,807 ....D 1
Boca del Río, 27,884 ....Q 1
Buenaventura, 14,629 ....F 2
Burgos, 5,529 ....K 4
Cadereyta, 28,093 ....K 6
Cadereyta Jiménez, 30,429 ....K 4
Calera, 13,030 ....H 5
Calkiní, 24,503 ....O 6
Calpulalpan, 14,633 ....M 1
Calvillo, 24,039 ....H 6
Campeche, 81,147 ....O 7
Cananea, 21,824 ....D 1
Canatlán, 63,871 ....G 4
Cancún ....Q 6
Candela, 2,202 ....J 3
Carbo, 3,242 ....D 2
Cárdenas, S. Luis Potosí, 18,091 ....K 6
Cárdenas, Tabasco, 78,477 ....N 8
Carmen, 71,240 ....N 7
Casas Grandes, 11,207....F 1
Catemaco, 23,671 ....M 7
Cedral, 12,426 ....J 5
Celaya, 143,703 ....J 6
Celestún, 1,535 ....O 6
Cerralvo, 6,831 ....J 3
Cerritos, 18,868 ....K 5
Chalchihuites, 11,347 ....G 5
Chalco, 41,145 ....M 1
Champotón, 27,581 ....O 7
Chapulco, 2,807 ....O 2
Charcas, 22,388 ....J 5
Chetumal, 34,237 ....Q 7
Chiapa de Corzo, 22,640 ....N 8
Chiautempan, 33,820 ....N 1
Chicoloapan de Juárez, 8,995 ....M 1
Chietla, 26,921 ....M 2
Chignahuapan, 29,556 ....N 1
Chignautla, 8,348 ....N 1
Chihuahua, 363,850 ....G 2
Chilapa, 53,263 ....K 8
Chilpancingo, 56,904 ....K 8
China, 9,018 ....K 4
Chocamán, 7,270 ....P 2
Choix, 27,515 ....E 3
Cholula, 20,913 ....M 1
Cihuatlán, 16,314 ....G 7
Cintalapa, 31,252 ....M 8
Ciudad Acuña, 32,760 ....J 2
Ciudad Camargo, Chihuahua, 29,185 ....G 3
Ciudad Camargo, Tamaulipas, 16,097 ....K 3
Ciudad Delicias, 64,385 ....G 2
Ciudad del Maíz, 35,502 ....K 5
Ciudad de Valles, 71,098 ....K 5
Ciudad Guerrero, 35,631 ....F 2
Ciudad Guzmán, 48,142 ....H 7
Ciudad Juárez, 436,054 ....F 1
Ciudad Lerdo, 53,551 ....H 4
Ciudad Madero, 89,994 ....L 5
Ciudad Mante, 79,130 ....K 5
Ciudad Miguel Alemán, 18,134 ....K 3
Ciudad Obregón, 181,972 ....E 3
Ciudad Río Bravo, 70,814 ....K 4
Ciudad Serdán, 25,288 ....O 2
Ciudad Victoria, 94,304 ....K 5
Coalcomán de Matamoros, 13,480 ....H 7
Coatepec, 34,161 ....P 1
Coatzacoalcos, 108,818 ....M 7
Cocula, 20,273 ....G 6
Colima, 72,074 ....H 7
Colón, 20,392 ....K 6
Colotlán, 14,316 ....H 5
Comala, 13,715 ....G 7
Comalcalco, 71,651 ....N 7
Comitán, 38,137 ....O 8
Comondú, 30,872 ....D 3
Compostela, 59,422 ....G 6
Concepción del Oro, 15,711....J 4
Concordia, 21,023 ....G 5
Córdoba, 92,870 ....P 2
Cosalá, 16,202 ....F 4
Cosamaloapan de Carpio, 75,412 ....M 7
Cosautlán de Carvajal, 8,015 ....P 1
Coscomatepec de Bravo, 19,890 ....P 2
Cosío, 7,031 ....H 5
Cosoleacaque, 20,251 ....M 7
Cotija, 17,296 ....H 7
Coyame, 3,798 ....G 2
Coyoacán, 338,850 ....L 1
Coyotepec, 8,658 ....L 1
Coyuca, 25,128 ....J 7
Coyuca de Benítez, 36,032....J 8
Coyutla, 12,008 ....L 6
Cozumel, 12,634 ....Q 6
Cuatrociénegas de Carranza, 9,512 ....H 3
Cuauhtémoc, 65,160 ....F 2
Cuautitlán, 40,622 ....L 1
Cuautla Morelos, 67,869....L 2
Cuencamé, 31,170 ....H 4
Cuernavaca, 159,909 ....L 2
Cuicatlán, 45,013 ....L 8
Cuitlahuac, 13,078 ....P 2
Culiacán, 358,812 ....F 4
Cumpas, 6,186 ....D 2
Cuna de la Independencia Nacional, 71,212 ....J 6
Cunduacán, 42,872 ....N 7
Doctor Arroyo, 45,889 ....K 5
Durango, 192,934 ....G 4
Ejutla de Crespo, 34,890 ....L 8
El Ebano, 20,571 ....K 5
El Fuerte, 62,001 ....E 3
El Oro, Durango, 18,668 ....G 4
El Oro, México, 17,086 ....K 7
El Salto, 19,604 ....G 5
Empalme, 32,541 ....D 2
Encarnación de Díaz, 29,533 ....H 6
Ensenada, 113,320 ....A 1
Escuinapa de Hidalgo, 30,763 ....G 5
Escuintla, 13,754 ....N 9
Etchojoa, 53,767 ....E 3
Fortín de las Flores, 21,370....P 2
Fresnillo, 101,316 ....H 5
Frontera, 43,007 ....N 7
Galeana, Chihuahua, 3,176 ....F 1
Galeana, Nuevo León, 39,143....J 4
García de la Cadena, 4,755....H 6
General Bravo, 6,063 ....K 4
General Cepeda, 13,332 ....J 4
Gómez Palacio, 135,743 ....G 4
González, 23,748 ....K 5
Guadalajara, 1,196,218 ....H 6
Guadalupe, Nvo. León, 153,454 ....J 4
Guadalupe, Zacatecas, 31,976 ....H 5
Guadalupe-Bravos, 9,649 ....F 1
Guadalupe Victoria, 27,450 ....G 4
Guadalupe y Calvo, 31,131 ....F 2
Guanacevi, 12,035 ....G 4
Guanajuato, 65,258 ....J 6
Guasave, 148,475 ....E 4
Guaymas, 84,730 ....D 3
Gutiérrez Zamora, 20,534 ....L 6
Halachó, 8,547 ....O 6
Hecelchakán, 10,974 ....O 6
Hermosillo, 206,663 ....D 2
Heroica Caborca, 29,486 ....C 1
Heroica Huamantla, 26,191 ....N 1
Heroica Nogales, 52,865 ....D 1
Hidalgo, 21,434 ....K 4
Hopelchén, 23,509 ....P 7
Huajuapan de León, 83,939....L 8
Huaquechula, 16,702 ....M 2
Huatabampo, 43,963 ....D 3
Huatusco de Chicuellar, 20,621 ....P 2
Huauchinango, 37,211 ....L 6
Huehuetlán, 6,962 ....M 2
Huejotzingo, 21,728 ....M 1
Huejutla de Reyes, 45,771 ....K 6
Huetamo de Núñez, 35,414 ....J 7
Hueyotlipan, 6,786 ....M 1
Huimanguillo, 70,525 ....N 8
Huitzuco, 28,159 ....K 7
Huixtla, 25,884 ....N 9
Hunucmá, 10,600 ....O 6
Ignacio de la Llave, 16,345 ....Q 2
Iguala, 60,980 ....K 7
Imuris, 5,853 ....D 1
Indé, 11,969 ....G 4
Irapuato, 175,966 ....J 6
Isla de Aguada ....O 7
Isla Mujeres, 10,469 ....Q 6
Ixmiquilpan, 35,851 ....K 6
Ixtacalco, 474,700 ....L 1
Ixtapalapa, 533,569 ....L 1
Ixtlán del Río, 16,228 ....G 6
Izamal, 16,188 ....P 6
Izúcar de Matamoros, 44,074 ....M 2
Jala, 11,174 ....G 6
Jalacingo, 15,436 ....P 1
Jalapa Enríquez, 127,081 ....P 1
Jalpa, Tabasco, 29,904....N 7
Jalpa, Zacatecas, 26,050 ....H 6
Jalpan, 15,319 ....K 6
Jáltipan, 19,676 ....M 8
Jaumave, 13,504 ....K 5
Jerez de Garcia Salinas, 49,202 ....H 5
Jico, 14,153 ....P 1
Jilotepec, 34,866 ....K 7
Jiménez, Chihuahua, 27,044 ....G 3
Jiménez, Coahuila, 8,019 ....J 2
Jojutla de Juárez, 31,196....L 2
Jonatatepec, 7,478 ....M 2
Jonuta, 14,227 ....N 7
Juan Aldama, 13,661 ....H 4
Juárez, 1,664 ....J 3
Juchipila, 14,517 ....H 6
Juchique de Ferrer, 14,094 ....Q 1
Juchitán de Zaragoza, 178,388 ....M 8
La Barca, 40,331 ....H 6
La Concordia, 15,296 ....N 9
La Cruz, Chihuahua, 3,899 ....G 3
La Cruz, Sinaloa, 19,055 ....F 5
Lagos, 66,273 ....J 6
La Paz, 49,637 ....D 5
La Piedad, 51,484 ....H 6
La Trinitaria, 28,028 ....N 9
La Yesca, 9,010 ....G 6
León, 453,976 ....J 6
Libres, 12,973 ....O 1
Linares, 49,397 ....K 4
Llera de Canales, 21,117 ....K 5
Loreto, 21,544 ....J 5
Los Mochis, 165,612 ....E 4
Los Reyes, 33,879 ....H 7
Macuspana, 75,013 ....N 8
Madera, 32,367 ....F 2
Magdalena, 13,485 ....D 1
Manuel Benavides, 5,135 ....H 2
Manzanillo, 46,170 ....G 7
Mapastepec, 16,911 ....N 9
Mapimí, 19,053 ....G 4
Martínez de la Torre, 62,707 ....L 6
Mascota, 15,260 ....G 6
Matamoros, Coahuila, 44,103 ....H 4
Matamoros, Tamaulipas, 182,887 ....L 4
Matehuala, 48,368 ....J 5
Maxcanú, 10,620 ....O 6
Mazapil, 28,656 ....J 4
Mazatán, 1,561 ....E 2
Mazatlán, 171,835 ....F 5
Melchor Múzquiz, 45,945 ....J 3
Melchor Ocampo, 4,180 ....H 4
Melchor Ocampo del Balsas, 23,248 ....H 8
Meoquí, 27,000 ....G 2
Mérida, 253,856 ....P 6
Mexicali, 390,411 ....B 1
Mexico City (México) (capital), 3,025,564 ....L 1
Mexico City, *7,157,000 ....L 1
Mezquital, 4,663 ....G 5
Miacatlán, 12,579 ....L 2
Mier, 5,916 ....K 3
Miguel Azua, 15,330 ....H 4
Minatitlán, 89,412 ....M 8
Mineral del Monte, 10,943 ....K 6
Miquihuana, 3,099 ....K 5
Misantla, 44,268 ....P 1
Mocorito, 49,957 ....F 4
Moctezuma, S. L. Potosí, 13,628 ....J 5
Moctezuma, Sonora, 3,476 ....E 2
Monclova, 80,252 ....J 3
Montemorelos, 34,067 ....K 4
Monterrey, 830,336 ....J 4
Morelia, 209,507 ....J 7
Morelos, 4,721 ....J 2
Morelos Cañada, 11,463 ....O 2
Moroleón, 33,765 ....J 6
Motozintla de Mendoza, 31,518 ....N 9
Motul, 21,087 ....P 6
Mulegé, 19,282 ....C 3
Muna, 6,147 ....P 6
Naco, 3,639 ....D 1
Nacozari de García, 3,483 ....E 1
Nadadores, 3,869 ....J 3
Nanacamilpa, 8,658 ....M 1
Naolinco de Victoria, 11,077 ....P 1
Naranjos, 21,371 ....L 6
Naucalpan, 373,605 ....L 1
Nautla, 9,425 ....L 6
Nava, 5,669 ....J 2
Navojoa, 69,792 ....E 3
Nazas, 13,189 ....G 4
Nieves, 19,938 ....H 5
Nochistlán, Oaxaca, 58,609 ....L 8
Nochistlán, Zacatecas, 28,463 ....H 6
Nogales, 19,158 ....P 2
Nombre de Dios, 17,742 ....G 5
Nonoava, 4,054 ....F 3
Nopalucan, 8,401 ....O 1
Nueva Casas Grandes, 5,333 ....F 1
Nueva Ciudad Guerrero, 4,065 ....K 3
Nuevo Laredo, 150,922 ....J 3
Nuevo Morelos, 2,245 ....K 5
Oaxaca, 156,587 ....L 8
Ocampo, Chihuahua, 4,947 ....E 2
Ocampo, Coahuila, 10,072 ....H 3
Ocampo, Tamaulipas, 15,998 ....K 5
Ocotlán, 43,394 ....H 6
Ocotlán de Morelos, 45,752 ....L 8
Ojinaga, 23,854 ....G 2
Ojocaliente, 20,280 ....H 5
Ometepec, 23,604 ....K 8
Opódepe, 3,312 ....D 2
Oriental, 7,375 ....O 1
Orizaba, 92,728 ....P 2
Otumba de Gómez Farías, 11,960 ....M 1
Oxkutzcab, 10,295 ....P 7
Ozuluama, 22,382 ....L 6
Ozumba, 11,013 ....M 1
Pachuca, 84,543 ....K 6
Padilla, 13,643 ....K 5
Palenque, 22,684 ....O 8
Palizada, 7,445 ....O 7
Palmar de Bravo, 15,898 ....O 2
Palmillas, 2,420 ....K 5
Pánuco, 49,077 ....K 6
Papantla de Olarte, 94,623 ....L 6
Paraíso, 30,439 ....N 7
Parral, 61,729 ....G 3
Parras, 32,664 ....H 4
Pátzcuaro, 44,591 ....J 7
Pedro Montoya, 10,760 ....K 6
Pénjamo, 89,548 ....J 6
Peñón Blanco, 10,541....H 4
Perote, 23,556 ....P 1
Petatlán, 31,088 ....J 8
Peto, 11,986 ....P 6
Piedras Negras, 65,883 ....J 2
Pijijiapan, 20,350 ....N 9
Pitiquito, 6,100 ....D 1
Pochutla, 84,033 ....L 9
Poza Rica de Hidalgo, 121,341 ....L 6
Progreso, 22,100 ....P 6

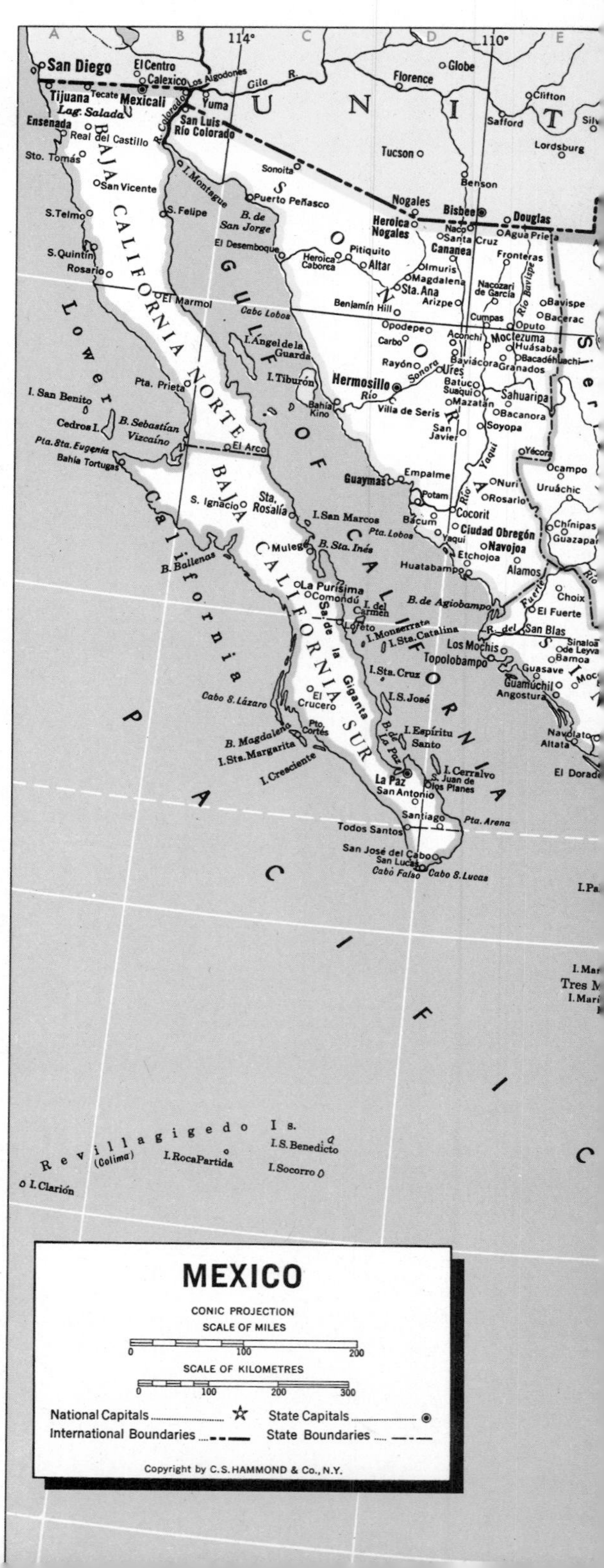
MEXICO
CONIC PROJECTION
SCALE OF MILES
0 100 200
SCALE OF KILOMETRES
0 100 200 300
National Capitals
State Capitals
International Boundaries
State Boundaries
Copyright by C.S. HAMMOND & Co., N.Y.
San Diego
El Centro
Calexico
Tijuana
Tecate
Mexicali
Yuma
Ensenada
San Luis Río Colorado
Tucson
Nogales
Bisbee
Douglas
Heroica Nogales
Cananea
Hermosillo
Guaymas
Ciudad Obregón
Navojoa
Los Mochis
La Paz
BAJA CALIFORNIA NORTE
BAJA CALIFORNIA SUR
GULF OF CALIFORNIA
Lower California
PACIFIC
Revillagigedo Is.

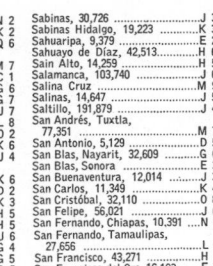

AREA 761,601 sq. mi.
POPULATION 48,313,438
CAPITAL Mexico City
LARGEST CITY Mexico City
HIGHEST POINT Citlaltépetl 18,855 ft.
MONETARY UNIT Mexican peso
MAJOR LANGUAGE Spanish
MAJOR RELIGION Roman Catholicism

States Indicated by Numbers

1	Tlaxcala	6	Querétaro
2	Morelos	7	Guanajuato
3	Distrito Federal	8	Aguascalientes
4	México	9	Nayarit
5	Hidalgo	10	Colima

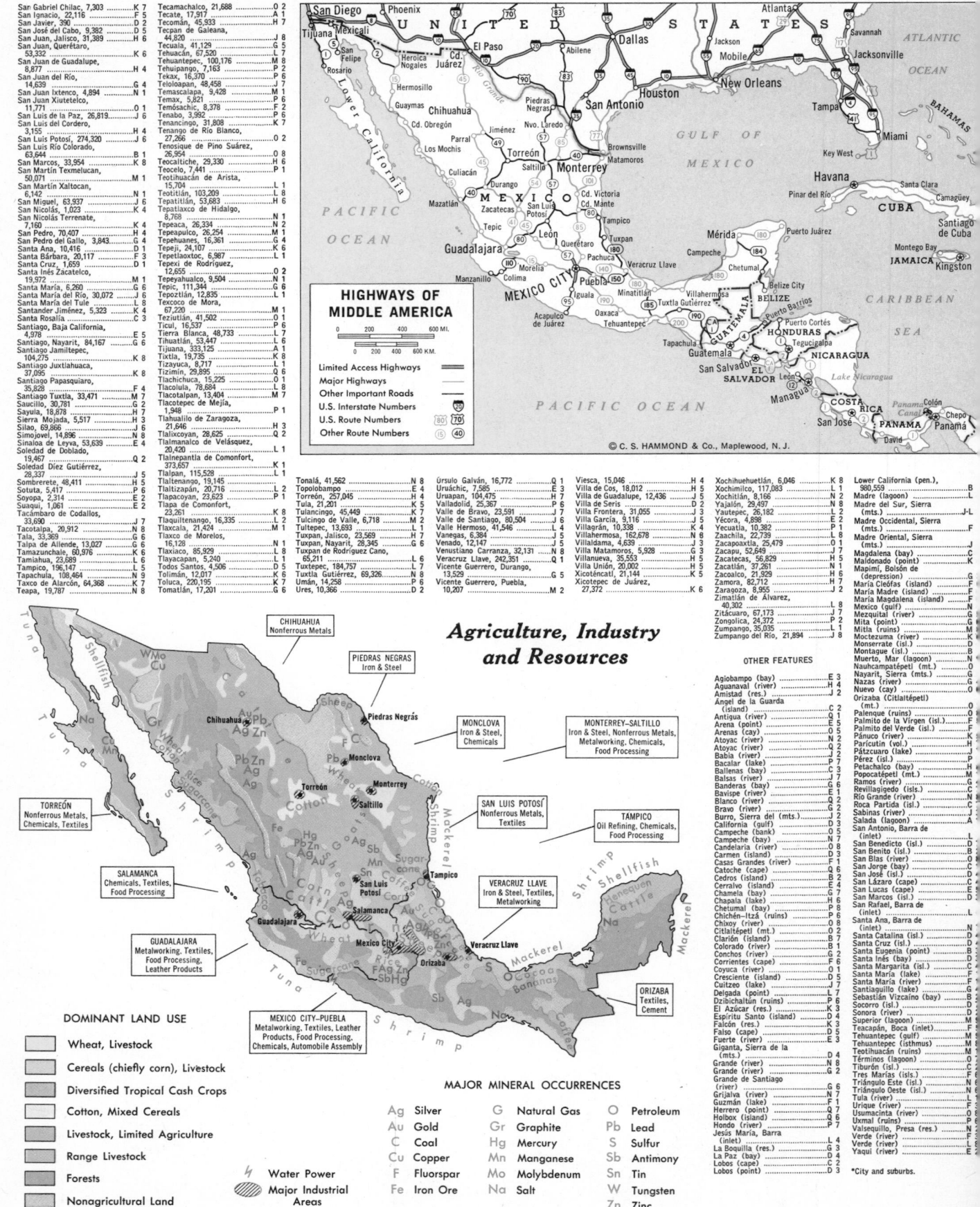

HIGHWAYS OF MIDDLE AMERICA

© C. S. HAMMOND & Co., Maplewood, N.J.

Agriculture, Industry and Resources

CHIHUAHUA
Nonferrous Metals

PIEDRAS NEGRAS
Iron & Steel

MONCLOVA
Iron & Steel,
Chemicals

MONTERREY–SALTILLO
Iron & Steel, Nonferrous Metals,
Metalworking, Chemicals,
Food Processing

TORREÓN
Nonferrous Metals,
Chemicals, Textiles

SAN LUIS POTOSÍ
Nonferrous Metals,
Textiles

TAMPICO
Oil Refining, Chemicals,
Food Processing

SALAMANCA
Chemicals, Textiles,
Food Processing

VERACRUZ LLAVE
Iron & Steel, Textiles,
Metalworking

GUADALAJARA
Metalworking, Textiles,
Food Processing,
Leather Products

ORIZABA
Textiles,
Cement

MEXICO CITY–PUEBLA
Metalworking, Textiles, Leather
Products, Food Processing,
Chemicals, Automobile Assembly

DOMINANT LAND USE

- Wheat, Livestock
- Cereals (chiefly corn), Livestock
- Diversified Tropical Cash Crops
- Cotton, Mixed Cereals
- Livestock, Limited Agriculture
- Range Livestock
- Forests
- Nonagricultural Land

Water Power
Major Industrial Areas

MAJOR MINERAL OCCURRENCES

Ag Silver
Au Gold
C Coal
Cu Copper
F Fluorspar
Fe Iron Ore
G Natural Gas
Gr Graphite
Hg Mercury
Mn Manganese
Mo Molybdenum
Na Salt
O Petroleum
Pb Lead
S Sulfur
Sb Antimony
Sn Tin
W Tungsten
Zn Zinc

GUATEMALA
AREA 42,042 sq. mi.
POPULATION 5,200,000
CAPITAL Guatemala
LARGEST CITY Guatemala
HIGHEST POINT Tajumulco 13,845 ft.
MONETARY UNIT quetzal
MAJOR LANGUAGES Spanish, Quiché
MAJOR RELIGION Roman Catholicism

BELIZE
AREA 8,867 sq. mi.
POPULATION 122,000
CAPITAL Belmopan
LARGEST CITY Belize City
HIGHEST POINT Victoria Peak, 3,681 ft.
MONETARY UNIT Belize dollar
MAJOR LANGUAGES English, Spanish, Mayan
MAJOR RELIGIONS Protestantism, Roman Catholicism

EL SALVADOR
AREA 8,260 sq. mi.
POPULATION 3,418,455
CAPITAL San Salvador
LARGEST CITY San Salvador
HIGHEST POINT Santa Ana 7,825 ft.
MONETARY UNIT colón
MAJOR LANGUAGE Spanish
MAJOR RELIGION Roman Catholicism

HONDURAS
AREA 43,277 sq. mi.
POPULATION 2,495,000
CAPITAL Tegucigalpa
LARGEST CITY Tegucigalpa
HIGHEST POINT Las Minas 9,347 ft.
MONETARY UNIT lempira
MAJOR LANGUAGE Spanish
MAJOR RELIGION Roman Catholicism

NICARAGUA
AREA 45,698 sq. mi.
POPULATION 1,984,000
CAPITAL Managua
LARGEST CITY Managua
HIGHEST POINT Cerro Mocotón 6,913 ft.
MONETARY UNIT córdoba
MAJOR LANGUAGE Spanish
MAJOR RELIGION Roman Catholicism

COSTA RICA
AREA 19,575 sq. mi.
POPULATION 1,800,000
CAPITAL San José
LARGEST CITY San José
HIGHEST POINT Chirripó Grande 12,530 ft.
MONETARY UNIT colón
MAJOR LANGUAGE Spanish
MAJOR RELIGION Roman Catholicism

PANAMA
AREA 29,209 sq. mi.
POPULATION 1,425,343
CAPITAL Panamá
LARGEST CITY Panamá
HIGHEST POINT Vol. Chiriquí 11,401 ft.
MONETARY UNIT balboa
MAJOR LANGUAGE Spanish
MAJOR RELIGION Roman Catholicism

CANAL ZONE
AREA 647 sq. mi.
POPULATION 44,650
CAPITAL Balboa Heights

Agriculture, Industry and Resources

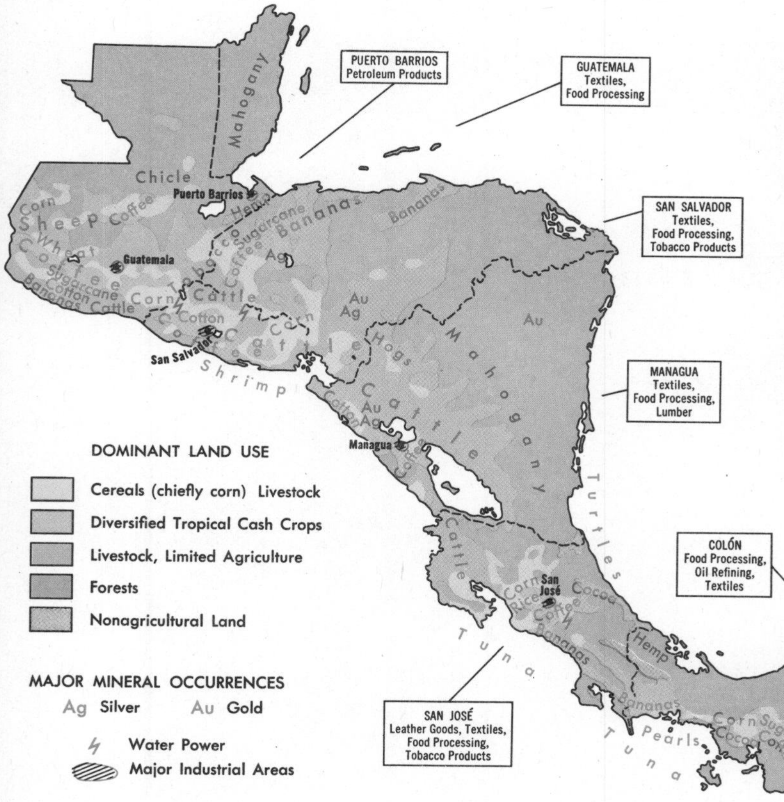

PUERTO BARRIOS
Petroleum Products

GUATEMALA
Textiles,
Food Processing

SAN SALVADOR
Textiles,
Food Processing,
Tobacco Products

MANAGUA
Textiles,
Food Processing,
Lumber

PANAMÁ
Food Processing,
Textiles

COLÓN
Food Processing,
Oil Refining,
Textiles

SAN JOSÉ
Leather Goods, Textiles,
Food Processing,
Tobacco Products

DOMINANT LAND USE

- Cereals (chiefly corn) Livestock
- Diversified Tropical Cash Crops
- Livestock, Limited Agriculture
- Forests
- Nonagricultural Land

MAJOR MINERAL OCCURRENCES

Ag Silver   Au Gold

Water Power

Major Industrial Areas

GUATEMALA

HONDURAS

EL SALVADOR

NICARAGUA

COSTA RICA

PANAMA

BELIZE

CITIES and TOWNS

Belize City, 37,000	C 2	
Belize City, *48,421	C 2	
Belmopan (capital)	C 2	
Benque Viejo, 1,607	C 2	
Cayo, 1,890	C 2	
Corozal Town, 3,171	C 1	
Hill Bank, 78	C 2	
Monkey River Town, 417	C 2	
Orange Walk Town, 2,157	C 1	
Punta Gorda, 1,789	C 2	

San José, 365	C 2	
San Pedro, 170	D 2	
Stann Creek Town, 5,287	C 2	

OTHER FEATURES

Ambergris (cay), †572	D 1	
Belize (river)	C 2	
Bokel (cay)	D 2	
Cockscomb (mts.)	C 2	
Corker (cay), †360	D 2	
Glovers (reef)	D 2	
Half Moon (cay)	D 2	
Hondo (river)	C 1	

Honduras (gulf)	D 2	
Mauger (cay)	D 2	
New (river)	C 2	
Saint Georges (cay), 134	C 2	
Sarstún (river)	C 3	
Turneffe (isls.), 99	D 2	

CANAL ZONE

CITIES and TOWNS

Balboa, 2,568	H 6	
Cristóbal, 817	G 6	

COSTA RICA

CITIES and TOWNS

Alajuela, 25,195	E 6	
Atenas, 963	E 6	
Atlanta	F 6	
Bagaces, 1,175	E 5	
Beverly	F 6	
Boruca, †1,049	F 6	
Buenos Aires, †4,624	F 6	
Cañas, 2,991	E 5	
Carmen	F 5	
Cartago, 19,038	F 6	
Chomes, †1,991	E 5	

Ciudad Quesada, 3,696	E 5	
El Salvador	F 6	
Esparta, 2,860	E 5	
Filadelfia, 1,574	E 5	
Golfito, 6,859	F 6	
Grecia, 4,862	E 5	
Guácimo, 5,731	E 5	
Guápiles, 983	F 5	
Heredia, 20,523	F 6	
Las Juntas, 827	E 5	
Liberia, 11,171	E 5	
Limón, 30,676	F 6	
Miramar, 1,122	E 6	
Nicoya, 3,196	E 5	
Orotina, 1,749	E 6	

Palmares, 1,529	F 6	
Paquera	F 6	
Paraíso, 4,427	F 6	
Pejivalle	F 6	
Platanilla	F 6	
Playa Bonita	F 6	
Puerto Cortés, 1,757	F 6	
Puntarenas, 27,527	E 6	
Quepos, 1,858	E 6	
San Ignacio, 315	E 6	
San José (cap.), 182,961	F 5	
San José, *408,000	F 5	
San Marcos, 411	F 6	
San Ramón, 6,444	E 5	
Santa Cruz, 3,849	E 5	

Santa Rosa, †1,750	E 5	
Santo Domingo, 3,333	F 6	
Sibube	F 6	
Siquirres, 2,157	F 5	
Turrialba, 8,629	F 6	
Vesta	F 6	

OTHER FEATURES

Blanca (point)	F 5	
Blanco (cape)	F 6	
Blanco (mt.)	F 6	
Burica (point)	F 6	
Cahuita (point)	F 6	
Caño (isl.)	F 6	

(continued on following page)

Topography

0   75   150
MILES

5,000 m. 2,000 m. 1,000 m. 500 m. 200 m. 100 m. Sea
16,404 ft. 6,562 ft. 3,281 ft. 1,640 ft. 656 ft. 328 ft. Level Below

El Paraíso, Copán, 1,787	C 3	
El Paraíso, El Paraíso, 5,758	D 4	
El Porvenir, 529	D 3	
El Progreso, 8,718	D 3	
El Triunfo, 2,136	D 4	
Goascorán, 1,184	D 4	
Gracias, 2,484	C 3	
Guaimaca, 2,620	E 3	
Gualpatanta	E 2	
Guanaja, 1,253	E 2	
Guarita, 599	C 3	
Guayape, 610	D 3	
Iriona, 119	E 2	
Jacaleapa, 992	D 3	
Jesús de Otoro, 2,775	C 3	
Jutiapa, 1,711	D 3	
Juticalpa, 7,912	D 3	
La Ceiba, 33,934	D 2	
La Concepción	E 3	
La Esperanza, 2,000	C 3	
La Guata, 281	D 3	
La Paz, 5,542	D 3	
La Protección	C 3	
Lauterique, 272	D 4	
Limón, 1,934	E 3	
Manto, 943	D 3	
Marcala, 1,968	C 3	
Melcher	D 3	
Morazán, 3,924	D 3	
Morocelí, 1,472	D 4	
Nacaome, 4,376	D 4	
Namasigüe, 1,024	D 4	
Naranjito, 3,291	C 3	
Nueva Armenia, 866	C 3	
Nueva Ocotepeque, 4,608	C 3	
Olanchito, 5,008	D 3	
Omoa, 1,384	C 2	
Paso Real	E 3	
Patuca	D 3	
Pespire, 1,758	D 4	
Puerto Castilla	E 2	
Puerto Cortés, 21,600	D 2	
Roatán, 1,883	D 2	
Sabanagrande, 1,657	D 4	
Salado	D 2	
San Esteban, 763	D 3	
San Francisco, 1,122	D 3	
San Francisco de la Paz, 1,971	D 3	
San Juan de Flores, 1,174	D 3	
San Luis, 2,631	C 3	
San Marcos, 1,576	C 3	
San Pedro Sula, 90,538	C 3	
San Pedro Zacapa, 765	C 3	
Santa Bárbara, 6,129	C 3	
Santa Cruz de Yojoa, 1,833	D 3	

JAMAICA — Montego Bay, Falmouth, St. Ann's Bay, Annotto Bay, Port María, Port Antonio, S. Negril Pt., Savanna la Mar, Ewarton, Spanish Town, Kingston, Morant Point, Black River, Portland Point, Blue Mountain Pk. 7,388, Walton Bank, Pedro Bank, Pedro Cays (Jamaica), Morant Cays (Jamaica)

Serranilla Bank (Col.), Bajo Nuevo (Col.), Serrana Bank (Col.), Roncador Bank (Col.)

Santa Rita, 3,976	D 3	
Santa Rosa de Aguán, 1,701	E 2	
Santa Rosa de Copán, 9,109	C 3	
Siguatepeque, 9,462	D 3	
Sinuapa, 882	C 3	
Sonaguera, 1,344	D 3	
Sulaco, 1,071	D 3	
Tegucigalpa (cap.), 253,283	D 3	
Tela, 14,103	D 3	
Teupasenti, 829	D 3	
Tocoa, 1,605	E 3	
Trinidad, 2,817	C 3	
Trujillo, 4,656	E 2	
Uji	F 3	
Utila, 967	D 2	
Villa de San Antonio, 2,287	D 3	
Yocón, 269	D 3	
Yorito, 869	D 3	
Yoro, 4,129	D 3	
Yuscarán, 1,854	D 4	

OTHER FEATURES

Aguán (river)	E 3	
Bahía (isls.), 9,702	D 2	
Bonacca (Guanaja) (isl.), 2,039	E 2	
Brus (lagoon)	E 2	
Camarón (cape)	E 2	
Caratasca (cays)	F 2	
Caratasca (lagoon)	F 3	
Choluteca (river)	D 4	
Cisne (isls.), 28	F 2	
Coco (river)	E 3	
Colón (mts.)	E 3	
Esperanza (mts.)	F 3	
Falso (cape)	F 3	
Fonseca (gulf)	D 4	
Gorda (cay)	F 3	
Guanaja (isl.), 2,039	E 2	
Half Moon (reefs)	F 3	
Honduras (cape)	E 2	
Honduras (gulf)	D 2	
Patuca (point)	E 3	
Patuca (river)	E 3	
Paulaya (river)	E 3	
Pigeon (cays)	E 3	
Pija (mts.)	D 3	
Roatán (isl.), 6,552	D 2	
San Pablo, Sierra de (mts.)	E 3	
Segovia (Coco) (river)	F 3	
Sico (river)	E 3	
Sulaco (river)	D 3	
Swan (Cisne) (isls.), 28	F 2	
Ulúa (river)	D 3	
Utila (isl.), 1,111	D 2	
Vivario (cays)	F 3	
Wanks (Coco) (river)	D 3	
Yojoa (lake)	D 3	

NICARAGUA

CITIES and TOWNS

Acoyapa, 1,755	E 5	
Barra de Río Grande	F 4	
Bilwaskarma	E 3	
Bluefields, 9,292	F 4	
Boaco, 4,656	E 4	
Bocay	E 3	
Bonanza, 2,175	E 4	
Bragman's Bluff (Puerto Cabezas), 5,983	F 3	
Cabo Gracias a Dios, 511	F 3	
Camoapa, 2,617	E 4	

Chichigalpa, 6,657	D 4	
Chinandega, 22,409	D 4	
Ciudad Darío, 3,851	E 4	
Comalapa, 441	E 4	
Condega, 2,229	D 4	
Corinto, 9,177	D 4	
Cuicuina	E 4	
Cuyu Tigni	F 3	
Diriamba, 10,499	D 5	
El Gallo	E 4	
El Jicaral, 239	D 4	
El Jícaro, 1,114	D 4	
El Sauce, 2,944	D 4	
El Viejo, 7,190	D 4	
Esquipulas, 1,636	E 4	
Estelí, 12,742	D 4	
Granada, 28,507	E 5	
Greytown (San Juan del Norte), 199	F 5	
Jalapa, 1,868	E 4	
Jinotega, 7,693	E 4	
Jinotepe, 9,113	D 5	
Juigalpa, 6,146	E 4	
La Conquista, 364	D 5	
La Cruz, 155	E 4	
Laguna de Perlas	F 4	
La Libertad, 1,355	E 4	
La Paz Central, 441	D 4	
La Paz de Oriente, 828	D 4	
La Trinidad, 2,340	D 4	
León, 44,053	D 4	
Managua (capital), 262,047	D 4	
Masatepe, 4,831	D 5	
Masaya, 23,402	D 5	
Matagalpa, 15,030	D 4	
Mateare, 1,254	D 4	
Morrito, 324	E 5	
Moyogalpa, 1,252	E 5	
Muluculca	E 4	
Muy Muy, 691	E 4	
Muy Muy Viejo	E 4	
Nagarote, 5,241	D 4	
Nandaime, 5,051	E 5	
Ocotal, 4,339	D 4	
Ocotal	E 4	
Palsagua	E 4	
Playa Grande	D 4	
Poneloya, 995	D 4	
Poteca	E 4	
Prinzapolka, 230	F 4	
Puerto Cabezas, 5,983	F 3	
Quilalí, 710	E 4	
Rama (El Rama), 600	E 4	
Rivas, 7,721	E 5	
San Carlos, 1,547	E 5	
Sandy Bay	F 3	
San Francisco	E 5	
San Jorge, 1,657	E 5	
San Juan del Norte, 199	F 5	
San Juan del Sur, 2,103	D 5	
San Miguelito, 885	E 5	
San Pedro	E 4	
San Rafael del Norte, 1,298	E 4	
San Rafael del Sur, 2,411	D 5	
San Ramón, 436	E 4	
Santa Cruz	E 4	
Santo Domingo, 1,779	E 4	
Santo Tomás, 1,530	E 4	
Siuna, 3,743	E 4	
Somotillo, 1,435	D 4	
Somoto, 3,967	D 4	
Telpaneca, 1,019	D 4	
Terrabona, 690	E 4	
Teustepe, 764	E 4	
Tipitapa, 3,600	E 4	
Tunki	E 3	
Waspán, 973	E 3	
Yablis	F 4	

OTHER FEATURES

Alargate (reef)	F 3	
Coco (river)	E 3	
Coseguina (point)	D 4	
Dariense (range)	E 4	
Dipilto (range)	D 4	
Escondido (river)	F 4	
Fonseca (gulf)	D 4	
Gorda (point)	F 5	
Gracias a Dios (cape)	F 3	
Grande (river)	E 4	
Great Corn (isl.), 1,896	F 4	
Huapí (mts.)	E 4	
Isabella (range)	E 4	
King (cays)	F 4	
Kukalaya (river)	F 4	
Little Corn (isl.)	F 4	
Managua (lake)	E 4	
Miskito (cays)	F 3	
Monkey (point)	F 4	
Mosquito Coast (reg.)	E 4	
Nicaragua (lake)	E 5	
Ometepe (isl.), 12,556	E 5	
Pearl (cays)	F 4	
Perlas (lagoon)	F 4	
Prinzapolca (river)	F 4	
Salinas (bay)	D 5	
San Juan (river)	E, F 5	
San Juan del Norte (bay)	F 5	
Solentiname (isls.)	E 5	
Tuma (river)	E 4	
Tyra (river)	F 4	
Waspuk (river)	E 3	
Wawa (river)	F 3	
Zapatera (isl.)	E 5	

PANAMA

CITIES and TOWNS

Aguadulce, 8,192	G 6	
Alanje, †1,544	F 6	
Almirante, 4,134	F 6	
Antón, 3,022	G 6	
Bajo Boquete, 2,625	F 6	
Belén	G 6	
Bocas del Toro, 2,462	F 6	
Calobre, 11,933	G 6	
Cañazas, 15,516	G 6	
Capira, 12,168	G 6	
Carreto	J 6	
Chepo, †598	H 6	
Chimán, †972	H 6	
Chiriquí Grande, 11,517	F 6	
Chitré, 12,575	G 6	
Chorrera, 26,026	H 6	
Coclé del Norte, 11,329	G 6	
Colón, 67,641	H 6	
David, 35,538	F 6	
Dolega, †3,710	F 6	
El Real	J 6	
Garachiné, †1,471	H 6	
Guabito, †3,531	F 6	
Gualaca, †3,125	F 6	
Horconcitos	F 6	
La Concepción, 9,179	F 6	
La Palma, 1,945	H 6	
Las Palmas, †3,115	G 6	
Las Tablas, 3,571	G 7	
Loma Escobar (La Pintada)	G 6	
Los Santos, 3,940	G 7	
Mandinga	H 6	
Miguel de la Borda	H 6	
Miramar, †132	H 6	
Montijo, †3,600	G 6	
Natá, 3,195	G 6	
Nuevo Chagres	G 6	
Ocú, 15,267	G 7	

Olá, †987	G 6	
Panamá (cap.), 418,013	H 6	
Parita, †2,320	G 7	
Pedasí, †1,302	G 7	
Penonomé, 5,067	G 6	
Playón Chico	H 6	
Playón Grande	H 6	
Portobelo, 1626	H 6	
Potrerillos	F 6	
Puerto Armuelles, 12,022	F 6	
Puerto Obaldía	J 6	
San Carlos, †1,421	G 6	
San Cristóbal	H 6	
San Félix, †1,314	G 6	
San Francisco, 11,576	G 6	
Santa Fé, 11,768	G 6	
Santiago, 14,391	G 6	
Soná, 4,066	G 6	
Tocumen, 15,905	H 6	
Tolé, 14,734	F 6	
Tonosí, 11,301	G 7	

OTHER FEATURES

Azuero (pen.)	G 7	
Bastimentos (isl.), 574	G 6	
Brewster (mt.)	H 6	
Burica (point)	F 6	
Cébaco (isl.)	G 7	
Chepo (river)	H 6	
Chiriquí (gulf)	F 7	
Chiriquí (lagoon)	F 6	
Chiriquí (volcano)	F 6	
Chucunaque (river)	J 6	
Coiba (isl.)	F 7	
Colón (isl.)	F 6	
Contreras (isls.)	G 7	
Darién (mts.)	J 6	
Escudo de Veraguas (isl.)	G 6	
Gatún (lake)	H 6	
Gorda (point)	H 6	
Jicarón (isl.)	F 7	
Ladrones (isls.)	F 7	
Manzanillo (point)	H 6	
Montijo (gulf)	G 6	
Mosquito (gulf)	G 6	
Mulatas (arch.)	H 6	
Panamá (gulf)	H 7	
Pando (mt.)	F 6	
Parida (isl.)	F 6	
Parita (gulf)	G 6	
Perlas (arch.)	H 7	
Puercos (prom.)	H 7	
Rey (isl.)	H 6	
Rincón (point)	G 6	
San Blas (gulf)	H 6	
San Blas (range)	H 6	
San José (isl.)	H 6	
San Miguel (bay)	H 6	
Santiago (mt.)	G 7	
Secas (isls.)	F 7	
Tabasará (mts.)	G 6	
Taboga (isl.), 1,747	H 6	
Tiburón (cape)	J 6	
Urabá (gulf)	J 7	
Valiente (pen.)	G 6	

City and suburbs.
†Population of sub-district.
‡Population of district.

124 West Indies

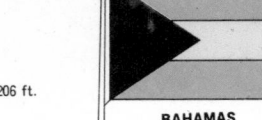
BAHAMAS

CUBA

HAITI

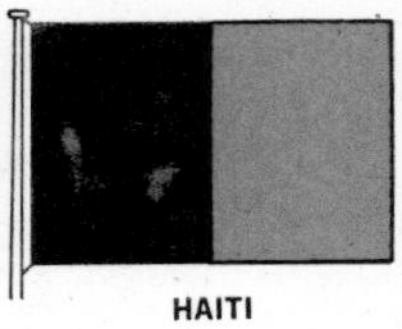

DOMINICAN REPUBLIC

JAMAICA

BAHAMAS
AREA 4,404 sq. mi.
POPULATION 168,838
CAPITAL Nassau
LARGEST CITY Nassau
HIGHEST POINT Mt. Alvernia (Cat. I.) 206 ft.
MONETARY UNIT Bahaman dollar
MAJOR LANGUAGE English
MAJOR RELIGIONS Roman Catholicism,
Protestantism

CUBA
AREA 44,206 sq. mi.
POPULATION 8,553,395
CAPITAL Havana
LARGEST CITY Havana
HIGHEST POINT Pico Turquino 6,561 ft.
MONETARY UNIT Cuban peso
MAJOR LANGUAGE Spanish
MAJOR RELIGION Roman Catholicism

JAMAICA
AREA 4,411 sq. mi.
POPULATION 1,972,000
CAPITAL Kingston
LARGEST CITY Kingston
HIGHEST POINT Blue Mountain Peak, 7,402 ft.
MONETARY UNIT Jamaican pound
MAJOR LANGUAGE English
MAJOR RELIGIONS Protestantism, Roman
Catholicism

GRENADA
AREA 133 sq. mi.
POPULATION 96,000
CAPITAL Saint George's
LARGEST CITY Saint George's
HIGHEST POINT Mt. St. Catherine
2,757 ft.
MONETARY UNIT East Caribbean dollar
MAJOR LANGUAGES English, French patois
MAJOR RELIGIONS Roman Catholicism,
Protestantism

DOMINICA
AREA 290 sq. mi.
POPULATION 70,302
CAPITAL Roseau
HIGHEST POINT Morne Diablotin 4,747
MONETARY UNIT East Caribbean dollar
MAJOR LANGUAGES English,
French patois
MAJOR RELIGIONS Roman Catholicism,
Protestantism

HAITI
AREA 10,694 sq. mi.
POPULATION 4,867,190
CAPITAL Port-au-Prince
LARGEST CITY Port-au-Prince
HIGHEST POINT Pic La Selle 8,793 ft.
MONETARY UNIT gourde
MAJOR LANGUAGES Creole French, French
MAJOR RELIGION Roman Catholicism

TRINIDAD AND TOBAGO
AREA 1,980 sq. mi.
POPULATION 1,040,000
CAPITAL Port of Spain
LARGEST CITY Port of Spain
HIGHEST POINT Mt. Aripo 3,084 ft.
MONETARY UNIT Trinidad and Tobago dollar
MAJOR LANGUAGES English, Hindi
MAJOR RELIGIONS Roman Catholicism, Prot.
Hinduism, Islam

DOMINICAN REPUBLIC
AREA 18,704 sq. mi.
POPULATION 4,011,589
CAPITAL Santo Domingo
LARGEST CITY Santo Domingo
HIGHEST POINT Pico Duarte 10,417 ft.
MONETARY UNIT Dominican peso
MAJOR LANGUAGE Spanish
MAJOR RELIGION Roman Catholicism

BARBADOS
AREA 166 sq. mi.
POPULATION 253,620
CAPITAL Bridgetown
LARGEST CITY Bridgetown
HIGHEST POINT Mt. Hillaby 1,104 ft.
MONETARY UNIT East Caribbean dollar
MAJOR LANGUAGE English
MAJOR RELIGION Protestantism

BARBADOS

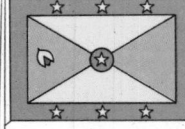
GRENADA

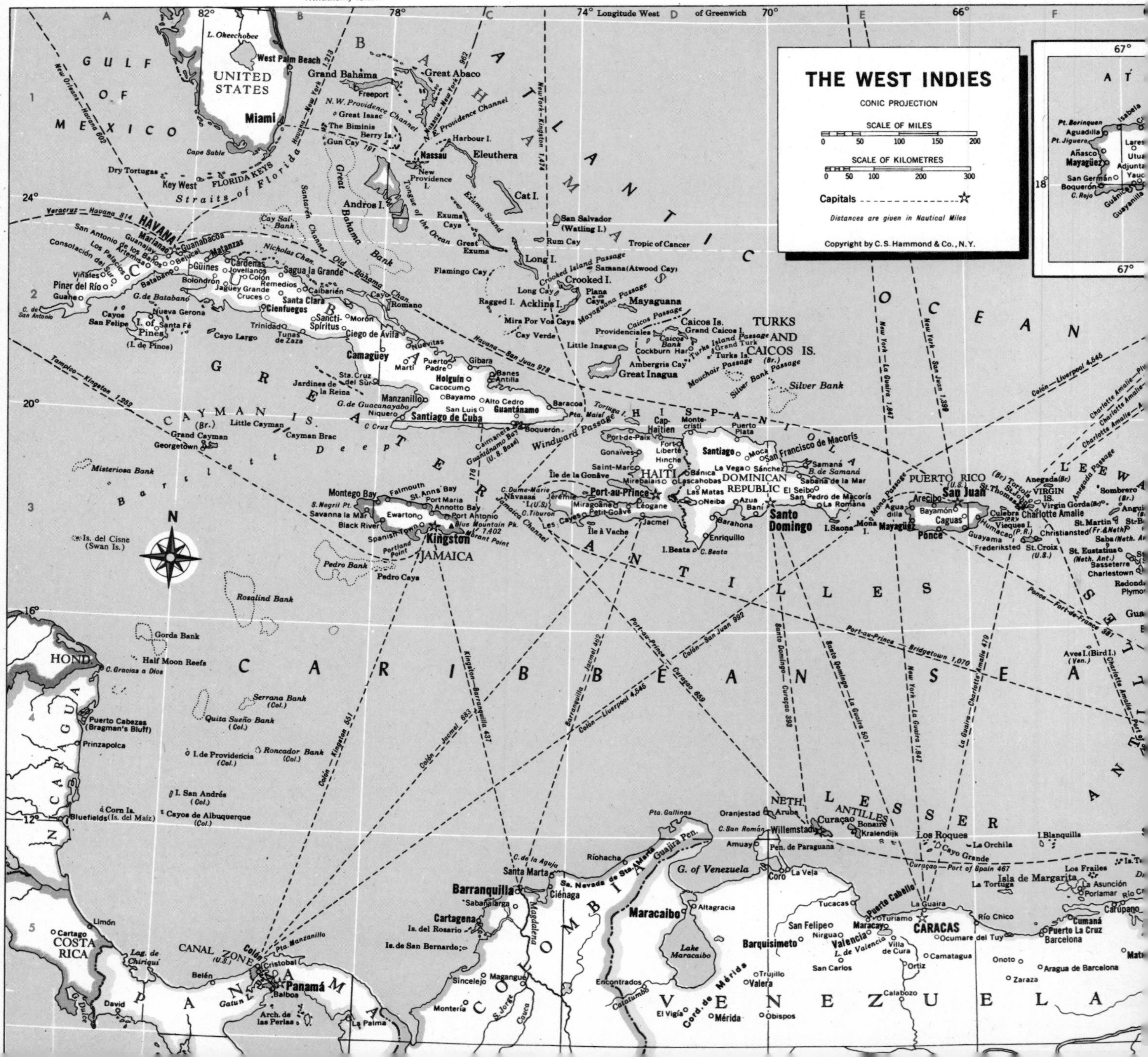

THE WEST INDIES

CONIC PROJECTION

SCALE OF MILES
0   50   100   150   200

SCALE OF KILOMETRES
0   50   100   200   300

Capitals - - - - - - - - - ☆

Distances are given in Nautical Miles

Copyright by C.S. Hammond & Co., N.Y.

Agriculture, Industry and Resources

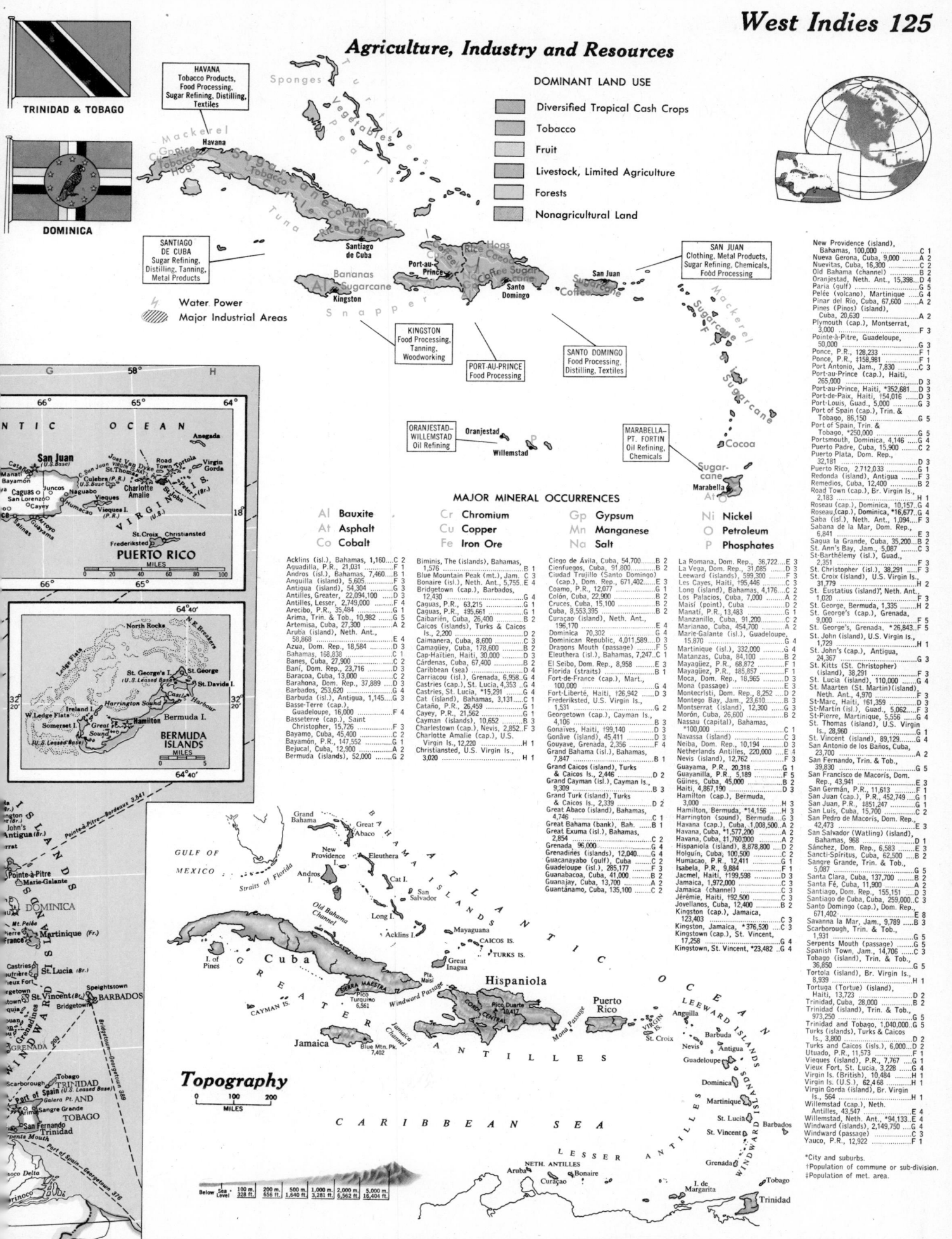

TRINIDAD & TOBAGO

DOMINICA

HAVANA
Tobacco Products, Food Processing, Sugar Refining, Distilling, Textiles

SANTIAGO DE CUBA
Sugar Refining, Distilling, Tanning, Metal Products

SAN JUAN
Clothing, Metal Products, Sugar Refining, Chemicals, Food Processing

KINGSTON
Food Processing, Tanning, Woodworking

PORT-AU-PRINCE
Food Processing

SANTO DOMINGO
Food Processing, Distilling, Textiles

ORANJESTAD–WILLEMSTAD
Oil Refining

MARABELLA–PT. FORTIN
Oil Refining, Chemicals

DOMINANT LAND USE

- Diversified Tropical Cash Crops
- Tobacco
- Fruit
- Livestock, Limited Agriculture
- Forests
- Nonagricultural Land

Water Power
Major Industrial Areas

MAJOR MINERAL OCCURRENCES

Al Bauxite	Cr Chromium	Gp Gypsum	Ni Nickel
At Asphalt	Cu Copper	Mn Manganese	O Petroleum
Co Cobalt	Fe Iron Ore	Na Salt	P Phosphates

PUERTO RICO

BERMUDA ISLANDS

Topography

Acklins (isl.), Bahamas, 1,160....C 2
Aguadilla, P.R., 21,031 ....F 1
Andros (isl.), Bahamas, 7,460...B 1
Anguilla (island), 5,605...........F 3
Antigua (island), 54,304 ....G 3
Antilles, Greater, 22,094,100....D 3
Antilles, Lesser, 2,749,000 ......F 4
Arecibo, P.R., 35,484 ....G 1
Arima, Trin. & Tob., 10,982 .....G 5
Artemisa, Cuba, 27,300 ....A 2
Aruba (island), Neth. Ant.,
  58,868 ....E 4
Azua, Dom. Rep., 18,584 ....D 3
Bahamas, 168,838 ....C 1
Banes, Cuba, 45,400 ....C 2
Baní, Dom. Rep., 23,716 ....D 3
Baracoa, Cuba, 13,000 ....C 2
Barahona, Dom. Rep., 37,889 ...D 3
Barbados, 253,620 ....G 4
Barbuda (isl.), Antigua, 1,145...G 3
Basse-Terre (cap.),
  Guadeloupe, 16,000 ....F 4
Basseterre (cap.), Saint
  Christopher, 15,726 ....F 3
Bayamo, Cuba, 45,400 ....C 2
Bayamón, P.R., 147,552 ....G 1
Bejucal, Cuba, 12,900 ....A 2
Bermuda (islands), 52,000 ......G 2

Biminis, The (islands), Bahamas,
  1,576 ....B 1
Blue Mountain Peak (mt.), Jam. ..C 3
Bonaire (isl.), Neth. Ant., 5,755..E 4
Bridgetown (cap.), Barbados,
  12,430 ....G 4
Caguas, P.R., 63,215 ....G 1
Caguas, P.R., ‡95,661 ....G 1
Caibarién, Cuba, 26,400 ....B 2
Caicos (islands), Turks & Caicos
  Is., 2,200 ....D 2
Caimanera, Cuba, 8,600 ....C 2
Camagüey, Cuba, 178,600 ....B 2
Cap-Haïtien, Haiti, 30,000 ......D 3
Cárdenas, Cuba, 67,400 ....B 2
Caribbean (sea) ....
Carriacou (isl.), Grenada, 6,958..G 4
Castries (cap.), St. Lucia, 4,353 ..G 4
Castries, St. Lucia, *15,291 .....G 4
Cat (island), Bahamas, 3,131....C 1
Cataño, P.R., 26,459 ....G 1
Cayey, P.R., 21,562 ....G 1
Cayman (islands), 10,652 ....B 3
Charlestown (cap.), Nevis, 2,852..F 3
Charlotte Amalie (cap.), U.S.
  Virgin Is., 12,220 ....H 1
Christiansted, U.S. Virgin Is.,
  3,020 ....H 1

Ciego de Ávila, Cuba, 54,700 ....B 2
Cienfuegos, Cuba, 91,800 ....B 2
Ciudad Trujillo (Santo Domingo)
  (cap.), Dom. Rep., 671,402....E 3
Coamo, P.R., 12,077 ....G 1
Colón, Cuba, 22,900 ....B 2
Cruces, Cuba, 15,100 ....B 2
Cuba, 8,553,395 ....B 2
Curaçao (island), Neth. Ant.,
  196,170 ....E 4
Dominica, 70,302 ....G 4
Dominican Republic, 4,011,589...D 3
Eleuthera (isl.), Bahamas, 7,247..C 1
El Seibo, Dom. Rep., 8,958 ......E 3
Florida (straits) ....B 1
Fort-de-France (cap.), Mart.,
  100,000 ....G 4
Fort-Liberté, Haiti, 126,942 .....D 3
Frederiksted, U.S. Virgin Is.,
  1,531 ....H 1
Georgetown (cap.), Cayman Is.,
  4,106 ....B 2
Gonaïves, Haiti, ‡99,140 ....D 3
Gonâve (island), 45,411 ....D 3
Gouyave, Grenada, 2,356 ....F 4
Grand Bahama (isl.), Bahamas,
  7,847 ....B 1
Grand Caicos (island), Turks
  & Caicos Is., 2,446 ....D 2
Grand Cayman (isl.), Cayman Is.,
  9,309 ....B 3
Grand Turk (island), Turks
  & Caicos Is., 2,339 ....D 2
Great Abaco (island), Bahamas,
  4,746 ....B 1
Great Bahama (bank), Bah. .....B 1
Great Exuma (isl.), Bahamas,
  2,854 ....C 2
Grenada, 96,000 ....G 4
Grenadines (islands), 12,040 ...G 4
Guacanayabo (gulf), Cuba ......C 2
Guadeloupe (isl.), 285,177 .....F 3
Guanabacoa, Cuba, 41,000 .....B 2
Guanajay, Cuba, 13,700 ....A 2
Guantánamo, Cuba, 135,100 ...C 2

La Romana, Dom. Rep., 36,722...E 3
La Vega, Dom. Rep., 31,085 .....D 3
Leeward (islands), 599,300 ......F 3
Les Cayes, Haiti, 195,446 ....C 3
Long (island), Bahamas, 4,176...C 2
Los Palacios, Cuba, 7,000 ....A 2
Maisí (point), Cuba ....C 2
Manatí, P.R., 13,483 ....G 1
Manzanillo, Cuba, 91,200 ....C 2
Marianao, Cuba, 454,700 ....A 2
Marie-Galante (isl.), Guadeloupe,
  15,870 ....G 4
Martinique (isl.), 332,000 ....G 4
Matanzas, Cuba, 84,100 ....B 2
Mayagüez, P.R., 68,872 ....F 1
Mayagüez, P.R., ‡85,857 ....F 1
Mayarí, Dom. Rep., 18,965 ......D 3
Mona (passage) ....E 3
Montecristi, Dom. Rep., 8,252...D 2
Montego Bay, Jam., 23,610 .....B 3
Montserrat (island), 12,300 .....G 3
Morón, Cuba, 26,600 ....B 2
Nassau (capital), Bahamas,
  *100,000 ....C 1
Navassa (island) ....
Neiba, Dom. Rep., 10,194 ....D 3
Netherlands Antilles, 220,000 ..E 4
Nevis (island), 12,762 ....F 3
Nueva Gerona, Cuba, 20,318 ...G 1
Guayama, P.R., 20,318 ....G 1
Guayanilla, P.R., 5,189 ....F 5
Güines, Cuba, 45,000 ....B 2
Haiti, 4,867,190 ....D 3
Hamilton (cap.), Bermuda ....H 3
Hamilton, Bermuda, *14,156 ....H 3
Harrington (sound), Bermuda ...H 3
Havana (cap.), Cuba, 1,008,500..A 2
Havana, Cuba, *1,577,200 ......A 2
Havana, Cuba, †1,760,900 ......A 2
Hispaniola (island), 8,878,800 ..D 2
Holguín, Cuba, 100,500 ....C 2
Humacao, P.R., 12,411 ....G 1
Isabela, P.R., 9,884 ....F 1
Jacmel, Haiti, ‡199,598 ....D 3
Jamaica, 1,972,000 ....C 3
Jamaica (channel) ....C 3
Jérémie, Haiti, 192,500 ....C 3
Jovellanos, Cuba, 12,400 ....B 2
Kingston (cap.), Jamaica,
  123,403 ....C 3
Kingston, Jamaica, *376,520 ...C 3
Kingstown (cap.), St. Vincent,
  17,258 ....G 4
Kingstown, St. Vincent, *23,482..G 4

New Providence (island),
  Bahamas, 100,000 ....C 1
Nueva Gerona, Cuba, 9,000 .....A 2
Nuevitas, Cuba, 16,300 ....B 2
Old Bahama (channel) ....B 2
Oranjestad, Neth. Ant., 15,398...D 4
Paria (gulf) ....G 5
Pelée (volcano), Martinique .....G 4
Pinar del Río, Cuba, 67,600 .....A 2
Pines (Pinos) (island),
  Cuba, 20,630 ....A 2
Plymouth (cap.), Montserrat,
  3,000 ....F 3
Pointe-à-Pitre, Guadeloupe,
  50,000 ....G 3
Ponce, P.R., 128,233 ....F 1
Ponce, P.R., ‡158,981 ....F 1
Port Antonio, Jam., 7,830 ....C 3
Port-au-Prince (cap.), Haiti,
  265,000 ....D 3
Port-au-Prince, Haiti, *352,681...D 3
Port-de-Paix, Haiti, 154,016 ....D 3
Port-Louis, Cuba, 5,000 ....G 4
Port of Spain (cap.), Trin. &
  Tobago, 86,150 ....G 5
Port of Spain, Trin. &
  Tobago, †250,000 ....G 5
Portsmouth, Dominica, 4,146 ...G 4
Puerto Padre, Cuba, 15,900 ....C 2
Puerto Plata, Dom. Rep.,
  32,181 ....D 3
Puerto Rico, 2,712,033 ....G 1
Redonda (island), Antigua ......F 3
Remedios, Cuba, 12,400 ....B 2
Road Town (cap.), Br. Virgin Is.,
  2,183 ....H 1
Roseau (cap.), Dominica, 10,157..G 4
Roseau (cap.), Dominica, *16,677..G 4
Saba (isl.), Neth. Ant., 1,094....F 3
Sabana de la Mar, Dom. Rep.,
  6,841 ....E 3
Sagua la Grande, Cuba, 35,200..B 2
St. Ann's Bay, Jam., 5,087 ......C 3
St-Barthélemy (isl.), Guad.,
  2,351 ....F 3
St. Christopher (isl.), 38,291 ....F 3
St. Croix (island), U.S. Virgin Is.,
  31,779 ....H 2
St. Eustatius (island), Neth. Ant.,
  1,020 ....F 3
St. George, Bermuda, 1,335 .....H 2
St. George's (cap.), Grenada,
  9,000 ....F 5
St. George's, Grenada, *26,843..F 5
St. John (island), U.S. Virgin Is.,
  1,729 ....H 1
St. John's (cap.), Antigua,
  24,367 ....G 3
St. Kitts (St. Christopher)
  (island), 38,291 ....F 3
St. Lucia (island), 110,000 .....G 4
St. Maarten (St. Martin) (island),
  Neth. Ant., 4,470 ....F 3
St-Marc, Haiti, 161,359 ....D 3
St-Martin (St. Martin), Guad.,
  5,062 ....F 3
St-Pierre, Martinique, 5,556 ....G 4
St. Thomas (island), U.S. Virgin
  Is., 28,960 ....G 1
St. Vincent (island), 89,129 .....G 4
San Antonio de los Baños, Cuba,
  23,700 ....A 2
San Fernando, Trin. & Tob.,
  39,830 ....G 5
San Francisco de Macorís, Dom.
  Rep., 43,941 ....E 3
San Germán, P.R., 11,613 ....F 1
San Juan (cap.), P.R., 452,749...G 1
San Juan, P.R., ‡851,247 ....G 1
San Luis, Cuba, 15,700 ....C 2
San Pedro de Macorís, Dom. Rep.,
  42,473 ....E 3
San Salvador (Watling) (island),
  Bahamas, 968 ....D 1
Sánchez, Dom. Rep., 6,583 .....E 3
Sancti-Spíritus, Cuba, 62,500 ..B 2
Sangre Grande, Trin. & Tob.,
  5,087 ....G 5
Santa Clara, Cuba, 137,700 ....B 2
Santa Fé, Cuba, 11,900 ....A 2
Santiago, Dom. Rep., 155,151 ..D 3
Santiago de Cuba, Cuba, 259,000..C 2
Santo Domingo (cap.), Dom. Rep.,
  671,402 ....E 8
Savanna la Mar, Jam., 9,789 ...B 3
Scarborough, Trin. & Tob.,
  1,931 ....G 5
Serpents Mouth (passage) ......G 5
Spanish Town, Jam., 14,706 ....C 3
Tobago (island), Trin. & Tob.,
  36,850 ....G 5
Tortola (island), Br. Virgin Is.,
  8,939 ....H 1
Tortuga (Tortue) (island),
  Haiti, 13,723 ....D 2
Trinidad, Cuba, 28,000 ....B 2
Trinidad (isl.), Trin. & Tob.,
  973,250 ....G 5
Trinidad and Tobago, 1,040,000..G 5
Turks (islands), Turks & Caicos
  Is., 3,800 ....D 2
Turks and Caicos (isls.), 6,000...D 2
Utuado, P.R., 11,573 ....F 1
Vieques (island), P.R., 7,767 ...G 1
Vieux Fort, St. Lucia, 3,228 .....G 4
Virgin Is. (British), 10,484 ......H 1
Virgin Is. (U.S.), 62,468 ....H 1
Virgin Gorda (island), Br. Virgin
  Is., 564 ....H 1
Willemstad (cap.), Neth.
  Antilles, 43,547 ....E 4
Willemstad, Neth. Ant., *94,133..E 4
Windward (islands), 2,149,750 ..G 4
Windward (passage) ....C 3
Yauco, P.R., 12,922 ....F 1

*City and suburbs.
†Population of commune or sub-division.
‡Population of met. area.

UNITED STATES

POLYCONIC PROJECTION

SCALE

0 50 100 200 300 400 MI.

0 50 100 200 300 400 KM.

Capitals of Countries .... ⋆
State Capitals .... △
International Boundaries .... —·—·—
State Boundaries .... — — —

© C.S. HAMMOND & Co., N.Y.

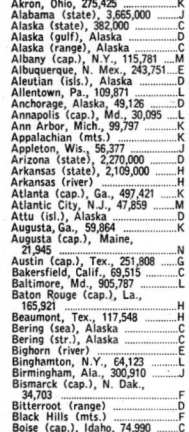

Akron, Ohio, 275,425 ....K 2
Alabama (state), 3,665,000 ...J 4
Alaska (state), 382,000 .....D 6
Alaska (gulf), Alaska ......D 6
Alaska (range), Alaska .....C 5
Albany (cap.), N.Y., 115,781 ..M 2
Albuquerque, N. Mex., 243,751...E 3
Aleutian (isls.), Alaska .....D 6
Allentown, Pa., 109,871 ....L 2
Anchorage, Alaska, 49,126 ...D 6
Annapolis (cap.), Md., 30,095 ..L 3
Ann Arbor, Mich., 99,797 ....K 2
Appalachian (mts.) .....K 3
Appleton, Wis., 56,377 ....J 2
Arizona (state), 2,270,000 ...D 4
Arkansas (state), 2,109,000 ..H 3
Arkansas (river) .....H 3
Atlanta (cap.), Ga., 497,421 ..K 4
Atlantic City, N.J., 47,859 ...M 3
Attu (isl.), Alaska .....
Augusta, Ga., 59,864 ....K 4
Augusta (cap.), Maine, 21,945 ..N 2
Austin (cap.), Tex., 251,808 ..G 4
Bakersfield, Calif., 69,515 ...C 3
Baltimore, Md., 905,787 ....L 3
Baton Rouge (cap.), La., 165,921 ..H 4
Beaumont, Tex., 117,548 ...H 4
Bering (sea), Alaska .....B 5
Bering (str.), Alaska .....C 5
Bighorn (river) .....E 2
Binghamton, N.Y., 64,123 ...L 2
Birmingham, Ala., 300,910 ...J 4
Bismarck (cap.), N. Dak., 34,703 ..F 1
Bitterroot (range) ....D 1
Black Hills (mts.) .....F 2
Boise (cap.), Idaho, 74,990 ..C 2

Borah (peak), Idaho .....D 2
Boston (cap.), Mass., 641,071...M 2
Brazos (river), Tex. .....G 4
Bridgeport, Conn., 156,542 ...M 2
Brooks (range), Alaska ....C 5
Buffalo, N.Y., 462,768 ....L 2
California (state), 21,520,000 ..B 3
Canadian (river) .....F 3
Canaveral (cape), Fla. ....K 5
Canton, Ohio, 110,053 ....K 2
Cape Fear (river), N.C. ....L 4
Carson City (cap.), Nev., 15,468..C 3
Cascade (range) .....B 1
Cedar Rapids, Iowa, 110,642 ..H 2
Champlain (lake) .....M 2
Charleston, S.C. 66,945 ....L 4
Charleston (cap.), W. Va., 71,505 ..K 3
Charlotte, N.C., 241,178 ....K 3
Chattahoochee (river) ....J 4
Chattanooga, Tenn., 119,923 ..J 3
Chesapeake (bay) .....L 3
Cheyenne (cap.), Wyo., 40,914 ..E 2
Chicago, Ill., 3,369,357 ....J 2
Cimarron (river) .....G 3
Cincinnati, Ohio, 451,455 ...K 3
Cleveland, Ohio, 750,879 ....K 2
Cod (cape), Mass. .....N 2
Colorado (state), 2,583,000 ..E 3
Colorado (river) .....D 4
Colorado (river), Tex. ....G 4
Colorado Spgs., Colo., 135,060..F 3
Columbia (cap.), S.C., 113,542..L 4
Columbia (river) .....B 1
Columbus, Ga., 167,377 ....J 4
Columbus (cap.), Ohio, 540,025..K 3
Concord (cap.), N.H., 30,022 ..M 2

Connecticut (state), 3,117,000 ..M 2
Connecticut (river) .....M 2
Corpus Christi, Tex., 204,525 ..G 4
Cumberland (river) .....J 3
Dallas, Tex., 844,401 ....G 4
Davenport, Iowa, 98,469 ....H 2
Dayton, Ohio, 242,917 ....K 3
Death Valley (depr.), Calif. ..C 3
Delaware (state), 582,000 ...L 3
Delaware (bay) .....L 3
Denver (cap.), Colo., 514,678...F 3
Des Moines (cap.), Iowa, 201,404 ..H 2
Detroit, Mich., 1,513,601 ....K 2
District of Columbia, 702,000 ..L 3
Dover (cap.), Del., 17,488 ...L 3
Duluth, Minn., 100,578 ....H 1
Durham, N.C., 95,438 ....L 3
El Paso, Tex., 322,261 ....E 4
Elbert (mt.), Colo. .....E 3
Erie, Pa., 129,231 .....K 2
Erie (lake) .....K 2
Eugene, Oreg., 79,028 ....B 2
Evansville, Ind., 138,764 ....J 3
Everglades (swamp), Fla. ...K 5
Fayetteville, N.C., 53,510 ...L 3
Flint, Mich., 193,717 ....K 2
Florida (state), 8,421,000 ...K 5
Florida (keys), Fla. .....K 6
Ft. Smith, Ark., 62,802 ....H 3
Ft. Wayne, Ind., 178,021 ...J 2
Ft. Worth, Tex., 393,476 ....G 4
Frankfort (cap.), Ky., 21,902...K 3
Fresno, Calif., 165,972 ....C 3
Galveston, Tex., 61,809 ....H 5
Gary, Ind., 175,415 .....J 2
Georgia (state), 4,970,000 ...K 4
Gila (river) .....D 4

Glacier Nat'l Park, Mont. ....D 1
Golden Gate (chan.), Calif. ..B 3
Grand Canyon Nat'l Park, Ariz. ..D 3
Grand Rapids, Mich., 197,649 ..J 2
Great Salt (lake), Utah ....D 2
Greensboro, N.C., 144,076 ...L 3
Greenville, S.C., 61,436 ....K 4
Hamilton, Ohio, 67,865 ....J 3
Harrisburg (cap.), Pa., 68,061..L 2
Hartford (cap.), Conn., 158,017 ..M 2
Hatteras (cape), N.C. .....M 3
Havasu (lake) .....D 4
Hawaii (state), 887,000 ....H 4
Hawaii (isl.), Hawaii .....H 4
Helena (cap.), Mont., 22,730 ..D 1
Honolulu (cap.), Hawaii, 324,871 ..F 5
Houston, Tex., 1,232,802 ....G 5
Huntington, W. Va., 74,315 ...K 3
Huntsville, Ala., 139,282 ...J 4
Huron (lake), Mich. .....K 2
Idaho (state), 831,000 ....D 2
Illinois (state), 11,229,000 ..J 2
Indiana (state), 5,302,000 ...J 3
Indianapolis (cap.), Ind., 746,302 ..J 3
Iowa (state), 2,870,000 ....H 2
Jackson (cap.), Miss., 153,968..H 4
Jacksonville, Fla., 528,865 ...K 4
Jefferson City (cap.), Mo., 32,407 ..H 3
Jersey City, N.J., 260,350 ...M 2
Johnstown, Pa., 42,476 ....L 2
Juneau (cap.), Alaska, 13,556...E 6
Kalamazoo, Mich., 85,555 ...J 2
Kansas (state), 2,310,000 ...G 3
Kansas City, Kans.-Mo., 675,543 ..H 3

Kauai (isl.), Hawaii .....E 5
Kentucky (state), 3,428,000 ..J 3
Knoxville, Tenn., 174,587 ...K 3
Lancaster, Pa., 57,690 ....L 2
Lansing (cap.), Mich., 131,403..K 2
Las Vegas, Nev., 125,787 ...C 3
Lawrence, Mass., 66,915 ....M 2
Lexington, Ky., 108,137 ....K 3
Lima, Ohio, 53,734 .....K 2
Lincoln (cap.), Nebr., 149,518..G 2
Little Rock (cap.), Ark., 132,483 ..H 4
Long (isl.), N.Y. .....M 2
Long Beach, Calif., 358,879 ..C 4
Los Angeles, Calif., 2,809,813..C 4
Louisiana (state), 3,841,000 ..H 4
Louisville, Ky., 361,706 ....J 3
Lowell, Mass., 94,239 ....M 2
Lubbock, Tex., 149,101 ....F 4
Macon, Ga., 122,423 .....K 4
Madison (cap.), Wis., 171,769..H 2
Maine (state), 1,070,000 ....N 1
Maryland (state), 4,144,000 ...L 3
Massachusetts (state), 5,809,000 ..M 2
Maui (isl.), Hawaii .....H 4
Mauna Kea (mt.), Hawaii ....G 6
Mauna Loa (mt.), Hawaii ....G 6
May (cape), N.J. .....M 3
McKinley (mt.), Alaska ....D 5
Mead (lake) .....D 3
Memphis, Tenn., 623,530 ....J 3
Mendocino (cape), Calif. ...B 3
Mexico (gulf) .....J 5
Miami, Fla., 334,859 ....K 5
Michigan (state), 9,104,000 ..J 1
Michigan (lake) .....J 1

Milwaukee, Wis., 717,372 ...J 2
Minneapolis, Minn., 434,400 ..H 1
Minnesota (state), 3,965,000 ..H 1
Mississippi (state), 2,354,000..J 4
Mississippi (river) .....H 3
Missouri (state), 4,778,000 ..H 3
Missouri (river) .....H 3
Mitchell (mt.), N.C. .....K 3
Mobile, Ala., 190,026 ....J 4
Montana (state), 753,000 ....E 1
Montgomery (cap.), Ala., 133,386 ..J 4
Montpelier (cap.), Vt., 8,609 ..M 2
Nantucket (isl.), Mass. ....N 2
Nashville (cap.), Tenn., 447,877..J 3
Nebraska (state), 1,553,000 ..F 2
Nevada (state), 610,000 ....C 3
Newark, N.J., 381,930 ....M 2
New Hampshire (state), 822,000..M 2
New Haven, Conn., 137,707 ...M 2
New Jersey (state), 7,336,000..M 2
New Mexico (state), 1,143,000..E 4
New Orleans, La., 593,471 ...H 5
Newport News, Va., 138,177 ..L 3
New York (state), 18,084,000 ..L 2
New York, N.Y., 7,895,563 ...M 2
Norfolk, Va., 307,951 ....L 3
North Carolina (state), 5,469,000..L 3
North Dakota (state), 643,000..F 1
Oahu (isl.), Hawaii .....F 5
Oakland, Calif., 361,561 ....B 3
Ohio (state), 10,690,000 ....K 2
Ohio (river) .....J 3
Oklahoma (state), 2,766,000 ..G 3
Oklahoma City (cap.), Okla., 368,377 ..G 3
Olympia (cap.), Wash., 23,296..B 1
Olympic Nat'l Park, Wash. ...A 1
Omaha, Nebr., 346,929 ....G 2

Ontario (lake), N.Y. .....L 2
Oregon (state), 2,329,000 ...B 2
Orlando, Fla., 99,006 ....K 5
Ozark (mts.) .....H 3
Paterson, N.J., 144,824 ....M 2
Pennsylvania (state), 11,862,000..L 2
Pensacola, Fla., 59,507 ....J 4
Peoria, Ill., 126,963 .....J 2
Philadelphia, Pa., 1,949,996 ..M 2
Phoenix (cap.), Ariz., 582,500..D 4
Pierre (cap.), S. Dak., 9,699 ..F 2
Pikes (peak), Colo. .....F 3
Pittsburgh, Pa., 520,117 ....L 2
Platte (river), Nebr. .....G 2
Pontchartrain (lake), La. ...H 5
Portland, Maine, 65,116 ....N 2
Portland, Oreg., 379,967 ....B 2
Potomac (river) .....L 3
Providence (cap.), R.I., 179,116 ..M 2
Racine, Wis., 95,162 .....J 2
Rainier (mt.), Wash. .....B 1
Raleigh (cap.), N.C., 123,793..L 3
Reading, Pa., 87,643 .....L 2
Red (river) .....G 4
Red River of the North (river)..G 1
Rhode Island (state), 927,000..M 2
Richmond (cap.), Va., 249,431..L 3
Rio Grande (river) .....F 4
Roanoke, Va., 92,115 .....L 3
Rochester, N.Y., 296,233 ...L 2
Rockford, Ill., 147,370 ....J 2
Rocky (mts.) .....E 3
Sacramento (cap.), Calif., 257,105 ..B 3
Saginaw, Mich., 91,849 ....K 2
Saint Clair (lake), Mich. ...K 2
Saint Lawrence (river), N.Y. ..N 1
Saint Louis, Mo., 622,236 ...H 3

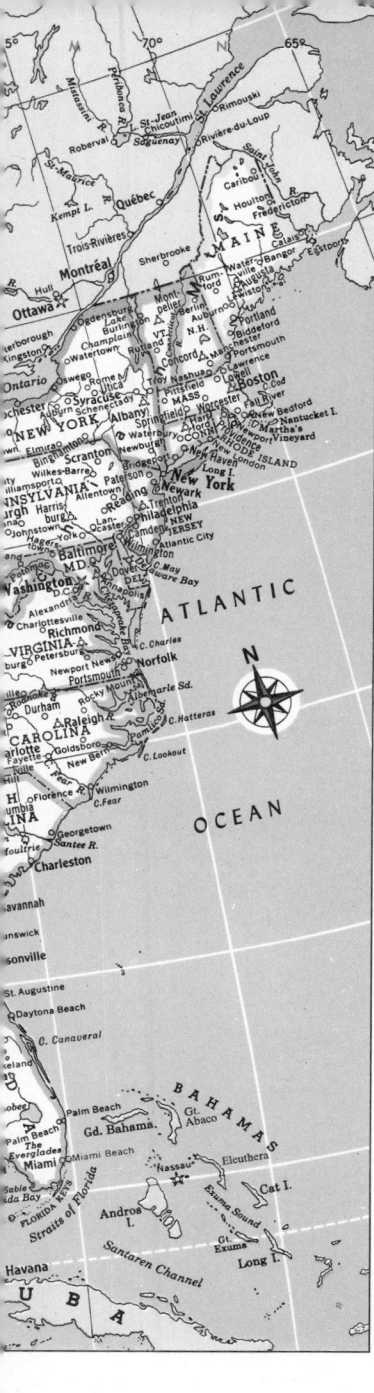

AREA 3,615,123 sq. mi.
POPULATION 217,739,000
CAPITAL Washington
LARGEST CITY New York
HIGHEST POINT Mt. McKinley 20,320 ft.
MONETARY VALUE U.S. dollar
MAJOR LANGUAGE English
MAJOR RELIGIONS Protestantism, Roman Catholicism, Judaism

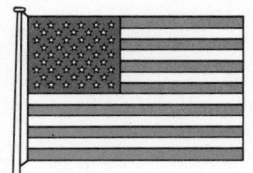

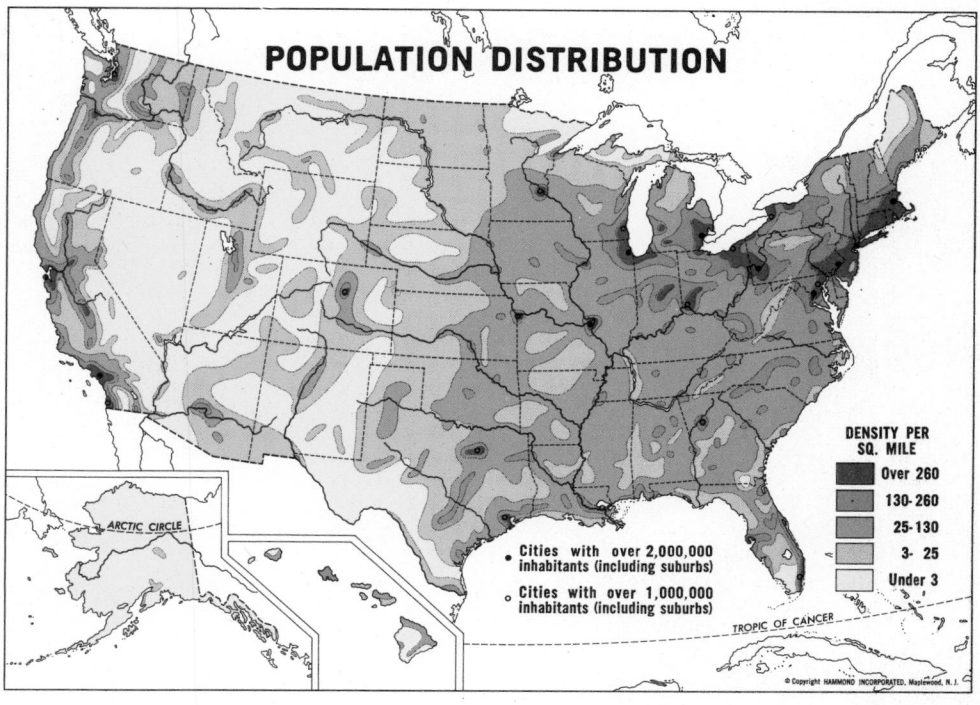

POPULATION DISTRIBUTION

DENSITY PER SQ. MILE

Over 260
130- 260
25- 130
3- 25
Under 3

• Cities with over 2,000,000 inhabitants (including suburbs)
○ Cities with over 1,000,000 inhabitants (including suburbs)

ARCTIC CIRCLE

TROPIC OF CANCER

© Copyright HAMMOND INCORPORATED, Maplewood, N.J.

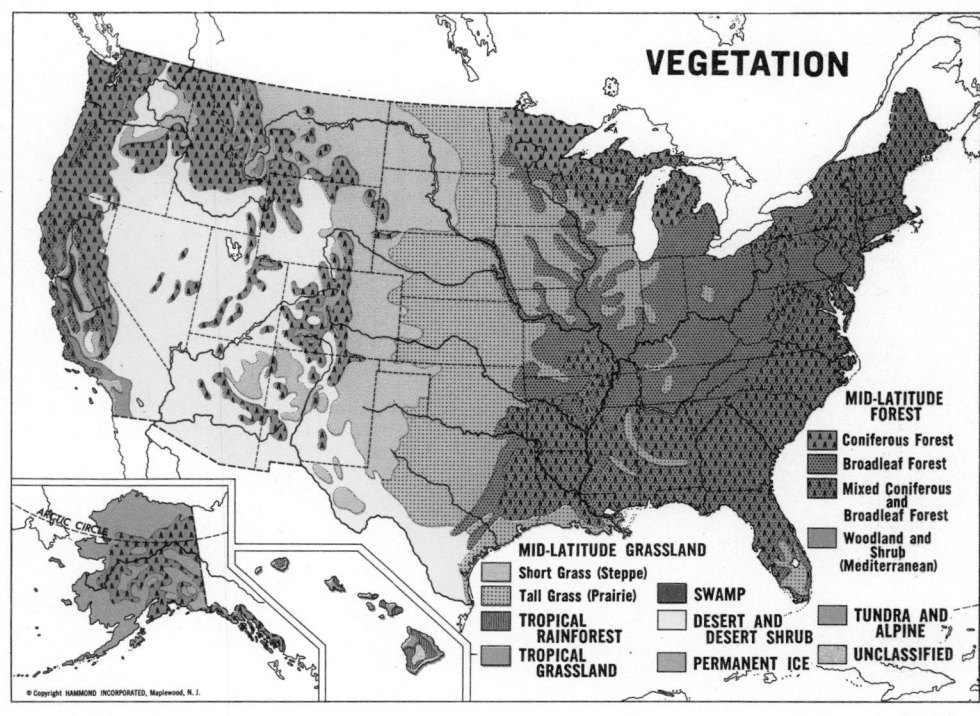

VEGETATION

MID-LATITUDE FOREST
Coniferous Forest
Broadleaf Forest
Mixed Coniferous and Broadleaf Forest
Woodland and Shrub (Mediterranean)

MID-LATITUDE GRASSLAND
Short Grass (Steppe)
Tall Grass (Prairie)
TROPICAL RAINFOREST
TROPICAL GRASSLAND
SWAMP
DESERT AND DESERT SHRUB
PERMANENT ICE
TUNDRA AND ALPINE
UNCLASSIFIED

ARCTIC CIRCLE

© Copyright HAMMOND INCORPORATED, Maplewood, N.J.

Topography

0   200   400
MILES

Agriculture, Industry and Resources

SEATTLE–TACOMA
Aircraft, Lumber, Wood &
Paper Products, Food Processing

PORTLAND
Lumber, Wood &
Paper Products

SAN FRANCISCO–SAN JOSE
Food Processing,
Machinery, Metal &
Electrical Products,
Primary Metals

**LOS ANGELES–
SAN BERNARDINO**
Aircraft, Clothing,
Motion Pictures, Food
Processing, Metals &
Machinery, Electrical &
Metal Products

SAN DIEGO
Aircraft, Food Processing

DENVER
Food Processing,
Machinery,
Metal Products,
Missile Parts

KANSAS CITY
Food Processing,
Automobile Assembly

ST. LOUIS
Chemicals, Metals,
Food & Beverages,
Aircraft

DALLAS–FT. WORTH
Aircraft, Machinery,
Food Processing

**HOUSTON–
GULF COAST**
Chemicals, Oil Refining,
Machinery, Metal Products

NEW ORLEANS
Food Processing,
Shipbuilding, Chemicals,
Wood & Paper Products

MINNEAPOLIS–ST. PAUL
Food Processing, Metal Products,
Farm & Electrical Machinery

CHICAGO–GARY–MILWAUKEE
Machinery, Metal & Electrical
Products, Iron & Steel, Chemicals,
Food Processing, Printing & Publishing

INDIANAPOLIS–CINCINNATI–DAYTON
Transportation Equipment,
Electrical & Metal Products,
Machinery, Chemicals

CLEVELAND–PITTSBURGH
Iron & Steel, Machinery,
Electrical & Metal Products

DETROIT–TOLEDO
Automobiles, Machinery,
Metal & Glass Products,
Chemicals

BUFFALO–CENTRAL NEW YORK
Electrical & Metal Products, Machinery,
Automobile & Aircraft Parts, Chemicals,
Iron & Steel, Food Processing,
Precision Equipment

**BOSTON–
NEW ENGLAND**
Electrical & Metal
Products, Machinery
Textiles

**NEW YORK–
N.E. NEW JERSEY**
Clothing, Electrical
Products, Machinery
Printing & Publishing
Chemicals, Oil Refining
Food Processing

**PHILADELPHIA–EASTERN
PENNSYLVANIA–BALTIMORE**
Iron & Steel, Electrical &
Metal Products, Machinery,
Chemicals, Oil Refining,
Clothing, Shipbuilding

**WINSTON-SALEM–
GREENSBORO**
Tobacco Products,
Textiles, Furniture

CHARLOTTE–PIEDMONT
Textiles, Clothing

LOUISVILLE
Tobacco Products,
Chemicals,
Electrical Products

BIRMINGHAM
Iron & Steel,
Metal Products

ATLANTA
Transportation Equipment,
Food Processing

DOMINANT LAND USE

- Wheat and Small Grains
- Feed Grains and Livestock
- Dairy
- General Farming
- Cotton
- Fruit, Truck and Mixed Farming
- Tobacco and General Farming
- Special Crops and General Farming
- Range Livestock
- Forests
- Swampland
- Nonagricultural Land

MAJOR MINERAL OCCURRENCES

Ab	Asbestos	Gp	Gypsum	Sb	Antimony
Ag	Silver	Hg	Mercury	Tc	Talc
Al	Bauxite	K	Potash	Ti	Titanium
Au	Gold	Mi	Mica	U	Uranium
Bx	Borax	Mo	Molybdenum	V	Vanadium
C	Coal	Na	Salt	W	Tungsten
Cl	Clay	O	Petroleum	Zn	Zinc
Cu	Copper	P	Phosphates		
F	Fluorspar	Pb	Lead	⚡	Water Power
Fe	Iron Ore	Pt	Platinum	▨	Major Industrial Areas
G	Natural Gas	S	Sulfur		

COUNTIES

Autauga, 24,460 .... E 5
Baldwin, 59,382 .... C 9
Barbour, 22,543 .... H 7
Bibb, 13,812 .... D 5
Blount, 26,853 .... E 3
Bullock, 11,824 .... G 6
Butler, 22,007 .... E 7
Calhoun, 103,092 .... G 3
Chambers, 36,356 .... H 5
Cherokee, 15,606 .... G 2
Chilton, 25,180 .... E 5
Choctaw, 16,589 .... B 6
Clarke, 26,724 .... C 7
Clay, 12,636 .... G 4
Cleburne, 10,996 .... G 3
Coffee, 34,872 .... G 8
Colbert, 49,632 .... C 1
Conecuh, 15,645 .... E 8
Coosa, 10,662 .... F 5
Covington, 34,079 .... F 8
Crenshaw, 13,188 .... F 7
Cullman, 52,445 .... E 2
Dale, 52,938 .... G 8
Dallas, 55,296 .... D 6
De Kalb, 41,981 .... G 2
Elmore, 33,535 .... F 5
Escambia, 34,906 .... D 8
Etowah, 94,144 .... F 2
Fayette, 16,252 .... C 3
Franklin, 21,933 .... C 2
Geneva, 21,924 .... G 8
Greene, 10,650 .... C 5
Hale, 15,888 .... C 5
Henry, 13,254 .... H 7
Houston, 56,574 .... H 8
Jackson, 39,202 .... F 1
Jefferson, 644,991 .... E 3
Lamar, 14,335 .... B 3
Lauderdale, 68,111 .... C 1
Lawrence, 27,281 .... D 1
Lee, 61,268 .... H 5
Limestone, 41,699 .... E 1
Lowndes, 12,897 .... E 6
Macon, 24,841 .... G 6
Madison, 186,540 .... E 1
Marengo, 23,819 .... C 6
Marion, 23,788 .... C 2
Marshall, 54,211 .... F 2
Mobile, 317,308 .... B 9
Monroe, 20,883 .... D 7
Montgomery, 167,790 .... F 6
Morgan, 77,306 .... E 2
Perry, 15,388 .... D 5
Pickens, 20,326 .... B 4
Pike, 25,038 .... G 7
Randolph, 18,331 .... H 4
Russell, 45,394 .... H 6
Saint Clair, 27,956 .... F 3
Shelby, 38,037 .... E 4
Sumter, 16,974 .... B 5
Talladega, 65,280 .... F 4
Tallapoosa, 33,840 .... G 5
Tuscaloosa, 116,029 .... C 4
Walker, 56,246 .... D 3
Washington, 16,241 .... B 8
Wilcox, 16,303 .... D 7
Winston, 16,654 .... D 2

CITIES and TOWNS

Zip	Name/Pop.	Key
36310	Abbeville◉, 2,996	H 7
35440	Abernant, 602	D 4
35005	Adamsville, 2,412	D 3
35540	Addison, 692	D 2
35006	Adger, 1,550	D 4
35441	Akron, 535	C 5
35007	Alabaster, 2,642	E 4
35950	Albertville, 9,963	F 2
† 35115	Aldrich, 476	E 4
35010	Alexander City, 12,358	G 5
36250	Alexandria, 600	G 3
35442	Aliceville, 2,807	B 4
35013	Allgood, 272	F 3
† 35616	Allsboro, 300	B 1
35015	Alton, 500	E 4
35952	Altoona, 781	F 2
36420	Andalusia◉, 10,092	E 8
35610	Anderson, 400	D 1
36201	Anniston◉, 31,533	G 3
35016	Arab, 4,399	E 2
35805	Ardmore, 761	E 1
36311	Ariton, 643	G 7
35033	Arkadelphia, 325	E 3
† 35035	Ashby, 500	E 4
36312	Ashford, 1,980	H 8
36251	Ashland◉, 1,921	G 4
35953	Ashville, 986	F 3
35611	Athens◉, 14,360	E 1
36502	Atmore, 8,293	C 8
35954	Attalla, 7,510	F 2
36830	Auburn, 22,767	H 5
36003	Autaugaville, 870	E 6
† 36312	Avon, 374	H 8
36505	Axis, 400	B 9
35019	Baileyton, 500	E 2
36004	Baker Hill, 350	H 7
36506	Barlow Bend, 300	C 8
† 36532	Barnwell, 700	C 10
36533	Battles Wharf, 300	C 10
36507	Bay Minette◉, 6,727	C 9
36509	Bayou La Batre, 2,664	B 10
35543	Bear Creek, 336	C 2
36425	Beatrice, 455	D 7
35544	Beaverton, 265	B 3
† 35653	Belgreen, 500	C 2
36901	Bellamy, 700	B 6
35546	Berry, 679	C 3
35020	Bessemer, 33,428	D 4
* 35201	Birmingham◉, 300,910	D 3
	Birmingham, ‡739,274	D 3
36902	Bladon Springs, 300	B 7
† 36874	Bleecker, 250	H 5
35031	Blountsville, 1,254	E 2
36201	Blue Mountain, 446	G 3
35226	Bluff Park, 12,372	E 4

35957	Boaz, 5,621	F 2
36903	Bolinger, 250	B 7
36007	Bolling, 250	E 7
36511	Bon Secour, 850	C 10
36110	Boylston, 2,943	F 7
36009	Brantley, 1,066	F 7
35034	Brent, 2,093	D 5
36426	Brewton◉, 6,747	D 8
36427	Bridgeport, 2,908	G 1
35035	Brierfield, 950	E 4
35020	Brighton, 2,277	D 4
35048	Brilliant, 726	C 2
36429	Brooklyn, 350	E 8
35036	Brookside, 990	E 3
35444	Brookwood, 450	D 4
35445	Brownville, 300	C 4
36010	Brundidge, 2,709	G 7
35446	Buhl, 500	C 4
36725	Burkville, 250	E 6
36431	Burnt Corn, 250	D 7
36904	Butler◉, 2,064	B 6
† 36767	Cahaba, 50	D 6
35040	Calera, 1,655	E 4
36012	Calhoun, 990	F 6
36513	Calvert, 500	B 8
36726	Camden◉, 1,742	D 7
36850	Camp Hill, 1,554	G 5
36514	Canoe, 560	D 8
36726	Canton Bend, 250	D 6
35549	Carbon Hill, 1,929	C 3
36515	Carlton, 275	C 8
35447	Carrollton◉, 923	B 4
36023	Carrville, 895	G 5
† 36548	Carson, 250	C 8
36432	Castleberry, 666	D 8
36013	Cecil, 300	F 6
35959	Cedar Bluff, 956	G 2
36014	Central, 300	F 5
35960	Centre◉, 2,418	G 2
35042	Centreville◉, 2,233	C 5
36729	Chance, 350	C 7
36015	Chapman, 400	E 7
36518	Chatom◉, 1,059	B 8
35043	Chelsea, 615	E 4
35616	Cherokee, 1,484	C 1
36611	Chickasaw, 8,447	B 9
35044	Childersburg, 4,831	F 4
36254	Choccolocco, 300	G 3
36905	Choctaw, 600	B 6
36520	Chrysler, 300	C 8
36521	Chunchula, 400	B 9
36522	Citronelle, 1,935	B 8
35045	Clanton◉, 5,868	E 5
36015	Clayton◉, 1,626	G 7
36049	Cleveland, 413	E 3
36017	Clio, 1,065	G 7
35617	Cloverdale, 650	C 1
35449	Coaling, 500	D 4
36523	Coden, 500	B 10
36318	Coffee Springs, 329	G 8
36524	Coffeeville, 441	C 7
35452	Coker, 800	C 4
35444	Collinsville, 1,300	G 2
36319	Columbia, 891	H 8
35051	Columbiana◉, 2,248	E 4

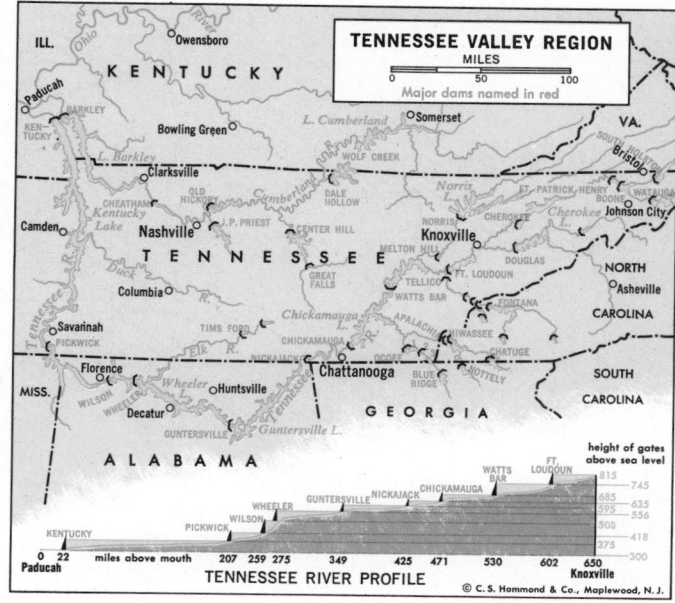

AREA 51,609 sq. mi.
POPULATION 3,444,165
CAPITAL Montgomery
LARGEST CITY Birmingham
HIGHEST POINT Cheaha Mtn. 2,407 ft.
SETTLED IN 1702
ADMITTED TO UNION December 14, 1819
POPULAR NAME Heart of Dixie; Cotton State
STATE FLOWER Camellia
STATE BIRD Yellowhammer

TENNESSEE VALLEY REGION
MILES
0   50   100
Major dams named in red

TENNESSEE RIVER PROFILE

height of gates above sea level

© C. S. Hammond & Co., Maplewood, N.J.

Agriculture, Industry and Resources

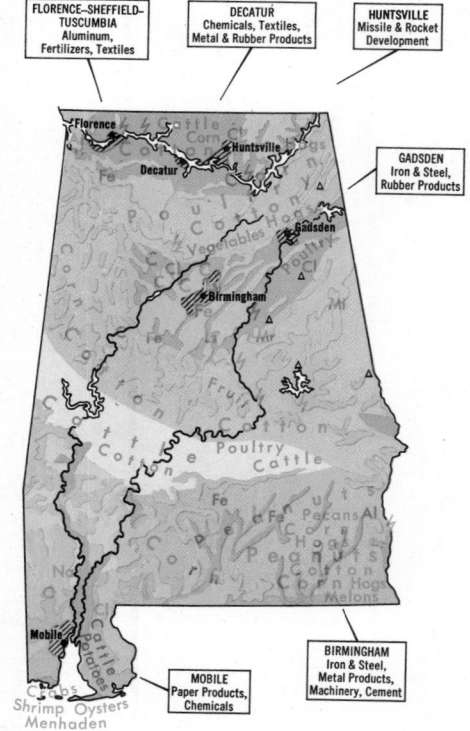

FLORENCE–SHEFFIELD–TUSCUMBIA
Aluminum, Fertilizers, Textiles

DECATUR
Chemicals, Textiles, Metal & Rubber Products

HUNTSVILLE
Missile & Rocket Development

GADSDEN
Iron & Steel, Rubber Products

BIRMINGHAM
Iron & Steel, Metal Products, Machinery, Cement

MOBILE
Paper Products, Chemicals

DOMINANT LAND USE

- Specialized Cotton
- Cotton, Livestock
- Cotton, General Farming
- Cotton, Hogs, Peanuts
- Cotton, Forest Products
- Peanuts, General Farming
- Truck and Mixed Farming
- Forests
- Swampland, Limited Agriculture

MAJOR MINERAL OCCURRENCES

Al	Bauxite	Ls	Limestone
At	Asphalt	Mi	Mica
C	Coal	Mr	Marble
Cl	Clay	Na	Salt
Fe	Iron Ore	O	Petroleum

⚡ Water Power

▨ Major Industrial Areas

△ Major Textile Manufacturing Centers

36019	Cooper, 250	E 5
36020	Coosada, 600	F 5
35550	Cordova, 2,750	D 3
† 35546	Corona, 300	C 3
35088	Cottage Grove, 300	F 5
35453	Cottondale, 600	D 4
36851	Cottonton, 415	H 6
36320	Cottonwood, 1,149	H 8
35618	Courtland, 547	D 1
36321	Cowarts, 350	H 8
36435	Coy, 950	D 7
36525	Creola, 950	B 9
36906	Cromwell, 700	B 6
35962	Crossville, 1,035	G 2
36907	Cuba, 386	B 6
35055	Cullman◉, 12,601	E 2
36920	Cullomburg, 325	B 7
36852	Cusseta, 250	H 5
36853	Dadeville◉, 2,847	G 5
36322	Daleville, 5,182	G 8
35619	Danville, 400	D 2
36526	Daphne, 2,382	C 9
36528	Dauphin Island, 950	B 10
36256	Daviston, 247	G 4
36022	Deatsville, 350	F 5
35601	Decatur◉, 38,044	D 1
36529	Deer Park, 300	B 8
36732	Demopolis, 7,651	C 6
36436	Dickinson, 350	C 7
36736	Dixons Mills, 285	C 6
35601	Dolomite, 1,237	D 4
35062	Dora, 1,862	D 3
36301	Dothan◉, 36,733	H 8
35553	Double Springs◉, 957	D 2
35964	Douglas, 527	F 2
36028	Dozier, 304	F 7
36259	Duke, 250	A 3
35744	Dutton, 423	G 1
† 36507	Dyas, 250	C 9
36260	Eastaboga, 500	F 3
36426	East Brewton, 2,336	E 8
35457	Echola, 300	C 4
36024	Eclectic, 1,184	F 5
† 36317	Edwin, 296	H 7
36323	Elba◉, 4,634	F 8
36530	Elberta, 395	C 10
35554	Eldridge, 350	C 3
35620	Elkmont, 394	E 1
36025	Elmore, 656	F 5
35458	Elrod, 600	C 4
35459	Emelle, 300	B 5
35063	Empire, 400	D 3
36330	Enterprise, 15,591	G 8
35460	Epes, 293	B 5
36027	Eufaula, 9,102	H 7
35462	Eutaw◉, 2,805	C 5
36401	Evergreen◉, 3,924	D 8
36439	Excel, 422	D 8
35746	Fackler, 250	G 1

36854	Fairfax, 2,772	H 5
35064	Fairfield, 14,369	E 3
36532	Fairhope, 5,720	C 10
35208	Fairview, 313	E 2
35622	Falkville, 966	E 2
35555	Fayette◉, 4,568	C 3
36440	Finchburg, 300	D 7
36855	Five Points, 247	H 4
† 35129	Flat Creek-Wegra, 1,066	D 3
35966	Flat Rock, 750	G 1
35790	Flatwood, 300	C 6
† 35601	Flint City, 404	D 1
36441	Flomaton, 1,584	D 8
36442	Florala, 2,701	F 8
35630	Florence◉, 34,031	C 1
36535	Foley, 3,368	C 10
35214	Forestdale, 6,091	E 3
36030	Forest Home, 450	E 7
36740	Forkland, 400	C 6
36031	Fort Davis, 500	G 6
36032	Fort Deposit, 1,438	E 7
36856	Fort Mitchell, 2,400	H 6
35967	Fort Payne◉, 8,435	G 2
35463	Fosters, 400	C 4
36444	Franklin, 500	D 7
36538	Frankville, 550	B 7
† 31833	Fredonia, 300	H 5
36445	Frisco City, 1,286	D 8
36539	Fruitdale, 275	B 8
35068	Fultondale, 5,163	E 3
36741	Furman, 300	E 6
35971	Fyffe, 311	G 2
* 35901	Gadsden◉, 53,928	G 2
	Gadsden, ‡94,144	G 2
36540	Gainestown, 300	C 8
35464	Gainesville, 255	B 5
35972	Gallant, 475	F 2
36038	Gantt, 380	F 8
35070	Garden City, 746	E 2
35071	Gardendale, 6,502	E 3
36340	Geneva◉, 4,398	G 8
36033	Georgiana, 2,148	E 7
35974	Geraldine, 610	G 2
35559	Glen Allen, 276	C 3
35905	Glencoe, 2,901	G 2
36034	Glenwood, 378	F 7
† 36024	Good Hope, 840	E 2
35072	Goodwater, 2,172	F 4
35466	Gordo, 1,991	C 4
36343	Gordon, 312	H 8
35561	Gorgas, 500	D 3
36035	Goshen, 279	F 7
36450	Gosport, 400	C 7
36036	Grady, 298	F 7
36541	Grand Bay, 950	B 10
35747	Grant, 382	F 1
35073	Graysville, 3,182	D 3
35074	Green Pond, 500	D 4
35746	Greensboro◉, 3,371	C 5

(continued on following page)

ALABAMA

SCALE

0 5 10   20   30   40 MI.

0 5 10 20 30 40 KM.

State Capitals........ ⊛

County Seats......... ◉

© C.S. Hammond & Co., N.Y.

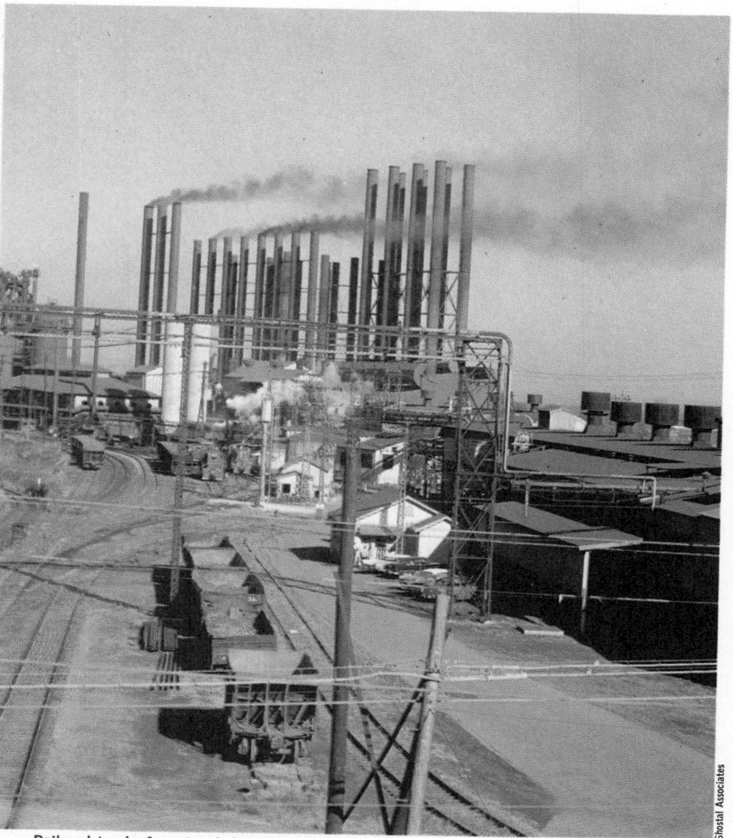

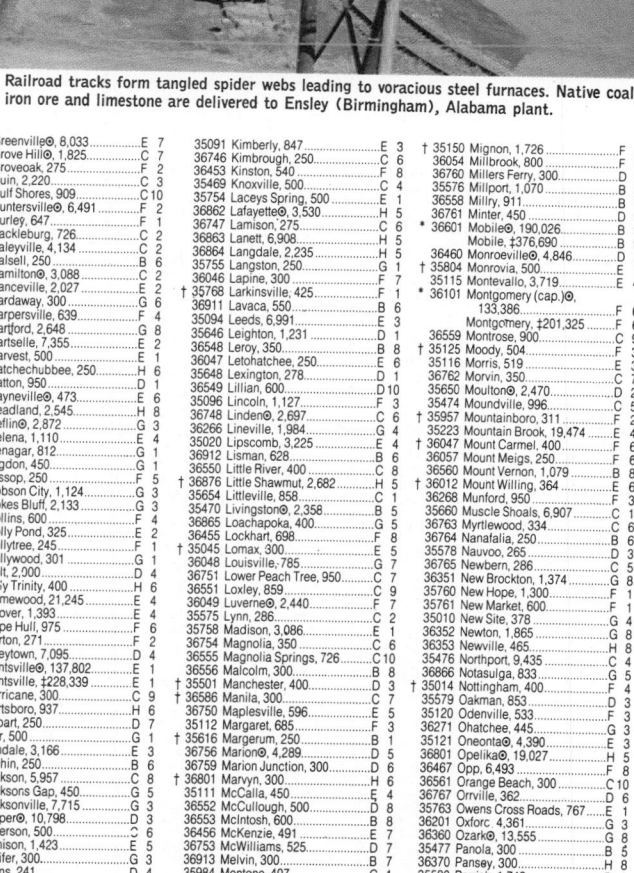

Railroad tracks form tangled spider webs leading to voracious steel furnaces. Native coal, iron ore and limestone are delivered to Ensley (Birmingham), Alabama plant.

Shostal Associates

Topography

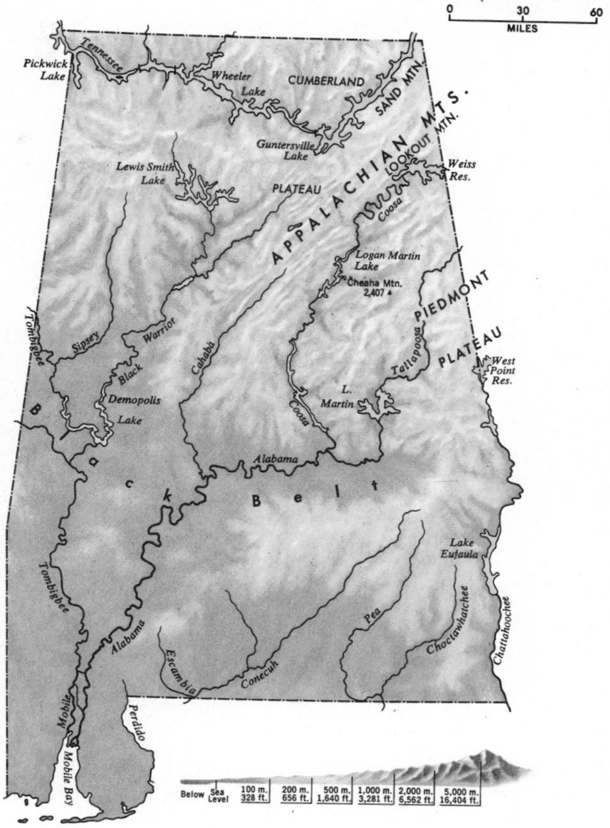
0 30 60
MILES
Pickwick Lake
Tennessee
Wheeler Lake
CUMBERLAND
SAND MTN.
Guntersville Lake
LOOKOUT MTN.
Weiss Res.
Lewis Smith Lake
PLATEAU
APPALACHIAN MTS.
Coosa
Logan Martin Lake
Cheaha Mtn. 2,407
PIEDMONT
PLATEAU
West Point Res.
Tallapoosa
L. Martin
Coosa
Cahaba
Warrior
Black
Sipsey
Tombigbee
Demopolis Lake
Alabama
Black Belt
Lake Eufaula
Tombigbee
Alabama
Escambia
Conecuh
Pea
Choctawhatchee
Chattahoochee
Mobile
Perdido
Mobile Bay
Below Sea Level
100 m. 328 ft.
200 m. 656 ft.
500 m. 1,640 ft.
1,000 m. 3,281 ft.
2,000 m. 6,562 ft.
5,000 m. 16,404 ft.

36037 Greenville⊙, 8,033 .... E 7
36451 Grove Hill⊙, 1,825 .... C 7
35975 Groveoak, 275 .... F 2
35563 Guin, 2,220 .... C 3
36542 Gulf Shores, 909 .... C 10
35976 Guntersville⊙, 6,491 .... F 2
35748 Gurley, 647 .... F 1
35564 Hackleburg, 726 .... C 2
35565 Haleyville, 4,134 .... C 2
36909 Halsell, 250 .... B 6
35570 Hamilton⊙, 3,088 .... C 2
35077 Hanceville, 2,027 .... E 2
36039 Hardaway, 300 .... G 6
35078 Harpersville, 639 .... F 4
36344 Hartford, 2,648 .... G 8
35640 Hartselle, 7,355 .... E 2
35749 Harvest, 500 .... E 1
36858 Hatchechubbee, 250 .... H 6
35672 Hatton, 950 .... D 1
36040 Hayneville⊙, 473 .... E 6
36345 Headland, 2,545 .... H 8
36264 Heflin⊙, 2,872 .... G 3
35080 Helena, 1,110 .... E 4
35978 Henagar, 812 .... G 1
35979 Higdon, 450 .... G 1
35081 Hissop, 250 .... F 5
36201 Hobson City, 1,124 .... G 3
35903 Hokes Bluff, 2,133 .... G 3
35082 Hollins, 600 .... F 4
35083 Holly Pond, 325 .... E 2
35751 Hollytree, 245 .... F 1
35752 Hollywood, 301 .... G 1
35401 Holt, 2,000 .... D 4
36859 Holy Trinity, 400 .... H 6
35209 Homewood, 21,245 .... E 4
35226 Hoover, 1,393 .... E 4
36043 Hope Hull, 975 .... F 6
35980 Horton, 271 .... F 2
35020 Hueytown, 7,095 .... D 4
35801 Huntsville⊙, 137,802 .... E 1
Huntsville, ‡228,339 .... E 1
36507 Hurricane, 300 .... C 9
36860 Hurtsboro, 937 .... H 6
36452 Hybart, 250 .... D 7
35981 Ider, 500 .... G 1
35210 Irondale, 3,166 .... E 3
36910 Jachin, 250 .... B 6
36545 Jackson, 5,957 .... C 8
36861 Jacksons Gap, 450 .... G 5
36265 Jacksonville, 7,715 .... G 3
35501 Jasper⊙, 10,798 .... D 3
36745 Jefferson, 500 .... C 6
35085 Jemison, 1,423 .... E 5
36268 Jenifer, 300 .... G 3
35086 Johns, 241 .... D 4
35087 Joppa, 350 .... E 2
35089 Kellyton, 500 .... F 5
35574 Kennedy, 415 .... B 3
36045 Kent, 500 .... G 5
35645 Killen, 683 .... D 1
35091 Kimberly, 847 .... E 3
36746 Kimbrough, 250 .... C 6
36453 Kinston, 540 .... F 8
35469 Knoxville, 500 .... C 4
35754 Laceys Spring, 500 .... E 1
36862 Lafayette⊙, 3,530 .... H 5
36747 Lamison, 275 .... C 6
36863 Lanett, 6,908 .... H 5
36864 Langdale, 2,235 .... H 5
35755 Langston, 250 .... G 1
36046 Lapine, 300 .... F 7
† 35768 Larkinsville, 425 .... F 1
36911 Lavaca, 550 .... B 6
35094 Leeds, 6,991 .... E 3
35646 Leighton, 1,231 .... D 1
36548 Leroy, 350 .... B 8
36047 Letohatchee, 250 .... E 6
35648 Lexington, 278 .... D 1
36549 Lillian, 600 .... D 10
35096 Lincoln, 1,127 .... F 3
36748 Linden⊙, 2,697 .... C 6
36266 Lineville, 1,984 .... G 4
35020 Lipscomb, 3,225 .... E 4
36912 Lisman, 628 .... B 6
36550 Little River, 400 .... C 8
† 36876 Little Shawmut, 2,682 .... H 5
35654 Littleville, 858 .... C 1
35470 Livingston⊙, 2,358 .... B 5
36865 Loachapoka, 400 .... G 5
36455 Lockhart, 698 .... F 8
† 35045 Lomax, 300 .... E 5
36048 Louisville, 785 .... G 7
36751 Lower Peach Tree, 950 .... C 7
36551 Loxley, 859 .... C 9
36049 Luverne⊙, 2,440 .... F 7
35575 Lynn, 286 .... C 2
35758 Madison, 3,086 .... E 1
36754 Magnolia, 350 .... C 6
36555 Magnolia Springs, 726 .... C 10
36556 Malcolm, 300 .... B 8
† 35501 Manchester, 400 .... D 3
† 36586 Manila, 300 .... C 7
36750 Maplesville, 596 .... E 5
35112 Margaret, 685 .... F 3
† 35616 Margerum, 250 .... B 1
36756 Marion⊙, 4,289 .... D 5
36759 Marion Junction, 300 .... D 6
† 36801 Marvyn, 300 .... H 6
35111 McCalla, 450 .... E 4
36552 McCullough, 500 .... D 8
36553 McIntosh, 600 .... B 8
36456 McKenzie, 491 .... E 7
36753 McWilliams, 525 .... D 7
36913 Melvin, 300 .... B 7
35984 Mentone, 407 .... G 1
35759 Meridianville, 950 .... F 1
36458 Mexia, 250 .... D 8
35228 Midfield, 6,399 .... E 4
36350 Midland City, 1,172 .... H 8
36053 Midway, 558 .... H 6
† 35150 Mignon, 1,726 .... F 4
36054 Millbrook, 800 .... F 6
36760 Millers Ferry, 300 .... D 6
35576 Millport, 1,070 .... B 3
36558 Millry, 911 .... B 7
36761 Minter, 450 .... D 6
* 36601 Mobile⊙, 190,026 .... B 9
Mobile, ‡376,690 .... B 9
36460 Monroeville⊙, 4,846 .... D 7
† 35804 Monrovia, 500 .... E 1
35115 Montevallo, 3,719 .... E 4
* 36101 Montgomery (cap.)⊙, 133,386 .... F 6
Montgomery, ‡201,325 .... F 6
36559 Montrose, 900 .... C 9
† 35125 Moody, 504 .... F 3
35116 Morris, 519 .... E 3
36762 Morvin, 350 .... C 7
35650 Moulton⊙, 2,470 .... D 2
35474 Moundville, 996 .... C 5
† 35957 Mountainboro, 311 .... F 2
35223 Mountain Brook, 19,474 .... E 4
† 36047 Mount Carmel, 400 .... F 6
36057 Mount Meigs, 250 .... F 6
36560 Mount Vernon, 1,079 .... B 8
† 36012 Mount Willing, 364 .... E 6
36268 Munford, 950 .... F 3
35660 Muscle Shoals, 6,907 .... C 1
36763 Myrtlewood, 334 .... C 6
36764 Nanafalia, 250 .... B 6
35578 Nauvoo, 265 .... D 3
36765 Newbern, 286 .... C 5
36351 New Brockton, 1,374 .... G 8
35760 New Hope, 1,300 .... F 1
35761 New Market, 600 .... F 1
35010 New Site, 378 .... G 4
36352 Newton, 1,865 .... G 8
36353 Newville, 465 .... H 8
35476 Northport, 9,435 .... C 4
36866 Notasulga, 833 .... G 5
† 35014 Nottingham, 400 .... F 4
35579 Oakman, 853 .... D 3
35120 Odenville, 533 .... F 3
36271 Ohatchee, 445 .... G 3
35121 Oneonta⊙, 4,390 .... E 3
36801 Opelika⊙, 19,027 .... H 5
36467 Opp, 6,493 .... F 8
36561 Orange Beach, 300 .... C 10
36767 Orrville, 362 .... D 6
35763 Owens Cross Roads, 767 .... E 1
36201 Oxford, 4,361 .... G 3
36360 Ozark⊙, 13,555 .... G 8
35477 Panola, 300 .... B 5
36370 Pansey, 300 .... H 8
35580 Parrish, 1,742 .... D 3
35124 Pelham, 931 .... E 4
35125 Pell City⊙, 5,381 .... F 3
36916 Pennington, 276 .... B 6
36562 Perdido, 325 .... C 8
36530 Perdido Beach, 300 .... C 10
36471 Peterman, 750 .... D 7
35478 Peterson, 1,040 .... D 4
36867 Phenix City⊙, 25,281 .... H 6
35581 Phil Campbell, 1,230 .... C 2
36272 Piedmont, 5,063 .... G 3
36371 Pinckard, 609 .... G 8
36768 Pine Apple, 347 .... E 7
36769 Pine Hill, 697 .... C 7
36065 Pine Level, 300 .... F 6
35126 Pinson, 2,500 .... E 3
35765 Pisgah, 519 .... G 1
36871 Pittsview, 400 .... H 6
36758 Plantersville, 550 .... E 5
36564 Point Clear, 850 .... C 10
36067 Prattville⊙, 13,116 .... E 6
36610 Prichard, 41,578 .... B 9
35766 Princeton, 250 .... F 1
36772 Putnam, 305 .... B 6
† 36507 Rabun, 300 .... C 8
35131 Ragland, 1,239 .... F 3
35901 Rainbow City, 3,107 .... F 3
35986 Rainsville, 2,099 .... G 2
35480 Ralph, 500 .... C 4
36069 Ramer, 750 .... F 6
36273 Ranburne, 371 .... H 3
36473 Range, 275 .... D 8
35582 Red Bay, 2,464 .... B 2
36474 Red Level, 616 .... E 8
† 35954 Reece City, 496 .... G 2
35481 Reform, 1,893 .... C 4
† 36720 Rehoboth, 300 .... D 6
† 35160 Renfroe, 400 .... F 4
36475 Repton, 277 .... D 8
† 35203 Republic, 500 .... E 3
36918 Riderwood, 400 .... B 6
36476 River Falls, 580 .... E 8
35135 Riverside, 351 .... F 3
36872 River View, 1,109 .... H 5
36274 Roanoke, 5,251 .... H 4
36567 Robertsdale, 2,078 .... C 9
35136 Rockford⊙, 603 .... F 5
36274 Rock Mills, 800 .... H 4
35652 Rogersville, 950 .... D 1
† 35020 Roosevelt City, 3,663 .... E 4
35653 Russellville⊙, 7,814 .... C 2
36071 Rutledge, 353 .... F 7
35137 Saginaw, 300 .... E 4
35138 Saint Bernard, 896 .... E 2
† 35146 Saint Clair Springs, 300 .... F 3
36568 Saint Elmo, 650 .... B 10
36569 Saint Stephens, 400 .... B 7
36874 Salem, 475 .... H 5
36570 Salitpa, 500 .... C 7
36477 Samson, 2,257 .... F 8
36478 Sanford, 256 .... F 8
35583 Saragossa, 300 .... D 3
36571 Saraland, 7,840 .... B 9
36775 Sardis, 300 .... E 6
36775 Sardis, 368 .... F 2
36572 Satsuma, 2,035 .... B 9
35139 Sayre, 700 .... E 3
35768 Scottsboro⊙, 9,324 .... F 1
36875 Seale, 400 .... H 6
35771 Section, 702 .... G 1
36701 Selma⊙, 27,379 .... E 6
† 36701 Selmont, 2,270 .... E 6
36574 Seminole, 275 .... D 10
36575 Semmes, 800 .... B 9
36876 Shawmut, 2,181 .... H 5
35660 Sheffield, 13,115 .... C 1
35143 Shelby, 500 .... E 4
36075 Shorter, 500 .... G 6
36373 Shorterville, 330 .... H 7
36733 Shortleaf, 253 .... C 6
36919 Silas, 345 .... B 7
35144 Siluria, 678 .... E 4
36576 Silverhill, 552 .... C 9
† 36268 Silver Run, 250 .... G 3
35584 Sipsey, 608 .... D 3
36375 Slocomb, 1,883 .... G 8
36877 Smiths, 2,500 .... H 5
35952 Snead, 347 .... F 2
† 36104 Snowdoun, 250 .... F 6
36778 Snow Hill, 500 .... E 7
35901 Southside, 983 .... F 3
36527 Spanish Fort, 983 .... C 9
† 35674 Spring Valley, 600 .... C 1
35146 Springville, 1,153 .... E 3
35585 Spruce Pine, 600 .... C 2
36878 Standing Rock, 500 .... H 4
36578 Stapleton, 975 .... C 9
35987 Steele, 798 .... F 3
35147 Sterrett, 450 .... F 4
35772 Stevenson, 2,390 .... G 1
† 35150 Stewartville, 250 .... F 4
36579 Stockton, 1,400 .... C 9
35586 Sulligent, 1,762 .... B 3
35148 Sumiton, 2,374 .... D 3
36580 Summerdale, 550 .... C 10
36780 Sunny South, 250 .... C 7
36781 Suttle, 256 .... D 5
36782 Sweet Water, 265 .... C 6
35149 Sycamore, 800 .... F 4
35150 Sylacauga, 12,255 .... F 4
35988 Sylvania, 476 .... G 1
35160 Talladega⊙, 17,662 .... F 4
36078 Tallassee, 4,809 .... G 5
35671 Tanner, 600 .... E 1
35217 Tarrant, 6,835 .... E 3
36582 Theodore, 1,950 .... B 9
36783 Thomaston, 824 .... C 6
36784 Thomasville, 3,769 .... C 7
35171 Thorsby, 944 .... E 5
35672 Town Creek, 1,203 .... D 1
35587 Townley, 500 .... D 3
36921 Toxey, 304 .... B 7
35172 Trafford, 628 .... E 3
35673 Trinity, 881 .... D 1
36081 Troy⊙, 11,482 .... G 7
35173 Trussville, 2,985 .... E 3
36479 Tunnel Springs, 300 .... D 7
35401 Tuscaloosa⊙, 65,773 .... C 4
Tuscaloosa, ‡116,029 .... C 4
35674 Tuscumbia⊙, 8,828 .... C 1
36083 Tuskegee⊙, 11,028 .... G 6
36088 Tuskegee Institute, 5,800 .... G 6
36089 Union Springs⊙, 4,324 .... G 6
36786 Uniontown, 2,133 .... D 6
36480 Uriah, 1,200 .... D 8
35775 Valhermoso Springs, 500 .... E 2
35989 Valley Head, 470 .... G 1
35176 Vandiver, 700 .... F 4
36091 Verbena, 350 .... E 5
35592 Vernon⊙, 2,190 .... B 3
35216 Vestavia Hills, 8,311 .... E 4
35593 Vina, 366 .... B 2
35178 Vincent, 1,419 .... F 4
35179 Vinemont, 480 .... E 2
36481 Vredenburgh, 622 .... D 7
36276 Wadley, 626 .... G 4
36585 Wagarville, 350 .... B 8
36586 Walker Springs, 500 .... C 7
35180 Warrior, 2,621 .... E 3
35677 Waterloo, 262 .... B 1
35182 Wattsville, 500 .... F 3
36879 Waverly, 247 .... G 5
36277 Weaver, 2,091 .... G 3
36376 Webb, 354 .... H 8
36278 Wedowee⊙, 842 .... H 4
† 35129 Wegra-Flat Creek, 1,066 .... D 3
35183 Weogufka, 350 .... F 4
35184 West Blocton, 1,172 .... D 4
† 36201 West End-Cobb Town, 5,515 .... G 3
35185 Westover, 1,400 .... E 4
36092 Wetumpka⊙, 3,786 .... F 5
36482 Whatley, 500 .... C 7
† 35618 Wheeler, 300 .... D 1
† 36040 White Hall, 300 .... E 6
† 36862 White Plains, 350 .... G 3
† 35094 Whites Chapel, 334 .... F 3
36923 Whitfield, 500 .... B 6
† 36352 Wicksburg, 400 .... G 8
36587 Wilmer, 720 .... B 9
35186 Wilsonville, 659 .... E 4
35187 Wilton, 573 .... E 4
35594 Winfield, 3,292 .... C 3
35188 Woodstock, 320 .... D 4
35776 Woodville, 322 .... F 1
36924 Yantley, 500 .... B 6
36789 Yellow Bluff, 350 .... C 7
36925 York, 3,044 .... B 6

⊙ County seat.
‡ Population of metropolitan area.
† Zip of nearest p.o.
* Multiple zips

132 Alaska

SENATORIAL DISTRICTS

District	Pop.	Key
Central	70,996	H 2
Northwestern	16,763	E 2
South Central	170,058	G 3
Southeastern	42,565	L 3

CITIES and TOWNS

Zip Name/Pop. Key

99615 Akhiok, 115 .... H 3
99551 Akiachak, 312 .... F 2
99552 Akiak, 171 .... F 2
99553 Akutan, 101 .... E 4
99554 Alakanuk, 265 .... E 2
99555 Aleknagik, 128 .... G 3
99720 Allakaket, 174 .... H 1
99786 Ambler, 169 .... G 1
99721 Anaktuvuk Pass, 99 .... H 1
* 99501 Anchorage⊙, 48,029 .... B 1
99556 Anchor Point, 102 .... B 2
† 99760 Anderson, 362 .... H 2
† 99658 Andreafski (Saint Marys), 384 .... E 2
99820 Angoon, 400 .... M 1
99557 Aniak, 205 .... G 2
99920 Annette, 195 .... N 2
99558 Anvik, 83 .... F 2
99722 Arctic Village, 85 .... K 1
† 99701 Aurora Lodge, 250 .... J 2
99723 Barrow, 2,104 .... G 1
† 99747 Barter Island (Kaktovik),123 .... K 1
99724 Beaver, 101 .... J 1
† 99612 Belkofski, 59 .... F 3
99559 Bethel, 2,416 .... F 2
† 99726 Bettles, 65 .... H 1
99726 Bettles Field, 49 .... H 1
† 99740 Birch Creek, 45 .... J 1
99567 Birchwood, 1,219 .... C 1
99785 Brevig Mission, 123 .... E 1
99727 Buckland, 104 .... F 1
99729 Cantwell, 62 .... J 2
† 99901 Cape Pole, 123 .... M 2
99730 Central, 26 .... J 1
99788 Chalkyitsik, 130 .... K 1
99620 Chaneliak, 100 .... F 2
99561 Chefornak, 146 .... F 2
99563 Chevak, 387 .... E 2
99732 Chicken, 25 .... K 2
99564 Chignik, 83 .... G 3
99565 Chignik Lagoon, 70 .... G 3
99564 Chignik Lake, 117 .... G 3
99586 Chistochina, 33 .... K 2
99566 Chitina, 38 .... K 2
99567 Chugiak, 489 .... C 1
99733 Circle, 54 .... K 1
99568 Clam Gulch, 47 .... B 1
99569 Clarks Point, 95 .... G 3
99704 Clear, 504 .... J 2
99570 Cohoe, 60 .... B 1
99571 Cold Bay, 256 .... F 3
99701 College, 3,434 .... J 1
99572 Cooper Landing, 31 .... C 1
99573 Copper Center, 206 .... J 2
99574 Cordova, 1,164 .... D 1
99921 Craig, 272 .... M 2
99575 Crooked Creek, 59 .... G 2
† 99746 Cutoff (Huslia), 159 .... G 1
99736 Deering, 85 .... F 1
99737 Delta Junction, 703 .... J 2
99576 Dillingham, 914 .... G 3
† 99762 Diomede, 84 .... E 1
99737 Dot Lake, 42 .... K 2
99685 Dutch Harbor, 30 .... E 4
99738 Eagle, 36 .... K 2
99577 Eagle River, 2,437 .... C 1
† 99901 Edna Bay, 112 .... M 2
99578 Eek, 186 .... F 2
99579 Egegik, 148 .... G 3
99569 Ekuk, 51 .... G 3
99580 Ekwok, 103 .... G 3
99825 Elfin Cove, 49 .... M 1
99739 Elim, 174 .... F 2
99581 Emmonak, 439 .... E 2
† 99603 English Bay, 58 .... B 2
99674 Eska, 50 .... B 1
99725 Ester, 264 .... J 2
99701 Fairbanks⊙, 14,771 .... J 2
99583 False Pass, 62 .... F 4
99585 Fortuna Ledge, 175 .... F 2
99740 Fort Yukon, 448 .... J 1
99586 Gakona, 88 .... K 2
99741 Galena, 302 .... G 2
99742 Gambell, 372 .... D 2
99587 Girdwood, 144 .... D 1
99588 Glennallen, 363 .... D 1
99762 Golovin, 117 .... F 2
99589 Goodnews Bay, 218 .... F 3
99586 Gulkana, 53 .... J 2
99826 Gustavus, 64 .... M 1
99827 Haines, 463 .... M 1
99743 Healy, 79 .... H 2
99665 Holikachuk, 100 .... G 2
99602 Holy Cross, 199 .... G 2
99603 Homer, 1,083 .... B 2
99829 Hoonah, 748 .... M 1
99604 Hooper Bay, 490 .... E 2
99605 Hope, 51 .... C 1
99687 Houston, 69 .... B 1
99745 Hughes, 85 .... H 1
99746 Huslia, 159 .... G 1
99922 Hydaburg, 214 .... M 2
99923 Hyder, 49 .... P 2
99625 Igiugig, 36 .... G 3
99606 Iliamna, 58 .... G 3
† 99801 Juneau (cap.)⊙, 6,050 .... N 1
† 99663 Kachemak, 76 .... B 2
99608 Kaguyak, 59 .... H 3
99830 Kake, 448 .... M 1
99647 Kakhonak, 88 .... H 3
99747 Kaktovik, 123 .... K 1
99607 Kalskag, 122 .... F 2
99748 Kaltag, 206 .... G 2
99924 Kasaan, 30 .... N 2
99668 Kashegelok, 200 .... G 2
99609 Kasigluk, 526 .... F 2
99610 Kasilof, 71 .... B 1
99611 Kenai, 3,533 .... B 1
99901 Ketchikan, 6,994 .... N 2
99749 Kiana, 278 .... F 1
99612 King Cove, 283 .... F 4
† 99762 King Island, 100 .... E 1
99613 King Salmon, 202 .... G 3
99614 Kipnuk, 325 .... F 2
99750 Kivalina, 188 .... E 1
99925 Klawock, 213 .... M 2
99827 Klukwan, 103 .... M 1
99751 Kobuk, 98 .... G 1
99615 Kodiak, 3,798 .... H 3
99576 Koliganek, 142 .... G 3
99620 Kotlik, 228 .... F 2
99752 Kotzebue, 1,696 .... F 1
99753 Koyuk, 122 .... F 1
99754 Koyukuk, 124 .... G 1
† 99625 Kvichak, 75 .... G 3
99621 Kwethluk, 408 .... F 2
99622 Kwigillingok, 148 .... F 3
† 99655 Kwinhagak (Quinhagak), 340 .... F 2
99624 Larsen Bay, 109 .... H 3
99625 Levelock, 74 .... G 3
† 99566 Lower Tonsina, 65 .... J 2
99756 Manley Hot Springs, 34 .... J 1
99628 Manokotak, 214 .... G 3
† 99585 Marshall (Fortuna Ledge), 175 .... F 2
99627 McGrath, 279 .... H 2
99630 Mekoryuk, 249 .... E 2
† 99579 Meshik, 75 .... G 3
99926 Metlakatla, 1,050 .... N 2
99903 Meyers Chuck, 37 .... N 2
99758 Minto, 168 .... J 1
99676 Montana, 33 .... J 2
99631 Moose Pass, 53 .... C 1
99901 Mountain Point, 459 .... N 2
99632 Mountain Village, 419 .... F 2
99835 Mount Edgecumbe, 835 .... M 1
† 99589 Mumtrak (Goodnews Bay), 218 .... F 3
† 99764 Nabesna, 40 .... K 2
99633 Naknek, 178 .... G 3
99559 Napaiskak, 259 .... F 2
99634 Napakiak, 270 .... F 2
99760 Nenana, 362 .... J 2
† 99606 Newhalen, 88 .... H 3
99636 New Stuyahok, 216 .... G 3
99559 Newtok, 114 .... E 2
† 99603 Nikolaevsk, 70 .... B 2
99691 Nikolai, 112 .... H 2
99638 Nikolski, 57 .... E 3
99639 Ninilchik, 134 .... B 2
99761 Noatak, 293 .... F 1
99762 Nome⊙, 2,488 .... E 1
99640 Nondalton, 184 .... G 3
99763 Noorvik, 461 .... F 1
99705 North Pole, 265 .... J 2
99704 Northway, 40 .... K 2
99765 Nulato, 308 .... G 2
99641 Nunapitchuk, 400 .... F 2
99643 Old Harbor, 290 .... H 3
99559 Oscarville, 41 .... F 2
† 99644 Ouzinkie, 160 .... H 3
99645 Palmer, 1,140 .... C 1
99646 Paulof Harbor, 39 .... F 3
99737 Paxson, 32 .... J 2
99647 Pedro Bay, 65 .... H 3
99832 Pelican, 133 .... M 1
99648 Perryville, 94 .... G 3
99833 Petersburg, 2,042 .... N 1
99649 Pilot Point, 68 .... G 3
99650 Pilot Station, 290 .... F 2
† 99658 Pitkas Point, 70 .... F 2
99651 Platinum, 55 .... F 3
99766 Point Hope, 386 .... E 1
99587 Portage, 80 .... C 1
99834 Port Alexander, 36 .... M 2
† 99827 Port Chilkoot, 220 .... M 1
† 99603 Port Graham, 107 .... B 2
† 99579 Port Heiden, 66 .... G 3
99550 Port Lions, 227 .... H 3

Agriculture, Industry and Resources

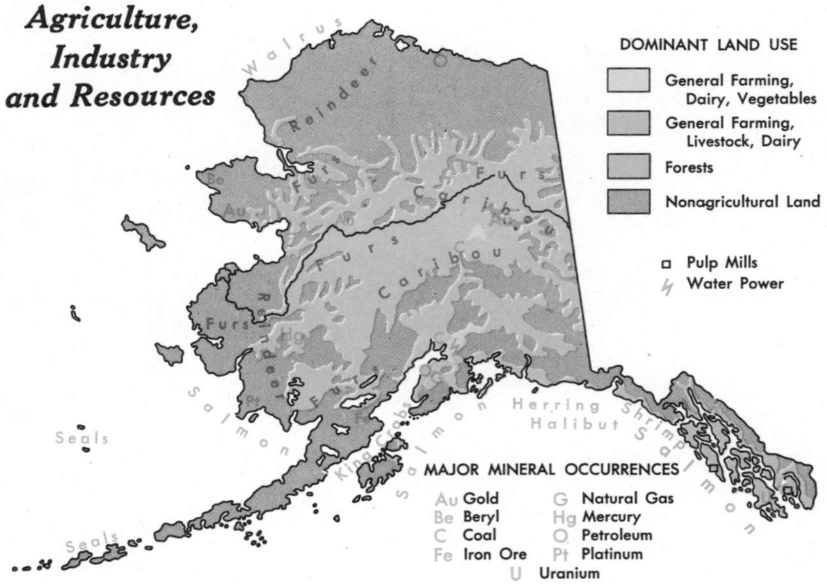

DOMINANT LAND USE

- General Farming, Dairy, Vegetables
- General Farming, Livestock, Dairy
- Forests
- Nonagricultural Land

□ Pulp Mills
⚡ Water Power

MAJOR MINERAL OCCURRENCES

Au Gold
Be Beryl
C Coal
Fe Iron Ore
G Natural Gas
Hg Mercury
O Petroleum
Pt Platinum
U Uranium

Topography

MILES
0   200   400

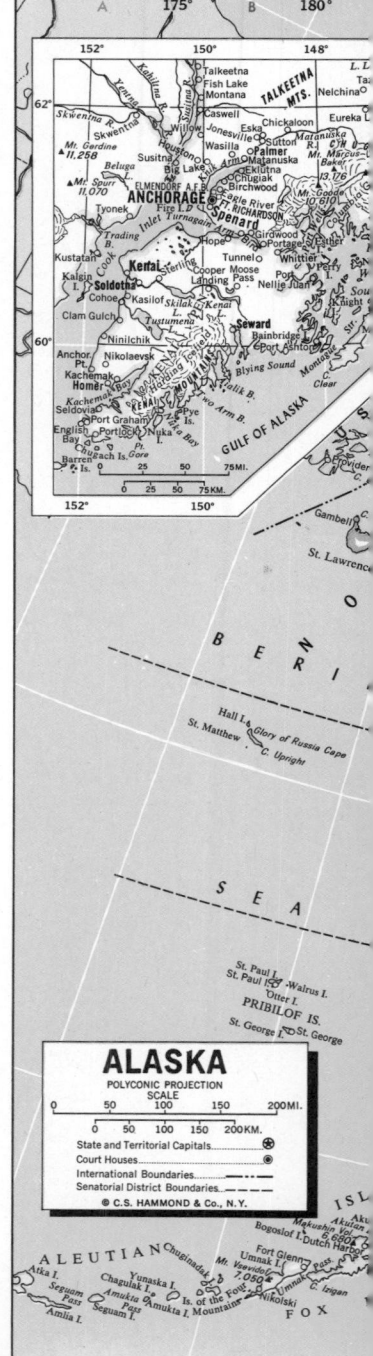

ALASKA

POLYCONIC PROJECTION
SCALE

⊕ State and Territorial Capitals
⊙ Court Houses
— · — · International Boundaries
— — — Senatorial District Boundaries

© C.S. HAMMOND & Co., N.Y.

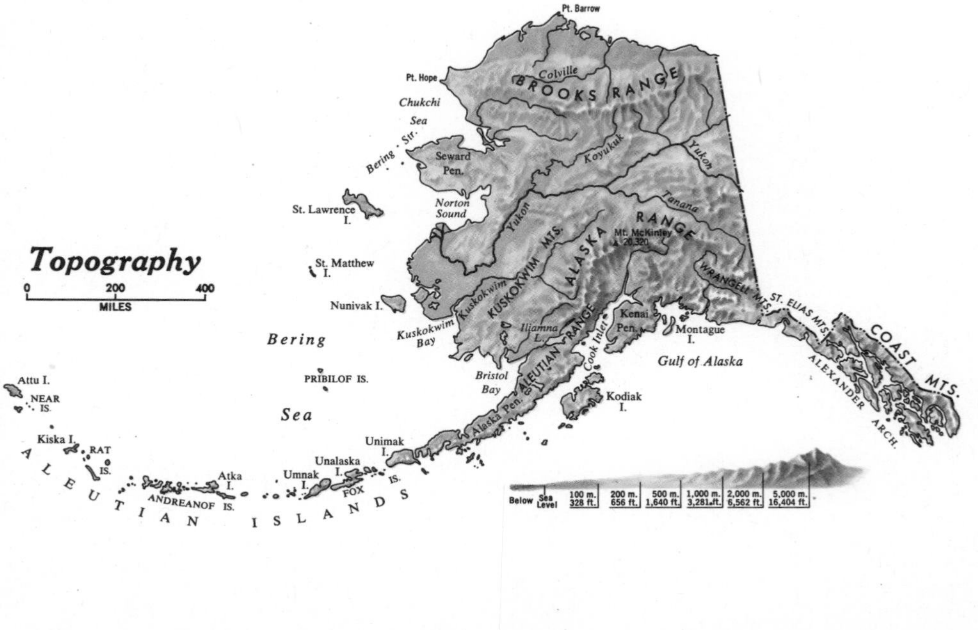

Despite its deceptively calm exterior, the Vaughan Lewis Glacier is actually a river of ice, hundreds of feet deep, flowing steadily. Ridges (eskers) are formed by streams under the ice.

Arthur A. Twomey—Shostal Associates

AREA 586,412 sq. mi.
POPULATION 302,173
CAPITAL Juneau
LARGEST CITY Anchorage
HIGHEST POINT Mt. McKinley 20,320 ft.
SETTLED IN 1801
ADMITTED TO UNION January 3, 1959
POPULAR NAME Great Land
STATE FLOWER Forget-me-not
STATE BIRD Willow Ptarmigan

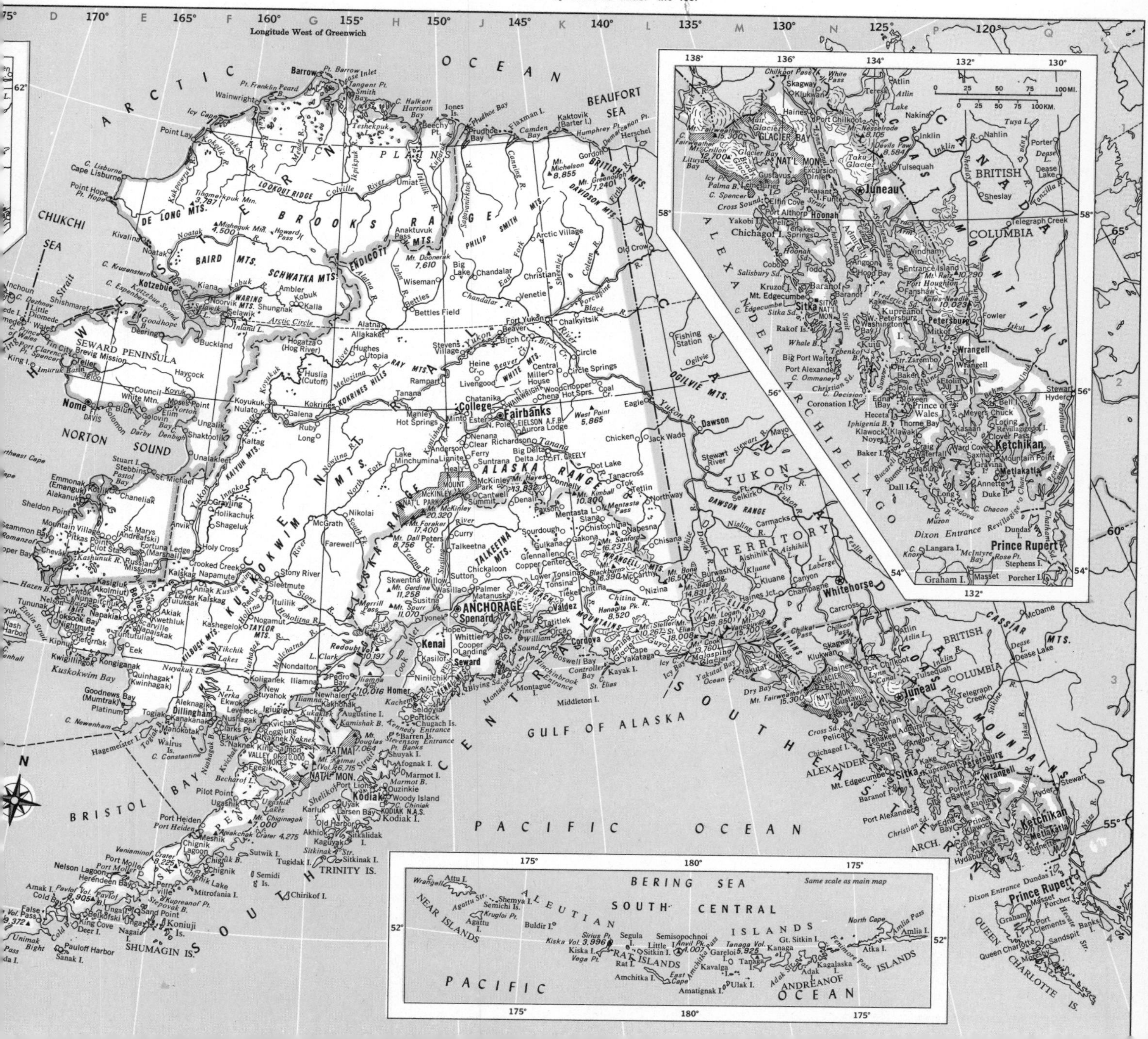

ARIZONA

SCALE

0 5 10   20   30   40   50   60 MI.

0 5 10 20 30 40 50 60 KM.

State Capitals.......... ⊛

County Seats.......... ◉

© C.S. HAMMOND & Co., N.Y.

Topography

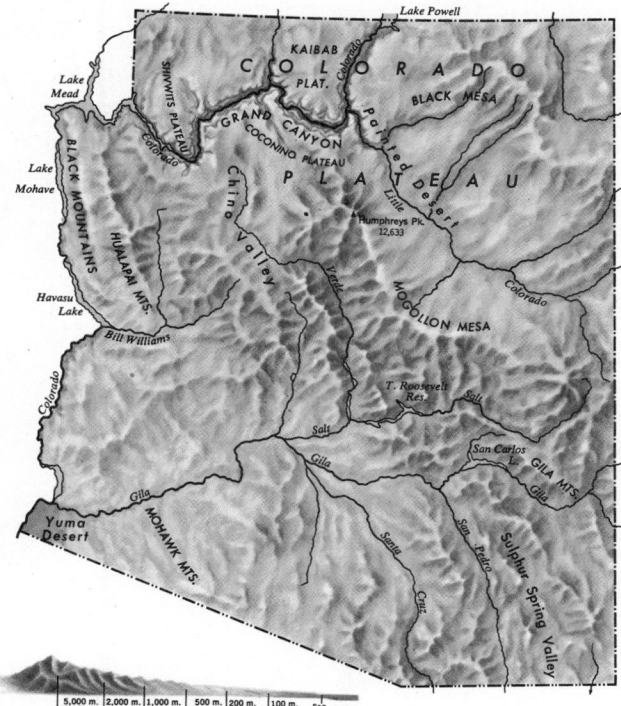

0   50   100
MILES

5,000 m. | 2,000 m. | 1,000 m. | 500 m. | 200 m. | 100 m. | Sea | Below
16,404 ft. | 6,562 ft. | 3,281 ft. | 1,640 ft. | 656 ft. | 328 ft. | Level

AREA 113,909 sq. mi.
POPULATION 1,772,482
CAPITAL Phoenix
LARGEST CITY Phoenix
HIGHEST POINT Humphreys Pk. 12,633 ft.
SETTLED IN 1580
ADMITTED TO UNION February 14, 1912
POPULAR NAME Grand Canyon State
STATE FLOWER Saguaro Cactus Blossom
STATE BIRD Cactus Wren

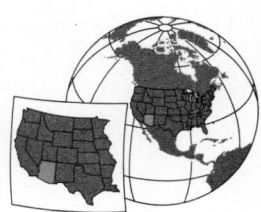

Agriculture, Industry and Resources

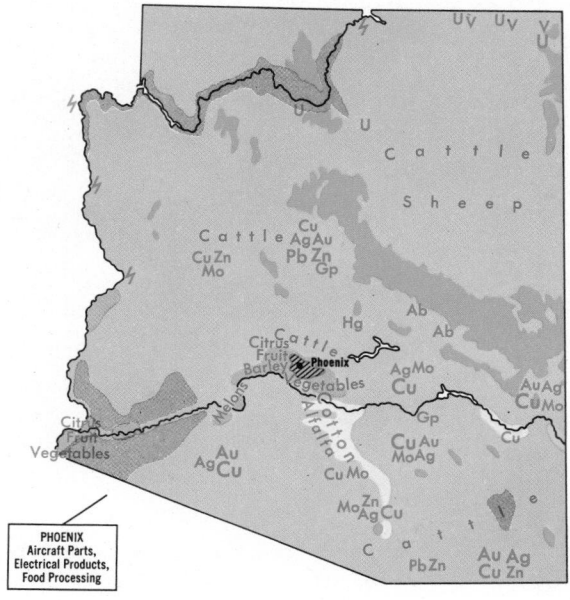

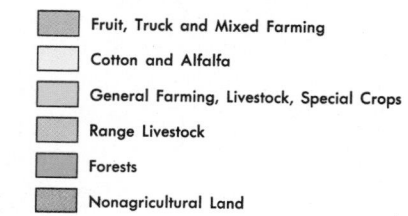

PHOENIX
Aircraft Parts,
Electrical Products,
Food Processing

MAJOR MINERAL OCCURRENCES

Ab	Asbestos	Gp	Gypsum	U	Uranium
Ag	Silver	Hg	Mercury	V	Vanadium
Au	Gold	Mo	Molybdenum	Zn	Zinc
Cu	Copper	Pb	Lead		

DOMINANT LAND USE

- Fruit, Truck and Mixed Farming
- Cotton and Alfalfa
- General Farming, Livestock, Special Crops
- Range Livestock
- Forests
- Nonagricultural Land

⚡ Water Power

▨ Major Industrial Areas

COUNTIES

Apache, 32,298	F 3
Cochise, 61,910	F 7
Coconino, 48,326	C 3
Gila, 29,255	E 5
Graham, 16,578	E 6
Greenlee, 10,330	F 5
Maricopa, 967,522	C 5
Mohave, 25,857	A 3
Navajo, 47,715	E 3
Pima, 351,667	D 6
Pinal, 67,916	D 6
Santa Cruz, 13,966	E 7
Yavapai, 36,733	C 4
Yuma, 60,827	A 5

CITIES and TOWNS

Zip	Name/Pop.	Key
† 85333	Agua Caliente, 30	B 6
85320	Aguila, 450	B 5
85321	Ajo, 5,881	C 6
85920	Alpine, 450	F 5
85640	Amado, 75	D 7
85220	Apache Junction, 2,390	D 5
† 85901	Aripine, 25	E 4
85601	Arivaca, 165	D 7
85322	Arlington, 950	C 5
85320	Ash Fork, 800	C 3
85323	Avondale, 6,304	C 5
† 85333	Aztec, 20	B 6
86321	Bagdad, 2,079	B 4
85221	Bapchule, 300	D 5
86001	Bellemont, 6	D 3
85602	Benson, 2,839	E 7
85603	Bisbee⊙, 8,328	F 7
85324	Black Canyon City, 600	C 4
85922	Blue, 50	F 5
† 85643	Bonita, 20	E 6
85325	Bouse, 200	A 5
85605	Bowie, 600	F 6
85326	Buckeye, 2,599	C 5
86430	Bullhead City, 2,900	A 3
85327	Bumble Bee, 15	C 4
85530	Bylas, 1,125	E 5
† 85530	Calva, 10	E 5
86020	Cameron, 600	D 3
86322	Camp Verde, 1,500	D 4
† 86022	Cane Beds, 30	B 2
85331	Carefree, 350	D 5
† 85640	Carmen, 200	D 7
85222	Casa Grande, 10,536	D 6
85329	Cashion, 2,705	C 5
† 85342	Castle Hot Springs, 50	C 5
85331	Cave Creek, 300	D 5
† 85501	Central Heights, 2,289	E 5
86502	Chambers, 500	F 3

85224	Chandler, 13,763	D 5
† 86327	Cherry, 20	C 4
86503	Chinle, 500	F 2
86323	Chino Valley, 970	C 4
86431	Chloride, 225	A 3
† 85292	Christmas, 201	E 5
85901	Cibecue, 100	E 4
86324	Clarkdale, 892	C 4
85532	Claypool, 2,245	E 5
85934	Clay Springs, 225	E 4
86326	Clemenceau, 300	C 4
85533	Clifton⊙, 5,087	F 5
85606	Cochise, 150	F 6
86021	Colorado City, 350	B 2
85924	Concho, 100	F 4
85332	Congress, 350	C 4
† 85640	Continental, 250	D 7
85228	Coolidge, 4,651	D 6
85542	Coolidge Dam, 42	E 5
† 86505	Cornfields, 200	F 3
86325	Cornville, 425	D 4
85230	Cortaro, 75	D 6
86326	Cottonwood, 2,815	D 4
86333	Crown King, 100	C 4
85333	Dateland, 100	B 6
† 86430	Davis Dam, 125	A 3
86327	Dewey, 90	C 4
† 86047	Dilkon, 90	E 3
85364	Dome, 48	A 6
† 85643	Dos Cabezas, 30	F 6
85607	Douglas, 12,462	F 7
85609	Dragoon, 150	F 6
85534	Duncan, 773	F 6
85925	Eagar, 1,279	F 4
85535	Eden, 89	F 4
85334	Ehrenburg, 93	A 5
† 85617	Elfrida, 700	F 7
† 85637	Elgin, 247	E 7
85335	El Mirage, 3,258	C 5
85231	Eloy, 5,381	D 6
85612	Fairbank, 100	E 7
86001	Flagstaff⊙, 26,117	D 3
85232	Florence⊙, 2,173	D 5
85233	Florence Junction, 35	D 5
85234	Gilbert, 1,971	D 5
85926	Fort Apache, 500	F 5
86504	Fort Defiance, 900	F 3
85643	Fort Grant, 240	E 6
85613	Fort Huachuca, 159	E 7
85536	Fort Thomas, 450	F 5
85534	Franklin, 300	F 6
86022	Fredonia, 798	C 2
85336	Gadsden, 250	A 6
86505	Ganado, 300	F 3
† 85536	Geronimo, 25	F 5
85337	Gila Bend, 1,795	C 6
† 85617	Gleeson, 15	F 7
85301	Glendale, 36,228	C 5
85501	Globe⊙, 7,333	E 5

85338	Goodyear, 2,140	C 5
86023	Grand Canyon, 1,011	C 2
† 85637	Greaterville, 15	E 7
85614	Green Valley, 5,971	D 7
85927	Greer, 60	F 4
† 85634	Gu-Achi, 339	C 6
86401	Hackberry, 250	B 3
86024	Happy Jack, 50	D 4
85235	Hayden, 1,283	E 5
85928	Heber, 750	E 4
85615	Hereford, 10	E 7
85236	Higley, 500	D 5
† 86301	Hillside, 100	B 4
† 85632	Hilltop, 9	F 6
86025	Holbrook⊙, 4,759	E 4
86030	Hotevilla, 600	E 3
86506	Houck, 325	F 3
85616	Huachuca City, 1,233	E 7
86329	Humboldt, 424	C 4
86031	Indian Wells, 100	E 3
85537	Inspiration, 500	D 5
86330	Iron Springs, 175	C 4
86022	Jacob Lake, 16	C 2
86025	Jeddito, 20	E 3
86331	Jerome, 290	C 4
86032	Joseph City, 650	E 4
86044	Kaibito, 275	D 2
† 86401	Katherine Landing, 102	A 3
86033	Kayenta, 500	E 2
86034	Keams Canyon, 400	E 3
85237	Kearny, 2,829	E 5
86401	Kingman⊙, 7,312	A 3
86027	Kirkland, 100	C 4
† 86505	Klagetoh, 200	F 3
85643	Klondyke, 86	E 6
85538	Kohls Ranch, 100	D 4
† 85339	Komatke, 300	C 5
86403	Lake Havasu City, 5,700	A 4
85929	Lakeside, 700	E 4
85339	Laveen, 800	C 5
† 86036	Lees Ferry, 10	D 2
86035	Leupp, 150	E 3
† 85326	Liberty, 150	C 5
† 85901	Linden, 50	E 4
85340	Litchfield Park, 1,664	C 5
86432	Littlefield, 40	B 2
86507	Lukachukai, 350	F 2
85341	Lukeville, 50	C 7
86508	Lupton, 250	F 3
† 85637	Madera Canyon, 75	E 7
85618	Mammoth, 1,953	F 6
86503	Many Farms, 250	F 2
85238	Marana, 2,900	D 6
86036	Marble Canyon, 6	D 2
85239	Maricopa, 750	C 5
† 85920	Maverick, 50	F 5
86333	Mayer, 810	C 4
85930	McNary, 950	F 4
85617	McNeal, 100	F 7

(continued on following page)

Indigo-blue Lake Mead is surrounded by color-streaked cliffs and ranges, set off by the bright concrete of Arizona's Hoover Dam. One of the world's largest man-made lakes, Lake Mead provides water storage, dependable water supply and water sports.

Ray Manley — Shostal Associates

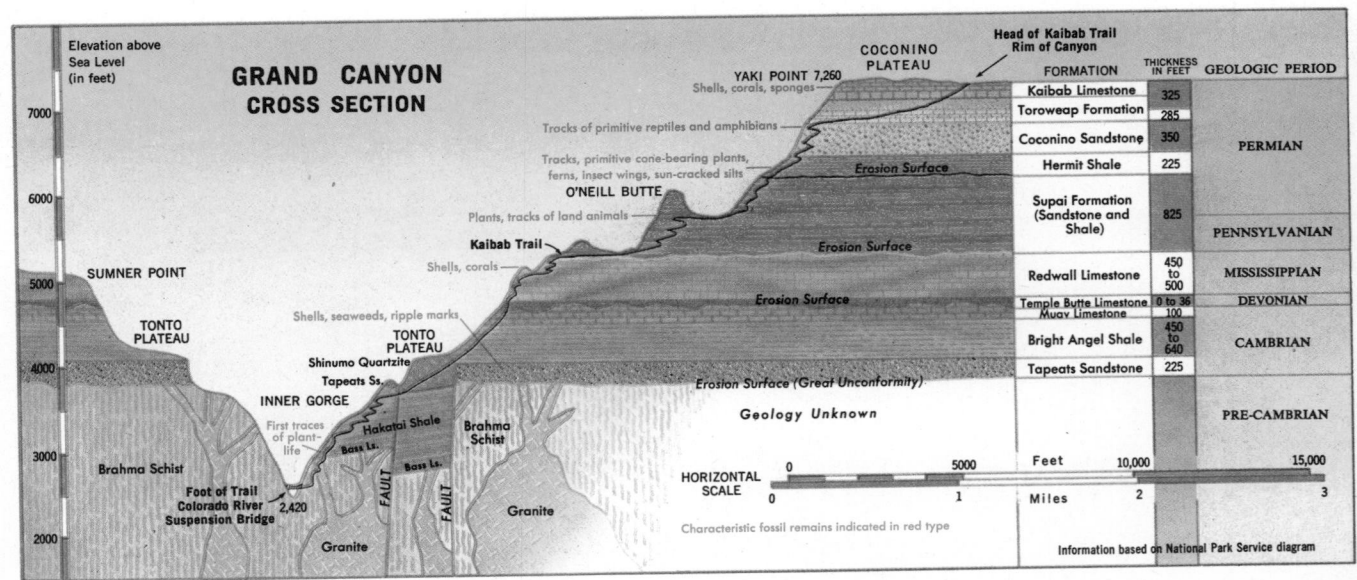

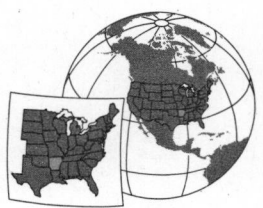

COUNTIES

Arkansas, 23,347	H 5	
Ashley, 24,976	G 7	
Baxter, 15,319	F 1	
Benton, 50,476	B 1	
Boone, 19,073	D 1	
Bradley, 12,778	F 7	
Calhoun, 5,573	E 6	
Carroll, 12,301	C 1	
Chicot, 18,164	H 7	
Clark, 21,537	D 5	
Clay, 18,771	K 1	
Cleburne, 10,349	F 2	
Cleveland, 6,605	F 6	
Columbia, 25,952	D 7	
Conway, 16,805	E 3	
Craighead, 52,068	J 2	
Crawford, 25,677	B 2	
Crittenden, 48,106	K 3	
Cross, 19,783	J 3	
Dallas, 10,022	E 6	
Desha, 18,761	H 6	
Drew, 15,157	G 6	
Faulkner, 31,572	F 3	

Franklin, 11,301	C 2	
Fulton, 7,699	G 1	
Garland, 54,131	D 4	
Grant, 9,711	F 5	
Greene, 24,765	J 1	
Hempstead, 19,308	C 6	
Hot Spring, 21,963	E 5	
Howard, 11,412	C 5	
Independence, 22,723	G 2	
Izard, 7,381	G 1	
Jackson, 20,452	H 2	
Jefferson, 85,329	G 5	
Johnson, 13,630	C 2	
Lafayette, 10,018	C 7	
Lawrence, 16,320	H 1	
Lee, 18,884	J 4	
Lincoln, 12,913	G 6	
Little River, 11,194	B 6	
Logan, 16,789	C 3	
Lonoke, 26,249	G 4	
Madison, 9,453	C 1	
Marion, 7,000	E 1	
Miller, 33,385	C 7	
Mississippi, 62,060	K 2	
Monroe, 15,657	H 4	
Montgomery, 5,821	C 4	

Nevada, 10,111	D 6	
Newton, 5,844	D 2	
Ouachita, 30,896	E 6	
Perry, 5,634	E 4	
Phillips, 40,046	J 5	
Pike, 8,711	C 5	
Poinsett, 26,822	J 2	
Polk, 13,297	B 5	
Pope, 28,607	D 3	
Prairie, 10,249	G 4	
Pulaski, 287,189	F 4	
Randolph, 12,645	H 1	
Saint Francis, 30,799	J 4	
Saline, 36,107	E 4	
Scott, 8,207	B 4	
Searcy, 7,731	E 2	
Sebastian, 79,237	B 3	
Sevier, 11,272	B 6	
Sharp, 8,233	G 1	
Stone, 6,838	F 2	
Union, 45,428	E 7	
Van Buren, 8,275	E 2	
Washington, 77,370	B 2	
White, 39,253	G 3	
Woodruff, 11,566	H 3	
Yell, 14,208	D 3	

AREA 53,104 sq. mi.
POPULATION 1,923,295
CAPITAL Little Rock
LARGEST CITY Little Rock
HIGHEST POINT Magazine Mtn. 2,753 ft.
SETTLED IN 1685
ADMITTED TO UNION June 15, 1836
POPULAR NAME Land of Opportunity; Wonder State
STATE FLOWER Apple Blossom
STATE BIRD Mockingbird

DOMINANT LAND USE

Fruit and Mixed Farming

Specialized Cotton

Cotton, General Farming

Rice, General Farming

General Farming, Livestock, Truck Farming, Cotton

Forests

Swampland, Limited Agriculture

MAJOR MINERAL OCCURRENCES

Al	Bauxite		G	Natural Gas
Ba	Barite		Gp	Gypsum
C	Coal		Mr	Marble
Cl	Clay		O	Petroleum
D	Diamonds		Sp	Soapstone
		Zn	Zinc	

⚡ Water Power   ▨ Major Industrial Areas

Agriculture, Industry and Resources

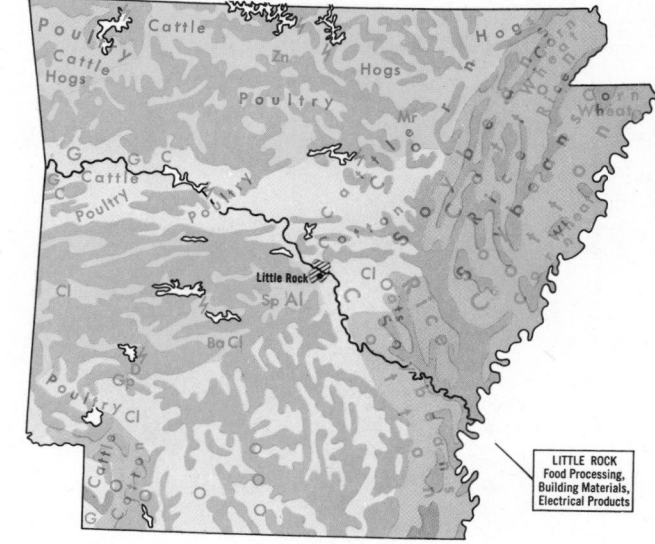

LITTLE ROCK
Food Processing,
Building Materials,
Electrical Products

Soybeans, Arkansas' leading cash crop, valued primarily as high protein food and feed, also has a wide range of uses, including plastics and agricultural sprays.

Eric Carle — Shostal Associates

CITIES and TOWNS

Zip	Name/Pop.	Key
72920	Abbott, 210	B 3
72001	Adona, 130	E 3
72510	Agnos, 130	G 1
72002	Alexander, 297	F 4
72410	Alicia, 246	H 2
72820	Alix, 250	C 3
† 72046	Allport, 307	G 4
72921	Alma, 1,613	B 3
72003	Almyra, 220	H 5
72611	Alpena, 309	D 1
72004	Altheimer, 1,037	G 5
72821	Altus, 418	C 3
72005	Amagon, 136	H 2
71921	Amity, 614	D 5
71922	Antoine, 182	D 5
72822	Appleton, 150	E 3
71923	Arkadelphia⊙, 9,841	D 5
71630	Arkansas City⊙, 615	H 6
† 72055	Arkansas Post, 15	H 5
72310	Armorel, 300	L 2
71822	Ashdown⊙, 3,522	B 6
72513	Ash Flat⊙, 211	G 1
72823	Atkins, 2,015	E 3
72311	Aubrey, 351	J 4
72006	Augusta⊙, 2,777	H 3
72007	Austin, 236	G 4
72008	Auvergne, 150	H 2
72711	Avoca, 173	B 1
72010	Bald Knob, 2,094	G 3
71631	Banks, 189	F 6
72923	Barling, 1,739	B 3
72312	Barton, 400	J 4
72313	Bassett, 265	K 2
72501	Batesville⊙, 7,209	G 2
72411	Bay, 751	J 2
71720	Bearden, 1,199	E 6
72012	Beebe, 2,805	G 3
72014	Beedeville, 144	H 3
71721	Beirne, 140	D 6
72712	Bella Vista, 500	B 1
† 72601	Bellefonte, 300	D 1
72824	Belleville, 379	D 3
71823	Ben Lomond, 155	B 6
72015	Benton⊙, 16,499	E 4
72712	Bentonville⊙, 5,508	B 1
72615	Bergman, 249	E 1
72616	Berryville⊙, 2,271	C 1
† 72764	Bethel Heights, 284	B 1
† 72501	Bethesda, 285	G 2
72016	Bigelow, 258	E 3
72617	Bigflat, 189	F 1
72413	Biggers, 372	J 1
† 72386	Birdsong, 150	K 3
72017	Biscoe, 340	H 4
71929	Bismarck, 200	D 5

Zip	Name/Pop.	Key
72414	Black Oak, 272	K 2
72415	Black Rock, 498	H 1
† 72069	Blackton, 175	H 4
71825	Blevins, 265	C 6
† 72933	Bloomer, 150	B 3
71722	Bluff City, 244	D 6
72827	Bluffton, 198	C 4
72315	Blytheville⊙, 24,752	L 2
† 71858	Bodcaw, 158	D 6
72926	Boles, 163	B 4
† 72901	Bonanza, 342	B 3
72416	Bono, 428	J 2
72927	Booneville⊙, 3,239	C 3
72020	Bradford, 826	G 3
71826	Bradley, 706	C 7
72928	Branch, 325	C 3
† 72017	Brasfield, 200	H 4
72828	Briggsville, 200	C 4
72021	Brinkley, 5,275	H 4
72618	Bruno, 130	E 1
72022	Bryant, 1,199	F 4
71827	Buckner, 392	D 7
72619	Bull Shoals, 430	E 1
72321	Burdette, 173	L 2
72023	Cabot, 2,903	F 4
72322	Caldwell, 292	J 3
72519	Calico Rock, 723	F 1
71724	Calion, 535	E 7
71701	Camden⊙, 15,147	E 6
† 72201	Cammack Village, 1,165	E 4
† 72473	Campbell Station, 218	H 2
71829	Canfield, 365	C 7
72419	Caraway, 952	K 2
72024	Carlisle, 2,048	G 4
71725	Carthage, 566	E 5
72025	Casa, 208	D 3
72421	Cash, 265	J 2
72026	Casscoe, 200	H 4
† 72951	Caulksville, 208	C 3
72521	Cave City, 807	G 2
72718	Cave Springs, 469	B 1
72930	Cecil, 234	C 3
72450	Center Hill, 1,201	J 1
71830	Center Point, 144	C 5
72027	Center Ridge, 220	E 3
72719	Centerton, 312	B 1
71901	Central City, 150	B 3
† 71832	Chapel Hill, 154	B 5
72933	Charleston⊙, 1,497	B 3
72522	Charlotte, 158	H 2
72323	Cherokee Village, 1,300	K 3
72542	Cherokee Village, 1,300	G 1
† 71953	Cherry Hill, 250	B 4
72324	Cherry Valley, 556	J 3
71726	Chidester, 232	D 6
72029	Clarendon⊙, 2,563	H 4

Zip	Name/Pop.	Key
72325	Clarkedale, 250	K 3
72830	Clarksville⊙, 4,616	D 3
72031	Clinton⊙, 1,029	F 2
72832	Coal Hill, 733	C 3
72476	College City, 645	J 1
71655	College Heights, 2,050	G 6
72326	Colt, 301	J 3
71831	Columbus, 258	C 6
72523	Concord, 163	G 2
72032	Conway⊙, 15,510	F 3
72422	Corning⊙, 2,705	J 1
72626	Cotter, 858	E 1
72036	Cotton Plant, 1,657	H 3
71937	Cove, 334	B 5
72037	Coy, 240	G 4
72327	Crawfordsville, 831	K 3
71635	Crossett, 6,191	G 7
71728	Curtis, 500	D 5
72526	Cushman, 427	G 2
† 71923	Dalark, 132	E 5
72039	Damascus, 255	F 3
72833	Danville⊙, 1,362	D 3
72834	Dardanelle⊙, 3,297	D 3
72424	Datto, 142	J 1
72722	Decatur, 847	A 1
72723	Delaney, 150	C 2
72425	Delaplaine, 145	J 1
72835	Delaware, 200	D 3
71940	Delight, 439	C 5
72426	Dell, 358	K 2
72836	Denning, 203	C 3
71832	De Queen⊙, 3,863	B 5
71638	Dermott, 4,250	H 7
72040	Des Arc⊙, 1,714	G 4
72041	De Valls Bluff⊙, 622	H 4
72042	De Witt⊙, 3,728	H 5
72644	Diamond City, 282	E 1
72043	Diaz, 283	H 2
71833	Dierks, 1,101	B 5
71834	Doddridge, 125	C 7
71941	Donaldson, 500	E 5
72837	Dover, 662	D 3
72530	Drasco, 300	G 2
† 72943	Driggs, 125	C 3
71639	Dumas, 4,600	H 6
72935	Dyer, 486	B 3
71729	Eagle Mills, 149	E 6
72331	Earle, 3,146	K 3
71701	East Camden, 589	E 6
72044	Edgemont, 125	F 2
72332	Edmondson, 412	K 3
72333	Elaine, 1,210	J 5
71730	El Dorado, 25,283	E 7
72727	Elkins, 418	C 1
72728	Elm Springs, 260	B 1
72045	El Paso, 131	F 3
71740	Emerson, 393	D 7
71835	Emmet, 433	D 6

(continued on following page)

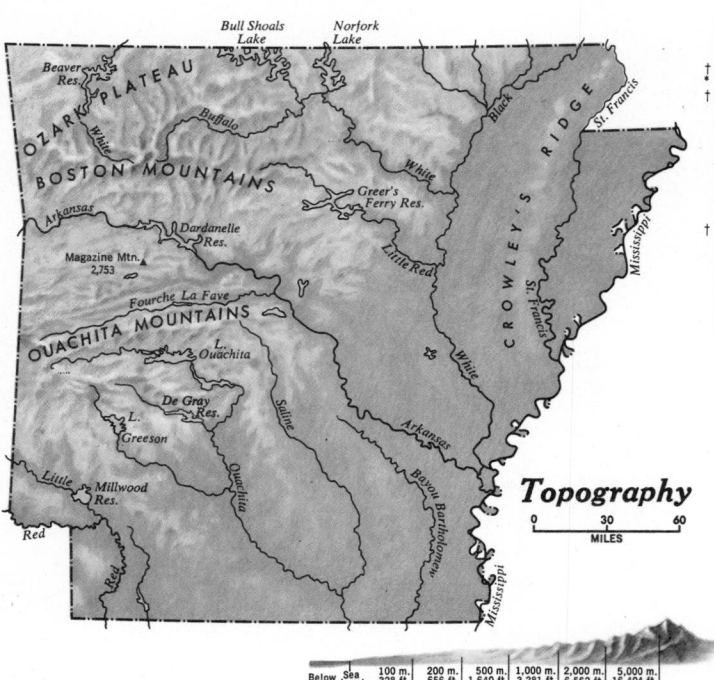

Topography

0   30   60
MILES

Below Sea Level | 100 m. 328 ft. | 200 m. 656 ft. | 500 m. 1,640 ft. | 1,000 m. 3,281 ft. | 2,000 m. 6,562 ft. | 5,000 m. 16,404 ft.

72658 Norfork, 266......F 1
71960 Norman, 360......C 5
71759 Norphlet, 755......E 7
71635 North Crossett, 2,891......J 7
*72114 North Little Rock, 60,040......F 4
72386 Norvell, 440......K 3
†72660 Oakgrove, 236......C 1
71961 Oden, 141......C 4
71853 Ogden, 286......B 6
72564 Oil Trough, 524......G 2
72449 O'Kean, 244......J 1
71962 Okolona, 233......D 5
72662 Omaha, 160......D 1
72369 Oneida, 300......J 5
72110 Oppelo, 147......E 3
72370 Osceola⊙, 7,204......K 2
72565 Oxford, 271......G 1
71855 Ozan, 134......C 6
72949 Ozark⊙, 2,592......C 3
72372 Palestine, 755......J 4
72121 Pangburn, 654......G 3
72450 Paragould⊙, 10,639......J 1

72855 Paris⊙, 3,646......C 3
71661 Parkdale, 459......H 7
72373 Parkin, 1,731......J 3
72950 Parks, 358......B 4
72123 Patterson, 417......H 3
72453 Peach Orchard, 256......J 1
71964 Pearcy, 200......D 5
72751 Pea Ridge, 1,088......C 1
71965 Pencil Bluff, 200......C 4
72124 Perla, 227......D 5
72125 Perry, 218......E 3
71801 Perrytown, 148......C 6
72126 Perryville⊙, 815......E 3
72752 Pettigrew, 300......C 2
71662 Pickens, 200......H 6
72454 Piggott⊙, 3,087......K 1
72669 Pindall, 154......D 1
71601 Pine Bluff⊙, 57,389......F 5
      Pine Bluff, ‡85,329......F 5
72857 Plainview, 677......D 4
72568 Pleasant Plains, 162......G 2
72127 Plumerville, 724......E 3
72455 Pocahontas⊙, 4,544......H 1

72456 Pollard, 253......K 1
72374 Poplar Grove, 255......J 4
72457 Portia, 381......H 1
71663 Portland, 662......H 7
72858 Pottsville, 411......D 3
72569 Poughkeepsie, 130......H 1
72128 Poyen, 265......E 5
72753 Prairie Grove, 1,582......B 2
72859 Prairie View, 150......C 3
72129 Prattsville, 299......F 5
71857 Prescott⊙, 3,921......D 6
72672 Pyatt, 137......E 1
72131 Quitman, 354......F 3
72951 Ratcliff, 184......C 3
†72333 Ratio, 200......J 5
72459 Ravenden, 219......H 1
71726 Reader, 143......D 6
72461 Readland, 225......H 7
72461 Rector, 1,990......K 1
72132 Redfield, 277......F 5
71670 Reed, 403......H 6
72462 Reyno, 356......H 1
71665 Rison⊙, 1,214......F 6

72046 England, 3,075......G 4
72047 Enola, 150......F 3
72048 Ethel, 350......H 5
72428 Etowah, 150......K 2
71640 Eudora, 3,687......H 7
72632 Eureka Springs⊙, 1,670......C 1
72729 Evansville, 427......B 2
72532 Evening Shade, 309......G 1
†72936 Excelsior, 160......B 3
72397 Fair Oaks, 270......J 3
72049 Fargo, 206......H 4
72730 Farmington, 908......B 1
72701 Fayetteville⊙, 30,729......B 1
71747 Felsenthal, 150......F 7
72429 Fisher, 361......J 2
72634 Flippen, 626......E 1
72534 Floral, 165......G 2
71742 Fordyce⊙, 4,837......F 6
71836 Foreman, 1,173......B 6
†72031 Formosa, 224......E 3
72335 Forrest City⊙, 12,521......J 3
72901 Fort Smith⊙, 62,802......B 3
      Fort Smith, ‡160,421......B 3
71837 Fouke, 506......C 7
71642 Fountain Hill, 266......G 7
72051 Fox, 200......F 2
72017 Fredonia (Biscoe), 340......H 4
71942 Friendship, 150......E 5
71838 Fulton, 323......C 6
72732 Garfield, 163......C 1
71839 Garland, 321......C 7
72052 Garner, 150......G 3
72635 Gassville, 434......F 1
71840 Genoa, 125......C 7
72734 Gentry, 1,022......A 1
72054 Georgetown, 137......G 3
72055 Gillett, 860......H 5
71841 Gillham, 200......B 6
72339 Gilmore, 461......K 3
71943 Glenwood, 1,212......C 5
72340 Goodwin, 125......J 4
†72315 Gosnell, 1,386......K 2
71643 Gould, 1,683......G 5
71644 Grady, 688......G 5
71944 Grannis, 177......B 4
72838 Gravelly, 300......C 4
72736 Gravette, 1,154......B 1
72058 Greenbrier, 582......F 3
72638 Green Forest, 1,354......D 1
72737 Greenland, 650......B 1
72430 Greenway, 240......K 1
72936 Greenwood⊙, 2,032......B 3
†72067 Greers Ferry, 389......F 2
72059 Gregory, 311......H 3
72060 Griffithville, 227......G 3
72431 Grubbs, 442......J 2
72540 Guion, 213......G 2
†71923 Gum Springs, 269......D 5
71743 Gurdon, 2,075......D 6
72061 Guy, 179......F 3
72937 Hackett, 462......B 3
71645 Halley, 204......H 6
71646 Hamburg⊙, 3,102......H 7
71744 Hampton⊙, 1,252......F 6
72542 Hardy, 692......H 1
71745 Harrell, 269......F 7
72432 Harrisburg⊙, 1,931......J 2
72601 Harrison⊙, 7,239......D 1
72938 Hartford, 616......B 3
72840 Hartman, 400......C 3
72062 Haskell, 239......E 4
71945 Hatfield, 377......B 5
72063 Hattieville, 163......E 3
72842 Havana, 308......D 3
72341 Haynes, 375......J 4

72064 Hazen, 1,605......G 4
72543 Heber Springs⊙, 2,497......G 2
72843 Hector, 387......E 3
72342 Helena⊙, 10,415......J 4
72065 Hensley, 350......F 4
71647 Hermitage, 399......F 7
72066 Hickory Plains, 200......G 3
72347 Hickory Ridge, 410......J 3
72068 Higginson, 225......G 3
72739 Hiwasse, 175......B 1
†72857 Hollis, 275......D 4
72069 Holly Grove, 840......H 4
71923 Hollywood, 175......D 5
72939 Hon, 250......B 4
71801 Hope⊙, 8,810......C 6
71842 Horatio, 748......B 6
72536 Horseshoe Bend, 321......G 1
71901 Hot Springs National Park⊙,
      35,631......D 4
72070 Houston, 200......E 3
72433 Hoxie, 2,265......H 1
†72315 Huffman, 150......L 2
72348 Hughes, 1,872......J 4
72349 Hulbert, 500......K 3
72072 Humnoke, 398......G 4
72073 Humphrey, 818......G 5
72074 Hunter, 131......H 3
72940 Huntington, 627......B 3
72740 Huntsville⊙, 1,287......C 1
71747 Huttig, 822......F 7
72434 Imboden, 496......H 1
72075 Jacksonport, 306......H 2
72076 Jacksonville, 19,832......F 4
72641 Jasper⊙, 394......D 1
72079 Jefferson, 250......F 5
71649 Jennie, 172......H 7
72901 Jenny Lind, 250......B 3
†72327 Jericho, 150......K 3
72080 Jerusalem, 250......E 3
71949 Jessieville, 248......D 4
72741 Johnson, 274......B 1
72350 Joiner, 839......K 3
72401 Jonesboro⊙, 27,050......J 2
72105 Jones Mill, 850......E 5
72081 Judsonia, 1,667......G 3
71749 Junction City, 763......E 7
72351 Keiser, 688......K 2
72082 Kensett, 1,444......G 3
72083 Keo, 226......G 4
†72956 Kibler, 611......B 3
71652 Kingsland, 304......F 6
72742 Kingston, 200......C 1
71950 Kirby, 300......C 5
72436 Knobel, 375......J 1
72845 Knoxville, 202......D 3
72436 Lafe, 160......J 1
72352 La Grange, 350......J 4
72437 Lake City⊙, 948......K 2
71653 Lake Village⊙, 3,310......H 7
72846 Lamar, 589......D 3
71929 Lambert, 200......D 5
71844 Laneburg, 150......D 6
71952 Langley, 200......C 5
72941 Lavaca, 532......B 3
71750 Lawson, 300......E 7
72438 Leachville, 1,582......K 2
72644 Lead Hill, 143......D 1
72084 Leola, 390......E 5
72354 Lepanto, 1,846......K 2
72645 Leslie, 563......E 2
72085 Letona, 191......G 3
71845 Lewisville⊙, 1,653......C 7
72355 Lexa, 500......J 4
72646 Limestone, 200......D 2
72744 Lincoln, 1,023......B 2

*72201 Little Rock (cap.)⊙
      132,483......F 4
      Little Rock-North Little Rock
      ‡323,296......F 4
71846 Lockesburg, 620......B 6
72550 Locust Grove, 225......G 2
72847 London, 539......D 3
72086 Lonoke⊙, 3,140......G 4
71751 Louann, 245......E 7
72545 Lowell, 653......B 1
†72856 Lurton, 150......D 2
72358 Luxora, 1,566......K 2
72440 Lynn, 274......H 1
72103 Mabelvale, 350......F 4
†71753 Macedonia, 150......D 7
72359 Madison, 984......J 3
72943 Magazine, 677......C 3
72553 Magness, 139......H 2
†72104 Magnet, 230......E 5
71753 Magnolia⊙, 11,303......D 7
72104 Malvern⊙, 8,739......E 5
72554 Mammoth Spring, 1,072......G 1
72442 Manila, 1,961......K 2
72944 Mansfield, 981......B 3
72555 Marcella, 136......G 2
72114 Marche, 150......F 4
72360 Marianna⊙, 6,196......J 4
72364 Marion⊙, 1,634......K 3
72365 Marked Tree, 3,208......K 2
72443 Marmaduke, 821......K 1
72650 Marshall⊙, 1,397......E 2
72366 Marvell, 1,980......J 4
72106 Mayflower, 469......F 4
72444 Maynard, 224......J 1
72747 Maysville, 200......A 1
†72006 McClelland, 200......H 3
72101 McCrory, 1,378......H 3
72441 McDougal, 328......K 1
71654 McGehee, 4,683......H 6
71849 McNab, 201......C 6
71752 McNeil, 684......D 7
72102 McRae, 643......G 3
72556 Melbourne⊙, 1,043......G 1
71953 Mena⊙, 4,530......B 4
72107 Menifee, 251......E 3
72945 Midland, 294......B 3
71851 Mineral Springs, 761......C 6
†71639 Mitchellville, 494......H 6
72447 Monette, 1,076......K 2
72108 Monroe, 200......H 4
71655 Monticello⊙, 5,085......G 6
71658 Montrose, 558......H 7
72558 Moorefield, 127......G 2
72109 Morganton, 144......F 3
72368 Moro, 489......J 4
72110 Morrilton⊙, 6,814......E 3
71659 Moscow, 250......G 5
72946 Mountainburg, 524......B 2
72653 Mountain Home⊙, 3,936......F 1
71956 Mountain Pine, 800......D 4
72560 Mountain View⊙, 1,866......F 2
71758 Mount Holly, 300......E 7
71957 Mount Ida⊙, 819......C 4
72655 Mount Judea, 500......D 2
72561 Mount Pleasant, 346......G 2
72111 Mount Vernon, 200......F 3
72947 Mulberry, 1,340......C 2
71958 Murfreesboro⊙, 1,350......C 5
71852 Nashville⊙, 4,016......C 6
72562 Newark, 849......H 2
71660 New Edinburg, 304......F 6
71959 Newhope, 130......C 5
72112 Newport⊙, 7,725......H 2
72448 Nimmons, 135......K 1
†71601 Noble Lake, 350......G 5

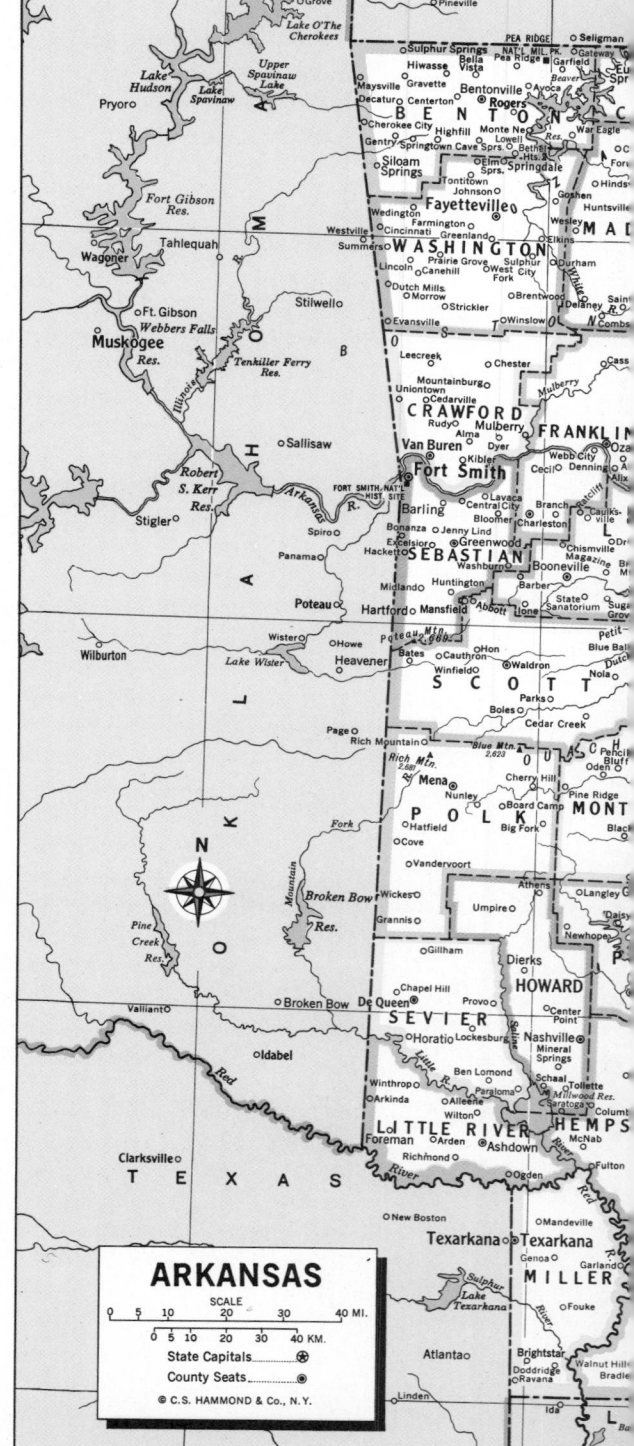

ARKANSAS
SCALE
0 5 10   20   30   40 MI.
0 5 10 20   30   40 KM.
State Capitals......⊛
County Seats......⊙

© C.S. HAMMOND & Co., N.Y.

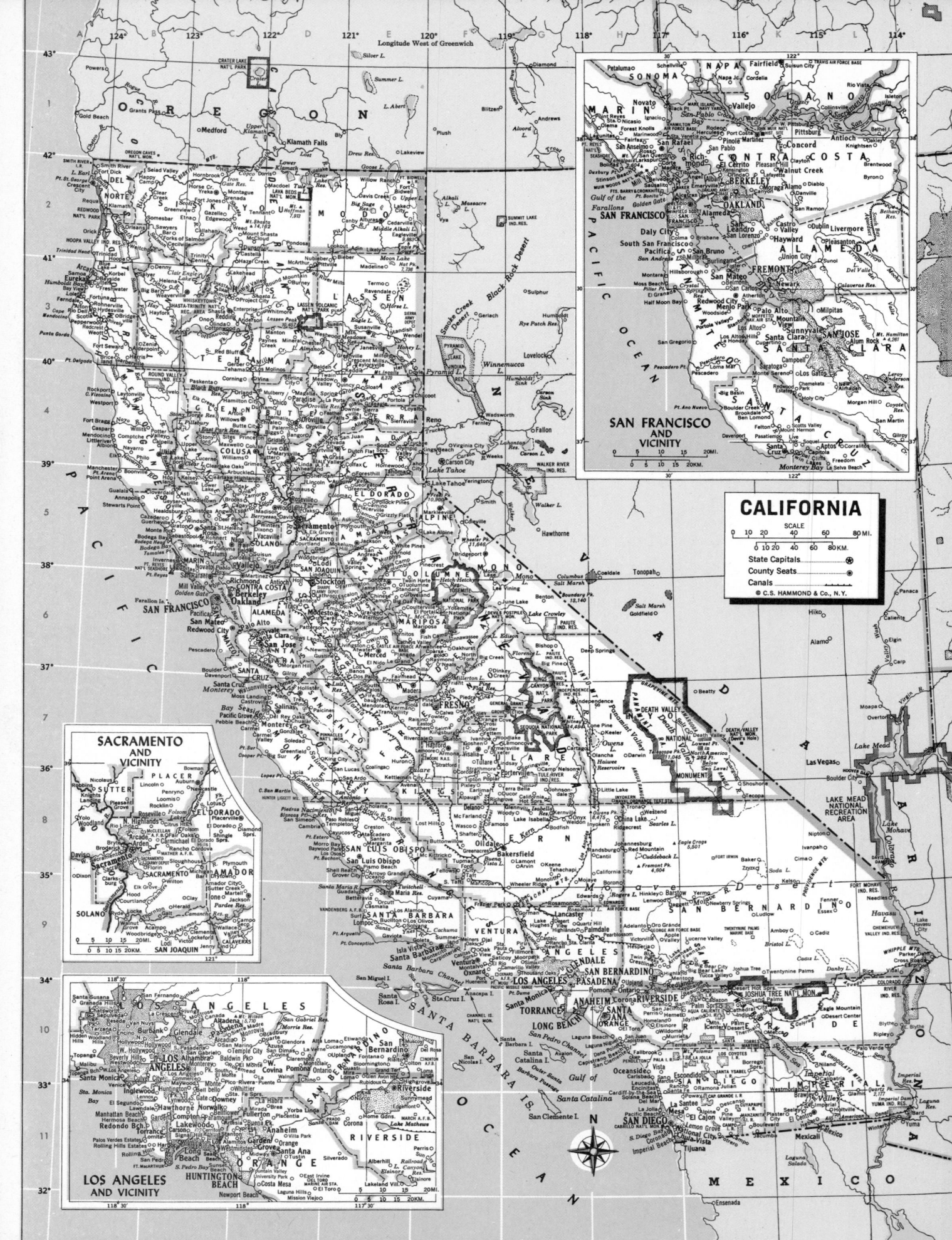

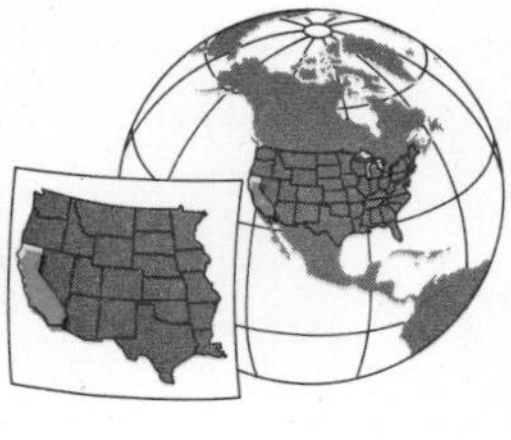

AREA 158,693 sq. mi.
POPULATION 19,953,134
CAPITAL Sacramento
LARGEST CITY Los Angeles
HIGHEST POINT Mt. Whitney 14,494 ft.
SETTLED IN 1769
ADMITTED TO UNION September 9, 1850
POPULAR NAME Golden State
STATE FLOWER Golden Poppy
STATE BIRD California Valley Quail

COUNTIES

Alameda, 1,073,184 D 6
Alpine, 484 F 5
Amador, 11,821 E 5
Butte, 101,969 D 4
Calaveras, 13,585 E 5
Colusa, 12,430 C 4
Contra Costa, 558,389 D 6
Del Norte, 14,580 B 2
El Dorado, 43,833 E 5
Fresno, 413,053 E 7
Glenn, 17,521 C 4
Humboldt, 99,692 B 3
Imperial, 74,492 K 10
Inyo, 15,571 H 7
Kern, 329,162 G 8
Kings, 64,610 F 8
Lake, 19,548 C 4
Lassen, 14,960 E 3
Los Angeles, 7,032,075 G 9
Madera, 41,519 F 6
Marin, 206,038 C 5
Mariposa, 6,015 E 6
Mendocino, 51,101 B 4
Merced, 104,629 E 6
Modoc, 7,469 E 2
Mono, 4,016 F 5
Monterey, 250,071 D 7
Napa, 79,140 C 5
Nevada, 26,346 E 4
Orange, 1,420,386 H 10
Placer, 77,306 E 4
Plumas, 11,707 E 4
Riverside, 459,074 J 10
Sacramento, 631,498 D 5
San Benito, 18,226 D 7
San Bernardino, 684,072 J 9
San Diego, 1,357,854 J 10
San Francisco (city county), 715,674 J 2
San Joaquin, 290,208 D 6
San Luis Obispo, 105,690 E 8
San Mateo, 556,234 C 6
Santa Barbara, 264,324 E 9
Santa Clara, 1,064,714 D 6
Santa Cruz, 123,790 C 6
Shasta, 77,640 C 3
Sierra, 2,365 E 4
Siskiyou, 33,225 C 2
Solano, 169,941 D 5
Sonoma, 204,885 C 5
Stanislaus, 194,506 D 6
Sutter, 41,935 D 4
Tehama, 29,517 C 3
Trinity, 7,615 B 3
Tulare, 188,322 G 7
Tuolumne, 22,169 F 5
Ventura, 376,430 F 9
Yolo, 91,788 D 5
Yuba, 44,736 D 4

CITIES and TOWNS

Zip Name/Pop. Key

92301 Adelanto, 2,115 H 9
96006 Adin, 550 E 2
93601 Ahwahnee, 503 F 6
94501 Alameda, 70,968 J 2
94507 Alamo-Danville, 14,059 K 2
94706 Albany, 14,674 J 2
* 91801 Alhambra, 62,125 C 10
93201 Alpaugh, 800 F 8
92001 Alpine, 1,570 J 11
91001 Altadena, 42,380 C 10
91701 Alta Loma, 6,100 E 10
96101 Alturas⊙, 2,799 E 2
† 95101 Alum Rock, 18,355 L 3
* 92801 Anaheim, 166,701 D 11
Anaheim-Santa Ana-Garden Grove, ‡1,420,386 D 11
96007 Anderson, 5,492 C 3
95222 Angels Camp, 1,710 E 5
94508 Angwin, 2,690 C 5
94509 Antioch, 28,060 L 1
92307 Apple Valley, 6,702 H 9
95003 Aptos, 8,704 K 4
95912 Arbuckle, 1,037 C 4
95825 Arcade-Arden, 82,498 B 8
91006 Arcadia, 42,868 C 10
95521 Arcata, 8,985 A 3
93202 Armona, 1,392 F 7
93420 Arroyo Grande, 7,454 E 8
90701 Artesia, 14,757 C 11
† 94578 Ashland, 14,810 K 2
95413 Asti, 50 C 5
93422 Atascadero, 10,290 E 8
94025 Atherton, 8,085 K 3
95301 Atwater, 11,640 E 6
93602 Auberry, 515 F 6
95603 Auburn⊙, 6,570 C 8
90704 Avalon, 1,520 G 10
93204 Avenal, 3,035 E 8
91702 Azusa, 25,217 D 10
92309 Baker, 600 J 8
* 93301 Bakersfield⊙, 69,515 G 8
Bakersfield, ‡329,271 G 8
91706 Baldwin Park, 47,285 D 10
92220 Banning, 12,034 J 10
92311 Barstow, 17,442 H 9
† 95501 Bayview, 2,340 A 3
† 93401 Baywood Park-Los Osos, 3,487 E 8
92223 Beaumont, 5,484 J 10
90201 Bell, 21,836 C 11
90706 Bellflower, 51,454 C 11
94002 Belmont, 23,667 J 3
94920 Belvedere, 2,599 H 2
94510 Benicia, 8,783 K 1
95005 Ben Lomond, 2,793 K 4
* 94701 Berkeley, 116,716 J 2
94511 Bethel Island, 1,398 L 1
* 90210 Beverly Hills, 33,416 B 10
92314 Big Bear City, 850 J 9
92315 Big Bear Lake, 5,268 J 9
95917 Biggs, 1,115 D 4
93513 Big Pine, 839 G 6
93920 Big Sur, 500 D 7
93606 Biola, 950 E 7
93514 Bishop, 3,498 G 6
† 94947 Black Point, 500 J 1
92316 Bloomington, 11,957 E 10
95525 Blue Lake, 1,112 A 3
92225 Blythe, 7,047 L 10
94923 Bodega Bay, 700 B 5
94924 Bolinas, 700 H 1
95415 Boonville, 715 B 5
93516 Boron, 1,999 H 8
92004 Borrego Springs, 860 J 10
95006 Boulder Creek, 1,806 J 4
95707 Bowman, 2,089 C 8
91010 Bradbury, 1,098 D 10
92227 Brawley, 13,746 K 11
92621 Brea, 18,447 D 11
94513 Brentwood, 2,649 L 2
93517 Bridgeport⊙, 525 F 5
94005 Brisbane, 3,003 J 2
95605 Broderick-Bryte, 12,782 B 8
95007 Brookdale, 630 J 4
95605 Bryte-Broderick, 12,782 B 8
93427 Buellton, 1,402 E 9
90620 Buena Park, 63,646 D 11
* 91501 Burbank, 88,871 C 10
94010 Burlingame, 27,320 J 2
96013 Burney, 2,190 D 3
93206 Buttonwillow, 1,193 F 8
94514 Byron, 800 L 2
92230 Cabazon, 598 J 10
92231 Calexico, 10,625 K 11
93501 California City, 1,309 H 8
92233 Calipatria, 1,824 K 10
94515 Calistoga, 1,882 C 5
95418 Calpella, 900 B 4
93745 Calwa, 5,191 F 7
93010 Camarillo, 19,219 F 9
93428 Cambria, 1,716 D 8
95709 Camino, 800 E 5
95008 Campbell, 24,770 K 3
92006 Campo, 850 J 11
95226 Campo Seco, 700 D 9
* 91303 Canoga Park, 109,127 B 10
92672 Capistrano Beach, 4,149 H 10
95010 Capitola, 5,080 K 4
92007 Cardiff-by-the-Sea, 5,724 H 10
92008 Carlsbad, 14,944 H 10
93921 Carmel, 4,525 D 7
93924 Carmel Valley, 3,026 D 7
95608 Carmichael, 37,625 C 8
93013 Carpinteria, 6,982 F 9
90744 Carson, 71,150 C 11
93609 Caruthers, 950 E 7
* 93001 Casitas Springs, 1,113 F 9
95420 Caspar, 578 B 4
91310 Castaic, 800 G 9
94546 Castro Valley, 44,760 K 2
95012 Castroville, 3,235 D 7
92234 Cathedral City, 3,640 J 10
93430 Cayucos, 1,772 E 8
96104 Cedarville, 825 E 2
96019 Central Valley, 2,361 C 3
95307 Ceres, 6,029 D 6
90701 Cerritos, 15,856 C 11
91311 Chatsworth, 24,000 B 10
95044 Chemeketa Park-Redwood Estates, 1,452 K 4
† 94521 Cherryland, 9,969 K 2
96020 Chester, 1,531 D 3
95926 Chico, 19,580 D 4
93555 China Lake, 11,105 H 8
95309 Chinese Camp, 150 E 6
91710 Chino, 20,411 D 10
93610 Chowchilla, 4,349 E 6
* 92010 Chula Vista, 67,901 J 11
95610 Citrus Heights, 21,760 C 8
91711 Claremont, 23,464 D 10
95612 Clarksburg, 554 B 9
94517 Clayton, 1,385 K 2
95422 Clearlake Highlands, 2,836 C 5
95423 Clearlake Oaks, 975 C 4
95425 Cloverdale, 3,251 B 5
92236 Coachella, 8,353 J 10
93210 Coalinga, 6,161 E 7
95713 Colfax, 798 E 4
94014 Colma, 537 J 2
92324 Colton, 19,974 E 10
95932 Colusa⊙, 3,842 C 4
† 90001 Commerce, 10,536 C 10
* 90220 Compton, 78,611 C 11
* 94520 Concord, 85,164 K 1
93212 Corcoran, 5,249 F 7
96021 Corning, 3,573 C 4
91720 Corona, 27,519 E 11
92118 Coronado, 20,910 H 11
95076 Corralitos, 600 L 4
94925 Corte Madera, 8,464 J 2
* 92626 Costa Mesa, 72,660 D 11
96022 Cottonwood, 1,288 C 3
95428 Covelo, 900 B 4
91722 Covina, 30,380 D 10
95531 Crescent City⊙, 2,586 A 2
92325 Crestline, 3,509 H 9
94525 Crockett, 2,900 J 1
91730 Cucamonga, 5,796 E 10
90230 Culver City, 31,035 B 10
95014 Cupertino, 18,216 K 3
93615 Cutler, 2,503 F 7
95534 Cutten, 2,228 A 3
90630 Cypress, 31,026 D 11
92327 Daggett, 950 H 9
* 94014 Daly City, 66,922 H 2
92629 Dana Point, 4,745 H 10
94526 Danville-Alamo, 14,059 K 2
95616 Davis, 23,488 B 8
94576 Deer Park, 975 C 5
93215 Delano, 14,559 F 8
95315 Delhi, 2,063 E 6
92014 Del Mar, 3,956 H 11
93940 Del Rey Oaks, 1,823 D 7
92404 Del Rosa, 8,000 E 10
92240 Desert Hot Springs, 2,738 J 9
† 93550 Desert View Highlands, 2,172 G 9
94528 Diablo, 950 K 2
95619 Diamond Springs, 900 D 8
93618 Dinuba, 7,917 F 7
95620 Dixon, 4,432 B 9
96023 Dorris, 840 D 2
93620 Dos Palos, 2,496 E 6
* 90240 Downey, 88,445 C 11
95936 Downieville⊙, 375 E 4
91010 Duarte, 14,981 D 10
94566 Dublin, 13,641 K 2
95937 Dunnigan, 550 C 5
96025 Dunsmuir, 2,214 C 2
95938 Durham, 700 D 4
92241 Eagle Mountain, 2,453 K 10
93219 Earlimart, 3,080 F 8
† 92225 East Blythe, 1,252 L 10
90804 East Los Angeles, 105,033 C 10
93706 Easton, 1,065 F 7
93523 Edwards, 900 G 9
* 92020 El Cajon, 52,273 J 11
92243 El Centro⊙, 19,272 K 11
94530 El Cerrito, 25,190 J 2
95623 El Dorado, 900 C 8
95630 El Dorado Hills, 2,000 C 8
94018 El Granada, 1,473 H 3
95624 Elk Grove, 3,721 B 9
* 91731 El Monte, 69,837 D 10
95318 El Portal, 675 F 6
93030 El Rio, 6,173 F 9
90245 El Segundo, 15,620 B 11
92330 Elsinore, 3,530 F 11
92630 El Toro, 8,654 E 11
94608 Emeryville, 2,681 J 2
95319 Empire, 2,016 D 6
92024 Encinitas, 5,375 H 10
91316 Encino, 40,000 B 10
96001 Enterprise, 11,486 C 3
95320 Escalon, 2,366 E 6
92025 Escondido, 36,792 J 10
95627 Esparto, 1,088 C 5
91739 Etiwanda, 900 E 10
96027 Etna, 667 C 2
95501 Eureka⊙, 24,337 A 3
93221 Exeter, 4,475 F 7
94930 Fairfax, 7,661 H 1
94533 Fairfield⊙, 44,146 K 1
95628 Fair Oaks, 11,256 C 8
92028 Fallbrook, 6,945 H 10
96028 Fall River Mills, 600 D 3
93223 Farmersville, 3,456 F 7
93224 Fellows, 530 F 8
95018 Felton, 2,062 K 4
95536 Ferndale, 1,352 A 3
93015 Fillmore, 6,285 G 9
93622 Firebaugh, 2,517 E 7
95828 Florin, 9,646 B 8
95630 Folsom, 5,810 C 8
92335 Fontana, 20,673 E 10
† 93268 Ford City, 3,503 F 8
† 95703 Foresthill, 900 E 4
94933 Forest Knolls, 900 H 1
95437 Fort Bragg, 4,455 B 4
95538 Fort Dick, 850 A 2
96032 Fort Jones, 515 C 2
95540 Fortuna, 4,203 A 3
94404 Foster City, 9,327 J 2
92708 Fountain Valley, 31,826 D 11
93625 Fowler, 2,239 F 7
93225 Frazier Park, 1,167 F 9
95019 Freedom, 5,563 L 4
* 94536 Fremont, 100,869 K 3
† 93701 Fresno⊙, 165,972 F 7
Fresno, ‡413,053 F 7
* 92631 Fullerton, 85,987 D 11
95632 Galt, 3,200 C 9
* 90247 Gardena, 41,021 C 11
* 92640 Garden Grove, 122,524 D 11
95634 Georgetown, 700 E 5
96035 Gerber, 800 C 3
95441 Geyserville, 887 B 5
95020 Gilroy, 12,665 D 6
† 92501 Glen Avon Heights, 5,759 E 10
* 91201 Glendale, 132,752 C 10
91740 Glendora, 31,349 D 10
93017 Goleta, 3,500 F 9
93926 Gonzales, 2,575 D 7
93227 Goshen, 1,324 F 7
91344 Granada Hills, 50,000 B 10
92324 Grand Terrace, 5,901 E 10
95945 Grass Valley, 5,149 D 4
95444 Graton, 975 C 5
93308 Greenacres, 2,116 F 8
93927 Greenfield, 2,608 D 7
95947 Greenville, 1,073 E 3
95948 Gridley, 3,534 D 4
93433 Grover City, 5,939 E 8
93434 Guadalupe, 3,145 E 9
95445 Gualala, 585 B 5
95446 Guerneville, 900 B 5
95322 Gustine, 2,793 D 6
94019 Half Moon Bay, 4,023 H 3
95951 Hamilton City, 961 C 4
93230 Hanford⊙, 15,179 F 7
96039 Happy Camp, 925 B 2
90710 Harbor City, 17,500 C 11
90250 Hawthorne, 53,304 C 11
96041 Hayfork, 900 B 3
* 94541 Hayward, 93,058 K 2
95448 Healdsburg, 5,438 B 5
92249 Heber, 875 K 11
92343 Hemet, 12,252 H 10
96113 Herlong, 900 E 3
90254 Hermosa Beach, 17,412 B 11
92345 Hesperia, 4,592 H 9
† 91302 Hidden Hills, 1,529 B 10
92507 Highgrove, 2,158 E 10
92346 Highland, 13,290 H 9
95324 Hilmar, 813 E 6
92347 Hinkley, 900 H 9
95023 Hollister⊙, 7,663 D 7
90028 Hollywood, 85,047 C 10
92250 Holtville, 3,496 K 11
† 91720 Home Gardens, 5,116 E 11
92348 Homeland, 1,187 H 10
95546 Hoopa, 850 B 2
95449 Hopland, 817 B 5
95326 Hughson, 2,144 E 6
* 92646 Huntington Beach, 115,960 C 11
90255 Huntington Park, 33,744 C 11
93234 Huron, 1,525 E 7
92349 Idyllwild, 950 J 10
94947 Ignacio, 4,500 H 1
92251 Imperial, 3,094 K 11
92032 Imperial Beach, 20,244 H 11
93526 Independence⊙, 748 H 7
92201 Indio, 14,459 J 10
* 90301 Inglewood, 89,985 B 11
94937 Inverness, 800 B 5
95640 Ione, 2,369 C 9
93017 Isla Vista, 13,441 E 9
95641 Isleton, 909 L 1
93235 Ivanhoe, 1,595 F 7
95642 Jackson⊙, 1,924 C 9
92034 Jacumba, 700 J 11
95327 Jamestown, 950 E 6
92252 Joshua Tree, 1,211 J 9
95451 Kelseyville, 950 C 5
† 94701 Kensington, 5,823 J 2
93600 Kerman, 2,667 E 7
93238 Kernville, 900 G 8
93239 Kettleman City, 600 E 7
95328 Keyes, 1,875 E 6
93930 King City, 3,717 D 7
95719 Kings Beach, 600 F 4
93631 Kingsburg, 3,843 F 7
95645 Knights Landing, 846 B 8
91011 La Canada, 20,652 C 10
91214 La Crescenta-Montrose, 19,594 C 10
94549 Lafayette, 20,484 K 2
* 92651 Laguna Beach, 14,550 G 10
92653 Laguna Hills, 13,676 D 11
92677 Laguna Niguel, 4,644 H 10
90631 La Habra, 41,350 D 11
94020 La Honda, 650 J 3
92037 La Jolla, 30,000 H 11
92352 Lake Arrowhead, 2,682 H 9
93532 Lake Hughes, 750 G 9
93240 Lake Isabella, 850 G 8
† 92330 Lakeland Village, 1,724 E 11
95453 Lakeport⊙, 3,005 C 4
* 90712 Lakewood, 82,973 C 11
92041 La Mesa, 39,178 H 11
90638 La Mirada, 30,808 D 11
93241 Lamont, 7,007 G 8
93534 Lancaster, 30,948 G 9
* 91744 La Puente, 31,092 D 10
94939 Larkspur, 10,487 H 1
95076 La Selva Beach, 1,171 K 4
95330 Lathrop, 2,137 D 6
93242 Laton, 1,071 F 7
91750 La Verne, 12,965 D 10

(continued on following page)

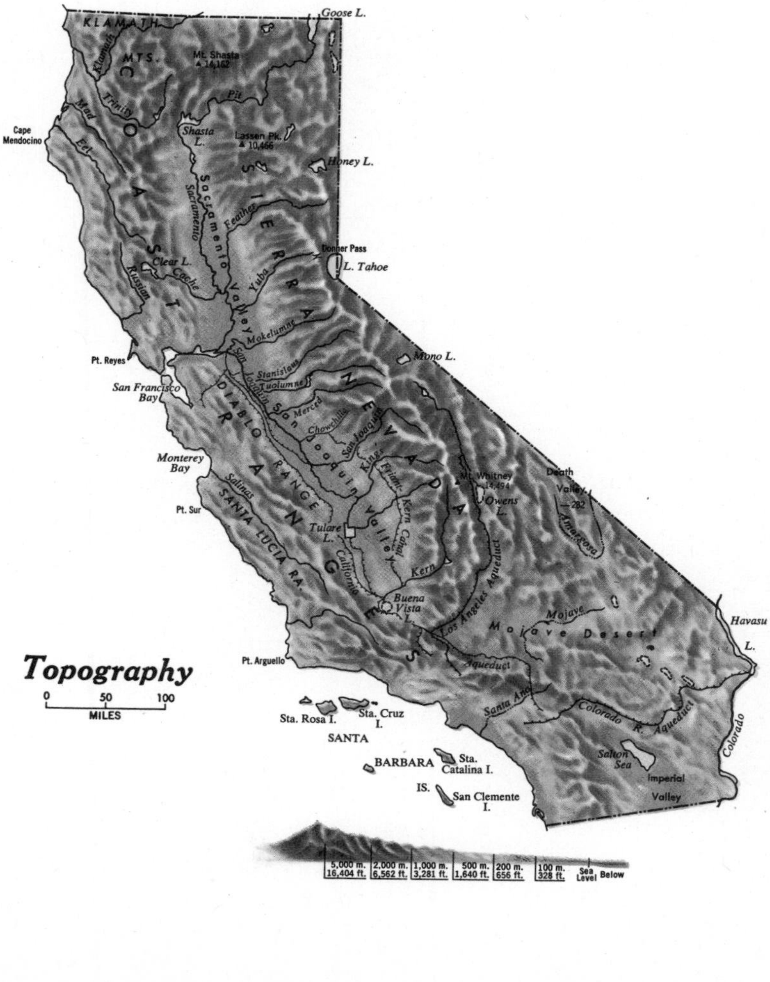

(continued)

90260 Lawndale, 24,825 .... B 11
95454 Laytonville, 917 .... B 4
95333 Le Grand, 995 .... E 6
92045 Lemon Grove, 19,690 .... J 11
93245 Lemoore, 4,219 .... F 7
90304 Lennox, 16,121 .... B 11
92311 Lenwood, 3,834 .... H 9
92024 Leucadia, 5,900 .... H 10
95648 Lincoln, 3,176 .... B 8
† 95901 Linda, 7,731 .... D 4
93247 Lindsay, 5,206 .... F 7
95953 Live Oak, 2,645 .... D 4
95953 Live Oak, 6,443 .... K 4
94550 Livermore, 37,703 .... L 2
95334 Livingston, 2,588 .... E 6
95237 Lockeford, 890 .... C 9
95240 Lodi, 28,691 .... C 9
95551 Loleta, 800 .... A 3
92354 Loma Linda, 9,797 .... F 10
90717 Lomita, 19,784 .... C 11
93436 Lompoc, 25,284 .... E 9
93545 Lone Pine, 1,241 .... H 7
* 90801 Long Beach, 358,633 .... C 11
95650 Loomis, 1,108 .... C 8
90720 Los Alamitos, 11,346 .... D 11
93440 Los Alamos, 750 .... E 9
94022 Los Altos, 24,956 .... K 3
94022 Los Altos Hills, 6,865 .... J 3
* 90001 Los Angeles⊙, 2,816,061 .... C 10
Los Angeles-Long Beach, ‡7,032,075 .... C 10
93635 Los Banos, 9,188 .... E 6
95030 Los Gatos, 23,735 .... K 4
96055 Los Molinos, 900 .... D 3
† 93401 Los Osos-Baywood Park, 3,487 .... E 8
95457 Lower Lake, 850 .... C 5
96118 Loyalton, 945 .... E 4
95458 Lucerne, 1,300 .... C 4
92356 Lucerne Valley, 850 .... J 9
90262 Lynwood, 43,353 .... C 11
93637 Madera⊙, 16,044 .... E 7
90265 Malibu, 15,000 .... B 10
90266 Manhattan Beach, 35,352 .... B 11
95336 Manteca, 13,845 .... D 6
93252 Maricopa, 740 .... F 8
† 94901 Marinwood, 6,000 .... H 1
95338 Mariposa⊙, 900 .... F 6
96120 Markleeville⊙, 150 .... F 5
94553 Martinez⊙, 16,506 .... K 1
95901 Marysville⊙, 9,353 .... D 4
95955 Maxwell, 850 .... C 4
90270 Maywood, 16,996 .... C 10
96057 McCloud, 1,643 .... C 2
93250 McFarland, 4,177 .... F 8
92254 Mecca, 900 .... K 10
93023 Meiners Oaks, 7,025 .... F 9
95460 Mendocino, 975 .... B 4
93640 Mendota, 2,705 .... E 7
94025 Menlo Park, 26,734 .... J 3
92359 Mentone, 2,900 .... H 9
95340 Merced⊙, 22,670 .... E 6
95461 Middletown, 800 .... C 5
92655 Midway City, 5,900 .... D 11
94030 Millbrae, 20,781 .... J 2
94941 Mill Valley, 12,942 .... H 2
95035 Milpitas, 27,149 .... L 3
91752 Mira Loma, 8,482 .... E 10
92675 Mission Viejo, 11,933 .... D 11
* 95350 Modesto⊙, 61,712 .... D 6
93501 Mojave, 2,573 .... G 8
95245 Mokelumne Hill, 560 .... E 5
91016 Monrovia, 30,015 .... D 10
96064 Montague, 890 .... C 2
93003 Montalvo, 2,400 .... F 9
94037 Montara, 1,459 .... H 3
91763 Montclair, 22,546 .... D 10
90640 Montebello, 42,807 .... C 10
93103 Montecito, 4,900 .... F 9
93940 Monterey, 26,302 .... D 7
91754 Monterey Park, 49,166 .... C 10
95462 Monte Rio, 900 .... B 5
95030 Monte Sereno, 3,089 .... K 4
91020 Montrose-La Crescenta, 19,594 .... C 10
93021 Moorpark, 3,380 .... G 9
94556 Moraga, 14,205 .... K 2
95037 Morgan Hill, 6,485 .... L 4
93442 Morro Bay, 7,109 .... D 8
94038 Moss Beach, 700 .... H 3
95039 Moss Landing, 600 .... C 7
94040 Mountain View, 51,092 .... K 3
96067 Mount Shasta, 2,163 .... C 2
† 95926 Mulberry, 1,795 .... D 4
95247 Murphys, 780 .... E 5
92362 Murrieta, 850 .... H 10
92405 Muscoy, 7,091 .... E 10
94558 Napa⊙, 35,978 .... C 5
92050 National City, 43,184 .... J 11
92363 Needles, 4,051 .... L 9
95959 Nevada City⊙, 2,314 .... D 4
94560 Newark, 27,153 .... K 3
92365 Newberry Springs, 710 .... J 9
95658 Newcastle, 900 .... C 8
91321 Newhall, 9,651 .... G 9
95360 Newman, 2,505 .... D 6
* 92660 Newport Beach, 49,422 .... D 11
92257 Niland, 900 .... K 10
93444 Nipomo, 3,642 .... E 8
91760 Norco, 14,511 .... E 11
93643 North Fork, 575 .... F 6
95660 North Highlands, 31,854 .... B 8
* 91601 North Hollywood, 190,000 .... B 10
90650 Norwalk, 91,827 .... C 11
94947 Novato, 31,006 .... H 1
95361 Oakdale, 6,594 .... E 6
93644 Oakhurst, 800 .... F 6
* 94601 Oakland⊙, 361,561 .... J 2
94561 Oakley, 1,306 .... L 1
93022 Oak View, 4,872 .... F 9
93445 Oceano, 2,564 .... E 8
92054 Oceanside, 40,494 .... H 10
93308 Oildale, 20,879 .... F 8
93023 Ojai, 5,591 .... F 9
* 91761 Ontario, 64,118 .... D 10
95060 Opal Cliffs, 5,425 .... K 4
* 92666 Orange, 77,374 .... D 11

93646 Orange Cove, 3,392 .... F 7
93454 Orcutt, 8,500 .... E 9
95555 Orick, 950 .... A 2
94563 Orinda, 6,790 .... J 2
95963 Orland, 2,884 .... C 4
95556 Orleans, 850 .... B 2
92368 Oro Grande, 700 .... H 9
93647 Orosi, 2,757 .... F 7
95965 Oroville⊙, 7,536 .... D 4
93030 Oxnard, 71,225 .... F 9
Oxnard-Ventura, ‡376,430 .... F 9
94044 Pacifica, 36,020 .... H 2
92109 Pacific Beach, 59,000 .... H 11
93950 Pacific Grove, 13,505 .... C 7
† 95076 Pajaro, 1,407 .... D 7
95968 Palermo, 1,966 .... D 4
93550 Palmdale, 8,511 .... G 9
92260 Palm Desert, 6,171 .... J 10
92262 Palm Springs, 20,936 .... J 10
* 94301 Palo Alto, 55,966 .... K 3
90274 Palos Verdes Estates, 13,641 .... B 11
95969 Paradise, 14,539 .... D 4
90723 Paramount, 34,734 .... C 11
93648 Parlier, 1,993 .... F 7
* 91101 Pasadena, 113,327 .... C 10
† 95060 Pastiempo, 1,115 .... K 4
93446 Paso Robles, 7,168 .... E 8
95363 Patterson, 3,147 .... D 6
93553 Pearblossom, 900 .... H 9
93953 Pebble Beach, 5,000 .... C 7
92370 Perris, 4,228 .... F 11
94060 Pescadero, 625 .... J 4
94952 Petaluma, 24,870 .... H 1
95466 Philo, 700 .... B 4
90660 Pico Rivera, 54,170 .... C 10
94611 Piedmont, 10,917 .... J 2
93650 Pinedale, 1,900 .... F 7
94564 Pinole, 15,850 .... J 1
93040 Piru, 975 .... G 9
93449 Pismo Beach, 4,043 .... E 8
94565 Pittsburg, 20,651 .... L 1
93256 Pixley, 1,584 .... F 8
92670 Placentia, 21,948 .... D 11
95667 Placerville⊙, 5,416 .... C 8
95365 Planada, 2,056 .... E 6
94523 Pleasant Hill, 24,610 .... K 2
94566 Pleasanton, 18,328 .... L 2
95669 Plymouth, 501 .... C 8
95726 Pollock Pines, 850 .... E 5
* 91766 Pomona, 87,384 .... D 10
93257 Poplar, 1,239 .... F 7
93257 Porterville, 12,602 .... G 7
93041 Port Hueneme, 14,295 .... F 9
96122 Portola, 1,625 .... E 4
94025 Portola Valley, 4,999 .... J 3
95469 Potter Valley, 975 .... B 4
92064 Poway, 9,422 .... J 11
96079 Project City, 1,431 .... C 3
93534 Quartz Hill, 4,935 .... G 9
95971 Quincy⊙, 3,343 .... E 4
92065 Ramona, 3,554 .... J 10
95670 Rancho Cordova, 30,451 .... C 8
† 91321 Rancho Santa Clarita, 4,860 .... G 9
92067 Rancho Santa Fe, 975 .... H 10
96080 Red Bluff⊙, 7,676 .... C 3
96001 Redding⊙, 16,659 .... C 3
92373 Redlands, 36,355 .... H 9
* 90277 Redondo Beach, 56,075 .... B 11
* 94061 Redwood City⊙, 55,686 .... J 3
95044 Redwood Estates-Chemeketa Park, 1,452 .... K 4
93654 Reedley, 8,131 .... F 7
91335 Reseda, 60,862 .... B 10
92376 Rialto, 28,370 .... E 10
93261 Richgrove, 1,023 .... F 8
* 94801 Richmond, 79,043 .... J 1
93555 Ridgecrest, 7,629 .... H 8
95562 Rio Dell, 2,817 .... A 3
95673 Rio Linda, 7,524 .... B 8
94571 Rio Vista, 3,135 .... L 1
95366 Ripon, 2,679 .... D 6
95367 Riverbank, 3,949 .... E 6
93656 Riverdale, 1,722 .... E 7
* 92501 Riverside⊙, 140,089 .... E 11
95677 Rocklin, 3,039 .... B 8
94572 Rodeo, 5,356 .... J 1
94928 Rohnert Park, 6,133 .... C 5
95540 Rohnerville, 2,781 .... B 3
90274 Rolling Hills, 2,050 .... B 11
90274 Rolling Hills Estates, 6,027 .... B 11
93560 Rosamond, 2,281 .... G 9
91770 Rosemead, 40,972 .... C 10
95678 Roseville, 17,895 .... B 8
94957 Ross, 2,742 .... H 1
92509 Rubidoux, 13,969 .... E 10
* 95801 Sacramento (cap.)⊙, 254,413 .... B 8
Sacramento, ‡800,592 .... B 8
94574 Saint Helena, 3,173 .... C 5
93901 Salinas⊙, 58,896 .... D 7
Salinas-Monterey, ‡250,071 .... D 7
95563 Salyer, 700 .... B 3
95564 Samoa, 585 .... A 3
95249 San Andreas⊙, 1,564 .... E 5
94960 San Anselmo, 13,031 .... H 1
93450 San Ardo, 750 .... E 7
* 92401 San Bernardino⊙, 104,251 .... E 10
San Bernardino-Riverside-Ontario, ‡1,143,146 .... E 10
94066 San Bruno, 36,254 .... J 2
94070 San Carlos, 25,924 .... J 3
92672 San Clemente, 17,063 .... H 10
* 92101 San Diego⊙, 696,769 .... H 11
San Diego, ‡1,357,854 .... H 11
91773 San Dimas, 15,692 .... D 10
* 91340 San Fernando, 16,571 .... C 10
* 94101 San Francisco⊙, 715,674 .... H 2
San Francisco-Oakland, ‡3,109,519 .... H 2
* 91775 San Gabriel, 29,176 .... C 10
93657 Sanger, 10,088 .... F 7
92383 San Jacinto, 4,385 .... H 10
93660 San Joaquin, 1,506 .... E 7
* 95101 San Jose⊙, 445,779 .... L 3
San Jose, ‡1,064,714 .... L 3

Agriculture, Industry and Resources

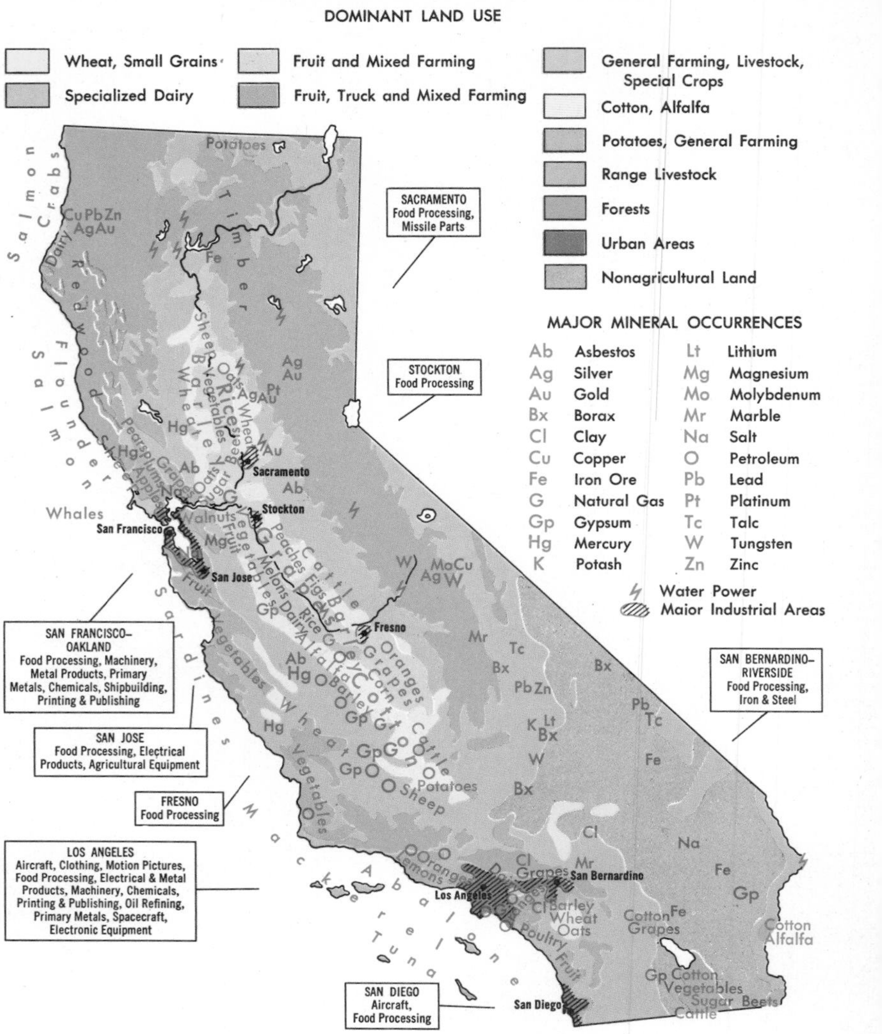
DOMINANT LAND USE
Wheat, Small Grains
Specialized Dairy
Fruit and Mixed Farming
Fruit, Truck and Mixed Farming
General Farming, Livestock, Special Crops
Cotton, Alfalfa
Potatoes, General Farming
Range Livestock
Forests
Urban Areas
Nonagricultural Land
MAJOR MINERAL OCCURRENCES
Ab Asbestos
Ag Silver
Au Gold
Bx Borax
Cl Clay
Cu Copper
Fe Iron Ore
G Natural Gas
Gp Gypsum
Hg Mercury
K Potash
Lt Lithium
Mg Magnesium
Mo Molybdenum
Mr Marble
Na Salt
O Petroleum
Pb Lead
Pt Platinum
Tc Talc
W Tungsten
Zn Zinc
Water Power
Major Industrial Areas
SACRAMENTO
Food Processing, Missile Parts
STOCKTON
Food Processing
SAN FRANCISCO–OAKLAND
Food Processing, Machinery, Metal Products, Primary Metals, Chemicals, Shipbuilding, Printing & Publishing
SAN JOSE
Food Processing, Electrical Products, Agricultural Equipment
FRESNO
Food Processing
LOS ANGELES
Aircraft, Clothing, Motion Pictures, Food Processing, Electrical & Metal Products, Machinery, Chemicals, Printing & Publishing, Oil Refining, Primary Metals, Spacecraft, Electronic Equipment
SAN DIEGO
Aircraft, Food Processing
SAN BERNARDINO–RIVERSIDE
Food Processing, Iron & Steel
Sacramento
Stockton
San Francisco
San Jose
Fresno
Los Angeles
San Bernardino
San Diego
Whales
Salmon
Crabs
Timber
Potatoes
Sheep
Cattle
Oranges
Grapes
Cotton
Alfalfa
Vegetables
Sugar Beets
Poultry
Fruit
Barley
Wheat
Oats
Rice

95045 San Juan Bautista, 1,164 .... D 7
92675 San Juan Capistrano, 3,781 .... H 10
* 94577 San Leandro, 68,698 .... J 2
94580 San Lorenzo, 24,633 .... K 2
93401 San Luis Obispo⊙, 28,036 .... E 8
92069 San Marcos, 3,896 .... H 10
91108 San Marino, 14,177 .... D 10
95046 San Martin, 1,392 .... L 4
* 94401 San Mateo, 78,911 .... J 3
93451 San Miguel, 600 .... E 8
94806 San Pablo, 21,461 .... J 1
* 90731 San Pedro, 91,000 .... C 11
* 94901 San Rafael⊙, 38,977 .... J 1
94583 San Ramon, 4,084 .... K 2
* 92701 Santa Ana⊙, 156,601 .... D 11
* 93101 Santa Barbara⊙, 70,215 .... F 9
Santa Barbara, ‡264,324 .... F 9
* 95050 Santa Clara, 87,717 .... K 3
95060 Santa Cruz⊙, 32,076 .... K 4
90670 Santa Fe Springs, 14,750 .... C 11
93453 Santa Margarita, 750 .... E 8
93454 Santa Maria, 32,749 .... E 9
* 90401 Santa Monica, 88,289 .... B 10
93060 Santa Paula, 18,001 .... F 9
* 95401 Santa Rosa⊙, 50,006 .... C 5
93063 Santa Susana, 2,900 .... B 10
† 94901 Santa Venetia, 2,500 .... J 1
92071 Santee, 21,107 .... J 11
95070 Saratoga, 27,110 .... K 4
93003 Saticoy, 2,400 .... F 9
94965 Sausalito, 6,158 .... H 2
95565 Scotia, 950 .... A 3
95060 Scotts Valley, 3,621 .... K 4
90740 Seal Beach, 24 441 .... C 11
93955 Seaside, 35,935 .... D 7
95472 Sebastopol, 3,993 .... C 5
92273 Seeley, 952 .... K 11
93662 Selma, 7,459 .... F 7
91343 Sepulveda, 40,000 .... B 10
93263 Shafter, 5,327 .... F 8
96087 Shasta, 750 .... C 3
93449 Shell Beach, 1,900 .... E 8
91024 Sierra Madre, 12,140 .... D 10
90806 Signal Hill, 5,582 .... C 11

92676 Silverado, 950 .... E 11
93065 Simi Valley, 56,464 .... G 9
92075 Solana Beach, 5,023 .... H 11
93960 Soledad, 6,843 .... D 7
93463 Solvang, 2,004 .... E 9
95476 Sonoma, 4,112 .... C 5
95370 Sonora⊙, 3,100 .... E 6
95073 Soquel, 5,795 .... K 4
93665 South Dos Palos, 850 .... E 7
91733 South El Monte, 13,443 .... C 10
90280 South Gate, 56,909 .... C 11
95705 South Lake Tahoe, 12,921 .... F 5
† 95965 South Oroville, 4,111 .... D 4
91030 South Pasadena, 22,979 .... C 10
† 95801 South Sacramento, 28,574 .... B 8
94080 South San Francisco, 46,646 .... J 2
† 93268 South Taft, 2,214 .... F 8
93265 Springville, 720 .... G 7
94305 Stanford, 8,691 .... J 3
90680 Stanton, 17,947 .... D 11
94970 Stinson Beach, 800 .... H 2
* 95201 Stockton⊙, 107,644 .... D 6
Stockton, ‡290,208 .... D 6
93266 Stratford, 750 .... F 7
93267 Strathmore, 1,221 .... F 7
94585 Suisun City, 2,917 .... K 1
93067 Summerland, 781 .... F 9
92381 Sun City, 5,519 .... F 11
96089 Summit City, 900 .... C 3
91040 Sunland, 22,200 .... C 10
92388 Sunnymead, 6,708 .... F 11
* 94086 Sunnyvale, 95,408 .... K 3
94586 Sunol, 750 .... L 2
90742 Sunset Beach, 1,900 .... C 11
96130 Susanville⊙, 6,608 .... E 3
95982 Sutter, 1,488 .... D 4
95685 Sutter Creek, 1,508 .... C 9
93268 Taft, 4,285 .... F 8
95730 Tahoe City, 1,394 .... E 4
91356 Tarzana, 24,165 .... B 10
93561 Tehachapi, 4,211 .... G 8
91780 Temple City, 29,673 .... D 10
93465 Templeton, 900 .... E 8

93270 Terra Bella, 1,037 .... G 8
92274 Thermal, 975 .... J 10
† 95965 Thermalito, 4,217 .... D 4
95686 Thornton, 850 .... B 9
91360 Thousand Oaks. 36,334 .... G 9
92276 Thousand Palms, 600 .... J 10
94920 Tiburon, 6,209 .... J 2
93272 Tipton, 969 .... F 7
90290 Topanga, 4,800 .... B 10
† 90290 Topanga Beach, 4,500 .... B 10
* 90501 Torrance, 134,584 .... C 11
95376 Tracy, 14,724 .... D 6
93668 Tranquillity, 800 .... E 7
93562 Trona, 975 .... H 8
95734 Truckee, 1,392 .... E 4
91042 Tujunga, 22,000 .... C 10
93274 Tulare, 16,235 .... F 7
96134 Tulelake, 857 .... D 2
95379 Tuolumne, 1,365 .... E 6
95380 Turlock, 13,992 .... E 6
92680 Tustin, 21,178 .... D 11
95383 Twain Harte, 1,484 .... E 6
92277 Twentynine Palms, 5,667 .... K 9
† 95060 Twin Lakes, 3,012 .... K 4
95482 Ukiah⊙, 10,095 .... B 4
94587 Union City, 14,724 .... K 2
90007 University Park, 3,100 .... D 11
91786 Upland, 32,551 .... E 10
95485 Upper Lake, 975 .... C 4
95688 Vacaville, 21,690 .... D 5
91355 Valencia, 4,243 .... G 9
94590 Vallejo, 66,733 .... J 1
Vallejo-Napa, ‡249,081 .... J 1
95252 Valley Springs, 800 .... C 9
* 91401 Van Nuys, 231,600 .... B 10
90291 Venice, 80,500 .... B 11
* 93001 Ventura⊙, 55,797 .... F 9
92392 Victorville, 10,845 .... H 9
92667 Villa Park, 2,723 .... D 11
93277 Visalia⊙, 27,268 .... F 7
92083 Vista, 24,688 .... H 10
91789 Walnut, 5,992 .... D 10
* 94595 Walnut Creek, 39,844 .... K 2
95690 Walnut Grove, 800 .... B 9

93280 Wasco, 8,269 .... F
95386 Waterford, 2,243 .... E
95076 Watsonville, 14,569 .... D
96093 Weaverville⊙, 1,489 .... B
96094 Weed, 2,983 C
* 91790 West Covina, 68,034 .... D
† 90025 West Hollywood, 29,448 .... B
90025 West Los Angeles, 38,805 .... B
92683 Westminster, 59,865 .... D
92281 Westmorland, 1,175 .... K
94565 West Pittsburg, 5,969 .... K
95255 West Point, 950 .... E
95691 West Sacramento, 12,002 .... B
96137 Westwood, Lassen, 1,862 .... D
90024 Westwood, L.A., 45,000 .... B
95692 Wheatland, 1,280 .... D
* 90601 Whittier, 72,863 .... D
95987 Williams, 1,571 C
95490 Willits, 3,091 .... B
95988 Willows⊙, 4,085 C
90744 Wilmington, 38,000 C
95492 Windsor, 2,359 C
92283 Winterhaven, 850 L
95694 Winters, 2,419 .... D
95388 Winton, 3,393 .... E
95258 Woodbridge, 1,397 .... B
93286 Woodlake, 3,371 .... G
95695 Woodland⊙, 20,677 .... B
91364 Woodland Hills, 56,420 .... B
94062 Woodside, 4,731 .... J
92398 Yermo, 1,304 .... J
92686 Yorba Linda, 11,856 .... D
95389 Yosemite National Park, 857 .... F
94599 Yountville, 2,332 C
96097 Yreka⊙, 5,394 C
95991 Yuba City⊙, 13,986 .... D
92399 Yucaipa, 19,284 .... J
92284 Yucca Valley, 3,893 .... J

⊙ County seat.
‡ Population of metropolitan area.
† Zip of nearest p.o.
* Multiple zips

AREA 104,247 sq. mi
POPULATION 2,207,259
CAPITAL Denver
LARGEST CITY Denver
HIGHEST POINT Mt. Elbert 14,433 ft.
SETTLED IN 1858
ADMITTED TO UNION August 1, 1876
POPULAR NAME Centennial State
STATE FLOWER Mountain Columbine
STATE BIRD Lark Bunting

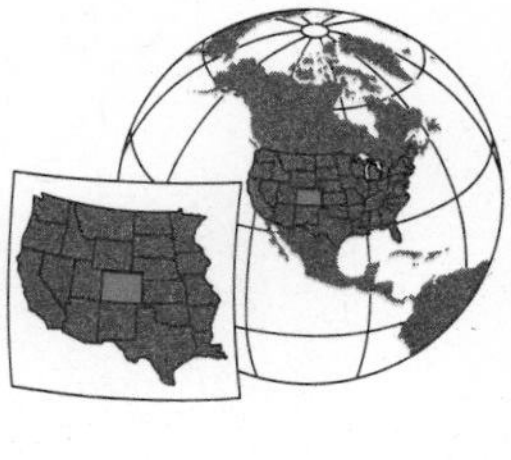

COUNTIES

dams, 185,789 ... L 3
lamosa, 11,422 ... H 7
rapahoe, 162,142 ... L 3
rchuleta, 2,733 ... E 8
aca, 5,674 ... O 8
ent, 6,493 ... N 7
oulder, 131,889 ... J 2
haffee, 10,162 ... G 5
heyenne, 2,396 ... O 5
lear Creek, 4,819 ... H 3
onejos, 7,846 ... G 8
ostilla, 3,091 ... J 8
rowley, 3,086 ... M 6
uster, 1,120 ... J 6
elta, 15,286 ... D 5
enver, 514,678 ... K 3
olores, 1,641 ... C 7
ouglas, 8,407 ... K 4
agle, 7,498 ... F 3
lbert, 3,903 ... L 4
l Paso, 235,972 ... K 5
remont, 21,942 ... J 5
arfield, 14,821 ... C 3
ilpin, 1,272 ... H 3
rand, 4,107 ... G 2
unnison, 7,578 ... E 5
insdale, 202 ... E 7
uerfano, 6,590 ... K 7
ackson, 1,811 ... G 1
efferson, 233,031 ... J 3
iowa, 2,029 ... O 6
it Carson, 7,530 ... O 4
ake, 8,282 ... G 4
a Plata, 19,199 ... D 8
arimer, 89,900 ... H 1
as Animas, 15,744 ... L 8
ncoln, 4,836 ... M 5
ogan, 18,852 ... N 1
esa, 54,374 ... B 5
ineral, 786 ... F 7
offat, 6,525 ... C 1
ontezuma, 12,952 ... B 8
ontrose, 18,366 ... C 6
organ, 20,105 ... M 2
tero, 23,523 ... M 7
uray, 1,546 ... D 6
ark, 2,185 ... H 4
hillips, 4,131 ... P 1
tkin, 6,185 ... F 4
owers, 13,258 ... P 7
ueblo, 118,238 ... K 6
o Blanco, 4,842 ... C 3
o Grande, 10,494 ... G 7
outt, 6,592 ... E 1
aguache, 3,827 ... G 6
an Juan, 831 ... D 7
an Miguel, 1,949 ... C 6
edgwick, 3,405 ... P 1
ummit, 2,665 ... G 3
eller, 3,316 ... J 5
ashington, 5,550 ... N 3
eld, 89,297 ... L 1
uma, 8,544 ... P 2

CITIES and TOWNS

Zip *Name/Pop.* *Key*

80101 Agate, 120 ... M 4
81020 Aguilar, 699 ... K 8
80720 Akron⊙, 1,775 ... N 2
81101 Alamosa⊙, 6,985 ... H 8
80510 Allenspark, 100 ... J 2
80420 Alma, 73 ... G 4
81210 Almont, 15 ... F 5
80721 Amherst, 105 ... P 1
80801 Anton, 65 ... N 3
81120 Antonito, 1,113 ... H 8
80802 Arapahoe, 100 ... P 5
81021 Arlington, 10 ... N 6
80804 Arriba, 254 ... N 4
† 81323 Arriola, 50 ... B 8
80002 Arvada, 46,814 ... J 3
81611 Aspen⊙, 2,404 ... F 4
80722 Atwood, 75 ... N 1
80610 Ault, 841 ... K 1
80010 Aurora, 74,974 ... K 3
81410 Austin, 1,163 ... D 5
81620 Avon, 50 ... F 3
81022 Avondale, 750 ... L 6
80421 Bailey, 200 ... H 4
† 80624 Barnesville, 20 ... L 2
81621 Basalt, 419 ... E 4
81122 Bayfield, 320 ... D 8
81411 Bedrock, 20 ... B 6
† 80758 Beecher Island, 5 ... P 3
80512 Bellvue, 335 ... J 1
80102 Bennett, 613 ... L 3
80513 Berthoud, 1,446 ... J 2
† 80438 Berthoud Pass, 200 ... H 3
80805 Bethune, 99 ... P 4
81023 Beulah, 425 ... K 6
80908 Black Forest, 700 ... K 4
80422 Black Hawk, 217 ... J 3
81123 Blanca, 212 ... H 8
† 81001 Blende, 950 ... K 6
† 80424 Blue River, 8 ... G 4
† 81155 Bonanza, 10 ... G 6
81024 Boncarbo, 50 ... K 8
80423 Bond, 63 ... F 3
81025 Boone, 448 ... L 6
* 80301 Boulder⊙, 66,870 ... J 2
† 81428 Bowie, 18 ... D 5
80806 Boyero, 25 ... N 5
81026 Brandon, 10 ... P 6
81027 Branson, 70 ... M 8
80424 Breckenridge⊙, 548 ... G 4
80611 Briggsdale, 440 ... L 1
80601 Brighton⊙, 8,309 ... K 3
81028 Bristol, 250 ... P 6
† 80901 Broadmoor, 3,871 ... K 5
† 81212 Brookside, 173 ... J 6
80020 Broomfield, 7,261 ... J 3
80723 Brush, 3,377 ... M 2
† 80742 Buckingham, 6 ... L 1
81211 Buena Vista, 1,962 ... G 5
80425 Buffalo Creek, 150 ... J 4
80807 Burlington⊙, 2,828 ... P 4
80426 Burns, 100 ... F 3
80103 Byers, 490 ... L 3
81320 Cahone, 125 ... B 7
80808 Calhan, 465 ... L 4
81029 Campo, 206 ... O 8
81212 Canon City⊙, 9,206 ... J 6
81124 Capulin, 600 ... G 8
81623 Carbondale, 726 ... E 4
80612 Carr, 47 ... K 1
80809 Cascade, 950 ... K 5
80104 Castle Rock⊙, 1,531 ... K 4
81413 Cedaredge, 581 ... D 5
81125 Center, 1,470 ... G 7
80427 Central City⊙, 228 ... J 3
81126 Chama, 400 ... J 8
81030 Cheraw, 129 ... N 6
80810 Cheyenne Wells⊙, 982 ... P 5
81127 Chimney Rock, 51 ... E 8
81031 Chivington, 15 ... O 6
81128 Chromo, 150 ... F 8
81220 Cimarron, 25 ... D 6
80428 Clark, 55 ... F 1
† 80731 Clarkville, 4 ... P 2
81520 Clifton, 950 ... C 4
80429 Climax, 975 ... G 4
81221 Coal Creek, 225 ... J 6
81222 Coaldale, 104 ... H 6
80430 Coalmont, 12 ... F 1
81032 Cokedale, 101 ... K 8
81624 Collbran, 225 ... C 4
† 81401 Colona, 54 ... D 6
81004 Colorado City, 411 ... K 6
* 80901 Colorado Springs⊙, 135,060 ... K 5
Colorado Springs, ‡235,972 ... K 5
† 80428 Columbine, 12 ... E 1
80022 Commerce City, 17,407 ... K 3
80432 Como, 35 ... H 4
81129 Conejos⊙, 100 ... G 8
80812 Cope, 125 ... O 3
80611 Cornish, 2 ... L 2
81321 Cortez⊙, 6,032 ... B 8
81223 Cotopaxi, 150 ... H 6
80434 Cowdrey, 10 ... G 1
81625 Craig⊙, 4,205 ... D 2
81415 Crawford, 171 ... D 5
81130 Creede⊙, 653 ... E 7
81224 Crested Butte, 372 ... E 5
81131 Crestone, 34 ... H 7
80813 Cripple Creek⊙, 425 ... J 5
80726 Crook, 199 ... O 1
81033 Crowley, 216 ... M 6
81055 Cuchara, 43 ... J 8
80514 Dacono, 360 ... K 2
† 80728 Dailey, 20 ... O 1
81630 De Beque, 155 ... C 4
† 80135 Deckers, 4 ... J 4
80105 Deer Trail, 374 ... M 3
81034 Delhi, 10 ... M 7
81132 Del Norte⊙, 1,569 ... G 7
81416 Delta⊙, 3,694 ... D 5
* 80201 Denver (cap.)⊙, 514,678 ... K 3
Denver, ‡1,227,529 ... K 3
81035 Deora, 2 ... O 7
80435 Dillon, 182 ... H 3
81610 Dinosaur, 247 ... B 2
80814 Divide, 50 ... J 5
81323 Dolores, 820 ... C 8
81324 Dove Creek⊙, 619 ... A 7
† 81239 Doyleville, 75 ... F 6
80515 Drake, 75 ... J 2
81301 Durango⊙, 10,333 ... D 8
81036 Eads⊙, 795 ... O 6
81631 Eagle⊙, 790 ... F 3
† 81212 East Canon, 1,805 ... J 6
80615 Eaton, 1,389 ... K 1
81418 Eckert, 850 ... C 5
80727 Eckley, 193 ... P 2
80214 Edgewater, 4,866 ... J 3
81632 Edwards, 100 ... F 3
81325 Egnar, 84 ... B 7
80106 Elbert, 150 ... L 4
80437 Eldora, 100 ... H 3
80107 Elizabeth, 493 ... K 4
81633 Elk Springs, 56 ... C 2
80438 Empire, 249 ... H 3
80110 Englewood, 33,695 ... K 3
80516 Erie, 1,090 ... K 2
80517 Estes Park, 1,616 ... J 2
† 81433 Eureka, 25 ... D 7
80620 Evans, 2,570 ... K 2
80439 Evergreen, 2,321 ... J 3
80440 Fairplay⊙, 419 ... H 4
81037 Farisita, 45 ... J 7
† 80030 Federal Heights, 1,502 ... J 3
80520 Firestone, 570 ... K 2
† 80810 Firstview, 6 ... O 5
80815 Flagler, 615 ... N 4
80728 Fleming, 349 ... O 1
81226 Florence, 2,846 ... J 6
80816 Florissant, 75 ... J 5
80521 Fort Collins⊙, 43,337 ... J 1
81133 Fort Garland, 400 ... J 8
80621 Fort Lupton, 2,489 ... K 2
81038 Fort Lyon, 135 ... N 6
80701 Fort Morgan⊙, 7,594 ... M 2
80817 Fountain, 3,515 ... K 5
81039 Fowler, 1,241 ... L 6
80441 Foxton, 75 ... J 4
80116 Franktown, 157 ... K 4
80442 Fraser, 221 ... H 3
80530 Frederick, 696 ... K 2
80820 Freshwater (Guffey), 24 ... H 5
80443 Frisco, 471 ... G 3
81521 Fruita, 1,822 ... B 4
† 81501 Fruitvale, 950 ... C 4
80622 Galeton, 200 ... K 1
81134 Garcia, 90 ... J 8
81040 Gardner, 75 ... J 7
81227 Garfield, 11 ... G 5
81522 Gateway, 250 ... B 5
80818 Genoa, 161 ... N 4
80444 Georgetown⊙, 542 ... H 3
80623 Gilcrest, 382 ... K 2
80624 Gill, 250 ... L 2
81634 Gilman, 400 ... G 3
81523 Glade Park, 69 ... B 5
80485 Glendevey, 50 ... H 1
80532 Glen Haven, 50 ... H 2
81601 Glenwood Springs⊙, 4,106 ... E 4
80401 Golden⊙, 9,817 ... J 3
80625 Goodrich, 85 ... M 2
80445 Gould, 12 ... G 2
81041 Granada, 551 ... P 6
80446 Granby, 554 ... H 2
81501 Grand Junction⊙, 20,170 ... B 4
80447 Grand Lake, 189 ... H 2
81635 Grand Valley, 270 ... D 4
81228 Granite, 23 ... G 4
80448 Grant, 50 ... H 4
80631 Greeley⊙, 38,902 ... K 2
† 80118 Greenland, 47 ... K 4
80819 Green Mountain Falls, 359 ... K 5
81636 Greystone, 2 ... B 1
80729 Grover, 121 ... L 1
80820 Guffey, 24 ... H 5
81042 Gulnare, 100 ... K 8
81230 Gunnison⊙, 4,613 ... E 5
81637 Gypsum, 420 ... F 3
80730 Hale, 12 ... P 3
81638 Hamilton, 30 ... D 2
81043 Hartman, 129 ... P 6
80449 Hartsel, 75 ... H 4
81044 Hasty, 150 ... O 6
81045 Haswell, 135 ... N 6
80731 Haxtun, 899 ... O 1
81639 Hayden, 763 ... E 2
80732 Hereford, 50 ... L 1
81326 Hesperus, 78 ... C 8
80733 Hillrose, 121 ... N 2
81232 Hillside, 79 ... H 6
81046 Hoehne, 400 ... L 8
81047 Holly, 993 ... P 6
80734 Holyoke⊙, 1,640 ... P 1
81136 Hooper, 80 ... H 7
81419 Hotchkiss, 507 ... D 5
80451 Hot Sulphur Springs⊙, 220 ... H 2
81233 Howard, 175 ... H 6
80641 Hoyt, 175 ... L 2
80642 Hudson, 518 ... K 2
80821 Hugo⊙, 759 ... N 4
80533 Hygiene, 400 ... J 2
80452 Idaho Springs, 2,003 ... H 3
80735 Idalia, 100 ... P 3
81137 Ignacio, 613 ... D 8
80736 Iliff, 193 ... N 1
81427 Ironton ... D 7
† 80901 Ivywild, 12,000 ... K 5
80455 Jamestown, 185 ... J 2
81048 Jansen, 267 ... K 8
81138 Jaroso, 56 ... H 8
80456 Jefferson, 45 ... H 4
80822 Joes, 100 ... O 3
80534 Johnstown, 1,191 ... K 2
80737 Julesburg⊙, 1,578 ... P 1
80823 Karval, 70 ... N 5
80643 Keenesburg, 427 ... L 2
80738 Keota, 6 ... L 1
80644 Kersey, 474 ... L 2
81049 Kim, 200 ... N 8
80117 Kiowa⊙, 235 ... L 4
80824 Kirk, 100 ... P 3
80825 Kit Carson, 220 ... O 5
† 80435 Kokomo, 75 ... G 4
80459 Kremmling, 764 ... G 2
80826 Kutch, 2 ... M 5
80026 Lafayette, 3,498 ... K 3
81139 La Garita, 50 ... G 7
80739 Laird, 105 ... P 2
81140 La Jara, 768 ... H 8
81050 La Junta⊙, 7,938 ... M 7
81235 Lake City⊙, 91 ... E 6
80827 Lake George, 29 ... J 5
80215 Lakewood, 92,787 ... J 3
81052 Lamar⊙, 7,797 ... O 6
80535 Laporte, 950 ... J 1
80118 Larkspur, 350 ... K 4
80645 La Salle, 1,227 ... K 2
81054 Las Animas⊙, 3,148 ... N 6
† 81151 Lasauces, 120 ... H 8
† 81153 Lavalley, 237 ... J 8
81055 La Veta, 589 ... J 8
† 80452 Lawson, 108 ... H 3
81625 Lay, 8 ... D 2
81420 Lazear, 60 ... D 5
80461 Leadville⊙, 4,314 ... G 4
† 81323 Lebanon, 50 ... B 8
81327 Lewis, 350 ... B 8
80828 Limon, 1,814 ... M 4
† 81212 Lincoln Park, 2,984 ... J 6
80740 Lindon, 50 ... N 3
80120 Littleton⊙, 26,466 ... K 3
80536 Livermore, 20 ... J 1
† 80701 Log Lane Village, 329 ... M 2
81524 Loma, 100 ... B 4
80501 Longmont, 23,209 ... J 2
† 80135 Longview, 10 ... J 4
80027 Louisville, 2,409 ... J 3
80131 Louviers, 306 ... K 4
80537 Loveland, 16,220 ... J 2
80646 Lucerne, 150 ... K 2
81056 Lycan, 4 ... P 7
80540 Lyons, 958 ... J 2
81525 Mack, 175 ... B 4
81421 Maher, 80 ... D 5
† 80461 Malta, 200 ... G 4
81141 Manassa, 814 ... H 8
81328 Mancos, 709 ... C 8
80829 Manitou Springs, 4,278 ... J 5
81058 Manzanola, 451 ... M 6
† 81623 Marble, 1 ... E 4
81329 Marvel, 100 ... C 8
80541 Masonville, 200 ... J 2
† 80649 Masters, 50 ... L 2
80830 Matheson, 100 ... M 4
81640 Maybell, 82 ... C 2
81057 McClave, 165 ... O 6
80463 McCoy, 14 ... F 3
80542 Mead, 195 ... K 2
81641 Meeker⊙, 1,597 ... D 2
81642 Meredith, 48 ... F 4
80741 Merino, 260 ... N 2
81005 Mesa, 295 ... C 4
81330 Mesa Verde National Park, 70 ... C 8
81142 Mesita, 50 ... H 8
80543 Milliken, 702 ... K 2
80477 Milner, 75 ... F 2
81645 Minturn, 706 ... G 3
81059 Model, 19 ... L 8
81143 Moffat, 98 ... H 6
81646 Molina, 120 ... D 4
81144 Monte Vista, 3,909 ... G 7
80464 Montezuma, 6 ... H 3

(continued on following page)

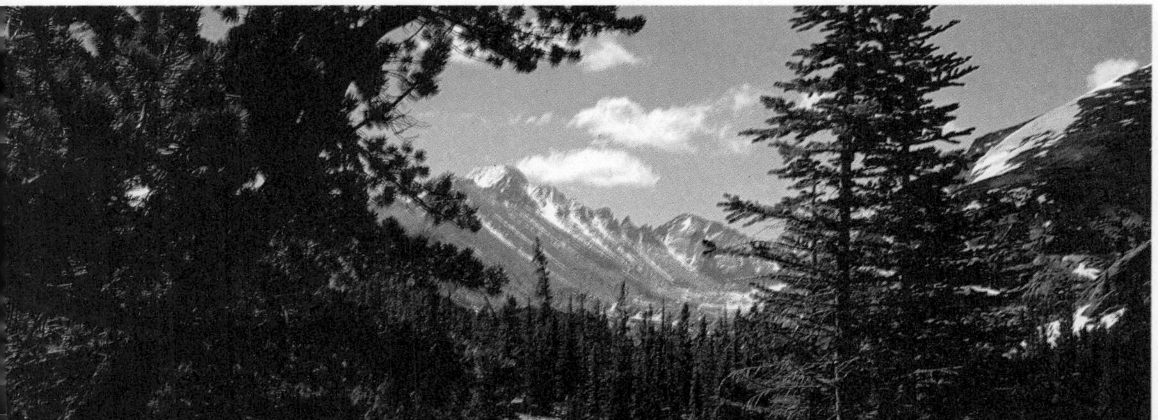

Colorado Department of Public Relations

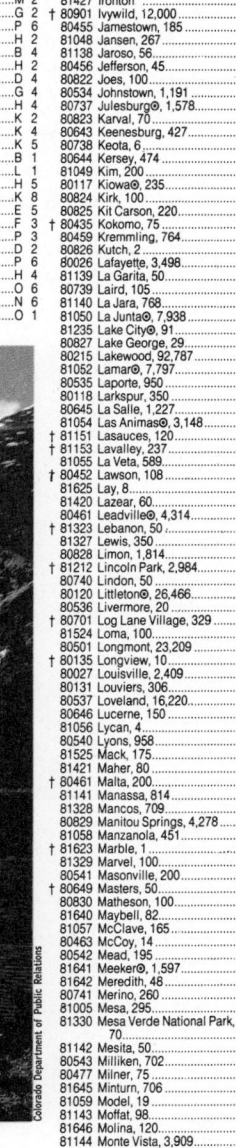

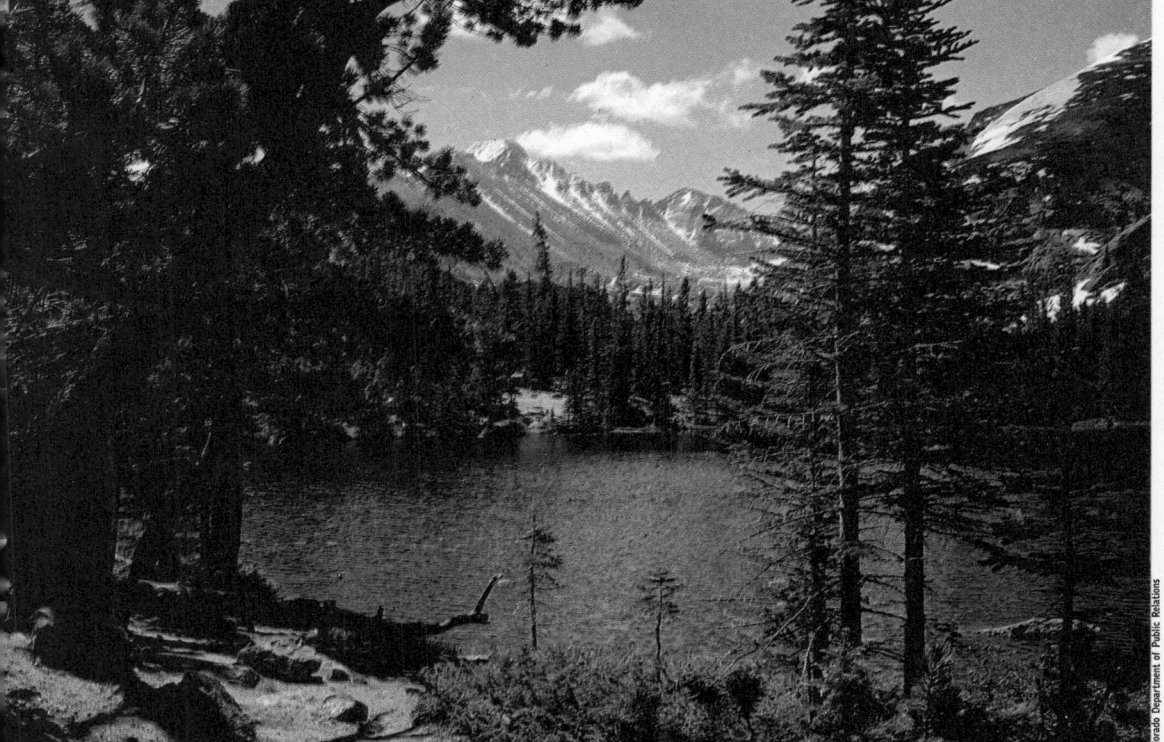

This view of Bear Lake and Longs Peak is typical of the beautiful mountain scenery found in Rocky Mountain National Park, an area which many call "the roof of America."

Topography

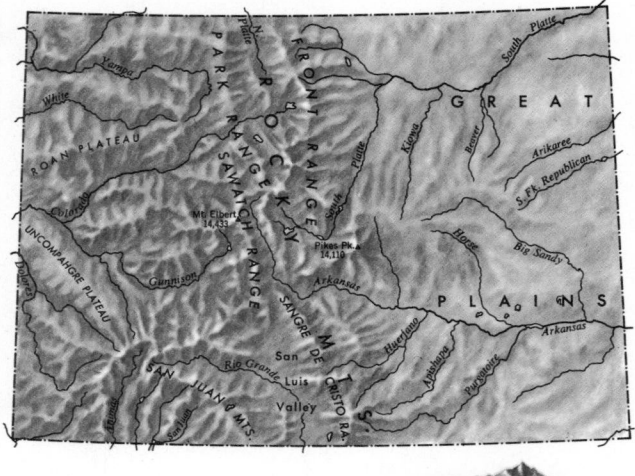

0   50   100
MILES

Below Sea Level | 100 m. 328 ft. | 200 m. 656 ft. | 500 m. 1,640 ft. | 1,000 m. 3,281 ft. | 2,000 m. 6,562 ft. | 5,000 m. 16,404 ft.

Agriculture, Industry and Resources

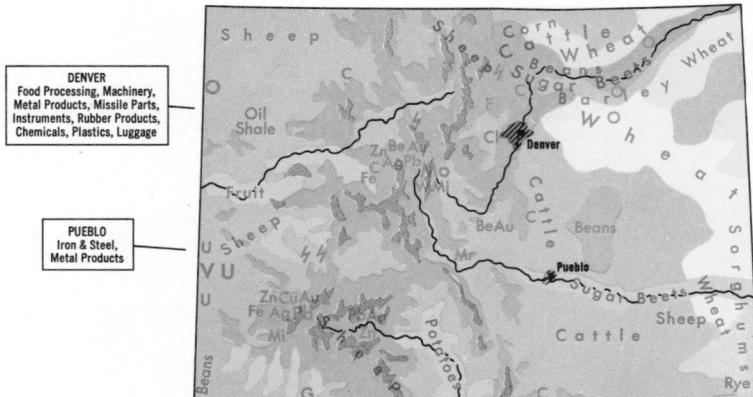

DENVER
Food Processing, Machinery, Metal Products, Missile Parts, Instruments, Rubber Products, Chemicals, Plastics, Luggage

PUEBLO
Iron & Steel, Metal Products

DOMINANT LAND USE

- Specialized Wheat
- Wheat, Range Livestock
- Wheat, Grain Sorghums, Range Livestock
- Dry Beans, General Farming
- Sugar Beets, Dry Beans, Livestock, General Farming
- Fruit, Mixed Farming
- General Farming, Livestock, Special Crops
- Range Livestock
- Forests
- Urban Areas
- Nonagricultural Land

MAJOR MINERAL OCCURRENCES

Ag	Silver	Mi	Mica
Au	Gold	Mo	Molybdenum
Be	Beryl	Mr	Marble
C	Coal	O	Petroleum
Cl	Clay	Pb	Lead
Cu	Copper	U	Uranium
F	Fluorspar	V	Vanadium
Fe	Iron Ore	W	Tungsten
G	Natural Gas	Zn	Zinc

↯ Water Power

▨ Major Industrial Areas

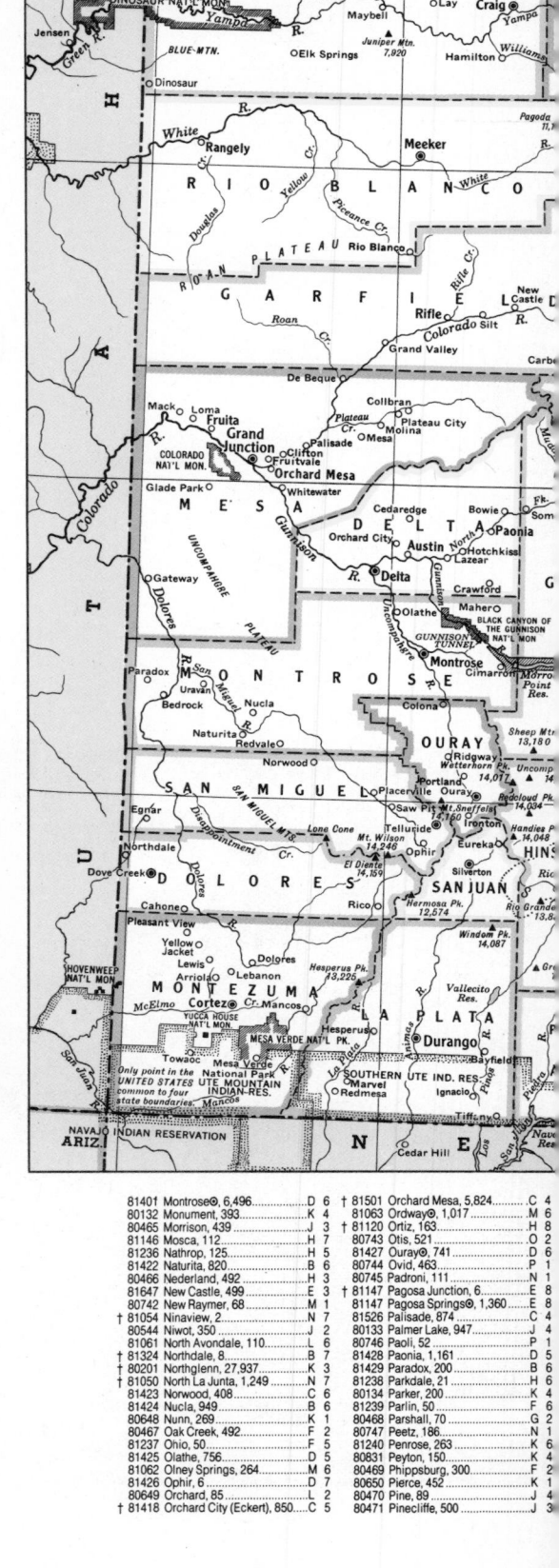

COLORADO

SCALE
0 5 10   20   30   40 MI.
0 5 10 20   30   40 KM.

State Capitals......⊛ County Seats......◉
© C.S. HAMMOND & Co., N.Y.

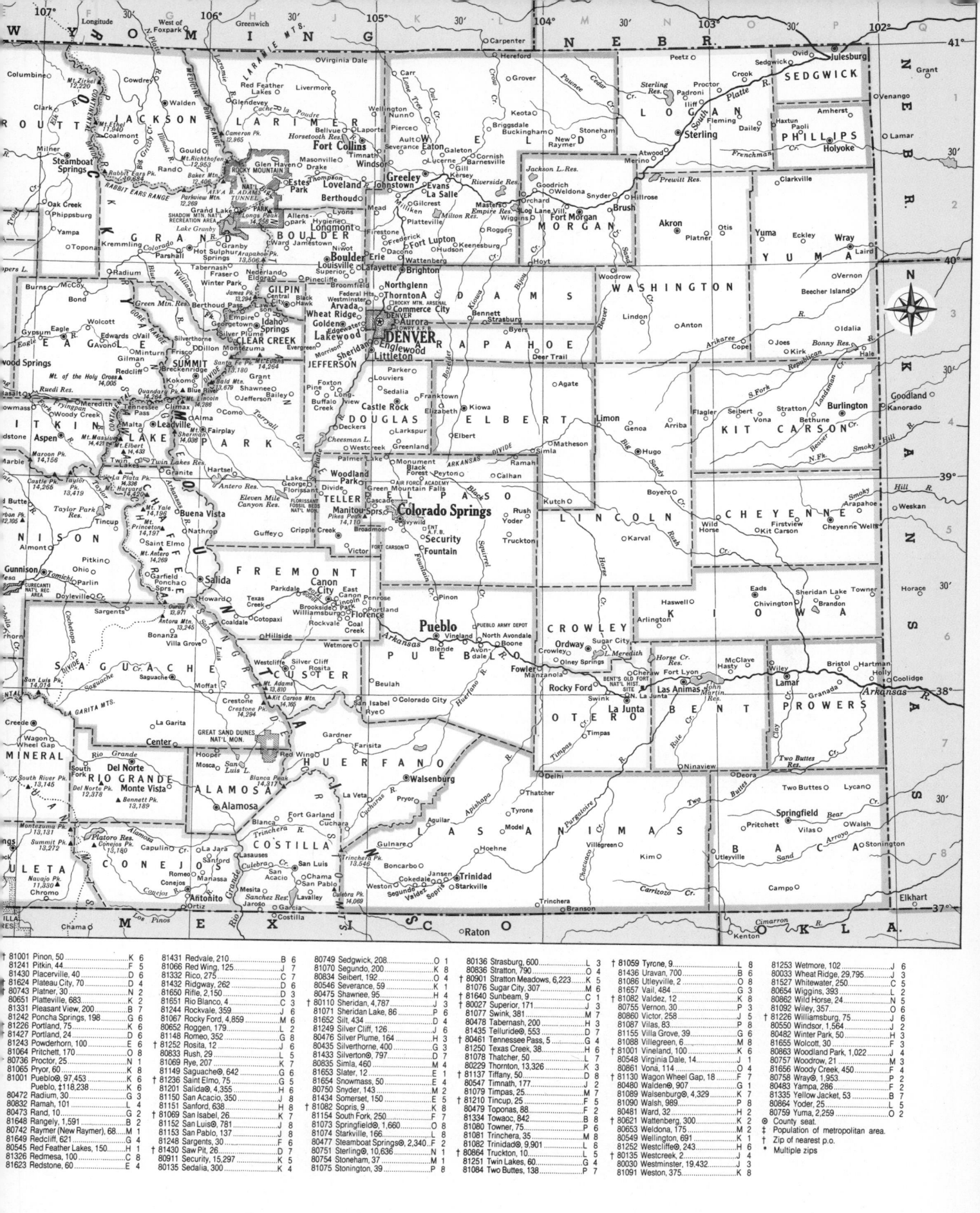

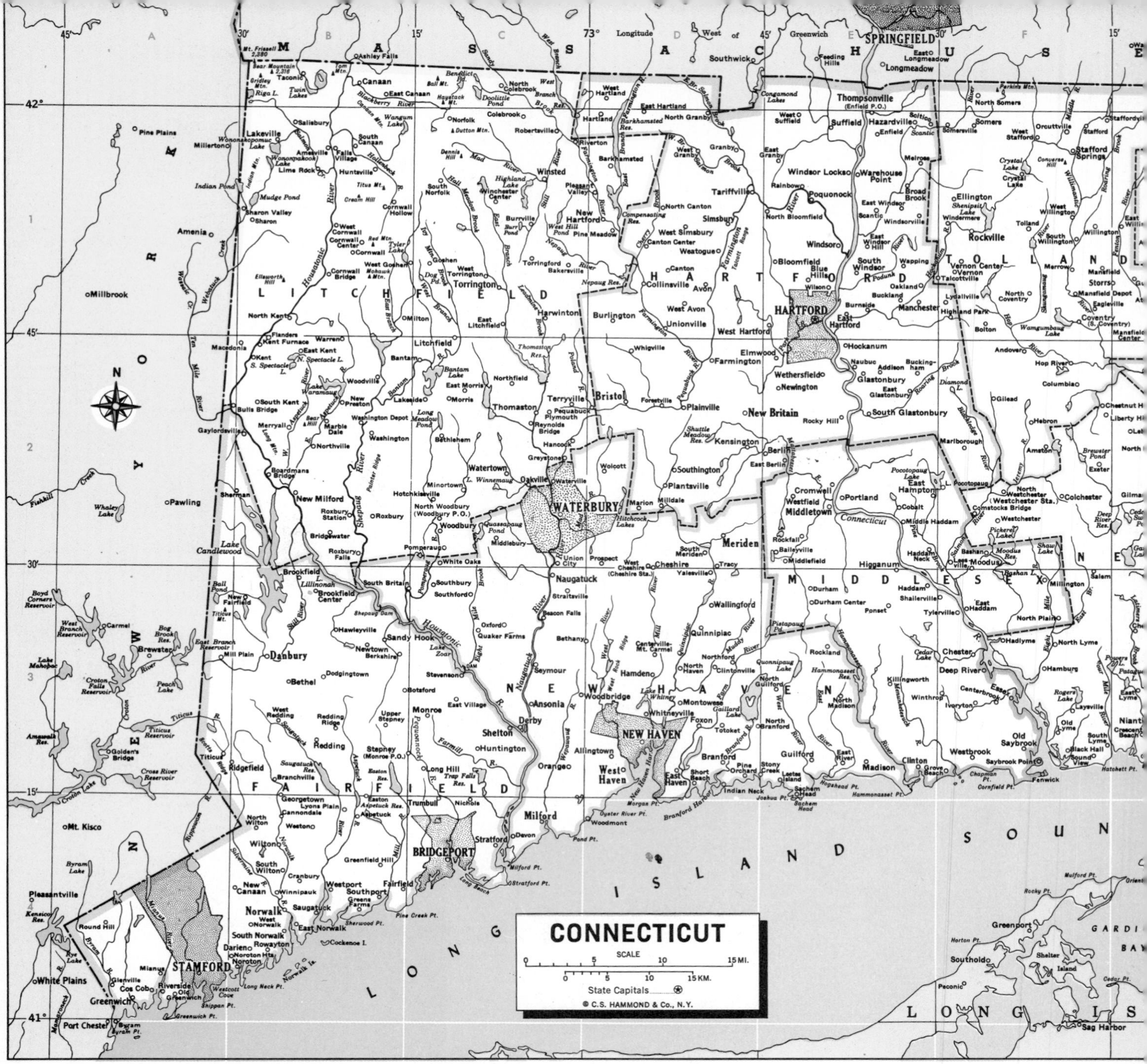

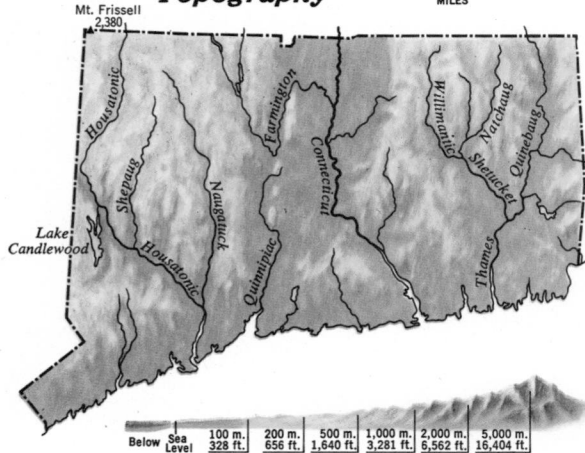

CONNECTICUT

SCALE

0   5   10   15 MI.

0   5   10   15 KM.

State Capitals ⊕

© C.S. HAMMOND & Co., N.Y.

Topography

Mt. Frissell 2,380

MILES   0   15   30

	100 m.	200 m.	500 m.	1,000 m.	2,000 m.	5,000 m.
Below Sea Level	328 ft.	656 ft.	1,640 ft.	3,281 ft.	6,562 ft.	16,404 ft.

COUNTIES

Name/Pop.	Key
Fairfield, 792,814	B 3
Hartford, 816,737	D 1
Litchfield, 144,091	B 1
Middlesex, 114,816	E 3
New Haven, 744,948	D 3
New London, 230,348	G 2
Tolland, 103,440	F 1
Windham, 84,515	H 1

CITIES and TOWNS

Zip	Name/Pop.	Key
† 06516	Allingtown, 7,000	D 3
06231	Amston, 1,963	F 2
06232	Andover, 2,099	F 2
06401	Ansonia, 21,160	C 3
† 06250	Ashford, 2,156	G 1
06001	Avon, △8,352	D 1
06330	Baltic, 1,500	G 2
† 06063	Barkhamsted, △2,066	D 1
06403	Beacon Falls, △3,546	C 3
06037	Berlin, △14,149	E 2
† 06501	Bethany, △3,857	C 3
06801	Bethel, △10,945	B 3
06751	Bethlehem, △1,923	C 2
06002	Bloomfield, △18,301	E 1
06002	Bloomfield, 8,000	E 1
06112	Blue Hills, 5,000	E 1
06640	Bolton, △3,691	F 1
06405	Branford, △20,444	D 3
06405	Branford, 2,080	D 3
* 06601	Bridgeport, 156,542	C 4
	Bridgeport, ‡388,953	C 4
06752	Bridgewater, △1,277	B 2
06010	Bristol, 55,487	D 2
06016	Broad Brook, 1,548	E 1
06804	Brookfield, △9,688	B 3
06804	Brookfield, 6,000	B 3
06805	Brookfield Center, 3,000	B 3
06234	Brooklyn, △4,965	H 1
06085	Burlington, △4,070	D 1
06085	Burlington, 950	D 1
10573	Byram, 5,631	A 4
06018	Canaan, △931	B 1
06018	Canaan, 1,083	B 1
06331	Canterbury, △2,673	H 2
06019	Canton, △6,868	D 1
06332	Central Village, 1,200	H 2
06235	Chaplin, △1,621	G 1
06410	Cheshire, △19,051	D 2
06412	Chester, △2,982	F 3
06412	Chester, 1,569	F 3
06413	Clinton, △10,267	E 3
06413	Clinton, 5,957	E 3
† 06473	Clintonville, 1,300	D 3
06415	Colchester, △6,603	F 2
06415	Colchester, 3,529	F 2
06021	Colebrook, △1,020	C 1
06022	Collinsville, 2,897	D 1
06238	Coventry, △8,140	F 1
06238	Coventry, 3,735	F 1
06416	Cromwell, △7,400	E 2
06810	Danbury, 50,781	B 3
06239	Danielson, 4,580	H 1
06820	Darien, △20,411	B 4
06241	Dayville, 950	H 1
06417	Deep River, △3,690	F 3
06417	Deep River, 2,333	F 3
06418	Derby, 12,599	C 3
† 06460	Devon, 2,750	C 3
06422	Durham, △4,489	E 2
06023	East Berlin, 1,100	E 2
† 06239	East Brooklyn, 1,377	H 1
06242	Eastford, △922	G 1
06026	East Granby, △3,352	E 1
06423	East Haddam, △4,474	F 2
06424	East Hampton, △7,078	E 2
06424	East Hampton, 1,982	E 2
06108	East Hartford, △57,583	E 1
06512	East Haven, 25,120	D 3
06333	East Lyme, △11,399	G 2
† 06856	East Norwalk, 9,500	B 4
06425	Easton, △4,885	B 3
† 06088	East Windsor, △8,513	E 1
06029	Ellington, △7,707	F 1
06110	Elmwood, 18,500	D 1
06082	Enfield, △46,189	E 1
06082	Enfield P.O. (Thompsonville), 27,000	E 1
06426	Essex, △4,911	F 3
06426	Essex, 2,473	F 3
06430	Fairfield, △56,487	B 3
06032	Farmington, △14,390	D 1
† 06010	Forestville, 20,000	D 2

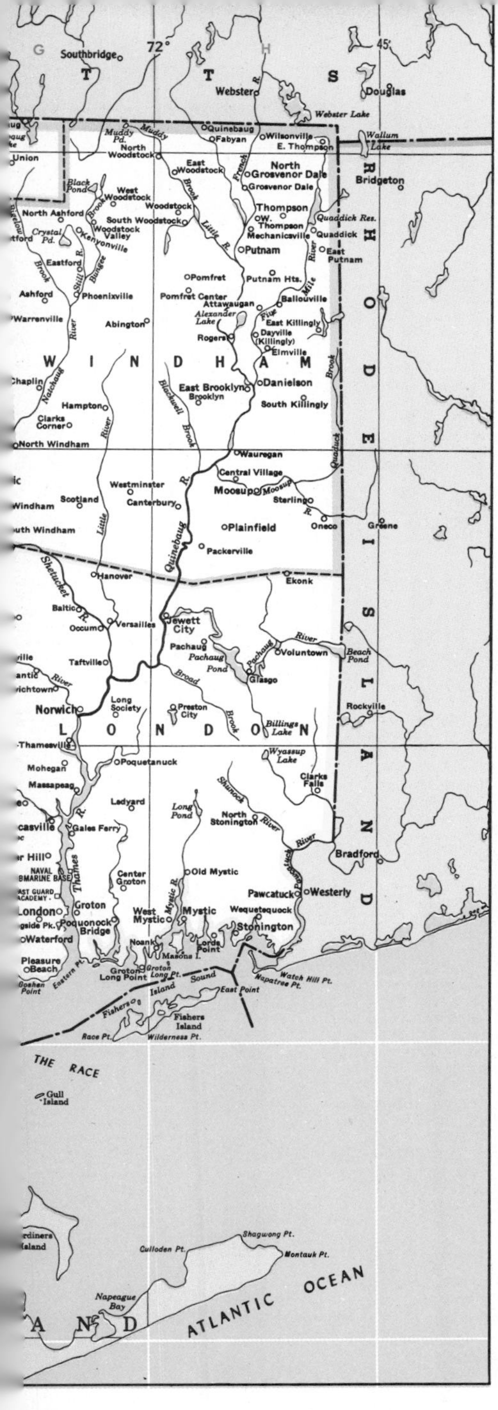
Southbridge
72°
T
S
Webster
Douglas
Webster Lake
Quinebaug
Fabyan
Wilsonville
E. Thompson
Wallum Lake
North Woodstock
East Woodstock
North Grosvenor Dale
Grosvenor Dale
Bridgeton
West Woodstock
Woodstock
Thompson
South Woodstock
Quaddick Res.
North Ashford
Woodstock Valley
Mechanicsville
Quaddick
Putnam
East Putnam
Eastford
Pomfret
Putnam Hts.
Ashford
Phoenixville
Pomfret Center
Ballouville
Abington
Alexander Lake
East Killingly
Dayville
Rogers
Elmville
W I N D H A M
East Brooklyn
Danielson
Brooklyn
South Killingly
Hampton
Clarks Corner
North Windham
Wauregan
Central Village
Westminster
Scotland
Canterbury
Moosup
Sterling
Windham
Oneco
South Windham
Plainfield
Greene
Packerville
Hanover
Ekonk
Baltic
Versailles
Jewett City
Occum
Pachaug
Voluntown
Beach Pond
Taftville
Pachaug Pond
Glasgo
Long Society
Preston City
Rockville
Norwich
L O N D O N
Billings Lake
Thamesville
Poquetanuck
Wyassup Lake
Mohegan
Massapeag
Clarks Falls
Ledyard
Long Pond
North Stonington
Gales Ferry
Bradford
Old Mystic
Center Groton
Pawcatuck
Westerly
Groton
West Mystic
Mystic
Wequetequock
Poquonock Bridge
Stonington
Waterford
Noank
Masons I.
Lords Point
Pleasure Beach
Groton Long Point
Watch Hill Pt.
Napatree Pt.
East Point
Fishers Island
Race Pt.
Wilderness Pt.
THE RACE
Gull Island
Shagwong Pt.
Culloden Pt.
Montauk Pt.
Napeague Bay
ATLANTIC OCEAN

†	06254	Franklin, ▵1,356	G 2
	06335	Gales Ferry, 6,200	G 3
	06829	Georgetown, 1,101	B 4
	06033	Glastonbury, ▵20,651	E 2
	06756	Goshen, ▵1,351	C 1
	06035	Granby, ▵6,150	D 1
†	06430	Greenfield Hill, 2,500	B 4
	06436	Greens Farms, 3,147	B 4
	06830	Greenwich, ▵59,755	A 4
	06340	Groton, ▵38,523	G 3
	06340	Groton, 8,933	G 3
	06437	Guilford, ▵12,033	E 3
	06437	Guilford, 3,632	E 3
	06438	Haddam, ▵4,934	E 3
	06438	Haddam, 950	E 3
	06514	Hamden, ▵49,357	D 3
	06247	Hampton, ▵1,129	G 1
*	06101	Hartford (cap.), 158,017	E 1
		Hartford, ‡663,891	E 1
†	06091	Hartland, ▵1,303	D 1
	06790	Harwinton, ▵4,318	C 1
	06082	Hazardville, 10,000	E 1
	06248	Hebron, ▵3,815	F 2
	06441	Higganum, 2,600	E 2
†	06108	Hockanum, 6,500	E 2
†	06484	Huntington, 2,000	C 3
†	06405	Indian Neck, 1,500	D 3
	06442	Ivoryton, 1,500	F 3
	06351	Jewett City, 3,372	H 2
	06037	Kensington, 6,000	D 2
	06757	Kent, ▵1,990	B 2
†	06241	Killingly, ▵13,573	H 1
†	06413	Killingworth, ▵2,435	E 3
†	06424	Lake Pocotopaug, 1,515	F 2
	06039	Lakeville, 2,100	B 1
	06249	Lebanon, ▵3,804	G 2
	06339	Ledyard, ▵14,558	G 3
	06759	Litchfield, ▵7,399	C 2
	06759	Litchfield, 1,559	C 2
	06443	Madison, ▵9,768	E 3
	06443	Madison, 4,310	E 3
	06040	Manchester, ▵47,994	E 1
†	06250	Mansfield, ▵19,994	F 1
	06444	Marion, 1,800	D 2
†	06424	Marlborough, ▵2,991	F 2
	06450	Meriden, 55,959	D 2
		Meriden, ‡55,959	D 2
	06762	Middlebury, ▵5,542	C 2
	06455	Middlefield, ▵4,132	E 2
	06457	Middletown, 36,924	E 2
	06460	Milford, 50,858	C 4
	06467	Milldale, 1,175	D 2
	06468	Monroe, ▵12,047	C 3
	06468	Monroe P.O. (Stepney), 3,000	B 3
†	06473	Montowese, 2,500	D 3
	06353	Montville, 1,688	G 3
	06353	Montville, ▵15,662	G 3
	06469	Moodus, 1,352	F 2
.	06354	Moosup, 3,376	H 2
†	06385	Morningside Park, 3,458	G 3
	06763	Morris, ▵1,609	C 2
	06355	Mystic, 2,568	H 3
	06770	Naugatuck, 23,034	C 3
*	06050	New Britain, 83,441	E 2
		New Britain, ‡145,269	E 2
	06840	New Canaan, ▵17,455	B 4
	06810	New Fairfield, ▵6,991	B 3
	06057	New Hartford, ▵3,970	C 1
	06057	New Hartford, 1,076	C 1
*	06501	New Haven, 137,707	D 3
		New Haven, ‡355,538	D 3
	06111	Newington, ▵26,037	E 2
	06320	New London, 31,630	G 3
		New London-Groton-Norwich, ‡208,412	G 3
	06776	New Milford, ▵14,601	B 2
	06776	New Milford, 4,606	B 2
	06470	Newtown, ▵16,942	B 3
	06470	Newtown, 1,963	B 3
	06357	Niantic, 3,422	G 3
†	06611	Nichols, 5,000	C 4
	06340	Noank, 950	G 3
	06058	Norfolk, ▵2,073	C 1
†	06820	Noroton, 4,000	B 4
†	06820	Noroton Heights, 7,000	B 4
	06471	North Branford, ▵10,778	E 3
	06472	Northford, 4,950	D 3
	06060	North Granby, 1,500	D 1
	06255	North Grosvenor Dale, 2,156	H 1
	06473	North Haven, ▵22,194	D 3
	06359	North Stonington, ▵3,748	H 3
*	06850	Norwalk, 79,113	B 4
		Norwalk, ‡120,099	B 4
	06360	Norwich, 41,433	G 2
†	06360	Norwichtown, 6,500	G 2
	06779	Oakville, 8,000	C 2
†	06360	Occum, 1,500	G 2
	06870	Old Greenwich, 5,000	A 4
	06371	Old Lyme, ▵4,964	F 3
	06371	Old Lyme, 1,200	F 3
	06475	Old Saybrook, ▵8,468	F 3
	06475	Old Saybrook, 2,281	F 3
	06477	Orange, ▵13,524	C 3
	06483	Oxford, ▵4,480	C 3
	06483	Oxford, 950	C 3
	02891	Pawcatuck, 5,255	H 3
†	06405	Pine Orchard, 2,000	D 3
	06374	Plainfield, ▵11,957	H 2
	06374	Plainfield, 2,923	H 2
	06062	Plainville, ▵16,733	D 2
	06479	Plantsville, 3,900	D 2
†	06385	Pleasure Beach, 1,394	G 3
	06782	Plymouth, ▵10,321	C 2
	06258	Pomfret, ▵2,529	H 1
	06064	Poquonock, 2,000	E 1
†	06340	Poquonock Bridge, 3,165	G 3
	06480	Portland, ▵8,812	E 2
†	06360	Preston, ▵3,593	H 2
	06712	Prospect, ▵6,543	D 2
	06260	Putnam, ▵8,598	H 1
	06260	Putnam, 6,918	H 1
	06375	Quaker Hill, 2,068	G 3
	06262	Quinebaug, 1,350	H 1
†	06492	Quinnipiac, 7,500	D 3
	06875	Redding, ▵5,590	B 3
	06876	Redding Ridge, 1,500	B 3
	06877	Ridgefield, ▵18,188	B 3
	06877	Ridgefield, 5,878	B 3
	06878	Riverside, 10,719	A 4
	06066	Rockville, 12,500	F 1
	06067	Rocky Hill, ▵11,103	E 2
	06853	Rowayton, 4,210	B 4
	06783	Roxbury, ▵1,238	B 2
†	06415	Salem, ▵1,453	F 3
	06068	Salisbury, ▵3,573	B 1
	06482	Sandy Hook, 3,900	B 3
†	06880	Saugatuck, 3,311	B 4
	06264	Scotland, ▵1,022	G 2
	06483	Seymour, ▵12,776	C 3
	06069	Sharon, ▵2,491	B 1
	06484	Shelton, 27,165	C 3
	06784	Sherman, ▵1,459	B 2
†	06405	Short Beach, 2,500	D 3
	06070	Simsbury, ▵17,475	D 1
	06070	Simsbury, 4,994	D 1
	06071	Somers, ▵6,893	F 1
	06071	Somers, 1,274	F 1
	06488	Southbury, ▵7,852	C 3
†	06238	South Coventry (Coventry), 3,735	F 1
	06073	South Glastonbury, 3,000	E 2
	06489	Southington, ▵30,946	D 2
†	06850	South Norwalk, 21,000	B 4
	06490	Southport, 3,500	B 4
†	06897	South Wilton, 1,400	B 4
	06074	South Windsor, ▵15,553	E 1
	06075	Stafford, ▵8,680	F 1
	06076	Stafford Springs, 3,339	F 1
	06077	Staffordville, 1,200	G 1
*	06901	Stamford, 108,798	A 4
		Stamford, ‡206,419	A 4
†	06468	Stepney, 2,300	B 3
	06377	Sterling, ▵1,853	H 2
	06491	Stevenson, 1,500	C 3
	06378	Stonington, ▵15,940	H 3
	06378	Stonington, 1,413	H 3
†	06405	Stony Creek, 2,800	E 3
	06268	Storrs, 10,691	F 1
	06497	Stratford, ▵49,775	C 4
	06078	Suffield, ▵8,634	E 1
	06380	Taftville, 2,000	G 2
	06081	Tariffville, 1,337	D 1
	06786	Terryville, 6,900	C 2
†	06360	Thamesville, 1,500	G 2
	06787	Thomaston, ▵6,233	C 2
	06277	Thompson, ▵7,580	H 1
	06277	Thompson, 1,200	H 1
†	06082	Thompsonville, 27,000	E 1
	06084	Tolland, ▵7,857	F 1
†	06790	Torringford, 3,500	C 1
	06790	Torrington, 31,952	C 1
†	06405	Totoket, 950	D 3
	06611	Trumbull, ▵31,394	C 4
	06611	Trumbull, 10,000	C 4
	06382	Uncasville, 1,750	G 3
†	06076	Union, ▵443	G 1
†	06770	Union City, 5,000	C 2
	06085	Unionville, 2,900	D 1
	06086	Vernon, ▵27,237	F 1
	06384	Voluntown, ▵1,452	H 2
	06492	Wallingford, ▵35,714	D 3
†	06074	Wapping, 1,600	E 1
	06088	Warehouse Point, 2,400	E 1
	06754	Warren, ▵827	B 2
	06793	Washington, ▵3,121	B 2
*	06701	Waterbury, 108,033	C 2
		Waterbury, ‡208,956	C 2
	06385	Waterford, ▵17,227	G 3
	06795	Watertown, ▵18,610	C 2
	06795	Watertown, 9,000	C 2
	06714	Waterville, 4,295	C 2
	06387	Wauregan, 1,100	H 2
	06089	Weatogue, 2,396	D 1
†	06001	West Avon, 4,500	D 1
	06498	Westbrook, ▵3,820	F 3
	06498	Westbrook, 1,507	F 3
†	06410	West Cheshire, 2,000	D 3
†	06457	Westfield, 9,000	E 2
	06107	West Hartford, ▵68,031	D 1
	06516	West Haven, 52,851	D 3
	06388	West Mystic, 3,694	H 3
†	06856	West Norwalk, 950	B 4
	06880	Weston, ▵7,417	B 4
	06880	Weston, 3,000	B 4
	06880	Westport, ▵27,414	B 4
	06896	West Redding, 1,200	B 3
	06092	West Simsbury, 1,419	D 1
	06093	West Suffield, 2,400	E 1
	06109	Wethersfield, 26,662	E 2
	06517	Whitneyville, 18,438	D 3
	06226	Willimantic, 14,402	G 2
†	06279	Willington, ▵3,755	F 1
	06897	Wilton, ▵13,572	B 4
	06897	Wilton, 4,200	B 4
	06094	Winchester, ▵11,106	C 1
	06094	Winchester Center, 350	C 1
	06280	Windham, ▵19,626	G 2
	06095	Windsor, ▵22,502	E 1
	06096	Windsor Locks, ▵15,080	E 1
	06098	Winsted, 8,954	C 1
	06716	Wolcott, ▵12,495	D 2
†	06501	Woodbridge, ▵7,673	D 3
	06798	Woodbury, ▵5,869	C 2
	06798	Woodbury, 1,800	C 2
	06798	Woodbury P.O. (North Woodbury), 1,342	C 2
†	06460	Woodmont, 2,400	D 4
	06281	Woodstock, ▵4,311	H 1
†	06492	Yalesville, 3,500	D 3
	06389	Yantic, 1,200	G 2

‡ Population of metropolitan area.
▵ Population of town or township.
† Zip of nearest p.o.
* Multiple zips

AREA 5,009 sq. mi.
POPULATION 3,032,217
CAPITAL Hartford
LARGEST CITY Hartford
HIGHEST POINT Mt. Frissell (S. Slope) 2,380 ft.
SETTLED IN 1635
ADMITTED TO UNION January 9, 1788
POPULAR NAME Constitution State; Nutmeg State
STATE FLOWER Mountain Laurel
STATE BIRD Robin

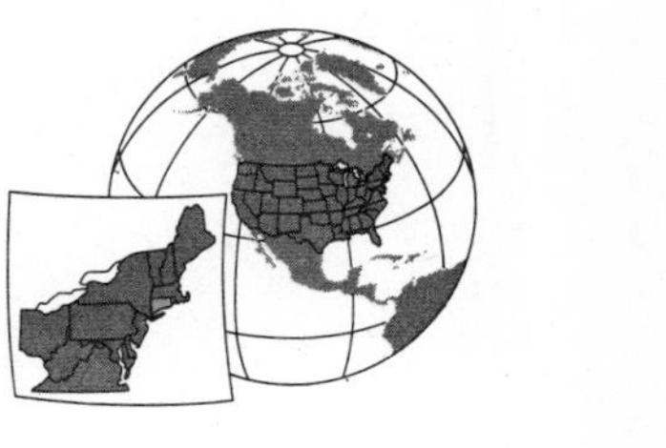

Agriculture, Industry and Resources

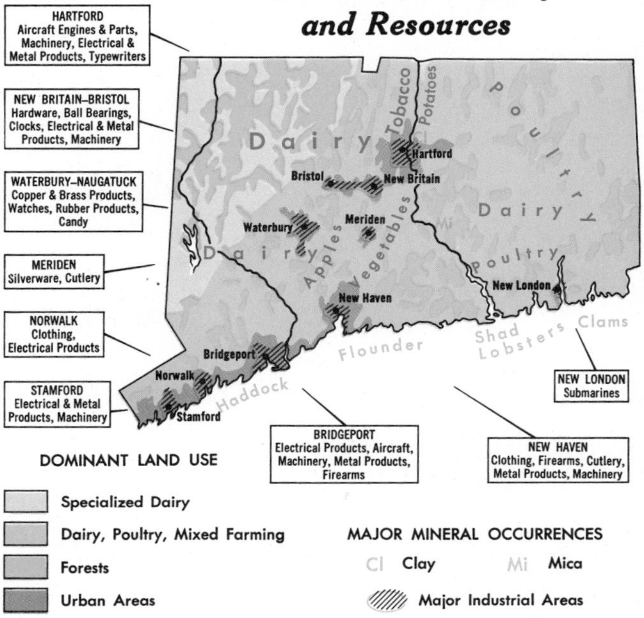
HARTFORD
Aircraft Engines & Parts, Machinery, Electrical & Metal Products, Typewriters
NEW BRITAIN–BRISTOL
Hardware, Ball Bearings, Clocks, Electrical & Metal Products, Machinery
WATERBURY–NAUGATUCK
Copper & Brass Products, Watches, Rubber Products, Candy
MERIDEN
Silverware, Cutlery
NORWALK
Clothing, Electrical Products
STAMFORD
Electrical & Metal Products, Machinery
BRIDGEPORT
Electrical Products, Aircraft, Machinery, Metal Products, Firearms
NEW HAVEN
Clothing, Firearms, Cutlery, Metal Products, Machinery
NEW LONDON
Submarines
Dairy
Tobacco
Potatoes
Poultry
Hartford
Bristol
New Britain
Waterbury
Meriden
Apples
Vegetables
New Haven
New London
Bridgeport
Norwalk
Stamford
Flounder
Haddock
Shad
Lobsters
Clams
DOMINANT LAND USE
Specialized Dairy
Dairy, Poultry, Mixed Farming
Forests
Urban Areas
MAJOR MINERAL OCCURRENCES
Cl Clay
Mi Mica
Major Industrial Areas

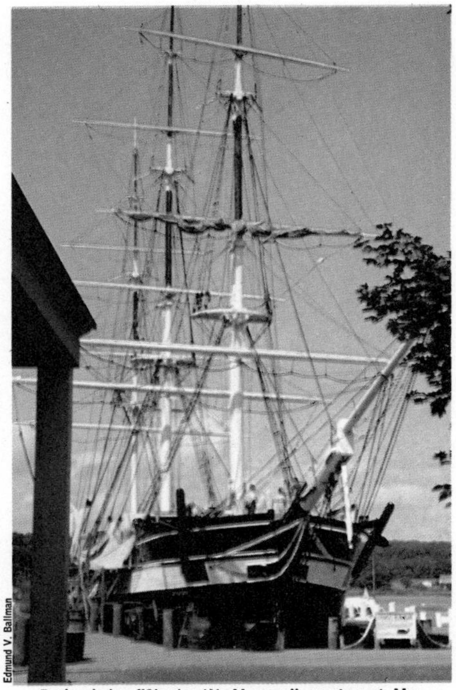
Edmund V. Ballman

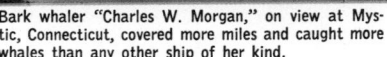

Bark whaler "Charles W. Morgan," on view at Mystic, Connecticut, covered more miles and caught more whales than any other ship of her kind.

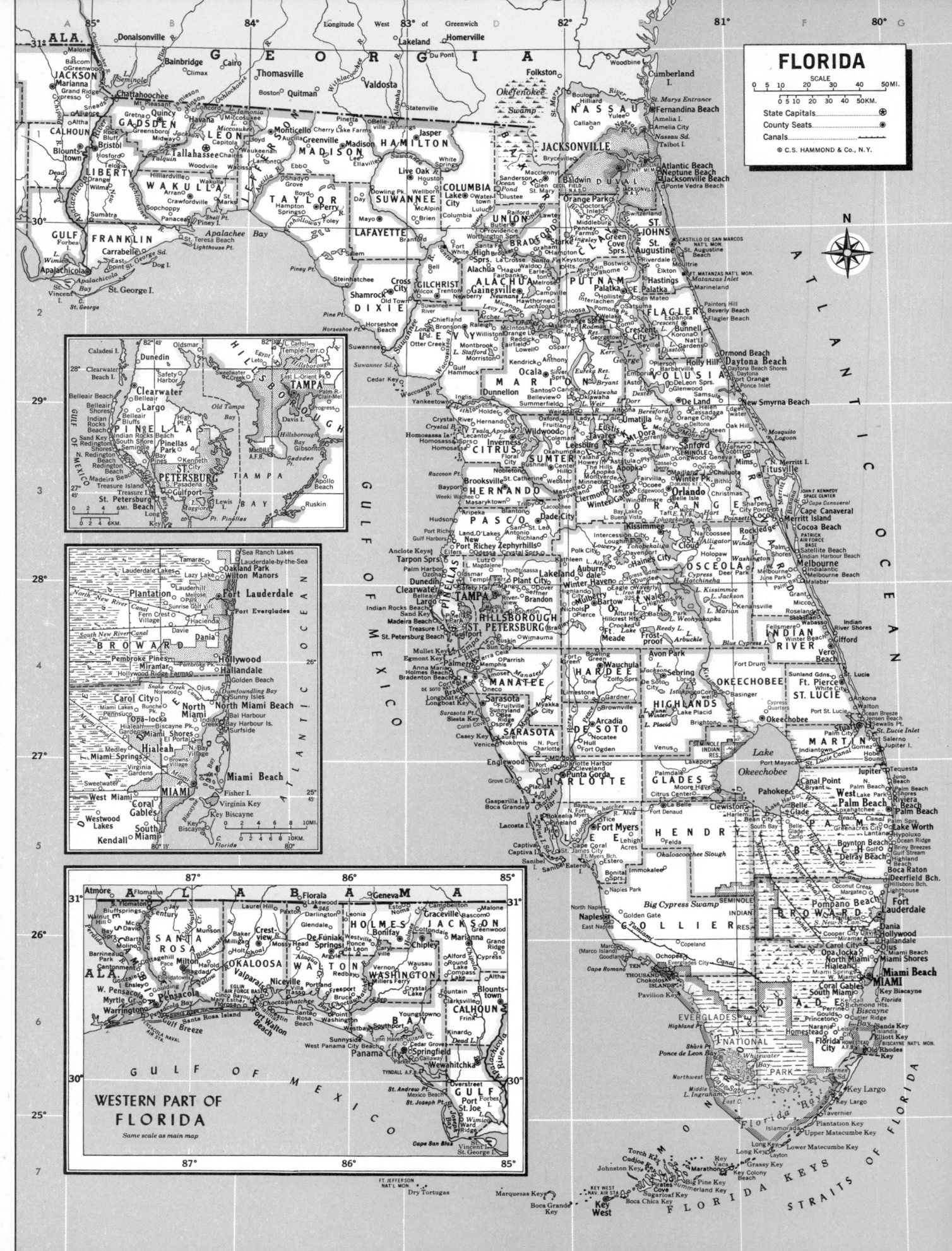

COUNTIES

Alachua, 104,764 ....D 2
Baker, 9,242 ....D 1
Bay, 75,283 ....C 6
Bradford, 14,625 ....D 2
Brevard, 230,006 ....F 3
Broward, 620,100 ....F 5
Calhoun, 7,624 ....D 6
Charlotte, 27,559 ....E 5
Citrus, 19,196 ....D 3
Clay, 32,059 ....E 2
Collier, 38,040 ....E 5
Columbia, 25,250 ....D 1
Dade, 1,287,792 ....F 6
De Soto, 13,060 ....E 4
Dixie, 5,480 ....C 2
Duval, 528,865 ....E 1
Escambia, 205,334 ....A 6
Flagler, 4,454 ....E 2
Franklin, 7,065 ....C 2
Gadsden, 39,184 ....B 1
Gilchrist, 3,551 ....D 2
Glades, 3,669 ....E 5
Gulf, 10,096 ....D 7
Hamilton, 7,787 ....D 1
Hardee, 14,889 ....E 4
Hendry, 11,859 ....E 5
Hernando, 17,004 ....E 3
Highlands, 29,507 ....E 4
Hillsborough, 490,265 .....D 4
Holmes, 10,720 ....C 5
Indian River, 35,992 .....F 4
Jackson, 34,434 ....D 5
Jefferson, 8,778 ....C 1
Lafayette, 2,892 ....C 2
Lake, 69,305 ....E 3
Lee, 105,216 ....E 5
Leon, 103,047 ....B 1
Levy, 12,756 ....D 2
Liberty, 3,379 ....B 1
Madison, 13,481 ....C 1
Manatee, 97,115 ....D 4
Marion, 69,030 ....D 2
Martin, 28,035 ....F 4
Monroe, 52,586 ....E 7
Nassau, 20,626 ....E 1
Okaloosa, 88,187 ....C 6
Okeechobee, 11,233 ....F 4
Orange, 344,311 ....E 3
Osceola, 25,267 ....E 3
Palm Beach, 348,753 ....F 5
Pasco, 75,955 ....D 3
Pinellas, 522,329 ....D 4
Polk, 227,222 ....E 4
Putnam, 36,290 ....E 2
Saint Johns, 30,727 ....E 2
Saint Lucie, 50,836 ....F 4
Santa Rosa, 37,741 ....B 6
Sarasota, 120,413 ....D 4
Seminole, 83,692 ....E 3
Sumter, 14,839 ....D 3

Suwannee, 15,559 ....C 1
Taylor, 13,641 ....C 1
Union, 8,112 ....D 1
Volusia, 169,487 ....E 2
Wakulla, 6,308 ....B 1
Walton, 16,087 ....C 6
Washington, 11,453 ....C 6

CITIES and TOWNS

Zip	Name/Pop.	Key
32615	Alachua, 2,252	D 2
32420	Alford, 402	D 6
32421	Altha, 423	A 1
32702	Altoona, 800	E 3
33820	Alturas, 468	E 4
33920	Alva, 900	E 5
33501	Anna Maria, 1,137	D 4
32617	Anthony, 500	D 2
32320	Apalachicola⊙, 3,102	A 2
33570	Apollo Beach, 1,042	D 4
32703	Apopka, 4,045	E 3
33821	Arcadia⊙, 5,658	E 4
32422	Argyle, 155	C 6
33502	Aripeka, 300	D 3
† 32327	Arran, 160	B 1
32705	Astatula, 388	E 3
32002	Astor, 300	E 2
33823	Auburndale, 5,386	E 3
† 32344	Aucilla, 150	C 1
33825	Avon Park, 6,712	E 4
33827	Babson Park, 950	E 4
32530	Bagdad, 850	B 6
32531	Baker, 500	C 5
32234	Baldwin, 1,272	E 1
† 33101	Bal Harbour, 2,038	C 4
32005	Barberville, 300	E 2
† 32533	Barrineau Park, 150	B 6
32532	Barth, 200	B 6
33830	Bartow⊙, 12,891	A 1
32423	Bascom, 300	E 4
33428	Basinger, 300	F 4
† 33101	Bay Harbour Islands, 4,619	B 3
33504	Bay Pines, 1,100	F 4
33902	Bayshore, 150	B 5
† 36502	Bay Springs, 125	B 6
33429	Bean City, 155	F 5
33578	Bee Ridge, 2,100	D 4
32619	Bell, 227	D 2
33540	Belleair, 2,962	B 2
† 33540	Belleair Beach, 952	B 2
33540	Belleair Bluffs, 1,910	B 3
33430	Belle Glade, 15,949	F 5
33430	Belle Glade Camp, 1,892	F 5
† 32801	Belle Isle, 2,705	E 2
32620	Belleview, 916	D 2
33152	Biscayne Park, 2,717	B 4
† 32801	Bithlo, 684	E 3
32424	Blountstown⊙, 2,384	A 1
32621	Bronson⊙, 698	D 2
32622	Brooker, 340	D 2
33512	Brooksville⊙, 4,060	D 3

33432	Boca Raton, 28,506	F 5
33922	Bokeelia, 750	D 5
32425	Bonifay⊙, 2,068	C 5
33923	Bonita Springs, 1,932	E 5
32007	Bostwick, 500	E 2
33834	Bowling Green, 1,357	E 4
33435	Boynton Beach, 18,115	F 5
33505	Bradenton⊙, 21,040	D 4
33510	Bradenton Beach, 1,370	D 4
33835	Bradley, 1,276	D 4
33511	Brandon, 12,749	D 4
32008	Branford, 820	D 2
† 33435	Briny Breezes, 481	G 5
32321	Bristol⊙, 626	B 1

AREA 58,560 sq. mi.
POPULATION 6,789,443
CAPITAL Tallahassee
LARGEST CITY Jacksonville
HIGHEST POINT 345 ft. (Walton County)
SETTLED IN 1565
ADMITTED TO UNION March 3, 1845
POPULAR NAME Sunshine State; Peninsula State
STATE FLOWER Orange Blossom
STATE BIRD Mockingbird

Topography

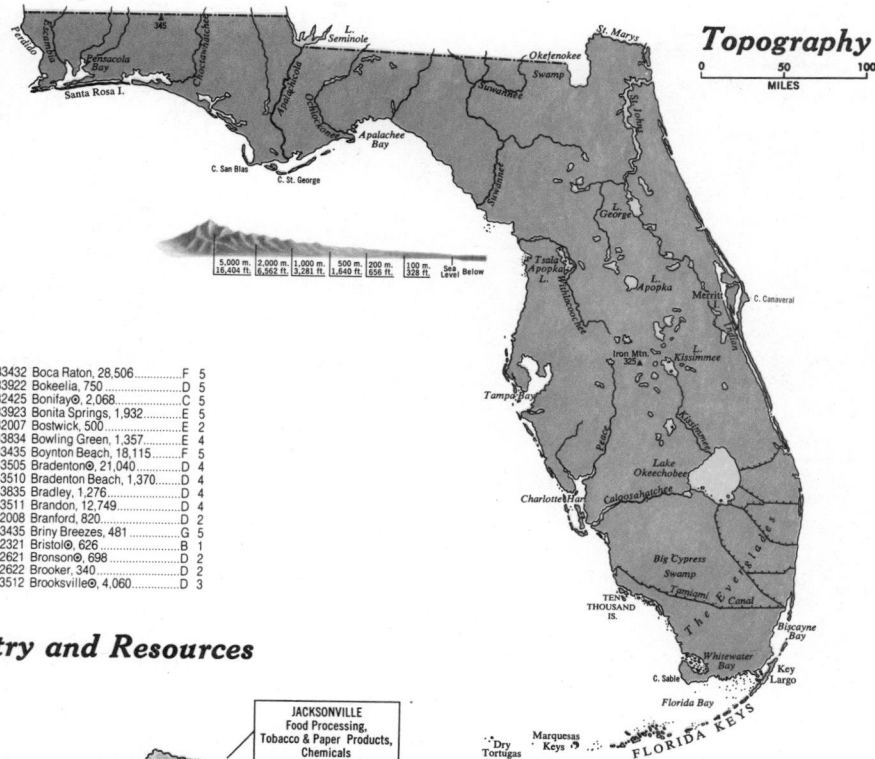

0   50   100
MILES

5,000 m. 2,000 m. 1,000 m. 500 m. 200 m. 100 m. Sea Below
16,404 ft. 6,562 ft. 3,281 ft. 1,640 ft. 656 ft. 328 ft. Level

Agriculture, Industry and Resources

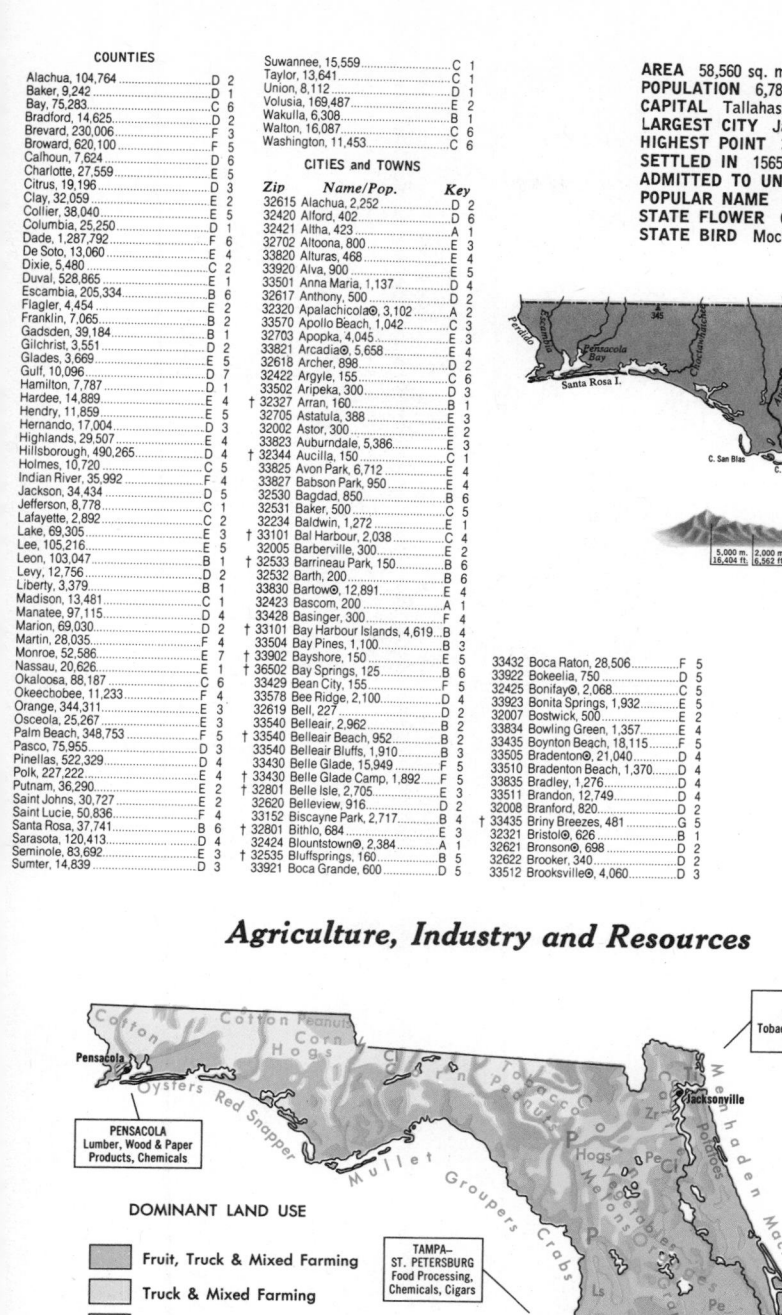

JACKSONVILLE
Food Processing,
Tobacco & Paper Products,
Chemicals

PENSACOLA
Lumber, Wood & Paper
Products, Chemicals

**TAMPA–
ST. PETERSBURG**
Food Processing,
Chemicals, Cigars

**MIAMI–
WEST PALM BEACH**
Aircraft, Metal & Electrical
Products, Food Processing,
Clothing, Furniture

DOMINANT LAND USE

Fruit, Truck & Mixed Farming

Truck & Mixed Farming

Truck Farming

Cotton, Tobacco, Hogs, Peanuts

Peanuts, General Farming

General Farming, Forest Products,
Truck Farming, Cotton

Livestock Grazing

Forests

Swampland, Limited Agriculture

Urban Areas

Nonagricultural Land

MAJOR MINERAL OCCURRENCES

Cl	Clay	Pe	Peat
Ls	Limestone	Ti	Titanium
P	Phosphates	Zr	Zirconium
⚡	Water Power		

▨ Major Industrial Areas

† 33103	Browns Village, 23,442	B 4
32455	Bruce, 221	C 6
33439	Bryant, 400	F 5
† 33054	Bunche Park, 5,773	B 4
32010	Bunnell⊙, 1,687	E 2
33513	Bushnell⊙, 700	D 3
32011	Callahan, 772	E 1
32401	Callaway, 3,240	D 6
32426	Campbellton, 304	D 5
33438	Canal Point, 900	F 5
32624	Candler, 500	E 2
32533	Cantonment, 3,241	B 6
32920	Cape Canaveral, 4,258	F 3
33904	Cape Coral, 10,193	E 5
33924	Captiva, 150	D 5
33022	Carol City, 27,361	B 4
32322	Carrabelle, 1,044	A 2
32427	Caryville, 724	C 6
32706	Cassadaga, 250	E 3
32707	Casselberry, 9,438	E 3
† 32401	Cedar Grove, 689	D 6
32625	Cedar Key, 714	C 2
33514	Center Hill, 371	D 3
32535	Century, 2,679	B 5
† 32302	Chaires, 150	B 1
33950	Charlotte Harbor, 990	E 5
32324	Chattahoochee, 7,944	B 1
32350	Cherry Lake Farms, 400	C 1
32626	Chiefland, 1,965	D 2
32428	Chipley⊙, 3,347	D 6
33925	Chokoloskee, 230	E 6
32709	Christmas, 800	E 3
† 32548	Cinco Bayou, 362	B 6
32627	Citra, 500	D 2
† 32922	City Point, 350	F 3
32430	Clarksville, 250	D 6
* 33515	Clearwater⊙, 52,074	B 2
32711	Clermont, 3,661	E 3
† 33950	Cleveland, 150	E 5
33440	Clewiston, 3,896	E 5
32922	Cocoa, 16,110	F 3
32931	Cocoa Beach, 9,952	F 3
33060	Coconut Creek, 1,359	F 5
33521	Coleman, 614	D 3
32448	Compass Lake, 200	D 6
† 32333	Concord, 300	B 1
33314	Cooper City, 2,535	F 5
33926	Copeland, 500	E 6
† 83559	Coral Cove, 700	D 4
33134	Coral Gables, 42,494	B 5
33836	Cornwell, 700	E 4
33522	Cortez, 600	D 4

32533	Cottagehill, 500	B 6
32431	Cottondale, 765	D 6
32327	Crawfordville⊙, 750	B 1
32012	Crescent City, 1,734	E 2
32536	Crestview⊙, 7,952	C 6
32628	Cross City⊙, 2,268	C 2
32463	Crystal Lake, 125	D 6
32629	Crystal River, 1,696	D 3
33524	Crystal Springs, 300	D 3
33157	Cutler Ridge, 17,441	F 6
32432	Cypress, 266	A 1
33880	Cypress Gardens, 3,757	E 4
† 33472	Cypress Quarters, 1,310	F 4
33525	Dade City⊙, 4,241	D 3
33004	Dania, 9,013	B 4
† 32464	Darlington, 175	C 5
33837	Davenport, 828	E 3
33314	Davie, 2,856	B 4
32013	Day, 200	C 1
* 32014	Daytona Beach, 45,327	F 2
32016	Daytona Beach Shores, 768	F 2
32713	De Bary, 3,154	E 3
33441	Deerfield Beach, 17,130	F 5
32433	De Funiak Springs⊙, 4,966	C 6
32720	De Land⊙, 11,641	E 2
32028	De Leon Springs, 1,134	E 2
33444	Delray Beach, 19,366	F 5
32763	Deltona, 4,868	E 3
† 33870	De Soto City, 250	E 4
32541	Destin, 1,536	C 6
32030	Doctors Inlet, 800	D 4
† 32060	Dowling Park, 200	C 1
33838	Dundee, 1,660	E 3
33528	Dunedin, 17,639	B 2
32630	Dunnellon, 1,146	D 2
33839	Eagle Lake, 1,373	E 4
32631	Earleton, 350	D 2
† 33601	East Lake-Orient Park, 5,697	C 2
† 33940	East Naples, 6,152	E 5
32031	East Palatka, 1,446	E 2
32328	Eastpoint, 1,188	B 2
32437	Ebro, 125	C 6
32032	Edgewater, 3,348	F 3
32801	Edgewood, 392	E 3
† 33601	Egypt Lake, 7,556	C 2
33531	Elfers, 500	D 3
32033	Elkton, 240	E 2
† 33101	El Portal, 2,068	B 4
33533	Englewood, 5,182	D 5
32504	Ensley, 2,400	B 6

(continued on following page)

(continued)

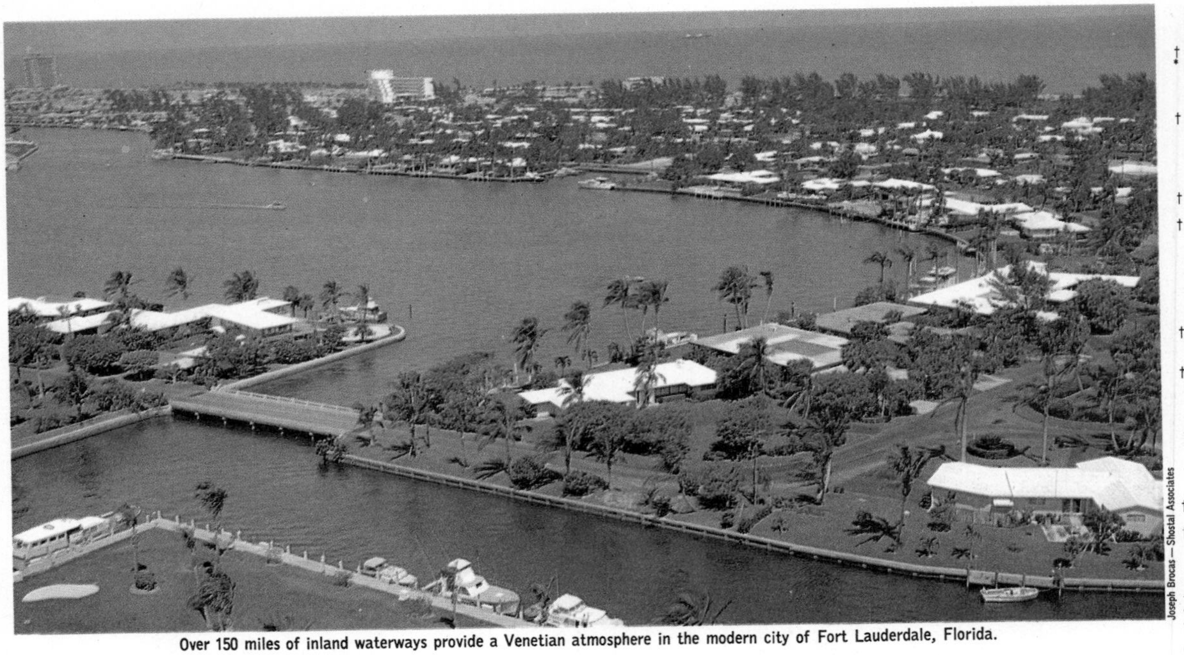

Over 150 miles of inland waterways provide a Venetian atmosphere in the modern city of Fort Lauderdale, Florida.

Joseph Brocas — Shostal Associates

† 32010 Espanola, 300 .... E 2
33928 Estero, 950 .... E 5
32425 Esto, 210 .... C 5
32726 Eustis, 6,722 .... E 3
33929 Everglades City, 462 .... E 6
† 32601 Fairbanks, 380 .... D 2
† 32804 Fairvilla, 950 .... E 3
33930 Felda, 125 .... E 5
32948 Fellsmere, 813 .... F 4
32034 Fernandina Beach⊙, 6,955 .... E 1
† 33301 Fern Crest Village, 1,009 .... B 4
32036 Flagler Beach, 1,042 .... E 2
32635 Florahome, 400 .... E 2
32636 Floral City, 975 .... D 3
33030 Florida City, 5,133 .... F 6
† 32570 Floridatown, 297 .... B 6
† 32569 Florosa, 200 .... B 6
† 32347 Foley, 500 .... C 1
† 33935 Fort Denaud, 300 .... E 5
† 33472 Fort Drum, 100 .... F 4
33834 Fort Green, 300 .... E 4
* 33301 Fort Lauderdale⊙, 139,590 .... C 4
Fort Lauderdale-Hollywood, ‡620,100 .... C 4
32637 Fort McCoy, 900 .... E 2
33841 Fort Meade, 4,374 .... E 4
* 33901 Fort Myers⊙, 27,351 .... E 5
33931 Fort Myers Beach, 4,305 .... E 5
33842 Fort Ogden, 700 .... E 4
33450 Fort Pierce⊙, 29,721 .... F 4
32548 Fort Walton Beach, 19,994 .... C 6
32038 Fort White, 365 .... D 2
32438 Fountain, 650 .... D 6
32439 Freeport, 950 .... C 6
† 32430 Frink, 275 .... D 6
33843 Frostproof, 2,814 .... E 4
32731 Fruitland Park, 1,359 .... D 3
33578 Fruitville, 1,531 .... D 4
32601 Gainesville⊙, 64,510 .... D 2
32732 Geneva, 950 .... E 3
32039 Georgetown, 687 .... E 2
33534 Gibsonton, 1,900 .... C 3
32960 Gifford, 5,772 .... F 4
32040 Glen Saint Mary, 357 .... D 1
32722 Glenwood, 400 .... E 2
33160 Golden Beach, 849 .... C 4
33940 Golden Gate, 1,410 .... E 5
† 33455 Gomez, 400 .... F 4
32560 Gonzalez, 750 .... B 6
33933 Goodland, 500 .... E 6
† 32502 Goulding, 500 .... B 6
33170 Goulds, 6,690 .... F 6
32440 Graceville, 2,560 .... D 5
32042 Graham, 150 .... D 2
32638 Grandin, 150 .... E 2
32442 Grand Ridge, 512 .... A 1
32949 Grant, 500 .... F 4
33460 Greenacres City, 1,731 .... F 5
32043 Green Cove Springs⊙, 3,857 .... E 2
32330 Greensboro, 716 .... B 1
32331 Greenville, 1,141 .... C 1
32443 Greenwood, 515 .... A 1
32332 Gretna, 883 .... B 1
33533 Grove City, 1,178 .... F 5
32736 Groveland, 1,928 .... E 3
32561 Gulf Breeze, 4,190 .... B 6
32639 Gulf Hammock, 300 .... D 2
† 33552 Gulf Harbors, 1,177 .... D 3
33737 Gulfport, 9,730 .... B 3
† 33444 Gulf Stream, 408 .... F 5
† 32601 Hague, 200 .... D 2
33844 Haines City, 8,956 .... E 3
33009 Hallandale, 23,849 .... B 4
32044 Hampton, 386 .... D 2
33440 Harlem, 2,006 .... F 5
32563 Harold, 150 .... B 6
32045 Hastings, 320 .... E 2

32333 Havana, 2,022 .... B 1
32640 Hawthorne, 1,126 .... D 2
32642 Hernando, 524 .... D 3
* 33010 Hialeah, 102,297 .... B 4
† 33010 Hialeah Gardens, 492 .... B 4
33846 Highland City, 900 .... E 4
† 33515 High Point, 800 .... B 3
32643 High Springs, 2,787 .... D 2
32401 Hiland Park, 3,691 .... C 6
† 33827 Hillcrest Heights, 154 .... E 4
32046 Hilliard, 1,205 .... E 1
† 32327 Hilliardville, 150 .... B 1
† 33060 Hillsboro Beach, 713 .... F 5
† 32333 Hinson, 250 .... B 1
33455 Hobe Sound, 2,029 .... F 4
32645 Holder, 134 .... D 3
32047 Hollister, 500 .... E 2
32017 Holly Hill, 8,191 .... E 2
* 33020 Hollywood, 106,873 .... B 4
† 33020 Hollywood Ridge Farms, 302 .... B 4
33509 Holmes Beach, 2,699 .... D 4
32564 Holt, 850 .... C 6
33030 Homestead, 13,674 .... F 6
32646 Homosassa, 850 .... D 3
32647 Homosassa Springs, 550 .... D 3
32334 Hosford, 975 .... B 1
32737 Howey In The Hills, 466 .... E 3
33568 Hudson, 2,278 .... D 3
† 33460 Hypoluxo, 336 .... F 5
33934 Immokalee, 3,764 .... E 5
32901 Indialantic, 2,685 .... F 3
32935 Indian Harbour Beach, 5,371 .... F 3
33535 Indian Rocks Beach, 2,666 .... B 3
† 33535 Indian Rocks Beach South Shore, 791 .... B 3
33456 Indiantown, 2,283 .... F 4
32649 Inglis, 449 .... D 2
33848 Intercession City, 600 .... E 3
32048 Interlachen, 478 .... E 2
32650 Inverness⊙, 2,299 .... D 3
33036 Islamorada, 1,251 .... F 7
32654 Island Grove, 200 .... D 2
* 32201 Jacksonville⊙, 528,865 .... E 1
Jacksonville, ‡528,865 .... E 1
32250 Jacksonville Beach, 12,049 .... E 1
32052 Jasper⊙, 2,221 .... D 1
32565 Jay, 646 .... B 5
32053 Jennings, 582 .... C 1
33457 Jensen Beach, 3,000 .... F 4
† 32901 June Park, 3,090 .... F 3
† 33404 Juno Beach, 747 .... F 5
33458 Jupiter, 3,136 .... F 5
† 33455 Jupiter Island, 295 .... F 4
33849 Kathleen, 900 .... D 3
32739 Kenansville, 450 .... F 4
33156 Kendall, 35,497 .... B 5
† 32670 Kendrick, 200 .... D 2
33709 Kenneth City, 3,862 .... B 3
33149 Key Biscayne, 4,563 .... B 5
33051 Key Colony Beach, 371 .... F 7
33037 Key Largo, 2,866 .... F 6
32656 Keystone Heights, 800 .... E 2
33040 Key West⊙, 27,563 .... E 7
32449 Kinard, 450 .... D 6
32741 Kissimmee⊙, 7,119 .... E 3
† 32010 Korona, 200 .... E 2
33935 La Belle⊙, 1,823 .... E 5
33537 Lacoochee, 1,380 .... D 3
32658 La Crosse, 365 .... D 2
32659 Lady Lake, 382 .... E 3
33850 Lake Alfred, 2,847 .... E 3
32054 Lake Butler⊙, 1,598 .... D 1
† 33601 Lake Carroll, 5,577 .... C 2
32055 Lake City⊙, 10,575 .... D 1
32057 Lake Como, 340 .... E 2
33459 Lake Harbor, 300 .... F 5

32744 Lake Helen, 1,303 .... E 3
32745 Lake Jem, 314 .... E 3
* 33801 Lakeland, 41,550 .... D 3
† 33601 Lake Magdalene, 9,266 .... D 3
32746 Lake Mary, 900 .... E 3
32747 Lake Monroe, 500 .... E 3
33403 Lake Park, 6,993 .... F 5
33852 Lake Placid, 656 .... E 4
† 33471 Lakeport, 375 .... E 5
33853 Lake Wales, 8,240 .... E 4
32566 Lakewood, 525 .... C 5
33460 Lake Worth, 23,714 .... G 5
32336 Lamont, 500 .... C 1
33539 Land O'Lakes, 900 .... D 3
33460 Lantana, 7,126 .... F 5
33540 Largo, 22,031 .... B 3
33308 Lauderdale-by-the-Sea, 2,879 .... C 3
† 33301 Lauderdale Lakes, 10,577 .... B 4
33313 Lauderhill, 8,465 .... B 4
32567 Laurel Hill, 418 .... C 5
33545 Laurel-Nokomis, 3,238 .... D 4
32058 Lawtey, 636 .... D 1
32661 Lecanto, 125 .... D 3
32059 Lee, 240 .... C 1
32748 Leesburg, 11,869 .... E 3
33936 Lehigh Acres, 4,394 .... E 5
33030 Leisure City, 2,900 .... F 6
† 33601 Leto, 8,458 .... C 2
33064 Lighthouse Point, 9,071 .... F 5
† 33865 Limestone, 200 .... E 4
32060 Live Oak⊙, 6,830 .... D 1
32337 Lloyd, 225 .... C 1
32662 Lochloosa, 175 .... E 2
33548 Longboat Key, 2,850 .... D 4
33001 Long Key, 150 .... F 7
32750 Longwood, 3,203 .... E 3
33857 Lorida, 950 .... E 4
33858 Loughman, 950 .... E 3
32663 Lowell, 350 .... D 2
33470 Loxahatchee, 950 .... F 5
33549 Lutz, 950 .... D 3
32444 Lynn Haven, 4,044 .... C 6
32063 Macclenny⊙, 2,733 .... D 1
33738 Madeira Beach, 4,158 .... B 3
32340 Madison⊙, 3,737 .... C 1
32751 Maitland, 7,157 .... E 3
32950 Malabar, 634 .... F 3
32445 Malone, 667 .... A 1
33550 Mango, 950 .... D 4
33050 Marathon, 4,397 .... E 7
33937 Marco, 900 .... E 6
33063 Margate, 8,867 .... F 5
32446 Marianna⊙, 6,741 .... A 1
† 32084 Marineland, 13 .... E 2
32569 Mary Esther, 3,192 .... B 6
33512 Masaryktown, 389 .... D 3
32753 Mascotte, 966 .... E 3
32066 Mayo⊙, 793 .... C 1
32568 McDavid, 500 .... B 5
32664 McIntosh, 287 .... D 2
† 33101 Medley, 351 .... B 4
32901 Melbourne, 40,236 .... F 3
32951 Melbourne Beach, 2,262 .... F 3
32666 Melrose, 950 .... D 2
† 33301 Melrose Park, 6,111 .... B 4
† 33561 Memphis, 3,207 .... D 4
32952 Merritt Island, 29,233 .... F 3
32410 Mexico Beach, 588 .... D 6
* 33101 Miami⊙, 334,859 .... B 5
Miami, ‡1,267,792 .... B 5
33139 Miami Beach, 87,072 .... C 5
† 33101 Miami Lakes, 3,500 .... B 4
33153 Miami Shores, 9,425 .... B 4
33166 Miami Springs, 13,279 .... B 5
32667 Micanopy, 759 .... D 2
† 32960 Micco, 400 .... F 4
32309 Miccosukee, 275 .... B 1

32068 Middleburg, 950 .... E 1
32343 Midway, 900 .... B 1
32537 Milligan, 950 .... C 6
32570 Milton⊙, 5,360 .... B 6
32754 Mims, 8,309 .... F 3
32755 Minneola, 878 .... E 3
33023 Miramar, 23,973 .... B 4
32577 Molino, 850 .... B 6
† 32696 Montbrook, 250 .... D 2
32344 Monticello⊙, 2,473 .... C 1
32756 Montverde, 308 .... E 3
33471 Moore Haven⊙, 974 .... E 5
32434 Mossy Head, 160 .... C 6
32757 Mount Dora, 4,543 .... E 3
32352 Mount Pleasant, 150 .... B 1
33860 Mulberry, 2,701 .... E 4
33551 Myakka City, 672 .... D 4
32506 Myrtle Grove, 16,186 .... B 6
33940 Naples⊙, 12,042 .... E 5
† 33940 Naples Park, 1,522 .... E 5
33030 Naranja, 2,900 .... F 6
32233 Neptune Beach, 2,868 .... E 1
32669 Newberry, 1,247 .... D 2
33552 New Port Richey, 6,098 .... D 3
32069 New Smyrna Beach, 10,580 .... F 2
32578 Niceville, 4,024 .... C 6
33863 Nichols, 300 .... E 4
33864 Nocatee, 950 .... E 4
33555 Nokomis-Laurel, 3,238 .... D 4
32452 Noma, 234 .... C 5
33141 North Bay Village, 4,831 .... B 4
33903 North Fort Myers, 8,798 .... E 5
33161 North Miami, 34,767 .... B 4
33161 North Miami Beach, 30,723 .... C 4
† 33940 North Naples, 3,201 .... E 5
33403 North Palm Beach, 9,035 .... F 5
33595 North Port Charlotte, 2,244 .... D 4
† 33708 North Redington Beach, 768 .... B 3
† 33054 Norwood, 14,973 .... B 4
32759 Oak Hill, 747 .... F 3
32760 Oakland, 672 .... E 3
33307 Oakland Park, 16,261 .... B 3
32071 O'Brien, 200 .... D 1
32670 Ocala⊙, 22,583 .... D 2
† 33457 Ocean Breeze, 714 .... F 4
33444 Ocean Ridge, 1,074 .... F 5
33943 Ochopee, 200 .... E 6
32761 Ocoee, 3,937 .... E 3
33556 Odessa, 500 .... D 3
33163 Ojus, 12,000 .... B 4
32762 Okahumpka, 470 .... D 3
33472 Okeechobee⊙, 3,715 .... F 4
32679 Oklawaha, 700 .... E 2
33557 Oldsmar, 1,538 .... B 2
32680 Old Town, 500 .... C 2
32072 Olustee, 400 .... D 1
33865 Ona, 236 .... E 4
33558 Oneco, 3,246 .... D 4
33054 Opa-locka, 11,902 .... B 4
32763 Orange City, 1,777 .... E 3
32681 Orange Lake, 900 .... D 2
32073 Orange Park, 7,619 .... E 1
32682 Orange Springs, 500 .... E 2
* 32801 Orlando⊙, 99,006 .... E 3
Orlando, ‡428,003 .... E 3
32074 Ormond Beach, 14,063 .... E 2
33559 Osprey, 1,115 .... D 4
32764 Osteen, 875 .... E 3
32683 Otter Creek, 400 .... D 2
32765 Oviedo, 1,870 .... E 3
32684 Oxford, 490 .... D 3
33560 Ozona, 900 .... D 3
32570 Pace, 1,776 .... B 6
33476 Pahokee, 5,663 .... F 5
32077 Palatka⊙, 9,310 .... E 2
32901 Palm Bay, 6,927 .... F 3
33480 Palm Beach, 9,086 .... G 4

† 33404 Palm Beach Shores, 1,214 .... G 5
33490 Palm City, 900 .... F 4
33561 Palmetto, 7,422 .... D 4
33563 Palm Harbor, 1,763 .... D 3
33619 Palm River-Clair Mel, 8,536 .... C 3
32935 Palm Shores, 202 .... F 3
33460 Palm Springs, 4,340 .... F 5
32346 Panacea, 950 .... B 1
32401 Panama City⊙, 32,096 .... C 6
32401 Parker, 4,212 .... C 6
33564 Parrish, 950 .... D 4
32538 Paxton, 243 .... C 5
† 33023 Pembroke Park, 2,949 .... B 4
33023 Pembroke Pines, 15,520 .... B 4
32079 Penney Farms, 561 .... E 2
* 32501 Pensacola⊙, 59,507 .... B 6
Pensacola, ‡243,075 .... B 6
33157 Perrine, 10,257 .... F 6
32347 Perry⊙, 7,701 .... C 1
33867 Pierce, 500 .... E 4
32080 Pierson, 654 .... E 2
33565 Pinellas Park, 22,287 .... B 3
32350 Pinetta, 300 .... C 1
† 33042 Pirates Cove, 150 .... E 7
33946 Placida, 250 .... D 5
33314 Plantation, 23,523 .... B 4
33566 Plant City, 15,451 .... D 3
32768 Plymouth, 950 .... E 3
33868 Polk City, 151 .... E 3
32081 Pomona Park, 578 .... E 2
* 33060 Pompano Beach, 37,724 .... F 5
32455 Ponce de Leon, 288 .... C 6
† 32019 Ponce Inlet, 328 .... F 2
32082 Ponte Vedra Beach, 2,100 .... E 1
33950 Port Charlotte, 10,769 .... D 5
† 32439 Portland, 228 .... C 6
† 33438 Port Mayaca, 400 .... F 5
32019 Port Orange, 3,781 .... F 2
33568 Port Richey, 1,259 .... D 3
32456 Port Saint Joe, 4,401 .... D 6
33450 Port Saint Lucie, 330 .... F 4
33492 Port Salerno, 1,161 .... F 4
33171 Princeton, 1,900 .... F 6
† 33619 Progress, 1,328 .... C 3
† 32061 Providence, 150 .... D 2
33950 Punta Gorda⊙, 3,879 .... E 5
32351 Quincy⊙, 8,334 .... B 1
32083 Raiford, 500 .... D 1
† 32696 Raleigh, 275 .... D 2
32455 Redbay, 500 .... C 6
32686 Reddick, 305 .... D 2
33708 Redington Beach, 1,583 .... B 3
† 33708 Redington Shores, 1,733 .... B 3
† 33599 Richland, 928 .... D 3
† 33158 Richmond Heights, 6,663 .... F 6
33569 Riverview, 2,225 .... D 4
33404 Riviera Beach, 21,401 .... G 5
32955 Rockledge, 10,523 .... F 3
32957 Roseland, 550 .... F 4
32447 Round Lake, 275 .... D 6
33570 Ruskin, 2,414 .... C 3
33572 Safety Harbor, 3,103 .... B 2
32084 Saint Augustine⊙, 12,352 .... E 2
32084 Saint Augustine Beach, 632 .... E 2
33573 Saint Catherine, 350 .... D 3
32769 Saint Cloud, 5,041 .... E 3
33956 Saint James City, 500 .... D 5
33574 Saint Leo, 1,145 .... D 3
† 33450 Saint Lucie, 428 .... F 4
32355 Saint Marks, 366 .... B 1
* 33701 Saint Petersburg, 216,232 .... B 3
33736 Saint Petersburg Beach, 8,024 .... B 3
32356 Salem, 150 .... C 2
33505 Samoset, 4,070 .... D 4
† 32069 Samsula, 270 .... E 2
33576 San Antonio, 473 .... D 3
32087 Sanderson, 150 .... D 1

32771 Sanford⊙, 17,393 .... E 3
33957 Sanibel, 750 .... D 5
32088 San Mateo, 975 .... E 2
† 32670 Santos, 150 .... D 2
* 33577 Sarasota⊙, 40,237 .... D 4
32935 Satellite Beach, 6,558 .... F 3
32089 Satsuma, 610 .... E 2
32775 Scottsmoor, 850 .... F 3
† 33301 Sea Ranch Lakes, 660 .... C 3
32958 Sebastian, 825 .... F 4
33870 Sebring⊙, 7,223 .... E 4
33584 Seffner, 2,000 .... D 4
33540 Seminole, 2,410 .... B 3
32090 Seville, 500 .... E 2
† 33457 Sewalls Point, 298 .... F 4
32579 Shalimar, 578 .... C 6
† 32628 Shamrock, 200 .... C 2
32959 Sharpes, 427 .... F 3
32688 Silver Springs, 500 .... D 2
32460 Sneads, 1,550 .... B 1
32358 Sopchoppy, 460 .... B 1
32776 Sorrento, 500 .... E 3
33493 South Bay, 2,958 .... F 5
32021 South Daytona, 4,979 .... F 2
† 36441 South Flomaton, 329 .... B 5
33143 South Miami, 19,571 .... B 5
33707 South Pasadena, 2,063 .... B 3
† 32401 Southport, 1,560 .... C 6
32690 Sparr, 450 .... D 2
32401 Springfield, 5,949 .... D 6
32091 Starke⊙, 4,848 .... D 2
32359 Steinhatchee, 800 .... C 2
33494 Stuart⊙, 4,820 .... F 4
32335 Sumatra, 150 .... B 1
32691 Summerfield, 450 .... D 2
33042 Summerland Key, 350 .... E 7
33586 Sun City, 2,143 .... D 4
† 33450 Sunland Gardens, 1,900 .... F 4
33160 Sunny Isles, 950 .... C 4
† 33577 Sunnyland, 4,900 .... D 4
32461 Sunnyside, 370 .... C 6
33313 Sunrise Golf Village, 7,403 .... B 4
33154 Surfside, 3,614 .... B 4
32692 Suwannee, 203 .... C 2
† 33144 Sweetwater, 3,307 .... B 5
† 33601 Sweetwater Creek, 19,453 .... B 2
† 32043 Switzerland, 500 .... E 1
32809 Taft, 1,183 .... E 3
* 32301 Tallahassee (cap.)⊙, 71,897 .... B 1
Tallahassee, ‡103,047 .... B 1
† 33301 Tamarac, 5,078 .... B 3
* 33601 Tampa⊙, 277,767 .... C 2
Tampa-Saint Petersburg, ‡1,012,594 .... C 2
33589 Tarpon Springs, 7,118 .... D 3
32778 Tavares⊙, 3,261 .... E 3
33070 Tavernier, 900 .... F 6
32360 Telogia, 300 .... B 1
33617 Temple Terrace, 7,347 .... C 2
33458 Tequesta, 2,642 .... F 5
33591 Terra Ceia, 450 .... D 4
33592 Thonotosassa, 900 .... D 3
33905 Tice, 7,254 .... E 5
32780 Titusville⊙, 30,515 .... F 3
33740 Treasure Island, 6,120 .... B 3
32693 Trenton⊙, 1,074 .... D 2
33593 Trilby, 930 .... D 3
32784 Umatilla, 1,600 .... E 3
32580 Valparaiso, 6,504 .... C 6
33595 Venice, 6,648 .... D 4
33960 Venus, 300 .... E 4
32462 Vernon, 691 .... C 6
32960 Vero Beach⊙, 11,908 .... F 4
† 32548 Villa Tasso, 200 .... C 6
† 33166 Virginia Gardens, 2,524 .... B 5
32970 Wabasso, 950 .... F 4
32361 Wacissa, 275 .... B 1
† 32327 Wakulla, 225 .... B 1
32694 Waldo, 800 .... D 2
32568 Walnut Hill, 500 .... B 5
32507 Warrington, 15,848 .... B 6
† 32055 Watertown, 3,624 .... D 1
33873 Wauchula⊙, 3,007 .... E 4
32463 Wausau, 288 .... D 6
33877 Waverly, 1,172 .... E 4
33597 Webster, 739 .... D 3
32695 Weirsdale, 995 .... D 3
32093 Welaka, 496 .... E 2
32094 Wellborn, 600 .... D 1
32401 Westbay, 350 .... C 6
† 32901 West Melbourne, 3,050 .... F 3
† 33101 West Miami, 5,494 .... B 5
* 33401 West Palm Beach⊙, 57,375 .... F 5
West Palm Beach, ‡348,753 .... F 5
32401 West Panama City Beach, 1,052 .... C 6
32505 West Pensacola, 20,924 .... B 6
32464 Westville, 475 .... C 6
† 33101 Westwood Lakes, 12,811 .... B 5
32465 Wewahitchka⊙, 1,733 .... D 6
† 32465 White City, 600 .... F 4
32096 White Springs, 767 .... D 1
32785 Wildwood, 2,082 .... D 3
32696 Williston, 1,939 .... D 2
33305 Wilton Manors, 10,948 .... B 3
33598 Wimauma, 650 .... D 4
32786 Windermere, 894 .... E 3
32971 Winter Beach, 350 .... F 4
32787 Winter Garden, 5,153 .... E 3
33880 Winter Haven, 16,136 .... E 3
32789 Winter Park, 21,895 .... E 3
32362 Woodville, 900 .... B
32697 Worthington Springs, 214 .... D
32797 Yalaha, 675 .... E
32698 Yankeetown, 490 .... D
32466 Youngstown, 400 .... D
32097 Yulee, 950 .... E
32798 Zellwood, 550 .... E
33599 Zephyrhills, 3,369 .... D
33890 Zolfo Springs, 1,117 .... E

⊙ County seat.
‡ Population of metropolitan area.
† Zip of nearest p.o.
* Multiple zips

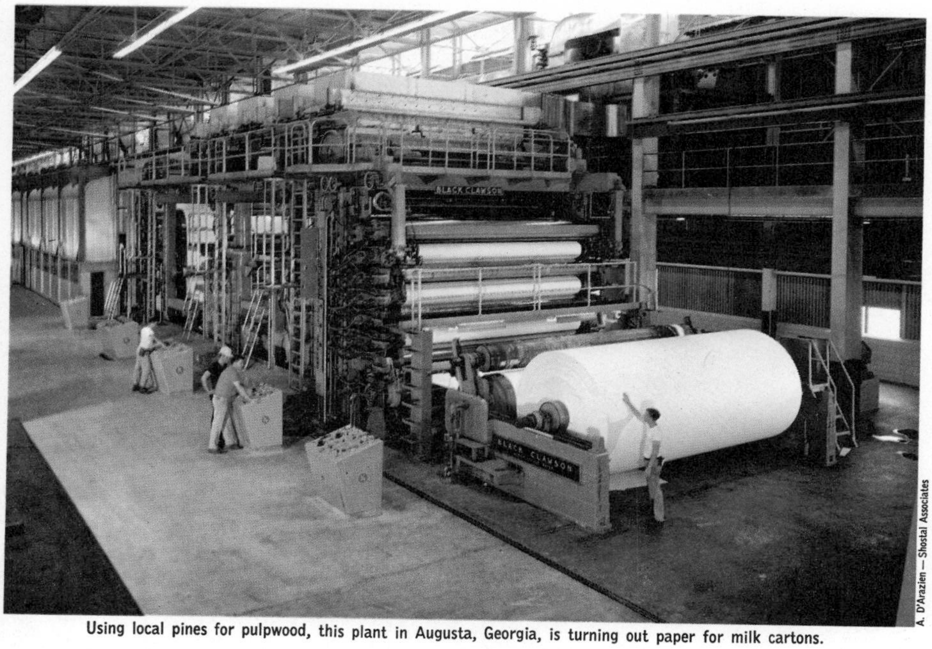

A. D'Arazien — Shostal Associates

Using local pines for pulpwood, this plant in Augusta, Georgia, is turning out paper for milk cartons.

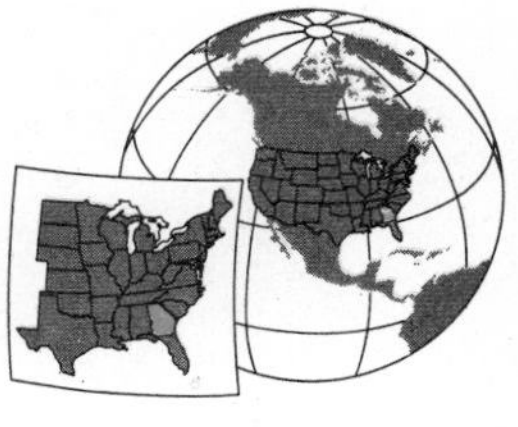

AREA 58,876 sq. mi.
POPULATION 4,589,575
CAPITAL Atlanta
LARGEST CITY Atlanta
HIGHEST POINT Brasstown Bald 4,784 ft.
SETTLED IN 1733
ADMITTED TO UNION January 2, 1788
POPULAR NAME Empire State of the South; Peach State
STATE FLOWER Cherokee Rose
STATE BIRD Brown Thrasher

COUNTIES

Name/Pop.	Key
Appling, 12,726	H 7
Atkinson, 5,879	G 8
Bacon, 8,233	G 7
Baker, 3,875	D 8
Baldwin, 34,240	F 4
Banks, 6,833	E 2
Barrow, 16,859	E 2
Bartow, 32,663	C 2
Ben Hill, 13,171	F 7
Berrien, 11,556	F 8
Bibb, 143,418	E 5
Bleckley, 10,291	F 6
Brantley, 5,940	J 8
Brooks, 13,739	E 9
Bryan, 6,539	K 6
Bulloch, 31,585	J 6
Burke, 18,255	J 4
Butts, 10,560	E 4
Calhoun, 6,606	C 7
Camden, 11,334	J 9
Candler, 6,412	H 6
Carroll, 45,404	B 3
Catoosa, 28,271	B 1
Charlton, 5,680	H 9
Chatham, 187,767	K 6
Chattahoochee, 25,813	C 6
Chattooga, 20,541	B 1
Cherokee, 31,059	D 2
Clarke, 65,177	F 3
Clay, 3,636	B 7
Clayton, 98,043	D 3
Clinch, 6,405	G 9
Cobb, 196,793	C 3
Coffee, 22,828	G 8
Colquitt, 32,200	E 8
Columbia, 22,327	H 3
Cook, 12,129	F 8
Coweta, 32,310	C 4
Crawford, 5,748	E 5
Crisp, 18,087	E 7
Dade, 9,910	A 1
Dawson, 3,639	D 2
Decatur, 22,310	C 9
De Kalb, 415,387	D 3
Dodge, 15,658	F 6
Dooly, 10,404	E 6
Dougherty, 89,639	D 7
Douglas, 28,659	C 3
Early, 12,682	C 8
Echols, 1,924	G 9
Effingham, 13,632	K 6
Elbert, 17,262	G 2
Emanuel, 18,189	H 5
Evans, 7,290	J 6
Fannin, 13,357	D 1
Fayette, 11,364	C 4
Floyd, 73,742	B 2
Forsyth, 16,928	D 2
Franklin, 12,784	F 2
Fulton, 607,592	D 3
Gilmer, 8,956	D 1
Glascock, 2,280	G 4
Glynn, 50,528	J 8
Gordon, 23,570	C 2
Grady, 17,826	D 9
Greene, 10,212	F 3
Gwinnett, 72,349	D 2
Habersham, 20,691	E 1
Hall, 59,405	E 2
Hancock, 9,019	G 4
Haralson, 15,927	B 3
Harris, 11,520	C 5
Hart, 15,814	G 2
Heard, 5,354	B 4
Henry, 23,724	D 4
Houston, 62,924	E 6
Irwin, 8,036	F 7
Jackson, 21,093	E 2
Jasper, 5,760	E 4
Jeff Davis, 9,425	G 7
Jefferson, 17,174	H 4
Jenkins, 8,332	J 5
Johnson, 7,727	G 5
Jones, 12,218	E 5
Lamar, 10,688	D 4
Lanier, 5,031	F 8
Laurens, 32,738	G 6
Lee, 7,044	D 7
Liberty, 17,569	J 7
Lincoln, 5,895	H 3
Long, 3,746	J 7
Lowndes, 55,112	F 9
Lumpkin, 8,728	D 1
Macon, 12,933	D 6
Madison, 13,517	F 2
Marion, 5,099	C 6
McDuffie, 15,276	H 4
McIntosh, 7,371	K 7
Meriwether, 19,461	C 4
Miller, 6,397	C 8
Mitchell, 18,956	D 8
Monroe, 10,991	E 4
Montgomery, 6,099	G 6
Morgan, 9,904	F 3
Murray, 12,986	C 1
Muscogee, 167,377	C 6
Newton, 26,282	E 3
Oconee, 7,915	F 3
Oglethorpe, 7,598	F 3
Paulding, 17,520	C 3
Peach, 15,990	E 5
Pickens, 9,620	D 2
Pierce, 9,281	H 8
Pike, 7,316	D 4
Polk, 29,656	B 3
Pulaski, 8,066	E 6
Putnam, 8,394	F 4
Quitman, 2,180	B 7
Rabun, 8,327	F 1
Randolph, 8,734	C 7
Richmond, 162,437	H 4
Rockdale, 18,152	D 3
Schley, 3,097	D 6
Screven, 12,591	J 5
Seminole, 7,059	C 9
Spalding, 39,514	D 4
Stephens, 20,331	F 1
Stewart, 6,511	C 6
Sumter, 26,931	D 6
Talbot, 6,625	C 5
Taliaferro, 2,423	G 3
Tattnall, 16,557	J 6
Taylor, 7,865	D 5
Telfair, 11,381	G 7
Terrell, 11,416	D 7
Thomas, 34,515	E 9
Tift, 27,288	E 7
Toombs, 19,151	H 6
Towns, 4,565	E 1
Treutlen, 5,647	G 6
Troup, 44,466	B 4
Turner, 8,790	E 7
Twiggs, 8,222	F 5
Union, 6,811	E 1
Upson, 23,505	D 5
Walker, 50,691	B 1
Walton, 23,404	E 3
Ware, 33,525	H 8
Warren, 6,669	G 4
Washington, 17,480	G 4
Wayne, 17,858	J 7
Webster, 2,362	C 6
Wheeler, 4,596	G 6
White, 7,742	E 1
Whitfield, 55,108	B 1
Wilcox, 6,998	F 7
Wilkes, 10,184	G 3
Wilkinson, 9,393	F 5
Worth, 14,770	E 8

CITIES and TOWNS

	Zip	Name/Pop.	Key
	31001	Abbeville⊙, 781	F 7
	30101	Acworth, 3,929	C 2
	30103	Adairsville, 1,676	C 2
	31620	Adel⊙, 4,972	F 8
	31002	Adrian, 705	G 5
	30410	Ailey, 487	G 6
	30411	Alamo⊙, 833	G 6
	31622	Alapaha, 633	F 8
*	31701	Albany⊙, 72,623	D 7
		Albany, ‡89,639	D 7
†	30204	Aldora, 322	D 4
	30801	Alexander, 200	J 4
	31301	Allenhurst, 230	J 7
	31003	Allentown, 295	F 5
	31510	Alma⊙, 3,756	G 7
†	30209	Almon, 400	E 3
	30201	Alpharetta, 2,455	D 2
	30510	Alto, 372	E 2
†	30161	Alto Park, 2,963	B 2
	31512	Ambrose, 253	G 7
	31709	Americus⊙, 16,091	D 6
	31711	Andersonville, 274	D 6
	30802	Appling⊙, 212	H 3
	31712	Arabi, 305	E 7
	30104	Aragon, 850	B 2
†	30549	Arcade, 229	E 2
	31520	Arco, 6,009	J 8
	31623	Argyle, 206	G 8
	31713	Arlington, 1,698	C 8
	30105	Armuchee, 600	B 2
	31714	Ashburn⊙, 4,209	E 7
†	30521	Ashland, 350	F 2
	30601	Athens⊙, 44,342	F 3
*	30301	Atlanta (cap.)⊙, 496,973	D 3
		Atlanta, ‡1,390,164	D 3
	31715	Attapulgus, 513	D 9
	30203	Auburn, 361	E 2
*	30901	Augusta⊙, 59,864	J 4
		Augusta, ‡253,460	J 4
	30001	Austell, 2,632	C 3
†	30557	Avalon, 204	F 1
	30803	Avera, 217	G 4
	30002	Avondale Estates, 1,735	D 3
	31624	Axson, 250	G 8
	31716	Baconton, 710	D 8
	31717	Bainbridge⊙, 10,887	C 9
	30511	Baldwin, 772	E 2
	30107	Ball Ground, 617	D 2
	30204	Barnesville⊙, 4,935	D 4
†	31601	Barretts, 275	F 8
	30413	Bartow, 333	G 5
	31720	Barwick, 381	E 9
	31513	Baxley⊙, 3,503	H 7
†	31792	Beachton, 200	D 9
	30414	Bellville, 234	H 6
†	31601	Bemiss, 325	F 9
	31722	Berlin, 422	E 8
	30748	Berryton, 200	B 2
	30620	Bethlehem, 304	E 3
	31904	Bibb City, 812	B 5
	30621	Bishop, 235	F 3
	31516	Blackshear⊙, 2,624	H 8
	30512	Blairsville⊙, 491	E 1
	31723	Blakely⊙, 5,267	C 8
†	31308	Blitchton, 256	J 6
	31302	Bloomingdale, 1,588	K 6
	30513	Blue Ridge⊙, 1,602	D 1
	30805	Blythe, 333	H 4
	30622	Bogart, 667	E 3
	31626	Boston, 1,443	E 9
	30623	Bostwick, 289	E 3
	30108	Bowdon, 1,753	B 3
	30109	Bowdon Junction, 200	B 3
	30516	Bowersville, 301	G 2
	30624	Bowman, 724	G 2
	31801	Box Springs, 600	C 5
	30517	Braselton, 386	E 2
	30110	Bremen, 3,484	B 3
	31701	Bridgeboro, 250	E 8
	31725	Brinson, 231	C 9
	31726	Bronwood, 500	D 7
	31727	Brookfield, 860	F 8
	30415	Brooklet, 683	J 6
	31519	Broxton, 957	G 7
	31520	Brunswick⊙, 19,585	K 8
	30113	Buchanan⊙, 800	B 3
	31803	Buena Vista⊙, 1,486	C 6
	30518	Buford, 4,640	D 2
†	31020	Bullard, 230	F 5
	31006	Butler⊙, 1,589	D 5
	31007	Byromville, 419	E 6
	31008	Byron, 1,368	E 5
	31009	Cadwell, 354	G 6
	31728	Cairo⊙, 8,061	D 9
	30701	Calhoun⊙, 4,748	C 1
	31729	Calvary, 500	D 9
	30807	Camak, 224	G 4
	31730	Camilla⊙, 4,987	D 8
	30520	Canon, 709	F 2
	30114	Canton⊙, 3,654	C 2
†	30720	Carbondale, 300	B 1
	30203	Carl, 234	E 3
	30627	Carlton, 294	F 2
	30521	Carnesville⊙, 510	F 2
	30117	Carrollton⊙, 13,520	C 3
†	30540	Cartecay, 250	D 1
	30120	Cartersville⊙, 9,929	C 2
	30123	Cassville, 350	C 2
	31804	Cataula, 500	C 5
	30124	Cave Spring, 1,305	B 2
	31627	Cecil, 265	F 8
	30125	Cedartown⊙, 9,253	B 2
†	30601	Center, 213	F 2
	31093	Centerville, 1,725	E 5
†	31816	Chalybeate Springs, 266	C 5
	30341	Chamblee, 9,127	D 3
	30705	Chatsworth⊙, 2,706	C 1
	31011	Chauncey, 308	F 6
	31012	Chester, 409	F 6
	30707	Chickamauga, 1,842	B 1
†	30512	Choestoe, 215	E 1
	31733	Chula, 300	E 7
	30523	Clarkesville⊙, 1,294	F 1
	30021	Clarkston, 3,127	D 3
	30417	Claxton⊙, 2,669	J 6
	30525	Clayton⊙, 1,569	F 1
	30128	Clem, 350	B 3
	30527	Clermont, 290	E 2
	30528	Cleveland⊙, 1,353	E 1
	31734	Climax, 275	D 9
	31604	Clyattville, 500	F 9
	31303	Clyo, 300	K 6
	30420	Cobbtown, 321	H 6
	31014	Cochran⊙, 5,161	F 6
	30710	Cohutta, 300	C 1
	30628	Colbert, 532	F 2
	30337	College Park, 18,203	C 3
	30421	Collins, 574	H 6
	31737	Colquitt⊙, 2,026	C 8
*	31901	Columbus⊙, 154,168	C 6
		Columbus, ‡238,584	C 6
	30629	Comer, 828	F 2
	30529	Commerce, 3,702	E 2
	30206	Concord, 312	D 4
	30207	Conyers⊙, 4,890	D 3
	31738	Coolidge, 717	E 8
	30129	Coosa, 600	B 2
	31015	Cordele⊙, 10,733	E 7
	30531	Cornelia, 3,014	E 1
	30209	Covington⊙, 10,267	E 3
	30630	Crawford, 624	F 3
	30631	Crawfordville⊙, 735	G 3
†	30105	Crystal Springs, 500	B 2
	31016	Culloden, 272	D 5
	30130	Cumming⊙, 2,031	D 2
	31805	Cusseta⊙, 1,251	C 6
	31740	Cuthbert⊙, 3,972	C 7
	30211	Dacula, 782	E 3
	30533	Dahlonega⊙, 2,658	D 1
	30132	Dallas⊙, 2,133	C 3
	30720	Dalton⊙, 18,872	C 1
	31741	Damascus, 272	C 8
	30633	Danielsville⊙, 378	F 2
	31017	Danville, 515	F 5
	31305	Darien⊙, 1,826	K 8
	31601	Dasher, 452	F 9
	31018	Davisboro, 476	G 5
	31742	Dawson⊙, 5,383	D 7
	30534	Dawsonville⊙, 288	D 2
	30808	Dearing, 555	H 4
*	30030	Decatur⊙, 21,943	D 3
†	31501	Deenwood, 3,015	H 8
	30535	Demorest, 1,070	F 1
	31532	Denton, 244	G 7
	31743	De Soto, 321	D 7
	31019	Dexter, 438	G 6
†	31520	Dock Junction (Arco), 6,009	J 8
	31744	Doerun, 1,157	E 8
	31745	Donalsonville⊙, 2,907	C 8
	30340	Doraville, 9,039	D 3
	31533	Douglas⊙, 10,195	G 7
	30134	Douglasville⊙, 5,472	C 3
	31020	Dry Branch, 700	F 5
	31021	Dublin⊙, 15,143	G 5
	31022	Dudley, 423	F 5
	30136	Duluth, 1,810	D 2
	31630	Du Pont, 252	G 9
	30538	Eastanollee, 365	F 1
	31021	East Dublin, 1,986	G 5
	30539	East Ellijay, 488	C 1
	31023	Eastman⊙, 5,416	F 6
†	30263	East Newnan, 1,634	C 4
	30344	East Point, 39,315	C 3
	31024	Eatonton⊙, 4,125	F 4
	31307	Eden, 300	K 6
	31746	Edison, 1,210	C 7
†	31093	Elberta, 500	E 5
	30635	Elberton⊙, 6,438	G 2
	30060	Elizabeth, 950	C 2
	31025	Elko, 450	E 6
	31308	Ellabell, 400	K 6
	31806	Ellaville⊙, 1,391	D 6
	31747	Ellenton, 337	E 8
	31807	Ellerslie, 615	C 5
	30540	Ellijay⊙, 1,326	C 1
	30137	Emerson, 813	C 2
	31026	Empire, 325	F 6
	31749	Enigma, 505	F 8
†	30217	Ephesus, 212	B 4
	30541	Epworth, 300	D 1
	30724	Eton, 286	C 1
†	31331	Eulonia, 500	K 7
	30809	Evans, 1,500	H 3
	31536	Everett, 300	J 8
	30212	Experiment, 2,256	D 4
	30213	Fairburn, 3,143	C 3
	30139	Fairmount, 623	C 2
	31631	Fargo, 800	G 9
	30214	Fayetteville⊙, 2,160	C 4
	30140	Felton, 300	B 3
	31750	Fitzgerald⊙, 8,015	F 7
†	31313	Flemington, 265	K 7
	30215	Flippen, 600	D 3
	30216	Flovilla, 289	E 4
	30542	Flowery Branch, 779	E 2
	31537	Folkston⊙, 2,112	H 9
	30050	Forest Park, 19,994	D 3
	31029	Forsyth⊙, 3,736	E 4
	31751	Fort Gaines⊙, 1,255	C 7
	30741	Fort Oglethorpe, 3,869	B 1
	31030	Fort Valley⊙, 9,251	E 5
	31752	Fowlstown, 400	D 9
	30217	Franklin⊙, 749	B 4
	30639	Franklin Springs, 501	F 2
	37317	Fry, 300	D 1
	31753	Funston, 293	E 8
	30501	Gainesville⊙, 15,459	E 2
	31408	Garden City, 5,741	K 6
	30425	Garfield, 214	H 5
	31810	Geneva, 250	C 5
	31754	Georgetown⊙, 578	B 7
	30810	Gibson⊙, 701	G 4
	30426	Girard, 241	J 4
	30427	Glennville, 2,965	J 7
	30428	Glenwood, 670	G 6
	30641	Good Hope, 202	E 3
	31031	Gordon, 2,553	F 5
	30811	Gough, 300	H 4
	30812	Gracewood, 1,200	H 4
	30220	Grantville, 1,128	C 4
	31032	Gray⊙, 2,014	F 4
	30221	Grayson, 366	E 3
	30642	Greensboro⊙, 2,583	F 3
	30222	Greenville⊙, 1,085	C 4
†	31620	Greggs, 250	F 8
	30223	Griffin⊙, 22,734	D 4
†	31036	Grovania, 300	E 6
	30813	Grovetown, 3,169	H 4
	31312	Guyton, 742	K 6
	30544	Habersham, 225	F 1
	31033	Haddock, 600	F 4
	30429	Hagan, 572	J 6
	31632	Hahira, 1,326	F 9
	31811	Hamilton⊙, 357	C 5
	30228	Hampton, 1,551	D 4
	30354	Hapeville, 9,567	D 3
	31034	Hardwick, 14,047	F 4
	30814	Harlem, 1,540	H 4
	31035	Harrison, 329	G 5
	30643	Hartwell⊙, 4,865	G 2
	31036	Hawkinsville⊙, 4,077	E 6
	31539	Hazlehurst⊙, 4,065	G 7
	30545	Helen, 252	E 1
	31037	Helena, 1,230	G 6
	30815	Hephzibah, 987	H 4
	30546	Hiawassee⊙, 415	E 1
	31038	Hillsboro, 250	E 4
	30467	Hilltonia, 294	J 5
	31313	Hinesville⊙, 4,115	J 7
	30141	Hiram, 441	C 3
	31542	Hoboken, 424	H 8
	30230	Hogansville, 3,075	C 4
	30142	Holly Springs, 575	D 2
	30523	Hollywood, 300	E 1
†	31537	Homeland, 595	H 9
	30547	Homer⊙, 365	F 2
	31634	Homerville⊙, 3,025	G 8
	31543	Hortense, 400	J 8
	30548	Hoschton, 509	E 2
	30646	Hull, 222	F 2
	30561	Hurst, 216	D 1
	31041	Ideal, 543	D 6
	30647	Ila, 202	F 2
	30231	Indian Springs, 300	E 4
	30232	Inman, 475	D 4
	31759	Iron City, 351	C 8
	31042	Irwinton⊙, 757	F 5
	31760	Irwinville, 550	F 7
	31406	Isle of Hope, 975	K 7
†	31031	Ivey, 245	F 5
	30233	Jackson⊙, 3,778	E 4
	31544	Jacksonville, 214	G 7
	30143	Jasper⊙, 1,202	D 2

(continued on following page)

GEORGIA

SCALE
0 5 10   20   30   40 MI.
0 5 10   20   30   40 KM.

State Capitals .... ⊛
County Seats .... ⊙

© C.S. HAMMOND & Co., N.Y.

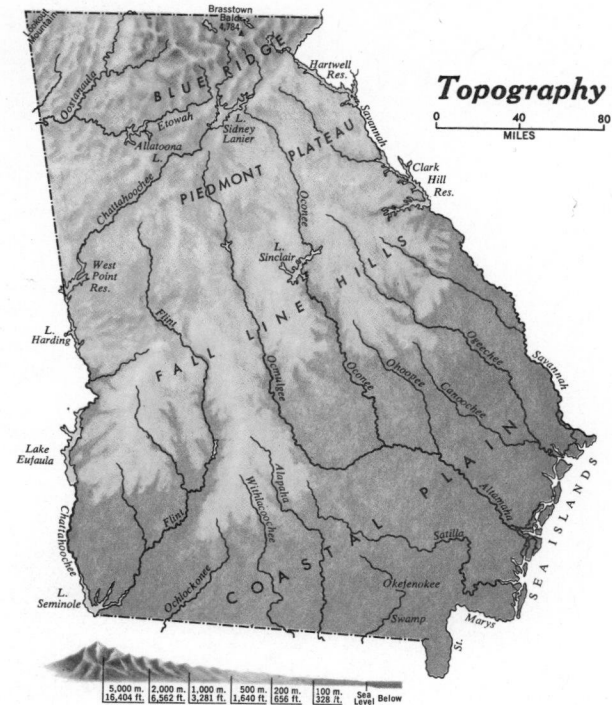

Topography

0   40   80
MILES

5,000 m. | 2,000 m. | 1,000 m. | 500 m. | 200 m. | 100 m. | Sea Level
16,404 ft. | 6,562 ft. | 3,281 ft. | 1,640 ft. | 656 ft. | 328 ft. | Below

Agriculture, Industry and Resources

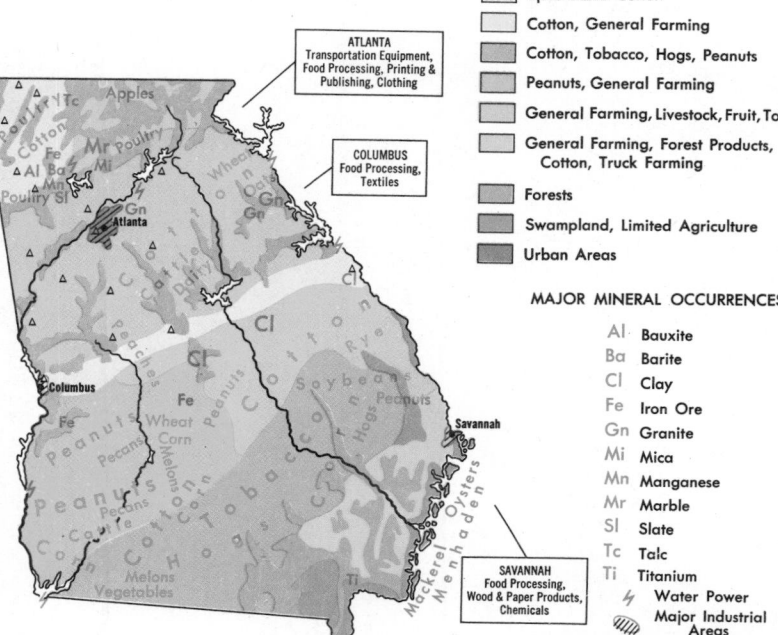

DOMINANT LAND USE

Specialized Cotton
Cotton, General Farming
Cotton, Tobacco, Hogs, Peanuts
Peanuts, General Farming
General Farming, Livestock, Fruit, Tobacco
General Farming, Forest Products, Cotton, Truck Farming
Forests
Swampland, Limited Agriculture
Urban Areas

MAJOR MINERAL OCCURRENCES

Al Bauxite
Ba Barite
Cl Clay
Fe Iron Ore
Gn Granite
Mi Mica
Mn Manganese
Mr Marble
Sl Slate
Tc Talc
Ti Titanium
⚡ Water Power
▨ Major Industrial Areas
△ Major Textile Manufacturing Centers

ATLANTA
Transportation Equipment, Food Processing, Printing & Publishing, Clothing

COLUMBUS
Food Processing, Textiles

SAVANNAH
Food Processing, Wood & Paper Products, Chemicals

Topography

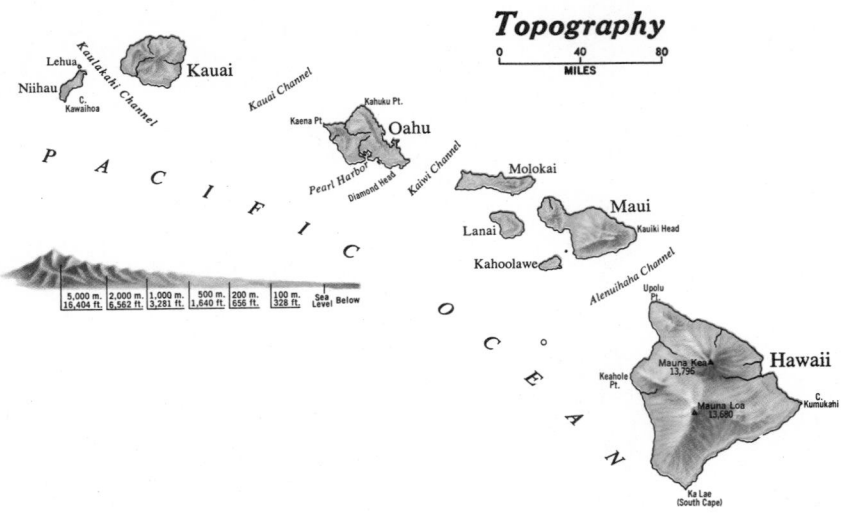

0 40 80
MILES

P A C I F I C   O C E A N

Lehua
Niihau
C. Kawaihoa
Kaulakahi Channel
Kauai
Kauai Channel
Kaena Pt.
Kahuku Pt.
Oahu
Pearl Harbor
Diamond Head
Kaiwi Channel
Molokai
Maui
Kauiki Head
Lanai
Kahoolawe
Alenuihaha Channel
Upolu Pt.
Keahole Pt.
Mauna Kea 13,796
Mauna Loa 13,680
Hawaii
C. Kumukahi
Ka Lae (South Cape)

| 5,000 m. 16,404 ft. | 2,000 m. 6,562 ft. | 1,000 m. 3,281 ft. | 500 m. 1,640 ft. | 200 m. 656 ft. | 100 m. 328 ft. | Sea Level | Below |

Sharp spikes bristle protectively around their precious fruit crop on Pineapple Hill, west Maui. Second only to sugarcane, pineapples rank high in Hawaii's economy.

David Muench — Shostal Associates

Agriculture, Industry and Resources

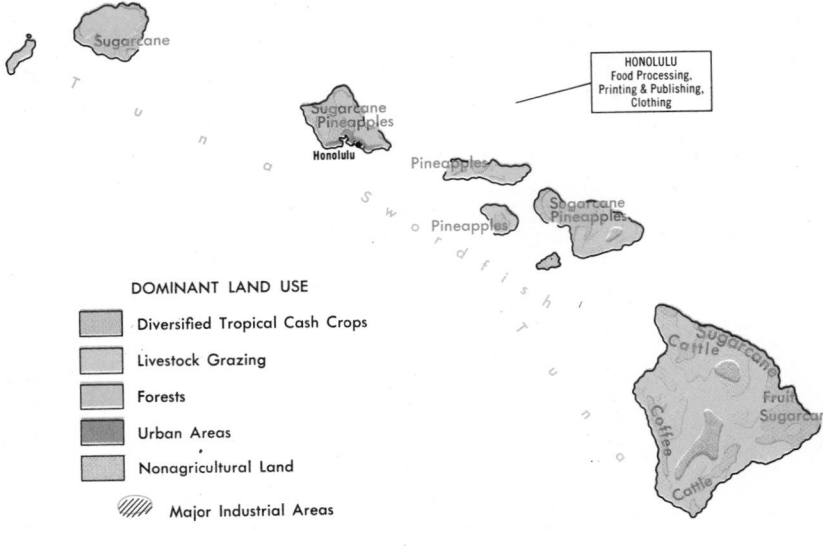

Sugarcane
Tuna
Sugarcane Pineapples
Honolulu
Pineapples
Pineapples
Swordfish
Tuna
Sugarcane Pineapples
Sugarcane Cattle
Coffee
Fruit Sugarcane
Cattle

HONOLULU
Food Processing,
Printing & Publishing,
Clothing

DOMINANT LAND USE

Diversified Tropical Cash Crops

Livestock Grazing

Forests

Urban Areas

Nonagricultural Land

Major Industrial Areas

KAUAI COUNTY

SCALE
0 5 10 15MI.
0 5 10 15KM.

160° Longitude West of Greenwich 159°3

Kaulakahi Channel

Hanalei Bay
Haena Pt.
Haena
Wainiha
Wainiha R.
Makaha Pt.
Nohili Pt.
Kawaikini Pk. 5,170
K A U A I
Mana
Waimea R.
Kekaha
Waimea
Waimea Bay
Makaweli
Kaumakani
Eleele
Kalah
Hanapepe
Hanapepe Bay
Lehua
Paniau Pk. 1,281
Kaunuopou Pt.
Kokole Pt.
Kolo Pt.
Puolo Pt.
Puuwai
Pueo Pt.
NIIHAU
Kamalino
Halalii Lake
Cape Kawaihoa

Waipahu
158°
Pearl City
Waimalu
Halawa Hts.
Middle Loch
East Loch
Ford I.
Aiea
Halawa Stream
Honouliuli
West Loch
FORD I. N.A.S.
Foster Village
Salt Lake
FT. SHAFTER
Ewa
PEARL
Waipio Pen.
HARBOR
Southeast Loch
Hickam Housing
Kalihi
O
Waipio
HICKAM A.F.B.
HONOLULU INTERN'L AIRPORT
Keehi Lagoon
Kalihi
Iroquois Point
Keahi Pt.
Keahi Entrance
Ahua Pt.
Honolulu
Ewa Beach
M A M A L A
Kalihi Entrance
Honolulu Harbor
Punchbowl
Palama
B A Y

HONOLULU &
PEARL HARBOR

SCALE
0 1 2MI.
0 1 2KM.

180° Kure 176° Eastern I. Sand I. Midway Is. (U.S.) 172° 168°

International Date Line

H A W A I I A N

Pearl and Hermes Reef

Lisianski I.

Layson I.
Maro Reef

French Frigate Shoals

Garden Pinnacles

P A C I F I C   O C E A N

HAWAII

State Capital .... ⊛

County Seats .... ⦿

© C.S. HAMMOND & CO., N.Y.

Johnston Atoll (U.S.)

† 96750 Kainaliu, 450 ....G 5
† 96757 Kalae, 150 ....G 1
  96741 Kalaheo, 1,514 ....C 2
† 96740 Kalaoa, 300 ....G 5
  96742 Kalaupapa⊙, 164 ....G 1
  96817 Kalihi, 32,650 ....E 2
† 96748 Kaluaaha, 300 ....H 1
† 96748 Kamalo, 300 ....H 1
  96743 Kamuela, 756 ....G 3
  96744 Keneohe, 29,903 ....F 2
  96746 Kapaa, 3,794 ....D 1
† 96778 Kapaahu, 850 ....J 6
  96755 Kapaau, 237 ....G 3
† 96778 Kapoho, 300 ....K 5
† 96758 Kapulena, 125 ....H 4
  96747 Kaumakani, 1,014 ....C 2
† 96748 Kaunakakai, 1,070 ....C 1
† 96708 Kaupakulua, 100 ....K 2
  96743 Kawaihae, 50 ....G 4
† 96712 Kawailoa, 900 ....E 1
  96749 Keaau, 951 ....J 5
† 96750 Kealakekua, 740 ....G 5
  96751 Kealia, 600 ....D 1
  96751 Kealia, 550 ....G 6
  96752 Kekaha, 2,404 ....C 2
† 96704 Keokea, 500 ....G 6
  96704 Keokea, 750 ....J 2
† 96753 Kihei, 1,450 ....J 2
  96754 Kilauea, 671 ....C 1
† 96713 Koali, 100 ....K 2
† 96755 Kohala (Kapaau), 237 ....G 3

† 96708 Kokomo, 200 ....K 2
  96756 Koloa, 1,368 ....C 2
  96757 Kualapuu, 441 ....G 1
† 96758 Kukuihaele, 310 ....H 3
  96790 Kula, 800 ....J 2
  96759 Kunia, 545 ....E 2
  96760 Kurtistown, 900 ....J 5
  96761 Lahaina, 3,718 ....H 2
  96762 Laie, 3,009 ....E 1
  96763 Lanai City, 2,122 ....H 2
  96764 Laupahoehoe, 452 ....J 4
  96765 Lawai, 950 ....C 2
  96766 Lihue⊙, 3,124 ....C 2
† 96779 Lower Paia, 1,105 ....J 1
  96753 Maalaea, 80 ....J 2
  96792 Maili, 4,397 ....D 2
  96792 Makaha, 4,644 ....D 2
  96706 Makakilo City, 3,499 .....E 2
† 96711 Makaula, 201 ....G 3
  96768 Makawao, 1,066 ....K 2
  96769 Makaweli, 900 ....C 2
  96770 Maunaloa, 872 ....G 1
† 96744 Maunawili, 5,303 ....F 2
  96786 Mililani, 2,035 ....E 2
  96704 Miloli, 120 ....G 6
  96734 Mokapu, 7,860 ....F 2
† 96791 Mokuleia, 880 ....D 1
  96771 Mountainview, 419 ....J 5
  96772 Naalehu, 1,014 ....H 7
  96792 Nanakuli, 6,506 ....D 2
  96773 Ninole, 75 ....J 4

  96761 Olowalu, 750 ....H 2
  96781 Onomea, 500 ....J 4
  96774 Ookala, 486 ....J 4
† 96778 Opihikao, 125 ....K 6
  96778 Paauhau, 400 ....H 4
  96776 Paauilo, 710 ....H 4
  96801 Pacific Heights, 5,305 ...C 4
  96782 Pacific Palisades, 7,846 .E 2
  96777 Pahala, 1,507 ....H 6
  96778 Pahoa, 900 ....J 5
  96779 Paia, 541 ....J 2
  96801 Palama, 15,307 ....C 4
  96704 Papa, 100 ....G 6
  96780 Papaaloa, 319 ....J 4
  96781 Papaikou, 1,888 ....J 4
  96781 Paukaa, 450 ....J 4
† 96708 Pauwela, 355 ....K 2
  96782 Pearl City, 19,552 ....B 3
  96783 Pepeekeo, 1,150 ....J 4
  96756 Poipu, 466 ....C 2
  96766 Puhi, 700 ....C 2
  96788 Pukalani, 1,629 ....J 2
† 96748 Pukoo, 300 ....H 1
  96784 Punene, 1,132 ....J 2
  96801 Puunui, 10,082 ....C 4
  96769 Puuwai, 200 ....A 2
  96786 Schofield Barracks, 13,516 .E 2
  96779 Spreckelsville, 350 ......J 2
† 96790 Ulupalakua, 75 ....J 2
  96785 Volcano, 400 ....J 6
  96766 Wahiawa, 17,598 ....E 2

  96788 Waiakoa, 1,050 ....J 2
† 96731 Waialee, 80 ....E 1
  96791 Waialua, Oahu, 4,047 ..E 1
  96792 Waianae, 3,302 ....D 2
  96793 Waihee, 346 ....J 2
  96793 Waikapu, 598 ....J 2
  96815 Waikiki, 35,000 ....C 4
† 96748 Wailau, 300 ....H 1
  96710 Wailea, 315 ....J 4
  96746 Wailua, 1,379 ....D 2
  96793 Wailuku⊙, 7,979 ....J 2
  96701 Waimalu, 2,982 ....B 3
  96795 Waimanalo, 2,081 ......F 2
† 96795 Waimanalo Beach, 3,045 .F 2
† 96743 Waimea (Kamuela), Hawaii
           756 ....G 3
  96796 Waimea, Kauai, 1,569 ..C 2
  96712 Waimea, Oahu, 200 .....E 1
† 96772 Waiohinu, 200 ....G 7
  96797 Waipahu, 22,798 ....A 3
† 96786 Waipio Acres, 2,146 ....E 2
  96786 Whitmore Village, 2,015 .E 1
† 96801 Woodlawn, 5,569 ....D 4

MIDWAY ISLANDS
Total Population
2,356

⊙ County seat.
‡ Population of metropolitan area.
† Zip of nearest p.o.
* Multiple zips

AREA 6,450 sq. mi.
POPULATION 769,913
CAPITAL Honolulu
LARGEST CITY Honolulu
HIGHEST POINT Mauna Kea 13,796 ft.
SETTLED IN —
ADMITTED TO UNION August 21, 1959
POPULAR NAME Aloha State; Paradise of the Pacific
STATE FLOWER Red Hibiscus
STATE BIRD Nene (Hawaiian Goose)

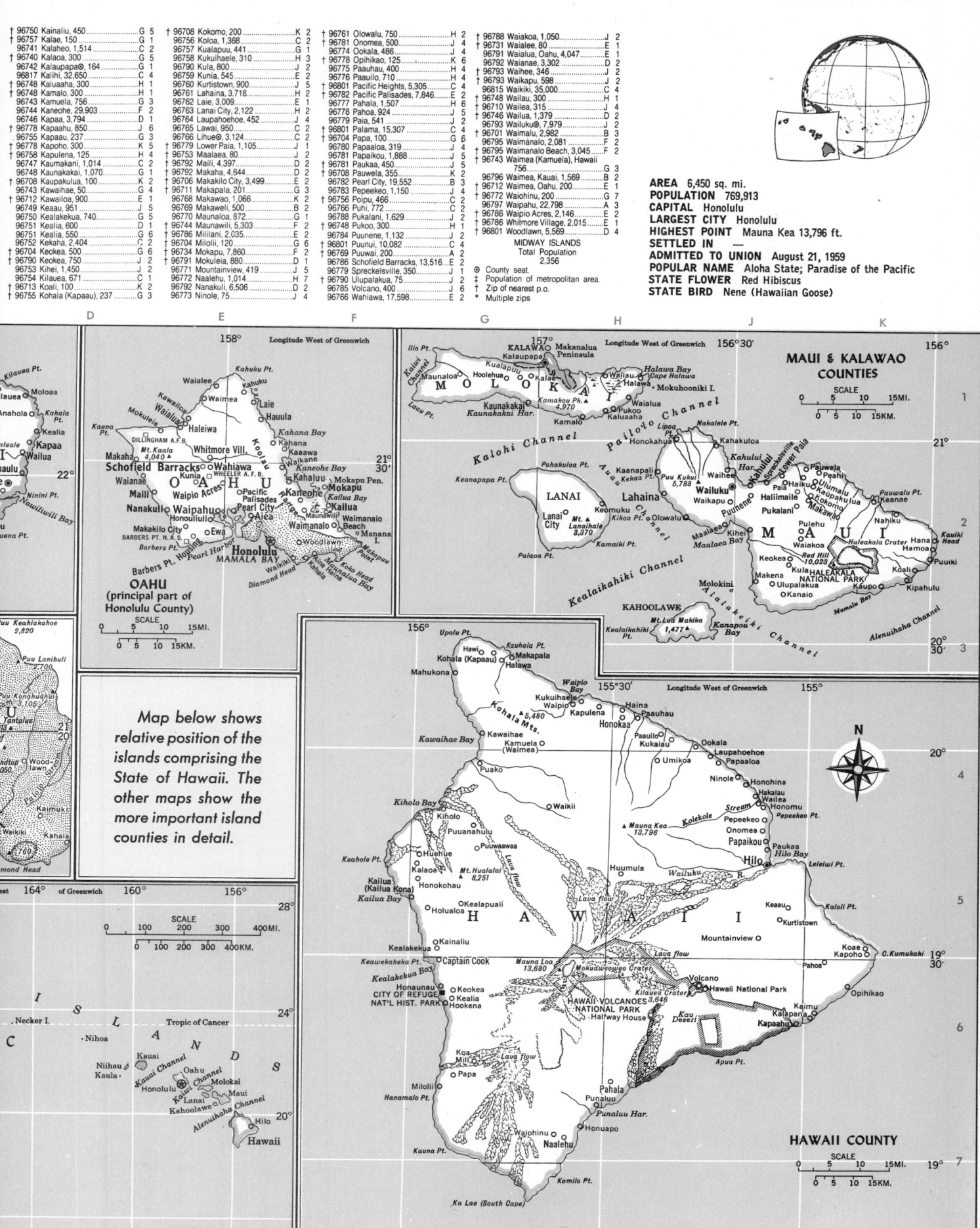

Map below shows relative position of the islands comprising the State of Hawaii. The other maps show the more important island counties in detail.

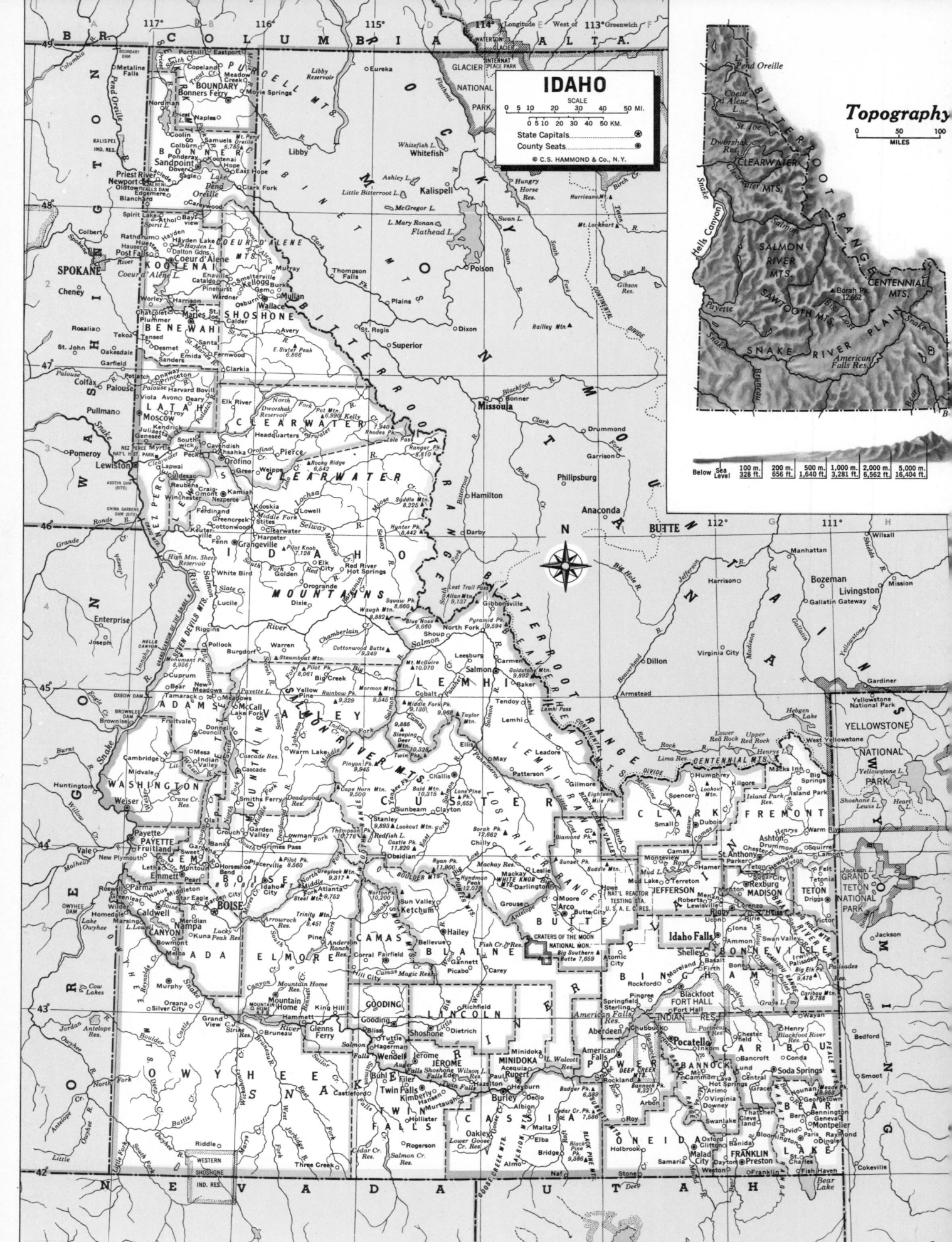

IDAHO

SCALE
0 5 10   20   30   40   50 MI.
0 5 10   20   30   40   50 KM.

State Capitals .... ⊛
County Seats .... ⊛

© C.S. HAMMOND & Co., N.Y.

Topography

0   50   100
MILES

| Below Sea Level | 100 m. 328 ft. | 200 m. 656 ft. | 500 m. 1,640 ft. | 1,000 m. 3,281 ft. | 2,000 m. 6,562 ft. | 5,000 m. 16,404 ft. |

COUNTIES

Name/Pop.	Key
Ada, 112,230	B 6
Adams, 2,877	B 5
Bannock, 52,200	F 7
Bear Lake, 5,801	G 7
Benewah, 6,230	B 2
Bingham, 29,167	F 6
Blaine, 5,749	D 6
Boise, 1,763	C 6
Bonner, 15,560	B 1
Bonneville, 51,250	G 6
Boundary, 6,371	B 1
Butte, 2,925	E 6
Camas, 728	D 6
Canyon, 61,288	B 6
Caribou, 6,534	G 7
Cassia, 17,017	E 7
Clark, 741	F 5
Clearwater, 10,871	C 3
Custer, 2,967	D 5
Elmore, 17,479	C 6
Franklin, 7,373	G 7
Fremont, 8,710	G 5
Gem, 9,387	B 6
Gooding, 8,645	D 6
Idaho, 12,891	C 4
Jefferson, 11,619	F 6
Jerome, 10,253	D 7
Kootenai, 35,332	B 2
Latah, 24,891	B 3
Lemhi, 5,566	D 4
Lewis, 3,867	B 3
Lincoln, 3,057	D 6
Madison, 13,452	G 6
Minidoka, 15,731	E 7
Nez Perce, 30,376	B 3
Oneida, 2,864	F 7
Owyhee, 6,422	B 7
Payette, 12,401	B 5
Power, 4,864	F 7
Shoshone, 19,718	B 2
Teton, 2,351	G 6
Twin Falls, 41,807	D 7
Valley, 3,609	C 5
Washington, 7,633	B 5

CITIES and TOWNS

Zip	Name/Pop.	Key
83210	Aberdeen, 1,542	F 7
83310	Acequia, 107	E 7
83520	Ahsahka, 500	B 3
83311	Albion, 229	E 7
83312	Almo, 170	E 7
83211	American Falls⊙, 2,769	E 7
83401	Ammon, 1,338	G 6
83212	Arbon, 75	F 7
83213	Arco⊙, 1,244	E 6
83214	Arimo, 252	F 7
83420	Ashton, 1,187	G 5
83801	Athol, 190	B 2
83601	Atlanta, 50	C 6
83215	Atomic City, 24	F 6
83802	Avery, 250	C 2
83461	Baker, 98	E 4
83217	Bancroft, 366	G 7
83264	Banida, 76	G 7
83602	Banks, 49	B 5
83218	Basalt, 349	F 6
83803	Bayview, 300	B 2
83313	Bellevue, 537	D 6
83219	Bennington, 60	G 7
83220	Bern, 135	G 7
83221	Blackfoot⊙, 8,716	F 6
83804	Blanchard, 120	A 1
83314	Bliss, 114	D 7
83223	Bloomington, 186	G 7
83701	Boise (cap.)⊙, 74,990	B 6
	Boise, ‡112,230	B 6
83805	Bonners Ferry⊙, 2,796	B 1
83806	Bovill, 343	B 3
83651	Bowmont, 100	B 6
83315	Bridge, 140	E 7
83604	Bruneau, 150	C 7
83316	Buhl, 2,975	D 7
83807	Burke, 150	C 2
83318	Burley⊙, 8,279	E 7
83213	Butte City, 42	E 6
83808	Calder, 140	B 2
83605	Caldwell⊙, 14,219	B 6
83610	Cambridge, 383	B 5
83320	Carey, 750	E 6
83809	Careywood, 60	B 1
83462	Carmen, 40	E 4
83611	Cascade⊙, 833	C 5
83321	Castleford, 174	C 7
83810	Cataldo, 275	B 2
83241	Central, 60	G 7
83226	Challis⊙, 784	D 5
83851	Chatcolet, 95	B 2
83421	Chester, 206	G 5
83217	Chesterfield, 50	G 7
83201	Chubbuck, 2,924	F 7
83811	Clark Fork, 367	B 1
83812	Clarkia, 147	B 2
83227	Clayton, 36	D 5
83521	Clearwater, 110	C 3
83263	Cleveland, 60	G 7
83228	Clifton, 137	F 7
83229	Cobalt, 35	D 4
83814	Coeur d'Alene⊙, 16,228	B 2
83865	Colburn, 200	B 1
83230	Conda, 250	G 7
83821	Coolin, 110	B 1
83322	Corral, 21	D 6
83522	Cottonwood, 867	B 3
83612	Council⊙, 899	B 5
83523	Craigmont, 554	B 3
83622	Crouch, 71	B 5
83524	Culdesac, 211	B 3
83814	Dalton Gardens, 1,559	B 2
3232	Dayton, 198	F 7
3823	Deary, 411	B 3
3323	Declo, 251	E 7
3824	Desmet, 154	B 2
3324	Dietrich, 84	D 7
83233	Dingle, 300	G 7
83615	Donnelly, 114	B 5
83825	Dover, 300	B 1
83234	Downey, 586	F 7
83422	Driggs⊙, 727	G 6
83423	Dubois⊙, 400	F 5
83616	Eagle, 525	B 6
† 83836	East Hope, 175	B 1
83826	Eastport, 83	B 1
83325	Eden, 343	D 7
83326	Elba, 87	E 7
83525	Elk City, 500	C 4
83827	Elk River, 383	B 3
83235	Ellis, 75	D 5
83828	Emida, 135	B 2
83617	Emmett⊙, 3,945	B 6
83829	Enaville, 90	B 2
83327	Fairfield⊙, 157	D 6
83424	Felt, 90	G 6
83531	Fenn, 45	B 4
83526	Ferdinand, 157	B 3
83830	Fernwood, 360	B 2
83328	Filer, 1,173	D 7
83236	Firth, 362	F 6
83261	Fish Haven, 120	G 7
83203	Fort Hall, 750	F 6
83237	Franklin, 402	G 7
83619	Fruitland, 1,576	B 6
83620	Fruitvale, 90	B 5
83621	Gardena, 44	B 5
83704	Garden City, 2,368	B 6
83622	Garden Valley, 100	C 5
† 83873	Gem, 50	C 2
83832	Genesee, 619	B 3
83238	Geneva, 200	G 7
83239	Georgetown, 421	G 7
83463	Gibbonsville, 85	E 4
83623	Glenns Ferry, 1,386	C 7
83330	Gooding⊙, 2,599	D 7
83241	Grace, 826	G 7
83624	Grand View, 450	B 7
83530	Grangeville⊙, 3,636	B 4
83533	Greencreek, 72	B 3
83626	Greenleaf, 425	B 6
† 83544	Greer, 70	B 3
83332	Hagerman, 436	D 7
83333	Hailey⊙, 1,425	D 6
83425	Hamer, 81	F 6
83627	Hammett, 653	C 7
83334	Hansen, 415	D 7
† 83521	Harpster, 250	C 4
83833	Harrison, 249	B 2
83834	Harvard, 50	B 3
† 83854	Hauser, 349	A 2
† 83835	Hayden, 1,285	B 2
83835	Hayden Lake, 260	B 2
83335	Hazelton, 396	E 7
83534	Headquarters, 350	C 3
† 83443	Heise, 84	G 6
83336	Heyburn, 1,637	E 7
83337	Hill City, 30	D 6
83243	Holbrook, 100	F 7
† 83301	Hollister, 57	D 7
83628	Homedale, 1,411	A 6
83836	Hope, 63	B 1
83629	Horseshoe Bend, 511	B 6
83244	Howe, 428	F 6
† 83854	Huetter, 49	B 2
83631	Idaho City⊙, 164	C 6
83401	Idaho Falls⊙, 35,776	F 6
83632	Indian Valley, 72	B 5
83245	Inkom, 522	F 7
83427	Iona, 890	G 6
83428	Irwin, 228	G 6
83429	Island Park, 136	G 5
83338	Jerome⊙, 4,183	D 7
83535	Juliaetta, 423	B 3
83536	Kamiah, 1,307	B 3
83837	Kellogg, 3,811	B 2
83537	Kendrick, 426	B 3
83340	Ketchum, 1,454	D 6
83538	Keuterville, 26	B 3
† 83423	Kilgore, 50	G 5
83341	Kimberly, 1,557	D 7
83633	King Hill, 150	C 6
83539	Kooskia, 809	C 3
83840	Kootenai, 168	B 1
83634	Kuna, 593	B 6
83841	Laclede, 200	B 1
83635	Lake Fork, 141	B 5
83430	Lamont, 30	G 6
83540	Lapwai, 400	B 3
83246	Lava Hot Springs, 516	F 7
83464	Leadore, 111	E 5
83465	Lemhi, 36	E 5
83249	Leslie, 100	E 6
83636	Letha, 115	B 6
83501	Lewiston⊙, 26,068	A 3
83431	Lewisville, 468	F 6
83432	Lorenzo, 125	G 6
† 83242	Lost River, 58	E 6
83637	Lowman, 45	C 5
83542	Lucile, 105	B 4
† 83241	Lund, 100	G 7
83251	Mackay, 539	E 6
83433	Macks Inn, 150	G 5
83252	Malad City⊙, 1,848	F 7
83342	Malta, 196	E 7
83639	Marsing, 610	B 6
83253	May, 120	E 5
83638	McCall, 1,758	C 5
83250	McCammon, 623	F 7
83640	Meadows, 250	B 5
83641	Melba, 197	B 6
83434	Menan, 545	F 6
83642	Meridian, 2,616	B 6
83643	Mesa, 25	B 5
83644	Middleton, 739	B 6
83645	Midvale, 176	B 5
83343	Minidoka, 131	E 7
83435	Monteview, 110	F 6
83646	Montour, 138	B 6
83254	Montpelier, 2,604	G 7
83255	Moore, 156	E 6
83256	Moreland, 500	F 6
83843	Moscow⊙, 14,146	B 3
83647	Mountain Home⊙, 6,451	C 6
83845	Moyie Springs, 203	B 1
† 83450	Mud Lake, 194	F 6
83846	Mullan, 1,279	C 2
83650	Murphy⊙, 75	B 6
83874	Murray, 100	C 2
83344	Murtaugh, 124	D 7
83345	Naf, 42	E 7
83651	Nampa, 20,768	B 6
83847	Naples, 463	B 1
83436	Newdale, 267	G 6
83654	New Meadows, 605	B 4
83655	New Plymouth, 986	B 6
83543	Nezperce⊙, 555	B 3
83848	Nordman, 168	B 1
83466	North Fork, 150	D 4
83656	Notus, 304	B 6
† 83254	Nounan, 92	G 7
83346	Oakley, 656	D 7
83259	Obsidian, 22	D 6
83657	Ola, 78	B 5
† 99156	Oldtown, 161	A 1
† 83855	Onaway, 166	B 3
83659	Oreana, 115	B 6
83544	Orofino⊙, 3,883	B 3
† 83525	Orogrande, 34	C 4
83849	Osburn, 2,248	B 2
83260	Ovid, 150	G 7
† 83263	Oxford, 75	F 7
83437	Palisades, 95	G 6
83261	Paris⊙, 615	G 7
83438	Parker, 266	G 6
83660	Parma, 1,228	B 6
83347	Paul, 911	E 7
83661	Payette⊙, 4,521	B 5
83545	Peck, 238	B 3
83348	Picabo, 50	D 6
83546	Pierce, 1,218	C 3
83850	Pinehurst, 1,934	B 2
83262	Pingree, 115	F 6
83851	Plummer, 443	B 2
83201	Pocatello⊙, 40,036	F 7
83547	Pollock, 50	B 4
83852	Ponderay, 275	B 1
83853	Porthill, 39	B 1
83854	Post Falls, 2,371	A 2
83855	Potlatch, 871	A 3
83263	Preston⊙, 3,310	G 7
83856	Priest River, 1,493	A 1
83857	Princeton, 124	B 3
83858	Rathdrum, 741	A 2
† 83114	Raymond, 65	G 7
83548	Reubens, 81	B 3
83440	Rexburg⊙, 8,272	G 6
83349	Richfield, 290	D 6
† 89832	Riddle, 44	B 7
83442	Rigby⊙, 2,293	F 6
83549	Riggins, 533	B 4
83443	Ririe, 575	G 6
83444	Roberts, 393	F 6
† 83221	Rockford, 150	F 6
83271	Rockland, 209	F 7
83302	Rogerson, 45	D 7
† 83660	Roswell, 65	A 6
83350	Rupert⊙, 4,563	E 7
83860	Sagle, 100	B 1
83445	Saint Anthony⊙, 2,877	G 6
83272	Saint Charles, 200	G 7
† 83861	Saint Joe, 50	B 2
83861	Saint Maries⊙, 2,571	B 2
83467	Salmon⊙, 2,910	D 4
83252	Samaria, 137	F 7
83862	Samuels, 467	B 1
83863	Sanders, 27	B 2
83864	Sandpoint⊙, 4,144	B 1
83866	Santa, 100	B 2
83274	Shelley, 2,614	F 6
83352	Shoshone⊙, 1,233	D 7
† 83650	Silver City, 1	B 6
† 83423	Small, 35	F 5
83868	Smelterville, 967	B 2
83276	Soda Springs⊙, 2,977	G 7
83550	Southwick, 38	B 3
83446	Spencer, 45	F 5
83869	Spirit Lake, 622	A 2
83277	Springfield, 180	F 6
83447	Squirrel, 43	G 5
83278	Stanley, 47	D 5
83669	Star, 500	B 6
83279	Sterling, 73	F 6
83552	Stites, 263	C 3
83280	Stone, 114	F 7
83448	Sugar City, 617	G 6
83353	Sun Valley, 180	D 6
83281	Swanlake, 145	F 7
83449	Swan Valley, 235	G 6
83670	Sweet, 120	B 6
83468	Tendoy, 150	E 5
83870	Tensed, 151	B 2
83450	Terreton, 42	F 6
83451	Teton, 390	G 6
83452	Tetonia, 176	G 6
83283	Thatcher, 300	G 7
83453	Thornton, 177	G 6
83871	Troy, 541	B 3
83354	Tuttle, 53	D 7
83301	Twin Falls⊙, 21,914	D 7
83454	Ucon, 664	F 6
83455	Victor, 241	G 6
83872	Viola, 300	B 3
† 83234	Virginia, 100	F 7
83873	Wallace⊙, 2,206	C 2
83875	Wardner, 492	B 2
83611	Warm Lake, 200	C 5
83285	Wayan, 50	G 7
83553	Weippe, 713	C 3
83672	Weiser⊙, 4,108	B 5
83355	Wendell, 1,122	D 7
83286	Weston, 230	F 7
83554	White Bird, 185	B 4
83676	Wilder, 564	A 6
83555	Winchester, 274	B 3
83876	Worley, 235	B 2
83677	Yellow Pine, 45	C 4

⊙ County seat.
‡ Population of metropolitan area.
† Zip of nearest p.o.
* Multiple zips

AREA 83,557 sq. mi.
POPULATION 713,008
CAPITAL Boise
LARGEST CITY Boise
HIGHEST POINT Borah Pk. 12,662 ft.
SETTLED IN 1842
ADMITTED TO UNION July 3, 1890
POPULAR NAME Gem State
STATE FLOWER Syringa
STATE BIRD Mountain Bluebird

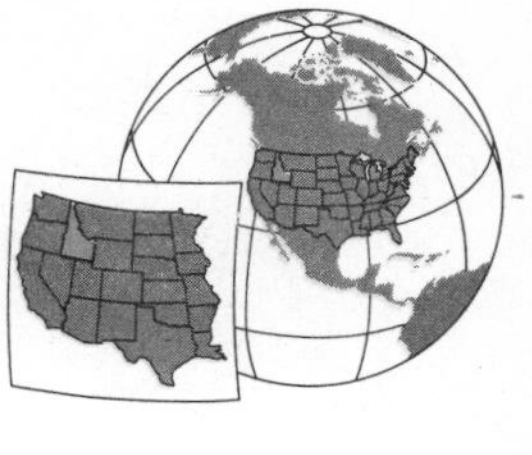

Agriculture, Industry and Resources

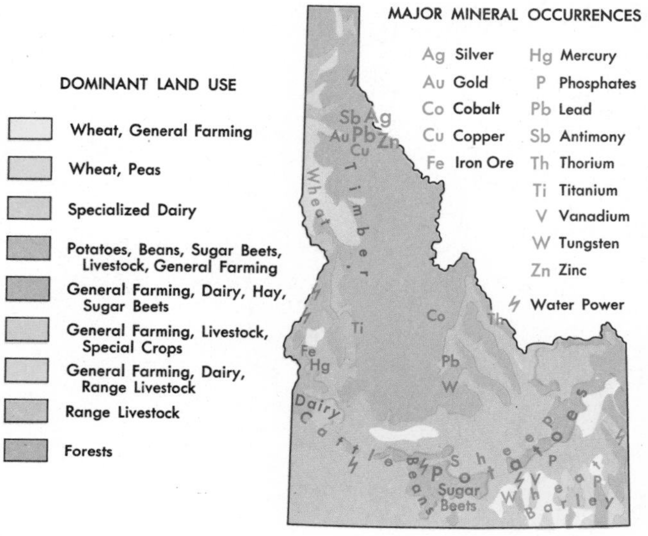
DOMINANT LAND USE
Wheat, General Farming
Wheat, Peas
Specialized Dairy
Potatoes, Beans, Sugar Beets, Livestock, General Farming
General Farming, Dairy, Hay, Sugar Beets
General Farming, Livestock, Special Crops
General Farming, Dairy, Range Livestock
Range Livestock
Forests
MAJOR MINERAL OCCURRENCES
Ag Silver
Au Gold
Co Cobalt
Cu Copper
Fe Iron Ore
Hg Mercury
P Phosphates
Pb Lead
Sb Antimony
Th Thorium
Ti Titanium
V Vanadium
W Tungsten
Zn Zinc
Water Power
Wheat
Timber
Dairy
Cattle
Beans
Sheep
Potatoes
Sugar Beets
Wheat
Barley

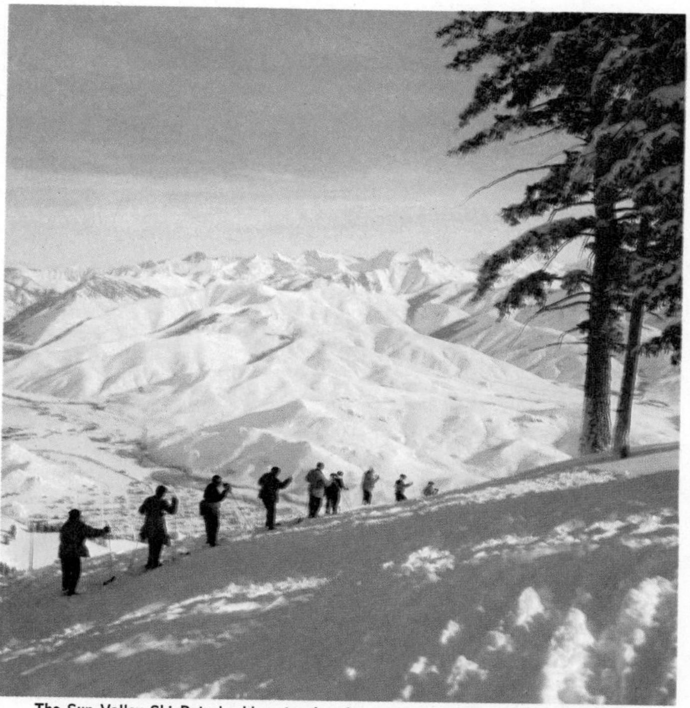
Bob Lee,—Shostal Associates

The Sun Valley Ski Patrol adds a touch of color to the slopes of Baldy Mountain. Here, in one of the country's most popular resorts, visitors acquire tropical tans while swimming in heated pools, skiing, skijoring, dogsledding or just sunbathing in the glacial air.

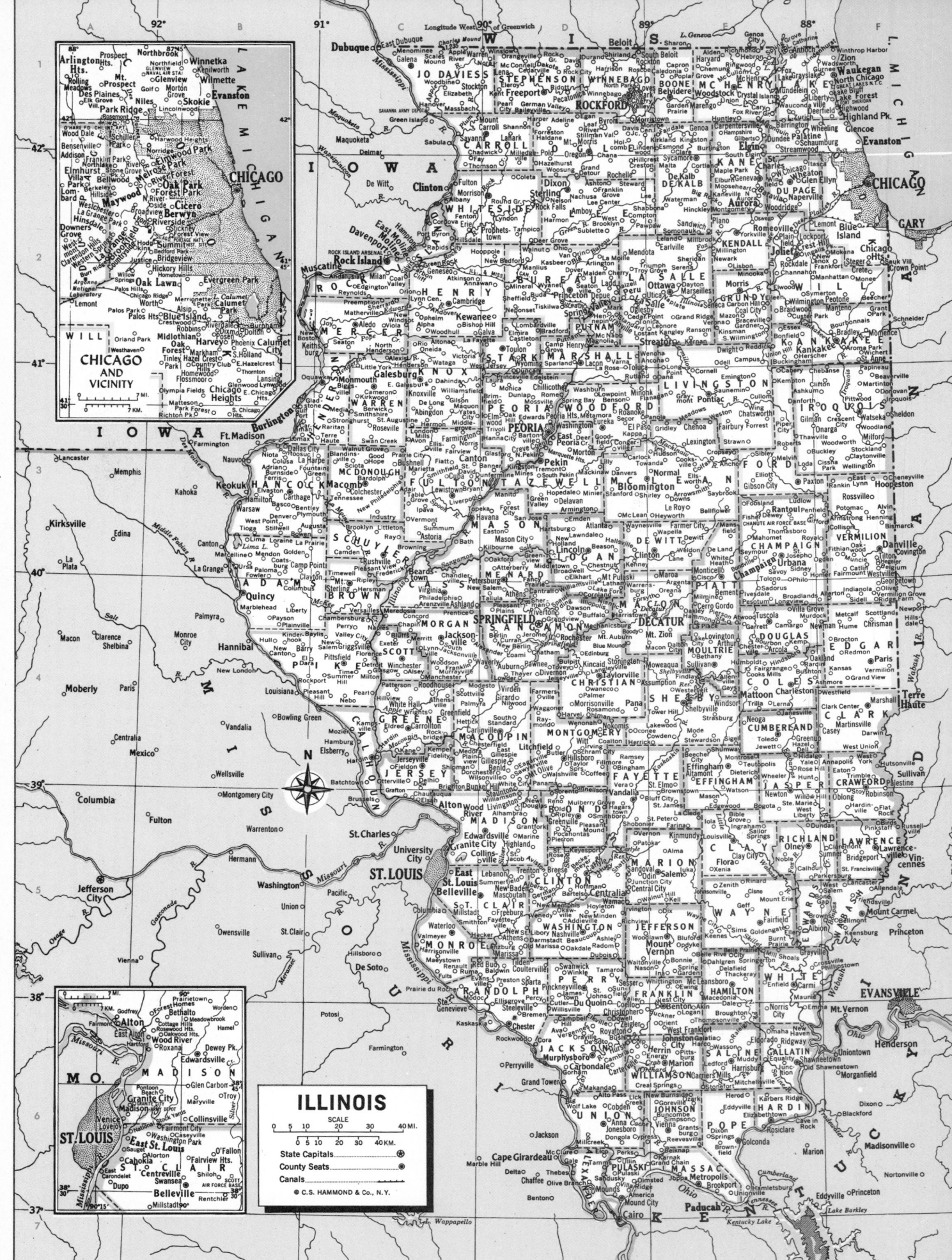

CHICAGO
AND VICINITY

ST. LOUIS

ILLINOIS
SCALE
0   5 10   20   30   40 MI.
0 5 10   20   30   40 KM.
State Capitals
County Seats
Canals
© C.S. HAMMOND & CO., N.Y.

Illinois 159

COUNTIES

County	Key
dams, 70,861	B 4
lexander, 12,015	D 6
ond, 14,012	D 5
oone, 25,440	E 1
rown, 5,586	C 4
ureau, 38,541	D 2
alhoun, 5,675	C 4
arroll, 19,276	D 1
ass, 14,219	C 4
hampaign, 163,281	E 3
hristian, 35,948	D 4
lark, 16,216	F 4
lay, 14,735	E 5
linton, 28,315	D 5
oles, 47,815	E 4
ook, 5,492,369	F 2
rawford, 19,824	F 4
umberland, 9,772	E 4
e Kalb, 71,654	E 2
e Witt, 16,975	E 3
ouglas, 18,997	E 4
u Page, 491,882	E 2
dgar, 21,591	F 4
dwards, 7,090	E 5
ffingham, 24,608	E 4
ayette, 20,752	D 4
ord, 16,382	E 3
ranklin, 38,329	E 5
ulton, 41,890	C 3
allatin, 7,418	E 6
reene, 17,014	C 4
rundy, 26,535	E 2
amilton, 8,665	E 5
ancock, 23,645	B 3
ardin, 4,914	E 6
enderson, 8,451	C 3
enry, 53,217	C 2
oquois, 33,532	F 3
ackson, 55,008	D 6
asper, 10,741	E 4
efferson, 31,446	E 5
ersey, 18,492	C 4
o Daviess, 21,766	C 1
ohnson, 7,550	E 6
ane, 251,005	E 2
ankakee, 97,250	F 2
endall, 26,374	E 2
nox, 61,280	C 3
ake, 382,638	E 1
a Salle, 111,409	E 2
awrence, 17,522	F 5
ee, 37,947	D 2
ivingston, 40,690	E 3
ogan, 33,538	D 3
Macon, 125,010	E 4
Macoupin, 44,557	D 4
Madison, 250,934	D 5
Marion, 38,986	E 5
Marshall, 13,302	D 2
Mason, 16,161	D 3
Massac, 13,889	E 6
McDonough, 36,653	C 3
McHenry, 111,555	E 1
McLean, 104,389	E 3
Menard, 9,685	D 3
Mercer, 17,294	C 2
Monroe, 18,831	C 5
Montgomery, 30,260	D 4
Morgan, 36,174	C 4
Moultrie, 13,263	E 4
Ogle, 42,867	D 1
Peoria, 195,318	D 3
Perry, 19,757	D 5
Piatt, 15,509	E 4
Pike, 19,185	C 4
Pope, 3,857	E 6
Pulaski, 8,741	D 6
Putnam, 5,007	D 2
Randolph, 31,379	D 5
Richland, 16,829	E 5
Rock Island, 166,734	C 2
Saint Clair, 285,176	D 5
Saline, 25,721	E 6
Sangamon, 161,335	D 4
Schuyler, 8,135	C 3
Scott, 6,096	C 4
Shelby, 22,589	E 4
Stark, 7,510	D 2
Stephenson, 48,861	D 1
Tazewell, 118,649	D 3
Union, 16,071	D 6
Vermilion, 97,047	F 3
Wabash, 12,841	F 5
Warren, 21,595	C 3
Washington, 13,780	D 5
Wayne, 17,004	E 5
White, 17,312	E 5
Whiteside, 62,877	D 2
Will, 249,498	F 2
Williamson, 49,021	E 6
Winnebago, 246,623	D 1
Woodford, 28,012	D 3

CITIES and TOWNS

	Zip	Name/Pop.	Key
	61410	Abingdon, 3,936	C 3
	60101	Addison, 24,482	A 2
	61230	Albany, 942	C 2
	62215	Albers, 656	D 5
	62806	Albion⊙, 1,791	E 5
	61231	Aledo⊙, 3,325	C 2
	61412	Alexis, 946	C 2
	60102	Algonquin, 3,515	E 1
	62001	Alhambra, 594	D 5
†	62207	Alorton, 3,573	B 6
	61413	Alpha, 771	C 2
†	60601	Alsip, 11,141	B 2
	62411	Altamont, 1,929	E 4
	62002	Alton, 39,700	A 6
	61310	Amboy, 2,184	D 2
	61232	Andalusia, 950	C 2
	62906	Anna, 4,766	D 6
	61234	Annawan, 787	C 2
	60002	Antioch, 3,189	E 1
	61910	Arcola, 2,276	E 4
	62501	Argenta, 1,034	E 4
*	60004	Arlington Heights, 64,884	A 1
	60910	Aroma Park, 896	F 2
	61911	Arthur, 2,214	E 4
	60911	Ashkum, 590	E 3
	62612	Ashland, 1,128	C 4
	62808	Ashley, 655	D 5
	61006	Ashton, 1,112	D 2
	62510	Assumption, 1,487	E 4
	61501	Astoria, 1,281	C 3
	62613	Athens, 1,158	D 4
	61235	Atkinson, 1,053	C 2
	61723	Atlanta, 1,640	D 3
	61913	Atwood, 1,264	E 4
	62615	Auburn, 2,594	D 4
	62311	Augusta, 824	C 3
*	60504	Aurora, 74,182	E 2
	62907	Ava, 728	D 6
	62216	Aviston, 828	D 5
	61415	Avon, 1,013	C 3
	61007	Baileyville, 600	D 1
	60010	Barrington, 7,701	E 1
	62312	Barry, 1,444	B 4
	61607	Bartonville, 7,221	D 3
	60510	Batavia, 8,994	E 2
	62618	Beardstown, 6,222	C 3
	62219	Beckemeyer, 1,069	D 5
†	60601	Bedford Park, 583	B 2
	60401	Beecher, 1,770	F 2
†	61883	Belgium, 578	F 3
*	62220	Belleville⊙, 41,699	B 6
	60104	Bellwood, 22,096	A 2
	61008	Belvidere⊙, 14,061	E 1
	61813	Bement, 1,638	E 4
	62009	Benld, 1,736	D 4
	60106	Bensenville, 12,833	A 1
	62812	Benton⊙, 6,833	E 6
	60162	Berkeley, 6,152	A 2
	60402	Berwyn, 52,502	B 2
	62010	Bethalto, 7,074	B 6
	61914	Bethany, 1,235	E 4
	61420	Blandinsville, 922	C 3
	61701	Bloomington⊙, 39,992	D 3
		Bloomington-Normal, ‡104,389	D 3
	60406	Blue Island, 22,958	B 2
	62513	Blue Mound, 1,181	D 4
	62621	Bluffs, 866	C 4
	60914	Bourbonnais, 5,909	F 2
	60407	Braceville, 668	E 2
	61421	Bradford, 885	D 2
	60915	Bradley, 9,881	F 2
	60408	Braidwood, 2,323	E 2
	62230	Breese, 2,885	D 5
	62417	Bridgeport, 2,262	F 5
	60455	Bridgeview, 12,522	B 2
	62012	Brighton, 1,889	C 4
	61517	Brimfield, 729	D 3
	60153	Broadview, 9,307	A 2
	60513	Brookfield, 20,284	A 2
†	62059	Brooklyn (Lovejoy), 1,702	A 6
	62910	Brookport, 1,046	E 6
	62418	Brownstown, 689	E 5
	60918	Buckley, 680	F 3
	61314	Buda, 675	D 2
	62014	Bunker Hill, 1,465	D 4
†	60601	Burnham, 3,634	B 2
†	60558	Burr Ridge, 1,637	A 2
	61422	Bushnell, 3,703	C 3
	61010	Byron, 1,749	D 1
	62606	Cahokia, 20,649	B 6
	62914	Cairo⊙, 6,277	D 6
	60409	Calumet City, 32,956	B 2
†	60601	Calumet Park, 10,069	B 2
	62915	Cambria, 798	D 6
	61238	Cambridge⊙, 2,095	C 2
	62320	Camp Point, 1,143	B 3
	61520	Canton, 14,217	C 3
	61012	Capron, 654	E 1
	61239	Carbon Cliff, 1,369	C 2
	62901	Carbondale, 22,816	D 6
	62626	Carlinville⊙, 5,675	D 4
	62231	Carlyle⊙, 3,139	D 5
	62821	Carmi⊙, 6,033	E 5
	60110	Carpentersville, 24,059	E 1
	62917	Carriers Mills, 2,013	E 6
	62016	Carrollton⊙, 2,866	C 4
	62918	Carterville, 3,061	D 6
	62321	Carthage⊙, 3,350	B 3
	60013	Cary, 4,358	E 1
	62420	Casey, 2,994	F 4
	62232	Caseyville, 3,411	B 6
	61817	Catlin, 2,093	F 3
	61013	Cedarville, 578	D 1
†	62801	Central City, 1,377	D 5
	62801	Centralia, 15,217	D 5
	62206	Centreville, 11,378	B 6
	61818	Cerro Gordo, 1,368	E 4
	61014	Chadwick, 605	D 1
	61820	Champaign, 56,532	E 3
		Champaign-Urbana, ‡163,281	E 3
	62627	Chandlerville, 762	C 3
	60410	Channahon, 1,505	E 2
	62628	Chapin, 552	C 4
	61920	Charleston⊙, 16,421	E 4
	62629	Chatham, 2,788	D 4
	60921	Chatsworth, 1,255	E 3
	60922	Chebanse, 1,185	F 3
	61726	Chenoa, 1,860	E 3
	61016	Cherry Valley, 952	D 1
	62233	Chester⊙, 5,310	D 6
*	60601	Chicago⊙, 3,366,957	B 2
		Chicago, ‡6,978,947	B 2
	60411	Chicago Heights, 40,900	B 3
	60415	Chicago Ridge, 9,187	A 2
	61523	Chillicothe, 6,052	D 3
	61924	Chrisman, 1,285	F 4
	62822	Christopher, 2,910	D 6
	60650	Cicero, 67,058	B 2
	62823	Cisne, 615	E 5
	60924	Cissna Park, 773	F 3
	60514	Clarendon Hills, 6,750	A 2
	62824	Clay City, 1,049	E 5
	62324	Clayton, 727	B 3
	60927	Clifton, 1,339	F 3
	61727	Clinton⊙, 7,570	E 3
	60416	Coal City, 3,040	E 2
	61240	Coal Valley, 3,088	C 2
	62920	Cobden, 1,114	D 6
	62017	Coffeen, 641	D 4
	62326	Colchester, 1,747	C 3
	61728	Colfax, 935	E 3
	62234	Collinsville, 17,773	B 6
	62236	Columbia, 4,188	C 5
	61242	Cordova, 589	C 2
	62018	Cottage Hills, 1,261	B 6
	62237	Coulterville, 1,186	D 5
	60477	Country Club Hills, 6,920	B 3
†	60525	Countryside, 2,888	A 2
	62922	Creal Springs, 830	E 6
	60928	Crescent City, 597	F 3
	60435	Crest Hill, 7,460	E 2
	60113	Creston, 595	D 2
	60445	Crestwood, 5,543	B 2
	60417	Crete, 4,656	F 2
	61611	Creve Coeur, 6,440	D 3
	62827	Crossville, 860	F 5
	60014	Crystal Lake, 14,541	E 1
	61427	Cuba, 1,581	C 3
	60929	Cullom, 572	E 3
	62330	Dallas City, 1,284	B 3
	61320	Dalzell, 579	D 2
	61732	Danvers, 854	D 3
	61832	Danville⊙, 42,570	F 3
*	62521	Decatur⊙, 90,397	E 4
		Decatur, ‡125,010	E 4

(continued on following page)

AREA 56,400 sq. mi.
POPULATION 11,113,976
CAPITAL Springfield
LARGEST CITY Chicago
HIGHEST POINT Charles Mound 1,235 ft.
SETTLED IN 1720
ADMITTED TO UNION December 3, 1818
POPULAR NAME Prairie State
STATE FLOWER Violet
STATE BIRD Cardinal

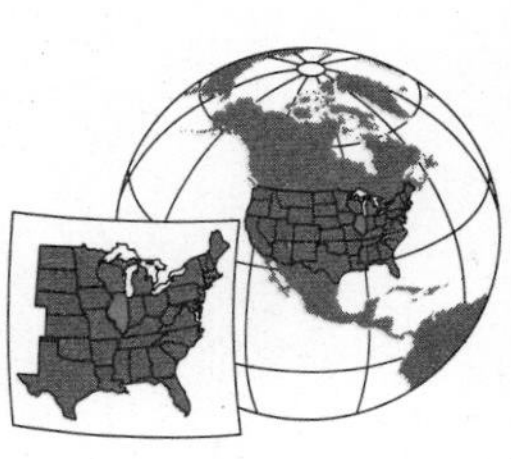

Agriculture, Industry and Resources

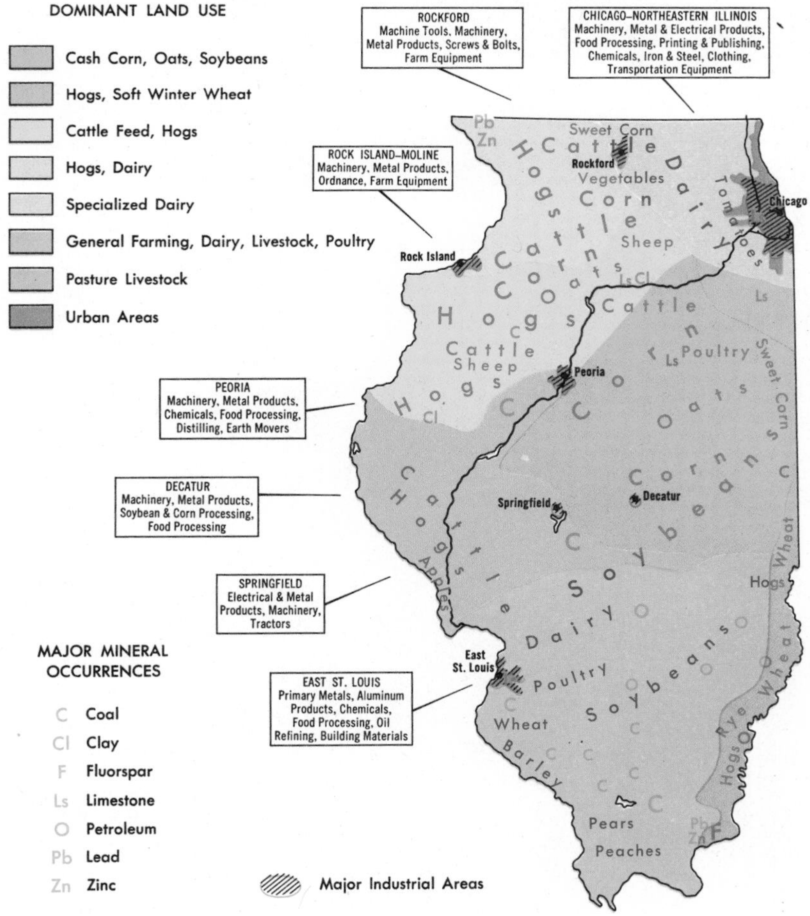
DOMINANT LAND USE
Cash Corn, Oats, Soybeans
Hogs, Soft Winter Wheat
Cattle Feed, Hogs
Hogs, Dairy
Specialized Dairy
General Farming, Dairy, Livestock, Poultry
Pasture Livestock
Urban Areas
MAJOR MINERAL OCCURRENCES
C Coal
Cl Clay
F Fluorspar
Ls Limestone
O Petroleum
Pb Lead
Zn Zinc
Major Industrial Areas
ROCKFORD
Machine Tools, Machinery, Metal Products, Screws & Bolts, Farm Equipment
CHICAGO–NORTHEASTERN ILLINOIS
Machinery, Metal & Electrical Products, Food Processing, Printing & Publishing, Chemicals, Iron & Steel, Clothing, Transportation Equipment
ROCK ISLAND–MOLINE
Machinery, Metal Products, Ordnance, Farm Equipment
PEORIA
Machinery, Metal Products, Chemicals, Food Processing, Distilling, Earth Movers
DECATUR
Machinery, Metal Products, Soybean & Corn Processing, Food Processing
SPRINGFIELD
Electrical & Metal Products, Machinery, Tractors
EAST ST. LOUIS
Primary Metals, Aluminum Products, Chemicals, Food Processing, Oil Refining, Building Materials
Rockford
Chicago
Rock Island
Peoria
Springfield
Decatur
East St. Louis
Sweet Corn
Cattle
Vegetables
Dairy
Corn
Sheep
Tomatoes
Hogs
Oats
Poultry
Soybeans
Wheat
Apples
Barley
Rye
Pears
Peaches

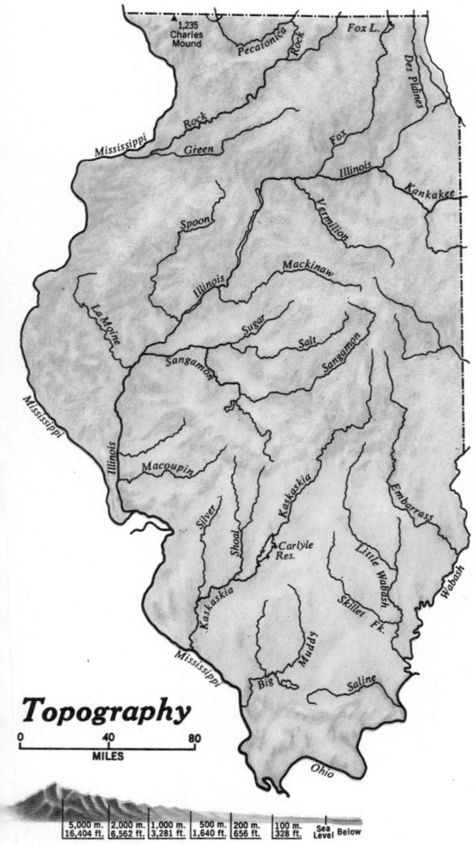
1,235 Charles Mound
Pecatonica
Rock
Fox L.
Des Plaines
Mississippi
Green
Fox
Illinois
Kankakee
Spoon
Vermilion
Mackinaw
La Moine
Sugar
Salt
Sangamon
Macoupin
Kaskaskia
Embarrass
Silver
Shoal
Carlyle Res.
Little Wabash
Skillet Fk.
Wabash
Big Muddy
Saline
Ohio
0 40 80
MILES
5,000 m. 16,404 ft.
2,000 m. 6,562 ft.
1,000 m. 3,281 ft.
500 m. 1,640 ft.
200 m. 656 ft.
100 m. 328 ft.
Sea Level
Below

Topography

(continued)

61733 Deer Creek, 647 D 3
60015 Deerfield, 18,949 F 1
60115 De Kalb, 32,949 E 2
61734 Delavan, 1,844 D 3
61322 Depue, 1,919 D 2
62924 De Soto, 966 D 6
* 60016 Des Plaines, 57,239 A 1
† 62025 Dewey Park, 2,029 B 6
62530 Divernon, 1,010 D 4
† 60469 Dixmoor, 4,735 B 2
61021 Dixon⊙, 18,147 D 2
60419 Dolton, 25,937 B 2
62926 Dongola, 825 D 6
60515 Downers Grove, 32,751 A 2
61736 Downs, 651 E 3
60118 Dundee (East and West Dundee), 6,215 E 1
61525 Dunlap, 656 D 3
62239 Dupo, 2,842 A 6
62832 Du Quoin, 6,691 D 5
61024 Durand, 972 D 1
60420 Dwight, 3,841 E 2
60518 Earlville, 1,410 E 2
62024 East Alton, 7,309 B 6
† 60411 East Chicago Heights, 5,000 B 3
61025 East Dubuque, 2,408 C 1
† 60118 East Dundee (Dundee), 2,920 E 1
61430 East Galesburg, 706 C 3
† 60429 East Hazelcrest, 1,885 B 2
61244 East Moline, 20,832 C 2
61611 East Peoria, 18,455 D 3
* 62201 East Saint Louis, 69,996 B 6
62531 Edinburg, 1,153 D 4
62025 Edwardsville⊙, 11,070 B 6
62401 Effingham⊙, 9,458 E 4
60119 Elburn, 1,122 E 2
62930 Eldorado, 3,876 E 6
60120 Elgin, 55,691 E 1
61028 Elizabeth, 707 C 1
62931 Elizabethtown⊙, 436 E 6
60007 Elk Grove Village, 24,516 A 1
62932 Elkville, 850 D 6
60126 Elmhurst, 50,547 A 2
61529 Elmwood, 2,014 D 3
60635 Elmwood Park, 26,160 B 2
61738 El Paso, 2,291 D 3
60421 Elwood, 794 E 2
62635 Emden, 552 D 3
62933 Energy, 812 E 6
62835 Enfield, 764 E 5
62934 Equality, 732 E 6
61250 Erie, 1,566 C 2
61530 Eureka⊙, 3,028 D 3
* 60201 Evanston, 79,808 B 1
62242 Evansville, 838 D 5
60642 Evergreen Park, 25,487 B 2
61739 Fairbury, 3,359 E 3
62837 Fairfield⊙, 5,897 E 5
† 62002 Fairmont, 1,521 A 6
† 62201 Fairmont City, 2,769 B 6
61841 Fairmount, 785 F 3
61432 Fairview 601 C 3
62232 Fairview Heights, 8,625 B 6
62838 Farina, 634 E 5
61842 Farmer City, 2,217 E 3
61531 Farmington, 2,959 C 3
62534 Findlay, 809 E 4
61843 Fisher, 1,525 E 3
61844 Fithian, 562 F 3
61740 Flanagan, 878 E 3
62839 Flora, 5,283 E 5
60422 Flossmoor, 7,846 B 3
† 62018 Forest Homes, 1,998 B 6
60130 Forest Park, 15,472 B 2
† 60402 Forest View, 927 B 2
61741 Forrest, 1,219 E 3
61030 Forreston, 1,227 D 1
60020 Fox Lake, 4,511 E 1
60021 Fox River Grove, 2,245 E 1
60423 Frankfort, 2,325 F 2
62638 Franklin, 565 C 4
61031 Franklin Grove, 968 D 2
60131 Franklin Park, 20,497 A 2
62243 Freeburg, 2,495 D 5
61032 Freeport⊙, 27,736 D 1
61252 Fulton, 3,630 C 2
62935 Galatia, 792 E 6
61036 Galena⊙, 3,930 C 1
61401 Galesburg⊙, 36,290 C 3
61434 Galva, 3,061 D 2
60424 Gardner, 1,212 E 2
61254 Geneseo, 5,840 C 2
60134 Geneva⊙, 9,115 E 2
60135 Genoa, 3,003 E 1
61846 Georgetown, 3,984 F 4
62245 Germantown, 1,108 D 5
60936 Gibson City, 3,454 E 3
61847 Gifford, 814 E 3
62033 Gillespie, 3,457 D 4
60938 Gilman, 1,786 E 3
62640 Girard, 1,881 D 4
61533 Glasford, 1,066 D 3
62034 Glen Carbon, 1,897 B 6
60022 Glencoe, 10,542 F 1
60137 Glen Ellyn, 21,909 F 2
60025 Glenview, 24,880 B 1
60425 Glenwood, 7,416 B 3
62035 Godfrey, 1,225 A 6
62938 Golconda⊙, 922 E 6
62339 Golden, 571 B 3
62939 Goreville, 1,109 E 6
62037 Grafton, 1,018 C 5
61325 Grand Ridge, 698 E 2
62942 Grand Tower, 664 D 6
† 62701 Grandview, 2,242 D 4
62040 Granite City, 40,440 B 6
60940 Grant Park, 801 F 2
61326 Granville, 1,232 D 2
60030 Grayslake, 4,907 E 1
62844 Grayville, 2,035 E 5
62044 Greenfield, 1,179 C 4
† 61241 Green Rock, 2,744 C 2
62428 Greenup, 1,618 E 4
61534 Green Valley, 617 D 3
62642 Greenview, 740 D 3
62246 Greenville⊙, 4,631 D 5
61744 Gridley, 1,007 E 3
62340 Griggsville, 1,245 C 4
60031 Gurnee, 2,738 F 1
62341 Hamilton, 2,764 B 3
60140 Hampshire, 1,611 E 1
61256 Hampton, 1,612 C 2
61536 Hanna City, 1,282 D 3
61041 Hanover, 1,243 C 1
62047 Hardin⊙, 1,035 C 4
62946 Harrisburg⊙, 9,535 E 6
62048 Hartford, 2,243 B 6
60033 Harvard, 5,177 E 1
60426 Harvey, 34,636 B 2
60656 Harwood Heights, 9,060 B 1
62644 Havana⊙, 4,376 D 3
60429 Hazel Crest, 10,329 B 2
60034 Hebron, 781 E 1
† 61832 Hegeler, 1,595 F 3
61327 Hennepin⊙, 535 D 2
61537 Henry, 2,610 D 2
62948 Herrin, 9,623 E 6
60941 Herscher, 988 E 2
61745 Heyworth, 1,441 E 3
60457 Hickory Hills, 13,176 B 2
62249 Highland, 5,981 D 5
60035 Highland Park, 32,263 F 1
60040 Highwood, 4,973 F 1
61244 Hillcrest, 630 D 2
62049 Hillsboro⊙, 4,267 D 4
60162 Hillside, 8,888 A 2
60520 Hinckley, 1,053 E 2
60521 Hinsdale, 15,918 A 2
60525 Hodgkins, 2,270 A 2
61849 Homer, 1,354 F 3
60456 Hometown, 6,729 B 2
60430 Homewood, 18,871 B 3
60942 Hoopeston, 6,461 F 3
61747 Hopedale, 923 D 3
61748 Hudson, 802 E 3
62343 Hull, 585 B 4
60142 Huntley, 1,432 E 1
62949 Hurst, 934 D 6
62539 Illiopolis, 1,122 D 4
61440 Industry, 558 C 3
† 60431 Ingalls Park, 5,615 F 2
61441 Ipava, 608 C 3
62051 Irving, 599 D 4
60042 Island Lake, 1,973 E 1
60143 Itasca, 4,638 F 2
62650 Jacksonville⊙, 20,553 C 4
† 62701 Jerome, 1,673 D 4
62052 Jerseyville⊙, 7,446 C 4
62951 Johnston City, 3,928 E 6
* 60431 Joliet⊙, 80,378 E 2
62952 Jonesboro⊙, 1,676 D 6
† 60453 Justice, 9,473 A 2
60901 Kankakee⊙, 30,944 F 2
61933 Kansas, 779 F 4
62956 Karnak, 641 E 6
† 63673 Kaskaskia, 79 C 6
61442 Keithsburg, 836 B 2
60043 Kenilworth, 2,980 B 1
61443 Kewanee, 15,762 C 2
62540 Kincaid, 1,424 D 4
62854 Kinmundy, 759 E 5
60146 Kirkland, 1,138 E 1
61447 Kirkwood, 817 C 3
61448 Knoxville, 2,930 C 3
61540 Lacon⊙, 2,147 D 2
61329 Ladd, 1,328 D 2
60525 La Grange, 16,773 A 2
60525 La Grange Park, 15,626 A 2
61450 La Harpe, 1,240 C 3
60044 Lake Bluff, 4,979 F 1
† 60002 Lake Catherine, 1,219 E 1
60045 Lake Forest, 15,642 F 1
60047 Lake Zurich, 4,082 E 1
61330 La Moille, 669 D 2
61046 Lanark, 1,495 D 1
60438 Lansing, 25,805 B 3
61301 La Salle, 10,736 E 2
62439 Lawrenceville⊙, 5,863 F 5
61047 Leaf River, 633 D 1
62254 Lebanon, 3,564 D 5
60531 Leland, 743 E 2
60439 Lemont, 5,080 A 2
61048 Lena, 1,691 D 1
61752 Le Roy, 2,435 E 3
61542 Lewistown⊙, 2,706 C 3
61753 Lexington, 1,615 E 3
60048 Libertyville, 11,684 F 1
62656 Lincoln⊙, 17,582 D 3
† 60601 Lincolnwood, 12,929 B 1
60046 Lindenhurst, 3,141 F 1
62056 Litchfield, 7,190 D 4
62058 Livingston, 916 D 5
60441 Lockport, 9,985 F 2
61454 Lomax, 565 B 3
60148 Lombard, 35,977 A 2
61544 London Mills, 600 C 3
62858 Louisville⊙, 1,020 E 5
62059 Lovejoy, 1,702 A 6
61111 Loves Park, 12,390 E 1
61937 Lovington, 1,303 E 4
61261 Lyndon, 673 D 2
† 60411 Lynwood, 1,042 B 3
60534 Lyons, 11,124 B 2
61755 Mackinaw, 1,293 D 3
61455 Macomb⊙, 19,643 C 3
62544 Macon, 1,249 E 4
62060 Madison, 7,042 B 6
61853 Mahomet, 1,296 E 3
60150 Malta, 961 E 2
60442 Manhattan, 1,530 F 2
61546 Manito, 1,334 D 3
61854 Mansfield, 870 E 3
60950 Manteno, 2,864 F 2
60151 Maple Park, 660 E 2
60152 Marengo, 4,235 E 1
62061 Marine, 882 D 5
62059 Marion⊙, 11,724 E 6
62257 Marissa, 2,004 D 5
60426 Markham, 15,987 B 2
61756 Maroa, 1,467 E 3
† 61554 Marquette Heights, 2,758 D 3
61341 Marseilles, 4,320 E 2
62441 Marshall⊙, 3,468 F 4
62442 Martinsville, 1,374 F 4
62062 Maryville, 809 B 6
62258 Mascoutah, 5,045 D 5
62664 Mason City, 2,611 D 3
61263 Matherville, 699 C 2
60443 Matteson, 4,741 B 3
61938 Mattoon, 19,681 E 4
60153 Maywood, 30,036 A 2
60444 Mazon, 727 E 2
62957 McClure, 800 D 6
† 60050 McCullom Lake, 873 E 1
60050 McHenry, 6,772 E 1
61754 McLean, 820 D 3
62859 McLeansboro⊙, 2,630 E 5
† 62010 Meadowbrook, 1,295 B 6
* 60160 Melrose Park, 22,706 A 2
62351 Mendon, 883 B 3
61342 Mendota, 6,902 D 2
62665 Meredosia, 1,178 C 4
† 60601 Merrionette Park, 2,303 B 2
61548 Metamora, 2,176 D 3
62960 Metropolis⊙, 6,940 E 6
62666 Middletown, 626 D 3
60445 Midlothian, 15,939 B 2
61264 Milan, 4,873 C 2
60953 Milford, 1,656 F 3
61051 Milledgeville, 1,130 D 1
62260 Millstadt, 2,168 B 6
61759 Minier, 986 D 3
61760 Minonk, 2,267 D 3
60447 Minooka, 768 E 2
60448 Mokena, 1,643 F 2
61265 Moline, 46,237 C 2
60954 Momence, 2,836 F 2
60449 Monee, 940 F 2
61462 Monmouth⊙, 11,022 C 3
60538 Montgomery, 3,278 E 2
61856 Monticello⊙, 4,130 E 3
60539 Mooseheart, 850 E 2
60450 Morris⊙, 8,194 E 2
61270 Morrison⊙, 4,387 C 2
62546 Morrisonville, 1,178 D 4
† 61101 Morristown, 669 D 1
61550 Morton, 10,419 D 3
60053 Morton Grove, 26,369 B 1
62963 Mound City⊙, 1,177 D 6
62964 Mounds, 1,718 D 6
62863 Mount Carmel⊙, 8,096 F 5
61053 Mount Carroll⊙, 2,143 D 1
61054 Mount Morris, 3,173 D 1
62069 Mount Olive, 2,288 D 4
60056 Mount Prospect, 34,995 A 1
62548 Mount Pulaski, 1,677 D 3
62353 Mount Sterling⊙, 2,182 C 4
62864 Mount Vernon⊙, 15,980 E 5
62549 Mount Zion, 2,343 E 4
62550 Moweaqua, 1,687 E 4
62262 Mulberry Grove, 697 D 5
60060 Mundelein, 16,128 E 1
62966 Murphysboro⊙, 10,013 D 6
62668 Murrayville, 595 C 4
60540 Naperville, 23,885 E 2
† 61350 Naplate, 686 E 2
62263 Nashville⊙, 3,027 D 5
62354 Nauvoo, 1,047 B 3
62447 Neoga, 1,270 E 4
60541 Newark, 590 E 2
62264 New Athens, 2,000 D 5
62265 New Baden, 1,953 D 5
62670 New Berlin, 754 D 4
61272 New Boston, 706 B 2
62867 New Haven, 606 E 6
60451 New Lenox, 2,855 F 2
61942 Newman, 1,018 F 4
62448 Newton⊙, 3,024 E 5
61465 New Windsor, 723 C 2
62551 Niantic, 705 D 4
60648 Niles, 31,432 A 1
62868 Noble, 719 E 5
62075 Nokomis, 2,532 D 4
61761 Normal, 26,396 E 3
† 60601 Norridge, 16,880 B 1
62869 Norris City, 1,319 E 6
60542 North Aurora, 4,833 E 2
60062 Northbrook, 27,297 A 1
60064 North Chicago, 47,275 F 1
60093 Northfield, 5,010 B 1
60164 Northlake, 14,212 A 2
† 61101 North Park, 15,679 D 1
† 61554 North Pekin, 1,886 D 3
60546 North Riverside, 8,097 B 2
† 61373 North Utica (Utica), 974 E 2
60452 Oak Forest, 17,870 B 2
61943 Oakland, 1,012 F 4
* 60453 Oak Lawn, 60,305 B 2
60303 Oak Park, 62,511 B 2
61858 Oakwood, 1,367 F 3
† 62095 Oakwood Heights, 3,229 B 6
62449 Oblong, 1,860 F 5
60460 Odell, 1,076 E 2
62870 Odin, 1,263 D 5
62269 O'Fallon, 7,268 B 6
61348 Oglesby, 4,175 D 2
62271 Okawville, 992 D 5
62969 Olive Branch, 600 D 6
62450 Olney⊙, 8,974 E 5
60461 Olympia Fields, 3,478 B 3
60955 Onarga, 1,436 F 3
61467 Oneida, 728 C 2
61469 Oquawka⊙, 1,352 C 3
62554 Oreana, 1,092 E 4
61061 Oregon⊙, 3,539 D 1
61273 Orion, 1,801 C 2
60462 Orland Park, 6,391 A 2
60543 Oswego, 1,862 E 2
61350 Ottawa⊙, 18,716 E 2
60067 Palatine, 25,904 E 1
62451 Palestine, 1,640 F 4
62674 Palmyra, 776 C 4
60463 Palos Heights, 9,915 A 2
60465 Palos Hills, 6,629 A 2
60464 Palos Park, 3,297 A 2
62557 Pana, 6,326 D 4
61944 Paris⊙, 9,971 F 4
60466 Park Forest, 30,638 B 3
60068 Park Ridge, 42,466 A 1
62875 Patoka, 562 D 5
62558 Pawnee, 1,936 D 4
61353 Pawpaw, 846 E 2
60957 Paxton⊙, 4,373 E 3
62360 Payson, 589 B 4
61063 Pecatonica, 1,781 D 1
61554 Pekin⊙, 31,375 D 3
* 61601 Peoria⊙, 126,963 D 3
Peoria, ‡341,979 D 3
61614 Peoria Heights, 7,943 D 3
60468 Peotone, 2,345 F 2
62272 Percy, 967 D 5
61354 Peru, 11,772 D 2
62675 Petersburg⊙, 2,632 D 4
61864 Philo, 1,022 E 3
† 60426 Phoenix, 3,596 B 2
62274 Pinckneyville⊙, 3,377 D 5
60959 Piper City, 817 E 3
62363 Pittsfield⊙, 4,244 C 4
60544 Plainfield, 2,928 E 2
60545 Plano, 4,664 E 2
62366 Pleasant Hill, 1,064 C 4
62677 Pleasant Plains, 644 D 4
62367 Plymouth, 740 C 3
62275 Pocahontas, 764 D 5
61074 Polo, 2,542 D 1
61764 Pontiac⊙, 9,031 E 3
61065 Poplar Grove, 607 E 1
61275 Port Byron, 1,222 C 2
60469 Posen, 5,498 B 2
61865 Potomac, 909 F 3
61470 Prairie City, 630 C 3
62277 Prairie du Rocher, 658 C 5
61356 Princeton⊙, 6,959 D 2
61559 Princeville, 1,455 D 3
61277 Prophetstown, 1,915 D 2
60070 Prospect Heights, 13,333 A 1
62301 Quincy⊙, 45,288 B 4
62080 Ramsey, 830 D 4
60960 Rankin, 727 F 3
61866 Rantoul, 25,562 E 3
61278 Rapids City, 656 C 2
62560 Raymond, 890 D 4
62278 Red Bud, 2,559 D 5
61279 Reynolds, 610 C 2
60071 Richmond, 1,153 E 1
60471 Richton Park, 2,558 B 3
61870 Ridge Farm, 1,015 F 4
62979 Ridgway, 1,160 E 6
60627 Riverdale, 15,806 B 2
60305 River Forest, 13,402 B 2
60171 River Grove, 11,465 A 2
60546 Riverside, 10,432 B 2
62561 Riverton, 2,090 D 4
61561 Roanoke, 2,040 D 3
60472 Robbins, 9,641 B 2
62454 Robinson⊙, 7,178 F 5
61068 Rochelle, 8,594 D 2
62563 Rochester, 1,667 D 4
60436 Rockdale, 2,085 E 2
61071 Rock Falls, 10,287 D 2
* 61101 Rockford⊙, 147,370 D 1
Rockford, ‡272,063 D 1
61201 Rock Island⊙, 50,166 C 2
Rock Island-Moline-Davenport, ‡362,638 C 2
61072 Rockton, 2,099 E 1
60008 Rolling Meadows, 19,178 A 1
61562 Rome, 1,919 D 3
† 60441 Romeoville, 12,674 E 2
62082 Roodhouse, 2,357 C 4
61073 Roscoe, 949 D 1
60018 Rosemont, 4,360 A 1
61473 Roseville, 1,111 C 3
† 62024 Rosewood Heights, 3,391 B 6
62982 Rosiclare, 1,421 E 6
60963 Rossville, 1,420 F 3
62084 Roxana, 1,882 B 6
62983 Royalton, 1,166 D 6
62681 Rushville⊙, 3,300 C 3
60964 Saint Anne, 1,271 F 2
60174 Saint Charles, 12,928 E 2
61563 Saint David, 773 C 3
62458 Saint Elmo, 1,676 E 4
62460 Saint Francisville, 997 F 5
62281 Saint Jacob, 659 D 5
61873 Saint Joseph, 1,554 E 3
62881 Salem⊙, 6,187 E 5
62882 Sandoval, 1,332 D 5
60548 Sandwich, 5,056 E 2
62682 San Jose, 681 D 3
60411 Sauk Village, 7,479 F 2
61074 Savanna, 4,942 C 1
61874 Savoy, 592 E 3
61770 Saybrook, 814 E 3
60172 Schaumburg, 18,730 E 1
60176 Schiller Park, 12,712 A 1
† 62049 Schram City, 657 D 4
61360 Seneca, 1,781 E 2
62884 Sesser, 2,125 D 5
61875 Seymour, 850 E 3
60550 Shabbona, 730 E 2
61078 Shannon, 848 D 1
62984 Shawneetown⊙, 1,742 E 6
61361 Sheffield, 1,038 D 2
62565 Shelbyville⊙, 4,597 E 4
60966 Sheldon, 1,455 F 3
60551 Sheridan, 724 E 2
61281 Sherrard, 808 C 2
† 62220 Shiloh, 945 B 6
61876 Sidell, 645 F 4
61877 Sidney, 915 E 3
61282 Silvis, 5,907 C 2
60076 Skokie, 68,627 B 1
62285 Smithton, 847 C 5
60552 Somonauk, 1,112 E 2
62086 Sorento, 625 D 5
61080 South Beloit, 3,804 E 1
60411 South Chicago Heights, 4,923 B 3
60177 South Elgin, 4,289 E 2
60473 South Holland, 23,931 B 2
62650 South Jacksonville, 2,950 C 4
61564 South Pekin, 955 D 3
60474 South Wilmington, 725 E 2
61565 Sparland, 585 D 2
62286 Sparta, 4,307 D 5
* 62701 Springfield (cap.)⊙, 91,753 D 4
Springfield, ‡161,335 D 4
61362 Spring Valley, 5,605 D
61774 Stanford, 657 D
62088 Staunton, 4,396 D
62288 Steeleville, 1,957 D
60475 Steger, 8,104 F
61081 Sterling, 16,113 D
62463 Stewardson, 729 E
60402 Stickney, 6,601 B
61084 Stillman Valley, 871 D
61085 Stockton, 1,930 C
60165 Stone Park, 4,451 A
62567 Stonington, 1,096 D
60103 Streamwood, 18,176 E
61364 Streator, 15,600 E
61480 Stronghurst, 836 C
61951 Sullivan⊙, 4,112 E
60501 Summit, 11,569 B
62466 Sumner, 1,201 F
62221 Swansea, 5,432 B
60178 Sycamore⊙, 7,843 E
62468 Tallula, 643 D
62888 Tamaroa, 799 D
62988 Tamms, 645 D
61283 Tampico, 838 D
62089 Taylor Springs, 620 D
62568 Taylorville⊙, 10,644 D
62467 Teutopolis, 1,249 E
62689 Thayer, 616 D
61878 Thomasboro, 806 E
61285 Thomson, 617 C
60476 Thornton, 3,714 B
62292 Tilden, 909 D
† 61832 Tilton, 2,544 F
60477 Tinley Park, 12,382 B
61368 Tiskilwa, 973 D
62468 Toledo⊙, 1,068 E
61880 Tolono, 2,027 E
61369 Toluca, 1,319 D
61370 Tonica, 821 E
61483 Toulon⊙, 1,207 D
61776 Towanda, 578 E
62571 Tower Hill, 683 E
61376 Tremont, 1,942 D
62293 Trenton, 2,328 D
62294 Troy, 2,144 B
61953 Tuscola⊙, 3,917 E
60180 Union, 579 E
61801 Urbana⊙, 32,800 E
61373 Utica, 974 E
62891 Valier, 628 D
62295 Valmeyer, 733 C
62471 Vandalia⊙, 5,160 D
62090 Venice, 4,680 A
61484 Vermont, 947 C
61485 Victoria, 782 C
62995 Vienna⊙, 1,325 E
61956 Villa Grove, 2,605 E
60181 Villa Park, 25,891 A
61486 Viola, 946 C
62690 Virden, 3,504 D
62691 Virginia⊙, 1,814 C
60083 Wadsworth, 756 F
61376 Walnut, 1,295 D
† 62801 Wamac, 1,347 D
61777 Wapella, 572 E
61087 Warren, 1,523 C
62573 Warrensburg, 738 D
62379 Warsaw, 1,758 B
61570 Washburn, 1,173 D
61571 Washington, 6,790 D
62204 Washington Park, 9,524 B
61488 Wataga, 570 C
62298 Waterloo⊙, 4,546 C
60556 Waterman, 990 E
60970 Watseka⊙, 5,294 F
60084 Wauconda, 5,460 E
60085 Waukegan⊙, 65,269 F
62692 Waverly, 1,442 D
62895 Wayne City, 985 E
61882 Weldon, 553 E
61377 Wenona, 1,080 E
60153 Westchester, 20,033 A
60185 West Chicago, 10,111 E
† 62812 West City, 637 E
† 60118 West Dundee (Dundee), 3,295 E
60558 Western Springs, 12,147 A
62474 Westfield, 678 F
62896 West Frankfort, 8,836 E
60559 Westmont, 8,482 A
62476 West Salem, 979 F
61883 Westville, 3,655 F
60187 Wheaton⊙, 31,138 E
60090 Wheeling, 14,746 F
62092 White Hall, 2,979 C
61489 Williamsfield, 552 C
62693 Williamsville, 923 D
62997 Willisville, 659 D
60480 Willow Springs, 3,318 A
60091 Wilmette, 32,134 B
60481 Wilmington, 4,335 E
62093 Wilsonville, 691 D
62694 Winchester⊙, 1,788 C
61957 Windsor, 1,126 E
† 61465 Windsor (New Windsor), 723 C
62090 Winfield, 4,285 E
61088 Winnebago, 1,285 D
60093 Winnetka, 14,131 B
60096 Winthrop Harbor, 4,794 F
62094 Witt, 1,040 D
60191 Wood Dale, 8,831 A
61490 Woodhull, 898 C
60515 Woodridge, 11,028 E
62095 Wood River, 13,186 B
60098 Woodstock⊙, 10,226 E
62097 Worden, 1,091 B
60482 Worth, 11,999 A
61379 Wyanet, 1,005 D
61491 Wyoming, 1,563 D
61572 Yates City, 840 C
60560 Yorkville⊙, 2,049 E
62999 Zeigler, 1,940 D
60099 Zion, 17,268 F

⊙ County seat.
‡ Population of metropolitan area.
† Zip of nearest p.o.
* Multiple zips

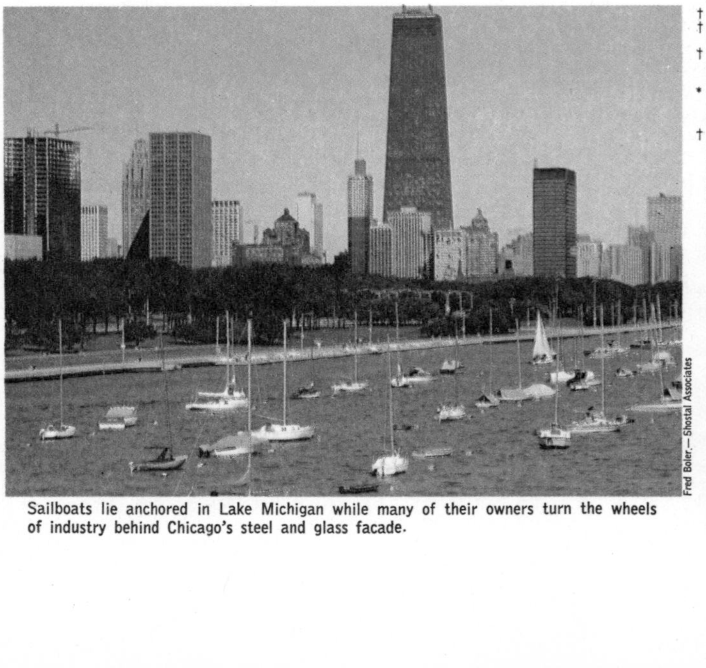

Fred Boler—Shostal Associates

Sailboats lie anchored in Lake Michigan while many of their owners turn the wheels of industry behind Chicago's steel and glass facade.

AREA 36,291 sq. mi.
POPULATION 5,193,669
CAPITAL Indianapolis
LARGEST CITY Indianapolis
HIGHEST POINT 1,257 ft. (Wayne County)
SETTLED IN 1730
ADMITTED TO UNION December 11, 1816
POPULAR NAME Hoosier State
STATE FLOWER Peony
STATE BIRD Cardinal

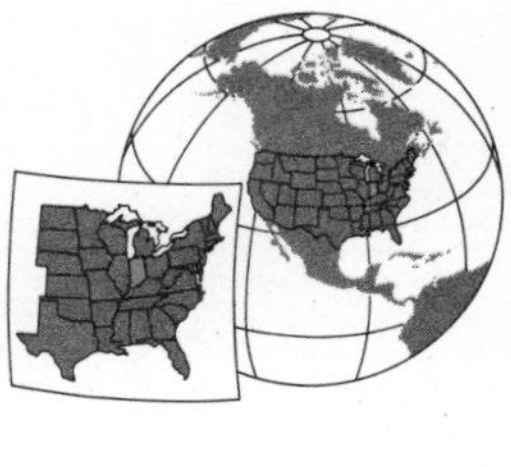

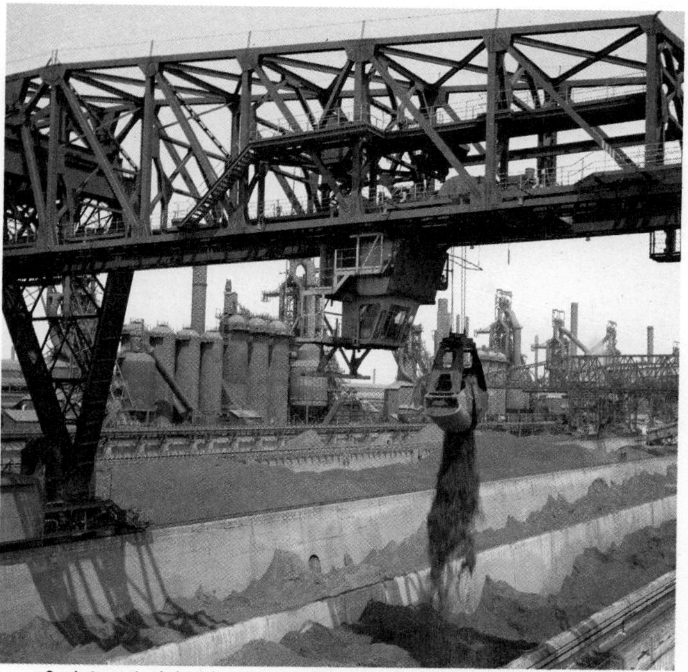

D'Arazien — Shostal Associates

Ore being unloaded in the storage yard at steel plant docks in Gary, Indiana. Aided by the state's outstanding natural supply of limestone, mills in the Lake Michigan area produce more than 15 million tons of steel yearly.

COUNTIES

Adams, 26,871 .... H 3
Allen, 280,455 .... G 2
Bartholomew, 57,022 .... F 6
Benton, 11,262 .... C 3
Blackford, 15,888 .... G 4
Boone, 30,870 .... E 4
Brown, 9,057 .... E 6
Carroll, 17,734 .... D 3
Cass, 40,456 .... E 3
Clark, 75,876 .... F 8
Clay, 23,933 .... C 6
Clinton, 30,547 .... E 4
Crawford, 8,033 .... E 8
Daviess, 26,602 .... C 7
Dearborn, 29,430 .... H 6
Decatur, 22,738 .... G 6
De Kalb, 30,837 .... H 2
Delaware, 129,219 .... G 4
Dubois, 30,934 .... D 8
Elkhart, 126,529 .... F 1
Fayette, 26,216 .... G 5
Floyd, 55,622 .... F 8
Fountain, 18,257 .... C 4
Franklin, 16,943 .... G 6
Fulton, 16,984 .... E 2
Gibson, 30,444 .... B 8
Grant, 83,955 .... F 3
Greene, 26,894 .... D 6
Hamilton, 54,532 .... E 4
Hancock, 35,096 .... F 5
Harrison, 20,423 .... E 8
Hendricks, 53,974 .... D 5
Henry, 52,603 .... G 5
Howard, 83,198 .... E 4
Huntington, 34,970 .... G 3
Jackson, 33,187 .... E 7
Jasper, 20,429 .... C 2
Jay, 23,575 .... G 4
Jefferson, 27,006 .... G 7
Jennings, 19,454 .... F 7
Johnson, 61,138 .... E 6
Knox, 41,546 .... C 7
Kosciusko, 48,127 .... F 2
Lagrange, 20,890 .... G 1
Lake, 546,253 .... C 2
LaPorte, 105,342 .... D 1
Lawrence, 38,038 .... E 7
Madison, 138,451 .... F 4
Marion, 792,299 .... E 5
Marshall, 34,986 .... E 2
Martin, 10,969 .... D 7
Miami, 39,246 .... E 3
Monroe, 84,849 .... D 6
Montgomery, 33,930 .... D 4
Morgan, 44,176 .... E 6
Newton, 11,606 .... C 3
Noble, 31,382 .... G 2
Ohio, 4,289 .... H 7
Orange, 16,968 .... E 7
Owen, 12,163 .... D 6
Parke, 14,600 .... C 5
Perry, 19,075 .... D 8
Pike, 12,281 .... C 8
Porter, 87,114 .... C 2
Posey, 21,740 .... B 8
Pulaski, 12,534 .... D 2
Putnam, 26,932 .... D 5
Randolph, 28,915 .... G 4
Ripley, 21,138 .... G 6
Rush, 20,352 .... G 5
Saint Joseph, 245,045 .... E 1
Scott, 17,144 .... F 7
Shelby, 37,797 .... F 5
Spencer, 17,134 .... C 9
Starke, 19,280 .... D 2
Steuben, 20,159 .... G 1
Sullivan, 19,889 .... C 6
Switzerland, 6,306 .... G 7
Tippecanoe, 109,378 .... D 4
Tipton, 16,650 .... E 4
Union, 6,582 .... H 5
Vanderburgh, 168,772 .... B 8
Vermillion, 16,793 .... C 5
Vigo, 114,528 .... C 6
Wabash, 35,553 .... F 3
Warren, 8,705 .... C 4
Warrick, 27,972 .... C 8
Washington, 19,278 .... E 7
Wayne, 79,109 .... G 5
Wells, 23,821 .... G 3
White, 20,995 .... D 3
Whitley, 23,395 .... F 2

CITIES and TOWNS

Zip *Name/Pop.* *Key*
47240 Adams, 300 .... F 6
46947 Adamsboro, 325 .... E 3
46102 Advance, 561 .... D 5
46910 Akron, 1,019 .... E 2
47320 Albany, 2,293 .... G 4
46701 Albion⊙, 1,498 .... G 2
47283 Alert, 210 .... F 6
46001 Alexandria, 5,097 .... F 4
46738 Altona, 209 .... G 2
47917 Ambia, 300 .... C 4
46911 Amboy, 473 .... F 3
46131 Amity, 400 .... E 6
46103 Amo, 422 .... D 5
46011 Anderson⊙, 70,787 .... F 4
Anderson, ‡138,451 .... F 4
47024 Andersonville, 250 .... G 5
46702 Andrews, 1,207 .... F 3
46703 Angola⊙, 5,117 .... G 1
46030 Arcadia, 1,338 .... E 4
46704 Arcola, 325 .... G 2
46624 Ardmore, 800 .... E 1
46501 Argos, 1,393 .... E 2
46104 Arlington, 550 .... F 5
46705 Ashley, 721 .... G 1
46031 Atlanta, 620 .... E 4
47918 Attica, 4,262 .... C 4
46502 Atwood, 300 .... F 2
46706 Auburn⊙, 7,337 .... G 2
47001 Aurora, 4,293 .... H 6
47102 Austin, 4,902 .... F 7
46710 Avilla, 881 .... G 2
47420 Avoca, 400 .... D 7
46105 Bainbridge, 703 .... D 5
46106 Bargersville, 873 .... E 5
47006 Batesville, 3,799 .... G 6
47920 Battle Ground, 818 .... D 3
47421 Bedford⊙, 13,087 .... E 7
46107 Beech Grove, 13,468 .... E 5
† 46526 Benton, 221 .... F 2
46711 Berne, 2,988 .... H 3
46301 Beverly Shores, 946 .... C 1
47512 Bicknell, 3,717 .... C 7
46713 Bippus, 220 .... F 3
47513 Birdseye, 404 .... D 8
† 46401 Blackoak, 9,624 .... C 1
47831 Blanford, 700 .... B 5
47170 Blocher, 350 .... F 7
47424 Bloomfield⊙, 2,565 .... D 6
47832 Bloomingdale, 391 .... C 5
47401 Bloomington⊙, 42,890 .... D 6
† 47360 Blountsville, 220 .... G 4
† 46176 Blue Ridge, 236 .... F 5
46714 Bluffton⊙, 8,297 .... G 3
46110 Boggstown, 200 .... F 5
46302 Boone Grove, 225 .... C 2
47601 Boonville⊙, 5,736 .... C 8
47106 Borden, 337 .... F 8
47324 Boston, 210 .... H 5
47921 Boswell, 998 .... C 3
46504 Bourbon, 1,606 .... E 2
47833 Bowling Green, 200 .... D 6
47107 Bradford, 400 .... E 8
47834 Brazil⊙, 8,163 .... C 5
46506 Bremen, 3,487 .... E 2
47836 Bridgeton, 350 .... C 5
† 45030 Bright, 450 .... H 6
46720 Brimfield, 258 .... G 2
46913 Bringhurst, 250 .... E 3
46507 Bristol, 1,100 .... F 1
† 47354 Bronson (Losantville), 212 .... G 4
47922 Brook, 919 .... C 3
46111 Brooklyn, 911 .... E 5
47923 Brookston, 1,232 .... D 3
47012 Brookville⊙, 2,864 .... G 6
46112 Brownsburg, 5,186 .... E 5
47220 Brownstown⊙, 2,376 .... F 7
47325 Brownsville, 285 .... H 5
47516 Bruceville, 627 .... C 7
47326 Bryant, 320 .... G 3
47924 Buck Creek, 260 .... D 4
47517 Buckskin, 275 .... C 8
47925 Buffalo, 350 .... D 3
46914 Bunker Hill, 956 .... E 3
46508 Burket, 210 .... F 2
46915 Burlington, 685 .... E 4
47926 Burnettsville, 510 .... D 3
47222 Burney, 344 .... F 6
† 46401 Burns Harbor, 1,284 .... C 1
46916 Burrows, 259 .... E 3
46721 Butler, 2,394 .... H 2
47223 Butlerville, 275 .... F 6
† 46371 Byron, 200 .... C 5
† 47362 Cadiz, 207 .... G 5
47327 Cambridge City, 2,481 .... G 5
46917 Camden, 577 .... D 3
47108 Campbellsburg, 678 .... E 7
47520 Cannelton⊙, 2,280 .... D 9
47837 Carbon, 344 .... C 5
47838 Carlisle, 714 .... C 7
46032 Carmel, 6,568 .... E 5
46114 Cartersburg, 400 .... E 5
46115 Carthage, 946 .... F 5
† 47460 Cataract, 200 .... D 6
47928 Cayuga, 1,090 .... C 5
47016 Cedar Grove, 248 .... H 6
46303 Cedar Lake, 7,589 .... C 2
47521 Celestine, 300 .... D 8
† 47842 Centenary, 225 .... B 5
46918 Center, 310 .... E 4
47840 Centerpoint, 275 .... C 6
46116 Centerton, 250 .... E 5
47330 Centerville, 2,380 .... H 5
47929 Chalmers, 544 .... D 3
47610 Chandler, 2,032 .... C 8
47111 Charlestown, 5,890 .... F 8
46117 Charlottesville, 500 .... F 5
† 47138 Chelsea, 200 .... F 7
46017 Chesterfield, 3,001 .... F 4
46304 Chesterton, 6,177 .... D 1
47611 Chrisney, 550 .... C 8
46723 Churubusco, 1,528 .... G 2
46034 Cicero, 1,378 .... E 4
47225 Clarksburg, 347 .... G 6
47930 Clarks Hill, 741 .... D 4
47130 Clarksville, 13,806 .... F 8
47841 Clay City, 900 .... C 6
46510 Claypool, 468 .... F 2
46118 Clayton, 736 .... D 5
47426 Clear Creek, 250 .... E 6
† 46737 Clear Lake, 271 .... H 1
47226 Clifford, 275 .... F 6
47842 Clinton, 5,340 .... C 5
46120 Cloverdale, 870 .... D 5
47427 Coal City, 300 .... D 6
47845 Coalmont, 400 .... C 6
46121 Coatesville, 453 .... D 5
47931 Colburn, 300 .... D 3
46035 Colfax, 633 .... D 4
47978 Collegeville, 1,700 .... C 3
46725 Columbia City⊙, 4,911 .... G 2
47201 Columbus⊙, 27,141 .... E 6
47331 Connersville⊙, 17,604 .... G 5
46919 Converse, 1,163 .... F 3
47228 Cortland, 200 .... F 7
46730 Corunna, 359 .... G 2
47112 Corydon⊙, 2,719 .... E 8
47932 Covington⊙, 2,641 .... C 4
† 47302 Cowan, 428 .... G 4
47522 Crane, 339 .... D 7
47933 Crawfordsville⊙, 13,842 .... D 4
46732 Cromwell, 475 .... F 2
47229 Crothersville, 1,663 .... F 7
46307 Crown Point⊙, 10,931 .... C 2
46511 Culver, 1,783 .... E 2
46229 Cumberland, 479 .... E 5
47612 Cynthiana, 793 .... B 8
47523 Dale, 1,113 .... D 8
47334 Daleville, 1,730 .... F 4
47847 Dana, 720 .... C 5
46122 Danville⊙, 3,771 .... D 5
47940 Darlington, 802 .... D 4
47941 Dayton, 840 .... D 4
46733 Decatur⊙, 8,445 .... H 3
47524 Decker, 268 .... B 7
† 46917 Deer Creek, 250 .... E 3
46923 Delphi⊙, 2,582 .... D 3
46310 Demotte, 1,697 .... C 2
46926 Denver, 566 .... E 3
47230 Deputy, 255 .... F 7
47302 Desoto, 385 .... G 4
47018 Dillsboro, 840 .... G 6
46513 Donaldson, 250 .... E 2
† 47118 Doolittle Mills, 200 .... D 8
47335 Dublin, 1,021 .... G 5
47525 Dubois, 500 .... D 8
47848 Dugger, 1,150 .... C 6
† 46304 Dune Acres, 301 .... C 1
47336 Dunkirk, 3,465 .... G 4
† 46514 Dunlap, 1,900 .... F 1
47337 Dunreith, 200 .... F 5
47231 Dupont, 357 .... G 7
46311 Dyer, 4,906 .... C 1
† 46074 Eagletown, 365 .... E 4
47942 Earl Park, 478 .... C 3
46312 East Chicago, 46,982 .... C 1
47019 East Enterprise, 250 .... H 7
46405 East Gary, 9,858 .... C 1
† 47370 East Germantown (Pershing), 447 .... G 5
47338 Eaton, 1,594 .... G 4
47116 Eckerty, 200 .... D 8
47339 Economy, 285 .... G 5
† 46011 Edgewood, 2,326 .... F 4
46124 Edinburg, 4,906 .... E 6
47528 Edwardsport, 482 .... C 7
† 47150 Edwardsville, 700 .... F 8
47613 Elberfeld, 834 .... C 8
47232 Elizabethtown, 519 .... F 6
46514 Elkhart, 43,152 .... F 1
47429 Ellettsville, 1,627 .... D 6
47529 Elnora, 873 .... C 7
† 47018 Elrod, 200 .... G 6
† 47901 Elston, 500 .... D 4
46036 Elwood, 11,196 .... F 4
46125 Eminence, 200 .... D 5
47118 English⊙, 664 .... E 8
46524 Etna Green, 516 .... E 2
† 47928 Eugene, 300 .... B 5
* 47701 Evansville⊙, 138,764 .... C 9
Evansville, ‡232,775 .... C 9
46126 Fairland, 950 .... F 5
46928 Fairmount, 3,427 .... F 4
† 47842 Fairview Park, 1,067 .... C 5
47850 Farmersburg, 962 .... C 6
47340 Farmland, 1,262 .... G 4
47532 Ferdinand, 1,432 .... D 8
46128 Fillmore, 600 .... D 5
46129 Finly, 350 .... F 5
46038 Fishers, 628 .... E 5
47234 Flat Rock, 289 .... F 6
46929 Flora, 1,877 .... E 3
47119 Floyds Knobs, 350 .... F 8
47851 Fontanet, 200 .... C 5
46039 Forest, 400 .... E 4
47533 Fort Branch, 2,535 .... B 8
46040 Fortville, 2,460 .... F 5
* 46801 Fort Wayne⊙, 177,671 .... G 2
Fort Wayne, ‡280,455 .... G 2
47341 Fountain City, 852 .... H 5
46130 Fountaintown, 225 .... F 5
47944 Fowler⊙, 2,643 .... C 3
46930 Fowlerton, 337 .... F 4
47946 Francesville, 1,015 .... D 3
47534 Francisco, 621 .... B 8
46041 Frankfort⊙, 14,956 .... E 4
46131 Franklin⊙, 11,477 .... E 6
46044 Frankton, 1,796 .... F 4
47120 Fredericksburg, 207 .... E 8
47431 Freedom, 262 .... D 6
47535 Freelandville, 710 .... C 7
47235 Freetown, 550 .... E 7
46737 Fremont, 1,043 .... H 1
47432 French Lick, 2,059 .... D 7
46931 Fulton, 372 .... E 3
† 47119 Galena, 250 .... F 8
46932 Galveston, 1,284 .... E 3
46738 Garrett, 4,715 .... G 2
* 46401 Gary, 175,415 .... C 1
Gary-Hammond-East Chicago, ‡633,367 .... C 1
46933 Gas City, 5,742 .... F 4
47342 Gaston, 928 .... G 4
46740 Geneva, 1,100 .... H 3
47537 Gentryville, 281 .... C 8
47122 Georgetown, 1,273 .... F 8
47343 Glenwood, 452 .... G 5
† 47567 Glezen, 300 .... C 8
46045 Goldsmith, 235 .... E 4
47948 Goodland, 1,176 .... C 3
46526 Goshen⊙, 17,171 .... F 1
47433 Gosport, 692 .... D 6
46741 Grabill, 570 .... H 2
47615 Grandview, 696 .... C 9
46530 Granger, 200 .... E 1
46135 Greencastle⊙, 8,852 .... D 5
† 47025 Greendale, 3,783 .... H 6
46140 Greenfield⊙, 9,986 .... F 5
47344 Greensboro, 225 .... G 5
47240 Greensburg⊙, 8,620 .... G 6
47345 Greens Fork, 444 .... H 5
46936 Greentown, 1,870 .... E 4
47124 Greenville, 611 .... F 8
46142 Greenwood, 11,408 .... E 5
46319 Griffith, 18,168 .... C 1
46144 Gwynneville, 240 .... F 5
47346 Hagerstown, 2,059 .... G 5
46742 Hamilton, 537 .... H 1
46532 Hamlet, 761 .... D 2
* 46320 Hammond, 107,790 .... B 1
46340 Hanna, 500 .... D 2
47243 Hanover, 3,018 .... F 7
47125 Hardinsburg, 263 .... E 8
46743 Harlan, 840 .... H 2
47853 Harmony, 750 .... C 5
47434 Harrodsburg, 400 .... D 6
47348 Hartford City⊙, 8,207 .... G 4
47244 Hartsville, 434 .... F 6
47617 Hatfield, 800 .... C 9
47539 Haubstadt, 1,171 .... B 8
† 47546 Haysville, 585 .... D 8
47540 Hazleton, 416 .... B 8
46341 Hebron, 1,624 .... C 2
47436 Heltonville, 400 .... E 7
46937 Hemlock, 200 .... F 4
47126 Henryville, 1,500 .... F 7
46322 Highland, 24,947 .... B 1
46046 Hillisburg, 225 .... E 4
47949 Hillsboro, 505 .... C 4
47854 Hillsdale, 500 .... C 5
46745 Hoagland, 530 .... H 3
46342 Hobart, 21,485 .... C 1
46047 Hobbs, 400 .... F 4
47541 Holland, 662 .... C 8
47023 Holton, 610 .... G 6
46146 Homer, 245 .... F 5
47246 Hope, 1,603 .... F 6
† 46069 Hortonville, 240 .... E 4
46746 Howe, 800 .... G 1
46747 Hudson, 464 .... G 1
46552 Hudson Lake, 1,134 .... D 1
46748 Huntertown, 775 .... G 2
47542 Huntingburg, 4,794 .... D 8
46750 Huntington⊙, 16,217 .... G 3
† 46064 Huntsville, 450 .... G 4
47437 Huron, 580 .... D 7
47855 Hymera, 907 .... C 6
47950 Idaville, 600 .... D 3
* 46201 Indianapolis (cap.)⊙ 744,624 .... E 5
Indianapolis, ‡1,109,882 .... E 5
46048 Ingalls, 888 .... F 5
47545 Ireland, 527 .... C 8
46147 Jamestown, 938 .... D 5
47438 Jasonville, 2,335 .... C 6
47546 Jasper⊙, 8,641 .... D 8
47130 Jeffersonville⊙, 20,008 .... F 8
† 47565 Johnson, 250 .... B 8
† 46074 Jolietville, 265 .... E 4
46938 Jonesboro, 2,466 .... F 4
47247 Jonesville, 202 .... F 6
46049 Kempton, 469 .... E 4
46755 Kendallville, 6,838 .... G 2
47351 Kennard, 518 .... G 5
47951 Kentland⊙, 1,864 .... C 3
46939 Kewanna, 614 .... E 2
46759 Keystone, 200 .... G 3
46760 Kimmell, 350 .... F 2
47952 Kingman, 530 .... C 5
46345 Kingsbury, 314 .... D 1
46346 Kingsford Heights, 1,200 .... D 2
46050 Kirklin, 736 .... E 4
46148 Knightstown, 2,456 .... F 5
47857 Knightsville, 788 .... C 5
46534 Knox⊙, 3,519 .... D 2
46901 Kokomo⊙, 44,042 .... E 4
† 46574 Koontz Lake, 900 .... D 2
46347 Kouts, 1,388 .... C 2
46348 La Crosse, 696 .... D 2
47954 Ladoga, 1,099 .... D 5
* 47901 Lafayette⊙, 44,955 .... D 4
Lafayette-West Lafayette, ‡109,378 .... D 4
46940 La Fontaine, 793 .... F 3
46761 Lagrange⊙, 2,053 .... F 1
46941 Lagro, 552 .... F 3
† 46703 Lake James, 400 .... H 1
46943 Laketon, 500 .... F 3
46349 Lake Village, 600 .... C 2
46536 Lakeville, 712 .... E 1
† 46567 Lake Wawasee, 600 .... F 2
47136 Lanesville, 586 .... E 8
46763 Laotto, 312 .... G 2
46537 Lapaz, 604 .... E 2
46051 Lapel, 1,725 .... F 4
46350 LaPorte⊙, 22,140 .... D 1
46764 Larwill, 324 .... F 2
47024 Laurel, 753 .... G 6
46226 Lawrence, 16,646 .... E 5
47025 Lawrenceburg⊙, 4,636 .... H 6
47137 Leavenworth, 330 .... E 8
46052 Lebanon⊙, 9,766 .... D 4
46538 Leesburg, 561 .... F 2
46945 Leiters Ford, 250 .... E 2
46765 Leo, 500 .... G 2
46355 Leroy, 350 .... C 2
† 47240 Letts, 247 .... F 6
47352 Lewisville, 530 .... G 5
47138 Lexington, 400 .... F 7
47353 Liberty⊙, 1,831 .... H 5
46766 Liberty Center, 300 .... G 3
46946 Liberty Mills, 200 .... F 2
46767 Ligonier, 3,034 .... F 2
47955 Linden, 713 .... D 4
46769 Linn Grove, 300 .... H 3
47441 Linton, 5,450 .... C 6
† 46755 Lisbon, 200 .... G 2
46149 Lizton, 397 .... D 5
46947 Logansport⊙, 19,255 .... E 3
† 46360 Long Beach, 2,740 .... D 1
47553 Loogootee, 2,953 .... D 7
47354 Losantville, 212 .... G 4
46356 Lowell, 3,839 .... C 2
† 46601 Lydick, 1,341 .... E 1
† 47874 Lyford, 400 .... C 5
47355 Lynn, 1,360 .... H 4
47619 Lynnville, 556 .... C 8
47443 Lyons, 702 .... C 7
46951 Macy, 273 .... E 3
47250 Madison⊙, 13,081 .... G 7
† 47001 Manchester, 250 .... H 6
46150 Manilla, 300 .... F 5
† 47872 Mansfield, 200 .... C 5
47140 Marengo, 767 .... E 8
47556 Mariah Hill, 275 .... D 8
† 46176 Marietta, 280 .... F 6
46952 Marion⊙, 39,607 .... F 3
46770 Markle, 963 .... G 3
46056 Markleville, 457 .... F 5
47859 Marshall, 365 .... C 5
46151 Martinsville⊙, 9,723 .... D 6
46957 Matthews, 728 .... F 4
46154 Maxwell, 245 .... F 5
46055 McCordsville, 500 .... F 5
47860 Mecca, 800 .... C 5
47957 Medaryville, 732 .... D 2
47260 Medora, 788 .... E 7
47958 Mellott, 325 .... C 4
47143 Memphis, 324 .... F 8
46539 Mentone, 830 .... E 2
47861 Merom, 305 .... B 6
46410 Merrillville, 15,918 .... C 2
47030 Metamora, 400 .... G 6
† 46703 Metz, 200 .... H 1
46958 Mexico, 850 .... E 3
46959 Miami, 420 .... E 3
46360 Michigan City, 39,369 .... C 1

(continued on following page)

162 Indiana

(continued)

46057 Michigantown, 457 ..... E 4
46540 Middlebury, 1,055 ..... F 1
47356 Middletown, 2,046 ..... F 4
47445 Midland, 220 ..... C 6
47031 Milan, 1,260 ..... G 6
46542 Milford, 1,264 ..... F 2
46543 Millersburg, 618 ..... F 1
47261 Millhousen, 252 ..... G 6
47145 Milltown, 829 ..... E 8
† 47362 Millville, 275 ..... G 5
46156 Milroy, 750 ..... G 6
47357 Milton, 694 ..... G 5
46544 Mishawaka, 35,517 ..... E 1
47446 Mitchell, 4,092 ..... E 7
47358 Modoc, 275 ..... G 4
46771 Mongo, 225 ..... G 1
47959 Monon, 1,548 ..... D 3
46772 Monroe, 622 ..... H 3
47557 Monroe City, 603 ..... C 7
46773 Monroeville, 1,353 ..... H 3
46157 Monrovia, 750 ..... E 5
46960 Monterey, 268 ..... D 2
47862 Montezuma, 1,192 ..... C 5
47558 Montgomery, 411 ..... C 7
47960 Monticello⊙, 4,869 ..... D 3
47962 Montmorenci, 350 ..... D 4
47359 Montpelier, 2,093 ..... G 3
47360 Mooreland, 495 ..... G 5
47032 Moores Hill, 616 ..... G 6
46158 Mooresville, 5,800 ..... E 5
46160 Morgantown, 1,134 ..... E 6
47963 Morocco, 1,285 ..... C 3
47033 Morris, 435 ..... G 6
46161 Morristown, 838 ..... F 5
47361 Mount Summit, 395 ..... G 4
47620 Mount Vernon⊙, 6,770 ..... B 9
46058 Mulberry, 1,075 ..... D 4
* 47302 Muncie⊙, 69,080 ..... G 4
Muncie, ‡129,219 ..... G 4
46321 Munster, 16,514 ..... B 1
47147 Nabb, 204 ..... F 7
47034 Napoleon, 282 ..... G 6
46550 Nappanee, 4,159 ..... F 2
47448 Nashville⊙, 527 ..... E 6
† 47421 Needmore, 200 ..... E 7
47150 New Albany⊙, 38,402 ..... F 8
47449 Newberry, 295 ..... C 7
47630 Newburgh, 2,302 ..... C 9
46552 New Carlisle, 1,434 ..... E 1
47362 New Castle⊙, 21,215 ..... G 5
† 46342 New Chicago, 2,231 ..... C 1
47863 New Goshen, 500 ..... B 5
47631 New Harmony, 971 ..... B 8
46774 New Haven, 5,728 ..... H 2
47366 New Lisbon, 350 ..... G 5
† 46979 New London, 200 ..... E 4
47965 New Market, 640 ..... D 5
46163 New Palestine, 863 ..... F 5
46553 New Paris, 1,080 ..... F 2
† 47165 New Pekin, 912 ..... F 7
47263 New Point, 381 ..... G 6
47966 Newport⊙, 708 ..... C 5
† 47106 New Providence (Borden), 337 ..... F 8
47967 New Richmond, 381 ..... D 4
47968 New Ross, 318 ..... D 5
† 46173 New Salem, 270 ..... G 5
47161 New Salisbury, 350 ..... E 8
47969 Newtown, 286 ..... C 4
47035 New Trenton, 200 ..... H 6
47162 New Washington, 1,100 ..... F 7
46184 New Whiteland, 4,200 ..... E 5
46060 Noblesville⊙, 7,548 ..... F 4
46366 North Judson, 1,738 ..... D 2
46554 North Liberty, 1,259 ..... E 1
46962 North Manchester, 5,791 ..... F 3
46165 North Salem, 601 ..... D 5
47805 North Terre Haute, 1,400 ..... C 5
47265 North Vernon, 4,582 ..... F 6
46555 North Webster, 456 ..... F 2
† 47960 Norway, 250 ..... D 3
46556 Notre Dame, 8,400 ..... E 1
† 47331 Nulltown, 250 ..... G 5
46965 Oakford, 300 ..... E 4
47560 Oakland City, 3,289 ..... C 8
47561 Oaktown, 726 ..... C 7
47367 Oakville, 250 ..... G 4
47562 Odon, 1,433 ..... C 7
† 46401 Ogden Dunes, 1,361 ..... C 1
47036 Oldenburg, 758 ..... G 6
47451 Oolitic, 1,155 ..... E 7
† 47343 Orange, 200 ..... G 5
46063 Orestes, 519 ..... F 4
46776 Orland, 457 ..... G 1
47452 Orleans, 1,834 ..... D 7
46561 Osceola, 1,572 ..... E 1
47037 Osgood, 1,346 ..... G 6
46777 Ossian, 1,538 ..... G 3
46367 Otis, 300 ..... D 1
47163 Otisco, 375 ..... F 7
47970 Otterbein, 899 ..... C 4
47564 Otwell, 850 ..... C 8
47453 Owensburg, 700 ..... D 7
47565 Owensville, 1,056 ..... B 8
47971 Oxford, 1,098 ..... C 3
† 46508 Palestine, 200 ..... F 2
47164 Palmyra, 483 ..... E 8
47454 Paoli⊙, 3,281 ..... E 7
46166 Paragon, 538 ..... D 6
47368 Parker, 1,179 ..... G 4
47566 Patoka, 529 ..... B 8
47455 Patricksburg, 265 ..... D 6
47038 Patriot, 216 ..... H 7
47865 Paxton, 250 ..... C 6
47165 Pekin, 950 ..... E 7
46064 Pendleton, 2,243 ..... F 5
47369 Pennville, 798 ..... G 4
† 46011 Perkinsville, 300 ..... F 4
47974 Perrysville, 510 ..... C 4
47370 Pershing, 447 ..... G 5
† 46975 Pershing, 425 ..... E 2
46970 Peru⊙, 14,139 ..... E 3
47567 Petersburg⊙, 2,697 ..... C 7
46778 Petroleum, 200 ..... G 3
46562 Pierceton, 1,175 ..... F 2
47866 Pimento, 200 ..... C 6
† 46350 Pine Lake, 1,954 ..... D 1
47975 Pine Village, 291 ..... C 4
46167 Pittsboro, 867 ..... D 5
46168 Plainfield, 8,211 ..... E 5
47568 Plainville, 538 ..... C 7
46779 Pleasant Lake, 650 ..... H 1
46563 Plymouth⊙, 7,661 ..... E 2
47868 Poland, 300 ..... C 6
46781 Poneto, 286 ..... G 3
46368 Portage, 19,127 ..... C 1
46304 Porter, 3,058 ..... C 1
47371 Portland⊙, 7,115 ..... H 4
47633 Poseyville, 1,035 ..... B 8
† 46360 Pottawattamie Park, 374 ..... C 1
47869 Prairie Creek, 225 ..... C 6
47870 Prairieton, 400 ..... B 6
† 46164 Princes Lakes, 597 ..... E 6
47570 Princeton⊙, 7,431 ..... B 8
46170 Putnamville, 200 ..... D 5
47456 Quincy, 250 ..... D 6
47573 Ragsdale, 200 ..... C 7
46737 Ray, 200 ..... H 1
† 47274 Reddington, 245 ..... F 6
47373 Redkey, 1,667 ..... G 4
46171 Reelsville, 210 ..... D 5
47977 Remington, 1,127 ..... C 3
47978 Rensselaer⊙, 4,688 ..... C 3
47980 Reynolds, 641 ..... D 3
47634 Richland, 650 ..... C 9
47374 Richmond⊙, 43,999 ..... H 5
47380 Ridgeville, 924 ..... G 4
47871 Riley, 257 ..... C 6
47040 Rising Sun⊙, 2,305 ..... H 7
46172 Roachdale, 1,004 ..... D 5
46974 Roann, 509 ..... F 3
46783 Roanoke, 858 ..... G 3
46975 Rochester⊙, 4,631 ..... E 2
46977 Rockfield, 300 ..... D 3
47635 Rockport⊙, 2,565 ..... C 9
47872 Rockville⊙, 2,820 ..... C 5
46371 Rolling Prairie, 2,500 ..... D 1
47574 Rome, 1,354 ..... D 9
46784 Rome City, 1,385 ..... G 1
47981 Romney, 420 ..... D 4
47874 Rosedale, 817 ..... C 5
† 46601 Roseland, 895 ..... E 1
46372 Roselawn, 200 ..... C 2
46065 Rossville, 830 ..... D 4
46978 Royal Center, 987 ..... E 3
† 47302 Royerton, 411 ..... G 4
46173 Rushville⊙, 6,686 ..... G 5
46175 Russellville, 390 ..... D 5
46975 Russiaville, 844 ..... E 4
47575 Saint Anthony, 460 ..... D 8
47875 Saint Bernice, 900 ..... C 5
46785 Saint Joe, 564 ..... H 2
46373 Saint John, 1,757 ..... C 2
† 45030 Saint Leon, 435 ..... H 6
47876 Saint Mary-of-the-Woods, 1,200 ..... B 6
† 46556 Saint Marys, 1,600 ..... E 1
47577 Saint Meinrad, 1,100 ..... D 8
47272 Saint Paul, 785 ..... F 6
† 47012 Saint Peter, 200 ..... H 6
† 47620 Saint Philip, 400 ..... B 9
† 47638 Saint Wendel, 250 ..... B 8
47167 Salem⊙, 5,041 ..... E 7
47578 Sandborn, 528 ..... C 7
† 47401 Sanders, 200 ..... E 6
46374 San Pierre, 300 ..... D 2
47579 Santa Claus, 125 ..... D 8
47382 Saratoga, 406 ..... H 4
† 47283 Sardinia, 225 ..... F 6
46375 Schererville, 3,663 ..... C 2
46376 Schneider, 426 ..... C 2
47273 Scipio, 250 ..... F 6
47170 Scottsburg⊙, 4,791 ..... F 7
47878 Seelyville, 1,195 ..... C 6
47172 Sellersburg, 3,177 ..... F 8
47383 Selma, 890 ..... G 4
47274 Seymour, 13,352 ..... F 7
46068 Sharpsville, 672 ..... E 4
47879 Shelburn, 1,281 ..... C 6
46377 Shelby, 400 ..... C 2
46176 Shelbyville⊙, 15,094 ..... F 6
47880 Shepardsville, 325 ..... B 5
46069 Sheridan, 2,137 ..... E 4
† 47338 Shideler, 275 ..... G 4
46565 Shipshewana, 448 ..... F 1
47384 Shirley, 958 ..... F 5

Topography

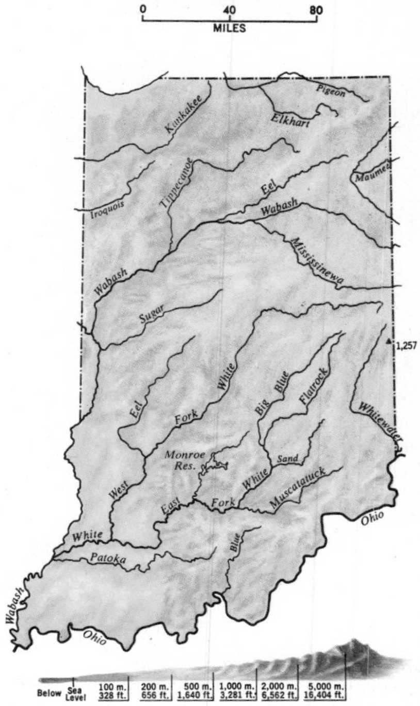

0
40
80
MILES
Pigeon
Elkhart
Kankakee
Maumee
Iroquois
Tippecanoe
Eel
Wabash
Mississinewa
Wabash
Sugar
Eel
Fork
White
Big Blue
Flatrock
Whitewater
1,257
Monroe Res.
Sand
West
East
Fork
White
Muscatatuck
Ohio
White
Patoka
Blue
Wabash
Ohio
Below Sea Level
100 m. 328 ft.
200 m. 656 ft.
500 m. 1,640 ft.
1,000 m. 3,281 ft.
2,000 m. 6,562 ft.
5,000 m. 16,404 ft.

Agriculture, Industry and Resources

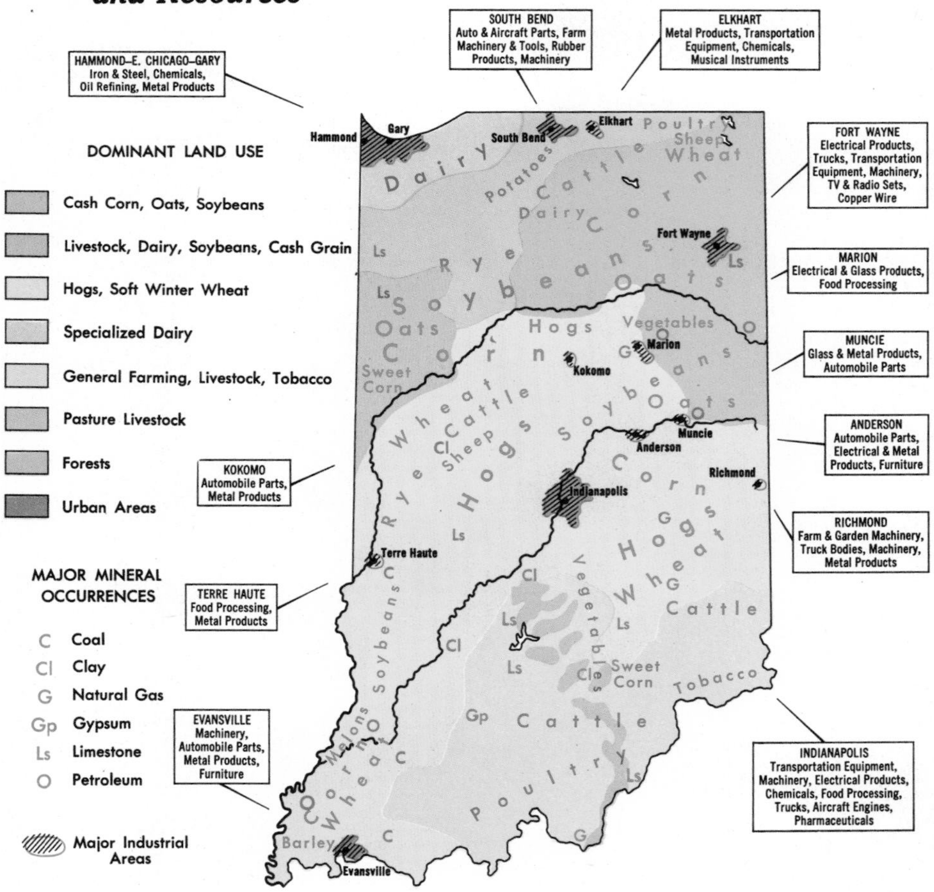

HAMMOND–E. CHICAGO–GARY
Iron & Steel, Chemicals, Oil Refining, Metal Products
SOUTH BEND
Auto & Aircraft Parts, Farm Machinery & Tools, Rubber Products, Machinery
ELKHART
Metal Products, Transportation Equipment, Chemicals, Musical Instruments
FORT WAYNE
Electrical Products, Trucks, Transportation Equipment, Machinery, TV & Radio Sets, Copper Wire
MARION
Electrical & Glass Products, Food Processing
MUNCIE
Glass & Metal Products, Automobile Parts
ANDERSON
Automobile Parts, Electrical & Metal Products, Furniture
RICHMOND
Farm & Garden Machinery, Truck Bodies, Machinery, Metal Products
INDIANAPOLIS
Transportation Equipment, Machinery, Electrical Products, Chemicals, Food Processing, Trucks, Aircraft Engines, Pharmaceuticals
KOKOMO
Automobile Parts, Metal Products
TERRE HAUTE
Food Processing, Metal Products
EVANSVILLE
Machinery, Automobile Parts, Metal Products, Furniture
DOMINANT LAND USE
Cash Corn, Oats, Soybeans
Livestock, Dairy, Soybeans, Cash Grain
Hogs, Soft Winter Wheat
Specialized Dairy
General Farming, Livestock, Tobacco
Pasture Livestock
Forests
Urban Areas
MAJOR MINERAL OCCURRENCES
C Coal
Cl Clay
G Natural Gas
Gp Gypsum
Ls Limestone
O Petroleum
Major Industrial Areas
Hammond
Gary
South Bend
Elkhart
Fort Wayne
Marion
Kokomo
Muncie
Anderson
Richmond
Indianapolis
Terre Haute
Evansville
Dairy
Potatoes
Cattle
Poultry
Sheep
Wheat
Corn
Rye
Soybeans
Oats
Hogs
Vegetables
Sweet Corn
Cattle
Sheep
Melons
Barley
Tobacco

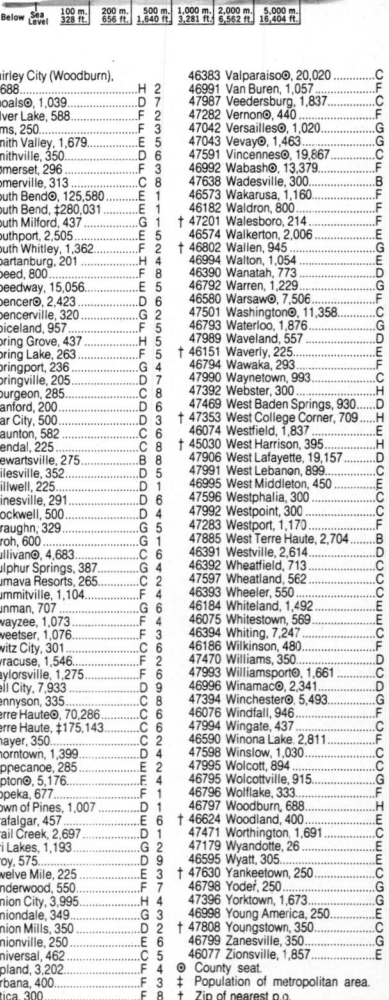

† 46797 Shirley City (Woodburn), 688 ..... H 2
47581 Shoals⊙, 1,039 ..... D 7
46982 Silver Lake, 588 ..... F 2
46983 Sims, 250 ..... F 3
† 46142 Smith Valley, 1,679 ..... E 5
47458 Smithville, 350 ..... D 6
46984 Somerset, 296 ..... F 3
47583 Somerville, 313 ..... C 8
* 46601 South Bend⊙, 125,580 ..... E 1
South Bend, ‡280,031 ..... E 1
46786 South Milford, 437 ..... G 1
† 46201 Southport, 2,505 ..... E 5
46787 South Whitley, 1,362 ..... F 2
† 47355 Spartanburg, 201 ..... H 4
47172 Speed, 800 ..... F 8
46224 Speedway, 15,056 ..... E 5
47460 Spencer⊙, 2,423 ..... D 6
46788 Spencerville, 320 ..... G 2
47385 Spiceland, 957 ..... F 5
† 47374 Spring Grove, 437 ..... H 5
† 46140 Spring Lake, 263 ..... F 5
47386 Springport, 236 ..... G 4
47462 Springville, 205 ..... D 7
47584 Spurgeon, 285 ..... C 8
47463 Stanford, 200 ..... D 6
46985 Star City, 500 ..... D 3
47881 Staunton, 582 ..... C 6
47585 Stendal, 225 ..... C 8
47636 Stewartsville, 275 ..... B 8
46180 Stilesville, 352 ..... D 5
46351 Stillwell, 225 ..... D 1
47464 Stinesville, 291 ..... D 6
47983 Stockwell, 500 ..... D 4
47387 Straughn, 329 ..... G 5
46789 Stroh, 600 ..... G 1
47882 Sullivan⊙, 4,683 ..... C 6
47388 Sulphur Springs, 387 ..... G 4
46379 Sumava Resorts, 265 ..... C 2
46070 Summitville, 1,104 ..... F 4
47041 Sunman, 707 ..... G 6
46986 Swayzee, 1,073 ..... F 4
46987 Sweetser, 1,076 ..... F 3
47465 Switz City, 301 ..... C 6
46567 Syracuse, 1,546 ..... F 2
47280 Taylorsville, 1,275 ..... F 6
47586 Tell City, 7,933 ..... D 9
47637 Tennyson, 335 ..... C 8
* 47801 Terre Haute⊙, 70,286 ..... C 6
Terre Haute, ‡175,143 ..... C 6
46381 Thayer, 350 ..... C 2
46071 Thorntown, 1,399 ..... D 4
46570 Tippecanoe, 285 ..... E 2
46072 Tipton⊙, 5,176 ..... F 4
46571 Topeka, 677 ..... F 1
† 46360 Town of Pines, 1,007 ..... D 1
46181 Trafalgar, 457 ..... E 6
† 46360 Trail Creek, 2,697 ..... D 1
† 46725 Tri Lakes, 1,193 ..... G 2
47588 Troy, 575 ..... D 9
46988 Twelve Mile, 225 ..... E 3
47177 Underwood, 550 ..... F 7
47390 Union City, 3,995 ..... H 4
46791 Uniondale, 349 ..... G 3
46382 Union Mills, 350 ..... D 2
47468 Unionville, 250 ..... E 6
47884 Universal, 462 ..... C 5
46989 Upland, 3,202 ..... F 4
46990 Urbana, 400 ..... F 3
† 47130 Utica, 300 ..... F 8
47281 Vallonia, 600 ..... E 7
46383 Valparaiso⊙, 20,020 ..... C 2
46991 Van Buren, 1,057 ..... F 3
47987 Veedersburg, 1,837 ..... C 4
47282 Vernon⊙, 440 ..... F 7
47042 Versailles⊙, 1,020 ..... G 6
47043 Vevay⊙, 1,463 ..... G 7
47591 Vincennes⊙, 19,867 ..... C 7
46992 Wabash⊙, 13,379 ..... F 3
47638 Wadesville, 300 ..... B 8
46573 Wakarusa, 1,160 ..... F 1
46182 Waldron, 800 ..... F 6
† 47201 Walesboro, 214 ..... F 6
46574 Walkerton, 2,006 ..... E 2
† 46802 Wallen, 945 ..... G 2
46994 Walton, 1,054 ..... E 3
46390 Wanatah, 773 ..... D 2
46792 Warren, 1,229 ..... G 3
46580 Warsaw⊙, 7,506 ..... F 2
47501 Washington⊙, 11,358 ..... C 7
46793 Waterloo, 1,876 ..... G 2
47989 Waveland, 557 ..... D 5
† 46151 Waverly, 225 ..... E 5
46794 Wawaka, 293 ..... F 2
47990 Waynetown, 993 ..... C 4
47392 Webster, 300 ..... H 5
47469 West Baden Springs, 930 ..... D 7
† 47353 West College Corner, 709 ..... H 5
46074 Westfield, 1,837 ..... E 4
† 45030 West Harrison, 395 ..... H 6
47906 West Lafayette, 19,157 ..... D 4
47991 West Lebanon, 899 ..... C 4
46995 West Middleton, 450 ..... E 4
47596 Westphalia, 300 ..... C 7
47992 Westpoint, 300 ..... C 4
47283 Westport, 1,170 ..... F 6
47885 West Terre Haute, 2,704 ..... B 6
46391 Westville, 2,614 ..... D 1
46392 Wheatfield, 713 ..... C 2
47597 Wheatland, 562 ..... C 7
46393 Wheeler, 550 ..... C 1
46184 Whiteland, 1,492 ..... E 5
46075 Whitestown, 569 ..... E 5
46394 Whiting, 7,247 ..... C 1
46186 Wilkinson, 480 ..... F 5
47470 Williams, 350 ..... D 7
47993 Williamsport⊙, 1,661 ..... C 4
46996 Winamac⊙, 2,341 ..... D 2
47394 Winchester⊙, 5,493 ..... G 4
46076 Windfall, 946 ..... F 4
47994 Wingate, 437 ..... C 4
46590 Winona Lake, 2,811 ..... F 2
47598 Winslow, 1,030 ..... C 8
47995 Wolcott, 894 ..... C 3
46795 Wolcottville, 915 ..... G 1
46796 Wolflake, 333 ..... F 2
46797 Woodburn, 688 ..... H 2
† 46624 Woodland, 400 ..... E 1
47471 Worthington, 1,691 ..... C 6
47179 Wyandotte, 26 ..... E 8
46595 Wyatt, 305 ..... E 1
† 47630 Yankeetown, 250 ..... C 9
46798 Yoder, 250 ..... G 3
47396 Yorktown, 1,673 ..... G 4
46998 Young America, 250 ..... E 3
† 47808 Youngstown, 350 ..... C 6
46799 Zanesville, 350 ..... G 3
46077 Zionsville, 1,857 ..... E 5

⊙ County seat.
‡ Population of metropolitan area.
† Zip of nearest p.o.
* Multiple zips

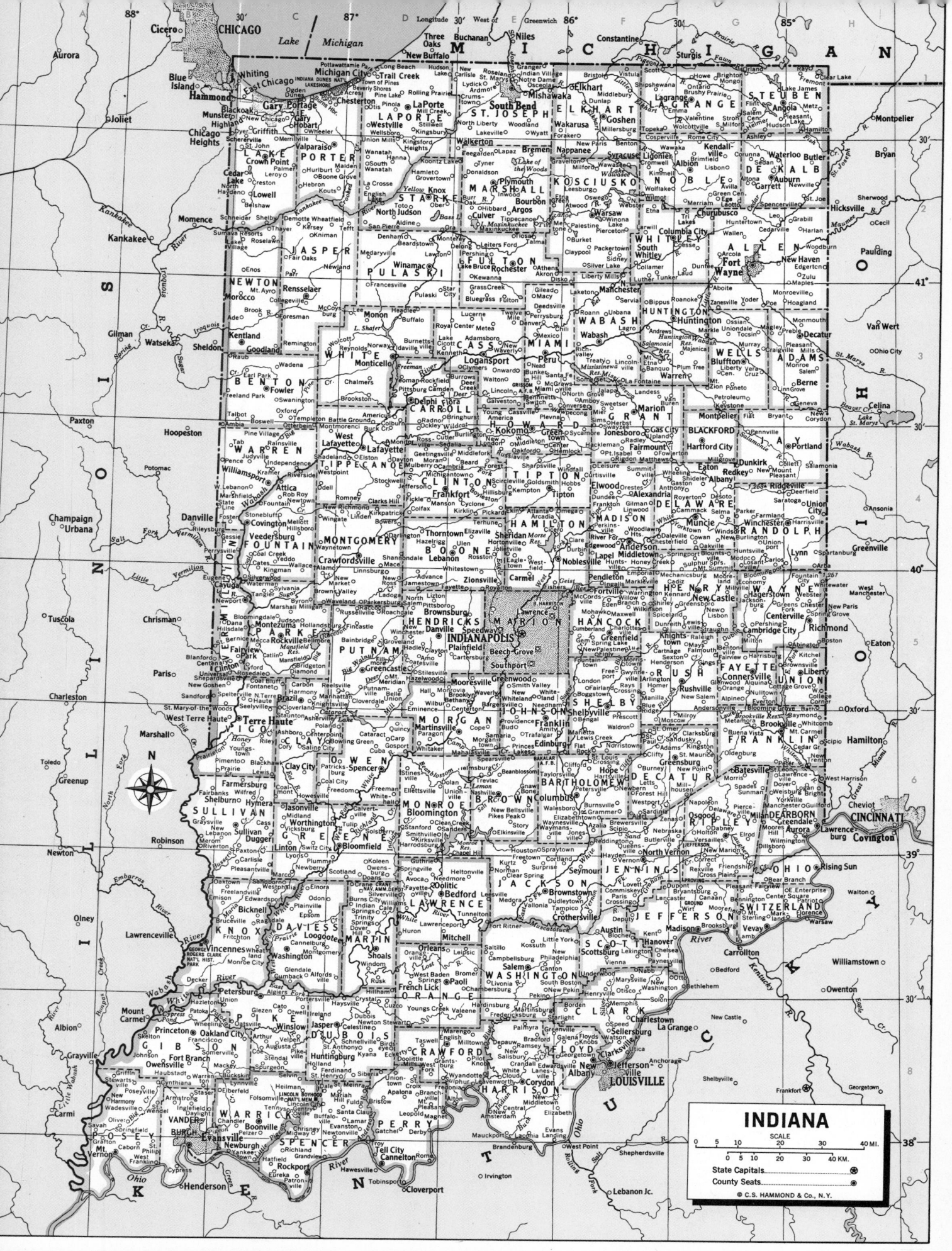

INDIANA

SCALE

0   5   10   20   30   40 MI.
0 5 10   20   30   40 KM.

State Capitals .... ⊛
County Seats .... ⊙

© C.S. HAMMOND & Co., N.Y.

164 Iowa

COUNTIES

Adair, 9,487 .... E 6
Adams, 6,322 .... D 6
Allamakee, 14,968 .... L 2
Appanoose, 15,007 .... H 7
Audubon, 9,595 .... D 5
Benton, 22,885 .... J 4
Black Hawk, 132,916 .... J 4
Boone, 26,470 .... F 5
Bremer, 22,737 .... J 3
Buchanan, 21,746 .... K 4
Buena Vista, 20,693 .... C 3
Butler, 16,953 .... H 3
Calhoun, 14,287 .... D 4
Carroll, 22,912 .... D 6
Cedar, 17,655 .... L 5
Cerro Gordo, 49,335 .... G 2
Cherokee, 17,269 .... B 3
Chickasaw, 14,969 .... J 2
Clarke, 7,581 .... F 6
Clay, 18,464 .... C 2
Clayton, 20,606 .... L 3
Clinton, 56,749 .... M 5
Crawford, 18,780 .... C 4
Dallas, 26,085 .... E 5

Davis, 8,207 .... J 7
Decatur, 9,737 .... F 7
Delaware, 18,770 .... L 4
Des Moines, 46,982 .... L 6
Dickinson, 12,565 .... C 2
Dubuque, 90,609 .... M 4
Emmet, 14,009 .... D 2
Fayette, 25,488 .... K 3
Floyd, 19,860 .... H 2
Franklin, 13,255 .... G 3
Fremont, 9,282 .... B 7
Greene, 12,716 .... E 5
Grundy, 14,119 .... H 4
Guthrie, 12,243 .... D 5
Hamilton, 18,383 .... F 4
Hancock, 13,227 .... F 2
Hardin, 22,248 .... G 4
Harrison, 16,240 .... B 5
Henry, 18,114 .... K 6
Howard, 11,442 .... J 2
Humboldt, 12,519 .... E 3
Ida, 9,190 .... C 4
Iowa, 15,419 .... J 5
Jackson, 20,839 .... M 4
Jasper, 35,425 .... H 5
Jefferson, 15,774 .... K 6
Johnson, 72,127 .... K 5

Jones, 19,868 .... L 4
Keokuk, 13,943 .... J 6
Kossuth, 22,937 .... E 2
Lee, 42,996 .... L 7
Linn, 163,213 .... K 4
Louisa, 10,163 .... L 6
Lucas, 10,163 .... G 6
Lyon, 13,340 .... A 2
Madison, 11,558 .... E 6
Mahaska, 22,177 .... H 6
Marion, 26,352 .... G 6
Marshall, 41,076 .... G 4
Mills, 11,606 .... B 6
Mitchell, 13,108 .... H 2
Monona, 12,069 .... B 4
Monroe, 9,357 .... H 7
Montgomery, 12,781 .... C 6
Muscatine, 37,181 .... L 5
O'Brien, 17,522 .... B 2
Osceola, 8,555 .... B 2
Page, 18,507 .... C 7
Palo Alto, 13,289 .... D 2
Plymouth, 24,312 .... A 3
Pocahontas, 12,729 .... D 3
Polk, 286,101 .... F 5
Pottawattamie, 86,991 .... B 6
Poweshiek, 18,803 .... H 5

Ringgold, 6,373 .... E 7
Sac, 15,573 .... C 3
Scott, 142,687 .... M 5
Shelby, 15,528 .... C 5
Sioux, 27,996 .... A 2
Story, 62,783 .... G 5
Tama, 20,147 .... H 4
Taylor, 8,790 .... D 7
Union, 13,557 .... E 6
Van Buren, 8,643 .... K 7
Wapello, 42,149 .... J 6
Warren, 27,432 .... G 6
Washington, 18,967 .... K 6
Wayne, 8,405 .... G 7
Webster, 48,391 .... E 4
Winnebago, 12,990 .... F 2
Winneshiek, 21,758 .... K 2
Woodbury, 103,052 .... B 4
Worth, 9,981 .... G 2
Wright, 17,294 .... F 3

CITIES and TOWNS

Zip	Name/Pop.	Key
50601	Ackley, 1,794	G 3
50002	Adair, 750	D 6
50003	Adel⊙, 2,419	E 5
50601	Ackley, 1,794	G 3
50606	Arlington, 481	K 3
50830	Afton, 823	E 6
52530	Agency, 610	J 7
52201	Ainsworth, 455	K 6
51001	Akron, 1,324	A 3
50510	Albert City, 683	C 3
52531	Albia⊙, 4,151	H 6
52202	Alburnett, 418	K 4
50006	Alden, 876	G 4
50420	Alexander, 249	G 3
50511	Algona⊙, 6,032	E 2
50008	Allerton, 643	G 7
50602	Allison⊙, 1,071	H 3
51002	Alta, 1,717	C 3
50603	Alta Vista, 283	J 2
51003	Alton, 1,018	A 3
50009	Altoona, 2,854	G 5
52203	Amana, 610	K 5
50010	Ames, 39,505	G 4
52205	Anamosa⊙, 4,389	L 4
50020	Andrew, 335	M 4
50020	Anita, 1,101	D 6
50210	Ankeny, 9,151	F 5
51004	Anthon, 711	B 4

50514	Armstrong, 1,061	D 2
51331	Arnolds Park, 970	C 2
51431	Arthur, 273	C 4
† 52001	Asbury, 410	M 4
51232	Ashton, 483	B 2
52720	Atalissa, 244	L 5
52206	Atkins, 581	K 4
50022	Atlantic⊙, 7,306	D 6
51433	Auburn, 329	D 5
50025	Audubon⊙, 2,907	D 5
51005	Aurelia, 1,065	C 3
50607	Aurora, 229	K 3
51521	Avoca, 1,535	C 5
50516	Ayrshire, 243	D 2
50518	Badger, 465	E 3
50026	Bagley, 365	E 5
50517	Bancroft, 1,103	E 2
52720	Barnes City, 238	H 6
52533	Batavia, 525	J 7
51006	Battle Creek, 837	C 4
50028	Baxter, 788	G 5
50029	Bayard, 628	D 5
52534	Beacon, 338	H 6
50609	Beaman, 222	H 4
50833	Bedford⊙, 1,733	D 7
52208	Belle Plaine, 2,810	J 5
52031	Bellevue, 2,336	M 4

50421 Belmond, 2,358 ...... F 3
52721 Bennett, 385 ...... L 5
52722 Bettendorf, 22,126 ...... N 5
52535 Birmingham, 452 ...... K 7
50034 Blairsburg, 287 ...... F 4
52209 Blairstown, 612 ...... J 5
52536 Blakesburg, 403 ...... H 7
51523 Blencoe, 255 ...... A 5
50036 Blockton, 273 ...... D 7
52537 Bloomfield⊙, 2,718 ...... J 7
52726 Blue Grass, 1,032 ...... M 5
50519 Bode, 372 ...... E 3
52620 Bonaparte, 517 ...... K 7
50035 Bondurant, 462 ...... G 5
50036 Boone⊙, 12,468 ...... F 4
50040 Boxholm, 242 ...... E 4
51234 Boyden, 670 ...... B 2
52210 Brandon, 432 ...... K 4
51436 Breda, 518 ...... C 4
52540 Brighton, 632 ...... K 6
50611 Bristow, 230 ...... H 3
50423 Britt, 2,069 ...... F 2
52211 Brooklyn, 1,410 ...... J 5
52728 Buffalo, 1,513 ...... M 6
50424 Buffalo Center, 1,118 ...... F 2
52601 Burlington⊙, 32,366 ...... L 7
50522 Burt, 608 ...... E 3

50044 Bussey, 498 ...... H 6
52729 Calamus, 396 ...... M 5
50523 Callender, 421 ...... E 4
52132 Calmar, 1,941 ...... K 2
51009 Calumet, 219 ...... B 3
52730 Camanche, 3,470 ...... N 5
50046 Cambridge, 661 ...... G 5
50047 Carlisle, 2,246 ...... G 6
51401 Carroll⊙, 8,716 ...... D 4
51525 Carson, 756 ...... C 6
† 68101 Carter Lake, 3,268 ...... B 6
52033 Cascade, 1,744 ...... L 3
50048 Casey, 561 ...... D 5
52133 Castalia, 210 ...... K 2
51010 Castana, 211 ...... B 4
50613 Cedar Falls, 29,597 ...... H 4
* 52401 Cedar Rapids⊙, 110,642 ...... K 5
   Cedar Rapids, ‡163,213 ...... K 5
52213 Center Point, 1,456 ...... K 4
52544 Centerville⊙, 6,531 ...... H 7
52214 Central City, 1,116 ...... K 4
50049 Chariton⊙, 5,009 ...... G 6
50616 Charles City⊙, 9,268 ...... H 3
52731 Charlotte, 444 ...... M 4
51439 Charter Oak, 715 ...... C 4
52215 Chelsea, 381 ...... J 5

51012 Cherokee⊙, 7,272 ...... B 3
50050 Churdan, 598 ...... D 4
52549 Cincinnati, 570 ...... G 7
50524 Clare, 249 ...... E 3
52216 Clarence, 915 ...... M 5
51632 Clarinda⊙, 5,420 ...... C 7
50525 Clarion⊙, 2,972 ...... F 3
50619 Clarksville, 1,185 ...... H 3
50840 Clearfield, 430 ...... D 7
50428 Clear Lake, 6,430 ...... G 2
51014 Cleghorn, 274 ...... B 3
52135 Clermont, 582 ...... K 3
52732 Clinton⊙, 34,719 ...... N 5
50053 Clive, 3,005 ...... F 5
52217 Clutier, 275 ...... J 4
† 50501 Coalville, 275 ...... E 4
52218 Coggon, 656 ...... K 4
50056 Colesburg, 379 ...... L 3
50054 Colfax, 2,293 ...... G 5
51637 College Springs, 295 ...... C 7
50055 Collins, 404 ...... G 5
50056 Colo, 606 ...... G 5
52737 Columbus City, 312 ...... L 6
52738 Columbus Junction, 1,205 ...... L 6
52739 Conesville, 295 ...... L 6
50631 Conrad, 932 ...... H 4

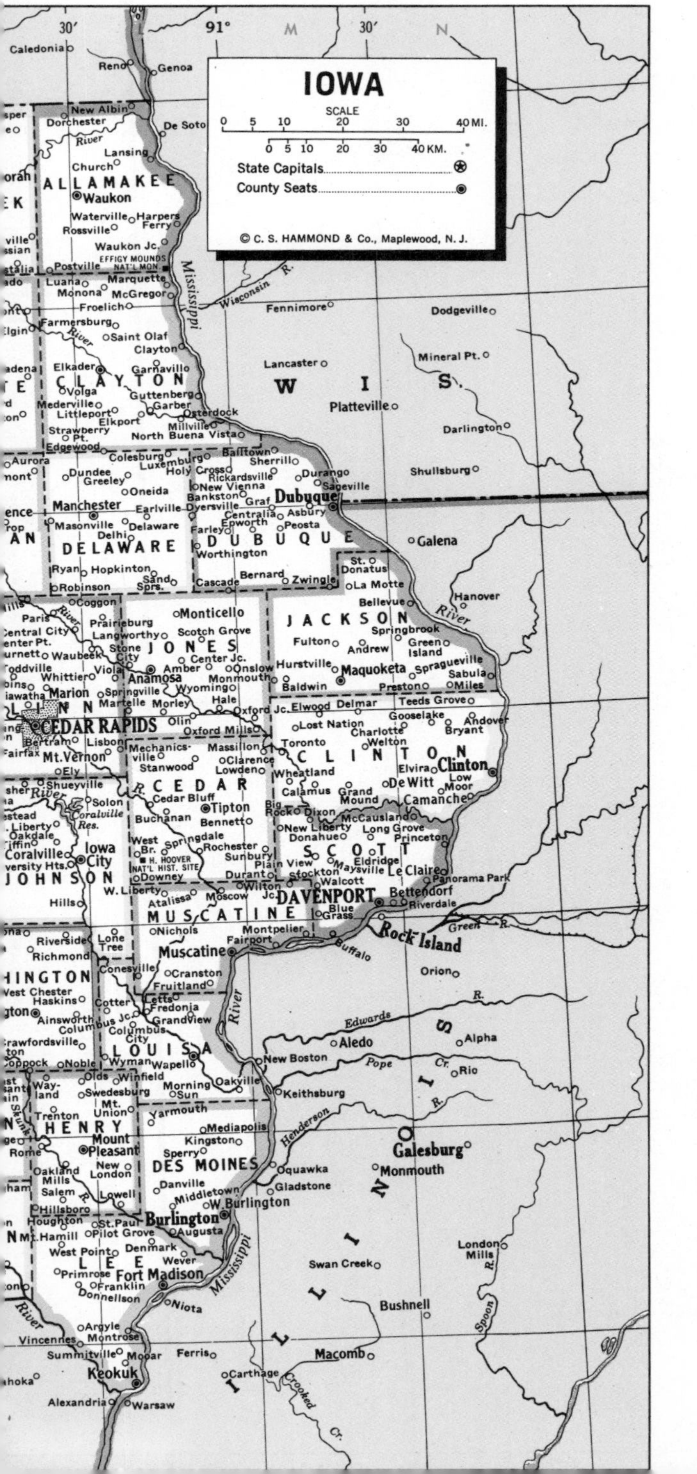

AREA 56,290 sq. mi.
POPULATION 2,825,041
CAPITAL Des Moines
LARGEST CITY Des Moines
HIGHEST POINT 1670 ft. (Osceola Co.)
SETTLED IN 1788
ADMITTED TO UNION December 28, 1846
POPULAR NAME Hawkeye State
STATE FLOWER Wild Rose
STATE BIRD Eastern Goldfinch

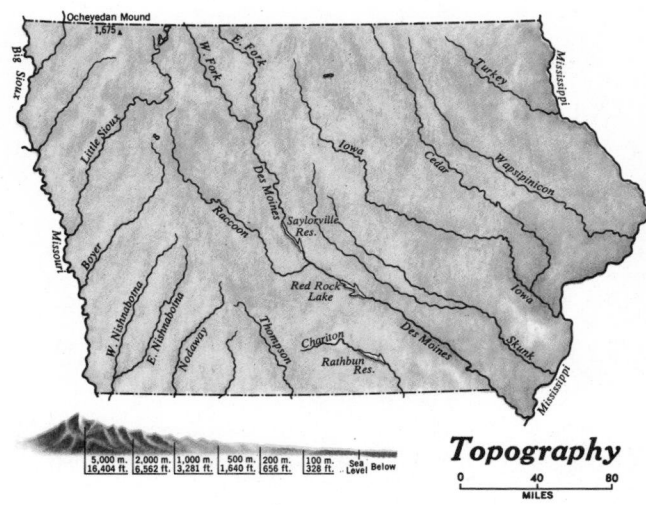

Topography

50058 Coon Rapids, 1,381 ...... D 5
52240 Coralville, 6,130 ...... K 5
50841 Corning⊙, 2,095 ...... D 7
51016 Correctionville, 870 ...... B 4
50430 Corwith, 407 ...... F 3
50060 Corydon⊙, 1,745 ...... G 7
50431 Coulter, 262 ...... G 3
51501 Council Bluffs⊙, 60,348 ...... B 6
52621 Crawfordsville, 288 ...... K 6
51526 Crescent, 284 ...... B 6
52136 Cresco⊙, 3,927 ...... J 2
50801 Creston⊙, 8,234 ...... E 6
50432 Crystal Lake, 276 ...... F 2
50843 Cumberland, 385 ...... D 6
50529 Dakota City⊙, 746 ...... E 3
50062 Dallas, 438 ...... G 6
50063 Dallas Center, 1,128 ...... E 5
52623 Danville, 948 ...... L 7
51019 Danbury, 527 ...... B 4
52801 Davenport⊙, 98,469 ...... M 5
   Davenport-Rock Island-
   Moline, ‡362,638 ...... M 5
50065 Davis City, 301 ...... F 7
50066 Dawson, 232 ...... E 5
50530 Dayton, 909 ...... E 4
52101 Decorah⊙, 7,458 ...... K 2
51440 Dedham, 325 ...... D 5
52222 Deep River, 323 ...... J 5
51527 Defiance, 392 ...... C 5
52223 Delhi, 527 ...... L 4
52037 Delmar, 599 ...... M 4
51441 Deloit, 279 ...... C 4
52550 Delta, 475 ...... J 6
51442 Denison⊙, 5,882 ...... C 4
52624 Denmark, 375 ...... L 7
50622 Denver, 1,169 ...... J 3
50301 Des Moines (cap.)⊙,
   200,587 ...... G 5
   Des Moines, ‡286,101 ...... G 5
50069 De Soto, 369 ...... E 5
52742 De Witt, 3,647 ...... N 5
50070 Dexter, 652 ...... E 5
50845 Diagonal, 327 ...... E 7
51333 Dickens, 240 ...... C 2
50624 Dike, 794 ...... H 4
52745 Dixon, 276 ...... M 5
52746 Donahue, 216 ...... M 5
52625 Donnellson, 798 ...... K 7
51235 Doon, 437 ...... A 2
52551 Douds, 247 ...... J 7
51528 Dow City, 571 ...... B 5
50071 Dows, 777 ...... G 3
52001 Dubuque⊙, 62,309 ...... M 3
   Dubuque, ‡90,609 ...... M 3
50625 Dumont, 724 ...... H 3
50532 Duncombe, 418 ...... E 4
50626 Dunkerton, 563 ...... J 3
51529 Dunlap, 1,292 ...... B 5
52747 Durant, 1,472 ...... M 5
52040 Dyersville, 3,437 ...... L 3
52224 Dysart, 1,251 ...... J 4
52533 Eagle Grove, 4,489 ...... F 3
50072 Earlham, 974 ...... E 6
51530 Earling, 573 ...... C 5
52041 Earlville, 751 ...... L 4
50535 Early, 727 ...... C 4

52553 Eddyville, 945 ...... H 6
52042 Edgewood, 786 ...... K 3
52554 Eldon, 1,319 ...... J 7
50627 Eldora⊙, 3,223 ...... G 4
52748 Eldridge, 1,535 ...... M 5
52141 Elgin, 613 ...... K 3
52043 Elkader⊙, 1,592 ...... L 3
50073 Elkhart, 269 ...... F 5
51531 Elk Horn, 667 ...... C 5
† 50700 Elk Run Heights, 1,175 ...... J 4
51532 Elliott, 423 ...... C 6
50075 Ellsworth, 443 ...... F 4
50628 Elma, 601 ...... J 2
52227 Ely, 275 ...... K 5
51533 Emerson, 484 ...... C 6
50536 Emmetsburg⊙, 4,150 ...... D 2
52045 Epworth, 1,132 ...... M 4
51638 Essex, 770 ...... C 7
51334 Estherville⊙, 8,108 ...... D 2
50707 Evansdale, 5,038 ...... J 4
51338 Everly, 699 ...... C 2
50076 Exira, 966 ...... D 5
52555 Exline, 224 ...... H 7
50629 Fairbank, 810 ...... K 3
52228 Fairfax, 635 ...... K 5
52556 Fairfield⊙, 8,715 ...... J 6
52046 Farley, 1,096 ...... L 4
52047 Farmersburg, 232 ...... L 3
52626 Farmington, 800 ...... K 7
50538 Farnhamville, 393 ...... D 4
51639 Farragut, 521 ...... C 7
52142 Fayette, 1,947 ...... K 3
50599 Fenton, 403 ...... E 2
50434 Fertile, 394 ...... G 2
50435 Floyd, 380 ...... H 2
50540 Fonda, 980 ...... D 3
50846 Fontanelle, 752 ...... E 6
50436 Forest City⊙, 3,841 ...... F 2
52144 Fort Atkinson, 339 ...... J 2
50501 Fort Dodge⊙, 31,263 ...... E 3
52627 Fort Madison⊙, 13,996 ...... L 7
51340 Fostoria, 219 ...... C 2
50630 Fredericksburg, 912 ...... J 3
52561 Fremont, 480 ...... H 6
51020 Galva, 319 ...... C 4
50103 Garden Grove, 285 ...... F 7
52049 Garnavillo, 634 ...... L 3
50438 Garner⊙, 2,217 ...... F 2
52229 Garrison, 383 ...... J 4
50632 Garwin, 563 ...... H 4
51237 George, 1,194 ...... B 2
50105 Gilbert, 521 ...... F 4
50634 Gilbertville, 655 ...... J 4
50106 Gilman, 513 ...... H 5
50541 Gilmore City, 766 ...... D 3
50635 Gladbrook, 961 ...... H 4
51534 Glenwood⊙, 4,195 ...... B 6
51443 Glidden, 964 ...... D 4
50542 Goldfield, 722 ...... F 3
50439 Goodell, 241 ...... F 3
52750 Gooselake, 218 ...... N 5
50543 Gowrie, 1,225 ...... D 4
51342 Graettinger, 907 ...... D 2
50440 Grafton, 254 ...... G 2
50107 Grand Junction, 967 ...... E 4
52751 Grand Mound, 627 ...... M 5

50108 Grand River, 211 ...... F 7
52752 Grandview, 357 ...... L 6
50109 Granger, 661 ...... F 5
51022 Granville, 383 ...... B 3
50848 Gravity, 286 ...... D 7
52050 Greeley, 323 ...... L 3
50636 Greene, 1,363 ...... H 3
50849 Greenfield⊙, 2,212 ...... D 6
50111 Grimes, 834 ...... F 5
50112 Grinnell, 8,402 ...... H 5
51535 Griswold, 1,181 ...... C 6
50638 Grundy Center⊙, 2,712 ...... H 4
50115 Guthrie Center⊙, 1,834 ...... D 5
52052 Guttenberg, 2,177 ...... L 3
51444 Halbur, 235 ...... D 4
51640 Hamburg, 1,649 ...... B 7
50441 Hampton⊙, 4,376 ...... G 3
51536 Hancock, 228 ...... C 6
50544 Harcourt, 305 ...... E 4
51537 Harlan⊙, 5,049 ...... C 5
52146 Harpers Ferry, 227 ...... L 2
50118 Hartford, 582 ...... G 6
51346 Hartley, 1,694 ...... C 2
50119 Harvey, 217 ...... H 6
51540 Hastings, 229 ...... C 6
50546 Havelock, 220 ...... D 3
51023 Hawarden, 2,789 ...... A 2
52147 Hawkeye, 529 ...... J 3
50641 Hazleton, 626 ...... K 3
52563 Hedrick, 790 ...... J 6
51541 Henderson, 211 ...... B 6
52233 Hiawatha, 2,416 ...... K 4
52235 Hills, 507 ...... K 5
52630 Hillsboro, 252 ...... K 7
51024 Hinton, 488 ...... A 3
50642 Holland, 258 ...... H 4
51025 Holstein, 1,445 ...... B 4
52053 Holy Cross, 290 ...... L 3
52237 Hopkinton, 852 ...... L 4
51026 Hornick, 250 ...... A 4
51238 Hospers, 646 ...... B 2
50122 Hubbard, 846 ...... G 4
50643 Hudson, 1,535 ...... H 4
51239 Hull, 1,523 ...... A 2
50548 Humboldt⊙, 4,665 ...... E 3
50123 Humeston, 673 ...... G 7
50124 Huxley, 937 ...... F 5
51445 Ida Grove⊙, 2,261 ...... B 4
50644 Independence⊙, 5,910 ...... K 4
50125 Indianola⊙, 8,852 ...... F 6
51240 Inwood, 644 ...... A 2
50126 Iona, 270 ...... J 2
52240 Iowa City⊙, 46,850 ...... L 5
50126 Iowa Falls, 6,454 ...... G 3
51027 Ireton, 582 ...... A 3
51446 Irwin, 446 ...... C 5
50128 Jamaica, 271 ...... E 5
52647 Janesville, 741 ...... J 3
50129 Jefferson⊙, 4,735 ...... E 4
50648 Jesup, 1,662 ...... J 4
50130 Jewell, 1,152 ...... F 4
50131 Johnston, 222 ...... F 5
52247 Kalona, 1,488 ...... K 6
50132 Kamrar, 243 ...... F 4
50447 Kanawha, 705 ...... F 3
50133 Kellerton, 299 ...... E 7

(continued on following page)

Agriculture, Industry and Resources

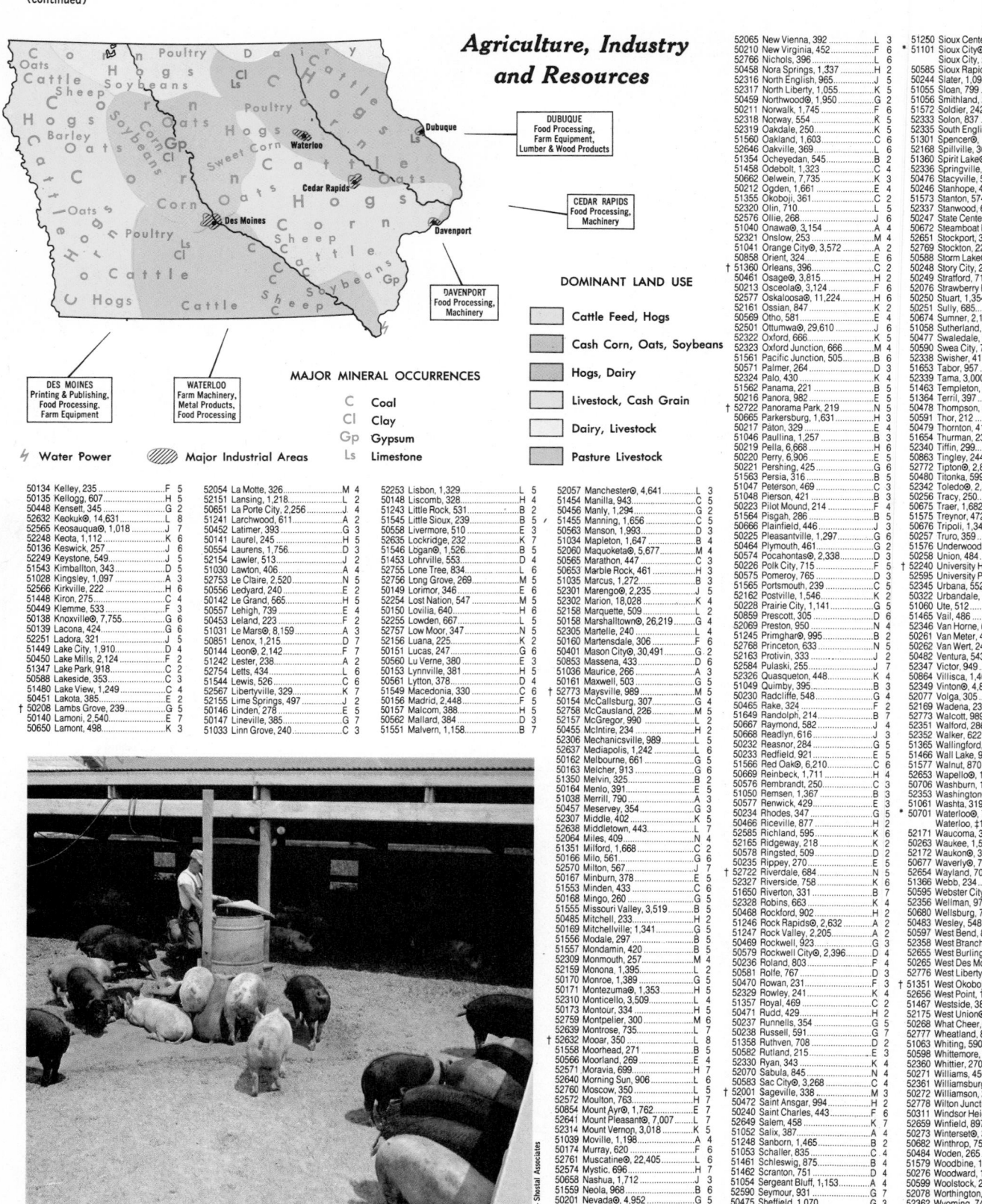

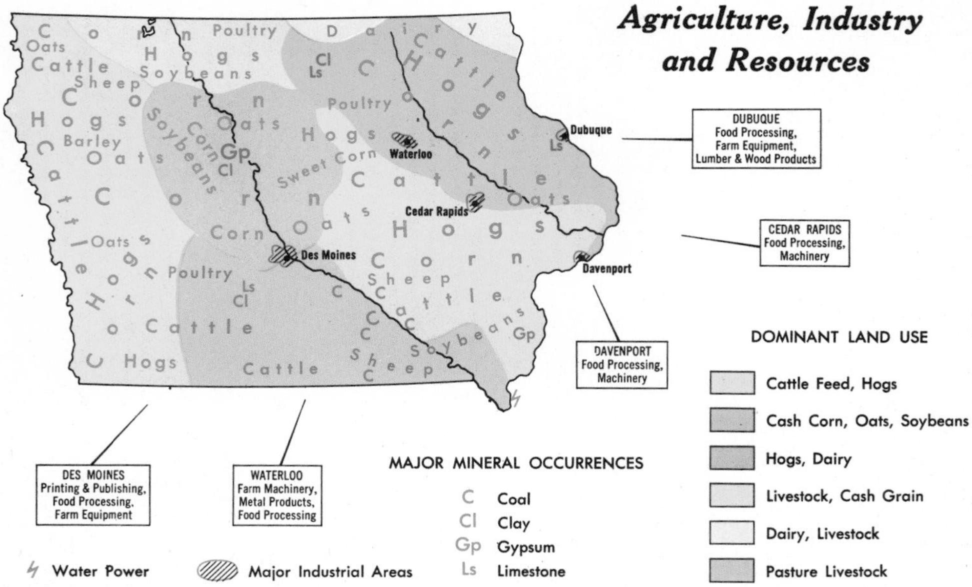
Corn
Oats
Cattle
Sheep
Hogs
Soybeans
Poultry
Dairy
Barley
Sweet Corn
Cl
Ls
C
Gp
Dubuque
Waterloo
Cedar Rapids
Des Moines
Davenport
DUBUQUE
Food Processing,
Farm Equipment,
Lumber & Wood Products
CEDAR RAPIDS
Food Processing,
Machinery
DAVENPORT
Food Processing,
Machinery
DES MOINES
Printing & Publishing,
Food Processing,
Farm Equipment
WATERLOO
Farm Machinery,
Metal Products,
Food Processing
DOMINANT LAND USE
Cattle Feed, Hogs
Cash Corn, Oats, Soybeans
Hogs, Dairy
Livestock, Cash Grain
Dairy, Livestock
Pasture Livestock
MAJOR MINERAL OCCURRENCES
C Coal
Cl Clay
Gp Gypsum
Ls Limestone
Water Power
Major Industrial Areas

50134	Kelley, 235	F	5
50135	Kellogg, 607	H	5
50448	Kensett, 345	G	2
52632	Keokuk⊙, 14,631	L	8
52565	Keosauqua⊙, 1,018	J	7
52248	Keota, 1,112	K	6
50136	Keswick, 257	J	6
52249	Keystone, 549	J	5
51543	Kimballton, 343	D	5
51028	Kingsley, 1,097	A	3
52566	Kirkville, 222	H	6
51448	Kiron, 275	C	4
50449	Klemme, 533	F	3
50138	Knoxville⊙, 7,755	G	6
50139	Lacona, 424	G	6
52251	Ladora, 321	J	5
51449	Lake City, 1,910	D	4
50450	Lake Mills, 2,124	F	2
51347	Lake Park, 918	C	2
50588	Lakeside, 353	C	3
51480	Lake View, 1,249	C	4
50451	Lakota, 385	E	2
† 50208	Lambs Grove, 239	G	5
50140	Lamoni, 2,540	E	7
50650	Lamont, 498	K	3
52054	La Motte, 326	M	4
52151	Lansing, 1,218	L	2
50651	La Porte City, 2,256	J	4
51241	Larchwood, 611	A	2
50452	Latimer, 393	G	3
50141	Laurel, 245	H	5
50554	Laurens, 1,756	D	3
52154	Lawler, 513	J	2
51030	Lawton, 406	A	4
52753	Le Claire, 2,520	N	5
50556	Ledyard, 240	E	2
50142	Le Grand, 565	H	5
50557	Lehigh, 739	E	4
50453	Leland, 223	F	2
51031	Le Mars⊙, 8,159	A	3
50851	Lenox, 1,215	D	7
50144	Leon⊙, 2,142	F	7
51242	Lester, 238	A	2
52754	Letts, 434	L	6
51544	Lewis, 526	C	6
52567	Libertyville, 329	K	7
52155	Lime Springs, 497	J	2
50146	Linden, 278	E	5
50147	Lineville, 385	G	7
51033	Linn Grove, 240	C	3
52253	Lisbon, 1,329	L	5
50148	Liscomb, 328	H	4
51243	Little Rock, 531	B	2
51545	Little Sioux, 239	B	5
50558	Livermore, 510	E	3
52635	Lockridge, 232	K	7
51546	Logan⊙, 1,526	B	5
51453	Lohrville, 553	D	4
52755	Lone Tree, 834	L	6
52756	Long Grove, 269	M	5
50149	Lorimor, 346	E	6
52254	Lost Nation, 547	M	5
50150	Lovilia, 640	H	6
52255	Lowden, 667	L	5
52757	Low Moor, 347	N	5
52156	Luana, 225	K	2
50151	Lucas, 247	G	6
50560	Lu Verne, 380	E	3
50153	Lynnville, 381	H	5
50561	Lytton, 378	D	4
51549	Macedonia, 330	C	6
50156	Madrid, 2,448	F	5
50157	Malcom, 388	H	5
50562	Mallard, 384	D	3
51551	Malvern, 1,158	B	7
52057	Manchester⊙, 4,641	L	3
51454	Manilla, 943	C	5
50456	Manly, 1,294	G	2
51455	Manning, 1,656	C	5
50563	Manson, 1,993	D	3
51034	Mapleton, 1,647	B	4
52060	Maquoketa⊙, 5,677	M	4
50565	Marathon, 447	C	3
50653	Marble Rock, 461	H	3
51035	Marcus, 1,272	B	3
52301	Marengo⊙, 2,235	J	5
52302	Marion, 18,028	K	4
52158	Marquette, 509	L	2
50158	Marshalltown⊙, 26,219	G	4
52305	Martelle, 240	L	4
50160	Martensdale, 306	F	6
50401	Mason City⊙, 30,491	G	2
50853	Massena, 433	D	6
51036	Maurice, 266	A	3
50161	Maxwell, 503	G	5
† 52773	Maysville, 989	M	5
50154	McCallsburg, 307	G	4
52758	McCausland, 226	M	5
52157	McGregor, 990	L	2
50455	McIntire, 234	H	2
52306	Mechanicsville, 989	L	5
52637	Mediapolis, 1,242	L	6
50162	Melbourne, 661	G	5
50163	Melcher, 913	G	6
51350	Melvin, 325	B	2
50164	Menlo, 391	E	5
51038	Merrill, 790	A	3
50457	Meservey, 354	G	3
52307	Middle, 402	K	5
52638	Middletown, 443	L	7
52064	Miles, 409	N	4
51351	Milford, 1,668	C	2
50166	Milo, 561	G	6
52570	Milton, 567	J	7
50167	Minburn, 378	E	5
51553	Minden, 433	C	6
50168	Mingo, 260	G	5
51555	Missouri Valley, 3,519	B	5
50485	Mitchell, 233	H	2
50169	Mitchellville; 1,341	G	5
51556	Modale, 297	B	5
51557	Mondamin, 420	B	5
52309	Monmouth, 257	M	4
52159	Monona, 1,395	L	2
50170	Monroe, 1,389	G	5
50171	Montezuma⊙, 1,353	H	5
52310	Monticello, 3,509	L	4
50173	Montour, 334	H	5
52759	Montpelier, 300	M	6
52639	Montrose, 735	L	7
† 52632	Mooar, 350	L	8
51558	Moorhead, 271	B	5
50566	Moorland, 269	E	4
52571	Moravia, 699	H	7
52640	Morning Sun, 906	L	6
52760	Moscow, 350	L	5
52572	Moulton, 763	H	7
50854	Mount Ayr⊙, 1,762	E	7
52641	Mount Pleasant⊙, 7,007	L	7
52314	Mount Vernon, 3,018	K	5
51039	Moville, 1,198	A	4
50174	Murray, 620	F	6
52761	Muscatine⊙, 22,405	L	6
52574	Mystic, 696	H	7
50658	Nashua, 1,712	J	3
51559	Neola, 968	B	6
50201	Nevada⊙, 4,952	G	5
52160	New Albin, 644	L	2
50568	Newell, 877	D	3
52315	Newhall, 701	K	5
50659	New Hampton⊙, 3,621	J	2
50660	New Hartford, 690	H	3
52645	New London, 1,900	L	7
51646	New Market, 501	D	7
50206	New Providence, 208	G	4
50207	New Sharon, 944	H	6
50208	Newton⊙, 15,619	H	5
52065	New Vienna, 392	L	3
50210	New Virginia, 452	F	6
52766	Nichols, 396	L	6
50458	Nora Springs, 1,337	H	2
52316	North English, 965	J	5
52317	North Liberty, 1,055	K	5
50459	Northwood⊙, 1,950	G	2
50211	Norwalk, 1,745	F	6
52318	Norway, 554	K	5
52319	Oakdale, 250	K	5
51560	Oakland, 1,603	C	6
52646	Oakville, 369	L	6
51354	Ocheyedan, 545	B	2
51458	Odebolt, 1,323	C	4
50662	Oelwein, 7,735	K	3
50212	Ogden, 1,661	E	4
51355	Okoboji, 361	C	2
52320	Olin, 710	L	5
52576	Ollie, 268	J	6
51040	Onawa⊙, 3,154	A	4
52321	Onslow, 253	M	4
51041	Orange City⊙, 3,572	A	2
50858	Orient, 324	E	6
† 51360	Orleans, 396	C	2
50461	Osage⊙, 3,815	H	2
50213	Osceola⊙, 3,124	F	6
52577	Oskaloosa⊙, 11,224	H	6
52161	Ossian, 847	K	2
50569	Otho, 581	E	4
52501	Ottumwa⊙, 29,610	J	6
52322	Oxford, 666	K	5
52323	Oxford Junction, 666	M	4
51561	Pacific Junction, 505	B	6
50571	Palmer, 264	D	3
52324	Palo, 430	K	4
51562	Panama, 221	B	5
50216	Panora, 982	E	5
† 52722	Panorama Park, 219	N	5
50665	Parkersburg, 1,631	H	3
50217	Paton, 329	E	4
51046	Paullina, 1,257	B	3
50219	Pella, 6,668	H	6
50220	Perry, 6,906	E	5
50221	Pershing, 425	G	6
51563	Persia, 316	B	5
51047	Peterson, 469	C	3
51048	Pierson, 421	B	3
50223	Pilot Mound, 214	F	4
51564	Pisgah, 286	B	5
50666	Plainfield, 446	J	3
50225	Pleasantville, 1,297	G	6
50464	Plymouth, 461	G	2
50574	Pocahontas⊙, 2,338	D	3
50226	Polk City, 715	F	5
50575	Pomeroy, 765	D	3
51565	Portsmouth, 239	C	5
52162	Postville, 1,546	K	2
50228	Prairie City, 1,141	G	5
50859	Prescott, 305	D	6
52069	Preston, 950	N	4
51245	Primghar⊙, 995	B	2
52768	Princeton, 633	N	5
52163	Protivin, 333	J	2
52584	Pulaski, 255	J	7
52326	Quasqueton, 448	K	4
51049	Quimby, 395	B	3
50230	Radcliffe, 548	G	4
50465	Rake, 324	F	2
51649	Randolph, 214	B	7
50667	Raymond, 582	J	4
50668	Readlyn, 616	J	3
50232	Reasnor, 284	G	5
50233	Redfield, 921	E	5
51566	Red Oak⊙, 6,210	C	6
50669	Reinbeck, 1,711	H	4
50576	Rembrandt, 250	C	3
51050	Remsen, 1,367	B	3
50577	Renwick, 429	E	3
50234	Rhodes, 347	G	5
50466	Riceville, 877	H	2
52585	Richland, 595	K	6
52165	Ridgeway, 218	K	2
50578	Ringsted, 509	D	2
50235	Rippey, 270	E	5
† 52722	Riverdale, 684	N	5
52327	Riverside, 758	K	6
51650	Riverton, 331	B	7
52328	Robins, 663	K	4
50468	Rockford, 902	H	2
51246	Rock Rapids⊙, 2,632	A	2
51247	Rock Valley, 2,205	A	2
50469	Rockwell, 923	G	3
50579	Rockwell City⊙, 2,396	D	4
50236	Roland, 803	F	4
50581	Rolfe, 767	D	3
50470	Rowan, 231	F	3
52329	Rowley, 241	K	4
51357	Royal, 469	C	2
50471	Rudd, 429	H	2
50237	Runnells, 354	G	5
50238	Russell, 591	G	7
51358	Ruthven, 708	D	2
50582	Rutland, 215	E	3
52330	Ryan, 343	K	4
52070	Sabula, 845	N	4
50583	Sac City⊙, 3,268	C	4
† 52001	Sageville, 338	M	3
50472	Saint Ansgar, 994	H	2
50240	Saint Charles, 443	F	6
52649	Salem, 458	K	7
51052	Salix, 387	A	4
51248	Sanborn, 1,465	B	2
51053	Schaller, 835	C	4
51461	Schleswig, 875	B	4
51462	Scranton, 751	D	4
51054	Sergeant Bluff, 1,153	A	4
52590	Seymour, 931	G	7
50475	Sheffield, 1,070	G	3
51570	Shelby, 868	C	5
50243	Sheldahl, 285	F	5
51201	Sheldon, 4,535	B	2
50670	Shell Rock, 1,159	H	3
52332	Shellsburg, 740	K	4
51601	Shenandoah, 5,968	C	7
51249	Sibley⊙, 2,749	B	2
51652	Sidney⊙, 1,061	B	7
52591	Sigourney⊙, 2,319	J	6
51571	Silver City, 272	B	6
51250	Sioux Center, 3,450	A	
* 51101	Sioux City⊙, 85,925	A	
	Sioux City, ‡116,189	A	
50585	Sioux Rapids, 813	C	
50244	Slater, 1,094	F	
51055	Sloan, 799	A	
51056	Smithland, 293	B	
51572	Soldier, 242	B	
52333	Solon, 837	L	
52335	South English, 218	J	
51301	Spencer⊙, 10,278	C	
52168	Spillville, 361	J	
51360	Spirit Lake⊙, 3,014	C	
52336	Springville, 970	L	
50476	Stacyville, 598	H	
50246	Stanhope, 482	F	
51573	Stanton, 574	C	
52337	Stanwood, 642	L	
50247	State Center, 1,232	G	
50672	Steamboat Rock, 394	G	
52651	Stockport, 334	K	
52769	Stockton, 222	M	
50588	Storm Lake⊙, 8,591	C	
50248	Story City, 2,104	F	
50249	Stratford, 710	F	
52076	Strawberry Point, 1,281	K	
50250	Stuart, 1,354	E	
50251	Sully, 685	H	
50674	Sumner, 2,174	J	
51058	Sutherland, 875	B	
50477	Swaledale, 222	G	
50590	Swea City, 774	E	
52338	Swisher, 417	K	
51653	Tabor, 957	B	
52339	Tama, 3,000	H	
51463	Templeton, 312	D	
51364	Terril, 397	C	
50478	Thompson, 600	F	
50591	Thor, 212	E	
50479	Thornton, 410	G	
51654	Thurman, 230	B	
52340	Tiffin, 299	K	
50863	Tingley, 244	E	
52772	Tipton⊙, 2,877	L	
50480	Titonka, 599	E	
52342	Toledo⊙, 2,361	H	
50256	Tracy, 250	H	
50675	Traer, 1,682	J	
51575	Treynor, 472	B	
50676	Tripoli, 1,345	J	
50257	Truro, 359	F	
51576	Underwood, 424	B	
50258	Union, 484	G	
† 52240	University Heights, 1,265	K	
52595	University Park, 534	H	
52345	Urbana, 552	K	
50322	Urbandale, 14,434	F	
51060	Ute, 512	B	
51465	Vail, 486	C	
52346	Van Horne, 613	J	
50261	Van Meter, 464	E	
50262	Van Wert, 244	F	
50482	Ventura, 543	F	
52347	Victor, 949	J	
50864	Villisca, 1,402	C	
52349	Vinton⊙, 4,845	J	
52077	Volga, 305	L	
52169	Wadena, 237	K	
52773	Walcott, 989	M	
52351	Walford, 286	K	
52352	Walker, 622	K	
51365	Wallingford, 245	D	
51466	Wall Lake, 936	C	
51577	Walnut, 870	C	
52653	Wapello⊙, 1,873	L	
50706	Washburn, 1,408	J	
52353	Washington⊙, 6,317	K	
51061	Washta, 319	B	
* 50701	Waterloo⊙, 75,533	J	
	Waterloo, ‡132,916	J	
52171	Waucoma, 357	J	
50263	Waukee, 1,577	F	
52172	Waukon⊙, 3,883	L	
50677	Waverly⊙, 7,205	J	
52654	Wayland, 702	K	
51366	Webb, 234	D	
50595	Webster City⊙, 8,488	F	
52356	Wellman, 977	K	
50680	Wellsburg, 754	H	
50483	Wesley, 548	E	
50597	West Bend, 865	D	
52358	West Branch, 1,322	L	
52655	West Burlington, 3,139	L	
50265	West Des Moines, 16,441	F	
52776	West Liberty, 2,296	L	
† 51351	West Okoboji, 210	C	
52656	West Point, 1,045	K	
51467	Westside, 389	C	
52175	West Union⊙, 2,624	K	
50268	What Cheer, 868	J	
52777	Wheatland, 832	M	
51063	Whiting, 590	A	
50598	Whittemore, 658	E	
52360	Whittier, 270	K	
50271	Williams, 456	F	
52361	Williamsburg, 1,544	J	
50272	Williamson, 216	G	
52778	Wilton Junction, 1,873	M	
50311	Windsor Heights, 6,303	F	
52659	Winfield, 897	L	
50273	Winterset⊙, 3,654	E	
50682	Winthrop, 750	K	
50484	Woden, 265	F	
51579	Woodbine, 1,349	B	
50276	Woodward, 1,010	E	
50599	Woolstock, 222	F	
52078	Worthington, 365	L	
52362	Wyoming, 746	L	
50277	Yale, 301	E	
50278	Zearing, 535	G	

⊙ County seat.
‡ Population of metropolitan area.
† Zip of nearest p.o.
* Multiple zips

A. M. Wettach — Shostal Associates

This Iowa farmer confines his hogs to concrete pens as a more efficient and sanitary method of raising healthy animals for market. Iowa's record-breaking hog production is due largely to the availability of corn for fodder.

Agriculture, Industry and Resources

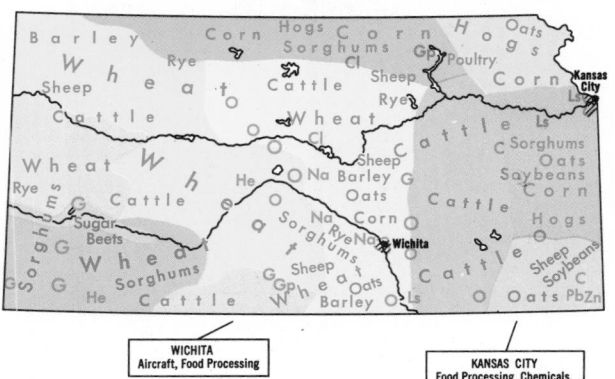

DOMINANT LAND USE

- Specialized Wheat
- Wheat, General Farming
- Wheat, Range Livestock
- Wheat, Grain Sorghums, Range Livestock
- Cattle Feed, Hogs
- Livestock, Cash Grain
- Livestock, Cash Grain, Dairy
- General Farming, Livestock, Cash Grain
- General Farming, Livestock, Special Crops
- Range Livestock

WICHITA
Aircraft, Food Processing

KANSAS CITY
Food Processing, Chemicals, Automobiles, Machinery, Metal Products

MAJOR MINERAL OCCURRENCES

C	Coal	Ls	Limestone
Cl	Clay	Na	Salt
G	Natural Gas	O	Petroleum
Gp	Gypsum	Pb	Lead
He	Helium	Zn	Zinc

▨ Major Industrial Areas

AREA 82,264 sq. mi.
POPULATION 2,249,071
CAPITAL Topeka
LARGEST CITY Wichita
HIGHEST POINT Mt. Sunflower 4,039 ft.
SETTLED IN 1831
ADMITTED TO UNION January 29, 1861
POPULAR NAME Sunflower State
STATE FLOWER Sunflower
STATE BIRD Western Meadowlark

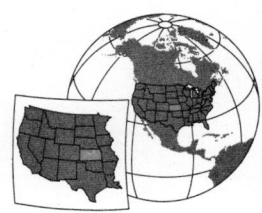

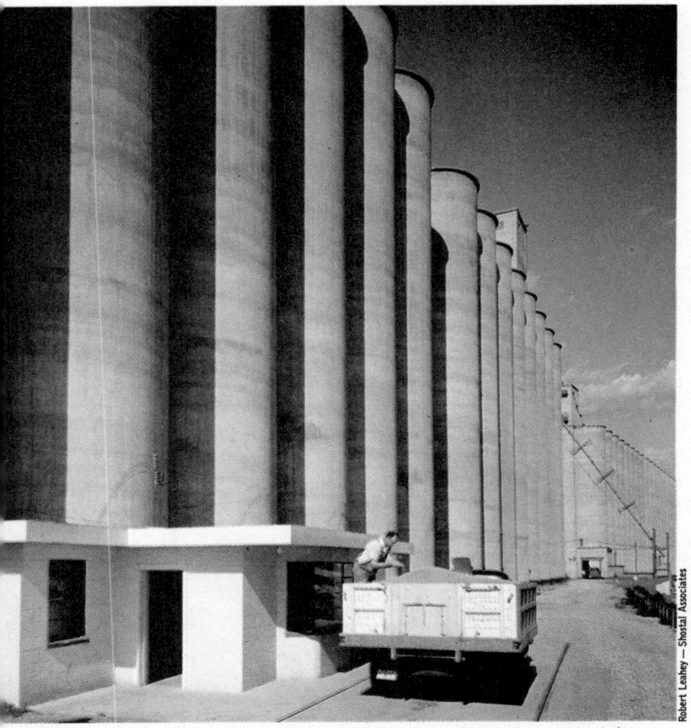

McPherson, 24,778	E 3
Meade, 4,912	B 4
Miami, 19,254	H 3
Mitchell, 8,010	D 2
Montgomery, 39,949	G 4
Morris, 6,432	F 3
Morton, 3,576	A 4
Nemaha, 11,825	F 2
Neosho, 18,812	G 4
Ness, 4,791	C 3
Norton, 7,279	C 2
Osage, 13,352	G 3
Osborne, 6,416	D 2
Ottawa, 6,183	E 2
Pawnee, 8,484	C 3
Phillips, 7,888	C 2
Pottawatomie, 11,755	F 2
Pratt, 10,056	D 4
Rawlins, 4,393	B 2
Reno, 60,765	D 4
Republic, 8,498	E 2
Rice, 12,320	D 3
Riley, 56,788	F 2
Rooks, 7,628	C 2
Rush, 5,117	C 3
Russell, 9,428	D 3
Saline, 46,592	E 3
Scott, 5,606	B 3
Sedgwick, 350,694	E 4
Seward, 15,744	B 4
Shawnee, 155,322	G 2
Sheridan, 3,859	B 2
Sherman, 7,792	A 2
Smith, 6,757	D 2
Stafford, 5,943	D 3
Stanton, 2,287	A 4
Stevens, 4,198	A 4
Sumner, 23,553	E 4
Thomas, 7,501	A 2
Trego, 4,436	C 3
Wabaunsee, 6,397	F 3
Wallace, 2,215	A 3
Washington, 9,249	E 2
Wichita, 3,274	A 3
Wilson, 11,317	G 4
Woodson, 4,789	G 4
Wyandotte, 186,845	H 2

COUNTIES

Allen, 15,043	G 4
Anderson, 8,501	G 3
Atchison, 19,165	G 2
Barber, 7,016	D 4
Barton, 30,663	D 3
Bourbon, 15,215	H 4
Brown, 11,685	G 2
Butler, 38,658	F 4
Chase, 3,408	F 3
Chautauqua, 4,642	F 4
Cherokee, 21,549	H 4
Cheyenne, 4,256	A 2
Clark, 2,896	C 4
Clay, 9,890	E 2
Cloud, 13,466	E 2
Coffey, 7,397	G 3
Comanche, 2,702	C 4
Cowley, 35,012	F 4
Crawford, 37,850	H 4
Decatur, 4,988	B 2
Dickinson, 19,993	E 3
Doniphan, 9,107	G 2
Douglas, 57,932	G 3
Edwards, 4,581	C 4
Elk, 3,858	F 4
Ellis, 24,730	C 3
Ellsworth, 6,146	D 3
Finney, 18,947	B 3
Ford, 22,587	C 4
Franklin, 20,007	G 3
Geary, 28,111	F 3
Gove, 3,940	B 3
Graham, 4,751	C 2
Grant, 5,961	A 4
Gray, 4,516	B 4
Greeley, 1,819	A 3
Greenwood, 9,141	F 4
Hamilton, 2,747	A 3
Harper, 7,871	D 4
Harvey, 27,236	E 3
Haskell, 3,672	B 4
Hodgeman, 2,662	C 3
Jackson, 10,342	G 2
Jefferson, 11,945	G 2
Jewell, 6,099	D 2
Johnson, 217,662	H 3
Kearny, 3,047	A 3
Kingman, 8,886	D 4
Kiowa, 4,088	C 4
Labette, 25,775	G 4
Lane, 2,707	B 3
Leavenworth, 53,340	H 2
Lincoln, 4,582	D 2
Linn, 7,770	H 3
Logan, 3,814	A 3
Lyon, 32,071	F 3
Marion, 13,935	E 3
Marshall, 13,139	F 2

CITIES and TOWNS

Zip	Name/Pop.	Key
67510	Abbyville, 143	D 4
67410	Abilene⊙, 6,661	E 3
67414	Ada, 120	E 2
66830	Admire, 144	F 3
66930	Agenda, 107	E 2
67621	Agra, 294	C 2
67511	Albert, 235	D 3
67512	Alden, 238	D 3
67513	Alexander, 129	C 3
66833	Allen, 175	F 3
67401	Alma⊙, 905	F 2
67622	Almena, 489	C 2
67330	Altamont, 845	G 4
66834	Alta Vista, 402	F 3
67623	Alton, 214	D 2
66710	Altoona, 475	G 4
66835	Americus, 441	F 3
67001	Andale, 500	E 4
67002	Andover, 1,880	E 4
67003	Anthony⊙, 2,653	D 4
66711	Arcadia, 388	H 4
67004	Argonia, 591	E 4
67005	Arkansas City, 13,216	E 4
67514	Arlington, 503	D 4
66712	Arma, 1,348	H 4
67831	Ashland⊙, 1,244	C 4
67416	Assaria, 303	E 3
66002	Atchison⊙, 12,565	G 2
66932	Athol, 108	D 2
67008	Atlanta, 216	F 4
67009	Attica, 639	D 4
67730	Atwood⊙, 1,658	B 2
66402	Auburn, 261	G 3
67010	Augusta, 5,977	F 4
67417	Aurora, 120	E 2
66403	Axtell, 456	F 2
66404	Baileyville, 110	F 2
66006	Baldwin City, 2,520	G 3
67418	Barnard, 190	D 2
66933	Barnes, 209	F 2
67332	Bartlett, 138	G 4
66007	Basehor, 724	G 2
66713	Baxter Springs, 4,489	H 4
67516	Bazine, 386	C 3
66406	Beattie, 288	F 2
67012	Beaumont, 135	F 4
67013	Belle Plaine, 1,553	E 4
66935	Belleville⊙, 3,063	E 2
67420	Beloit⊙, 4,121	D 2
67519	Belpre, 191	C 4
66407	Belvue, 161	F 2
67422	Bennington, 561	E 3
67016	Bentley, 260	E 4
67017	Benton, 517	E 4
66408	Bern, 191	F 2
67423	Beverly, 193	E 2
67731	Bird City, 671	A 2

67520	Bison, 285	C 3
66010	Blue Mound, 308	H 3
66411	Blue Rapids, 1,148	F 2
67018	Bluff City, 109	E 4
67625	Bogue, 257	C 2
66012	Bonner Springs, 3,662	H 2
67732	Brewster, 320	A 2
66716	Bronson, 397	H 4
67425	Brookville, 238	E 3
67834	Bucklin, 771	C 4
66013	Bucyrus, 196	H 3
66717	Buffalo, 321	G 4
67522	Buhler, 1,019	E 3
67626	Bunker Hill, 181	D 3
67019	Burden, 685	F 4
67523	Burdett, 285	C 3
66838	Burdick, 120	F 3
66413	Burlingame, 999	G 3
66839	Burlington⊙, 2,099	G 3
66840	Burns, 268	F 3
66936	Burr Oak, 426	D 2
67020	Burrton, 808	E 3
67427	Bushton, 397	D 3
67022	Caldwell, 1,540	E 4
67023	Cambridge, 110	F 4
67333	Caney, 2,192	G 4
67428	Canton, 893	E 3
66414	Carbondale, 1,041	G 3
66842	Cassoday, 123	F 3
67627	Catharine, 126	C 3
67430	Cawker City, 726	D 2
67024	Cedar Vale, 665	F 4
66415	Centralia, 511	F 2
66720	Chanute, 10,341	G 4
67431	Chapman, 1,132	E 3
67524	Chase, 800	D 3
67334	Chautauqua, 137	F 4
67025	Cheney, 1,160	E 4
66724	Cherokee, 790	H 4
67335	Cherryvale, 2,609	G 4
67336	Chetopa, 1,596	G 4
† 66762	Chicopee, 300	H 4
87835	Cimarron⊙, 1,373	B 4
66416	Circleville, 178	G 2
67525	Claflin, 887	D 3
67432	Clay Center⊙, 4,963	E 2
67629	Clayton, 127	B 2
67026	Clearwater, 1,435	E 4
66938	Clifton, 718	E 2
67028	Coats, 152	D 4
67337	Coffeyville, 15,116	G 4
67701	Colby⊙, 4,658	A 2
67029	Coldwater⊙, 1,016	C 4
67631	Collyer, 182	B 2
66015	Colony, 382	G 3
66725	Columbus⊙, 3,356	H 4
67030	Colwich, 879	E 4
66901	Concordia⊙, 7,221	E 2
67031	Conway Springs, 1,153	E 4
67836	Coolidge, 102	A 3
67837	Copeland, 267	B 4
66417	Corning, 162	F 2
66845	Cottonwood Falls⊙, 987	F 3
66846	Council Grove⊙, 2,403	F 3
66939	Courtland, 403	E 2
66728	Crestline, 102	H 4
66940	Cuba, 290	E 2
† 67124	Cullison, 117	D 4
67435	Culver, 148	E 3
66016	Cummings, 826	G 2
67035	Cunningham, 483	D 4
67632	Damar, 245	C 2
67340	Dearing, 338	G 4
67838	Deerfield, 474	A 4
66418	Delia, 168	G 2
67436	Delphos, 599	E 2
66419	Denison, 248	G 2
67341	Dennis, 120	G 4
66017	Denton, 162	G 2
67037	Derby, 7,947	E 4
66018	De Soto, 1,839	H 3
67038	Dexter, 286	F 4
67839	Dighton⊙, 1,540	B 3
66020	Easton, 435	G 2
66021	Edgerton, 513	H 3
67342	Edna, 418	G 4
66022	Edwardsville, 619	H 2
66023	Effingham, 605	G 2
67041	Elbing, 128	E 3
67042	El Dorado⊙, 12,308	F 4
67361	Elgin, 115	F 4
67344	Elk City, 432	G 4
67345	Elk Falls, 124	F 4
67950	Elkhart⊙, 2,089	A 4
67526	Ellinwood, 2,416	D 3
67637	Ellis, 2,137	C 3

(continued on following page)

Loaded with wheat for storage, a truck pulls onto a weighing platform at the Salina grain elevators. Wheat is grown here on such a scale that Kansas is known as the Breadbasket of the World.

Robert Leahey – Shostal Associates

66449 Leonardville, 412 .....F 3
67861 Leoti●, 1,916 .....A 3
66857 Le Roy, 551 .....G 3
67743 Levant, 425 .....A 2
67552 Lewis, 525 .....D 4
67901 Liberal●, 13,471 .....B 4
67351 Liberty, 185 .....G 4
67553 Liebenthal, 169 .....C 3
67455 Lincoln●, 1,582 .....D 2
66858 Lincolnville, 218 .....F 3
67456 Lindsborg, 2,764 .....E 3
66953 Linn, 388 .....E 2
66052 Linwood, 323 .....G 2
67457 Little River, 493 .....E 3
67646 Logan, 760 .....C 2
67647 Long Island, 195 .....C 2
67352 Longton, 304 .....F 4
67459 Lorraine, 153 .....D 3
66859 Lost Springs, 103 .....F 3
66053 Louisburg, 1,033 .....H 3
66450 Louisville, 204 .....F 2
67648 Lucas, 524 .....D 2
67649 Luray, 303 .....D 2
66451 Lyndon●, 958 .....G 3
67554 Lyons●, 4,355 .....D 3
67557 Macksville, 484 .....D 4

66860 Madison, 1,061 .....F 3
66955 Mahaska, 122 .....E 2
67101 Maize, 785 .....E 4
66502 Manhattan●, 27,575 .....F 2
66956 Mankato●, 1,287 .....D 2
67862 Manter, 219 .....A 4
66507 Maple Hill, 327 .....F 2
66754 Mapleton, 112 .....H 3
67863 Marienthal, 120 .....A 3
66861 Marion●, 2,052 .....F 3
67464 Marquette, 578 .....E 3
66508 Marysville●, 3,588 .....F 2
66509 Mayetta, 246 .....G 2
67103 Mayfield, 110 .....E 4
67556 McCracken, 333 .....C 3
66753 McCune, 487 .....G 4
67745 McDonald, 269 .....A 2
66501 McFarland, 209 .....F 2
66054 McLouth, 623 .....G 2
67460 McPherson●, 10,851 .....E 3
67864 Meade●, 1,899 .....B 4
67104 Medicine Lodge●, 2,545 .....D 4
67558 Medora, 110 .....E 4
66510 Melvern, 455 .....G 3
66512 Meriden, 472 .....G 2
66203 Merriam, 10,851 .....H 3

Topography

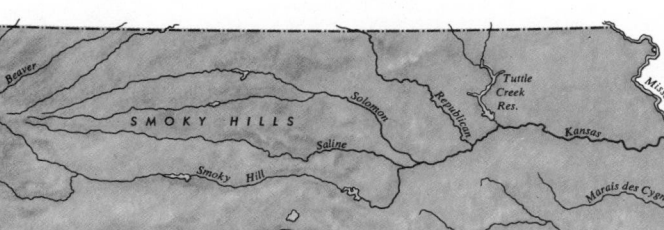

5,000 m.	2,000 m.	1,000 m.	500 m.	200 m.	100 m.	Sea
16,404 ft.	6,562 ft.	3,281 ft.	1,640 ft.	656 ft.	328 ft.	Level Below

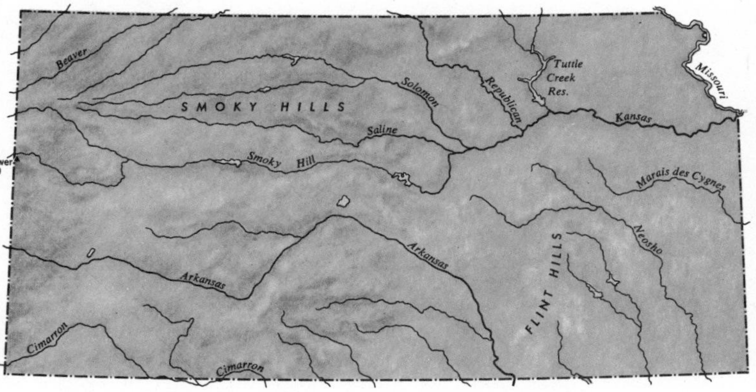

67105 Milan, 162 .....E 4
66514 Milford, 296 .....F 2
67466 Miltonvale, 718 .....E 2
67467 Minneapolis●, 1,971 .....E 2
67865 Minneola, 630 .....C 4
66222 Mission, 8,376 .....H 2
67353 Moline, 555 .....F 4
67867 Montezuma, 606 .....B 4
66755 Moran, 550 .....G 4
67468 Morganville, 257 .....E 2
67650 Morland, 300 .....B 2
66515 Morrill, 308 .....G 2
66958 Morrowville, 201 .....E 2
67952 Moscow, 228 .....A 4
66056 Mound City●, 714 .....H 3
67107 Moundridge, 1,271 .....E 3
67354 Mound Valley, 467 .....G 4
67108 Mount Hope, 665 .....E 4
66758 Mulberry, 622 .....H 4
67109 Mullinville, 376 .....C 4
67110 Mulvane, 3,185 .....E 4
66959 Munden, 123 .....E 2
† 67601 Munjor, 200 .....C 3
66058 Muscotah, 206 .....G 2
66960 Narka, 130 .....E 2
67112 Nashville, 107 .....D 4
67651 Natoma, 603 .....D 2
66757 Neodesha, 3,295 .....G 4
66758 Neosho Falls, 184 .....G 3
66864 Neosho Rapids, 234 .....F 3
67560 Ness City●, 1,756 .....C 3
66516 Netawaka, 192 .....G 2
67470 New Cambria, 160 .....E 3
67114 Newton●, 15,439 .....E 3
67561 Nickerson, 1,187 .....D 3
67653 Norcatur, 284 .....B 2
67117 North Newton, 963 .....E 3
67654 Norton●, 3,627 .....C 2
66060 Nortonville, 727 .....G 2
67118 Norwich, 414 .....E 4
67748 Oakley●, 2,327 .....B 2
67749 Oberlin●, 2,291 .....B 2
67562 Odin, 117 .....D 3
67563 Offerle, 212 .....C 4
67656 Ogallah, 110 .....C 3
66517 Ogden, 1,491 .....F 2
66518 Oketo, 133 .....F 2
66061 Olathe●, 37,917 .....H 2
67564 Olmitz, 161 .....D 3
66865 Olpe, 453 .....F 3
66520 Olsburg, 151 .....F 2
66521 Onaga, 761 .....F 2
66522 Oneida, 112 .....G 2
66760 Opolis, 160 .....H 4
66523 Osage City●, 2,600 .....G 3
66064 Osawatomie, 4,294 .....H 3
67473 Osborne●, 1,980 .....D 2
66066 Oskaloosa●, 955 .....G 2
67356 Oswego●, 2,827 .....G 4
67565 Otis, 387 .....C 3
66067 Ottawa●, 11,036 .....G 3
66524 Overbrook, 748 .....G 3
66204 Overland Park, 76,623 .....H 2
67119 Oxford, 1,113 .....E 4
66070 Ozawkie, 137 .....G 2
67657 Palco, 398 .....C 2
66962 Palmer, 166 .....E 2
66071 Paola●, 4,622 .....H 3
66758 Paradise, 145 .....D 2
67751 Park, 178 .....B 2
67219 Park City, 2,529 .....E 4
66072 Parker, 255 .....H 3
67357 Parsons, 13,015 .....G 4
67566 Partridge, 302 .....D 4
66619 Pauline, 800 .....G 3
67567 Pawnee Rock, 442 .....C 3
66526 Paxico, 216 .....F 2
66866 Peabody, 1,368 .....E 3
67120 Peck, 150 .....E 4
66073 Perry, 664 .....G 2
67360 Peru, 289 .....F 4
67660 Pfeifer, 175 .....C 3
67661 Phillipsburg●, 3,241 .....C 2
67122 Piedmont, 116 .....F 4
67868 Pierceville, 175 .....B 4

66761 Piqua, 107 .....G 4
66762 Pittsburg, 20,171 .....H 4
67869 Plains, 857 .....B 4
67663 Plainville, 2,627 .....C 2
66075 Pleasanton, 1,216 .....H 3
67568 Plevna, 124 .....D 4
66076 Pomona, 541 .....G 3
67474 Portis, 178 .....D 2
67123 Potwin, 497 .....E 3
67468 Powhattan, 111 .....G 2
67664 Prairie View, 201 .....C 2
66208 Prairie Village, 28,138 .....H 2
67124 Pratt●, 6,736 .....D 4
66767 Prescott, 222 .....H 3
67569 Preston, 239 .....D 4
67570 Pretty Prairie, 561 .....D 4
66078 Princeton, 159 .....G 3
67127 Protection, 673 .....C 4
66528 Quenemo, 429 .....G 3
67752 Quinter, 930 .....B 2
67475 Ramona, 121 .....E 3
66963 Randall, 195 .....D 2
66554 Randolph, 106 .....F 2
67572 Ransom, 416 .....C 3
66079 Rantoul, 163 .....G 3
67573 Raymond, 133 .....D 3
66868 Reading, 247 .....F 3
67660 Redfield, 138 .....H 4
66964 Republic, 243 .....E 2
66529 Reserve, 117 .....G 2
67753 Rexford, 231 .....B 2
66080 Richmond, 464 .....G 3
66531 Riley, 668 .....F 2
66770 Riverton, 500 .....H 4
67532 Robinson, 278 .....G 2
† 66205 Roeland Park, 9,974 .....H 2
67954 Rolla, 400 .....A 4
67132 Rosalia, 130 .....F 4
67133 Rose Hill, 387 .....E 4
66533 Rossville, 934 .....G 2
67476 Roxbury, 110 .....E 3
67574 Rozel, 236 .....C 3
67575 Rush Center, 237 .....C 3
67665 Russell●, 5,371 .....D 3
66534 Sabetha, 2,376 .....G 2
67756 Saint Francis●, 1,725 .....A 2
66535 Saint George, 241 .....F 2
67576 Saint John●, 1,477 .....D 3
66536 Saint Marys, 1,434 .....G 2
67571 Saint Paul, 804 .....G 4
67401 Salina●, 37,714 .....E 3
67870 Satanta, 1,161 .....A 4
66772 Savonburg, 109 .....G 4
67134 Sawyer, 164 .....D 4
66773 Scammon, 457 .....H 4
66966 Scandia, 567 .....E 2
67667 Schoenchen, 182 .....C 3
67871 Scott City●, 4,001 .....B 3
66537 Scranton, 575 .....G 3
67361 Sedan●, 1,555 .....F 4
67135 Sedgwick, 1,083 .....E 4
67757 Selden, 271 .....B 2
66538 Seneca●, 2,182 .....F 2
66081 Severance, 128 .....G 2
67137 Severy, 384 .....F 4
67138 Sharon, 265 .....D 4
67758 Sharon Springs●, 1,012 .....A 3
66203 Shawnee, 20,482 .....H 2
67874 Shields, 110 .....B 3
66539 Silver Lake, 811 .....G 2
67478 Simpson, 131 .....E 2
66967 Smith Center●, 2,389 .....D 2
67479 Smolan, 175 .....E 3
66540 Soldier, 173 .....G 2
67480 Solomon, 973 .....E 3
67140 South Haven, 413 .....E 4
† 67501 South Hutchinson, 1,879 .....D 3
67876 Spearville, 738 .....C 4
66083 Spring Hill, 1,186 .....H 3
67578 Stafford, 1,414 .....D 4
66084 Stanley, 450 .....H 3
66775 Stark, 124 .....G 4
67579 Sterling, 2,312 .....D 3
66085 Stilwell, 350 .....H 3

67669 Stockton●, 1,818 .....C 2
66869 Strong City, 545 .....F 3
67877 Sublette●, 1,208 .....B 4
66541 Summerfield, 254 .....F 2
67143 Sun City, 119 .....D 4
66019 Sunflower, 1,744 .....H 3
67363 Sycamore, 125 .....G 4
67581 Sylvia, 390 .....D 4
67878 Syracuse●, 1,720 .....A 3
67482 Talmage, 125 .....E 2
67483 Tampa, 154 .....E 3
66542 Tecumseh, 270 .....G 2
67484 Tescott, 393 .....E 2
66776 Thayer, 430 .....G 4
67582 Timken, 123 .....C 3
67485 Tipton, 315 .....D 2
67086 Tonganoxie, 1,717 .....G 2
* 66601 Topeka (cap.)●, 125,011 .....G 2
Topeka, ‡155,322 .....G 2
66777 Toronto, 431 .....F 4
67144 Towanda, 1,190 .....E 4
66778 Treece, 225 .....H 4
67879 Tribune●, 1,013 .....A 3
66087 Troy●, 1,047 .....G 2
67583 Turon, 430 .....D 4
67364 Tyro, 206 .....G 4
67146 Udall, 668 .....E 4
67880 Ulysses●, 3,779 .....A 4
66779 Uniontown, 286 .....G 4
67584 Utica, 297 .....B 3
67147 Valley Center, 2,551 .....E 4
66088 Valley Falls, 1,169 .....G 2
66544 Vermillion, 191 .....F 2
67671 Victoria, 1,246 .....C 3
67149 Viola, 193 .....E 4
66870 Virgil, 179 .....F 4
67672 WaKeeney●, 2,334 .....C 2
67487 Wakefield, 583 .....E 2
67673 Waldo, 123 .....D 2
67761 Wallace, 112 .....A 3
67151 Walton, 211 .....E 3
66547 Wamego, 2,507 .....F 2
66968 Washington●, 1,584 .....F 2
66548 Waterville, 632 .....F 2
66090 Wathena, 1,150 .....H 2
67781 Waverly, 510 .....G 3
66781 Weir, 740 .....H 4
66091 Welda, 149 .....G 3
67152 Wellington●, 8,072 .....E 4
66092 Wellsville, 1,183 .....G 3
67762 Weskan, 350 .....A 3
66782 West Mineral, 232 .....H 4
66549 Westmoreland●, 485 .....F 2
66093 Westphalia, 185 .....G 3
67869 West Plains (Plains), 857 .....B 4
66550 Wetmore, 392 .....G 2
66551 Wheaton, 106 .....F 2
66872 White City, 458 .....F 3
66094 White Cloud, 210 .....G 2
67154 Whitewater, 520 .....E 4
66552 Whiting, 256 .....G 2
* 67201 Wichita●, 276,554 .....E 4
Wichita, ‡389,352 .....E 4
† 66601 Willard, 124 .....G 2
66095 Williamsburg, 286 .....G 3
66873 Wilsey, 169 .....F 3
67490 Wilson, 870 .....D 3
66097 Winchester, 492 .....G 2
67491 Windom, 183 .....E 3
67156 Winfield●, 11,405 .....F 4
67764 Winona, 293 .....A 2
67492 Woodbine, 170 .....E 3
67675 Woodston, 211 .....C 2
67882 Wright, 173 .....C 4
66783 Yates Center●, 1,967 .....G 3
67585 Yoder, 155 .....D 4
67159 Zenda, 142 .....D 4
67676 Zurich, 189 .....C 2

● County seat.
‡ Population of metropolitan area.
† Zip of nearest p.o.
* Multiple zips

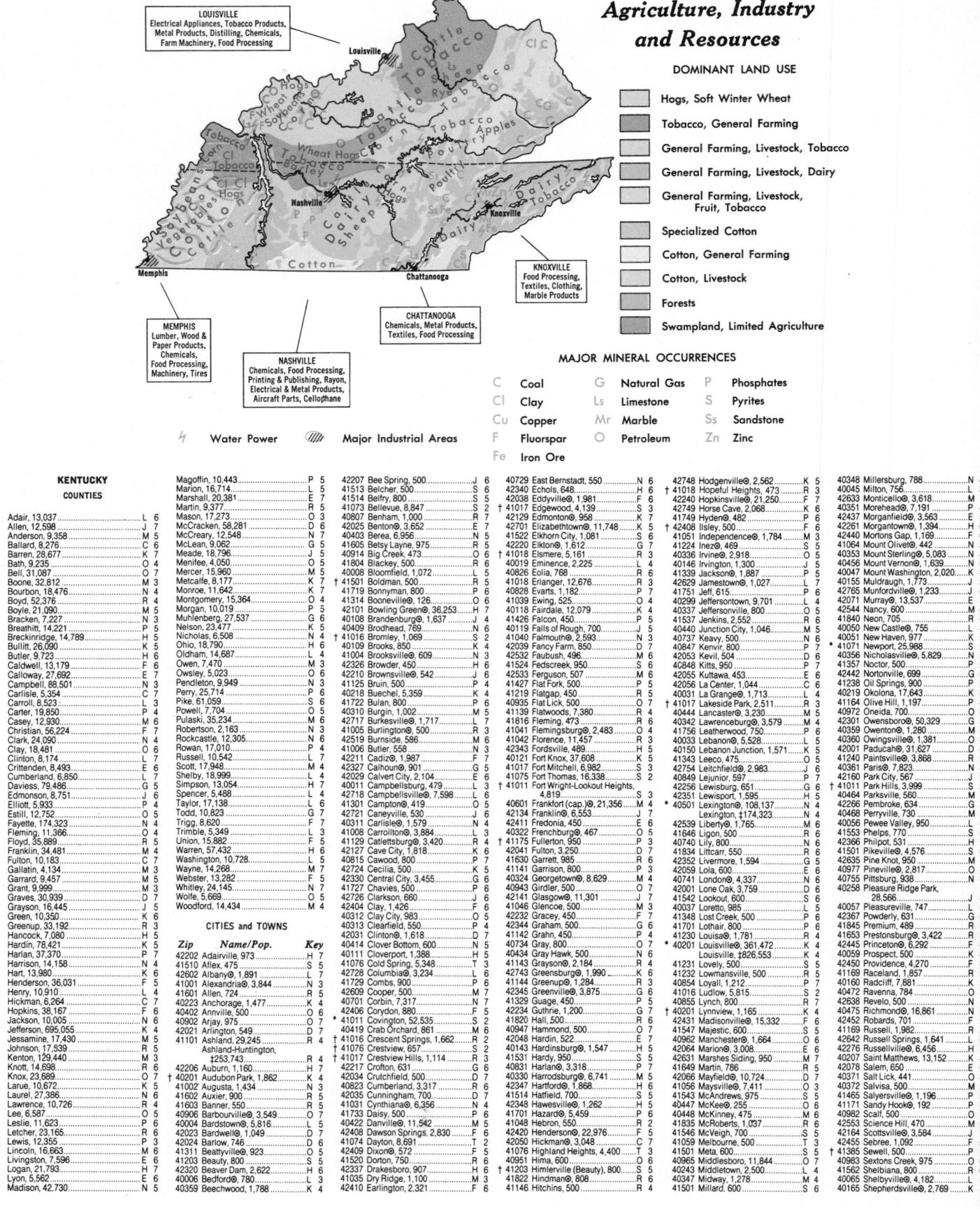

Agriculture, Industry and Resources

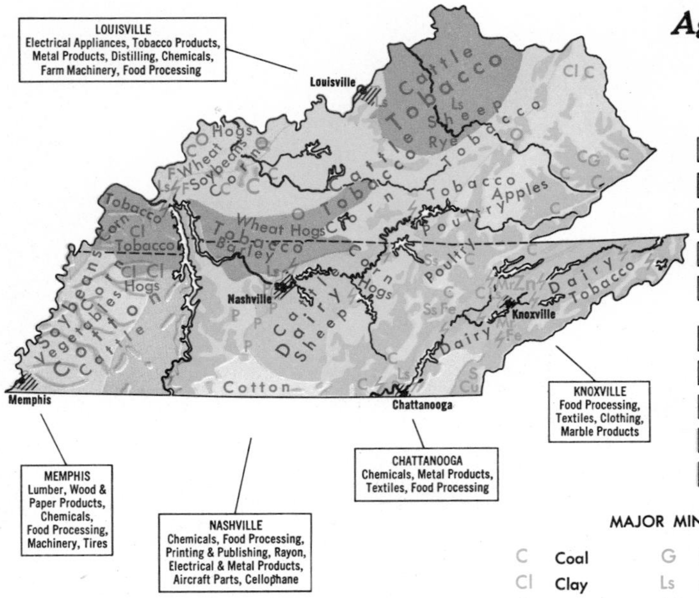
LOUISVILLE
Electrical Appliances, Tobacco Products, Metal Products, Distilling, Chemicals, Farm Machinery, Food Processing
Louisville
Nashville
Knoxville
Memphis
Chattanooga
Cotton
KNOXVILLE
Food Processing, Textiles, Clothing, Marble Products
CHATTANOOGA
Chemicals, Metal Products, Textiles, Food Processing
MEMPHIS
Lumber, Wood & Paper Products, Chemicals, Food Processing, Machinery, Tires
NASHVILLE
Chemicals, Food Processing, Printing & Publishing, Rayon, Electrical & Metal Products, Aircraft Parts, Cellophane

DOMINANT LAND USE

- Hogs, Soft Winter Wheat
- Tobacco, General Farming
- General Farming, Livestock, Tobacco
- General Farming, Livestock, Dairy
- General Farming, Livestock, Fruit, Tobacco
- Specialized Cotton
- Cotton, General Farming
- Cotton, Livestock
- Forests
- Swampland, Limited Agriculture

MAJOR MINERAL OCCURRENCES

C	Coal	G	Natural Gas	P	Phosphates
Cl	Clay	Ls	Limestone	S	Pyrites
Cu	Copper	Mr	Marble	Ss	Sandstone
F	Fluorspar	O	Petroleum	Zn	Zinc
Fe	Iron Ore				

Water Power — Major Industrial Areas

KENTUCKY

COUNTIES

Adair, 13,037 L 6
Allen, 12,598 J 7
Anderson, 9,358 M 5
Ballard, 8,276 C 6
Barren, 28,677 K 7
Bath, 9,235 O 4
Bell, 31,087 O 7
Boone, 32,812 M 3
Bourbon, 18,476 N 4
Boyd, 52,376 R 4
Boyle, 21,090 M 5
Bracken, 7,227 N 3
Breathitt, 14,221 P 5
Breckinridge, 14,789 H 5
Bullitt, 26,090 K 5
Butler, 9,723 H 6
Caldwell, 13,179 F 6
Calloway, 27,692 E 7
Campbell, 88,501 N 3
Carlisle, 5,354 C 7
Carroll, 8,523 L 3
Carter, 19,850 P 4
Casey, 12,930 M 6
Christian, 56,224 F 7
Clark, 24,090 N 4
Clay, 18,481 O 6
Clinton, 8,174 L 7
Crittenden, 8,493 E 6
Cumberland, 6,850 L 7
Daviess, 79,486 G 5
Edmonson, 8,751 J 6
Elliott, 5,933 P 4
Estill, 12,752 O 5
Fayette, 174,323 N 4
Fleming, 11,366 O 4
Floyd, 35,889 R 5
Franklin, 34,481 M 4
Fulton, 10,183 C 7
Gallatin, 4,134 M 3
Garrard, 9,457 M 5
Grant, 9,999 M 3
Graves, 30,939 D 7
Grayson, 16,445 J 5
Green, 10,350 K 6
Greenup, 33,192 R 3
Hancock, 7,080 H 5
Hardin, 78,421 K 5
Harlan, 37,370 P 7
Harrison, 14,158 N 4
Hart, 13,980 K 6
Henderson, 36,031 F 5
Henry, 10,910 L 4
Hickman, 6,264 C 7
Hopkins, 38,167 F 6
Jackson, 10,005 N 6
Jefferson, 695,055 K 4
Jessamine, 17,430 M 5
Johnson, 17,539 R 5
Kenton, 129,440 M 3
Knott, 14,698 R 6
Knox, 23,689 O 7
Larue, 10,672 K 5
Laurel, 27,386 N 6
Lawrence, 10,726 R 4
Lee, 6,587 O 5
Leslie, 11,623 P 6
Letcher, 23,165 R 6
Lewis, 12,355 P 3
Lincoln, 16,663 M 6
Livingston, 7,596 E 6
Logan, 21,793 H 7
Lyon, 5,562 E 6
Madison, 42,730 N 5
Magoffin, 10,443 P 5
Marion, 16,714 L 5
Marshall, 20,381 E 7
Martin, 9,377 R 5
Mason, 17,273 O 3
McCracken, 58,281 D 6
McCreary, 12,548 N 7
McLean, 9,062 G 5
Meade, 18,796 J 5
Menifee, 4,050 O 5
Mercer, 15,960 M 5
Metcalfe, 8,177 K 7
Monroe, 11,642 K 7
Montgomery, 15,364 O 4
Morgan, 10,019 P 5
Muhlenberg, 27,537 G 6
Nelson, 23,477 K 5
Nicholas, 6,508 N 4
Ohio, 18,790 H 6
Oldham, 14,687 L 4
Owen, 7,470 M 3
Owsley, 5,023 O 6
Pendleton, 9,949 N 3
Perry, 25,714 P 6
Pike, 61,059 S 6
Powell, 7,704 O 5
Pulaski, 35,234 M 6
Robertson, 2,163 N 3
Rockcastle, 12,305 N 6
Rowan, 17,010 P 4
Russell, 10,542 L 7
Scott, 17,948 M 4
Shelby, 18,999 L 4
Simpson, 13,054 H 7
Spencer, 5,488 L 4
Taylor, 17,138 L 6
Todd, 10,823 G 7
Trigg, 8,620 F 7
Trimble, 5,349 L 3
Union, 15,882 F 5
Warren, 57,432 H 6
Washington, 10,728 L 5
Wayne, 14,268 M 7
Webster, 13,282 F 5
Whitley, 24,145 N 7
Wolfe, 5,669 O 5
Woodford, 14,434 M 4

CITIES and TOWNS

Zip *Name/Pop.* *Key*

42202 Adairville, 973 H 7
41510 Aflex, 475 S 5
42602 Albany⊙, 1,891 L 7
41001 Alexandria⊙, 3,844 N 3
41601 Allen, 724 R 5
40223 Anchorage, 1,477 K 4
40402 Annville, 500 O 6
40902 Arjay, 975 O 7
42021 Arlington, 549 D 7
41101 Ashland, 29,245 R 4
Ashland-Huntington, ‡253,743 R 4
42206 Auburn, 1,160 H 7
† 40201 Audubon Park, 1,862 K 4
41002 Augusta, 1,434 N 3
41602 Auxier, 900 R 5
41603 Banner, 550 R 5
40906 Barbourville⊙, 3,549 O 7
40004 Bardstown⊙, 5,816 L 5
42023 Bardwell⊙, 1,049 D 7
42024 Barlow, 746 D 6
41311 Beattyville⊙, 923 O 5
41203 Beauty, 800 S 5
42320 Beaver Dam, 2,622 H 6
40006 Bedford⊙, 780 L 3
40359 Beechwood, 1,788 K 4
42207 Bee Spring, 500 J 6
41513 Belcher, 500 S 6
41514 Belfry, 800 S 5
41073 Bellevue, 8,847 S 2
40807 Benham, 1,000 R 7
42025 Benton⊙, 3,652 E 7
40403 Berea, 6,956 N 5
41605 Betsy Layne, 975 R 5
40914 Big Creek, 473 O 6
41804 Blackey, 500 R 6
40008 Bloomfield, 1,072 L 5
† 41501 Boldman, 500 R 5
41719 Bonnyman, 800 P 6
41314 Booneville⊙, 126 O 6
42101 Bowling Green⊙, 36,253 H 7
40108 Brandenburg⊙, 1,637 J 4
40409 Brodhead, 769 N 6
† 41016 Bromley, 1,069 S 2
40109 Brooks, 850 K 4
41004 Brooksville⊙, 609 N 3
42326 Browder, 450 H 6
42210 Brownsville⊙, 542 J 6
41125 Bruin, 500 P 4
40218 Buechel, 5,359 K 4
41722 Bulan, 800 P 6
40310 Burgin, 1,002 M 5
42717 Burkesville⊙, 1,717 L 7
41005 Burlington⊙, 500 R 3
42519 Burnside, 586 M 6
41006 Butler, 558 N 3
42211 Cadiz⊙, 1,987 F 7
42327 Calhoun⊙, 901 G 5
42029 Calvert City, 2,104 E 6
40011 Campbellsburg, 479 L 3
42718 Campbellsville⊙, 7,598 L 6
41301 Campton⊙, 419 O 5
42721 Caneyville, 530 J 6
40311 Carlisle⊙, 1,579 N 4
41008 Carrollton⊙, 3,884 L 3
41129 Catlettsburg⊙, 3,420 R 4
42127 Cave City, 1,818 K 6
40815 Cawood, 800 P 7
42724 Cecilia, 500 K 5
42330 Central City, 3,455 G 6
41727 Chavies, 500 P 6
42726 Clarkson, 660 J 6
42404 Clay, 1,426 F 6
40312 Clay City, 983 O 5
40313 Clearfield, 550 P 4
42031 Clinton⊙, 1,618 D 7
40414 Clover Bottom, 600 N 5
40111 Cloverport, 1,388 H 5
41076 Cold Spring, 5,348 T 3
42728 Columbia⊙, 3,234 L 6
41729 Combs, 900 P 6
42609 Cooper, 500 M 7
40701 Corbin, 7,317 N 7
42406 Corydon, 880 F 5
* 41011 Covington, 52,535 S 2
40419 Crab Orchard, 861 M 6
† 41016 Crescent Springs, 1,662 R 2
† 41076 Crestview, 657 S 2
† 41017 Crestview Hills, 1,114 R 3
42217 Crofton, 631 G 6
42034 Crutchfield, 500 D 7
40823 Cumberland, 3,317 R 6
42035 Cunningham, 700 D 7
41031 Cynthiana⊙, 6,356 N 4
41733 Daisy, 500 P 6
40422 Danville⊙, 11,542 M 5
42408 Dawson Springs, 2,830 F 6
41074 Dayton, 8,691 T 2
42409 Dixon⊙, 572 F 5
41520 Dorton, 750 R 6
42337 Drakesboro, 907 H 6
41035 Dry Ridge, 1,100 M 3
42410 Earlington, 2,321 F 6
40729 East Bernstadt, 550 N 6
42340 Echols, 648 H 6
42038 Eddyville⊙, 1,981 F 6
† 41017 Edgewood, 4,139 S 3
42129 Edmonton⊙, 958 K 7
42701 Elizabethtown⊙, 11,748 K 5
41522 Elkhorn City, 1,081 S 6
42220 Elkton⊙, 1,612 G 7
† 41018 Elsmere, 5,161 R 3
40019 Eminence, 2,225 L 4
40826 Eolia, 768 R 6
41018 Erlanger, 12,676 R 3
40828 Evarts, 1,182 P 7
41039 Ewing, 525 O 4
40118 Fairdale, 12,079 K 4
41426 Falcon, 450 P 5
40119 Falls of Rough, 700 J 5
41040 Falmouth⊙, 2,593 N 3
42039 Fancy Farm, 850 D 7
42532 Faubush, 496 M 6
41524 Fedscreek, 950 S 6
42533 Ferguson, 507 M 6
41427 Flat Fork, 500 P 5
41219 Flatgap, 450 R 5
40935 Flat Lick, 500 O 7
41139 Flatwoods, 7,380 R 4
41816 Fleming, 473 R 6
41041 Flemingsburg⊙, 2,483 O 4
41042 Florence, 11,457 R 3
42343 Fordsville, 489 H 5
40121 Fort Knox, 37,608 K 5
41017 Fort Mitchell, 6,982 S 3
41075 Fort Thomas, 16,338 S 2
† 41011 Fort Wright-Lookout Heights, 4,819 S 3
40601 Frankfort (cap.)⊙, 21,356 M 4
42134 Franklin⊙, 6,553 J 7
42411 Fredonia, 450 E 6
40322 Frenchburg⊙, 467 O 5
† 41175 Fullerton, 950 P 3
42041 Fulton, 3,250 D 7
41630 Garrett, 985 R 6
41141 Garrison, 800 P 3
40324 Georgetown⊙, 8,629 M 4
40943 Girdler, 500 O 7
42141 Glasgow⊙, 11,301 J 7
41046 Glencoe, 500 M 3
42232 Gracey, 450 F 7
42344 Graham, 500 G 6
41142 Grahn, 450 P 4
40734 Gray, 800 O 7
40434 Gray Hawk, 500 N 6
41143 Grayson⊙, 2,184 R 4
42743 Greensburg⊙, 1,990 K 6
41144 Greenup⊙, 1,284 R 3
42345 Greenville⊙, 3,875 G 6
41329 Guage, 450 P 5
42234 Guthrie, 1,200 G 7
41820 Hall, 500 R 6
40947 Hammond, 500 O 7
42048 Hardin, 522 E 7
40143 Hardinsburg⊙, 1,547 H 5
41531 Hardy, 950 S 5
40831 Harlan⊙, 3,318 P 7
40330 Harrodsburg⊙, 6,741 M 5
42347 Hartford⊙, 1,868 H 6
41514 Hatfield, 700 S 5
42348 Hawesville⊙, 1,262 H 5
41701 Hazard⊙, 5,459 P 6
41048 Hebron, 550 R 2
42420 Henderson⊙, 22,976 F 5
42050 Hickman⊙, 3,048 C 7
41076 Highland Heights, 4,400 T 3
40951 Hima, 600 O 6
† 41203 Himlerville (Beauty), 800 S 5
41822 Hindman⊙, 808 R 6
41146 Hitchins, 500 R 4
42748 Hodgenville⊙, 2,562 K 5
† 41018 Hopeful Heights, 473 R 3
42240 Hopkinsville⊙, 21,250 F 7
42749 Horse Cave, 2,068 K 6
41749 Hyden⊙, 482 P 6
† 42408 Ilsley, 500 F 6
41051 Independence⊙, 1,784 M 3
41224 Inez⊙, 469 S 5
40336 Irvine⊙, 2,918 O 5
40146 Irvington, 1,300 J 5
41339 Jackson⊙, 1,887 P 5
42629 Jamestown⊙, 1,027 L 7
41751 Jeff, 615 P 6
40299 Jeffersontown, 9,701 L 4
40337 Jeffersonville, 800 O 5
41537 Jenkins, 2,552 R 6
40440 Junction City, 1,046 M 5
40737 Keavy, 500 N 6
40847 Kenvir, 800 P 7
42053 Kevil, 504 D 6
40848 Kitts, 950 P 7
42055 Kuttawa, 453 E 6
42056 La Center, 1,044 C 6
40031 La Grange⊙, 1,713 L 4
† 41017 Lakeside Park, 2,511 R 3
40444 Lancaster⊙, 3,230 M 5
40342 Lawrenceburg⊙, 3,579 M 4
41756 Leatherwood, 750 P 6
40033 Lebanon⊙, 5,528 L 5
40150 Lebanon Junction, 1,571 K 5
41343 Leeco, 475 O 5
42754 Leitchfield⊙, 2,983 J 6
40849 Lejunior, 597 P 7
42256 Lewisburg, 651 G 6
42351 Lewisport, 1,595 H 5
* 40501 Lexington⊙, 108,137 N 4
Lexington, ‡174,323 N 4
42539 Liberty⊙, 1,765 M 6
41646 Ligon, 500 R 6
40740 Lily, 800 N 6
41834 Littcarr, 550 R 6
42352 Livermore, 1,594 G 5
42059 Lola, 600 E 6
40741 London⊙, 4,337 N 6
42001 Lone Oak, 3,759 D 6
41542 Lookout, 600 S 6
40037 Loretto, 985 L 5
41348 Lost Creek, 500 P 6
41701 Lothair, 800 P 6
41230 Louisa⊙, 1,781 R 4
* 40201 Louisville⊙, 361,472 K 4
Louisville, ‡826,553 K 4
41231 Lovely, 500 S 5
41232 Lowmansville, 500 R 5
40854 Loyall, 1,212 P 7
41016 Ludlow, 5,815 S 2
40855 Lynch, 800 R 7
† 40201 Lynnview, 1,165 K 4
42431 Madisonville⊙, 15,332 F 6
41547 Majestic, 600 S 5
40962 Manchester⊙, 1,664 O 6
42064 Marion⊙, 3,008 E 6
42631 Marshes Siding, 950 M 7
41649 Martin, 786 R 5
42066 Mayfield⊙, 10,724 D 7
41056 Maysville⊙, 7,411 O 3
41543 McAndrews, 975 S 5
40447 McKee⊙, 255 O 6
40448 McKinney, 475 M 6
41835 McRoberts, 1,037 R 6
41546 McVeigh, 700 S 5
41059 Melbourne, 500 T 3
41501 Meta, 600 S 5
40965 Middlesboro, 11,844 O 7
40243 Middletown, 2,500 L 4
40347 Midway, 1,278 M 4
41501 Millard, 600 S 6
40348 Millersburg, 788 N 4
40045 Milton, 756 L 3
42633 Monticello⊙, 3,618 M 7
40351 Morehead⊙, 7,191 P 4
42437 Morganfield⊙, 3,563 E 5
42261 Morgantown⊙, 1,394 H 6
42440 Mortons Gap, 1,169 F 6
41064 Mount Olivet⊙, 442 N 3
40353 Mount Sterling⊙, 5,083 N 4
40456 Mount Vernon⊙, 1,639 N 6
40047 Mount Washington, 2,020 K 4
40155 Muldraugh, 1,773 J 5
42765 Munfordville⊙, 1,233 J 6
42071 Murray⊙, 13,537 E 7
42544 Nancy, 600 M 6
41840 Neon, 705 R 6
40050 New Castle⊙, 755 L 4
40051 New Haven, 977 K 5
* 41071 Newport, 25,988 S 2
40356 Nicholasville⊙, 5,829 N 5
41357 Noctor, 500 P 5
42442 Nortonville, 699 G 6
41238 Oil Springs, 900 P 5
40219 Okolona, 17,643 K 4
41164 Olive Hill, 1,197 P 4
40972 Oneida, 700 O 6
42301 Owensboro⊙, 50,329 G 5
40359 Owenton⊙, 1,280 M 3
40360 Owingsville⊙, 1,381 O 4
42001 Paducah⊙, 31,627 D 6
41240 Paintsville⊙, 3,868 R 5
40361 Paris⊙, 7,823 N 4
42160 Park City, 567 J 6
† 41011 Park Hills, 3,999 S 2
40464 Parksville, 560 M 5
42266 Pembroke, 634 G 7
40468 Perryville, 730 M 5
40056 Pewee Valley, 950 L 4
41553 Phelps, 770 S 6
42366 Philpot, 531 H 5
41501 Pikeville⊙, 4,576 S 6
42635 Pine Knot, 950 M 7
40977 Pineville⊙, 2,817 O 7
40755 Pittsburg, 938 N 6
40258 Pleasure Ridge Park, 28,566 J 4
40057 Pleasureville, 747 L 4
42367 Powderly, 631 G 6
41845 Premium, 489 R 6
41653 Prestonsburg⊙, 3,422 R 5
42445 Princeton⊙, 6,292 F 6
40059 Prospect, 500 K 4
42450 Providence, 4,270 F 6
41169 Raceland, 1,857 R 3
40160 Radcliff, 7,881 K 5
40472 Ravenna, 784 O 5
42638 Revelo, 500 N
40475 Richmond⊙, 16,861 N 5
42452 Robards, 701 F
41169 Russell, 1,982 R
42642 Russell Springs, 1,641 L
42276 Russellville⊙, 6,456 H
40207 Saint Matthews, 13,152 K
42078 Salem, 650 E
40371 Salt Lick, 441 O
40372 Salvisa, 500 M
41465 Salyersville⊙, 1,196 P
41171 Sandy Hook⊙, 192 P
40982 Scalf, 500 O
42553 Science Hill, 470 M
42164 Scottsville⊙, 3,584 J
42455 Sebree, 1,092 F
† 41385 Sewell, 500 P
40983 Sextons Creek, 975 O
41562 Shelbiana, 800 R
40065 Shelbyville⊙, 4,182 L
40165 Shepherdsville⊙, 2,769 K

KENTUCKY

AREA 40,395 sq. mi.
POPULATION 3,219,311
CAPITAL Frankfort
LARGEST CITY Louisville
HIGHEST POINT Black Mtn. 4,145 ft.
SETTLED IN 1774
ADMITTED TO UNION June 1, 1792
POPULAR NAME Blue Grass State
STATE FLOWER Goldenrod
STATE BIRD Cardinal

TENNESSEE

AREA 42,244 sq. mi.
POPULATION 3,924,164
CAPITAL Nashville
LARGEST CITY Memphis
HIGHEST POINT Clingmans Dome 6,643 ft.
SETTLED IN 1757
ADMITTED TO UNION June 1, 1796
POPULAR NAME Volunteer State
STATE FLOWER Iris
STATE BIRD Mockingbird

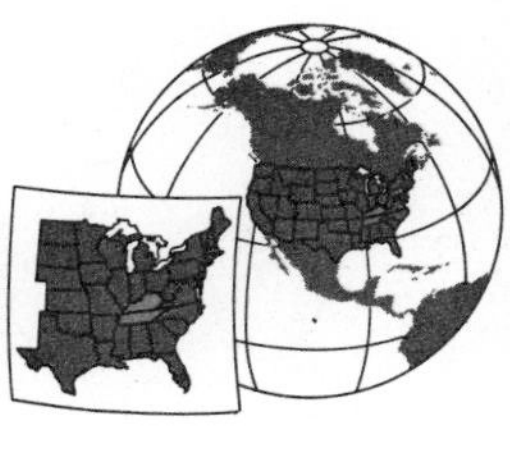

40216	Shively, 19,223	K 4
40984	Sibert, 500	O 6
41085	Silver Grove, 1,365	T 3
40067	Simpsonville, 628	L 4
41763	Slemp, 500	P 6
41764	Smilax, 856	P 6
42081	Smithland⊙, 514	E 6
42171	Smiths Grove, 756	J 6
42646	Smith Town, 500	M 7
41173	Soldier, 600	P 4
42501	Somerset⊙, 10,436	M 6
41071	Southgate, 3,212	S 2
41174	South Portsmouth, 950	P 3
41175	South Shore, 676	R 3
25661	South Williamson, 850	S 5
42458	Spottsville, 914	G 5
40069	Springfield⊙, 2,961	L 5
41256	Staffordsville, 700	R 5
40484	Stanford⊙, 2,474	M 5
40380	Stanton⊙, 2,037	O 5
42647	Stearns, 900	N 7
40170	Stephensport, 500	H 5
41567	Stone, 850	S 5
42459	Sturgis, 2,210	F 5
42558	Tateville, 680	M 7
41011	Taylor Mill, 3,253	S 3
40071	Taylorsville⊙, 897	L 4
41259	Thealka, 550	R 5
41189	Tollesboro, 500	O 3
42167	Tompkinsville⊙, 2,207	K 7
42286	Trenton, 496	G 7
40486	Tyner, 590	O 6
41091	Union, 500	M 3
42461	Uniontown, 1,255	F 5
42784	Upton, 552	K 6
40272	Valley Station, 24,471	K 4
41179	Vanceburg⊙, 1,773	P 3
41265	Van Lear, 1,033	R 5
40872	Verda, 950	P 7
41092	Verona, 500	M 3
40383	Versailles⊙, 5,679	M 4
41017	Villa Hills, 1,647	R 2
40175	Vine Grove, 2,987	K 5
41572	Virgie, 600	R 6
41094	Walton, 1,801	M 3
41095	Warsaw⊙, 1,232	M 3
41667	Weeksbury, 950	R 6
41472	West Liberty⊙, 1,387	P 5
40177	West Point, 1,741	J 4
42564	West Somerset, 850	M 6
41268	West Van Lear, 975	R 5
41101	Westwood, 2,900	R 4
41669	Wheelwright, 793	R 6
42464	White Plains, 729	G 6
41858	Whitesburg⊙, 1,137	R 6
42378	Whitesville, 752	H 5
42653	Whitley City⊙, 1,060	N 7
42087	Wickliffe⊙, 1,211	C 7
41071	Wilders, 823	S 3
40769	Williamsburg⊙, 3,687	N 7
41097	Williamstown⊙, 2,063	M 3
40390	Wilmore, 3,466	M 5
40391	Winchester⊙, 13,402	N 4
42088	Wingo, 593	D 7
41011	Winston Park, 578	S 3
41394	Wolverine, 500	P 5
40771	Woodbine, 700	N 7
42001	Woodlawn, 1,639	D 6
41071	Woodlawn, 525	S 2
41776	Wooton, 750	P 6
41183	Worthington, 1,364	R 3
41501	Zebulon, 800	R 5

TENNESSEE

COUNTIES

Anderson, 60,300	N 8
Bedford, 25,039	J 9
Benton, 12,126	E 8
Bledsoe, 7,643	L 9
Blount, 63,744	O 9
Bradley, 50,686	M 10
Campbell, 26,045	N 8
Cannon, 8,467	J 9
Carroll, 25,741	E 9
Carter, 42,575	S 8
Cheatham, 13,199	G 8
Chester, 9,927	D 10
Claiborne, 19,420	O 8
Clay, 6,624	K 7
Cocke, 25,283	P 9
Coffee, 32,572	J 9
Crockett, 14,402	C 9
Cumberland, 20,733	L 9
Davidson, 447,877	H 8
Decatur, 9,457	E 9
De Kalb, 11,151	K 9
Dickson, 21,977	G 8
Dyer, 30,427	C 8
Fayette, 22,692	C 10
Fentress, 12,593	M 8
Franklin, 27,244	J 10
Gibson, 47,871	D 9
Giles, 22,138	G 10
Grainger, 13,948	O 8
Greene, 47,630	R 8
Grundy, 10,631	K 10
Hamblen, 38,696	P 8
Hamilton, 254,236	L 10
Hancock, 6,719	P 7
Hardeman, 22,435	C 10
Hardin, 18,212	E 10
Hawkins, 33,726	P 8
Haywood, 19,596	C 9
Henderson, 17,291	E 9
Henry, 23,749	E 8
Hickman, 12,096	G 9
Houston, 5,845	F 8
Humphreys, 13,560	F 8
Jackson, 8,141	K 8
Jefferson, 24,940	P 8
Johnson, 11,569	T 7
Knox, 276,293	O 9
Lake, 7,896	B 8
Lauderdale, 20,271	B 9
Lawrence, 29,097	G 10
Lewis, 6,761	F 9
Lincoln, 24,318	H 10
Loudon, 24,266	N 9
Macon, 12,315	J 7
Madison, 65,727	D 9
Marion, 20,577	K 10
Marshall, 17,319	H 10
Maury, 43,376	G 9
McMinn, 35,462	M 10
McNairy, 18,369	D 10
Meigs, 5,219	M 9
Monroe, 23,475	N 10
Montgomery, 62,721	G 8
Moore, 3,568	J 10
Morgan, 13,619	M 8
Obion, 29,936	C 8
Overton, 14,866	L 8
Perry, 5,238	F 9
Pickett, 3,774	M 7
Polk, 11,669	N 10
Putnam, 35,487	K 8
Rhea, 17,202	M 9
Roane, 38,881	M 9
Robertson, 29,102	H 7
Rutherford, 59,428	J 9
Scott, 14,762	M 8
Sequatchie, 6,331	L 10
Sevier, 28,241	O 9
Shelby, 722,014	B 10
Smith, 12,509	J 8
Stewart, 7,319	F 7
Sullivan, 127,329	S 7
Sumner, 56,106	J 8
Tipton, 28,001	B 9
Trousdale, 5,155	J 8
Unicoi, 15,254	S 8
Union, 9,072	O 8
Van Buren, 3,758	L 9
Warren, 26,972	K 9
Washington, 73,924	R 8
Wayne, 12,365	F 10
Weakley, 28,827	D 8
White, 17,088	L 9
Williamson, 34,330	H 9
Wilson, 36,999	J 8

CITIES and TOWNS

	Zip	*Name/Pop.*	*Key*
	37010	Adams, 458	G 7
	38310	Adamsville, 1,344	E 10
	37616	Afton, 550	R 8
	38001	Alamo⊙, 2,499	C 9
	37701	Alcoa, 7,739	N 9
	37012	Alexandria, 680	J 8
	38501	Algood, 1,808	K 8
	38504	Allardt, 610	M 8
	38541	Allons, 600	L 8
	37301	Altamont⊙, 546	K 10
	38449	Ardmore, 601	H 10
	38002	Arlington, 1,349	B 10
	38506	Armathwaite, 625	M 8
	37707	Arthur, 500	O 7
	37015	Ashland City⊙, 2,027	G 8
	37303	Athens⊙, 11,790	M 10
	38004	Atoka, 446	B 10
	38220	Atwood, 937	D 9
	37304	Bakewell, 600	L 10
†	37650	Banner Hill, 2,517	R 8
	38005	Bartlett, 1,150	B 10
	38311	Bath Springs, 725	E 10
	38544	Baxter, 1,229	K 8
	37708	Bean Station, 500	P 8
	37018	Beechgrove, 600	J 9
	37305	Beersheba Springs, 560	K 10
	37205	Belle Meade	H 8
	38006	Bells, 1,474	C 9
	38314	Bemis, 1,883	D 9
	37307	Benton⊙, 749	M 10
†	37201	Berry Hill	H 8
†	37027	Berry's Chapel, 1,345	H 9
	38315	Bethel Springs, 781	D 10
	38221	Big Sandy, 539	E 8
	37308	Birchwood, 900	M 10
	37709	Blaine, 650	O 8
	37660	Bloomingdale, 3,120	R 7
	38545	Bloomington Springs, 800	K 8
	37617	Blountville⊙, 900	S 7
	37618	Bluff City, 947	S 8
	38008	Bolivar⊙, 6,674	C 10
	38316	Bradford, 968	D 8
	37658	Braemar-Hampton, 1,100	S 8
	37027	Brentwood, 1,091	H 8
	37710	Briceville, 850	N 8
	38011	Brighton, 952	B 10
	37620	Bristol, 20,064	S 7
	38012	Brownsville⊙, 7,011	C 9
	38317	Bruceton, 1,450	E 8
	38014	Brunswick, 500	B 10
	38318	Buena Vista, 500	E 9
	37711	Bulls Gap, 774	P 8
	37640	Butler, 500	T 8
	38549	Byrdstown⊙, 582	L 7
	37309	Calhoun, 624	M 10
	38320	Camden⊙, 3,052	E 8
	38129	Capleville, 450	B 10
	37030	Carthage⊙, 2,491	K 8
	37714	Caryville, 648	N 8
	38551	Celina⊙, 1,370	K 7
	37033	Centerville⊙, 2,592	G 9
	37034	Chapel Hill, 752	H 9
	37310	Charleston, 792	M 10
	37036	Charlotte⊙, 610	G 8
*	37401	Chattanooga⊙, 119,082	K 10
		Chattanooga, ‡304,927	K 10
	37642	Church Hill, 2,822	R 7
	37715	Clairfield, 650	O 7
	38553	Clarkrange, 675	L 8
	37040	Clarksville⊙, 31,719	G 7
	37311	Cleveland⊙, 20,651	M 10
	38425	Clifton, 737	F 10
	37716	Clinton⊙, 4,794	N 8
	37719	Coalfield, 712	N 8
	37313	Coalmont, 518	K 10
	37314	Cokercreek, 500	N 10
	37315	Collegedale, 3,031	M 10
	38017	Collierville, 3,625	B 10
	38450	Collinwood, 922	F 10
	37663	Colonial Heights, 3,027	R 8
	38401	Columbia⊙, 21,471	G 9
	37720	Concord, 500	N 9
	38501	Cookeville⊙, 14,270	L 8
	37317	Copperhill, 563	N 10
	38018	Cordova, 600	B 10
	37047	Cornersville, 655	H 10
	37721	Corryton, 500	O 8
	38326	Counce, 975	E 10
	38019	Covington⊙, 5,801	B 9
	37318	Cowan, 1,772	K 10
	37723	Crab Orchard, 900	M 9
	38555	Crossville⊙, 5,381	L 9
	37051	Cumberland Furnace, 800	G 8
	38452	Cypress Inn, 500	F 10
	37725	Dandridge⊙, 1,270	O 8
	37321	Dayton⊙, 4,361	L 9
	37322	Decatur⊙, 698	M 9
	38329	Decaturville⊙, 958	E 9
	37324	Decherd, 2,148	J 10
	37055	Dickson, 5,665	G 8
	37214	Donelson	H 8
	37058	Dover⊙, 1,179	F 8
	38559	Doyle, 1,205	K 9
	38225	Dresden⊙, 1,939	D 8
	38023	Drummonds, 700	A 10
	37326	Ducktown, 562	N 10
	37327	Dunlap⊙, 1,672	L 10
	38330	Dyer, 2,501	D 8
	38024	Dyersburg⊙, 14,523	C 8
†	37801	Eagleton, 5,345	O 9
†	37311	East Cleveland, 1,870	M 10
	37412	East Ridge, 21,799	L 11
	37732	Elgin, 500	M 8
	37643	Elizabethton⊙, 12,269	S 8
	37734	Elk Valley, 750	N 7
	38029	Ellendale, 1,500	B 10
†	37601	Embreeville Junction, 1,293	R 8
	37735	Emory Gap, 500	M 9
	37329	Englewood, 1,878	M 10
	37061	Erin⊙, 1,157	F 8
	37650	Erwin⊙, 4,715	S 8
	37330	Estill Springs, 919	J 10
	38456	Ethridge, 600	G 10
	37331	Etowah, 3,736	M 10
	37332	Evensville, 475	M 9
	37062	Fairview, 1,630	G 9
	37656	Fall Branch, 825	R 8
	37334	Fayetteville⊙, 7,030	H 10
	38030	Finley, 950	B 8
	37335	Flintville, 500	H 10
	38031	Forest Hill, 850	B 10
†	37201	Forest Hills	H 8
	38032	Fort Pillow, 700	B 9
	37064	Franklin⊙, 9,404	H 9
	38034	Friendship, 441	C 9
	37737	Friendsville, 575	N 9
	38337	Gadsden, 523	D 9
	38562	Gainesboro⊙, 1,101	K 8
	37066	Gallatin⊙, 13,093	H 8
	38037	Gates, 523	C 9
	37738	Gatlinburg, 2,329	O 9
	38038	Germantown, 3,474	B 10
	37071	Gladeville, 500	J 8
	38229	Gleason, 1,314	D 8
	37072	Goodlettsville	H 8
	38563	Gordonsville, 601	K 8
	37337	Grandview, 1,250	M 9
	37338	Graysville, 951	L 10
	37073	Green Brier, 2,279	H 8
	37743	Greeneville⊙, 13,722	R 8
	38230	Greenfield, 2,050	D 8
	38565	Grimsley, 500	L 2
	37339	Gruetli, 910	K 10
†	37766	Habersham, 800	N 8
	38040	Halls, 2,323	C 9
	38461	Hampshire, 500	G 9
	37658	Hampton-Braemar, 1,100	S 8
	37748	Harriman, 8,734	M 9
	37341	Harrison, 500	L 10
	37752	Harrogate, 950	O 8
	37074	Hartsville⊙, 2,243	J 8
	37755	Helenwood, 675	M 8
	38340	Henderson⊙, 3,581	D 10
	38041	Henning, 605	B 9
	37343	Hixson, 6,188	L 10
	38462	Hohenwald⊙, 3,385	F 9
	38342	Hollow Rock, 722	E 8
	38343	Humboldt, 10,066	D 9
	38344	Huntingdon⊙, 3,661	E 8
	37345	Huntland, 849	J 10
	37756	Huntsville⊙, 337	N 8
	37079	Indian Mound, 600	F 7
†	37201	Inglewood ■	H 8
	38463	Iron City, 504	F 10
	37757	Jacksboro⊙, 689	N 8
	38301	Jackson⊙, 39,996	D 9
	38556	Jamestown⊙, 1,899	M 8
	37347	Jasper⊙, 1,811	K 10
	37760	Jefferson City, 5,124	P 8
	37762	Jellico, 2,235	N 7
	37601	Johnson City, 33,770	S 8
	37659	Jonesboro⊙, 1,510	R 8
	37921	Karns, 1,105	N 9
	38233	Kenton, 1,439	C 8
†	34347	Kimball, 807	K 10
*	37660	Kingsport, 31,938	R 7
	37763	Kingston⊙, 4,142	N 9
*	37901	Knoxville⊙, 174,587	O 9
		Knoxville, ‡400,337	O 9
	37349	Laager, 675	K 10
	37083	Lafayette⊙, 2,583	J 7
	37766	La Follette, 6,902	N 8
	37769	Lake City, 1,923	N 8
	37416	Lake Hills-Murray Hills, 7,806	L 10
†	37138	Lakewood, 2,500	H 8
	37086	La Vergne, 2,825	H 9
	38464	Lawrenceburg⊙, 8,889	G 10
	37087	Lebanon⊙, 12,492	J 8
	37771	Lenoir City, 5,324	N 9
	37091	Lewisburg⊙, 7,207	H 10
	38351	Lexington⊙, 4,955	E 9
	37681	Limestone, 500	R 8
	37096	Linden⊙, 1,062	F 9
	38570	Livingston⊙, 3,050	L 8
	37097	Lobelville, 773	F 9
†	37662	Long Island, 1,352	S 7
	37350	Lookout Mountain, 1,741	L 11
	38469	Loretto, 1,375	G 10
	37774	Loudon⊙, 3,728	N 9
	37777	Louisville, 500	N 9
	37351	Lupton City, 750	L 10
	37779	Luttrell, 819	O 8
	38471	Lutts, 850	F 10

(continued on following page)

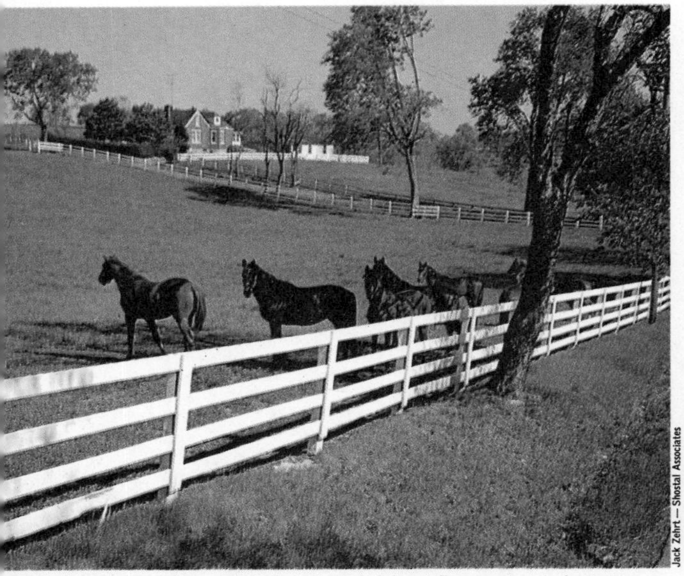

Jack Zehrt — Shostal Associates

Sleek racehorses enjoy a patch of shade on a Calumet Farm pasture in Lexington, Kentucky. More than half the country's winning racehorses are from Inner Bluegrass area farms.

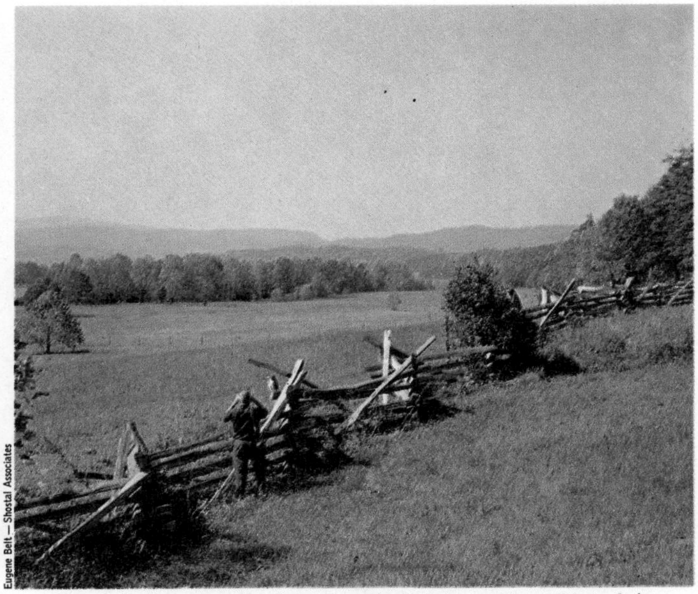

Eugene Bell — Shostal Associates

Using field glasses to bridge the gap, a naturalist observes the wildlife in Cades Cove, Tennessee. Mist-shrouded Great Smoky Mountains are in the distance.

Topography

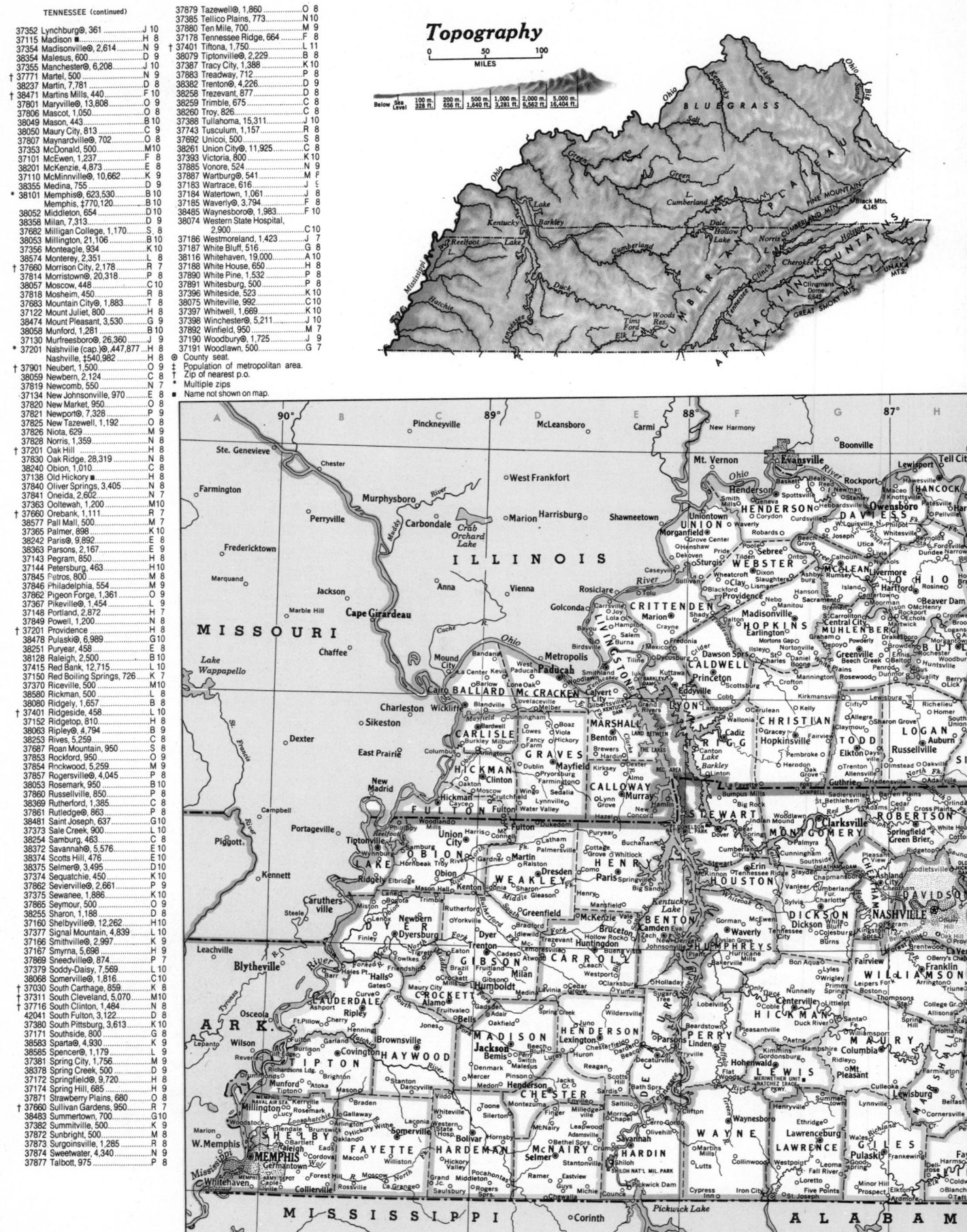

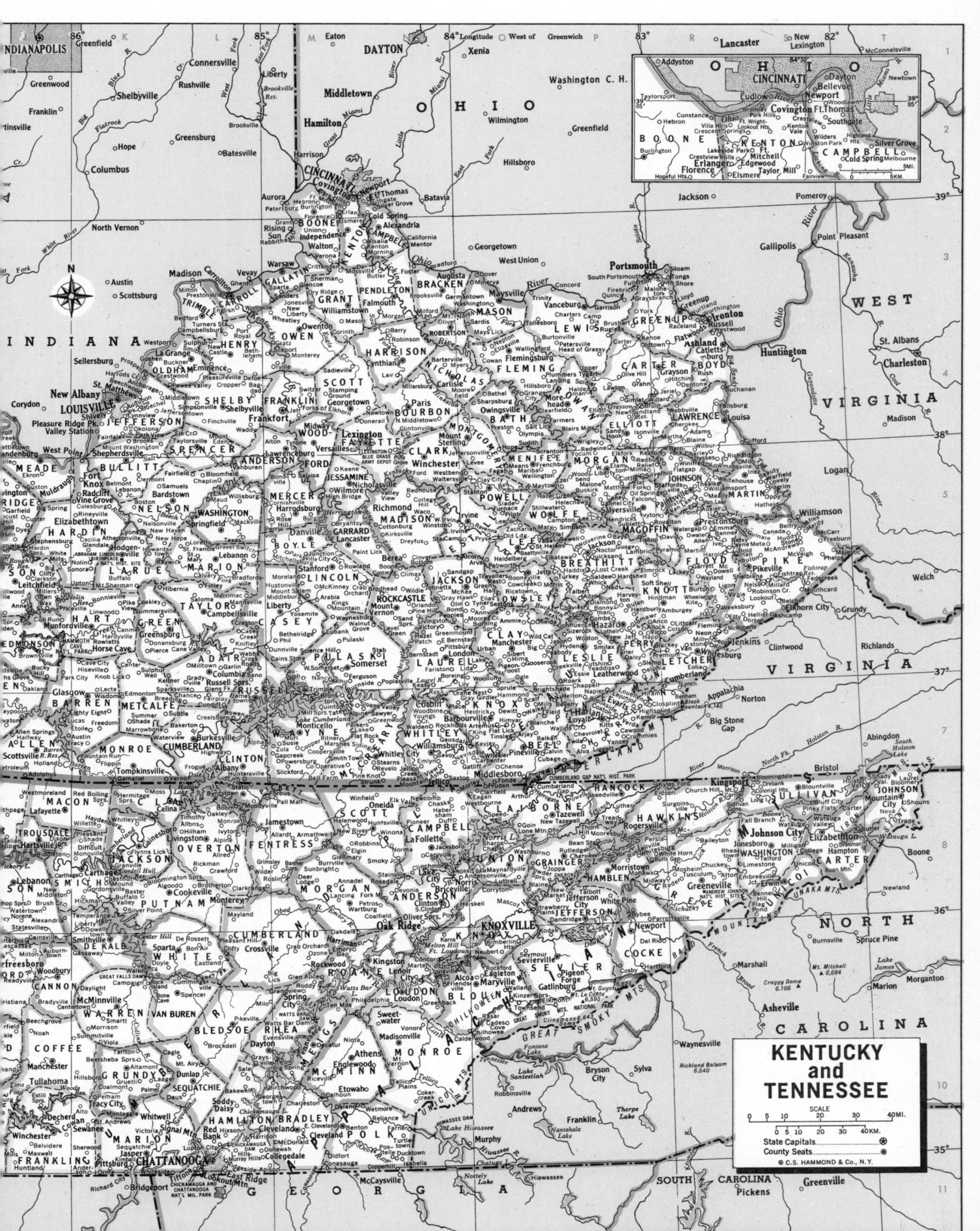

KENTUCKY
and
TENNESSEE

SCALE

0 5 10   20   30   40 MI.

0 5 10 20 30 40 KM.

State Capitals............................⊛
County Seats..............................⊛

© C.S. HAMMOND & Co., N.Y.

Topography

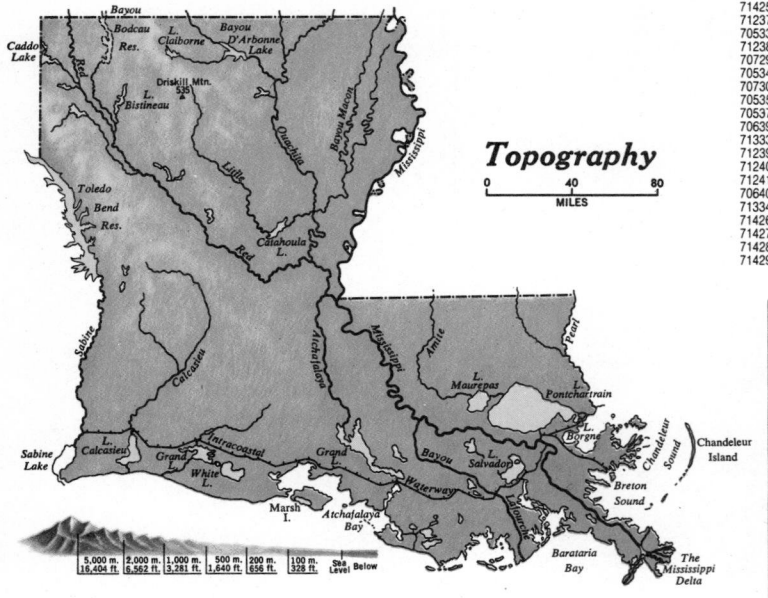

0   40   80
MILES

LOUISIANA

SCALE
0 5 10   20   30   40 MI.

0 5 10   20   30   40 KM.

State Capitals............⊛
Parish Seats.............⊚
Canals....................

© C.S. HAMMOND & Co., N.Y.

644 Grant, 225 ....E 5
359 Gray, 750 ....J 7
435 Grayson, 516 ....F 2
441 Greensburg◉, 652 ......J 5
739 Greenwell Springs, 225 .K 1
033 Greenwood, 212 ....O 4
053 Gretna◉, 24,875 ....O 7
740 Grosse Tete, 710 ......G 6
542 Gueydan, 1,984 ....D 7
730 Gurley, 150 ....H 5
645 Hackberry, 750 ....B 7
057 Hahnville◉, 2,483 .....N 4
246 Haile, 300 ....F 1
034 Hall Summit, 190 ......D 2
401 Hammond, 12,487 ....K 5
083 Happy Jack, 800 ....L 7
123 Harahan, 13,037 ....N 4
340 Harrisonburg◉, 626 ....G 3
058 Harvey, 6,347 ....O 7
037 Haughton, 885 ....C 1

70646 Hayes, 800 ....E 6
71038 Haynesville, 3,055 ..D 1
70462 Head of Island, 420 .L 2
71436 Hebert, 150 ....G 2
71039 Heflin, 314 ....D 2
71341 Hessmer, 454 ....F 4
70743 Hester, 280 ....L 3
71437 Hicks, 369 ....E 4
71247 Hodge, 818 ....E 2
† 70663 Hollywood, 2,328 ..D 6
70744 Holden, 750 ....M 1
70546 Holly Ridge, 200 ....G 2
† 70083 Homeplace, 600 ....L 8
71040 Homer◉, 4,483 ....D 1
71439 Hornbeck, 525 ....D 4
71043 Hosston, 428 ....C 1
70360 Houma◉, 30,922 ......J 7
† 70356 Humphreys, 900 ....J 7
70746 Iberville, 221 ......K 2
71044 Ida, 370 ....C 1

70443 Independence, 1,770 .M 1
70747 Innis, 300 ....G 5
70543 Iota, 1,271 ....E 6
70647 Iowa, 1,944 ....D 6
† 70427 Isabel, 365 ....K 5
70748 Jackson, 4,697 ......H 5
71045 Jamestown, 153 ......D 2
70544 Jeanerette, 6,322 ...G 7
70121 Jefferson Heights, 16,489 ....O 4
71342 Jena◉, 2,389 ....F 3
70546 Jennings◉, 11,783 ...E 6
71249 Jigger, 400 ....G 2
† 70631 Johnsons Bayou, 300 .C 7
71250 Jones, 200 ....E 1
71251 Jonesboro◉, 5,072 ...E 2
71343 Jonesville, 2,761 ...G 3
71440 Joyce, 365 ....E 3
71749 Junction City, 733 ..E 1
70548 Kaplan, 5,540 ....F 6
71046 Keatchie, 328 ....C 2

(continued on following page)

AREA 48,523 sq. mi.
POPULATION 3,643,180
CAPITAL Baton Rouge
LARGEST CITY New Orleans
HIGHEST POINT Driskill Mtn. 535 ft.
SETTLED IN 1699
ADMITTED TO UNION April 30, 1812
POPULAR NAME Pelican State
STATE FLOWER Magnolia
STATE BIRD Eastern Brown Pelican

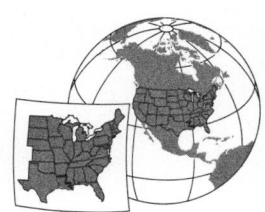

176 Louisiana

(continued)

Agriculture, Industry and Resources

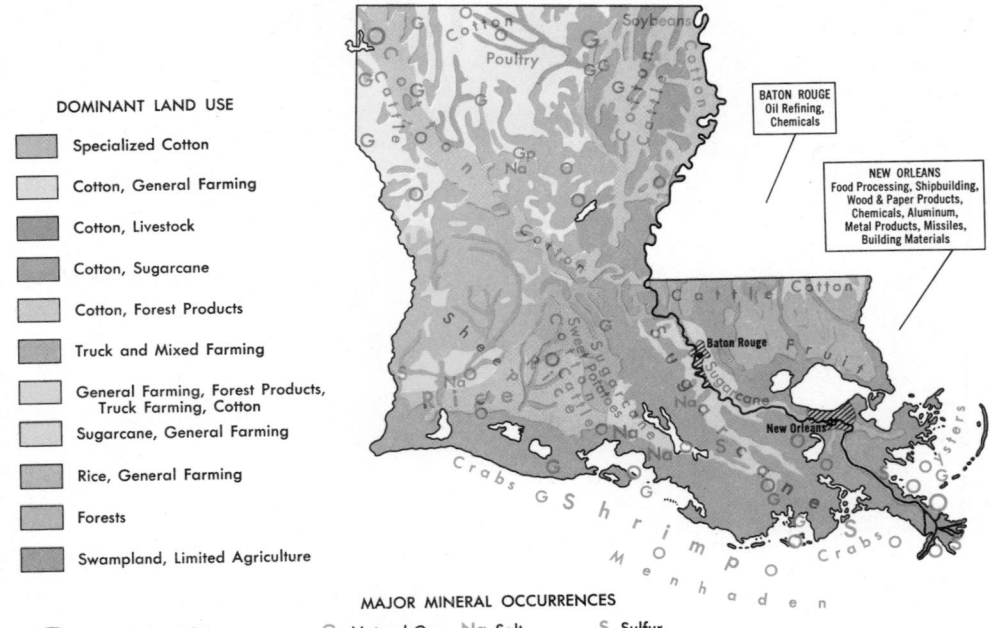

DOMINANT LAND USE

- Specialized Cotton
- Cotton, General Farming
- Cotton, Livestock
- Cotton, Sugarcane
- Cotton, Forest Products
- Truck and Mixed Farming
- General Farming, Forest Products, Truck Farming, Cotton
- Sugarcane, General Farming
- Rice, General Farming
- Forests
- Swampland, Limited Agriculture

Major Industrial Areas

BATON ROUGE Oil Refining, Chemicals

NEW ORLEANS Food Processing, Shipbuilding, Wood & Paper Products, Chemicals, Aluminum, Metal Products, Missiles, Building Materials

MAJOR MINERAL OCCURRENCES

G Natural Gas	Na Salt	S Sulfur
Gp Gypsum	O Petroleum	

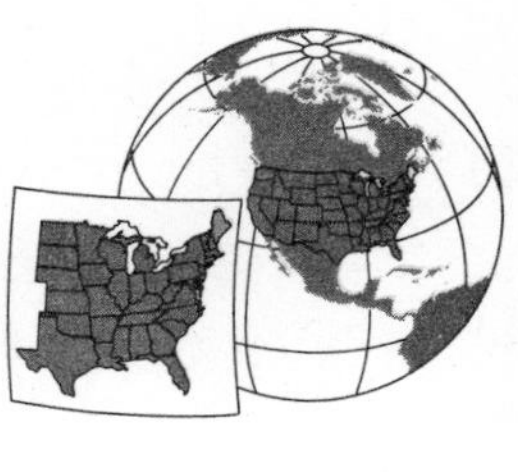

AREA 33,215 sq. mi.
POPULATION 993,663
CAPITAL Augusta
LARGEST CITY Portland
HIGHEST POINT Katahdin 5,268 ft.
SETTLED IN 1624
ADMITTED TO UNION March 15, 1820
POPULAR NAME Pine Tree State
STATE FLOWER Pine Cone & Tassel
STATE BIRD Chickadee

COUNTIES

Androscoggin, 91,279	C 7
Aroostook, 92,463	F 2
Cumberland, 192,528	C 8
Franklin, 22,444	B 5
Hancock, 34,590	G 6
Kennebec, 95,247	D 7
Knox, 29,013	E 7
Lincoln, 20,537	D 7
Oxford, 43,457	B 7
Penobscot, 125,393	F 5
Piscataquis, 16,285	E 4
Sagadahoc, 23,452	D 7
Somerset, 40,597	C 4
Waldo, 23,328	E 6
Washington, 29,859	H 6
York, 111,576	B 9

CITIES and TOWNS

Zip	*Name/Pop.*	*Key*
04406	Abbot Village, ▵453	D 5
04001	Acton, ▵697	B 8
04606	Addison, ▵773	H 6
04910	Albion, ▵1,056	E 6
† 04610	Alexander, ▵169	H 5
04002	Alfred⊙, ▵1,211	B 9
† 04774	Allagash, ▵456	F 1
† 04938	Allens Mills, 150	C 6
04535	Alna, ▵315	D 7
† 04468	Alton, ▵340	F 5
† 04408	Amherst, ▵148	G 6
04216	Andover, ▵791	B 6
04216	Andover, 350	B 6
04911	Anson. ▵2,168	D 6
04911	Anson, 950	D 6
† 04862	Appleton, ▵628	E 7
04732	Ashland, ▵1,761	G 2
04732	Ashland, 750	G 2
04912	Athens, ▵592	D 6
04912	Athens, 200	D 6
† 04426	Atkinson, ▵213	E 5
04210	Auburn⊙, 24,151	C 7
04330	Augusta (cap.)⊙, 21,945	D 7
04408	Aurora, ▵72	G 6
04003	Bailey Island, 400	D 8
04409	Bancroft, ▵53	H 4
04401	Bangor⊙, 33,168	F 6
04609	Bar Harbor, ▵3,716	G 7
04609	Bar Harbor, 2,392	G 7
04610	Baring, 150	J 5
04004	Bar Mills, 800	C 8
04653	Bass Harbor, 413	G 7
04530	Bath⊙, 9,679	D 8
04915	Bayside, 238	F 7
04611	Beals, ▵663	H 7
04622	Beddington, ▵32	H 6
04915	Belfast⊙, 5,957	F 7
04917	Belgrade, ▵1,302	D 7
04917	Belgrade, 300	D 7
04918	Belgrade Lakes, 700	D 6
04915	Belmont, ▵349	E 7
04733	Benedicta, ▵177	G 4
04919	Benton, ▵1,729	D 6
03901	Berwick, ▵3,136	B 9
03901	Berwick, 1,765	B 9
04285	Berry Mills, 245	C 6
04217	Bethel, ▵2,220	B 7
04217	Bethel, 750	B 7
04005	Biddeford, 19,983	B 9
04006	Biddeford Pool, 500	C 9
04920	Bingham, ▵1,254	D 5
04920	Bingham, 1,184	D 5
04613	Birch Harbor, 210	H 7
04734	Blaine, ▵903	H 2
04734	Blaine-Mars Hill, 1,854	H 2
04406	Blanchard, ▵56	D 5
04614	Blue Hill, ▵1,367	F 7
04615	Blue Hill Falls, 850	F 7
04040	Bolsters Mills, 150	B 7
04537	Boothbay, ▵1,814	D 8
04537	Boothbay, 700	D 8
04538	Boothbay Harbor, 2,320	D 8
04008	Bowdoinham, ▵1,294	D 7
04481	Bowerbank, ▵29	E 5
04410	Bradford, ▵569	F 5
04410	Bradford, 150	F 5
04411	Bradley, ▵1,010	F 6
04412	Brewer, 9,300	F 6
04735	Bridgewater, ▵895	H 3
04009	Bridgton, ▵2,967	B 7
04009	Bridgton, 1,779	B 7
† 04990	Brighton, ▵58	D 5
04539	Bristol, ▵1,721	D 8
04539	Bristol, 160	D 8
04616	Brooklin, ▵598	F 7
04921	Brooks, ▵751	E 6
04617	Brooksville, ▵673	F 7
04413	Brookton, 225	H 4
04010	Brownfield, ▵478	B 8
04010	Brownfield, 200	B 8
04414	Brownville, ▵1,490	E 5
04414	Brownville, 1,641	E 5
04415	Brownville Junction, 950	E 5
04011	Brunswick, ▵16,195	C 8
04011	Brunswick, 10,867	C 8
04219	Bryant Pond, 350	B 7
04220	Buckfield, ▵929	C 7
04618	Bucks Harbor, 161	J 6
04416	Bucksport, ▵3,756	F 6
04416	Bucksport, 2,456	F 6
04417	Burlington, ▵266	G 5
04922	Burnham, ▵802	E 6
† 04093	Buxton, ▵3,135	C 8
† 04275	Byron, ▵132	B 6
04619	Calais, 4,044	J 5
04923	Cambridge, ▵281	E 5
04843	Camden, ▵4,115	F 7
04843	Camden, 3,492	F 7
04924	Canaan, ▵904	D 6
04221	Canton, ▵742	C 7
03902	Cape Neddick, 850	B 9
04014	Cape Porpoise, 500	C 9
04925	Caratunk, ▵96	C 5
04418	Cardville, 223	F 5
04736	Caribou, 10,419	G 2
04419	Carmel, ▵1;301	E 6
04420	Carroll, ▵132	G 5
† 04224	Carthage, ▵354	C 6
† 04465	Cary, ▵184	H 4
04015	Casco, ▵1,256	B 7
04015	Casco, 250	B 7
04421	Castine, ▵1,080	F 7
† 04623	Centerville, ▵19	H 6
† 04757	Chapman, ▵328	G 2
04422	Charleston, ▵909	F 5
† 04666	Charlotte, ▵199	J 5
04017	Chebeague Island, 400	C 8
† 04345	Chelsea, ▵2,095	D 7
04622	Cherryfield, ▵771	H 6
† 04458	Chester, ▵255	F 5
† 04938	Chesterville, ▵643	C 6
04926	China, ▵1,850	E 7
04926	China, 336	E 7
04222	Chisholm, 1,530	C 7
† 04428	Clifton, ▵233	G 6
04927	Clinton, ▵1,971	D 6
04927	Clinton, 1,124	D 6
† 04623	Columbia, ▵162	H 6
04623	Columbia Falls, ▵367	H 6
† 04638	Cooper, ▵88	H 6
04341	Coopers Mills, 200	E 7
04624	Corea, 300	H 7
04928	Corinna, ▵1,700	E 6
04020	Cornish, ▵839	B 8
† 04976	Cornville, ▵623	D 6
04423	Costigan, 200	F 5
04625	Cranberry Isles, ▵186	G 7
† 04610	Crawford, ▵74	H 5
† 04015	Crescent Lake, 175	C 7
04738	Crouseville, 300	G 2
† 04747	Crystal, ▵281	G 4
04021	Cumberland Center, ▵4,096	C 8
04021	Cumberland Center, 950	C 8
04011	Cundys Harbor, 150	D 8
† 04563	Cushing, ▵522	E 7
04626	Cutler, ▵588	J 6
04626	Cutler, 153	J 6
04543	Damariscotta, ▵1,264	E 7
04543	Damariscotta-Newcastle, 1,188	E 7
04424	Danforth, ▵794	H 4
04424	Danforth, 650	H 4
† 04622	Deblois, ▵20	H 6
† 04429	Dedham, ▵522	F 6
04627	Deer Isle, ▵1,211	F 7
04627	Deer Isle, 600	F 7
04022	Denmark, ▵397	B 8
04628	Dennysville, ▵278	J 6
04425	Derby, 300	E 5
04929	Detroit, ▵663	E 6
04930	Dexter, ▵3,725	E 5
04936	Dexter, 2,732	E 5
04224	Dixfield, ▵2,188	C 6
04224	Dixfield, 1,535	C 6
04932	Dixmont, ▵559	E 6
04426	Dover-Foxcroft, ▵4,178	E 5
04426	Dover-Foxcroft⊙, 3,102	E 5
04342	Dresden, ▵787	D 7
04225	Dryden, 675	C 6
† 04039	Dry Mills, 700	C 8
† 04747	Dyer Brook, ▵165	G 3
04739	Eagle Lake, ▵908	F 1
04739	Eagle Lake, 675	F 1
04226	East Andover, 194	B 6
04024	East Baldwin, 175	B 8
04629	East Blue Hill, 150	G 7
04544	East Boothbay, 400	D 8
04427	East Corinth, 525	F 5
04227	East Dixfield, 288	C 6
04428	East Eddington, 200	F 6
04026	East Hiram, 198	B 8
04429	East Holden, 450	F 6
04027	East Lebanon, 950	B 9
† 04049	East Limington, 200	B 8
04228	East Livermore, 290	C 7
04630	East Machias, ▵1,057	J 6
04630	East Machias, 750	J 6
† 04950	East Madison, 400	D 6
04430	East Millinocket, ▵2,567	F 4
04430	East Millinocket, 2,564	F 4
04740	Easton, ▵1,305	H 2
† 04270	East Otisfield, 200	B 7
04229	East Peru, 350	C 7
04230	East Poland, 700	C 7
04631	Eastport, 1,989	K 6
04231	East Stoneham, 150	B 7
04632	East Sullivan, 300	G 6
† 04862	East Union, 220	E 7
04935	East Vassalboro, 300	D 7
04030	East Waterboro, 365	B 8
04234	East Wilton, 650	C 6
† 04428	Eddington, ▵1,358	F 6
† 04428	Eddington, 250	F 6
04545	Edgecomb, ▵549	D 8
† 04628	Edmunds, 229	J 6
03903	Eliot, ▵3,497	B 9
04605	Ellsworth⊙, 4,603	F 6
04433	Enfield, ▵1,148	F 5
04433	Enfield, 150	F 5
04434	Etna, ▵526	E 6
04936	Eustis, ▵595	B 5
04435	Exeter, ▵663	E 6
† 04938	Fairbanks, 300	C 6
04937	Fairfield, ▵5,684	D 6
04937	Fairfield, 3,694	D 6
† 04937	Fairfield Center, 975	D 6
04105	Falmouth, ▵6,291	C 8
04105	Falmouth, 1,621	C 8
† 04105	Falmouth Foreside (Falmouth), 1,621	C 8
† 04345	Farmingdale, ▵2,423	D 7
† 04345	Farmingdale, 1,832	D 7
04938	Farmington, ▵5,657	C 6
04938	Farmington⊙, 3,096	C 6
04940	Farmington Falls, 500	C 6
04344	Fayette, ▵447	C 7
04546	Five Islands, 161	D 8
04742	Fort Fairfield, ▵4,859	H 2
04742	Fort Fairfield, 2,322	H 2
04743	Fort Kent, ▵4,575	F 1
04743	Fort Kent, 2,876	F 1
04744	Fort Kent Mills, 300	F 1
04438	Frankfort, ▵620	F 6
04634	Franklin, ▵708	G 6
04634	Franklin, 350	G 6
04941	Freedom, ▵373	E 7
04032	Freeport, ▵4,781	C 8
04032	Freeport, 1,822	C 8
04745	Frenchville, ▵1,375	G 1
04745	Frenchville, 800	G 1
04547	Friendship, ▵834	E 7
04547	Friendship, 700	E 7
04037	Fryeburg, ▵2,208	A 7
04037	Fryeburg, 1,075	A 7
04345	Gardiner, 6,685	D 7
04939	Garland, ▵596	E 5
04939	Garland, 300	E 5
04548	Georgetown, ▵464	D 8
04548	Georgetown, 190	D 8
† 04217	Gilead, ▵153	B 7
† 04401	Glenburn, ▵1,196	F 6
04846	Glen Cove, 300	E 7
† 04005	Goodwins Mills, 340	B 8
† 04046	Goose Rocks Beach, 200	C 9
04038	Gorham, ▵7,839	C 8
04038	Gorham, 3,337	C 8
04636	Gouldsboro, ▵1,310	H 7
04636	Gouldsboro, 296	H 7
04746	Grand Isle, ▵797	G 1
04746	Grand Isle, 400	G 1
04637	Grand Lake Stream, ▵186	H 5
04039	Gray, ▵2,939	C 8
04039	Gray, 525	C 8
04236	Greene, ▵1,772	C 7
04441	Greenville, ▵1,894	D 5
04441	Greenville, 1,714	D 5
04442	Greenville Junction, 150	D 5
04443	Guilford, ▵1,694	E 5
04443	Guilford, 1,216	E 5
04347	Hallowell, 2,814	D 7
† 04785	Hamlin, ▵357	H 1
04444	Hampden, ▵4,693	F 6
04444	Hampden, 2,207	F 6
04445	Hampden Highlands, 950	F 6
04640	Hancock, ▵1,070	G 6
04237	Hanover, ▵275	B 7
04942	Harmony, ▵650	D 6
04942	Harmony, 350	D 6
† 04011	Harpswell, ▵2,552	D 8
04643	Harrington, ▵553	H 6
04040	Harrison, ▵1,045	B 7
† 04221	Hartford, ▵312	C 7
04943	Hartland, ▵1,414	D 6
04943	Hartland, 975	D 6
04446	Haynesville, ▵157	G 4
04238	Hebron, ▵532	C 7
† 04401	Hermon, ▵2,376	F 6
† 04082	Highland Lake, 600	C 8
04944	Hinckley, 317	D 6
04041	Hiram, ▵686	B 8
04041	Hiram, 175	B 8
04730	Hodgdon, ▵933	H 3
† 04429	Holden, ▵1,789	H 3
† 04429	Holden, 900	H 3
04042	Hollis Center, ▵1,560	B 8
04847	Hope, ▵500	E 7
04847	Hope, 175	E 7
04730	Houlton, ▵8,111	H 3
04730	Houlton⊙, 6,760	H 3
04448	Howland, ▵1,468	F 5
04448	Howland, 1,418	F 5
04449	Hudson, ▵482	F 5
04644	Hulls Cove, 200	G 7
04747	Island Falls, ▵913	G 3
04645	Isle au Haut, ▵45	F 7
04848	Islesboro, ▵421	F 7
04848	Islesboro, 200	F 7
04945	Jackman, ▵848	C 4
04945	Jackman, 700	C 4
04647	Jacksonville, 200	J 6
04239	Jay, ▵3,954	C 7
04239	Jay, 850	C 7
04348	Jefferson, ▵1,242	D 7
04648	Jonesboro, ▵448	J 6
04649	Jonesport, ▵1,326	H 6
04649	Jonesport, 1,073	H 6
04748	Keegan, 450	G 1
04450	Kenduskeag, ▵733	E 6
04043	Kennebunk, ▵5,646	B 9
04043	Kennebunk, 2,764	B 9
04046	Kennebunkport, ▵2,160	C 9
04046	Kennebunkport, 1,097	C 9
04349	Kents Hill, 250	D 7
04047	Kezar Falls, 680	B 8
04947	Kingfield, ▵877	C 6
04451	Kingman, 250	G 4
† 04990	Kingsbury, ▵7	D 5
03904	Kittery, ▵11,028	B 9
03904	Kittery, 7,363	B 9
03905	Kittery Point, 1,172	B 9
† 04986	Knox, ▵443	E 6
04453	La Grange, ▵393	F 5
04453	La Grange, 250	F 5
† 04463	Lake View, ▵16	F 5
† 04605	Lamoine, ▵615	G 7
04455	Lee, ▵599	G 5
† 04263	Leeds, ▵1,031	C 7
04456	Levant, ▵862	F 6
04240	Lewiston, 41,779	C 7
	Lewiston-Auburn, ‡72,474	C 7
04949	Liberty, ▵515	E 7
04949	Liberty, 200	E 7
04749	Lille, 300	G 1
04048	Limerick, ▵963	B 8
04750	Limestone, ▵8,745	H 2
04750	Limestone, 1,572	H 2
04049	Limington, ▵1,066	B 8
04049	Limington, 250	B 8
04457	Lincoln, ▵4,759	G 5
04457	Lincoln, 3,482	G 5
04458	Lincoln Center, 325	G 5
04849	Lincolnville, ▵955	E 7
04849	Lincolnville, 800	E 7
04755	Linneus, ▵608	H 3
04250	Lisbon, ▵6,544	C 7
• 04250	Lisbon-Lisbon Center, 1,475	C 7
04252	Lisbon Falls, 3,257	D 7
04350	Litchfield, ▵1,222	D 7
04650	Little Deer Isle, 275	F 7
† 04760	Littleton, ▵958	H 3
04253	Livermore, ▵1,610	C 7
04253	Livermore, 280	C 7
04254	Livermore Falls, ▵3,450	C 7
04254	Livermore Falls, 2,378	C 7
04255	Locke Mills, 300	B 7
04051	Lovell, ▵607	B 7
04051	Lovell, 180	B 7
† 04433	Lowell, ▵154	F 5
04652	Lubec, ▵1,949	K 6
04652	Lubec, 900	K 6
† 04730	Ludlow, ▵259	G 3
04654	Machias, ▵2,441	J 6
04654	Machias⊙, 1,368	J 6
04655	Machiasport, ▵887	H 6
04655	Machiasport, 374	H 6
† 04451	Macwahoc, ▵126	G 4
04756	Madawaska, ▵5,585	G 1
04756	Madawaska, 4,452	G 1
04950	Madison, ▵4,278	D 6
04950	Madison, 2,920	D 6
† 04966	Madrid, ▵107	B 6
04351	Manchester, ▵1,331	D 7
04757	Mapleton, ▵1,598	G 2
04758	Mars Hill, ▵1,875	H 2
04758	Mars Hill-Blaine, 1,854	H 2
04759	Masardis, ▵317	G 3
04459	Mattawamkeag, ▵988	G 5
04256	Mechanic Falls, ▵2,193	C 7
04256	Mechanic Falls, 1,872	C 7
04657	Meddybemps, ▵76	J 5
† 04453	Medford, ▵146	F 5
04460	Medway, ▵1,491	G 4
04957	Mercer, ▵313	D 6
04257	Mexico, ▵4,309	B 6
04257	Mexico, 3,325	B 6
04658	Milbridge, ▵1,154	H 6
04461	Milford, ▵1,828	F 6
04461	Milford, 1,519	F 6
04462	Millinocket, ▵7,742	F 4
04462	Millinocket, 7,558	F 4
04463	Milo, ▵2,572	F 5
04463	Milo, 1,514	F 5
04258	Minot, ▵919	C 7
04258	Minot, 250	C 7
04852	Monhegan, ▵44	E 8
04259	Monmouth. ▵2,062	D 7

(continued on following page)

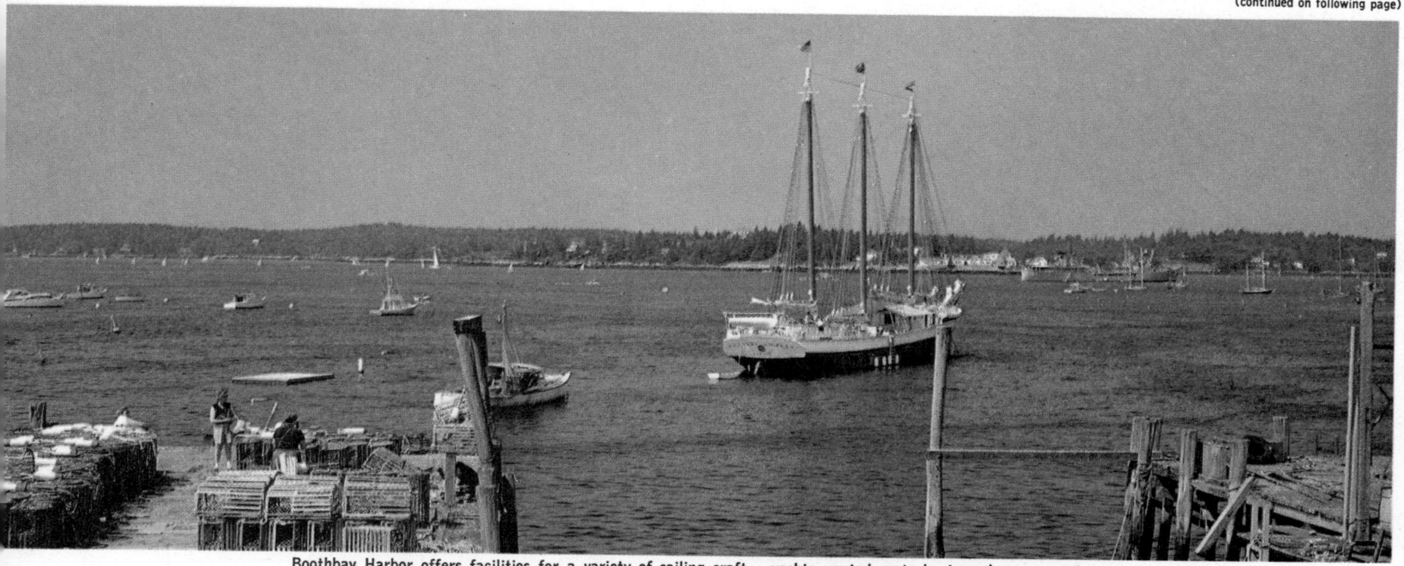

Boothbay Harbor offers facilities for a variety of sailing craft — yachts, rented party boats and commercial fishermen, all seen here at anchor. This active port rates high among Maine's popular coastal resort towns.

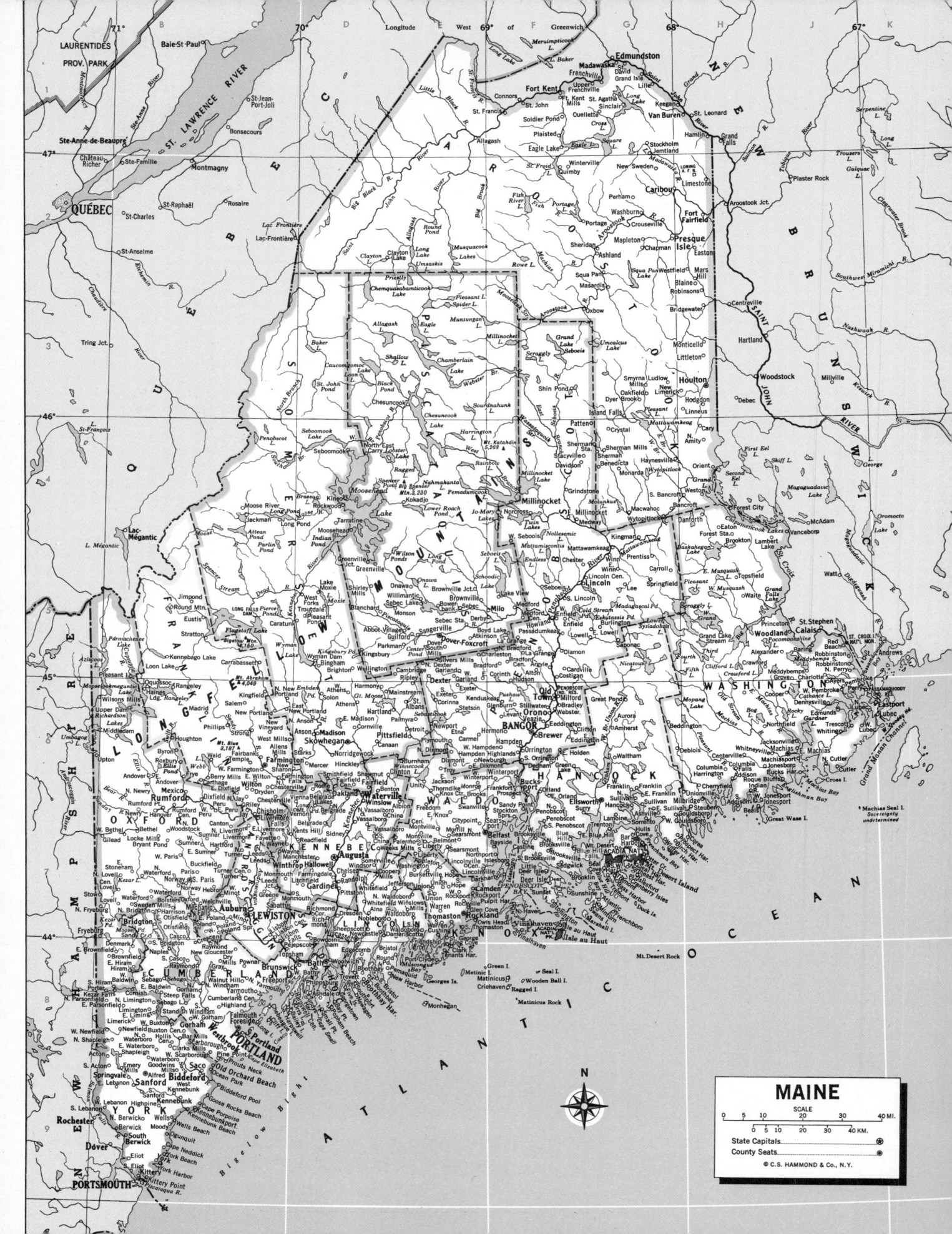

MAINE

SCALE

0 5 10 20 30 40 MI.

0 5 10 20 40 KM.

State Capitals .... ⊗

County Seats .... ⊙

© C.S. Hammond & Co., N.Y.

Agriculture, Industry and Resources

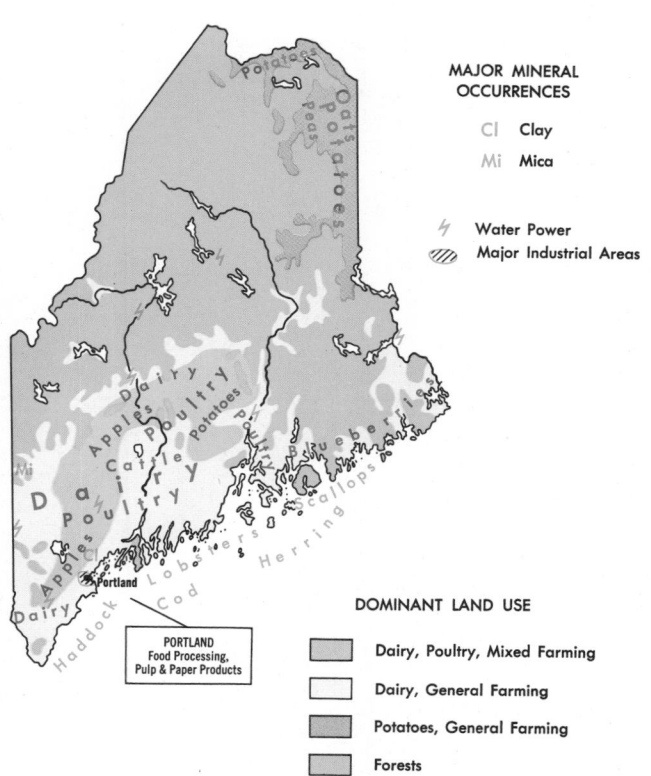

MAJOR MINERAL OCCURRENCES

Cl Clay

Mi Mica

⚡ Water Power

▨ Major Industrial Areas

PORTLAND
Food Processing,
Pulp & Paper Products

DOMINANT LAND USE

▨ Dairy, Poultry, Mixed Farming

☐ Dairy, General Farming

▨ Potatoes, General Farming

▨ Forests

Topography

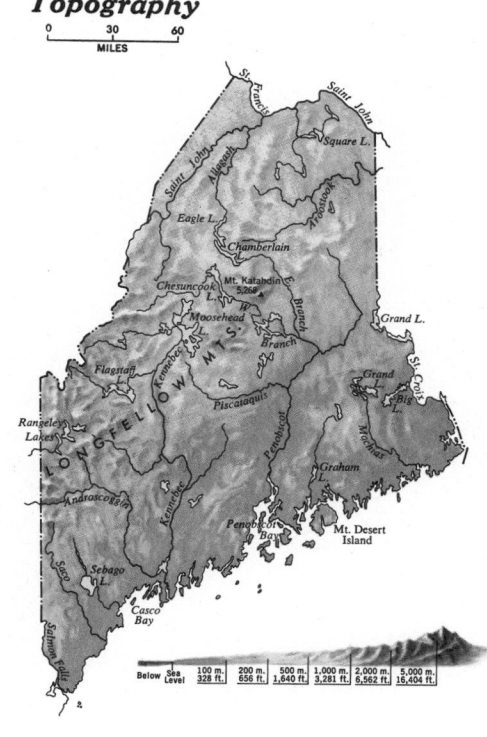

0 30 60
MILES

| Below Sea Level | 100 m. 328 ft. | 200 m. 656 ft. | 500 m. 1,640 ft. | 1,000 m. 3,281 ft. | 2,000 m. 6,562 ft. | 5,000 m. 16,404 ft. |

MARYLAND
COUNTIES

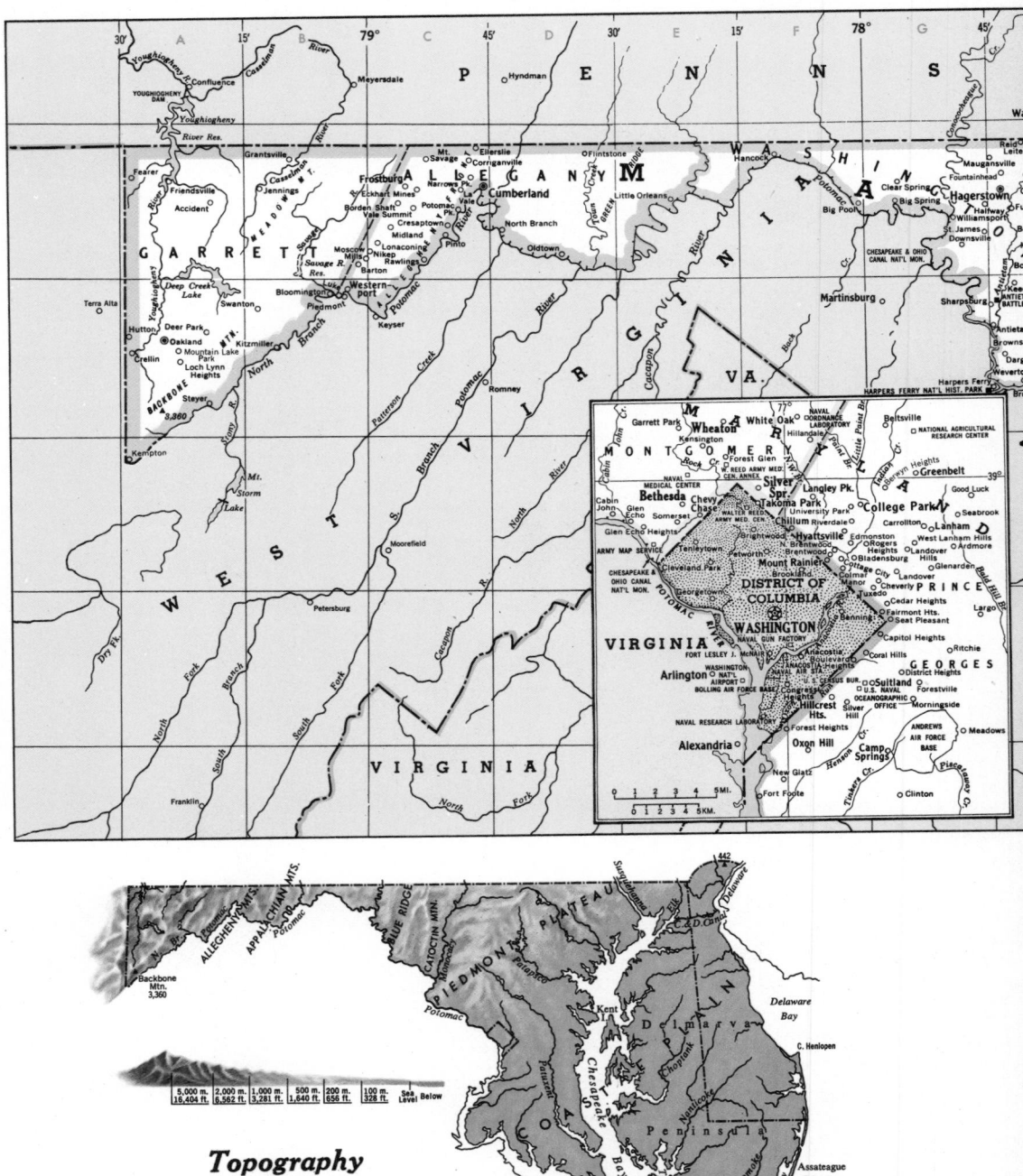

Topography

| 5,000 m. 16,404 ft. | 2,000 m. 6,562 ft. | 1,000 m. 3,281 ft. | 500 m. 1,640 ft. | 200 m. 656 ft. | 100 m. 328 ft. | Sea Level | Below |

0 30 60
MILES

MARYLAND

AREA 10,577 sq. mi.
POPULATION 3,922,399
CAPITAL Annapolis
LARGEST CITY Baltimore
HIGHEST POINT Backbone Mtn. 3,360 ft.
SETTLED IN 1634
ADMITTED TO UNION April 28, 1788
POPULAR NAME Old Line State; Free State
STATE FLOWER Black-eyed Susan
STATE BIRD Baltimore Oriole

DELAWARE

AREA 2,057 sq. mi.
POPULATION 548,104
CAPITAL Dover
LARGEST CITY Wilmington
HIGHEST POINT Ebright Road 442 ft.
SETTLED IN 1631
ADMITTED TO UNION December 7, 1787
POPULAR NAME First State; Diamond State
STATE FLOWER Peach Blossom
STATE BIRD Blue Hen Chicken

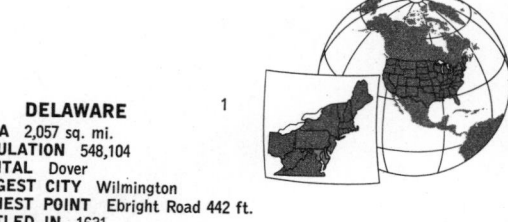

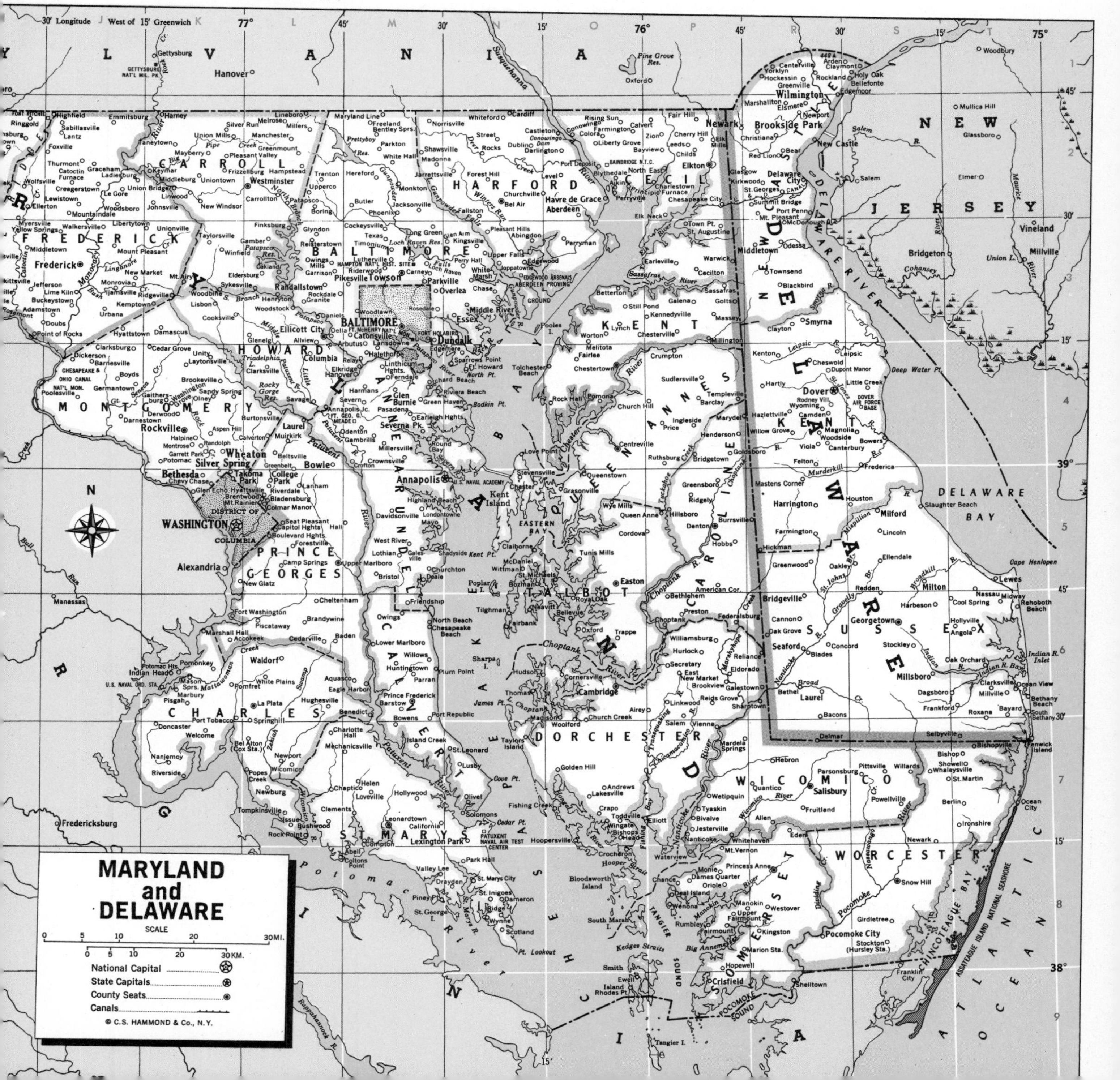

1

(continued on following page)

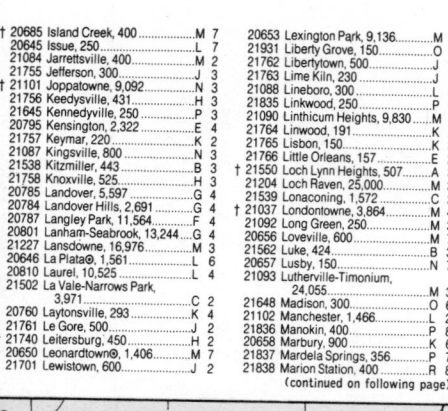

MARYLAND and DELAWARE

SCALE

| 0 | 5 | 10 | 20 | 30 MI. |

| 0 | 5 | 10 | 20 | 30 KM. |

National Capital ....⊛
State Capitals ....⊛
County Seats ....⊙
Canals ....

© C.S. HAMMOND & Co., N.Y.

182 *Maryland and Delaware*
(continued)

MARYLAND (continued)

† 20616 Marshall Hall, 325 .... K 6
21649 Marydel, 176 .... P 4
21105 Maryland Line, 250 .... M 2
21650 Massey, 220 .... P 3
21767 Maugansville, 1,069 .... H 2
21106 Mayo, 2,154 .... M 5
21647 McDaniel, 325 .... N 5
† 20870 Meadows, 200 .... G 5
20659 Mechanicsville, 784 .... M 7
21768 Middleburg, 200 .... K 2
21220 Middle River, 19,935 .... N 3
21769 Middletown, 1,262 .... J 3
21542 Midland, 665 .... C 2
21108 Millersville, 380 .... M 4
21651 Millington, 474 .... P 3
21111 Monkton, 307 .... M 2
21770 Monrovia, 300 .... J 3
† 20850 Montrose, 6,140 .... K 4
† 20028 Morningside, 1,665 .... G 5
† 21521 Moscow Mills, 275 .... B 2
21701 Mountaindale, 400 .... C 2
21550 Mountain Lake Park, 1,263 .... A 3
21771 Mount Airy, 1,825 .... K 3
† 21701 Mount Pleasant, 400 .... J 3
20822 Mount Rainier, 8,180 .... F 4
21545 Mount Savage, 1,413 .... C 2
† 21853 Mount Vernon, 900 .... P 8
† 20705 Muirkirk, 950 .... L 4
21773 Myersville, 450 .... H 3
20662 Nanjemoy, 238 .... K 7
21840 Nanticoke, 400 .... P 8
† 21522 Narrows Park-La Vale, 3,971 .... C 2
21652 Neavitt, 241 .... N 6
21841 Newark, 800 .... S 7
20664 Newburg, 550 .... L 7
† 20013 New Glatz, 950 .... F 4
21774 New Market, 339 .... J 3
21776 New Windsor, 788 .... K 2
21546 Nikep, 400 .... C 2
20831 North Beach, 761 .... N 6
† 20722 North Brentwood, 758 .... F 4
21901 North East, 1,818 .... P 2
21550 Oakland⊙, 1,786 .... A 3
21550 Oakland, 1,256 .... L 3
21842 Ocean City, 1,493 .... T 7
21113 Odenton, 5,989 .... M 4
† 21043 Oella, 600 .... L 3
21555 Oldtown, 400 .... D 2
20832 Olney, 2,138 .... K 4
† 21122 Orchard Beach, 200 .... M 4
21206 Overlea, 13,086 .... N 3
20836 Owings, 700 .... M 6
21117 Owings Mills, 7,360 .... L 3
21654 Oxford, 750 .... O 6
20021 Oxon Hill, 11,974 .... F 4
20667 Park Hall, 600 .... N 8
21120 Parkton, 290 .... M 2
21234 Parkville, 33,897 .... M 3
† 20639 Parran, 200 .... M 6
21849 Parsonsburg, 200 .... R 7
21122 Pasadena, 2,380 .... M 4
21127 Patapsco, 160 .... L 2
21128 Perry Hall, 5,446 .... N 3
21130 Perryman, 665 .... O 3
21903 Perryville, 2,091 .... O 2
21131 Phoenix, 165 .... M 2
21208 Pikesville, 25,395 .... M 3
20674 Piney Point, 950 .... M 8
21556 Pinto, 165 .... C 2
20640 Pisgah, 650 .... K 6
21850 Pittsville, 477 .... S 7
† 21087 Pleasant Hills, 1,754 .... N 3
21851 Pocomoke City, 3,573 .... R 8
21777 Point of Rocks, 400 .... J 3
20675 Pomfret, 600 .... L 6
20837 Poolesville, 349 .... J 4
21904 Port Deposit, 906 .... O 2
20677 Port Tobacco, 590 .... K 6
20854 Potomac (Potomac Valley), 5,094 .... K 4
20640 Potomac Heights, 1,983 .... K 6
† 21502 Potomac Park, 2,253 .... C 2
21852 Powellville, 450 .... S 7
21655 Preston, 509 .... P 6
20678 Prince Frederick⊙, 950 .... M 6
21853 Princess Anne⊙, 975 .... P 8
21856 Quantico, 200 .... R 7
21657 Queen Anne, 292 .... O 5
21658 Queenstown, 387 .... O 5
21133 Randallstown, 33,683 .... L 3
† 20853 Randolph, 13,233 .... K 4
21557 Rawlings, 600 .... C 2
21136 Reisterstown-Glyndon, 14,037 .... L 3
21139 Riderwood, 8,000 .... M 3
20680 Ridge, 550 .... N 8
21660 Ridgely, 822 .... P 5
21911 Rising Sun, 956 .... O 2
† 20013 Ritchie, 950 .... G 5
20840 Riverdale, 5,724 .... F 4
21122 Riviera Beach, 7,464 .... N 4
21661 Rock Hall, 1,125 .... O 4
20682 Rock Point, 300 .... L 7
* 20850 Rockville⊙, 41,564 .... K 4
† 20780 Rogers Heights, 3,000 .... G 4
21779 Rohrersville, 500 .... H 3
21237 Rosedale, 19,417 .... M 3
21662 Royal Oak, 600 .... O 6
21780 Sabillasville, 200 .... J 2
20684 Saint Inigoes, 750 .... N 8
21781 Saint James, 400 .... G 2
20685 Saint Leonard, 244 .... N 7
20686 Saint Marys City, 1,900 .... N 8
21663 Saint Michaels, 1,456 .... N 5
21801 Salisbury⊙, 15,252 .... R 7
20860 Sandy Spring, 500 .... K 4
20863 Savage, 2,116 .... L 4
20687 Scotland, 660 .... N 8
20801 Seabrook-Lanham, 13,244 .... G 4
20027 Seat Pleasant, 7,217 .... G 5
21664 Secretary, 352 .... P 6
21146 Severna Park, 16,358 .... M 4
20867 Shady Side, 1,562 .... N 5
21782 Sharpsburg, 833 .... G 3
21861 Sharptown, 660 .... R 6

Antietam Battlefield, near Sharpsburg, Maryland, the scene of the country's bloodiest one-day battle on September 17, 1862. A national battlefield site today, it is surrounded by farms, some of whose cattle graze among the cannons and monuments.

In Lewes, Delaware, settled by the Dutch in 1631, the Thompson Country Store sign establishes its origin as c.1800. The home of generations of Delaware River ship pilots, this seafaring town survives a history of shipwreck, bombardment and plundering.

21862 Showell, 250 .... T 7
20023 Silver Hill-Suitland, 30,355 .... F 5
* 20901 Silver Spring, 77,496 .... F 4
21783 Smithsburg, 671 .... H 2
21863 Snow Hill⊙, 2,201 .... S 8
20688 Solomons, 250 .... N 7
20015 Somerset, 1,303 .... E 4
21666 Stevensville, 500 .... N 5
21667 Still Pond, 250 .... O 3
21864 Stockton, 500 .... S 8
21154 Street, 200 .... N 2
21668 Sudlersville, 417 .... P 4
20023 Suitland-Silver Hill, 30,355 .... F 5
21561 Swanton, 223 .... A 3
21784 Sykesville, 1,399 .... K 3
20012 Takoma Park, 18,455 .... F 4
21787 Taneytown, 1,731 .... K 2
21669 Taylors Island, 375 .... N 7
21788 Thurmont, 2,359 .... J 2
21671 Tilghman, 950 .... N 6
21093 Timonium-Lutherville, 24,055 .... M 3
21672 Toddville, 300 .... O 7
21204 Towson⊙, 77,809 .... M 3
21673 Trappe, 426 .... O 6
20781 Tuxedo, 500 .... G 5
21791 Union Bridge, 904 .... K 2
21157 Uniontown, 250 .... K 2
21792 Unionville, 400 .... K 2
† 20740 University Park, 2,926 .... F 4
21155 Upperco, 500 .... L 2
21867 Upper Fairmount, 300 .... P 8

21156 Upper Falls, 900 .... N 3
20870 Upper Marlboro⊙, 646 .... M 5
20692 Valley Lee, 600 .... M 8
21869 Vienna, 358 .... P 7
20601 Waldorf, 7,368 .... L 6
21793 Walkersville, 1,269 .... J 3
21912 Warwick, 550 .... P 3
20880 Washington Grove, 688 .... K 4
20693 Welcome, 438 .... K 7
21870 Wenona, 323 .... P 8
21562 Westernport, 3,106 .... B 3
† 20784 West Lanham Hills, 950 .... G 4
21157 Westminster⊙, 7,207 .... L 2
21871 Westover, 450 .... R 8
20881 West River, 796 .... M 5
20902 Wheaton, 66,247 .... E 3
21160 Whiteford, 500 .... N 2
21161 White Hall, 350 .... M 2
21162 White Marsh, 500 .... N 3
† 20901 White Oak, 19,769 .... F 3
20695 White Plains, 1,600 .... L 6
21874 Willards, 494 .... S 7
21674 Williamsburg, 300 .... P 6
21672 Williamsport, 2,270 .... G 2
21675 Wingate, 200 .... O 7
21676 Wittman, 500 .... N 5
21797 Woodbine, 872 .... K 3
† 21201 Woodlawn, 28,811 .... M 3
21798 Woodsboro, 439 .... J 2
21163 Woodstock, 700 .... L 3
21677 Woolford, 295 .... O 7
21678 Worton, 315 .... O 3

21679 Wye Mills, 300 .... O 5
† 21701 Yellow Springs, 940 .... H 3

DELAWARE

COUNTIES

Kent, 81,892 .... R 4
New Castle, 385,856 .... R 2
Sussex, 80,356 .... S 6

CITIES and TOWNS

Zip	Name/Pop.	Key
† 19801	Arden, 3,340	R 1
19701	Bear, 200	R 2
19809	Bellefonte, 1,442	S 1
19930	Bethany Beach, 189	T 6
19931	Bethel, 219	R 6
† 19973	Blades, 632	R 6
19993	Bridgeville, 1,317	R 6
19711	Brookside Park, 7,856	R 2
19934	Camden, 1,241	R 4
† 19801	Centreville, 1,260	R 1
19938	Cheswold, 286	R 4
19702	Christiana, 550	R 2
19937	Clarksville, 350	T 6
19703	Claymont, 6,584	S 1
19938	Clayton, 1,015	R 3
19930	Dagsboro, 375	S 6
19706	Delaware City, 2,024	R 2
19940	Delmar, 943	R 7

19901 Dover (cap.)⊙, 17,488 .... R 4
† 19901 Dupont Manor, 1,256 .... R 4
† 19801 Edgemoor, 2,100 .... S 1
19941 Ellendale, 399 .... S 5
† 19801 Elsmere, 8,415 .... R 2
19943 Felton, 495 .... R 4
19945 Frankford, 635 .... S 6
19946 Frederica, 878 .... S 4
† 19947 Georgetown⊙, 1,844 .... S 6
19807 Greenville, 230 .... R 1
19950 Greenwood, 654 .... R 5
19951 Harbeson, 312 .... S 6
19952 Harrington, 2,407 .... R 5
19953 Hartly, 180 .... R 4
19707 Hockessin, 950 .... R 1
† 19801 Holly Oak, 1,140 .... S 1
19954 Houston, 317 .... S 5
19955 Kenton, 205 .... R 4
19708 Kirkwood, 450 .... R 2
19956 Laurel, 2,408 .... R 6
19958 Lewes, 2,563 .... T 5
19960 Lincoln, 757 .... S 5
19961 Little Creek, 215 .... S 4
19962 Magnolia, 319 .... R 4
19808 Marshallton, 1,240 .... R 2
19709 Middletown, 2,644 .... R 3
19963 Milford, 5,314 .... S 5
19966 Millsboro, 1,073 .... S 6
19967 Millville, 224 .... T 6
19968 Milton, 1,490 .... S 5
19711 Newark, 20,757 .... P 2
19720 New Castle, 4,814 .... R 2

19804 Newport, 1,366 .... R
19970 Ocean View, 411 .... T
19730 Odessa, 547 .... R
19731 Port Penn, 325 .... R
19971 Rehoboth Beach, 1,614 .... T
19901 Rodney Village, 2,127 .... R
19733 Saint Georges, 450 .... R
19973 Seaford, 5,537 .... R
19975 Selbyville, 1,099 .... S
19977 Smyrna, 4,243 .... R
19734 Townsend, 505 .... R
19979 Viola, 154 .... R
† 19801 Wilmington⊙, 80,386 .... R
19801 Wilmington, ‡498,977 .... R
19980 Woodside, 223 .... R
19934 Wyoming, 1,062 .... R
19736 Yorklyn, 300 .... R

DISTRICT OF COLUMBIA

CITIES and TOWNS

Zip	Name/Pop.	Key
20007	Georgetown	E
* 20001	Washington, D.C. (cap.), U.S. 756,510	F
	Washington, ‡2,861,123	F

⊙ County seat.
‡ Population of metropolitan area.
† Zip of nearest p.o.
* Multiple zips

Agriculture, Industry and Resources

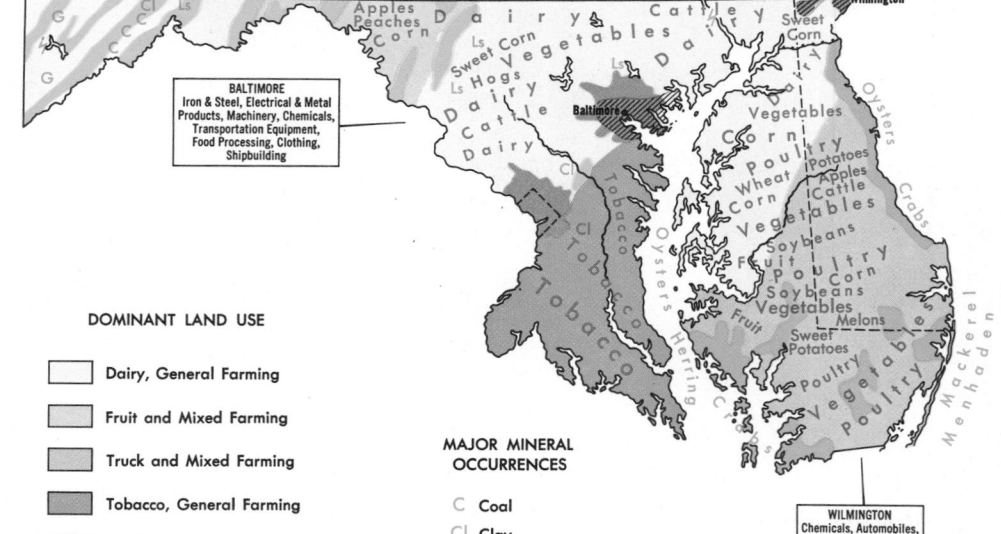

BALTIMORE
Iron & Steel, Electrical & Metal Products, Machinery, Chemicals, Transportation Equipment, Food Processing, Clothing, Shipbuilding

WILMINGTON
Chemicals, Automobiles, Metal Products, Textiles

DOMINANT LAND USE

- Dairy, General Farming
- Fruit and Mixed Farming
- Truck and Mixed Farming
- Tobacco, General Farming
- Forests
- Swampland, Limited Agriculture
- Urban Areas

MAJOR MINERAL OCCURRENCES

- C Coal
- Cl Clay
- G Natural Gas
- Ls Limestone

⚡ Water Power
▨ Major Industrial Areas

MASSACHUSETTS

AREA 8,257 sq. mi.
POPULATION 5,689,170
CAPITAL Boston
LARGEST CITY Boston
HIGHEST POINT Mt. Greylock 3,491 ft.
SETTLED IN 1620
ADMITTED TO UNION February 6, 1788
POPULAR NAME Bay State; Old Colony
STATE FLOWER Mayflower
STATE BIRD Chickadee

RHODE ISLAND

AREA 1,214 sq. mi.
POPULATION 949,723
CAPITAL Providence
LARGEST CITY Providence
HIGHEST POINT Jerimoth Hill 812 ft.
SETTLED IN 1636
ADMITTED TO UNION May 29, 1790
POPULAR NAME Little Rhody
STATE FLOWER Violet
STATE BIRD Rhode Island Red

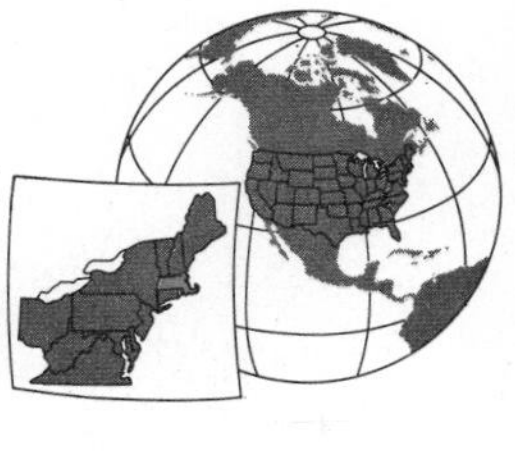

Agriculture, Industry and Resources

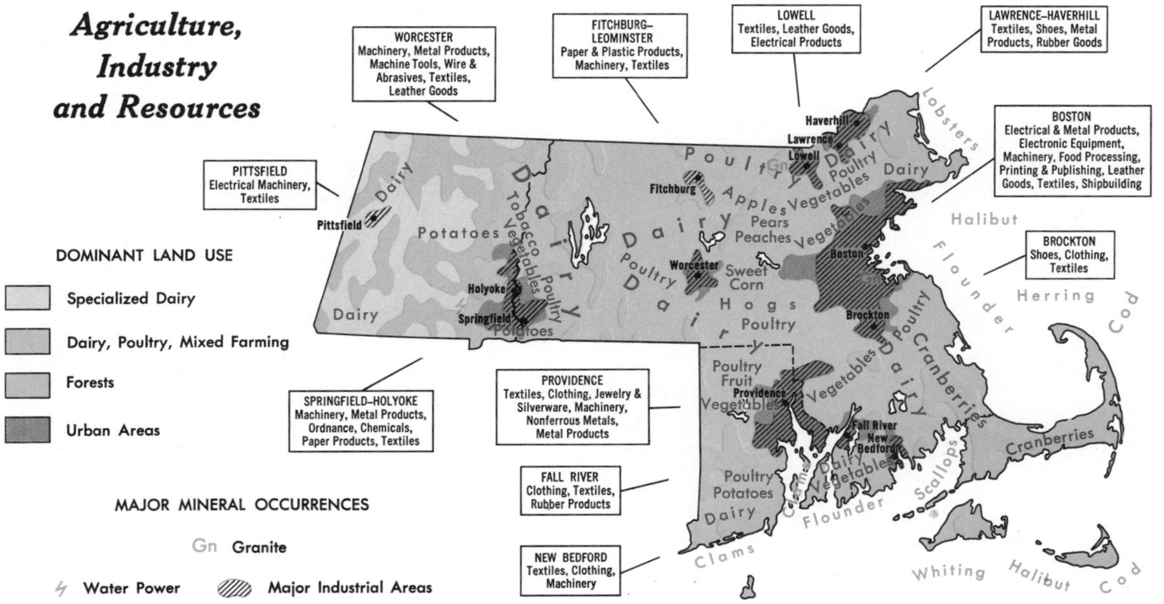
WORCESTER
Machinery, Metal Products, Machine Tools, Wire & Abrasives, Textiles, Leather Goods
FITCHBURG–LEOMINSTER
Paper & Plastic Products, Machinery, Textiles
LOWELL
Textiles, Leather Goods, Electrical Products
LAWRENCE–HAVERHILL
Textiles, Shoes, Metal Products, Rubber Goods
BOSTON
Electrical & Metal Products, Electronic Equipment, Machinery, Food Processing, Printing & Publishing, Leather Goods, Textiles, Shipbuilding
PITTSFIELD
Electrical Machinery, Textiles
BROCKTON
Shoes, Clothing, Textiles
SPRINGFIELD–HOLYOKE
Machinery, Metal Products, Ordnance, Chemicals, Paper Products, Textiles
PROVIDENCE
Textiles, Clothing, Jewelry & Silverware, Machinery, Nonferrous Metals, Metal Products
FALL RIVER
Clothing, Textiles, Rubber Products
NEW BEDFORD
Textiles, Clothing, Machinery
DOMINANT LAND USE
Specialized Dairy
Dairy, Poultry, Mixed Farming
Forests
Urban Areas
MAJOR MINERAL OCCURRENCES
Gn Granite
Water Power
Major Industrial Areas
Haverhill
Lawrence
Lowell
Fitchburg
Pittsfield
Worcester
Holyoke
Springfield
Boston
Brockton
Providence
Fall River
New Bedford
Dairy
Potatoes
Tobacco
Vegetables
Poultry
Apples
Pears
Peaches
Vegetables
Sweet Corn
Hogs
Fruit
Cranberries
Lobsters
Halibut
Flounder
Herring
Cod
Scallops
Clams
Whiting

MASSACHUSETTS

COUNTIES

Barnstable, 96,656 ... N 6
Berkshire, 149,402 ... B 3
Bristol, 444,301 ... K 5
Dukes, 6,117 ... M 7
Essex, 637,887 ... L 2
Franklin, 59,210 ... D 2
Hampden, 459,050 ... D 4
Hampshire, 123,981 ... D 3
Middlesex, 1,397,268 ... J 3
Nantucket, 3,774 ... O 7
Norfolk, 605,051 ... K 4
Plymouth, 333,314 ... L 5
Suffolk, 735,190 ... K 3
Worcester, 637,969 ... G 3

CITIES and TOWNS

Zip	Name/Pop.	Key
02351	Abington, ▵12,334	L 4
02351	Abington, 5,900	L 4
01720	Acton, ▵14,770	J 3
01220	Adams, ▵11,772	B 2
01220	Adams, 11,256	B 2
01001	Agawam, ▵21,717	D 4
01261	Alford, ▵302	A 4
01913	Amesbury, ▵11,388	L 1
01913	Amesbury, 10,088	L 1
01002	Amherst, ▵26,331	E 3
01002	Amherst, 17,926	E 3
01810	Andover, ▵23,695	K 2
02174	Arlington, ▵53,524	C 6
01430	Ashburnham, ▵3,484	G 2
01431	Ashby, ▵2,274	G 2
01330	Ashfield, ▵1,274	C 2
01721	Ashland, ▵8,882	J 3
01331	Athol, ▵11,185	F 2
01331	Athol, 9,723	F 2
02703	Attleboro, 32,907	J 5
02763	Attleboro Falls, 5,000	J 5
01501	Auburn, ▵15,347	G 4
02166	Auburndale, 7,235	B 7
02322	Avon, ▵5,295	K 4
01432	Ayer, ▵7,393	H 2
02630	Barnstable⊙, ▵19,842	N 6
01005	Barre, ▵3,825	F 3
01223	Becket, ▵929	B 3
01730	Bedford, ▵13,513	B 6
01007	Belchertown, ▵5,936	E 3
02019	Bellingham, ▵13,967	J 4
02019	Bellingham, 4,228	J 4
02178	Belmont, ▵28,285	C 6
02780	Berkley, ▵2,027	K 5
01503	Berlin, ▵2,099	H 3
01337	Bernardston, ▵1,659	D 2
01915	Beverly, 38,348	E 5
01821	Billerica, ▵31,648	J 2
01504	Blackstone, ▵6,566	H 4
01008	Blandford, ▵863	C 4
01740	Bolton, ▵1,905	H 3
* 02101	Boston (cap.)⊙, 641,071	D 7
	Boston, ‡2,753,700	D 7
02532	Bourne, ▵12,636	M 6
† 01720	Boxborough, ▵1,451	H 3
01921	Boxford, ▵4,032	L 2
01505	Boylston, ▵2,774	H 3
02184	Braintree, ▵35,050	D 8
02631	Brewster, ▵1,790	O 5
02324	Bridgewater, ▵11,829	K 5
02324	Bridgewater, 4,032	K 5
01010	Brimfield, ▵1,907	F 4
* 02401	Brockton, 89,040	K 4
	Brockton, ‡189,820	K 4
01506	Brookfield, ▵2,063	F 4
02147	Brookline, ▵58,886	C 7
01338	Buckland, ▵1,892	C 2
01803	Burlington, ▵21,980	C 5
† 02138	Cambridge⊙, 100,361	C 7
02021	Canton, ▵17,100	C 8
01741	Carlisle, ▵2,871	J 2
02330	Carver, ▵2,420	M 5
01339	Charlemont, ▵897	C 2
01507	Charlton, ▵4,654	F 4
02633	Chatham, ▵4,554	P 6
01824	Chelmsford, ▵31,432	J 2
02150	Chelsea, 30,625	D 6
01225	Cheshire, ▵3,006	B 2
01011	Chester, ▵1,025	C 3
01012	Chesterfield, ▵704	C 3
* 01013	Chicopee, 66,676	D 4
02535	Chilmark, ▵340	M 7
01510	Clinton, ▵13,383	H 3
01778	Cochituate, 6,000	A 7
02025	Cohasset, ▵6,954	F 7
02025	Cohasset, 3,900	F 7
† 01826	Collinsville, 4,000	J 2
01340	Colrain, ▵1,420	D 2
01742	Concord, ▵16,148	B 6
01742	Concord, 5,900	B 6
01341	Conway, ▵998	D 2
01026	Cummington, ▵562	C 3
01226	Dalton, ▵7,505	B 3
01923	Danvers, ▵26,151	D 5
02714	Dartmouth, ▵18,800	K 6
02026	Dedham⊙, ▵26,938	C 7
01342	Deerfield, ▵3,850	D 2
02638	Dennis, ▵6,454	O 5
02715	Dighton, ▵4,667	K 5
† 02122	Dorchester, 153,061	D 7
† 01516	Douglas, ▵2,947	H 4
02030	Dover, ▵4,529	B 7
01826	Dracut, ▵18,214	J 2
01570	Dudley, ▵8,087	G 4
01827	Dunstable, ▵1,292	J 2
02332	Duxbury, ▵7,636	M 4
02332	Duxbury, 2,477	M 4
† 02184	East Braintree, 12,000	D 8
02333	East Bridgewater, ▵8,347	L 4
01515	East Brookfield, ▵1,800	G 4
02642	Eastham, ▵2,043	O 5
01027	Easthampton, ▵13,012	D 3
01028	East Longmeadow, ▵13,029	E 4
† 02186	East Milton, 9,500	D 7
02334	Easton, ▵12,157	K 4
01437	East Pepperell, 4,200	H 2
† 01906	East Saugus, 4,200	D 6
02032	East Walpole, 4,500	C 8
† 02189	East Weymouth, 20,000	E 8
02539	Edgartown, ▵1,481	M 7
02539	Edgartown⊙, 1,006	M 7
01344	Erving, ▵1,260	E 2
02112	Essex, ▵2,670	L 2
02149	Everett, 42,485	D 6
02719	Fairhaven, ▵16,332	L 6
* 02720	Fall River, 96,898	K 6
	Fall River, ‡149,976	K 6
* 02540	Falmouth, ▵15,942	M 6
* 02540	Falmouth, 5,806	M 6
01030	Feeding Hills, 9,500	D 4
01420	Fitchburg, 43,343	G 2
	Fitchburg-Leominster, ‡97,164	G 2
† 01247	Florida, ▵672	B 2
02035	Foxboro, ▵14,218	J 4
02035	Foxboro, 4,090	J 4
01701	Framingham, 64,048	A 7
01701	Framingham Center, 16,000	J 3
02038	Franklin, ▵17,830	J 4
02038	Franklin, 8,863	J 4
01440	Gardner, 19,748	G 2
† 02535	Gay Head, ▵118	L 7
01830	Georgetown, ▵5,290	L 2
† 01376	Gill, ▵1,100	D 2
01930	Gloucester, 27,941	M 2
01032	Goshen, ▵483	C 3
01519	Grafton, ▵11,659	H 4
01033	Granby, ▵5,473	E 3
01034	Granville, ▵1,008	C 4
01230	Great Barrington, ▵7,537	A 4
01301	Greenfield, ▵18,116	D 2
01301	Greenfield⊙, 14,642	D 2
01880	Greenwood, 7,500	D 6
01450	Groton, ▵5,109	H 2
01830	Groveland, ▵5,382	L 1
01035	Hadley, ▵3,750	D 3
02338	Halifax, ▵3,537	L 5
01936	Hamilton, ▵6,373	L 2
01036	Hampden, ▵4,572	E 4
01237	Hancock, ▵675	A 2
02339	Hanover, ▵10,107	L 4
02341	Hanson, ▵7,148	L 4
01037	Hardwick, ▵2,379	F 3
01451	Harvard, ▵13,426	H 2
02645	Harwich, ▵5,892	O 6
02645	Harwich, 3,842	O 6
01038	Hatfield, ▵2,825	D 3
01830	Haverhill, 46,120	K 1
01346	Heath, ▵383	C 2
02043	Hingham, ▵18,845	E 8
01235	Hinsdale, ▵1,588	B 3
02343	Holbrook, ▵11,775	D 8
01520	Holden, ▵12,564	G 3
† 01550	Holland, ▵931	F 4
01746	Holliston, ▵12,069	A 8
01746	Holliston, 3,900	A 8
01040	Holyoke, 50,112	D 4
01747	Hopedale, ▵4,292	H 4
01748	Hopkinton, ▵5,981	J 4
01452	Hubbardston, ▵1,437	F 3
01749	Hudson, ▵16,084	H 3
01749	Hudson, 14,283	H 3
02045	Hull, ▵9,961	E 7
01050	Huntington, ▵1,593	C 4
02601	Hyannis, 6,847	N 6
02136	Hyde Park, 25,000	C 7
01938	Ipswich, ▵10,750	L 2
01938	Ipswich, 5,022	L 2
02090	Islington, 3,800	C 8
02130	Jamaica Plain, 50,000	C 7
02360	Kingston, ▵5,999	M 5
02360	Kingston, 3,772	M 5
02346	Lakeville, ▵4,376	L 5
01523	Lancaster, ▵6,095	H 3
01237	Lanesboro, ▵2,972	A 2
* 01840	Lawrence, 66,915	K 2
	Lawrence-Haverhill, ‡232,395	K 2
01238	Lee, ▵6,426	B 3
01524	Leicester, ▵9,140	G 4
01240	Lenox, ▵5,804	A 3
01240	Lenox, 2,208	A 3
01453	Leominster, 32,939	G 2
01054	Leverett, ▵1,005	E 3
02173	Lexington, ▵31,886	B 6
† 01301	Leyden, ▵376	D 2
01773	Lincoln, ▵7,567	B 6
01460	Littleton, ▵6,380	H 2
01106	Longmeadow, ▵15,630	D 4
* 01850	Lowell, 94,239	J 2
	Lowell, ‡212,860	J 2
01056	Ludlow, ▵17,580	E 4
02745	Lunds Corner, 7,020	L 6
01462	Lunenburg, ▵7,419	H 2
* 01901	Lynn, 90,294	D 6
01940	Lynnfield, ▵10,826	D 5
† 01940	Lynnfield Center (Lynnfield P.O.), 6,500	C 5
02148	Malden, 56,127	D 6
01944	Manchester, ▵5,151	F 5
02048	Mansfield, ▵9,939	J 4
02048	Mansfield, 4,778	J 4
01945	Marblehead, ▵21,295	E 7
02738	Marion, ▵3,466	L 6
01752	Marlborough, 27,936	H 3
02050	Marshfield, ▵15,223	M 4
02649	Mashpee, ▵1,288	M 6
02126	Mattapan, 18,500	C 7
02739	Mattapoisett, ▵4,500	L 6
01754	Maynard, ▵9,710	J 3
02052	Medfield, ▵9,821	B 8
02052	Medfield, 3,900	B 8
02155	Medford, 64,397	C 6
02053	Medway, ▵7,938	J 4
02053	Medway, 3,716	J 4
02176	Melrose, 33,180	D 6
01756	Mendon, ▵2,524	H 4
01860	Merrimac, ▵4,245	L 1
01844	Methuen, 35,456	K 2
02346	Middleboro, ▵13,607	L 5
02346	Middleboro, 6,259	L 5
01243	Middlefield, ▵288	B 3
01949	Middleton, ▵4,044	K 2
01757	Milford, ▵19,352	H 4
01757	Milford, 13,740	H 4
01527	Millbury, ▵11,987	H 4
02054	Millis, ▵5,686	A 8
01529	Millville, ▵1,764	H 4
02186	Milton, ▵27,190	D 7
01057	Monson, ▵7,355	E 4
01351	Montague, ▵8,451	E 2
01245	Monterey, ▵600	B 4
† 12517	Mount Washington, ▵52	A 4
01908	Nahant, ▵4,119	E 6
02554	Nantucket, ▵3,774	O 7
02554	Nantucket⊙, 2,461	O 7
01760	Natick, ▵31,057	A 7
02192	Needham, ▵29,748	B 7
02194	Needham Heights, 10,000	B 7
† 02122	Neponset, 25,000	D 7
* 02740	New Bedford, 101,777	K 6
	New Bedford, ‡152,642	K 6
01531	New Braintree, ▵631	F 3
01950	Newbury, ▵3,804	L 1
01950	Newburyport, 15,807	L 1
† 01230	New Marlboro, ▵1,031	B 4
01355	New Salem, ▵474	E 2
† 02158	Newton, 91,066	C 7
† 02159	Newton Center, 20,790	C 7
† 02161	Newton Highlands, 6,900	C 7
† 02160	Newtonville, 14,000	C 7
02790	Noquochoke P.O. (Westport), ▵950	K 6
02056	Norfolk, ▵4,656	J 4
02351	North Abington, 6,200	L 4
01247	North Adams, 19,195	B 2
01060	Northampton⊙, 29,664	D 3
01845	North Andover, ▵16,284	K 2
* 02760	North Attleboro, ▵18,665	J 5
01862	North Billerica, 4,900	J 2
01532	Northboro, ▵9,218	H 3
01532	Northboro, 3,900	H 3
01536	Northbridge, ▵11,795	H 4
01535	North Brookfield, ▵3,967	F 3
01863	North Chelmsford, 3,700	J 2
02747	North Dartmouth, 6,000	K 6
02356	North Easton, 6,000	K 4
01360	Northfield, ▵2,631	E 2
01536	North Grafton, 5,500	H 4
01864	North Reading, ▵11,264	C 5
02060	North Scituate, 5,507	F 8
† 02191	North Weymouth, 13,000	D 8
01067	North Wilbraham, 5,700	E 4
02766	Norton, ▵9,487	K 5
02061	Norwell, ▵7,796	F 8
02062	Norwood, ▵30,815	B 8
02557	Oak Bluffs, ▵1,385	M 7
01068	Oakham, ▵730	F 3
† 01566	Old Sturbridge Village, 500	F 4
01364	Orange, ▵6,104	E 2
01364	Orange, 3,847	E 2
02653	Orleans, ▵3,055	O 5
01253	Otis, ▵820	B 4
01540	Oxford, ▵10,345	G 4
01540	Oxford, 6,109	G 4
01069	Palmer, ▵11,680	E 4
01069	Palmer, 3,649	E 4
01612	Paxton, ▵3,731	G 3
01960	Peabody, 48,080	E 5
† 01002	Pelham, ▵937	E 3
02359	Pembroke, ▵11,193	L 4
01463	Pepperell, ▵5,887	H 2
01366	Petersham, ▵1,014	F 3
† 01331	Phillipston, ▵872	F 2
01866	Pinehurst, 5,681	B 5
01201	Pittsfield⊙, 57,020	A 3
	Pittsfield, ‡79,727	A 3
01070	Plainfield, ▵287	C 2
02762	Plainville, ▵4,953	J 4
* 02360	Plymouth, ▵18,606	M 5
* 02360	Plymouth⊙, 6,940	M 5
02367	Plympton, ▵1,224	L 5
† 02726	Pottersville, 3,722	K 6
01541	Princeton, ▵1,681	G 3
02657	Provincetown, ▵2,911	O 4
† 02169	Quincy, 87,966	D 7
02368	Randolph, ▵27,035	D 8
02767	Raynham, ▵6,705	K 5
01867	Reading, ▵22,539	C 5
02137	Readville, 10,000	C 8
02769	Rehoboth, ▵6,512	K 5
02151	Revere, 43,159	D 6
01254	Richmond, ▵1,461	A 3
02770	Rochester, ▵1,770	L 6
02370	Rockland, ▵15,674	L 4
01966	Rockport, ▵5,636	M 2
01966	Rockport, 4,166	M 2
01367	Rowe, ▵277	C 2
01969	Rowley, ▵3,040	L 2
† 02119	Roxbury, 200,000	C 7
01368	Royalston, ▵809	F 2
01071	Russell, ▵1,382	C 4
01543	Rutland, ▵3,198	G 3
01970	Salem⊙, 40,556	E 5
01950	Salisbury, ▵4,179	L 1
01255	Sandisfield, ▵547	B 4
02563	Sandwich, ▵5,239	N 5
01906	Saugus, ▵25,110	D 6
01256	Savoy, ▵322	B 2
01701	Saxonville, 15,000	A 7
02066	Scituate, ▵16,973	F 8
02066	Scituate, 3,738	F 8
02771	Seekonk, ▵11,116	J 5
02067	Sharon, ▵12,367	K 4
01810	Shawsheen Village, 5,200	K 2
01257	Sheffield, ▵2,374	A 4
01770	Sherborn, ▵3,309	A 8
01464	Shirley, ▵4,909	H 2
01545	Shrewsbury, ▵19,196	H 3
01072	Shutesbury, ▵489	E 3
02726	Somerset, ▵18,088	K 5
† 02143	Somerville, 88,779	C 6
01073	Southampton, ▵3,069	C 4
01772	Southborough, ▵5,798	H 3
† 02185	South Braintree, 6,000	D 8

(continued on following page)

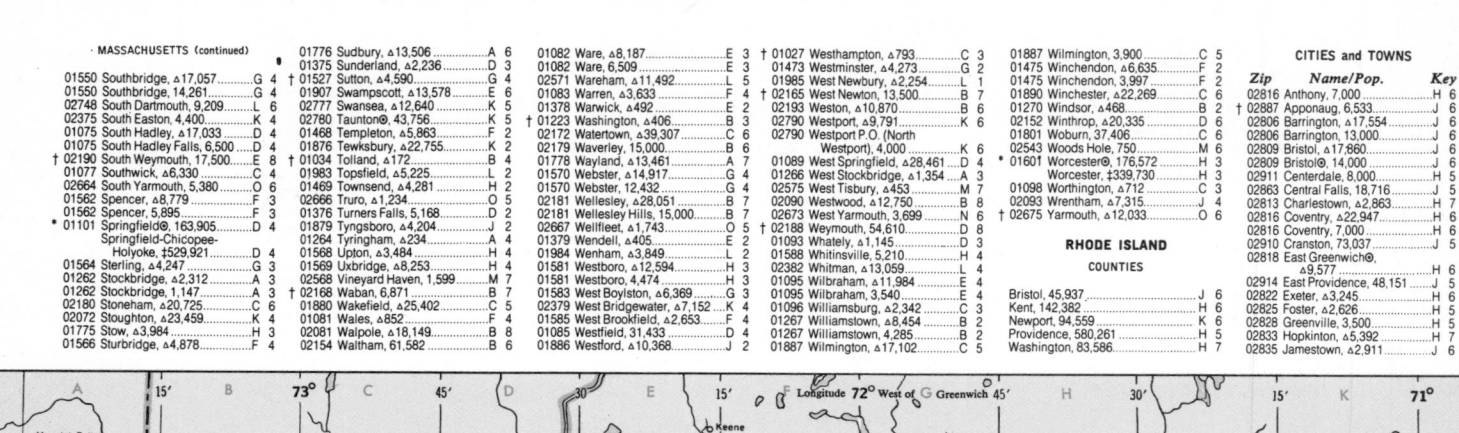

MASSACHUSETTS (continued)

01550 Southbridge, Δ17,057 G 4
01550 Southbridge, 14,261 G 4
02748 South Dartmouth, 9,209 L 6
02375 South Easton, 4,400 K 4
01075 South Hadley, Δ17,033 D 4
01075 South Hadley Falls, 6,500 D 4
† 02190 South Weymouth, 17,500 E 8
01077 Southwick, Δ6,330 C 4
02664 South Yarmouth, 5,380 O 6
01562 Spencer, Δ8,779 F 3
01562 Spencer, 5,895 F 3
* 01101 Springfield⊙, 163,905 D 4
Springfield-Chicopee-Holyoke, ‡529,921 D 4
01564 Sterling, Δ4,247 G 3
01262 Stockbridge, Δ2,312 A 3
01262 Stockbridge, 1,147 A 3
02180 Stoneham, Δ20,725 C 6
02072 Stoughton, Δ23,459 K 4
01775 Stow, Δ3,984 H 3
01566 Sturbridge, Δ4,878 F 4
01776 Sudbury, Δ13,506 A 6
01375 Sunderland, Δ2,236 D 3
† 01527 Sutton, Δ4,590 G 4
01907 Swampscott, Δ13,578 E 6
02777 Swansea, Δ12,640 K 5
02780 Taunton⊙, 43,756 K 5
01468 Templeton, Δ5,863 F 2
01876 Tewksbury, Δ22,755 K 2
† 01034 Tolland, Δ172 B 4
01983 Topsfield, Δ5,225 L 2
01469 Townsend, Δ4,281 H 2
02666 Truro, Δ1,234 O 5
01376 Turners Falls, 5,168 D 2
01879 Tyngsboro, Δ4,204 J 2
01264 Tyringham, Δ234 A 4
01568 Upton, Δ3,484 H 4
01569 Uxbridge, Δ8,253 H 4
02568 Vineyard Haven, 1,599 M 7
† 02168 Waban, 6,871 B 7
01880 Wakefield, Δ25,402 C 5
01081 Wales, Δ852 F 4
02081 Walpole, Δ18,149 B 8
02154 Waltham, 61,582 B 6
01082 Ware, Δ8,187 E 3
01082 Ware, 6,509 E 3
02571 Wareham, Δ11,492 L 5
01083 Warren, Δ3,633 F 4
01378 Warwick, Δ492 E 2
† 01223 Washington, Δ406 B 3
02172 Watertown, Δ39,307 C 6
02179 Waverley, 15,000 B 6
01778 Wayland, Δ13,461 A 7
01570 Webster, Δ14,917 G 4
01570 Webster, 12,432 G 4
02181 Wellesley, Δ28,051 B 7
02181 Wellesley Hills, 15,000 B 7
02667 Wellfleet, Δ1,743 O 5
01379 Wendell, Δ405 E 2
01984 Wenham, Δ3,849 L 2
01581 Westboro, Δ12,594 H 3
01581 Westboro, 4,474 H 3
01583 West Boylston, Δ6,369 G 3
02379 West Bridgewater, Δ7,152 K 4
01585 West Brookfield, Δ2,653 F 4
01085 Westfield, 31,433 D 4
01886 Westford, Δ10,368 J 2
† 01027 Westhampton, Δ793 C 3
01473 Westminster, Δ4,273 G 2
01985 West Newbury, Δ2,254 L 1
† 02165 West Newton, 13,500 B 7
02193 Weston, Δ10,870 B 6
02790 Westport, Δ9,791 K 6
02790 Westport P.O. (North Westport), 4,000 K 6
01089 West Springfield, Δ28,461 D 4
01266 West Stockbridge, Δ1,354 A 3
02575 West Tisbury, Δ453 M 7
02090 Westwood, Δ12,750 B 8
02673 West Yarmouth, 3,699 N 6
† 02188 Weymouth, 54,610 D 8
01093 Whately, Δ1,145 D 3
01588 Whitinsville, 5,210 H 4
02382 Whitman, Δ13,059 L 4
01095 Wilbraham, Δ11,984 E 4
01095 Wilbraham, 3,540 E 4
01096 Williamsburg, Δ2,342 C 3
01267 Williamstown, Δ8,454 B 2
01267 Williamstown, 4,285 B 2
01887 Wilmington, Δ17,102 C 5
01887 Wilmington, 3,900 C 5
01475 Winchendon, Δ6,635 F 2
01475 Winchendon, 3,997 F 2
01890 Winchester, Δ22,269 C 6
01270 Windsor, Δ468 B 2
02152 Winthrop, Δ20,335 D 6
01801 Woburn, 37,406 C 6
02543 Woods Hole, 750 M 6
* 01601 Worcester⊙, 176,572 H 3
Worcester, ‡339,730 H 3
01098 Worthington, Δ712 C 3
02093 Wrentham, Δ7,315 J 4
† 02675 Yarmouth, Δ12,033 O 6

RHODE ISLAND

COUNTIES

Bristol, 45,937 J 6
Kent, 142,382 H 6
Newport, 94,559 K 6
Providence, 580,261 H 5
Washington, 83,586 H 7

CITIES and TOWNS

Zip	Name/Pop.	Key
02816	Anthony, 7,000	H 6
† 02887	Apponaug, 6,533	J 6
02806	Barrington, Δ17,554	J 6
02806	Barrington, 13,000	J 6
02809	Bristol, Δ17,860	J 6
02809	Bristol⊙, 14,000	J 6
02911	Centerdale, 8,000	H 5
02863	Central Falls, 18,716	J 5
02813	Charlestown, Δ2,863	H 7
02816	Coventry, Δ22,947	H 6
02816	Coventry, 7,000	H 6
02910	Cranston, 73,037	J 5
02818	East Greenwich⊙, Δ9,577	H 6
02914	East Providence, 48,151	J 5
02822	Exeter, Δ3,245	H 6
02825	Foster, Δ2,626	H 5
02828	Greenville, 3,500	H 5
02833	Hopkinton, Δ5,392	H 7
02835	Jamestown, Δ2,911	J 6

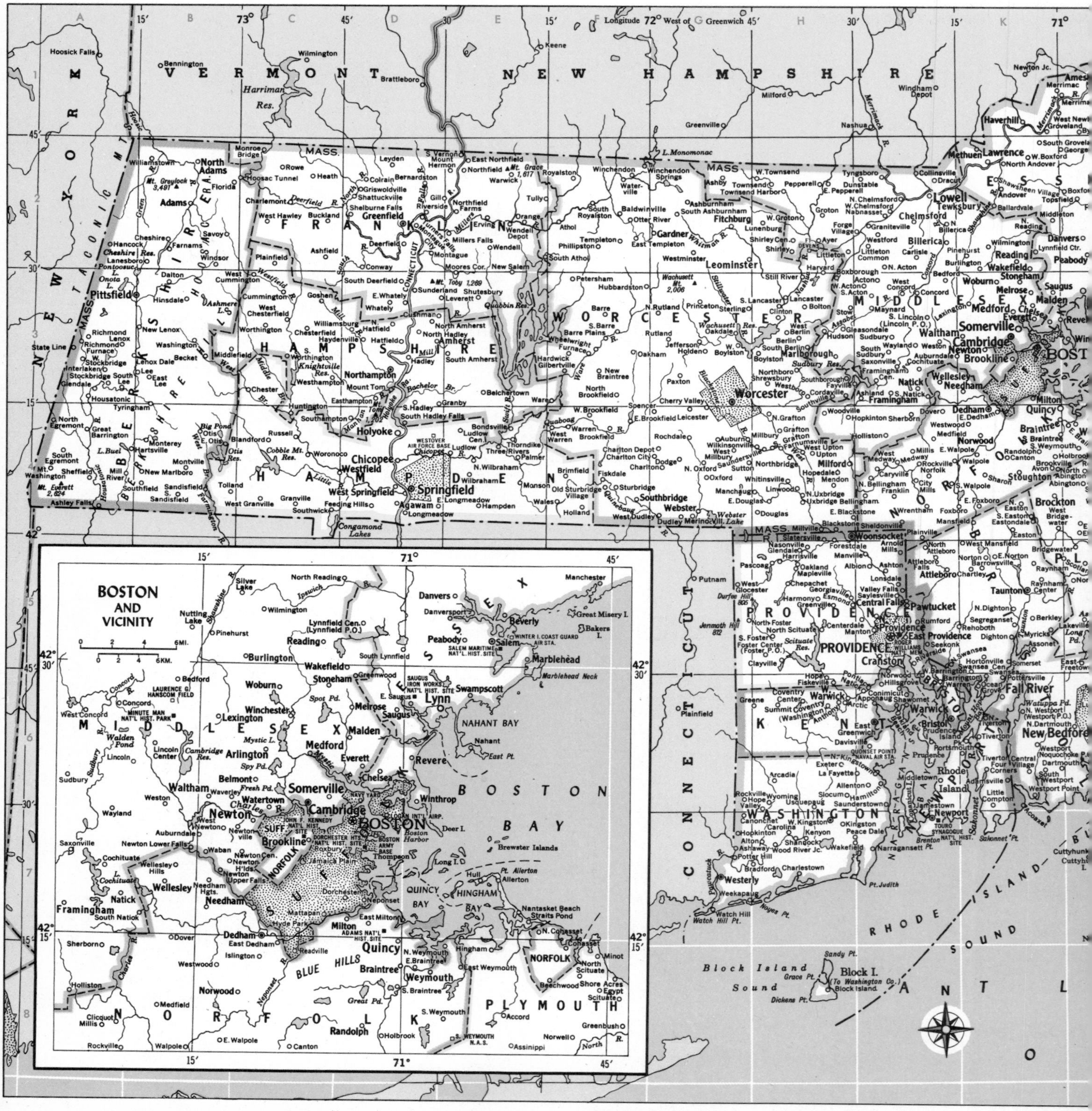

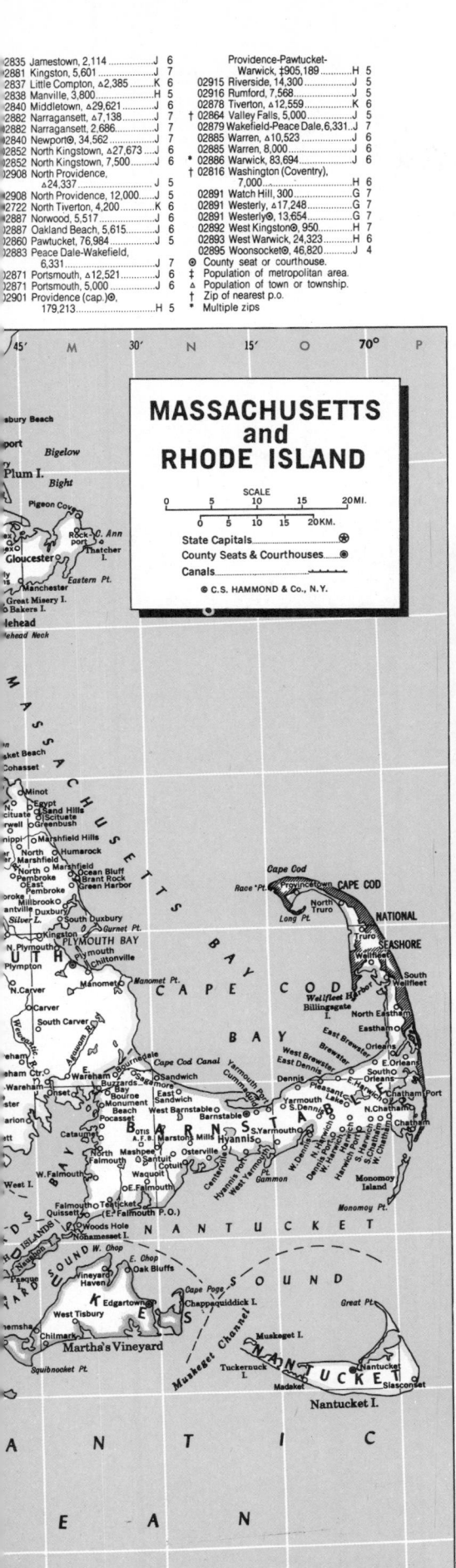

MASSACHUSETTS and RHODE ISLAND

SCALE
0 5 10 15 20MI.
0 5 10 15 20KM.

State Capitals.............................⊛
County Seats & Courthouses.......⊙
Canals

© C.S. HAMMOND & Co., N.Y.

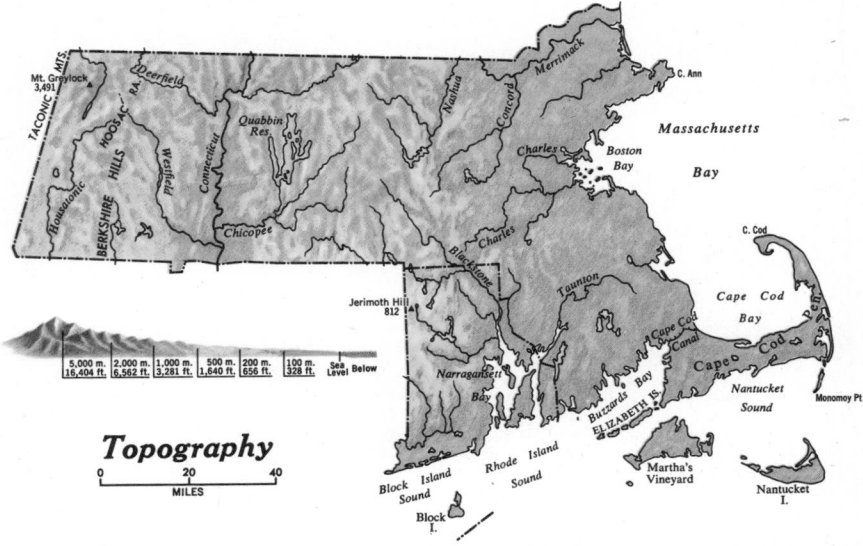

Topography

Marking the site of the first battle of the Revolutionary War on April 19, 1775, the Minuteman Statue faces the line of advancing Redcoats at Lexington, Massachusetts.

Typical Newport turn-of-the-century grandeur in a French chalet-style mansion, with mansard roof and wrought iron gates.

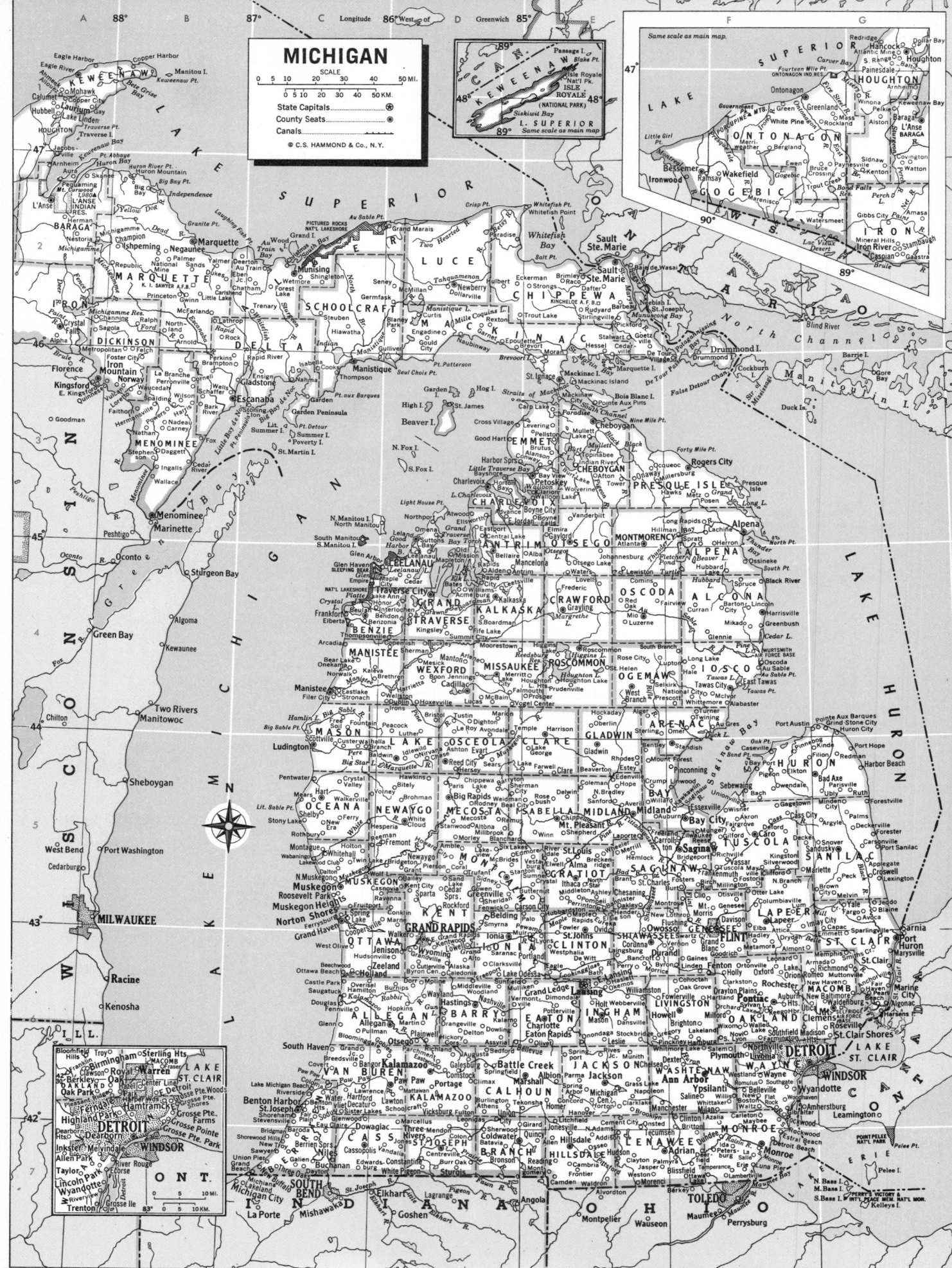

AREA 58,216 sq. mi.
POPULATION 8,875,083
CAPITAL Lansing
LARGEST CITY Detroit
HIGHEST POINT Mt. Curwood 1,980 ft.
SETTLED IN 1650
ADMITTED TO UNION January 26, 1837
POPULAR NAME Wolverine State
STATE FLOWER Apple Blossom
STATE BIRD Robin

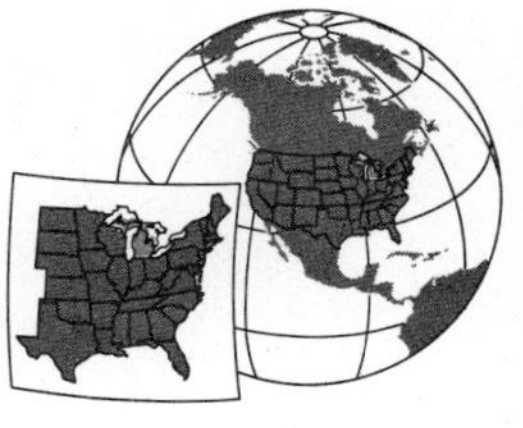

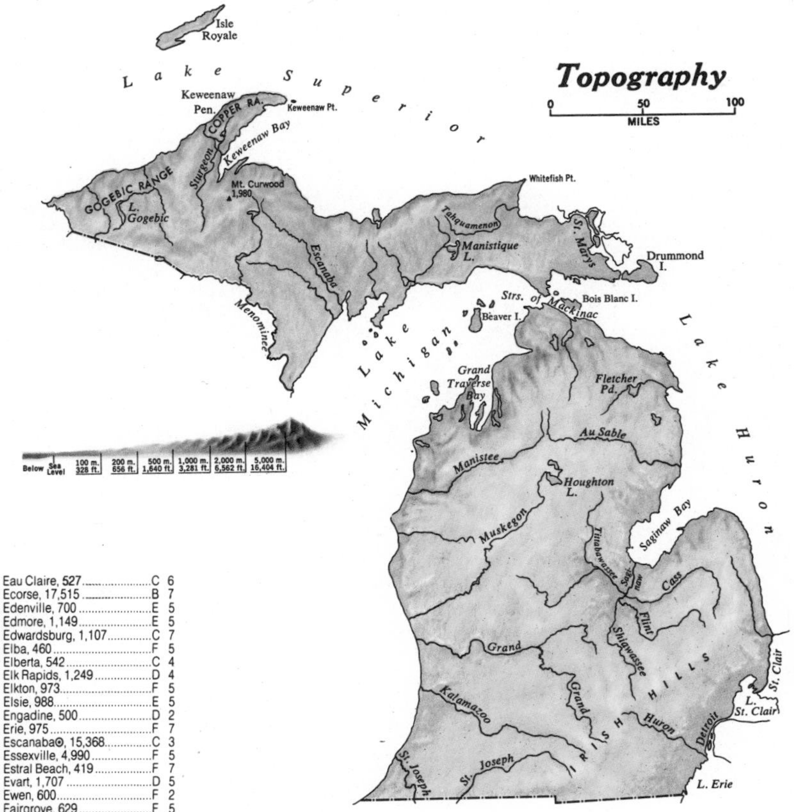

COUNTIES

Alcona, 7,113 F 4
Alger, 8,568 C 2
Allegan, 66,575 D 6
Alpena, 30,708 F 4
Antrim, 12,612 D 3
Arenac, 11,149 F 4
Baraga, 7,789 A 2
Barry, 38,166 D 6
Bay, 117,339 E 5
Benzie, 8,593 C 4
Berrien, 163,875 C 7
Branch, 37,906 D 7
Calhoun, 141,963 D 6
Cass, 43,312 C 7
Charlevoix, 16,541 D 3
Cheboygan, 16,573 E 3
Chippewa, 32,412 E 2
Clare, 16,695 E 5
Clinton, 48,492 E 6
Crawford, 6,482 E 4
Delta, 35,924 C 2
Dickinson, 23,753 B 2
aton, 68,892 E 6
mmet, 18,331 E 3
Genesee, 444,341 F 5
Gladwin, 13,471 E 4
Gogebic, 20,676 F 2
Grand Traverse, 39,175 D 4
Gratiot, 39,246 E 5
Hillsdale, 37,171 E 7
Houghton, 34,652 G 1
Huron, 34,083 F 5
ngham, 261,039 E 6
onia, 45,848 D 6
osco, 24,905 F 4
on, 13,813 G 2
sabella, 44,594 E 5
ackson, 143,274 E 6
Kalamazoo, 201,550 D 6
alkaska, 5,272 D 4
ent, 411,044 D 5
eweenaw, 2,264 A 1
ake, 5,661 D 5
apeer, 52,317 F 5
eelanau, 10,872 D 4
enawee, 81,609 E 7
ivingston, 58,967 F 6
uce, 6,789 D 2
Mackinac, 9,660 D 2
Macomb, 625,309 G 6
Manistee, 20,094 C 4
Marquette, 64,686 B 2
Mason, 22,612 C 4
Mecosta, 27,992 D 5
Menominee, 24,587 B 3
Midland, 63,769 E 5
Missaukee, 7,126 D 4
Monroe, 118,479 F 7
Montcalm, 39,660 D 5
Montmorency, 5,247 E 3
Muskegon, 157,246 C 5
ewaygo, 27,992 D 5
akland, 907,871 F 6
Oceana, 17,984 C 5
Ogemaw, 11,903 E 4
Ontonagon, 10,548 F 1
Osceola, 14,838 D 5
Oscoda, 4,726 E 4
Otsego, 10,422 E 3
Ottawa, 128,181 C 6
resque Isle, 12,836 F 3
oscommon, 9,892 E 4
aginaw, 219,743 E 5
aint Clair, 120,175 G 6
aint Joseph, 47,392 D 7
anilac, 34,889 G 5
choolcraft, 8,226 C 2
hiawassee, 63,075 E 6
uscola, 48,603 F 5
an Buren, 56,173 C 6
Washtenaw, 234,103 F 6
Wayne, 2,666,751 F 6
Wexford, 19,717 D 4

CITIES and TOWNS

Zip *Name/Pop.* *Key*

9220 Addison, 595 E 7
9221 Adrian⊙, 20,382 F 7
8701 Akron, 525 F 5
8764 Alabaster, 46 F 4
9224 Albion, 12,112 E 6
8001 Algonac, 3,684 G 6
9010 Allegan⊙, 4,516 D 6
8101 Allen Park, 40,747 B 7
8801 Alma, 9,790 E 5
8003 Almont, 1,634 F 6
9707 Alpena⊙, 13,805 F 3
9903 Amasa, 450 G 2
8004 Anchorville, 440 G 6
8103 Ann Arbor⊙, 99,797 F 6
Ann Arbor, ‡234,103 F 6
9659 Antrim, 475 D 4
8410 Argyle, 800 G 5
8005 Armada, 1,352 G 6
8806 Ashley, 521 E 5
9011 Athens, 996 D 6
9709 Atlanta⊙, 475 E 3
9905 Atlantic Mine, 785 G 1
8611 Auburn, 1,919 F 5
8057 Auburn Heights, 7,500 F 6
8703 Au Gres, 564 F 4
9012 Augusta, 1,025 D 6
8750 Au Sable-Oscoda, 3,475 F 4
8640 Averill, 800 E 5
8413 Bad Axe⊙, 2,999 G 5
9304 Baldwin⊙, 612 D 5
8414 Bancroft, 724 E 6
9013 Bangor, 2,050 C 6
9908 Baraga, 1,116 G 1
9807 Bark River, 550 B 3
9101 Baroda, 439 C 7
8808 Bath, 600 E 6
9014 Battle Creek, 38,931 D 6
48706 Bay City⊙, 49,449 F 5
Bay City, ‡117,339 F 5
48720 Bay Port, 600 F 5
49770 Bay View, 500 E 3
48612 Beaverton, 954 E 5
49020 Bedford, 450 D 6
† 49423 Beechwood, 2,714 C 6
48809 Belding, 5,121 D 5
49615 Bellaire⊙, 897 D 4
48111 Belleville, 2,406 F 6
49021 Bellevue, 1,297 E 6
49022 Benton Harbor, 16,481 C 6
† 49022 Benton Heights, 8,067 C 6
49910 Bergland, 635 F 1
48072 Berkley, 22,618 B 6
49103 Berrien Springs, 1,951 C 7
49911 Bessemer⊙, 2,805 F 2
49617 Beulah⊙, 461 C 4
49307 Big Rapids⊙, 11,995 D 5
48415 Birch Run, 932 F 5
* 48008 Birmingham, 26,170 B 6
49228 Blissfield, 2,753 F 7
48013 Bloomfield Hills, 3,672 B 6
49026 Bloomingdale, 496 C 6
49712 Boyne City, 2,969 E 3
48615 Breckenridge, 1,257 E 5
48722 Bridgeport, 1,900 F 5
49106 Bridgman, 1,621 C 7
48116 Brighton, 2,457 F 6
49715 Brimley, 490 E 2
49229 Britton, 697 F 6
49028 Bronson, 2,390 D 7
49230 Brooklyn, 1,112 E 6
48416 Brown City, 1,142 G 5
49716 Brutus, 431 E 3
49107 Buchanan, 4,645 C 7
49314 Burnips, 725 D 6
49030 Burr Oak, 873 D 7
48418 Byron, 655 E 6
49315 Byron Center, 900 D 6
49601 Cadillac⊙, 9,990 D 4
49316 Caledonia, 716 D 6
49913 Calumet, 1,007 A 1
48014 Capac, 1,279 G 5
48117 Carleton, 1,503 F 6
48723 Caro⊙, 3,701 F 5
48724 Carrollton, 7,300 E 5
48811 Carson City, 1,217 E 5
48419 Carsonville, 621 G 5
48725 Caseville, 607 F 5
49915 Caspian, 1,165 G 2
48726 Cass City, 1,974 F 5
49031 Cassopolis⊙, 2,108 C 7
49422 Castle Park, 500 C 6
49319 Cedar Springs, 1,807 D 5
49719 Cedarville, 800 E 2
49233 Cement City, 531 E 6
48015 Center Line, 10,379 B 6
49622 Central Lake, 741 D 3
49032 Centreville⊙, 1,044 D 7
49814 Champion, 550 B 2
49815 Channing, 550 B 2
49720 Charlevoix⊙, 3,519 D 3
48813 Charlotte⊙, 8,244 E 6
49623 Chase, 534 D 5
49721 Cheboygan⊙, 5,553 E 3
48118 Chelsea, 3,858 E 6
48616 Chesaning, 2,876 E 5
48617 Clare, 2,639 E 5
49234 Clarklake, 500 E 6
48016 Clarkston, 1,034 F 6
48017 Clawson, 17,617 B 6
49235 Clayton, 505 E 7
48727 Clifford, 472 F 5
49034 Climax, 594 D 6
49236 Clinton, 1,677 F 6
48420 Clio, 2,357 F 5
49036 Coldwater⊙, 9,099 D 7
48618 Coleman, 1,295 E 5
49038 Coloma, 1,814 C 6
49040 Colon, 1,172 D 7
48421 Columbiaville, 935 F 5
49041 Comstock, 5,003 D 6
49237 Concord, 983 E 6
49042 Constantine, 1,733 D 7
49722 Conway, 560 E 3
49404 Coopersville, 2,129 C 5
49818 Cornell, 640 B 3
48817 Corunna⊙, 2,829 E 6
49043 Covert, 650 C 6
48422 Croswell, 1,954 G 5
48818 Crystal, 649 E 5
49920 Crystal Falls⊙, 2,000 A 2
† 49501 Cutlerville, 6,267 D 6
48819 Dansville, 486 E 6
48423 Davison, 5,259 F 5
* 48120 Dearborn, 104,199 B 7
48127 Dearborn Heights, 80,069 B 7
49045 Decatur, 1,764 C 6
48427 Deckerville, 817 G 5
49238 Deerfield, 834 F 7
49725 De Tour Village, 494 E 3
* 48201 Detroit⊙, 1,511,482 B 7
Detroit, ‡4,199,931 B 7
† 48161 Detroit Beach, 2,053 F 7
48820 De Witt, 1,829 E 6
48130 Dexter, 1,729 F 6
48821 Dimondale, 970 E 6
49922 Dollar Bay, 950 G 1
49323 Dorr, 550 D 6
49406 Douglas, 813 C 6
49047 Dowagiac, 6,583 D 6
48020 Drayton Plains, 16,462 F 6
49726 Drummond Island, 700 F 3
48428 Dryden, 654 F 6
48131 Dundee, 2,472 F 7
48429 Durand, 3,678 E 6
49924 Eagle River⊙, 36 A 1
48021 East Detroit, 45,920 B 6
† 49506 East Grand Rapids, 12,565 D 6
49727 East Jordan, 2,041 D 3
† 49801 East Kingsford, 1,155 A 3
49626 Eastlake, 512 C 4
48823 East Lansing, 47,540 E 6
48730 East Tawas, 2,372 F 4
† 49001 Eastwood, 9,682 D 6
48827 Eaton Rapids, 4,494 E 6
49111 Eau Claire, 527 C 6
48229 Ecorse, 17,515 B 7
48620 Edenville, 700 E 5
48829 Edmore, 1,149 E 5
49112 Edwardsburg, 1,107 C 7
† 48446 Elba, 460 F 5
49628 Elberta, 542 C 4
49629 Elk Rapids, 1,249 D 4
48731 Elkton, 973 F 5
48831 Elsie, 988 E 5
49827 Engadine, 500 D 2
48133 Erie, 975 F 7
49829 Escanaba⊙, 15,368 C 3
48732 Essexville, 4,990 F 5
† 48166 Estral Beach, 419 F 7
49631 Evart, 1,707 D 5
49925 Ewen, 600 F 2
48733 Fairgrove, 629 F 5
48023 Fair Haven, 550 G 6
49022 Fair Plain, 3,680 C 6
48621 Fairview, 600 F 4
48024 Farmington, 13,337 F 6
48622 Farwell, 777 E 5
49408 Fennville, 811 C 6
48430 Fenton, 8,284 F 6
48220 Ferndale, 30,850 B 6
49409 Ferrysburg, 2,196 C 5
48134 Flat Rock, 5,643 F 6
* 48501 Flint⊙, 193,317 F 6
Flint, ‡496,658 F 6
48433 Flushing, 7,190 F 5
48835 Fowler, 1,020 E 5
48836 Fowlerville, 1,978 F 6
48734 Frankenmuth, 2,834 F 5
49635 Frankfort, 1,660 C 4
48025 Franklin, 3,344 B 6
48026 Fraser, 11,868 B 6
48623 Freeland, 1,303 E 5
49325 Freeport, 501 D 6
49412 Fremont, 3,465 D 5
49415 Fruitport, 1,409 C 5
49052 Fulton, 500 D 6
49927 Gaastra, 479 G 2
49053 Galesburg, 1,355 D 6
49113 Galien, 691 C 7
49735 Gaylord⊙, 3,012 E 3
48437 Genesee, 950 F 5
49836 Germfask, 750 C 2
48173 Gibraltar, 3,325 F 6
49837 Gladstone, 5,237 C 3
48624 Gladwin⊙, 2,071 E 5
49055 Gobles, 801 D 6
49737 Good Hart, 500 D 3
48438 Goodrich, 774 F 6
48439 Grand Blanc, 5,132 F 6
49417 Grand Haven⊙, 11,884 C 5
48837 Grand Ledge, 6,032 E 6
49839 Grand Marais, 650 D 2
* 49501 Grand Rapids⊙, 197,649 D 5
Grand Rapids, ‡539,225 D 5
49418 Grandville, 10,764 D 6
49327 Grant, 772 D 5
49240 Grass Lake, 1,061 E 6
49738 Grayling⊙, 2,143 E 4
48738 Greenbush, 650 F 4
48838 Greenville, 7,493 D 5
48138 Grosse Ile, 7,799 B 7
48236 Grosse Pointe, 6,637 B 7
† 48236 Grosse Pointe Farms, 11,701 B 6
† 48236 Grosse Pointe Park, 15,585 B 7
† 48236 Grosse Pointe Shores, 3,042 B 6
† 48236 Grosse Pointe Woods, 21,878 B 6
49840 Gulliver, 962 D 2
49841 Gwinn, 1,054 B 2
48739 Hale, 500 F 4
48139 Hamburg, 500 F 6
49419 Hamilton, 950 C 6
48212 Hamtramck, 27,245 B 6
49930 Hancock, 4,820 G 1
49241 Hanover, 513 E 6
48441 Harbor Beach, 2,134 G 5
49740 Harbor Springs, 1,662 D 3
48236 Harper Woods, 20,186 B 6
48625 Harrison⊙, 1,460 E 4
48740 Harrisville⊙, 541 F 4
48028 Harsens Island, 750 G 6
49420 Hart⊙, 2,139 C 5
49057 Hartford, 2,508 C 6
48840 Haslett, 3,492 E 6
49058 Hastings⊙, 6,501 D 6
48030 Hazel Park, 23,784 B 6
48626 Hemlock, 900 E 5
48841 Henderson, 600 E 5
49847 Hermansville, 950 B 3
49744 Herron, 950 F 3
49421 Hesperia, 877 D 5
49745 Hessel, 500 E 2
48203 Highland Park, 35,444 B 6
49242 Hillsdale⊙, 7,728 E 7
49423 Holland, 26,337 C 6
48442 Holly, 4,355 F 6
48842 Holt, 6,980 E 6
49425 Holton, 500 C 5
49245 Homer, 1,617 E 6
49328 Hopkins, 566 D 6
49931 Houghton⊙, 6,067 G 1
48629 Houghton Lake, 500 E 4
48630 Houghton Lake Heights, 1,252 E 4
49329 Howard City, 1,060 D 5
48843 Howell⊙, 5,224 E 6
49934 Hubbell, 1,251 A 1
49247 Hudson, 2,618 E 7
49426 Hudsonville, 3,523 D 6
48140 Ida, 970 F 7
49642 Idlewild, 800 D 5
48444 Imlay City, 1,980 F 5
49749 Indian River, 950 E 3
48141 Inkster, 38,595 B 7
49643 Interlochen, 800 D 4
48846 Ionia⊙, 6,361 D 6
49801 Iron Mountain⊙, 8,702 B 3
49935 Iron River, 2,684 G 2
49938 Ironwood, 8,711 F 2
49849 Ishpeming, 8,245 B 2
48847 Ithaca⊙, 2,749 E 5
* 49201 Jackson⊙, 45,484 E 6
Jackson, ‡143,274 E 6
49428 Jenison, 11,266 D 6
49061 Jones, 420 D 7
49250 Jonesville, 2,081 E 6
* 49001 Kalamazoo⊙, 85,555 D 6
Kalamazoo, ‡201,550 D 6
49646 Kalkaska⊙, 1,475 D 4
48631 Kawkawlin, 450 F 5
48030 Keego Harbor, 3,092 F 6
49330 Kent City, 686 D 5
49508 Kentwood, 20,310 D 6
48445 Kinde, 618 G 5
49801 Kingsford, 5,276 A 3
49649 Kingsley, 632 D 4
48741 Kingston, 464 F 5
48848 Laingsburg, 1,159 E 6
48632 Lake, 600 E 5
49651 Lake City⊙, 704 D 4
48143 Lakeland, 720 F 6
49945 Lake Linden, 1,214 A 1
† 49039 Lake Michigan Beach, 1,201 C 6
48849 Lake Odessa, 1,924 D 6
48850 Lakeview, 1,198 D 5
† 49440 Lakewood Club, 590 C 5
48144 Lambertville, 5,721 F 7
49946 L'Anse⊙, 2,538 G 1
* 48901 Lansing (cap.), 131,546 E 6
Lansing, ‡378,423 E 6
48446 Lapeer⊙, 6,270 F 5
49913 Laurium, 2,868 A 1
49064 Lawrence, 790 C 6
49065 Lawton, 1,358 D 6
49654 Leland⊙, 776 D 3
49251 Leslie, 1,894 E 6
49755 Levering, 967 E 3
49756 Lewiston, 750 E 4
48450 Lexington, 834 G 5
48146 Lincoln Park, 52,984 B 7
48451 Linden, 1,546 F 6
48634 Linwood, 950 F 5
49252 Litchfield, 1,167 E 6
49833 Little Lake, 950 B 2
* 48150 Livonia, 110,109 F 6
48743 Long Lake, 900 F 4
49331 Lowell, 3,068 D 6
49431 Ludington⊙, 9,021 C 5
48157 Luna Pier, 1,418 F 7
48851 Lyons, 758 E 6
49757 Mackinac Island, 517 E 3
49701 Mackinaw City, 810 E 3
48071 Madison Heights, 38,599 F 6
49659 Mancelona, 1,255 E 4
48158 Manchester, 1,650 E 6
49660 Manistee⊙, 7,723 C 4
49854 Manistique⊙, 4,324 C 3
49663 Manton, 1,107 D 4
48853 Maple Rapids, 683 E 5
49067 Marcellus, 1,139 D 6
49947 Marenisco, 865 F 2
48039 Marine City, 4,567 G 6
49665 Marion, 891 D 4
48453 Marlette, 1,706 G 5
49435 Marne, 950 D 5
49855 Marquette⊙, 21,967 B 2
49068 Marshall⊙, 7,253 E 6
49070 Martin, 502 D 6
48040 Marysville, 5,610 G 6
48854 Mason⊙, 5,468 E 6
49948 Mass, 850 G 1
49071 Mattawan, 1,569 D 6
48159 Maybee, 485 F 6
48744 Mayville, 872 F 5
49657 McBain, 520 D 4
48122 Melvindale, 13,862 B 7
48041 Memphis, 1,121 G 6
49072 Mendon, 949 D 7
49858 Menominee⊙, 10,748 B 3

(continued on following page)

Recognized as the country's leading automotive center, Detroit, with its fine harbor on the Detroit River, is also one of the busiest ports in the United States.

Michigan Travel Bureau

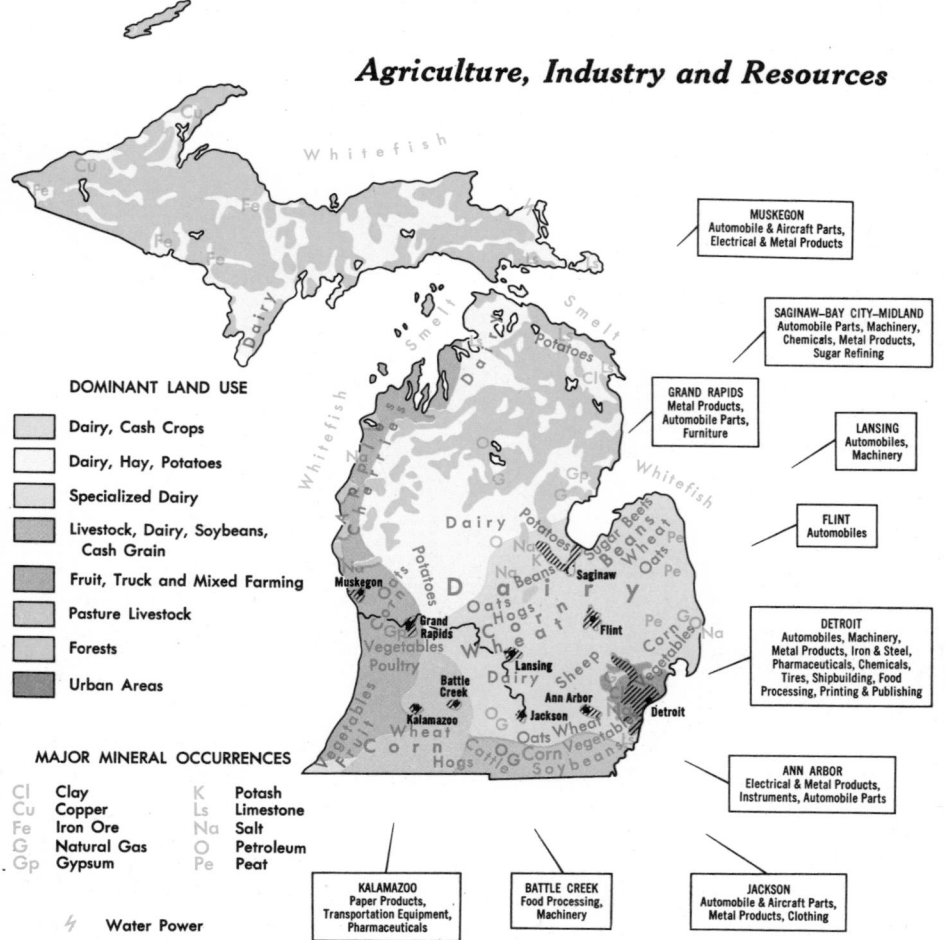

Agriculture, Industry and Resources

DOMINANT LAND USE

- Dairy, Cash Crops
- Dairy, Hay, Potatoes
- Specialized Dairy
- Livestock, Dairy, Soybeans, Cash Grain
- Fruit, Truck and Mixed Farming
- Pasture Livestock
- Forests
- Urban Areas

MAJOR MINERAL OCCURRENCES

Cl	Clay	K	Potash
Cu	Copper	Ls	Limestone
Fe	Iron Ore	Na	Salt
G	Natural Gas	O	Petroleum
Gp	Gypsum	Pe	Peat

⚡ Water Power

▨ Major Industrial Areas

MUSKEGON
Automobile & Aircraft Parts, Electrical & Metal Products

SAGINAW–BAY CITY–MIDLAND
Automobile Parts, Machinery, Chemicals, Metal Products, Sugar Refining

GRAND RAPIDS
Metal Products, Automobile Parts, Furniture

LANSING
Automobiles, Machinery

FLINT
Automobiles

DETROIT
Automobiles, Machinery, Metal Products, Iron & Steel, Pharmaceuticals, Chemicals, Tires, Shipbuilding, Food Processing, Printing & Publishing

ANN ARBOR
Electrical & Metal Products, Instruments, Automobile Parts

KALAMAZOO
Paper Products, Transportation Equipment, Pharmaceuticals

BATTLE CREEK
Food Processing, Machinery

JACKSON
Automobile & Aircraft Parts, Metal Products, Clothing

48637 Merrill, 961 ....E 5
48455 Metamora, 468 ....F 6
49758 Metz, 495. ....F 3
49254 Michigan Center, 4,900. ....E 6
48856 Middleton, 500. ....E 5
49333 Middleville, 1,865 ....D 6
48640 Midland⊙, 35,176 ....E 5
48160 Milan, 4,533 ....F 6
48042 Milford, 4,699 ....F 6
48746 Millington, 1,099 ....F 5
48647 Mio⊙, 975 ....E 4
48950 Mohawk, 800 ....A 1
49335 Moline, 750. ....D 6
48161 Monroe⊙, 23,894 ....F 7
49437 Montague, 2,396 ....C 5
48457 Montrose, 1,789 ....F 5
49256 Morenci, 2,132 ....E 7
49336 Morley, 481. ....D 5
48857 Morrice, 734 ....E 5
48043 Mount Clemens⊙, 20,476 ....G 6
48458 Mount Morris, 3,778 ....F 5
48858 Mount Pleasant⊙, 20,504 ....E 5
48860 Muir, 617 ....D 5
48861 Mulliken, 454 ....E 5
48747 Munger, 432 ....F 5
49862 Munising⊙, 3,677 ....C 3
*49440 Muskegon⊙, 44,631 ....C 5
  Muskegon-Muskegon
  Heights, ‡157,426 ....C 5
49444 Muskegon Heights, 17,304 ....C 5
49261 Napoleon, 950 ....E 6
49073 Nashville, 1,558 ....D 6
49865 National Mine, 565 ....B 2
49866 Negaunee, 5,248 ....B 2
49337 Newaygo, 1,381 ....D 5
48047 New Baltimore, 4,132 ....G 6
49868 Newberry⊙, 2,334 ....D 2
48164 New Boston, 800 ....F 6
49117 New Buffalo, 2,784 ....C 7
49446 New Era, 466 ....C 5
48048 New Haven, 1,855 ....G 6
48460 New Lothrop, 596 ....F 5
49119 New Troy, 430 ....C 7
49120 Niles, 12,988 ....C 7
49262 North Adams, 574 ....E 7
48461 North Branch, 932 ....F 5
49445 North Muskegon, 4,243 ....C 5
49670 Northport, 594 ....D 3
48167 Northville, 5,400 ....F 6
*49444 Norton Shores, 22,271 ....C 5
49870 Norway, 3,033 ....B 3
48050 Novi, 9,668 ....F 6
48237 Oak Park, 36,762 ....B 6
49763 Ocqueoc, 500. ....F 3
48864 Okemos, 7,770 ....E 6
49076 Olivet, 1,629 ....E 6
49765 Onaway, 1,262 ....E 3
49675 Onekama, 638 ....C 4
49265 Onsted, 555 ....E 6
49953 Ontonagon⊙, 2,432 ....F 1
48033 Orchard Lake, 1,487 ....F 6
48462 Ortonville, 983 ....F 6
48750 Oscoda-Au Sable, 3,475 ....F 4
48463 Otisville, 724 ....F 5
49078 Otsego, 3,957 ....D 6
†49735 Otsego Lake, 500 ....E 4
48464 Otter Lake, 551 ....F 5
48866 Ovid, 1,650 ....E 5
48867 Owosso, 17,179 ....E 5
48051 Oxford, 2,536 ....F 6
49955 Painesdale, 600 ....G 1
49871 Palmer, 950 ....B 2
49268 Palmyra, 600 ....E 7
49004 Parchment, 2,027 ....D 6
49269 Parma, 880 ....E 6
†49079 Paw Paw⊙, 3,160 ....D 6
†49038 Paw Paw Lake, 3,726 ....C 6
48052 Pearl Beach, 1,744 ....G 6
48466 Peck, 580 ....G 5
49769 Pellston, 469 ....E 3
49449 Pentwater, 993 ....C 5
48871 Perrinton, 489 ....E 5
48872 Perry, 1,531 ....E 5
49270 Petersburg, 1,227 ....F 7
49770 Petoskey⊙, 6,342 ....E 3
48873 Pewamo, 498 ....E 5
49774 Pickford, 800 ....E 2
48755 Pigeon, 1,174 ....F 5
48169 Pinckney, 921 ....F 6
48650 Pinconning, 1,320 ....F 5
49271 Pittsford, 610 ....E 7
49080 Plainwell, 3,195 ....D 6
48170 Plymouth, 11,758 ....F 6
48069 Pleasant Ridge, 3,989 ....B 6
*48053 Pontiac⊙, 85,279 ....F 6
49081 Portage, 33,590 ....D 6
48467 Port Austin, 883 ....F 4
48060 Port Huron⊙, 35,794 ....G 6
48875 Portland, 3,817 ....E 5
48469 Port Sanilac, 493 ....G 5
48876 Potterville, 1,280 ....E 6
49874 Powers, 560 ....B 3
48651 Prudenville, 500 ....E 4
49082 Quincy, 1,540 ....E 7
49876 Quinnesec, 770 ....A 3
49959 Ramsay, 1,068 ....F 2
49676 Rapid City, 450 ....D 4
49878 Rapid River, 950 ....C 3
49451 Ravenna, 1,048 ....C 5
49274 Reading, 1,125 ....E 7
49677 Reed City⊙, 2,286 ....D 5
48757 Reese, 1,050 ....F 5
49340 Remus, 425 ....D 5
49879 Republic, 900 ....B 2
49083 Richland, 728 ....D 6
48062 Richmond, 3,234 ....G 6
48758 Richville, 650 ....F 5
48218 River Rouge, 15,947 ....B 7
49084 Riverside, 650 ....C 6
48192 Riverview, 11,342 ....B 7
48063 Rochester, 7,054 ....F 6
49341 Rockford, 2,428 ....D 5
49960 Rockland, 450 ....G 1
48173 Rockwood, 3,119 ....F 6
49779 Rogers City⊙, 4,275 ....F 3
48065 Romeo, 4,012 ....F 6
48174 Romulus, 3,900 ....F 6
49444 Roosevelt Park, 4,176 ....C 5

48653 Roscommon⊙, 810 ....E 4
48878 Rosebush, 439 ....E 5
48654 Rose City, 530 ....E 4
48066 Roseville, 60,529 ....G 6
*48067 Royal Oak, 85,499 ....B 6
49780 Rudyard, 950 ....E 2
*48601 Saginaw⊙, 91,849 ....F 5
  Saginaw, ‡219,743 ....F 5
48655 Saint Charles, 2,046 ....E 5
48079 Saint Clair, 4,770 ....G 6
*48080 Saint Clair Shores, 88,093 ....G 6
48656 Saint Helen, 700 ....E 4
49781 Saint Ignace⊙, 2,892 ....E 3
48879 Saint Johns⊙, 6,672 ....E 6
49085 Saint Joseph⊙, 11,042 ....C 6
48880 Saint Louis, 4,101 ....E 5
48176 Saline, 4,811 ....F 6
48471 Sandusky⊙, 2,071 ....G 5
48657 Sanford, 818 ....E 5
48881 Saranac, 1,223 ....D 6
49453 Saugatuck, 1,022 ....C 6
49783 Sault Sainte Marie⊙, 15,136 ....E 2
49125 Sawyer, 650 ....C 7
49087 Schoolcraft, 1,277 ....D 6
49454 Scottville, 1,202 ....C 5
48759 Sebewaing, 2,053 ....F 5
49455 Shelby, 1,703 ....C 5
48883 Shepherd, 1,416 ....E 5
48884 Sheridan, 653 ....D 5
†49085 Shoreham, 666 ....C 6
49125 Shorewood Hills, 1,629 ....C 7
49047 Sister Lakes, 700 ....C 6
48075 Southfield, 69,285 ....F 6
48192 Southgate, 33,909 ....F 6
49090 South Haven, 6,471 ....C 6
48178 South Lyon, 2,675 ....F 6
*48161 South Monroe, 3,012 ....F 7
49963 South Range, 898 ....G 1
48179 South Rockwood, 1,477 ....F 7
49886 Spalding, 600 ....B 3
†48060 Sparlingville, 1,845 ....G 6
49345 Sparta, 3,094 ....D 5
49283 Spring Arbor, 1,832 ....E 6
49015 Springfield, 3,994 ....D 6
49456 Spring Lake, 3,034 ....C 5
49284 Springport, 723 ....E 6
49964 Stambaugh, 1,458 ....G 2
48658 Standish⊙, 1,184 ....F 5
48888 Stanton⊙, 1,089 ....D 5
49887 Stephenson, 800 ....B 3
48659 Sterling, 507 ....E 4
*48077 Sterling Heights, 61,365 ....B 6
49127 Stevensville, 1,107 ....C 6
49285 Stockbridge, 1,190 ....E 6
49681 Stronach, 500 ....C 4
49790 Strongs, 450 ....E 2
49091 Sturgis, 9,295 ....D 7
49890 Sunfield, 497 ....D 6
49682 Suttons Bay, 522 ....D 3
48473 Swartz Creek, 4,928 ....F 6
†48053 Sylvan Lake, 2,219 ....F 6
48763 Tawas City⊙, 1,666 ....F 4
48180 Taylor, 70,020 ....B 7
49286 Tecumseh, 7,120 ....E 7
49092 Tekonsha, 739 ....E 6
48182 Temperance, 2,900 ....F 7
49128 Three Oaks, 1,750 ....C 7
49093 Three Rivers, 7,355 ....D 7
49792 Tower, 425 ....E 3
49684 Traverse City⊙, 18,048 ....D 4
48183 Trenton, 24,127 ....B 7
48084 Troy, 39,419 ....B 6
49347 Trufant, 600 ....D 5
48475 Ubly, 899 ....G 5
49094 Union City, 1,740 ....D 6
49129 Union Pier, 900 ....C 7
48767 Unionville, 647 ....F 5
48087 Utica, 3,504 ....F 6
49095 Vandalia, 427 ....D 7
49795 Vanderbilt, 522 ....E 3
48768 Vassar, 2,802 ....F 5
49096 Vermontville, 857 ....E 6
48476 Vernon, 818 ....E 5
49097 Vicksburg, 2,139 ....D 6
49892 Vulcan, 975 ....B 3
49968 Wakefield, 2,757 ....F 2
49288 Waldron, 564 ....E 7
49504 Walker, 11,492 ....D 6
48088 Walled Lake, 3,759 ....F 6
49796 Walloon Lake, 550 ....E 3
*48089 Warren, 179,260 ....B 6
49969 Watersmeet, 700 ....G 2
49098 Watervliet, 2,059 ....C 6
49348 Wayland, 2,054 ....D 6
48184 Wayne, 21,054 ....F 6
48892 Webberville, 1,251 ....E 6
48893 Weidman, 450 ....D 5
48894 Wells, 1,085 ....B 3
48661 West Branch⊙, 1,912 ....E 4
48185 Westland, 86,749 ....F 6
48894 Westphalia, 806 ....E 6
49349 White Cloud⊙, 1,044 ....D 5
49461 Whitehall, 3,017 ....C 5
49099 White Pigeon, 1,455 ....D 7
49971 White Pine, 1,218 ....F 1
48189 Whitmore Lake, 2,763 ....F 6
48190 Whittaker, 500 ....F 6
48770 Whittemore, 460 ....F 4
48895 Williamston, 2,600 ....E 6
48191 Willis, 500 ....F 6
49896 Wilson, 500 ....B 3
48096 Wixom, 2,010 ....F 6
49896 Winn, 600 ....E 5
49442 Wolf Lake, 2,258 ....D 5
48183 Woodhaven, 3,330 ....F 6
48897 Woodland, 473 ....D 6
48192 Wyandotte, 41,061 ....B 7
49509 Wyoming, 56,560 ....D 6
48097 Yale, 1,505 ....G 5
48197 Ypsilanti, 29,538 ....F 6
49464 Zeeland, 4,734 ....D 6
†48601 Zilwaukee, 2,072 ....F 5

⊙ County seat.
⊛ Population of metropolitan area.
‡ Population of metropolitan area.
† Zip of nearest p.o.
* Multiple zips

AREA 84,068 sq. mi.
POPULATION 3,805,069
CAPITAL St. Paul
LARGEST CITY Minneapolis
HIGHEST POINT Eagle Mtn. 2,301 ft.
SETTLED IN 1805
ADMITTED TO UNION May 11, 1858
POPULAR NAME North Star State; Gopher State
STATE FLOWER Lady-slipper
STATE BIRD Loon

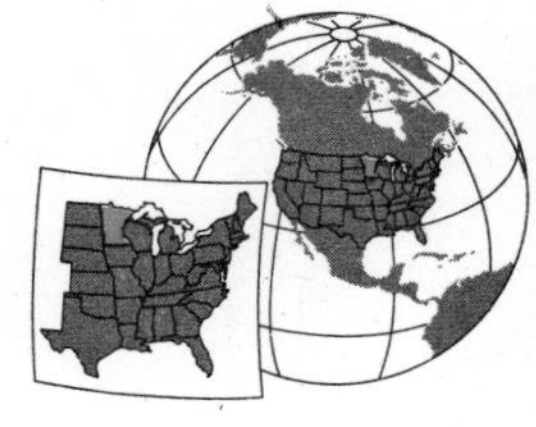

COUNTIES

Aitkin, 11,403	E 4
Anoka, 154,556	E 5
Becker, 24,372	C 4
Beltrami, 26,373	C 2
Benton, 20,841	D 5
Big Stone, 7,941	B 5
Blue Earth, 52,322	D 6
Brown, 28,887	D 6
Carlton, 28,072	F 4
Carver, 28,310	E 6
Cass, 17,323	D 4
Chippewa, 15,109	C 5
Chisago, 17,492	F 5
Clay, 46,585	B 4
Clearwater, 8,013	C 3
Cook, 3,423	H 3
Cottonwood, 14,887	C 6
Crow Wing, 34,826	D 4
Dakota, 139,808	E 6
Dodge, 13,037	F 7
Douglas, 22,892	C 5
Faribault, 20,896	D 7
Fillmore, 21,916	F 7
Freeborn, 38,064	E 7
Goodhue, 34,763	F 6
Grant, 7,462	B 5
Hennepin, 960,080	E 5
Houston, 17,556	G 7
Hubbard, 10,583	D 3
Isanti, 16,560	E 5
Itasca, 35,530	E 3
Jackson, 14,352	C 7
Kanabec, 9,775	E 5
Kandiyohi, 30,548	C 5
Kittson, 6,853	B 2
Koochiching, 17,731	E 2
Lac qui Parle, 11,164	B 6
Lake, 13,351	G 3
Lake of the Woods, 3,987	D 2
Le Sueur, 21,332	E 6
Lincoln, 8,143	B 6
Lyon, 24,273	C 6
Mahnomen, 5,638	C 3
Marshall, 13,060	B 2
Martin, 24,316	D 7
McLeod, 27,662	D 6
Meeker, 18,810	D 5
Mille Lacs, 15,703	E 5
Morrison, 26,949	D 4
Mower, 43,783	F 7
Murray, 12,508	C 6
Nicollet, 24,518	D 6
Nobles, 23,208	C 7
Norman, 10,008	B 3
Olmsted, 84,104	F 7
Otter Tail, 46,097	C 4
Pennington, 13,266	B 2
Pine, 16,821	F 4
Pipestone, 12,791	B 6
Polk, 34,435	B 3
Pope, 11,107	C 5
Ramsey, 476,255	E 5
Red Lake, 5,388	B 3
Redwood, 20,024	C 6
Renville, 21,139	C 6
Rice, 41,582	E 6
Rock, 11,346	B 7
Roseau, 11,569	C 2
Saint Louis, 220,693	F 3
Scott, 32,423	E 6
Sherburne, 18,344	E 5
Sibley, 15,845	D 6
Stearns, 95,400	D 5
Steele, 26,931	E 7
Stevens, 11,218	B 5
Swift, 13,177	C 5
Todd, 22,114	D 4
Traverse, 6,254	B 5
Wabasha, 17,224	F 6
Wadena, 12,412	D 4
Waseca, 16,663	E 6
Washington, 82,948	F 5
Watonwan, 13,298	D 7
Wilkin, 9,389	B 4
Winona, 44,409	G 6
Wright, 38,933	D 5
Yellow Medicine, 14,418	B 6

CITIES and TOWNS

Zip	Name/Pop.	Key
56510	Ada⊙, 2,076	B 3
55909	Adams, 771	F 7
56110	Adrian, 1,350	C 7
55001	Afton, 248	F 6
56430	Ah-Gwah-Ching, 500	D 3
56431	Aitkin⊙, 1,553	E 4
56433	Akeley, 468	D 3
56307	Albany, 1,599	D 5
56207	Alberta, 140	B 5
56007	Albert Lea⊙, 19,418	E 7
55301	Albertville, 451	E 5
56009	Alden, 713	E 7
56308	Alexandria⊙, 6,973	C 5
55002	Almelund, 150	F 5
56111	Alpha, 179	D 7
55910	Altura, 334	G 6
56710	Alvarado, 302	B 2
56010	Amboy, 571	D 7
55703	Angora, 287	F 3
55302	Annandale, 1,234	D 5
55303	Anoka⊙, 13,489	E 5
56208	Appleton, 1,789	C 5
55378	Apple Valley, 8,502	G 6
56113	Arco, 121	B 6
56713	Argyle, 739	B 2
55307	Arlington, 1,823	D 6
55801	Arnold, 750	F 4
56309	Ashby, 415	C 4
55704	Askov, 287	F 4
56209	Atwater, 956	D 5
56511	Audubon, 297	C 4
55705	Aurora, 2,531	F 3
55912	Austin⊙, 25,074	E 7
56114	Avoca, 203	C 7
56310	Avon, 725	D 5
55706	Babbitt, 3,076	G 3
56435	Backus, 257	D 4
56714	Badger, 327	B 2
56621	Bagley⊙, 1,314	C 3
56115	Balaton, 649	C 6
56622	Ball Club, 150	E 3
56514	Barnesville, 1,782	B 4
55707	Barnum, 382	F 4
56311	Barrett, 342	B 5
56515	Battle Lake, 772	C 4
56623	Baudette⊙, 1,547	D 2
† 56401	Baxter, 1,556	D 4
† 56444	Bay Lake, 250	E 4
55003	Bayport, 2,987	F 5
56211	Beardsley, 366	B 5
† 55723	Bear River, 250	E 3
55601	Beaver Bay, 362	G 3
56116	Beaver Creek, 235	B 7
55308	Becker, 365	E 5
56516	Bejou, 157	B 3
56312	Belgrade, 713	C 5
† 55027	Bellechester, 199	F 6
56011	Belle Plaine, 2,328	E 6
56212	Bellingham, 263	B 5
56517	Beltrami, 171	B 3
56214	Belview, 429	C 6
56601	Bemidji⊙, 11,490	D 3
56626	Bena, 169	D 3
56215	Benson⊙, 3,484	C 5
56437	Bertha, 512	C 4
56117	Bigelow, 262	C 7
56627	Big Falls, 534	E 2
56628	Bigfork, 399	E 3
55309	Big Lake, 1,015	E 5
56118	Bingham Lake, 214	C 7
55310	Bird Island, 1,309	D 6
55708	Biwabik, 1,483	F 3
56630	Blackduck, 595	D 3
† 55303	Blaine, 20,640	G 5
† 56011	Blakeley, 125	E 6
56216	Blomkest, 172	D 6
55917	Blooming Prairie, 1,804	E 7
55420	Bloomington, 81,970	G 6
56013	Blue Earth⊙, 3,965	D 7
56518	Bluffton, 195	C 4
56519	Borup, 128	B 3
55709	Bovey, 858	E 3
56314	Bowlus, 268	D 5
56218	Boyd, 311	C 6
55006	Braham, 744	E 5
56401	Brainerd⊙, 11,667	D 4
† 55056	Branch, 880	F 5
56315	Brandon, 414	C 5
56520	Breckenridge⊙, 4,200	B 4
† 56472	Breezy Point Village, 233	D 4
56119	Brewster, 563	C 7
56014	Bricelyn, 470	E 7
55710	Britt, 175	F 3
55429	Brooklyn Center, 35,173	G 5
† 55401	Brooklyn Park, 26,230	G 5
56715	Brooks, 163	B 3
55711	Brookston, 137	F 4
56316	Brooten, 615	C 5
56438	Browerville, 665	D 4
55918	Brownsdale, 625	F 7
56219	Browns Valley, 906	B 5
55919	Brownsville, 417	G 7
55312	Brownton, 688	D 6
55712	Bruno, 130	F 4
† 55051	Brunswick, 144	E 5
56317	Buckman, 158	D 5
55313	Buffalo⊙, 3,275	E 5
55314	Buffalo Lake, 758	D 6
55713	Buhl, 1,303	F 3
55378	Burnsville, 19,940	E 6
56318	Burtrum, 135	D 5
56120	Butterfield, 619	D 7
† 56723	Bygland, 475	B 3
55920	Byron, 1,419	F 6
55921	Caledonia⊙, 2,619	G 7
56521	Callaway, 233	C 3
55716	Calumet, 460	E 3
55008	Cambridge⊙, 3,467	E 5
56522	Campbell, 339	B 4
56220	Canby, 2,081	B 6
55009	Cannon Falls, 2,072	F 6
55922	Canton, 391	F 7
55717	Canyon, 125	F 3
56319	Carlos, 260	C 5
55718	Carlton⊙, 884	F 4
55315	Carver, 669	E 6
56633	Cass Lake, 1,317	D 3
55010	Castle Rock, 150	E 6
55012	Center City⊙, 324	F 5
† 55038	Centerville, 534	E 5
56121	Ceylon, 487	D 7
55316	Champlin, 2,275	G 5
56122	Chandler, 319	C 7
55317	Chanhassen, 4,879	F 6
55318	Chaska⊙, 4,352	F 6
55923	Chatfield, 1,885	F 7
55013	Chisago City, 1,068	E 5
55719	Chisholm, 5,913	E 3
56221	Chokio, 455	B 5
55014	Circle Pines, 3,918	G 5
56222	Clara City, 1,491	C 6
55924	Claremont, 520	E 6
56440	Clarissa, 599	C 4
56223	Clarkfield, 1,084	C 6
56016	Clarks Grove, 480	E 7
56634	Clearbrook, 599	C 3
55319	Clear Lake, 280	E 5
55320	Clearwater, 282	D 5
56224	Clements, 252	D 6
56017	Cleveland, 492	E 6
56523	Climax, 255	B 3
56225	Clinton, 608	B 5
56524	Clitherall, 131	C 4
56226	Clontarf, 147	C 5
55720	Cloquet, 8,699	F 4
55015	Cloverton, 150	F 4
55721	Cohasset, 536	E 3
55321	Cokato, 1,735	D 5
56320	Cold Spring, 2,006	D 5
55722	Coleraine, 1,086	E 3
56321	Collegeville, 1,600	D 5
55322	Cologne, 518	E 6
55421	Columbia Heights, 23,997	G 5
56019	Comfrey, 525	D 6
56525	Comstock, 135	B 4
56020	Conger, 167	E 7
55723	Cook, 687	F 3
55433	Coon Rapids, 30,505	G 5
† 55340	Corcoran, 1,656	F 5
56228	Cosmos, 570	D 6
55016	Cottage Grove, 13,419	F 6
55724	Cotton, 350	F 3
56229	Cottonwood, 794	C 6
56021	Courtland, 360	D 6
55725	Crane Lake, 350	F 2
55726	Cromwell, 181	F 4
56716	Crookston⊙, 8,312	B 3
56441	Crosby, 2,241	D 4
56442	Crosslake, 358	E 4
† 55005	Crown, 200	E 5
† 55401	Crystal, 30,925	G 5
55323	Crystal Bay, 6,787	F 5
56123	Currie, 368	C 6
56323	Cyrus, 289	C 5
55925	Dakota, 369	G 7
56324	Dalton, 221	C 4
56230	Danube, 497	C 6
56231	Danvers, 136	C 5
56022	Darfur, 179	D 6
55324	Darwin, 224	D 5
55325	Dassel, 1,058	D 5
56232	Dawson, 1,699	B 6
55327	Dayton, 517	E 5
55391	Deephaven, 3,853	G 5
56527	Deer Creek, 287	C 4
56636	Deer River, 815	E 3
56444	Deerwood, 448	E 4
56233	De Graff, 195	C 5
55328	Delano, 1,851	E 5
56023	Delavan, 281	D 7
56234	Delhi, 154	C 6
† 55110	Dellwood, 514	F 5
55018	Dennison, 162	E 6
56528	Dent, 156	C 4
56501	Detroit Lakes⊙, 5,797	C 4
55926	Dexter, 252	F 7
56529	Dilworth, 2,321	B 4
55927	Dodge Center, 1,603	F 6
56235	Donnelly, 252	B 5
55929	Dover, 321	F 7
55930	Dresbach, 250	G 7
* 55801	Duluth⊙, 100,578	F 4
	Duluth-Superior, ‡265,350	F 4
56236	Dumont, 204	B 5
55019	Dundas, 460	E 6
56126	Dundee, 138	C 7
56127	Dunnell, 237	D 7
56446	Eagle Bend, 557	D 4
† 55005	East Bethel, 2,586	E 5
56024	Eagle Lake, 839	E 6
† 56031	East Chain, 171	D 7
56721	East Grand Forks, 7,607	B 3
† 56401	East Gull Lake, 440	D 4
56025	Easton, 352	E 7
56237	Echo, 356	C 6
55343	Eden Prairie, 6,938	G 6
55329	Eden Valley, 776	D 5
56128	Edgerton, 1,119	B 7
55424	Edina, 44,046	G 5
56639	Effie, 165	E 3
55931	Eitzen, 208	G 7
† 55910	Elba, 158	F 6
56531	Elbow Lake⊙, 1,484	B 5
55932	Elgin, 580	F 6
56533	Elizabeth, 188	B 4
55330	Elk River⊙, 2,252	E 5
55933	Elkton, 134	F 7
56026	Ellendale, 569	E 7
56129	Ellsworth, 588	C 7
56027	Elmore, 910	D 7
56325	Elrosa, 203	C 5
55731	Ely, 4,904	G 3
56028	Elysian, 445	E 6
55732	Embarrass, 195	F 3
56447	Emily, 386	E 4
56029	Emmons, 412	E 7
56534	Erhard, 748	B 4
56640	Ericsburg, 300	E 2
56535	Erskine, 571	B 3
55733	Esko, 500	F 4
56722	Euclid, 130	B 3
56238	Evan, 126	D 6
56326	Evansville, 553	C 4
55734	Eveleth, 4,721	F 3
55331	Excelsior, 2,563	E 6
55934	Eyota, 639	F 7
55332	Fairfax, 1,432	D 6
55383	Fairhaven, 129	D 5
56031	Fairmont⊙, 10,751	D 7
55113	Falcon Heights, 5,507	G 5
55021	Faribault⊙, 16,595	E 6
55024	Farmington, 3,104	E 6
56641	Federal Dam, 147	D 3
56536	Felton, 232	B 3
56537	Fergus Falls⊙, 12,443	B 4
56540	Fertile, 955	B 3
56448	Fifty Lakes, 143	D 4
55603	Finland, 300	G 3
55735	Finlayson, 192	F 4
56723	Fisher, 383	B 3
56328	Flensburg, 259	D 5
55736	Floodwood, 650	E 4
† 55792	Florenton, 635	F 3
56329	Foley⊙, 1,271	D 5
† 56308	Forada, 158	C 5
55738	Forbes, 225	F 3
55025	Forest Lake, 3,207	F 5
56330	Foreston, 273	E 5
56542	Fosston, 1,684	C 3
55935	Fountain, 347	F 7
56543	Foxhome, 185	B 4
55333	Franklin, 557	D 6
56544	Frazee, 1,015	C 4
56032	Freeborn, 296	E 7
56331	Freeport, 593	D 5
† 55801	French River, 200	G 4
55421	Fridley, 29,233	G 5
55026	Frontenac, 223	F 6
56033	Frost, 290	D 7
56131	Fulda, 1,226	C 7
56034	Garden City, 270	D 6
56332	Garfield, 198	C 5
56450	Garrison, 125	E 4
56132	Garvin, 201	C 6
56545	Gary, 265	B 3
55334	Gaylord⊙, 1,720	D 6
56035	Geneva, 358	E 7
56717	Gentilly, 163	B 3
56546	Georgetown, 141	B 3
55740	Gheen, 145	F 3
56239	Ghent, 301	C 6
55335	Gibbon, 877	D 6
55741	Gilbert, 2,287	F 3
† 56431	Glen, 125	E 4
55336	Glencoe⊙, 4,217	D 6
56036	Glenville, 740	E 7
56334	Glenwood⊙, 2,584	C 5
56547	Glyndon, 674	B 4
55427	Golden Valley, 24,246	G 5
56644	Gonvick, 344	C 3
55027	Goodhue, 539	F 6
55742	Goodland, 175	E 3
56725	Goodridge, 144	C 2
56037	Good Thunder, 489	D 6
55027	Goodview, 1,829	G 6
56240	Graceville, 735	B 5
56039	Granada, 381	D 7
55604	Grand Marais⊙, 1,301	G 2
55936	Grand Meadow, 869	F 7
55744	Grand Rapids⊙, 7,247	E 3
55029	Grandy, 155	E 5
56241	Granite Falls⊙, 3,225	C 6
55030	Grasston, 132	E 5
56726	Greenbush, 787	B 2
† 55373	Greenfield, 977	F 5
55338	Green Isle, 363	E 6
56242	Green Valley, 129	C 6
56335	Greenwald, 244	D 5
56336	Grey Eagle, 325	D 5
56243	Grove City, 502	D 5
56727	Grygla, 211	C 2
56452	Hackensack, 220	D 4
56133	Hadley, 119	C 7
56728	Hallock⊙, 1,477	A 2
56548	Halstad, 598	B 3
55339	Hamburg, 377	D 6
55340	Hamel, 2,396	F 5
55938	Hammond, 179	F 6
55031	Hampton, 369	E 6
56244	Hancock, 806	C 5
56245	Hanley Falls, 265	C 6
55341	Hanover, 365	E 5
56041	Hanska, 442	D 6
56364	Harding, 119	E 4
56134	Hardwick, 274	B 7
55939	Harmony, 1,130	F 7
55032	Harris, 559	F 5
56042	Hartland, 331	E 7
† 55374	Hassan, 778	E 5
55033	Hastings⊙, 12,195	F 6
56549	Hawley, 1,371	B 4
55940	Hayfield, 939	F 7
56043	Hayward, 261	E 7
55342	Hector, 1,178	D 6
56044	Henderson, 730	E 6
56136	Hendricks, 712	B 6
56550	Hendrum, 311	B 3
56551	Henning, 850	C 4
56248	Herman, 619	B 5
56137	Heron Lake, 777	C 7
56453	Hewitt, 198	C 4
55746	Hibbing, 16,104	F 3
55748	Hill City, 357	E 4
56138	Hills, 571	B 7
55037	Hinckley, 885	E 4
56552	Hitterdal, 178	B 4
56339	Hoffman, 627	C 5
55941	Hokah, 697	G 7
56340	Holdingford, 551	D 5
56139	Holland, 263	B 6
56045	Hollandale, 287	E 7
56249	Holloway, 146	C 5
55749	Holyoke, 190	F 4
55942	Homer, 150	G 6
56045	Hope, 125	E 7
55343	Hopkins, 13,428	G 5
55943	Houston, 1,090	G 7
55606	Hovland, 150	G 2
55349	Howard Lake, 1,162	D 5
55750	Hoyt Lakes, 3,634	F 3
55038	Hugo, 751	E 5
56047	Huntley, 139	D 7
55350	Hutchinson, 8,031	D 6
56140	Ihlen, 132	B 7
† 55359	Independence, 1,993	F 5
56649	International Falls⊙, 6,439	E 2
55075	Inver Grove Heights, 12,148	E 6
56141	Iona, 260	C 7
55751	Iron, 150	F 3
56455	Ironton, 562	D 4
55040	Isanti, 679	E 5
56342	Isle, 551	E 4
56142	Ivanhoe⊙, 738	B 6
56143	Jackson⊙, 3,550	C 7
55752	Jacobson, 225	E 4
56048	Janesville, 1,557	E 6
56144	Jasper, 754	B 7
56145	Jeffers, 436	C 6
56456	Jenkins, 148	D 4
55352	Jordan, 1,836	E 6
† 56669	Kabetogama, 150	F 2
56251	Kandiyohi, 295	D 5
56732	Karlstad, 727	B 2
56050	Kasota, 732	D 6
55944	Kasson, 1,883	F 6
55753	Keewatin, 1,382	E 3
56650	Kelliher, 289	D 3
55945	Kellogg, 403	G 6
55754	Kelly Lake, 950	F 3
55755	Kelsey, 151	F 3
56733	Kennedy, 424	B 2
56343	Kensington, 308	C 5
56553	Kent, 139	B 4
55946	Kenyon, 1,575	E 6
56252	Kerkhoven, 641	C 5
55757	Kettle River, 173	E 4
56051	Kiester, 681	E 7
56052	Kilkenny, 182	E 6
55353	Kimball, 567	D 5
55758	Kinney, 325	F 3
55609	Knife River, 350	G 4
55947	La Crescent, 3,142	G 7
56054	Lafayette, 498	D 6
56149	Lake Benton, 759	B 6
56734	Lake Bronson, 325	B 2
55041	Lake City, 3,594	F 6
56055	Lake Crystal, 1,807	D 6
55042	Lake Elmo, 4,032	F 6
56150	Lakefield, 1,820	C 7
† 55398	Lake Fremont (Zimmerman), 495	E 5
56458	Lake George, 200	D 3
55043	Lakeland, 962	F 6
56253	Lake Lillian, 316	C 6
56554	Lake Park, 658	B 4
† 55043	Lake Saint Croix Beach, 1,111	F 6
† 56401	Lake Shore, 410	D 4
55044	Lakeville, 7,556	E 6
56151	Lake Wilson, 378	B 7
56152	Lamberton, 962	C 6
56735	Lancaster, 382	B 2
55949	Lanesboro, 850	G 7
55950	Lansing, 300	F 7
56461	Laporte, 154	D 3
† 55744	La Prairie, 413	E 3
56056	La Salle, 132	D 6

(continued on following page)

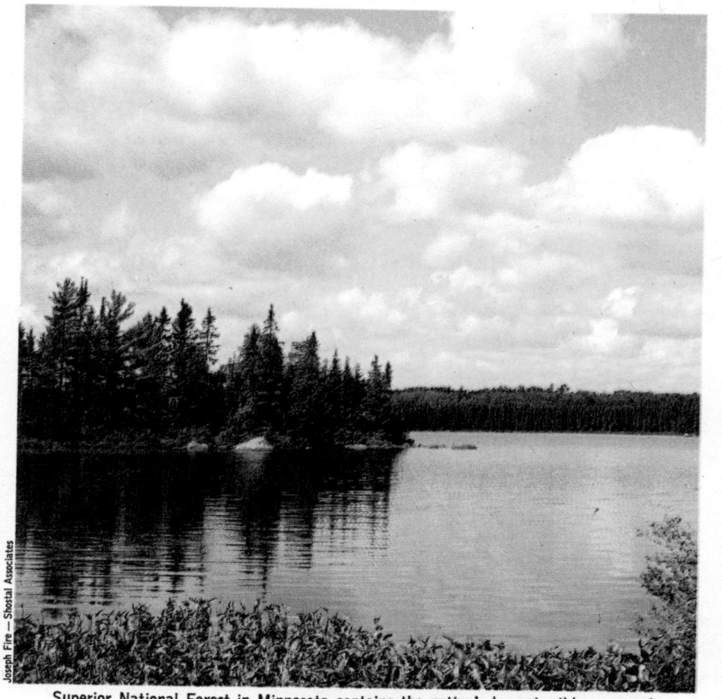
Joseph Fire — Shostal Associates

Superior National Forest in Minnesota contains the nation's largest wilderness park with primitive virgin timberlands, protected wildlife and 5,000 restocked lakes.

56344 Lastrup, 161 ... D 4
† 55101 Lauderdale, 2,419 ... G 5
56057 Le Center⊙, 1,890 ... E 6
56651 Lengby, 140 ... C 3
† 55734 Leonidas, 157 ... F 3
56153 Leota, 285 ... C 7
55951 Le Roy, 870 ... F 7
55354 Lester Prairie, 1,162 ... D 6
56058 Le Sueur, 3,745 ... E 6
55952 Lewiston, 1,000 ... G 7
56060 Lewisville, 291 ... D 7
† 55014 Lexington, 1,926 ... G 5
† 55050 Lilydale, 664 ... G 5
55045 Lindstrom, 1,260 ... F 5
† 55038 Lino Lakes, 3,692 ... G 5
56155 Lismore, 323 ... B 7
55355 Litchfield⊙, 5,262 ... D 5
56345 Little Falls⊙, 7,467 ... D 5
56653 Littlefork, 824 ... E 2
55611 Little Marais, 175 ... G 3
56334 Long Beach, 219 ... C 5
55356 Long Lake, 1,506 ... F 5
56347 Long Prairie⊙, 2,416 ... D 5
56655 Longville, 171 ... D 4
55046 Lonsdale, 622 ... E 6
55357 Loretto, 340 ... F 5
56349 Lowry, 257 ... C 5
56255 Lucan, 254 ... C 6
55612 Lutsen, 620 ... F 2
56156 Luverne⊙, 4,703 ... B 7
55953 Lyle, 522 ... F 7
56157 Lynd, 267 ... C 6
55954 Mabel, 888 ... G 7
56062 Madelia, 2,316 ... D 6
56256 Madison⊙, 2,242 ... B 5
56063 Madison Lake, 587 ... E 6
56158 Magnolia, 233 ... B 7
56557 Mahnomen⊙, 1,313 ... C 3
55115 Mahtomedi, 2,640 ... F 5
55762 Mahtowa, 167 ... F 4
56001 Mankato⊙, 30,895 ... E 6
55955 Mantorville⊙, 479 ... F 6
55369 Maple Grove, 6,275 ... F 5
55358 Maple Lake, 1,124 ... D 5
55359 Maple Plain, 1,169 ... F 5
56065 Mapleton, 1,307 ... E 7
55912 Mapleview, 328 ... E 7
55109 Maplewood, 25,222 ... G 5
55764 Marble, 682 ... E 3
56657 Marcell, 350 ... E 3
56257 Marietta, 264 ... B 5
55047 Marine on Saint Croix, 513 ... F 5
56258 Marshall⊙, 9,886 ... C 6
55360 Mayer, 325 ... E 6
56260 Maynard, 455 ... C 6
55956 Mazeppa, 498 ... F 6
55760 McGregor, 331 ... E 4
56556 McIntosh, 753 ... C 3
55761 McKinley, 317 ... F 3
55765 Meadowlands, 128 ... F 3
55049 Medford, 690 ... E 6
55427 Medicine Lake, 930 ... G 5
55340 Medina (Hamel), 2,396 ... F 5
† 56352 Meire Grove, 171 ... C 5
56352 Melrose, 2,273 ... D 5
56464 Menahga, 835 ... C 4
55050 Mendota, 327 ... G 5
† 55050 Mendota Heights, 6,165 ... G 6
56736 Mentor, 236 ... B 3
56465 Merrifield, 300 ... D 4
56737 Middle River, 369 ... B 2
† 55033 Miesville, 192 ... F 6
56353 Milaca⊙, 1,940 ... E 5
56262 Milan, 427 ... C 5
55957 Millville, 139 ... F 6
56263 Milroy, 247 ... C 6
56354 Miltona, 172 ... C 4
* 55401 Minneapolis⊙, 434,400 ... G 5
Minneapolis-Saint Paul, ‡1,813,647 ... G 5
56264 Minneota, 1,320 ... C 6
55959 Minnesota City, 301 ... G 6
56068 Minnesota Lake, 738 ... E 7
55343 Minnetonka, 35,776 ... G 5
† 55364 Minnetrista, 2,878 ... F 5
56265 Montevideo⊙, 5,661 ... C 6
56069 Montgomery, 2,281 ... E 6
55362 Monticello, 1,636 ... E 5
55363 Montrose, 379 ... E 5
56560 Moorhead⊙, 29,687 ... B 4
Moorhead-Fargo, ‡120,238 ... B 4
55767 Moose Lake, 1,400 ... F 4
56266 Mora⊙, 2,582 ... E 5
56266 Morgan, 972 ... D 6
56267 Morris⊙, 5,366 ... C 5
55052 Morristown, 659 ... E 6
56270 Morton, 591 ... C 6
56466 Motley, 351 ... D 4
55364 Mound, 7,572 ... E 6
† 55112 Mounds View, 9,988 ... G 5
55768 Mountain Iron, 1,698 ... F 3
56159 Mountain Lake, 1,986 ... D 7
56271 Murdock, 358 ... C 5
55769 Nashwauk, 1,341 ... E 3
56272 Nassau, 126 ... B 5
56566 Naytahwaush, 350 ... C 3
56355 Nelson, 175 ... C 5
55053 Nerstrand, 231 ... E 6
55772 Nett Lake, 470 ... E 2
56467 Nevis, 308 ... D 4
55366 New Auburn, 274 ... D 6
55112 New Brighton, 19,507 ... G 5
56738 Newfolden, 390 ... B 2
55367 New Germany, 303 ... E 6
56273 New London, 736 ... C 5
55054 New Market, 215 ... E 6
56356 New Munich, 307 ... D 5
55055 Newport, 2,922 ... F 6
56071 New Prague, 2,680 ... E 6
56072 New Richland, 1,113 ... E 7
† 55031 New Trier, 153 ... F 6
56073 New Ulm⊙, 13,051 ... D 6
56567 New York Mills, 791 ... C 4
† 56431 Nichols, 125 ... E 4
56074 Nicollet, 618 ... D 6
56568 Nielsville, 156 ... B 3
56468 Nisswa, 1,011 ... D 4
55770 Nopeming, 268 ... F 4
56274 Norcross, 137 ... B 5
55056 North Branch, 1,106 ... F 5
† 56442 North Crosslake, 362 ... D 4
55057 Northfield, 10,235 ... E 6
56001 North Mankato, 7,347 ... D 6
56661 Northome, 351 ... D 3
56275 North Redwood, 155 ... D 6
56075 Northrop, 188 ... D 7
55109 North Saint Paul, 11,950 ... E 5
55368 Norwood, 1,058 ... E 6
56276 Odessa, 194 ... B 5
56160 Odin, 166 ... D 7
56569 Ogema, 236 ... C 3
56358 Ogilvie, 384 ... E 5
56161 Okabena, 237 ... C 7
56742 Oklee, 536 ... C 3
56277 Olivia⊙, 2,553 ... C 6
56359 Onamia, 670 ... E 4
† 55044 Orchard Lake, 200 ... E 6
56162 Ormsby, 199 ... D 7
† 55323 Orono (Crystal Bay), 6,787 ... F 5
55960 Oronoco, 564 ... F 6
55771 Orr, 315 ... F 2
56278 Ortonville⊙, 2,665 ... B 5
56570 Osage, 175 ... C 4
56360 Osakis, 1,306 ... C 5
56744 Oslo, 417 ... A 2
55369 Osseo, 2,908 ... G 5
55961 Ostrander, 216 ... F 7
† 56058 Ottawa, 125 ... E 6
56571 Ottertail, 180 ... C 4
56662 Outing, 425 ... E 4
55060 Owatonna⊙, 15,341 ... E 6
56469 Palisade, 149 ... E 4
† 55801 Palmers, 150 ... G 4
† 55705 Palo, 158 ... F 3
56361 Parkers Prairie, 882 ... C 4
56470 Park Rapids⊙, 2,772 ... D 4
56362 Paynesville, 1,920 ... D 5
56363 Pease, 187 ... E 5
† 56472 Pelican Lakes (Breezy Point Village), 233 ... D 4
56572 Pelican Rapids, 1,835 ... B 4
56078 Pemberton, 128 ... E 7
55775 Pengilly, 625 ... E 3
56279 Pennock, 255 ... C 5
56472 Pequot Lakes, 499 ... D 4
56573 Perham, 1,933 ... C 4
56574 Perley, 149 ... B 3
55962 Peterson, 269 ... G 7
† 55948 Pickwick, 150 ... G 7
56364 Pierz, 893 ... D 5
56473 Pillager, 374 ... D 4
55063 Pine City⊙, 2,143 ... F 5
55963 Pine Island, 1,640 ... F 6
56474 Pine River, 803 ... D 4
56164 Pipestone⊙, 5,328 ... B 7
55964 Plainview, 2,093 ... F 6
55370 Plato, 303 ... D 6
56748 Plummer, 285 ... B 3
† 55401 Plymouth, 17,593 ... G 5
56666 Ponemah, 531 ... D 2
56280 Porter, 207 ... B 6
55965 Preston⊙, 1,413 ... F 7
55371 Princeton, 2,531 ... E 5
56281 Prinsburg, 448 ... C 6
55372 Prior Lake, 1,114 ... E 6
55810 Proctor, 3,123 ... F 4
† 55752 Rabey, 125 ... E 4
55967 Racine, 197 ... F 7
56475 Randall, 536 ... D 4
55065 Randolph, 350 ... E 6
56668 Ranier, 255 ... E 2
56669 Ray, 200 ... E 2
56282 Raymond, 589 ... C 5
56165 Reading, 150 ... C 7
55968 Reads Landing, 150 ... F 6
56670 Redby, 475 ... D 3
56671 Redlake, 300 ... C 3
56750 Red Lake Falls⊙, 1,740 ... B 3
55066 Red Wing⊙, 10,441 ... F 6
56283 Redwood Falls⊙, 4,774 ... C 6
56672 Remer, 403 ... E 3
56284 Renville, 1,252 ... C 6
56166 Revere, 166 ... C 6
56367 Rice, 366 ... D 5
55423 Richfield, 47,231 ... G 6
56368 Richmond, 866 ... D 5
55422 Robbinsdale, 16,845 ... G 5
55901 Rochester⊙, 53,766 ... F 6
55067 Rock Creek, 805 ... F 5
55373 Rockford, 730 ... F 5
56369 Rockville, 302 ... D 5
55374 Rogers, 544 ... E 5
55969 Rollingstone, 450 ... G 6
56371 Roscoe, 195 ... D 5
56751 Roseau⊙, 2,552 ... C 2
55970 Rose Creek, 390 ... F 7
† 56216 Roseland, 123 ... C 6
55068 Rosemount, 1,337 ... E 6
55113 Roseville, 34,518 ... G 5
56579 Rothsay, 448 ... B 4
56167 Round Lake, 506 ... C 7
56373 Royalton, 534 ... D 5
55069 Rush City, 1,130 ... F 5
55971 Rushford, 1,318 ... G 7
56168 Rushmore, 394 ... C 7
56169 Russell, 398 ... C 6
56170 Ruthton, 405 ... B 6
55778 Rutledge, 123 ... F 4
56580 Sabin, 333 ... B 4
56285 Sacred Heart, 707 ... C 6
55779 Saginaw, 407 ... F 4
55414 Saint Anthony Falls, 9,239 ... G 5
55375 Saint Bonifacius, 685 ... F 5
55972 Saint Charles, 1,942 ... F 7
56080 Saint Clair, 488 ... E 6
56301 Saint Cloud⊙, 39,691 ... D 5
55070 Saint Francis, 897 ... E 5
56554 Saint Hilaire, 337 ... B 2
56081 Saint James⊙, 4,027 ... D 7
56374 Saint Joseph, 1,786 ... D 5
55426 Saint Louis Park, 48,883 ... G 5
56376 Saint Martin, 188 ... D 5
55376 Saint Michael, 1,021 ... E 5
* 55101 Saint Paul (cap.)⊙, 309,980 ... G 6
55071 Saint Paul Park, 5,587 ... G 6
56082 Saint Peter⊙, 8,339 ... E 6
56375 Saint Stephen, 331 ... D 5
56755 Saint Vincent, 177 ... A 2
56083 Sanborn, 505 ... C 6
55072 Sandstone, 1,641 ... F 4
56377 Sartell, 1,323 ... D 5
56378 Sauk Centre, 3,750 ... C 5
56379 Sauk Rapids, 5,051 ... D 5
55378 Savage, 3,611 ... G 6
55780 Sawyer, 200 ... F 4
55073 Scandia, 200 ... F 5
† 55720 Scanlon, 1,132 ... F 4
55613 Schroeder, 550 ... G 3
56287 Seaforth, 132 ... C 6
56084 Searles, 160 ... D 6
56477 Sebeka, 668 ... C 4
55074 Shafer, 149 ... F 5
55379 Shakopee⊙, 6,876 ... F 6
56581 Shelly, 260 ... B 3
56171 Sherburn, 1,190 ... D 7
56676 Shevlin, 185 ... C 3
† 55021 Shieldsville, 150 ... E 6
† 55331 Shorewood, 4,223 ... F 5
55614 Silver Bay, 3,504 ... G 3
55380 Silver Creek, 125 ... D 5
55381 Silver Lake, 694 ... D 6
† 56001 Skyline, 400 ... D 6
56172 Slayton⊙, 2,351 ... C 7
56085 Sleepy Eye, 3,461 ... D 6
† 56345 Sobieski, 189 ... D 5
55782 Soudan, 900 ... F 3
55382 South Haven, 238 ... D 5
56679 South International Falls, 2,116 ... E 2
55075 South Saint Paul, 25,016 ... G 6
56288 Spicer, 586 ... C 5
56087 Springfield, 2,530 ... C 6
55974 Spring Grove, 1,290 ... G 7
55432 Spring Lake Park, 6,417 ... E 5
55384 Spring Park, 1,087 ... F 5
55975 Spring Valley, 2,572 ... F 7
55079 Stacy, 278 ... E 5
55080 Stanchfield, 155 ... E 5
56479 Staples, 2,657 ... D 4
56381 Starbuck, 1,138 ... C 5
56173 Steen, 191 ... B 7
56757 Stephen, 904 ... A 2
55385 Stewart, 666 ... D 6
55976 Stewartville, 2,802 ... F 7
55082 Stillwater⊙, 10,191 ... F 5
55988 Stockton, 346 ... G 6
56174 Storden, 364 ... C 6
56758 Strandquist, 138 ... B 2
55783 Sturgeon Lake, 167 ... F 4
56289 Sunburg, 144 ... C 5
† 55075 Sunfish Lake, 269 ... E 6
56290 Svea, 125 ... C 6
56382 Swanville, 300 ... D 5
55785 Swatara, 250 ... E 4
55786 Taconite, 352 ... E 3
56291 Taunton, 195 ... B 6
55084 Taylors Falls, 587 ... F 5
56683 Tenstrike, 138 ... D 3
56701 Thief River Falls⊙, 8,618 ... B 2
† 56319 Thomson, 159 ... F 4
56583 Tintah, 167 ... B 5
55615 Tofte, 400 ... H 3
55789 Toivola, 185 ... F 3
† 55331 Tonka Bay, 1,397 ... F 5
55790 Tower, 699 ... F 3
56175 Tracy, 2,516 ... C 6
56176 Trimont, 835 ... D 7
56088 Truman, 1,137 ... D 7
55791 Twig, 165 ... F 4
56089 Twin Lakes, 230 ... E 7
56584 Twin Valley, 868 ... B 3
55616 Two Harbors⊙, 4,437 ... G 3
56178 Tyler, 1,069 ... B 6
56585 Ulen, 486 ... B 3
56586 Underwood, 278 ... C 4
56384 Upsala, 312 ... D 5
† 56361 Urbank, 125 ... C 4
55979 Utica, 240 ... G 7
† 55101 Vadnais Heights, 3,391 ... G 5
56587 Vergas, 281 ... C 4
55085 Vermillion, 359 ... F 6
56481 Verndale, 570 ... C 4
† 55752 Verndon, 135 ... E 4
56090 Vernon Center, 347 ... D 7
55086 Veseli, 150 ... E 6
56292 Vesta, 330 ... C 6
55386 Victoria, 850 ... F 6
56385 Villard, 221 ... C 5
56588 Vining, 121 ... C 4
55792 Virginia, 12,450 ... F 3
55981 Wabasha⊙, 2,371 ... G 6
56293 Wabasso, 738 ... C 6
55387 Waconia, 2,445 ... E 6
56482 Wadena⊙, 4,640 ... C 4
56386 Wahkon, 208 ... E 4
56387 Waite Park, 2,824 ... D 5
56091 Waldorf, 285 ... E 7
56484 Walker⊙, 2,073 ... D 3
56180 Walnut Grove, 756 ... C 6
56092 Walters, 152 ... E 7
55982 Waltham, 189 ... F 7
55983 Wanamingo, 574 ... F 6
56294 Wanda, 124 ... C 6
55743 Warba, 148 ... E 3
56762 Warren⊙, 1,999 ... B 2
56763 Warroad, 1,086 ... C 2
55087 Warsaw, 200 ... E 6
56093 Waseca⊙, 6,789 ... E 6
55388 Watertown, 1,390 ... E 6
56096 Waterville, 1,539 ... E 6
55389 Watkins, 785 ... D 5
56295 Watson, 228 ... C 5
56589 Waubun, 345 ... C 3
55390 Waverly, 546 ... E 5
55391 Wayzata, 3,700 ... G 5
55088 Webster, 175 ... E 6
56181 Welcome, 694 ... D 7
56097 Wells, 2,791 ... E 7
56590 Wendell, 247 ... B 4
56183 Westbrook, 990 ... C 6
55985 West Concord, 718 ... F 6
55118 West Saint Paul, 18,799 ... G 5
56296 Wheaton⊙, 2,029 ... B 5
56485 Whipholt, 142 ... D 3
55110 White Bear Lake, 23,313 ... G 5
56591 White Earth, 150 ... C 3
56184 Wilder, 132 ... C 7
55090 Willernie, 697 ... G 5
56686 Williams, 220 ... D 2
56201 Willmar⊙, 12,869 ... C 5
55795 Willow River, 331 ... F 4
56185 Wilmont, 390 ... C 7
56687 Wilton, 119 ... C 3
56101 Windom⊙, 3,952 ... C 7
56592 Winger, 228 ... B 3
56098 Winnebago, 1,791 ... D 7
55987 Winona⊙, 26,438 ... G 6
55395 Winsted, 1,266 ... D 6
55396 Winthrop, 1,391 ... D 6
55796 Winton, 193 ... G 3
56594 Wolverton, 171 ... B 4
† 55798 Woodbury, 6,184 ... F 6
56297 Wood Lake, 418 ... C 6
56186 Woodstock, 217 ... B 7
56187 Worthington⊙, 9,825 ... C 7
55797 Wrenshall, 147 ... F 4
55798 Wright, 132 ... E 4
55990 Wykoff, 450 ... F 7
55092 Wyoming, 695 ... F 5
55397 Young America, 611 ... E 6
55799 Zim, 608 ... F 3
55398 Zimmerman, 495 ... E 5
55991 Zumbro Falls, 203 ... F 6
55992 Zumbrota, 1,929 ... F 6

⊙ County seat.
‡ Population of metropolitan area.
† Zip of nearest p.o.
* Multiple zips

Agriculture, Industry and Resources

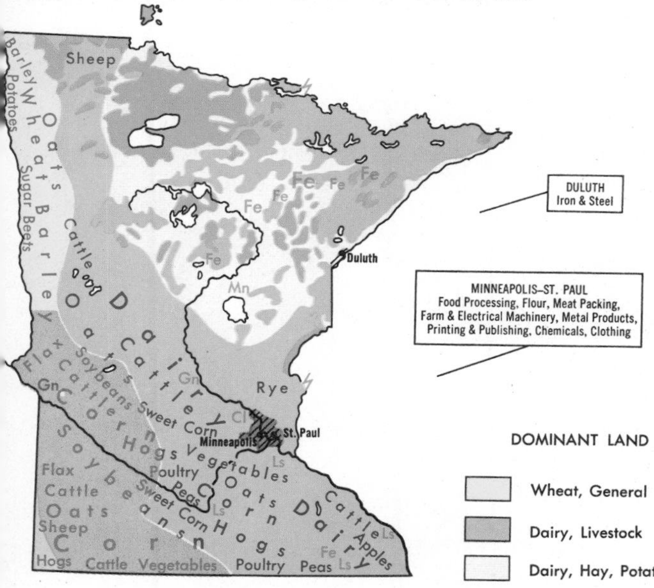

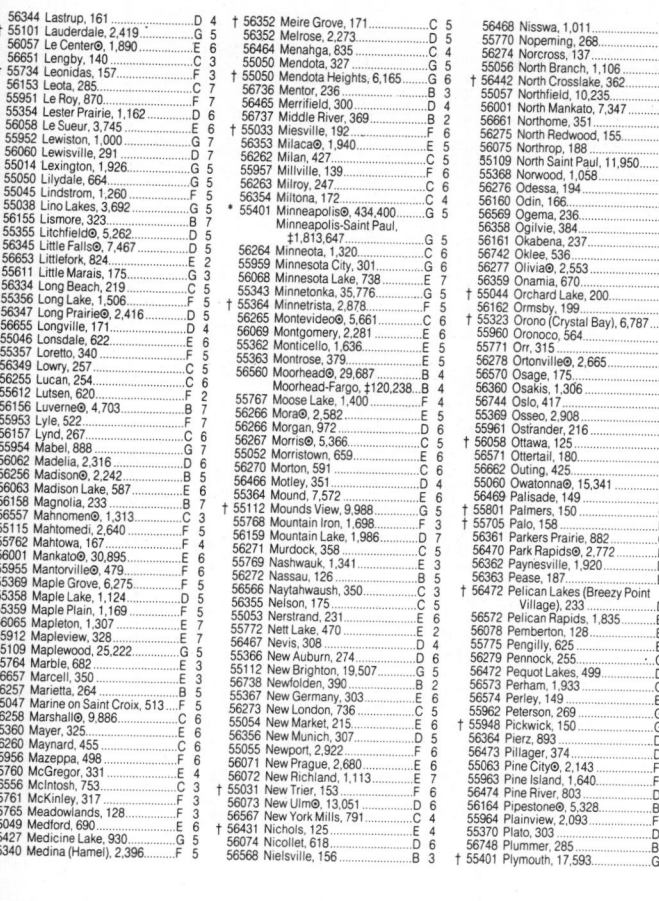

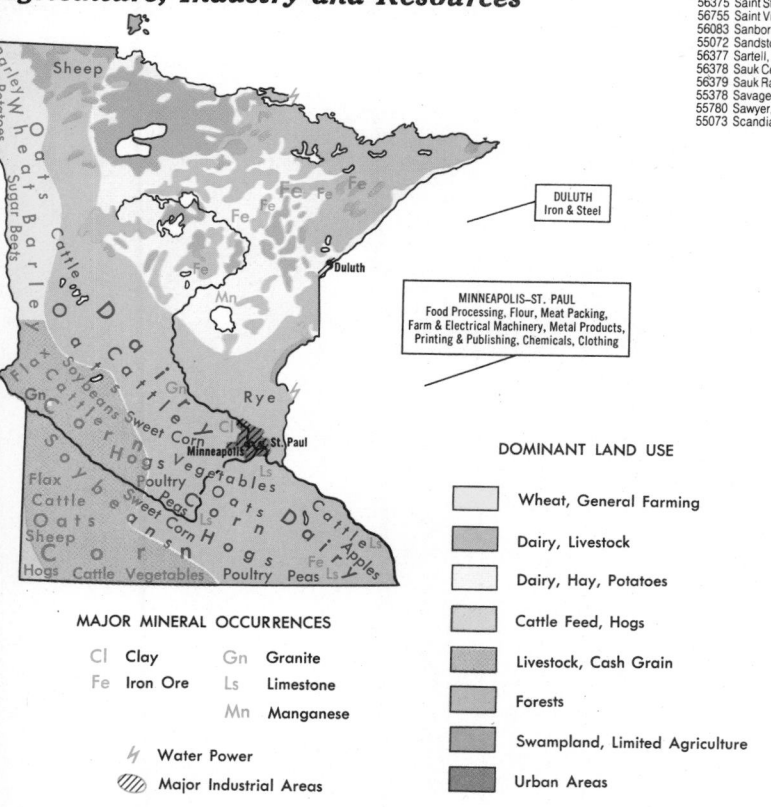

Sheep
Barley
Wheat
Potatoes
Oats
Sugar Beets
Cattle
Dairy
Flax
Soybeans
Corn
Hogs
Rye
Sweet Corn
Vegetables
Poultry
Peas
Apples
Fe
Mn
Gn
Cl
Ls
Duluth
Minneapolis
St. Paul
DULUTH
Iron & Steel
MINNEAPOLIS–ST. PAUL
Food Processing, Flour, Meat Packing, Farm & Electrical Machinery, Metal Products, Printing & Publishing, Chemicals, Clothing

DOMINANT LAND USE

- Wheat, General Farming
- Dairy, Livestock
- Dairy, Hay, Potatoes
- Cattle Feed, Hogs
- Livestock, Cash Grain
- Forests
- Swampland, Limited Agriculture
- Urban Areas

MAJOR MINERAL OCCURRENCES

- Cl Clay
- Fe Iron Ore
- Gn Granite
- Ls Limestone
- Mn Manganese
- Water Power
- Major Industrial Areas

Topography

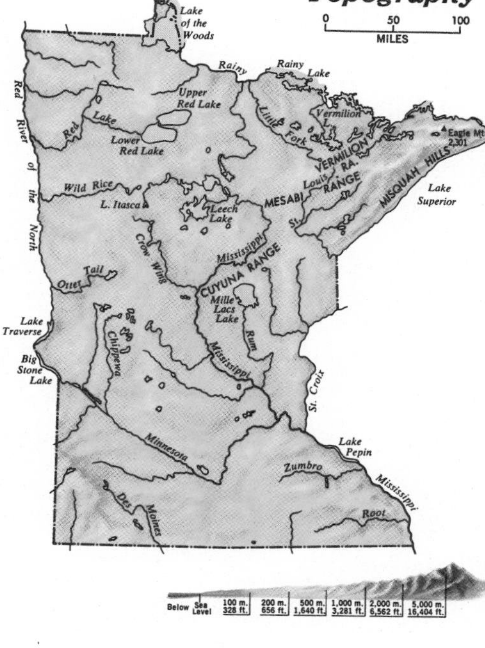

0
50
100
MILES
Lake of the Woods
Rainy
Rainy Lake
Upper Red Lake
Red Lake
Lower Red Lake
Red River of the North
Vermilion
Little Fork
Eagle Mtn. 2,301
VERMILION RA.
MESABI RANGE
MISQUAH HILLS
Lake Superior
St. Louis
Wild Rice
L. Itasca
Leech Lake
Mississippi
Crow Wing
CUYUNA RANGE
Mille Lacs Lake
Otter Tail
Lake Traverse
Big Stone Lake
Chippewa
Rum
St. Croix
Minnesota
Lake Pepin
Zumbro
Root
Des Moines
Below Sea Level
100 m. 328 ft.
200 m. 656 ft.
500 m. 1,640 ft.
1,000 m. 3,281 ft.
2,000 m. 6,562 ft.
5,000 m. 16,404 ft.

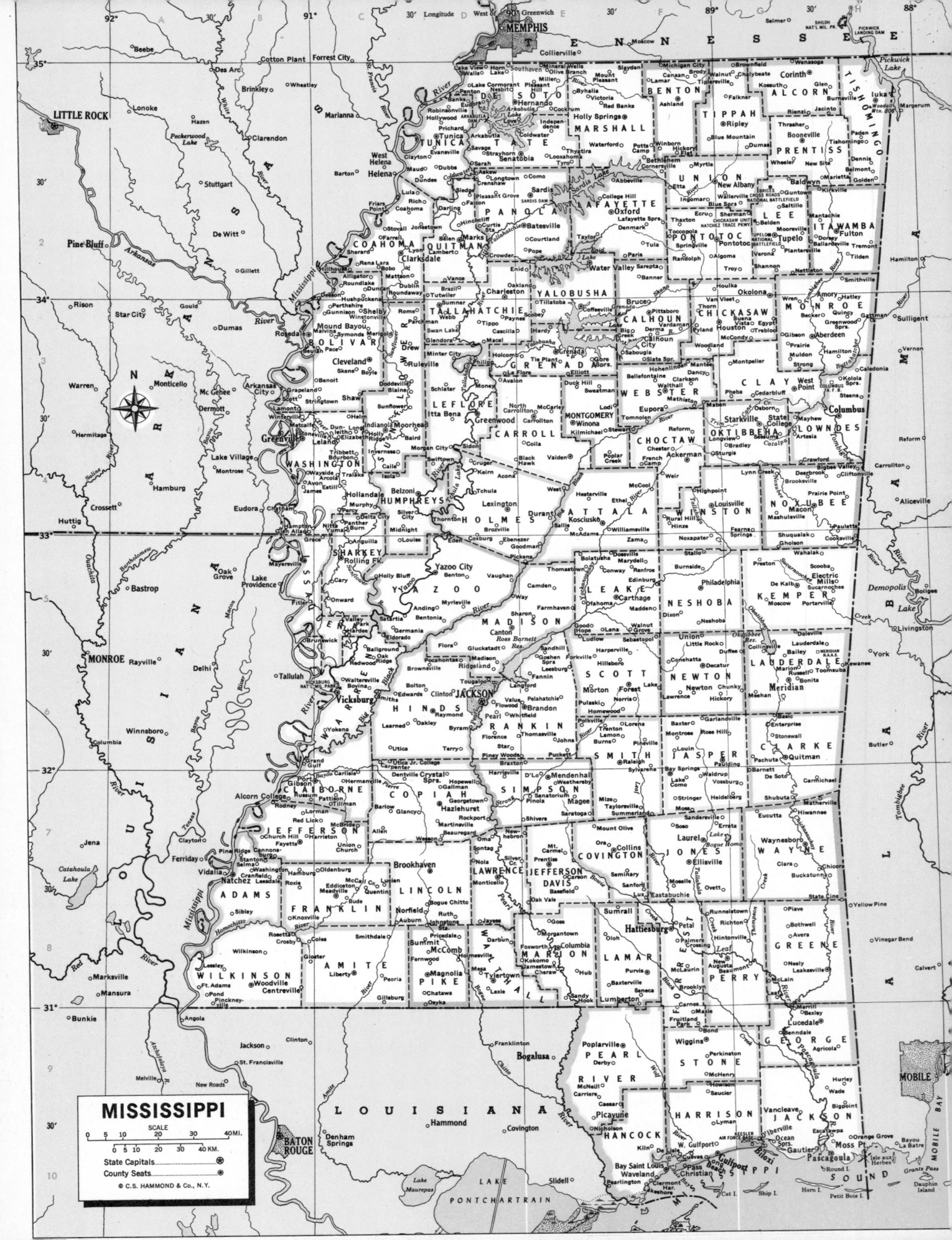

MISSISSIPPI

SCALE
0 5 10   20   30   40 MI.
0 5 10   20   30   40 KM.

State Capitals................⊛
County Seats.................◉

© C.S. HAMMOND & Co., N.Y.

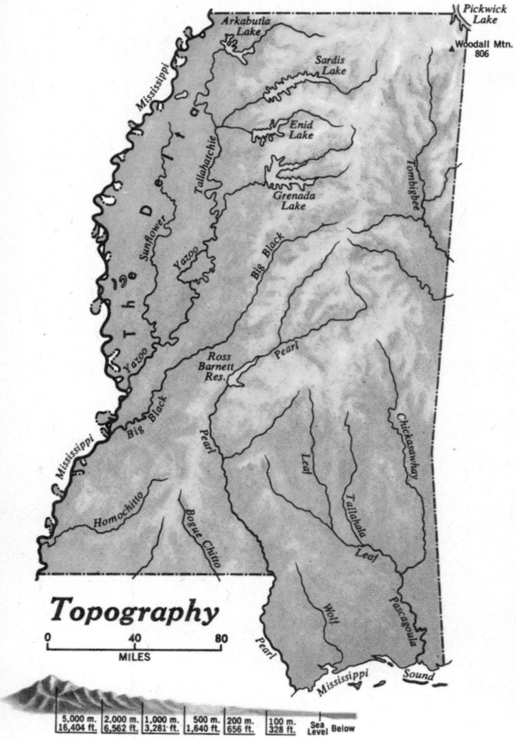

AREA 47,716 sq. mi.
POPULATION 2,216,912
CAPITAL Jackson
LARGEST CITY Jackson
HIGHEST POINT Woodall Mtn. 806 ft.
SETTLED IN 1716
ADMITTED TO UNION December 10, 1817
POPULAR NAME Magnolia State
STATE FLOWER Magnolia
STATE BIRD Mockingbird

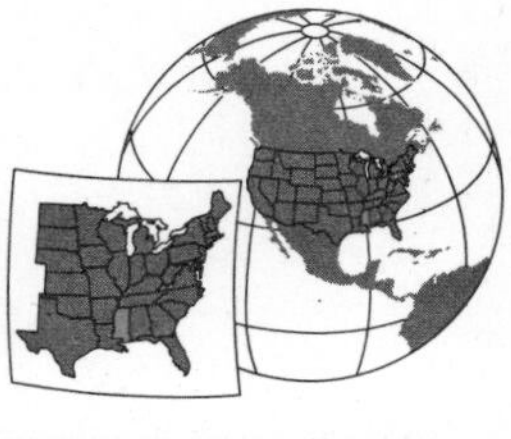

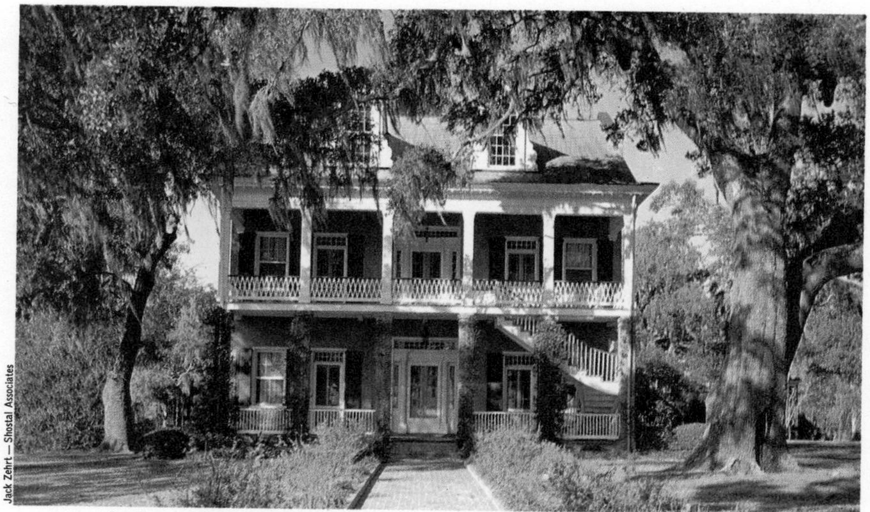

Jack Zehrt — Shostal Associates

Gracious antebellum houses of brick and stucco, shaded by moss-draped oaks, add a sense of permanence to the older section of Biloxi, Mississippi.

COUNTIES

Adams, 37,293 B 8
Alcorn, 27,179 G 1
Amite, 13,763 C 8
Attala, 19,570 E 4
Benton, 7,505 F 1
Bolivar, 49,409 C 3
Calhoun, 14,623 F 3
Carroll, 9,397 E 4
Chickasaw, 16,805 G 3
Choctaw, 8,440 F 4
Claiborne, 10,086 C 7
Clarke, 15,049 G 6
Clay, 18,840 G 3
Coahoma, 40,447 C 2
Copiah, 24,749 D 7
Covington, 14,002 E 7
De Soto, 35,885 E 1
Forrest, 57,849 F 8
Franklin, 8,011 C 8
George, 12,459 G 9
Greene, 8,545 G 8
Grenada, 19,854 E 3
Hancock, 17,387 E 10
Harrison, 134,582 F 10
Hinds, 214,973 D 6
Holmes, 23,120 D 4
Humphreys, 14,601 C 4
Issaquena, 2,737 B 5
Itawamba, 16,847 H 2
Jackson, 87,975 G 9
Jasper, 15,994 F 6
Jefferson, 9,295 B 7
Jefferson Davis, 12,936 E 7
Jones, 56,357 F 7
Kemper, 10,233 G 5
Lafayette, 24,181 E 2
Lamar, 15,209 E 8
Lauderdale, 67,087 G 6
Lawrence, 11,137 D 7
Leake, 17,085 E 5
Lee, 46,148 G 2
Leflore, 42,111 D 3
Lincoln, 26,198 D 8
Lowndes, 49,700 H 4
Madison, 29,737 D 5
Marion, 22,871 E 8
Marshall, 24,027 E 1
Monroe, 34,043 H 3
Montgomery, 12,918 E 4
Neshoba, 20,802 F 5
Newton, 18,983 F 6
Noxubee, 14,288 G 4
Oktibbeha, 28,752 G 4
Panola, 26,829 E 2
Pearl River, 27,802 E 9
Perry, 9,065 G 8
Pike, 31,756 D 8
Pontotoc, 17,363 F 2
Prentiss, 20,133 G 1
Quitman, 15,888 D 2
Rankin, 43,933 E 6
Scott, 21,369 E 6
Sharkey, 8,937 C 5
Simpson, 19,947 E 7
Smith, 13,561 E 6
Stone, 8,101 F 9
Sunflower, 37,047 C 3
Tallahatchie, 19,338 D 3
Tate, 18,544 E 1
Tippah, 15,852 G 1
Tishomingo, 14,940 H 1
Tunica, 11,854 D 1
Union, 19,096 F 2
Walthall, 12,500 D 8
Warren, 44,981 C 6
Washington, 70,581 C 4
Wayne, 16,650 G 7
Webster, 10,047 F 3
Wilkinson, 11,099 B 8
Winston, 18,406 F 4
Yalobusha, 11,915 E 2
Yazoo, 27,304 D 5

CITIES and TOWNS

Zip *Name/Pop.* *Key*

38601 Abbeville, 600 F 2
39730 Aberdeen⊙, 6,157 H 3
39735 Ackerman⊙, 1,502 F 4
† 39095 Acona, 200 D 4
† 39452 Agricola, 200 G 9
39096 Alcorn College, 2,380 B 7
38820 Algoma, 150 G 2
38720 Alligator, 280 C 2
38821 Amory, 7,236 H 3
38721 Anguilla, 612 C 5
38722 Arcola, 517 C 4
38602 Arkabutla, 195 D 1
39736 Artesia, 444 G 4
38603 Ashland⊙, 348 F 1
38604 Askew, 200 D 1
† 39664 Auburn, 500 C 8
38912 Avalon, 275 D 3
† 39456 Avera, 150 G 8
38723 Avon, 400 B 4
39320 Bailey, 320 G 6
38724 Baird, 212 C 4
38824 Baldwyn, 2,366 G 2
† 38801 Ballardsville, 105 H 2
† 38664 Banks, 100 D 1
38913 Banner, 200 F 2
39421 Bassfield, 354 E 8
38606 Batesville⊙, 3,796 E 2
† 39343 Baxter, 225 F 6
† 39455 Baxterville, 100 E 8
39520 Bay Saint Louis⊙, 6,752 F 10
39422 Bay Springs⊙, 1,801 F 7
39423 Beaumont, 1,061 G 8
† 39191 Beauregard, 199 D 7
38825 Becker, 450 G 3
38826 Belden, 241 G 2
38609 Belen, 500 D 2
39737 Bellefontaine, 360 F 3
38827 Belmont, 968 H 1
39038 Belzoni⊙, 3,146 C 4
† 39450 Benndale, 500 G 9
38725 Benoit, 473 C 3
39039 Benton, 500 D 5
39040 Bentonia, 544 D 5
† 38659 Bethlehem, 210 F 1
38726 Beulah, 443 B 3
39453 Bexley, 130 G 9
39738 Bigbee Valley, 370 H 4
38914 Big Creek, 148 F 3
† 39567 Bigpoint, 100 H 9
* 39530 Biloxi, 48,486 G 10
Biloxi-Gulfport, ‡134,582 G 10
38918 Black Hawk, 100 E 4
38610 Blue Mountain, 677 G 1
38828 Blue Springs, 125 G 2
38728 Bobo, 200 C 2
39629 Bogue Chitto, 658 D 8
39041 Bolton, 787 D 6
39550 Bond, 350 F 9
39321 Bonita, 300 G 6
38829 Booneville⊙, 5,895 G 1
† 39456 Bothwell, 100 G 8
38729 Bourbon, 350 C 4
38730 Boyle, 861 C 3
39042 Brandon⊙, 2,685 E 6
39044 Braxton, 180 D 6
38956 Brazil, 229 D 2
39601 Brookhaven⊙, 10,700 C 7
39425 Brooklyn, 750 F 8
39739 Brooksville, 978 G 4
† 38683 Brownfield, 300 G 1
† 39041 Brownsville, 200 D 6
† 39095 Brozville, 150 D 4
38915 Bruce, 2,033 F 3
† 39180 Brunswick, 90 C 5
39322 Buckatunna, 500 G 7
39630 Bude, 1,146 C 8
† 39153 Burns, 100 E 6
38833 Burnsville, 435 H 1
38611 Byhalia, 702 E 1
† 39205 Byram, 250 D 6
† 38754 Caile, 350 C 4
39740 Caledonia, 245 H 3
38916 Calhoun City, 1,847 F 3
39045 Camden, 248 E 5
38612 Canaan, 200 F 1
† 39120 Cannonsburg, 240 B 7
39046 Canton⊙, 10,503 D 5
39049 Carlisle, 350 C 7
† 39360 Carmichael, 150 G 7
39426 Carriere, 900 E 9
38917 Carrollton⊙, 295 E 4
39427 Carson, 285 E 7
39051 Carthage⊙, 3,031 E 5
39054 Cary, 517 C 5
38920 Cascilla, 150 D 3
39741 Cedarbluff, 180 G 3
39631 Centreville, 1,819 B 8
38684 Chalybeate, 350 G 1
38921 Charleston⊙, 2,821 D 2
39632 Chatawa, 300 D 8
† 39483 Cheraw, 100 E 8
39323 Chunky, 280 G 6
39324 Clara, 400 G 7
38614 Clarksdale⊙, 21,673 D 2
† 39752 Clarkson, 100 F 3
39551 Clermont Harbor, 200 F 10
38732 Cleveland⊙, 13,327 C 3
39742 Cliftonville, 280 H 4
39056 Clinton, 7,246 D 6
38617 Coahoma, 350 C 2
38922 Coffeeville⊙, 1,024 E 3
38618 Coldwater, 1,450 E 1
39639 Coles, 195 C 8
† 38655 College Hill, 175 E 2
39428 Collins⊙, 1,934 E 7
39325 Collinsville, 700 G 6
39429 Columbia⊙, 7,587 E 8
39701 Columbus⊙, 25,795 H 3
38619 Como, 1,003 E 1
† 39051 Conway, 125 E 5
38834 Corinth⊙, 11,581 G 1
† 38659 Cornersville, 235 F 1
38620 Courtland, 316 E 2
† 39095 Coxburg, 300 D 5
† 39120 Cranfield, 100 B 7
39743 Crawford, 391 G 4
38621 Crenshaw, 1,271 D 2
39633 Crosby, 491 B 8
38622 Crowder, 815 D 2
38924 Cruger, 415 D 4
39059 Crystal Springs, 4,180 D 7
† 39571 Cuevas, 200 F 10
† 38606 Curtis Station, 200 D 2
† 39751 Dancy, 116 F 3
† 39643 Darbun, 100 D 8
38623 Darling, 250 D 2
39327 Decatur⊙, 1,311 F 6
39328 De Kalb⊙, 1,072 G 5
† 39571 De Lisle, 450 F 10
39061 Delta City, 300 C 4
38838 Dennis, 175 H 1
† 39470 Derby, 189 E 9
38839 Derma, 660 F 3
39360 De Soto, 150 G 7
39532 D'Iberville, 7,288 G 10
† 39350 Dixon, 125 F 5
39062 D'Lo, 485 E 7
38736 Doddsville, 276 C 3
38840 Dorsey, 100 H 2
38737 Drew, 2,574 C 3
38739 Dublin, 385 C 2
38925 Duck Hill, 809 E 3
† 39337 Duffee, 100 G 6
38625 Dumas, 200 G 1
38740 Duncan, 599 C 2
† 38756 Dunleith, 140 C 4
39063 Durant, 2,752 E 4
39436 Eastabuchie, 200 F 8
39064 Ebenezer, 150 D 5
38841 Ecru, 417 F 2
39634 Eddiceton, 175 C 8
39065 Eden, 152 D 5
† 39051 Edinburg, 200 F 5
39066 Edwards, 1,236 C 6
38842 Egypt, 100 G 3
39329 Electric Mills, 200 G 5
38742 Elizabeth, 540 C 4
38926 Elliott, 200 E 3
39437 Ellisville⊙, 4,643 F 7
39330 Enterprise, 458 G 6
39552 Escatawpa, 1,579 G 10
† 38748 Estill, 100 C 4
39067 Ethel, 560 F 4
38627 Etta, 100 F 2
† 38632 Eudora, 200 D 1
39744 Eupora, 1,792 F 3
38628 Falcon, 230 D 2
38629 Falkner, 500 G 1
† 39042 Fannin, 250 E 6
38630 Farrell, 400 C 2
39069 Fayette⊙, 1,725 B 7
39635 Fernwood, 600 D 8
39070 Fitler, 800 B 5
39071 Flora, 987 D 5
39073 Florence, 404 D 6
† 39201 Flowood, 352 D 6
39074 Forest⊙, 4,085 F 6
39076 Forkville, 180 E 6
39636 Fort Adams, 129 B 8
39483 Foxworth, 950 E 8
39745 French Camp, 174 F 4
38631 Friars Point, 1,177 C 2
38843 Fulton⊙, 2,899 H 2
† 39345 Garlandville, 150 F 6
38844 Gattman, 175 H 3
39553 Gautier, 2,087 G 10
39078 Georgetown, 339 D 7
† 39083 Glancy, 120 C 7
38846 Glen, 250 H 1
38744 Glen Allan, 400 B 4
38928 Glendora, 201 D 3
39638 Gloster, 1,401 B 8
† 39110 Gluckstadt, 150 D 5
38847 Golden, 115 H 2
† 39094 Good Hope, 125 E 5
39079 Goodman, 1,194 E 5
38929 Gore Springs, 120 E 3
† 39042 Goshen Springs, 100 E 6
† 39429 Goss, 100 E 8
38745 Grace, 325 C 5
† 38725 Grapeland, 200 B 3
38701 Greenville⊙, 39,648 B 4
38930 Greenwood⊙, 22,400 D 4
38848 Greenwood Springs, 170 H 3
38901 Grenada⊙, 9,944 E 3
39501 Gulfport⊙, 40,791 F 10
38746 Gunnison, 545 C 3
38849 Guntown, 304 G 2
39746 Hamilton, 350 H 3
† 38744 Hampton, 200 B 4
† 39177 Hardee, 100 C 5
39080 Harperville, 260 E 6
39081 Harriston, 500 C 7
39082 Harrisville, 500 D 7
† 38821 Hatley, 500 H 3
39401 Hattiesburg⊙, 38,277 F 8
39083 Hazlehurst⊙, 4,577 D 7
39439 Heidelberg, 1,112 F 7
39086 Hermanville, 500 C 7
38632 Hernando⊙, 2,499 E 1
† 39192 Hesterville, 100 E 4
39332 Hickory, 570 F 6
38633 Hickory Flat, 354 F 1
39087 Hillsboro, 350 E 6
† 38646 Hinchcliff, 125 D 2
† 39462 Hintonville, 100 F 8
† 39108 Hinze, 140 F 4
39333 Hiwannee, 250 G 7
† 39751 Hohenlinden, 96 F 3
38748 Hollandale, 3,260 C 4
39088 Holly Bluff, 250 C 5
38749 Holly Ridge, 375 C 4
38635 Holly Springs⊙, 5,728 E 1
† 38676 Hollywood, 125 D 1
† 39648 Holmesville, 200 D 8
† 39059 Hopewell, 300 D 7
38637 Horn Lake, 850 D 1
38850 Houlka, 646 G 2
38851 Houston⊙, 2,720 G 3
39555 Hurley, 500 H 9
† 38774 Hushpuckena, 100 C 2
38638 Independence, 150 E 1
38751 Indianola⊙, 8,947 C 4
† 38652 Ingomar, 150 F 2
38753 Inverness, 1,119 C 4
38754 Isola, 458 C 4
38941 Itta Bena, 2,489 D 4
38852 Iuka⊙, 2,389 H 1
† 38865 Jacinto, 150 H 1
* 39201 Jackson (cap.)⊙, 153,968 D 6
Jackson, ‡258,906 D 6
† 38748 James, 100 B 4
39641 Jayess, 150 D 8
† 39042 Johns, 90 E 6
38639 Jonestown, 1,110 D 2
39334 Kewanee, 100 H 6
39747 Kilmichael, 543 E 4
39556 Kiln, 750 F 10
† 38856 Kirkville, 200 H 2
† 39661 Knoxville, 100 B 8
39643 Kokomo, 150 E 8
† 39740 Kolola Springs, 150 H 3
39090 Kosciusko⊙, 7,266 E 4
38834 Kossuth, 227 G 1
39092 Lake, 441 F 6
† 39422 Lake Como, 150 F 7
38641 Lake Cormorant, 300 D 1
39558 Lakeshore, 550 F 10
† 38680 Lake View, 125 D 1
38642 Lamar, 135 F 1
38643 Lambert, 1,511 D 2
38755 Lamont, 450 B 3
† 39042 Langford, 100 E 6
39335 Lauderdale, 600 G 5
39440 Laurel⊙, 24,145 F 7
39336 Lawrence, 200 F 6
39450 Leaf, 350 G 8
39451 Leakesville⊙, 1,090 G 8
39093 Learned, 116 C 6
38942 Le Flore, 99 D 3
38756 Leland, 6,000 C 4
† 39074 Lemon, 90 E 6
39094 Lena, 233 E 5
39644 Lessley, 100 B 8
† 39667 Lexie, 270 D 8
39095 Lexington⊙, 2,756 D 4
39645 Liberty⊙, 612 C 8
39337 Little Rock, 130 F 5
† 38828 Long, 110 C 4
39560 Long Beach, 6,170 F 10
† 38665 Longtown, 150 D 1
39749 Longview, 800 G 4
† 38668 Looxahoma, 200 E 1
† 39153 Lorena, 90 F 6
39096 Lorman, 500 B 7
39338 Louin, 382 F 6
39097 Louise, 444 C 5
39339 Louisville⊙, 6,626 G 4
39452 Lucedale⊙, 2,083 G 9
39098 Ludlow, 300 E 5
38644 Lula, 445 C 2
39455 Lumberton, 2,084 E 8
† 39501 Lyman, 500 F 10
38645 Lyon, 383 D 2
39750 Maben, 862 F 3
39341 Macon⊙, 2,612 G 4
39109 Madden, 450 F 5
39110 Madison, 853 D 6
39111 Magee, 2,973 E 7
39652 Magnolia⊙, 1,913 D 8

(continued on following page)

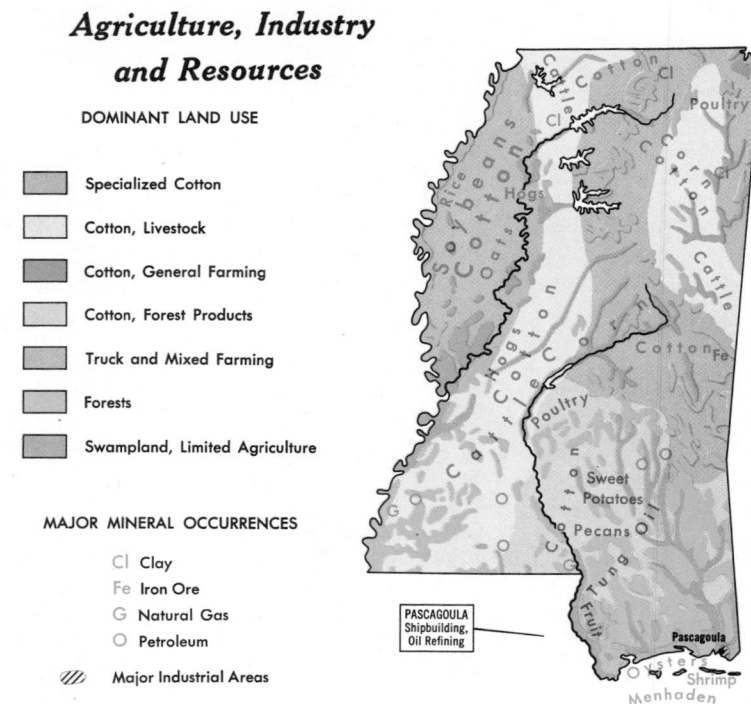

Agriculture, Industry and Resources

DOMINANT LAND USE

- Specialized Cotton
- Cotton, Livestock
- Cotton, General Farming
- Cotton, Forest Products
- Truck and Mixed Farming
- Forests
- Swampland, Limited Agriculture

MAJOR MINERAL OCCURRENCES

- Cl Clay
- Fe Iron Ore
- G Natural Gas
- O Petroleum
- ▨ Major Industrial Areas

PASCAGOULA
Shipbuilding,
Oil Refining

---

† 38769 Malvina, 100......C 3
38855 Mantachie, 200......H 2
39751 Mantee, 142......F 3
38856 Marietta, 250......H 2
39342 Marion, 550......G 6
38646 Marks©, 2,609......D 2
† 39083 Martinsville, 250......D 7
† 39051 Marydell, 125......F 5
39341 Mashulaville, 227......G 4
† 39360 Matherville, 150......G 7
39752 Mathiston, 570......F 3
38758 Mattson, 200......C 2
† 39425 Maxie, 100......F 9
39113 Mayersville©, 500......B 5
39753 Mayhew, 200......G 4
39107 McAdams, 240......E 4
39647 McCall Creek, 250......C 7
38943 McCarley, 250......E 3
39648 McComb, 11,969......D 8
38854 McCondy, 150......G 3
39108 McCool, 225......F 4
39561 McHenry, 550......F 9
39456 McLain, 632......G 8
† 39401 McLaurin, 100......F 8
39457 McNeill, 800......E 9
39653 Meadville©, 594......C 8
† 39301 Meehan, 150......G 6
39114 Mendenhall©, 2,402......E 7
39301 Meridian©, 45,083......G 6
38759 Merigold, 772......C 3
39452 Merrill, 100......G 9
38760 Metcalfe, 600......B 4
38647 Michigan City, 350......F 1
39115 Midnight, 450......C 4
38648 Mineral Wells, 250......E 1
38944 Minter City, 300......D 3
39116 Mize, 372......E 7
38945 Money, 350......D 3
39654 Monticello©, 1,790......D 7
39754 Montpelier, 200......G 3
39343 Montrose, 160......F 6
38857 Mooreville, 200......G 2
38761 Moorhead, 2,284......C 4
38946 Morgan City, 300......D 4
39484 Morgantown, 305......E 8
39117 Morton, 2,672......E 6
39459 Moselle, 525......F 8
39460 Moss, 150......F 7
39563 Moss Point, 19,321......G 10
38762 Mound Bayou, 2,134......C 3
39119 Mount Olive, 923......E 7
38649 Mount Pleasant, 250......E 1
† 38748 Murphy, 100......C 4
38650 Myrtle, 308......F 1
39120 Natchez©, 19,704......B 7
39461 Neely, 200......G 8
38651 Nesbit, 300......D 1
39344 Neshoba, 250......F 5
38858 Nettleton, 1,591......G 2
38652 New Albany©, 6,426......G 2
39462 New Augusta©, 511......F 8
39140 Newhebron, 456......D 7
39345 Newton, 3,556......F 6
39463 Nicholson, 400......E 10
38763 Nitta Yuma, 150......C 4
39665 Nola, 120......D 7
† 39629 Norfield, 225......C 8
38947 North Carrollton, 611......E 3

39346 Noxapater, 554......F 5
38948 Oakland, 493......E 2
† 39154 Oakley, 420......D 6
† 39180 Oak Ridge, 350......C 5
39656 Oak Vale, 166......E 8
39564 Ocean Springs, 9,580......G 10
39141 Ofahoma, 850......E 5
38860 Okolona©, 3,002......G 2
38654 Olive Branch, 1,513......E 1
† 39482 Oloh, 100......E 8
39142 Oma, 100......D 7
† 39428 Ora, 140......E 7
39501 Orange Grove, 200......H 10
39657 Osyka, 628......D 8
39464 Ovett, 250......F 8
38655 Oxford©, 13,846......F 2
38764 Pace, 629......C 3
39347 Pachuta, 271......G 6
38861 Paden, 97......H 1
† 39401 Palmers Crossing, 250......F 8
38765 Panther Burn, 400......C 4
38738 Parchman, 200......D 3
38949 Paris, 253......F 2
39144 Pattison, 540......C 7
39348 Paulding©, 769......F 6
39349 Paulette, 230......H 4
† 38920 Paynes, 100......D 3
39208 Pearl, 9,623......D 6
39572 Pearlington, 500......E 10
39145 Pelahatchie, 1,306......E 6
† 38664 Penton, 175......D 1
39645 Peoria, 100......C 8
39573 Perkinston, 950......F 9
39465 Petal, 6,986......F 8
39755 Pheba, 280......G 3
39350 Philadelphia©, 6,274......F 5
38850 Philipp, 975......D 3
39476 Piave, 250......G 8
39146 Pickens, 1,012......E 5
† 39120 Pine Ridge, 175......B 7
39148 Piney Woods, 300......D 6
39149 Pinola, 102......E 7
38951 Pittsboro©, 188......F 3
38862 Plantersville, 910......G 2
38657 Pleasant Grove, 150......D 2
38651 Pleasant Hill, 400......E 1
39118 Polkville, 500......E 6
38863 Pontotoc©, 3,453......G 2
38568 Pope, 210......E 2
39747 Poplar Creek, 100......F 4
39470 Poplarville©, 2,312......E 9
39352 Porterville, 150......G 5
39150 Port Gibson©, 2,589......B 7
38659 Potts Camp, 459......F 1
39353 Prairie Point, 150......H 4
39474 Prentiss©, 1,789......E 7
39354 Preston, 120......G 5
39666 Pricedale, 400......D 8
38660 Prichard, 150......D 1
39152 Puckett, 333......E 6
39152 Pulaski, 108......E 6
39475 Purvis©, 1,860......F 8
38851 Pyland, 120......F 3
39660 Quentin, 150......C 8
39355 Quitman©, 2,702......G 6

39153 Raleigh©, 1,018......F 6
38864 Randolph, 205......F 2
39154 Raymond©, 1,620......D 6
38661 Red Banks, 350......F 1
† 39096 Red Lick, 250......B 7
39156 Redwood, 400......C 6
39757 Reform, 150......F 4
38767 Rena Lara, 400......C 2
† 39051 Renfroe, 100......F 5
39476 Richton, 1,110......G 8
39475 Ridgeland, 1,650......D 6
38865 Rienzi, 363......G 1
38663 Ripley©, 3,482......G 1
38664 Robinsonville, 285......D 1

39083 Rockport, 100......D 7
39096 Rodney, 200......B 7
39159 Rolling Fork©, 2,034......C 5
38768 Rome, 171......C 3
38769 Rosedale©, 2,599......B 3
39356 Rose Hill, 300......F 6
38614 Roundaway, 175......C 2
† 38740 Roundlake, 105......C 2
39661 Roxie, 662......B 8
38771 Ruleville, 2,351......D 3
† 39401 Runnelstown, 200......F 8
39108 Rural Hill, 125......F 4
39357 Russell, 300......G 6
39662 Ruth, 150......D 8

† 38955 Sabougla, 100......F 3
39160 Sallis, 213......E 4
38866 Saltillo, 836......G 2
39112 Sanatorium, 400......E 7
39477 Sandersville, 694......F 7
39161 Sandhill, 392......E 5
39478 Sandy Hook, 108......E 8
38665 Sarah, 300......D 1
38667 Sardis©, 2,391......E 2
38867 Sarepta, 650......F 2
39574 Saucier, 100......F 9
38667 Savage, 100......D 1
38952 Schlater, 398......D 3
38953 Scobey, 100......E 3
39358 Scooba, 626......G 5
38772 Scott, 500......B 3
39359 Sebastopol, 268......F 5
39479 Seminary, 269......E 7
38668 Senatobia©, 4,247......E 1
39758 Sessums, 100......G 4
38868 Shannon, 575......G 2
38773 Shaw, 2,513......C 3
38774 Shelby, 2,645......C 3
38669 Sherard, 160......C 2
38869 Sherman, 468......G 2
39164 Shivers, 100......E 7
39360 Shubuta, 602......G 7
39361 Shuqualak, 591......G 5
39165 Sibley, 250......B 8
38954 Sidon, 348......D 4
39166 Silver City, 370......C 4
39663 Silver Creek, 257......D 7
38775 Skene, 300......C 3
38955 Slate Spring, 105......F 3
† 38642 Slayden, 310......F 1
38670 Sledge, 516......D 2
39664 Smithdale, 200......C 8
38870 Smithville, 552......H 2
39665 Sontag, 200......D 7
39480 Soso, 230......F 7
38671 Southaven, 8,931......E 1
38863 Springville, 100......F 2
† 39350 Stallo, 100......F 5
39167 Star, 575......D 6
39759 Starkville©, 11,369......G 4
39762 State College, 4,595......G 4
39362 State Line, 598......G 8
39766 Steens, 125......H 3
39767 Stewart, 150......F 4
38776 Stoneville, 700......C 4
39363 Stonewall, 1,161......G 6
38672 Stovall, 260......C 2
38665 Strayhorn, 800......D 1
39481 Stringer, 340......F 7
38777 Stringtown, 300......C 3
39769 Sturgis, 321......G 4
39168 Summerland, 150......F 7
39666 Summit, 1,640......D 8
38957 Sumner©, 533......D 3
39482 Sumrall, 955......E 8
38778 Sunflower, 983......C 3
38958 Swan Lake, 250......D 3
38959 Swiftown, 400......D 4
39153 Sylvarena, 115......F 6
† 38769 Symonds, 200......C 3
38673 Taylor, 92......F 2
39168 Taylorsville, 1,299......F 7
39169 Tchula, 1,729......D 4
39170 Terry, 546......D 6
38871 Thaxton, 250......F 2
39171 Thomastown, 350......E 5
38872 Thorn, 125......F 3
39172 Thornton, 120......D 4

38829 Thrasher, 800......G 1
† 38668 Thyatira, 100......E 1
38960 Tie Plant, 950......E 3
† 38843 Tilden, 250......H 2
38961 Tillatoba, 102......E 3
38674 Tiplersville, 120......G 1
38962 Tippo, 200......D 3
38873 Tishomingo, 410......H 1
38874 Toccopola, 175......F 2
39770 Tomnolen, 225......F 4
38364 Toomsuba, 500......G 6
39174 Tougaloo, 1,720......D 6
38757 Tralake, 200......C 4
38875 Trebloc, 750......G 3
38876 Tremont, 250......H 2
38779 Tribbett, 200......C 4
† 38663 Troy, 150......G 2
38675 Tula, 100......F 2
38676 Tunica©, 1,685......D 1
38801 Tupelo©, 20,471......G 2
38963 Tutwiler, 1,103......D 2
39667 Tylertown©, 1,736......D 8
39365 Union, 1,856......F 5
39668 Union Church, 194......C 7
39175 Utica, 1,019......C 6
39175 Utica Junior College, 700......C 6
39176 Vaiden©, 716......E 4
39177 Valley Park, 350......C 5
39178 Value, 327......F 5
38964 Vance, 500......D 2
39564 Vancleave, 505......G 9
† 38851 Van Vleet, 300......G 3
38878 Vardaman, 777......F 3
38879 Verona, 1,877......G 2
39180 Vicksburg©, 25,478......C 6
38679 Victoria, 400......E 1
39366 Vossburg, 250......F 7
39575 Wade, 800......G 9
38683 Walnut, 458......G 1
39189 Walnut Grove, 398......F 5
39180 Waltersville, 150......C 6
39771 Walthall©, 161......F 3
39190 Washington, 250......B 7
38685 Waterford, 375......E 1
38965 Water Valley©, 3,285......E 2
39576 Waveland, 3,108......F 10
39367 Waynesboro©, 4,368......G 7
38780 Wayside, 250......C 4
38966 Webb, 751......D 3
39772 Weir, 573......F 4
38886 Wenasoga, 125......F 1
39191 Wesson, 1,253......D 7
39192 West, 305......E 4
39501 West Gulfport, 6,996......F 10
39773 West Point©, 8,714......G 3
38880 Wheeler, 600......G 1
39193 Whitfield, 6,200......E 6
39577 Wiggins©, 2,995......F 9
39090 Williamsville, 250......F 1
38659 Winborn, 122......F 1
38967 Winona©, 5,521......E 4
38781 Winstonville, 536......C 3
38782 Winterville, 500......B 4
39776 Woodland, 130......F 3
39669 Woodville©, 1,734......B 8
† 39730 Wren, 150......G 3
39194 Yazoo City©, 10,796......D 5
39090 Zama, 125......F 5

© County seat.
‡ Population of metropolitan area.
† Zip of nearest p.o.
▲ Multiple zips

MISSISSIPPI-MISSOURI RIVER SYSTEM

MILES
0   100   200   300

Navigable Waterways
over 9 feet deep
Major River Ports ©

© Copyright HAMMOND INCORPORATED.

COUNTIES

Adair, 22,472 G 2
Andrew, 11,913 C 3
Atchison, 9,240 B 2
Audrain, 25,362 J 4
Barry, 19,597 E 9
Barton, 10,431 D 7
Bates, 15,468 D 6
Benton, 9,695 F 6
Bollinger, 8,820 M 8
Boone, 80,911 H 4
Buchanan, 86,915 C 3
Butler, 33,529 M 9
Caldwell, 8,351 E 3
Callaway, 25,850 J 5
Camden, 13,315 G 6
Cape Girardeau, 49,350 N 8
Carroll, 12,565 F 4
Carter, 3,878 L 9
Cass, 39,448 D 5
Cedar, 9,424 E 7
Chariton, 11,084 F 3
Christian, 15,124 F 9
Clark, 8,260 J 2
Clay, 123,322 D 4
Clinton, 12,462 D 3
Cole, 46,228 H 6
Cooper, 14,732 G 5
Crawford, 14,828 K 7
Dade, 6,850 E 8
Dallas, 10,054 F 7
Daviess, 8,420 E 3
De Kalb, 7,305 D 3
Dent, 11,457 J 7
Douglas, 9,268 G 9
Dunklin, 33,742 M10
Franklin, 55,116 K 6
Gasconade, 11,878 J 6
Gentry, 8,060 D 2
Greene, 152,929 F 8
Grundy, 11,819 E 2
Harrison, 10,257 E 2
Henry, 18,451 E 6
Hickory, 4,481 F 7
Holt, 6,654 B 2
Howard, 10,561 G 4
Howell, 23,521 J 9
Iron, 9,529 L 7
Jackson, 654,558 D 5
Jasper, 79,852 D 8
Jefferson, 105,248 L 6
Johnson, 34,172 E 5
Knox, 5,692 H 2
Laclede, 19,944 G 7
Lafayette, 26,626 E 4
Lawrence, 24,585 E 8
Lewis, 10,993 J 2
Lincoln, 18,041 L 4
Linn, 15,125 F 3
Livingston, 15,368 E 3
Macon, 15,432 G 3
Madison, 8,641 M 8
Maries, 6,851 J 6
Marion, 28,121 J 3
McDonald, 12,357 D 9
Mercer, 4,910 E 2
Miller, 15,026 H 6
Mississippi, 16,647 O 9
Moniteau, 10,742 G 5
Monroe, 9,542 H 3
Montgomery, 11,000 K 5
Morgan, 10,068 G 6
New Madrid, 23,420 N 9
Newton, 32,901 D 9
Nodaway, 22,467 C 2
Oregon, 9,180 K 9
Osage, 10,994 J 6
Ozark, 6,226 H 9
Pemiscot, 26,373 N10
Perry, 14,393 N 7
Pettis, 34,137 F 5
Phelps, 29,481 J 7
Pike, 16,928 K 4
Platte, 32,081 C 4
Polk, 15,415 F 7
Pulaski, 53,781 H 7
Putnam, 5,916 F 2
Ralls, 7,764 J 3
Randolph, 22,434 G 3
Ray, 17,599 E 4
Reynolds, 6,106 L 8
Ripley, 9,803 L 9
Saint Charles, 92,954 L 5
Saint Clair, 7,667 E 6
Sainte Genevieve, 12,867 M 7
Saint Francois, 36,818 M 7
Saint Louis, 951,353 M 5
Saint Louis (city county), 622,236 M 5
Saline, 24,633 F 4
Schuyler, 4,665 G 2
Scotland, 5,499 H 2
Scott, 33,250 N 8
Shannon, 7,196 K 8
Shelby, 7,906 H 3
Stoddard, 25,771 N 9
Stone, 9,921 F 9
Sullivan, 7,572 F 2
Taney, 13,023 F 9
Texas, 18,320 J 8
Vernon, 19,065 D 7
Warren, 9,699 K 5
Washington, 15,086 L 7
Wayne, 8,546 L 8
Webster, 15,562 G 8
Worth, 3,359 D 2
Wright, 13,667 H 8

CITIES and TOWNS

Zip Name/Pop. Key
64720 Adrian, 1,259 D 6
63730 Advance, 903 N 8
63123 Affton, 24,067 P 3
64836 Airport Drive, 300 C 8
63830 Alba, 365 D 8
64402 Albany⊙, 1,804 D 2
63430 Alexandria, 453 K 2
63001 Allenton, 800 N 3
64001 Alma, 380 E 4
64620 Altamont, 225 D 3
63732 Altenburg, 277 O 7
65606 Alton⊙, 715 K 9
64421 Amazonia, 326 C 3
64722 Amoret, 219 C 6
64831 Anderson, 1,065 D 9
63620 Annapolis, 330 L 8
63820 Anniston, 515 O 9
64724 Appleton City, 1,058 D 6
63821 Arbyrd, 575 M10
63621 Arcadia, 627 L 7
64725 Archie, 525 D 5
65001 Argyle, 262 J 6
65230 Armstrong, 354 G 4
63010 Arnold, 11,994 P 4
65604 Ash Grove, 934 E 8
65010 Ashland, 769 H 5
63530 Atlanta, 377 H 3
63332 Augusta, 259 M 3
65605 Aurora, 5,359 E 9
65231 Auxvasse, 808 J 4
65608 Ava⊙, 2,504 G 9
64010 Avondale, 748 P 5
63011 Ballwin, 10,656 O 3
63531 Baring, 206 H 2
64423 Barnard, 206 C 2
64011 Bates City, 229 E 5
† 65619 Battlefield, 291 F 8
63622 Belgrade, 349 L 7
63735 Bell City, 424 N 8
65013 Belle, 1,133 J 6
† 63101 Bellefontaine Neighbors, 13,987 R 2
63623 Belleview, 225 L 7
63333 Bellflower, 360 K 4
64012 Belton, 9,783 C 5
63736 Benton⊙, 640 O 8
63014 Berger, 226 K 5
63134 Berkeley, 19,743 P 2
63822 Bernie, 1,641 M 9
63823 Bertrand, 604 O 9
64424 Bethany⊙, 2,914 E 2
63532 Bevier, 806 G 3
65610 Billings, 760 F 8
65438 Birch Tree, 573 K 9
† 64068 Birmingham, 266 P 5
63624 Bismarck, 1,387 L 7
65321 Blackburn, 294 F 4
† 63031 Black Jack, 3,500 P 2
65322 Blackwater, 249 G 5
65014 Bland, 621 J 6
63824 Blodgett, 220 O 8
63825 Bloomfield⊙, 1,584 M 9
63627 Bloomsdale, 411 M 6
64015 Blue Springs, 6,779 R 6
† 64101 Blue Summit, 1,283 R 5
64426 Blythedale, 213 E 2
64622 Bogard, 294 E 4
65612 Bois D'Arc, 250 F 8
64427 Bolckow, 225 C 2
65613 Bolivar⊙, 4,769 F 7
63628 Bonne Terre, 3,622 L 7
65016 Bonnots Mill, 210 J 5
65233 Boonville⊙, 7,514 G 5
64723 Bosworth, 386 F 4
65441 Bourbon, 955 K 6
63334 Bowling Green⊙, 2,936 K 4
63826 Braggadocio, 285 N10
63827 Bragg City, 210 N10
65616 Branson, 2,175 F 9
63533 Brashear, 316 H 2
64624 Braymer, 919 E 3
64625 Breckenridge, 598 E 3
† 63101 Breckenridge Hills, 7,011 O 2
63144 Brentwood, 11,248 P 3
63044 Bridgeton, 19,992 O 2
64728 Bronaugh, 203 C 7
64628 Brookfield, 5,491 F 3
64630 Browning, 412 F 2
65236 Brunswick, 1,870 F 4
64631 Bucklin, 654 G 3
64016 Buckner, 1,695 R 5
65622 Buffalo⊙, 1,915 F 7
65237 Bunceton, 437 G 5
63629 Bunker, 447 K 8
64428 Burlington Junction, 634 B 2
64730 Butler⊙, 3,984 D 6
65689 Cabool, 1,848 H 8
63630 Cadet, 300 L 6
64632 Cainsville, 454 E 2
65239 Cairo, 248 H 4
65323 Calhoun, 360 E 6
65018 California⊙, 3,105 H 5
63534 Callao, 373 G 3
64017 Camden, 286 D 4
65020 Camdenton⊙, 1,636 G 6
64429 Cameron, 3,960 D 3
63933 Campbell, 1,979 M 9
63828 Canalou, 358 N 9
63435 Canton, 2,680 J 2
63701 Cape Girardeau, 31,282 O 8
63829 Cardwell, 859 M10
64834 Carl Junction, 1,661 C 8
64633 Carrollton⊙, 4,847 E 4
64835 Carterville, 1,716 D 8
64836 Carthage⊙, 11,035 D 8
63830 Caruthersville⊙, 7,350 N10
65625 Cassville⊙, 1,910 E 9
63015 Catawissa, 250 N 4
65022 Cedar City, 454 H 5
63016 Cedar Hill, 500 L 6
63436 Center, 588 J 3
65023 Centertown, 277 H 5
64019 Centerview, 234 E 5
63633 Centerville⊙, 209 L 8
65240 Centralia, 3,618 H 4
63740 Chaffee, 2,793 N 8
65024 Chamois, 615 J 5
63834 Charleston⊙, 5,131 O 9
63017 Chesterfield, 13,000 O 3
64733 Chilhowee, 297 E 5
64601 Chillicothe⊙, 9,519 E 3
64635 Chula, 244 F 3
63437 Clarence, 1,050 H 3
65243 Clark, 271 H 4
65025 Clarksburg, 343 G 5
64430 Clarksdale, 248 D 3
63336 Clarksville, 668 K 4
63837 Clarkton, 1,177 M10
64119 Claycomo, 1,841 P 5
63105 Clayton⊙, 16,222 P 3
64431 Clearmont, 226 C 1
64734 Cleveland, 256 C 5
65631 Clever, 430 F 8
64735 Clinton⊙, 7,504 E 6
65325 Cole Camp, 1,038 F 6
65201 Columbia⊙, 58,804 H 5
63742 Commerce, 234 O 8
64434 Conception Junction, 237 C 2
64020 Concordia, 1,854 E 5
65632 Conway, 547 G 7
63839 Cooter, 414 N10
64021 Corder, 476 E 4
63338 Cottleville, 275 N 2
† 64501 Country Club Village, 221 C 3
64637 Cowgill, 232 E 3
64437 Craig, 369 B 2
65633 Crane, 1,003 E 9
64739 Creighton, 294 D 6
63018 Crescent, 425 N 3
† 63011 Crestwood, 15,398 O 3
63141 Creve Coeur, 8,967 O 3
65452 Crocker, 814 H 7
65634 Cross Timbers, 204 F 6
63019 Crystal City, 3,898 M 6
65453 Cuba, 2,070 K 6
63339 Curryville, 337 K 4
64439 Dearborn, 543 C 3
64740 Deepwater, 565 E 6
64440 De Kalb, 287 C 3
63744 Delta, 462 N 8
63636 Des Arc, 222 L 8
63601 Desloge, 2,818 M 7
63020 De Soto, 5,984 M 6
63131 Des Peres, 5,333 O 3
63841 Dexter, 6,024 N 9
64840 Diamond, 554 D 9
65459 Dixon, 1,387 H 6
63637 Doe Run, 900 M 7
63935 Doniphan⊙, 1,850 L 9
† 65550 Doolittle, 509 J 7
63844 Dorena, 500 O 9
63536 Downing, 406 H 2
64742 Drexel, 723 C 6
63936 Dudley, 248 M 9
64841 Duenweg, 656 D 8
† 64801 Duquesne, 738 D 8
64442 Eagleville, 388 D 2
64743 East Lynne, 255 D 5
63845 East Prairie, 3,275 O 9
65462 Edgar Springs, 450 J 7
64444 Edgerton, 477 C 4
63537 Edina⊙, 1,574 H 2
65026 Eldon, 3,520 G 6
64744 El Dorado Springs, 3,300 E 7
63638 Ellington, 1,094 L 8
63011 Ellisville, 4,681 N 3
63937 Ellsinore, 342 L 9
63343 Elsberry, 1,398 L 4
63639 Elvins, 1,603 L 7
65466 Eminence⊙, 520 K 8
65327 Emma, 224 F 5
63344 Eolia, 321 L 4
63846 Essex, 493 N 9
* 63601 Esther, 1,040 M 7
63025 Eureka, 2,384 N 3
65646 Everton, 264 E 8
63440 Ewing, 330 J 2
64024 Excelsior Springs, 9,411 R 4
65647 Exeter, 434 D 9
64446 Fairfax, 835 B 2
65648 Fair Grove, 431 F 8
65649 Fair Play, 328 E 7
64842 Fairview, 263 D 9
63345 Farber, 470 J 4
63640 Farmington⊙, 6,590 M 7
65248 Fayette⊙, 3,520 G 4
63026 Fenton, 2,275 P 3
63135 Ferguson, 28,915 P 2
63028 Festus, 7,530 M 6
64449 Fillmore, 251 C 2
63940 Fisk, 503 M 9
63601 Flat River, 4,550 M 7
* 63031 Florissant, 65,908 P 2
63347 Foley, 224 L 4
65652 Fordland, 399 G 8
64451 Forest City, 365 B 3
63348 Foristell, 273 M 2
65653 Forsyth⊙, 803 F 9
63441 Frankford, 472 K 4
65250 Franklin, 252 G 4
63645 Fredericktown⊙, 3,799 M 7
65035 Freeburg, 577 J 6
64746 Freeman, 417 C 5
63748 Frohna, 225 N 7
† 63101 Frontenac, 3,920 O 3
65251 Fulton⊙, 12,148 J 5
65655 Gainesville⊙, 627 G 9
65656 Galena⊙, 391 F 9
64640 Gallatin⊙, 1,833 E 3
64641 Galt, 261 F 2
64747 Garden City, 633 D 5
65036 Gasconade, 235 J 5
63037 Gerald, 762 K 6
63848 Gideon, 1,112 N10
65330 Gilliam, 248 F 4
64642 Gilman City, 376 D 2
64118 Gladstone, 23,128 P 5
65254 Glasgow, 1,336 G 4
† 64068 Glenaire, 505 R 5
63038 Glencoe, 2,500 N 3
63122 Glendale, 6,891 P 3
64748 Golden City, 810 D 8
63843 Goodman, 565 C 9
63543 Gorin, 220 H 1
64454 Gower, 758 C 3
64455 Graham, 213 C 2
64029 Grain Valley, 709 S 6
64844 Granby, 1,678 D 9
63943 Grandin, 243 L 9
64030 Grandview, 17,456 P 6

AREA 69,686 sq. mi.
POPULATION 4,677,399
CAPITAL Jefferson City
LARGEST CITY St. Louis
HIGHEST POINT Taum Sauk Mtn. 1,772 ft.
SETTLED IN 1764
ADMITTED TO UNION August 10, 1821
POPULAR NAME Show Me State
STATE FLOWER Hawthorn
STATE BIRD Bluebird

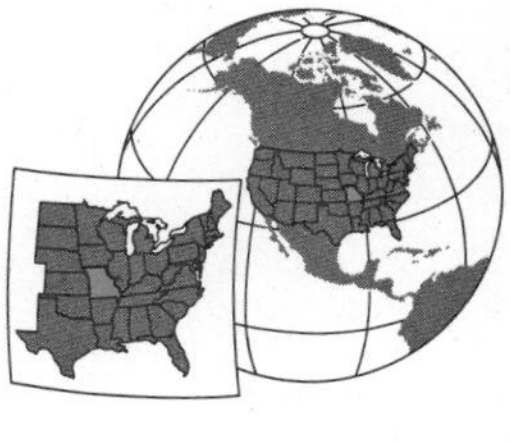

63650 Graniteville, 375 L 7
64456 Grant City⊙, 1,095 D 2
65037 Gravois Mills, 994 G 6
63850 Grayridge, 300 N 9
63039 Gray Summit, 950 M 3
63544 Green Castle, 235 G 2
63545 Green City, 629 F 2
65661 Greenfield⊙, 1,172 E 8
65332 Green Ridge, 403 F 5
63546 Greentop, 351 H 2
63944 Greenville⊙, 328 M 8
64034 Greenwood, 925 R 6
63040 Grover, 550 O 3
64643 Hale, 461 F 3
65255 Hallsville, 790 H 4
64644 Hamilton, 1,645 E 3
63401 Hannibal, 18,609 K 3
64035 Hardin, 683 E 4
64701 Harrisonville⊙, 4,928 D 5
65667 Hartville⊙, 524 G 8
63349 Hawk Point, 354 K 5
63851 Hayti, 3,841 N10
* 63042 Hazelwood, 14,082 P 2
63047 Hematite, 300 L 6
64460 Hemple, 350 D 3
64036 Henrietta, 466 E 4
63048 Herculaneum, 1,885 M 6
65041 Hermann⊙, 2,658 K 5
65668 Hermitage⊙, 284 F 7
65257 Higbee, 641 H 4
64037 Higginsville, 4,318 E 4
63049 High Ridge, 350 O 4
63050 Hillsboro⊙, 432 L 6
63852 Holcomb, 593 N10
64040 Holden, 2,089 E 5
63853 Holland, 329 N10
65672 Hollister, 906 F 9
64048 Holt, 319 D 4
64461 Hopkins, 656 C 1
† 63070 Horine, 850 M 6
63855 Hornersville, 693 M10
63051 House Springs, 500 O 4
65483 Houston⊙, 2,178 J 8
65333 Houstonia, 312 F 5
65674 Humansville, 825 E 7
64752 Hume, 350 C 6
63443 Hunnewell, 304 J 3
65259 Huntsville⊙, 1,442 H 4
63547 Hurdland, 225 H 2
65486 Iberia, 741 H 6
63754 Illmo, 1,232 O 8
63052 Imperial, 900 P 4
* 64050 Independence⊙, 111,662 R 5
63648 Irondale, 319 L 7
63650 Ironton⊙, 1,452 L 7
63755 Jackson⊙, 5,896 N 8
64648 Jamesport, 614 E 3
65046 Jamestown, 243 G 5
64755 Jasper, 796 D 8
65101 Jefferson City (cap.)⊙, 32,407 H 5
63136 Jennings, 19,379 P 2
63351 Jonesburg, 479 K 5
64801 Joplin, 39,256 C 8
† 63385 Josephville, 250 N 2
63445 Kahoka⊙, 2,207 J 2
* 64101 Kansas City, 507,087 P 5
Kansas City, ‡1,253,916 P 5
64060 Kearney, 984 D 4
63758 Kelso, 401 O 8
63857 Kennett⊙, 9,852 M10
65261 Keytesville⊙, 730 G 4
64649 Kidder, 231 D 3
63053 Kimmswick, 268 M 6
64463 King City, 1,023 D 2
64650 Kingston⊙, 291 E 3
64061 Kingsville, 284 D 5
63140 Kinloch, 5,629 P 2
63501 Kirksville⊙, 15,560 H 2
63122 Kirkwood, 31,890 O 3
65336 Knob Noster, 2,264 E 5
63446 Knox City, 284 H 2
63054 Koch, 600 P 4
65692 Koshkonong, 216 J 9
† 63090 Krakow, 300 K 6
63055 Labadie, 350 N 3
63447 La Belle, 848 J 2
64651 Laclede, 430 F 3
63352 Laddonia, 745 J 4
† 64758 Ladue, 10,491 P 3
63448 La Grange, 1,237 K 2
64063 Lake Lotawana, 1,786 R 6
65049 Lake Ozark, 507 G 6
† 64015 Lake Tapawingo, 867 R 6
† 64034 Lake Winnebago, 432 R 6
64759 Lamar⊙, 3,760 D 8
65337 La Monte, 814 F 5
64847 Lanagan, 374 C 9
63548 Lancaster⊙, 821 H 1
63549 La Plata, 1,377 H 2
64652 Laredo, 383 E 2
64465 Lathrop, 1,268 D 3
64062 Lawson, 1,034 D 4
† 63060 Leadington, 299 M 7
63653 Leadwood, 1,397 L 7
65535 Leasburg, 218 K 6
65536 Lebanon⊙, 8,616 G 7
64063 Lee's Summit, 16,230 R 6
64761 Leeton, 425 E 5
63125 Lemay, 40,115 P 3
63654 Lesterville, 275 L 8
64066 Levasy, 283 S 5
63452 Lewistown, 615 J 2
64067 Lexington⊙, 5,388 E 4
64762 Liberal, 644 D 7
64068 Liberty⊙, 13,679 R 5
65542 Licking, 1,002 J 8
63862 Lilbourn, 1,152 N 9
65338 Lincoln, 574 F 6
65051 Linn⊙, 1,289 J 5
65052 Linn Creek, 268 G 6
64653 Linneus⊙, 400 F 3
65682 Lockwood, 887 E 8
65054 Loose Creek, 370 J 5
63353 Louisiana, 4,533 K 4
64763 Lowry City, 520 E 6
63762 Lutesville, 626 M 8
63552 Macon⊙, 5,301 H 3
65263 Madison, 540 H 4
64466 Maitland, 319 B 2
63863 Malden, 5,374 M 9
65339 Malta Bend, 342 F 4
65704 Mansfield, 1,056 G 8
63143 Maplewood, 12,785 P 3
63764 Marble Hill⊙, 589 N 8
64658 Marceline, 2,622 F 3
65705 Marionville, 1,496 E 8
63655 Marquand, 400 M 8
65340 Marshall⊙, 11,847 F 4
65706 Marshfield⊙, 2,961 G 8
63866 Marston, 666 N 9
63357 Marthasville, 415 L 5
65264 Martinsburg, 318 J 4
64468 Maryville⊙, 9,970 C 2
63857 Matthews, 538 N 9
64469 Maysville⊙, 1,045 D 3
64071 Mayview, 330 E 4
64657 McFall, 203 D 2
64659 Meadville, 409 F 3
63555 Memphis⊙, 2,081 H 2
64660 Mendon, 289 F 3
64661 Mercer, 364 F 2
65058 Meta, 387 H 6
65265 Mexico⊙, 11,807 J 4
65344 Miami, 205 F 4
63359 Middletown, 235 J 4
63556 Milan⊙, 1,794 F 2
65707 Miller, 676 E 8
63952 Mill Spring, 207 L 8
64769 Mindenmines, 279 D 8
63659 Mine La Motte, 200 M 7
† 63801 Miner, 640 N 9
63660 Mineral Point, 369 L 7
64072 Missouri City, 375 R 5
65270 Moberly, 12,988 G 4

(continued on following page)

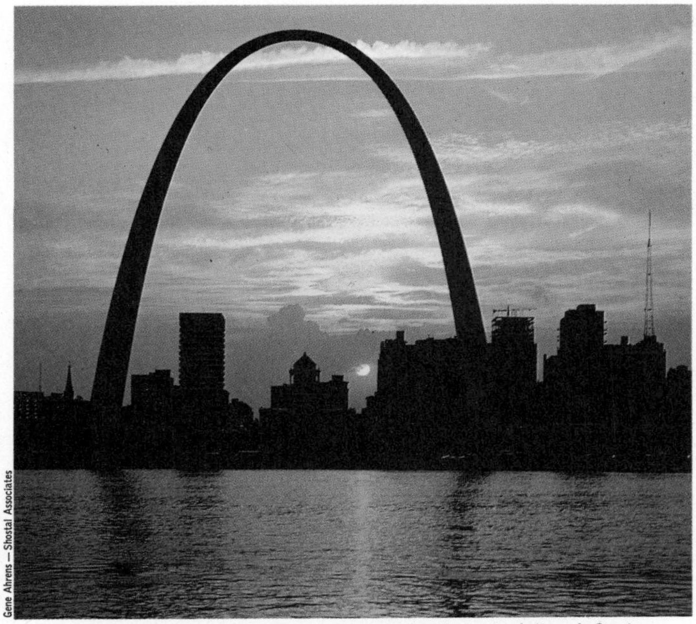

Gene Ahrens—Shostal Associates

The Gateway Arch soars in silhouette against the St. Louis skyline. A Saarinen design, the monument is the centerpiece of the Jefferson National Expansion Memorial. Internal passenger trains carry sightseers up either leg to the long observation room.

Agriculture, Industry and Resources

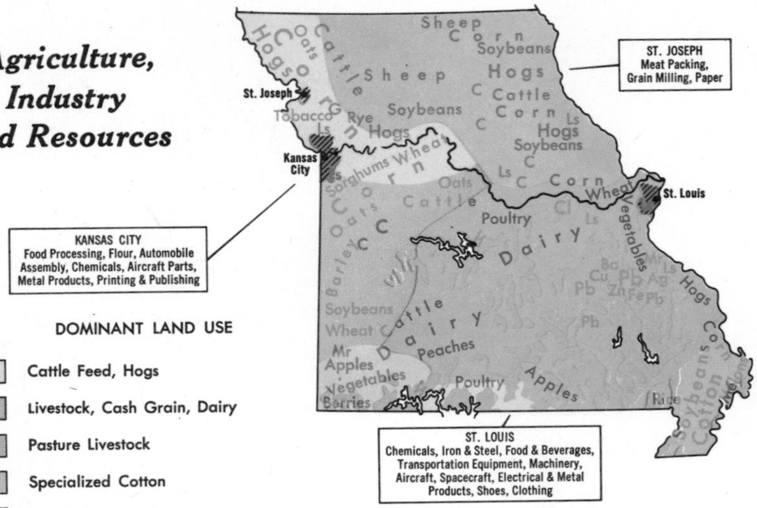

DOMINANT LAND USE
- Cattle Feed, Hogs
- Livestock, Cash Grain, Dairy
- Pasture Livestock
- Specialized Cotton
- General Farming, Dairy, Livestock, Poultry
- General Farming, Livestock, Truck Farming, Cotton
- Fruit and Mixed Farming
- Forests
- Urban Areas

ST. JOSEPH
Meat Packing, Grain Milling, Paper

KANSAS CITY
Food Processing, Flour, Automobile Assembly, Chemicals, Aircraft Parts, Metal Products, Printing & Publishing

ST. LOUIS
Chemicals, Iron & Steel, Food & Beverages, Transportation Equipment, Machinery, Aircraft, Spacecraft, Electrical & Metal Products, Shoes, Clothing

MAJOR MINERAL OCCURRENCES
- Ag Silver
- Ba Barite
- C Coal
- Cl Clay
- Cu Copper
- Fe Iron Ore
- G Natural Gas
- Ls Limestone
- Mr Marble
- Pb Lead
- Zn Zinc
- Water Power
- Major Industrial Areas

Topography
0 40 80 MILES

OZARK PLATEAU
ST. FRANCOIS MTS.
Taum Sauk Mtn. 1,772
Clearwater Lake
L. Wappapello
Table Rock Lake
Bull Shoals Lake
Stockton Res.

5,000 m. 16,404 ft. | 2,000 m. 6,562 ft. | 1,000 m. 3,281 ft. | 500 m. 1,640 ft. | 200 m. 656 ft. | 100 m. 328 ft. | Sea Level | See Below

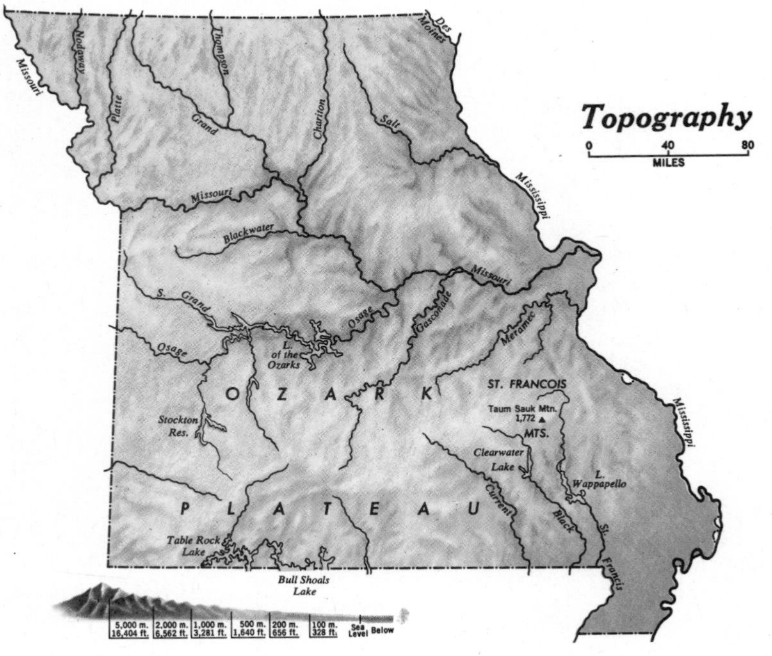

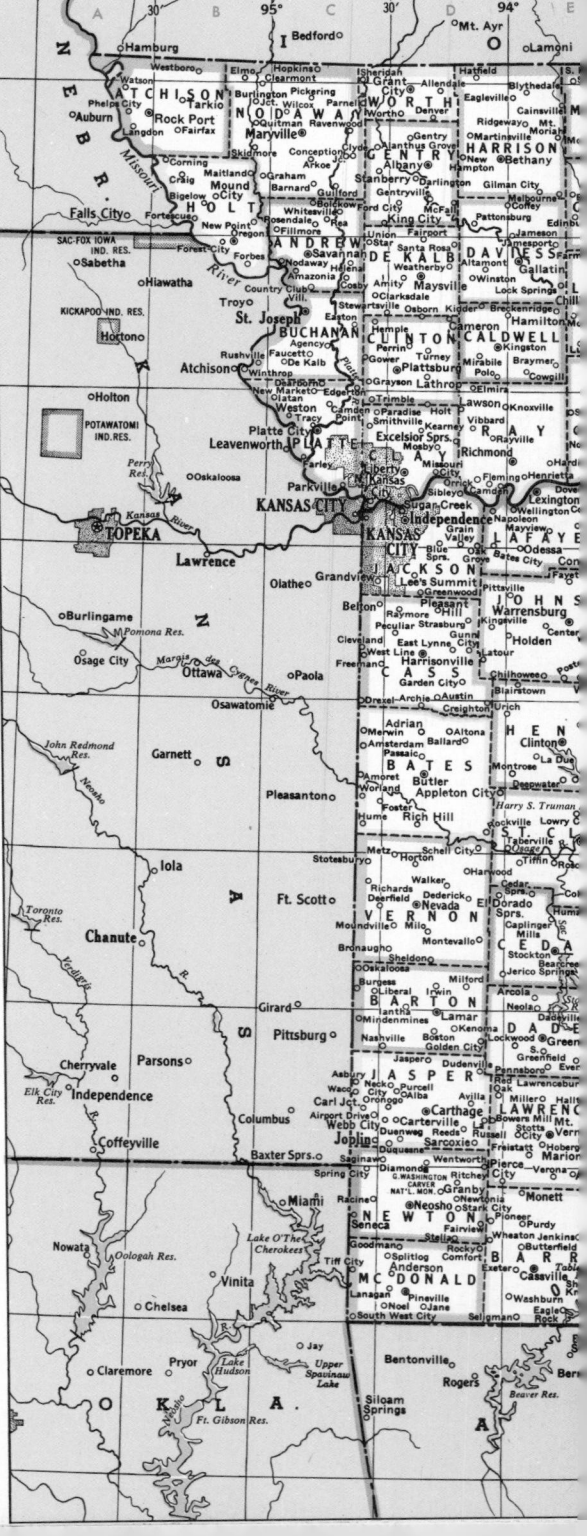

COUNTIES

Beaverhead, 8,187 .... C 5
Big Horn, 10,057 .... J 5
Blaine, 6,727 .... H 2
Broadwater, 2,526 .... E 4
Carbon, 7,080 .... G 5
Carter, 1,956 .... M 5
Cascade, 81,804 .... E 3
Chouteau, 6,473 .... F 3
Custer, 12,174 .... L 4
Daniels, 3,083 .... L 2
Dawson, 11,269 .... M 3
Deer Lodge, 15,652 .... C 5
Fallon, 4,050 .... M 4
Fergus, 12,611 .... G 3
Flathead, 39,460 .... B 2
Gallatin, 32,505 .... E 5
Garfield, 1,796 .... J 3
Glacier, 10,783 .... C 2
Golden Valley, 931 .... G 4
Granite, 2,737 .... C 4
Hill, 17,358 .... F 2
Jefferson, 5,238 .... D 4
Judith Basin, 2,667 .... F 3
Lake, 14,445 .... B 3
Lewis and Clark, 33,281 .... D 3
Liberty, 2,359 .... E 2
Lincoln, 18,063 .... A 2
Madison, 5,014 .... D 5
McCone, 2,875 .... L 3
Meagher, 2,122 .... E 4
Mineral, 2,958 .... B 3
Missoula, 58,263 .... C 3
Musselshell, 3,734 .... H 4
Park, 11,197 .... F 5
Petroleum, 675 .... H 3
Phillips, 5,386 .... J 2
Pondera, 6,611 .... D 2
Powder River, 2,862 .... L 5
Powell, 6,660 .... C 4
Prairie, 1,752 .... L 4
Ravalli, 14,409 .... B 4
Richland, 9,837 .... M 3
Roosevelt, 10,365 .... L 2
Rosebud, 6,032 .... K 4
Sanders, 7,093 .... A 3
Sheridan, 5,779 .... M 2
Silver Bow, 41,981 .... D 5
Stillwater, 4,632 .... G 5
Sweet Grass, 2,980 .... G 5

Teton, 6,116 .... D 3
Toole, 5,839 .... E 2
Treasure, 1,069 .... J 4
Valley, 11,471 .... K 2
Wheatland, 2,529 .... G 4
Wibaux, 1,465 .... M 4
Yellowstone, 87,367 .... H 4
Yellowstone Nat'l Park, 64 .... F 6

CITIES and TOWNS

Zip	Name/Pop.	Key
59001	Absarokee, 700	G 5
59820	Alberton, 363	B 3
59710	Alder, 100	D 5
† 59634	Alhambra, 50	E 4
† 59741	Amsterdam, 200	E 5
59711	Anaconda◎, 9,771	C 4
59221	Antelope, 95	M 2
59821	Arlee, 220	C 3
† 59412	Armington, 62	F 3
59003	Ashland, 200	K 5
59410	Augusta, 400	D 3
59713	Avon, 250	D 4
59411	Babb, 50	C 2
59212	Bainville, 217	M 2
59313	Baker◎, 2,584	M 4
59006	Ballantine, 200	J 5
† 59725	Bannack, 20	C 5
59613	Basin, 230	D 4
59007	Bearcreek, 31	G 5
† 59441	Becket, 35	G 3
59008	Belfry, 250	H 5
59714	Belgrade, 1,307	E 5
† 59046	Belmont, 75	G 4
59412	Belt, 656	E 3
† 59462	Benchland, 100	F 3
59314	Biddle, 83	L 5
59910	Big Arm, 150	B 3
59911	Bigfork, 500	C 2
59010	Bighorn, 40	J 4
59520	Big Sandy, 827	G 2
† 59011	Big Timber◎, 1,592	G 5
* 59101	Billings◎, 61,581	H 5
	Billings, †87,367	H 5
59414	Black Eagle, 1,500	E 3
59415	Blackfoot, 100	D 2
59823	Bonner, 250	C 4
59632	Boulder◎, 1,342	E 4
59521	Box Elder, 200	F 2
59715	Bozeman◎, 18,670	E 5

59416	Brady, 230	E 2
59014	Bridger, 717	H 5
59317	Broadus◎, 799	L 5
59015	Broadview, 123	H 4
59213	Brockton, 401	M 2
59214	Brockway, 80	L 3
59417	Browning, 1,700	C 2
59016	Busby, 600	J 5
59701	Butte◎, 23,368	D 5
† 59857	Camas Prairie, 160	B 3
† 59601	Canyon Ferry, 100	E 4
59721	Cardwell, 36	E 5
59420	Carter, 100	E 3
59347	Cartersville, 140	K 4
59421	Cascade, 714	E 3
† 59701	Centerville, 2,284	D 4
59824	Charlo, 150	B 3
59522	Chester◎, 936	E 2
59523	Chinook◎, 1,813	G 2
59422	Choteau◎, 1,586	D 3
59423	Christina, 44	G 3
59215	Circle◎, 964	L 3
59634	Clancy, 550	E 4
59825	Clinton, 250	C 4
59018	Clyde Park, 244	F 5
59424	Coffee Creek, 79	F 3
59323	Colstrip, 160	K 5
59912	Columbia Falls, 2,652	B 2
59019	Columbus◎, 1,173	G 5
59826	Condon, 200	C 3
59827	Conner, 150	C 4
59425	Conrad◎, 2,770	D 2
59020	Cooke City, 45	G 5
59913	Coram, 450	C 2
59828	Corvallis, 467	C 4
59648	Craig, 100	D 3
59217	Crane, 152	M 3
59022	Crow Agency, 975	J 5
59831	Dixon, 300	B 3
59524	Dodson, 196	H 2
59832	Drummond, 494	D 4
59432	Dupuyer, 105	D 2
59219	Dagmar, 55	M 2
59829	Darby, 538	B 4
59914	Dayton, 60	B 3
59028	Dean, 32	G 5
59830	De Borgia, 95	A 3
59722	Deer Lodge◎, 4,306	D 4
59724	Dell, 50	D 6
59053	Delpine, 33	F 4
59430	Denton, 398	G 3
59431	Devon, 33	E 2

59725	Dillon◎, 4,548	D 5
59727	Divide, 105	D 5
59524	Culbertson, 821	M 2
59427	Cut Bank◎, 4,004	D 2
59434	East Glacier Park, 340	C 2
59635	East Helena, 1,651	E 4
59026	Edgar, 150	H 5
59324	Ekalaka◎, 663	M 5
† 59701	Elk Park, 53	D 4
59728	Elliston, 300	D 4
59915	Elmo, 150	B 3
59729	Ennis, 501	E 5
59325	Epsie, 60	L 5
59916	Essex, 35	C 2
59917	Eureka, 1,195	B 2
59436	Fairfield, 638	D 3
59028	Fishtail, 52	G 5
59222	Flaxville, 185	L 2
59833	Florence, 500	B 4
59440	Floweree, 90	E 3
59441	Forestgrove, 90	H 3
59327	Forsyth◎, 1,873	K 4
59526	Fort Belknap, 185	H 2
59442	Fort Benton◎, 1,863	F 3
59918	Fortine, 250	A 2
59223	Fort Peck, 975	K 2
59443	Fort Shaw, 450	E 3
† 59075	Fort Smith, 300	J 5
59224	Four Buttes, 50	L 2
59225	Frazer, 300	K 2
59834	Frenchtown, 200	B 3
59016	Froid, 330	M 2
59029	Fromberg, 364	H 5
59444	Galata, 48	E 2
† 59722	Galen, 210	D 4
59730	Gallatin Gateway, 200	E 5
59030	Gardiner, 479	F 5
59445	Garneill, 55	G 3
59731	Garrison, 350	D 4
59446	Geraldine, 370	F 3
59447	Geyser, 567	F 3
59525	Gildford, 285	F 2

Topography

| Below Sea Level | 100 m. 328 ft. | 200 m. 656 ft. | 500 m. 1,640 ft. | 1,000 m. 3,281 ft. | 2,000 m. 6,562 ft. | 5,000 m. 16,404 ft. |

0 ——— 75 ——— 150
MILES

MONTANA

SCALE
0 5 10 20 40 60 MI.
0 5 10 20 40 60KM.

State Capitals .... ⊛
County Seats .... ◎

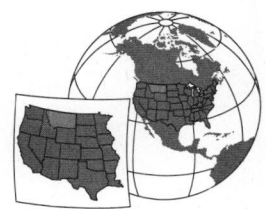

AREA 147,138 sq. mi.
POPULATION 694,409
CAPITAL Helena
LARGEST CITY Billings
HIGHEST POINT Granite Pk. 12,799 ft.
SETTLED IN 1809
ADMITTED TO UNION November 8, 1889
POPULAR NAME Treasure State
STATE FLOWER Bitterroot
STATE BIRD Western Meadowlark

Agriculture, Industry and Resources

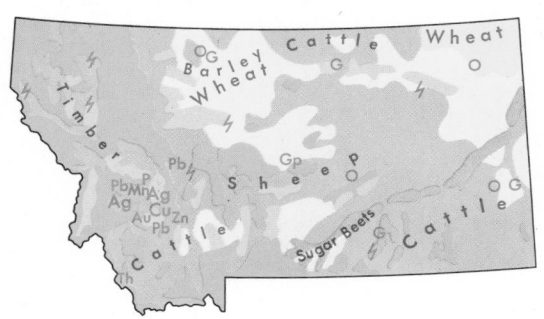

DOMINANT LAND USE

- Specialized Wheat
- Wheat, Range Livestock
- General Farming, Dairy, Range Livestock
- General Farming, Livestock, Special Crops
- Range Livestock
- Sugar Beets, Beans, Livestock, General Farming
- Forests

MAJOR MINERAL OCCURRENCES

Ag Silver
Au Gold
Cu Copper
G Natural Gas
Gp Gypsum
Mn Manganese

O Petroleum
P Phosphates
Pb Lead
Th Thorium
Zn Zinc

⚡ Water Power

Surrounded by the wide open spaces, a Montana ranch basks in the reflected glory of the Rocky Mountains while it awaits cattle returning from the range. Ranches accommodate so many head of cattle that the state's residents are outnumbered six to one.

Ray Manley — Shostal Associates

COUNTIES

Adams, 30,553 ....F 4
Antelope, 9,047 ....F 2
Arthur, 606 ....C 3
Banner, 1,034 ....A 3
Blaine, 847 ....E 3
Boone, 8,190 ....F 3
Box Butte, 10,094 ....A 2
Boyd, 3,752 ....F 2
Brown, 4,021 ....D 2
Buffalo, 31,222 ....E 4
Burt, 8,247 ....H 3
Butler, 9,461 ....G 3
Cass, 18,076 ....H 4
Cedar, 12,192 ....G 2
Chase, 4,129 ....C 4
Cherry, 6,846 ....C 2
Cheyenne, 10,778 ....A 3
Clay, 8,266 ....F 4
Colfax, 9,498 ....G 3
Cuming, 12,034 ....H 3
Custer, 14,092 ....E 3
Dakota, 13,137 ....H 2
Dawes, 9,693 ....A 2
Dawson, 19,467 ....E 4
Deuel, 2,717 ....B 3
Dixon, 7,453 ....H 2
Dodge, 34,782 ....H 3
Douglas, 389,455 ....H 3
Dundy, 2,926 ....C 4
Fillmore, 8,137 ....G 4
Franklin, 4,566 ....F 4
Frontier, 3,982 ....D 4
Furnas, 6,897 ....D 4
Gage, 25,719 ....H 4
Garden, 2,929 ....B 3
Garfield, 2,411 ....E 3
Gosper, 2,178 ....E 4
Grant, 1,019 ....C 3
Greeley, 4,000 ....F 3
Hall, 42,851 ....F 4
Hamilton, 8,867 ....F 4
Harlan, 4,357 ....E 4
Hayes, 1,530 ....C 4
Hitchcock, 4,051 ....C 4
Holt, 12,933 ....F 2
Hooker, 939 ....C 3
Howard, 6,807 ....F 3
Jefferson, 10,436 ....G 4
Johnson, 5,743 ....H 4
Kearney, 6,707 ....E 4
Keith, 8,487 ....C 3
Keya Paha, 1,340 ....E 2
Kimball, 6,009 ....A 3
Knox, 11,723 ....G 2
Lancaster, 167,972 ....H 4
Lincoln, 29,538 ....D 4
Logan, 991 ....D 3
Loup, 854 ....E 3
Madison, 27,402 ....G 3
McPherson, 623 ....C 3
Merrick, 8,751 ....F 3
Morrill, 5,813 ....A 3
Nance, 5,142 ....F 3
Nemaha, 8,976 ....J 4
Nuckolls, 7,404 ....F 4
Otoe, 15,576 ....H 4
Pawnee, 4,473 ....H 4
Perkins, 3,423 ....B 4
Phelps, 9,553 ....E 4
Pierce, 8,493 ....G 2
Platte, 26,508 ....G 3
Polk, 6,468 ....G 3
Red Willow, 12,191 ....D 4
Richardson, 12,277 ....J 4
Rock, 2,231 ....E 2
Saline, 12,809 ....G 4
Sarpy, 63,696 ....H 3
Saunders, 17,018 ....H 3
Scotts Bluff, 36,432 ....A 3
Seward, 14,460 ....G 4
Sheridan, 7,285 ....B 2
Sherman, 4,725 ....F 3

Sioux, 2,034 ....A 2
Stanton, 5,758 ....G 3
Thayer, 7,779 ....G 4
Thomas, 954 ....D 3
Thurston, 6,942 ....H 2
Valley, 5,783 ....E 3
Washington, 13,310 ....H 3
Wayne, 10,400 ....G 2
Webster, 6,477 ....F 4
Wheeler, 1,054 ....F 3
York, 13,685 ....G 4

CITIES and TOWNS

Zip	Name/Pop.	Key
68301	Adams, 463	H 4
69210	Ainsworth⊙, 2,073	D 2
68620	Albion⊙, 2,074	F 3
68810	Alda, 456	F 4
68710	Allen, 309	H 2
69301	Alliance⊙, 6,862	A 2
68920	Alma⊙, 1,299	E 4
68814	Ansley, 631	E 3
68922	Arapahoe, 1,147	E 4
68815	Arcadia, 418	F 3
68002	Arlington, 910	H 3
69120	Arnold, 752	D 3
69121	Arthur⊙, 175	C 3
68003	Ashland, 2,176	H 3
68713	Atkinson, 1,406	E 2
68305	Auburn⊙, 3,650	J 4
68818	Aurora⊙, 3,180	F 4
68924	Axtell, 500	E 4
68004	Bancroft, 545	H 2
68622	Bartlett⊙, 193	F 3
69020	Bartley, 283	D 4
68714	Bassett⊙, 983	E 2
68715	Battle Creek, 1,158	G 3
69334	Bayard, 1,338	A 3
68310	Beatrice⊙, 12,389	H 4
68926	Beaver City⊙, 802	E 4
68313	Beaver Crossing, 400	G 4
68716	Beemer, 699	H 3
68005	Bellevue, 19,449	J 3
68624	Bellwood, 361	G 3
69021	Benkelman⊙, 1,349	C 4
68317	Bennet, 489	H 4
68007	Bennington, 683	H 4
68927	Bertrand, 662	E 4
69122	Big Springs, 472	B 3
68928	Bladen, 293	F 4
68008	Blair⊙, 6,106	H 3
68718	Bloomfield, 1,287	G 2
68930	Blue Hill, 1,201	F 4
68318	Blue Springs, 494	H 4
68010	Boys Town, 989	H 3
68819	Bradshaw, 347	G 4
69123	Brady, 311	D 3
68626	Brainard, 309	G 3
68821	Brewster⊙, 54	D 3
69336	Bridgeport⊙, 1,490	A 3
68822	Broken Bow⊙, 3,734	E 3
68321	Brownville, 174	J 4
69127	Brule, 423	C 3
68322	Bruning, 315	G 4
68823	Burwell⊙, 1,341	E 3
68722	Butte⊙, 575	F 2
68824	Cairo, 686	F 3
68825	Callaway, 523	D 3
69022	Cambridge, 1,145	D 4
68932	Campbell, 447	F 4
68015	Cedar Bluffs, 616	H 3
68627	Cedar Rapids, 449	F 3
68724	Center⊙, 111	G 2
68826	Central City⊙, 2,803	F 3
68017	Ceresco, 995	H 3
68826	Chadron⊙, 5,853	B 2
68725	Chambers, 321	F 2
68827	Chapman, 371	F 3
69129	Chappell⊙, 1,204	B 3
68327	Chester, 459	G 4
68628	Clarks, 480	F 3
68629	Clarkson, 805	G 3

68933	Clay Center⊙, 952	F 4
68726	Clearwater, 398	F 2
68727	Coleridge, 608	G 2
68601	Columbus⊙, 15,471	G 3
68329	Cook, 328	H 4
68331	Cortland, 326	H 4
69130	Cozad, 4,219	E 4
68019	Craig, 295	H 3
69339	Crawford, 1,291	A 2
68729	Creighton, 1,461	G 2
68333	Crete, 4,444	G 4
68730	Crofton, 677	G 2
69024	Culbertson, 801	C 4
69025	Curtis, 1,166	D 4
68731	Dakota City⊙, 1,057	H 2
69131	Dalton, 354	B 3
68831	Dannebrog, 384	F 3
68335	Davenport, 427	G 4
68632	David City⊙, 2,380	G 3
68020	Decatur, 679	H 2
68340	Deshler, 937	G 4
68341	De Witt, 651	G 4
68342	Diller, 287	H 4
69133	Dix, 342	A 3
68633	Dodge, 704	H 3
68832	Doniphan, 542	F 4
68343	Dorchester, 492	G 4
68634	Duncan, 298	G 3
68347	Eagle, 441	H 4
68935	Edgar, 707	F 4
68636	Elgin, 917	F 3
68022	Elkhorn, 1,184	H 3
68836	Elm Creek, 798	E 4
68349	Elmwood, 548	H 4
68937	Elwood⊙, 601	E 4
68733	Emerson, 850	H 2
69028	Eustis, 400	D 4
68735	Ewing, 552	F 2
68351	Exeter, 759	G 4
68352	Fairbury⊙, 5,265	G 4
68938	Fairfield, 487	G 4
68354	Fairmont, 761	G 4
68355	Falls City⊙, 5,444	J 4
68358	Firth, 328	H 4
68023	Fort Calhoun, 642	J 3
68939	Franklin⊙, 1,193	F 4
68025	Fremont⊙, 22,962	H 3
68359	Friend, 1,126	G 4
68638	Fullerton⊙, 1,444	F 3
68361	Geneva⊙, 2,275	G 4
68640	Genoa, 1,174	F 3
69341	Gering⊙, 5,639	A 3
68840	Gibbon, 1,388	F 4
68841	Giltner, 408	F 4
68941	Glenvil, 332	F 4
69343	Gordon, 2,106	B 2
69138	Gothenburg, 3,154	D 4
68801	Grand Island⊙, 31,269	F 4
69140	Grant⊙, 1,099	C 4
68842	Greeley⊙, 580	F 3
68366	Greenwood, 506	H 3
68028	Gretna, 1,557	H 3
68942	Guide Rock, 318	F 4
68843	Hampton, 387	G 4
69345	Harrisburg⊙, 80	A 3
69346	Harrison⊙, 377	A 2
68739	Hartington⊙, 1,581	G 2
68944	Harvard, 1,230	F 4
68901	Hastings⊙, 23,580	F 4
69032	Hayes Center⊙, 237	C 4
69347	Hay Springs, 682	B 2
68370	Hebron⊙, 1,667	G 4
69348	Hemingford, 734	A 2
68371	Henderson, 901	G 4
68029	Herman, 323	H 3
69143	Hershey, 526	D 3
68372	Hickman, 415	H 4
68947	Hildreth, 352	E 4
68948	Holbrook, 307	D 4
68949	Holdrege⊙, 5,635	E 4
68030	Homer, 457	H 2
68031	Hooper, 895	H 3
68641	Howells, 682	H 3
68376	Humboldt, 1,194	J 4

Miles of pens hold thousands of head of cattle in the Union Stockyards, Omaha. Next stop — the meat packers' plant.

J. Gordon Miller — Shostal Associates

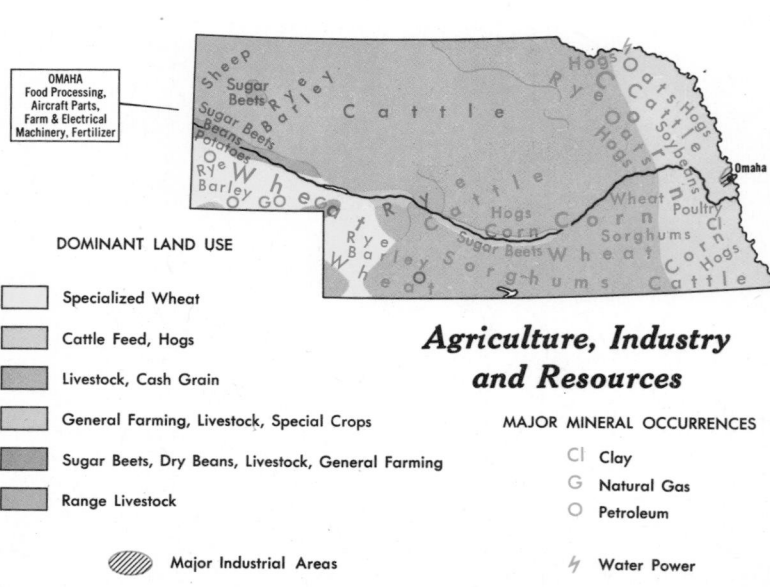

OMAHA
Food Processing,
Aircraft Parts,
Farm & Electrical
Machinery, Fertilizer

DOMINANT LAND USE

- Specialized Wheat
- Cattle Feed, Hogs
- Livestock, Cash Grain
- General Farming, Livestock, Special Crops
- Sugar Beets, Dry Beans, Livestock, General Farming
- Range Livestock
- Major Industrial Areas

Agriculture, Industry and Resources

MAJOR MINERAL OCCURRENCES

Cl Clay
G Natural Gas
O Petroleum
⚡ Water Power

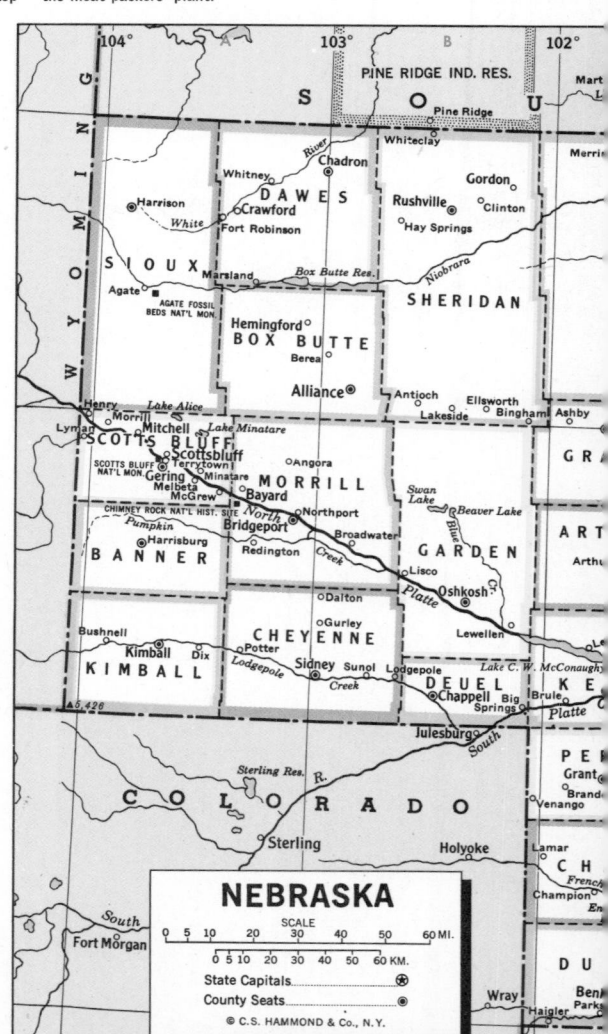

NEBRASKA

SCALE
0 5 10 20 30 40 50 60 MI.
0 5 10 20 30 40 50 60 KM.

State Capitals .... ⊛
County Seats .... ⊛

© C.S. HAMMOND & Co., N.Y.

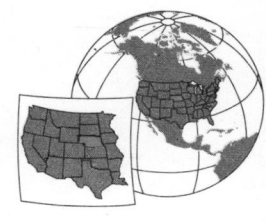

AREA 77,227 sq. mi.
POPULATION 1,483,791
CAPITAL Lincoln
LARGEST CITY Omaha
HIGHEST POINT 5,426 ft. (Kimball Co.)
SETTLED IN 1847
ADMITTED TO UNION March 1, 1867
POPULAR NAME Cornhusker State
STATE FLOWER Goldenrod
STATE BIRD Western Meadowlark

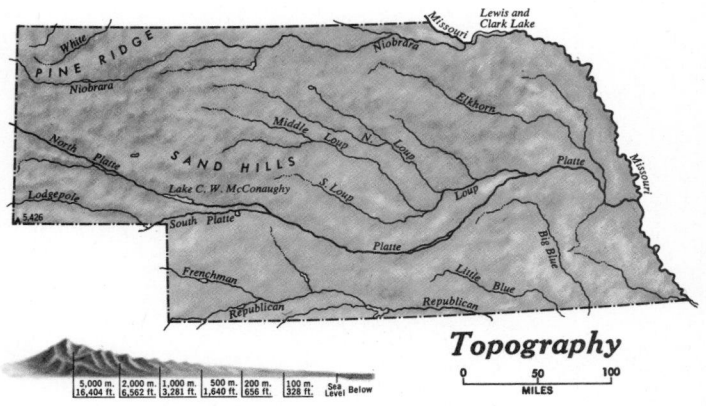

Topography

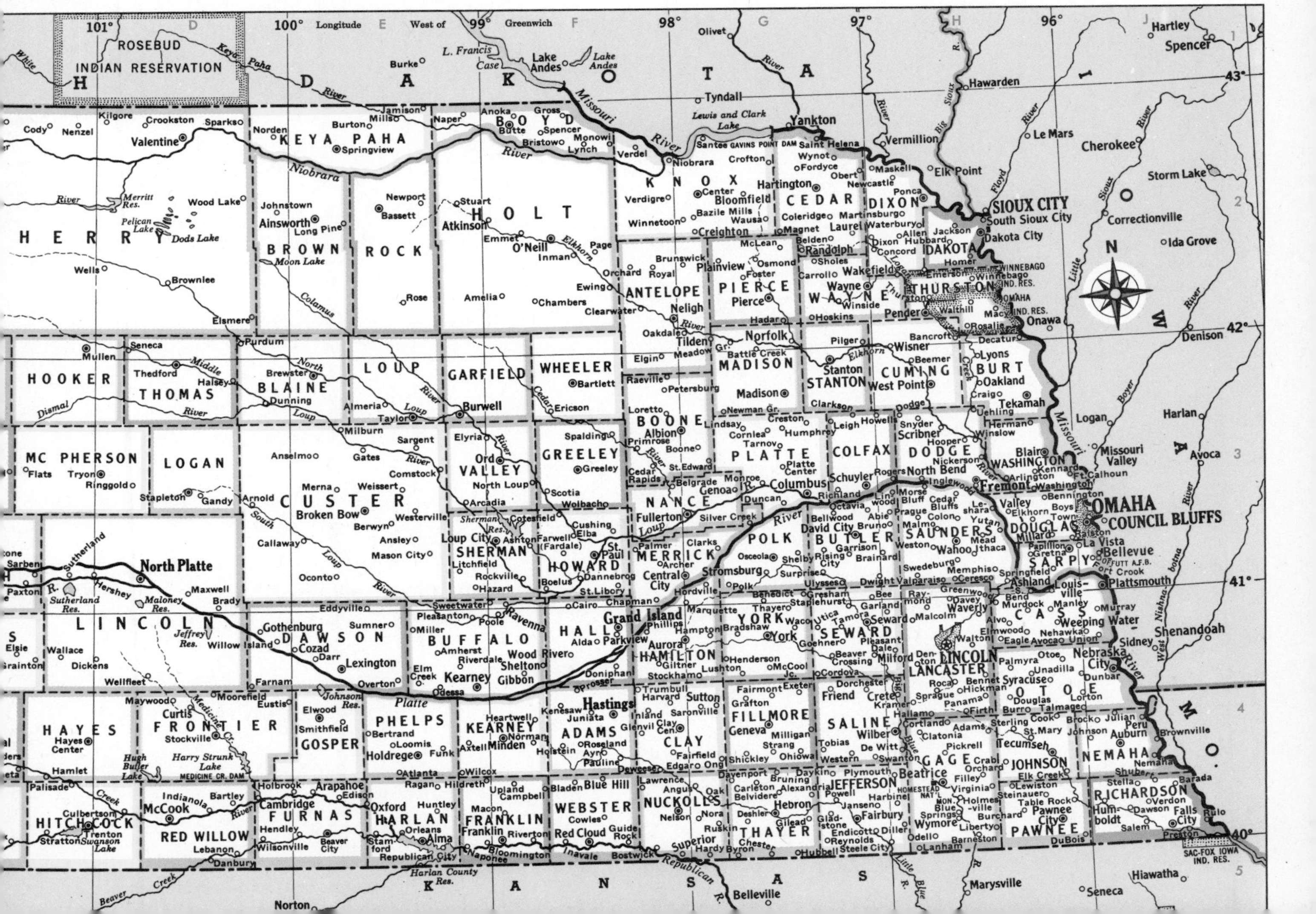

5,000 m. 2,000 m. 1,000 m. 500 m. 200 m. 100 m. Sea
16,404 ft. 6,562 ft. 3,281 ft. 1,640 ft. 656 ft. 328 ft. Level Below

0   50   100
MILES

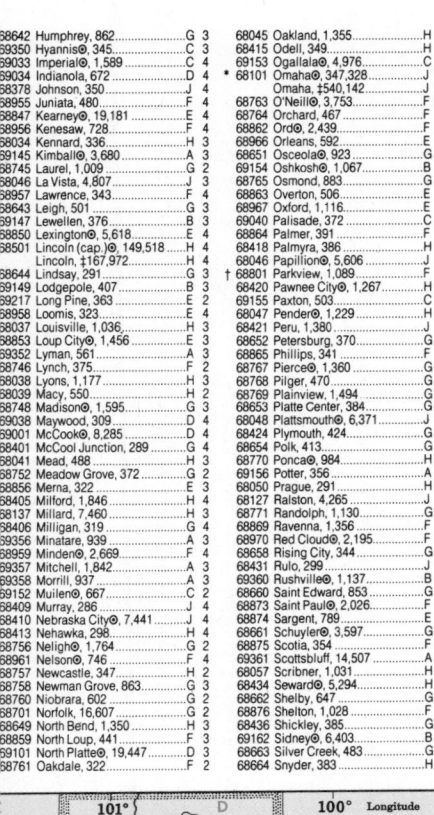

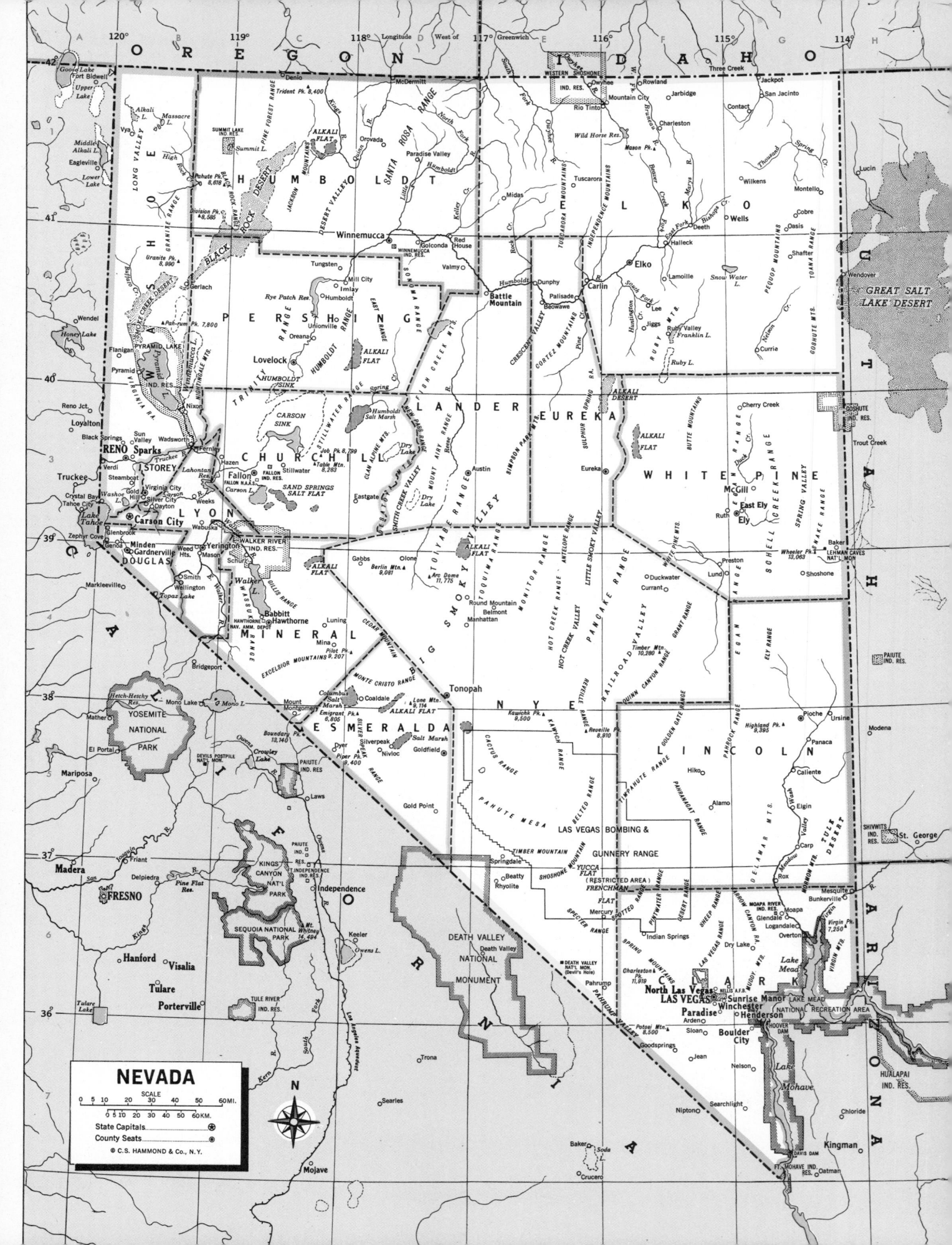

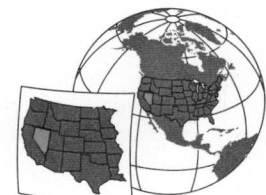

COUNTIES

Carson City (city), 15,468	B 3
Churchill, 10,513	C 3
Clark, 273,288	F 6
Douglas, 6,882	B 4
Elko, 13,958	F 1
Esmeralda, 629	D 5
Eureka, 948	E 3
Humboldt, 6,375	C 1
Lander, 2,666	D 3
Lincoln, 2,557	F 5
Lyon, 8,221	B 3
Mineral, 7,051	C 4
Nye, 5,599	E 4
Pershing, 2,670	C 2
Storey, 695	B 3
Washoe, 121,068	B 2
White Pine, 10,150	F 3

CITIES and TOWNS

Zip	Name/Pop.	Key
89001	Alamo, 300	F 5
89310	Austin⊙, 300	E 3
89416	Babbitt, 1,579	C 4
89311	Baker, 75	G 3
89820	Battle Mountain, 1,856	E 2
89003	Beatty, 570	E 6
89045	Belmont, 25	E 4
89821	Beowawe, 104	E 2
89508	Black Springs, 2,500	B 3
89005	Boulder City, 5,223	G 7
89007	Bunkerville, 150	G 6
89008	Caliente, 916	G 5
89822	Carlin, 1,313	E 2
89009	Carp, 32	G 5
89701	Carson City (cap.), 15,468	B 3
89801	Charleston, 1	F 1
89312	Cherry Creek, 75	G 3
89049	Coaldale, 31	D 4
89830	Cobre, 14	G 1
89825	Contact, 9	G 1
89402	Crystal Bay, 950	A 3
89314	Currant, 30	F 4
89313	Currie, 15	G 2
89403	Dayton, 350	B 3
89823	Deeth, 27	F 1
89404	Denio, 28	C 1
89040	Dry Lake, 5	G 6
89314	Duckwater, 85	F 4
89821	Dunphy, 90	E 2
89010	Dyer, 60	C 5
89315	East Ely, 1,992	G 3
89406	Eastgate, 17	D 3
89112	East Las Vegas, 6,501	F 6
89009	Elgin, 8	G 5
89801	Elko⊙, 7,621	F 2
89301	Ely⊙, 4,176	G 3
89316	Eureka⊙, 300	E 3
89406	Fallon⊙, 2,959	C 3
89408	Fernley, 750	B 3
89409	Gabbs, 874	D 4
89410	Gardnerville, 800	B 4
89411	Genoa, 170	B 4
89412	Gerlach, 150	B 2
89413	Glenbrook, 800	B 3
89025	Glendale, 20	G 6
89013	Goldfield⊙, 213	D 5
89440	Gold Hill, 50	B 3
89013	Gold Point, 10	D 5
89019	Goodsprings, 120	F 7
89824	Halleck, 50	F 2
89415	Hawthorne⊙, 3,539	C 4
89417	Hazen, 60	C 3

Zip	Name/Pop.	Key
89015	Henderson, 16,395	G 6
89017	Hiko, 150	F 5
† 89418	Humboldt, 12	C 2
96104	Vya, 12	B 1
89018	Indian Springs, 500	F 6
† 89310	Ione, 15	D 4
89825	Jackpot, 400	G 1
89826	Jarbidge, 25	F 1
89019	Jean, 100	F 7
89827	Jiggs, 6	F 2
89828	Lamoille, 51	F 2
* 89101	Las Vegas⊙, 125,787	F 6
	Las Vegas, ‡273,288	F 6
89829	Lee, 180	F 2
89021	Logandale, 410	G 6
89419	Lovelock⊙, 1,571	C 2
89317	Lund, 300	F 4
89420	Luning, 55	C 4
89022	Manhattan, 28	E 4
† 89447	Mason, 200	B 4
89421	McDermitt, 300	D 1
89318	McGill, 2,164	G 3
89023	Mercury, 2,200	E 6
89024	Mesquite, 500	G 6
† 89414	Midas, 6	E 1
† 89418	Mill City, 4	D 2
89422	Mina, 375	C 4
89423	Minden⊙, 520	B 4
89025	Moapa, 250	G 6
89830	Montello, 150	G 1
89831	Mountain City, 80	F 1
† 89422	Mount Montgomery, 10	C 5
89046	Nelson, 67	G 7
89424	Nixon, 300	B 3
89030	North Las Vegas, 36,216	F 6
89830	Oasis, 5	G 1
† 89419	Oreana, 18	C 2
89425	Orovada, 250	D 1
89040	Overton, 900	G 6
89832	Owyhee, 100	F 1
89041	Pahrump, 400	E 6
† 89822	Palisade, 5	E 2
89042	Panaca, 500	G 5
† 89101	Paradise, 24,477	F 6
89426	Paradise Valley, 110	D 1
89043	Pioche⊙, 525	G 5
89301	Preston, 44	G 4
† 89414	Red House, 4	D 2
89501	Reno⊙, 72,863	B 3
	Reno, ‡121,068	B 3
† 89003	Rhyolite, 8	E 6
† 89831	Rio Tinto, 5	E 1
89045	Round Mountain, 100	E 4
† 89831	Rowland, 10	F 1
89009	Rox, 12	G 6
89833	Ruby Valley, 225	F 2
89319	Ruth, 750	F 3
† 89825	San Jacinto, 8	G 1
89046	Searchlight, 279	F 7
† 89835	Shafter, 7	G 2
85301	Shoshone, 15	G 4
89428	Silver City, 100	B 3
89047	Silverpeak, 80	D 5
† 89114	Sloan, 25	F 7
89430	Smith, 300	B 4
89431	Sparks, 24,187	B 3
89436	Steamboat, 560	B 3
89406	Stillwater, 30	C 3
89101	Sunrise Manor, 10,886	F 6
† 89431	Sun Valley, 2,414	B 3
89049	Tonopah⊙, 1,716	D 4
89834	Tuscarora, 15	E 1
† 89418	Unionville, 18	C 2
† 89043	Ursine, 40	G 5
89438	Valmy, 50	D 2

Zip	Name/Pop.	Key
89439	Verdi, 100	B 3
89440	Virginia City⊙, 300	B 3
† 89418	Humboldt, 12	C 2
89018	Imlay, 150	C 2
89442	Wadsworth, 375	B 3
89447	Wabuska, 50	B 3
89442	Wadsworth, 375	B 3
89443	Weed Heights, 750	B 4
89447	Weeks, 15	B 3
89444	Wellington, 100	B 4
89835	Wells, 1,081	G 1
† 89835	Wilkins, 6	G 1
89101	Winchester, 13,981	F 6
89445	Winnemucca⊙, 3,587	D 2
89447	Yerington⊙, 2,010	B 4
89447	Zephyr Cove, 400	A 3

⊙ County seat.
‡ Population of metropolitan area.
† Zip of nearest p.o.
* Multiple zips

- **AREA** 110,540 sq. mi.
- **POPULATION** 488,738
- **CAPITAL** Carson City
- **LARGEST CITY** Las Vegas
- **HIGHEST POINT** Boundary Pk. 13,140 ft.
- **SETTLED IN** 1850
- **ADMITTED TO UNION** October 31, 1864
- **POPULAR NAME** Silver State
- **STATE FLOWER** Sagebrush
- **STATE BIRD** Mountain Bluebird

An incandescent oasis in the Nevada desert, Reno beckons travelers to its varied diversions — from games of chance and nightclub entertainment to annual rodeos and skiing in the Sierra Nevada.

Agriculture, Industry and Resources

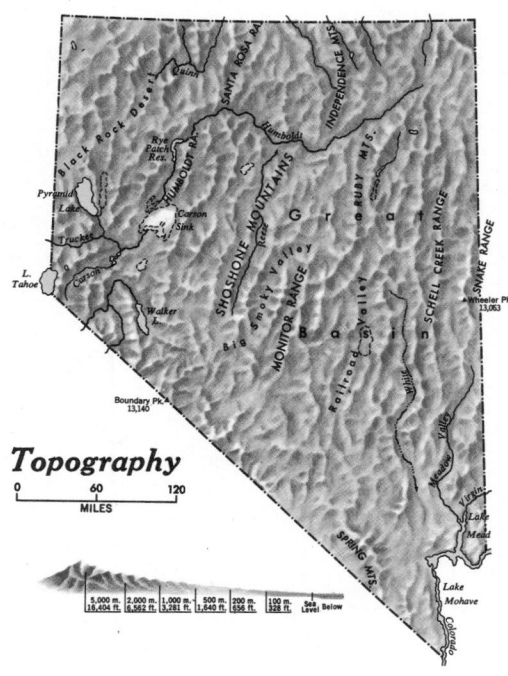

Topography

```
0      60     120
      MILES
```

```
5,000 m.  2,000 m.  1,000 m.  500 m.  200 m.  100 m.  Sea
16,404 ft. 6,562 ft. 3,281 ft. 1,640 ft. 656 ft. 328 ft. Level
                                                      Below
```

MAJOR MINERAL OCCURRENCES

- Ag Silver
- Au Gold
- Ba Barite
- Cu Copper
- Gp Gypsum
- Hg Mercury
- Lt Lithium
- Mg Magnesium
- Mo Molybdenum
- Na Salt
- O   Petroleum
- Pb Lead
- S   Sulfur
- W   Tungsten   ⚡ Water Power
- Zn Zinc

DOMINANT LAND USE

- General Farming, Dairy, Livestock
- General Farming, Livestock, Special Crops
- Range Livestock
- Forests
- Nonagricultural Land

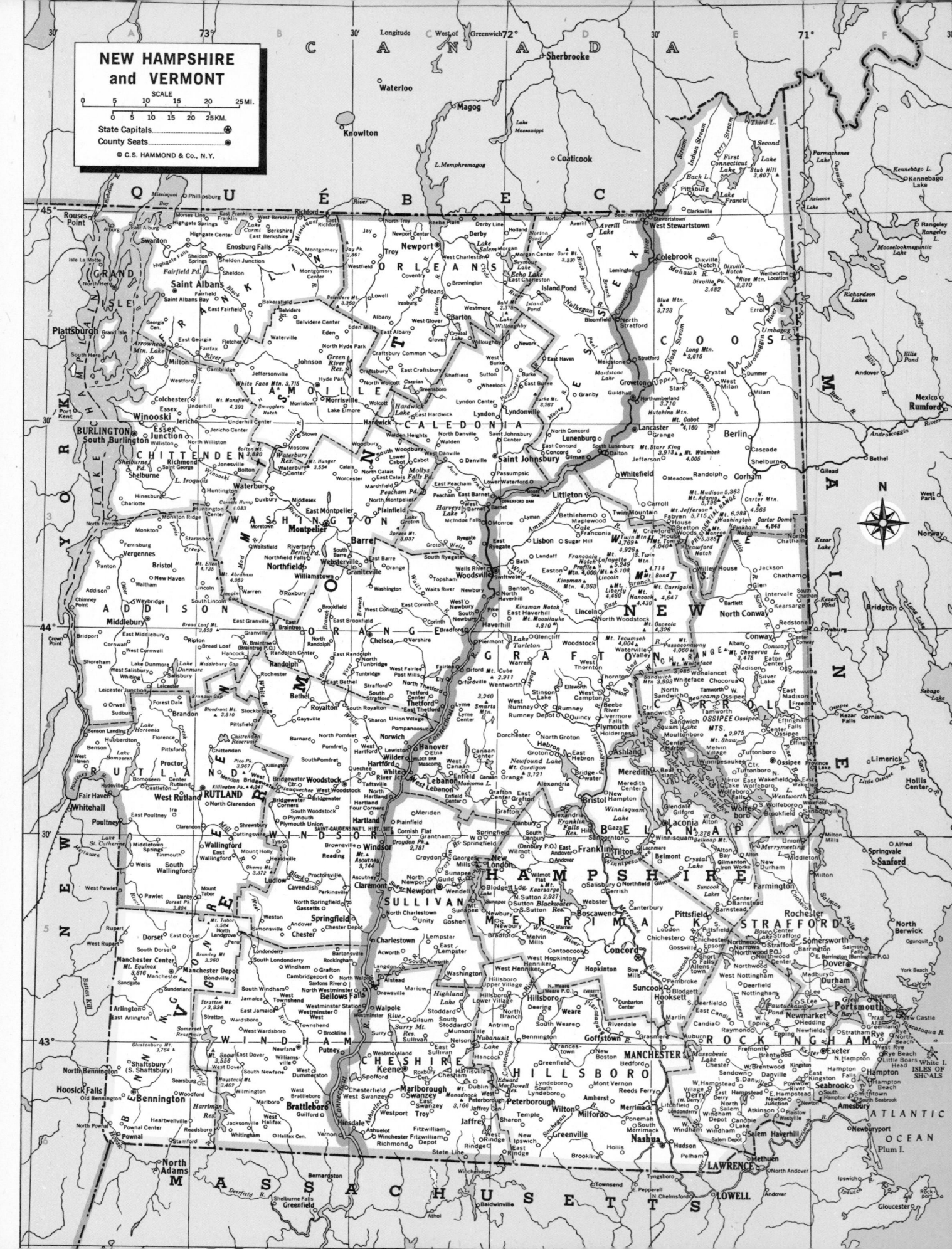

NEW HAMPSHIRE
COUNTIES

Belknap, 32,367 .... D 4
Carroll, 18,548 .... D 4
Cheshire, 52,364 .... C 6
Coos, 34,291 .... E 2
Grafton, 54,914 .... C 4
Hillsboro, 223,941 .... D 6
Merrimack, 80,925 .... D 5
Rockingham, 138,951 .... E 5
Strafford, 70,431 .... E 5
Sullivan, 30,949 .... C 5

CITIES and TOWNS

Zip	Name/Pop.	Key
03601	Acworth, △459	C 5
† 03864	Albany, △259	E 4
‡ 03222	Alexandria, △466	D 4
03275	Allenstown, △2,732	E 5
03602	Alstead, △1,185	C 5
03602	Alstead, 450	C 5
03809	Alton, △1,647	E 5
03809	Alton, 450	E 5
03031	Amherst, △4,605	D 6
03810	Amherst, 600	D 6
03216	Andover, △1,138	D 5
03216	Andover, 500	D 5
03440	Antrim, △2,122	D 5
03440	Antrim, 750	D 5
03217	Ashland, △1,599	D 4
03217	Ashland, 1,391	D 4
03441	Ashuelot, 750	C 6
03811	Atkinson, △2,291	E 6
03032	Auburn, △2,035	E 5
03218	Barnstead, △1,119	E 5
03218	Barnstead, 400	E 5
03825	Barrington, △1,865	F 5
03812	Bartlett, △1,098	E 3
03812	Bartlett, 600	E 3
03740	Bath, △607	D 3
03102	Bedford, △5,859	D 6
03220	Belmont, △2,493	E 5
03220	Belmont, 900	E 5
03442	Bennington, △639	D 5

† 03785	Benton, △194	D 3
03570	Berlin, 15,256	E 3
03574	Bethlehem, △1,142	D 3
03574	Bethlehem, 500	D 3
03301	Boscawen, △3,162	D 5
† 03301	Bow Mills, 600	D 5
03221	Bradford, △679	D 5
† 03833	Brentwood, △1,468	E 5
03575	Bretton Woods, 6	E 3
† 03222	Bridgewater, △398	D 4
03222	Bristol, △1,670	D 4
03222	Bristol, 1,080	D 4
03872	Brookfield, △198	E 4
03033	Brookline, △1,167	D 6
03223	Campton, △1,171	D 4
03741	Canaan, △1,923	C 4
03741	Canaan, 500	C 4
† 03079	Canobie Lake, 500	E 6
03224	Canterbury, △895	D 5
† 03595	Carroll, △310	D 3
03813	Center Conway, 450	E 4
03226	Center Harbor, △540	E 4
03814	Center Ossipee, 550	E 4
03603	Charlestown, △3,274	C 5
03603	Charlestown, 1,285	C 5
† 04037	Chatham, △134	E 3
03036	Chester, △1,382	E 6
03443	Chesterfield, △1,817	C 6
03443	Chesterfield, 450	C 6
† 03258	Chichester, △1,083	E 5
03743	Claremont, 14,221	C 5
† 05902	Clarksville, △166	E 1
03576	Colebrook, △2,094	E 1
03576	Colebrook, 1,070	E 1
03301	Concord (cap.) ⊙, △30,022	D 5
03229	Contoocook, 975	D 5
03818	Conway, △4,865	E 4
03818	Conway, 1,489	E 4
03753	Croydon, △396	C 5
03598	Dalton, △425	D 3
03230	Danbury, △489	D 4
03819	Danville, △924	E 6
03037	Deerfield, △1,178	E 5
† 03244	Deering, △578	D 5
03038	Derry, △11,712	E 6
03038	Derry, 6,090	E 6

† 03266	Dorchester, △141	D 4
03820	Dover⊙, 20,850	F 5
03444	Dublin, △837	C 6
† 03588	Dummer, △225	E 2
† 03301	Dunbarton, △825	D 5
03824	Durham, △8,869	F 5
03824	Durham, 7,221	F 5
03231	East Andover, 450	D 5
03041	East Derry, 600	E 6
03827	East Kingston, △838	F 6
03580	Easton, △92	D 3
03446	East Swanzey, 500	C 6
03894	East Wolfeboro, 400	E 4
03832	Eaton, △221	E 4
03264	Ellsworth, △13	D 4
03748	Enfield, △2,345	C 4
03748	Enfield, 1,408	C 4
03042	Epping, △2,356	E 5
03042	Epping, 1,097	E 5
03234	Epsom, △1,469	E 5
03579	Errol, △199	E 2
03750	Etna, 550	C 4
03833	Exeter, △8,892	F 6
03833	Exeter⊙, 6,439	F 6
03835	Farmington, △3,588	E 5
03835	Farmington, 2,884	E 5
03447	Fitzwilliam, △1,362	C 6
03447	Fitzwilliam, 750	C 6
03043	Francestown, △525	D 6
03580	Franconia, △655	D 3
03235	Franklin, 7,292	D 5
03836	Freedom, △387	E 4

NEW HAMPSHIRE
AREA 9,304 sq. mi.
POPULATION 737,681
CAPITAL Concord
LARGEST CITY Manchester
HIGHEST POINT Mt. Washington 6,288 ft.
SETTLED IN 1623
ADMITTED TO UNION June 21, 1788
POPULAR NAME Granite State
STATE FLOWER Purple Lilac
STATE BIRD Purple Finch

VERMONT
AREA 9,609 sq. mi.
POPULATION 444,732
CAPITAL Montpelier
LARGEST CITY Burlington
HIGHEST POINT Mt. Mansfield 4,393 ft.
SETTLED IN 1764
ADMITTED TO UNION March 4, 1791
POPULAR NAME Green Mountain State
STATE FLOWER Red Clover
STATE BIRD Hermit Thrush

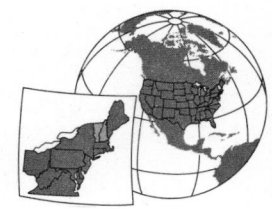

Topography

0   20   40
MILES

(Topographic map labels: Connecticut, Lake Memphremagog, Lake Champlain, Grand Isle, Missisquoi, Lamoille, Black, Winooski, Umbagog L., Mt. Mansfield 4,393, GREEN MOUNTAINS, Passumpsic, Moore Res., Ammonoosuc, Connecticut, Mt. Washington 6,288, WHITE MOUNTAINS, Saco, Squam, Lake Ossipee, Lake Winnipesaukee, Newfound L., Lake Bomoseen, Black, TACONIC MTS., Otter, White, Sunapee, L. Sunapee, Merrimack, Salmon Falls, Great Bay, Ashuelot, Contoocook, Mt. Monadnock 3,166, West, Connecticut)

5,000 m. 16,404 ft.	2,000 m. 6,562 ft.	1,000 m. 3,281 ft.	500 m. 1,640 ft.	200 m. 656 ft.	100 m. 328 ft.	Sea Level	Below

---

Agriculture, Industry and Resources

DOMINANT LAND USE

(Map labels: Dairy, Potatoes, Maple Syrup, Apples, Mr, Gn, Tc, Be, Mi, Th, Manchester, Vegetables, Poultry, Ab, Gn)

- Specialized Dairy
- Dairy, General Farming
- Dairy, Poultry, Mixed Farming
- Forests

⚡ Water Power
▨ Major Industrial Areas

MANCHESTER Leather Goods, Textiles, Electrical Products

MAJOR MINERAL OCCURRENCES

Ab	Asbestos		Mr	Marble
Be	Beryl		Sl	Slate
Gn	Granite		Tc	Talc
Mi	Mica		Th	Thorium

03044	Fremont, △993	E 6
† 03246	Gilford, △3,219	E 4
03237	Gilmanton, △1,010	E 5
03448	Gilsum, △570	C 5
03045	Goffstown, △9,284	D 5
03045	Goffstown, 2,272	D 5
03581	Gorham, △2,998	E 3
03581	Gorham, 2,020	E 3
03752	Goshen, △395	C 5
03239	Gossville, 800	E 5
03240	Grafton, △370	D 4
03753	Grantham, △366	D 5
03045	Grasmere, 513	D 5
03047	Greenfield, △1,058	D 6
03840	Greenland, △1,784	F 5
03048	Greenville, △1,587	D 6
03048	Greenville, 1,332	D 6
† 03241	Groton, △120	D 4
03582	Groveton, 1,597	D 2
03841	Hampstead, △2,401	E 6
03841	Hampstead, 500	E 6
03842	Hampton, △8,011	F 6
03842	Hampton, 5,407	F 6
03842	Hampton Beach, 975	F 6
03844	Hampton Falls, △1,254	F 6
03449	Hancock, △909	C 6
03755	Hanover, △8,494	C 4
03755	Hanover, 6,147	C 4
03450	Harrisville, △584	C 6
03765	Haverhill, △3,090	C 3
03765	Haverhill, 400	C 3
03241	Hebron, △234	D 4
03242	Henniker, △2,348	D 5
03242	Henniker, 950	D 5
03243	Hill, △450	D 4
03244	Hillsboro, △2,775	D 5
03244	Hillsboro, 1,784	D 5
03451	Hinsdale, △3,276	C 6
03451	Hinsdale, 1,059	C 6
03245	Holderness, △1,048	D 4
03049	Hollis, △2,616	D 6
03049	Hollis, 500	D 6
03106	Hooksett, △5,564	E 5
03106	Hooksett, 1,303	E 5

03301	Hopkinton, △3,007	D 5
03301	Hopkinton, 500	D 5
03051	Hudson, △10,638	E 6
03051	Hudson, 4,900	E 6
03845	Intervale, 500	E 3
03846	Jackson, △404	E 3
03452	Jaffrey, △3,353	C 6
03452	Jaffrey, 1,922	C 6
03583	Jefferson, △714	D 3
03431	Keene⊙, 20,467	C 6
03848	Kingston, △2,882	E 6
03246	Laconia⊙, 14,888	D 4
03584	Lancaster, △3,166	D 3
03584	Lancaster⊙, 2,120	D 3
† 03585	Landaff, △292	D 3
03602	Langdon, △337	C 5
03766	Lebanon, 9,725	C 4
03857	Lee, △1,481	F 5
03606	Lempster, △360	C 5
03251	Lincoln, △1,341	D 3
03251	Lincoln, 900	D 3
03585	Lisbon, △1,480	D 3
03585	Lisbon, 1,247	D 3
† 03051	Litchfield, △1,420	E 6
03561	Littleton, △5,290	D 3
03561	Littleton, 4,180	D 3
03252	Lochmere, 500	D 5
03053	Londonderry, △5,346	E 6
03301	Loudon, △1,707	E 5
† 03585	Lyman, △213	D 3
03768	Lyme, △1,112	C 4
03768	Lyme, 400	C 4
† 03082	Lyndeboro, △789	D 6
03820	Madbury, △704	F 5
03849	Madison, △572	E 4
* 03101	Manchester⊙, 87,754	E 6
	Manchester, △108,461	E 6
03455	Marlborough, △1,671	C 6
03455	Marlborough, 1,231	C 6
03456	Marlow, △390	C 5
03253	Meredith, △2,904	D 4
03253	Meredith, 1,017	D 4
03770	Meriden, 495	C 4
03054	Merrimack, △8,595	D 6

03054	Merrimack, 850	D 6
† 03887	Middleton, △430	E 5
03588	Milan, △713	E 2
03055	Milford, △6,622	D 6
03055	Milford, 4,997	D 6
03851	Milton, △1,859	F 5
03851	Milton, 750	F 5
03771	Monroe, △385	C 3
03057	Mont Vernon, △906	D 6
03254	Moultonboro, △1,310	E 4
03060	Nashua⊙, 55,820	D 6
† 03457	Nelson, △304	C 5
03070	New Boston, △1,390	D 6
03070	New Boston, 450	D 6
03255	Newbury, △509	C 5
03854	New Castle, △975	F 5
03855	New Durham, △583	E 5
03856	Newfields, △843	F 5
03256	New Hampton, △946	D 4
† 03801	Newington, △798	F 5
03071	New Ipswich, △1,803	D 6
03257	New London, △2,236	D 5
03257	New London, 1,347	D 5
03857	Newmarket, △3,361	F 5
03857	Newmarket, 2,645	F 5
03773	Newport, △5,899	C 5
03773	Newport, 3,296	C 5
03858	Newton, △1,920	E 6
03858	Newton, 483	E 6
03859	Newton Junction, 500	E 6
03258	North Chichester, 450	E 5
03860	North Conway, 1,723	E 3
† 03276	Northfield, △2,193	D 5
03276	Northfield-Tilton, 2,420	D 5
03862	North Hampton, △3,259	F 6
03862	North Hampton, 750	F 6
03774	North Haverhill, 750	D 3
† 03773	North Newport, 500	C 5
03073	North Salem, 650	E 6
03590	North Stratford, 650	D 2
† 03582	Northumberland, △2,493	D 2
03608	North Walpole, 950	C 5
† 03281	North Weare, 483	D 5
03261	Northwood, △1,526	E 5

(continued on following page)

(continued)

NEW HAMPSHIRE (continued)

	Zip	Name/Pop.	Key
	03262	North Woodstock, 650	D 3
	03290	Nottingham, ▵952	E 5
†	03741	Orange, ▵103	D 4
	03777	Orford, ▵793	C 4
	03864	Ossipee⊙, ▵1,647	E 4
	03076	Pelham, ▵5,408	E 6
†	03275	Pembroke, ▵4,261	E 5
	03458	Peterborough, ▵3,807	D 6
	03458	Peterborough, 2,078	D 6
	03779	Piermont, ▵462	C 4
	03592	Pittsburg, ▵726	E 1
	03263	Pittsfield, ▵2,517	E 5
	03263	Pittsfield, 1,662	E 5
	03781	Plainfield, ▵1,323	C 4
	03865	Plaistow, ▵4,712	E 6
	03865	Plaistow, 950	E 6
	03264	Plymouth, ▵4,225	D 4
	03264	Plymouth, 3,109	D 4
	03801	Portsmouth, 25,717	F 5
	03593	Randolph, ▵169	E 3
	03077	Raymond, ▵3,003	E 5
†	03470	Richmond, ▵287	C 6
	03461	Rindge, ▵2,175	C 6
	03867	Rochester, 17,938	E 5
†	03431	Roxbury, ▵161	C 6
	03266	Rumney, ▵870	D 4
	03870	Rye, ▵4,083	F 5
	03870	Rye, 750	F 5
	03871	Rye Beach, 750	F 6
†	03870	Rye North Beach, 700	F 5
	03079	Salem, ▵20,142	E 6
	03079	Salem, 950	E 6
†	03079	Salem Depot, 975	E 6
	03268	Salisbury, ▵589	D 5
†	03820	Salmon Falls, 950	F 5
	03269	Sanbornton, ▵1,022	D 5
	03872	Sanbornville, 550	F 4
	03873	Sandown, ▵741	E 6
	03270	Sandwich, ▵666	E 4
	03874	Seabrook, ▵3,053	F 6
	03874	Seabrook, 950	F 6
†	03458	Sharon, ▵136	D 6
†	03581	Shelburne, ▵199	E 3
	03878	Somersworth, 9,026	F 5
†	03037	South Deerfield, 500	E 5
†	01913	South Hampton, ▵558	F 6
	03083	South Merrimack, 650	D 6
†	03874	South Seabrook, 500	F 6
	03462	Spofford, 631	C 6
†	03284	Springfield, ▵310	C 4
†	03582	Stark, ▵343	E 2
†	03576	Stewartstown, ▵1,008	E 2
	03464	Stoddard, ▵242	C 5
	03884	Strafford, ▵965	E 5
†	03590	Stratford, ▵980	D 2
	03885	Stratham, ▵1,512	F 5
	03585	Sugar Hill, ▵336	D 3
†	03445	Sullivan, ▵376	C 5
	03782	Sunapee, ▵1,384	C 5
	03782	Sunapee, 750	C 5
	03275	Suncook, 4,280	D 5
	03431	Surry, ▵507	C 5
†	03260	Sutton, ▵642	D 5
†	03431	Swanzey, ▵4,254	C 6
†	03431	Swanzey, 950	C 6
	03886	Tamworth, ▵1,054	E 4
	03084	Temple, ▵441	D 6
†	03285	Thornton, ▵594	D 4
	03276	Tilton, ▵2,579	D 5
	03276	Tilton-Northfield, 2,420	D 5
	03465	Troy, ▵1,713	C 6
†	03816	Tuftonboro, ▵910	E 4
†	03743	Unity, ▵709	C 5
	03888	Wakefield, ▵1,420	F 4
	03608	Walpole, ▵2,966	C 5
	03608	Walpole, 900	C 5
	03278	Warner, ▵1,441	D 5
	03278	Warner, 600	D 5
	03279	Warren, ▵539	D 4
	03280	Washington, ▵248	C 5
	03223	Waterville Valley, ▵109	D 4
	03281	Weare, ▵1,851	D 5
	03281	Weare P.O. (North Weare), 600	D 5
†	03301	Webster, ▵680	D 5
	03282	Wentworth, ▵376	D 4
†	03579	Wentworths Location, ▵37	E 2
†	03038	West Derry (Derry), 6,090	E 6
	03784	West Lebanon, 4,200	C 4
	03467	Westmoreland, ▵998	C 6
	03597	West Stewartstown, 600	E 2
	03469	West Swanzey, 950	C 6
	03892	Westville, 500	E 6
	03598	Whitefield, ▵1,538	D 3
	03598	Whitefield, 1,093	D 3
†	03287	Wilmot, ▵516	D 5
	03086	Wilton, ▵2,276	D 6
	03086	Wilton, 1,161	D 6
	03470	Winchester, ▵2,869	C 6
	03470	Winchester, 938	C 6
	03087	Windham, ▵3,008	E 6
	03289	Winnisquam, 500	E 5
	03894	Wolfeboro, ▵3,036	E 4
	03894	Wolfeboro, 1,718	E 4
	03896	Wolfeboro Falls, 650	E 4
	03293	Woodstock, ▵897	D 4
	03785	Woodsville⊙, 1,336	C 3

VERMONT

COUNTIES

Addison, 24,266	A 3
Bennington, 29,282	A 6
Caledonia, 22,789	C 2
Chittenden, 99,131	A 3
Essex, 5,416	D 2
Franklin, 31,282	B 2
Grand Isle, 3,574	A 2
Lamoille, 13,309	B 2
Orange, 17,676	C 3
Orleans, 20,153	C 2
Rutland, 52,637	A 4
Washington, 47,659	B 3
Windham, 33,074	B 5
Windsor, 44,082	B 4

CITIES and TOWNS

	Zip	Name/Pop.	Key
†	05491	Addison, ▵717	A 3
	05820	Albany, ▵528	C 2
	05440	Alburg, ▵1,271	A 2
	05440	Alburg, 520	A 2
†	05143	Andover, ▵239	B 5
	05250	Arlington, ▵1,934	A 5
	05250	Arlington, 1,212	A 5
	05030	Ascutney, 500	C 5
	05901	Averill, ▵8	D 2
	05441	Bakersfield, ▵635	B 2
	05031	Barnard, ▵569	B 4
	05821	Barnet, ▵1,342	C 3
	05641	Barre, 10,209	C 3
	05641	Barre, ▵6,509	C 3
	05822	Barton, ▵2,874	C 2
	05822	Barton, 1,051	C 2
	05902	Beecher Falls, 640	D 2
	05101	Bellows Falls, 3,505	C 5
	05442	Belvidere, ▵189	B 2
	05201	Bennington, ▵14,586	A 6
	05201	Bennington⊙, 7,950	A 6
	05731	Benson, ▵583	A 4
†	05476	Berkshire, ▵931	B 2
	05032	Bethel, ▵1,347	B 4
†	03590	Bloomfield, ▵196	D 2
†	05466	Bolton, ▵427	B 3
	05732	Bomoseen, 500	A 4
	05033	Bradford, ▵1,627	C 3
	05033	Bradford, 709	C 3
	05646	Braintree, ▵751	B 4
	05733	Brandon, ▵3,697	A 4
	05733	Brandon, 1,720	A 4
	05301	Brattleboro, ▵12,239	B 6
	05301	Brattleboro, 9,055	B 6
	05034	Bridgewater, ▵783	B 4
	05734	Bridport, ▵809	A 4
	05443	Bristol, ▵2,744	A 3
	05443	Bristol, 1,737	A 3
	05036	Brookfield, ▵606	B 3
†	05345	Brookline, ▵180	B 5
†	05860	Brownington, ▵522	C 2
†	05871	Burke, ▵1,053	D 2
	05401	Burlington⊙, 38,633	A 3
	05647	Cabot, ▵663	C 3
	05648	Calais, ▵749	B 3
	05444	Cambridge, ▵1,528	B 2
	05903	Canaan, ▵949	D 2
	05735	Castleton, ▵2,837	A 4
	05735	Castleton, 450	A 4
	05142	Cavendish, ▵1,264	B 5
	05736	Center Rutland, 500	A 4
	05445	Charlotte, ▵1,802	A 3
	05038	Chelsea⊙, ▵983	C 4
	05038	Chelsea, 525	C 4
	05143	Chester, ▵2,371	B 5
	05143	Chester, 950	B 5
	05144	Chester Depot, 500	B 5
	05737	Chittenden, ▵646	B 4
	05737	Chittenden, 525	B 4
†	05759	Clarendon, ▵1,537	A 4
	05446	Colchester, ▵8,776	A 2
	05824	Concord, ▵896	D 3
	05039	Corinth, ▵683	C 3
†	05753	Cornwall, ▵900	A 4
	05825	Coventry, ▵492	C 2
	05826	Craftsbury, ▵632	C 2
	05739	Danby, ▵910	A 5
	05828	Danville, ▵1,405	C 3
	05828	Danville, 450	C 3
	05829	Derby, ▵3,252	C 2
	05829	Derby (Derby Center), 547	C 2
	05830	Derby Line, 834	C 2
	05251	Dorset, ▵1,293	A 5
	05251	Dorset, 450	A 5
†	05676	Duxbury, ▵621	B 3
	05252	East Arlington, 500	A 5
	05649	East Barre, 950	C 3
	05448	East Fairfield, 700	B 2
	05837	East Haven, ▵197	D 2
	05740	East Middlebury, 500	A 4
	05651	East Montpelier, ▵1,597	B 3
	05651	East Montpelier, 550	B 3
	05652	Eden, ▵513	B 2
	05450	Enosburg Falls, 1,266	B 2
	05451	Essex, ▵10,951	A 2
	05451	Essex, 850	A 2
	05452	Essex Junction, 6,511	A 3
	05454	Fairfax, ▵1,366	B 2
	05455	Fairfield, ▵1,285	B 2
	05743	Fair Haven, ▵2,777	A 4
	05743	Fair Haven, 2,287	A 4
	05045	Fairlee, ▵604	C 4
	05045	Fairlee, 425	C 4
	05456	Ferrisburg, ▵1,875	A 3
†	05444	Fletcher, ▵456	B 2
	05745	Forest Dale, 500	A 4
	05457	Franklin, ▵821	B 2
†	05478	Georgia, ▵1,711	A 2
	05904	Gilman, 700	D 3
	05839	Glover, ▵649	C 2
	05146	Grafton, ▵465	B 5
	05840	Granby, ▵52	D 2
	05458	Grand Isle, ▵809	A 2
	05654	Graniteville, 1,120	C 3
	05747	Granville, ▵255	B 4
	05841	Greensboro, ▵593	C 2
	05046	Groton, ▵666	C 3
	05046	Groton, 438	C 3
	05905	Guildhall⊙, ▵169	D 2
†	05301	Guilford, ▵1,108	B 6
†	05358	Halifax, ▵295	B 6
	05748	Hancock, ▵283	B 4
	05843	Hardwick, ▵2,466	C 2
	05843	Hardwick, 1,503	C 2
	05047	Hartford, ▵6,477	C 4
	05047	Hartford, 650	C 4
	05047	Hartland, ▵1,806	C 4
†	05459	Highgate, ▵1,936	B 2
	05459	Highgate Center, 927	B 2
	05461	Hinesburg, ▵1,775	A 3
†	05830	Holland, ▵383	D 2
	05749	Hubbardton, ▵228	A 4
	05462	Huntington, ▵748	B 3
	05655	Hyde Park, ▵1,347	B 2
	05655	Hyde Park⊙, 418	B 2
	05750	Hydeville, 450	A 4
†	05777	Ira, ▵284	A 4
	05845	Irasburg, ▵775	C 2
	05846	Island Pond, 1,123	D 2
	05463	Isle La Motte, ▵262	A 2
	05343	Jamaica, ▵590	B 5
†	05859	Jay, ▵182	C 2
	05465	Jericho, ▵2,343	B 3
	05465	Jericho, 450	A 2
	05656	Johnson, ▵1,927	B 2
	05656	Johnson, 1,296	B 2
†	05752	Leicester, ▵583	A 4
†	03576	Lemington, ▵120	D 2
†	05443	Lincoln, ▵599	B 3
	05148	Londonderry, ▵1,037	B 5
	05847	Lowell, ▵515	C 2
	05149	Ludlow, ▵2,463	B 5
	05149	Ludlow, 1,508	B 5
	05906	Lunenburg, ▵1,061	D 3
	05849	Lyndon, ▵3,705	C 2
	05851	Lyndonville, 1,415	D 2
†	05905	Maidstone, ▵94	D 2
	05254	Manchester, ▵2,919	A 5
	05254	Manchester⊙, 435	A 5
	05255	Manchester Center, 900	A 5
	05256	Manchester Depot, 1,560	B 5
	05344	Marlboro, ▵592	B 6
	05658	Marshfield, ▵1,033	C 3
†	05701	Mendon, ▵743	B 4
	05753	Middlebury, ▵6,532	A 3
	05753	Middlebury⊙, 4,500	A 3
†	05602	Middlesex, ▵857	B 3
	05757	Middletown Springs, ▵426	A 5
	05468	Milton, ▵4,495	A 2
	05468	Milton, 1,164	A 2
	05469	Monkton, ▵765	A 3
	05470	Montgomery, ▵651	B 2
	05602	Montpelier (cap.)⊙, 8,609	B 3
	05660	Moretown, ▵904	B 3
	05853	Morgan, ▵286	D 2
†	05661	Morristown, ▵4,052	B 2
	05661	Morrisville, 2,116	B 2
	05758	Mount Holly, ▵687	B 5
†	05739	Mount Tabor, ▵184	B 5
†	05871	Newark, ▵144	D 2
	05051	Newbury, ▵1,440	C 3
	05051	Newbury, 450	C 3
	05345	Newfane, ▵900	B 6
	05345	Newfane⊙, 183	B 6
	05472	New Haven, ▵1,039	A 3
	05855	Newport, ▵1,125	C 2
	05855	Newport⊙, 4,664	C 2
	05257	North Bennington, 984	A 6
	05759	North Clarendon, 750	B 4
	05663	Northfield, ▵4,870	B 3
	05663	Northfield, 2,139	B 3
	05664	Northfield Falls, 700	B 3
	05474	North Hero⊙, ▵364	A 2
	05260	North Pownal, 600	A 6
	05150	North Springfield, 1,100	B 5
	05859	North Troy, 774	C 2
	05907	Norton, ▵207	D 2
	05055	Norwich, ▵1,966	C 4
	05055	Norwich, 500	C 4
†	05649	Orange, ▵540	C 3
	05860	Orleans, 1,138	C 2
	05760	Orwell, ▵851	A 4
†	05491	Panton, ▵416	A 3
	05761	Pawlet, ▵1,184	A 5
	05862	Peacham, ▵446	C 3
	05152	Peru, ▵243	B 5
	05762	Pittsfield, ▵249	B 4
	05763	Pittsford, ▵2,306	A 4
	05763	Pittsford, 682	A 4
	05667	Plainfield, ▵1,399	C 3
	05667	Plainfield, 949	C 3
	05056	Plymouth, ▵283	B 4
†	05067	Pomfret, ▵620	B 4
	05764	Poultney, ▵3,217	A 4
	05764	Poultney, 1,914	A 4
	05261	Pownal, ▵2,441	A 6
	05261	Pownal, 700	A 6
	05765	Proctor, ▵2,095	A 4
	05765	Proctor, 1,950	A 4
	05153	Proctorsville, 512	B 5
	05346	Putney, ▵1,727	B 6
	05346	Putney, 1,115	B 6
	05059	Quechee, 420	C 4
	05060	Randolph, ▵3,882	B 4
	05060	Randolph, 2,115	B 4
	05062	Reading, ▵564	B 5
	05350	Readsboro, ▵638	B 6
	05350	Readsboro, 469	B 6
	05476	Richford, ▵2,116	B 2
	05476	Richford, 1,527	B 2
	05477	Richmond, ▵2,249	A 3
	05477	Richmond, 935	A 3
	05766	Ripton, ▵187	A 4
	05767	Rochester, ▵884	B 4
†	05101	Rockingham, ▵5,501	C 5
	05669	Roxbury, ▵354	B 3
	05063	Royalton, ▵1,399	B 4
	05768	Rupert, ▵582	A 5
	05701	Rutland, ▵2,248	B 4
	05701	Rutland⊙, 19,293	B 4
	05042	Ryegate, ▵830	C 3
	05478	Saint Albans, ▵3,270	A 2
	05478	Saint Albans⊙, 8,082	A 2
†	05401	Saint George, ▵477	A 2
	05819	Saint Johnsbury, ▵8,409	D 3
	05819	Saint Johnsbury⊙, 7,000	D 3
	05769	Salisbury, ▵649	A 4
†	05250	Sandgate, ▵127	A 5
	05154	Saxtons River, 581	B 5
†	05363	Searsburg, ▵84	A 6
	05262	Shaftsbury, ▵2,411	A 6
	05065	Sharon, ▵541	C 4
	05866	Sheffield, ▵307	C 2
	05482	Shelburne, ▵3,728	A 3
	05482	Shelburne, 2,591	A 3
	05483	Sheldon, ▵1,481	B 2
	05770	Shoreham, ▵790	A 4
†	05738	Shrewsbury, ▵570	B 4
	05670	South Barre, 865	B 3
	05401	South Burlington, ▵10,032	A 3
	05486	South Hero, ▵868	A 2
	05155	South Londonderry, 600	B 5
	05068	South Royalton, 625	C
	05156	Springfield, ▵10,063	B
	05156	Springfield, 5,632	B
†	01247	Stamford, ▵752	A
	05487	Starksboro, ▵668	A
	05772	Stockbridge, ▵389	B
	05672	Stowe, ▵2,388	B
	05672	Stowe, 435	B
	05072	Strafford, ▵536	C
†	05360	Stratton, ▵104	B
†	05733	Sudbury, ▵253	A
†	05250	Sunderland, ▵601	A
	05867	Sutton, ▵438	C
	05488	Swanton, ▵4,622	A
	05488	Swanton, 2,630	A
	05074	Thetford, ▵1,422	C
†	05773	Tinmouth, ▵268	A
	05076	Topsham, ▵686	C
	05353	Townshend, ▵668	B
	05868	Troy, ▵1,457	C
	05077	Tunbridge, ▵791	C
	05489	Underhill, ▵1,198	B
	05491	Vergennes, 2,242	A
	05354	Vernon, ▵1,024	B
	05079	Vershire, ▵299	C
	05673	Waitsfield, ▵837	B
†	05873	Walden, ▵442	C
	05773	Wallingford, ▵1,676	B
	05773	Wallingford, 815	B
†	05491	Waltham, ▵265	A
	05355	Wardsboro, ▵391	B
	05674	Warren, ▵588	B
	05675	Washington, ▵667	C
	05676	Waterbury, ▵4,614	B
	05676	Waterbury, 2,840	B
	05677	Waterbury Center, 900	B
	05492	Waterville, ▵397	B
	05678	Websterville, 700	B
	05774	Wells, ▵560	A
	05081	Wells River, 419	C
	05301	West Brattleboro, 2,200	B
	05083	West Fairlee, ▵337	C
	05874	Westfield, ▵375	C
	05494	Westford, ▵991	A
†	05743	West Haven, ▵240	A
	05158	Westminster, ▵1,875	C
†	05860	Westmore, ▵195	C
	05161	Weston, ▵507	B
	05161	Weston, 450	B
	05777	West Rutland, ▵2,381	A
	05777	West Rutland, 1,875	A
†	05753	Weybridge, ▵618	A
†	05851	Wheelock, ▵238	C
	05001	White River Junction, 2,379	C
	05778	Whiting, ▵359	A
	05361	Whitingham, ▵1,011	B
	05088	Wilder, 1,328	C
	05679	Williamstown, ▵1,822	B
	05679	Williamstown, 650	B
	05495	Williston, ▵3,187	A
	05363	Wilmington, ▵1,184	B
	05363	Wilmington, 544	B
†	05359	Windham, ▵174	B
	05089	Windsor, ▵4,158	C
	05089	Windsor, 3,400	C
	05404	Winooski, 7,309	A
	05680	Wolcott, ▵676	C
†	05681	Woodbury, ▵399	C
†	05201	Woodford, ▵286	A
	05091	Woodstock, ▵2,608	B
	05091	Woodstock⊙, 1,154	B
	05682	Worcester, ▵505	B

⊙ County seat.
▵ Population of town or townsnip
‡ Population of metropolitan area.
† Zip of nearest p.o.
* Multiple zips

Edmund V. Ballman

Designed to protect wooden structures from the ravages of weather, a few early covered bridges are still standing in New Hampshire. This barn-red relic is in Jackson.

Located in the heart of Vermont, Barre rightfully boasts of its granite quarries which provide a sculptured panorama set off by surrounding green hills.

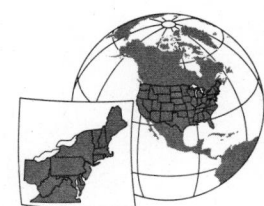

AREA 7,836 sq. mi.
POPULATION 7,168,164
CAPITAL Trenton
LARGEST CITY Newark
HIGHEST POINT High Point 1,803 ft.
SETTLED IN 1617
ADMITTED TO UNION December 18, 1787
POPULAR NAME Garden State
STATE FLOWER Violet
STATE BIRD Eastern Goldfinch

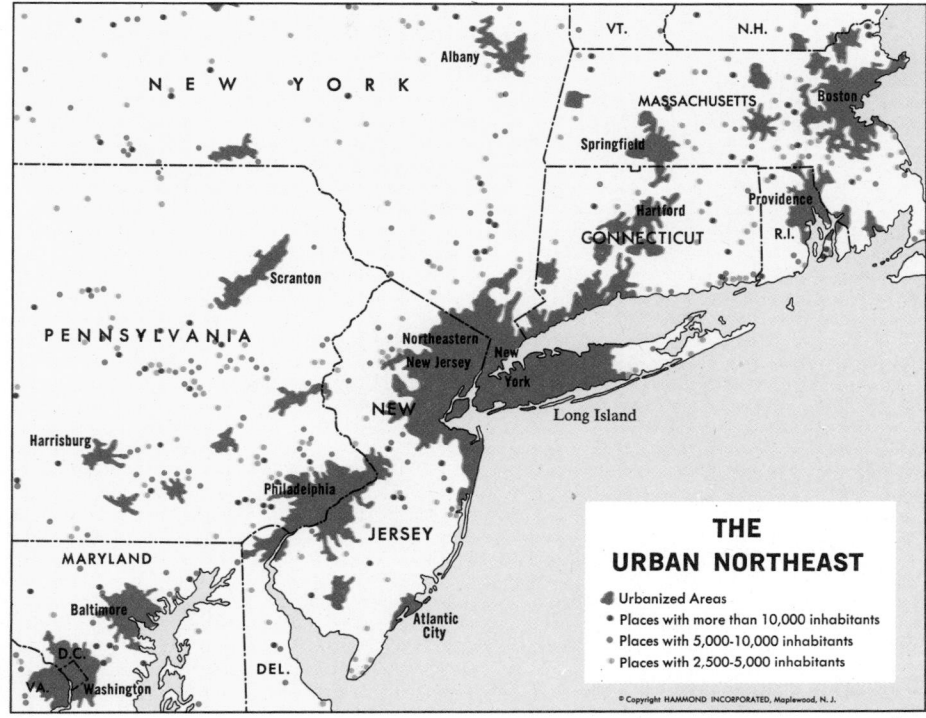

THE URBAN NORTHEAST

◤ Urbanized Areas
● Places with more than 10,000 inhabitants
• Places with 5,000-10,000 inhabitants
• Places with 2,500-5,000 inhabitants

© Copyright HAMMOND INCORPORATED, Maplewood, N. J.

Agriculture, Industry and Resources

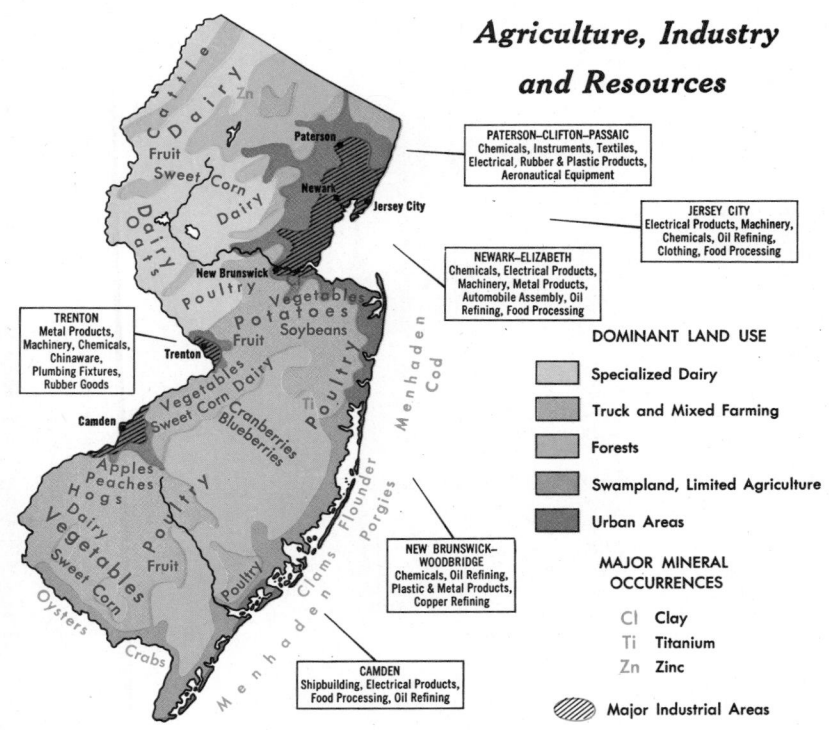

PATERSON–CLIFTON–PASSAIC
Chemicals, Instruments, Textiles, Electrical, Rubber & Plastic Products, Aeronautical Equipment

JERSEY CITY
Electrical Products, Machinery, Chemicals, Oil Refining, Clothing, Food Processing

NEWARK–ELIZABETH
Chemicals, Electrical Products, Machinery, Metal Products, Automobile Assembly, Oil Refining, Food Processing

TRENTON
Metal Products, Machinery, Chemicals, Chinaware, Plumbing Fixtures, Rubber Goods

NEW BRUNSWICK–WOODBRIDGE
Chemicals, Oil Refining, Plastic & Metal Products, Copper Refining

CAMDEN
Shipbuilding, Electrical Products, Food Processing, Oil Refining

DOMINANT LAND USE

Specialized Dairy
Truck and Mixed Farming
Forests
Swampland, Limited Agriculture
Urban Areas

MAJOR MINERAL OCCURRENCES

Cl Clay
Ti Titanium
Zn Zinc

▨ Major Industrial Areas

(continued on following page)

(continued)

	08732	Island Heights, 1,397	E 4
	08527	Jackson, ▵18,276	E 3
	08831	Jamesburg, 4,584	E 3
*	07301	Jersey City⊙, 260,545	B 2
		Jersey City, ‡609,266	B 2
	07734	Keansburg, 9,720	E 3
	07032	Kearny, 37,585	B 2
	08832	Keasbey, 1,200	E 2
	08824	Kendall Park, 7,412	D 3
	07033	Kenilworth, 9,165	E 2
	07735	Keyport, 7,205	E 3
	08528	Kingston, 1,200	D 3
	07405	Kinnelon, 7,600	E 2
	08043	Kirkwood, 800	B 4
	07848	Lafayette, 900	D 1
	07034	Lake Hiawatha, 11,389	E 2
	07849	Lake Hopatcong, 1,941	D 2
	08733	Lakehurst, 2,641	E 3
†	07871	Lake Mohawk, 6,262	D 1
	08701	Lakewood, 17,874	E 3
	08530	Lambertville, 4,359	D 3
	07850	Landing, 2,370	D 2
	08734	Lanoka Harbor, 1,066	E 4
	08021	Laurel Springs, 2,566	B 4
	08879	Laurence Harbor, 6,715	E 3
	08735	Lavallette, 1,509	E 4
	08045	Lawnside, 2,757	B 3
	08648	Lawrenceville, 1,464	D 3
	08833	Lebanon, 885	D 2
	07852	Ledgewood, 2,800	D 2
	08327	Leesburg, 800	D 5
	07737	Leonardo, 4,000	E 3
	07605	Leonia, 8,847	C 2
	07938	Liberty Corner, 1,900	D 2
	07035	Lincoln Park, 9,034	A 1
	07738	Lincroft, 4,900	E 3
	07036	Linden, 41,409	A 3
	08021	Lindenwold, 12,199	B 4
	08221	Linwood, 6,159	D 5
	07424	Little Falls, ▵11,727	B 2
	07643	Little Ferry, 9,042	B 2
	07739	Little Silver, 6,010	F 3
	07039	Livingston, ▵30,127	E 2
	07644	Lodi, 25,213	B 2
	08008	Long Branch, 31,774	F 3
	08403	Longport, 1,225	D 5
	07853	Long Valley, 1,645	D 2
	08048	Lumberton, 600	D 4
	07071	Lyndhurst, ▵22,729	B 2
	07939	Lyons, 3,900	D 2
	07940	Madison, 16,710	E 2
	08049	Magnolia, 5,893	B 3
	07430	Mahwah, ▵10,539	E 1
	08328	Malaga, 950	C 4
	08050	Manahawkin, 1,278	E 4
	08736	Manasquan, 4,971	E 3
	08051	Mantua, 5,530	C 4
	08835	Manville, 13,029	D 2
	08052	Maple Shade, ▵16,464	B 3
	07040	Maplewood, ▵24,932	E 2
†	07866	Marcella, 540	E 2
	08402	Margate City, 10,576	E 5
	07746	Marlboro, 2,380	E 3
	08053	Marlton, 10,180	D 4
	08223	Marmora, 650	D 5
	08836	Martinsville, 3,500	D 2
	08054	Masonville, 900	D 4
	07747	Matawan, 9,136	E 3
	08330	Mays Landing⊙, 1,272	D 5
	07607	Maywood, 11,087	B 2
	07428	McAfee, 800	D 1
†	08232	McKee City, 950	D 5
	08055	Medford, 1,448	D 4
	08055	Medford Lakes, 4,792	D 4
	07945	Mendham, 3,729	D 2
	08817	Menlo Park, 10,000	E 2
	08619	Mercerville, 5,456	D 3
	08109	Merchantville, 4,425	B 3
	08840	Metuchen, 16,031	E 2
	08056	Mickleton, 950	C 4
	08846	Middlesex, 15,038	E 2
	07748	Middletown, ▵54,623	E 3
	07432	Midland Park, 8,159	B 1
	08848	Milford, 1,230	C 2
	07041	Millburn, ▵21,307	E 2
	07946	Millington, 975	D 2
	08849	Millstone, 630	D 2
	08850	Milltown, 6,470	E 3
	08332	Millville, 21,366	C 5
	07438	Milton, 2,220	D 1
†	07801	Mine Hill, ▵3,557	D 2
	08342	Mizpah, 900	D 5
	07750	Monmouth Beach, 2,042	F 3
	08852	Monmouth Junction, 1,900	D 3
	07434	Monroe, ▵9,138	E 3
†	12771	Montague, 750	D 1
*	07042	Montclair, 44,043	B 2
	07645	Montvale, 7,327	B 1
	07045	Montville, 4,900	E 2
	07074	Moonachie, 2,937	B 2
	08057	Moorestown, 14,179	B 3
	07950	Morris Plains, 5,540	D 2
	07960	Morristown⊙, 17,662	D 2
	07046	Mountain Lakes, 4,739	E 2
	07092	Mountainside, 7,520	E 2
†	07470	Mountain View, 9,000	B 2
	07856	Mount Arlington, 3,590	D 2
	08059	Mount Ephraim, 5,625	B 3
	07970	Mount Freedom, 1,621	D 2
	08060	Mount Holly⊙, ▵12,713	D 4
†	07885	Mount Hope, 1,510	D 2
	08061	Mount Royal, 850	C 4
	08062	Mullica Hill, 800	C 4
†	08087	Mystic Islands, 900	E 4
	08063	National Park, 3,730	B 3
	07752	Navesink, 2,400	E 3
	07753	Neptune, ▵27,863	E 3
	07753	Neptune City, 5,502	E 3
†	08853	Neshanic, 752	D 3
	07857	Netcong, 2,858	D 2
*	07101	Newark⊙, 382,417	B 2
		Newark, ‡2,056,556	B 2
*	08901	New Brunswick⊙, 41,885	E 3
	08533	New Egypt, 1,769	E 3
	08344	Newfield, 1,487	D 4
	07435	Newfoundland, 900	D 1
	08224	New Gretna, 700	E 4
	07646	New Milford, 20,201	B 1
	08345	Newport, 700	C 5
	07974	New Providence, 13,796	E 2
	07724	New Shrewsbury, 5,925	E 3
	07860	Newton⊙, 7,297	D 1
	08346	Newtonville, 750	D 4
	07976	New Vernon, 1,900	D 2
	08817	Nixon, 12,000	E 2
	08347	Norma, 1,200	C 4
	07032	North Arlington, 18,096	B 2
	07047	North Bergen, ▵47,751	B 2
	08876	North Branch, 610	D 2
	08902	North Brunswick, ▵16,691	E 3
†	07006	North Caldwell, 6,425	B 2
	08204	North Cape May, 3,812	C 6
	08225	Northfield, 8,875	D 5
	07508	North Haledon, 7,614	B 1
	07060	North Plainfield, 21,796	E 2
	07647	Northvale, 5,177	F 1
	08260	North Wildwood, 3,914	D 6
	07648	Norwood, 4,398	C 1
	07110	Nutley, 32,099	B 2
	07755	Oakhurst, 5,558	E 3
	07436	Oakland, 14,420	B 1
	08107	Oaklyn, 4,626	B 3
	07438	Oak Ridge, 750	E 1
	08226	Ocean City, 10,575	D 5
	08740	Ocean Gate, 1,081	E 4
	07756	Ocean Grove, 7,000	F 3
	07757	Oceanport, 7,503	F 3
	08230	Ocean View, 950	D 5
	08231	Oceanville, 600	D 5
	07439	Ogdensburg, 2,222	D 1
	08857	Old Bridge, 25,176	E 3
	07675	Old Tappan, 3,917	C 1
	08858	Oldwick, 600	D 2
	07649	Oradell, 8,903	B 1
*	07050	Orange, 32,566	B 2
	08723	Osbornsville, 3,900	E 3
	07863	Oxford, 1,411	C 2
	07470	Packanack Lake, 4,000	B 1
†	08226	Palermo, 600	D 5
	07650	Palisades Park, 13,351	C 2
	08065	Palmyra, 6,969	B 3
	07652	Paramus, 29,495	B 1
†	08087	Parkertown, 600	E 4
	07656	Park Ridge, 8,709	B 1
	07054	Parsippany, ▵55,112	E 2
*	07055	Passaic, 55,124	E 2
*	07501	Paterson⊙, 144,824	B 2
		Paterson-Clifton-Passaic, ‡1,358,794	B 2
	08066	Paulsboro, 8,084	C 4
	07977	Peapack-Gladstone, 1,924	D 2
	08067	Pedricktown, 1,500	C 4
	08068	Pemberton, 1,344	D 4
	08534	Pennington, 2,151	D 3
	08110	Pennsauken, ▵36,394	B 3
	08069	Penns Grove, 5,727	C 4
	08070	Pennsville, 11,014	C 4
	07440	Pequannock, 4,900	B 1
*	08861	Perth Amboy, 38,798	E 2
	08865	Phillipsburg, 17,849	C 2
	08741	Pine Beach, 1,395	E 4
	07058	Pine Brook, 3,500	E 2
	08021	Pine Hill, 5,132	D 4
	08854	Piscataway, ▵36,418	D 2
	08071	Pitman, 10,257	C 4
*	07060	Plainfield, 46,862	E 2
	08536	Plainsboro, 1,200	D 3
	08232	Pleasantville, 13,778	D 5
	08742	Point Pleasant, 15,968	E 3
	08742	Point Pleasant Beach, 4,882	E 3
	08240	Pomona, 900	D 5
	07442	Pompton Lakes, 11,397	A 1
	07444	Pompton Plains, 9,500	B 1
	07758	Port Monmouth, 4,556	E 3
†	07850	Port Morris, 950	D 2
	07865	Port Murray, 800	D 2
	08349	Port Norris, 1,955	C 5
	07064	Port Reading, 4,900	E 2
	08241	Port Republic, 586	D 4
	08540	Princeton, 12,311	D 3
	08550	Princeton Junction, 950	D 3
†	07885	Prospect Park, 5,176	B 1
	08072	Quinton, 575	C 4
*	07065	Rahway, 29,114	E 2
†	07945	Ralston, 650	D 2
†	08057	Ramblewood, 5,556	D 4
	07446	Ramsey, 12,571	B 1
	08869	Raritan, 6,691	D 2
	07701	Red Bank, 12,847	E 3
	08350	Richland, 950	D 5
	07657	Ridgefield, 11,308	B 2
	07660	Ridgefield Park, 14,453	B 2
*	07450	Ridgewood, 27,547	B 1
	08551	Ringoes, 682	D 3
	07456	Ringwood, 10,393	E 1
	08242	Rio Grande, 1,203	D 5
	07457	Riverdale, 2,729	A 1
	07661	River Edge, 12,850	B 1
	08075	Riverside, ▵8,616	B 3
	08077	Riverton, 3,412	B 3
	08691	Robbinsville, 650	D 3
	07662	Rochelle Park, ▵6,380	B 2
	07866	Rockaway, ▵18,955	D 2
	07866	Rockaway, 6,383	D 2
	08553	Rocky Hill, 917	D 3
	08554	Roebling-Florence, 7,551	D 3
	08555	Roosevelt, 814	E 3
	07068	Roseland, 4,453	A 2
	07203	Roselle, 22,585	B 2
	07204	Roselle Park, 14,277	A 2
	08352	Rosenhayn, 950	C 5
†	07876	Roxbury, ▵15,754	D 2
	07760	Rumson, 7,421	F 3
	08078	Runnemede, 10,475	B 3
*	07070	Rutherford, 20.802	B 2
	07662	Saddle Brook, ▵15,098	B 1
	07458	Saddle River, 2,437	B 1
	08079	Salem⊙, 7,648	C 4
	08872	Sayreville, 32,508	E 3
	07076	Scotch Plains, ▵22,279	E 2
	07760	Sea Bright, 1,339	F 3
	08302	Seabrook, 1,569	C 5
	08750	Sea Girt, 2,207	E 3
	08243	Sea Isle City, 1,712	D 5
	08751	Seaside Heights, 1,248	E 4
	08752	Seaside Park, 1,432	E 4
	07094	Secaucus, 13,228	B 2
	07077	Sewaren, 3,200	E 2
	08080	Sewell, 2,210	C 4
	08353	Shiloh, 573	C 5
	08008	Ship Bottom, 1,079	E 4
	07078	Short Hills, 14,000	E 2
	07701	Shrewsbury, 3,315	E 3
	08081	Sicklerville, 1,700	D 4
†	07424	Singac, 3,942	B 2
	08558	Skillman, 1,955	D 3
†	07728	Smithburg, 750	E 3
	08083	Somerdale, 6,510	B 4
	08244	Somers Point, 7,919	D 5
	08876	Somerville⊙, 13,652	D 2
	08879	South Amboy, 9,338	E 3
†	07719	South Belmar, 1,490	E 3
	08880	South Bound Brook, 4,525	E 2
†	08852	South Brunswick, ▵14,058	E 3
	07079	South Orange, 16,971	A 2
	07080	South Plainfield, 21,142	E 2
	08882	South River, 15,428	E 3
	08246	South Seaville, 600	D 5
	08753	South Toms River, 3,981	E 4
	07871	Sparta, 3,000	D 1
	08884	Spotswood, 7,891	E 3
	07081	Springfield, ▵15,740	E 2
	07762	Spring Lake, 3,896	F 3
	07762	Spring Lake Heights, 4,602	E 3
	07874	Stanhope, 3,040	D 2
	08885	Stanton, 700	D 2
	08886	Stewartsville, 950	C 2
	07980	Stirling, 1,450	E 2
	07460	Stockholm, 1,477	D 1
	08559	Stockton, 619	D 3
	08247	Stone Harbor, 1,089	D 5
	08084	Stratford, 9,801	B 4
†	07747	Strathmore, 7,674	E 3
	07876	Succasunna, 5,000	D 2
	07901	Summit, 23,620	E 2
	08008	Surf City, 1,129	E 4
	07461	Sussex, 2,038	D 1
	08085	Swedesboro, 2,287	C 4
	07878	Tabor, 1,500	E 2
	07666	Teaneck, ▵42,355	B 2
	07670	Tenafly, 14,827	C 1
	07608	Teterboro, 14	B 2
	08086	Thorofare, 4,200	B 4
	08887	Three Bridges, 750	D 2
	08560	Titusville, 900	D 3
	08753	Toms River⊙, 7,303	E 4
	07511	Totowa, 11,580	B 1
	07082	Towaco, 2,500	E 2
*	08601	Trenton (cap.)⊙, 104,638	D 3
		Trenton, ‡303,968	D 3
	08087	Tuckerton, 1,926	E 4
	07083	Union, ▵53,077	A 2
	07735	Union Beach, 6,472	E 3
	07087	Union City, 58,537	C 2
†	07421	Upper Greenwood Lake 1,505	E 1
†	07458	Upper Saddle River, 7,949	B 1
†	07724	Vail Homes, 1,164	E 3
	07088	Vauxhall, 9,245	A 2
	08406	Ventnor City, 10,385	E 5
	07462	Vernon, 800	E 1
	07044	Verona, 15,067	B 2
	08251	Villas, 3,155	D 5
	08088	Vincentown, 900	D 4
	08360	Vineland, 47,399	C 5
		Vineland-Millville-Bridgeton, ‡121,374	C 5
	07463	Waldwick, 12,313	B 1
	07719	Wall, ▵16,498	E 3
	07055	Wallington, 10,284	B 2
†	07712	Wanamassa, 4,600	E 3
	07465	Wanaque, 8,636	B 1
	08758	Waretown, 1,800	E 4
	07882	Washington, 5,943	D 2
	07060	Watchung, 4,750	E 2
	08089	Waterford Works, 950	D 4
	07470	Wayne, ▵49,141	A 1
	07087	Weehawken, ▵13,383	C 2
	08090	Wenonah, 2,364	C 4
	07006	West Caldwell, 11,887	A 2
†	08204	West Cape May, 1,005	D 6
	08092	West Creek, 630	E 4
*	07090	Westfield, 33,720	E 2
	07764	West Long Branch, 6,845	F 3
	07480	West Milford, 950	E 1
	07093	West New York, 40,627	C 2
	07052	West Orange, 43,715	A 2
	07424	West Paterson, 11,692	B 2
	08628	West Trenton, 5,900	D 3
	08093	Westville, 5,170	B 3
	07675	Westwood, 11,105	B 1
	07885	Wharton, 5,535	D 2
	07981	Whippany, 7,500	E 2
	08888	Whitehouse, 800	D 2
	08889	White House Station, 1,019	D 2
	08252	Whitesboro, 700	D 5
†	08701	Whitesville, 600	E 3
	08759	Whiting, 750	E 4
	07765	Wickatunk, 950	E 3
	08260	Wildwood, 4,110	D 6
	08260	Wildwood Crest, 3,483	D 6
	08094	Williamstown, 4,075	D 4
	08046	Willingboro, ▵43,414	D 3
†	07036	Winfield, ▵2,184	B 2
	08270	Woodbine, 2,625	D 5
	07095	Woodbridge, ▵98,944	E 2
	08096	Woodbury⊙, 12,408	B 4
	08097	Woodbury Heights, 3,621	B 4
	07675	Woodcliff Lake, 5,506	B 1
	08107	Wood-Lynne, 3,101	B 3
†	07885	Woodport, 2,100	D 2
	07075	Wood-Ridge, 8,311	B 2
	08098	Woodstown, 3,137	C 4
	08562	Wrightstown, 2,719	D 3
	07481	Wyckoff, ▵16,039	B 1
	08620	Yardville, 9,500	D 3

⊙ County seat.
‡ Population of metropolitan area.
▵ Population of town or township.
† Zip of nearest p.o.
* Multiple zips

Topography

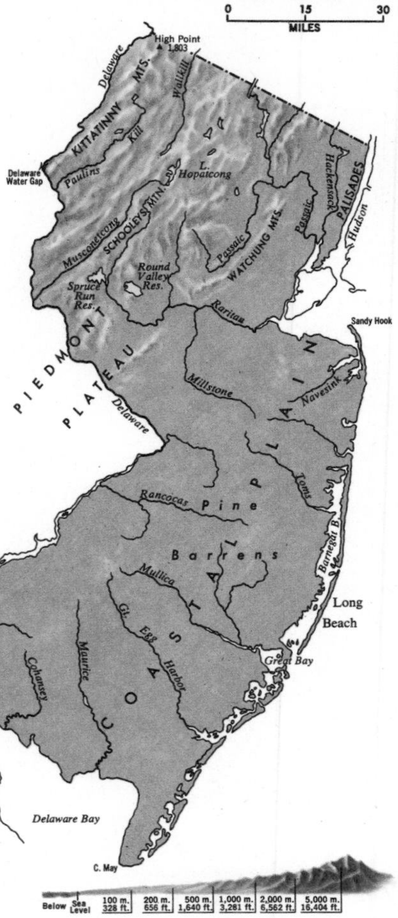
0 15 30
MILES
High Point 1,803
Delaware
KITTATINNY MTS.
Wallkill
Kill
Paulins
Delaware Water Gap
L. Hopatcong
SCHOOLEY'S MTN.
Musconetcong
Round Valley Res.
Spruce Run Res.
Passaic
WATCHUNG MTS.
Passaic
Hackensack
PALISADES
Hudson
Raritan
Sandy Hook
PIEDMONT PLATEAU
COASTAL PLAIN
Millstone
Navesink
Delaware
Rancocas
Pine Barrens
Toms
Barnegat B.
Long Beach
Mullica
Gt. Egg Harbor
Great Bay
Maurice
Cohansey
Delaware
Delaware Bay
C. May
Below Sea Level
100 m. 328 ft.
200 m. 656 ft.
500 m. 1,640 ft.
1,000 m. 3,281 ft.
2,000 m. 6,562 ft.
5,000 m. 16,404 ft.

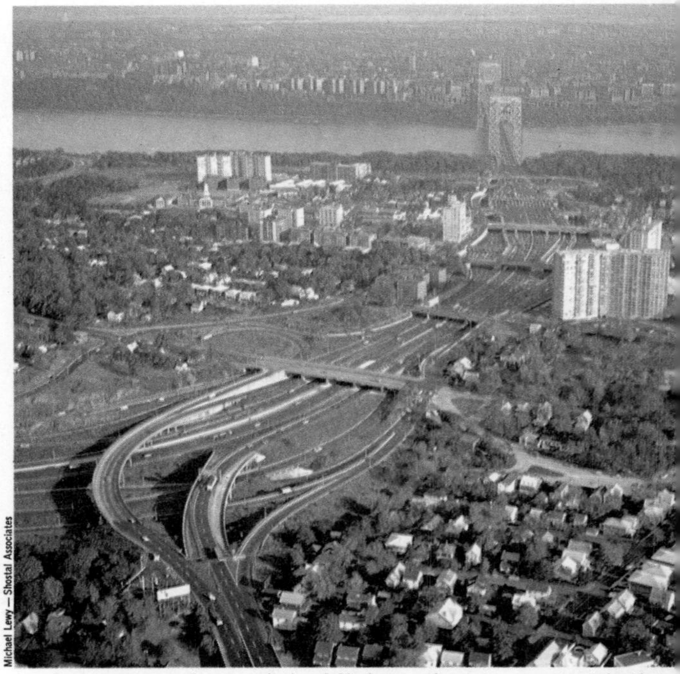

Michael Lewy — Shostal Associates

New Jersey towns become suburbs of Manhattan, thanks to connecting links like the Holland and Lincoln Tunnels and the George Washington Bridge. Scene above is the Fort Lee approach to the Bridge.

NEW JERSEY

SCALE

0   5   10   15   20 MI.

0   5   10   15   20 KM.

State Capitals .... ⊗

County Seats .... ◉

Canals ....

© C.S. HAMMOND & Co., N.Y.

210 New Mexico

COUNTIES

Bernalillo, 315,774..............C 4
Catron, 2,198.......................A 4
Chaves, 43,335....................E 5
Colfax, 12,170......................E 2
Curry, 39,517.......................F 4
De Baca, 2,547....................E 4
Dona Ana, 69,773...............C 6
Eddy, 41,119.......................E 6
Grant, 22,030.....................A 5
Guadalupe, 4,969...............E 4
Harding, 1,348....................F 3
Hidalgo, 4,734....................A 7
Lea, 49,554.........................F 6
Lincoln, 7,560.....................D 5
Los Alamos, 15,198...........B 3
Luna, 11,706.......................B 6
McKinley, 43,208................A 3
Mora, 4,673.........................E 3
Otero, 41,097......................D 6
Quay, 10,903.......................F 3
Rio Arriba, 25,170..............B 2

Roosevelt, 16,479...............F 4
Sandoval, 17,492................C 3
San Juan, 52,517...............A 2
San Miguel, 21,951............D 3
Santa Fe, 53,756...............C 3
Sierra, 7,189.......................B 5
Socorro, 9,763.....................C 5
Taos, 17,516.......................D 2
Torrance, 5,290..................D 4
Union, 4,925........................F 2
Valencia, 40,539.................A 4

CITIES and TOWNS

Zip   Name/Pop.   Key

87510 Abiquiu, 310.............C 2
† 87049 Acoma, 150............B 4
87049 Acomita, 975............B 3
87114 Alameda, 5,000........C 3
88310 Alamogordo⊙, 23,035...C 6
* 87101 Albuquerque⊙, 243,751...C 3
    Alburquerque, ‡315,774...C 3
87511 Alcalde, 975.............C 2

87001 Algodones, 195.........C 3
88312 Alto, 104..................D 5
87512 Amalia, 200..............D 1
88020 Animas, 75...............A 7
88021 Anthony, 1,728.........C 7
87930 Anton Chico, 600......D 3
† 88351 Arabela, 65.............D 5
87820 Aragon, 85...............A 4
87930 Arrey, 367................B 6
87513 Arroyo Hondo, 400....D 2
87514 Arroyo Seco, 500......D 2
88210 Artesia, 10,315.........E 6
87410 Aztec⊙, 3,354...........A 1
88023 Bayard, 2,908...........A 6
87002 Belen, 4,823.............C 4
88314 Bent, 157..................D 5
88024 Berino, 300...............C 7
87004 Bernalillo, 2,016........C 3
87815 Bingham, 60..............C 5
87412 Blanco, 150...............B 2
87413 Bloomfield, 1,574.......A 2
87005 Bluewater, 300..........A 3
87006 Bosque, 300..............C 4

87712 Buena Vista, 178........D 3
87515 Canjilon, 300..............C 2
87516 Canones, 200.............C 2
88414 Capitan, 439..............D 5
88414 Capulin, 100...............F 2
88220 Carlsbad⊙, 21,297.....E 6
88301 Carrizozo⊙, 1,123......D 5
87007 Casa Blanca, 560........B 4
88113 Causey, 150...............F 5
87518 Cebolla, 150...............C 2
87008 Cedar Crest, 600........C 3
† 87410 Cedar Hill, 145..........D 1
88026 Central, 1,864............A 6
87010 Cerrillos, 118..............D 3
87519 Cerro, 400..................D 2
87713 Chacon, 200...............D 2
87520 Chama, 899...............C 2
88027 Chamberino, 400........C 6
87521 Chamisal, 637............D 2
† 87059 Chilili, 80..................C 4
87522 Chimayo, 900.............D 2
87714 Cimarron, 927............E 2
88415 Clayton⊙, 2,931.........F 2

87715 Cleveland, 500...........D 2
88028 Cliff, 350...................A 6
88317 Cloudcroft, 525..........D 6
88101 Clovis⊙, 28,495.........F 4
† 87041 Cochiti, 300...............C 3
88029 Columbus, 241...........B 7
88416 Conchas Dam, 192......E 3
87523 Cordova, 600.............D 2
88318 Corona, 262...............D 4
87048 Corrales, 975.............C 3
87524 Costilla, 400...............D 2
87012 Coyote, 125...............C 2
87313 Crownpoint, 876.........A 3
† 86504 Crystal, 200.............A 2
87013 Cubero, 300..............B 4
88417 Cuervo, 150..............E 3
87522 Cundiyo, 98...............D 3
87821 Datil, 150..................B 4
88030 Deming⊙, 8,343........B 6
87933 Derry, 350................B 6
88418 Des Moines, 204........F 2
88230 Dexter, 746..............E 5

† 87711 Dilia, 125..................D 3
87527 Dixon, 640...............D 2
88032 Dona Ana, 800..........C 6
88115 Dora, 196.................F 5
87528 Dulce, 450...............B 2
88319 Duran, 100...............D 4
87718 Eagle Nest, 300.........E 2
87015 Edgewood, 75............C 3
87935 Elephant Butte, 75.....B 5
88116 Elida, 233................E 5
† 88731 El Porvenir, 90..........D 3
87529 El Prado, 200............D 2
88530 El Rito, 475..............C 2
88531 Embudo, 400............D 2
88321 Encino, 250..............D 4
87014 Eunice, 2,641...........F 6
87016 Estancia⊙, 721..........D 4
88231 Eunice, 2,641...........F 6
88033 Fairacres, 500...........C 6
87720 Farley, 81.................E 2
87401 Farmington, 21,979.....A 2
88034 Faywood, 75..............A 6
† 88041 Fierro, 200...............A 6

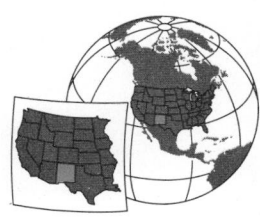

AREA 121,666 sq. mi.
POPULATION 1,016,000
CAPITAL Santa Fe
LARGEST CITY Albuquerque
HIGHEST POINT Wheeler Pk. 13,161 ft.
SETTLED IN 1605
ADMITTED TO UNION January 6, 1912
POPULAR NAME Land of Enchantment
STATE FLOWER Yucca
STATE BIRD Road Runner

Stephen Vovrick — Shostal Associates

Golden adobe against the blue Sangre de Cristo Mountains. Clear, pure colors, magnificent surroundings and congenial atmosphere combine to draw artists and writers to Taos, New Mexico.

Topography

0   50   100
MILES

Below Sea Level | 100 m. 328 ft. | 200 m. 656 ft. | 500 m. 1,640 ft. | 1,000 m. 3,281 ft. | 2,000 m. 6,562 ft. | 5,000 m. 16,404 ft.

Agriculture, Industry and Resources

DOMINANT LAND USE

- Wheat, Grain Sorghums, Range Livestock
- General Farming, Livestock, Special Crops
- General Farming, Livestock, Cash Grain
- Dry Beans, General Farming
- Cotton, Forest Products
- Range Livestock
- Forests
- Nonagricultural Land

MAJOR MINERAL OCCURRENCES

Ag Silver	Gp Gypsum			
Au Gold	K Potash		U Uranium
C Coal	Mo Molybdenum		V Vanadium
Cu Copper	Mr Marble	O Petroleum	Zn Zinc
G Natural Gas	Na Salt	Pb Lead	⚡ Water Power

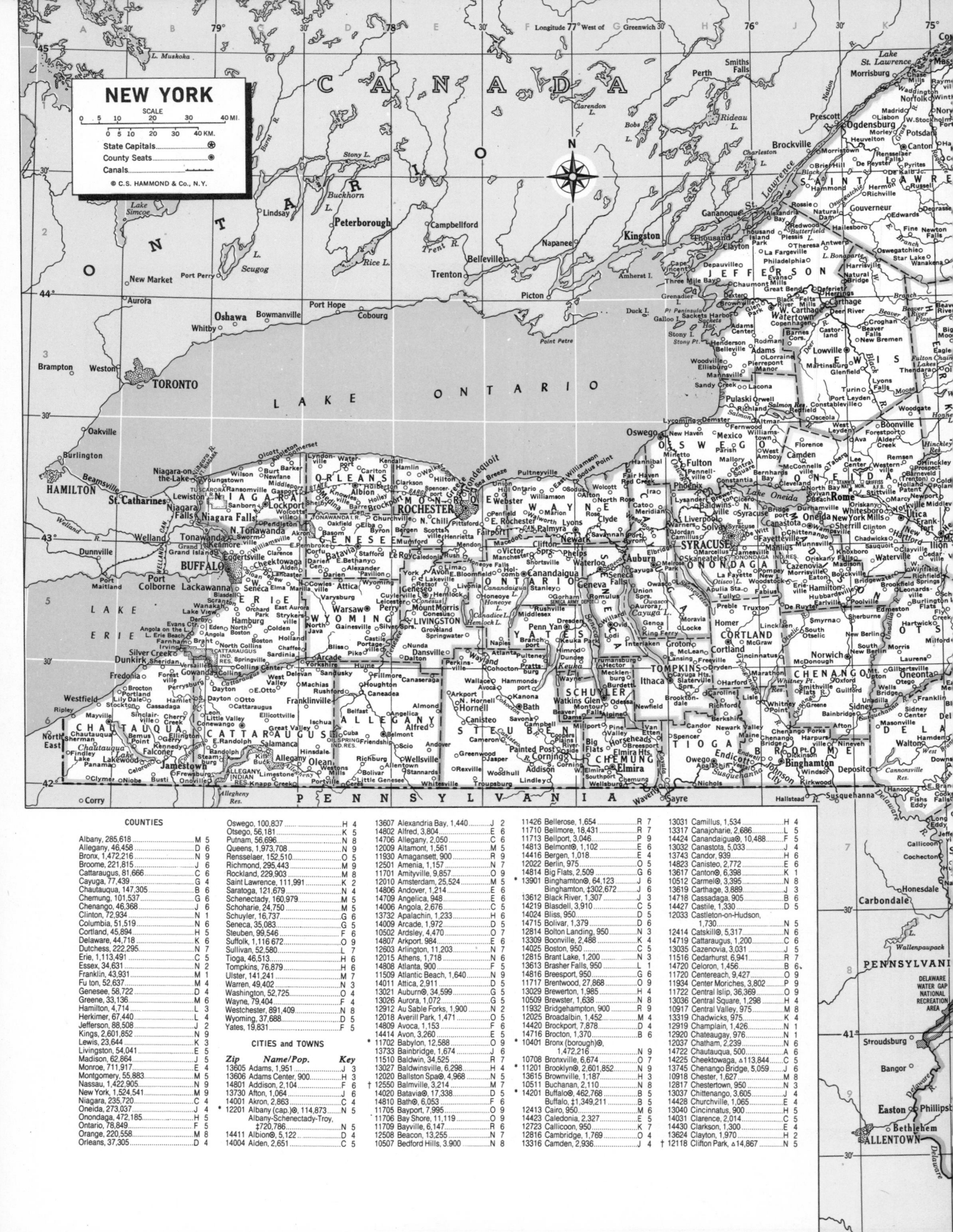

NEW YORK

SCALE
0 5 10 20 30 40 MI.
0 5 10 20 30 40 KM.

State Capitals............................⊛
County Seats.............................◉
Canals

© C.S. HAMMOND & CO., N.Y.

COUNTIES

Albany, 285,618 .... M 5
Allegany, 46,458 .... D 6
Bronx, 1,472,216 .... N 9
Broome, 221,815 .... J 6
Cattaraugus, 81,666 .... C 6
Cayuga, 77,439 .... G 4
Chautauqua, 147,305 .... B 6
Chemung, 101,537 .... G 6
Chenango, 46,368 .... J 5
Clinton, 72,934 .... N 1
Columbia, 51,519 .... N 5
Cortland, 45,894 .... H 5
Delaware, 44,718 .... K 6
Dutchess, 222,295 .... N 7
Erie, 1,113,491 .... C 5
Essex, 34,631 .... N 2
Franklin, 43,931 .... M 1
Fu ton, 52,637 .... M 4
Genesee, 58,722 .... D 4
Greene, 33,136 .... M 6
Hamilton, 4,714 .... L 3
Herkimer, 67,440 .... L 3
Jefferson, 88,508 .... J 2
Kings, 2,601,852 .... N 9
Lewis, 23,644 .... K 3
Livingston, 54,041 .... E 5
Madison, 62,864 .... J 5
Monroe, 711,917 .... E 4
Montgomery, 55,883 .... M 5
Nassau, 1,422,905 .... N 9
New York, 1,524,541 .... N 9
Niagara, 235,720 .... C 4
Oneida, 273,037 .... J 4
Onondaga, 472,185 .... H 5
Ontario, 78,849 .... F 5
Orange, 220,558 .... M 8
Orleans, 37,305 .... D 4
Oswego, 100,807 .... H 4
Otsego, 56,181 .... K 5
Putnam, 56,696 .... N 8
Queens, 1,973,708 .... N 9
Rensselaer, 152,510 .... O 5
Richmond, 295,443 .... M 9
Rockland, 229,903 .... M 8
Saint Lawrence, 111,991 .... K 2
Saratoga, 121,679 .... N 4
Schenectady, 160,979 ...... M 5
Schoharie, 24,750 .... M 5
Schuyler, 16,737 .... G 6
Seneca, 35,083 .... G 5
Steuben, 99,546 .... F 6
Suffolk, 1,116,672 .... O 9
Sullivan, 52,580 .... L 7
Tioga, 49,515 .... H 6
Tompkins, 76,879 .... H 6
Ulster, 141,241 .... M 7
Warren, 49,402 .... N 3
Washington, 52,725 .... O 4
Wayne, 79,404 .... F 4
Westchester, 891,409 ...... N 8
Wyoming, 37,688 .... D 5
Yates, 19,831 .... F 5

CITIES and TOWNS

Zip	Name/Pop.	Key
13605	Adams, 1,951	J 3
13606	Adams Center, 900	H 3
14801	Addison, 2,104	F 6
13730	Afton, 1,064	J 6
14001	Akron, 2,863	C 4
* 12201	Albany (cap.)◉, 114,873	N 5
	Albany-Schenectady-Troy, ‡720,786	N 5
14411	Albion◉, 5,122	C 5
14004	Alden, 2,651	C 5
13607	Alexandria Bay, 1,440	J 2
14802	Alfred, 3,804	E 6
14706	Allegany, 2,050	C 6
12009	Altamont, 1,561	M 5
11930	Amagansett, 900	R 9
12501	Amenia, 1,157	N 7
11701	Amityville, 9,857	O 9
12010	Amsterdam, 25,524	M 5
14806	Andover, 1,214	E 6
14709	Angelica, 948	D 6
14006	Angola, 2,676	C 5
13732	Apalachin, 1,233	H 6
14009	Arcade, 1,972	D 5
10502	Ardsley, 4,470	O 5
14807	Arkport, 984	E 6
12603	Arlington, 11,203	N 7
12015	Athens, 1,718	N 6
14808	Atlanta, 900	F 5
11509	Atlantic Beach, 1,640	N 9
14011	Attica, 2,911	D 5
13021	Auburn◉, 34,599	G 5
13026	Aurora, 1,072	G 5
12912	Au Sable Forks, 1,900	N 2
12018	Averill Park, 1,471	O 5
14809	Avoca, 1,153	F 6
14414	Avon, 3,260	E 5
* 11702	Babylon, 12,588	O 9
13733	Bainbridge, 1,674	J 6
11510	Baldwin, 34,525	R 7
13027	Baldwinsville, 6,298	H 4
12020	Ballston Spa◉, 4,968	N 5
12550	Balmville, 3,214	M 7
14020	Batavia◉, 17,338	D 5
14810	Bath◉, 6,053	F 6
11705	Bayport, 7,995	O 9
11706	Bay Shore, 11,119	O 9
11709	Bayville, 6,147	N 9
12508	Beacon, 13,255	N 7
10507	Bedford Hills, 3,900	N 8
11426	Bellerose, 1,654	R 7
11710	Bellmore, 18,431	R 7
11713	Bellport, 3,046	P 9
14813	Belmont◉, 1,102	E 6
14416	Bergen, 1,018	E 4
12022	Berlin, 975	O 5
14814	Big Flats, 2,509	G 6
* 13901	Binghamton◉, 64,123	J 6
	Binghamton, ‡302,672	J 6
13612	Black River, 1,307	J 3
14219	Blasdell, 3,910	C 5
14024	Bliss, 950	D 5
14715	Bolivar, 1,379	D 6
12814	Bolton Landing, 950	N 3
13309	Boonville, 2,488	K 4
14025	Boston, 950	C 5
12815	Brant Lake, 1,200	N 3
13613	Brasher Falls, 950	L 1
14816	Breesport, 950	G 6
11717	Brentwood, 27,868	O 9
13029	Brewerton, 1,985	H 4
10509	Brewster, 1,638	N 8
11932	Bridgehampton, 900	R 9
12025	Broadalbin, 1,452	M 4
14420	Brockport, 7,878	D 4
14716	Brocton, 1,370	B 6
* 10401	Bronx (borough)◉, 1,472,216	N 9
10708	Bronxville, 6,674	O 9
* 11201	Brooklyn◉, 2,601,852	N 9
13615	Brownville, 1,187	H 3
10511	Buchanan, 2,110	N 8
* 14201	Buffalo◉, 462,768	B 5
	Buffalo, ‡1,349,211	B 5
12413	Cairo, 950	M 6
14423	Caledonia, 2,327	E 5
12723	Callicoon, 950	K 7
12816	Cambridge, 1,769	O 4
13316	Camden, 2,936	J 4
13031	Camillus, 1,534	H 5
13317	Canajoharie, 2,686	L 5
14424	Canandaigua◉, 10,488	F 5
13032	Canastota, 5,033	J 4
13743	Candor, 939	H 6
14823	Canisteo, 2,772	E 6
13617	Canton◉, 6,398	K 1
10512	Carmel◉, 3,395	N 8
13619	Carthage, 3,889	J 3
14718	Cassadaga, 905	B 6
14427	Castile, 1,330	D 5
12033	Castleton-on-Hudson, 1,730	N 5
12414	Catskill◉, 5,317	N 6
14719	Cattaraugus, 1,200	C 6
13035	Cazenovia, 3,031	J 5
11516	Cedarhurst, 6,941	R 7
14720	Celoron, 1,456	B 6
11720	Centereach, 9,427	O 9
11934	Center Moriches, 3,802	P 9
11722	Central Islip, 36,369	O 9
13036	Central Square, 1,298	H 4
10917	Central Valley, 975	M 8
13319	Chadwicks, 975	K 4
12919	Champlain, 1,426	N 1
12920	Chateaugay, 976	N 1
12037	Chatham, 2,239	N 6
14722	Chautauqua, 500	A 6
14225	Cheektowaga, ∆113,844	C 5
13745	Chenango Bridge, 5,059	J 6
10918	Chester, 1,627	M 8
12817	Chestertown, 950	N 3
13037	Chittenango, 3,605	J 4
14428	Churchville, 1,065	E 4
13040	Cincinnatus, 900	J 5
14031	Clarence, 2,014	C 5
14430	Clarkson, 1,300	C 4
13624	Clayton, 1,970	H 2
† 12118	Clifton Park, ∆14,867	N 5

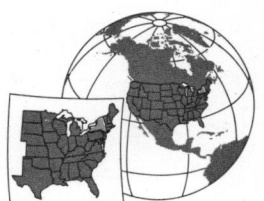

AREA 49,576 sq. mi.
POPULATION 18,241,266
CAPITAL Albany
LARGEST CITY New York
HIGHEST POINT Mt. Marcy 5,344 ft.
SETTLED IN 1614
ADMITTED TO UNION July 26, 1788
POPULAR NAME Empire State
STATE FLOWER Rose
STATE BIRD Bluebird

Topography

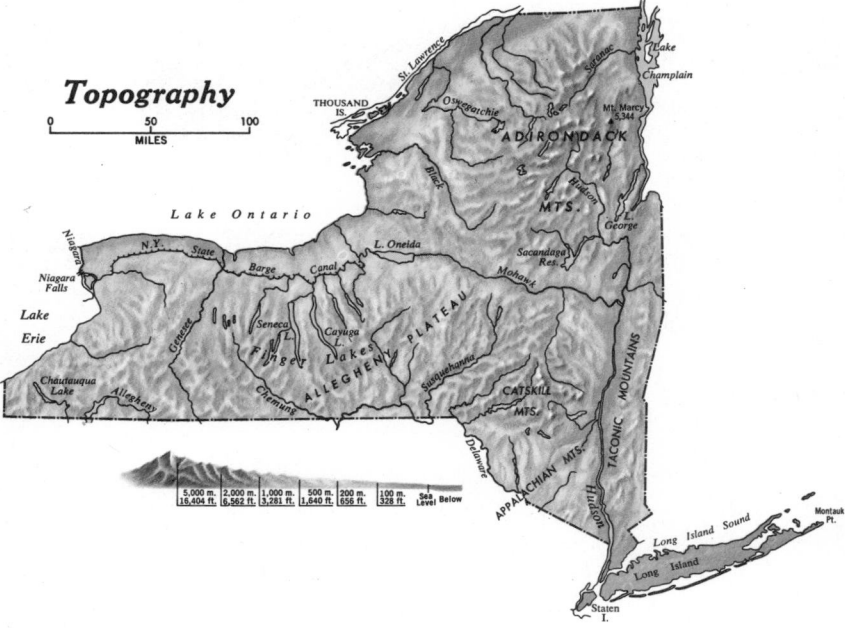

0   50   100
MILES

| 5,000 m. | 2,000 m. | 1,000 m. | 500 m. | 200 m. | 100 m. | Sea |
| 16,404 ft. | 6,562 ft. | 3,281 ft. | 1,640 ft. | 656 ft. | 328 ft. | Level Below |

(continued on following page)

(continued)

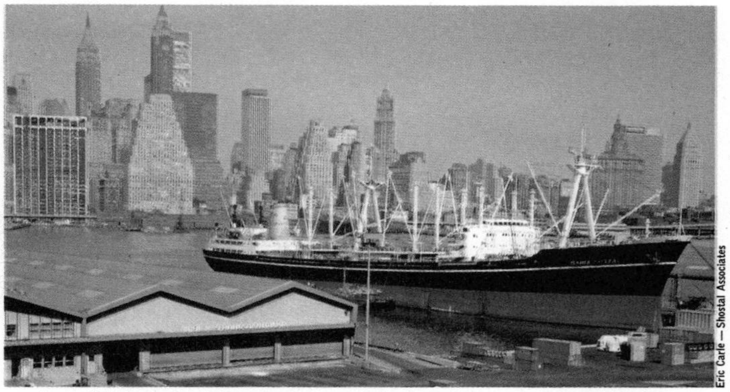

Lower Manhattan's skyline in an unusual view from a pier at the Brooklyn Port Authority Marine Terminal.

Eric Carle — Shostal Associates

11557 Hewlett, 6,796 .... R 7
* 11801 Hicksville, 48,075 .... R 7
12440 High Falls, 950 .... M 7
12528 Highland, 2,184 .... M 7
10928 Highland Falls, 4,638 .... M 8
10931 Hillburn, 1,058 .... M 8
14468 Hilton, 2,440 .... E 4
14080 Holland, 950 .... C 5
14470 Holley, 1,868 .... D 4
13077 Homer, 4,143 .... H 5
14472 Honeoye Falls, 2,248 .... F 5
12090 Hoosick Falls, 3,897 .... O 5
12533 Hopewell Junction, 2,055 .... N 7
14843 Hornell, 12,144 .... E 6
14845 Horseheads, 7,989 .... G 6
14744 Houghton, 1,620 .... D 6
12534 Hudson⊙, 8,940 .... N 6
12839 Hudson Falls⊙, 7,917 .... O 4
11743 Huntington, 12,130 .... O 9
11746 Huntington Station, 28,817 .... O 9
12443 Hurley, 4,081 .... M 7
12538 Hyde Park, 2,805 .... N 6
13357 Ilion, 9,808 .... K 5
12842 Indian Lake, 950 .... M 3
11696 Inwood, 8,433 .... R 7
14617 Irondequoit, ▵63,675 .... E 4
10533 Irvington, 5,878 .... O 6
11558 Island Park, 5,396 .... R 8
11751 Islip, 7,692 .... O 9
14850 Ithaca⊙, 26,226 .... G 6
* 11401 Jamaica⊙, 765,078 .... N 9
14701 Jamestown, 39,795 .... B 6
13078 Jamesville, 900 .... H 5
11753 Jericho, 14,010 .... S 7
13790 Johnson City, 18,025 .... J 6
12095 Johnstown⊙, 10,045 .... M 4
13080 Jordan, 1,493 .... H 4
10536 Katonah, 4,189 .... N 8
12944 Keeseville, 2,122 .... O 2
14271 Kenmore, 20,980 .... C 5
14747 Kennedy, 950 .... B 6
12446 Kerhonkson, 1,243 .... M 7
14478 Keuka Park, 990 .... F 5
12106 Kinderhook, 1,233 .... N 6
* 11201 Kings (Brooklyn) (borough), 2,601,852 .... N 9
11754 Kings Park, 5,555 .... O 9
11024 Kings Point, 5,525 .... R 7
12401 Kingston⊙, 25,544 .... M 7
14218 Lackawanna, 28,657 .... B 5
10512 Lake Carmel, 4,796 .... N 8
12845 Lake George⊙, 1,046 .... N 4
12449 Lake Katrine, 1,092 .... M 7
12846 Lake Luzerne, 900 .... N 4
12946 Lake Placid, 2,731 .... N 2
12108 Lake Pleasant⊙, 364 .... M 4
11040 Lake Success, 3,254 .... R 7
14085 Lake View, 6,000 .... B 5
14750 Lakewood, 3,864 .... B 6
14086 Lancaster, 13,365 .... C 5
10538 Larchmont, 7,203 .... P 7
11559 Lawrence, 6,566 .... R 7
14482 Le Roy, 5,118 .... E 5
11756 Levittown, 65,440 .... S 7
14092 Lewiston, 3,292 .... B 4
12754 Liberty, 4,293 .... L 7
14485 Lima, 1,686 .... E 5
11757 Lindenhurst, 28,338 .... O 9
13365 Little Falls, 7,629 .... L 4
14755 Little Valley⊙, 1,340 .... C 6
13088 Liverpool, 3,307 .... H 4
12758 Livingston Manor, 1,522 .... L 7
14487 Livonia, 1,278 .... E 5
14094 Lockport⊙, 25,399 .... C 4
11561 Long Beach, 33,127 .... R 8
13367 Lowville, 3,671 .... J 3
11563 Lynbrook, 23,776 .... R 7
12952 Lyon Mountain, 1,200 .... N 1
14489 Lyons⊙, 4,496 .... F 4
14502 Macedon, 1,168 .... F 4
13660 Madrid, 950 .... K 1
10541 Mahopac, 5,265 .... N 8
13103 Mallory, 900 .... H 4
12953 Malone⊙, 8,048 .... M 1
11565 Malverne, 10,036 .... R 7
10543 Mamaroneck, 18,909 .... P 7
14504 Manchester, 1,305 .... F 5
11030 Manhasset, 8,541 .... R 7
* 10001 Manhattan (borough), 1,524,541 .... M 9
13104 Manlius, 4,295 .... J 5
13803 Marathon, 1,053 .... J 6
13108 Marcellus, 1,456 .... H 5
13403 Marcy, 2,417 .... K 4

14505 Marion, 925 .... F 4
12542 Marlboro, 1,580 .... M 7
11758 Massapequa, 26,951 .... O 9
11762 Massapequa Park, 22,112 .... O 9
13662 Massena, 14,042 .... L 1
11950 Mastic Beach, 4,870 .... P 9
11952 Mattituck, 1,995 .... P 9
12543 Maybrook, 1,536 .... M 8
12117 Mayfield, 981 .... M 4
14757 Mayville⊙, 1,567 .... A 6
13101 McGraw, 1,319 .... H 5
12118 Mechanicville, 6,247 .... N 5
14103 Medina, 6,415 .... D 4
† 13021 Melrose Park, 2,189 .... G 5
† 12201 Menands, 3,449 .... N 5
11566 Merrick, 25,904 .... S 7
13114 Mexico, 1,555 .... H 4
12122 Middleburg, 1,410 .... M 5
12550 Middle Hope, 2,327 .... M 7
14105 Middleport, 2,132 .... C 4
10940 Middletown, 22,607 .... L 8
12545 Millbrook, 1,735 .... N 7
12546 Millerton, 1,042 .... O 7
11765 Mill Neck, 982 .... R 6
12547 Milton, 1,900 .... M 7
12547 Milton, 1,861 .... N 4
11501 Mineola⊙, 21,845 .... R 7
13115 Minetto, 950 .... H 4
12956 Mineville-Witherbee, 1,967 .... O 2
13407 Mohawk, 3,301 .... L 4
10950 Monroe, 4,439 .... M 8
12549 Montgomery, 1,533 .... M 7
12701 Monticello⊙, 5,991 .... L 7
14865 Montour Falls, 1,534 .... G 6
13118 Moravia, 1,642 .... H 5
12960 Moriah, 953 .... N 2
12962 Morrisonville, 1,276 .... N 1
13408 Morrisville, 2,296 .... J 5
12763 Mountain Dale, 950 .... L 7
10549 Mount Kisco, 8,172 .... N 8
14510 Mount Morris, 3,417 .... E 5
* 10550 Mount Vernon, 72,778 .... O 7
12458 Napanoch, 975 .... M 7
14512 Naples, 1,324 .... F 5
12123 Nassau, 1,466 .... N 5
14513 Newark, 11,644 .... G 4
13811 Newark Valley, 1,286 .... H 6
13411 New Berlin, 1,369 .... K 5
12550 Newburgh, 26,219 .... M 7
10956 New City⊙, 27,344 .... N 8
14108 Newfane, 2,588 .... C 4
13413 New Hartford, 2,433 .... K 4
11040 New Hyde Park, 10,116 .... R 7
12561 New Paltz, 6,058 .... M 7
13416 Newport, 908 .... K 4
* 10801 New Rochelle, 75,385 .... P 7
12550 New Windsor, 8,803 .... N 8
* 10001 New York (5 boroughs)⊙, 7,867,760 .... M 9
New York, ‡11,517,483 .... M 9
13417 New York Mills, 3,805 .... K 4
* 14301 Niagara Falls, 85,615 .... C 4
12309 Niskayuna, 6,186 .... N 5
13667 Norfolk, 1,379 .... K 1
14110 North Boston, 1,635 .... C 5
14514 North Chili, 3,163 .... E 4
14111 North Collins, 1,675 .... C 5
15853 North Creek, 950 .... M 3
14113 North Java, 950 .... D 5
11768 Northport, 7,440 .... O 9
13212 North Syracuse, 8,687 .... H 4
10591 North Tarrytown, 8,334 .... O 6
14120 North Tonawanda, 36,012 .... C 4
12134 Northville, 1,192 .... M 4
13815 Norwich⊙, 8,843 .... J 5
13668 Norwood, 2,098 .... L 1
14517 Nunda, 1,254 .... E 5
10960 Nyack, 6,659 .... N 8
14125 Oakfield, 1,964 .... D 4
11572 Oceanside, 35,028 .... R 7
13669 Ogdensburg, 14,554 .... K 1
14126 Olcott, 1,592 .... C 4
13420 Old Forge, 950 .... L 3
14760 Olean, 19,169 .... D 6
13421 Oneida, 11,658 .... J 4
13820 Oneonta, 16,030 .... K 6
14127 Orchard Park, 3,732 .... C 5
13424 Oriskany, 1,627 .... K 4
13425 Oriskany Falls, 927 .... J 5
10562 Ossining, 21,659 .... N 8
13126 Oswego⊙, 23,844 .... G 4
13825 Otego, 956 .... K 6
10963 Otisville, 933 .... L 8
14521 Ovid⊙, 779 .... G 5
13827 Owego⊙, 5,152 .... H 6

13830 Oxford, 1,944 .... J 6
11771 Oyster Bay, 14,330 .... S 6
14870 Painted Post, 2,496 .... F 6
14522 Palmyra, 3,776 .... F 4
12768 Parksville, 950 .... L 7
11772 Patchogue, 11,582 .... P 9
12563 Patterson, 975 .... N 7
12137 Pattersonville, 950 .... M 5
12564 Pawling, 1,914 .... N 7
10965 Pearl River, 17,146 .... M 8
10566 Peekskill, 18,881 .... N 8
† 10803 Pelham Manor, 6,673 .... O 7
14526 Penfield, 8,904 .... F 4
14527 Penn Yan⊙, 5,168 .... F 5
14530 Perry, 4,538 .... D 5
12972 Peru, 1,261 .... N 1
14532 Phelps, 1,989 .... F 5
12565 Philmont, 1,674 .... N 6
13135 Phoenix, 2,617 .... H 4
10968 Piermont, 2,386 .... M 8
12566 Pine Bush, 1,183 .... M 7
10969 Pine Island, 925 .... L 8
12567 Pine Plains, 950 .... N 7
14534 Pittsford, 1,755 .... E 4
11803 Plainview, 32,195 .... O 9

12901 Plattsburgh⊙, 18,715 .... O 1
10570 Pleasantville, 7,110 .... N 8
13140 Port Byron, 1,330 .... G 4
10573 Port Chester, 25,803 .... P 7
12466 Port Ewen, 2,882 .... N 7
12974 Port Henry, 1,532 .... O 2
11777 Port Jefferson, 5,515 .... P 9
12771 Port Jervis, 8,852 .... L 8
14770 Portville, 1,304 .... D 6
11050 Port Washington, 15,923 .... R 6
13676 Potsdam, 9,985 .... K 1
* 12601 Poughkeepsie⊙, 32,029 .... N 7
13142 Pulaski, 2,480 .... H 3
10577 Purchase, 2,900 .... P 7
10579 Putnam Valley, ▵975 .... N 8
* 11101 Queens (borough), 1,973,708 .... N 9
11429 Queens Village, 72,000 .... R 7
14772 Randolph, 1,498 .... C 6
14131 Ransomville, 1,034 .... C 4
12143 Ravena, 2,797 .... N 6
12571 Red Hook, 1,680 .... N 7
12144 Rensselaer, 10,136 .... N 5
12572 Rhinebeck, 2,336 .... N 7
13439 Richfield Springs, 1,540 .... K 5
14775 Ripley, 1,173 .... A 6
11901 Riverhead⊙, 7,585 .... P 9
† 14830 Riverside, 911 .... F 6
* 14601 Rochester⊙, 296,233 .... E 4
Rochester, ‡882,667 .... E 4
* 11570 Rockville Centre, 27,444 .... R 7
13440 Rome, 50,148 .... J 4
11779 Ronkonkoma, 7,284 .... O 9
11575 Roosevelt, 15,008 .... R 7
12776 Roscoe, 1,300 .... L 7
12472 Rosendale, 1,220 .... M 7
11576 Roslyn, 2,546 .... R 7
12979 Rouses Point, 2,250 .... O 1
10580 Rye, 15,869 .... P 7
13685 Sackets Harbor, 1,202 .... H 3
11963 Sag Harbor, 2,363 .... R 8
10301 Saint George⊙, 13,000 .... M 9
13452 Saint Johnsville, 2,089 .... L 5
14779 Salamanca, 7,877 .... C 6
12865 Salem, 1,025 .... O 4
† 11050 Sands Point, 2,916 .... N 9
12983 Saranac Lake, 6,086 .... M 2
12866 Saratoga Springs, 18,845 .... N 4
12477 Saugerties, 4,190 .... M 6
13456 Sauquoit, 1,900 .... K 5
14879 Savona, 933 .... F 6
11782 Sayville, 11,680 .... O 9
10583 Scarsdale, 19,229 .... P 7
* 12301 Schenectady⊙, 77,859 .... M 5
12157 Schoharie⊙, 1,125 .... M 5
12870 Schroon Lake, 950 .... N 3
12871 Schuylerville, 1,402 .... N 4
12302 Scotia, 8,224 .... N 5

14546 Scottsville, 1,967 .... E 4
† 14075 Scranton, 925 .... C 5
† 14617 Sea Breeze, 1,200 .... F 4
11579 Sea Cliff, 5,890 .... R 6
13148 Seneca Falls, 7,794 .... G 5
13460 Sherburne, 1,613 .... K 5
13461 Sherrill, 2,986 .... J 4
14548 Shortsville, 1,516 .... F 5
13838 Sidney, 4,789 .... K 6
14136 Silver Creek, 3,182 .... B 5
13152 Skaneateles, 3,055 .... H 5
† 14201 Sloan, 5,216 .... C 5
10974 Sloatsburg, 3,134 .... M 8
11787 Smithtown, 15,000 .... O 9
14551 Sodus, 1,813 .... G 4
14555 Sodus Point, 1,172 .... G 4
13209 Solvay, 8,280 .... H 4
11968 Southampton, 4,904 .... R 9
14830 South Corning, 1,414 .... F 6
12779 South Fallsburg, 1,590 .... L 7
† 12801 South Glens Falls, 4,013 .... N 4
11971 Southold, 2,030 .... P 8
† 14901 Southport, 8,685 .... G 6
14559 Spencerport, 2,929 .... E 4
10977 Spring Valley, 18,112 .... M 8
14141 Springville, 4,350 .... C 5
12167 Stamford, 1,286 .... L 6
* 10301 Staten Island (borough), 295,443 .... M 9
12170 Stillwater, 1,428 .... N 5
11790 Stony Brook, 6,391 .... O 9
10980 Stony Point, 8,270 .... M 8
12172 Stottville, 1,106 .... N 6
10901 Suffern, 8,273 .... M 8
11791 Syosset, 9,970 .... S 7
* 13201 Syracuse⊙, 197,208 .... H 4
Syracuse, ‡635,946 .... H 4
10591 Tarrytown, 11,115 .... O 6
13691 Theresa, 985 .... J 2
† 11020 Thomaston, 2,486 .... R 7
12883 Ticonderoga, 3,268 .... N 3
12486 Tillson, 1,256 .... M 7
14150 Tonawanda, 21,898 .... B 4
* 12180 Troy⊙, 62,918 .... N 5
14886 Trumansburg, 1,618 .... G 5
10707 Tuckahoe, 6,236 .... O 7
12986 Tupper Lake, 4,854 .... M 2
13849 Unadilla, 1,489 .... K 6
13160 Union Springs, 1,183 .... G 5
* 13501 Utica⊙, 91,611 .... K 4
Utica-Rome, ‡337,477 .... K 4
12184 Valatie, 1,288 .... N 6
10595 Valhalla, 6,000 .... P 6
* 11580 Valley Stream, 40,413 .... N 9
13850 Vestal, 8,303 .... H 6
14564 Victor, 2,187 .... F 5
12186 Voorheesville, 2,826 .... M 5
13694 Waddington, 955 .... K 1

11792 Wading River, 975 .... P 9
12586 Walden, 5,277 .... M 7
12589 Wallkill, 1,849 .... M 7
13856 Walton, 3,744 .... K 6
13163 Wampsville⊙, 586 .... J 4
† 14075 Wanakah, 1,600 .... C 5
11793 Wantagh, 21,873 .... N 9
12590 Wappingers Falls, 5,607 .... N 7
12885 Warrensburg, 2,743 .... N 3
14569 Warsaw⊙, 3,619 .... D 5
10990 Warwick, 3,604 .... M 8
12188 Waterford, 2,879 .... N 5
13165 Waterloo⊙, 5,418 .... G 5
13601 Watertown⊙, 30,787 .... J 3
13480 Waterville, 1,808 .... K 5
12189 Watervliet, 12,404 .... N 5
14891 Watkins Glen⊙, 2,716 .... G 6
14892 Waverley, 5,261 .... G 7
14572 Wayland, 2,022 .... E 5
14580 Webster, 5,037 .... F 4
13166 Weedsport, 1,900 .... G 4
14895 Wellsville, 5,815 .... E 6
11590 Westbury, 15,362 .... R 7
† 13619 West Carthage, 2,047 .... J 3
† 14901 West Elmira, 5,901 .... G 6
14787 Westfield, 3,651 .... A 6
† 12801 West Glens Falls, 3,363 .... N 4
11977 Westhampton, 1,156 .... P 9
11978 Westhampton Beach, 1,926 .... P 9
10996 West Point, 8,100 .... M 8
11796 West Sayville, 7,386 .... O 9
14224 West Seneca, ▵48,404 .... C 5
13491 West Winfield, 1,018 .... K 5
12887 Whitehall, 3,764 .... O 3
* 10601 White Plains⊙, 50,220 .... P 6
13492 Whitesboro, 4,805 .... K 4
13862 Whitney Point, 1,058 .... J 6
14589 Williamson, 1,991 .... F 4
14221 Williamsville, 6,835 .... C 5
11596 Williston Park, 9,154 .... R 7
12996 Willsboro, 950 .... N 2
14172 Wilson, 1,284 .... C 4
13865 Windsor, 1,098 .... J 6
12998 Witherbee-Mineville, 1,967 .... N 2
14590 Wolcott, 1,617 .... G 4
12788 Woodbourne, 1,155 .... M 7
11598 Woodmere, 19,831 .... R 7
12789 Woodridge, 1,071 .... L 7
12498 Woodstock, 1,073 .... M 6
* 10701 Yonkers, 204,370 .... O 7
† 10598 Yorktown, 9,008 .... N 8
13495 Yorkville, 3,425 .... K 4
14174 Youngstown, 2,169 .... C 4

⊙ County seat.
‡ Population of metropolitan area.
▵ Population of town or township.
† Zip of nearest p.o.
* Multiple zips

Agriculture, Industry and Resources

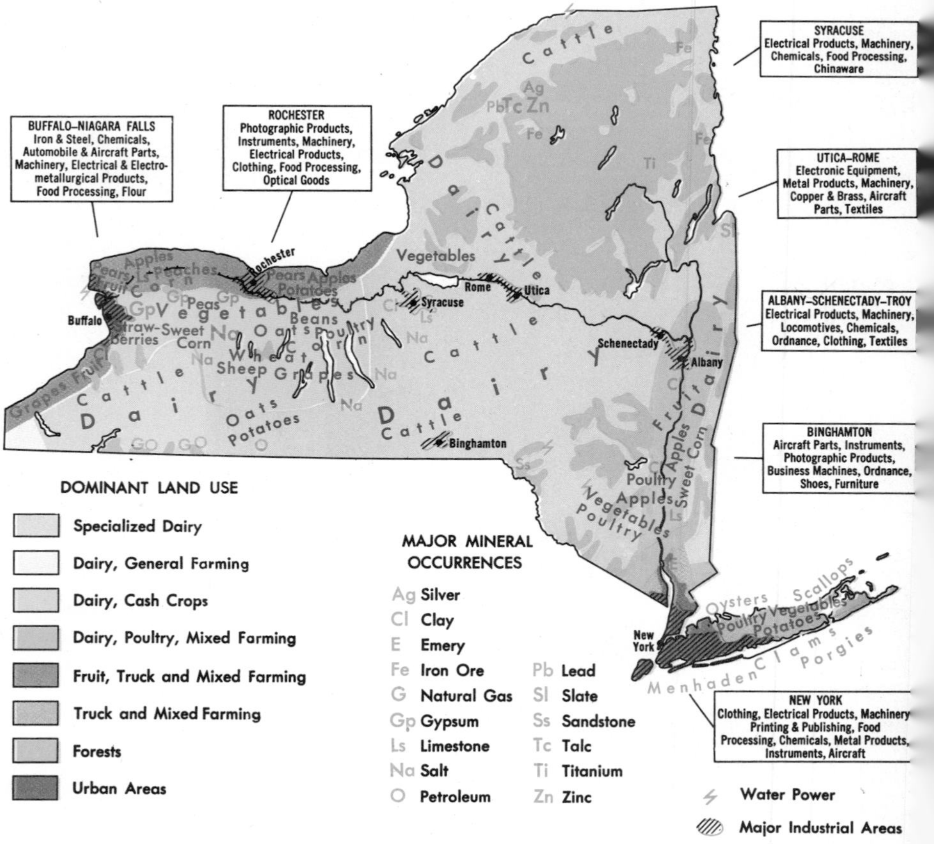
BUFFALO–NIAGARA FALLS
Iron & Steel, Chemicals, Automobile & Aircraft Parts, Machinery, Electrical & Electro-metallurgical Products, Food Processing, Flour
ROCHESTER
Photographic Products, Instruments, Machinery, Electrical Products, Clothing, Food Processing, Optical Goods
SYRACUSE
Electrical Products, Machinery, Chemicals, Food Processing, Chinaware
UTICA–ROME
Electronic Equipment, Metal Products, Machinery, Copper & Brass, Aircraft Parts, Textiles
ALBANY–SCHENECTADY–TROY
Electrical Products, Machinery, Locomotives, Chemicals, Ordnance, Clothing, Textiles
BINGHAMTON
Aircraft Parts, Instruments, Photographic Products, Business Machines, Ordnance, Shoes, Furniture
NEW YORK
Clothing, Electrical Products, Machinery, Printing & Publishing, Food Processing, Chemicals, Metal Products, Instruments, Aircraft
Buffalo
Rochester
Syracuse
Rome
Utica
Schenectady
Albany
Binghamton
New York
Cattle
Dairy
Vegetables
Pears
Apples
Peaches
Potatoes
Peas
Beans
Poultry
Oats
Corn
Wheat
Sheep
Grapes
Straw-berries
Sweet Corn
Fruit
Oysters
Scallops
Clams
Porgies
Menhaden
DOMINANT LAND USE
Specialized Dairy
Dairy, General Farming
Dairy, Cash Crops
Dairy, Poultry, Mixed Farming
Fruit, Truck and Mixed Farming
Truck and Mixed Farming
Forests
Urban Areas
MAJOR MINERAL OCCURRENCES
Ag Silver
Cl Clay
E Emery
Fe Iron Ore
G Natural Gas
Gp Gypsum
Ls Limestone
Na Salt
O Petroleum
Pb Lead
Sl Slate
Ss Sandstone
Tc Talc
Ti Titanium
Zn Zinc
Water Power
Major Industrial Areas

COUNTIES

Alamance, 96,362	L 3
Alexander, 19,466	G 3
Alleghany, 8,134	G 1
Anson, 23,488	J 4
Ashe, 19,571	F 2
Avery, 12,655	F 2
Beaufort, 35,980	R 4
Bertie, 20,528	P 2
Bladen, 26,477	M 5
Brunswick, 24,223	N 6
Buncombe, 145,056	D 3
Burke, 60,364	F 3
Cabarrus, 74,629	H 4
Caldwell, 56,699	F 3
Camden, 5,453	S 2
Carteret, 31,603	R 5
Caswell, 19,055	L 2
Catawba, 90,873	G 3
Chatham, 29,554	L 3
Cherokee, 16,330	A 4
Chowan, 10,764	R 2
Clay, 5,180	B 4
Cleveland, 72,556	F 4
Columbus, 46,937	M 6
Craven, 62,554	P 4
Cumberland, 212,042	M 4
Currituck, 6,976	S 2
Dare, 6,995	T 3
Davidson, 95,627	J 3
Davie, 18,855	H 3
Duplin, 38,015	O 5
Durham, 132,681	M 3
Edgecombe, 52,341	O 3
Forsyth, 214,348	J 2
Franklin, 26,820	N 2
Gaston, 148,415	G 4
Gates, 8,524	R 2
Graham, 6,562	B 4
Granville, 32,762	M 2
Greene, 14,967	O 3
Guilford, 288,590	K 3
Halifax, 53,884	O 2
Harnett, 49,667	M 4
Haywood, 41,710	C 3
Henderson, 42,804	D 4
Hertford, 23,529	P 2
Hoke, 16,436	L 4
Hyde, 5,571	S 3
Iredell, 72,197	H 3
Jackson, 21,593	C 4
Johnston, 61,737	N 4
Jones, 9,779	P 4
Lee 30,467	L 4
Lenoir, 55,204	O 4
Lincoln, 32,682	G 3
Macon, 15,788	B 4
Madison, 16,003	D 3
Martin, 24,730	P 3
McDowell, 30,648	E 3
Mecklenburg, 354,656	H 4
Mitchell, 13,447	E 2
Montgomery, 19,267	K 4
Moore, 39,048	L 4
Nash, 59,122	O 2
New Hanover, 82,996	O 6
Northampton, 24,009	P 2
Onslow, 103,126	P 5
Orange, 57,707	L 2
Pamlico, 9,467	R 4
Pasquotank, 26,824	S 2
Pender, 18,149	O 5
Perquimans, 8,351	S 2
Person, 25,914	M 2
Pitt, 73,900	P 3
Polk, 11,735	E 4
Randolph, 76,358	K 3
Richmond, 39,889	K 4
Robeson, 84,842	L 5
Rockingham, 72,402	K 2
Rowan, 90,035	H 3
Rutherford, 47,337	E 4
Sampson, 44,954	N 4
Scotland, 26,929	L 5
Stanly, 42,822	J 4
Stokes, 23,782	J 2
Surry, 51,415	H 2
Swain, 7,861	B 3
Transylvania, 19,713	D 4
Tyrrell, 3,806	S 3
Union, 54,714	H 4
Vance, 32,691	N 2
Wake, 228,453	M 3
Warren, 15,810	N 2
Washington, 14,038	R 3
Watauga, 23,404	F 2
Wayne, 85,408	N 4
Wilkes, 49,524	G 2
Wilson, 57,486	O 3
Yadkin, 24,599	H 2
Yancey, 12,629	E 3

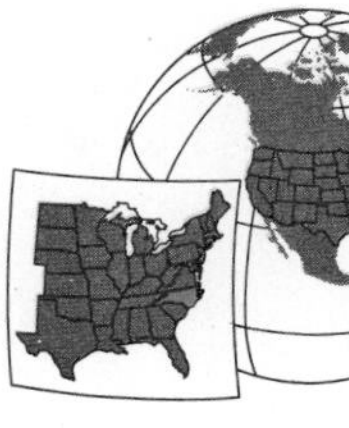

AREA 52,586 sq. mi.
POPULATION 5,082,059
CAPITAL Raleigh
LARGEST CITY Charlotte
HIGHEST POINT Mt. Mitchell 6,684 ft.
SETTLED IN 1650
ADMITTED TO UNION November 21, 1789
POPULAR NAME Tarheel State
STATE FLOWER Flowering Dogwood
STATE BIRD Cardinal

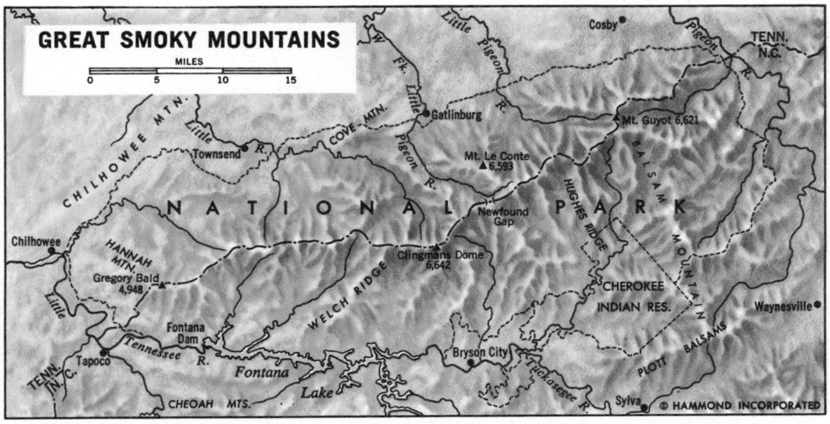
GREAT SMOKY MOUNTAINS
MILES
0
5
10
15
Cosby
TENN.
N.C.
Little Pigeon
W. Fk. Little Pigeon R.
Pigeon R.
CHILHOWEE MTN.
Little R.
Townsend
COVE MTN.
Gatlinburg
Mt. Guyot 6,621
Mt. Le Conte 6,593
BALSAM
NATIONAL PARK
Newfound Gap
HUGHES RIDGE
MOUNTAIN
Chilhowee
HANNAH MTN.
Gregory Bald 4,948
Clingmans Dome 6,642
WELCH RIDGE
CHEROKEE INDIAN RES.
Waynesville
Little
Fontana Dam
Tennessee R.
Fontana Lake
Bryson City
Tuckasegee R.
PLOTT BALSAMS
TENN. N.C.
Tapoco
CHEOAH MTS.
Sylva
© HAMMOND INCORPORATED

CITIES and TOWNS

Zip	Name/Pop.	Key
28321	Abbottsburg, 425	M 5
28315	Aberdeen, 1,592	L 4
27006	Advance, 206	J 3
27910	Ahoskie, 5,105	P 2
27201	Alamance, 450	K 2
† 28713	Alarka, 900	C 4
28001	Albemarle⊙, 11,126	J 4
† 27589	Alert, 200	N 2
28701	Alexander, 200	D 3
28509	Alliance, 577	R 4
† 28364	Alma, 200	L 5
28702	Almond, 200	B 4
27202	Altamahaw, 900	L 2
28901	Andrews, 1,384	B 4
27501	Angier, 1,431	M 4
28007	Ansonville, 694	J 4
27502	Apex, 2,192	M 3
28510	Arapahoe, 212	R 4
27263	Archdale, 6,103	K 3
27589	Arcola, 300	N 2
28704	Arden, 850	D 4
† 28642	Arlington, 711	H 2
28420	Ash, 250	N 6
27203	Asheboro⊙, 10,797	K 3
* 28801	Asheville⊙, 57,681	D 3
	Asheville, ‡145,056	D 3
28603	Ashford, 225	F 3
† 27983	Askewville, 247	R 2
28421	Atkinson, 325	N 5
28511	Atlantic, 950	S 5
28512	Atlantic Beach, 300	R 5
27805	Aulander, 947	P 2
27806	Aurora, 620	R 4
28318	Autryville, 213	M 4
27915	Avon, 400	U 4
† 28076	Avondale-Henrietta, 1,307	F 4
28513	Ayden, 3,450	P 4
28009	Badin, 1,626	J 4
27503	Bahama, 280	M 2
27807	Bailey, 724	N 3
28705	Bakersville⊙, 409	E 2
28706	Balfour, 2,014	E 4
† 27203	Balfours, 4,836	K 3
28707	Balsam, 300	C 4
† 27030	Bannertown, 1,138	H 1
27917	Barco, 325	T 2
† 28739	Barker Heights, 2,933	D 4
28710	Bat Cave, 400	E 4
27808	Bath, 231	R 4
27809	Battleboro, 688	O 2
28515	Bayboro⊙, 665	R 4
27207	Bear Creek, 500	L 3
28516	Beaufort⊙, 3,368	R 5
27810	Belhaven, 2,259	R 3
28012	Belmont, 4,814	H 4
27919	Belvidere, 275	S 2
† 28621	Benham, 400	G 2
27208	Bennett, 200	K 3
27504	Benson, 2,267	N 4
† 27565	Berea, 200	M 2
28016	Bessemer City, 5,217	G 4
† 28779	Beta, 500	C 4
27812	Bethel, 1,514	P 3
28518	Beulaville, 1,156	O 5
† 28803	Biltmore Forest, 1,298	E 3
27209	Biscoe, 1,244	K 4
27813	Black Creek, 449	O 3
28711	Black Mountain, 3,204	E 3
28320	Bladenboro, 783	M 5
27212	Blanch, 210	L 2
28605	Blowing Rock, 801	F 2
† 28438	Boardman, 233	M 6
28092	Boger City, 2,203	G 4
† 28570	Bogue, 600	R 5
28461	Boiling Spring Lakes, 245	N 7
28017	Boiling Springs, 2,284	F 4
28423	Bolton, 534	N 6
27213	Bonlee, 275	L 3
28606	Boomer, 212	G 2
28607	Boone⊙, 8,754	F 2
27011	Boonville, 687	H 2
28322	Bowdens, 250	N 4
28712	Brevard⊙, 5,243	D 4
28519	Bridgeton, 520	R 4
27505	Broadway, 694	L 4
28601	Brookford, 590	G 3
27214	Browns Summit, 500	K 2
28424	Brunswick, 206	M 6
28713	Bryson City⊙, 1,290	C 4
† 28377	Buies, 275	L 5
27506	Buies Creek, 2,024	M 4
27507	Bullock, 550	M 2
27508	Bunn, 284	N 3
28323	Bunnlevel, 200	M 4
28425	Burgaw⊙, 1,744	N 5
27215	Burlington, 35,930	K 2
28714	Burnsville⊙, 1,348	E 3
27509	Butner, 3,538	M 2
28324	Butters, 225	M 5
27920	Buxton, 700	U 4
27228	Bynum, 400	L 3
28325	Calypso, 462	N 4
27921	Camden⊙, 300	S 2
28326	Cameron, 204	L 4
28715	Candler, 950	D 3
27229	Candor, 561	K 4
28716	Canton, 5,158	D 3
28019	Caroleen, 975	F 4
28428	Carolina Beach, 1,663	O 6
27510	Carrboro, 3,472	L 3
28327	Carthage⊙, 1,034	K 4
27511	Cary, 7,430	M 3
28020	Casar, 350	F 3
28717	Cashiers, 230	C 4
27816	Castalia, 265	O 2
28429	Castle Hayne, 900	O 6
28609	Catawba, 565	G 3
† 28754	Catharine Lake, 500	O 5
27230	Cedar Falls, 500	K 3
28520	Cedar Island, 250	S 5
28718	Cedar Mountain, 250	D 4
28431	Chadbourn, 2,213	M 6
27514	Chapel Hill, 25,537	M 3
* 28201	Charlotte⊙, 241,178	H 4
	Charlotte, ‡409,370	H 4
28719	Cherokee, 975	C 4
28021	Cherryville, 5,258	G 4
28023	China Grove, 1,788	H 3
28521	Chinquapin, 350	O 5
27817	Chocowinity, 566	P 4
28610	Claremont, 788	G 3
28432	Clarendon, 300	M 6
28433	Clarkton, 662	M 6
27520	Clayton, 3,103	N 3
27012	Clemmons, 4,900	J 2
27013	Cleveland, 614	H 3
28024	Cliffside, 950	F 4
27233	Climax, 475	K 3
28328	Clinton⊙, 7,157	N 5
28721	Clyde, 900	D 3
27521	Coats, 1,051	M 4
27922	Cofield, 422	R 2
27923	Coinjock, 650	S 2
27924	Colerain, 373	R 2
27234	Coleridge, 600	K 3
28611	Collettsville, 275	F 3
27925	Columbia⊙, 902	S 3
28722	Columbus⊙, 731	E 4
28522	Comfort, 340	O 5
27818	Como, 211	P 1
28025	Concord⊙, 18,464	H 4
28612	Connellys Springs, 500	F 3
28613	Conover, 3,355	G 3
27820	Conway, 694	P 2
27014	Cooleemee, 1,115	H 3
28031	Cornelius, 1,296	H 4
28523	Cove City, 485	P 4
28032	Cramerton, 2,142	G 4
27522	Creedmoor, 1,405	M 2
27928	Creswell, 633	S 3
28033	Crouse, 850	G 4
† 28716	Cruso, 800	D 4
28723	Cullowhee, 6,300	C 4
28331	Cumberland, 800	M 5
28435	Currie, 294	N 6
27929	Currituck⊙, 500	T 2
27015	Cycle, 210	H 2
28034	Dallas, 4,059	G 4
† 27043	Dalton, 400	J 2
27016	Danbury⊙, 152	J 2
28036	Davidson, 2,931	H 4
28524	Davis, 600	R 5
28436	Delco, 450	N 6
27239	Denton, 1,017	J 3
28725	Dillsboro, 215	C 4
27017	Dobson⊙, 933	H 2
† 28685	Dockery, 300	G 2
28526	Dover, 585	P 4
28619	Drexel, 1,431	F 3
28332	Dublin, 283	M 5
28334	Dunn, 8,302	M 4
* 27701	Durham⊙, 95,438	M 2
	Durham, ‡190,388	M 2
† 28761	Dysartsville, 950	F 3
27242	Eagle Springs, 500	K 4
28038	Earl, 300	F 4
27018	East Bend, 485	H 2
28726	East Flat Rock, 2,627	E 4
28352	East Laurinburg, 487	L 5
† 28752	East Marion, 3,015	F 3
28039	East Spencer, 2,217	J 3
27288	Eden, 15,871	K 1
27932	Edenton⊙, 4,766	R 2
27243	Efland, 600	L 2
27909	Elizabeth City⊙, 14,069	S 2
28337	Elizabethtown⊙, 1,418	M 5
28621	Elkin, 2,899	H 2
28622	Elk Park, 503	F 2
28040	Ellenboro, 465	F 4
28338	Ellerbe, 913	K 4
27822	Elm City, 1,201	O 3
27244	Elon College, 2,150	L 2
27823	Enfield, 3,272	O 2
27824	Engelhard, 500	T 3
28728	Enka, 500	D 3
28527	Ernul, 350	P 4
28339	Erwin, 2,852	M 4
27247	Ether, 375	K 4
28729	Etowah, 700	D 4
27830	Eureka, 263	O 3
28438	Evergreen, 250	M 6
28439	Fair Bluff, 1,039	M 6
27826	Fairfield, 954	S 3
28340	Fairmont, 2,827	L 6
28730	Fairview, 800	D 3
28341	Faison, 598	N 4
28041	Faith, 506	J 3
28342	Falcon, 357	M 4
† 27028	Farmington, 300	H 3
27828	Farmville, 4,424	O 3
* 28301	Fayetteville⊙, 53,510	M 4
	Fayetteville, ‡212,042	M 4
28731	Flat Rock, 650	E 4
28732	Fletcher, 950	E 4
28043	Forest City, 7,179	E 4
† 27028	Fork, 250	J 3
27829	Fountain, 434	O 3
27524	Four Oaks, 1,057	M 4
28734	Franklin⊙, 2,336	C 4
27525	Franklinton, 1,459	N 2
27248	Franklinville, 794	K 3
28440	Freeland, 500	N 6
27830	Fremont, 1,596	N 3
27936	Frisco, 325	T 4
27526	Fuquay-Varina, 3,576	M 3
28441	Garland, 656	N 5
27529	Garner, 4,923	M 3
27831	Garysburg, 231	O 2

(continued on following page)

Agriculture, Industry and Resources

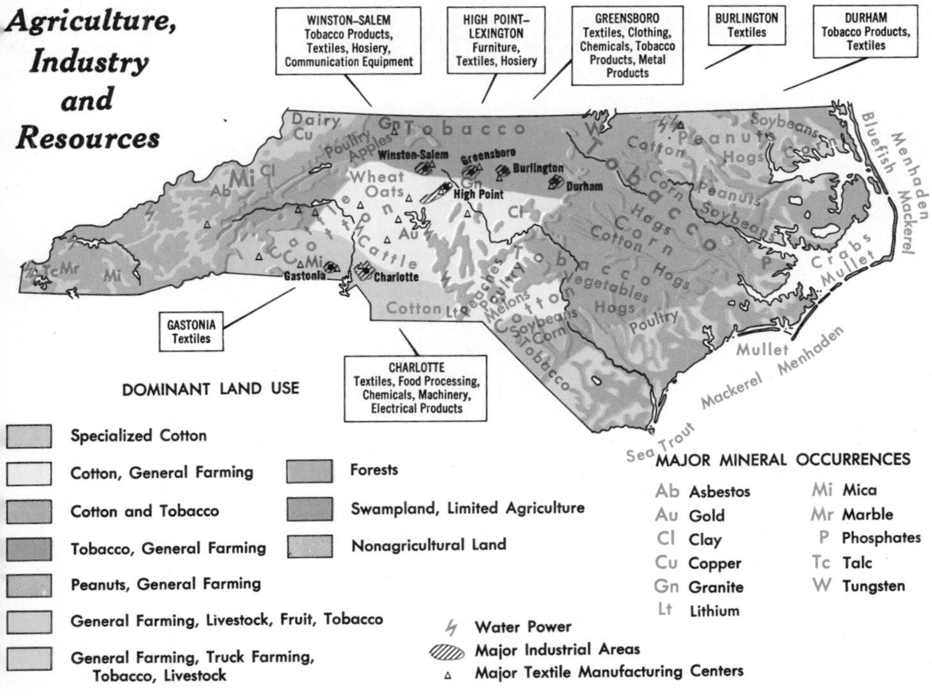
WINSTON-SALEM
Tobacco Products, Textiles, Hosiery, Communication Equipment
HIGH POINT–LEXINGTON
Furniture, Textiles, Hosiery
GREENSBORO
Textiles, Clothing, Chemicals, Tobacco Products, Metal Products
BURLINGTON
Textiles
DURHAM
Tobacco Products, Textiles
GASTONIA
Textiles
CHARLOTTE
Textiles, Food Processing, Chemicals, Machinery, Electrical Products
Dairy
Tobacco
Poultry
Apples
Winston-Salem
Greensboro
Burlington
Durham
High Point
Wheat
Oats
Cattle
Cotton
Peanuts
Hogs
Soybeans
Corn
Bluefish
Menhaden
Mackerel
Crabs
Mullet
Gastonia
Charlotte
Vegetables
Melons
Peaches
Mullet
Menhaden
Mackerel
Sea Trout
DOMINANT LAND USE
Specialized Cotton
Cotton, General Farming
Cotton and Tobacco
Tobacco, General Farming
Peanuts, General Farming
General Farming, Livestock, Fruit, Tobacco
General Farming, Truck Farming, Tobacco, Livestock
Forests
Swampland, Limited Agriculture
Nonagricultural Land
MAJOR MINERAL OCCURRENCES
Ab Asbestos
Au Gold
Cl Clay
Cu Copper
Gn Granite
Lt Lithium
Mi Mica
Mr Marble
P Phosphates
Tc Talc
W Tungsten
Water Power
Major Industrial Areas
Major Textile Manufacturing Centers

27832 Gaston, 1,105.............O 1
28052 Gastonia◉, 47,142.......G 4
27937 Gates, 225..............R 2
27938 Gatesville◉, 338........R 2
28343 Gibson, 502.............K 5
27249 Gibsonville, 2,019......K 2
28628 Glen Alpine, 797........F 3
27251 Glendon, 250............L 4
27215 Glen Raven, 2,848.......L 2
28736 Glenville, 400..........C 4
28737 Glenwood, 400...........F 3
28071 Gold Hill, 350..........J 3
27530 Goldsboro◉, 26,810......O 4
27252 Goldston, 364...........L 3
27939 Graham◉, 8,172..........L 2
28630 Granite Falls, 2,388....G 3
28072 Granite Quarry, 1,344...H 3
28529 Grantsboro, 900.........P 4
28740 Greenmountain, 500......E 3
* 27401 Greensboro◉, 144,076...K 2
Greensboro-Winston-Salem-
High Point, ‡603,895......K 2
27834 Greenville◉, 29,063.....P 3
28530 Grifton, 1,860..........P 3
27837 Grimesland, 394.........P 3
28073 Grover, 555.............G 4
27256 Gulf, 300...............L 3
27839 Halifax◉, 335...........O 2
28442 Hallsboro, 300..........M 6
27840 Hamilton, 579...........P 3
28345 Hamlet, 4,627...........K 5
28443 Hampstead, 400..........O 6
27020 Hamptonville, 250.......H 2
27941 Harbinger, 460..........T 2
28531 Harkers Island, 1,633...R 5
28634 Harmony, 377............H 3
28444 Harrells, 249...........N 5
28075 Harrisburg, 800.........H 4
27943 Hatteras, 800...........T 4
28532 Havelock, 5,283.........P 5
27258 Haw River, 1,542........L 2
28904 Hayesville◉, 428........B 4
† 28318 Hayne, 300.............M 5
28635 Hays, 750...............G 2
† 27559 Haywood, 550...........L 3
28738 Hazelwood, 2,057........C 4
27536 Henderson◉, 13,896......N 2
28739 Hendersonville◉, 6,443..E 3
28076 Henrietta-Avondale, 1,307...F 3
27944 Hertford◉, 2,023........S 2
28601 Hickory, 20,569.........G 3
28636 Hiddenite, 800..........G 3
28741 Highlands, 583..........C 4
* 27260 High Point, 63,204.....J 3
28077 High Shoals, 900........G 4
28637 Hildebran, 481..........F 3
27278 Hillsborough◉, 1,444....L 2
27843 Hobgood, 530............P 2
28537 Hobucken, 500...........S 4
28347 Hoffman, 434............K 4
27844 Hollister, 750..........O 2
28445 Holly Ridge, 415........P 6
27540 Holly Springs, 697......M 3
28538 Hookerton, 441..........O 4
28348 Hope Mills, 1,721.......M 5
28743 Hot Springs, 653........D 3
28539 Hubert, 980.............P 5
28638 Hudson, 2,820...........G 3
28078 Huntersville, 1,538.....H 4
28666 Icard, 1,100............G 3
28079 Indian Trail, 405.......H 4
27589 Inez, 250...............N 2
28080 Iron Station, 250.......G 4
27845 Jackson◉, 762...........P 2
27281 Jackson Springs, 225....K 4
28540 Jacksonville◉, 16,021...O 5
28550 James City, 2,577.......R 4
27282 Jamestown, 1,297........K 3
27846 Jamesville, 533.........R 3
27947 Jarvisburg, 350.........T 2
28640 Jefferson◉, 943.........G 2
† 28352 Johns, 250.............K 5
28642 Jonesville, 1,659.......H 2
27283 Julian, 300.............K 3
28787 Jupiter, 208............D 3
28081 Kannapolis, 36,293......H 4
27847 Kelford, 295............P 2
28349 Kenansville◉, 762.......O 5
27542 Kenly, 1,370............N 3
27284 Kernersville, 4,815.....J 2
27948 Kill Devil Hills, 357...T 3
27021 King, 1,033.............J 2
28086 Kings Mountain, 8,465...G 4
28501 Kinston◉, 22,309........O 4
27544 Kittrell, 427...........M 2
27949 Kitty Hawk, 600.........T 2

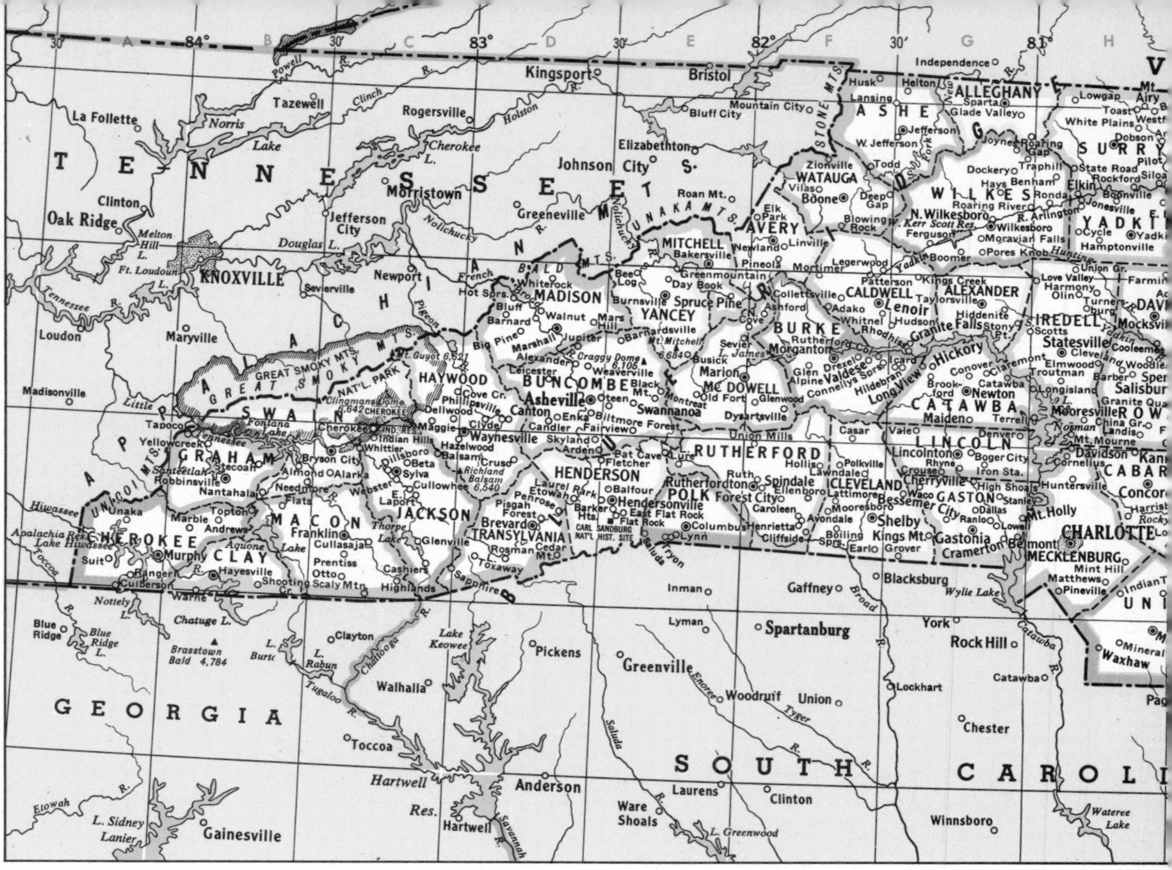

27545 Knightdale, 815.........N 3
27950 Knotts Island, 450......T 2
28449 Kure Beach, 394.........O 7
28551 La Grange, 2,558........O 4
28746 Lake Lure, 456..........E 4
28747 Lake Toxaway, 750.......D 4
28350 Lakeview, 449...........L 4
28450 Lake Waccamaw, 924......M 6
28088 Landis, 2,297...........H 3
28643 Lansing, 283............F 1
28089 Lattimore, 257..........F 4
† 28351 Laurel Hill, 1,215.....K 5
28739 Laurel Park, 581........D 4
28352 Laurinburg◉, 8,859......K 5
28090 Lawndale, 544...........F 4
27291 Leasburg, 250...........L 2
28748 Leicester, 265..........D 3
28451 Leland, 500.............N 6
28645 Lenoir◉, 14,705.........G 3
27849 Lewiston, 327...........P 2
27292 Lexington◉, 17,205......J 3
27298 Liberty, 2,167..........K 3
28091 Lilesville, 641.........J 4
27546 Lillington◉, 1,155......M 4
28092 Lincolnton◉, 5,293......G 4
28356 Linden, 205.............M 4
28646 Linville, 400...........F 2
27299 Linwood, 300............J 3
27850 Littleton, 903..........O 2
28461 Long Beach, 493.........N 7
27548 Longhurst, 1,485........L 2
28648 Longisland, 350.........H 3
28601 Long View, 3,360........G 3
27854 Longwood, 650...........N 6
† 28345 Longwood Park, 1,284...K 5
27549 Louisburg◉, 2,941.......N 2
28098 Lowell, 3,307...........G 4
27024 Lowgap, 660.............H 1
28552 Lowland, 538............S 4
27851 Lucama, 610.............N 3
28358 Lumberton◉, 16,961......L 5
28750 Lynn, 550...............E 4
27852 Macclesfield, 536.......O 3
27951 Mackeys, 250............R 3
27025 Madison, 2,018..........J 2
28751 Maggie, 400.............C 3
28453 Magnolia, 614...........O 5
28650 Maiden, 2,416...........G 3
27552 Mamers, 500.............L 4
† 28387 Manly, 225.............L 4
27953 Manns Harbor, 365.......T 3
27954 Manteo◉, 547............T 3
† 28510 Mapleton, 250..........P 2
28558 Marble, 950.............B 4
28752 Marion◉, 3,335..........E 3
28753 Marshall◉, 982..........D 3
28553 Marshallberg, 700.......S 5
28754 Mars Hill, 1,623........D 3
28103 Marshville, 1,405.......J 4
28105 Matthews, 783...........H 4
28554 Maury, 421..............O 4
28364 Maxton, 1,885...........L 5
27027 Mayodan, 2,875..........K 2
28555 Maysville, 912..........P 5
28361 McCain, 950.............L 4
27302 Mebane, 2,433...........L 2
† 28516 Merrimon, 500..........R 5
27555 Micro, 300..............N 3
28107 Midland, 950............J 4
† 28377 Midstate Mill, 925.....L 5
28544 Midway Park, 4,900......O 5
28601 Milton, 235.............L 1
27854 Milwaukee, 376..........P 2
28212 Mint Hill, 1,200........H 4
28109 Misenheimer, 1,450......J 4
27028 Mocksville◉, 2,529......H 3
27559 Moncure, 800............L 3
28110 Monroe◉, 11,282.........J 5
28757 Montreat, 450...........E 3

28114 Mooresboro, 275.........F 4
28115 Mooresville, 8,808......H 3
28654 Moravian Falls, 375.....G 2
28557 Morehead City, 5,233....R 5
28655 Morganton◉, 13,625......F 3
28119 Morven, 562.............J 4
27030 Mount Airy, 7,325.......H 1
27306 Mount Gilead, 1,286.....K 4
28120 Mount Holly, 5,107......H 4
28123 Mount Mourne, 950.......H 3
28365 Mount Olive, 4,914......O 4
28124 Mount Pleasant, 1,174...J 4
27345 Mount Vernon Springs, 225...L 3
27958 Moyock, 350.............S 1
27855 Murfreesboro, 3,508.....R 2
28906 Murphy◉, 2,082..........B 4
27856 Nashville◉, 1,670.......O 3
27561 Neuse, 500..............M 3
28560 New Bern◉, 14,660.......R 4
28657 Newland◉, 524...........F 2
28127 New London, 285.........J 4
28570 Newport, 1,735..........R 5
28658 Newton◉, 7,857..........G 3
28366 Newton Grove, 546.......N 4
27563 Norlina, 969............N 2
† 28752 North Cove, 257........F 3
28532 North Harlowe, 975......R 5
28669 North Wilkesboro, 3,357.G 2
27564 Northside, 400..........M 2
28128 Norwood, 1,896..........J 4
28129 Oakboro, 568............J 4
27857 Oak City, 559...........P 3
27310 Oak Ridge, 950..........K 2
27960 Ocracoke, 500...........T 4
27963 Old Fort, 676...........E 3
27961 Old Trap, 400...........T 2
28368 Olivia, 400.............L 4
28571 Oriental, 445...........R 4
28805 Oteen, 2,863............E 3

27565 Oxford◉, 7,178..........M 2
28860 Pantego, 218............R 3
28371 Parkton, 550............M 5
27861 Parmele, 373............P 3
28661 Patterson, 344..........F 3
28133 Peachland, 556..........J 5
† 28091 Pee Dee, 210...........K 5
27311 Pelham, 350.............L 1
28372 Pembroke, 1,982.........L 5
28766 Penrose, 600............D 4
† 28716 Phillipsville, 1,239...C 3
27863 Pikeville, 580..........N 4
27041 Pilot Mountain, 1,309...H 2
28373 Pinebluff, 570..........K 4
27042 Pine Hall, 550..........K 2
28374 Pinehurst, 1,056........K 4
27568 Pine Level, 983.........N 4
28662 Pineola, 875............F 2
27864 Pinetops, 1,379.........O 3
27865 Pinetown, 278...........R 3
28134 Pineville, 1,948........H 4
28572 Pink Hill, 522..........O 4
27043 Pinnacle, 725...........J 2
28768 Pisgah Forest, 850......D 4
27312 Pittsboro◉, 1,447.......L 3
27866 Pleasant Hill, 250......O 1
27962 Plymouth◉, 4,774........R 3
28135 Polkton, 845............J 4
28136 Polkville, 450..........F 4
28573 Pollocksville, 456......P 5
27965 Poplar Branch, 400......T 2
27966 Powells Point, 375......T 2
27967 Powellsville, 247.......R 2
27569 Princeton, 1,044........N 4
† 27886 Princeville, 654.......P 3
28376 Raeford◉, 3,180.........L 5
* 27601 Raleigh (cap.)◉, 121,577...M 3
Raleigh, ‡228,453.........M 3
27316 Ramseur, 1,328..........K 3
27317 Randleman, 2,312........K 3

† 28906 Ranger, 500............A 4
28052 Ranlo, 2,092............G 4
27868 Red Oak, 359............N 2
28377 Red Springs, 3,383......L 5
27320 Reidsville, 13,636......K 2
28838 Rex, 975................M 5
28667 Rhodhiss, 784...........F 3
* 2809? Rhyne, 2,273...........G 4
28137 Richfield, 306..........J 4
28574 Richlands, 935..........O 5
27869 Rich Square, 1,254......P 2
27570 Ridgeway, 500...........N 2
28456 Riegelwood, 459.........N 6
28870 Roanoke Rapids, 13,508..O 2
28668 Roaring Gap, 450........H 2
28669 Roaring River, 500......G 2
27325 Robbins, 1,059..........K 4
28771 Robbinsville◉, 777......B 4
28379 Roberdel, 350...........K 5
27871 Robersonville, 1,910....P 3
28379 Rockingham◉, 5,852......K 5
28138 Rockwell, 999...........J 4
27801 Rocky Mount, 34,284.....O 3
28457 Rocky Point, 975........O 6
27571 Rolesville, 529.........N 3
28670 Ronda, 465..............G 2
27970 Roper, 649..............R 3
28382 Roseboro, 1,235.........N 5
28458 Rose Hill, 1,448........O 5
28772 Rosman, 407.............D 4
27572 Rougemont, 400..........L 2
28383 Rowland, 1,358..........L 5
27573 Roxboro◉, 5,370.........L 2
27872 Roxobel, 347............P 2
27587 Royal Cotton Mills, 600.M 2
27326 Ruffin, 600.............K 2
27045 Rural Hall, 2,338.......J 2
28139 Ruth, 360...............E 4
28671 Rutherford College, 950.F 3
28139 Rutherfordton◉, 3,245...F 4

Topography

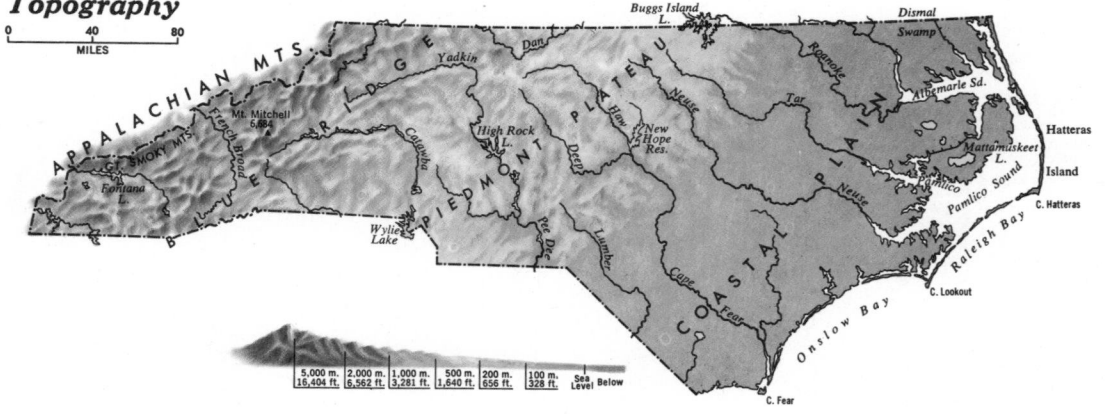

0   40   80
MILES

5,000 m. | 2,000 m. | 1,000 m. | 500 m. | 200 m. | 100 m. | Sea | Below
16,404 ft. | 6,562 ft. | 3,281 ft. | 1,640 ft. | 656 ft. | 328 ft. | Level |

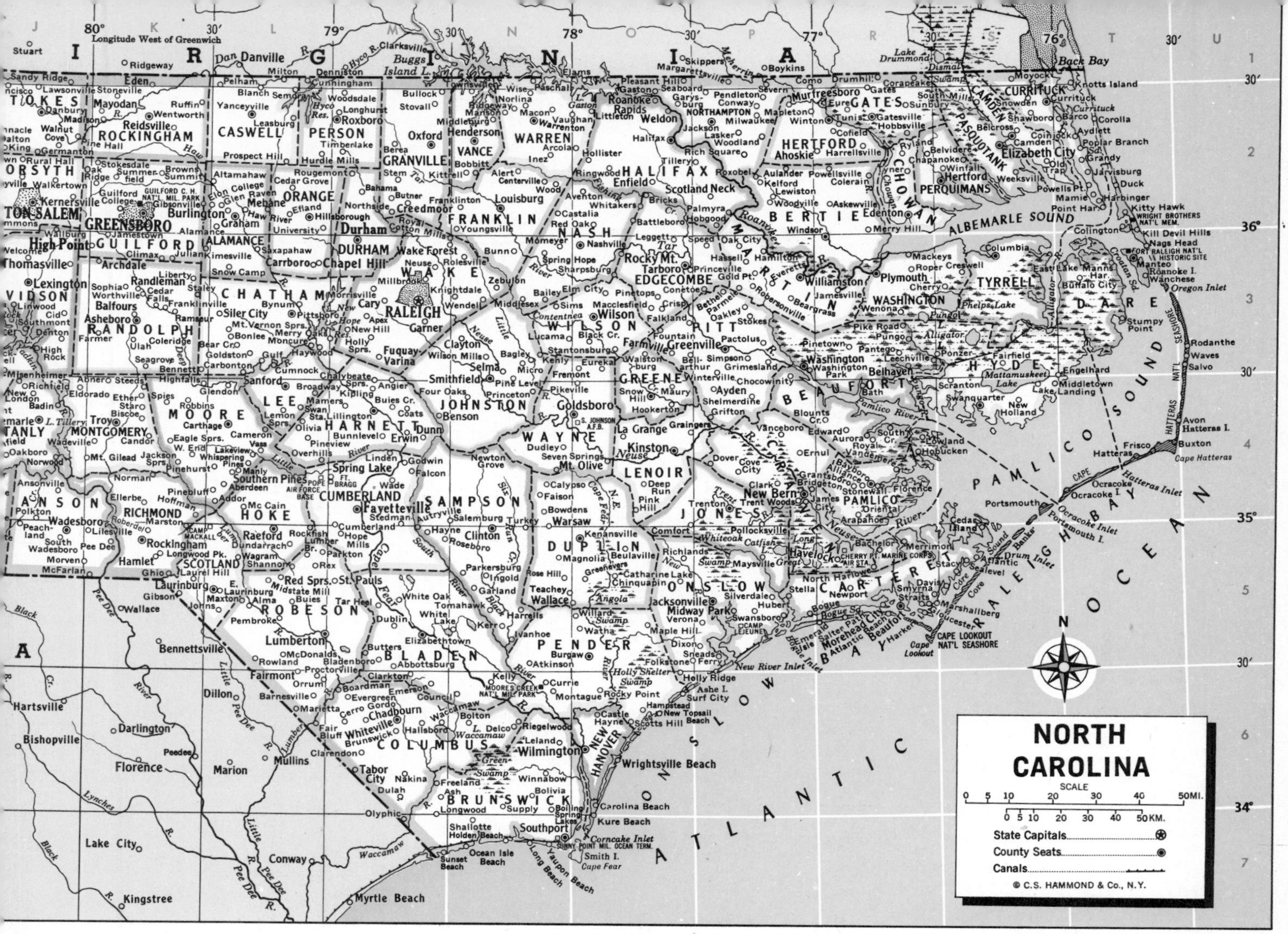

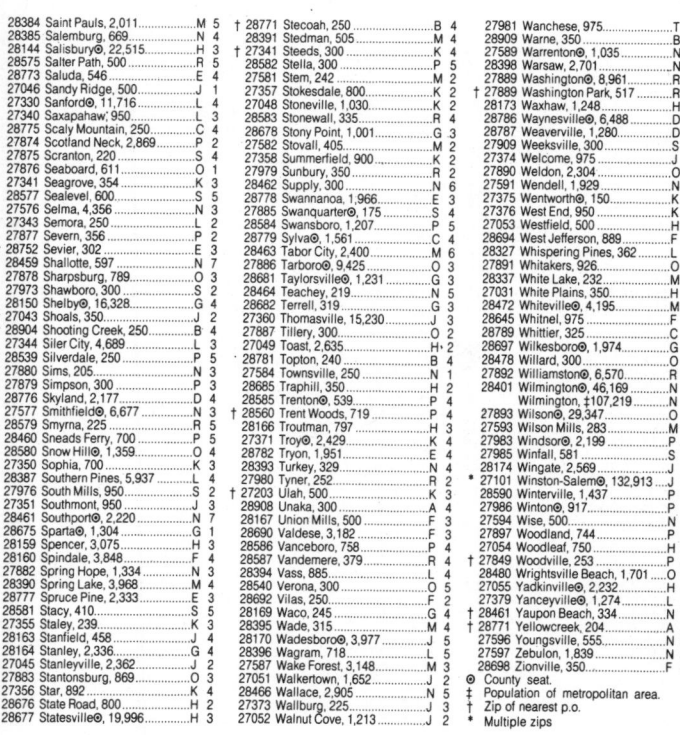

NORTH CAROLINA

SCALE
0 5 10 20 30 40 50 MI.
0 5 10 20 30 40 50 KM.

State Capitals.................⊛
County Seats.................⊙
Canals.................

© C.S. HAMMOND & Co., N.Y.

Zip	Place, Population	Grid	Zip	Place, Population	Grid	Zip	Place, Population	Grid
28384	Saint Pauls, 2,011	M 5	† 28771	Stecoah, 250	B 4	27981	Wanchese, 975	T 3
28385	Salemburg, 669	N 4	28391	Stedman, 505	M 4	28909	Warne, 350	B 5
28144	Salisbury⊙, 22,515	H 3	† 27341	Steeds, 300	K 4	27589	Warrenton⊙, 1,035	N 2
28575	Salter Path, 500	R 5	28582	Stella, 300	P 5	28398	Warsaw, 2,701	N 4
28773	Saluda, 546	E 4	27581	Stem, 242	M 2	27889	Washington⊙, 8,961	R 3
27046	Sandy Ridge, 500	J 1	27357	Stokesdale, 800	K 2	† 27889	Washington Park, 517	R 3
27330	Sanford⊙, 11,716	L 4	27048	Stoneville, 1,030	K 2	28173	Waxhaw, 1,248	H 5
27340	Saxapahaw, 950	L 3	28583	Stonewall, 335	R 4	28786	Waynesville⊙, 6,488	D 4
28775	Scaly Mountain, 250	C 4	28678	Stony Point, 1,001	G 3	28787	Weaverville, 1,280	D 3
27874	Scotland Neck, 2,869	P 2	27582	Stovall, 405	M 2	27909	Weeksville, 300	S 2
27875	Scranton, 220	S 4	27979	Sunbury, 350	R 2	27374	Welcome, 975	J 3
28576	Seaboard, 611	O 1	28462	Supply, 300	N 6	27890	Weldon, 2,304	O 2
27341	Seagrove, 354	K 3	28778	Swannanoa, 1,966	E 3	27591	Wendell, 1,929	N 3
28577	Sealevel, 600	S 5	27885	Swanquarter⊙, 175	S 4	27375	Wentworth⊙, 150	K 2
27576	Selma, 4,356	N 3	28584	Swansboro, 1,207	P 5	27376	West End, 950	K 4
27343	Semora, 250	L 2	28779	Sylva⊙, 1,561	C 4	27053	Westfield, 500	H 2
27877	Severn, 356	P 2	28463	Tabor City, 2,400	M 6	28694	West Jefferson, 889	F 2
† 28752	Sevier, 302	E 3	28681	Taylorsville⊙, 1,231	G 3	28327	Whispering Pines, 362	L 4
28459	Shallotte, 597	N 7	28464	Teachey, 219	N 5	27891	Whitakers, 926	O 2
27878	Sharpsburg, 789	O 3	28682	Terrell, 319	G 3	28337	White Lake, 232	M 5
27973	Shawboro, 300	S 1	27360	Thomasville, 15,230	J 3	27031	White Plains, 350	H 2
28150	Shelby⊙, 16,328	G 4	27887	Tillery, 300	P 2	28472	Whiteville⊙, 4,195	M 6
† 27043	Shoals, 350	J 2	27049	Toast, 2,635	H 2	28645	Whitnel, 975	F 3
† 28904	Shooting Creek, 250	B 4	28781	Topton, 240	B 4	28789	Whittier, 325	C 4
27344	Siler City, 4,689	L 3	27584	Townsville, 250	N 1	28697	Wilkesboro⊙, 1,974	G 2
† 28539	Silverdale, 250	P 5	28685	Traphill, 350	H 2	28478	Willard, 300	O 5
27880	Sims, 205	N 3	28585	Trenton⊙, 539	P 4	27892	Williamston⊙, 6,570	P 3
27879	Simpson, 300	P 3	† 28560	Trent Woods, 719	P 4	28401	Wilmington⊙, 46,169	N 6
28776	Skyland, 2,177	D 4	28166	Troutman, 797	H 3		Wilmington, ‡107,219	N 6
27577	Smithfield⊙, 6,677	N 3	27371	Troy⊙, 2,429	K 4	27893	Wilson⊙, 29,347	O 3
28579	Smyrna, 225	R 5	28782	Tryon, 1,951	E 4	27593	Wilson Mills, 283	N 3
28460	Sneads Ferry, 700	P 5	28393	Turkey, 252	N 4	27983	Windsor⊙, 2,199	P 2
28580	Snow Hill⊙, 1,359	O 4	27980	Tyner, 250	R 2	27985	Winfall, 581	S 2
27350	Sophia, 700	K 3	† 27203	Ulah, 500	K 3	28174	Wingate, 2,569	J 5
28387	Southern Pines, 5,937	L 4	28908	Unaka, 300	A 4	† 27101	Winston-Salem⊙, 132,913	J 2
27976	South Mills, 950	S 2	28167	Union Mills, 500	F 3	28590	Winterville, 1,437	P 3
27351	Southmont, 950	J 3	28690	Valdese, 3,182	F 3	27986	Winton⊙, 917	P 2
28461	Southport⊙, 2,220	N 7	28586	Vanceboro, 758	P 4	27594	Wise, 500	N 2
28675	Sparta⊙, 1,304	G 1	28587	Vandemere, 379	R 4	27897	Woodland, 744	P 2
28159	Spencer, 3,075	H 3	28394	Vass, 885	L 4	27054	Woodleaf, 750	H 3
28160	Spindale, 3,848	F 4	28540	Verona, 300	O 5	† 27849	Woodville, 253	P 2
27882	Spring Hope, 1,334	N 3	28692	Vilas, 250	E 2	28480	Wrightsville Beach, 1,701	O 6
28390	Spring Lake, 3,968	M 4	28169	Waco, 245	G 4	27055	Yadkinville⊙, 2,232	H 2
28777	Spruce Pine, 2,333	E 3	28395	Wade, 315	M 4	27379	Yanceyville⊙, 1,274	L 2
28581	Stacy, 410	S 5	28170	Wadesboro⊙, 3,977	J 5	28461	Yaupon Beach, 334	N 7
27355	Staley, 239	K 3	28396	Wagram, 718	L 5	† 28771	Yellowcreek, 204	B 4
28163	Stanfield, 458	J 4	27587	Wake Forest, 3,148	M 3	27596	Youngsville, 555	N 2
28164	Stanley, 2,336	G 4	27051	Walkertown, 1,652	J 2	27597	Zebulon, 1,839	N 3
† 27045	Stanleyville, 2,362	J 2	28466	Wallace, 2,905	N 5	28698	Zionville, 350	F 2
27883	Stantonsburg, 869	O 3	27373	Wallburg, 225	J 2			
28582	Star, 892	K 4	27052	Walnut Cove, 1,213	J 2			
28676	State Road, 800	H 2						
28677	Statesville⊙, 19,996	H 3						

⊙ County seat.
‡ Population of metropolitan area.
† Zip of nearest p.o.
* Multiple zips

Weeding "green gold" — tobacco is North Carolina's money crop.

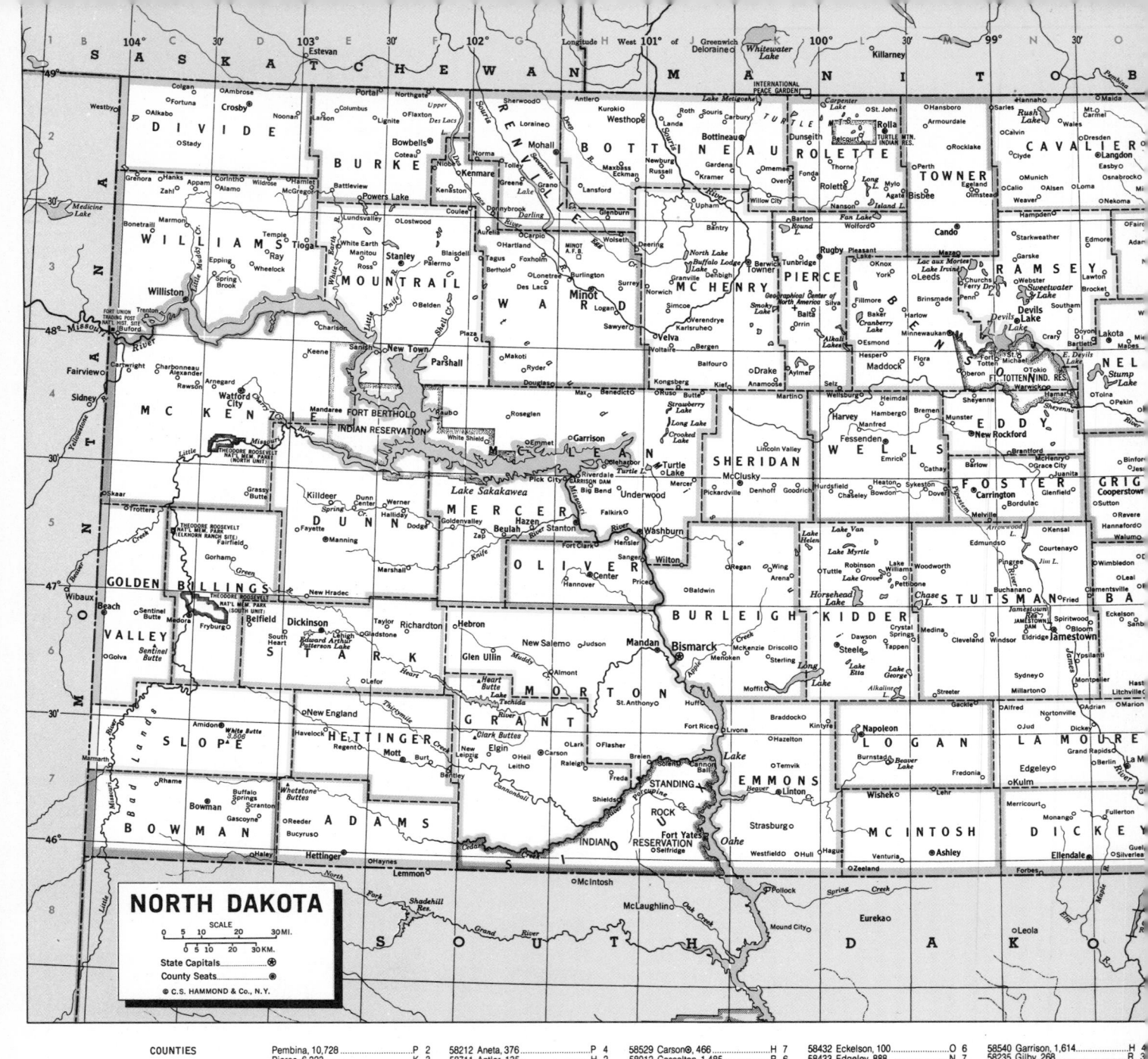

NORTH DAKOTA

SCALE
0 5 10 20 30 MI.
0 5 10 20 30 KM.

State Capitals ⊛
County Seats ⊙

Ⓒ C.S. HAMMOND & Co., N.Y.

COUNTIES

Adams, 3,832	F 7
Barnes, 14,669	O 5
Benson, 8,245	M 3
Billings, 1,198	D 5
Bottineau, 9,496	J 2
Bowman, 3,901	C 7
Burke, 4,739	E 2
Burleigh, 40,714	J 6
Cass, 73,653	R 5
Cavalier, 8,213	N 2
Dickey, 6,907	N 7
Divide, 4,564	C 2
Dunn, 4,895	E 5
Eddy, 4,103	N 4
Emmons, 7,200	K 7
Foster, 4,832	N 5
Golden Valley, 2,611	C 5
Grand Forks, 61,102	P 3
Grant, 5,009	G 6
Griggs, 4,184	O 5
Hettinger, 5,075	E 7
Kidder, 4,362	L 6
La Moure, 7,117	N 7
Logan, 4,245	L 7
McHenry, 8,977	J 3
McIntosh, 5,545	L 7
McKenzie, 6,127	D 4
McLean, 11,251	G 4
Mercer, 6,175	G 5
Morton, 20,310	H 6
Mountrail, 8,437	E 3
Nelson, 5,776	O 4
Oliver, 2,322	H 5
Pembina, 10,728	P 2
Pierce, 6,323	K 3
Ramsey, 12,915	N 3
Ransom, 7,102	P 7
Renville, 3,828	G 2
Richland, 18,089	R 7
Rolette, 11,549	L 2
Sargent, 5,937	P 7
Sheridan, 3,232	K 4
Sioux, 3,632	H 7
Slope, 1,484	C 6
Stark, 19,613	E 6
Steele, 3,749	P 4
Stutsman, 23,550	M 5
Towner, 4,645	M 2
Traill, 9,571	R 4
Walsh, 16,251	P 3
Ward, 58,560	G 3
Wells, 7,847	L 4
Williams, 19,301	C 3

CITIES and TOWNS

Zip	Name/Pop.	Key
58001	Abercrombie, 262	S 7
58210	Adams, 284	O 3
58830	Alamo, 124	D 2
58831	Alexander, 208	C 4
58003	Alice, 83	P 6
58520	Almont, 109	H 6
58311	Alsen, 201	N 2
58833	Ambrose, 109	D 2
58620	Amidon⊙, 54	D 7
58710	Anamoose, 401	K 4
58212	Aneta, 376	P 4
58711	Antler, 135	H 2
58005	Argusville, 118	R 5
58835	Arnegard, 141	D 4
58006	Arthur, 412	R 5
58214	Arvilla, 115	P 4
58413	Ashley⊙, 1,236	M 7
58313	Balta, 133	K 3
58712	Balfour, 93	J 4
58008	Barney, 81	S 7
58216	Bathgate, 133	P 2
58621	Beach⊙, 1,408	C 6
58316	Belcourt, 950	L 2
58622	Belfield, 1,130	D 6
58718	Berthold, 398	G 3
58523	Beulah, 1,344	G 5
58416	Binford, 242	O 4
58317	Bisbee, 305	M 2
58501	Bismarck (cap.)⊛, 34,703	J 6
58318	Bottineau⊙, 2,760	J 2
58721	Bowbells⊙, 584	F 2
58418	Bowdon, 229	L 5
58623	Bowman⊙, 1,762	D 7
58524	Braddock, 106	K 6
58321	Brocket, 95	O 3
58420	Buchanan, 100	N 5
58011	Buffalo, 241	R 6
58722	Burlington, 247	H 3
58723	Butte, 193	J 4
58218	Buxton, 235	R 4
58324	Cando⊙, 1,512	M 3
58532	Cannon Ball, 200	J 7
58725	Carpio, 215	G 3
58421	Carrington⊙, 2,491	M 5
58529	Carson⊙, 466	H 7
58012	Casselton, 1,485	R 6
58422	Cathay, 110	M 4
58220	Cavalier⊙, 1,381	P 2
58013	Cayuga, 116	R 7
58530	Center⊙, 619	H 5
58014	Chaffee, 99	R 6
58015	Christine, 108	S 6
58325	Church's Ferry, 139	M 3
58424	Cleveland, 128	M 6
58016	Clifford, 84	R 5
58017	Cogswell, 203	P 7
58727	Columbus, 465	E 2
58425	Cooperstown⊙, 1,485	O 5
58426	Courtenay, 125	N 5
58327	Crary, 150	N 3
58730	Crosby⊙, 1,545	D 2
58222	Crystal, 272	P 2
58021	Davenport, 147	R 6
58428	Dawson, 131	L 6
58429	Dazey, 128	O 5
58430	Denhoff, 85	K 5
58733	Des Lacs, 197	G 3
58301	Devils Lake⊙, 7,078	N 3
58431	Dickey, 118	N 6
58601	Dickinson⊙, 12,405	E 6
58625	Dodge, 151	F 5
58734	Donnybrook, 163	G 2
58735	Douglas, 144	H 4
58736	Drake, 636	K 4
58225	Drayton, 1,095	P 2
58532	Driscoll, 104	K 6
58626	Dunn Center, 107	E 5
58329	Dunseith, 811	K 2
58024	Dwight, 93	S 7
58432	Eckelson, 100	O 6
58433	Edgeley, 888	N 7
58227	Edinburg, 315	P 3
58330	Edmore, 398	O 3
58331	Egeland, 96	M 2
58533	Elgin, 839	G 7
58436	Ellendale⊙, 1,517	N 7
58228	Emerado, 515	R 4
58027	Enderlin, 1,343	P 6
58843	Epping, 140	D 3
58029	Erie, 100	R 5
58332	Esmond, 416	L 3
58229	Fairdale, 102	O 3
58030	Fairmount, 412	S 7
58102	Fargo⊙, 53,365	S 6
	Fargo-Moorhead ‡120,238	S 6
58438	Fessenden⊙, 815	L 4
58031	Fingal, 166	P 6
58230	Finley⊙, 809	P 4
58535	Flasher, 467	H 7
58737	Flaxton, 286	F 2
58439	Forbes, 88	N 8
58032	Forman⊙, 596	P 7
58033	Fort Ransom, 121	P 7
58335	Fort Totten, 550	M 4
58844	Fortuna, 216	C 2
58538	Fort Yates⊙, 1,153	J 7
58441	Fredonia, 100	M 7
58442	Fullerton, 110	O 7
58035	Galesburg, 134	R 5
58540	Garrison, 1,614	H 4
58235	Gilby, 268	R 3
58630	Gladstone, 222	H 2
58740	Glenburn, 381	H 2
58443	Glenfield, 127	N 6
58631	Glen Ullin, 1,070	G 6
58541	Goldenvalley, 235	F 5
58632	Golva, 104	C 5
58444	Goodrich, 300	L 5
58445	Grace City, 87	N 4
58237	Grafton⊙, 5,946	P 3
58201	Grand Forks⊙, 39,008	R 4
58038	Grandin, 187	R 5
58741	Granville, 282	J 3
58039	Great Bend, 86	S 7
58845	Grenora, 401	C 2
58040	Gwinner, 623	P 7
58542	Hague, 146	L 7
58636	Halliday, 413	F 5
58238	Hamilton, 110	R 2
58038	Hampden, 114	N 2
58041	Hankinson, 1,125	S 7
58448	Hannaford, 244	O 5
58239	Hannah, 145	N 2
58340	Harlow, 85	M 3
58341	Harvey, 2,361	L 4
58042	Harwood, 200	R 5
58240	Hatton, 808	R 4
58043	Havana, 156	P 8
58544	Hazelton, 374	K 7
58545	Hazen, 1,240	G 5
58638	Hebron, 1,103	G 6
58342	Heimdal, 101	L 4
58547	Hensler, 100	H 5
58639	Hettinger⊙, 1,655	E 7

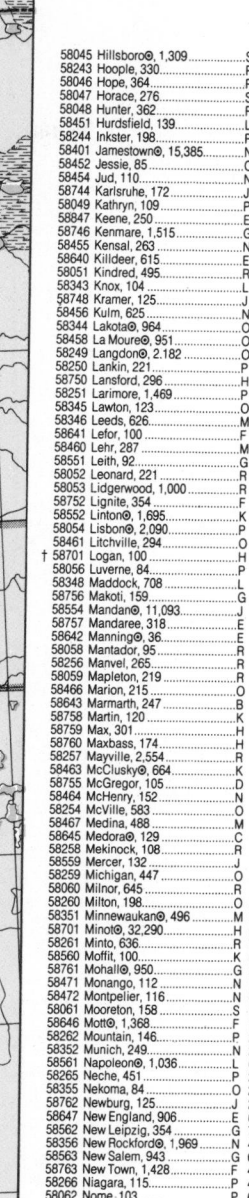

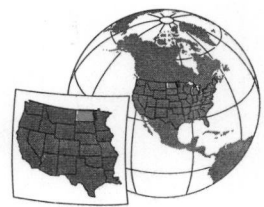

AREA 70,665 sq. mi.
POPULATION 617,761
CAPITAL Bismarck
LARGEST CITY Fargo
HIGHEST POINT White Butte 3,506 ft.
SETTLED IN 1780
ADMITTED TO UNION November 2, 1889
POPULAR NAME Flickertail State; Sioux State
STATE FLOWER Prairie Rose
STATE BIRD Meadowlark

58045 Hillsboro⊙, 1,309 .... S 5
58243 Hoople, 330 .... P 2
58046 Hope, 364 .... P 5
58047 Horace, 276 .... S 6
58048 Hunter, 362 .... R 5
58451 Hurdsfield, 139 .... L 4
58244 Inkster, 198 .... P 3
58401 Jamestown⊙, 15,385 .... N 6
58452 Jessie, 85 .... O 4
58454 Jud, 110 .... N 6
58744 Karlsruhe, 172 .... J 3
58049 Kathryn, 109 .... P 6
58847 Keene, 250 .... E 4
58746 Kenmare, 1,515 .... G 2
58455 Kensal, 263 .... N 5
58640 Killdeer, 615 .... E 5
58051 Kindred, 495 .... R 6
58343 Knox, 104 .... L 2
58748 Kramer, 125 .... J 2
58456 Kulm, 625 .... N 7
58344 Lakota⊙, 964 .... O 3
58458 La Moure⊙, 951 .... O 7
58249 Langdon⊙, 2,182 .... O 2
58250 Lankin, 221 .... P 3
58750 Lansford, 296 .... H 2
58251 Larimore, 1,469 .... P 4
58345 Lawton, 123 .... O 3
58346 Leeds, 626 .... M 3
58641 Lefor, 100 .... F 6
58460 Lehr, 287 .... M 7
58551 Leith, 92 .... G 7
58052 Leonard, 221 .... R 6
58053 Lidgerwood, 1,000 .... R 7
58752 Lignite, 354 .... F 2
58552 Linton⊙, 1,695 .... K 7
58054 Lisbon⊙, 2,090 .... P 7
58461 Litchville, 294 .... O 6
† 58701 Logan, 100 .... H 3
58056 Luverne, 84 .... N 5
58348 Maddock, 708 .... L 4
58756 Makoti, 159 .... G 4
58554 Mandan⊙, 11,093 .... J 6
58757 Mandaree, 318 .... E 4
58642 Manning⊙, 416 .... E 5
58058 Mantador, 95 .... R 7
58256 Manvel, 265 .... R 3
58059 Mapleton, 219 .... R 6
58466 Marion, 215 .... O 6
58643 Marmarth, 247 .... B 7
58758 Martin, 120 .... K 4
58759 Max, 301 .... H 4
58760 Maxbass, 174 .... H 2
58257 Mayville, 2,554 .... R 4
58463 McClusky⊙, 664 .... K 4
58755 McGregor, 105 .... D 2
58464 McHenry, 152 .... N 4
58254 McVille, 583 .... O 4
58467 Medina, 488 .... M 6
58645 Medora⊙, 129 .... C 6
58258 Mekinock, 108 .... R 4
58559 Mercer, 132 .... J 4
58259 Michigan, 447 .... O 3
58060 Milnor, 645 .... R 7
58260 Milton, 198 .... O 2
58351 Minnewaukan⊙, 496 .. M 3
58701 Minot⊙, 32,290 ...... H 3
58261 Minto, 636 .... R 3
58560 Moffit, 100 .... K 6
58761 Mohall⊙, 950 .... G 2
58471 Monango, 112 ...... N 7
58472 Montpelier, 116 .... N 6
58063 Mooreton, 158 ...... S 7
58646 Mott⊙, 1,368 .... F 7
58262 Mountain, 146 ...... P 2
58352 Munich, 249 .... N 2
58561 Napoleon⊙, 1,036 .. L 6
58265 Neche, 451 .... P 2
58355 Nekoma, 84 .... O 2
58762 Newburg, 125 ...... J 2
58647 New England, 906 .. E 6
58562 New Leipzig, 354 .. G 7
58356 New Rockford⊙, 1,969 .. M 4
58563 New Salem, 943 ... J 6
58763 New Town, 1,428 .. F 4
58266 Niagara, 115 .... P 4
58062 Nome, 103 .... P 6

58765 Noonan, 403 .... D 2
58267 Northwood, 1,189 .. P 4
58473 Nortonville, 90 .... N 6
58474 Oakes, 1,742 ...... O 7
† 58237 Oakwood, 91 .... R 3
58357 Oberon, 151 .... M 4
58063 Oriska, 128 .... O 6
58269 Osnabrock, 255 ... O 2
58064 Page, 367 .... R 5
58769 Palermo, 146 ..... F 3
58270 Park River, 1,680 . P 3
58770 Parshall, 1,246 ... F 4
58361 Pekin, 120 .... O 4
58271 Pembina, 741 ..... R 2
58272 Petersburg, 266 .. P 3
58475 Pettibone, 173 ... L 5
† 58545 Pick City, 119 .... G 5
58273 Pisek, 154 .... P 3
58771 Plaza, 291 .... G 3
58772 Portal, 251 .... E 2
58274 Portland, 534 .... R 5
58773 Powers Lake, 523 . E 2
58849 Ray, 776 .... D 3
58649 Reeder, 306 ...... E 7
58650 Regent, 344 ...... E 6
58275 Reynolds, 236 .... R 4
58651 Rhame, 206 .... C 7
58652 Richardton, 799 .. F 6
58565 Riverdale, 600 ... H 4
58478 Robinson, 125 ... L 5
58365 Rocklake, 270 ... M 2
58479 Rogers, 96 .... O 5
58366 Rolette, 579 ..... L 2
58367 Rolla⊙, 1,458 .... L 2
58776 Ross, 125 .... E 3
58368 Rugby⊙, 2,889 ... L 3
58067 Rutland, 225 ..... P 7

58779 Ryder, 211 .... G 4
58369 Saint John, 367 .. L 2
58276 Saint Thomas, 508 . R 2
58480 Sanborn, 255 .... O 6
58780 Sanish, 25 .... E 4
58372 Sarles, 148 ...... N 2
58781 Sawyer, 373 ..... H 3
58653 Scranton, 360 ... D 7
58568 Selfridge, 346 .. J 7
58373 Selz, 110 .... L 4
58654 Sentinel Butte, 125 . C 6
58277 Sharon, 201 ..... P 4
58068 Sheldon, 192 .... P 6
58782 Sherwood, 369 .. G 2
58374 Sheyenne, 362 .. M 4
58569 Shields, 125 ..... H 7
58570 Solen, 180 ...... J 7
58783 Souris, 151 ..... J 2
58655 South Heart, 132 . D 6
58481 Spiritwood, 100 . N 6
58784 Stanley⊙, 1,581 . F 3
58571 Stanton⊙, 517 .. H 5
58377 Starkweather, 193 . N 3
58482 Steele⊙, 696 .... L 6
58573 Strasburg, 642 .. K 7
58483 Streeter, 324 ... M 6
58785 Surrey, 361 ..... H 3
58484 Sutton, 87 ...... O 5
58486 Sykeston, 224 .. M 5
58487 Tappen, 294 .... L 6
58656 Taylor, 162 ..... E 6
58278 Thompson, 291 . R 4
58852 Tioga, 1,667 .... E 3
58379 Tokio, 130 ...... M 4
58787 Tolley, 163 ..... G 2
58380 Tolna, 247 ...... O 4
58071 Tower City, 289 . P 6

58788 Towner⊙, 870 ... K 3
58853 Trenton, 150 .... C 3
58575 Turtle Lake, 712 . J 4
58488 Tuttle, 216 ..... L 5
58576 Underwood, 781 . H 5
58789 Upham, 272 ..... J 3
58072 Valley City⊙, 7,843 . P 6
58790 Velva, 1,241 .... J 3
58490 Verona, 140 .... O 6
58075 Wahpeton⊙, 7,076 . S 7
58077 Warick, 175 ..... N 4
58281 Wales, 116 ...... N 2
58282 Walhalla, 1,471 . P 2
58577 Washburn⊙, 804 . J 5
58854 Watford City⊙, 1,768 . D 4
58078 West Fargo, 5,161 . S 6
† 58078 West Fargo Industrial Park, 104 .... S 6
58793 Westhope, 705 . H 2
58794 White Earth, 128 . E 3
58795 Wildrose, 235 .. D 2
58801 Williston⊙, 11,280 . C 3
58384 Willow City, 403 . K 2
58579 Wilton, 695 ..... J 5
58492 Wimbledon, 337 . O 5
58494 Wing, 223 .... K 5
58495 Wishek, 1,275 .. L 7
58496 Woodworth, 139 . M 5
58081 Wyndmere, 516 . R 7
58386 York, 102 .... L 3
58497 Ypsilanti, 139 .. N 6
58580 Zap, 271 .... G 5
58581 Zeeland, 313 ... L 8

⊙ County seat.
‡ Population of metropolitan area.
† Zip of nearest p.o.
* Multiple zips

Topography

5,000 m. 16,404 ft. / 2,000 m. 6,562 ft. / 1,000 m. 3,281 ft. / 500 m. 1,640 ft. / 200 m. 656 ft. / 100 m. 328 ft. / Sea Level / Below

0   50   100
MILES

North Dakota's wealth springs from her soil. The state has the largest farms and leads in production of barley, wheat and flaxseed.

COMPIX

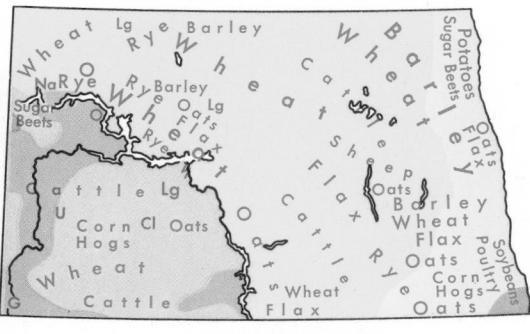

DOMINANT LAND USE

Specialized Wheat

Wheat, General Farming

Wheat, Range Livestock

Livestock, Cash Grain

Sugar Beets, Dry Beans, Livestock, General Farming

Range Livestock

⚡ Water Power

Agriculture, Industry and Resources

MAJOR MINERAL OCCURRENCES

Cl   Clay
G   Natural Gas
Lg   Lignite
Na   Salt
O   Petroleum
U   Uranium

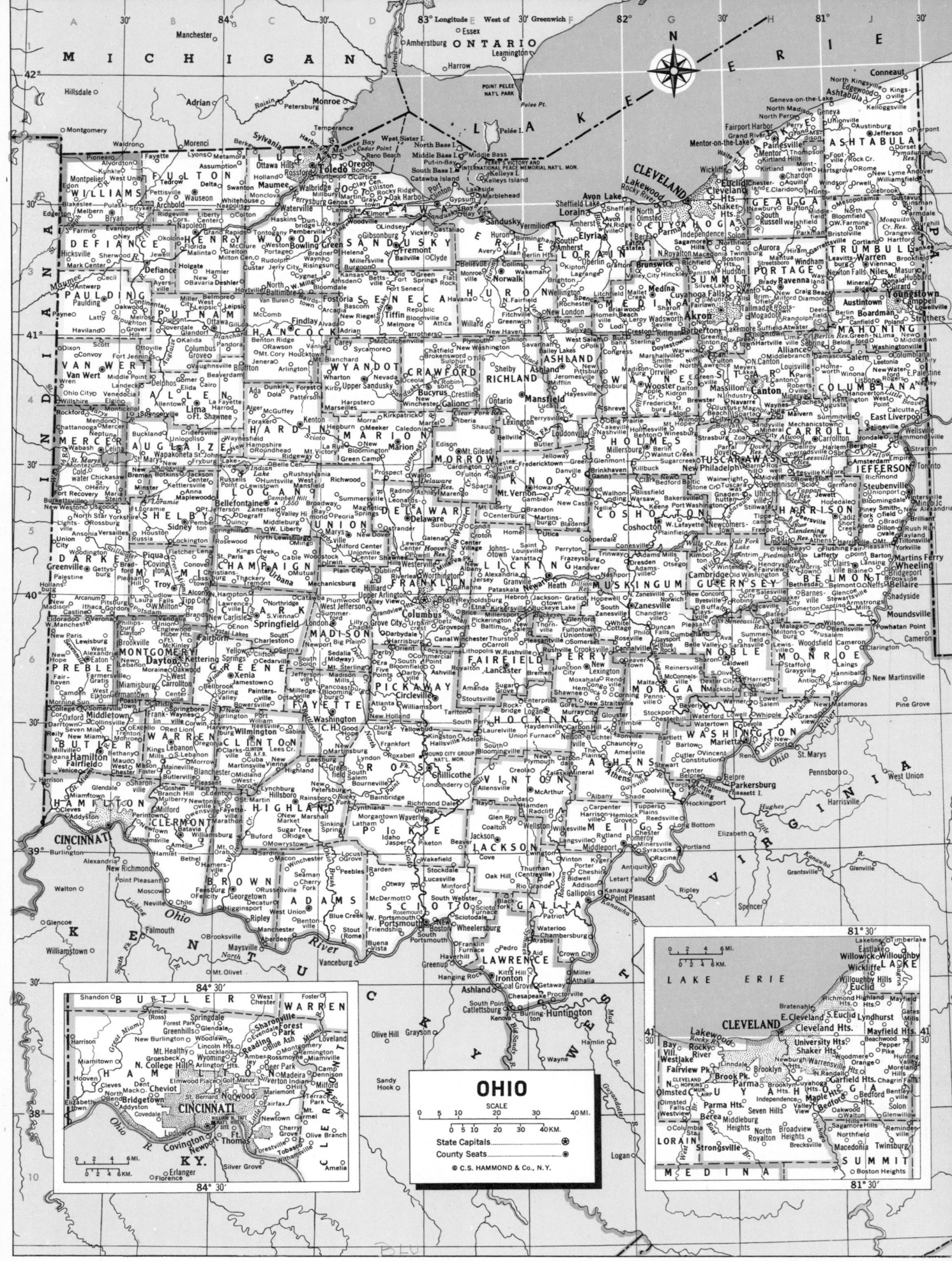

OHIO

SCALE

0   5   10   20   30   40 MI.

0   5 10   20   30   40KM.

State Capitals .... ⊛

County Seats .... ○

© C.S. HAMMOND & Co., N.Y.

COUNTIES

Adams, 18,957	D 8
Allen, 111,144	B 4
Ashland, 43,303	F 4
Ashtabula, 98,237	J 2
Athens, 54,889	F 7
Auglaize, 38,602	B 4
Belmont, 80,917	J 5
Brown, 26,635	C 8
Butler, 226,207	A 7
Carroll, 21,579	H 4
Champaign, 30,491	C 5
Clark, 157,115	C 6
Clermont, 95,725	B 7
Clinton, 31,464	C 7
Columbiana, 108,310	J 4
Coshocton, 33,486	G 5
Crawford, 50,364	E 4
Cuyahoga, 1,721,300	G 3
Darke, 49,141	A 5
Defiance, 36,949	A 3
Delaware, 42,908	D 5
Erie, 75,909	E 3
Fairfield, 73,301	E 6
Fayette, 25,461	D 6
Franklin, 833,249	E 5
Fulton, 33,071	B 2
Gallia, 25,239	F 8
Geauga, 62,977	H 3
Greene, 125,057	C 6
Guernsey, 37,665	H 5
Hamilton, 924,018	A 7
Hancock, 61,217	C 3
Hardin, 30,813	C 4
Harrison, 17,013	H 5
Henry, 27,058	B 3
Highland, 28,996	C 7
Hocking, 20,322	F 6
Holmes, 23,024	G 4
Huron, 49,587	E 3
Jackson, 27,174	E 7
Jefferson, 96,193	J 5
Knox, 41,795	F 5
Lake, 197,200	H 2
Lawrence, 56,868	E 8
Licking, 107,799	F 5
Logan, 35,072	C 5
Lorain, 256,843	F 3
Lucas, 484,370	C 2
Madison, 28,318	D 6
Mahoning, 303,424	J 4
Marion, 64,724	D 4
Medina, 82,717	G 3
Meigs, 19,799	F 7
Mercer, 35,265	A 4
Miami, 84,342	B 5
Monroe, 15,739	H 6
Montgomery, 606,148	B 6
Morgan, 12,375	G 6
Morrow, 21,348	E 4
Muskingum, 77,826	G 5
Noble, 10,428	G 6
Ottawa, 37,099	D 2
Paulding, 19,329	A 3
Perry, 27,434	F 6
Pickaway, 40,071	D 6
Pike, 19,114	D 7
Portage, 125,868	H 3
Preble, 34,719	A 6
Putnam, 31,134	B 3
Richland, 129,997	E 4
Ross, 61,211	D 7
Sandusky, 60,983	D 3
Scioto, 76,951	D 8
Seneca, 60,696	D 3
Shelby, 37,748	B 5
Stark, 372,210	H 4
Summit, 553,371	G 3
Trumbull, 232,579	J 3
Tuscarawas, 77,211	H 5
Union, 23,786	D 5
Van Wert, 29,194	A 4
Vinton, 9,420	E 7
Warren, 84,925	B 7
Washington, 57,160	H 7
Wayne, 87,123	G 4
Williams, 33,669	A 2
Wood, 89,722	C 3
Wyandot, 21,826	D 4

CITIES and TOWNS

	Zip	*Name/Pop.*	*Key*
	45101	Aberdeen, 1,165	C 8
	45810	Ada, 5,309	C 4
	45001	Addyston, 1,336	B 9
	43901	Adena, 1,134	J 5
*	44301	Akron⊙, 275,425	G 3
		Akron, ‡679,239	G 3
	45710	Albany, 899	F 7
	43001	Alexandria, 588	E 5
	45812	Alger, 1,071	C 4
	44601	Alliance, 26,547	H 4
	43102	Amanda, 788	E 6
†	45201	Amberley, 5,574	C 9
	45102	Amelia, 820	D 10
	44001	Amherst, 9,902	F 3
	43903	Amsterdam, 882	J 5
	44003	Andover, 1,179	J 2
	45302	Anna, 792	B 5
	45303	Ansonia, 1,044	A 5
	45813	Antwerp, 1,735	A 3
	44606	Apple Creek, 784	G 4
	44804	Arcadia, 689	D 3
	45304	Arcanum, 1,993	A 6
	43502	Archbold, 3,047	B 2
	45814	Arlington, 1,066	C 4
†	45201	Arlington Heights, 1,476	C 9
	44805	Ashland⊙, 19,872	F 4
	43003	Ashley, 1,034	E 5
	44004	Ashtabula, 24,313	J 2
	43103	Ashville, 1,772	E 6
	45701	Athens⊙, 23,310	F 7
	44807	Attica, 1,005	E 3
	44201	Atwater, 975	H 3
	44202	Aurora, 6,549	H 3
	44010	Austinburg, 900	J 2
	44515	Austintown, 29,393	J 3
	44011	Avon, 7,214	F 3
	44012	Avon Lake, 12,261	F 2
†	43512	Ayersville, 950	B 3
	45612	Bainbridge, 1,057	D 7
†	43420	Ballville, 1,652	D 3
	43804	Baltic, 571	G 5
	43105	Baltimore, 2,418	E 6
	44203	Barberton, 33,052	G 4
	43713	Barnesville, 4,292	H 6
	43905	Barton, 975	J 5
	45103	Batavia⊙, 1,894	B 7
†	44870	Bay View, 798	E 3
	44140	Bay Village, 18,163	G 9
	44608	Beach City, 1,133	G 4
†	44101	Beachwood, 9,631	J 9
	45808	Beaverdam, 525	C 4
	44146	Bedford, 17,552	H 9
†	44146	Bedford Heights, 13,063	J 9
	43906	Bellaire, 9,655	J 5
	45305	Bellbrook, 1,268	C 6
	43310	Belle Center, 985	C 4
	43311	Bellefontaine⊙, 11,255	C 5
	44811	Bellevue, 8,604	E 3
	44813	Bellville, 1,685	E 4
	43718	Belmont, 666	J 5
	44609	Beloit, 921	J 4
	45714	Belpre, 7,189	G 7
	44017	Berea, 22,396	G 10
	43908	Bergholz, 914	J 4
	44814	Berlin Heights, 828	F 3
	45106	Bethel, 2,214	B 8
	43719	Bethesda, 1,157	H 5
	44815	Bettsville, 833	D 3
	45715	Beverly, 1,396	G 6
	43209	Bexley, 14,888	E 6
	45107	Blanchester, 3,080	B 7
	44817	Bloomdale, 727	D 3
	43106	Bloomingburg, 895	D 6
	44818	Bloomville, 884	D 3
†	45201	Blue Ash, 8,324	C 9
	45817	Bluffton, 2,935	C 4
	44512	Boardman, 30,852	J 3
	44612	Bolivar, 1,084	G 4
†	44264	Boston Heights, 846	J 10
	45306	Botkins, 1,057	B 5
	43402	Bowling Green⊙, 21,760	C 3
	45308	Bradford, 2,163	B 5
	43406	Bradner, 1,140	C 3
†	44101	Bratenahl, 1,613	H 9
	44141	Brecksville, 9,137	H 10
	43107	Bremen, 1,413	F 6
	44613	Brewster, 2,020	G 4
†	44215	Briarwood Beach, 508	G 3
	43912	Bridgeport, 3,001	J 5
†	45201	Bridgetown, 13,352	B 9
	43913	Brilliant, 2,178	J 5
	44240	Brimfield, 950	H 3
	44402	Bristolville, 900	J 3
†	44141	Broadview Heights, 11,463	H 10
	44403	Brookfield, 1,200	J 3
	44144	Brooklyn, 13,142	H 9
†	44131	Brooklyn Heights, 1,527	H 9
	44142	Brook Park, 30.774	G 9
†	43912	Brookside, 939	J 5
	45309	Brookville, 4,403	B 6
	44212	Brunswick, 15,852	G 3
	43506	Bryan⊙, 7,008	A 3
	45716	Buchtel, 592	F 7
	43008	Buckeye Lake, 2,961	F 6
	44820	Bucyrus⊙, 13,111	E 4
	43722	Buffalo, 710	G 6
†	45680	Burlington, 900	F 9
	44021	Burton, 1,214	H 3
	44822	Butler, 1,052	F 4
	43723	Byesville, 2,097	G 6
	43907	Cadiz⊙, 3,060	J 5
	45820	Cairo, 587	B 4
	43920	Calcutta, 2,900	J 4
	43724	Caldwell⊙, 2,082	G 6
	43314	Caledonia, 792	D 4
	43725	Cambridge⊙, 13,656	G 5
	45311	Camden, 1,507	A 6
	44405	Campbell, 12,577	J 3
	45111	Camp Dennison, 550	D 9
	44614	Canal Fulton, 2,367	H 4
	43110	Canal Winchester, 2,412	E 6
	44406	Canfield, 4,997	J 3
*	44701	Canton⊙, 110,053	H 4
		Canton, ‡372,210	H 4
	43315	Cardington, 1,730	E 5
	43316	Carey, 3,523	D 4
	45005	Carlisle, 3,821	B 6
	43112	Carroll, 614	E 6
	44615	Carrollton⊙, 2,817	J 4
	44824	Castalia, 1,045	E 3
	45314	Cedarville, 2,342	C 6
	45822	Celina⊙, 7,779	A 4
	43011	Centerburg, 1,038	E 5
	45459	Centerville, 10,333	B 6
	44022	Chagrin Falls, 4,848	J 9
	44024	Chardon⊙, 3,991	H 2
	45719	Chauncey, 1,117	F 7
†	45202	Cherry Grove, 850	C 10
	45619	Chesapeake, 1,364	E 9
	44026	Chesterland, 11,500	H 2
†	45211	Cheviot, 11,135	B 9
	45601	Chillicothe⊙, 24,842	E 7
	45389	Christiansburg, 724	C 5
*	45201	Cincinnati⊙, 452,524	B 9
		Cincinnati, ‡1,384,851	B 9
	43113	Circleville⊙, 11,687	D 6
	45113	Clarksville, 574	C 7
	45315	Clayton, 773	B 6
*	44101	Cleveland⊙, 750,903	H 9
		Cleveland, ‡2,074,194	H 9
	44118	Cleveland Heights, 60,767	H 9
	45002	Cleves, 2,044	B 9
	44216	Clinton, 1,335	G 4
	43410	Clyde, 5,503	E 3
†	45638	Coal Grove, 2,759	E 9
	45621	Coalton, 550	E 7
	45828	Coldwater, 3,533	A 5
†	44034	Colebrook, 700	J 2
	44028	Columbia Station, 518	G 10
	44408	Columbiana, 4,959	J 4
*	43201	Columbus (cap.)⊙, 539,677	E 6
		Columbus, ‡916,228	E 6
	45830	Columbus Grove, 2,290	B 4

(continued on following page)

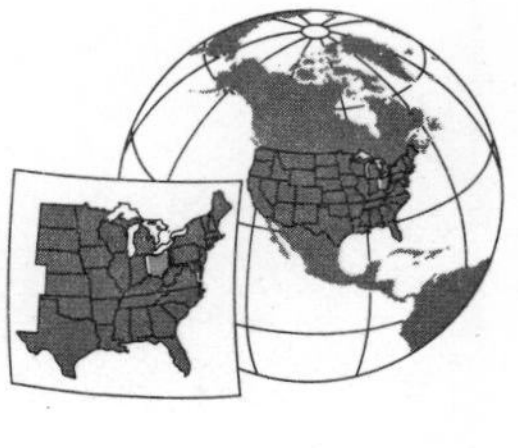

AREA 41,222 sq. mi.
POPULATION 10,652,017
CAPITAL Columbus
LARGEST CITY Cleveland
HIGHEST POINT Campbell Hill 1,550 ft.
SETTLED IN 1788
ADMITTED TO UNION March 1, 1803
POPULAR NAME Buckeye State
STATE FLOWER Scarlet Carnation
STATE BIRD Cardinal

Topography

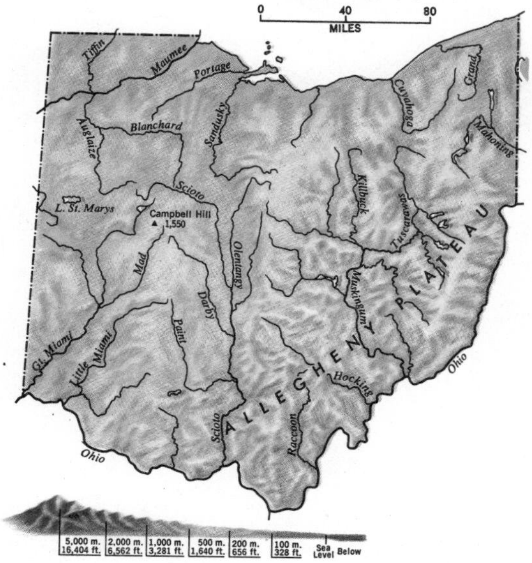
0 40 80
MILES
Tiffin
Maumee
Portage
Auglaize
Blanchard
Sandusky
Cuyahoga
Grand
Mahoning
Scioto
L. St. Marys
Campbell Hill 1,550
Mad
Olentangy
Killbuck
Walhonding
Tuscarawas
Muskingum
Darby
Paint
Gt. Miami
Little Miami
ALLEGHENY PLATEAU
Hocking
Raccoon
Ohio
5,000 m. 16,404 ft.
2,000 m. 6,562 ft.
1,000 m. 3,281 ft.
500 m. 1,640 ft.
200 m. 656 ft.
100 m. 328 ft.
Sea Level
Below

Agriculture, Industry and Resources

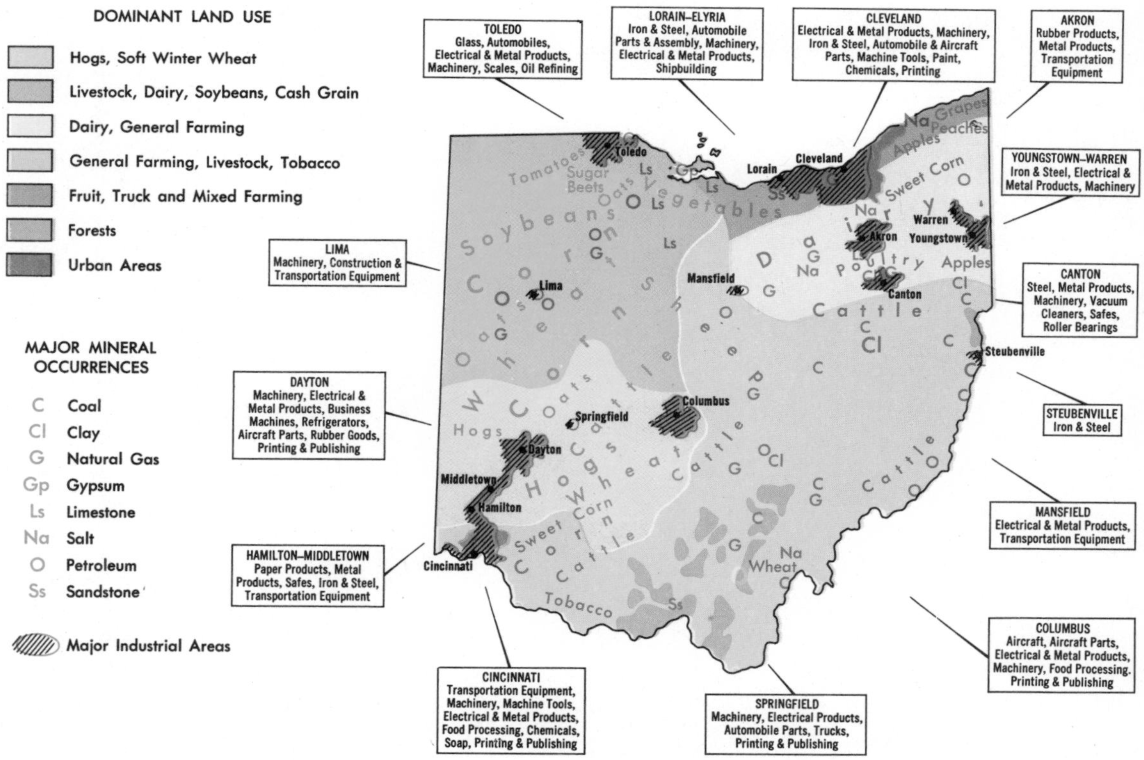
DOMINANT LAND USE
Hogs, Soft Winter Wheat
Livestock, Dairy, Soybeans, Cash Grain
Dairy, General Farming
General Farming, Livestock, Tobacco
Fruit, Truck and Mixed Farming
Forests
Urban Areas
MAJOR MINERAL OCCURRENCES
C Coal
Cl Clay
G Natural Gas
Gp Gypsum
Ls Limestone
Na Salt
O Petroleum
Ss Sandstone
Major Industrial Areas
TOLEDO Glass, Automobiles, Electrical & Metal Products, Machinery, Scales, Oil Refining
LORAIN–ELYRIA Iron & Steel, Automobile Parts & Assembly, Machinery, Electrical & Metal Products, Shipbuilding
CLEVELAND Electrical & Metal Products, Machinery, Iron & Steel, Automobile & Aircraft Parts, Machine Tools, Paint, Chemicals, Printing
AKRON Rubber Products, Metal Products, Transportation Equipment
YOUNGSTOWN–WARREN Iron & Steel, Electrical & Metal Products, Machinery
LIMA Machinery, Construction & Transportation Equipment
CANTON Steel, Metal Products, Machinery, Vacuum Cleaners, Safes, Roller Bearings
DAYTON Machinery, Electrical & Metal Products, Business Machines, Refrigerators, Aircraft Parts, Rubber Goods, Printing & Publishing
STEUBENVILLE Iron & Steel
MANSFIELD Electrical & Metal Products, Transportation Equipment
HAMILTON–MIDDLETOWN Paper Products, Metal Products, Safes, Iron & Steel, Transportation Equipment
COLUMBUS Aircraft, Aircraft Parts, Electrical & Metal Products, Machinery, Food Processing. Printing & Publishing
CINCINNATI Transportation Equipment, Machinery, Machine Tools, Electrical & Metal Products, Food Processing, Chemicals, Soap, Printing & Publishing
SPRINGFIELD Machinery, Electrical Products, Automobile Parts, Trucks, Printing & Publishing
Toledo
Lorain
Cleveland
Akron
Warren
Youngstown
Canton
Lima
Mansfield
Columbus
Springfield
Dayton
Middletown
Hamilton
Cincinnati
Steubenville
Tomatoes
Sugar Beets
Oats
Vegetables
Soybeans
Corn
Wheat
Sheep
Grapes
Peaches
Apples
Sweet Corn
Dairy
Poultry
Cattle
Hogs
Tobacco

(continued)

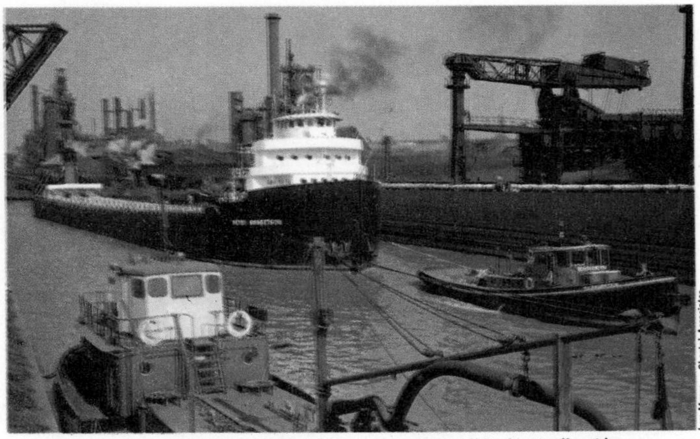

Lou Moore — Shostal Associates

Reminiscent of children's book illustrations, the tugboat "Washington" guides ore-carrier "Peter Robertson" through Cleveland's Industrial Flats, past a Milwaukee fuel tanker.

44030 Conneaut, 14,552 J 2
45831 Continental, 1,185 B 3
45832 Convoy, 991 A 4
45723 Coolville, 672 G 7
43730 Corning, 838 F 6
44410 Cortland, 2,525 J 3
43812 Coshocton⊙, 13,747 G 5
† 45201 Covedale, 6,639 B 10
45318 Covington, 2,575 B 5
† 44429 Craig Beach, 1,451 H 3
44827 Crestline, 5,947 E 4
44217 Creston, 1,632 G 3
45806 Cridersville, 1,103 B 4
43731 Crooksville, 2,828 F 6
† 45341 Crystal Lakes, 5,851 C 6
* 44221 Cuyahoga Falls, 49,678 G 3
† 44101 Cuyahoga Heights, 866 H 9
43413 Cygnet, 629 C 3
44618 Dalton, 1,177 G 4
43014 Danville, 1,025 F 5
43123 Darbydale, 743 D 6
* 45401 Dayton⊙, 243,601 B 6
Dayton, ‡850,266 B 6
44411 Deerfield, 800 H 3
45236 Deer Park, 7,415 C 9
43512 Defiance⊙, 16,281 B 3
43318 Degraff, 1,117 C 5
43015 Delaware⊙, 15,008 E 5
45833 Delphos, 7,608 B 4
43515 Delta, 2,544 B 2
44621 Dennison, 3,506 H 5
† 45202 Dent, 800 B 9
43516 Deshler, 1,938 C 3
45750 Devola, 1,989 H 7
43917 Dillonvale, 1,095 J 5
44622 Dover, 11,516 G 4
44230 Doylestown, 2,373 G 4
43821 Dresden, 1,516 G 5
43017 Dublin, 681 D 5
43734 Duncan Falls, 900 G 6
45836 Dunkirk, 1,036 C 4
44730 East Canton, 1,631 H 4
44112 East Cleveland, 39,600 H 9
44094 Eastlake, 19,690 J 8
43920 East Liverpool, 20,020 J 4
44413 East Palestine, 5,604 J 4
44626 East Sparta, 959 H 4
45320 Eaton⊙, 6,020 A 6
† 44035 Eaton Estates, 2,076 G 3
43517 Edgerton, 2,126 A 3
44004 Edgewood, 3,437 J 2
43320 Edison, 569 E 4
43518 Edon, 803 A 2
45807 Elida, 1,211 B 4
43416 Elmore, 1,316 D 3
45216 Elmwood Place, 3,525 B 9
* 44035 Elyria⊙, 53,427 F 3
45322 Englewood, 7,885 B 6
45323 Enon, 1,929 C 6
44117 Euclid, 71,552 J 9
† 45201 Evendale, 1,967 C 9
45042 Excello, 900 B 7
45324 Fairborn, 32,267 B 6
† 45201 Fairfax, 2,705 C 9
45014 Fairfield, 14,680 A 7
44313 Fairlawn, 6,102 G 3
44077 Fairport Harbor, 3,665 H 2
44126 Fairview Park, 21,681 G 9
45325 Farmersville, 865 A 6
43521 Fayette, 1,175 B 2
45120 Felicity, 786 B 8
45840 Findlay⊙, 35,800 C 3
45326 Fletcher, 539 B 5
43977 Flushing, 1,207 J 5
45843 Forest, 1,535 C 4
45405 Forest Park, 15,139 B 9
† 45202 Forestville, 950 C 10
45844 Fort Jennings, 533 B 4
45845 Fort Loramie, 744 B 5
† 45401 Fort McKinley, 11,536 B 6
45846 Fort Recovery, 1,348 A 5
† 45801 Fort Shawnee, 3,436 B 4
44830 Fostoria, 16,037 D 3
45628 Frankfort, 949 D 7
45005 Franklin, 10,075 B 6
45629 Franklin Furnace, 975 E 8
43822 Frazeysburg, 941 F 5
44627 Fredericksburg, 601 G 4
43019 Fredericktown, 1,935 F 5
43420 Fremont⊙, 18,490 D 3
45630 Friendship, 600 D 8
43230 Gahanna, 12,400 E 5
44833 Galion, 13,123 E 4
45631 Gallipolis⊙, 7,490 F 8
43022 Gambier, 1,571 F 5
44125 Garfield Heights, 41,417 J 9
44231 Garrettsville, 1,718 H 3
44040 Gates Mills, 2,378 J 9
44041 Geneva, 6,449 J 2
44043 Geneva-on-the-Lake, 877 H 2
43430 Genoa, 2,139 D 2
45121 Georgetown⊙, 2,949 C 8
45327 Germantown, 4,088 B 6
45328 Gettysburg, 526 A 5
43431 Gibsonburg, 2,585 D 3
44420 Girard, 14,119 J 3
45848 Glandorf, 732 B 3
45246 Glendale, 2,690 C 9
† 44139 Glenwillow, 526 J 10
45732 Glouster, 2,121 F 6
44629 Gnadenhutten, 1,466 G 5
† 45201 Golf Manor, 5,170 C 9
45122 Goshen, 1,174 B 7
44044 Grafton, 1,771 F 3
43522 Grand Rapids, 976 C 3
44045 Grand River, 613 H 2
† 43201 Grandview Heights, 8,460 D 6
43023 Granville, 3,963 E 5
45330 Gratis, 621 A 6
43322 Green Camp, 537 D 4
45123 Greenfield, 4,780 D 7
45218 Greenhills, 6,092 B 9
44232 Greensburg, 950 G 4
44836 Green Springs, 1,279 E 3
44630 Greentown, 1,150 H 4
45331 Greenville⊙, 12,380 A 5
44837 Greenwich, 1,473 E 3
45239 Groesbeck, 5,000 B 9
43123 Grove City, 13,911 D 6
43125 Groveport, 2,490 E 6
45849 Grover Hill, 536 B 3
45634 Hamden, 953 F 7
45130 Hamersville, 567 C 8
* 45011 Hamilton⊙, 67,865 A 7
Hamilton-Middletown, ‡226,207 A 7
43524 Hamler, 681 B 3
43931 Hannibal, 550 J 6
† 43055 Hanover, 626 F 5
43126 Harrisburg, 556 D 6
45030 Harrison, 4,408 A 9
45850 Harrod, 533 C 4
† 44085 Hartsgrove, 775 J 2
44632 Hartville, 1,752 H 4
43525 Haskins, 549 C 3
43127 Haydenville, 650 F 7
43055 Heath, 6,768 F 5
43025 Hebron, 1,699 E 6
43526 Hicksville, 3,461 A 3
† 44143 Highland Heights, 5,926 J 9
43026 Hilliard, 8,369 D 5
45133 Hillsboro⊙, 5,584 C 7
44234 Hiram, 1,484 H 3
43527 Holgate, 1,541 B 3
43528 Holland, 1,108 C 2
45033 Hooven, 550 A 9
43976 Hopedale, 916 J 5
44425 Hubbard, 8,583 J 3
45424 Huber Heights, 18,943 B 6
44236 Hudson, 3,933 H 3
† 44022 Hunting Valley, 797 J 9
44839 Huron, 6,896 E 3
44131 Independence, 7,034 H 9
† 45201 Indian Hill, 5,651 C 9
43932 Irondale, 602 J 4
45638 Ironton⊙, 15,030 E 8
45640 Jackson⊙, 6,843 E 7
45334 Jackson Center, 1,119 B 5
45740 Jacksonville, 545 F 7
45335 Jamestown, 1,790 C 6
44047 Jefferson⊙, 2,472 J 2
† 43162 Jefferson (West Jefferson), 3,664 D 6
43128 Jeffersonville, 1,031 C 6
44840 Jeromesville, 659 F 4
43986 Jewett, 901 H 5
43031 Johnstown, 3,208 E 5
43748 Junction City, 732 F 6
45853 Kalida, 900 B 4
44240 Kent, 28,183 H 3
43326 Kenton⊙, 8,315 C 4
45429 Kettering, 69,599 B 6
44637 Killbuck, 893 G 5
45034 Kings Mills, 800 B 7
45644 Kingston, 1,157 E 7
44048 Kingsville, 1,129 J 2
44428 Kinsman, 900 J 3
43033 Kirkersville, 578 E 6
44094 Kirtland, 5,530 H 2
43951 Lafferty, 900 H 5
44050 Lagrange, 1,074 F 3
44250 Lakemore, 2,708 H 3
43440 Lakeside, 850 E 2
43331 Lakeview, 1,026 C 4
44107 Lakewood, 70,173 G 9
43130 Lancaster⊙, 32,911 E 6
43934 Lansing, 950 J 5
43332 La Rue, 867 D 4
43135 Laurelville, 624 E 7
† 45501 Lawrenceville, 687 C 6
44430 Leavittsburg, 4,979 J 3
45036 Lebanon⊙, 7,934 B 7
45135 Leesburg, 984 D 7
44431 Leetonia, 2,342 J 4
45856 Leipsic, 2,072 C 3
44251 Leroy, 715 G 3
45338 Lewisburg, 1,553 A 6
44904 Lexington, 2,972 E 4
43532 Liberty Center, 1,007 B 3
* 45801 Lima⊙, 53,734 B 4
Lima, ‡171,472 B 4
† 45201 Lincoln Heights, 6,099 C 9
43442 Lindsey, 652 D 3
44432 Lisbon⊙, 3,521 J 4
44253 Litchfield, 650 F 3
43136 Lithopolis, 705 E 6
45742 Little Hocking, 520 G 7
45215 Lockland, 5,288 C 9
44254 Lodi, 2,399 F 3
43138 Logan⊙, 6,269 F 6
43140 London⊙, 6,481 C 6
* 44052 Lorain, 78,185 F 3
Lorain-Elyria, ‡256,843 F 3
44842 Loudonville, 2,865 F 4
44641 Louisville, 6,298 H 4
45140 Loveland, 7,144 D 9
45744 Lowell, 852 H 6
44436 Lowellville, 1,836 J 3
44843 Lucas, 771 F 4
45648 Lucasville, 900 E 8
43443 Luckey, 996 D 3
45142 Lynchburg, 1,186 C 7
44124 Lyndhurst, 19,749 J 9
43533 Lyons, 630 B 2
44056 Macedonia, 6,375 J 10
† 45202 Mack, 5,000 B 9
45243 Madeira, 6,713 C 9
44057 Madison, 1,678 H 2
44643 Magnolia, 1,064 H 4
43758 Malta, 1,017 G 6
44644 Malvern, 1,256 H 4
45144 Manchester, 2,195 C 8
* 44901 Mansfield⊙, 55,047 F 4
Mansfield, ‡129,997 F 4
44255 Mantua, 1,199 H 3
44137 Maple Heights, 34,093 H 9
† 43440 Marblehead, 726 E 2
45860 Maria Stein, 950 A 5
45227 Mariemont, 4,540 C 9
45750 Marietta⊙, 16,861 G 7
43302 Marion⊙, 38,646 D 4
44645 Marshallville, 693 G 4
43935 Martins Ferry, 10,757 J 5
43040 Marysville⊙, 5,744 D 5
45040 Mason, 5,677 B 7
44646 Massillon, 32,539 H 4
44438 Masury, 2,060 J 3
45069 Maud, 550 B 7
43537 Maumee, 15,937 C 2
† 44121 Mayfield, 3,548 J 9
† 44101 Mayfield Heights, 22,139 J 9
45651 McArthur⊙, 1,543 F 7
43534 McClure, 699 C 3
45858 McComb, 1,329 C 3
43756 McConnelsville⊙, 2,107 G 6
44437 McDonald, 3,177 J 3
45859 McGuffey, 704 C 4
43044 Mechanicsburg, 1,686 D 5
44256 Medina⊙, 10,913 G 3
45862 Mendon, 672 A 4
44060 Mentor, 36,912 H 2
44060 Mentor-on-the-Lake, 6,517 G 2
43540 Metamora, 594 C 2
45342 Miamisburg, 14,797 B 6
45041 Miamitown, 800 A 9
44652 Middlebranch, 600 H 4
† 44017 Middleburg Heights, 12,367 G 10
44062 Middlefield, 1,726 H 3
45863 Middle Point, 543 B 4
45760 Middleport, 2,784 F 7
45042 Middletown, 48,767 A 6
44653 Midvale, 636 H 5
44846 Milan, 1,405 E 3
45150 Milford, 4,828 D 9
43045 Milford Center, 753 D 5
43447 Millbury, 771 D 2
44654 Millersburg⊙, 2,979 F 4
43046 Millersport, 777 E 6
45013 Millville, 697 A 7
44656 Mineral City, 860 H 4
44440 Mineral Ridge, 1,500 J 3
44657 Minerva, 4,359 H 4
† 43201 Minerva Park, 1,402 E 5
43938 Mingo Junction, 5,278 J 5
45865 Minster, 2,405 B 5
44260 Mogadore, 3,858 H 3
45050 Monroe, 3,492 B 7
44847 Monroeville, 1,455 E 3
45242 Montgomery, 5,683 C 9
43543 Montpelier, 4,184 A 2
45439 Moraine, 4,898 B 6
† 44022 Moreland Hills, 3,000 J 9
45152 Morrow, 1,486 B 7
43338 Mount Gilead⊙, 2,971 E 4
45231 Mount Healthy, 7,446 B 9
45154 Mount Orab, 1,306 C 7
43939 Mount Pleasant, 635 J 5
43143 Mount Sterling, 1,536 D 6
43050 Mount Vernon⊙, 13,373 E 5
43340 Mount Victory, 633 D 4
44262 Munroe Falls, 3,794 H 3
43144 Murray City, 562 F 6
43545 Napoleon⊙, 7,791 B 3
44662 Navarre, 1,607 H 4
43940 Neffs, 900 J 5
44441 Negley, 600 J 4
45764 Nelsonville, 4,812 F 7
44849 Nevada, 917 D 4
43054 New Albany, 513 E 5
43055 Newark⊙, 41,836 F 5
45662 New Boston, 3,325 E 8
45869 New Bremen, 2,185 B 5
† 44101 Newburgh Heights, 3,396 H 9
† 45201 New Burlington, 900 B 9
45344 New Carlisle, 6,112 C 6
43832 Newcomerstown, 4,155 G 5
43762 New Concord, 2,318 G 6
43145 New Holland, 796 D 6
45871 New Knoxville, 852 B 5
45345 New Lebanon, 4,248 B 6
43764 New Lexington⊙, 4,921 F 6
44851 New London, 2,336 F 3
45346 New Madison, 959 A 6
45767 New Matamoras, 940 J 6
45011 New Miami, 3,273 A 7
44442 New Middletown, 1,664 J 4
45347 New Paris, 1,692 A 6
44663 New Philadelphia⊙, 15,184 G 5
45768 Newport, 975 H 7
45157 New Richmond, 2,650 B 8
43766 New Straitsville, 947 F 6
44444 Newton Falls, 5,378 J 3
45244 Newtown, 2,047 C 10
45159 New Vienna, 849 C 7
44854 New Washington, 1,251 E 4
44445 New Waterford, 735 J 4
44446 Niles, 21,581 J 3
45872 North Baltimore, 3,143 C 3
45052 North Bend, 638 B 9
44450 North Bloomfield, 650 J 3
44720 North Canton, 15,228 H 4
45239 North College Hill, 12,363 B 9
44855 North Fairfield, 540 E 3
44067 Northfield, 1,089 J 10
44707 North Industry, 2,000 H 4
44068 North Kingsville, 2,458 J 2
43060 North Lewisburg, 840 C 5
44452 North Lima, 800 J 4
44070 North Olmsted, 34,861 G 9
† 44081 North Perry, 851 H 2
† 44101 North Randall, 1,212 H 9
44035 North Ridgeville, 13,152 F 3
44133 North Royalton, 12,807 H 10
† 43601 Northwood, 4,222 D 2
† 43701 North Zanesville, 3,399 G 6
44203 Norton, 12,308 G 3
44857 Norwalk⊙, 13,386 E 3
45212 Norwood, 30,420 C 9
43449 Oak Harbor, 2,807 D 2
45656 Oak Hill, 1,642 E 8
45873 Oakwood, 10,095 B 6
45873 Oakwood, 3,127 H 9
45873 Oakwood, 804 B 3
44074 Oberlin, 8,761 F 3
43207 Obetz, 2,248 E 6
45874 Ohio City, 816 A 4
44138 Olmsted Falls, 2,504 G 9
44862 Ontario, 4,345 E 4
† 44101 Orange, 2,112 J 9
43616 Oregon, 16,563 D 2
44667 Orrville, 7,408 G 4
44076 Orwell, 965 J 2
45875 Ottawa⊙, 3,622 B 3
† 43601 Ottawa Hills, 4,270 C 2
45876 Ottoville, 914 B 4
45160 Owensville, 707 B 7
45056 Oxford, 15,868 A 6
44077 Painesville⊙, 16,536 H 2
45877 Pandora, 857 C 4
44080 Parkman, 750 H 3
44129 Parma, 100,216 H 9
† 44129 Parma Heights, 27,192 G 9
43062 Pataskala, 1,831 E 5
45879 Paulding⊙, 2,983 A 3
45880 Payne, 1,351 A 3
45660 Peebles, 1,629 D 8
43450 Pemberville, 1,301 C 3
44264 Peninsula, 692 G 3
44124 Pepper Pike, 5,933 J 9
44081 Perry, 917 H 2
43551 Perrysburg, 7,693 C 2
44864 Perrysville, 752 F 4
45354 Phillipsburg, 831 B 6
43771 Philo, 846 G 6
43147 Pickerington, 696 E 6
45661 Piketon, 1,347 E 7
43554 Pioneer, 968 A 2
45356 Piqua, 20,741 B 5
43064 Plain City, 2,254 D 5
45359 Pleasant Hill, 1,025 B 5
43148 Pleasantville, 754 F 6
44865 Plymouth, 1,993 E 4
† 45042 Poasttown, 650 B 6
44514 Poland, 3,097 J 3
45769 Pomeroy⊙, 2,672 G 7
43452 Port Clinton⊙, 7,202 E 2
45770 Portland, 550 G 7
45662 Portsmouth⊙, 27,633 D 8
43837 Port Washington, 550 G 5
43942 Powhatan Point, 2,167 J 6
45669 Proctorville, 881 F 9
43342 Prospect, 1,031 D 5
43456 Put-in-Bay, 135 E 2
43773 Quaker City, 510 H 6
43343 Quincy, 686 C 5
45771 Racine, 583 G 8
43066 Radnor, 950 D 5
44265 Randolph, 900 H 3
44266 Ravenna⊙, 11,780 H 3
43943 Rayland, 617 J 5
45215 Reading, 14,303 C 9
† 45202 Remington, 600 C 9
45773 Reno, 576 H 7
† 43412 Reno Beach, 1,049 D 2
44867 Republic, 705 D 3
43068 Reynoldsburg, 13,921 E 6
44286 Richfield, 3,228 G 3
43944 Richmond, 777 J 5
† 44045 Richmond (Grand River), 613 H 2
45673 Richmond Dale, 950 E 7
44143 Richmond Heights, 9,220 H 9
43344 Richwood, 2,072 D 5
45674 Rio Grande, 814 F 8
45167 Ripley, 2,745 C 8
43457 Risingsun, 730 C 3
44270 Rittman, 6,308 G 4
† 43085 Riverlea, 558 D 5
44670 Robertsville, 600 H 4
44084 Rock Creek, 731 J 2
45882 Rockford, 1,207 A 4
44116 Rocky River, 22,958 G 9
44085 Rome, 648 J 2
44272 Rootstown, 900 H 3
† 45662 Rosemount, 1,786 D 8
43777 Roseville, 1,767 F 6
45061 Ross (Venice), 1,661 B 9
43460 Rossford, 5,302 C 2
45236 Rossmoyne, 2,900 C 9
† 43943 Rush Run, 560 J 5
43347 Rushsylvania, 526 C 5
43348 Russells Point, 1,104 C 5
45775 Rutland, 663 F 7
45169 Sabina, 2,160 C 7
† 44067 Sagamore Hills, 4,100 J 10
45217 Saint Bernard, 6,080 B 9
43950 Saint Clairsville⊙, 4,754 J 5
45883 Saint Henry, 1,276 A 5
45885 Saint Marys, 7,699 B 4
43072 Saint Paris, 1,646 C 5
44460 Salem, 14,186 J 4
43945 Salineville, 1,686 J 4
44870 Sandusky⊙, 32,674 E 3
44671 Sandyville, 543 H 4
45171 Sardinia, 824 C 7
43946 Sardis, 700 J 6
43988 Scio, 1,002 H 5
† 45662 Sciotodale, 950 E 8
45679 Seaman, 866 C 8
44672 Sebring, 4,954 H 4
† 44101 Seven Hills, 12,700 H 9
45062 Seven Mile, 699 A 7
44273 Seville, 1,402 G 3
43947 Shadyside, 5,070 J 6
44120 Shaker Heights, 36,306 H 9
45241 Sharonville, 10,985 C 9
43782 Shawnee, 914 F 6
† 44052 Sheffield, 1,730 F 3
44054 Sheffield Lake, 8,734 F 3
44875 Shelby, 9,847 E 4
43556 Sherwood, 784 A 3
44878 Shiloh, 817 E 4
44676 Shreve, 1,635 F 4
45365 Sidney⊙, 16,332 B 5
† 44221 Silver Lake, 3,637 G 3
† 45201 Silverton, 6,588 C 9
43948 Smithfield, 1,245 J 5
44677 Smithville, 1,278 G 4
44139 Solon, 11,519 J 9
43783 Somerset, 1,417 F 6
† 44001 South Amherst, 2,913 F 3
† 43103 South Bloomfield, 610 D 6
45368 South Charleston, 1,500 C 6
44121 South Euclid, 29,579 H 9
45065 South Lebanon, 3,014 B 7
45680 South Point, 2,243 E 9
† 44022 South Russell, 2,673 H 3
45369 South Vienna, 545 C 6
45682 South Webster, 825 E 8
43701 South Zanesville, 1,436 F 6
44275 Spencer, 758 F 3
45887 Spencerville, 2,241 B 4
45066 Springboro, 2,799 B 6
45246 Springdale, 8,127 B 9
* 45501 Springfield⊙, 81,926 C 6
Springfield, ‡157,115 C 6
45370 Spring Valley, 667 C 6
44276 Sterling, 550 G 4
43952 Steubenville⊙, 30,771 J 5
Steubenville-Weirton, ‡165,627 J 5
43154 Stoutsville, 573 E 6
44224 Stow, 19,847 H 3
44680 Strasburg, 1,874 G 4
44240 Streetsboro, 7,966 H 3
44136 Strongsville, 15,182 G 10
44471 Struthers, 15,343 J 3
43557 Stryker, 1,296 B 3
† 44260 Suffield, 650 H 3
44681 Sugarcreek, 1,771 G 5
43074 Sunbury, 2,512 E 5
43558 Swanton, 2,927 C 2
44882 Sycamore, 1,096 D 4
43560 Sylvania, 12,031 C 2
45779 Syracuse, 684 G 7
44278 Tallmadge, 15,274 H 3
† 43771 Taylorsville (Philo), 846 G 6
45174 Terrace Park, 2,266 D 9
45780 The Plains, 1,568 F 7
43076 Thornville, 679 F 6
44883 Tiffin⊙, 21,596 D 3
43963 Tiltonsville, 2,123 J 5
† 44094 Timberlake, 964 J 8
45371 Tipp City, 5,090 B 6
† 45245 Tobasco, 950 C 10
* 43601 Toledo⊙, 383,818 D 2
Toledo, ‡692,571 D 2
43964 Toronto, 7,705 J 5
45067 Trenton, 5,278 B 7
45782 Trimble, 542 F 7
45373 Troy⊙, 17,186 B 5
44682 Tuscarawas, 830 H 5
44087 Twinsburg, 6,432 J 10
44683 Uhrichsville, 5,731 H 5
45322 Union, 3,654 B 6
† 47390 Union City, 1,808 A 5
44685 Uniontown, 875 H 4
44118 University Heights, 17,055 H 9
43221 Upper Arlington, 38,630 D 6
43351 Upper Sandusky⊙, 5,645 D 4
43078 Urbana⊙, 11,237 C 5
† 43123 Urbancrest, 754 D 6
43080 Utica, 1,977 F 5
† 43201 Valley View, 909 D 6
† 44101 Valley View, 1,422 H 9
45377 Vandalia, 10,796 B 6
45890 Vanlue, 539 C 4
45891 Van Wert⊙, 11,320 A 4
44870 Venice, 1,661 B 9
44089 Vermilion, 9,872 F 3
45378 Verona, 593 A 6
45380 Versailles, 2,441 A 5
44473 Vienna, 1,200 J 3
† 44473 Vienna (South Vienna), 545 C 6
44281 Wadsworth, 13,142 G 3
† 44094 Waite Hill, 514 H 2
44889 Wakeman, 514 F 3
43465 Walbridge, 3,208 C 2
44687 Walnut Creek, 550 G 4
† 44146 Walton Hills, 2,508 J 10
45895 Wapakoneta⊙, 7,324 B 4
* 44481 Warren⊙, 63,494 J 3
† 44100 Warrensville Heights, 18,925 H 9
43844 Warsaw, 725 G 5
43160 Washington Court House⊙, 12,495 D 6
44490 Washingtonville, 747 J 4
45786 Waterford, 600 G 6
43566 Waterville, 2,940 C 3
43567 Wauseon⊙, 4,932 B 2
45690 Waverly⊙, 4,858 D 7
43466 Wayne, 921 C 3
44688 Waynesburg, 1,337 H 4
45896 Waynesfield, 704 C 4
45068 Waynesville, 1,638 B 6
44090 Wellington, 4,137 F 3
45692 Wellston, 5,410 F
43968 Wellsville, 5,891 J 4
45381 West Alexandria, 1,553 A
45449 West Carrollton, 10,748 B
43081 Westerville, 12,530 D
44491 West Farmington, 650 J
43162 West Jefferson, 3,664 D
43845 West Lafayette, 1,719 G
44145 Westlake, 15,689 G
43357 West Liberty, 1,580 C
43358 West Mansfield, 753 C
45383 West Milton, 3,696 B
43569 Weston, 1,269 C
† 45662 West Portsmouth, 3,396 D
44287 West Salem, 1,058 F
45693 West Union⊙, 1,951 C
43570 West Unity, 1,589 B
† 44138 Westview, 2,523 G 1
45694 Wheelersburg, 3,709 E
43213 Whitehall, 25,263 E
43571 Whitehouse, 1,542 C
44092 Wickliffe, 21,354 J
44890 Willard, 5,510 E
45176 Williamsburg, 2,054 B
44093 Williamsfield, 950 J
43164 Williamsport, 857 D
44094 Willoughby, 18,634 J
† 44094 Willoughby Hills, 5,247 J
44094 Willowick, 21,237 J
45898 Willshire, 623 A
45177 Wilmington⊙, 10,051 C
45697 Winchester, 760 C
44288 Windham, 3,360 H
43952 Wintersville, 4,921 J
45245 Withamsville, 975 C 1
† 45201 Woodlawn, 3,251 C
† 44101 Woodmere, 976 J
43793 Woodsfield⊙, 3,239 H
43469 Woodville, 1,834 D
44691 Wooster⊙, 18,703 G
43085 Worthington, 15,326 E
45215 Wyoming, 9,089 C
45385 Xenia⊙, 25,373 C
45387 Yellow Springs, 4,624 C
43971 Yorkville, 1,656 J
* 44501 Youngstown⊙, 139,788 J
Youngstown-Warren, ‡536,003 J
43701 Zanesville⊙, 33,045 G

⊙ County seat.
‡ Population of metropolitan area.
† Zip of nearest p.o.
* Multiple zips

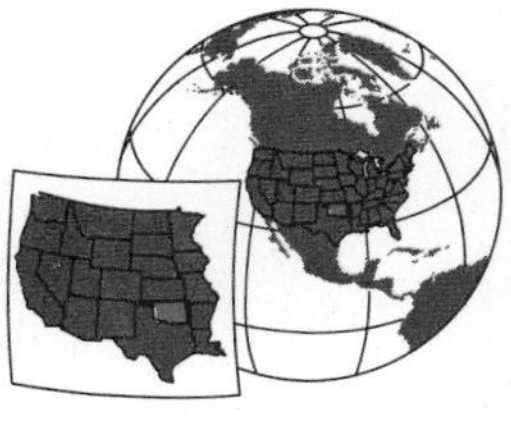

AREA 69,919 sq. mi.
POPULATION 2,559,253
CAPITAL Oklahoma City
LARGEST CITY Oklahoma City
HIGHEST POINT Black Mesa 4,973 ft.
SETTLED IN 1889
ADMITTED TO UNION November 16, 1907
POPULAR NAME Sooner State
STATE FLOWER Mistletoe
STATE BIRD Scissor-tailed Flycatcher

COUNTIES

Name/Pop.	Key
Adair, 15,141	S 3
Alfalfa, 7,224	K 1
Atoka, 10,972	O 6
Beaver, 6,282	E 1
Beckham, 15,754	G 4
Blaine, 11,794	K 3
Bryan, 25,552	O 7
Caddo, 28,931	K 4
Canadian, 32,245	K 3
Carter, 37,349	M 6
Cherokee, 23,174	R 3
Choctaw, 15,141	P 6
Cimarron, 4,145	A 1
Cleveland, 81,839	M 4
Coal, 5,525	O 5
Comanche, 108,144	K 5
Cotton, 6,832	K 6
Craig, 14,722	R 1
Creek, 45,532	O 3
Custer, 22,665	H 3
Delaware, 17,767	S 2
Dewey, 5,656	H 2
Ellis, 5,129	G 2
Garfield, 55,365	L 2
Garvin, 24,874	M 5
Grady, 29,354	L 5
Grant, 7,117	L 1
Greer, 7,979	G 5
Harmon, 5,136	G 5
Harper, 5,151	G 1
Haskell, 9,578	R 4
Hughes, 13,228	O 4
Jackson, 30,902	H 5
Jefferson, 7,125	L 6
Johnston, 7,870	N 6
Kay, 48,791	M 1
Kingfisher, 12,857	L 3
Kiowa, 12,532	J 5
Latimer, 8,601	R 5
Le Flore, 32,137	S 5
Lincoln, 19,482	N 3
Logan, 19,645	M 3
Love, 5,637	M 7
Major, 7,529	K 2
Marshall, 7,682	N 6
Mayes, 23,302	R 2
McClain, 14,157	M 5
McCurtain, 28,642	S 6
McIntosh, 12,472	P 4
Murray, 10,669	M 6
Muskogee, 59,542	R 3
Noble, 10,043	M 2
Nowata, 9,773	P 1
Okfuskee, 10,683	O 3
Oklahoma, 526,805	M 3
Okmulgee, 35,358	P 3
Osage, 29,750	O 1
Ottawa, 29,800	S 1
Pawnee, 11,338	N 2
Payne, 50,654	N 2
Pittsburg, 37,521	P 5
Pontotoc, 27,867	N 5
Pottawatomie, 43,134	N 4
Pushmataha, 9,385	R 6
Roger Mills, 4,452	G 3
Rogers, 28,425	P 2
Seminole, 25,144	N 4
Sequoyah, 23,370	S 3
Stephens, 35,902	L 6
Texas, 16,352	C 1
Tillman, 12,901	J 6
Tulsa, 401,663	P 2
Wagoner, 22,163	P 3
Washington, 42,277	P 1
Washita, 12,141	J 4
Woods, 11,920	J 1
Woodward, 15,537	H 2

CITIES and TOWNS

	Zip	Name/Pop.	Key
	74720	Achille, 382	O 7
	74820	Ada⊙, 14,859	N 5
	74330	Adair, 459	R 2
	73901	Adams, 175	D 1
	74520	Adamson, 150	P 5
	73520	Addington, 123	L 6
	74331	Afton, 1,022	S 1
	74824	Agra, 335	N 3
†	74955	Akins, 250	S 3
	74721	Albany, 100	O 7
	73001	Albert, 110	K 4
	74521	Albion, 186	R 5
	74522	Alderson, 215	P 5
	73002	Alex, 492	L 5
†	73015	Alfalfa, 70	J 4
	73716	Aline, 260	K 1
	74825	Allen, 974	O 5
	73521	Altus⊙, 23,302	H 5
	73717	Alva⊙, 7,440	J 1
	73004	Amber, 300	L 4
	73718	Ames, 227	K 2
†	73723	Amorita, 63	K 1
	73719	Anadarko⊙, 6,682	K 4
	74523	Antlers⊙, 2,685	P 6
	73006	Apache, 1,421	K 5
†	74633	Apperson, 40	N 1
	73620	Arapaho⊙, 531	H 3
	73007	Arcadia, 500	M 3
	73401	Ardmore⊙, 20,881	M 6
	74901	Arkoma, 2,098	T 4
	73832	Arnett⊙, 711	G 2
	74826	Asher, 437	N 5
	74524	Ashland, 73	O 5
	74525	Atoka⊙, 3,346	O 6
	74827	Atwood, 200	O 5
	74001	Avant, 439	O 2
	73833	Avard, 59	J 1
	74526	Bache, 100	P 5
	74420	Bacone, 786	R 3
	73930	Baker, 63	D 1
	73931	Balko, 100	E 1
	74002	Barnsdall, 1,579	O 1
†	74965	Baron, 100	S 3
	74003	Bartlesville⊙, 29,683	O 1
	74722	Battiest, 150	S 6
	74828	Bearden, 260	O 4
	73932	Beaver⊙, 1,853	F 1
	74421	Beggs, 1,107	P 3
†	74523	Belzoni, 50	R 6
	74929	Bengal, 75	R 5
	74723	Bennington, 288	P 7
	74527	Bentley, 125	O 6
†	73662	Berlin, 50	G 4
	74331	Bernice, 189	S 1
	73622	Bessie, 210	H 4
	73008	Bethany, 21,785	L 3
	74724	Bethel, 297	S 6
†	74801	Bethel Acres, 1,083	M 4
	74332	Big Cabin, 198	R 1
	74630	Billings, 618	M 1
	73009	Binger, 730	K 4
	73720	Bison, 80	L 2
	74008	Bixby, 3,973	P 3
	74058	Blackburn, 88	N 2
†	74962	Blackgum, 258	S 3
	74631	Blackwell, 8,645	M 1
	73526	Blair, 1,114	H 5
	73010	Blanchard, 1,580	L 4
	74528	Blanco, 200	P 5
	74529	Blocker, 151	P 4
	74725	Blue, 150	O 7
	74333	Bluejacket, 234	R 1
†	74525	Boggy Depot, 100	O 6
	73933	Boise City⊙, 1,993	B 1
	74726	Bokchito, 607	O 6
	74930	Bokoshe, 588	S 4
	74829	Boley, 514	O 4
	74727	Boswell, 755	P 6
	74830	Bowlegs, 540	N 4
	74009	Bowring, 100	O 1
	74422	Boynton, 522	P 3
	73011	Bradley, 247	L 5
	74423	Braggs, 325	R 3
	74632	Braman, 295	M 1
	73012	Bray, 90	L 5
	73721	Breckinridge, 70	L 2
	74424	Briartown, 100	R 4
	73013	Bridgeport, 142	K 3
	74010	Bristow, 4,653	O 3
	74012	Broken Arrow, 11,787	P 2
	74728	Broken Bow, 2,980	S 7
	74530	Bromide, 231	N 6
†	74873	Brooksville, 80	M 4
†	74437	Bryant, 86	P 4
	73834	Buffalo⊙, 1,579	G 1
	74931	Bunch, 90	S 3
	74633	Burbank, 188	N 1
	73722	Burlington, 165	K 1
	73430	Burneyville, 106	M 7
	73624	Burns Flat, 988	H 4
	73625	Butler, 315	H 3
	74831	Byars, 247	N 5
†	74820	Byng, 50	N 5
	73723	Byron, 72	K 1
	73527	Cache, 1,106	J 5
	74729	Caddo, 886	O 6
	74730	Calera, 1,063	O 7
	73014	Calumet, 386	K 3
	74531	Calvin, 359	O 5
	73835	Camargo, 236	H 2
	74932	Cameron, 311	T 4
	74425	Canadian, 304	P 4
	74533	Caney, 200	O 6
	73724	Canton, 844	J 2
	73626	Canute, 420	H 4
	73725	Capron, 80	J 1
	74335	Cardin, 950	S 1
	73726	Carmen, 519	J 1
	73015	Carnegie, 1,723	J 4
	74832	Carney, 396	N 3
	73727	Carrier, 125	K 2
	73627	Carter, 311	H 4
†	74633	Carter Nine, 50	N 1
	74934	Cartersville, 119	S 4
	73016	Cashion, 329	L 3
	74833	Castle, 212	O 4
	74015	Catoosa, 970	P 2
	73017	Cement, 892	K 5
†	74820	Center, 100	N 5
	74534	Centrahoma, 155	O 5
	74336	Centralia, 43	R 1
	74834	Chandler⊙, 2,529	N 3
	73528	Chattanooga, 302	J 6
	74426	Checotah, 3,074	R 4
	74016	Chelsea, 1,622	P 1
	73728	Cherokee⊙, 2,119	K 1
	73838	Chester, 135	J 2
	73628	Cheyenne⊙, 892	G 3
	73018	Chickasha⊙, 14,194	L 4
	74635	Chilocco, 712	M 1
	73020	Choctaw, 4,750	M 3
	74337	Chouteau, 1,046	R 2
†	74965	Christie, 70	S 3
	74017	Claremore⊙, 9,084	R 2
	74535	Clarita, 90	O 6
	74536	Clayton, 718	R 5
	74835	Clearview, 350	O 4
†	73437	Clemscot, 150	L 6
†	74331	Cleora, 87	S 1
	73729	Cleo Springs, 344	K 2
	74020	Cleveland, 2,573	O 2
	73601	Clinton, 8,513	H 3
	73632	Cloud Chief, 40	J 4
	74537	Cloudy, 175	R 6
	74538	Coalgate⊙, 1,859	O 5
†	73059	Cogar, 40	K 4
	74733	Colbert, 814	O 7
	74338	Colcord, 438	S 2
†	73010	Cole, 75	L 4
	73432	Coleman, 125	O 6
	74021	Collinsville, 3,009	P 2
	73021	Colony, 250	J 4
	73529	Comanche, 1,862	L 6
	74339	Commerce, 2,593	R 1
	73022	Concho, 500	L 3
	74836	Connerville, 150	N 6
	73023	Cooperton, 55	J 5
	74022	Copan, 558	P 1
	73632	Cordell⊙, 3,261	H 4
†	74751	Corinne, 100	R 6
	73024	Corn, 409	J 4
†	73456	Cornish, 90	L 6
	74428	Council Hill, 135	P 3
	73025	Countyline, 500	L 6
	73730	Covington, 605	L 2
	74429	Coweta, 2,457	P 3
†	74934	Cowlington, 751	S 4
	73082	Cox City, 285	L 5
	73027	Coyle, 303	M 3
	73028	Crescent, 1,568	L 3
	74837	Cromwell, 287	N 4
	74430	Crowder, 339	P 4
	73433	Cumberland, 150	N 6
	74023	Cushing, 7,529	N 3
	73639	Custer, 486	J 3
	73029	Cyril, 1,302	K 5
	73731	Dacoma, 226	J 1
	74540	Daisy, 250	P 5
	74838	Dale, 155	M 4
†	74523	Darwin, 50	P 6
	74026	Davenport, 831	N 3
	73530	Davidson, 515	J 6
	73030	Davis, 2,223	M 5
	74636	Deer Creek, 203	L 1
	74027	Delaware, 534	P 1
	73115	Del City, 27,133	L 4
	73640	Delhi, 41	G 4
	74028	Depew, 739	O 3
	73531	Devol, 129	J 6
	74431	Dewar, 933	P 4
	74029	Dewey, 3,958	P 1
†	74868	Dewright, 100	N 4
	73031	Dibble, 184	L 4
†	73401	Dickson, 798	M 6
	73641	Dill City, 578	H 4
	74340	Disney, 303	S 2
	73032	Dougherty, 211	M 6
	73733	Douglas, 79	L 2
	73734	Dover, 566	L 3
	74541	Dow, 300	P 5
	73735	Drummond, 326	L 2
	74030	Drumright, 2,931	O 3
	73532	Duke, 486	G 5
	73533	Duncan⊙, 19,718	L 5
	74701	Durant⊙, 11,118	O 6
	73642	Durham, 43	G 3
	74839	Dustin, 502	O 4
	73643	Eagle City, 56	J 3
	74734	Eagletown, 850	S 6
	73033	Eakly, 228	K 4
	74840	Earlsboro, 248	N 4
†	73532	East Duke, 250	H 5
	73034	Edmond, 16,633	M 3
	73537	Eldorado, 737	G 6
	73538	Elgin, 840	K 5
•	73644	Elk City, 7,323	G 4
	73539	Elmer, 138	H 6
	73035	Elmore City, 653	M 5
	73036	El Reno⊙, 14,510	K 3
	73701	Enid⊙, 44,008	L 2
†	74561	Enterprise, 130	R 4
	73645	Erick, 1,285	G 4
	74342	Eucha, 66	S 2
	74432	Eufaula⊙, 2,355	P 4
	74637	Fairfax, 1,889	N 1
	74343	Fairland, 814	S 1
	73736	Fairmont, 154	L 2
	73737	Fairview⊙, 2,894	J 2
	74935	Fanshawe, 199	S 5
	73840	Fargo, 262	G 2
	74542	Farris, 100	P 6
	73540	Faxon, 121	J 6
	73646	Fay, 75	J 3
†	74561	Featherston, 75	P 4
	73937	Felt, 105	A 1
	73434	Fillmore, 250	N 6
	74543	Finley, 400	R 6
	74842	Fittstown, 325	N 5
	74843	Fitzhugh, 212	N 5
	73541	Fletcher, 950	K 5
	74638	Foraker, 52	Q 1
†	73101	Forest Park, 835	M 3
	73938	Forgan, 496	E 1
	73038	Fort Cobb, 722	K 4
	74434	Fort Gibson, 1,418	R 3
	73841	Fort Supply, 550	G 1
	74735	Fort Towson, 430	R 7
	73647	Foss, 150	H 4
	73039	Foster, 50	M 5
	73435	Fox, 400	M 6
	74031	Foyil, 164	R 2
	74844	Francis, 283	N 5
	73542	Frederick⊙, 6,132	H 6
	73842	Freedom, 292	H 1
	73843	Gage, 536	G 2
	74936	Gans, 238	S 4
	73738	Garber, 1,011	M 2
	74736	Garvin, 117	S 7
	73844	Gate, 151	F 1
	73040	Geary, 1,380	K 3
	73436	Gene Autry, 120	N 6
	73543	Geronimo, 587	K 6
	74544	Gerty, 139	O 5
	74032	Glencoe, 421	M 2
	74033	Glenpool, 770	P 3
	74728	Glover, 244	S 6
	74737	Golden, 275	S 6
†	73093	Goldsby, 298	M 4
	73739	Goltry, 282	K 1
†	74740	Goodwater, 100	S 7
	73939	Goodwell, 1,467	C 1
	74435	Gore, 478	R 3
	73041	Gotebo, 376	J 4

(continued on following page)

Agriculture, Industry and Resources

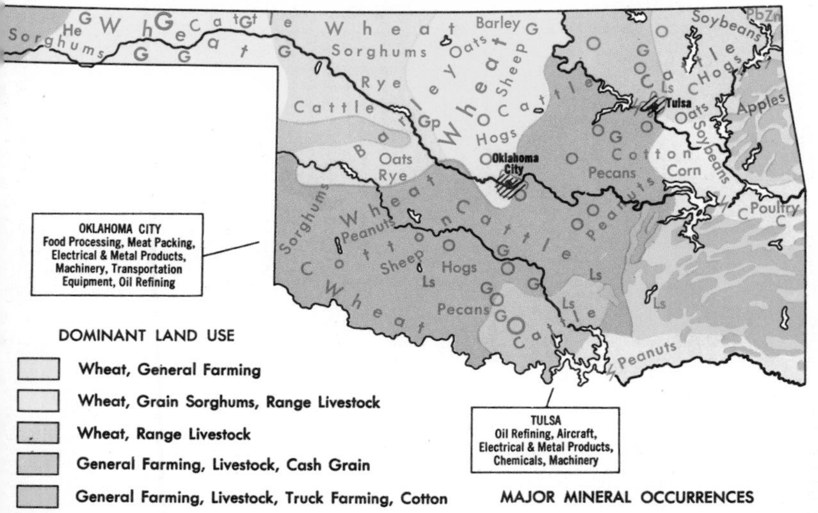
Oklahoma City
Tulsa
OKLAHOMA CITY
Food Processing, Meat Packing, Electrical & Metal Products, Machinery, Transportation Equipment, Oil Refining
TULSA
Oil Refining, Aircraft, Electrical & Metal Products, Chemicals, Machinery
Wheat
Sorghums
Cattle
Barley
Oats
Sheep
Hogs
Rye
Soybeans
Apples
Pecans
Cotton
Corn
Poultry
Peanuts

DOMINANT LAND USE

- Wheat, General Farming
- Wheat, Grain Sorghums, Range Livestock
- Wheat, Range Livestock
- General Farming, Livestock, Cash Grain
- General Farming, Livestock, Truck Farming, Cotton
- Cotton, General Farming
- Cotton, Wheat
- Fruit and Mixed Farming
- Range Livestock
- Forests

MAJOR MINERAL OCCURRENCES

C	Coal	Ls	Limestone
G	Natural Gas	O	Petroleum
Gp	Gypsum	Pb	Lead
He	Helium	Zn	Zinc

Water Power

Major Industrial Areas

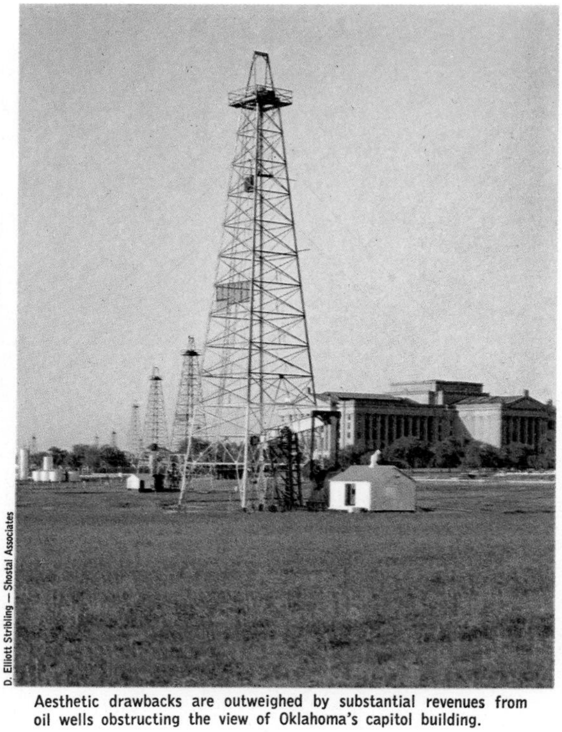

D. Elliott Stribling — Shostal Associates

Aesthetic drawbacks are outweighed by substantial revenues from oil wells obstructing the view of Oklahoma's capitol building.

73544 Gould, 368..................G 5
74545 Gowen, 350.................R 5
73042 Gracemont, 424............K 4
73437 Graham, 250...............M 6
74639 Grainola, 66...............N 1
73546 Grandfield, 1,524..........J 6
73547 Granite, 1,808.............H 5
74738 Grant, 273.................P 3
† 74437 Grayson (Wildcat), 142...P 3
73043 Greenfield, 143............K 3
74344 Grove, 2,000...............S 1
73044 Guthrie◉, 9,575...........M 3
73942 Guymon◉, 7,674............D 1
74546 Halleyville, 928...........P 5
74034 Hallett, 125...............N 2
73650 Hammon, 677................H 3
74845 Hanna, 181.................R 4
† 74955 Hanson, 250...............S 4
74846 Harden City, 150...........N 5
73944 Hardesty, 223..............D 1
73045 Harrah, 1,931..............M 4
74739 Harris, 200................S 5
74547 Hartshorne, 2,121..........R 4
74436 Haskell, 2,063.............P 3
73548 Hastings, 184..............K 6
74740 Haworth, 293...............S 7
74548 Haywood, 175...............P 5
73549 Headrick, 139..............J 6
73438 Healdton, 2,324............M 6
74937 Heavener, 2,566............S 5
73741 Helena, 769................K 1
74741 Hendrix, 117...............O 7
73046 Hennepin, 306..............M 5
73742 Hennessey, 2,181...........L 2
74437 Henryetta, 6,430...........Q 4
73539 Hess, 65...................H
† 73086 Hickory, 62...............N 5
73743 Hillsdale, 77..............K 1
73047 Hinton, 889................K 4
73744 Hitchcock, 160.............J 2
74438 Hitchita, 160..............P 3
73651 Hobart◉, 4,638............J 4
74345 Hockerville, 125...........S 1
74939 Hodgen, 150................S 5
74439 Hoffman, 262...............P 4
74848 Holdenville◉, 5,181.......O 4
73550 Hollis◉, 3,150............G 5
73551 Hollister, 105.............J 6
73745 Homestead, 75..............K 2
74035 Hominy, 2,274..............N 2
74549 Honobia, 250...............R 5
73945 Hooker, 1,615..............D 1
73746 Hopeton, 75................J 1
74940 Howe, 403..................S 5
74440 Hoyt, 110..................R 4
74743 Hugo◉, 6,585..............R 6
† 67333 Hulah, 50.................O 1
74441 Hulbert, 505...............R 2
† 73521 Humphreys, 44.............H 4
74640 Hunter, 274................L 1
73048 Hydro, 805.................J 3
74745 Idabel◉, 5,946...........S 7
73552 Indiahoma, 434.............J 5
74442 Indianola, 205.............P 4
74036 Inola, 948.................P 2
73747 Isabella, 89...............K 2
74346 Jay◉, 1,594..............S 1
73748 Jefferson, 128.............L 1
74037 Jenks, 1,997...............P 2
74038 Jennings, 338..............N 2
73749 Jet, 317...................K 1
73049 Jones, 1,666...............M 3
74551 Jumbo, 40..................P 6
74347 Kansas, 317................S 1
74641 Kaw, 283...................N 1
† 74401 Keefeton, 70..............R 3
74039 Kellyville, 685............O 3
74747 Kemp, 153..................O 7
† 74741 Kemp City (Hendrix), 117...O 7
74040 Kendrick, 126..............N 3
74748 Kenefic, 153...............O 6
74348 Kenwood, 125...............S 1
74941 Keota, 685.................S 4
74349 Ketchum, 238...............R 1
73947 Keyes, 569.................B 1
† 74574 Kiamichi, 100.............R 5
74401 Kiefer, 803................O 3
74642 Kildare, 79................M 1
73750 Kingfisher◉, 4,042.......L 3
73439 Kingston, 710..............N 7
74552 Kinta, 247.................R 4
74553 Kiowa, 754.................P 5

73847 Knowles, 52................F 1
74849 Konawa, 1,719..............N 5
† 74557 Kosoma, 50................P 6
74554 Krebs, 1,515...............P 5
73753 Kremlin, 200...............L 1
73754 Lahoma, 299................K 2
74850 Lamar, 153.................O 4
74643 Lamont, 478................L 1
74555 Lane, 218..................O 6
74350 Langley, 481...............R 2
73050 Langston, 486..............G 1
73848 Laverne, 1,373.............G 1
73501 Lawton◉, 74,470..........K 5
          Lawton, ‡108,144.......K 5
74351 Leach, 75..................S 2
73440 Lebanon, 240...............N 7
73654 Leedey, 465................H 3
74942 Leflore, 175...............S 5
74556 Lehigh, 296................O 5
74042 Lenapah, 325...............P 1
73441 Leon, 112..................M 7
74043 Leonard, 115...............P 3
74943 Lequire, 100...............R 4
73051 Lexington, 1,516...........M 4
† 74858 Lima (New Lima), 238......O 4
73052 Lindsay, 3,705.............L 5
74637 Little Chief, 40...........N 1
73446 Little City, 80............N 6
74352 Loco, 193..................L 6
74352 Locust Grove, 1,090........R 2
73443 Lone Grove, 1,240..........M 6
73655 Lone Wolf, 584.............H 5
73755 Longdale, 331..............K 2
73053 Lookeba, 165...............K 4
73756 Loyal, 107.................K 3

73757 Lucien, 150................M 2
73450 Milburn, 275...............O 6
† 74825 Lula, 40..................O 5
73054 Luther, 836................M 3
74578 Lutie, 250.................R 5
74852 Macomb, 41.................M 4
73446 Madill◉, 2,875...........N 6
73758 Manchester, 165............L 1
73554 Mangum◉, 4,066...........G 5
73555 Manitou, 308...............J 5
74044 Mannford, 892..............O 2
73447 Mannsville, 364............N 6
74045 Maramec, 128...............N 2
74945 Marble City, 299...........S 3
73448 Marietta◉, 2,013.........M 7
74644 Marland, 236...............M 1
73055 Marlow, 3,995..............K 5
73556 Marshall, 420..............L 2
73556 Martha, 268................H 5
74853 Mason, 75..................O 3
74854 Maud, 1,143................N 4
73851 May, 91....................G 1
73057 Maysville, 1,380...........M 5
74353 Mazie, 300.................R 2
74501 McAlester◉, 18,802.......P 5
74944 McCurtain, 575.............R 4
74851 McLoud, 2,159..............M 4
73449 Mead, 210..................N 6
73759 Medford◉, 1,304..........L 1
73557 Medicine Park, 562.........J 5
74855 Meeker, 683................N 3
74074 Mehan, 50..................N 3
73760 Meno, 115..................K 2
73058 Meridian, 104..............M 3
74354 Miami◉, 13,880...........S 1
74882 Micawber, 41...............N 3

73110 Midwest City, 48,114.......M 4
73450 Milburn, 275...............O 6
74046 Milfay, 150................N 3
74856 Mill Creek, 234............N 6
74750 Millerton, 350.............S 7
73451 Milo, 85...................M 6
74944 Milton, 90.................S 4
73059 Minco, 1,129...............L 4
74946 Moffett, 312...............S 4
74947 Monroe, 300................S 4
74444 Moodys, 200................S 2
† 71821 Moon, 50..................S 7
73060 Moore, 18,761..............M 4
73852 Mooreland, 1,196...........H 2
74445 Morris, 1,119..............P 3
73061 Morrison, 421..............M 2
74047 Mounds, 766................O 3
73559 Mountain Park, 458.........J 5
73062 Mountain View, 1,110.......J 4
74557 Moyers, 125................P 6
74948 Muldrow, 1,680.............S 4
73063 Mulhall, 307...............M 2
74949 Muse, 75...................S 5
74401 Muskogee◉, 37,331........P 3
73064 Mustang, 2,637.............L 4
73853 Mutual, 94.................H 2
74646 Nardin, 135................M 1
73761 Nash, 294..................K 1
74558 Nashoba, 100...............R 6
74056 Nelagoney, 62..............O 1
74857 Newalla, 350...............M 4
74049 New Alluwe, 116............R 1
73065 Newcastle, 1,271...........L 4
† 73632 New Cordell (Cordell)◉, 3,261...H 4

74647 Newkirk◉, 2,173..........N 1
74858 New Lima, 238..............O 4
† 74060 New Prue (Prue), 202......O 2
† 73466 New Woodville (Woodville), 118...N 7
73101 Nichols Hills, 4,478.......L 3
73066 Nicoma Park, 2,560.........M 4
73067 Ninnekah, 300..............L 5
73068 Noble, 2,241...............M 4
73069 Norman◉, 52,117..........M 4
73701 North Enid, 730............L 2
74358 North Miami, 503...........R 1
74048 Nowata◉, 3,679...........P 1
74050 Oakhurst, 500..............N 6
73452 Oakland, 317...............N 6
74359 Oaks, 219..................S 2
73658 Oakwood, 129...............J 3
74051 Ochelata, 330..............P 1
74958 Octavia, 40................S 5
73762 Okarche, 826...............L 3
74446 Okay, 419..................R 3
73763 Okeene, 1,421..............K 2
† 74003 Okesa, 165................O 1
73101 Oklahoma City (cap.)◉, 366,481...L 4
        Oklahoma City, ‡640,889...L 4
74447 Okmulgee◉, 15,180........O 3
74450 Oktaha, 193................R 3
74751 Oleta, 50..................R 6
74430 Olive, 110.................O 6
74538 Olney, 42..................O 6
73560 Olustee, 819...............H 5

73948 Optima, 103................D 1
73073 Orlando, 202...............M 2
74054 Osage, 170.................L 2
73561 Oscar, 61..................L 7
73453 Overbrook, 120.............M 6
74055 Owasso, 3,491..............P 2
74860 Paden, 442.................N 4
74951 Panama, 1,121..............S 4
74559 Panola, 100................R 5
73074 Paoli, 480.................M 5
74451 Park Hill, 125.............R 3
74824 Parkland, 55...............N 3
73075 Pauls Valley◉, 5,769.....M 5
74056 Pawhuska◉, 4,238.........O 1
74058 Pawnee◉, 2,443...........N 2
74861 Pearson, 60................N 4
74648 Peckham, 65................M 1
74452 Peggs, 82..................R 2
74301 Pensacola, 56..............R 2
66713 Peoria, 179................S 1
74059 Perkins, 1,029.............M 3
73076 Pernell, 117...............M 5
73077 Perry◉, 5,341............M 2
74862 Pharoah, 100...............O 4
74538 Phillips, 106..............O 6
74360 Picher, 2,363..............S 1
74752 Pickens, 350...............S 6
73078 Piedmont,·269..............L 3
74560 Pittsburg, 282.............P 5
74753 Platter, 275...............O 6
74952 Plunkettville, 125.........S 6
73079 Pocasset, 200..............L 4
74902 Pocola, 1,840..............T 4
74601 Ponca City, 25,940.........M 1
73766 Pondcreek, 903.............L 2

OKLAHOMA

SCALE
0 5 10   20   30   40 MI.
0 5 10   20   30   40 KM.

State Capitals...........◉
County Seats............◉

© C.S. HAMMOND & Co., N.Y.

Topography

MILES
0   50   100

5,000 m. / 2,000 m. / 1,000 m. / 500 m. / 200 m. / 100 m. / Sea Level / Below
16,404 ft. / 6,562 ft. / 3,281 ft. / 1,640 ft. / 656 ft. / 328 ft.

Zip	Place	Pop.	Loc.
74863	Pontotoc, 150		N 6
73454	Pooleville, 75		M 6
74454	Porter, 624		R 3
74953	Porum, 658		R 4
74953	Poteau⊙, 5,500		S 4
74864	Prague, 1,802		N 4
74456	Preston, 300		P 3
74457	Proctor, 175		S 3
74060	Prue, 202		O 2
74361	Pryor⊙, 7,057		M 4
73080	Purcell⊙, 4,076		M 4
73659	Putnam, 84		N 1
73454	Quapaw, 967		S 1
† 74085	Quay, 41		N 3
† 73852	Quinlan, 81		J 4
74561	Quinton, 1,262		R 4
74650	Ralston, 443		N 2
74061	Ramona, 600		P 3
73562	Randlett, 384		M 6
73081	Ratliff City, 250		K 6
74562	Rattan, 350		R 6
73455	Ravia, 373		N 6
† 73460	Reagan, 15		P 6
74458	Redbird, 230		P 3
74563	Red Oak, 609		R 4
74561	Redrock, 233		M 2
73563	Reed, 64		G 5
74459	Rentiesville, 96		R 4
73660	Reydon, 215		G 3
73456	Ringling, 1,206		L 6
73768	Ringwood, 241		K 2
74062	Ripley, 307		N 3
† 74701	Roberta, 45		O 7
74933	Rock Island, 97		T 4
73661	Rocky, 260		J 4
74865	Roff, 632		N 5
74954	Roland, 827		S 4
73564	Roosevelt, 353		J 5
74364	Rose, 120		M 4
74831	Rosedale, 98		M 5
73855	Rosston, 56		G 1
73457	Rubottom, 110		M 7
74755	Rufe, 54		R 6
73082	Rush Springs, 1,381		L 5
73565	Ryan, 1,011		L 6
† 74606	Sageeyah, 49		P 2
74866	Saint Louis, 207		N 4
74365	Salina, 1,024		R 2
74955	Sallisaw⊙, 4,888		S 4
74063	Sand Springs, 11,519		O 2
74066	Sapulpa⊙, 15,159		O 3
74564	Sardis, 58		R 5
74867	Sasakwa, 321		N 5
74565	Savanna, 948		P 5
74756	Sawyer, 210		R 7
73662	Sayre⊙, 2,712		G 4
74460	Schulter, 200		P 3
74566	Scipio, 100		P 4
73663	Seiling, 1,033		J 3
73856	Selman, 93		H 1
74868	Seminole, 7,878		N 4
73664	Sentinel, 984		H 4
74956	Shady Point, 350		S 4
74068	Shamrock, 204		N 3
73857	Sharon, 155		H 2
73858	Shattuck, 1,546		G 2
74801	Shawnee⊙, 25,075		N 4
74757	Sherwood, 60		S 6
74652	Shidler, 717		N 1
† 72955	Short, 200		S 3
74069	Skedee, 117		N 2
74070	Skiatook, 2,930		O 2
74071	Slick, 171		O 3
74957	Smithville, 144		S 6
74567	Snow, 150		R 6
73566	Snyder, 1,671		J 5
74759	Soper, 322		R 6
73770	Southard, 130		K 2
74072	South Coffeyville, 646		P 1
74869	Sparks, 181		N 3
74366	Spavinaw, 470		P 2
73084	Spencer, 3,603		M 3
74760	Spencerville, 275		R 6
74073	Sperry, 1,123		P 2
74959	Spiro, 2,057		S 4
73458	Springer, 256		M 6
73567	Sterling, 675		K 5
74461	Stidham, 53		P 4
74462	Stigler⊙, 2,347		R 4
74074	Stillwater⊙, 31,126		N 2
73571	Stillwell⊙, 2,134		S 3
† 74436	Stonebluff, 50		P 3
74871	Stonewall, 653		O 5
74367	Strang, 164		P 2
74872	Stratford, 1,278		M 5
74569	Stringtown, 397		P 5
74570	Stuart, 294		O 5
73565	Sugden, 54		L 6
73086	Sulphur⊙, 5,158		N 5
74966	Summerfield, 210		S 5
74761	Swink, 88		R 6
74463	Taft, 525		R 3
74464	Tahlequah⊙, 9,254		R 3
74080	Talala, 163		P 1
74571	Talihina, 1,227		S 5
73082	Tamaha, 363		J 2
† 74462	Tamaha, 83		S 4
73087	Tatums, 502		M 6
74873	Tecumseh, 4,451		N 4
73568	Temple, 1,354		K 6
74081	Terlton, 111		O 2
73569	Terral, 636		L 7
73949	Texhoma, 921		C 1
73668	Texola, 144		G 4
73459	Thackerville, 257		M 7
73120	The Village, 13,695		L 3
73669	Thomas, 1,336		J 3
74017	Tiawah, 119		P 2
73570	Tipton, 1,206		H 6
73460	Tishomingo⊙, 2,663		N 6
74762	Tom, 150		S 7
74653	Tonkawa, 3,337		N 1
† 74282	Tribbey, 60		M 4
74856	Troy, 92		M 4
74875	Tryon, 301		N 3
74466	Tullahassee, 183		P 3
* 74101	Tulsa⊙, 331,638		O 2
	Tulsa, ‡476,945		O 2
74572	Tupelo, 485		O 5
73950	Turpin, 295		E 1
74573	Tushka, 400		O 6
74574	Tuskahoma, 200		R 5
73088	Tussy, 150		L 6
73089	Tuttle, 1,640		L 4
73951	Tyrone, 863		D 1
74601	Uncas, 53		N 1
73090	Union, 306		L 4
74763	Utica, 177		O 7
† 73101	Valley Brook, 2,869		M 4
74764	Valliant, 840		R 6
74876	Vanoss, 130		N 5
73091	Velma, 611		L 6
73092	Verden, 439		K 4
74017	Verdigris, 307		P 2
74877	Vernon, 84		P 4
74962	Vian, 1,131		S 4
73859	Vici, 694		H 2
74301	Vinita⊙, 5,847		R 1
73571	Vinson, 77		G 4
74765	Wade, 50		O 7
74467	Wagoner⊙, 4,959		R 3
74468	Wainwright, 135		R 3
73771	Wakita, 426		L 1
73572	Walters⊙, 2,611		K 6
74878	Wanette, 303		M 5
74083	Wann, 135		P 1
73461	Wapanucka, 425		N 6
74576	Wardville, 100		P 5
74469	Warner, 1,217		R 4
73123	Warr Acres, 9,887		L 3
74879	Warwick, 146		M 3
73093	Washington, 322		M 4
73094	Washita, 160		K 4
73772	Watonga⊙, 3,696		K 3
74963	Watson, 48		S 6
74964	Watts, 326		S 2
73773	Waukomis, 241		K 2
73573	Waurika⊙, 1,833		L 6
73095	Wayne, 618		M 4
73860	Waynoka, 1,444		J 1
73096	Weatherford, 7,959		J 4
† 74560	Weathers, 100		P 5
74654	Webb City, 186		N 1
74470	Webbers Falls, 485		R 3
74369	Welch, 651		R 1
74880	Weleetka, 1,199		O 4
74471	Welling, 50		S 3
74881	Wellston, 789		M 3
74882	Welty, 89		O 3
† 72761	West Siloam Springs, 210		S 2
74965	Westville, 934		S 2
74883	Wetumka, 1,687		O 4
74884	Wewoka⊙, 5,284		O 4
74422	Whitefield, 250		R 4
74301	Whiteoak, 200		R 1
74577	Whitesboro, 300		S 5
74578	Wilburton⊙, 2,280		R 5
† 74437	Wildcat, 142		R 5
73462	Willis, 250		N 7
73673	Willow, 188		G 4
73463	Wilson, 1,569		M 6
73464	Wirt, 350		L 6
74966	Wister, 927		S 5
73466	Woodville, 118		N 7
73801	Woodward⊙, 8,710		H 2
74766	Wright City, 1,068		R 6
74370	Wyandotte, 297		S 1
73098	Wynnewood, 2,374		M 5
74084	Wynona, 547		O 1
74085	Yale, 1,239		N 3
74574	Yanush, 350		R 5
74885	Yeager, 107		O 4
74767	Yuba, 63		O 7
73099	Yukon, 8,411		L 3

⊙ County seat.
® Population of metropolitan area.
† Zip of nearest p.o.
* Multiple zips

COUNTIES

Baker, 14,919 .... K 3
Benton, 53,776 .... D 3
Clackamas, 166,088 ...... E 2
Clatsop, 28,473 .... D 1
Columbia, 28,790 .... D 2
Coos, 56,515 .... C 4
Crook, 9,985 .... G 3
Curry, 13,006 .... C 5
Deschutes, 30,442 .... F 4
Douglas, 71,743 .... D 4
Gilliam, 2,342 .... G 2
Grant, 6,996 .... J 3
Harney, 7,215 .... H 4
Hood River, 13,187 .... F 2
Jackson, 94,533 .... E 5
Jefferson, 8,548 .... F 3
Josephine, 35,746 .... D 5
Klamath, 50,021 .... F 5
Lake, 6,343 .... G 5
Lane, 213,358 .... E 4
Lincoln, 25,755 .... D 3
Linn, 71,914 .... E 3
Malheur, 23,169 .... K 4

Marion, 151,309 .... E 3
Morrow, 4,465 .... H 2
Multnomah, 556,667 .... E 2
Polk, 35,349 .... D 3
Sherman, 2,139 .... G 2
Tillamook, 17,930 .... D 2
Umatilla, 44,923 .... J 2
Union, 19,377 .... J 2
Wallowa, 6,247 .... K 2
Wasco, 20,133 .... F 2
Washington, 157,920 ...... D 2
Wheeler, 1,849 .... G 3
Yamhill, 40,213 .... D 2

CITIES and TOWNS

Zip Name/Pop. Key

97810 Adams, 219 .... J 2
97620 Adel, 200 .... H 5
97901 Adrian, 200 .... K 4
97320 Agate Beach, 975 ... C 3
97406 Agness, 120 .... C 5
† 97361 Airlie, 45 .... D 3
97321 Albany⊙, 18,181 ... D 3
† 97601 Algoma, 77 .... F 5
97811 Alicel, 30 .... J 2
97407 Allegany, 200 ...... D 4
97006 Aloha, 6,000 .... A 2
97408 Alpine, 80 .... D 3
97324 Alsea, 600 .... D 3
† 97601 Altamont, 15,746 .. F 5
97409 Alvadore, 350 ...... D 3
97101 Amity, 708 .... D 2
97001 Antelope, 50 .... G 3
97530 Applegate, 125 ..... D 5
97458 Arago, 200 .... C 4
97812 Arlington, 375 ..... G 2
97520 Ashland, 12,342 .... E 5
97813 Athena, 872 .... J 2
97325 Aumsville, 590 ..... E 3
97002 Aurora, 306 .... B 2
97814 Baker⊙, 9,354 ...... K 3
† 97378 Ballston, 120 ..... D 2
97459 Bancroft, 25 .... D 5
97411 Bandon, 1,832 ...... C 4
97106 Banks, 430 .... A 1

97003 Barlow, 105 .... B 2
† 97009 Barton, 100 .... B 2
97136 Bar View, 75 .... C 2
97817 Bates, 430 .... J 3
97107 Bay City, 898 ...... D 2
97621 Beatty, 50 .... F 5
97108 Beaver, 450 .... D 2
97004 Beavercreek, 708 ... B 2
97005 Beaverton, 18,577 .. A 2
97456 Bellfountain, 50 ... D 3
† 97701 Bend⊙, 13,710 ..... F 3
97058 Biggs, 50 .... G 2
97016 Birkenfeld, 45 ..... D 1
97412 Blachly, 425 .... D 3
† 97108 Blaine, 50 .... D 2
97326 Blodgett, 150 ...... D 3
97413 Blue River, 350 .... E 4
97622 Bly, 500 .... F 5
97818 Boardman, 192 ...... H 2
97623 Bonanza, 230 .... F 5
97008 Bonneville, 130 .... E 2
97009 Boring, 150 .... E 2
97021 Boyd, 26 .... F 2
97342 Breitenbush, 50 .... F 3
97820 Canyon City⊙, 600 .. J 3
97417 Canyonville, 940 ... D 5

97458 Bridge, 250 .... D 4
† 97819 Bridgeport, 45 .... K 3
† 97136 Brighton, 52 ...... C 2
97817 Brightwood, 420 .... E 2
97032 Broadacres, 80 ..... A 3
97414 Broadbent, 265 ..... C 4
97903 Brogan, 140 .... K 3
97415 Brookings, 2,720 ... C 5
97305 Brooks, 490 .... A 2
97840 Brownlee, 50 .... L 3
97524 Brownsboro, 50 ..... E 5
97327 Brownsville, 1,034 . E 3
97351 Buena Vista, 90 .... D 3
97420 Bunker Hill, 1,549 . C 4
97720 Burns⊙, 3,293 ...... H 4
97522 Butte Falls, 358 ... E 5
† 97002 Butteville, 385 ... A 2
97109 Buxton, 163 .... D 2
97416 Camas Valley, 665 .. D 4
97730 Camp Sherman, 87 ... F 3
† 97493 Canary, 50 .... D 3
97013 Canby, 3,813 .... B 2
97110 Cannon Beach, 779 .. D 2

97111 Carlton, 1,126 ..... D 2
† 97415 Carpenterville, 30 . C 5
† 97015 Carver, 500 .... B 2
97014 Cascade Locks, 574 . E 2
97329 Cascadia, 150 ...... E 3
97523 Cave Junction, 415 . D 5
97821 Cayuse, 300 .... J 2
97822 Cecil, 75 .... H 2
97225 Cedar Hills, 2,900 . A 2
† 97005 Cedar Mill, 1,500 . A 2
97058 Celilo, 50 .... F 2
97501 Central Point, 4,004 D 5
97420 Charleston, 500 .... C 4
97306 Chemawa, 900 .... A 3
97731 Chemult, 580 .... F 4
† 97058 Chenoweth, 2,329 .. F 2
97119 Cherry Grove, 200 .. D 2
97055 Cherryville, 280 ... E 2
97419 Cheshire, 750 ...... D 3
97624 Chiloquin, 826 ..... F 5
97015 Clackamas, 6,000 ... B 2
97016 Clatskanie, 1,286 .. D 1
97112 Cloverdale, 151 .... D 2
97401 Coburg, 665 .... E 3
97017 Colton, 305 .... B 3

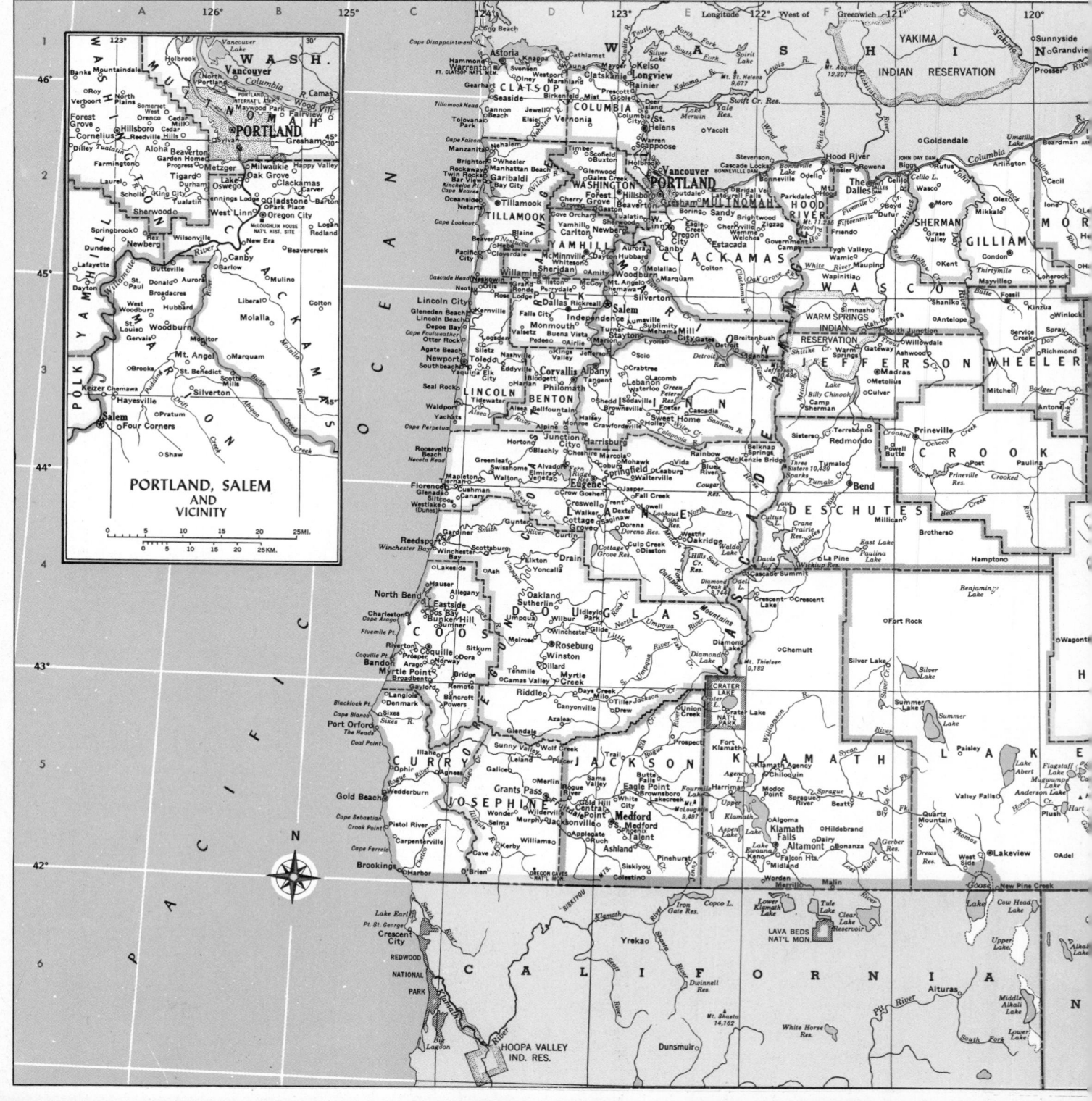

PORTLAND, SALEM AND VICINITY

AREA 96,981 sq. mi.
POPULATION 2,091,385
CAPITAL Salem
LARGEST CITY Portland
HIGHEST POINT Mt. Hood 11,235 ft.
SETTLED IN 1810
ADMITTED TO UNION February 14, 1859
POPULAR NAME Beaver State
STATE FLOWER Oregon Grape
STATE BIRD Western Meadowlark

Topography

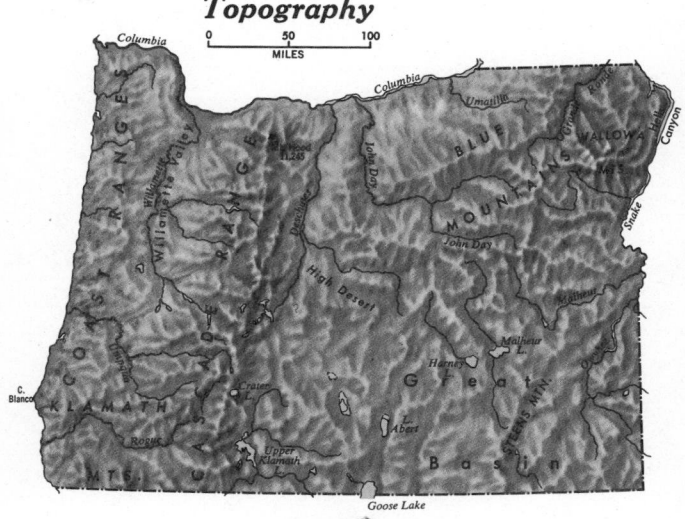

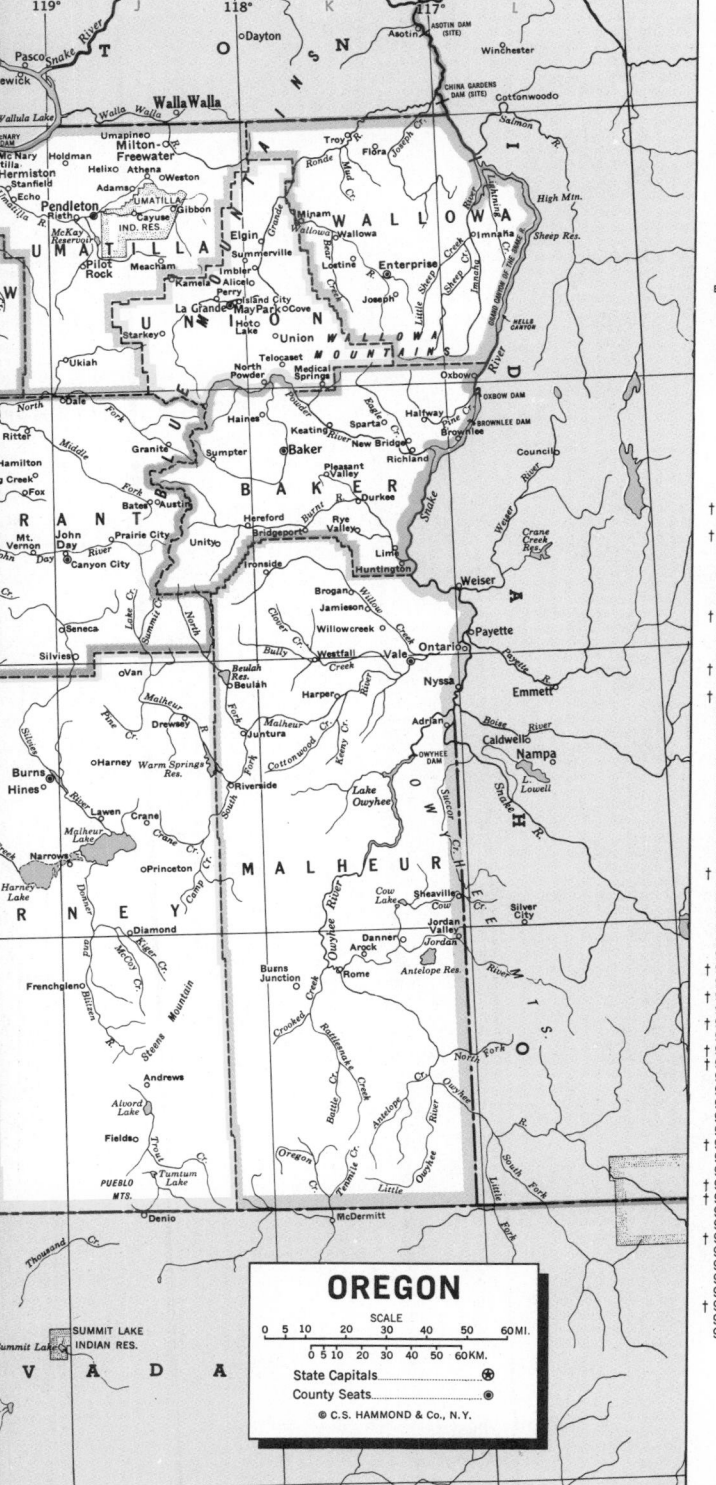

OREGON
SCALE
0 5 10 20 30 40 50 60 MI.
0 5 10 20 30 40 50 60 KM.
State Capitals ⊛
County Seats ◉
Ⓒ C.S. HAMMOND & CO., N.Y.

(continued on following page)

Agriculture, Industry and Resources

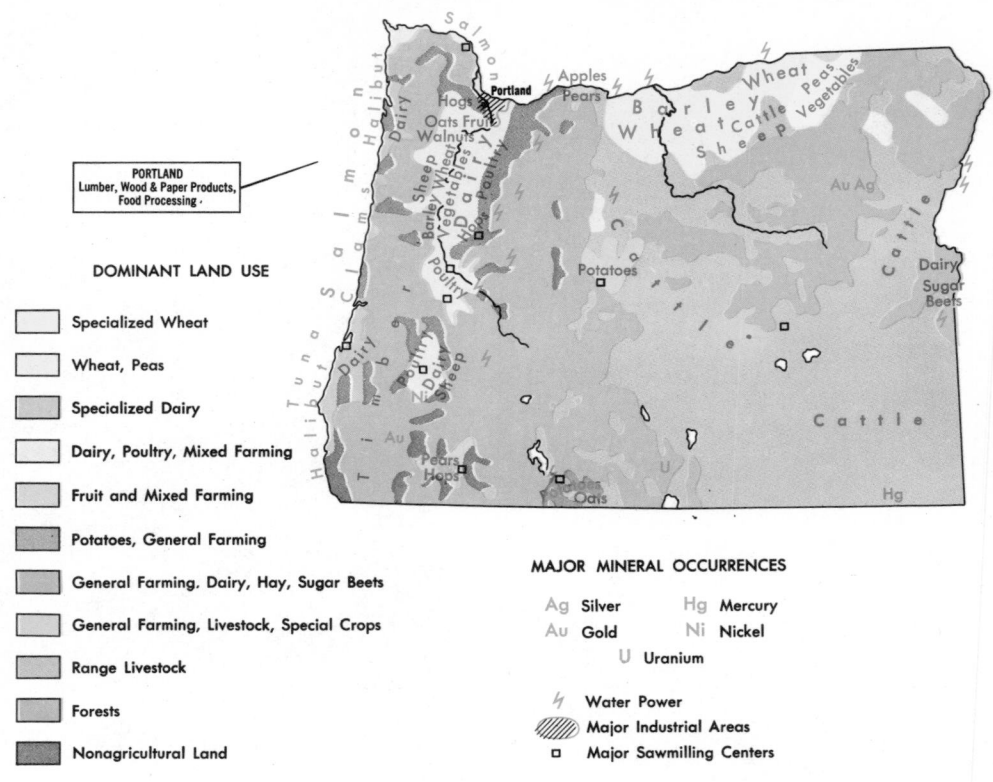

PORTLAND
Lumber, Wood & Paper Products,
Food Processing

DOMINANT LAND USE

Specialized Wheat

Wheat, Peas

Specialized Dairy

Dairy, Poultry, Mixed Farming

Fruit and Mixed Farming

Potatoes, General Farming

General Farming. Dairy, Hay, Sugar Beets

General Farming, Livestock, Special Crops

Range Livestock

Forests

Nonagricultural Land

MAJOR MINERAL OCCURRENCES

Ag Silver   Hg Mercury
Au Gold   Ni Nickel
       U Uranium

↯ Water Power
▨ Major Industrial Areas
□ Major Sawmilling Centers

Oregon's magnificently rugged coastline — sandy beaches interspersed with rock fragments ("stacks") torn from the cliffs.

Oregon State Highway Department

Agriculture, Industry and Resources

AREA 45,333 sq. mi.
POPULATION 11,793,909
CAPITAL Harrisburg
LARGEST CITY Philadelphia
HIGHEST POINT Mt. Davis 3,213 ft.
SETTLED IN 1682
ADMITTED TO UNION December 12, 1787
POPULAR NAME Keystone State
STATE FLOWER Mountain Laurel
STATE BIRD Ruffed Grouse

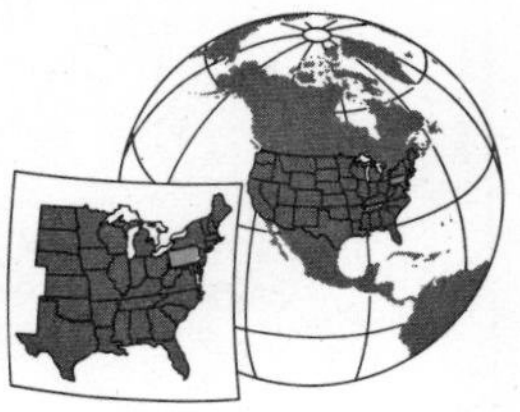

DOMINANT LAND USE

- Specialized Dairy
- Dairy, General Farming
- Fruit and Mixed Farming
- Fruit, Truck and Mixed Farming
- General Farming, Livestock, Tobacco
- General Farming, Livestock, Fruit, Tobacco
- Forests
- Urban Areas

MAJOR MINERAL OCCURRENCES

C	Coal	G	Natural Gas	Sl	Slate
Cl	Clay	Ls	Limestone	Ss	Sandstone
Co	Cobalt	O	Petroleum	Zn	Zinc
Fe	Iron Ore				

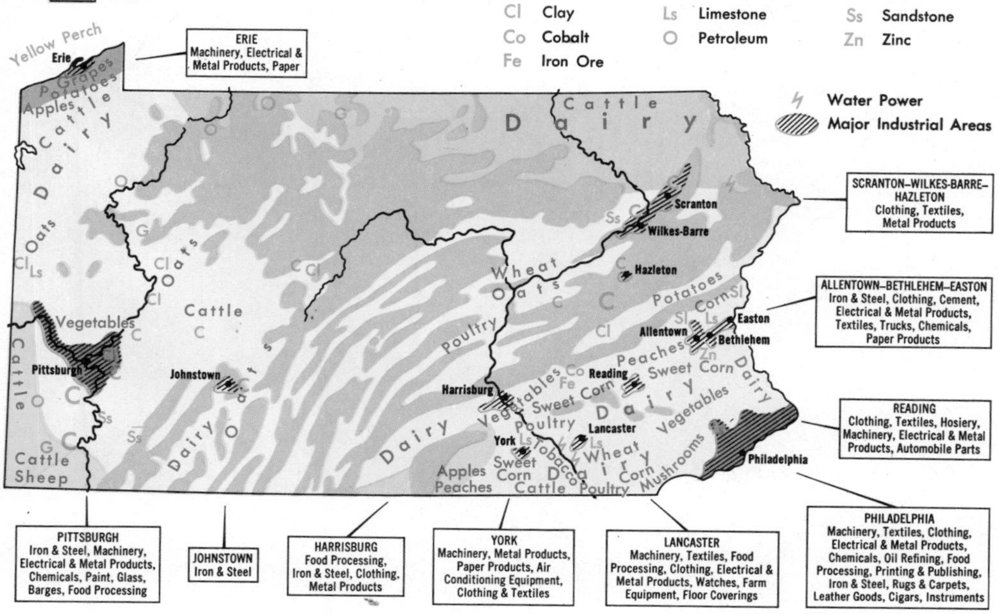
Water Power
Major Industrial Areas
ERIE
Machinery, Electrical & Metal Products, Paper
SCRANTON–WILKES-BARRE–HAZLETON
Clothing, Textiles, Metal Products
ALLENTOWN–BETHLEHEM–EASTON
Iron & Steel, Clothing, Cement, Electrical & Metal Products, Textiles, Trucks, Chemicals, Paper Products
READING
Clothing, Textiles, Hosiery, Machinery, Electrical & Metal Products, Automobile Parts
PHILADELPHIA
Machinery, Textiles, Clothing, Electrical & Metal Products, Chemicals, Oil Refining, Food Processing, Printing & Publishing, Iron & Steel, Rugs & Carpets, Leather Goods, Cigars, Instruments
PITTSBURGH
Iron & Steel, Machinery, Electrical & Metal Products, Chemicals, Paint, Glass, Barges, Food Processing
JOHNSTOWN
Iron & Steel
HARRISBURG
Food Processing, Iron & Steel, Clothing, Metal Products
YORK
Machinery, Metal Products, Paper Products, Air Conditioning Equipment, Clothing & Textiles
LANCASTER
Machinery, Textiles, Food Processing, Clothing, Electrical & Metal Products, Watches, Farm Equipment, Floor Coverings
Yellow Perch
Erie
Grapes
Potatoes
Apples
Cattle
Dairy
Oats
Vegetables
Pittsburgh
Johnstown
Cattle
Sheep
Scranton
Wilkes-Barre
Hazleton
Wheat
Poultry
Potatoes
Corn
Allentown
Easton
Bethlehem
Peaches
Sweet Corn
Reading
Harrisburg
Vegetables
Lancaster
York
Tobacco
Mushrooms
Philadelphia
Apples
Peaches

COUNTIES

County	Key
Adams, 56,937	H 6
Allegheny, 1,605,016	B 5
Armstrong, 75,590	D 4
Beaver, 208,418	B 4
Bedford, 42,353	E 6
Berks, 296,382	K 5
Blair, 135,356	F 4
Bradford, 57,962	J 2
Bucks, 415,056	M 5
Butler, 127,941	C 4
Cambria, 186,785	E 4
Cameron, 7,096	F 3
Carbon, 50,573	L 4
Centre, 99,267	G 4
Chester, 278,311	L 6
Clarion, 38,414	D 3
Clearfield, 74,619	F 3
Clinton, 37,721	G 3
Columbia, 55,114	K 3
Crawford, 81,342	B 2
Cumberland, 158,177	H 5
Dauphin, 223,834	J 5
Delaware, 600,035	M 6
Elk, 37,770	E 3
Erie, 263,654	B 2
Fayette, 154,667	C 6
Forest, 4,926	D 2
Franklin, 100,833	G 6
Fulton, 10,776	F 6
Greene, 36,090	B 6
Huntingdon, 39,108	F 5
Indiana, 79,451	D 4
Jefferson, 43,695	D 3
Juniata, 16,712	H 4
Lackawanna, 234,107	L 3
Lancaster, 319,693	K 5
Lawrence, 107,374	B 4
Lebanon, 99,665	K 5
Lehigh, 255,304	L 4
Luzerne, 342,301	L 3
Lycoming, 113,296	H 3
McKean, 51,915	E 2
Mercer, 127,175	B 3
Mifflin, 45,268	G 4
Monroe, 45,422	M 3
Montgomery, 623,799	M 5
Montour, 16,508	J 3
Northampton, 214,368	M 4
Northumberland, 99,190	J 4
Perry, 28,615	H 5
Philadelphia (city county), 1,948,609	M 6
Pike, 11,818	M 3
Potter, 16,395	G 2
Schuylkill, 160,089	K 4
Snyder, 29,269	H 4
Somerset, 76,037	D 6
Sullivan, 5,961	J 3
Susquehanna, 34,344	L 2
Tioga, 39,691	H 2
Union, 28,603	H 4
Venango, 62,353	C 3
Warren, 47,682	D 2
Washington, 210,876	B 5
Wayne, 29,581	M 2
Westmoreland, 376,935	D 5
Wyoming, 19,082	K 2
York, 272,603	J 6

CITIES and TOWNS

Zip	Name/Pop.	Key
19001	Abington, 8,594	M 5
19501	Adamstown, 1,202	K 5
17501	Akron, 3,149	K 5
16401	Albion, 1,768	B 2
18011	Alburtis, 1,142	L 5
19018	Aldan, 5,001	M 7
15001	Aliquippa, 22,277	B 4
* 18101	Allentown⊙, 109,527	L 4
	Allentown-Bethlehem-Easton, ‡543,551	L 4
15101	Allison Park, 7,500	C 4
* 16601	Altoona, 62,900	F 4
	Altoona, ‡135,356	F 4
19002	Ambler, 7,800	M 5
15003	Ambridge, 11,324	B 4
19020	Andalusia, 8,169	N 5
17003	Annville, 4,704	J 5
15613	Apollo, 2,308	C 4
18403	Archbald, 6,118	M 2
19003	Ardmore, 5,801	M 6
15068	Arnold, 8,174	C 4
17921	Ashland, 4,737	K 4
18706	Ashley, 4,095	L 3
15215	Aspinwall, 3,541	C 6
18810	Athens, 4,173	K 2
17851	Atlas, 1,527	K 4
15202	Avalon, 7,065	B 6
15312	Avella, 1,109	B 5
17721	Avis, 1,749	H 3
18641	Avoca, 3,543	L 3
19311	Avondale, 1,025	L 6
15618	Avonmore, 1,267	C 4
15005	Baden, 5,536	B 4
17502	Bainbridge, 950	J 5
19004	Bala-Cynwyd, 6,483	N 6
† 15201	Baldwin, 26,729	B 7
19503	Bally, 1,197	L 5
18013	Bangor, 5,425	M 4
15714	Barnesboro, 2,708	E 4
18014	Bath, 1,829	M 4
15009	Beaver⊙, 6,100	B 4
15921	Beaverdale, 1,579	E 5
15010	Beaver Falls, 14,375	B 4
18216	Beaver Meadows, 1,274	L 4
15522	Bedford⊙, 3,302	F 5
16823	Bellefonte⊙, 6,828	G 4
15012	Belle Vernon, 1,496	C 5
17004	Belleville, 1,817	G 4
15202	Bellevue, 11,586	B 6
16617	Bellwood, 2,395	F 4
† 15201	Ben Avon, 2,713	B 6
15314	Bentleyville, 2,714	B 5
17814	Benton, 1,027	K 3
15530	Berlin, 1,766	E 6
18603	Berwick, 12,274	K 3
19312	Berwyn, 14,000	L 5
16112	Bessemer, 1,427	B 4
19507	Bethel, 950	K 5
15102	Bethel Park, 34,791	B 7
* 18015	Bethlehem, 72,686	M 4
17307	Biglerville, 977	H 6
19508	Birdsboro, 3,196	L 5
15716	Black Lick, 1,074	D 4
15717	Blairsville, 4,411	D 5
18447	Blakely, 6,391	L 2
15238	Blawnox, 1,907	C 6
15224	Bloomfield (New Bloomfield)⊙, 1,032	H 5
17815	Bloomsburg⊙, 11,652	J 3
16912	Blossburg, 1,753	H 2
17214	Blue Ridge Summit, 950	G 6
16827	Boalsburg, 950	G 4
15315	Bobtown, 1,055	B 6
17007	Boiling Springs, 1,521	H 5
19061	Boothwyn, 8,900	L 7
15135	Boston, 2,500	C 7
15531	Boswell, 1,529	E 5
19512	Boyertown, 4,428	L 5
15014	Brackenridge, 4,796	C 4
15104	Braddock, 8,682	C 7
16701	Bradford, 12,672	E 2
15227	Brentwood, 13,732	B 7
19405	Bridgeport, 5,630	M 5
15017	Bridgeville, 6,717	B 5
15009	Bridgewater, 966	B 4
19007	Bristol (borough), 12,085	N 5
19007	Bristol (urban township), 67,498	N 5
15824	Brockway, 2,529	E 3
19015	Brookhaven, 7,370	M 7
15825	Brookville⊙, 4,314	D 3
19008	Broomall, 20,000	M 6
15236	Broughton, 3,276	B 7
15417	Brownsville, 4,856	C 5
19009	Bryn Athyn, 970	M 5
19010	Bryn Mawr, 5,737	M 5
15021	Burgettstown, 2,118	A 5
17009	Burnham, 2,607	H 4
16001	Butler⊙, 18,691	C 4
16212	Cadogan, ∆563	C 4
15419	California, 6,635	C 5
16403	Cambridge Springs, 1,998	C 2
17011	Camp Hill, 9,931	H 5
18325	Canadensis, 950	M 3
15317	Canonsburg, 11,439	B 5
17724	Canton, 2,037	J 2
18407	Carbondale, 12,808	L 2
17013	Carlisle⊙, 18,079	H 5
15106	Carnegie, 10,864	B 7
15722	Carrolltown, 1,507	E 4
15234	Castle Shannon, 11,899	B 7
18032	Catasauqua, 5,702	M 4
17820	Catawissa, 1,701	K 4
15321	Cecil, 1,900	B 5
16404	Centerville, 4,175	B 6
15926	Central City, 1,547	E 5
17927	Centralia, 1,165	K 4
16828	Centre Hall, 1,282	G 4
18914	Chalfont, 2,366	M 5
17201	Chambersburg⊙, 17,315	G 6
15022	Charleroi, 6,723	C 5
† 19380	Chatwood, 7,168	L 6
19012	Cheltenham, ∆40,238	M 5
* 19013	Chester, 56,331	L 7
19017	Chester Heights, 1,277	L 7
15024	Cheswick, 2,580	C 6
16025	Chicora, 1,166	C 4
17509	Christiana, 1,132	K 6
† 15201	Churchill, 4,690	C 7
15025	Clairton, 15,051	C 7
16214	Clarion⊙, 6,095	D 3
18411	Clarks Summit, 5,376	L 3
16625	Claysburg, 1,516	F 5
15323	Claysville, 951	B 5
16830	Clearfield⊙, 8,176	F 3
19018	Clifton Heights, 8,348	M 7
15728	Clymer, 2,054	E 4
18218	Coaldale, 3,023	L 4
19320	Coatesville, 12,331	L 5
16314	Cochranton, 1,229	B 2
19426	Collegeville, 3,191	M 5
19023	Collingdale, 10,605	N 7
18915	Colmar, 950	M 5
17512	Columbia, 11,237	K 5
16405	Columbus, 950	C 2
15927	Colver, 1,175	E 4
† 19023	Colwyn, 3,169	N 7
15424	Confluence, 954	D 6
16406	Conneautville, 1,032	A 2
15425	Connellsville, 11,643	C 5
19428	Conshohocken, 10,195	M 5
15027	Conway, 2,822	B 4
18219	Conyngham, 1,850	K 3
18036	Coopersburg, 2,326	M 5
18037	Coplay, 3,642	L 4
15108	Coraopolis, 8,435	B 4
17016	Cornwall, 2,111	K 5
16407	Corry, 7,435	C 2
16915	Coudersport⊙, 2,831	G 2
15624	Crabtree, 1,021	D 5
15205	Crafton, 8,233	B 7
16630	Cresson, 2,446	E 5
17929	Cressona, 1,814	K 4
19022	Crum Lynne, 3,700	M 7
15031	Cuddy, 2,500	B 5
16833	Curwensville, 3,189	E 4
† 15901	Dale, 2,274	E 5
18612	Dallas, 2,913	K 3
17313	Dallastown, 3,560	J 6
18414	Dalton, 1,282	L 2
17821	Danville⊙, 6,176	J 4
19023	Darby, 13,729	M 7
17018	Dauphin, 998	J 5
15626	Delmont, 1,934	D 5
17517	Denver, 2,248	K 5
15627	Derry, 3,338	D 5
18519	Dickson City, 7,698	L 3
17019	Dillsburg, 1,441	J 5
15734	Dixonville, 950	D 4
15033	Donora, 8,825	C 5
15216	Dormont, 12,856	B 7
19518	Douglassville, 975	L 5
17315	Dover, 1,168	J 6
19335	Downingtown, 7,437	L 5
18901	Doylestown⊙, 8,270	M 5
15034	Dravosburg, 2,916	C 7
19026	Drexel Hill, 50,000	M 6
18221	Drifton, 1,295	L 3
15801	DuBois, 10,112	E 3
† 17701	Duboistown, 1,468	H 3
15431	Dunbar, 1,499	C 6
17020	Duncannon, 1,739	H 5
16635	Duncansville, 2,210	F 5
18512	Dunmore, 17,300	L 3
15110	Duquesne, 11,410	C 7
18642	Duryea, 5,264	L 3
17316	East Berlin, 1.086	J 6
† 18603	East Berwick, 2,090	K 3
16028	East Brady, 1,218	C 3
15909	East Conemaugh, 2,710	E 5
† 17701	East Faxon, 4,175	J 3
18041	East Greenville, 2,003	L 5
† 19050	East Lansdowne, 3,186	M 7
18042	Easton⊙, 30,256	M 4
17520	East Petersburg, 3,407	K 5
18301	East Stroudsburg, 7,894	M 4
† 15301	East Washington, 2,198	B 5
15931	Ebensburg⊙, 4,318	E 5
† 15005	Economy, 7,176	B 4
19020	Eddington, 20,517	N 5
19013	Eddystone, 2,706	M 7
† 15201	Edgewood, 5,101	B 7
† 15143	Edgeworth, 2,200	B 4
16412	Edinboro, 4,871	B 2
16731	Eldred, 1,092	F 2
15037	Elizabeth, 2,206	C 5
17022	Elizabethtown, 8,072	J 5
17023	Elizabethville, 1,629	J 4
16920	Elkland, 1,942	H 1
15331	Ellsworth, 1,268	B 5
16117	Ellwood City, 10,857	B 4
15038	Elrama, 950	C 5
17824	Elysburg, 1,337	K 4
18049	Emmaus, 11,511	M 4
15834	Emporium⊙, 3,074	F 2
15202	Emsworth, 3,332	B 6
17025	Enola, 4,900	J 5
17522	Ephrata, 9,662	K 5
* 16501	Erie⊙, 129,231	B 1
	Erie, ‡263,654	B 1
17815	Espy, 1,652	K 4
19029	Essington, 3,100	M 7
15223	Etna, 5,819	B 6
16033	Evans City, 2,144	B 4
15537	Everett, 2,243	F 5
15631	Everson, 1,143	C 5
15632	Export, 1,402	C 5
15436	Fairchance, 1,906	C 6
19030	Fairless Hills, 16,000	N 5
16415	Fairview, 1,707	B 1
15840	Falls Creek, 1,255	E 3
16121	Farrell, 11,022	A 3
15438	Fayette City, 968	C 5
17222	Fayetteville, 2,449	G 6
18921	Ferndale, 2,482	E 5
19522	Fleetwood, 3,064	L 5
17745	Flemington, 1,519	G 3
† 17552	Florin, 975	J 5
19032	Folcroft, 9,610	M 7
19033	Folsom, 7,815	M 7
16226	Ford City, 4,749	D 4
18421	Forest City, 2,322	L 2
15221	Forest Hills, 9,561	C 7
18704	Forty Fort, 6,114	L 3
† 18015	Fountain Hill, 5,384	L 4
15238	Fox Chapel, 4,684	C 6
17931	Frackville, 5,445	K 4
16323	Franklin⊙, 8,629	C 3
17026	Fredericksburg, 1,073	B 2
17026	Fredericksburg, 950	J 5
15333	Fredericktown, 1,067	C 6
15042	Freedom, 2,643	B 4
18224	Freeland, 4,784	L 3
18017	Freemansburg, 1,681	M 4
16229	Freeport, 2,375	C 4
† 16117	Frisco, 950	B 4
16922	Galeton, 1,552	G 2
16641	Gallitzin, 2,496	E 4
17527	Gap, 1,022	L 6
† 17701	Garden View, 2,662	H 3
15904	Geistown, 3,633	E 5
17325	Gettysburg⊙, 7,275	H 6
17934	Gilberton, 1,293	K 4
16417	Girard, 2,613	B 2
17935	Girardville, 2,450	K 4
15045	Glassport, 7,450	C 7
18617	Glen Lyon, 3,408	K 3
19036	Glenolden, 8,697	M 7
19037	Glen Riddle, 950	L 7
17327	Glen Rock, 1,600	J 6
15116	Glenshaw, 19,500	C 6
19038	Glenside, 17,353	M 5
15634	Grapeville, 1,600	C 5
17225	Greencastle, 3,293	G 6
15601	Greensburg⊙, 15,870	D 5
† 15201	Greentree, 6,441	B 7
16125	Greenville, 8,704	B 3
16127	Grove City, 8,312	B 3
18822	Hallstead, 1,447	L 2
19526	Hamburg, 3,909	L 4
17331	Hanover, 15,623	J 6
† 15201	Harmarville, 1,900	C 6
16037	Harmony, 1,207	B 4
* 17101	Harrisburg (cap.)⊙, 68,061	H 5
	Harrisburg, ‡410,626	H 5
18618	Harveys Lake, 1,693	K 3
16646	Hastings, 1,791	E 4
19040	Hatboro, 8,880	M 5
19440	Hatfield, 2,385	M 5
19041	Haverford, ∆55,132	M 6
19083	Havertown, 42,500	M 6
16840	Hawk Run, 1,020	F 4
18428	Hawley, 1,331	M 3
18201	Hazleton, 30,426	L 4
15106	Heidelberg, 2,034	B 7
17406	Hellam, 1,825	J 6
18055	Hellertown, 6,613	M 4
15637	Herminie, 975	C 5
17033	Hershey, 7,407	J 5
† 17044	Highland Park, 1,704	H 4
17034	High Spire, 2,947	J 5
16132	Hillsville, 950	A 4
16648	Hollidaysburg⊙, 6,262	F 5
15748	Homer City, 2,465	D 4
15120	Homestead, 6,309	B 7
18431	Honesdale⊙, 5,224	M 2
19344	Honey Brook, 1,115	L 5
15936	Hooversville, 962	E 5
15445	Hopwood, 2,190	C 6

(continued on following page)

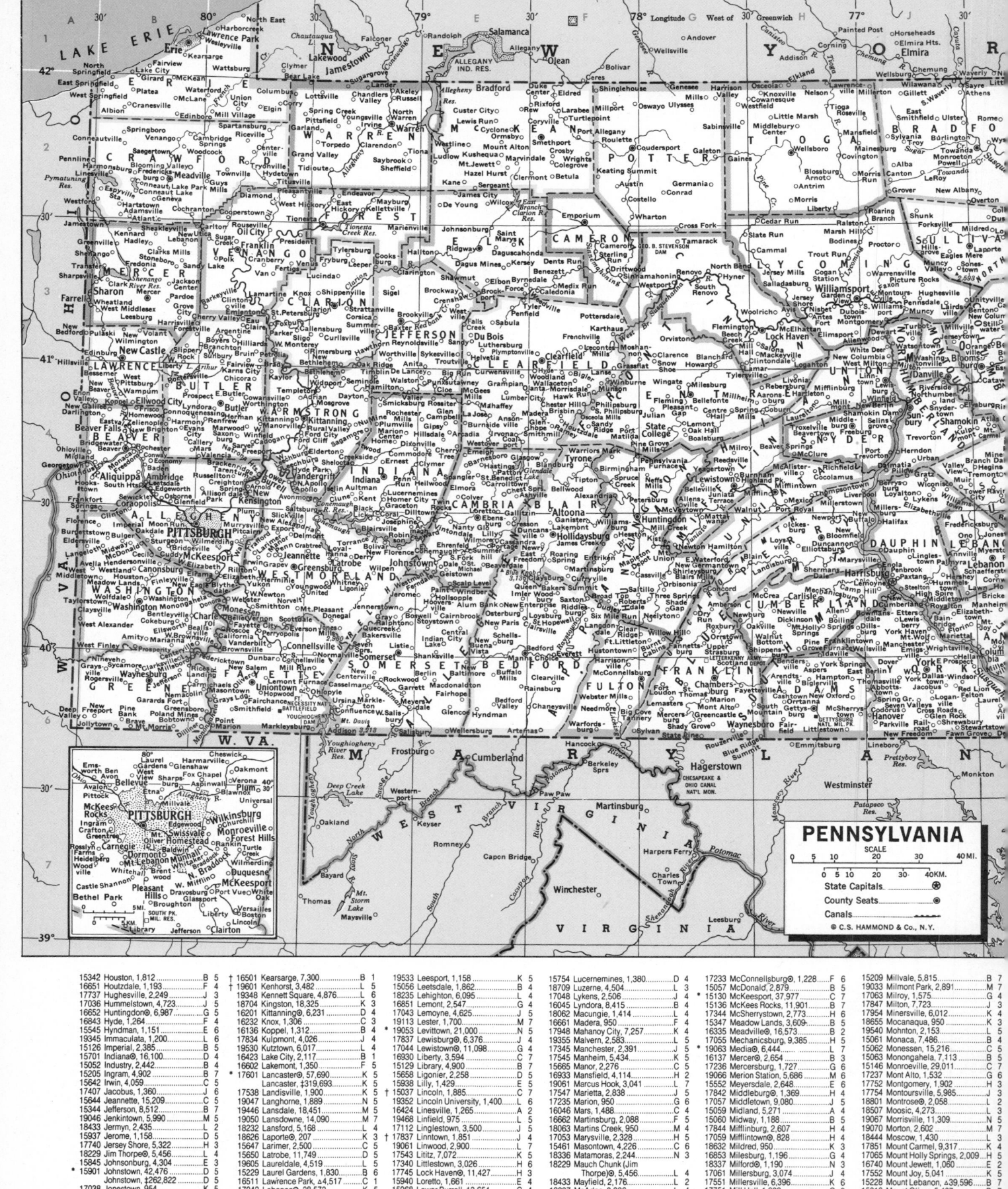

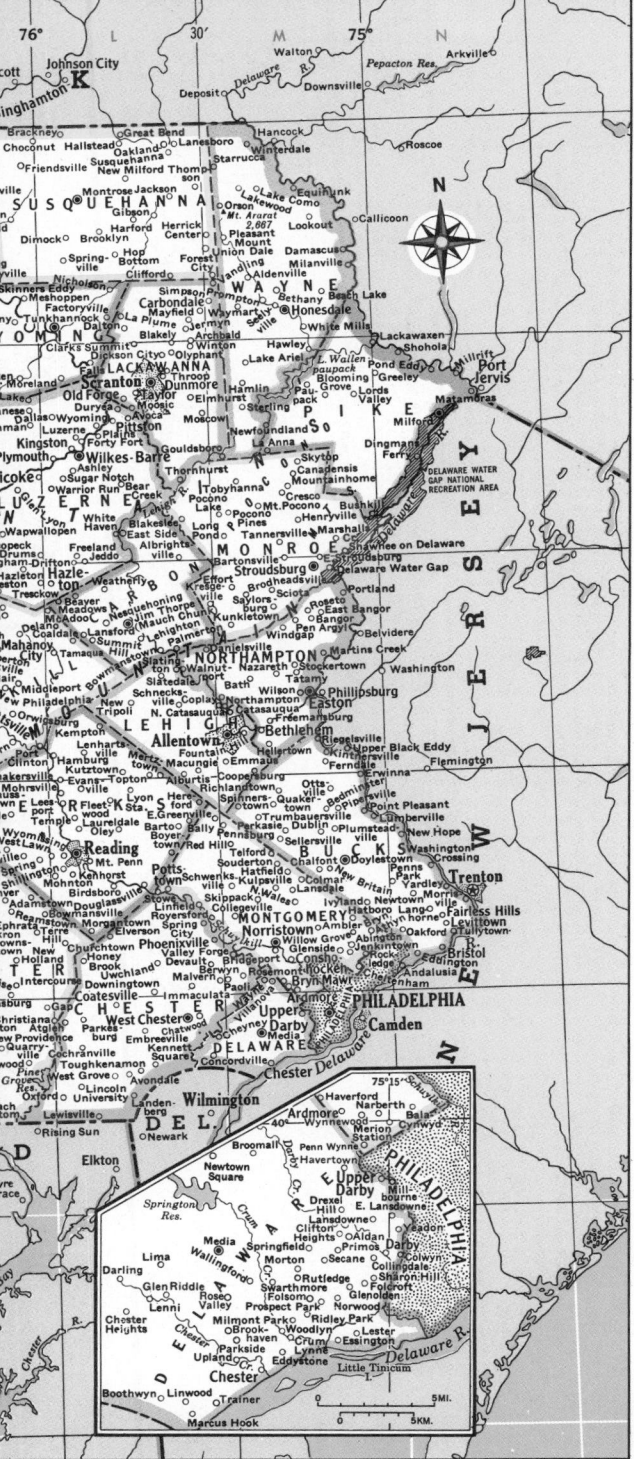

19074 Norwood, 7,229........M 7
18636 Noxen, 950........K 3
18241 Nuremberg, 950........K 4
15071 Oakdale, 1,614........B 5
† 19047 Oakford, 3,800........M 5
15139 Oakmont, 7,550........C 6
† 15059 Ohioville, 3,918........A 4
16301 Oil City, 15,033........C 3
18518 Old Forge, 9,522........L 4
15472 Oliver, 3,091........C 6
18447 Olyphant, 5,422........L 3
17961 Orwigsburg, 2,661........K 4
16666 Osceola Mills, 1,671........F 4
19363 Oxford, 3,658........L 6
† 15963 Paint, 1,233........E 5
18071 Palmerton, 5,620........K 4
17078 Palmyra, 7,615........J 5
19301 Paoli, 5,835........M 5
17562 Paradise, 975........L 6
19365 Parkesburg, 2,701........L 6
† 19013 Parkside, 2,343........M 7
† 17331 Parkville, 5,120........J 4
16668 Patton, 2,762........E 4
17111 Paxtang, 2,160........J 5
18072 Pen Argyl, 3,668........M 4
17103 Penbrook, 3,379........J 5
18073 Pennsburg, 2,260........L 5
† 19003 Penn Wynne, 6,038........M 6
18944 Perkasie, 5,451........L 5
15473 Perryopolis, 2,043........C 5
† 19101 Philadelphia⊙, 1,948,609......N 6
   Philadelphia, ‡4,817,914........N 6
16866 Philipsburg, 3,700........F 4
19460 Phoenixville, 14,823........L 5
17963 Pine Grove, 2,197........K 4
16868 Pine Grove Mills, 950........G 4
15140 Pitcairn, 4,741........C 6
† 15201 Pittsburgh⊙, 520,117......B 7
   Pittsburgh, ‡2,401,245........B 7
† 18640 Pittston, 11,113........L 3
18705 Plains, 6,606........L 3
16823 Pleasant Gap, 1,773........G 4
15236 Pleasant Hills, 10,409........B 7
16341 Pleasantville, 1,005........C 2
15239 Plum, 21,932........C 6
18651 Plymouth, 9,536........K 3
† 16830 Plymptonville, 1,040........E 3
15474 Point Marion, 1,750........C 6
16342 Polk, 3,673........C 3
15946 Portage, 4,151........E 5
16743 Port Allegany, 2,703........F 2
17965 Port Carbon, 2,717........K 4
15133 Port Vue, 5,862........C 7
19464 Pottstown, 25,355........L 5
17901 Pottsville⊙, 19,715........K 4
19018 Primos, 3,900........M 7
16052 Prospect, 973........B 4
19076 Prospect Park, 7,250........M 7
15767 Punxsutawney, 7,792........D 4
18951 Quakertown, 7,276........M 5
17566 Quarryville, 1,571........K 6
† 15104 Rankin, 3,817........C 7
† 19601 Reading⊙, 87,643........L 5
   Reading, ‡415,056........L 5
17567 Reamstown, 1,050........K 5
18076 Red Hill, 1,201........L 5
17356 Red Lion, 5,645........J 6
17084 Reedsville, 950........G 4
17764 Renovo, 2,620........G 3
15851 Reynoldsville, 2,771........D 3
17087 Richland, 1,444........K 5
15853 Ridgway⊙, 6,022........E 3
19078 Ridley Park, 9,025........M 7
18077 Riegelsville, 1,050........M 4
15678 Rillton, 975........C 6
16248 Rimersburg, 1,146........D 3
17868 Riverside, 1,905........J 4
16673 Roaring Spring, 2,811........F 5
19551 Robesonia, 1,685........K 5
15949 Robinson, 975........C 4
15074 Rochester, 4,819........B 4
19111 Rockledge, 2,564........M 5
15557 Rockwood, 1,051........D 6
15477 Roscoe, 1,176........C 5
19010 Rosemont, 4,900........M 6
18013 Roseto, 1,538........M 4
17250 Rouzerville, 1,419........G 6
† 17067 Royalton, 1,040........J 5
19468 Royersford, 4,235........L 5
16249 Rural Valley, 962........D 4

16345 Russell, 950........D 2
15076 Russellton, 1,597........C 4
19070 Rutledge, 1,167........M 7
16433 Saegertown, 1,348........B 2
17970 Saint Clair, 4,576........K 4
15857 Saint Marys, 7,470........E 3
15951 Saint Michael, 1,248........E 5
15681 Saltsburg, 1,037........C 4
† 16056 Sandy, 2,000........E 3
16056 Saxonburg, 1,191........C 4
18840 Sayre, 7,473........K 2
15963 Scalp Level, 1,353........E 5
17088 Schaefferstown, 1,027........K 5
18078 Schnecksville, 1,550........L 4
17972 Schuylkill Haven, 6,125........K 4
18354 Sciota, 950........M 4
15683 Scottdale, 5,818........C 5
* 18501 Scranton⊙, 103,564........L 3
   Scranton, ‡234,107........L 3
19018 Secane, 5,700........M 7
17870 Selinsgrove, 5,116........J 4
18960 Sellersville, 2,829........M 5
15143 Sewickley, 5,660........B 4
17872 Shamokin, 11,719........J 4
17876 Shamokin Dam, 1,562........J 4
16146 Sharon, 22,653........B 3
19079 Sharon Hill, 7,464........N 7
15215 Sharpsburg, 5,499........B 6
16150 Sharpsville, 6,126........A 3
16347 Sheffield, 1,564........D 2
15963 Shenandoah, 8,287........K 4
18655 Shickshinny, 1,685........K 3
19607 Shillington, 6,249........L 5
16748 Shinglehouse, 1,320........F 2
17257 Shippensburg, 6,536........H 5
19555 Shoemakersville, 1,427........K 4
17361 Shrewsbury, 1,716........J 6
18407 Simpson, 1,900........L 3
19608 Sinking Spring, 2,862........K 5
19474 Skippack, 975........M 5
18080 Slatington, 4,687........L 4
15684 Slickville, 1,066........C 5
16057 Slippery Rock, 4,949........B 3
16749 Smethport⊙, 1,883........F 2
15478 Smithfield, 966........C 6
15501 Somerset⊙, 6,269........D 6
18964 Souderton, 6,366........M 5
15425 South Connellsville, 2,385........C 6
15956 South Fork, 1,661........E 5
† 14892 South Waverly, 1,307........J 2
17701 South Williamsport, 7,153........J 3
15775 Spangler, 3,109........E 4
19475 Spring City, 3,578........L 5
15144 Springdale, 5,202........C 6
19064 Springfield, ▲2,446........M 7
17362 Spring Grove, 1,669........J 4
16801 State College, 33,778........G 4
17113 Steelton, 8,556........J 5
17363 Stewartstown, 1,157........K 6
16153 Stoneboro, 1,129........B 3
19464 Stowe, 3,596........L 5
17579 Strasburg, 1,897........K 6
18360 Stroudsburg⊙, 5,451........M 4
† 16323 Sugarcreek, 5,944........C 3
18706 Sugar Notch, 1,333........L 3
18250 Summit Hill, 3,811........L 4
18847 Susquehanna, 2,319........L 2
19081 Swarthmore, 6,156........M 7
15218 Swissvale, 13,821........C 7
15865 Sykesville, 1,311........E 3
18252 Tamaqua, 9,246........L 4
15084 Tarentum, 7,379........C 4
18517 Taylor, 6,977........L 3
18969 Telford, 3,409........M 5
19560 Temple, 1,667........L 5
16259 Templeton, 950........C 4
17581 Terre Hill, 1,129........L 5
18512 Throop, 4,307........L 3
16353 Tionesta⊙, 711........C 2
16354 Titusville, 7,331........C 2
19562 Topton, 1,744........L 5
19374 Toughkenamon, 1,233........L 6
18848 Towanda⊙, 4,224........J 2
17980 Tower City, 1,774........J 4
15085 Trafford, 4,383........C 5
† 19013 Trainer, 2,336........M 7
17981 Tremont, 1,833........K 4
18254 Trescow, 1,146........K 4
17881 Trevorton, 2,196........J 4

16947 Troy, 1,315........J 2
19007 Tullytown, 2,194........N 5
18657 Tunkhannock⊙, 2,251........L 2
15145 Turtle Creek, 8,308........C 7
15960 Twin Rocks, 975........E 4
16686 Tyrone, 7,072........F 4
16438 Union City, 3,631........C 2
15401 Uniontown⊙, 16,282........C 6
15689 United, 975........D 5
15235 Universal, 1,900........C 7
† 19013 Upland, 3,930........M 7
19082 Upper Darby, ▲95,910........M 6
19481 Valley Forge, 400........L 5
17983 Valley View, 1,585........J 4
15690 Vandergrift, 7,873........D 4
15147 Verona, 3,737........C 6
15132 Versailles, 2,754........C 7
19085 Villanova, 5,250........M 6
15148 Wall, 1,265........C 7
19086 Wallingford, 3,500........L 7
18088 Walnutport, 1,942........L 4
16157 Wampum, 1,189........B 4
16365 Warren⊙, 12,998........D 2
15301 Washington⊙, 19,827........B 5
16441 Waterford, 1,468........C 2
17777 Watsontown, 2,514........J 4
18472 Waymart, 1,122........M 2
19087 Wayne, 10,011........G 6
17268 Waynesboro, 10,011........G 6
15370 Waynesburg⊙, 5,152........B 6
18255 Weatherly, 2,554........L 4
16901 Wellsboro⊙, 4,003........H 2
19565 Wernersville, 1,761........K 5
16510 Wesleyville, 3,920........C 1
15417 West Brownsville, 1,426........C 5
19380 West Chester⊙, 19,301........L 6
16692 Westfield, 1,273........H 2
19390 West Grove, 1,870........L 6
18201 West Hazleton, 6,059........K 4
16201 West Kittanning, 956........C 4
19609 West Lawn, 1,973........K 5
15656 West Leechburg, 1,422........C 4
16159 West Middlesex, 1,293........B 3
15122 West Mifflin, 28,070........C 7
15901 Westmont, 6,673........D 5
15089 West Newton, 3,648........C 5
15229 West View, 8,312........B 6
17401 West York, 5,314........J 6
16161 Wheatland, 1,421........B 3
15120 Whitaker, 1,697........C 7
18052 Whitehall, 16,551........L 4
18661 White Haven, 2,134........L 3
15131 White Oak, 9,304........C 7
17097 Wiconisco, 1,236........J 4
16370 Wilcox, 950........E 3
* 18701 Wilkes-Barre⊙, 58,856........L 3
   Wilkes-Barre-Hazleton, ‡342,301........L 3
15221 Wilkinsburg, 26,780........C 7
16693 Williamsburg, 1,704........F 5
17701 Williamsport⊙, 37,918........H 3
17098 Williamstown, 1,919........J 4
19090 Willow Grove, 16,494........M 5
15148 Wilmerding, 3,218........C 7
15025 Wilson, 8,482........M 4
15963 Windber, 6,332........E 5
18091 Windgap, 2,270........M 4
17366 Windsor, 1,298........J 6
† 18434 Winton, 4,948........M 3
15301 Wolfdale, 1,202........B 5
19567 Womelsdorf, 1,551........K 5
19094 Woodlyn, 6,500........M 7
17368 Wrightsville, 2,668........J 5
19096 Wynnewood, 9,200........M 6
18644 Wyoming, 4,195........L 3
19610 Wyomissing, 7,136........K 5
19067 Yardley, 2,616........N 5
19050 Yeadon, 12,136........N 7
16901 Yeagertown, 1,363........G 4
* 17401 York⊙, 50,335........J 6
   York, ‡329,540........J 6
16371 Youngsville, 2,158........D 2
15697 Youngwood, 3,057........D 5
16063 Zelienople, 3,602........B 4

⊙ County seat.
‡ Population of metropolitan area.
▲ Population of town or township.
† Zip of nearest p.o.
* Multiple zips

15666 Mount Pleasant, 5,895........D 5
18344 Mount Pocono, 1,019........M 3
17066 Mount Union, 3,662........G 5
17554 Mountville, 1,454........K 5
17347 Mount Wolf, 1,811........J 5
17756 Muncy, 2,872........J 3
15120 Munhall, 16,674........C 7
15668 Murrysville, 3,900........C 5
17067 Myerstown, 3,645........K 5
18634 Nanticoke, 14,632........K 3
15943 Nanty Glo, 4,298........E 5
19072 Narberth, 5,151........M 6
15065 Natrona Heights, 15,000........C 4
18064 Nazareth, 5,815........M 4
15351 Nemacolin, 1,273........B 6
18635 Nescopeck, 1,897........K 3
18240 Nesquehoning, 3,338........L 4
16141 New Beaver, 1,426........A 4
16140 New Bedford, 950........A 3
16242 New Bethlehem, 1,406........D 3
† 17068 New Bloomfield, 1,032........H 5
15066 New Brighton, 7,637........B 4
18901 New Britain, 2,428........M 5
16101 New Castle⊙, 38,559........B 3
17070 New Cumberland, 9,803........J 5
15067 New Eagle, 2,497........B 5

17349 New Freedom, 1,495........J 6
17557 New Holland, 3,971........K 5
18938 New Hope, 978........N 5
15068 New Kensington, 20,312........C 4
18834 New Milford, 1,143........L 2
17350 New Oxford, 1,495........H 6
17959 New Philadelphia, 1,528........K 4
17074 Newport, 1,747........H 5
15468 New Salem, 1,337........C 6
15626 New Salem (Delmont), 1,934........D 5
18940 Newtown, 2,216........N 5
19073 Newtown Square, 16,000........L 6
17241 Newville, 1,631........H 5
16142 New Wilmington, 2,721........B 3
17759 Nisbet, 950........H 3
19401 Norristown⊙, 38,169........M 5
18067 Northampton, 8,389........M 4
18067 North Apollo, 1,618........D 4
15104 North Braddock, 10,838........C 7
* † 18032 North Catasauqua, 2,941........L 4
16428 North East, 3,846........C 1
17857 Northumberland, 4,102........J 4
19454 North Wales, 3,911........M 5
16365 North Warren, 1,360........D 2
15674 Norvelt, 2,588........C 5

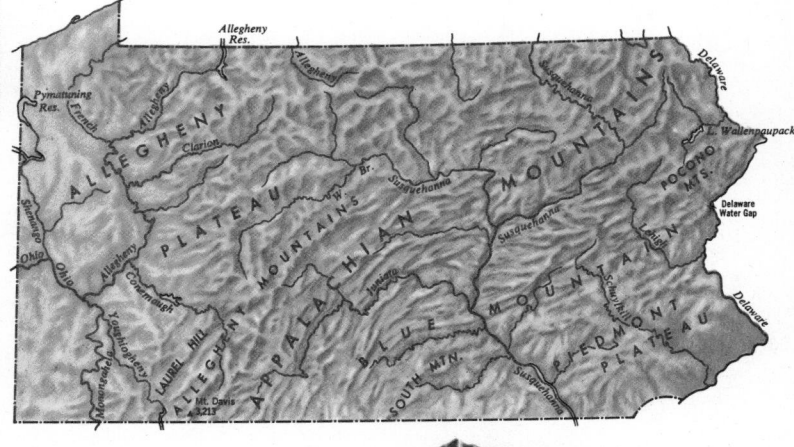

Topography

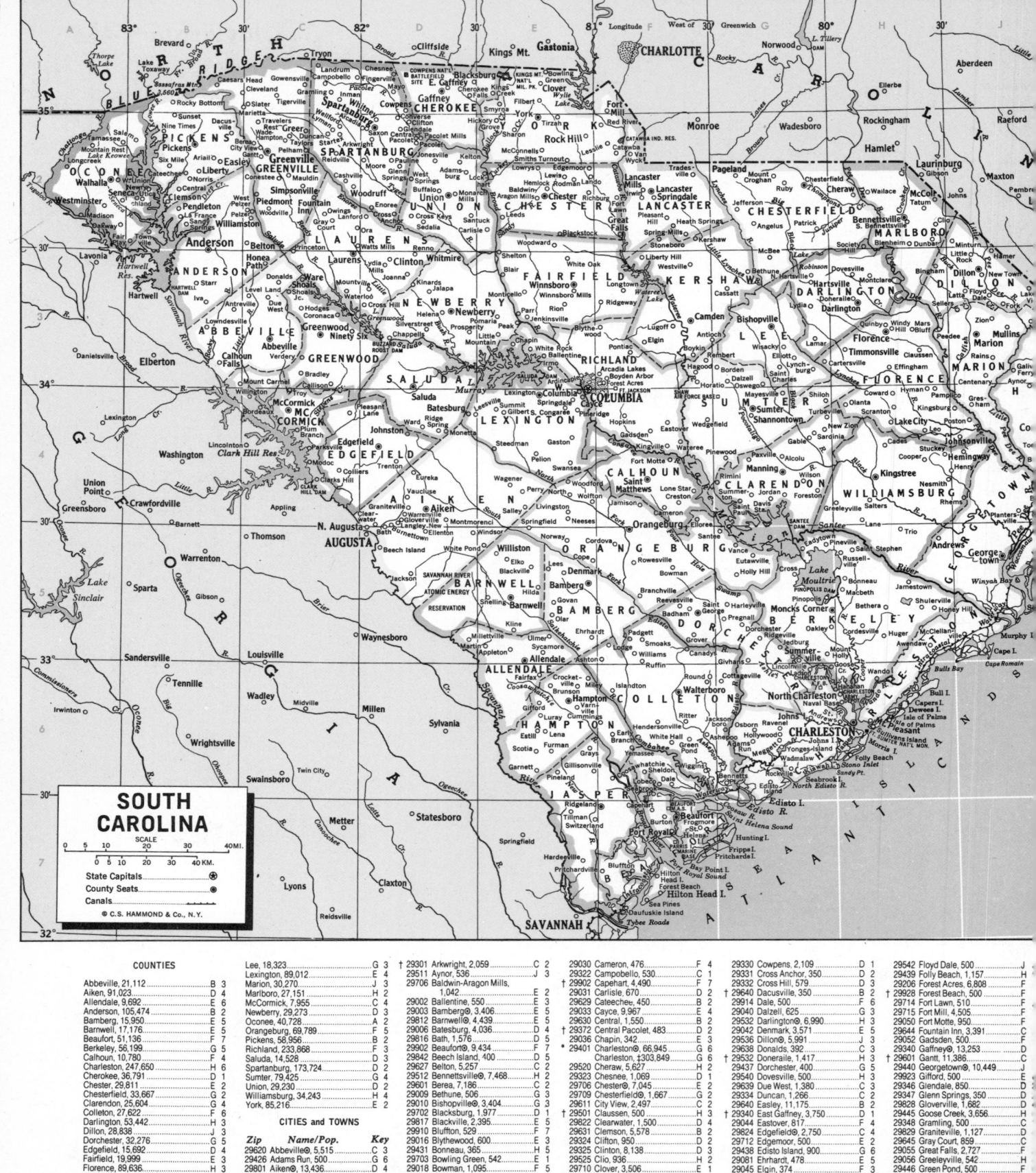

SOUTH CAROLINA

SCALE
0 5 10   20   30   40 MI.
0 5 10   20   30   40 KM.

State Capitals .... ⊛
County Seats .... ◉
Canals

® C.S. HAMMOND & Co., N.Y.

Agriculture, Industry and Resources

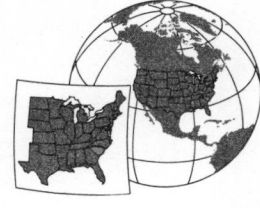

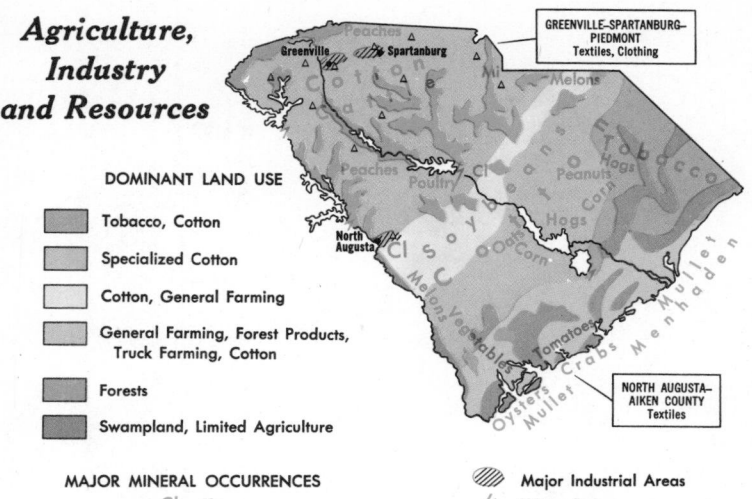

GREENVILLE-SPARTANBURG-
PIEDMONT
Textiles, Clothing

NORTH AUGUSTA-
AIKEN COUNTY
Textiles

DOMINANT LAND USE

- Tobacco, Cotton
- Specialized Cotton
- Cotton, General Farming
- General Farming, Forest Products, Truck Farming, Cotton
- Forests
- Swampland, Limited Agriculture

MAJOR MINERAL OCCURRENCES

Cl Clay
Mi Mica

- Major Industrial Areas
- ⚡ Water Power
- △ Major Textile Centers

AREA 31,055 sq. mi.
POPULATION 2,590,516
CAPITAL Columbia
LARGEST CITY Columbia
HIGHEST POINT Sassafras Mtn. 3,560 ft.
SETTLED IN 1670
ADMITTED TO UNION May 23, 1788
POPULAR NAME Palmetto State
STATE FLOWER Yellow Jessamine
STATE BIRD Carolina Wren

29656 La France, 875	B 2
29560 Lake City, 6,247	H 4
29563 Lake View, 949	J 3
29069 Lamar, 1,250	G 3
29720 Lancaster⊙, 9,186	F 2
† 29720 Lancaster Mills, 2,558	F 2
29724 Lando, 775	E 2
29356 Landrum, 1,859	C 1
29564 Lane, 517	H 5
29834 Langley, 975	D 4
29565 Latta, 1,764	J 3
29360 Laurens⊙, 10,298	C 3
29070 Leesville, 1,907	E 4
29734 Lesslie, 500	E 2
29072 Lexington⊙, 969	E 4
29657 Liberty, 2,860	B 2
† 29483 Lincolnville, 504	G 6
29566 Little River, 500	K 4
29569 Loris, 1,741	K 3
29078 Lugoff, 500	F 3
29079 Lydia, 400	G 3
29325 Lydia Mills, 925	D 3
29365 Lyman, 1,159	C 2
29080 Lynchburg, 546	G 3
29660 Madison, 388	A 2
29102 Manning⊙, 4,025	G 4
29661 Marietta-Slater, 1,764	C 1
29571 Marion⊙, 7,435	J 3
29662 Mauldin, 3,797	C 2
29104 Mayesville, 757	G 4
29368 Mayo, 800	D 1
29101 McBee, 592	G 3
29570 McColl, 2,524	H 2
29835 McCormick⊙, 1,864	C 4
† 29379 Monarch Mills, 1,726	D 2
29461 Moncks Corner⊙, 2,314	G 5
29105 Monetta, 400	D 4
29839 Montmorenci, 700	D 4
29664 Mountain Rest, 500	A 2
29464 Mount Pleasant, 6,155	H 6
29574 Mullins, 6,006	J 3
29576 Murrells Inlet, 850	K 4
29577 Myrtle Beach, 8,536	K 4
29408 Naval Base, 13,565	G 6
29107 Neeses, 388	E 4
29580 Nesmith, 350	H 4
29108 Newberry⊙, 9,218	D 3
29809 New Ellenton, 2,546	D 5
29665 Newry, 874	B 2
† 29536 New Town, 950	J 3
29581 Nichols, 500	J 3
29666 Ninety Six, 2,166	C 3
29667 Norris, 757	B 2
29112 North, 1,076	E 4
29841 North Augusta, 12,883	C 5
29406 North Charleston, 19,854	G 6
29550 North Hartsville, 1,485	G 3
29582 North Myrtle Beach, 1,957	K 4
29113 Norway, 579	E 4
29114 Olanta, 640	H 4
29843 Olar, 423	E 5
29115 Orangeburg⊙, 13,252	F 4
29372 Pacolet, 1,418	D 2
29373 Pacolet Mills, 1,504	D 2
29728 Pageland, 2,122	G 2
29583 Pamplico, 1,068	H 4
29584 Patrick, 421	G 2
29374 Pauline, 750	D 2
29585 Pawleys Island, 650	J 5
29670 Pendleton, 2,615	B 2
29671 Pickens⊙, 2,954	B 2
29673 Piedmont, 2,242	C 2
† 29169 Pineridge, 633	E 4
29468 Pineville, 900	H 5
29125 Pinewood, 687	G 4
29469 Pinopolis, 788	G 5
29935 Port Royal, 2,865	F 7
29127 Prosperity, 762	D 3
† 29501 Quinby, 788	H 3
29589 Rains, 600	J 3
29470 Ravenel, 931	G 6
29375 Reidville, 460	C 2
29128 Rembert, 350	G 3
29936 Ridgeland⊙, 1,165	E 7

29129 Ridge Spring, 644	D 4
29472 Ridgeville, 563	G 5
29130 Ridgeway, 437	F 3
29131 Rimini, 400	G 4
29473 Ritter, 350	F 6
29730 Rock Hill, 33,846	E 2
29740 Rodman, 500	E 2
29133 Rowesville, 392	F 5
29741 Ruby, 306	G 2
29475 Ruffin, 400	F 6
29407 Saint Andrews, 9,202	G 6
29134 Saint Charles, 350	G 3
29477 Saint George⊙, 1,806	F 5
29135 Saint Matthews⊙, 2,403	F 4
† 29148 Saint Paul, 725	G 4
29479 Saint Stephen, 1,506	H 5
29137 Salley, 450	E 4
† 29301 Saxon, 4,807	D 2
29591 Scranton, 732	H 4
29940 Seabrook, 500	E 7
29592 Sellers, 561	H 3
29678 Seneca, 6,027	A 2
† 29150 Shannontown, 7,491	G 4
29941 Sheldon, 950	F 6
29134 Shulerville, 375	H 5
29681 Simpsonville, 3,308	C 2
29682 Six Mile, 361	B 2
29683 Slater-Marietta, 1,764	C 1
29593 Society Hill, 806	H 2
† 29512 South Bennettsville, 1,726	H 2
† 29169 South Congaree, 1,434	E 4
* 29301 Spartanburg⊙, 44,546	C 1
29169 Springdale, 2,638	E 4
† 29720 Springdale, 3,193	F 2
29146 Springfield, 724	E 4
† 29067 Spring Mills, 975	F 2
29377 Startex, 1,203	C 2
29482 Sullivans Island, 1,426	H 6
29148 Summerton, 1,305	G 4
29483 Summerville, 3,839	G 5
29150 Sumter⊙, 24,435	G 4
29685 Sunset, 450	B 2
29577 Surfside Beach, 1,329	K 4
29160 Swansea, 691	E 4
29686 Tamassee, 420	A 2
29687 Taylors, 6,831	C 2
29688 Tigerville, 975	C 1
29161 Timmonsville, 2,246	H 3
29690 Travelers Rest, 2,241	C 2
29847 Trenton, 362	D 4
29162 Turbeville, 442	G 4
29379 Union⊙, 10,775	D 2
† 29678 Utica, 1,299	B 2
29944 Varnville, 1,555	E 6
29850 Vaucluse, 575	D 4
29607 Wade-Hampton, 17,152	C 2
29164 Wagener, 723	E 4
29691 Walhalla⊙, 3,662	A 2
29488 Walterboro⊙, 6,257	F 6
29692 Ware Shoals, 2,480	C 3
29851 Warrenville, 1,059	D 4
† 29360 Watts Mills, 1,181	D 2
29385 Wellford, 1,298	C 2
29169 West Columbia, 7,838	E 4
29180 Westminster, 2,521	A 2
29669 West Pelzer, 861	B 2
29696 West Union, 388	B 2
29178 Whitmire, 2,226	D 3
29303 Whitney, 2,891	D 1
29697 Williamston, 3,991	B 2
29853 Williston, 2,594	E 5
29856 Windsor, 590	D 4
† 29501 Windy Hill, 1,671	H 3
29180 Winnsboro⊙, 3,411	E 3
† 29180 Winnsboro Mills, 2,312	E 3
29388 Woodruff, 4,576	D 2
29945 Yemassee, 745	F 6
29494 Yonges Island, 350	G 6
29745 York⊙, 5,081	E 1
29574 Zion, 400	J 3

⊙ County seat.
‡ Population of metropolitan area.
⊙ Zip of nearest p.o.
† Multiple zips

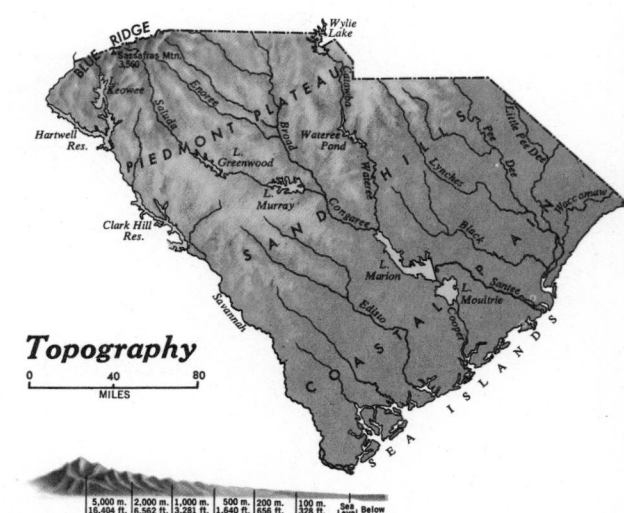

Colorful materials being Sanforized in a South Carolina textile mill. Textiles are by far the most important of the state's industries.

A. D'Arazien — Shostal Associates

Topography

0 40 80
MILES

5,000 m. 2,000 m. 1,000 m. 500 m. 200 m. 100 m. See
16,404 ft. 6,562 ft. 3,281 ft. 1,640 ft. 656 ft. 328 ft. Below

29927 Hardeeville, 853	E 7
29448 Harleyville, 704	G 5
29550 Hartsville, 8,017	G 3
29058 Heath Springs, 955	F 2
29554 Hemingway, 1,026	J 4
29706 Hemlock, 1,524	E 2
29717 Hickory Grove, 377	E 2
29813 Hilda, 331	E 5
29928 Hilton Head Island, 450	F 7
29059 Holly Hill, 1,178	G 5
29449 Hollywood, 339	G 6
29654 Honea Path, 3,707	C 3
29062 Horatio, 500	F 3
29450 Huger, 500	H 5
29349 Inman, 1,661	C 1
29063 Irmo, 517	E 3
† 29720 Irwin, 1,424	F 2
29451 Isle of Palms, 2,657	H 6
29655 Iva, 1,114	B 3
29831 Jackson, 1,928	D 5
29452 Jacksonboro, 550	G 6
† 29483 Jedburg, 900	G 5
29718 Jefferson, 709	G 2
29351 Joanna, 1,631	D 3
29455 Johns Island, 675	G 6
29555 Johnsonville, 1,267	J 4
29832 Johnston, 2,552	D 4
29353 Jonesville, 1,447	D 2
29067 Kershaw, 1,818	F 2
29556 Kingstree⊙, 3,381	H 4
29814 Kline, 305	E 5
29456 Ladson, 600	G 6

COUNTIES

Aurora, 4,183	M 6
Beadle, 20,877	N 5
Bennett, 3,088	F 7
Bon Homme, 8,577	O 7
Brookings, 22,158	R 5
Brown, 36,920	N 2
Brule, 5,870	L 6
Buffalo, 1,739	L 5
Butte, 7,825	B 4
Campbell, 2,866	J 2
Charles Mix, 9,994	M 7
Clark, 5,515	O 4
Clay, 12,923	P 8
Codington, 19,140	P 4
Corson, 4,994	G 2
Custer, 4,698	B 6
Davison, 17,319	N 6
Day, 8,713	O 3
Deuel, 5,686	R 4
Dewey, 5,170	G 3
Douglas, 4,569	N 7
Edmunds, 5,548	L 3
Fall River, 7,505	B 7
Faulk, 3,893	L 3

Grant, 9,005	R 3
Gregory, 6,710	L 7
Haakon, 2,802	F 5
Hamlin, 5,172	P 4
Hand, 5,883	L 4
Hanson, 3,781	O 6
Harding, 1,855	B 2
Hughes, 11,632	J 5
Hutchinson, 10,379	O 7
Hyde, 2,515	K 4
Jackson, 1,531	F 6
Jerauld, 3,310	M 5
Jones, 1,882	H 6
Kingsbury, 7,657	O 5
Lake, 11,456	P 5
Lawrence, 17,453	B 5
Lincoln, 11,761	R 7
Lyman, 4,060	J 6
Marshall, 5,965	O 2
McCook, 7,246	P 6
McPherson, 5,022	L 2
Meade, 16,618	D 5
Mellette, 2,420	H 6
Miner, 4,454	O 5
Minnehaha, 95,209	R 6
Moody, 7,622	R 5

Pennington, 59,349	C 6
Perkins, 4,769	D 3
Potter, 4,449	J 3
Roberts, 11,678	P 2
Sanborn, 3,697	N 5
Shannon, 8,198	D 7
Spink, 10,595	N 4
Stanley, 2,457	H 5
Sully, 2,362	J 4
Todd, 6,606	H 7
Tripp, 8,171	K 7
Turner, 9,872	P 7
Union, 9,643	R 8
Walworth, 7,842	J 3
Washabaugh, 1,389	F 6
Yankton, 19,039	P 7
Ziebach, 2,221	F 4

CITIES and TOWNS

Zip	Name/Pop.	Key
57401	Aberdeen◉, 26,476	M 3
57310	Academy, 17	M 7
57520	Agar, 156	J 4
57420	Akaska, 46	J 3
57210	Albee, 26	S 3
57001	Alcester, 627	R 7
57311	Alexandria◉, 598	O 6
57714	Allen, 150	F 7
57312	Alpena, 307	N 5
57211	Altamont, 54	R 4
57421	Amherst, 75	O 2
57422	Andover, 138	O 3
57715	Ardmore, 14	B 7
57212	Arlington, 954	P 5
57313	Armour◉, 925	N 7
57423	Artas, 73	K 2
57314	Artesian, 277	O 6
57424	Ashton, 137	N 3
57213	Astoria, 153	S 4
57425	Athol, 50	M 3
57002	Aurora, 237	R 5
57315	Avon, 610	N 8
57214	Badger, 122	P 5
57003	Baltic, 364	R 6
57316	Bancroft, 48	N 4
57426	Barnard, 72	N 2
57716	Batesland, 135	E 7
57427	Bath, 150	N 3
57717	Belle Fourche◉, 4,236	B 4
57521	Belvidere, 96	G 6

Zip	Name/Pop.	Key
57215	Bemis, 28	R 4
57004	Beresford, 1,655	R 7
57216	Big Stone City, 631	S 3
† 57310	Bijou Hills, 12	L 6
57620	Bison◉, 406	E 2
57718	Black Hawk, 550	C 5
57522	Blunt, 445	J 4
57317	Bonesteel, 354	M 7
57318	Bonilla, 33	N 4
57428	Bowdle, 667	K 3
57719	Box Elder, 607	D 5
57217	Bradley, 157	P 4
57005	Brandon, 1,431	R 6
57218	Brandt, 132	R 4
57429	Brentford, 94	N 3
57319	Bridgewater, 633	P 6
57219	Bristol, 470	O 3
57430	Britton◉, 1,465	O 2
† 57350	Broadland, 45	N 4
57006	Brookings◉, 13,717	R 5
57220	Bruce, 217	R 4
57221	Bryant, 502	P 4
57720	Buffalo◉, 393	C 2
57722	Buffalo Gap, 155	C 6
57621	Bullhead, 449	F 2
57010	Burbank, 96	R 8

Zip	Name/Pop.	Key
57523	Burke◉, 892	L 7
57011	Bushnell, 65	R 5
57222	Butler, 38	O 3
57724	Camp Crook, 150	B 2
57012	Canistota, 636	P 6
57524	Canning, 40	K 5
57321	Canova, 204	O 6
57013	Canton◉, 2,665	R 7
57725	Caputa, 43	D 5
† 57533	Carlock, 13	L 7
57322	Carpenter, 50	O 4
57526	Carter, 17	J 6
57431	Chelsea, 45	M 3
57223	Castlewood, 523	R 4
57323	Carthage, 362	O 5
57324	Cavour, 134	N 4
57014	Centerville, 910	R 7
† 57058	Center, 18	P 6
57727	Central City, 188	B 5
57325	Chamberlain◉, 2,626	L 6
57015	Chancellor, 220	R 7
57622	Cherry Creek, 275	F 4
57224	Claire City, 100	P 2
57016	Chester, 260	R 6
57432	Claremont, 214	N 2
57225	Clark◉, 1,356	O 4

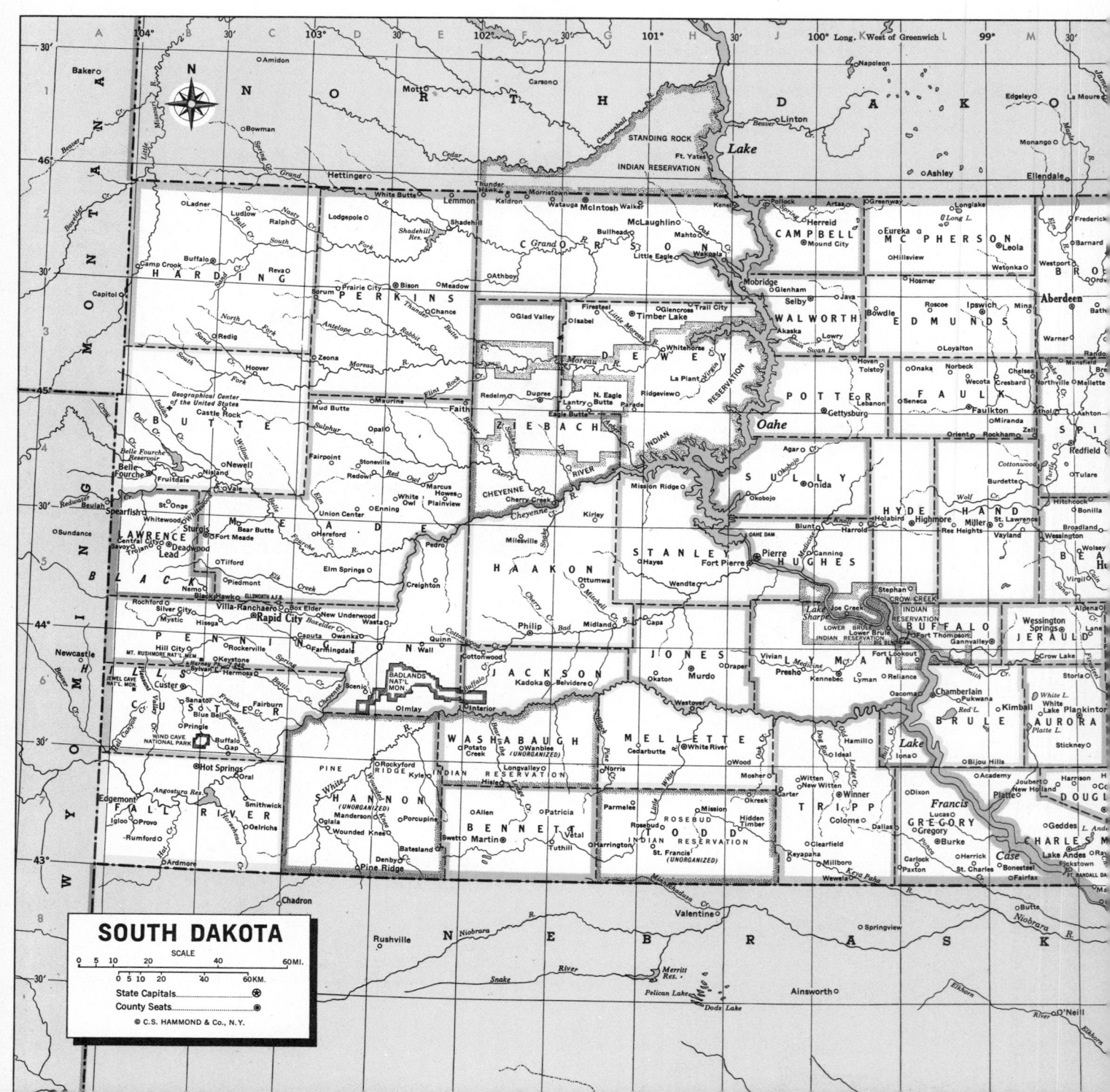

South Dakota 235

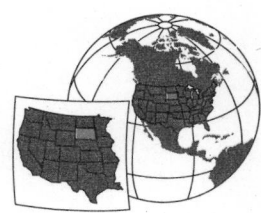

57332 Clayton, 13	O 7	
57581 Clearfield, 20	K 7	
57226 Clear Lake⊙ 1,157	R 4	
57017 Colman, 456	R 6	
57528 Colome, 375	K 7	
57018 Colton, 601	P 6	
57433 Columbia, 240	N 2	
57434 Conde, 279	N 3	
57227 Corona, 133	S 4	
57328 Corsica, 615	N 7	
57019 Corson, 101	R 6	
57728 Cottonwood, 16	F 6	
57228 Crandall, 107	O 3	
57435 Cresbard, 224	M 3	
57229 Crocker, 40	O 3 †	
57020 Crooks, 200	R 6	
57730 Custer⊙, 1,597	B 6	
57529 Dallas, 233	K 7	
57329 Dante, 88	N 7	
57021 Davis, 101	P 7	
57732 Deadwood⊙, 2,409	B 5	
57022 Dell Rapids, 1,991	R 6	
57330 Delmont, 260	N 7	
57230 Dempster, 75	R 4	
57231 De Smet⊙, 1,336	O 5	
57331 Dimock, 167	O 7	

57530 Dixon, 15	L 7	
57436 Doland, 430	N 4	
57023 Dolton, 60	P 7	
57531 Draper, 200	J 6	
57623 Dupree⊙, 523	F 3	
57625 Eagle Butte, 530	G 4	
57232 Eden, 132	P 2	
57735 Edgemont. 1.174	B 7	
57024 Egan, 281	R 6	
57025 Elk Point⊙, 1,372	R 8	
57026 Elkton, 541	S 5	
57736 Elm Springs, 16	D 5 †	
57332 Emery, 452	O 6	
57737 Enning, 35	E 4	
57321 Epiphany, 64	O 6 †	
57233 Erwin, 106	R 5	
57333 Esmond, 19	O 4	
57234 Estelline, 276	R 5	
57334 Ethan, 309	N 6	
57437 Eureka, 1,547	K 2	
57738 Fairburn, 50	C 6	
57335 Fairfax, 199	M 7	
57027 Fairview, 72	R 6	
57626 Faith, 576	E 4	
57336 Farmer, 58	O 6	
57740 Farmingdale, 30	D 6	

57438 Faulkton⊙, 955	L 3	
57337 Fedora, 75	O 5	
57439 Ferney, 72	N 3	
57628 Firesteel, 17	G 3	
57028 Flandreau⊙, 2,027	R 5	
57235 Florence, 175	P 3	
57338 Forestburg, 150	N 5	
57741 Fort Meade, 900	C 5	
57532 Fort Pierre⊙, 1,448	H 5	
57339 Fort Thompson, 750	L 5	
57042 Frankfort, 192	N 4	
57042 Franklin, 14	P 6 †	
57441 Frederick, 359	N 2	
57029 Freeman, 1,357	O 7	
57742 Fruitdale, 74	B 4	
57340 Fulton, 101	O 6	
57341 Gannvalley⊙, 80	L 5	
57236 Garden City, 126	O 4	
57030 Garretson, 847	S 6	
57237 Gary, 366	S 4	
57031 Gayville, 269	P 8	
57342 Geddes, 308	M 7	
57442 Gettysburg⊙, 1,915	K 3	
57630 Glencross, 75	H 3	
57631 Glenham, 178	J 2	
57238 Goodwin, 114	R 4	

(continued on following page)

AREA 77,047 sq. mi.
POPULATION 666,257
CAPITAL Pierre
LARGEST CITY Sioux Falls
HIGHEST POINT Harney Pk. 7,242 ft.
SETTLED IN 1856
ADMITTED TO UNION November 2, 1889
POPULAR NAME Coyote State; Sunshine State
STATE FLOWER Pasqueflower
STATE BIRD Ring-necked Pheasant

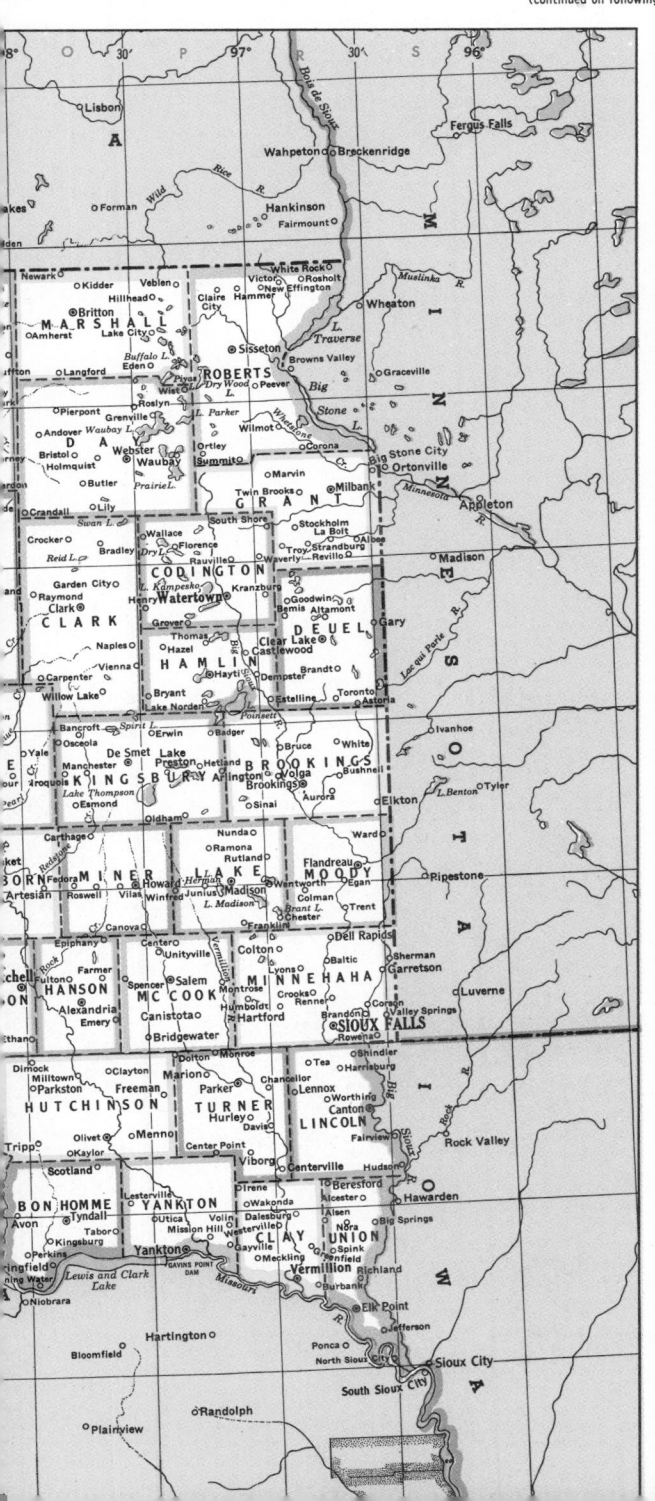

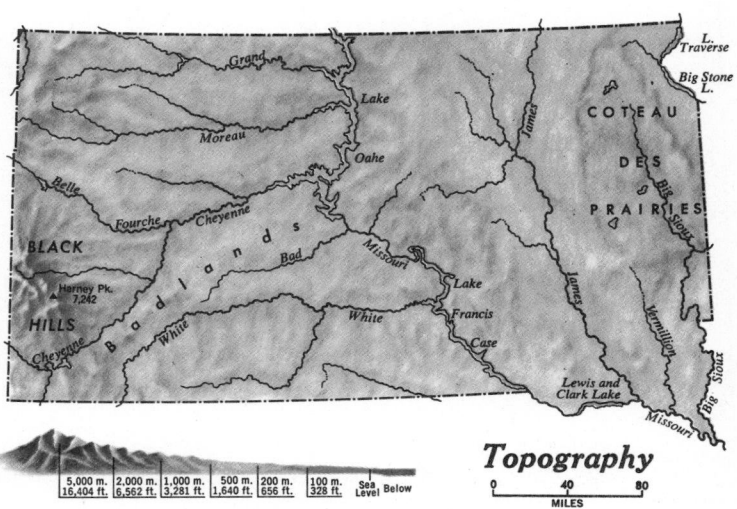

Topography

5,000 m. / 16,404 ft. — 2,000 m. / 6,562 ft. — 1,000 m. / 3,281 ft. — 500 m. / 1,640 ft. — 200 m. / 656 ft. — 100 m. / 328 ft. — Sea Level — Below

0 — 40 — 80 MILES

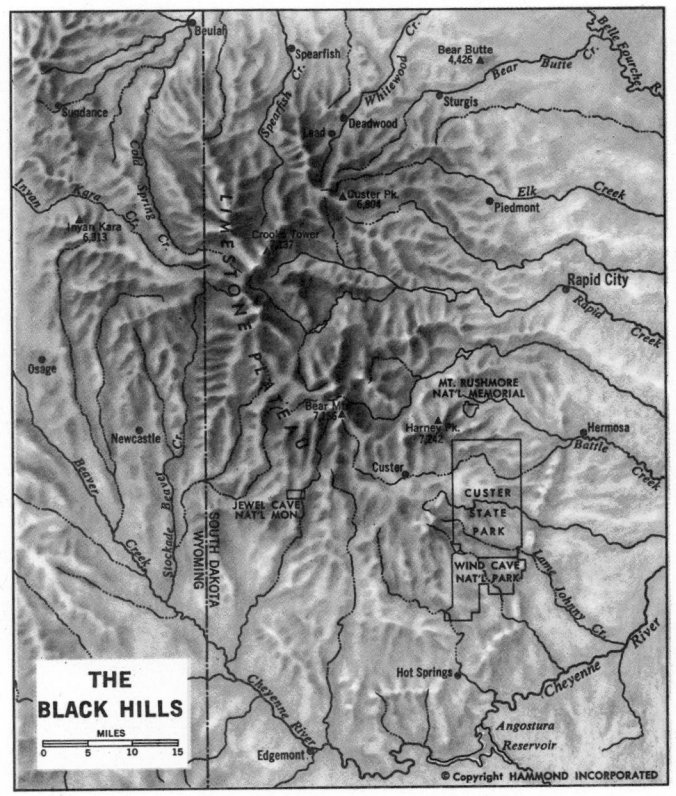

THE BLACK HILLS

MILES
0 — 5 — 10 — 15

© Copyright HAMMOND INCORPORATED

(continued)

† 57010 Greenfield, 12 ... R 8
† 57380 Greenwood, 90 ... N 8
57533 Gregory, 1,756 ... L 7
57239 Grenville, 154 ... O 3
57445 Groton, 1,021 ... N 3
† 57201 Grover, 12 ... P 4
57534 Hamill, 57 ... K 6
57240 Hammer, 30 ... R 2
57535 Harrington, 54 ... G 7
57032 Harrisburg, 338 ... R 7
57344 Harrison, 68 ... M 7
57536 Harrold, 184 ... K 4
57033 Hartford, 800 ... P 6
57537 Hayes, 28 ... H 5
57241 Hayti⊙, 393 ... P 4
57242 Hazel, 101 ... P 4
57446 Hecla, 407 ... N 2
57243 Henry, 182 ... P 4
57744 Hermosa, 150 ... C 6
57632 Herreid, 672 ... K 2
57538 Herrick, 126 ... L 7
57244 Hetland, 81 ... P 5
† 69501 Hidden Timber, 30 ... J 7
57345 Highmore⊙, 1,173 ... L 4
57745 Hill City, 389 ... B 6
† 57270 Hillhead, 26 ... O 2
† 57437 Hillsview, 19 ... L 2
† 57701 Hisega, 36 ... C 5
57348 Hitchcock, 150 ... M 4
57540 Holabird, 32 ... K 4
† 57274 Holmquist, 13 ... O 3
57448 Hosmer, 437 ... L 2
57747 Hot Springs⊙, 4,434 ... C 7
57449 Houghton, 90 ... N 2
57450 Hoven, 671 ... K 3
57349 Howard⊙, 1,175 ... P 5
57034 Hudson, 366 ... R 7
57035 Humboldt, 411 ... P 6
57036 Hurley, 399 ... P 7
57350 Huron⊙, 14,299 ... N 5
57541 Ideal, 135 ... K 6
† 57774 Igloo, 20 ... B 7
57750 Interior, 81 ... F 6
57451 Ipswich⊙, 1,187 ... L 3
57037 Irene, 461 ... P 7
57353 Iroquois, 375 ... O 5
57633 Isabel, 394 ... G 3
57452 Java, 305 ... K 3
57038 Jefferson, 474 ... S 8
† 57042 Junius, 50 ... P 6
57543 Kadoka⊙, 815 ... F 6
57354 Kaylor, 110 ... O 7
57634 Keldron, 35 ... F 2
57642 Kenel, 245 ... H 2
57544 Kennebec⊙, 372 ... K 6
57751 Keystone, 475 ... C 6
57453 Kidder, 140 ... O 2
57355 Kimball, 825 ... M 6
57245 Kranzburg, 143 ... R 4
57752 Kyle, 500 ... E 7
57246 La Bolt, 90 ... R 3
57356 Lake Andes⊙, 948 ... M 7
57247 Lake City, 44 ... O 2
57248 Lake Norden, 393 ... P 4
57249 Lake Preston, 812 ... P 5
57358 Lane, 94 ... N 5
57454 Langford, 328 ... O 2
57636 Lantry, 52 ... G 3
57637 La Plant, 165 ... H 3
57754 Lead, 5,420 ... B 5
57455 Lebanon, 182 ... K 3
57638 Lemmon, 1,997 ... E 2
57039 Lennox, 1,487 ... R 7
57456 Leola⊙, 787 ... M 2
57040 Lesterville, 181 ... O 7
57359 Letcher, 201 ... N 6
57250 Lily, 62 ... O 3
57639 Little Eagle, 975 ... H 2
57640 Lodgepole, 25 ... D 2
57457 Longlake, 128 ... L 2
57547 Longvalley, 16 ... F 7
57360 Loomis, 150 ... N 6
57548 Lower Brule, 500 ... K 5
57458 Lowry, 35 ... K 3
57549 Lucas, 13 ... L 7
† 57569 Lyman, 15 ... K 6
57041 Lyons, 89 ... R 6
57042 Madison⊙, 6,315 ... P 6
57643 Mahto, 23 ... H 2
† 57353 Manchester, 25 ... O 5
57756 Manderson, 350 ... D 7
57460 Mansfield, 150 ... N 3
57043 Marion, 844 ... P 7
57551 Martin⊙, 1,248 ... F 7
57361 Marty, 225 ... N 8
57251 Marvin, 65 ... R 3
57627 Maurine, 12 ... E 3
57641 McIntosh⊙, 563 ... G 2
57642 McLaughlin, 863 ... H 2
57044 Meckling, 100 ... R 8
57461 Mellette, 199 ... N 3
57045 Menno, 796 ... P 7
57552 Midland, 270 ... G 5
57252 Milbank⊙, 3,727 ... R 3
57362 Miller⊙, 2,148 ... L 4
† 57366 Milltown, 28 ... O 7
57462 Mina, 18 ... M 3
57463 Miranda, 60 ... M 4
57555 Mission, 739 ... H 7
57046 Mission Hill, 161 ... P 8
57301 Mitchell⊙, 13,425 ... N 6
57601 Mobridge, 4,545 ... J 2
57047 Monroe, 134 ... P 7
57048 Montrose, 377 ... P 6
57645 Morristown, 144 ... F 2
57558 Mosher, 19 ... J 7
57646 Mound City⊙, 164 ... K 2
57363 Mount Vernon, 398 ... N 6
57559 Murdo⊙, 865 ... H 6
† 57778 Mystic, 16 ... B 5
57254 Naples, 38 ... O 4
57759 Nemo, 100 ... B 5
† 57453 Newark, 25 ... O 2
57255 New Effington, 258 ... R 2
57760 Newell, 664 ... C 4
57364 New Holland, 131 ... M 7
57761 New Underwood, 416 ... D 5
† 57584 New Witten, 102 ... K 7

Agriculture, Industry and Resources

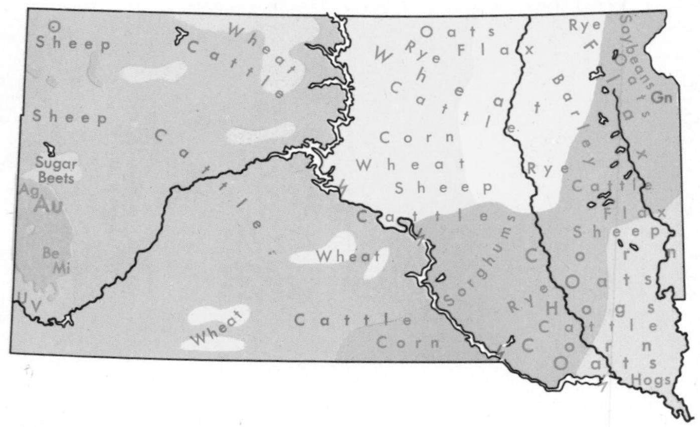

DOMINANT LAND USE

Specialized Wheat
Wheat, General Farming
Wheat, Range Livestock
Cattle Feed, Hogs
Livestock, Cash Grain
General Farming, Livestock, Special Crops
Range Livestock
Forests

Water Power

MAJOR MINERAL OCCURRENCES

Ag Silver
Au Gold
Be Beryl
Gn Granite
Mi Mica
O Petroleum
U Uranium
V Vanadium

57762 Nisland, 157 ... C 4
57560 Norris, 42 ... G 7
† 57625 North Eagle Butte, 1,351 ... G 3
57049 North Sioux City, 860 ... R 8
57465 Northville, 119 ... M 3
57050 Nunda, 85 ... P 5
57365 Oacoma, 215 ... L 6
57763 Oelrichs, 94 ... C 7
57764 Oglala, 250 ... D 7
57562 Okaton, 65 ... H 6
† 57501 Okobojo, 15 ... J 4
57563 Okreek, 300 ... J 7
57051 Oldham, 244 ... P 5
57052 Olivet⊙, 103 ... O 7
57466 Onaka, 69 ... L 3
57564 Onida⊙, 785 ... K 4
57766 Oral, 45 ... C 7
57467 Orient, 131 ... L 4
57256 Ortley, 111 ... P 3
† 57353 Osceola, 32 ... O 5
57053 Parker⊙, 1,005 ... P 7
57366 Parkston, 1,611 ... O 7
57566 Parmelee, 475 ... G 7
† 57529 Paxton, 18 ... L 7
† 57729 Pedro, 15 ... E 5
57257 Peever, 202 ... R 2
57567 Philip⊙, 983 ... F 5
57367 Pickstown, 300 ... M 7
57769 Piedmont, 650 ... C 5
57468 Pierpont, 241 ... O 3
57501 Pierre (cap.)⊙, 9,699 ... J 5
57770 Pine Ridge, 2,768 ... E 7
57368 Plankinton⊙, 613 ... N 6
57369 Platte, 1,351 ... M 7
57648 Pollock, 341 ... J 2
57772 Porcupine, 200 ... E 7
† 57750 Potato Creek, 40 ... F 6
57649 Prairie City, 55 ... D 2
57568 Presho, 922 ... J 6
57773 Pringle, 86 ... B 6
57774 Provo, 45 ... B 7
57370 Pukwana, 208 ... L 6
57402 Putney, 24 ... N 2
57775 Quinn, 105 ... E 5
57054 Ramona, 227 ... P 5
57701 Rapid City⊙, 43,836 ... C 5
57357 Ravinia, 109 ... N 7
57258 Raymond, 114 ... O 4
57469 Redfield⊙, 2,943 ... N 4
57776 Redig, 13 ... C 3
57777 Redowl, 14 ... D 4
57371 Ree Heights, 183 ... L 4
57569 Reliance, 204 ... K 6
57055 Renner, 260 ... R 6
57259 Revillo, 142 ... R 3
† 57025 Richland, 70 ... R 8
57652 Ridgeview, 65 ... H 3
57778 Rochford, 20 ... B 5
57701 Rockerville, 48 ... C 6
57470 Rockham, 60 ... M 4
† 57772 Rockyford, 50 ... E 7
57471 Roscoe, 398 ... L 3
57570 Rosebud, 650 ... H 7
57260 Rosholt, 456 ... R 2
57261 Roslyn, 250 ... P 2
57372 Roswell, 32 ... O 6
57056 Rowena, 76 ... R 6
57057 Rutland, 100 ... P 5
57571 Saint Charles, 33 ... L 7
57572 Saint Francis, 300 ... H 7
57373 Saint Lawrence, 249 ... M 4
57779 Saint Onge, 200 ... B 4
57058 Salem⊙, 1,391 ... P 6
† 57730 Sanator, 150 ... B 6
† 57754 Savoy, 15 ... B 5
57780 Scenic, 56 ... D 6
57059 Scotland, 984 ... O 7
57472 Selby⊙, 957 ... J 3
57473 Seneca, 118 ... L 3

57653 Shadehill, 186 ... E 2
57060 Sherman, 82 ... S 6
† 57101 Shindler, 20 ... R 7
57781 Silver City, 40 ... B 5
57061 Sinai, 147 ... P 5
* 57101 Sioux Falls⊙, 72,488 ... R 6
Sioux Falls, ‡95,209 ... R 6
57262 Sisseton⊙, 3,094 ... R 2
57782 Smithwick, 25 ... C 7
57263 South Shore, 199 ... P 3
57783 Spearfish, 4,661 ... B 5
57374 Spencer, 385 ... O 6
† 57010 Spink, 21 ... R 8
57062 Springfield, 1,566 ... N 8
57346 Stephan, 60 ... K 5
57375 Stickney, 421 ... M 6
57264 Stockholm, 116 ... R 3
† 57359 Storla, 75 ... M 6
57265 Strandburg, 98 ... R 3
57474 Stratford, 106 ... N 3
57785 Sturgis⊙, 4,536 ... B 5
57266 Summit, 332 ... P 3
† 57551 Swett, 20 ... E 7
57063 Tabor, 388 ... O 8
† 57433 Tacoma Park, 18 ... N 2
57064 Tea, 302 ... R 7
† 57242 Thomas, 15 ... P 4

57655 Thunder Hawk, 45 ... F 2
† 57769 Tilford, 162 ... C 5
57656 Timber Lake⊙, 625 ... H 3
57475 Tolstoy, 99 ... K 3
57268 Toronto, 216 ... R 4
57657 Trail City, 75 ... H 3
57065 Trent, 177 ... R 6
57376 Tripp, 851 ... N 7
† 57754 Trojan, 25 ... B 5
† 57265 Troy, 13 ... R 3
57476 Tulare, 211 ... N 4
57477 Turton, 121 ... N 3
57574 Tuthill, 73 ... G 7
57269 Twin Brooks, 122 ... R 3
57066 Tyndall⊙, 1,245 ... O 8
57787 Union Center, 50 ... D 4
† 57058 Unityville, 30 ... P 6
57067 Utica, 89 ... P 8
57788 Vale, 89 ... C 4
57068 Valley Springs, 566 ... S 6
57270 Veblen, 377 ... P 2
57478 Verdon, 18 ... N 3
57069 Vermillion⊙, 9,128 ... R 8
57575 Vetal, 17 ... G 7
57070 Viborg, 662 ... P 7
† 57260 Victor, 22 ... R 2
57271 Vienna, 119 ... O 4

† 57349 Vilas, 33 ... O 6
† 57701 Villa Ranchaero 3,171 ... C 5
57379 Virgil, 43 ... N 5
57576 Vivian, 200 ... J 6
57071 Volga, 982 ... R 5
57072 Volin, 157 ... P 8
57380 Wagner, 1,655 ... N 7
57073 Wakonda, 290 ... P 7
57658 Wakpala, 500 ... H 2
57790 Wall, 786 ... E 6
57272 Wallace, 95 ... P 3
57577 Wanblee, 500 ... F 6
57074 Ward, 57 ... R 5
57479 Warner, 175 ... M 3
57791 Wasta, 127 ... D 5
57660 Watauga, 76 ... F 2
57201 Watertown⊙, 13,388 ... P 4
57273 Waubay, 696 ... P 3
57202 Waverly, 40 ... R 3
57274 Webster⊙, 2,252 ... P 3
57480 Wecota, 50 ... L 3
† 57532 Wendte, 20 ... H 5
57075 Wentworth, 196 ... R 6
57881 Wessington, 380 ... M 5
57382 Wessington Springs⊙, 1,300 ... M 5

57481 Westport, 136 ... M 2
57482 Wetonka, 31 ... M 2
57578 Wewela, 16 ... K 7
57276 White, 418 ... R 5
† 57638 White Butte, 15 ... E 2
57661 Whitehorse, 100 ... H 3
57383 White Lake, 395 ... M 6
57579 White River⊙, 617 ... H 6
57277 White Rock, 35 ... R 2
57793 Whitewood, 689 ... B 5
57278 Willow Lake, 353 ... O 4
57279 Wilmot, 518 ... R 3
57076 Winfred, 110 ... P 6
57580 Winner⊙, 3,789 ... K 7
57584 Witten, 140 ... J 7
57384 Wolsey, 436 ... N 5
57585 Wood, 132 ... J 6
57385 Woonsocket⊙, 852 ... N 5
57077 Worthing, 294 ... R 7
57794 Wounded Knee, 500 ... D 7
57386 Yale, 148 ... O 5
57078 Yankton⊙, 11,919 ... P 8
57483 Zell, 87 ... M 4

⊙ County seat.
‡ Population of metropolitan area.
† Zip of nearest p.o.
* Multiple zips

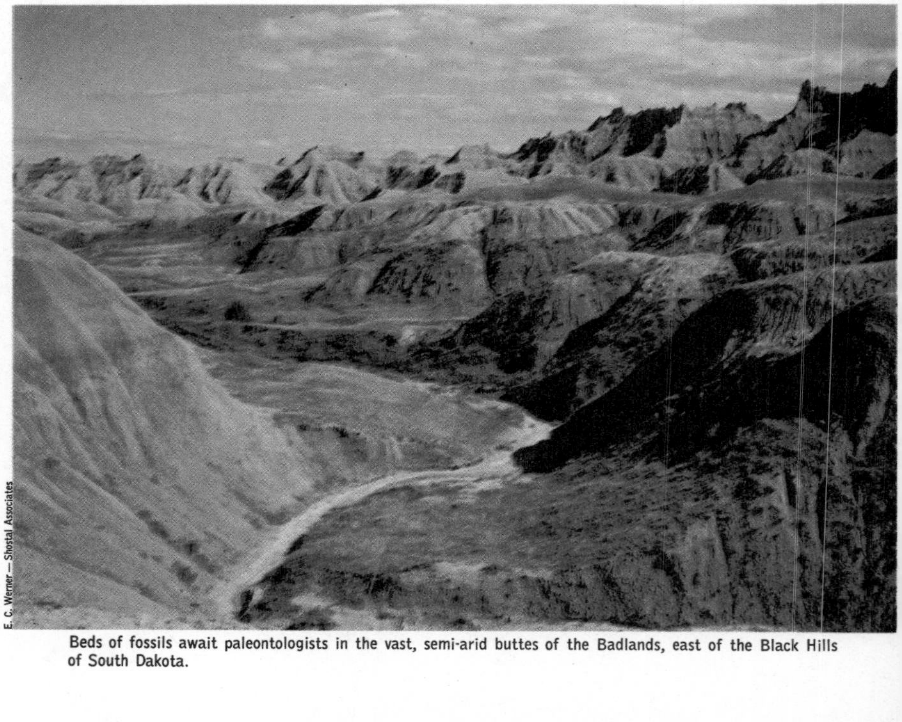

E. C. Werner—Shostal Associates

Beds of fossils await paleontologists in the vast, semi-arid buttes of the Badlands, east of the Black Hills of South Dakota.

Texas 237

COUNTIES

Anderson, 27,789 J 6
Andrews, 10,372 B 5
Angelina, 49,349 K 6
Aransas, 8,902 H 10
Archer, 5,759 F 4
Armstrong, 1,895 C 3
Atascosa, 18,696 F 9
Austin, 13,831 H 8
Bailey, 8,487 B 3
Bandera, 4,747 E 8
Bastrop, 17,297 G 7
Baylor, 5,221 E 4
Bee, 22,737 G 9
Bell, 124,483 G 6
Bexar, 830,460 F 8
Blanco, 3,567 F 7
Borden, 888 C 5
Bosque, 10,966 G 6
Bowie, 67,813 K 4
Brazoria, 108,312 J 8
Brazos, 57,978 H 7
Brewster, 7,780 A 8
Briscoe, 2,794 C 3
Brooks, 8,005 F 11
Brown, 25,877 F 6
Burleson, 9,999 H 7
Burnet, 11,420 F 7
Caldwell, 21,178 G 8
Calhoun, 17,831 H 9
Callahan, 8,205 E 5
Cameron, 140,368 G 11
Camp, 8,005 K 5
Carson, 6,358 C 2
Cass, 24,133 K 4
Castro, 10,394 B 3
Chambers, 12,187 K 8
Cherokee, 32,008 J 6
Childress, 6,605 D 3
Clay, 8,079 F 4
Cochran, 5,326 B 4
Coke, 3,087 D 6
Coleman, 10,288 E 6
Collin, 66,920 H 4
Collingsworth, 4,755 D 3
Colorado, 17,638 H 8
Comal, 24,165 F 8
Comanche, 11,898 F 5
Concho, 2,937 E 6
Cooke, 23,471 G 4
Coryell, 35,311 G 6
Cottle, 3,204 D 3
Crane, 4,172 B 6
Crockett, 3,885 C 7
Crosby, 9,085 C 4
Culberson, 3,429 C 11
Dallam, 6,012 B 1
Dallas, 1,327,321 H 5
Dawson, 16,604 C 5
Deaf Smith, 18,999 B 3
Delta, 4,927 J 4
Denton, 75,633 G 4
De Witt, 18,660 G 9
Dickens, 3,737 D 4
Dimmit, 9,039 E 9
Donley, 3,641 D 2
Duval, 11,722 F 10
Eastland, 18,092 F 5
Ector, 91,805 B 6
Edwards, 2,107 D 7
Ellis, 46,638 H 5
El Paso, 359,291 A 10
Erath, 18,141 F 5
Falls, 17,300 H 6
Fannin, 22,705 H 4
Fayette, 17,650 H 8
Fisher, 6,344 D 5
Floyd, 11,044 C 3
Foard, 2,211 E 3
Fort Bend, 52,314 J 8
Franklin, 5,291 J 4
Freestone, 11,116 H 6
Frio, 11,159 E 9
Gaines, 11,593 B 5
Galveston, 169,812 K 8
Garza, 5,289 C 4
Gillespie, 10,553 F 7
Glasscock, 1,155 C 6
Goliad, 4,869 G 9
Gonzales, 16,375 G 8
Gray, 26,949 D 2
Grayson, 83,225 H 4
Gregg, 75,929 K 5
Grimes, 11,855 J 7
Guadalupe, 33,554 G 8
Hale, 34,137 C 3
Hall, 6,015 D 3
Hamilton, 7,198 F 6
Hansford, 6,351 C 1
Hardeman, 6,795 E 3
Hardin, 29,996 K 7
Harris, 1,741,912 J 8
Harrison, 44,841 K 5
Hartley, 2,782 B 2
Haskell, 8,512 E 4
Hays, 27,642 F 7
Hemphill, 3,084 D 2
Henderson, 26,466 J 5
Hidalgo, 181,535 F 11
Hill, 22,596 G 5
Hockley, 20,396 B 4
Hood, 6,368 G 5
Hopkins, 20,710 J 4
Houston, 17,855 J 6
Howard, 37,796 C 5
Hudspeth, 2,392 B 10
Hunt, 47,948 H 4
Hutchinson, 24,443 C 2
Irion, 1,070 C 6
Jack, 6,711 F 4
Jackson, 12,975 H 9
Jasper, 24,692 K 7
Jeff Davis, 1,527 C 11
Jefferson, 244,773 K 8
Jim Hogg, 4,654 F 11
Jim Wells, 33,032 F 10
Johnson, 45,769 G 5
Jones, 16,106 E 5
Karnes, 13,462 G 9
Kaufman, 32,392 H 5
Kendall, 6,964 F 8
Kenedy, 678 G 11
Kent, 1,434 D 4
Kerr, 19,454 E 7
Kimble, 3,904 E 7
King, 464 D 4
Kinney, 2,006 D 8
Kleberg, 33,166 G 10
Knox, 5,972 E 4
Lamar, 36,062 J 4
Lamb, 17,770 B 3
Lampasas, 9,323 F 6
La Salle, 5,014 E 9
Lavaca, 17,903 H 8
Lee, 8,048 H 7
Leon, 8,738 J 6
Liberty, 33,014 K 7
Limestone, 18,100 H 6
Lipscomb, 3,486 D 1
Live Oak, 6,697 F 9
Llano, 6,979 F 7
Loving, 164 D 10
Lubbock, 179,295 C 4
Lynn, 9,107 C 4
Madison, 7,693 J 6
Marion, 8,517 K 5
Martin, 4,774 C 5
Mason, 3,356 E 7
Matagorda, 27,913 H 9
Maverick, 18,093 D 9
McCulloch, 8,571 E 6
McLennan, 147,553 G 6
McMullen, 1,095 F 9
Medina, 20,249 E 8
Menard, 2,646 E 7
Midland, 65,433 B 6
Milam, 20,028 H 7
Mills, 4,212 F 6
Mitchell, 9,073 D 5
Montague, 15,326 G 4
Montgomery, 49,479 J 7
Moore, 14,060 C 2
Morris, 12,310 K 4
Motley, 2,178 D 3
Nacogdoches, 36,362 K 6
Navarro, 31,150 H 5
Newton, 11,657 L 7
Nolan, 16,220 D 5
Nueces, 237,544 G 10
Ochiltree, 9,704 D 1
Oldham, 2,258 B 2
Orange, 71,170 L 7
Palo Pinto, 28,962 F 5
Panola, 15,894 K 5
Parker, 33,888 G 5
Parmer, 10,509 B 3
Pecos, 13,748 B 7
Polk, 14,457 K 7
Potter, 90,511 C 2
Presidio, 4,842 C 12
Rains, 3,752 J 5
Randall, 53,885 C 2
Reagan, 3,239 C 6
Real, 2,013 E 8
Red River, 14,298 J 4
Reeves, 16,526 D 11
Refugio, 9,494 G 9
Roberts, 967 D 2
Robertson, 14,389 H 6
Rockwall, 7,046 H 5
Runnels, 12,108 E 6
Rusk, 34,102 K 5
Sabine, 7,187 L 6
San Augustine, 7,858 K 6
San Jacinto, 6,702 J 7
San Patricio, 47,288 G 10
San Saba, 5,540 F 6
Schleicher, 2,277 D 7
Scurry, 15,760 D 5
Shackelford, 3,323 E 5
Shelby, 19,672 K 6
Sherman, 3,657 C 1
Smith, 97,096 J 5
Somervell, 2,793 G 5
Starr, 17,707 F 11
Stephens, 8,414 F 5
Sterling, 1,056 C 6
Stonewall, 2,397 D 4
Sutton, 3,175 D 7
Swisher, 10,373 C 3
Tarrant, 716,317 G 5
Taylor, 97,853 E 5
Terrell, 1,940 B 7
Terry, 14,118 B 4
Throckmorton, 2,205 E 4
Titus, 16,702 K 4
Tom Green, 71,047 D 6
Travis, 295,516 G 7
Trinity, 7,628 J 6
Tyler, 12,417 K 7
Upshur, 20,976 K 5
Upton, 4,697 B 6
Uvalde, 17,348 E 8
Val Verde, 27,471 C 8
Van Zandt, 22,155 J 5
Victoria, 53,766 H 9
Walker, 27,680 J 7
Waller, 14,285 J 8
Ward, 13,019 A 6
Washington, 18,842 H 7
Webb, 72,859 E 10
Wharton, 36,729 H 8
Wheeler, 6,434 D 2
Wichita, 121,862 F 3
Wilbarger, 15,355 E 3
Willacy, 15,570 G 11
Williamson, 37,305 G 7
Wilson, 13,041 F 8
Winkler, 9,640 A 6
Wise, 19,687 G 4
Wood, 18,589 J 5
Yoakum, 7,344 B 4
Young, 15,400 F 4
Zapata, 4,352 E 11
Zavala, 11,370 E 9

AREA 267,339 sq. mi.
POPULATION 11,196,730
CAPITAL Austin
LARGEST CITY Houston
HIGHEST POINT Guadalupe Pk. 8,751 ft.
SETTLED IN 1686
ADMITTED TO UNION December 29, 1845
POPULAR NAME Lone Star State
STATE FLOWER Bluebonnet
STATE BIRD Mockingbird

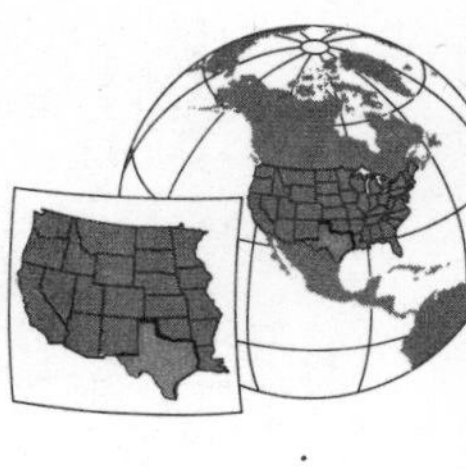

CITIES and TOWNS

	Zip	Name/Pop.	Key
	79311	Abernathy, 2,625	B 4
•	79601	Abilene⊙, 89,653	E 5
		Abilene, ‡113,959	E 5
	78516	Alamo, 4,291	F 11
	78209	Alamo Heights, 6,933	F 8
	76430	Albany⊙, 1,978	E 5
	78332	Alice⊙, 20,121	F 10
	79830	Alpine⊙, 5,971	D 11
	77510	Alta Loma, 1,536	K 3
	75925	Alto, 1,045	J 6
	76009	Alvarado, 2,129	G 5
	77511	Alvin, 10,671	J 3
•	79101	Amarillo⊙, 127,010	C 2
		Amarillo, ‡144,396	C 2
	77514	Anahuac⊙, 1,881	K 8
	77830	Anderson⊙, 500	J 7
	79714	Andrews⊙, 8,625	B 5
	77515	Angleton⊙, 9,770	J 8
	79501	Anson⊙, 2,615	E 5
	88021	Anthony, 2,154	A 10
	79313	Anton, 1,034	B 4
	78336	Aransas Pass, 5,813	G 10
	77517	Arcadia, 1,200	K 3
	76351	Archer City⊙, 1,722	F 4
•	76010	Arlington, 90,643	F 2
	78827	Asherton, 1,645	E 9
	79502	Aspermont⊙, 1,198	D 4
	75751	Athens⊙, 9,582	J 5
	75551	Atlanta, 5,007	K 4
•	78701	Austin (cap.)⊙, 251,808	G 7
		Austin, ‡295,516	G 7
	76020	Azle, 4,493	E 1
	77518	Bacliff, 1,900	K 2
	79504	Baird⊙, 1,538	E 5
	75149	Balch Springs, 10,464	H 2
	76821	Ballinger⊙, 4,203	E 6
	78003	Bandera⊙, 891	F 8
	76823	Bangs, 1,214	E 6
	77532	Barrett, 2,750	K 1
	76511	Bartlett, 1,622	G 7
	78602	Bastrop⊙, 3,112	G 7
	77414	Bay City⊙, 11,733	H 9
	77520	Baytown, 43,980	L 2
	77701	Beaumont⊙, 115,919	K 7
		Beaumont-Port Arthur-Orange, ‡315,943	K 7
	76021	Bedford, 10,049	F 2
	78102	Beeville⊙, 13,506	G 9
	77401	Bellaire, 19,009	J 2
	76705	Bellmead, 7,698	H 6
	77418	Bellville⊙, 2,371	H 8
	76513	Belton⊙, 8,696	G 7
	78341	Benavides, 2,112	F 10
	76126	Benbrook, 8,169	E 2
	79505	Benjamin⊙, 308	E 4
	76932	Big Lake⊙, 2,489	C 6
	79720	Big Spring⊙, 28,735	C 5
	78343	Bishop, 3,466	G 10
	77951	Bloomington, 1,676	H 9
	76131	Blue Mound, 1,283	F 1
	78006	Boerne⊙, 2,432	F 8
	75417	Bogata, 1,287	J 4
	75418	Bonham⊙, 7,698	H 4
	79007	Borger, 14,195	C 2
	75557	Boston⊙, 500	K 4
	79009	Bovina, 1,428	A 3
	76230	Bowie, 5,185	G 4
	78832	Brackettville⊙, 1,539	D 8
	76825	Brady⊙, 5,557	E 6
	77422	Brazoria, 1,681	J 9
	76024	Breckenridge⊙, 5,944	F 5
	77833	Brenham⊙, 8,922	H 7
	77611	Bridge City, 8,164	L 7
	76026	Bridgeport, 3,614	G 4
	77423	Brookshire, 1,683	J 8
	77581	Brookside Village, 1,507	J 2
	79316	Brownfield⊙, 9,647	B 4
	78520	Brownsville⊙, 52,522	G 12
		Brownsville-Harlingen-San Benito, ‡140,368	G 12
	76801	Brownwood⊙, 17,368	F 6
	77801	Bryan⊙, 33,719	H 7
		Bryan-College Station, ‡57,978	H 7
	75831	Buffalo, 1,242	J 6
	77612	Buna, 1,649	L 7
†	79007	Bunavista, 1,402	C 2
†	77001	Bunker Hill Village, 3,977	J 1
	76354	Burkburnett, 9,230	F 3
	76028	Burleson, 7,713	F 2
	78611	Burnet⊙, 2,864	F 7
	77836	Caldwell⊙, 2,308	H 7
	77837	Calvert, 2,072	H 7
	76520	Cameron⊙, 5,546	H 7
	79014	Canadian⊙, 2,292	D 2
	75103	Canton⊙, 2,283	J 5
	79835	Canutillo, 1,588	A 10
	79015	Canyon⊙, 8,333	C 3

(continued on following page)

Agriculture, Industry and Resources

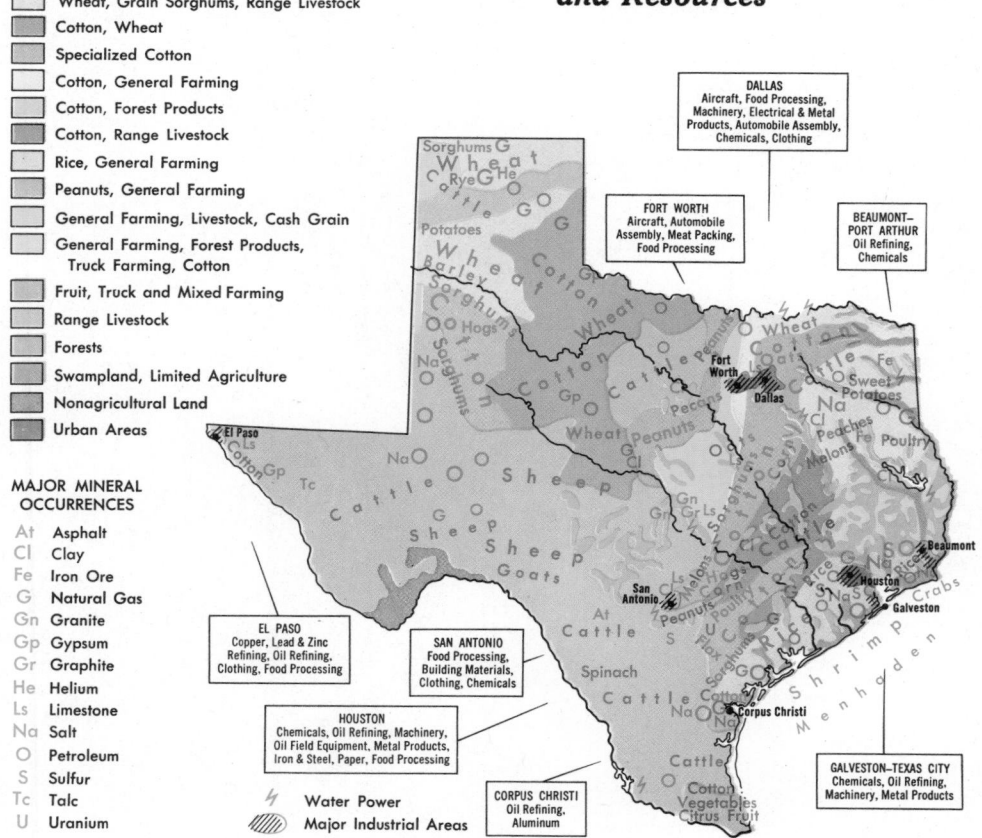

DOMINANT LAND USE

- Wheat, Grain Sorghums, Range Livestock
- Cotton, Wheat
- Specialized Cotton
- Cotton, General Farming
- Cotton, Forest Products
- Cotton, Range Livestock
- Rice, General Farming
- Peanuts, General Farming
- General Farming, Livestock, Cash Grain
- General Farming, Forest Products, Truck Farming, Cotton
- Fruit, Truck and Mixed Farming
- Range Livestock
- Forests
- Swampland, Limited Agriculture
- Nonagricultural Land
- Urban Areas

MAJOR MINERAL OCCURRENCES

At Asphalt
Cl Clay
Fe Iron Ore
G Natural Gas
Gn Granite
Gp Gypsum
Gr Graphite
He Helium
Ls Limestone
Na Salt
O Petroleum
S Sulfur
Tc Talc
U Uranium

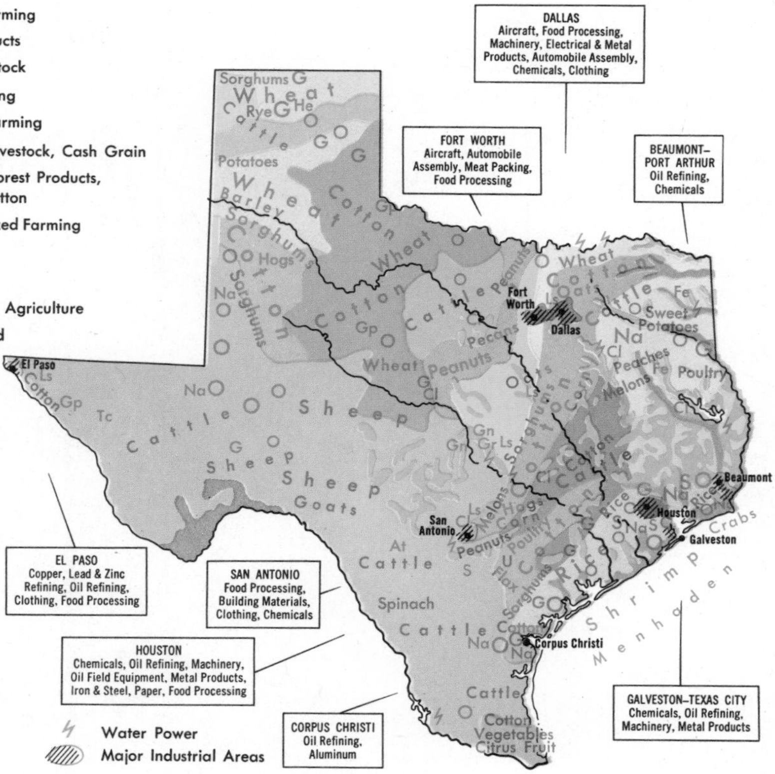
DALLAS
Aircraft, Food Processing, Machinery, Electrical & Metal Products, Automobile Assembly, Chemicals, Clothing
FORT WORTH
Aircraft, Automobile Assembly, Meat Packing, Food Processing
BEAUMONT–PORT ARTHUR
Oil Refining, Chemicals
EL PASO
Copper, Lead & Zinc Refining, Oil Refining, Clothing, Food Processing
SAN ANTONIO
Food Processing, Building Materials, Clothing, Chemicals
HOUSTON
Chemicals, Oil Refining, Machinery, Oil Field Equipment, Metal Products, Iron & Steel, Paper, Food Processing
CORPUS CHRISTI
Oil Refining, Aluminum
GALVESTON–TEXAS CITY
Chemicals, Oil Refining, Machinery, Metal Products
Water Power
Major Industrial Areas
El Paso
Fort Worth
Dallas
San Antonio
Houston
Galveston
Beaumont
Corpus Christi
Wheat
Cotton
Sorghums
Cattle
Sheep
Goats
Potatoes
Barley
Peanuts
Pecans
Hogs
Oats
Poultry
Sweet Potatoes
Peaches
Melons
Rice
Spinach
Flax
Corn
Shrimp
Crabs
Menhaden
Cotton
Vegetables
Citrus Fruit

TEXAS

State Capitals ⊛
County Seats ⊛

© C.S. HAMMOND & Co., N.Y.

0 20 40 60 80 100 MI.
0 20 40 60 80 100 KM.

WESTERN PART
OF
TEXAS
Same scale as main map

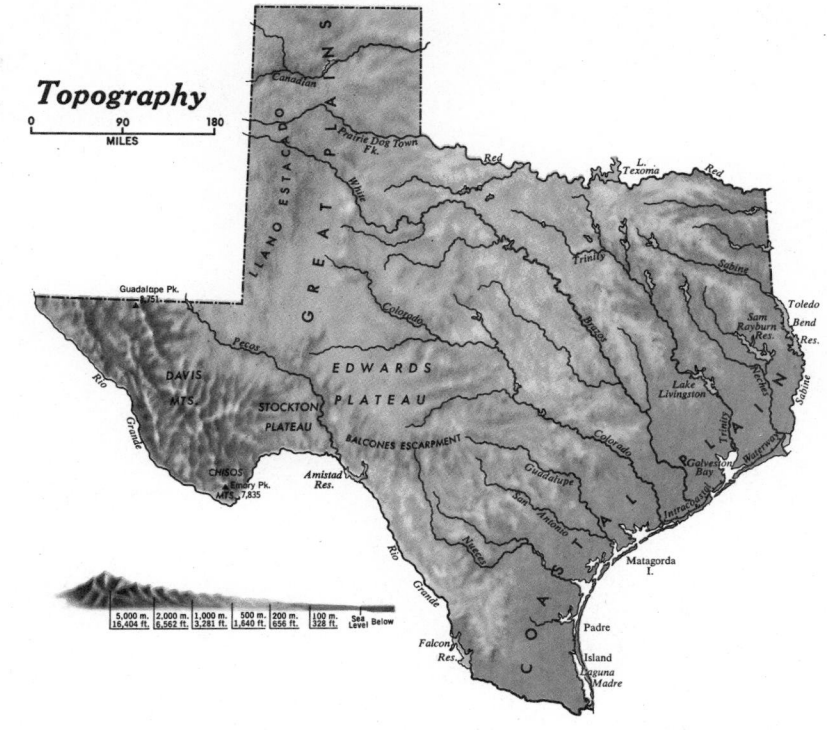

Topography

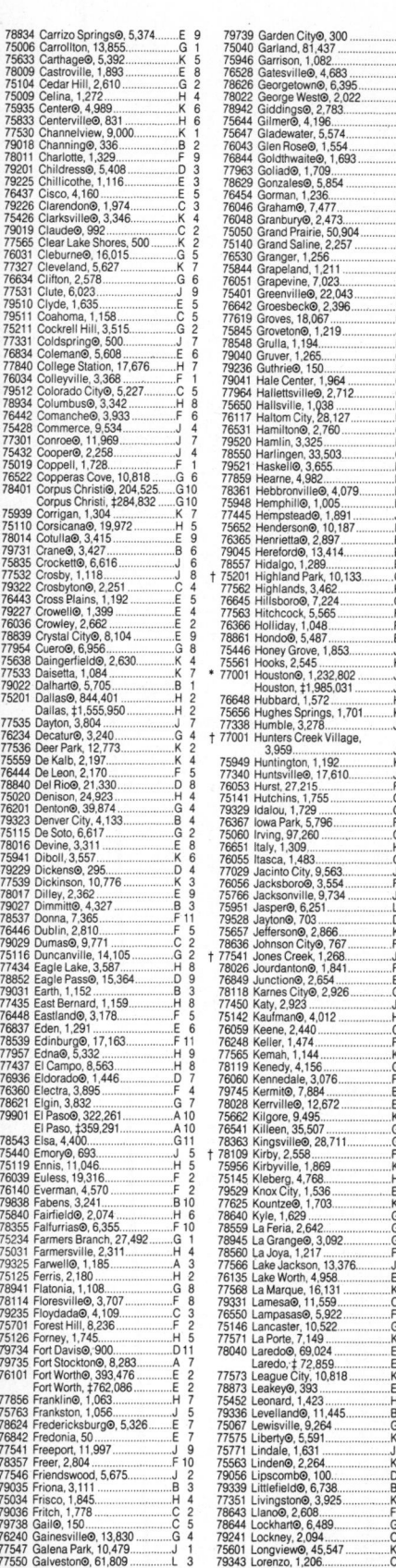

78834 Carrizo Springs⊙, 5,374......E 9
75006 Carrollton, 13,855......G 1
75633 Carthage⊙, 5,392......K 5
76009 Castroville, 1,893......E 8
75104 Cedar Hill, 2,610......G 2
75009 Celina, 1,272......H 4
75935 Center⊙, 4,989......K 6
75833 Centerville⊙, 831......H 6
77530 Channelview, 9,000......K 1
77090 Channing⊙, 336......B 2
78011 Charlotte, 1,329......F 9
79201 Childress⊙, 5,408......D 3
79225 Chillicothe, 1,116......E 3
76437 Cisco, 4,160......E 5
79226 Clarendon⊙, 1,974......C 3
75426 Clarksville⊙, 3,346......K 4
79019 Claude⊙, 992......C 2
77565 Clear Lake Shores, 500......K 2
76031 Cleburne⊙, 16,015......G 5
77327 Cleveland, 5,627......K 7
76634 Clifton, 2,578......G 6
77531 Clute, 6,023......J 9
76510 Clyde, 1,635......E 5
79511 Coahoma, 1,158......C 5
75211 Cockrell Hill, 3,515......G 2
77331 Coldspring⊙, 500......J 7
76834 Coleman⊙, 5,608......E 6
77840 College Station, 17,676......H 7
76034 Colleyville, 3,368......F 1
79512 Colorado City⊙, 5,227......C 5
78934 Columbus⊙, 3,342......H 8
76442 Comanche⊙, 3,933......F 6
75428 Commerce, 9,534......J 4
77301 Conroe⊙, 11,969......J 7
75432 Cooper⊙, 2,258......J 4
75019 Coppell, 1,728......F 1
76522 Copperas Cove, 10,818......G 6
78401 Corpus Christi⊙, 204,525......G10
 Corpus Christi, ‡284,832......G10
75939 Corrigan, 1,304......K 7
75110 Corsicana⊙, 19,972......H 5
78014 Cotulla⊙, 3,415......E 9
79731 Crane⊙, 3,427......B 6
75835 Crockett⊙, 6,616......J 6
77532 Crosby, 1,118......J 8
79322 Crosbyton⊙, 2,251......C 4
76443 Cross Plains, 1,192......C 5
79227 Crowell⊙, 1,399......E 4
76036 Crowley, 2,662......E 2
78839 Crystal City⊙, 8,104......E 9
77954 Cuero⊙, 6,956......G 8
75638 Daingerfield⊙, 2,630......K 4
77533 Daisetta, 1,084......K 7
75201 Dalhart⊙, 5,705......B 1
75201 Dallas⊙, 844,401......H 2
 Dallas, ‡1,555,950......H 2
77535 Dayton, 3,804......J 7
76234 Decatur⊙, 3,240......G 4
77536 Deer Park, 12,773......K 2
75006 De Kalb, 2,197......K 4
76444 De Leon, 2,170......F 5
78840 Del Rio⊙, 21,330......D 8
75020 Denison, 24,923......H 4
76201 Denton⊙, 39,874......G 4
79323 Denver City, 4,133......B 4
75115 De Soto, 6,617......G 2
78016 Devine, 3,311......E 8
75941 Diboll, 3,557......K 6
79229 Dickens⊙, 295......D 4
77539 Dickinson, 10,776......K 3
78017 Dilley, 2,362......E 9
79027 Dimmitt⊙, 4,327......B 3
78537 Donna, 7,365......F 11
76446 Dublin, 2,810......F 5
79029 Dumas⊙, 9,771......C 2
75116 Duncanville, 14,105......G 2
77434 Eagle Lake, 3,587......H 8
78852 Eagle Pass⊙, 15,364......D 9
79031 Earth, 1,152......B 3
77435 East Bernard, 1,159......H 8
76448 Eastland⊙, 3,178......F 5
76837 Eden, 1,291......E 6
78539 Edinburg⊙, 17,163......F 11
77957 Edna⊙, 5,332......H 8
77437 El Campo, 8,563......H 8
76936 Eldorado⊙, 1,446......D 7
76360 Electra, 3,895......F 4
78621 Elgin, 4,535......G 7
79901 El Paso⊙, 322,261......A 10
 El Paso, ‡359,291......A 10
78543 Elsa, 4,400......G11
75440 Emory⊙, 693......J 5
75119 Ennis, 11,046......H 5
76039 Euless, 19,316......F 2
76140 Everman, 4,570......F 2
79838 Fabens, 3,241......B 10
75840 Fairfield⊙, 2,074......H 6
78355 Falfurrias⊙, 6,355......F 10
75234 Farmers Branch, 27,492......G 1
75031 Farmersville, 2,311......H 4
79325 Farwell⊙, 1,185......A 3
75125 Ferris, 2,180......H 2
79041 Flatonia, 1,108......G 8
78114 Floresville⊙, 3,707......F 8
79235 Floydada⊙, 4,109......C 3
75126 Forest Hill, 8,236......F 2
75126 Forney, 1,745......H 4
79734 Fort Davis⊙, 900......D11
75857 Fort Stockton⊙, 8,283......A 7
76101 Fort Worth⊙, 393,476......E 2
 Fort Worth, ‡762,086......E 2
77856 Franklin⊙, 1,063......H 7
75763 Frankston, 1,056......J 5
78624 Fredericksburg⊙, 5,326......E 7
76842 Fredonia, 50......E 7
77541 Freeport, 11,997......J 9
78357 Freer, 2,804......F 10
77546 Friendswood, 5,675......J 2
79035 Friona, 3,111......B 3
75034 Frisco, 1,845......H 4
79036 Fritch, 1,778......C 2
79738 Gail, 150......C 5
76240 Gainesville⊙, 13,830......G 4
77547 Galena Park, 10,479......J 1
77550 Galveston⊙, 61,809......L 3
 Galveston-Texas City, ‡169,812......L 3
77962 Ganado, 1,640......H 8

79739 Garden City⊙, 300......C 6
75040 Garland, 81,437......H 1
75946 Garrison, 1,082......K 6
76528 Gatesville⊙, 4,683......G 6
78626 Georgetown⊙, 6,395......G 7
78022 George West⊙, 2,022......F 9
78942 Giddings⊙, 2,783......H 7
75644 Gilmer⊙, 4,196......J 5
75647 Gladewater, 5,574......K 5
76043 Glen Rose⊙, 1,554......G 5
76844 Goldthwaite⊙, 1,693......F 6
77963 Goliad⊙, 1,709......G 9
78629 Gonzales⊙, 5,854......G 8
76454 Gorman, 1,236......F 5
76046 Graham⊙, 7,477......F 4
76048 Granbury⊙, 2,473......G 5
75050 Grand Prairie, 50,904......G 2
75140 Grand Saline, 2,257......J 5
76530 Granger, 1,256......G 7
75844 Grapeland, 1,211......J 6
76051 Grapevine, 7,023......F 1
75401 Greenville⊙, 22,043......H 4
76642 Groesbeck⊙, 2,396......H 6
77619 Groves, 18,067......L 8
75845 Groveton⊙, 1,219......J 7
78548 Gruver, 1,194......F 11
79040 Gruver, 1,265......C 1
79236 Guthrie⊙, 150......D 4
79041 Hale Center, 1,964......C 3
77964 Hallettsville⊙, 2,712......G 8
75650 Hallsville, 1,038......K 5
76117 Haltom City, 28,127......F 2
76531 Hamilton⊙, 2,760......G 6
79520 Hamlin, 3,325......E 5
78550 Harlingen, 33,503......G11
75521 Haskell⊙, 3,655......E 4
77859 Hearne, 4,982......H 7
78361 Hebbronville⊙, 4,079......F 10
75948 Hemphill⊙, 1,005......L 6
77445 Hempstead⊙, 1,891......J 7
75652 Henderson⊙, 10,187......K 5
76365 Henrietta⊙, 2,897......F 4
79045 Hereford⊙, 13,414......B 3
78557 Hidalgo, 1,289......F 11
† 75201 Highland Park, 10,133......G 2
75562 Highlands, 3,462......K 1
76645 Hillsboro⊙, 7,224......G 5
77563 Hitchcock, 5,565......K 3
76366 Holliday, 1,048......F 4
78861 Hondo⊙, 5,487......E 8
75446 Honey Grove, 1,853......J 4
75561 Hooks, 2,545......K 4
* 77001 Houston⊙, 1,232,802......J 2
 Houston, ‡1,985,031......J 2
76648 Hubbard, 1,572......H 6
75656 Hughes Springs, 1,701......K 5
77338 Humble, 3,278......J 1
† 77001 Hunters Creek Village, 3,959......J 1
75949 Huntington, 1,192......K 6
75340 Huntsville⊙, 17,610......J 7
76053 Hurst, 27,215......F 2
75141 Hutchins, 1,755......G 2
79329 Idalou, 1,729......C 4
76367 Iowa Park, 5,796......F 4
75060 Irving, 97,260......G 2
76651 Italy, 1,309......H 5
76055 Itasca, 1,483......G 5
77029 Jacinto City, 9,563......J 1
76056 Jacksboro⊙, 3,554......F 4
75766 Jacksonville, 9,734......J 5
75951 Jasper⊙, 6,251......L 7
79528 Jayton⊙, 703......D 4
75657 Jefferson⊙, 2,866......K 5
78636 Johnson City⊙, 767......F 7
† 77541 Jones Creek, 1,268......J 9
78026 Jourdanton⊙, 1,841......F 9
76849 Junction⊙, 2,654......E 7
78118 Karnes City⊙, 2,926......G 9
77450 Katy, 2,923......J 8
75142 Kaufman⊙, 4,012......H 5
76059 Keene, 2,440......G 5
76248 Keller, 1,474......F 1
77565 Kemah, 1,144......K 2
76119 Kenedy, 4,156......G 9
76060 Kennedale, 3,076......F 2
79745 Kermit⊙, 7,884......B 6
78028 Kerrville⊙, 12,672......E 7
75662 Kilgore, 9,495......K 5
76541 Killeen, 35,507......G 6
78363 Kingsville⊙, 28,711......G10
† 78109 Kirby, 2,558......F 8
75956 Kirbyville, 1,869......K 7
75145 Kleberg, 4,768......H 2
79529 Knox City, 1,536......E 4
77625 Kountze⊙, 1,703......K 7
78640 Kyle, 1,629......G 8
78559 La Feria, 2,642......G11
78945 La Grange⊙, 3,092......G 8
78560 La Joya, 1,217......F 11
77566 Lake Jackson, 13,376......J 9
76135 Lake Worth, 4,958......E 2
77568 La Marque, 16,131......K 3
79331 Lamesa⊙, 11,559......C 5
76550 Lampasas⊙, 5,922......F 7
75146 Lancaster, 10,522......G 2
77571 La Porte, 7,149......K 2
78040 Laredo⊙, 69,024......E 10
 Laredo, ‡ 72,859......E 10
77573 League City, 10,818......K 2
78873 Leakey⊙, 393......E 8
75452 Leonard, 1,423......H 4
79336 Levelland⊙, 11,445......B 4
75067 Lewisville, 9,264......G 1
75775 Liberty⊙, 5,591......K 7
75771 Lindale, 1,631......J 5
75563 Linden⊙, 2,331......K 4
79056 Lipscomb⊙, 100......D 1
79339 Littlefield⊙, 6,738......B 4
77351 Livingston⊙, 3,925......K 7
78643 Llano⊙, 2,608......F 7
78644 Lockhart⊙, 6,489......G 8
79241 Lockney, 2,044......C 3
75601 Longview⊙, 45,547......K 5
79124 Lorenzo, 1,206......C 4
78566 Los Fresnos, 1,297......G11
* 79401 Lubbock⊙, 149,101......C 4
 Lubbock, ‡179,295......C 4

75901 Lufkin⊙, 23,049......K 6
78648 Luling, 4,719......G 8
78569 Lyford, 1,425......G11
78052 Lytle, 1,271......F 8
75147 Mabank, 1,239......H 5
77864 Madisonville⊙, 2,881......J 7
76063 Mansfield, 3,658......F 2
78654 Marble Falls, 2,209......F 7
79843 Marfa⊙, 2,647......C12
76661 Marlin⊙, 6,351......H 6
75670 Marshall⊙, 22,937......K 5
76664 Mart, 2,183......H 6
76856 Mason⊙, 1,806......E 7
79244 Matador⊙, 1,091......D 3
78368 Mathis, 5,351......G 9
75567 Maud, 1,107......K 4
78501 McAllen, 37,636......F 11
 McAllen-Pharr-Edinburg, ‡181,535......F 11
79752 McCamey, 2,647......B 6
79057 McGregor, 4,365......G 6
75069 McKinney⊙, 15,193......H 4
79057 McLean, 1,160......D 2
77520 McNair, 2,039......K 1
79245 Memphis⊙, 3,227......D 3
76859 Menard⊙, 1,740......E 7
79754 Mentone⊙, 50......D 10
78570 Mercedes, 9,355......F 12
76665 Meridian⊙, 1,162......G 6
79536 Merkel, 2,163......E 5
78941 Mertzon⊙, 513......C 6
75149 Mesquite, 55,131......H 2
76667 Mexia, 5,943......H 6
79059 Miami⊙, 611......D 2
79701 Midland⊙, 59,463......C 6
 Midland, ‡65,433......C 6
76065 Midlothian, 2,322......G 5
75773 Mineola, 3,843......J 5
76067 Mineral Wells, 18,411......F 5
78572 Mission, 13,043......F 11
77459 Missouri City, 4,136......J 2
79756 Monahans⊙, 8,333......B 6
76251 Montague⊙, 490......G 4
77580 Mont Belvieu, 1,144......L 1
76557 Moody, 1,286......G 6
79346 Morton⊙, 2,738......B 4
75455 Mount Pleasant⊙, 8,877......K 4
75457 Mount Vernon⊙, 1,806......J 4
78252 Muenster, 1,411......G 4
79347 Muleshoe⊙, 4,525......B 3
76371 Munday, 1,726......E 4
75961 Nacogdoches⊙, 22,544......J 6
75568 Naples, 1,226......K 4
75569 Nash, 1,961......K 4
78059 Natalia, 1,296......F 8
77868 Navasota, 5,111......J 7
77627 Nederland, 16,810......L 8
77461 Needville, 1,024......J 8
75570 New Boston, 3,699......K 4
78130 New Braunfels⊙, 17,859......F 8
75966 Newton⊙, 1,529......L 7
78140 Nixon, 1,925......G 8
75560 Nocona, 2,871......G 4
76118 North Richland Hills, 16,514......F 1
79760 Odessa⊙, 78,380......B 6
 Odessa, ‡91,805......B 6
79351 O'Donnell, 1,148......C 5
79064 Olney, 3,624......F 4
79064 Olton, 1,750......B 3
77630 Orange⊙, 24,457......L 7
78372 Orange Grove, 1,075......F 10
75684 Overton, 2,084......K 5

76943 Ozona⊙, 2,864......C 7
79248 Paducah⊙, 2,052......D 4
76066 Paint Rock⊙, 193......E 6
77465 Palacios, 3,642......H 9
75801 Palestine⊙, 14,525......J 6
76072 Palo Pinto⊙, 250......F 5
79065 Pampa⊙, 21,726......D 2
79068 Panhandle⊙, 2,141......C 2
75460 Paris⊙, 23,441......J 4
* 77501 Pasadena, 89,277......J 2
77581 Pearland, 6,444......J 2
78061 Pearsall⊙, 5,545......E 9
79772 Pecos⊙, 12,682......D 10
79070 Perryton⊙, 7,810......D 1
79250 Petersburg, 1,300......C 4
78577 Pharr, 15,829......F 11
79071 Phillips, 2,515......C 2
76258 Pilot Point, 1,663......H 4
75968 Pineland, 1,127......L 6
* 77001 Piney Point Village, 2,548......J 1
75686 Plains⊙, 1,087......B 4
79355 Plainview⊙, 19,096......C 3
75074 Plano, 17,872......H 4
77064 Pleasanton, 5,407......F 9
77978 Point Comfort, 1,446......H 9
78373 Port Aransas, 1,218......H10
77640 Port Arthur, 57,371......L 8
77365 Porter, 1,900......J 1
78578 Port Isabel, 3,067......G11
78374 Portland, 7,302......G10
77979 Port Lavaca⊙, 10,491......H 9
77651 Port Neches, 10,894......K 7
79356 Post⊙, 3,854......C 4
78065 Poteet, 3,013......F 8
78147 Poth, 1,296......F 8
77445 Prairie View, 3,589......J 7
78375 Premont, 3,282......F 10
79845 Presidio, 850......C12
79252 Quanah⊙, 3,948......E 3
75572 Queen City, 1,227......K 4
75783 Quitman⊙, 1,494......J 5
79357 Ralls, 1,962......C 4
76470 Ranger, 3,094......F 5
78377 Raymondville⊙, 7,987......G11
75080 Richardson, 48,582......G 1
76118 Richland Hills, 8,865......F 2
77469 Richmond⊙, 5,777......J 8
78582 Rio Grande City⊙, 5,676......F 11
78583 Rio Hondo, 1,671......G11
77019 River Oaks, 8,193......E 2
76945 Robert Lee⊙, 1,119......D 6
78380 Robstown, 11,217......G10
79543 Roby⊙, 784......D 5
76567 Rockdale, 4,655......G 7
78382 Rockport⊙, 3,879......H 9
78880 Rocksprings⊙, 1,221......D 8
75087 Rockwall⊙, 3,121......H 5
76569 Rogers, 1,030......G 7
78584 Roma-Los Saenz, 2,154......E 11
79545 Roscoe, 1,580......D 5
76570 Rosebud, 1,597......G 7
77471 Rosenberg, 12,098......J 8
75546 Rotan, 2,404......D 5
78664 Round Rock, 2,811......G 7
75189 Royse City, 1,535......H 4
78585 Rusk⊙, 4,914......J 6
78881 Sabinal, 1,554......E 8
76079 Saginaw, 2,382......E 2

78265 Saint Jo, 1,054......G 4
79901 San Angelo⊙, 63,884......D 6
 San Angelo, ‡71,047......D 6
* 78201 San Antonio⊙, 654,153......F 8
 San Antonio, ‡864,014......F 8
75972 San Augustine⊙, 2,539......K 6
78586 San Benito, 15,176......G12
79848 Sanderson⊙, 1,229......B 7
78266 Sanger, 1,603......G 4
78589 San Juan, 5,070......F 11
77539 San Leon, 1,500......L 2
78666 San Marcos⊙, 18,860......F 8
76955 San Saba⊙, 2,555......F 6
† 76101 Sansom Park Village, 4,771......E 2
76878 Santa Anna, 1,310......E 6
78385 Santa⊙, 250......G10
78154 Schertz, 4,061......F 8
78956 Schulenburg, 2,294......H 8
77586 Seabrook, 3,811......K 2
77983 Seadrift, 1,092......H 9
75159 Seagoville, 4,390......H 2
79359 Seagraves, 2,440......B 5
77474 Sealy, 2,603......H 8
78155 Seguin⊙, 15,934......G 8
79360 Seminole⊙, 5,007......B 5
76380 Seymour⊙, 3,469......E 4
79363 Shallowater, 1,339......B 4
79079 Shamrock, 2,644......D 2
77001 Sheldon, 1,665......K 1
75090 Sherman⊙, 29,061......H 4
 Sherman-Denison, ‡83,225......H 4
77984 Shiner, 2,102......G 8
77571 Shore Acres, 1,872......K 2
79851 Sierra Blanca⊙, 900......B 11
77656 Silsbee, 7,271......K 7
79257 Silverton⊙, 1,026......C 3
78387 Sinton⊙, 5,563......G 9
79364 Slaton, 6,583......C 4
78957 Smithville, 2,959......G 7
79549 Snyder⊙, 11,171......D 5
77879 Somerville, 1,250......H 7
76950 Sonora⊙, 2,149......D 7
77659 Sourlake, 1,694......K 7
75587 South Houston, 11,527......J 2
76051 Southlake, 2,031......F 1
† 77001 Southside Place, 1,466......J 2
79081 Spearman⊙, 3,435......C 1
77373 Spring, 1,900......J 1
76082 Springtown, 1,194......G 5
* 77001 Spring Valley, 3,170......J 1
79370 Spur, 1,747......D 4
77477 Stafford, 2,906......J 2
79553 Stamford, 4,558......E 5
79782 Stanton⊙, 2,117......C 5
79081 Stephenville⊙, 9,277......F 5
76951 Sterling City⊙, 780......C 6
79083 Stinnett⊙, 2,014......C 2
78160 Stockdale, 1,132......G 8
79084 Stratford⊙, 2,139......C 1
78478 Sugar Land, 3,318......J 8
75482 Sulphur Springs⊙, 10,642......J 4
79372 Sundown, 1,129......B 4
79086 Sunray, 1,854......C 1
77480 Sweeny, 3,191......J 9
75556 Sweetwater⊙, 12,020......D 5
78390 Taft, 3,274......G10
79373 Tahoka⊙, 2,956......C 4
76574 Taylor, 9,616......G 7
75860 Teague, 2,867......H 6
76501 Temple, 33,431......G 6
75974 Tenaha, 1,094......K 6
79852 Terlingua, 100......D12

78265 Terrell, 14,182......H 5
† 78201 Terrell Hills, 5,225......F 8
75501 Texarkana, 30,497......L 4
 Texarkana, ‡101,198......L 4
77590 Texas City, 38,908......K 3
73949 Texhoma, 356......C 1
76577 Thorndale, 1,031......G 7
78071 Three Rivers, 1,761......F 9
76083 Throckmorton⊙, 1,105......F 4
78072 Tilden⊙, 600......F 9
75975 Timpson, 1,254......K 6
77375 Tomball, 2,734......J 1
75163 Trinidad, 1,079......H 5
75862 Trinity, 2,512......J 7
75789 Troup, 1,668......J 5
79088 Tulia⊙, 5,033......C 3
75701 Tyler⊙, 57,770......J 5
 Tyler, ‡97,096......J 5
78228 University Park, 23,498......H 2
78801 Uvalde⊙, 10,764......E 8
75790 Van, 1,593......J 5
75095 Van Alstyne, 1,981......H 4
79855 Van Horn⊙, 2,240......C11
79092 Vega, 839......B 2
78384 Vernon⊙, 11,454......F 4
77901 Victoria⊙, 41,349......H 9
77662 Victor, 9,738......L 7
* 76701 Waco⊙, 95,326......G 6
 Waco, ‡147,553......G 6
78959 Waelder, 1,138......G 8
75501 Wake Village, 2,408......K 4
77485 Wallis, 1,028......H 8
75692 Waskom, 1,460......L 5
75165 Waxahachie⊙, 13,452......H 5
76086 Weatherford⊙, 11,750......G 5
77598 Webster, 2,231......K 2
78962 Weimar, 2,104......H 8
79095 Wellington⊙, 2,884......D 3
78596 Weslaco, 15,313......G11
76691 West, 2,406......G 6
77486 West Columbia, 3,335......J 8
77630 West Orange, 4,787......L 7
† 77001 West University Place, 13,317......J 2
† 76101 Westworth, 4,578......E 2
77488 Wharton⊙, 7,881......J 8
79096 Wheeler⊙, 1,116......D 2
79097 White Deer, 1,092......C 2
76273 Whitesboro, 2,927......H 4
78108 White Settlement, 13,449......E 2
75491 Whitewright, 1,742......H 4
76692 Whitney, 1,371......G 6
* 76301 Wichita Falls⊙, 97,564......F 4
 Wichita Falls, ‡127,621......F 4
77378 Willis, 1,577......J 7
75169 Wills Point, 2,636......J 5
75172 Wilmer, 1,922......H 2
76384 Wink, 1,543......A 6
75494 Winnsboro, 3,064......J 5
79567 Winters, 2,907......E 6
75496 Wolfe City, 1,433......J 4
79382 Wolfforth, 1,090......C 4
78393 Woodsboro⊙, 1,839......G 9
75979 Woodville⊙, 2,662......K 7
76693 Wortham, 1,036......H 6
75098 Wylie, 2,675......H 4
77995 Yoakum, 5,755......G 8
78164 Yorktown, 2,071......G 9
78076 Zapata⊙, 2,102......E 11

⊙ County seat.
‡ Population of metropolitan area.
† Zip of nearest p.o.
* Multiple zips

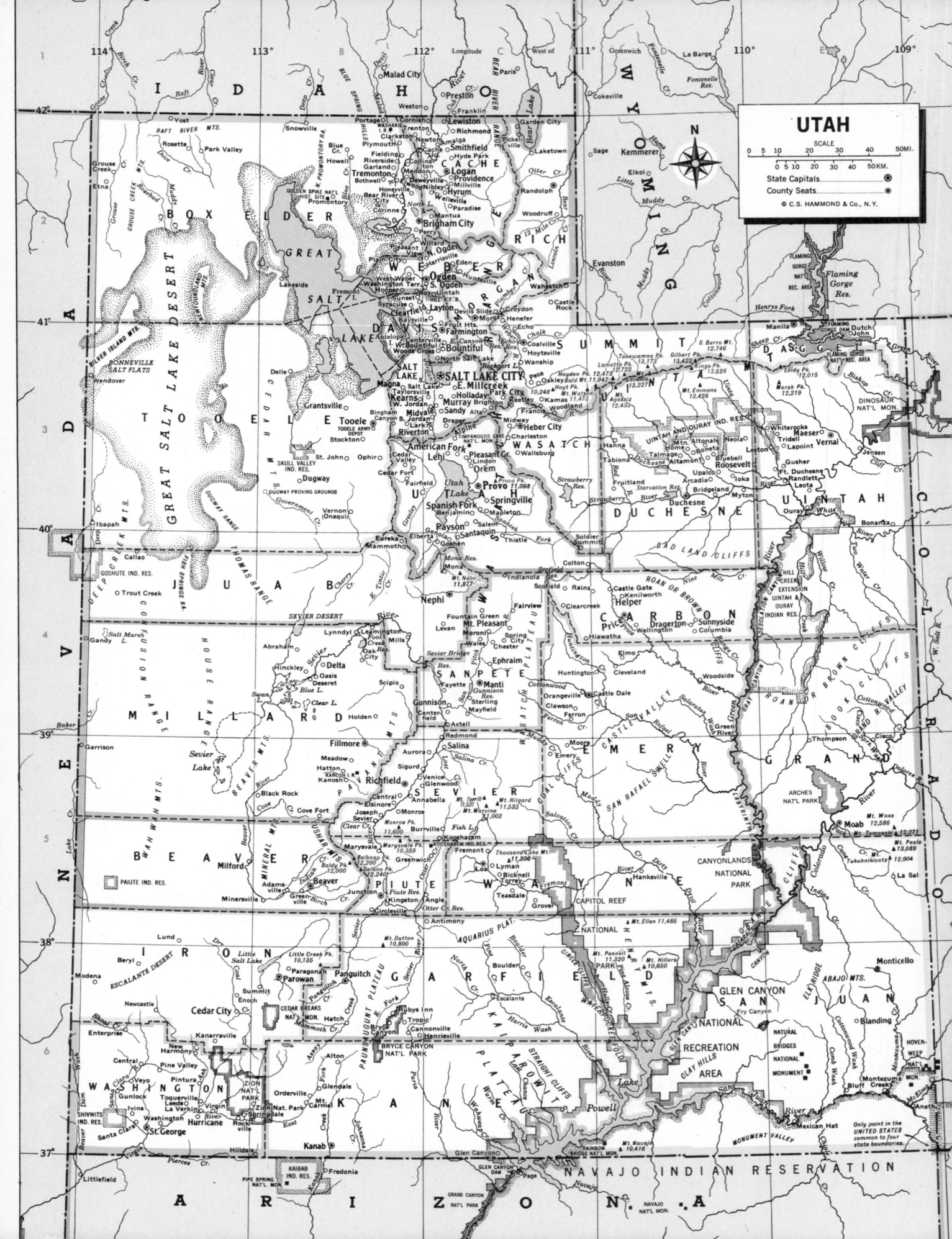

UTAH

SCALE

0 5 10   20   30   40   50MI.

0 5 10 20 30 40 50KM.

State Capitals............⊛

County Seats............◉

© C.S. HAMMOND & Co., N.Y.

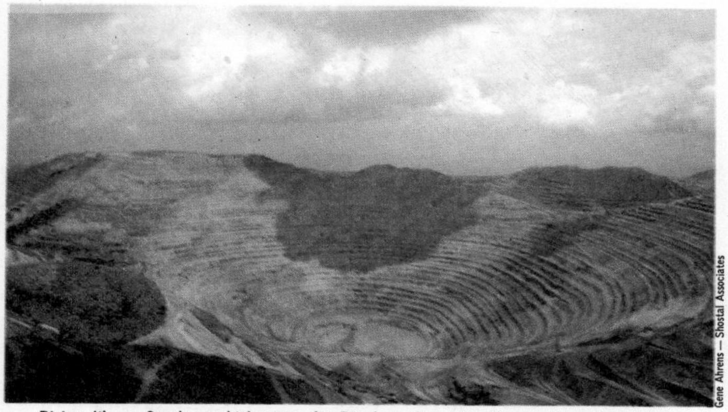

Gene Ahrens — Shostal Associates

Rising like a Greek amphitheater, the Bingham Open Pit Copper Mine in Utah is constantly changing as giant electric shovels remove seven tons of earth at a time.

AREA 84,916 sq. mi.
POPULATION 1,059,273
CAPITAL Salt Lake City
LARGEST CITY Salt Lake City
HIGHEST POINT Kings Pk. 13,528 ft.
SETTLED IN 1847
ADMITTED TO UNION January 4, 1896
POPULAR NAME Beehive State
STATE FLOWER Sego Lily
STATE BIRD Sea Gull

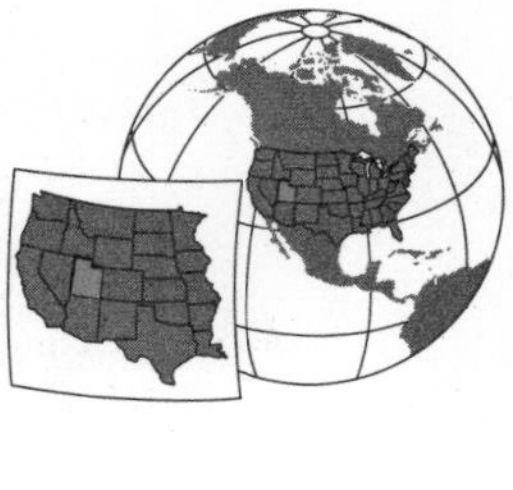

COUNTIES

Beaver, 3,800	A 5
Box Elder, 28,129	A 2
Cache, 42,331	C 2
Carbon, 15,647	D 4
Daggett, 666	E 3
Davis, 99,028	B 3
Duchesne, 7,299	D 3
Emery, 5,137	D 4
Garfield, 3,157	C 6
Grand, 6,688	E 5
Iron, 12,177	A 6
Juab, 4,574	A 4
Kane, 2,421	B 6
Millard, 6,988	A 4
Morgan, 3,983	C 2
Piute, 1,164	B 5
Rich, 1,615	C 2
Salt Lake, 458,607	B 3
San Juan, 9,606	E 6
Sanpete, 10,976	C 4
Sevier, 10,103	C 5
Summit, 5,879	D 3
Tooele, 21,545	A 3
Uintah, 12,684	E 3
Utah, 137,776	C 3
Wasatch, 5,863	C 3
Washington, 13,669	A 6
Wayne, 1,483	C 5
Weber, 126,278	B 2

CITIES and TOWNS

	Zip	*Name/Pop.*	*Key*
†	84003	Alpine, 1,047	C 3
	84001	Altamont, 129	D 3
	84002	Altonah, 225	D 3
†	84335	Amalga, 207	C 2
	84003	American Fork, 7,713	C 3
	84510	Aneth, 250	E 6
	84711	Annabella, 221	B 5
	84712	Antimony, 113	C 5
	84005	Arcadia, 150	D 3
	84620	Aurora, 493	B 5
	84621	Axtell, 150	C 4
	84301	Bear River City, 445	B 2
	84713	Beaver⊙, 1,453	B 5
†	84660	Benjamin, 503	C 3
	84715	Bicknell, 264	C 5
	84511	Blanding, 2,250	E 6
	84007	Bluebell, 210	D 3
	84512	Bluff, 300	E 6
	84008	Bonanza, 150	E 3
†	84337	Bothwell, 300	B 2
	84716	Boulder, 93	C 6
	84010	Bountiful, 27,853	C 3
	84012	Bridgeland, 150	D 3
	84302	Brigham City⊙, 14,007	C 2
	84117	Brighton, 150	C 3
	84717	Bryce Canyon, 229	B 6
	84718	Cannonville, 113	B 6
	84513	Castle Dale⊙, 541	D 4
	84514	Castle Gate, 205	D 4
	84720	Cedar City, 8,946	A 6
†	84013	Cedar Fort, 188	B 3
	84013	Cedar Valley, 290	B 3
	84622	Centerfield, 419	C 4
	84014	Centerville, 3,268	C 3
	84722	Central, 154	B 5
†	84032	Charleston, 196	C 3
	84623	Chester, 130	C 4
	84723	Circleville, 443	B 5
	84305	Clarkston, 420	B 2
	84516	Clawson, 95	C 4
	84015	Clearfield, 13,316	B 2
	84518	Cleveland, 244	D 4
	84017	Coalville⊙, 864	C 3
	84519	Columbia, 380	D 4
	84307	Corinne, 471	B 2
	84308	Cornish, 173	B 2
	84018	Croydon, 90	C 2
	84624	Delta, 1,610	B 4
	84625	Deseret, 215	B 4
	84309	Deweyville, 248	B 2
	84520	Dragerton, 1,614	D 4
	84020	Draper, 4,000	C 3
	84021	Duchesne⊙, 1,094	D 3
	84022	Dugway, 2,357	B 3
	84023	Dutch John, 263	E 3
†	84101	East Millcreek, 26,579	C 3
	84310	Eden, 421	C 2
	84626	Elberta, 325	B 4
	84521	Elmo, 141	D 4
	84724	Elsinore, 357	B 5
†	84337	Elwood, 294	B 2
	84522	Emery, 216	C 5
†	84720	Enoch, 120	A 6
	84725	Enterprise, 844	A 6
	84627	Ephraim, 2,127	C 4
	84726	Escalante, 638	C 6
	84628	Eureka, 753	B 4
	84629	Fairview, 696	C 4
	84025	Farmington⊙, 2,526	C 3
	84630	Fayette, 93	C 4
	84523	Ferron, 663	C 4
	84311	Fielding, 254	B 2
	84631	Fillmore⊙, 1,411	B 5
	84026	Fort Duchesne, 300	E 3
	84632	Fountain Green, 467	C 4
†	84036	Francis, 268	C 3
	84727	Fremont, 160	C 5
†	84037	Fruit Heights, 800	C 2
	84028	Garden City, 134	C 2
	84312	Garland, 1,187	B 2
†	84655	Genola, 424	C 4
	84729	Glendale, 200	B 6
	84730	Glenwood, 212	C 5
	84633	Goshen, 459	C 4
	84029	Grantsville, 2,931	B 3
	84525	Green River, 1,033	D 4
	84731	Greenville, 97	B 5
	84313	Grouse Creek, 100	A 2
	84733	Gunlock, 93	A 6
	84634	Gunnison, 1,073	C 4
	84030	Gusher, 125	E 3
	84734	Hanksville, 224	D 5
	84031	Hanna, 135	D 3
†	84401	Harrisville, 603	C 2
	84735	Hatch, 139	B 6
	84032	Heber City⊙, 3,245	C 3
	84526	Helper, 1,964	D 4
	84033	Henefer, 446	C 2
	84736	Henrieville, 145	C 6
	84527	Hiawatha, 166	D 4
†	84767	Hilldale, 480	B 6
	84635	Hinckley, 400	B 4
	84636	Holden, 351	B 4
	84117	Holladay, 23,014	C 3
	84314	Honeyville, 640	B 2
	84315	Hooper, 1,705	B 2
	84316	Howell, 146	B 2
†	84017	Hoytsville, 500	C 3
	84528	Huntington, 857	C 4
	84317	Huntsville, 553	C 2
	84737	Hurricane, 1,408	A 6
	84318	Hyde Park, 1,025	C 2
	84319	Hyrum, 2,340	C 2
	84034	Ibapah, 135	A 3
†	84052	Ioka, 115	D 3
	84738	Ivins, 137	A 6
	84035	Jensen, 360	E 3
	84739	Joseph, 125	B 5
	84740	Junction⊙, 135	B 5
	84036	Kamas, 806	C 3
	84741	Kanab⊙, 1,381	B 6
	84742	Kanarraville, 204	A 6
	84637	Kanosh, 319	B 5
	84037	Kaysville, 6,192	B 2
	84118	Kearns, 17,071	B 3
	84529	Kenilworth, 500	D 4
	84743	Kingston, 114	B 5
	84744	Koosharem, 141	C 5
	84038	Laketown, 208	C 2
	84039	Lapoint, 335	E 3
	84040	Lark, 728	B 3
	84530	La Sal, 200	E 5
	84745	La Verkin, 463	A 6
	84041	Layton, 13,603	C 2
	84638	Leamington, 112	B 4
	84746	Leeds, 151	A 6
	84043	Lehi, 4,659	C 3
	84639	Levan, 376	C 4
	84320	Lewiston, 1,244	C 2
†	84062	Lindon, 1,644	C 3
	84747	Loa⊙, 324	C 5
	84321	Logan⊙, 22,333	C 2
	84749	Lyman, 180	C 5
	84640	Lynndyl, 111	B 4
†	84078	Maeser, 1,248	E 3
	84044	Magna, 5,509	B 3
	84046	Manila⊙, 226	E 3
	84642	Manti⊙, 1,803	C 4
†	84302	Mantua, 413	C 2
†	84663	Mapleton, 1,980	C 3
	84750	Marysvale, 289	B 5
	84643	Mayfield, 267	C 4
	84644	Meadow, 238	B 5
	84325	Mendon, 345	B 2
	84531	Mexican Hat, 100	E 6
	84047	Midvale, 7,840	B 3
	84049	Midway, 804	C 3
	84751	Milford, 1,304	A 5
	84326	Millville, 441	C 2
	84752	Minersville, 448	A 5
	84532	Moab⊙, 4,793	E 5
	84645	Mona, 309	C 4
	84754	Monroe, 918	B 5
	84534	Montezuma Creek, 500	E 6
	84535	Monticello⊙, 1,431	E 6
	84050	Morgan⊙, 1,586	C 2
	84646	Moroni, 894	C 4
	84051	Mountain Home, 140	D 3
	84647	Mount Pleasant, 1,516	C 4
	84107	Murray, 21,206	C 3
	84052	Myton, 322	D 3
	84053	Neola, 600	D 3
	84648	Nephi⊙, 2,699	C 4
	84756	Newcastle, 150	A 6
	84327	Newton, 444	C 2
†	84321	Nibley, 367	C 2
†	84401	North Ogden, 5,257	C 2
	84054	North Salt Lake, 2,143	C 3
	84649	Oak City, 278	B 4
	84055	Oakley, 265	C 3
	84650	Oasis, 150	B 4
*	84401	Ogden⊙, 69,478	C 2
		Ogden, ‡126,278	C 4
†	84080	Onaqui (Vernon), 541	B 3
	84537	Orangeville, 511	C 4
	84758	Orderville, 399	B 6
	84057	Orem, 25,729	C 3
	84059	Ouray, 100	E 3
	84759	Panguitch⊙, 1,318	B 6
	84328	Paradise, 399	C 2
	84760	Paragonah, 275	B 6
	84060	Park City, 1,193	C 3
	84329	Park Valley, 100	A 2
	84761	Parowan⊙, 1,423	B 6
	84651	Payson, 4,501	C 3
	84061	Peoa, 230	C 3
†	84302	Perry, 909	C 2
†	84028	Pickleville, 106	C 2
†	84401	Plain City, 1,543	B 2
	84062	Pleasant Grove, 5,327	C 3
†	84401	Pleasant View, 2,028	B 2
	84330	Plymouth, 203	B 2
	84331	Portage, 144	B 2
	84501	Price⊙, 6,218	D 4
	84332	Providence, 1,608	C 2
	84601	Provo⊙, 53,131	C 3
		Provo-Orem, ‡137,776	C 3
	84063	Randlett, 350	E 3
	84064	Randolph⊙, 500	C 2
	84652	Redmond, 409	C 4
	84701	Richfield⊙, 4,471	B 5
	84333	Richmond, 1,000	C 2
	84334	Riverside, 290	B 2
	84065	Riverton, 2,820	B 3
	84763	Rockville, 110	A 6
	84066	Roosevelt, 2,005	D 3
	84067	Roy, 14,356	C 2
	84770	Saint George⊙, 7,097	A 6
	84069	Saint John, 200	B 3
	84653	Salem, 1,081	C 3
	84654	Salina, 1,494	C 5
*	84101	Salt Lake City (cap.)⊙, 175,885	B 3
		Salt Lake City, ‡557,635	B 3
	84070	Sandy, 6,438	C 3
	84765	Santa Clara, 271	A 6
	84655	Santaquin, 1,236	C 4
	84656	Scipio, 264	B 4
	84657	Sigurd, 291	B 5
	84335	Smithfield, 3,342	C 2
	84336	Snowville, 174	B 2
†	84065	South Jordan, 2,942	B 3
†	84401	South Ogden, 9,991	C 2
	84115	South Salt Lake, 7,810	C 3
	84660	Spanish Fork, 7,284	C 3
	84662	Spring City, 456	C 4
	84767	Springdale, 172	B 6
	84663	Springville, 8,790	C 3
	84665	Sterling, 144	C 4
	84071	Stockton, 469	B 3
	84772	Summit, 150	B 6
	84539	Sunnyside, 485	D 4
†	84015	Sunset, 6,268	B 2
†	84041	Syracuse, 1,843	B 2
	84072	Tabiona, 125	D 3
	84073	Talmage, 140	D 3
†	84101	Taylorsville, 12,522	B 3
	84773	Teasdale, 160	C 5
	84074	Tooele⊙, 12,539	B 3
	84774	Toquerville, 185	A 6
	84337	Tremonton, 2,794	B 2
	84338	Trenton, 390	B 2
	84076	Tridell, 212	E 3
	84776	Tropic, 329	B 6
†	84401	Uintah, 400	C 2
†	84007	Upalco, 150	D 3
	84777	Venice, 220	C 5
	84078	Vernal⊙, 3,908	E 3
	84080	Vernon, 541	B 3
†	84722	Veyo, 144	A 6
	84779	Virgin, 119	A 6
	84082	Wallsburg, 211	C 3
†	84017	Wanship, 175	C 3
	84780	Washington, 750	A 6
†	84401	Washington Terrace, 7,241	B 2
	84542	Wellington, 922	D 4
	84339	Wellsville, 1,267	C 2
	84083	Wendover, 781	A 3
†	84087	West Bountiful, 1,246	B 3
	84084	West Jordan, 4,221	B 3
†	84401	West Weber, 750	B 2
	84085	Whiterocks, 600	E 3
	84340	Willard, 1,045	C 2
†	84036	Woodland, 190	C 3
	84086	Woodruff, 173	C 2
	84087	Woods Cross, 3,124	B 3

⊙ County seat.
‡ Population of metropolitan area.
† Zip of nearest p.o.
* Multiple zips

Agriculture, Industry and Resources

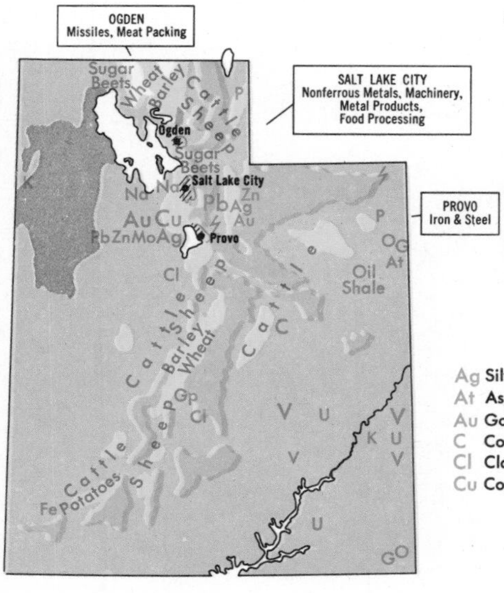
OGDEN
Missiles, Meat Packing
SALT LAKE CITY
Nonferrous Metals, Machinery, Metal Products, Food Processing
PROVO
Iron & Steel
Ogden
Salt Lake City
Provo
Sugar Beets
Wheat
Barley
Cattle
Sheep
Oil Shale

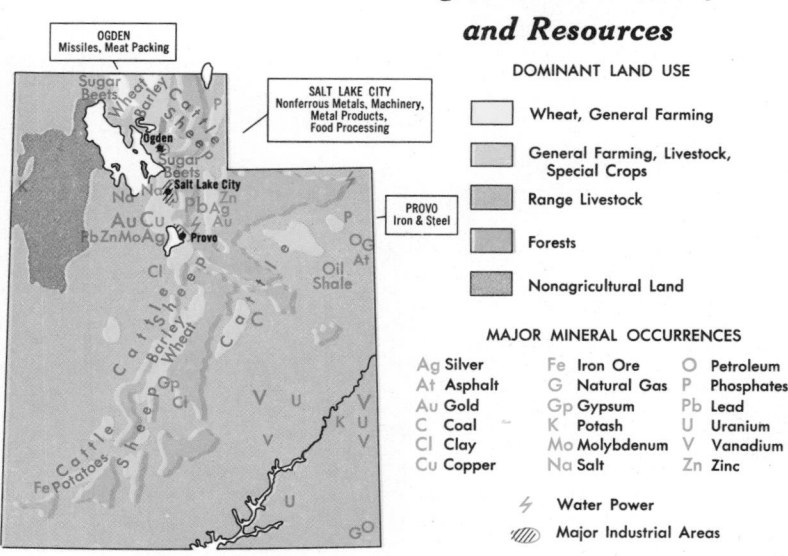

DOMINANT LAND USE

- Wheat, General Farming
- General Farming, Livestock, Special Crops
- Range Livestock
- Forests
- Nonagricultural Land

MAJOR MINERAL OCCURRENCES

Ag Silver	Fe Iron Ore	O Petroleum
At Asphalt	G Natural Gas	P Phosphates
Au Gold	Gp Gypsum	Pb Lead
C Coal	K Potash	U Uranium
Cl Clay	Mo Molybdenum	V Vanadium
Cu Copper	Na Salt	Zn Zinc

Water Power
Major Industrial Areas

Topography

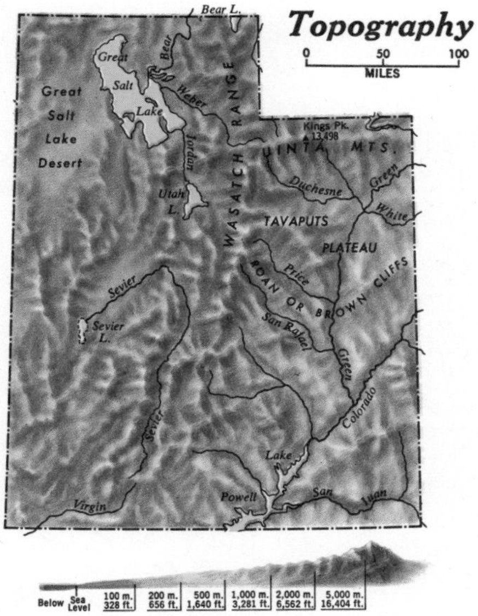
0 50 100
MILES
Bear L.
Great Salt Lake
Great Salt Lake Desert
Kings Pk. 13,498
UINTA MTS.
WASATCH RANGE
Utah L.
Sevier L.
TAVAPUTS PLATEAU
ROAN OR BROWN CLIFFS
Duchesne
Green
White
Price
San Rafael
Sevier
Colorado
Lake Powell
Virgin
San Juan
Below Sea Level
100 m. 328 ft.
200 m. 656 ft.
500 m. 1,640 ft.
1,000 m. 3,281 ft.
2,000 m. 6,562 ft.
5,000 m. 16,404 ft.

Topography

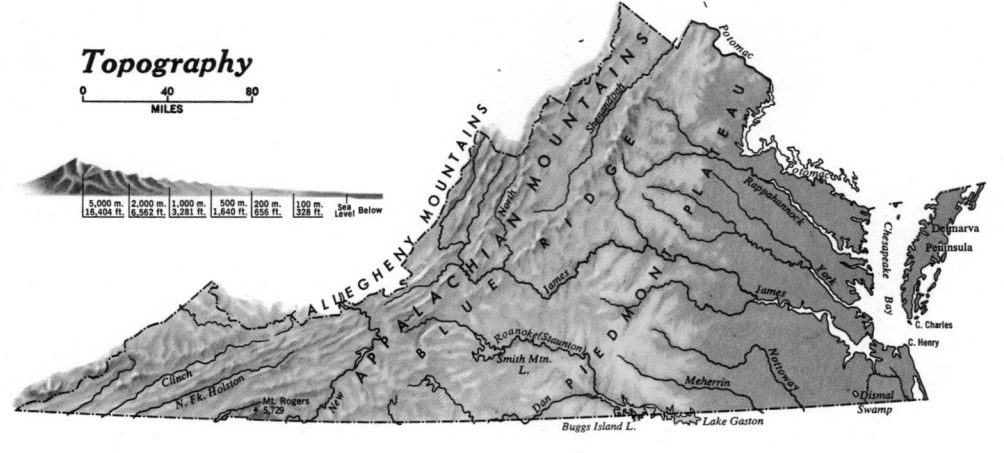

0   40   80
MILES

5,000 m. 2,000 m. 1,000 m. 500 m. 200 m. 100 m. Sea
16,404 ft. 6,562 ft. 3,281 ft. 1,640 ft. 656 ft. 328 ft. Level Below

COUNTIES

Accomack, 29,004..............S 5
Albemarle, 37,780............L 5
Alleghany, 12,461............H 5
Amelia, 7,592.................M 6
Amherst, 26,072..............K 5
Appomattox, 9,784...........L 6
Arlington, 174,284...........O 3
Augusta, 44,220..............K 4
Bath, 5,192...................J 4
Bedford, 26,728..............J 6
Bland, 5,423..................F 6
Botetourt, 18,193............J 5
Brunswick, 16,172...........N 7
Buchanan, 32,071............D 6
Buckingham, 10,597.........L 6
Campbell, 43,319............K 6
Caroline, 13,925.............O 4
Carroll, 23,092...............G 7
Charles City, 6,158..........O 6
Charlotte, 11,551.............L 6
Chesterfield, 76,855.........N 6
Clarke, 8,102.................M 2
Craig, 3,524..................H 6
Culpeper, 18,218.............M 3
Cumberland, 6,179..........M 6
Dickenson, 16,077...........D 6
Dinwiddie, 25,046...........N 6
Essex, 7,099.................P 5
Fairfax, 455,021.............O 3
Fauquier, 26,375............N 3
Floyd, 9,775.................H 7
Fluvanna, 7,621.............M 5
Franklin, 26,858.............J 6
Frederick, 28,893...........L 2
Giles, 16,741................G 6
Gloucester, 14,059..........P 6
Goochland, 10,069..........N 5
Grayson, 15,439.............F 7
Greene, 5,248...............M 4
Greensville, 9,604...........N 7
Halifax, 30,076..............L 7
Hanover, 37,479.............N 5
Henrico, 154,364............O 5
Henry, 50,901...............J 7
Highland, 2,529.............J 4
Isle of Wight, 18,285........P 7
James City, 17,853..........P 6
King and Queen, 5,491......O 5
King George, 8,039.........O 4
King William, 7,497.........O 5
Lancaster, 9,126.............R 5
Lee, 20,321..................B 7
Loudoun, 57,150............N 2
Louisa, 14,004..............N 5
Lunenburg, 11,687..........M 6
Madison, 8,638..............M 4
Mathews, 7,168.............R 6
Mecklenburg, 29,426........M 7
Middlesex, 6,295............R 5
Montgomery, 47,157........H 6
Nansemond, 35,166.........P 7
Nelson, 11,702..............L 5
New Kent, 5,300.............P 5
Northampton, 14,442........S 6
Northumberland, 9,239......R 5
Nottoway, 14,260............M 6
Orange, 13,792.............M 4
Page, 16,581................M 3
Patrick, 15,282..............J 7
Pittsylvania, 58,789.........K 7
Powhatan, 7,696............N 5
Prince Edward, 14,379.....M 6
Prince George, 29,092.....O 6
Prince William, 111,102....O 3
Pulaski, 29,564.............G 6
Rappahannock, 5,199.......M 3
Richmond, 5,841............P 5
Roanoke, 67,339............H 6
Rockbridge, 16,637.........K 5
Rockingham, 47,890........L 4
Russell, 24,533.............D 7
Scott, 24,376................C 7
Shenandoah, 22,852........L 3
Smyth, 31,349...............E 7
Southampton, 18,582.......O 7
Spotsylvania, 16,424........N 4
Stafford, 24,587............O 4
Surry, 5,882.................P 6
Sussex, 11,464..............O 6
Tazewell, 39,816............E 6
Warren, 15,301.............M 3
Washington, 40,835.........D 7
Westmoreland, 12,142.....P 4

Wise, 35,947................C 6
Wythe, 22,139..............F 7
York, 33,203................P 6

INDEPENDENT CITIES

Zip Name/Pop. Key
* 22301 Alexandria, 110,938......P 3
24523 Bedford⊙, 6,011...........J 6
24201 Bristol, 14,857............D 7
* 22901 Charlottesville⊙, 38,880...M 4
23320 Chesapeake, 89,580.......P 7
24422 Clifton Forge, 5,501.......J 5
23834 Colonial Heights, 15,097...O 6
24426 Covington⊙, 10,060.......H 5
24541 Danville, 46,391...........J 7
23847 Emporia⊙, 5,300..........N 7
22030 Fairfax⊙, 21,970..........O 3
22040 Falls Church, 10,772......O 3
23851 Franklin, 6,880............N 7
24401 Fredericksburg, 14,450....N 4
24333 Galax, 6,278...............G 7
23360 Hampton, 120,779.........R 6
22801 Harrisonburg⊙, 14,605...K 4
23860 Hopewell, 23,471..........O 6
24501 Lynchburg, 54,083.........K 6
24112 Martinsville⊙, 19,653.....J 7
23601 Newport News, 138,177...P 6

* 23501 Norfolk, 307,951.........R 7
24273 Norton, 4,001..............C 7
23803 Petersburg, 36,103.........N 6
* 23701 Portsmouth⊙, 110,963....R 7
24141 Radford, 11,596...........G 6
* 23201 Richmond (cap.)⊙, 249,621..O 5
24001 Roanoke, 92,115...........H 6
24153 Salem⊙, 21,982...........H 6
24592 South Boston, 6,889.......L 7
24401 Staunton⊙, 24,504........K 4
23434 Suffolk⊙, 9,858............P 7
* 23450 Virginia Beach, 172,106...S 7
22980 Waynesboro, 16,707......K 4
23185 Williamsburg⊙, 9,069.....P 6
22601 Winchester⊙, 14,643......M 2

CITIES and TOWNS

24210 Abingdon⊙, 4,376.........D 7
23301 Accomac⊙, 373............R 6
23001 Achilles, 525...............R 6
22920 Afton, 525.................L 4
† 22959 Alberene, 200..............L 5
23821 Alberta, 466................N 7
24310 Allisonia, 325...............G 7
24517 Altavista, 2,708.............K 6
24520 Alton, 300..................L 7
23002 Amelia Court House⊙, 537...N 6
24521 Amherst⊙, 1,106..........K 5
22002 Amissville, 150..............M 3

24601 Amonate, 500..............E 6
24215 Andover, 300...............C 7
22003 Annandale, 27,428.........O 3
24216 Appalachia, 2,161..........C 7
24522 Appomattox⊙, 1,400......L 6
24053 Ararat, 300.................J 7
22201 Arlington⊙, 174,284.......P 3
22922 Arrington, 350..............L 5
23004 Arvonia, 300...............M 5
22011 Ashburn, 345...............O 2
23005 Ashland, 2,934.............N 5
24311 Atkins, 500.................F 7
24411 Augusta Springs, 400......K 4
24312 Austinville, 750.............G 7
24054 Axton, 540.................J 7
23009 Aylett, 300.................O 5
24602 Bandy, 500.................E 6
24231 Banner, 350................D 7
22923 Barboursville, 207..........M 4
24313 Barren Springs, 150........G 7
24055 Bassett, 3,058..............J 7
24314 Bastian, 500................F 6
22924 Batesville, 450..............L 5
23016 Beaverlett, 178.............R 6
† 23201 Bellbluff, 3,900.............O 6
23306 Belle Haven, 504...........S 5
22307 Bellevue, 8,299............O 3
24218 Ben Hur, 300...............B 7
24059 Bent Mountain, 140........H 6
22610 Bentonville, 700............M 3

22811 Bergton, 150...............L 3
22611 Berryville⊙, 1,569.........M 2
24526 Big Island, 500.............K 5
24603 Big Rock, 350..............D 6
24219 Big Stone Gap, 4,153.....C 7
24220 Birchleaf, 650..............D 6
23307 Birdsnest, 250.............S 6
24604 Bishop, 400................E 6
23916 Blackridge, 140............M 7
24060 Blacksburg, 9,384.........H 6
23824 Blackstone, 3,412..........M 6
24221 Blackwater, 205............B 7
24527 Blairs, 500.................K 7
23308 Bloxom, 391...............S 5
24605 Bluefield, 5,286............E 6
22012 Bluemont, 310.............N 2
24064 Blue Ridge, 926............J 5
24606 Boissevain, 975............F 6
23235 Bon Air, 10,562...........N 5
24065 Boones Mill, 363...........J 6
24227 Bowling Green⊙, 528.....O 4
22620 Boyce, 378.................M 2
23917 Boydton⊙, 541............M 7
23827 Boykins, 742...............O 7
23828 Branchville, 189............O 7
22714 Brandy Station, 530........N 4
24607 Breaks, 500................D 6
23022 Bremo Bluff, 200...........M 5
22812 Bridgewater, 2,828........K 4

22715 Brightwood, 250...........M 4
24316 Broadford, 850.............E 7
22815 Broadway, 887.............L 3
23920 Brodnax, 569...............N 7
22430 Brooke, 275.................O 4
24528 Brookneal, 1,037...........L 6
24415 Brownsburg, 200...........K 5
22610 Browntown, 175............M 3
22622 Brucetown, 150.............M 2
† 22810 Bryce Mountain, 205........L 3
24066 Buchanan, 1,326..........J 5
23921 Buckingham⊙, 200........L 6
22432 Burgess, 300...............R 5
24608 Burkes Garden, 275.......F 6
23922 Burkeville, 703.............M 6
24420 Burnsville, 138.............J 4
22435 Callao, 500.................P 5
24067 Callaway, 191..............H 7
22016 Calverton, 200.............N 3
24317 Cana, 168..................G 7
23310 Cape Charles, 1,689.......R 6
23313 Capeville, 350..............R 6
23829 Capron, 314................O 7
23039 Cardwell, 200..............N 5
† 23315 Carrsville, 375..............P 7
23830 Carson, 275................O 6
22017 Casanova, 200.............N 3
24069 Cascade, 835...............J 7
24224 Castlewood, 799...........D 7
22019 Catlett, 500.................N 3
24609 Cedar Bluff, 1,050.........E 6
† 24368 Cedar Springs, 200........F 7
22630 Cedarville, 150.............M 3
22437 Center Cross, 360.........P 5
24438 Champlain, 160............O 4
22021 Chantilly, 620..............O 3
23030 Charles City⊙, 5...........O 6
23923 Charlotte Court House⊙,
       539.......................L 6
23924 Chase City, 2,909..........M 7
24531 Chatham⊙, 1,801.........K 7
23316 Cheriton, 655..............R 6
23831 Chester, 5,556.............O 6
23832 Chesterfield⊙, 950........N 6
22623 Chester Gap, 450..........M 3
24319 Chilhowie, 1,317..........E 7
23336 Chincoteague, 1,867.......S 5
24073 Christiansburg⊙, 7,857....H 6
23339 Chuckatuck, 500...........P 7
23032 Church View, 200..........P 5
24421 Churchville, 250............K 4
22928 Cismont, 400...............M 4
23899 Claremont, 383............O 6
23927 Clarksville, 1,641..........M 7
23924 Claudville, 180.............H 7
† 23061 Clay Bank, 200.............P 6
24225 Cleveland, 357.............D 7
24533 Clifford, 160................K 5
24321 Clinchburg, 250............D 7
24226 Clinchco, 900..............D 6
24227 Clinchport, 286............C 7
24226 Clintwood⊙, 1,320........D 6

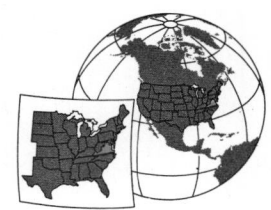

24534 Clover, 227 ....L 7	†24172 Dale City, 13,857 ....O 3	23845 Ebony, 150 ....N 7	23055 Fork Union, 350 ....M 5
24077 Cloverdale, 850 ....J 6	24083 Daleville, 450 ....J 6	23349 Eclipse, 295 ....R 7	24250 Fort Blackmore, 600 ....C 7
24535 Cluster Springs, 500 ...L 7	24236 Damascus, 1,230 ....E 7	†22485 Edgehill, 225 ....O 4	22578 Foxwells, 400 ....N 5
23035 Cobbs Creek, 600 ....R 6	24237 Dante, 1,153 ....D 7	22824 Edinburg, 766 ....M 3	24330 Fries, 885 ....F 7
24230 Coeburn, 2,362 ....D 7	24239 Davenport, 300 ....D 6	24086 Eggleston, 500 ....G 6	22630 Front Royal⊙, 8,211 .....M 3
24536 Coleman Falls, 250 .....H 6	22821 Dayton, 978 ....L 4	23846 Elberon, 200 ....P 6	22830 Fulks Run, 130 ....L 3
22442 Coles Point, 200 ....P 4	24432 Deerfield, 200 ....K 4	22827 Elkton, 1,511 ....L 4	22065 Gainesville, 600 ....N 3
†24450 Collierstown, 125 .....J 5	22025 Delaplane, 164 ....N 3	24087 Elliston, 700 ....H 6	22643 Garrisonville, 200 .....N 4
24078 Collinsville, 6,015 ....J 7	23043 Deltaville, 950 ....R 5	24327 Emory, 458 ....E 7	23857 Gasburg, 150 ....N 7
24101 Colonial Beach, 2,058 ..P 4	23839 Dendron, 336 ....P 6	22937 Esmont, 650 ....M 5	24251 Gate City⊙, 1,914 ....C 7
23038 Columbia, 125 ....M 5	23840 De Witt, 140 ....N 6	24974 Esserville, 975 ....G 2	†24228 Georges Fork, 500 .....C 6
24538 Concord, 400 ....K 6	23936 Dillwyn, 497 ....M 5	23803 Ettrick, 3,950 ....O 6	24248 Gibson Station, 200 ....A 7
24080 Copper Valley, 425 ......C 6	23841 Dinwiddie⊙, 500 ....N 6	23939 Evergreen, 300 ....L 6	24340 Glade Spring, 1,615 ....E 7
23837 Courtland⊙, 899 ....O 7	23842 Disputanta, 180 ....O 6	24550 Evington, 175 ....K 6	24554 Gladys, 312 ....K 6
22931 Covesville, 500 ....L 5	23047 Doswell, 200 ....N 5	24248 Ewing, 700 ....A 7	24555 Glasgow, 1,304 ....K 5
24230 Craigsville, 988 ....J 4	23937 Drakes Branch, 702 ......L 7	23350 Exmore, 1,421 ....S 5	23060 Glen Allen, 985 ....N 5
†24315 Crandon, 250 ....G 6	24324 Draper, 276 ....F 7	24435 Fairfield, 465 ....K 5	24093 Glen Lyn, 191 ....G 6
23930 Crewe, 1,433 ....M 6	23844 Drewryville, 250 ....O 7	24141 Fairlawn, 1,767 ....G 6	24438 Glen Wilton, 280 ....J 5
24431 Crimora, 450 ....L 4	24242 Drill, 192 ....E 6	†22539 Fairport, 175 ....R 5	24541 Glenwood, 1,295 ....K 7
24322 Cripple Creek, 200 ......F 7	23346 Driver, 250 ....P 7	24613 Falls Mills, 500 ....F 6	23061 Gloucester⊙, 750 ....P 6
24082 Critz, 150 ....H 7	24243 Dryden, 400 ....D 7	22401 Falmouth, 2,139 ....O 4	23062 Gloucester Point, 850 ..R 6
24323 Crockett, 300 ....E 7	24084 Dublin, 1,653 ....G 6	23901 Farmville⊙, 4,331 ....M 6	24094 Goochland⊙, 800 ....N 5
22625 Cross Junction, 200 .....M 2	22026 Dumfries, 1,890 ....O 3	22460 Farnham, 150 ....R 5	22720 Goldvein, 350 ....N 4
22932 Crozet, 1,433 ....L 4	23938 Dundas, 200 ....M 7	24088 Ferrum, 200 ....H 7	23063 Goochland⊙, 800 ....N 5
23039 Crozier, 300 ....N 5	24245 Dungannon, 282 ....C 7	24089 Fieldale, 1,337 ....H 7	24556 Goode, 200 ....K 6
24539 Crystal Hill, 475 ....L 7	22454 Dunnsville, 312 ....P 5	24090 Fincastle⊙, 397 ....J 6	22942 Gordonsville, 1,253 ....M 4
23934 Cullen, 140 ....L 6	24085 Eagle Rock, 750 ....J 5	22939 Fishersville, 975 ....L 4	22637 Gore, 150 ....M 2
22701 Culpeper⊙, 6,056 ....M 4	22936 Earlysville, 210 ....L 4	23937 Flint Hill, 200 ....M 3	23490 Grafton, 500 ....P 5
23040 Cumberland⊙, 500 ....M 6	24246 East Stone Gap, 500 .....C 7	24091 Floyd⊙, 474 ....H 7	23356 Greenbackville, 300 ....T 5
22448 Dahlgren, 950 ....O 4	23347 Eastville⊙, 203 ....R 6	24551 Forest, 497 ....K 6	23942 Green Bay, 150 ....M 6

(continued on following page)

AREA 40,817 sq. mi.
POPULATION 4,648,494
CAPITAL Richmond
LARGEST CITY Norfolk
HIGHEST POINT Mt. Rogers 5,729 ft.
SETTLED IN 1607
ADMITTED TO UNION June 26, 1788
POPULAR NAME Old Dominion
STATE FLOWER Dogwood
STATE BIRD Cardinal

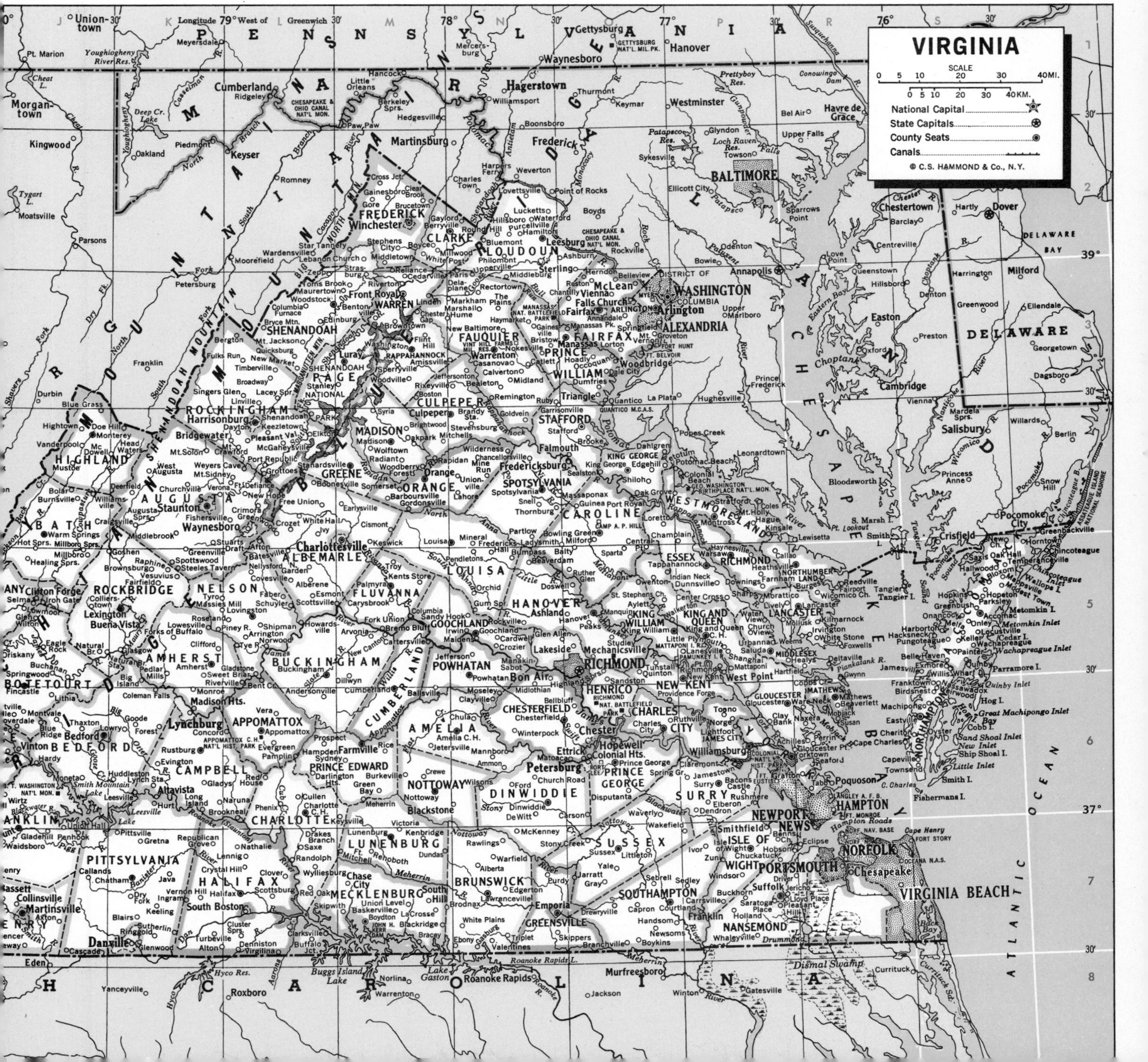

VIRGINIA

SCALE
0 5 10 20 30 40 MI.
0 5 10 20 30 40 KM.

National Capital ....★
State Capitals ....⊛
County Seats ....⊙
Canals ....

© C.S. HAMMOND & Co., N.Y.

Agriculture, Industry and Resources

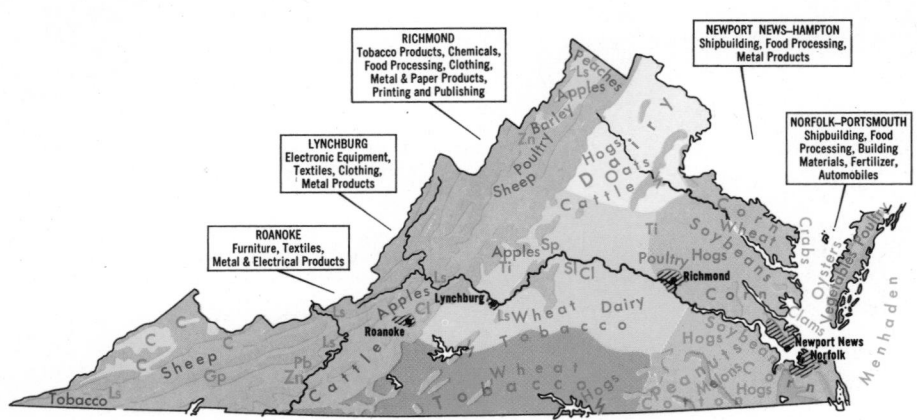

RICHMOND
Tobacco Products, Chemicals, Food Processing, Clothing, Metal & Paper Products, Printing and Publishing

LYNCHBURG
Electronic Equipment, Textiles, Clothing, Metal Products

ROANOKE
Furniture, Textiles, Metal & Electrical Products

NEWPORT NEWS–HAMPTON
Shipbuilding, Food Processing, Metal Products

NORFOLK–PORTSMOUTH
Shipbuilding, Food Processing, Building Materials, Fertilizer, Automobiles

DOMINANT LAND USE

- Dairy, General Farming
- General Farming, Livestock, Dairy
- General Farming, Livestock, Tobacco
- General Farming, Livestock, Fruit, Tobacco
- General Farming, Truck Farming, Tobacco, Livestock
- Tobacco, General Farming
- Peanuts, General Farming
- Fruit and Mixed Farming
- Truck and Mixed Farming
- Forests
- Swampland, Limited Agriculture

MAJOR MINERAL OCCURRENCES

C	Coal	Sl	Slate
Cl	Clay	Sp	Soapstone
Gp	Gypsum	Ti	Titanium
Ls	Limestone	Zn	Zinc
Pb	Lead		

⚡ Water Power

🗂 Major Industrial Areas

The Governor's Palace in Williamsburg, Virginia, typifies the splendor enjoyed by the royal governors in residence from 1720 to 1780.

Eric Carle — Shostal Associates

Agriculture, Industry and Resources

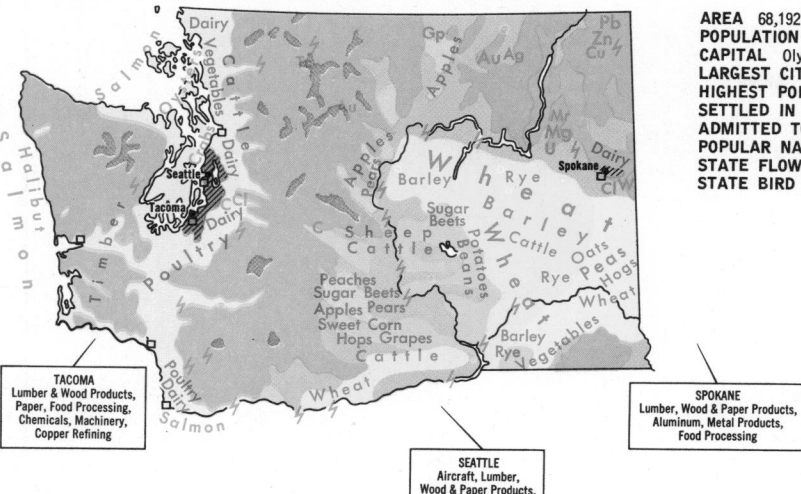

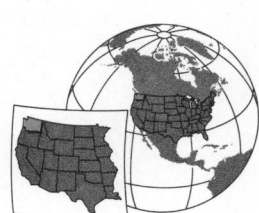

AREA 68,192 sq. mi.
POPULATION 3,409,169
CAPITAL Olympia
LARGEST CITY Seattle
HIGHEST POINT Mt. Rainier 14,410 ft.
SETTLED IN 1811
ADMITTED TO UNION November 11, 1889
POPULAR NAME Evergreen State
STATE FLOWER Coast Rhododendron
STATE BIRD Willow Goldfinch

TACOMA
Lumber & Wood Products, Paper, Food Processing, Chemicals, Machinery, Copper Refining

SPOKANE
Lumber, Wood & Paper Products, Aluminum, Metal Products, Food Processing

SEATTLE
Aircraft, Lumber, Wood & Paper Products, Food Processing, Metal Products

DOMINANT LAND USE

- Specialized Wheat
- Wheat, Peas
- Dairy, Poultry, Mixed Farming
- Fruit and Mixed Farming
- General Farming, Dairy, Range Livestock
- General Farming, Livestock, Special Crops
- Range Livestock
- Forests
- Urban Areas
- Nonagricultural Land

MAJOR MINERAL OCCURRENCES

Ag	Silver	Mr	Marble
Au	Gold	Pb	Lead
C	Coal	Tc	Talc
Cl	Clay	U	Uranium
Cu	Copper	W	Tungsten
Gp	Gypsum	Zn	Zinc
Mg	Magnesium		

- ⚡ Water Power
- ▨ Major Industrial Areas
- □ Major Sawmilling Centers

COUNTIES

Adams, 12,014 ....G 3
Asotin, 13,799 ....H 4
Benton, 67,540 ....F 4
Chelan, 41,355 ....E 3
Clallam, 34,770 ....B 2
Clark, 128,454 ....C 5
Columbia, 4,439 ....H 4
Cowlitz, 68,616 ....C 4
Douglas, 16,787 ....F 3
Ferry, 3,655 ....G 2
Franklin, 25,816 ....G 4
Garfield, 2,911 ....H 4
Grant, 41,881 ....F 3
Grays Harbor, 59,533 ....B 3
Island, 27,011 ....C 2
Jefferson, 10,661 ....B 3
King, 1,156,633 ....D 3
Kitsap, 101,732 ....C 3
Kittitas, 25,039 ....E 3
Klickitat, 12,138 ....E 5
Lewis, 45,467 ....C 4
Lincoln, 9,572 ....G 3
Mason, 20,918 ....B 3
Okanogan, 25,867 ....F 2
Pacific, 15,796 ....B 4
Pend Oreille, 6,025 ....H 2
Pierce, 411,027 ....C 3
San Juan, 3,856 ....C 2
Skagit, 52,381 ....D 2
Skamania, 5,845 ....D 5
Snohomish, 265,236 ....D 2
Spokane, 287,487 ....H 3
Stevens, 17,405 ....H 2
Thurston, 76,894 ....C 4
Wahkiakum, 3,592 ....B 4
Walla Walla, 42,176 ....G 4
Whatcom, 81,950 ....D 2
Whitman, 37,900 ....H 4
Yakima, 144,971 ....E 4

CITIES and TOWNS

Zip	Name/Pop.	Key
98520	Aberdeen, 18,489	B 3
98220	Acme, 170	C 2
99101	Addy, 141	H 2
98522	Adna, 150	B 4
98810	Aeneas, 85	F 2
99001	Airway Heights, 744	H 3
99102	Albion, 687	H 4
98301	Alder, 300	C 4
98002	Algona, 1,276	C 3
98524	Allyn, 850	C 3
99103	Almira, 376	G 3
98525	Aloha, 140	A 3
† 98643	Altoona, 66	B 4
98526	Amanda Park, 495	A 3
99002	Amber, 32	H 3
98601	Amboy, 480	C 5
98221	Anacortes, 7,701	C 2
99401	Anatone, 70	H 4
98602	Appleton, 40	D 5
† 99114	Arden, 30	H 2
98811	Ardenvoir, 350	E 3
98603	Ariel, 386	C 5
98223	Arlington, 2,261	C 2
98304	Ashford, 415	C 4
99402	Asotin◎, 637	H 4
98002	Auburn, 21,817	C 3
† 99348	Ayer, 70	G 4
98816	Azwell, 152	F 3
98110	Bainbridge Island-Winslow, 1,461	A 2
98224	Baring, 75	D 3
98604	Battle Ground, 1,438	C 5
98527	Bay Center, 350	A 4
† 98520	Bay City, 58	B 4
† 98004	Beaux Arts, 475	B 2
98305	Beaver, 450	A 2
98528	Belfair, 500	C 3
* 98004	Bellevue, 61,102	B 2
98225	Bellingham◎, 39,375	C 2
99104	Belmont, 59	H 3
99105	Benge, 45	G 4
99320	Benton City, 1,070	F 4
99321	Beverly, 86	F 4
99322	Bickleton, 200	E 5
† 98273	Biglake, 105	D
98605	Bingen, 671	D 5
98010	Black Diamond, 1,160	D 3
98230	Blaine, 1,955	C 2
98231	Blanchard, 200	C 2
99106	Bluecreek, 40	H 2
† 98382	Blyn, 350	B 3
† 98532	Boistfort, 55	B 4
† 98390	Bonney Lake, 2,313	C 3
99126	Bossburg, 66	H 2
98011	Bothell, 4,883	B 1
98232	Bow, 975	C 2
99107	Boyds, 68	G 2
98310	Bremerton, 35,307	A 2
98812	Brewster, 1,059	F 2
98813	Bridgeport, 952	F 3
98036	Brier, 3,093	C 3
98320	Brinnon, 500	B 3
† 98537	Brooklyn, 50	B 3
98920	Brownstown, 80	E 4
† 98310	Brownsville, 50	A 2
98606	Brush Prairie, 200	C 5
† 98101	Bryn Mawr, 4,589	B 2
98321	Buckley, 3,446	C 3
98530	Bucoda, 421	C 4
98921	Buena, 590	E 4
99323	Burbank, 800	G 4
98166	Burien, 2,000	A 2
98322	Burley, 200	C 3
98233	Burlington, 3,138	C 2
98013	Burton, 650	C 3
98607	Camas, 5,790	C 5
98323	Carbonado, 394	C 3
98324	Carlsborg, 500	B 2
98814	Carlton, 120	F 2
98014	Carnation, 530	D 3
98609	Carrolls, 400	C 4
98610	Carson, 500	D 5
98815	Cashmere, 1,976	E 3
98611	Castle Rock, 1,647	B 4
98612	Cathlamet◎, 647	B 4
† 98045	Cedar Falls, 200	D 3
98613	Centerville, 100	D 5
98531	Centralia, 10,054	C 4
98520	Central Park, 2,720	B 3
99003	Chattaroy, 250	H 3
98532	Chehalis◎, 5,727	C 4
98816	Chelan, 2,430	E 3
98817	Chelan Falls, 200	E 3
99004	Cheney, 6,358	H 3
98818	Chesaw, 32	G 2
99109	Chewelah, 1,365	H 2
98325	Chimacum, 275	C 3
98614	Chinook, 445	B 4
98533	Cinebar, 35	C 4
98326	Clallam Bay, 750	A 2
99403	Clarkston, 6,312	H 4
99110	Clayton, 204	H 3
98235	Clearlake, 750	C 2
98399	Clearwater, 155	A 3
98922	Cle Elum, 1,725	E 3
† 98937	Cliffdell, 50	E 4
98236	Clinton, 500	C 3
98244	Clipper, 25	C 2
† 99402	Cloverland, 80	H 4
† 98004	Clyde Hill, 2,987	B 2
† 98055	Coalfield, 500	B 2
99005	Colbert, 225	H 3
† 98366	Colby, 150	A 2
99111	Colfax◎, 2,664	H 4
99324	College Place, 4,510	G 4
99113	Colton, 279	H 4
† 98632	Columbia Heights, 1,572	C 4
99114	Colville◎, 3,742	H 2
98819	Conconully, 122	F 2
98237	Concrete, 573	D 2
99326	Connell, 1,161	G 4
98238	Conway, 420	C 2
98605	Cook, 240	D 5
98535	Copalis Beach, 481	A 3
98536	Copalis Crossing, 200	B 3
98537	Cosmopolis, 1,599	B 4
98616	Cougar, 76	C 4
99115	Coulee City, 558	F 3
99116	Coulee Dam, 1,425	G 3
98239	Coupeville◎, 678	C 2
98923	Cowiche, 150	E 4
99117	Creston, 325	G 3
98015	Cumberland, 250	D 3
99118	Curlew, 200	G 2
98538	Curtis, 200	B 4
99119	Cusick, 257	H 2
99240	Custer, 315	C 2
98617	Dallesport, 400	D 5
99121	Danville, 108	G 2
99241	Darrington, 1,094	D 2
99122	Davenport◎, 1,363	G 3
99328	Dayton◎, 2,596	H 4
† 99010	Deepcreek, 73	H 3
98618	Deep River, 500	B 4
98243	Deer Harbor, 200	B 2
99006	Deer Park, 1,295	H 3
99244	Deming, 250	C 2
† 99006	Denison, 100	H 3
98188	Des Moines, 3,871	B 2
98283	Diablo, 200	D 2
† 99111	Diamond, 49	H 4
99213	Dishman, 9,079	H 3
99329	Dixie, 200	G 4
† 98279	Doebay, 100	C 2
† 98951	Donald, 100	E 4
98539	Doty, 210	B 4
† 98858	Douglas, 27	F 3
† 98532	Dryad, 184	B 4
98821	Dryden, 550	E 3
† 98382	Dungeness, 675	B 2
98327	Du Pont, 384	C 3
98019	Duvall, 607	D 3
98540	East Olympia, 300	B 4
98925	Easton, 300	D 3
98245	Eastsound, 800	C 2
98801	East Wenatchee, 913	E 3
98328	Eatonville, 2,446	C 4
98246	Edison, 250	C 2
98020	Edmonds, 23,998	C 3

(continued on following page)

Pulpwood being rafted to the mills is a familiar sight in the Northwest, the region which leads the country in lumber production.

Warren Dick — Shostal Associates

WASHINGTON

SCALE
0 5 10 20 30 40 MI.
0 5 10 20 30 40 KM.

State Capitals..............⊛
County Seats..............⊙

© C.S. HAMMOND & Co., N.Y.

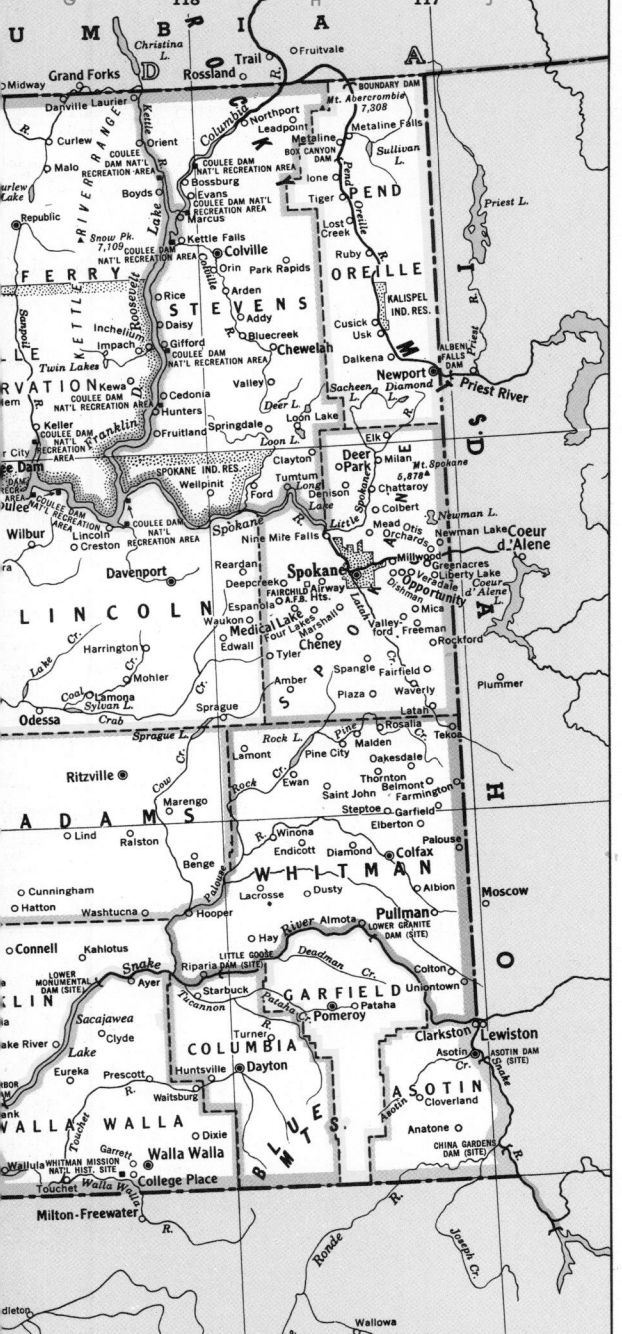

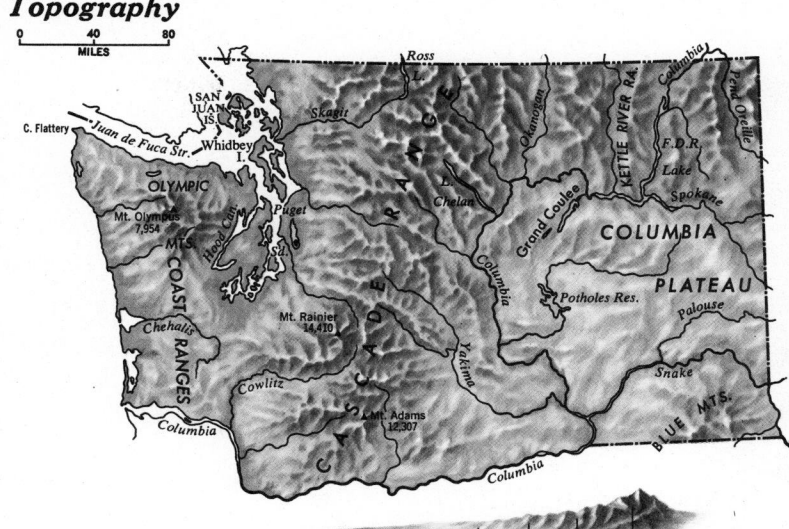

Topography

Scale: 0 — 40 — 80 MILES

Below Sea Level	100 m. 328 ft.	200 m. 656 ft.	500 m. 1,640 ft.	1,000 m. 3,281 ft.	2,000 m. 6,562 ft.	5,000 m. 16,404 ft.

98501 Olympia (cap.)◉, 23,111.....C 3
98841 Omak, 4,164.....F 2
98570 Onalaska, 288.....C 4
99214 Opportunity, 16,604.....H 3
98662 Orchards, 800.....C 5
98160 Orient, 200.....G 2
98843 Orondo, 130.....E 3
98844 Oroville, 1,555.....F 2
98360 Orting, 1,643.....C 3
98223 Oso, 150.....D 2
99344 Othello, 4,122.....F 4
99027 Otis Orchards, 900.....H 3
98938 Outlook, 300.....E 4
98641 Oysterville, 86.....A 4
† 98326 Ozette, 50.....A 2
98047 Pacific, 1,831.....C 3
98571 Pacific Beach, 975.....B 3
98361 Packwood, 800.....D 4
98845 Palisades, 90.....E 3
98048 Palmer, 250.....D 3
99161 Palouse, 948.....H 4
98398 Paradise Inn, 200.....D 4
98939 Parker, 700.....E 4
98444 Parkland, 21,012.....C 3
99301 Pasco◉, 13,920.....F 4
† 99347 Pataha, 97.....H 4
98846 Pateros, 472.....E 2
99345 Paterson, 50.....F 5
98572 Pe Ell, 582.....B 4
98847 Peshastin, 200.....E 3
99162 Pine City, 48.....H 3
† 98826 Plain, 75.....D 3
99028 Plaza, 50.....H 3
98346 Plymouth, 89.....F 5
98281 Point Roberts, 400.....B 2
99347 Pomeroy◉, 1,823.....H 4
98362 Port Angeles◉, 16,367.....B 2
98110 Port Blakely, 600.....A 2
98573 Porter, 200.....B 4
98364 Port Gamble, 425.....C 2
98365 Port Ludlow, 200.....C 3
98366 Port Orchard◉, 3,904.....A 2
98368 Port Townsend◉, 5,241.....C 2
98574 Potlatch, 350.....B 3
98370 Poulsbo, 1,856.....A 1
99348 Prescott, 242.....G 4
98050 Preston, 500.....D 3
† 98250 Prevost, 25.....B 2
99350 Prosser◉, 2,954.....F 4
99163 Pullman, 20,509.....H 4
98371 Puyallup, 14,742.....C 3
† 98399 Queets, 180.....A 3
98376 Quilcene, 900.....B 3
98575 Quinault, 340.....B 3
98848 Quincy, 3,237.....F 3
98576 Rainier, 382.....C 4
99165 Ralston, 35.....G 4
98377 Randle, 200.....D 4
98051 Ravensdale, 400.....D 3
98577 Raymond, 3,126.....B 4
99029 Reardan, 389.....H 3
98052 Redmond, 11,031.....B 1
98054 Redondo, 400.....B 2
98055 Renton, 25,258.....B 2
99166 Republic◉, 862.....G 2
98378 Retsil, 419.....A 2
98160 Richmond Beach, 2,550.....A 1
† 98133 Richmond Highlands, 6,854.....A 1
98642 Ridgefield, 1,004.....C 5
99169 Ritzville◉, 1,876.....G 3
98849 Riverside, 228.....F 2
† 98188 Riverton, 23,160.....B 2
98188 Riverton Heights, 34,800.....B 2
† 98250 Robe, 250.....D 2
98580 Roche Harbor, 175.....B 2
98579 Rochester, 325.....C 4
98030 Rockford, 250.....H 3
98057 Rock Island, 191.....E 3
98283 Rockport, 350.....D 2
98626 Rocky Point, 1,733.....A 2
98061 Rollingbay, 950.....A 2
99356 Roosevelt, 60.....E 5
99170 Rosalia, 569.....H 3
98643 Rosburg, 250.....B 4
98941 Roslyn, 1,031.....E 3
99357 Royal City, 477.....F 4
† 98832 Ruff, 40.....F 3
† 98401 Ruston, 668.....C 3
98581 Ryderwood, 345.....B 4
99171 Saint John, 575.....H 3
98582 Salkum, 298.....C 4
† 98239 San de Fuca, 80.....C 2
98379 Sappho, 200.....A 2
98583 Satsop, 300.....B 3
98283 Sauk, 50.....D 2
98370 Scandia, 75.....A 1
† 99321 Schawana, 100.....F 4
98380 Seabeck, 200.....C 3
† 98110 Seabold, 250.....A 1
98062 Seahurst, 3,000.....A 2
* 98101 Seattle◉, 530,831.....A 2
    Seattle-Everett, $1,421,869.....A 2
98644 Seaview, 950.....A 4
98284 Sedro-Woolley, 4,598.....C 2
98381 Sekiu, 500.....A 2
98942 Selah, 3,070.....E 4
* 98064 Selleck, 300.....D 3
98382 Sequim, 1,549.....B 2
98286 Shaw Island, 95.....B 2
98584 Shelton◉, 6,515.....B 3
† 98270 Shoultes, 4,754.....C 2
98287 Silvana, 300.....C 2
98585 Silver Creek, 382.....C 4
98383 Silverdale, 950.....A 2
98645 Silverlake, 42.....C 4
† 98852 Silverton, 65.....D 2
98646 Skamania, 250.....C 5
98647 Skamokawa, 500.....A 4
98288 Skykomish, 283.....D 3
† 99357 Smyrna, 70.....F 4
98290 Snohomish, 5,174.....D 2
98065 Snoqualmie, 1,260.....D 3
98066 Snoqualmie Falls, 250.....D 3
98851 Soap Lake, 1,064.....F 3
98586 South Bend◉, 1,795.....B 4
98901 South Broadway, 3,298.....E 4
98943 South Cle Elum, 374.....D 3
98384 South Colby, 450.....A 2
98385 South Prairie, 206.....D 3
98386 Southworth, 425.....A 2
98387 Spanaway, 5,768.....C 3
99031 Spangle, 179.....H 3
* 99201 Spokane◉, 170,516.....H 3
    Spokane, $287,487.....H 3
99032 Sprague, 550.....H 3
99173 Springdale, 215.....H 2
98292 Stanwood, 1,347.....C 2
99359 Starbuck, 216.....G 4
98293 Startup, 450.....D 3
98852 Stehekin, 65.....E 2
98388 Steilacoom, 2,850.....C 3
99174 Steptoe, 200.....H 3
98648 Stevenson◉, 916.....C 5
98853 Stratford, 160.....F 3
98294 Sultan, 1,119.....D 3
98295 Sumas, 689.....C 2
† 98101 Sunnydale, 1,850.....B 2
98944 Sunnyside, 6,751.....F 4
98392 Suquamish, 950.....A 2
* 98401 Tacoma◉, 154,581.....C 3
    Tacoma, ‡411,027.....C 3
98587 Taholah, 550.....A 3
98588 Tahuya, 260.....B 3
98033 Tekoa, 808.....H 3
† 98826 Tenina, 150.....E 3
98589 Tenino, 962.....C 4
98901 Terrace Heights, 1,033.....E 4
99176 Thornton, 97.....H 3
99946 Thorp, 350.....E 3
98947 Tieton, 415.....E 4
99177 Tiger, 69.....H 2
98492 Tillicum, 1,900.....C 3
98590 Tokeland, 300.....A 4
98591 Toledo, 654.....C 4
98855 Tonasket, 951.....F 2
98948 Toppenish, 5,744.....E 4
99360 Touchet, 250.....G 4
98649 Toutle, 813.....C 4
98393 Tracyton, 1,413.....A 2
† 98848 Trinidad, 30.....F 3
98650 Trout Lake, 500.....D 5
98188 Tukwila, 3,496.....C 2
98270 Tulalip, 325.....C 2
99034 Tumtum, 100.....H 3
98501 Tumwater, 5,373.....B 3
98328 Turner, 25.....H 4
98856 Twisp, 756.....E 2
99035 Tyler, 69.....H 3
98651 Underwood, 500.....D 5
98592 Union, 380.....B 3
98903 Union Gap, 2,040.....E 4
99179 Uniontown, 310.....H 4
99180 Usk, 250.....H 2
98593 Vader, 387.....B 4
99181 Valley, 156.....H 2
99036 Valleyford, 250.....H 3
* 98661 Vancouver◉, 42,493.....C 5
98950 Vantage, 125.....F 4
98244 Van Zandt, 25.....C 2
98070 Vashon, 350.....A 2
98394 Vaughn, 600.....C 3
98037 Veradale, 5,320.....H 3
98670 Wahkiacus, 65.....D 5
99361 Waitsburg, 953.....G 4
98297 Waldron, 75.....B 2
99362 Walla Walla◉, 23,619.....G 4
99363 Wallula, 89.....G 4
98951 Wapato, 2,841.....E 4
98857 Warden, 1,254.....F 4
† 98595 Warm Beach, 225.....C 2
98671 Washougal, 3,388.....C 5
99371 Washtucna, 314.....G 4
98858 Waterville◉, 919.....E 3
99038 Waukon, 41.....H 3
98395 Wauna, 300.....C 3
99039 Waverly, 48.....H 3
99040 Wellpinit, 125.....G 3
98801 Wenatchee◉, 16,912.....E 3
98837 Westlake, 258.....F 3
98595 Westport, 1,364.....A 4
99352 West Richland, 1,107.....F 4
98801 West Wenatchee, 2,134.....E 3
98837 Wheeler, 75.....F 3
98146 White Center, 17,300.....A 2
98541 Whites, 70.....B 3
98672 White Salmon, 1,585.....D 5
98952 White Swan, 770.....E 4
98285 Wickersham, 200.....C 2
99185 Wilbur, 1,074.....G 3
98906 Wiley City, 250.....E 4
98396 Wilkeson, 317.....D 3
98577 Willapa, 300.....B 4
98860 Wilson Creek, 184.....F 3
† 98848 Winchester, 70.....F 3
98596 Winlock, 890.....C 4
99186 Winona, 51.....H 3
98110 Winslow (Bainbridge Island-
    Winslow), 1,461.....A 2
98862 Winthrop, 371.....E 2
98672 Wishram, 575.....D 5
98863 Withrow, 30.....E 3
98072 Woodinville, 2,900.....B 1
98674 Woodland, 1,622.....C 4
98020 Woodway, 879.....A 1
98675 Yacolt, 488.....C 5
* 98901 Yakima◉, 45,588.....E 4
98904 Yarrow Point, 1,103.....B 2
98597 Yelm, 628.....C 4
98188 Zenith, 1,900.....C 2
98953 Zillah, 1,138.....E 4

◉ County seat.
‡ Population of metropolitan area.
⊛ Zip of nearest p.o.
* Multiple zips

98559 Malone, 175.....B 4
98829 Malott, 350.....F 2
98353 Manchester, 400.....A 2
98830 Mansfield, 273.....F 3
98831 Manson, 220.....E 3
98266 Maple Falls, 90.....D 2
98038 Maple Valley, 2,900.....D 3
98267 Marblemount, 387.....D 2
99151 Marcus, 142.....H 2
98268 Marietta, 300.....C 1
† 98520 Markham, 180.....A 4
98832 Marlin, 52.....F 3
99020 Marshall, 150.....H 3
98620 Maryhill, 90.....E 5
98870 Marysville, 4,343.....C 2
98560 Matlock, 250.....B 3
99344 Mattawa, 180.....F 4
98557 McCleary, 1,265.....B 4
98558 McKenna, 250.....C 4
† 98273 McMurray, 62.....C 2
99021 Mead, 1,099.....H 3
98841 Medical Lake, 3,529.....H 3
98039 Medina, 3,455.....B 2
† 98563 Melbourne, 200.....B 4
98561 Menlo, 200.....B 4
98040 Mercer Island (city), 19,047.....B 2

† 98826 Merritt, 150.....E 3
99343 Mesa, 274.....G 4
99152 Metaline, 197.....H 2
99153 Metaline Falls, 307.....H 2
98284 Newhalem, 350.....D 2
99023 Mica, 130.....H 3
99024 Milan, 90.....H 3
99212 Millwood, 1,770.....H 3
98354 Milton, 2,607.....C 3
98855 Mineral, 500.....C 4
98562 Moclips, 650.....A 3
98836 Monitor, 75.....E 3
98272 Monroe, 2,687.....D 3
† 98812 Monse, 29.....F 2
98563 Montesano◉, 2,847.....B 4
98356 Morton, 1,134.....C 4
98837 Moses Lake, 10,310.....F 3
98564 Mossyrock, 409.....C 4
98043 Mountlake Terrace, 16,600.....B 1
98273 Mount Vernon◉, 8,804.....C 2
98936 Moxee City, 600.....E 4
99275 Mukilteo, 1,369.....C 2
98937 Naches, 666.....E 4
98537 Nahcotta, 200.....A 4
98565 Napavine, 377.....C 4
98638 Naselle, 500.....B 4

† 98310 Navy Yard City, 2,827.....A 2
98357 Neah Bay, 750.....A 2
98566 Neilton, 250.....B 3
99155 Nespelem, 323.....G 2
† 98283 Newhalem, 94.....D 2
99025 Newman Lake, 102.....J 3
99156 Newport◉, 1,418.....H 2
99026 Nine Mile Falls, 150.....H 3
† 98501 Nisqually, 500.....C 3
98276 Nooksack, 322.....C 1
98358 Nordland, 500.....C 2
98100 Normandy Park, 4,208.....A 2
98045 North Bend, 1,625.....D 3
98639 North Bonneville, 459.....C 5
† 98590 North Cove, 50.....A 4
99157 Northport, 423.....H 2
98158 Oakesdale, 447.....H 4
98277 Oak Harbor, 9,167.....C 2
98568 Oakville, 460.....B 4
98569 Ocean City, 350.....A 3
98640 Ocean Park, 918.....A 4
98520 Ocosta, 300.....A 3
98159 Odessa, 1,074.....G 3
98840 Okanogan◉, 2,015.....F 2
98359 Olalla, 800.....A 2
98279 Olga, 150.....C 2

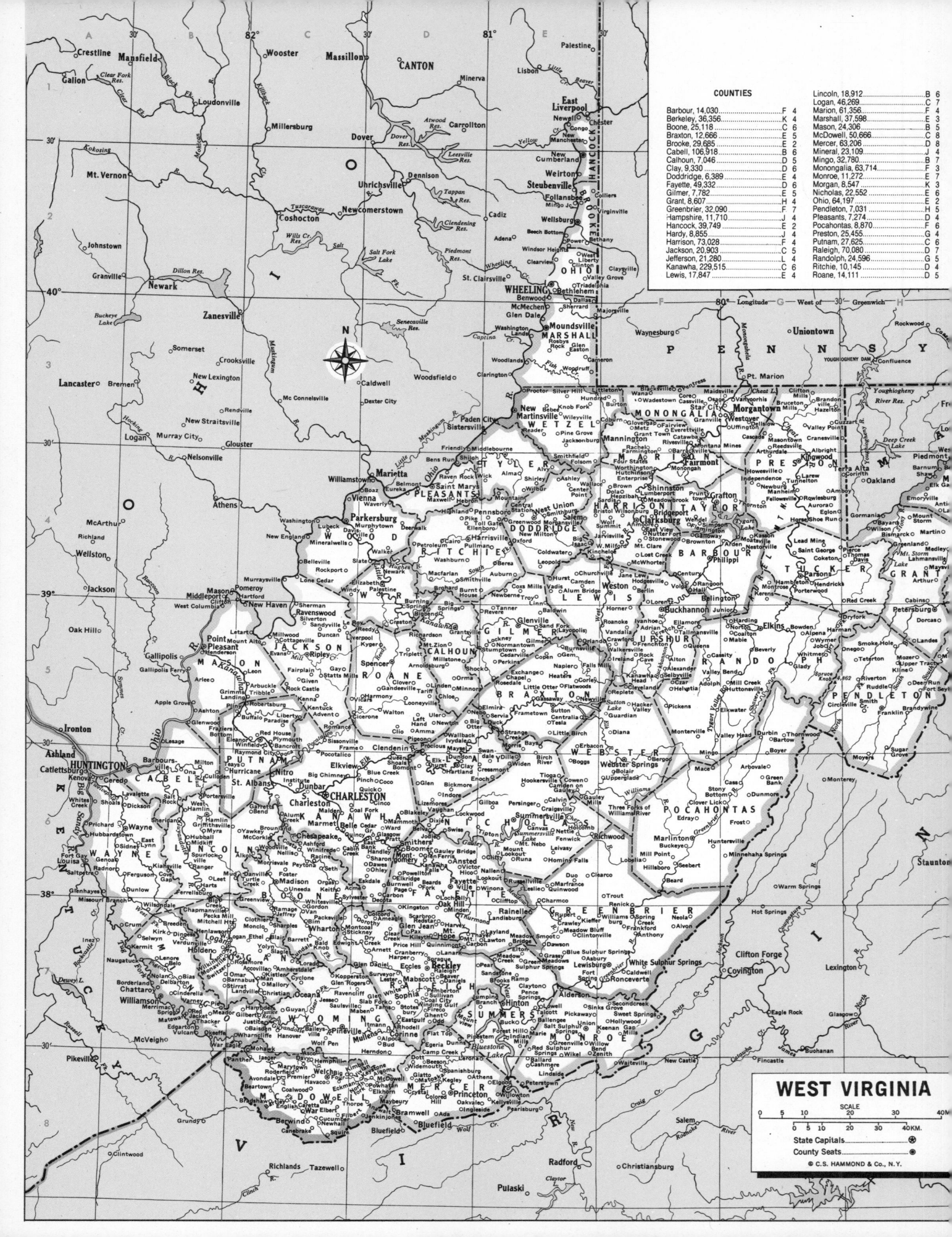

WEST VIRGINIA

SCALE

0 5 10 20 30 40M

0 5 10 20 30 40KM.

State Capitals ●
County Seats ◉

© C.S. HAMMOND & Co., N.Y.

Summers, 13,213	E 7
Taylor, 13,878	F 4
Tucker, 7,447	G 4
Tyler, 9,929	E 4
Upshur, 19,092	F 5
Wayne, 37,581	B 6
Webster, 9,809	F 6
Wetzel, 20,314	E 3
Wirt, 4,154	D 4
Wood, 86,818	D 4
Wyoming, 30,095	C 7

CITIES and TOWNS

Zip	Name/Pop.	Key
25606	Accoville, 975	C 7
† 24701	Ada, 250	D 8
† 26288	Addison (Webster Springs)⊙, 1,038	F 6
26210	Adrian, 500	F 5
26519	Albright, 319	G 3
24910	Alderson, 1,278	E 7
24807	Algoma, 400	D 8
25501	Alkol, 500	C 6
26320	Alma, 296	E 4
24710	Alpoca, 200	D 7
25003	Alum Creek, 900	C 6
25004	Ameagle, 210	D 7
25607	Amherstdale, 1,602	C 4
24808	Anawalt, 801	D 8
26323	Anmoore, 944	F 4
25812	Ansted, 1,511	D 6
24915	Arbovale, 300	G 6
25006	Arbuckle, 300	C 5
26324	Arden, 200	G 4
25007	Arnett, 300	D 7
25234	Arnoldsburg, 175	D 5
26816	Arthur, 200	H 4
26520	Arthurdale, 950	G 3
24916	Asbury, 280	E 7
24809	Asco, 200	C 8
25009	Ashford, 400	C 6
24712	Athens, 967	E 8
26704	Augusta, 550	J 4
26705	Aurora, 275	G 4
24811	Avondale, 250	C 8
24812	Baileysville, 800	C 7
25608	Baisden, 500	C 7
26801	Baker, 200	J 4
25410	Bakerton, 250	L 4
25010	Bald Knob, 356	C 7
24918	Ballard, 220	E 8
25011	Bancroft, 446	C 5
25504	Barboursville, 2,279	B 6
25609	Barnabus, 750	C 7
26559	Barrackville, 1,596	F 3
25013	Barrett, 950	C 7
24813	Bartley, 600	C 8
† 25411	Bath, 944	K 3
26707	Bayard, 475	H 4
† 26629	Bays, 186	E 5
25014	Beards Fork, 350	D 6
24814	Beartown, 500	C 8
25813	Beaver (Glen Hedrick), 1,711	D 7
25801	Beckley⊙, 19,884	D 7
26030	Beech Bottom, 544	E 2
24714	Beeson, 250	D 8
26250	Belington, 1,567	F 4

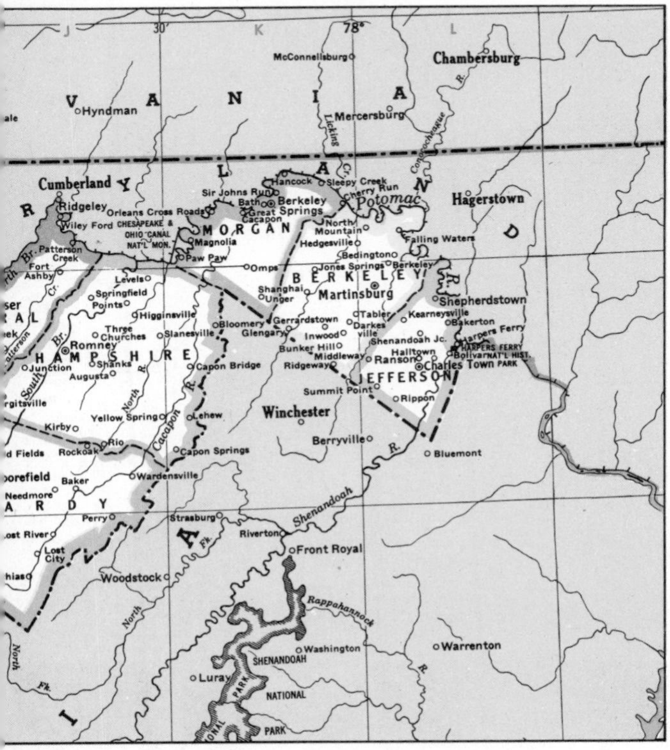

AREA 24,181 sq. mi.
POPULATION 1,744,237
CAPITAL Charleston
LARGEST CITY Huntington
HIGHEST POINT Spruce Knob 4,862 ft.
SETTLED IN 1774
ADMITTED TO UNION June 20, 1863
POPULAR NAME Mountain State
STATE FLOWER Rhododendron
STATE BIRD Cardinal

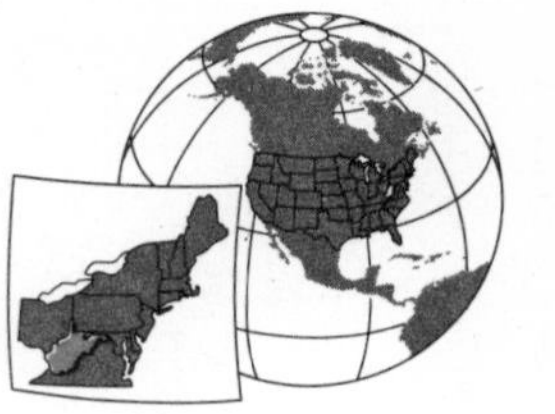

Zip	Name/Pop.	Key
25015	Belle, 1,786	C 6
26134	Belmont, 802	D 4
26656	Belva, 550	D 6
26031	Benwood, 2,737	E 2
26298	Bergoo, 260	F 6
† 25401	Berkeley, 600	L 4
25411	Berkeley Springs⊙, 2,200	K 3
24815	Berwind, 675	C 8
26032	Bethany, 602	E 2
† 26003	Bethlehem, 2,461	E 2
26253	Beverly, 470	G 5
25019	Bickmore, 375	D 6
25302	Big Chimney, 450	C 6
25505	Big Creek, 500	B 7
† 24853	Big Four, 200	C 8
25021	Bim, 395	C 7
26610	Birch River, 650	E 6
26521	Blacksville, 264	F 3
25022	Blair, 700	C 7
25023	Blakeley, 260	D 6
25026	Blue Creek, 300	D 6
24701	Bluefield, 15,921	D 8
26288	Bolair, 450	F 6
25426	Bolivar, 943	L 4
25030	Bomont, 412	D 6
25031	Boomer, 1,261	D 6
25665	Borderland, 250	B 7
24817	Bradshaw, 1,048	C 8
24715	Bramwell, 1,125	D 8
26802	Brandywine, 188	H 5
25666	Breeden, 300	B 7
26330	Bridgeport, 4,777	F 4
† 25314	Brounland, 900	C 6
26334	Brownton, 700	F 4
26525	Bruceton Mills, 209	G 3
26201	Buckhannon⊙, 7,261	F 5
24716	Bud, 400	D 7
25033	Buffalo, 831	C 5
25413	Bunker Hill, 500	K 4
26710	Burlington, 338	J 4
26335	Burnsville, 591	E 5
26562	Burton, 250	F 3
25035	Cabin Creek, 900	C 6
26855	Cabins, 300	H 4
26337	Cairo, 412	D 4
24925	Caldwell, 425	F 7
26660	Calvin, 200	E 6
26208	Camden on Gauley, 243	E 6
26033	Cameron, 1,537	E 3
25820	Camp Creek, 200	D 7
24819	Canebrake, 250	C 8
26662	Canvas, 300	E 6
26711	Capon Bridge, 211	K 4
26823	Capon Springs, 250	K 4
25037	Carbon, 200	D 6
24821	Caretta, 650	C 8
26527	Cassville, 800	F 3
26564	Catawba, 186	F 3
25039	Cedar Grove, 1,275	D 6
26340	Central Station, 275	E 4
26214	Century, 239	F 4
25507	Ceredo, 1,583	B 6
25508	Chapmanville, 1,175	B 7
* 25301	Charleston (cap.)⊙, 71,505	C 6
	Charleston, ‡229,515	C 6
25414	Charles Town⊙, 3,023	L 4
25958	Charmco, 900	E 6
25667	Chattaroy, 1,145	B 7
25315	Chesapeake, 2,428	C 6
26034	Chester, 3,614	E 1
25306	Cinco, 500	D 6
26804	Circleville, 180	H 5
26301	Clarksburg⊙, 24,864	F 4
25043	Clay⊙, 479	D 6
25044	Clear Creek, 300	D 7
† 26003	Clearview, 512	E 2
25045	Clendenin, 1,438	D 5
25237	Clifton, 358	B 5
† 25854	Clifty, 250	E 6
† 26058	Clinton, 350	E 2
25046	Clio, 300	D 5
25047	Clothier, 950	C 7
25238	Clover, 350	D 5
24929	Clover Lick, 250	F 6
25823	Coal City, 1,089	D 7
25306	Coal Fork, 950	D 6
26257	Coalton, 234	G 5
24824	Coalwood, 650	C 8
26565	Coburn, 230	F 3
25048	Colcord, 600	D 7
26035	Colliers, 500	E 2
† 24740	Colored Hill, 1,031	D 8
26615	Copen, 312	E 5
25826	Corinne, 1,090	D 7
26713	Corinth, 195	H 4
25051	Costa, 500	C 6
25239	Cottageville, 500	C 5
25509	Cove Gap, 650	B 6
26206	Cowen, 467	E 6
26205	Craigsville, 300	E 6
25828	Cranberry, 297	D 7
25669	Crum, 300	B 7
24826	Cucumber, 275	C 8
25510	Culloden, 1,033	B 6
24827	Cyclone, 500	C 7
25832	Daniels, 950	D 7
25053	Danville, 580	C 6
† 25428	Darkesville, 375	L 4
26260	Davis, 868	H 4
26142	Davisville, 200	C 4
24828	Davy, 993	C 8
25054	Dawes, 800	D 6
24932	Dawson, 200	E 7
25055	Decota, 800	D 6
25670	Delbarton, 903	B 7
26531	Dellslow, 500	G 3
26217	Diana, 600	F 5
† 25535	Dickson, 200	B 6
26617	Dille, 300	E 6
25671	Dingess, 600	B 7
25059	Dixie, 800	D 6
† 26386	Dola, 200	F 4
26835	Dorcas, 250	H 5
25060	Dorothy, 400	D 7
25062	Dry Creek, 290	D 7
26263	Dryfork, 208	H 5
25063	Duck, 500	E 5
25064	Dunbar, 9,151	C 6
24934	Dunmore, 200	G 6
26264	Durbin, 347	G 5
25067	East Bank, 1,025	D 6
25835	Eastgulf, 300	D 7
25512	East Lynn, 500	B 6
† 26301	East View, 1,618	F 4
25836	Eccles, 1,105	D 7
24829	Eckman, 850	C 8
25672	Edgarton, 415	B 7
† 24954	Edray, 175	F 6
24830	Elbert, 400	C 8
25070	Eleanor, 1,035	C 5
26143	Elizabeth⊙, 821	D 4
26717	Elk Garden, 291	H 4
26241	Elkins⊙, 8,287	G 5
† 24868	Elkridge, 500	D 6
25071	Elkview, 1,486	C 6
26267	Ellamore, 400	F 5
26346	Ellenboro, 267	D 4
25965	Elton, 320	E 7
24832	English, 500	C 8
26568	Enterprise, 975	F 4
26203	Erbacon, 350	E 5
25075	Eskdale, 500	D 6
25076	Ethel, 450	C 7
25241	Evans, 400	C 5
26533	Everettville, 200	F 3
26554	Fairmont, 26,093	F 4
† 25271	Fairplain, 200	C 5
26570	Fairview, 640	F 3
† 24966	Falling Springs (Renick), 255	F 6
26571	Farmington, 595	F 3
25840	Fayetteville⊙, 1,712	D 6
26202	Fenwick, 500	E 6
25513	Ferrellsburg, 300	B 6
25823	Fireco, 300	D 7
26818	Fisher, 250	H 4
25841	Flat Top, 550	D 7
26621	Flatwoods, 220	E 5
26347	Flemington, 458	F 4
26037	Follansbee, 3,883	E 2
26348	Folsom, 325	E 4
24935	Forest Hill, 314	E 7
26719	Fort Ashby, 1,225	J 4
25514	Fort Gay, 792	A 6
26806	Fort Seybert, 208	H 5
24936	Fort Spring, 250	E 7
26572	Four States, 300	F 4
25071	Frame, 200	C 5
26623	Frametown, 600	E 5
24938	Frankford, 200	F 7
26807	Franklin⊙, 695	H 5
26218	French Creek, 200	F 5
26219	Frenchton, 212	F 5
26146	Friendly, 190	D 3
25515	Gallipolis Ferry, 325	B 5
26349	Galloway, 289	F 4
25243	Gandeeville, 271	D 5
24836	Gary, 850	C 8
26624	Gassaway, 1,253	E 5
25085	Gauley Bridge, 1,800	D 6
25420	Gerrardstown, 258	K 4
25843	Ghent, 450	D 7
† 24736	Giatto, 400	D 8
25621	Gilbert, 778	C 7
26671	Gilboa, 375	E 6
25086	Glasgow, 904	D 6
26038	Glen Dale, 2,150	E 3
25844	Glen Daniel, 300	D 7
25090	Glen Ferris, 275	D 6
† 25813	Glen Hedrick (Beaver), 1,711	D 7
25846	Glen Jean, 1,510	D 7
25848	Glen Rogers, 500	D 7
26351	Glenville⊙, 2,183	E 5
25849	Glen White, 600	D 7
25520	Glenwood, 400	B 5
25093	Gordon, 500	C 7
26720	Gormania, 250	H 4
26354	Grafton⊙, 6,433	G 4
26147	Grantsville⊙, 795	D 5
26574	Grant Town, 946	F 3
26534	Granville, 1,027	F 3
25422	Great Cacapon, 750	K 3
25966	Green Sulphur Springs, 300	E 7
† 25166	Greenview, 250	C 6
26360	Greenwood, 460	E 4
25521	Griffithsville, 300	B 6
25095	Grimms Landing, 350	B 5
26221	Guardian, 200	F 5
24838	Guyan, 250	C 7
25423	Halltown, 325	L 4
26269	Hambleton, 328	G 4
25523	Hamlin⊙, 1,024	B 6
25623	Hampden, 251	C 7
25102	Handley, 500	D 6
24839	Hanover, 300	C 7
† 26250	Harding, 200	G 5
25851	Harper, 300	D 7
25425	Harpers Ferry, 423	L 4
26362	Harrisville⊙, 1,464	E 4
25247	Hartford, 527	C 4
25852	Harvey, 500	D 7
24841	Havaco, 329	C 8
26627	Heaters, 343	E 5
25427	Hedgesville, 274	K 3
26224	Helvetia, 269	F 5
24842	Hemphill, 785	C 8
25106	Henderson, 496	B 5
26271	Hendricks, 317	G 4
25624	Henlawson, 900	B 7
26369	Hepzibah, 600	F 4
24726	Herndon, 500	D 7
25854	Hico, 750	D 6
24946	Hillsboro, 267	F 6
25951	Hinton⊙, 4,503	E 7
26262	Holcomb, 200	E 6
25625	Holden, 2,325	B 7
† 26651	Hookersville, 250	E 6
26575	Hundred, 475	E 3
* 25701	Huntington⊙, 74,315	A 6
	Huntington-Ashland, ‡253,743	A 6
25526	Hurricane, 3,491	C 6
24844	Iaeger, 822	C 8
25111	Indore, 200	D 6
25112	Institute, 3,100	C 6
25428	Inwood, 600	K 4
24847	Itmann, 500	D 7
25113	Ivydale, 700	D 5
26377	Jacksonburg, 735	E 3
26378	Jane Lew, 397	F 4
† 26462	Jarvisville, 250	F 4
25114	Jeffrey, 900	C 7
24848	Jenkinjones, 800	D 8
26674	Jodie, 300	D 6
25969	Jumping Branch, 297	E 7
26275	Junior, 513	G 5
24851	Justice, 600	C 7
25430	Kearneysville, 250	L 4
24731	Kegley, 450	D 8
24732	Kellysville, 200	E 8
25248	Kenna, 380	C 5
25530	Kenova, 4,860	A 6
25674	Kermit, 716	B 7
26726	Keyser⊙, 6,586	J 4
24852	Keystone, 1,008	D 8
25859	Kilsyth, 450	D 7
24853	Kimball, 962	C 8
26537	Kingwood⊙, 2,550	G 4
† 25671	Kirk, 400	B 7
25628	Kistler, 750	C 7
24854	Kopperston, 900	C 7
25860	Lanark, 375	D 7
† 25831	Landisburg, 250	E 7
25629	Landville, 250	C 7
25535	Lavalette, 600	B 6
25864	Layland, 455	E 7
† 26430	Layopolis (Sand Fork), 252	E 5
25251	Left Hand, 200	D 5
26676	Leivasy, 450	E 6
25676	Lenore, 800	B 7
25123	Leon, 192	C 5
25971	Lerona, 350	D 8
25537	Lesage, 600	B 5
25972	Leslie, 500	E 6
25865	Lester, 507	D 7
25253	Letart, 250	C 5
24901	Lewisburg⊙, 2,407	E 7
24951	Lindside, 225	E 8
26384	Linn, 212	E 4
26629	Little Birch, 180	E 5
† 26624	Little Otter, 250	E 5
26581	Littleton, 333	F 3
25125	Lizemores, 400	D 6
26677	Lockwood, 300	D 6
25601	Logan⊙, 3,311	B 7
25868	Lookout, 200	E 6
25630	Lorado, 400	C 7
26385	Lost Creek, 571	F 4
† 26101	Lubeck, 500	C 4
26386	Lumberport, 957	F 4
25631	Lundale, 700	C 7
25870	Maben, 200	D 7
26278	Mabie, 366	G 5
25871	Mabscott, 1,254	D 7
25873	MacArthur, 1,614	D 7
25130	Madison⊙, 2,342	C 6
26541	Maidsville, 485	F 3
25306	Malden, 900	C 6
25634	Mallory, 1,240	C 7
25132	Mammoth, 576	D 6
25635	Man, 1,201	C 7
26582	Mannington, 2,747	F 3
25975	Marfrance, 240	E 6
24954	Marlinton⊙, 1,286	F 6
25315	Marmet, 2,339	C 6
25401	Martinsburg⊙, 14,626	K 4
25260	Mason, 1,319	B 4
26542	Masontown, 868	G 3
25678	Matewan, 651	B 7
24736	Matoaka, 608	D 8
24861	Maybeury, 850	D 8

(continued on following page)

Topography

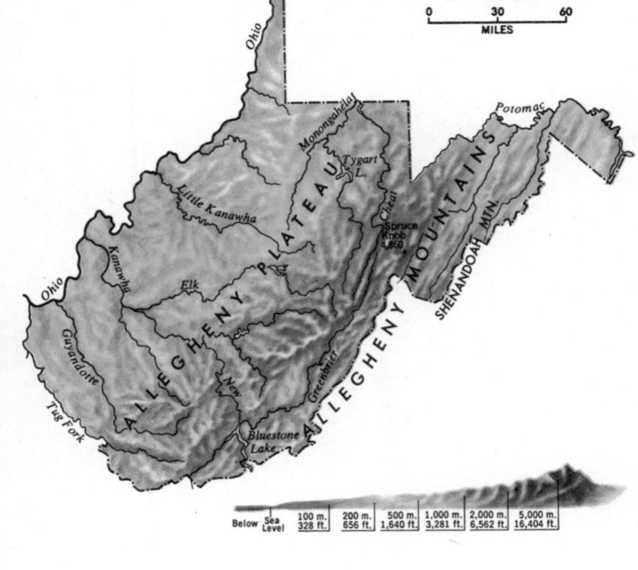

Agriculture, Industry and Resources

DOMINANT LAND USE

- Dairy, General Farming
- General Farming, Livestock, Dairy
- General Farming, Livestock, Tobacco
- General Farming, Livestock, Fruit, Tobacco
- Fruit and Mixed Farming
- Forests

MAJOR MINERAL OCCURRENCES

- C   Coal
- Cl   Clay
- G   Natural Gas
- Ls   Limestone
- Na   Salt
- O   Petroleum
- Water Power
- Major Industrial Areas

WEIRTON — Iron & Steel, Metal Products

WHEELING — Iron & Steel, Chemicals, Metal Products

HUNTINGTON — Chemicals, Glass & Metal Products, Clothing

CHARLESTON–KANAWHA VALLEY — Chemicals, Synthetic Fibers, Glass & Metal Products

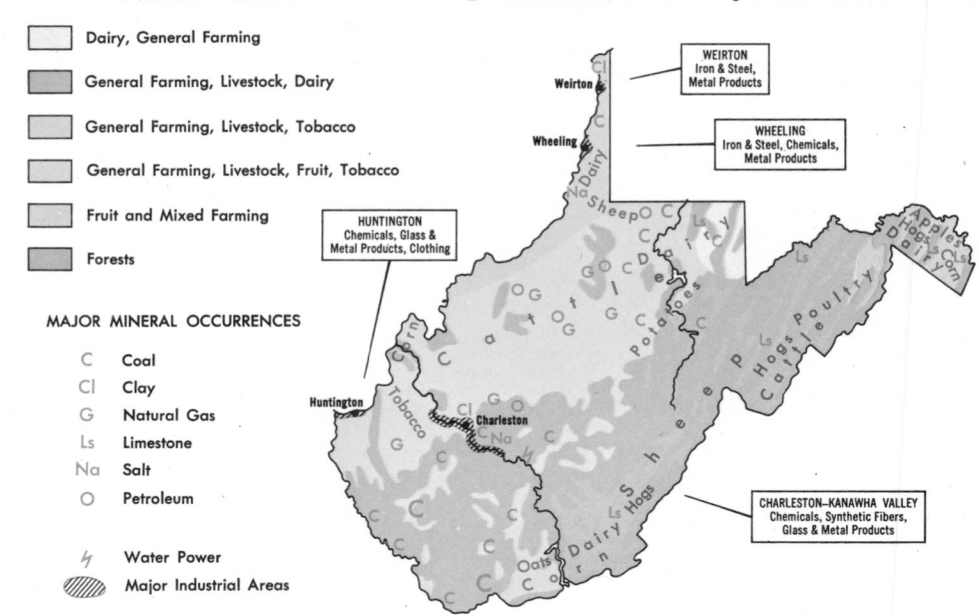

At one of Clarksburg, West Virginia's glass plants, liquid glass is poured into a machine and becomes beautifully textured stained-glass panels.

A. D'Arazien — Shostal Associates

AREA 56,154 sq. mi.
POPULATION 4,417,933
CAPITAL Madison
LARGEST CITY Milwaukee
HIGHEST POINT Timms Hill 1,952 ft.
SETTLED IN 1670
ADMITTED TO UNION May 29, 1848
POPULAR NAME Badger State
STATE FLOWER Wood Violet
STATE BIRD Robin

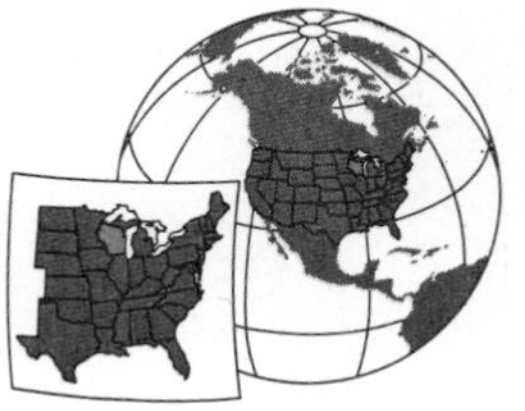

COUNTIES

Name/Pop.	Key
Adams, 9,234	G 8
Ashland, 16,743	E 3
Barron, 33,955	C 5
Bayfield, 11,683	D 3
Brown, 158,244	L 7
Buffalo, 13,743	C 7
Burnett, 9,276	B 4
Calumet, 27,604	K 7
Chippewa, 47,717	D 5
Clark, 30,361	E 6
Columbia, 40,150	H 9
Crawford, 15,252	E 9
Dane, 290,272	H 9
Dodge, 69,004	J 9
Door, 20,106	M 6
Douglas, 44,657	C 3
Dunn, 29,154	C 6
Eau Claire, 67,219	D 6
Florence, 3,298	K 4
Fond du Lac, 84,567	K 8
Forest, 7,691	J 4
Grant, 48,398	E 10
Green, 26,714	G 10
Green Lake, 16,878	H 8
Iowa, 19,306	F 9
Iron, 6,533	F 3
Jackson, 15,325	E 7
Jefferson, 60,060	J 9
Juneau, 18,455	F 8
Kenosha, 117,917	K 10
Kewaunee, 18,961	L 6
La Crosse, 80,468	D 8
Lafayette, 17,456	F 10
Langlade, 19,220	H 5
Lincoln, 23,499	G 5
Manitowoc, 82,294	L 7
Marathon, 97,457	G 6
Marinette, 35,810	K 5
Marquette, 8,865	H 8
Menominee, 2,607	J 5
Milwaukee, 1,054,063	L 9
Monroe, 31,610	E 8
Oconto, 25,553	K 6
Oneida, 24,427	G 4
Outagamie, 119,356	K 7
Ozaukee, 54,421	L 9
Pepin, 7,319	C 6
Pierce, 26,652	B 6
Polk, 26,666	B 5
Portage, 47,541	G 6
Price, 14,520	F 4
Racine, 170,838	K 10
Richland, 17,079	F 9
Rock, 131,970	H 10
Rusk, 14,238	D 5
Saint Croix, 34,354	B 5
Sauk, 39,057	G 9
Sawyer, 9,670	D 4
Shawano, 32,650	J 6
Sheboygan, 96,660	L 8
Taylor, 16,958	E 5
Trempealeau, 23,344	D 7
Vernon, 24,557	E 8
Vilas, 10,958	G 3
Walworth, 63,444	J 10
Washburn, 10,601	C 4
Washington, 63,839	K 9
Waukesha, 231,365	K 9
Waupaca, 37,780	J 6
Waushara, 14,795	H 7
Winnebago, 129,931	J 7
Wood, 65,362	F 7

CITIES and TOWNS

Zip	Name/Pop.	Key
54405	Abbotsford, 1,375	F 6
54101	Abrams, 300	L 6
53910	Adams, 1,440	G 8
53001	Adell, 380	L 8
53501	Afton, 250	H 10
53502	Albany, 875	G 10
53534	Albion, 250	H 10
54201	Algoma, 4,023	M 6
53002	Allenton, 584	K 9
† 54301	Allouez, 13,753	L 7
54610	Alma⊙, 956	C 7
54611	Alma Center, 495	E 7
54805	Almena, 423	B 5
54909	Almond, 440	G 7
54720	Altoona, 2,842	C 6
49936	Alvin, 160	J 4
54102	Amberg, 711	K 5
54001	Amery, 2,126	B 5
54406	Amherst, 585	H 7
† 54162	Angelica, 200	K 6
54408	Aniwa, 233	H 6
54409	Antigo⊙, 9,005	H 5
54911	Appleton⊙, 57,143	J 7
	Appleton-Oshkosh, ‡276,893	J 7
54510	Arbor Vitae, 950	G 4
54612	Arcadia, 2,159	D 7
53503	Arena, 377	G 9
54511	Argonne, 400	J 4
53504	Argyle, 673	G 10
54721	Arkansaw, 350	B 6
53911	Arlington, 379	H 9
54103	Armstrong Creek, 555	K 4
54410	Arpin, 355	G 6
53003	Ashippun, 400	H 1
54806	Ashland⊙, 9,615	E 2
54304	Ashwaubenon, 9,323	K 7
54411	Athens, 856	G 5
54412	Auburndale, 468	F 6
54722	Augusta, 1,242	D 6
54920	Auroraville, 250	H 7
53506	Avoca, 421	F 9
† 53520	Avon, 600	H 10
54413	Babcock, 260	F 7
53801	Bagley, 271	D 10
54202	Baileys Harbor, 900	M 5
54002	Baldwin, 1,399	B 6
54810	Balsam Lake⊙, 648	B 5
54921	Bancroft, 150	G 7
54614	Bangor, 974	E 8
53913	Baraboo⊙, 7,931	G 9
† 54873	Barnes, 450	D 3
53507	Barneveld, 528	F 10
54812	Barron⊙, 2,337	C 5
† 53001	Batavia, 160	K 8
54723	Bay City, 317	B 6
54814	Bayfield, 874	E 2
† 53201	Bayside, 4,461	M 1
54922	Bear Creek, 520	J 6
53916	Beaver Dam, 14,265	J 9
53802	Beetown, 170	E 10
53004	Belgium, 809	L 8
53508	Belleville, 1,063	G 10
53510	Belmont, 688	F 10
53511	Beloit, 35,729	H 10
54815	Bennett, 350	C 3
53803	Benton, 873	F 10
54923	Berlin, 5,338	H 8
† 53401	Berryville, 150	M 3
† 54410	Bethel, 210	F 6
† 54440	Bevent, 200	H 6
53103	Big Bend, 1,148	K 2
54817	Birchwood, 394	C 4
54414	Birnamwood, 632	H 6
† 54494	Biron, 771	G 7
54106	Black Creek, 921	K 7
53515	Black Earth, 1,114	G 9
54615	Black River Falls⊙, 3,273	E 7
† 54541	Blackwell, 350	J 4
54616	Blair, 1,036	D 7
53516	Blanchardville, 671	G 10
54724	Bloomer, 3,143	D 5
53804	Bloomington, 719	E 10
53517	Blue Mounds, 261	G 9
53518	Blue River, 369	E 9
54107	Bonduel, 995	K 6
53805	Boscobel, 2,510	E 9
54512	Boulder Junction, 500	G 3
54416	Bowler, 272	J 6
54725	Boyceville, 725	C 5
54726	Boyd, 574	E 6
54203	Branch, 225	L 7
53919	Brandon, 872	J 8
54513	Brantwood, 500	F 4
53920	Briggsville, 250	H 8
54110	Brillion, 2,588	L 7
53520	Brodhead, 2,515	G 10
54417	Brokaw, 312	G 5
53005	Brookfield, 32,140	K 1
53521	Brooklyn, 565	H 10
† 53201	Brown Deer, 12,622	L 1
† 53105	Browns Lake, 1,669	K 3
53006	Brownsville, 374	J 8
53522	Browntown, 253	G 10
54819	Bruce, 799	D 5
54820	Brule, 675	C 2
54204	Brussels, 306	L 6
† 54622	Buffalo, 671	C 7
53105	Burlington, 7,479	K 10
53922	Burnett, 241	J 9
53007	Butler, 2,261	K 1
54514	Butternut, 453	E 3
54821	Cable, 281	D 3
54727	Cadott, 977	D 6
53923	Cambria, 631	H 8
53523	Cambridge, 689	H 9
54822	Cameron, 893	C 5
† 53019	Campbellsport, 1,681	K 8
54618	Camp Douglas, 547	F 8
53109	Camp Lake, 1,898	K 10
54928	Caroline, 450	J 6
53011	Cascade, 603	K 8
54205	Casco, 481	L 6
54619	Cashton, 824	E 8
53806	Cassville, 1,343	E 10
54515	Catawba, 215	E 4
53924	Cazenovia, 335	F 8
54111	Cecil, 369	K 6
53012	Cedarburg, 7,697	L 9
53013	Cedar Grove, 1,276	L 8
54824	Centuria, 632	A 5
54621	Chaseburg, 224	D 8
† 53029	Chenequa, 642	J 1
54728	Chetek, 1,630	C 5
54420	Chili, 205	F 6
53014	Chilton⊙, 3,030	K 7
54729	Chippewa Falls⊙, 12,351	D 6
54004	Clayton, 306	B 5
54005	Clear Lake, 721	B 5
54518	Clearwater Lake, 200	H 4
53015	Cleveland, 761	L 8
53525	Clinton, 1,333	J 10
54929	Clintonville, 4,600	J 6
53016	Clyman, 328	J 9
53526	Cobb, 410	F 10
54622	Cochrane, 506	C 7
54421	Colby, 1,178	F 6
54112	Coleman, 683	L 5
54730	Colfax, 1,026	C 6
54930	Coloma, 336	H 7
53925	Columbus, 3,789	H 9
54113	Combined Locks, 2,734	K 7
† 53147	Como, 1,132	K 10
† 53066	Concord, 200	H 1
54519	Conover, 500	H 3
54623	Coon Valley, 596	E 8
54732	Cornell, 1,616	D 5
54827	Cornucopia, 250	D 2
54520	Crandon⊙, 1,582	H 4
54114	Crivitz, 985	L 5
53528	Cross Plains, 1,478	G 9
53807	Cuba City, 1,993	F 10
53110	Cudahy, 22,078	M 2
54829	Cumberland, 1,839	C 4
54931	Dale, 410	J 7
54733	Dallas, 359	C 5
53926	Dalton, 320	H 8
54830	Danbury, 350	B 3
53529	Dane, 486	G 9
53114	Darien, 839	J 10
53530	Darlington⊙, 2,351	F 10
53531	Deerfield, 1,067	H 9
54007	Deer Park, 217	B 5
53532	De Forest, 1,911	H 9
53018	Delafield, 3,182	J 1
53115	Delavan, 5,526	J 10
† 53115	Delavan Lake, 2,124	J 10
54856	Delta, 180	D 3
54208	Denmark, 1,364	L 7
54115	De Pere, 13,309	K 7
† 54663	De Soto, 295	D 9
53808	Dickeyville, 1,057	E 10
54625	Dodge, 204	D 7
53533	Dodgeville⊙, 3,255	F 10
54425	Dorchester, 491	F 5
53118	Dousman, 451	J 1
54734	Downing, 215	B 5
53928	Doylestown, 265	H 9
54009	Dresser, 533	A 5
54736	Durand⊙, 2,103	C 6
† 54217	Dyckesville, 300	L 6
53119	Eagle, 745	H 2
54521	Eagle River⊙, 1,326	H 4
54626	Eastman, 319	D 9
53120	East Troy, 1,711	J 2
54701	Eau Claire⊙, 44,619	D 6
53019	Eden, 376	K 8
54426	Edgar, 928	G 6
53534	Edgerton, 4,118	H 10
54209	Egg Harbor, 184	M 5
54427	Eland, 229	H 6
54428	Elcho, 500	H 5
54429	Elderon, 185	H 6
54932	Eldorado, 200	J 8
54738	Eleva, 574	D 6
53020	Elkhart Lake, 787	L 8
53121	Elkhorn⊙, 3,992	J 10
54739	Elk Mound, 471	C 6
54011	Ellsworth⊙, 1,983	A 6
53122	Elm Grove, 7,201	K 1
54740	Elmwood, 737	B 6
† 53401	Elmwood Park, 456	M 3
53929	Elroy, 1,513	F 8
54430	Elton, 250	J 5
54933	Embarrass, 472	J 6
53930	Endeavor, 328	G 8
54211	Ephraim, 236	M 5
54627	Ettrick, 463	D 7
54934	Eureka, 300	J 7
53536	Evansville, 2,992	H 10
54835	Exeland, 189	D 4
54741	Fairchild, 562	D 6
53931	Fair Water, 373	J 8
54742	Fall Creek, 825	D 6
53932	Fall River, 633	H 9
54120	Fence, 187	K 4
53809	Fennimore, 1,861	E 9
54628	Ferryville, 183	D 9
54524	Fifield, 287	F 4
54212	Fish Creek, 275	M 5
54121	Florence⊙, 800	K 4
54935	Fond du Lac⊙, 35,515	K 8
53125	Fontana, 1,464	J 10
53537	Footville, 698	H 10
54123	Forest Junction, 255	K 7
54213	Forestville, 349	L 6
53538	Fort Atkinson, 9,164	J 10
54629	Fountain City, 1,017	C 7
54836	Foxboro, 950	B 2
53933	Fox Lake, 1,242	J 8
53217	Fox Point, 7,937	M 1
54214	Francis Creek, 492	L 7
53132	Franklin, 12,247	L 2
53126	Franksville, 375	M 3
54837	Frederic, 908	B 4
53021	Fredonia, 1,045	L 8
54940	Fremont, 598	J 7
53934	Friendship⊙, 641	G 8
53935	Friesland, 301	H 8
54630	Galesville, 1,162	D 7
54631	Gays Mills, 623	E 9
† 53127	Genesee, 375	J 2
53127	Genesee Depot, 425	J 2
54632	Genoa, 305	D 8
53128	Genoa City, 1,085	K 11
53022	Germantown, 6,974	K 1
† 53085	Gibbsville, 408	L 8
54525	Gile, 450	F 3
54124	Gillett, 1,288	K 6
54433	Gilman, 328	E 5
54743	Gilmanton, 200	C 7
54435	Gleason, 300	G 5
53023	Glenbeulah, 496	L 8
† 53201	Glendale, 13,436	M 1
53810	Glen Haven, 250	E 10
54013	Glenwood City, 822	B 5
54527	Glidden, 860	E 3
54125	Goodman, 800	K 4
54838	Gordon, 350	C 3
53540	Gotham, 175	F 9
53024	Grafton, 5,998	L 9
53936	Grand Marsh, 200	G 8
54839	Grand View, 350	D 3
54436	Granton, 288	E 6
54840	Grantsburg⊙, 930	A 4
53541	Gratiot, 249	F 10
* 54301	Green Bay⊙, 87,809	K 6
	Green Bay, ‡158,244	K 6
53129	Greendale, 15,089	L 2
53220	Greenfield, 24,424	L 2
54941	Green Lake⊙, 1,109	H 8
54126	Greenleaf, 350	L 7
54942	Greenville, 900	J 7
54437	Greenwood, 1,036	E 6
54128	Gresham, 448	J 6
53130	Hales Corners, 7,771	K 2
† 54729	Hallie, 1,223	D 6
54438	Hamburg, 170	G 5
54015	Hammond, 768	A 6
54943	Hancock, 404	G 7
54529	Harshaw, 200	G 4
53027	Hartford, 6,499	K 9
53029	Hartland, 2,763	J 1
54440	Hatley, 315	H 6
54841	Haugen, 246	C 4
54530	Hawkins, 385	E 4
54843	Hayward⊙, 1,457	D 3
53811	Hazel Green, 982	F 11
54531	Hazelhurst, 334	G 4
† 53538	Hebron, 190	J 10
53137	Helenville, 230	J 10
54844	Herbster, 250	D 2
54441	Hewitt, 300	F 6
53543	Highland, 785	F 9
54129	Hilbert, 896	K 7
54533	Hiles, 260	J 4
54634	Hillsboro, 1,231	F 8
53031	Hingham, 210	K 8
54635	Hixton, 300	E 7
54745	Holcombe, 200	D 5
53544	Hollandale, 256	G 10
54636	Holmen, 1,081	D 8
53138	Honey Creek, 350	J 3
53032	Horicon, 3,356	J 9
54944	Hortonville, 1,524	J 7
† 55082	Houlton, 400	A 5
54303	Howard, 4,911	K 6
† 53081	Howards Grove-Millersville, 998	L 8
53033	Hubertus, 600	K 1
54016	Hudson⊙, 5,049	A 6
54746	Humbird, 219	E 6
54534	Hurley⊙, 2,418	F 3
53034	Hustisford, 789	J 9
54637	Hustler, 190	F 8
† 54450	Hutchins, 409	H 6
54747	Independence, 1,036	D 7
54945	Iola, 900	H 6
54536	Iron Belt, 425	F 3
53035	Iron Ridge, 480	K 9
54847	Iron River, 800	D 2
53938	Ironton, 195	F 8
† 53177	Ives Grove, 250	L 3
53036	Ixonia, 300	H 1
53037	Jackson, 561	K 9
54236	Jacksonport, 180	M 6
53545	Janesville⊙, 46,426	J 10
53549	Jefferson⊙, 5,429	J 10
54748	Jim Falls, 310	D 5
53038	Johnson Creek, 790	J 9
53550	Juda, 500	H 10
54443	Junction City, 396	G 6
53039	Juneau⊙, 2,043	J 9
53139	Kansasville, 300	L 3
54130	Kaukauna, 11,292	K 7
† 53050	Kekoskee, 233	J 8
54215	Kellnersville, 250	L 7
54638	Kendall, 468	F 8
54537	Kennan, 167	F 5
53140	Kenosha⊙, 78,805	M 3
	Kenosha, ‡117,917	M 3
54135	Keshena⊙, 980	J 6
53040	Kewaskum, 1,926	K 8
54216	Kewaunee⊙, 2,901	M 7
53042	Kiel, 2,848	L 8
53812	Kieler, 653	E 10
54136	Kimberly, 6,131	K 7
54946	King, 1,040	H 7
53939	Kingston, 343	H 8
54749	Knapp, 369	B 6
53044	Kohler, 1,738	L 8
53147	Krakow, 315	K 6
54538	Lac du Flambeau, 500	G 4
† 53066	Lac La Belle, 227	H 1
54601	La Crosse⊙, 51,153	D 8
	La Crosse, ‡80,468	D 8
54848	Ladysmith⊙, 3,674	D 5
54639	La Farge, 748	E 8
53940	Lake Delton, 1,059	G 8
53147	Lake Geneva, 4,890	K 10
53551	Lake Mills, 3,556	H 9
54849	Lake Nebagamon, 523	C 3
54539	Lake Tomahawk, 555	H 4
† 54494	Lake Wazeecha, 1,285	G 7
† 54729	Lake Wissota, 1,419	D 6
54138	Lakewood, 300	K 5
† 53065	Lamartine, 190	J 8
53813	Lancaster⊙, 3,756	E 10
54540	Land O'Lakes, 786	H 3
53046	Lannon, 1,056	K 1
54541	Laona, 1,500	J 4
54850	La Pointe, 300	E 2
53941	La Valle, 411	F 8
53047	Lebanon, 250	H 1
54139	Lena, 569	K 6
† 54656	Leon, 160	E 8
† 53190	Lima Center, 175	J 10
53942	Limeridge, 203	F 9
53553	Linden, 408	F 10
54140	Little Chute, 5,365	K 7
54141	Little Suamico, 190	L 6
53554	Livingston, 503	E 10
53555	Lodi, 1,831	G 9
53943	Loganville, 199	F 9
† 54970	Lohrville, 195	H 7
53048	Lomira, 1,084	J 8
† 53523	London, 317	H 9
53556	Lone Rock, 506	F 9
54852	Loretta, 200	E 4
53557	Lowell, 322	J 9
54446	Loyal, 1,126	E 6
54853	Luck, 848	B 4
54217	Luxemburg, 853	L 6
53944	Lyndon Station, 533	F 8
53148	Lyons, 550	K 10
* 53701	Madison (cap.)⊙, 173,258	H 9
	Madison, ‡290,272	H 9
54750	Maiden Rock, 172	B 6
54949	Manawa, 1,105	J 7
54220	Manitowoc⊙, 33,430	L 7
54226	Maplewood, 192	M 6
54448	Marathon, 1,214	G 6
54855	Marengo, 350	E 3
54227	Maribel, 316	L 7
54143	Marinette⊙, 12,696	L 5
54950	Marion, 1,218	J 6
53946	Markesan, 1,378	J 8
53947	Marquette, 161	H 8
53559	Marshall, 1,043	H 9
54449	Marshfield, 15,619	F 6
54450	Mattoon, 377	J 5
53948	Mauston⊙, 3,466	F 8
53050	Mayville, 4,139	K 9
53560	Mazomanie, 1,217	G 9
53558	McFarland, 2,386	H 10
54543	McNaughton, 350	H 4
54451	Medford⊙, 3,454	F 5
54546	Mellen, 1,168	E 3
54642	Melrose, 505	E 7
54952	Menasha, 14,905	J 7
53051	Menomonee Falls, 31,697	K 1
54751	Menomonie⊙, 11,275	C 6
53092	Mequon, 12,110	L 1
54547	Mercer, 1,100	F 3
54452	Merrill⊙, 9,502	G 5
54754	Merrillan, 612	E 7
53561	Merrimac, 376	G 9
53056	Merton, 646	K 1
54148	Middle Inlet, 200	K 5
53562	Middleton, 8,286	G 9
54857	Mikana, 215	C 4
54454	Milladore, 229	G 6
54643	Millston, 200	E 7
54858	Milltown, 634	B 4
53563	Milton, 3,699	J 10
* 53201	Milwaukee⊙, 717,099	M 1
	Milwaukee, ‡1,403,887	M 1
54644	Mindoro, 230	D 7
53565	Mineral Point, 2,305	F 10
54548	Minocqua, 950	G 4
54859	Minong, 420	C 3
54228	Mishicot, 938	L 7
54755	Mondovi, 2,338	C 6
54549	Monico, 285	H 4
53716	Monona, 10,420	H 9
53566	Monroe⊙, 8,654	G 10
53949	Montello⊙, 1,082	H 8
53569	Montfort, 518	E 10
53570	Monticello, 870	G 10
54550	Montreal, 877	F 3

(continued on following page)

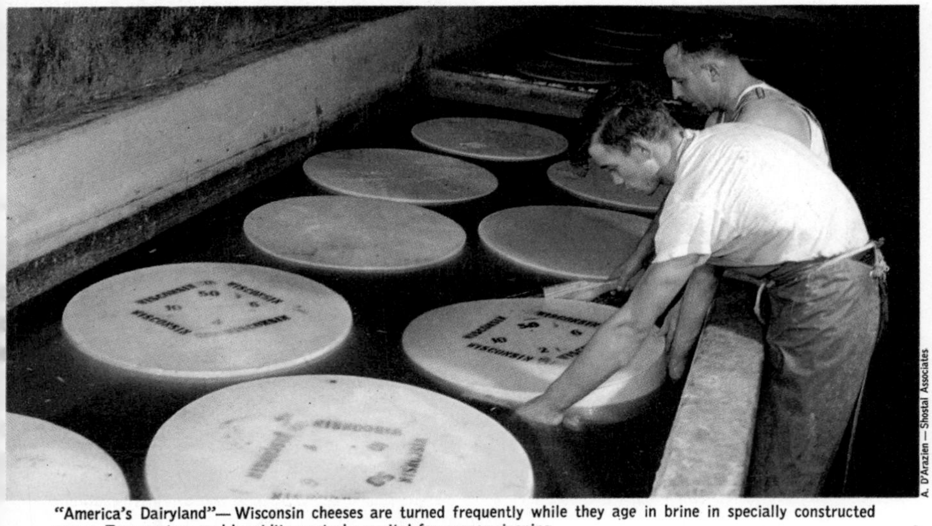

A. D'Arazien — Shostal Associates

"America's Dairyland"— Wisconsin cheeses are turned frequently while they age in brine in specially constructed rooms. Temperature and humidity control are vital for proper ripening.

(continued)

53571 Morrisonville, 350 G 9
54455 Mosinee, 2,395 G 6
54149 Mountain, 298 K 5
53057 Mount Calvary, 942 K 8
53816 Mount Hope, 176 D 10
53572 Mount Horeb, 2,402 G 10
54645 Mount Sterling, 181 D 9
† 53572 Mount Vernon, 250 G 10
53149 Mukwonago, 2,367 J 2
53573 Muscoda, 1,099 F 9
53150 Muskego, 11,573 K 2
53058 Nashotah, 410 J 1
54646 Necedah, 740 F 7
54956 Neenah, 22,892 J 7
54456 Neillsville⊙, 2,750 E 6
54457 Nekoosa, 2,409 G 7
54756 Nelson, 272 C 7
54458 Nelsonville, 152 H 7
54150 Neopit, 1,122 J 6
53059 Neosho, 400 J 9
54960 Neshkoro, 385 H 8
54551 Newald, 180 J 4
54757 New Auburn, 368 D 5
53151 New Berlin, 26,937 K 2
53060 Newburg, 425 K 9
† 61075 New Diggings, 224 F 10
54229 New Franken, 250 L 6
53574 New Glarus, 1,454 G 10
53061 New Holstein, 3,012 K 8
53950 New Lisbon, 1,361 F 8
54961 New London, 5,801 J 7
54017 New Richmond, 3,707 A 5
54151 Niagara, 2,347 K 4
54152 Nichols, 207 K 6
† 53401 North Bay, 263 M 3
54935 North Fond du Lac, 3,286 J 8
53951 North Freedom, 596 G 9
† 54016 North Hudson, 1,547 A 5
53064 North Lake, 525 J 1
53153 North Prairie, 669 J 2
54648 Norwalk, 432 E 8
53154 Oak Creek, 13,901 M 2
54649 Oakdale, 300 F 8
53065 Oakfield, 918 J 8
53066 Oconomowoc, 8,741 H 1
† 53066 Oconomowoc Lake, 599 H 1
54153 Oconto⊙, 4,667 L 6
54154 Oconto Falls, 2,517 K 6
54861 Odanah, 442 E 2
54962 Ogdensburg, 206 J 7
54459 Ogema, 280 F 5
53069 Okauchee, 3,134 J 1
† 53555 Okee, 300 H 9
† 54880 Oliver, 210 B 2
54963 Omro, 2,341 J 7
54650 Onalaska, 4,909 D 8
54155 Oneida, 900 K 7
54651 Ontario, 392 E 8
53070 Oostburg, 1,309 L 8
53575 Oregon, 2,553 H 10
53576 Orfordville, 888 H 10
54020 Osceola, 1,152 A 5
54901 Oshkosh⊙, 53,221 J 8
54758 Osseo, 1,356 D 6
54460 Owen, 1,031 F 6
53952 Oxford, 453 H 8
53953 Packwaukee, 250 G 8
† 53168 Paddock Lake, 1,470 K 10
53156 Palmyra, 1,341 H 2
53954 Pardeeville, 1,507 H 8
54552 Park Falls, 2,953 F 4
† 54481 Park Ridge, 817 H 6
53817 Patch Grove, 187 D 10
† 54514 Peeksville, 250 E 3
54156 Pembine, 500 L 4
54553 Pence, 315 F 3
† 54153 Pensaukee, 225 L 6
54759 Pepin, 747 B 7
† 53511 Perrygo Place, 5,912 J 10
54157 Peshtigo, 2,836 L 5
53072 Pewaukee, 3,271 K 1
54554 Phelps, 1,100 H 3
54555 Phillips⊙, 1,511 E 4
54464 Phlox, 235 J 5
54465 Pickerel, 400 J 5
54760 Pigeon Falls, 198 D 7
54466 Pittsville, 708 F 7
53577 Plain, 688 F 9
54966 Plainfield, 642 G 7
53818 Platteville, 9,599 F 10
53158 Pleasant Prairie, 950 L 10
54467 Plover, 1,900 G 7
54761 Plum City, 451 B 6
53073 Plymouth, 5,810 L 8
54864 Poplar, 455 C 2
53901 Portage⊙, 7,821 G 8
54469 Port Edwards, 2,126 G 7
53074 Port Washington⊙, 8,752 L 9
54865 Port Wing, 486 D 2
53820 Potosi, 713 E 10
54160 Potter, 320 K 7
54161 Pound, 284 L 5
53955 Poynette, 1,118 G 9
54967 Poy Sippi, 500 J 7
53821 Prairie du Chien⊙, 5,540 D 9
53578 Prairie du Sac, 1,902 G 9
54762 Prairie Farm, 426 C 5
54556 Prentice, 519 F 4
54021 Prescott, 2,331 A 6
54557 Presque Isle, 251 G 3
54968 Princeton, 1,446 H 8
54162 Pulaski, 1,717 K 6
* 53401 Racine⊙, 95,162 M 3
Racine, ‡170,838 M 3
54867 Radisson, 206 D 4
53956 Randolph, 1,582 H 8
53075 Random Lake, 1,068 K 8
† 53126 Raymond, 300 L 2
54969 Readfield, 200 J 7
54652 Readstown, 395 E 9
† 54814 Red Cliff, 250 E 2
54970 Redgranite, 645 J 7
53959 Reedsburg, 4,585 G 8
54230 Reedsville, 994 L 7
53579 Reeseville, 566 J 9
53580 Rewey, 232 F 10
54501 Rhinelander⊙, 8,218 H 4
54470 Rib Lake, 782 F 5
54868 Rice Lake, 7,278 C 5
53076 Richfield, 247 K 1
53581 Richland Center⊙, 5,086 F 9
54763 Ridgeland, 266 B 5
53582 Ridgeway, 463 F 10
53960 Rio, 792 H 9
54231 Rio Creek, 200 L 6
54971 Ripon, 7,053 J 8
54022 River Falls, 7,238 A 6
† 53201 River Hills, 1,561 M 1
54023 Roberts, 484 A 6
53167 Rochester, 436 K 3
† 53523 Rockdale, 172 J 10
54764 Rock Falls, 200 C 6
53077 Rockfield, 340 L 1
54653 Rockland, 278 D 8
53961 Rock Springs, 432 F 8
† 53178 Rome, 250 H 1
54974 Rosendale, 464 J 8
54473 Rosholt, 466 H 6
54474 Rothschild, 3,141 G 6
† 53583 Roxbury, 220 G 9
54975 Royalton, 200 J 7
53078 Rubicon, 261 K 9
54475 Rudolph, 349 G 7
53079 Saint Cloud, 550 K 8
54024 Saint Croix Falls, 1,425 A 5
† 53201 Saint Francis, 10,489 M 2
† 54601 Saint Joseph Ridge, 250 D 8
54232 Saint Nazianz, 718 L 7
54765 Sand Creek, 200 C 5
53583 Sauk City, 2,385 G 9
53080 Saukville, 1,389 L 9
54559 Saxon, 600 F 3
54560 Sayner, 300 H 4
54977 Scandinavia, 268 H 7
54476 Schofield, 2,577 H 6
† 53042 School Hill, 228 L 8
† 54843 Seeley, 213 D 3
54654 Seneca, 250 E 9
53584 Sextonville, 325 F 9
54165 Seymour, 2,194 K 6
53585 Sharon, 1,216 J 11
54166 Shawano⊙, 6,488 J 6
53081 Sheboygan⊙, 48,484 L 8
53085 Sheboygan Falls, 4,771 L 8
54766 Sheldon, 218 D 5
54871 Shell Lake⊙, 928 C 4
54169 Sherwood, 350 K 7
54170 Shiocton, 830 K 7
† 53525 Shopiere, 350 H 10
53211 Shorewood, 15,576 M 1
† 53701 Shorewood Hills, 2,206 G 9
53586 Shullsburg, 1,376 F 10
53170 Silver Lake, 1,210 K 10
54872 Siren, 639 B 4
54234 Sister Bay, 483 M 5
53086 Slinger, 1,022 K 9

Topography

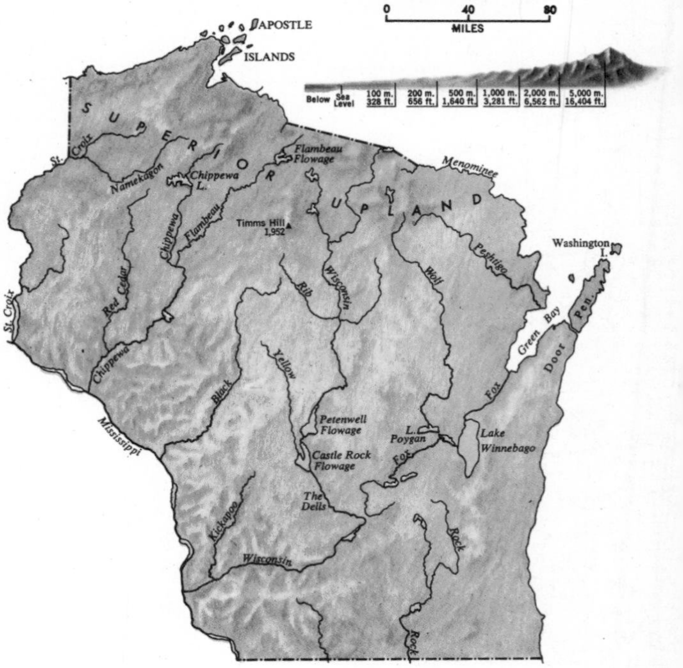

0 40 80
MILES
Below Sea Level
100 m. 328 ft.
200 m. 656 ft.
500 m. 1,640 ft.
1,000 m. 3,281 ft.
2,000 m. 6,562 ft.
5,000 m. 16,404 ft.
APOSTLE ISLANDS
SUPERIOR UPLAND
St. Croix
Namekagon
Chippewa L.
Flambeau Flowage
Menominee
Chippewa
Flambeau
Timms Hill 1,952
Red Cedar
Rib
Wisconsin
Wolf
Peshtigo
Washington I.
Green Bay
Door Pen.
Black
Yellow
Mississippi
Petenwell Flowage
Castle Rock Flowage
L. Poygan
Fox
Lake Winnebago
The Dells
Kickapoo
Rock

Agriculture, Industry and Resources

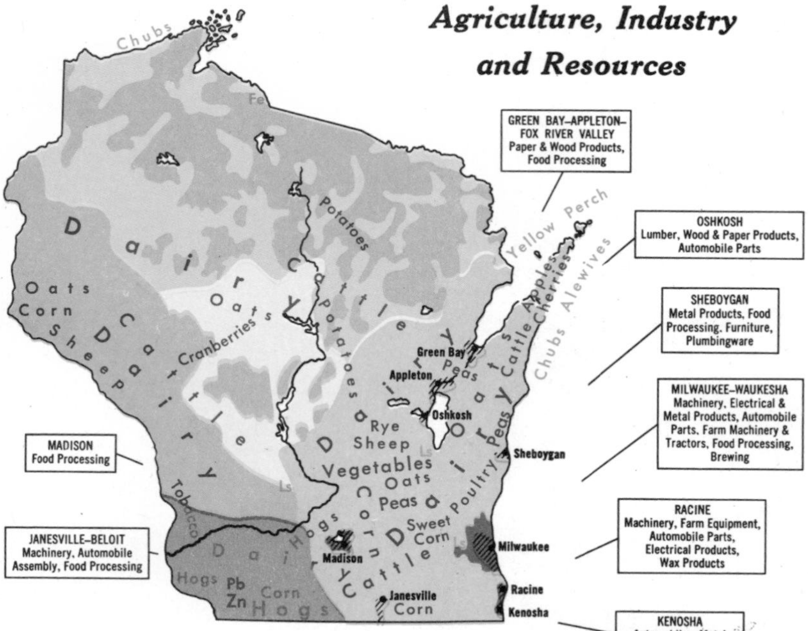

Chubs
Fe
Potatoes
Yellow Perch
Apples
Cherries
Alewives
Chubs
Dairy
Oats
Corn
Sheep
Cattle
Cranberries
Potatoes
Green Bay
Appleton
Peas
Oshkosh
Rye
Sheep
Vegetables
Oats
Peas
Poultry
Sweet Corn
Sheboygan
Tobacco
Ls
Hogs
Madison
Milwaukee
Racine
Kenosha
Pb
Zn
Corn
Hogs
Janesville Corn
GREEN BAY-APPLETON-FOX RIVER VALLEY
Paper & Wood Products, Food Processing
OSHKOSH
Lumber, Wood & Paper Products, Automobile Parts
SHEBOYGAN
Metal Products, Food Processing, Furniture, Plumbingware
MILWAUKEE-WAUKESHA
Machinery, Electrical & Metal Products, Automobile Parts, Farm Machinery & Tractors, Food Processing, Brewing
MADISON
Food Processing
RACINE
Machinery, Farm Equipment, Automobile Parts, Electrical Products, Wax Products
JANESVILLE-BELOIT
Machinery, Automobile Assembly, Food Processing
KENOSHA
Automobiles, Metal Products, Leather Goods

DOMINANT LAND USE

Specialized Dairy
Dairy, Hay, Potatoes
Dairy, General Farming
Hogs, Dairy
Dairy, Livestock
Forests
Urban Areas
Major Industrial Areas

MAJOR MINERAL OCCURRENCES

Fe Iron Ore
Pb Lead
Ls Limestone
Zn Zinc

54655 Soldiers Grove, 514 E 9
54873 Solon Springs, 598 C 3
53171 Somers, 400 M 3
54025 Somerset, 778 A 5
53172 South Milwaukee, 23,297 M 2
53587 South Wayne, 436 G 10
54656 Sparta⊙, 6,258 E 8
54479 Spencer, 1,181 F 6
54801 Spooner, 2,444 B 4
53588 Spring Green, 1,199 G 9
54767 Spring Valley, 995 B 6
54768 Stanley, 2,049 E 6
54026 Star Prairie, 362 A 5
54480 Stetsonville, 305 F 5
54657 Steuben, 179 E 9
54481 Stevens Point⊙, 23,479 G 7
54172 Stiles, 300 L 6
53825 Stitzer, 295 E 10
53088 Stockbridge, 582 K 7
54658 Stoddard, 750 D 8
† 53066 Stone Bank, 390 J 1
54876 Stone Lake, 190 C 4
53589 Stoughton, 6,081 H 10
54484 Stratford, 1,239 F 6
54770 Strum, 738 D 6
54235 Sturgeon Bay⊙, 6,776 M 6
53177 Sturtevant, 3,376 M 3
54173 Suamico, 900 K 6
53178 Sullivan, 467 H 1
54485 Summit Lake, 200 H 5
53590 Sun Prairie, 9,935 H 9
54880 Superior (city)⊙, 32,237 C 2
Superior-Duluth, ‡265,350 C 2
† 54880 Superior Village, 476 B 2
54174 Suring, 499 K 5
53089 Sussex, 2,758 K 1
53090 Taycheedah, 600 K 8
54659 Taylor, 322 E 7
† 53820 Tennyson, 402 E 10
53091 Theresa, 611 K 8
53092 Thiensville, 3,182 L 1
54771 Thorp, 1,469 E 6
54562 Three Lakes, 950 H 4
† 53185 Tichigan, 500 K 2
54486 Tigerton, 742 H 6
54240 Tisch Mills, 259 L 7
54660 Tomah, 5,647 F 8
54487 Tomahawk, 3,419 G 5
54175 Townsend, 450 K 5
54888 Trego, 200 C 4
54661 Trempealeau, 743 C 8
53180 Troy Center, 250 J 2
54662 Tunnel City, 226 E 7
54889 Turtle Lake, 637 B 5
53181 Twin Lakes, 2,276 K 11
54241 Two Rivers, 13,553 M 7
53962 Union Center, 205 F 8
53182 Union Grove, 2,703 L 3
54488 Unity, 363 F 6
54245 Valders, 821 L 7
53593 Verona, 2,334 G 9
54489 Vesper, 355 F 7
54664 Viola, 659 E 8
54665 Viroqua⊙, 3,739 D 8
54566 Wabeno, 800 J 5
53093 Waldo, 408 L 8
53183 Wales, 691 J 1
53184 Walworth, 1,637 J 10
54666 Warrens, 300 E 7
54890 Wascott, 200 C 3
54891 Washburn⊙, 1,957 D 2
54246 Washington Island, 550 M 5
53185 Waterford, 1,922 K 3
53594 Waterloo, 2,253 J 9
53094 Watertown, 15,683 J 9
53021 Waubeka, 300 L 9
54980 Waukau, 245 J 8
53186 Waukesha⊙, 40,258 K 1
53597 Waunakee, 2,181 G 9
54981 Waupaca⊙, 4,342 H 7
53963 Waupun, 7,946 J 8
54401 Wausau⊙, 32,806 G 6
54177 Wausaukee, 557 K 5
54982 Wautoma⊙, 1,624 H 7
53226 Wauwatosa, 58,676 L 1
53826 Wauzeka, 437 E 9
54893 Webster, 502 B 4
53214 West Allis, 71,723 L 1
† 53913 West Baraboo, 563 G 9
53095 West Bend⊙, 16,555 K 9
54490 Westboro, 950 F 5
54667 Westby, 1,568 E 8
53964 Westfield, 884 H 8
† 54601 West La Crosse, 950 D 8
† 53201 West Milwaukee, 4,405 L 1
† 54476 Weston, 3,375 G 6
54669 West Salem, 2,180 D 8
54983 Weyauwega, 1,377 H 7
54895 Weyerhauser, 285 D 5
54772 Wheeler, 212 C 5
53217 Whitefish Bay, 17,394 M 1
54773 Whitehall⊙, 1,486 D 7
54491 White Lake, 309 J 5
54247 Whitelaw, 557 L 7
53190 Whitewater, 12,038 J 10
† 54481 Whiting, 1,782 H 7
54984 Wild Rose, 585 H 7
53191 Williams Bay, 1,554 J 10
54670 Wilton, 516 F 8
54567 Winchester, 230 G 3
53185 Wind Lake, 900 K 2
† 53401 Wind Point, 1,251 M 2
53598 Windsor, 827 H 9
54985 Winnebago, 1,550 J 7
54986 Winneconne, 1,608 J 7
54896 Winter, 450 E 4
53965 Wisconsin Dells, 2,401 G 8
54494 Wisconsin Rapids⊙, 18,587 G 7
54498 Withee, 480 E 6
54499 Wittenberg, 895 H 6
53968 Wonewoc, 835 F 8
54568 Woodruff, 800 G 4
54028 Woodville, 522 B 6
54180 Wrightstown, 1,020 K 7
54671 Wyeville, 203 F 7
53969 Wyocena, 809 H 9
54182 Zachow, 160 K 6

⊙ County seat.
‡ Population of metropolitan area.
† Zip of nearest p.o.
* Multiple zips

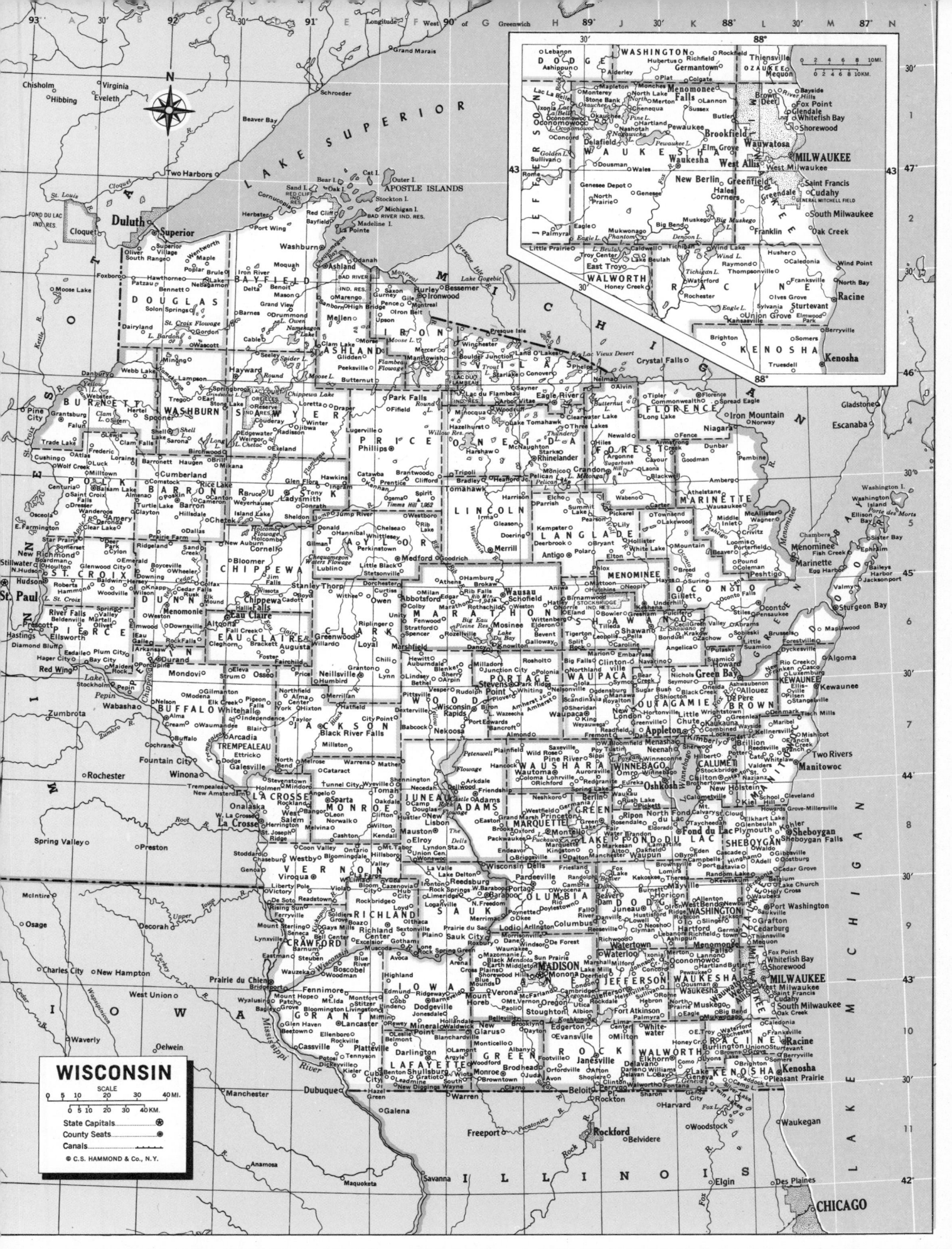

Agriculture, Industry and Resources

DOMINANT LAND USE

- Specialized Wheat
- Specialized Dairy
- General Farming, Livestock, Special Crops
- Sugar Beets, Dry Beans, Livestock, General Farming
- Range Livestock
- Forests
- Nonagricultural Land

MAJOR MINERAL OCCURRENCES

- C Coal
- Cl Clay
- Fe Iron Ore
- G Natural Gas
- O Petroleum
- U Uranium
- P Phosphates
- V Vanadium

⚡ Water Power

COUNTIES

Albany, 26,431	G
Big Horn, 10,202	E
Campbell, 12,957	G
Carbon, 13,354	F
Converse, 5,938	G
Crook, 4,535	H
Fremont, 28,352	D
Goshen, 10,885	H
Hot Springs, 4,952	F
Johnson, 5,587	F
Laramie, 56,360	H
Lincoln, 8,640	B
Natrona, 51,264	F
Niobrara, 2,924	H
Park, 17,752	C
Platte, 6,486	H
Sheridan, 17,852	F
Sublette, 3,755	C
Sweetwater, 18,391	D
Teton, 4,823	B
Uinta, 7,100	B
Washakie, 7,569	E
Weston, 6,307	H

CITIES and TOWNS

Zip	Name/Pop.	Key
82830	Acme, 98	E
83110	Afton, 1,290	B

WYOMING

SCALE
0 5 10 20 30 40 MI.
0 5 10 20 30 40 KM.

State Capitals .... ⊛
County Seats .... ◉

© C.S. HAMMOND & Co., N.Y.

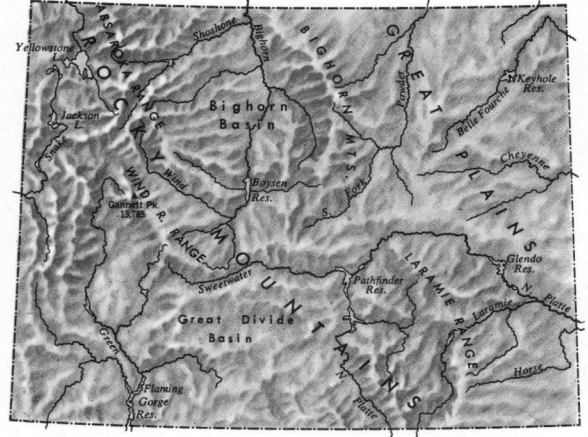

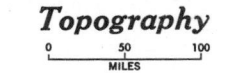

Topography

5,000 m. 2,000 m. 1,000 m. 500 m. 200 m. 100 m. Sea Below
16,404 ft. 6,562 ft. 3,281 ft. 1,640 ft. 656 ft. 328 ft. Level

0   50   100
MILES

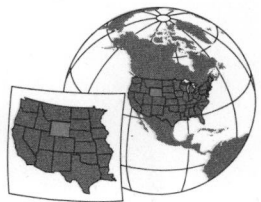

AREA 97,914 sq. mi.
POPULATION 332,416
CAPITAL Cheyenne
LARGEST CITY Cheyenne
HIGHEST POINT Gannett Pk. 13,785 ft.
SETTLED IN 1834
ADMITTED TO UNION July 10, 1890
POPULAR NAME Equality State
STATE FLOWER Indian Paintbrush
STATE BIRD Meadowlark

Jack Zehrt — Shostal Associates

Intrepid mountain climbers are challenged by the sheer granite cliffs of Wyoming's Teton Range. Lowland meadows and trails attract less ambitious sportsmen.

82710 Aladdin, 12.................H 1
82055 Albany, 50..................F 4
82050 Albin, 118..................H 4
82620 Alcova, 125.................F 3
83127 Alpine, 95..................B 2
82711 Alva, 45....................H 1
82510 Arapahoe, 682..............D 3
82831 Arvada, 50.................F 1
82520 Atlantic City, 25..........D 3
83111 Auburn, 240................A 3
82321 Baggs, 146.................E 4
83222 Bairoil, 150...............E 3
82832 Banner, 44.................F 1
82410 Basin◉, 1,145..............E 1
82836 Bear Lodge, 25.............E 1
82801 Beckton, 10................E 1
83112 Bedford, 290...............A 3
82712 Beulah, 85.................H 1
82833 Big Horn, 200..............E 1
83113 Big Piney, 570.............B 3
82923 Big Sandy, 20..............C 3
82442 Bigtrails, 25..............D 2
82921 Bitter Creek, 20...........D 4
82922 Bondurant, 90..............B 2
82649 Bonneville, 18.............E 2
82051 Bosler, 80.................G 4
82923 Boulder, 30................C 3
82834 Buffalo◉, 3,394............F 1
82052 Buford, 36.................G 4
82411 Burlington, 300............D 1

82053 Burns, 185.................H 4
82511 Burris, 30.................C 2
82412 Byron, 397.................D 1
† 83123 Calpet, 20...............B 3
82190 Canyon, 130................A 2
82054 Carpenter, 100.............H 4
† 82937 Carter, 31...............B 4
82601 Casper◉, 39,361............F 3
82055 Centennial, 160............F 4
82001 Cheyenne (cap.)◉, 40,914...H 4
82210 Chugwater, 187.............H 4
82213 Glendo, 210................G 3
82637 Glenrock, 1,515............G 3
82934 Granger, 137...............C 4
82059 Granite Canon, 72..........G 4
82425 Grass Creek, 130...........D 1
82935 Green River◉, 4,196........C 4
82426 Greybull, 1,953............D 1
83122 Grover, 120................A 3
82214 Guernsey, 793..............H 3
82427 Hamilton Dome, 106.........D 2
† 82701 Hampshire, 23............H 2
82327 Hanna, 460.................F 4
82215 Hartville, 246.............H 3
82217 Hawk Springs, 125..........H 4
82060 Hillsdale, 160.............H 4
82061 Horse Creek, 225...........G 4
82515 Hudson, 381................D 3
82720 Hulett, 318................H 1
82218 Huntley, 50................H 4
82428 Hyattville, 73.............E 1
82062 Iron Mountain, 12..........G 4

82324 Elk Mountain, 127..........F 4
† 82327 Elmo, 53.................F 4
82422 Emblem, 250................D 1
82325 Encampment, 321............F 4
82520 Ethete, 30.................D 2
83118 Etna, 400..................A 2
82930 Evanston◉, 4,462...........B 4
82636 Evansville, 832............F 3
83119 Fairview, 245..............B 3
82932 Farson, 210................C 3
† 82001 Federal, 15..............G 4
82933 Fort Bridger, 150..........B 4
† 82301 Fort Fred Steele, 15.....E 4
82212 Fort Laramie, 197..........H 3
82514 Fort Washakie, 140.........C 2
82001 Fox Farm, 1,329............H 4
82057 Foxpark, 110...............F 4
82423 Frannie, 139...............D 1
83120 Freedom, 497...............B 3
83121 Frontier, 246..............B 4
82424 Garland, 57................D 1
82058 Garrett, 10................G 3
82501 Gas Hills, 200.............E 3
82716 Gillette◉, 7,194...........G 1

83001 Jackson◉, 2,101............B 2
82219 Jay Em, 25.................H 3
82310 Jeffrey City, 702..........E 3
82063 Jelm, 29...................G 4
† 83012 Jenny Lake, 10...........B 2
82639 Kaycee, 272................F 2
† 82832 Kearney, 49..............F 1
82220 Keeline, 30................H 3
83011 Kelly, 35..................B 2
83101 Kemmerer◉, 2,292...........B 4
82516 Kinnear, 44................D 2
82430 Kirby, 75..................D 1
83123 La Barge, 375..............B 3
82221 Lagrange, 189..............H 4
† 82190 Lake-Fishing Bridge-Bridge
        Bay, 167..............B 1
† 82190 Lamar, 27................B 1
82328 Lamont, 30.................E 3
82222 Lance Creek, 175...........H 2
82520 Lander◉, 7,125.............D 2
82070 Laramie◉, 23,143...........G 4
82837 Leiter, 100................F 1
82640 Linch, 185.................F 2
82223 Lingle, 446................H 3
82929 Little America, 47.........C 4
† 82051 Lookout, 20..............G 4
82642 Lost Cabin, 25.............E 2
82431 Lovell, 2,371..............D 1
82443 Lucerne, 240...............D 2
82225 Lusk◉, 1,495...............H 3
82937 Lyman, 643.................B 4
82642 Lysite, 25.................E 2
† 82190 Madison, 42..............B 1
† 82190 Mammoth Hot Springs
        (Yellowstone Nat'l Park),
        162...................B 1
82432 Manderson, 117.............E 1
82227 Manville, 92...............H 3
† 83113 Marbleton, 223...........B 3
82080 McFadden, 150..............F 4
82938 McKinnon, 135..............C 4
82329 Medicine Bow, 455..........F 4
82433 Meeteetse, 459.............D 1
83115 Merna, 25..................B 3
82643 Midwest, 743...............F 2
82933 Millburne, 54..............B 4

82644 Mills, 1,724...............F 3
82721 Moorcroft, 981.............H 1
83012 Moose, 115.................B 2
83013 Moran, 600.................B 2
82701 Morrisey, 28...............H 1
82522 Morton, 35.................D 2
82939 Mountain View, 1,641.......F 3
82939 Mountain View, 500.........B 4
† 57735 Mule Creek, 10...........H 2
82701 Newcastle◉, 3,432..........H 2
82722 New Haven, 35..............H 1
† 82190 Norris, 20...............B 1
82190 Old Faithful, 134.........B 1
83124 Opal, 34...................B 4
82001 Orchard Valley, 1,015......H 4
82652 Orin, 20...................G 3
† 82633 Orpha, 12................G 3
82723 Osage, 346.................H 2
82434 Otto, 25...................D 1
82414 Pahaska, 75................C 1
† 82601 Paradise Valley, 1,764...F 3
82838 Parkman, 30................E 1
82523 Pavillion, 181.............D 2
† 82933 Piedmont, 25.............B 4
82082 Pine Bluffs, 937...........H 4
82941 Pinedale◉, 948.............C 3
82942 Point of Rocks, 20.........D 4
82648 Powder River, 75...........F 2
82435 Powell, 4,807..............D 1
82440 Ralston, 85................D 1
82839 Ranchester, 208............E 1
82301 Rawlins◉, 7,855............E 4
82725 Recluse, 25................G 1
82943 Reliance, 425..............C 4
82325 Riverside, 46..............F 4
82501 Riverton, 7,995............D 2
82944 Robertson, 30..............B 4
82701 Rochelle, 23...............H 2
82083 Rock River, 344............G 4
82901 Rock Springs, 11,657.......C 4
82726 Rockypoint, 22.............G 1
82727 Rozet, 50..................G 1
82330 Ryan Park, 18..............F 4
82840 Saddlestring, 100..........F 1
83125 Sage, 45...................B 4
82524 Saint Stephens, 100........D 3

82501 Sand Draw, 40..............D 3
82331 Saratoga, 1,181............F 4
† 82716 Savageton, 30............G 2
82332 Savery, 29.................E 4
† 82720 Seely, 10................H 1
82333 Seminoe Dam, 40............E 3
82229 Shawnee, 11................G 3
82441 Shell, 50..................E 1
82801 Sheridan◉, 10,856..........F 1
82601 Shirley Basin, 700.........F 3
82649 Shoshoni, 562..............D 2
82334 Sinclair, 445..............E 4
83126 Smoot, 200.................B 3
† 82945 South Superior, 197.......C 4
82842 Story, 637.................F 1
82729 Sundance◉, 1,056...........H 1
† 82215 Sunrise, 80..............H 3
82945 Superior, 2................D 4
82639 Sussex, 200................F 2
82442 Ten Sleep, 320.............E 1
82901 Thayer Junction, 15........D 4
83127 Thayne, 195................A 3
82443 Thermopolis◉, 3,063........D 2
82240 Torrington◉, 4,237.........H 3
82190 Tower, 24..................B 1
83112 Turnerville, 25............A 3
82835 Ucross, 17.................F 1
82190 Ulm, 25....................F 1
82730 Upton, 987.................H 1
82242 Van Tassell, 21............H 3
82243 Veteran, 34................H 4
82335 Walcott, 20................E 4
† 82648 Waltman, 20..............E 2
82236 Wamsutter, 139.............D 4
82450 Wapiti, 92.................C 1
† 82190 West Thumb-Grant Village,
        64....................B 1
82201 Wheatland◉, 2,498..........H 4
83014 Wilson, 550................B 2
82844 Wolf, 85...................E 1
82401 Worland◉, 5,055............E 2
82845 Wyarno, 12.................F 1
82190 Yellowstone Nat'l Park, 162..B 1
82244 Yoder, 101.................H 4

◉ County seat.

† Zip of nearest p.o.

82710 Aladdin, 12.................H 1
82055 Albany, 50..................F 4
82050 Albin, 118..................H 4
82620 Alcova, 125.................F 3

ACQUISITIONS OF TERRITORY

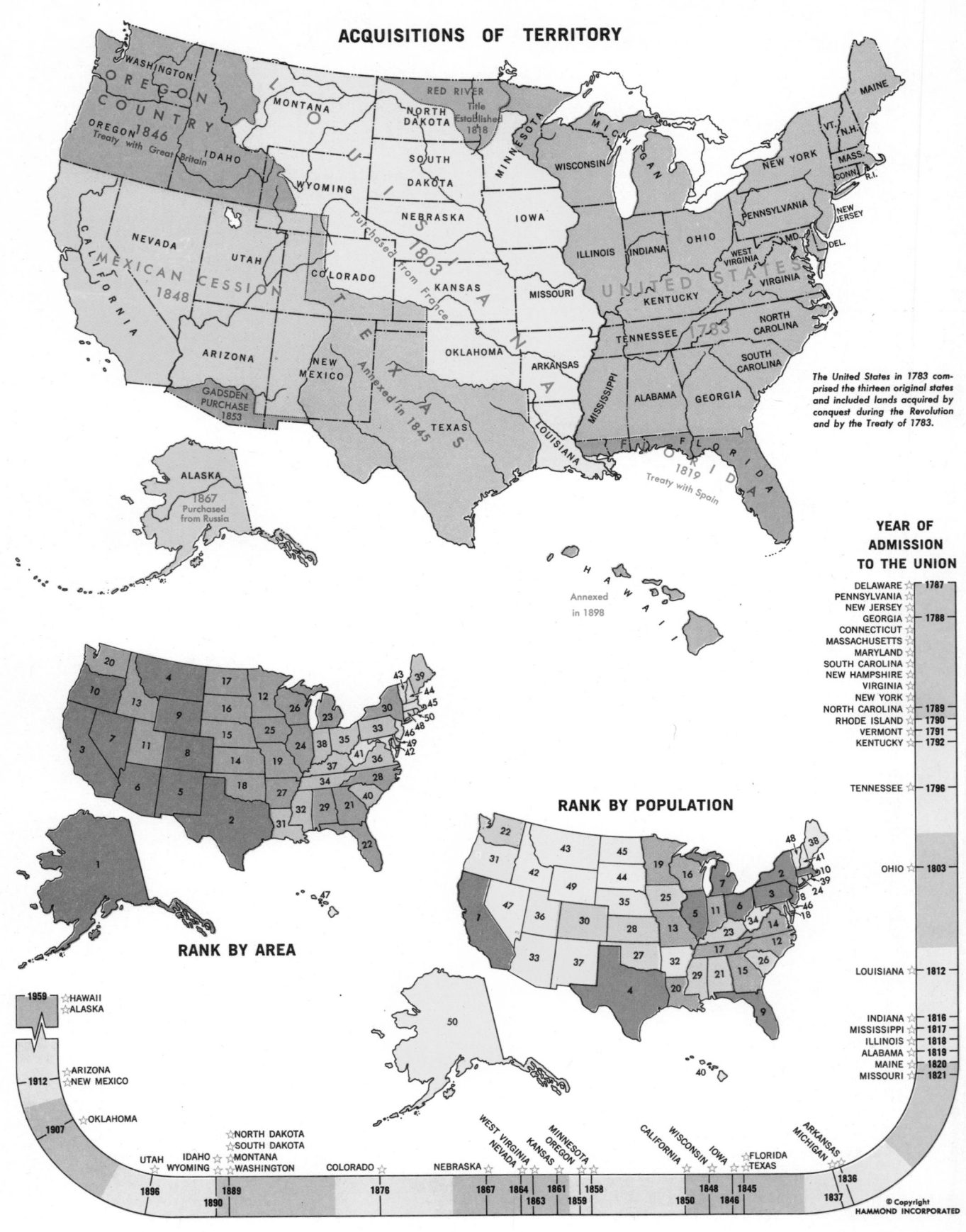

The United States in 1783 comprised the thirteen original states and included lands acquired by conquest during the Revolution and by the Treaty of 1783.

YEAR OF ADMISSION TO THE UNION

State	Year
DELAWARE ☆	1787
PENNSYLVANIA ☆	
NEW JERSEY ☆	
GEORGIA ☆	1788
CONNECTICUT ☆	
MASSACHUSETTS ☆	
MARYLAND ☆	
SOUTH CAROLINA ☆	
NEW HAMPSHIRE ☆	
VIRGINIA ☆	
NEW YORK ☆	
NORTH CAROLINA ☆	1789
RHODE ISLAND ☆	1790
VERMONT ☆	1791
KENTUCKY ☆	1792
TENNESSEE ☆	1796
OHIO ☆	1803
LOUISIANA ☆	1812
INDIANA ☆	1816
MISSISSIPPI ☆	1817
ILLINOIS ☆	1818
ALABAMA ☆	1819
MAINE ☆	1820
MISSOURI ☆	1821

RANK BY POPULATION

RANK BY AREA

© Copyright
HAMMOND INCORPORATED

INDEX
OF THE WORLD

A

B

Bayamón, P.R. G 1 124
Bay City, Mich. F 5 186
Bay City, Tex. H 9 238
Bayeux, France C 3 26
Baykal (lake), U.S.S.R. L 4 46

Baykonur, U.S.S.R. G 5 46
Bay Minette, Ala. C 9 130
Bayonne, France C 6 26
Bayonne, N.J. B 2 209
Bayreuth, W.Ger. D 4 20

Bay St. Louis, Miss. F10 192
Baytown, Tex. L 2 238
Bay Village, Ohio G 9 220
Bayville, N.Y. R 6 213
Beachwood, Ohio J 9 220

Beacon, N.Y. N 7 213
Bear (lake), U.S. C 2 240
Beardstown Ill. C 3 158
Bearpaw (mts.), Mont. G 2 198
Beatrice, Nebr. H 4 201

Beaufort (sea), N.A. D 2 94
Beaufort, S.C. F 7 232
Beaumaris, Wales C 4 11
Beaumont, Calif. J10 140
Beaumont, Tex. K 7 238

Beauvais, France E 3 26
Beaver, Pa. B 4 230
Beaver Dam, Wis. J 9 253
Beaver Falls, Pa. B 4 230
Beaverhead (mts.), Idaho E 4 156

Beaverton, Oreg. A 2 226
Beckley, W.Va. D 7 248
Bedford, Eng. G 5 11
Bedford, Ind. E 7 163
Bedford, Mass. B 6 184

Bedford, N.H. D 6 204
Bedford, Ohio H 9 220
Bedford, Tex. F 2 238
Bedford, Va. J 6 243
Bedford Hts., Ohio J 9 220

Beech Grove, Ind. E 5 163
Beersheba, Isr. B 5 67
Beeville, Tex. G 9 238
Beira, Moz. O15 57
Beirut (cap.), Leb. F 6 64

Bel Air, Md. N 2 181
Belchertown, Mass. E 3 184
Belém, Braz. L 4 90
Belfast, Maine F 7 178
Belfast (cap.), N.Ire. J 2 15

Belfort, France G 4 26
Belgium 25
Belgrade (cap.), Yugo. E 3 43
Belize C 2 122
Belize City, Belize C 2 122

Bell, Calif. C11 140
Bellaire, Ohio J 5 220
Bellaire, Tex. J 2 238
Bellary, India D 5 70
Bellefontaine, Ohio C 5 220

Bellefontaine Neighbors, Mo. R 2 197
Bellefonte, Pa. G 4 230
Belle Glade, Fla. F 5 148
Belleville, Ill. B 6 158

Belleville, N.J. B 2 209
Belleville, Ont. G 3 108
Bellevue, Ky. S 2 173
Bellevue, Nebr. J 3 201
Bellevue, Ohio E 3 220

Bellevue, Pa. B 6 230
Bellevue, Wash. B 2 246
Bellflower, Calif. C11 140
Bellingham, Mass. J 4 184
Bellingham, Wash. C 2 246

Bellingshausen (sea), Ant. C14 88
Bellmawr, N.J. B 3 209
Bellmead, Tex. H 6 238
Bellwood, Ill. A 2 158
Belmar, N.J. E 3 209

Belmont, Calif. J 3 140
Belmont, Mass. C 6 184
Belmont, N.C. H 4 216
Belmopan (cap.), Belize C 2 122
Belo Horizonte, Braz. M 7 90

Beloit, Wis. H10 253
Belpre, Ohio G 7 220
Belton, Mo. C 5 196
Belton, S.C. C 2 232
Belton, Tex. G 7 238

Belvidere, Ill. E 1 158
Bemidji, Minn. D 3 190
Benares (Varanasi), India E 3 70
Benbrook, Tex. E 2 238

Bend, Oreg. F 3 226
Bendigo, Aust. G 7 86
Benevento, Italy E 4 32
Bengal (bay), Asia F 5 70
Benghazi, Libya K 5 54

Benguela, Angola J14 57
Benicia, Calif. K 1 140
Benin G10 54
Bennettsville, S.C. H 2 232
Bennington, Vt. A 6 204

Bensenville, Ill. A 1 158
Benton, Ark. E 4 139
Benton, Ill. E 6 158
Benton Harbor, Mich. C 6 186
Bentonville, Ark. B 1 138

Bent's Old Fort N.H.S., Colo. M 6 145
Benue (riv.), Afr. H10 54
Berber, Sudan N 8 54
Berchtesgaden, W.Ger. E 5 20

Berea, Ky. N 5 173
Berea, Ohio G10 220
Bergen, Nor. D 6 16
Bergenfield, N.J. C 1 209
Bergerac, France D 5 26

Bering (sea) X 3 58
Bering (str.) E 1 133
Berkeley, Calif. J 2 140
Berkeley, Ill. A 2 158
Berkeley, Mo. P 2 197

Berkeley Hts., N.J. E 2 209
Berkley, Mich. B 6 186
Berkshire (hills), Mass. B 4 184
Berlin, Conn. E 2 146
Berlin, N.H. E 3 204

Berlin, Wis. H 8 253
Berlin, E. (cap.), E.Ger. F 4 20
Berlin, W., W.Ger. E 4 20
Bermuda H 3 125
Bern (cap.), Switz. D 3 37

Bernardsville, N.J. D 2 209
Berwick, Pa. K 3 230
Berwick-upon-Tweed, Eng. F 2 11
Berwyn, Ill. B 2 158
Besançon, France G 4 26

Bessemer, Ala. D 4 130
Bethalto, Ill. B 6 158
Bethany, Okla. L 3 225
Bethel, Conn. B 3 146
Bethel Park, Pa. B 7 230

Bethesda, Md. E 4 180
Bethlehem, Jordan C 4 67
Bethlehem, Pa. M 4 231
Bettendorf, Iowa N 5 165
Beverly, Mass. E 5 184

Beverly Hills, Calif. B10 140
Bexley, Ohio E 6 220
Bhagalpur, India F 4 70
Bhavnagar, India C 4 70
Bhopal, India D 4 70

Bhutan G 3 70
Biafra (bight), Afr. H11 57
Białystok, Pol. F 2 45
Biarritz, France C 6 26
Biddeford, Maine B 9 178

Big Bend N.P., Tex. A 8 238
Big Hole N.B., Mont. C 5 198
Bighorn (riv.), U.S. E 2 126
Bighorn Canyon N.R.A., U.S D 1 254
Big Rapids, Mich. D 5 186

Big Spring, Tex. C 5 238
Bihar (state), India F 4 70
Bikini (atoll), T.T.P.I. G 4 89
Bilbao, Spain E 1 31
Billerica, Mass. J 2 184

Billings, Mont. H 5 198
Biloxi, Miss. G10 192
Biminis, The (isls.), Bah. B 1 124
Binghamton, N.Y. J 6 212
Birkenhead, Eng. D 4 11

Birmingham, Ala. D 3 130
Birmingham, Eng. F 5 11
Birmingham, Mich. B 6 186
Bisbee, Ariz. F 7 134
Biscay (bay), Europe D 4 6

Biscayne N.M., Fla. F 6 148
Bismarck (cap.), N.Dak. J 6 218
Bismarck (arch.), P.N.G. E 6 89
Bissau (cap.), Guin.-Biss. C 9 54
Bitterroot (range), U.S. E 4 156

Bizerte, Tun. J 4 54
Black (sea) H 4 6
Black (for.), W.Ger. C 4 20
Black Canyon of the Gunnison N.M., Colo. D 5 144

Blackfoot, Idaho F 6 156
Black Hills (mts.), U.S. B 5 234
Blackpool, Eng. D 4 11
Blacksburg, Va. H 6 242
Blackstone, Mass. H 4 184

Blackwell, Okla. M 1 225
Bladensburg, Md. G 4 180
Blagoveshchensk, U.S.S.R. N 4 46
Blaine, Minn. G 5 190
Blair, Nebr. H 3 201

Blakely, Ga. C 8 152
Blakely, Pa. L 2 231
Blanc (mt.), Europe G 5 26
Blanca (peak), Colo. H 7 145
Blantyre, Malawi N15 57

Blarney, Ire. D 8 15
Block (isl.), R.I. H 8 184
Bloemfontein, S.Afr. L17 57
Blois, France D 4 26
Bloomfield, Conn. E 1 146

Bloomfield, N.J. B 2 209
Bloomingdale, N.J. E 1 209
Bloomington, Ill. D 3 158
Bloomington, Ind. D 6 163
Bloomington, Minn. G 6 190

Bloomsburg, Pa. J 3 230
Blue (mts.), Oreg. J 3 227
Blue Ash, Ohio C 9 220
Bluefield, Va. F 6 242
Bluefield, W.Va. D 8 248

Bluefields, Nic. F 4 122
Blue Island, Ill. B 2 158
Blue Mountains, Aust. H 6 86
Blue Nile (riv.), Afr. N 9 54
Blue Sprs., Mo. R 6 197

Bluffton, Ind. G 3 163
Blythe, Calif. L10 140
Blytheville, Ark. L 2 139
Boardman, Ohio J 3 220
Boaz, Ala. F 2 130

Boca Raton, Fla. F 5 148
Bogalusa, La. L 5 175
Bogotá (cap.), Col. F 3 90
Bogota, N.J. B 2 209
Bohemian (forest) B 2 38

Boise (cap.), Idaho B 6 156
Bolivar, Tenn. C10 172
Bolívar (mt.), Ven. F 2 90
Bolivia G-J 7 90
Bologna, Italy C 2 32

Boma, Zaire J13 57
Bombay, India B 7 70
Bon (cape), Tun. J 4 54
Bonaire (isl.), Neth.Ant. E 4 124

Bonham, Tex. H 4 238
Bonifacio (str.), Europe B 4 32
Bonin (isls.), Japan M 3 75
Bonn (cap.), W.Ger. B 3 20
Bonneville (dam), U.S. E 2 226

Booker T. Washington N.M., Va. J 6 243
Boone, Iowa F 4 164
Boone, N.C. F 2 216
Booneville, Miss. G 1 192

Boonville, Ind. C 8 163
Bophuthatswana (prov.), S. Afr. L17 57
Borabora (isl.), Fr.Poly. L 7 89
Borah (peak), Idaho E 5 156

Borås, Sweden H 8 16
Bordeaux, France C 5 26
Bordentown, N.J. D 3 209
Borger, Tex. C 2 238
Borneo (isl.), Asia E 5 83

Bornholm (isl.), Den. F 9 19
Bosporus (str.), Turkey D 5 64
Bossier City, La. C 1 174
Boston, Eng. G 5 11
Boston (cap.), Mass. D 7 184

Botany (bay), Aust. L 3 87
Bothell, Wash. B 1 246
Bothnia (gulf), Europe M 5 16
Botswana L16 57
Bouaké, I.C. F10 54

Bougainville (isl.), P.N.G. F 6 89
Boulder, Colo. J 2 145
Boulder City, Nev. G 7 202
Boulogne, France D 2 26
Bound Brook, N.J. D 2 209

Bountiful, Utah C 3 240
Bourbonnais, Ill. F 2 158
Bourg, France F 4 26
Bourges, France E 4 26
Bourne, Mass. M 6 185

Bowie, Md. L 4 181
Bowie, Tex. G 4 238
Bowling Green, Ky. H 7 172
Bowling Green, Ohio C 3 220
Bowmanville, Ont. F 4 108

Boynton Beach, Fla. F 5 148
Bozeman, Mont. E 5 198
Brabant (prov.), Belg. E 7 25
Braddock, Pa. C 7 230
Bradenton, Fla. D 4 148

Bradford, Eng. F 4 11
Bradford, Pa. E 2 230
Bradley, Ill. F 2 158
Brady, Tex. E 6 238
Braemar, Scot. E 3 13

Braga, Port. B 2 30
Bragança, Port. C 2 31
Brahmaputra (riv.), Asia G 3 70
Brăila, Rum. H 3 43
Brainerd, Minn. D 4 190

Braintree, Mass. D 8 184
Brandenburg (reg.), E.Ger. E 2 20
Brandon, Man. C 5 110
Branford, Conn. D 3 146
Brantford, Ont. D 4 108

Brasília (cap.), Braz. L 7 90
Brașov, Rum. G 3 43
Bratislava, Czech. D 2 39
Brattleboro, Vt. B 6 204
Brawley, Calif. K11 140

Brazil 90, 93
Brazil, Ind. C 5 163
Brazos (riv.), Tex. H 7 238
Brazzaville (cap.), Congo J12 57
Brea, Calif. D11 140

Breckenridge, Tex. F 5 238
Breckenridge Hills, Mo. O 2 197
Brecksville, Ohio H10 220
Breda, Neth. F 5 25
Bremen, W.Ger. C 2 20

Bremerhaven, W.Ger. C 2 20
Bremerton, Wash. A 2 246
Brenham, Tex. H 7 238
Brenner (pass), Europe A 3 38
Brentwood, Mo. P 3 197

Brentwood, N.Y. O 9 213
Brentwood, Pa. B 7 230
Breslau (Wrocław), Pol. F 3 6
Brest, France A 3 26
Breton (sound), La. M 7 175

Brevard, N.C. D 4 216
Brewer, Maine F 6 178
Brewton, Ala. D 8 130
Brices Cross Roads N.B.S., Miss. G 2 192

Bridgeport, Conn. C 4 146
Bridgeport, Pa. M 5 231
Bridgeton, Mo. O 2 197
Bridgeton, N.J. C 5 209
Bridgetown (cap.), Barb. G 4 125

Bridgeview, Ill. B 2 158
Bridgeville, Pa. B 5 230
Bridgewater, Mass. K 5 184
Brigantine, N.J. E 5 209
Brigham City, Utah C 2 240

Brighton, Colo. K 3 145
Brighton, Eng. G 7 11
Brinkley, Ark. H 4 139
Brindisi, Italy G 4 32
Brisbane, Aust. J 5 86

Bristol (bay), Alaska F 3 133
Bristol, Conn. D 2 146
Bristol, Eng. E 6 11
Bristol, Pa. N 5 231
Bristol, R.I. J 6 184

Bristol, Tenn. S 7 173
Bristol (chan.), U.K. C 6 11
Bristol, Va. D 7 242
British Columbia (prov.), Can. 116-117

British Indian Ocean Terr. L10 58
Brno, Czech. D 2 39
Broadview, Ill. A 2 158
Broadview Hts., Ohio H10 220
Brockport, N.Y. D 4 212

Brockton, Mass. K 4 184
Brockville, Ont. J 3 109
Broken Arrow, Okla. P 2 225
Broken Hill, Aust. G 6 86
Bronx (co.), N.Y. N 9 213

Bronxville, N.Y. O 7 213
Brookfield, Conn. B 3 146
Brookfield, Ill. A 2 158
Brookfield, Mo. F 3 197
Brookfield, Wis. K 1 253

Brookhaven, Miss. C 7 192
Brookhaven, Pa. M 7 231
Brookhaven N. Lab., N.Y. P 9 213
Brookings, S.Dak. R 5 235
Brookline, Mass. C 7 184

Brooklyn, N.Y. N 9 213
Brooklyn, Ohio H 9 220
Brooklyn Ctr., Minn. G 5 190
Brooklyn Park, Minn. G 5 190
Brook Park, Ohio G 9 220

Brooks (range), Alaska G 1 133
Broomfield, Colo. J 3 145
Brown Deer, Wis. L 1 253
Brownfield, Tex. B 4 238
Brownsburg, Ind. E 5 163

Brownsville, Tenn. C 9 172
Brownsville, Tex. G12 238
Brownwood, Tex. F 6 238
Bruges, Belg. C 6 25
Brunei E 4 83

Brunswick, Ga. K 8 152
Brunswick, Maine C 8 178
Brunswick, Ohio G 3 220
Brunswick, W.Ger. D 2 20
Brussels (cap.), Belg. C 9 25

Bryan, Ohio A 3 220
Bryan, Tex. H 7 238
Bryce Canyon N.P., Utah B 6 240
Bucaramanga, Col. F 2 90
Bucharest (cap.), Rum. G 3 43

Buckhannon, W.Va. F 5 248
Bucyrus, Ohio E 4 220
Budapest (cap.), Hung. E 3 39
Buea, Cameroon H11 54
Buena Park, Calif. D11 140

Buenaventura, Col. E 3 90
Buena Vista, Va. K 5 243
Buenos Aires (cap.), Arg. H10 93
Buffalo, N.Y. B 5 212
Bug (riv.), Europe F 2 45

Bujumbura (cap.), Burundi N12 57
Bukavu, Zaire M12 57
Bukhara, U.S.S.R. G 5 46
Bulawayo, Rhod. M16 57

Bulgaria F-H 4 43
Bunkie, La. F 5 175
Burbank, Calif. C10 140
Burgas, Bulg. H 4 43
Burgos, Spain E 1 31

Burkburnett, Tex. F 3 238
Burleson, Tex. F 2 238
Burley, Idaho E 7 156
Burlingame, Calif. J 2 140
Burlington, Iowa L 7 165

Burlington, Mass. C 5 184
Burlington, N.J. D 3 209
Burlington, N.C. K 2 217
Burlington, Ont. E 4 108
Burlington, Vt. A 3 204

Burlington, Wis. K10 253
Burma B-C 2 81
Burnsville, Minn. E 6 190
Bursa, Turkey C 2 64
Burundi M12 57

Buryat A.S.S.R., U.S.S.R. M 4 46
Bushire, Iran G 6 68
Butler, N.J. E 2 209
Butler, Pa. C 4 230

Butte, Mont. D 5 198
Buzzards (bay), Mass. L 7 184
Bydgoszcz, Pol. D 2 45
Bytom, Pol. B 4 45

C

Caatingas (reg.), Braz. L 6 90
Cabinda (dist.), Angola H13 57
Cabrillo N.M., Calif. H11 140
Cáceres, Spain C 3 31
Cadillac, Mich. D 4 186

Cádiz, Spain C 4 31
Caen, France C 3 26
Caernarfon, Wales C 4 11
Cagayan de Oro, Phil. G 4 83
Cagliari, Italy B 5 32

Caguas, P.R. G 1 125
Cahokia, Ill. B 6 158
Caicos (isls.), T.&C.Is. D 2 124
Cairns, Aust. H 3 86
Cairo (cap.), Egypt N 5 54

Cairo, Ga. D 9 152
Cairo, Ill. D 6 158
Calabria (reg.), Italy F 5 32
Calais, France D 2 26
Calais, Maine J 5 178

Calcasieu (lake), La. D 7 174
Calcutta, India F 2 70
Caldwell, Idaho B 6 156
Caldwell, N.J. B 2 209
Calexico, Calif. K11 140

Calgary, Alta. C 4 114
Cali, Col. E 3 90
Calicut (Kozhikode), India D 6 70
California (gulf), Mex. D 3 118
California, Pa. C 5 230

California (state), U.S. 140
Callao, Peru E 6 90
Calumet City, Ill. B 2 158
Calumet Park, Ill. B 2 158
Calvados (dept.), France C 3 26

Camarillo, Calif. F 9 140
Camas, Wash. C 5 246
Cambay (gulf), India C 4 70
Cambodia D 4 81
Cambrai, France E 2 26

Cambridge, Eng. G 5 11
Cambridge, Md. O 6 181
Cambridge, Mass. C 6 184
Cambridge, Ohio G 5 220
Cambridge Bay, N.W.T. F 2 96

Camden, Ark. E 6 139
Camden, N.J. B 3 209
Camden, S.C. F 3 232
Cameron, Tex. H 7 238
Cameroon J11 54

Campania (reg.), Italy E 4 32
Campbell, Calif. K 3 140
Campbell, Ohio J 3 220
Campbellsville, Ky. L 6 173
Campbellton, N.Br. D 1 102

Campeche (bay), Mex. N 7 119
Camp Hill, Pa. H 5 230
Campinas, Braz. L 8 93
Camp Lejeune, N.C. P 5 217
Campobello (isl.), N.Br. D 4 102

Campos (reg.), Braz. M 6 90
Camp Pendleton, Calif. H10 140
Cam Ranh (bay), Viet. F 5 81
Canada 96-97
Canadian (riv.), U.S. F 3 126

Çanakkale, Turkey B 6 64
Canal Zone G 6 123
Canandaigua, N.Y. F 5 212
Canary (isls.), Spain B 4 30
Canastota, N.Y. J 4 212

Canaveral (cape), Fla. F 3 148
Canavieiras, Braz. N 7 91
Canberra (cap.), Aust. H 7 86
Cancer, Tropic of 5
Canea (Khaniá), Greece G 8 43

Cannes, France G 6 26
Canoga Park, Calif. B10 140
Canon City, Colo. J 6 145
Canonsburg, Pa. B 5 230
Cantabrian (mts.), Spain C 1 31

Canterbury, Eng. H 6 11
Canton, China H 7 77
Canton, Conn. D 1 146
Canton (isl.), Gilb. Is. J 6 89
Canton, Ill. C 3 158

Canton, Mass. C 8 184
Canton, Miss. D 5 192
Canton, N.Y. K 1 212
Canton, N.C. D 3 216
Canton, Ohio H 4 220

Canyon, Tex. C 3 238
Canyon de Chelly N.M., Ariz. F 2 134
Canyonlands N.P., Utah D 5 240
Cape Breton (isl.), N.S. J 2 101

Cape Cod N.Sea., Mass. O 4 185
Cape Girardeau, Mo. O 8 197
Cape Hatteras N.Sea., N.C. T 4 217
Cape Lookout N.Sea., N.C. S 5 217

Cape May, N.J. D 6 209
Cape of Good Hope (prov.), S.Afr. K-M18 57
Cape Town (cap.), S.Afr. F19 57
Cape Verde 5

Cape York (pen.), Aust. G 2 86
Cap-Haïtien, Haiti D 3 124
Capitola, Calif. K 4 140
Capitol Reef N.P., Utah C 5 240
Capri (isl.), Italy E 4 32

Capricorn, Tropic of 5
Capulin Mtn. N.M., N.Mex. E 2 210
Caprivi Strip (reg.), S.W.Afr. L15 57
Caracas (cap.), Ven. G 1 90

Carbondale, Ill. D 6 158
Carbondale, Pa. L 2 231
Carcassonne, France D 6 26
Cárdenas, Cuba B 2 124
Cardiff, Wales B 7 11

Cardigan, Wales C 5 11
Caribbean (sea) B-F 4 124
Caribou, Maine G 2 178
Carlinville, Ill. D 4 158
Carlisle, Eng. D 3 11

Carlisle, Pa. H 5 230
Carl Sandburg Home N.H.S., N.C. E 4 216
Carlsbad, Calif. H10 140
Carlsbad, N.Mex. E 6 210

Carlsbad Caverns N.P., N.Mex. E 6 210
Carlstadt, N.J. B 2 209
Carmarthen, Wales C 6 11
Carmel, Ind. E 5 163

Carmel (mt.), Isr. C 2 67
Carmi, Ill. E 5 158
Carmichael, Calif. C 8 140
Carnegie, Pa. B 7 230
Caroline (isls.), T.T.P.I. E-F 5 89

Dansville, N.Y. E 5 212
Danube (riv.), Europe G 4 6
Danvers, Mass. D 5 184
Danville, Calif. K 2 140
Danville, Ill. F 3 158
Danville, Ind. D 5 163
Danville, Pa. J 4 230
Danville, Va. J 7 243
Danzig (gulf), Pol. D 1 45
Darby, Pa. M 7 231
Dardanelles (str.), Turkey B 6 64
Dar es Salaam (cap.), Tanz. O13 57
Darfur (prov.), Sudan L 9 54
Darien, Conn. B 4 146
Darién (mts.), Pan. J 6-7 123
Darjeeling, India F 3 70
Darlac (plat.), Viet. F 4 81
Darling (riv.), Aust. G 6 86
Darlington, S.C. H 3 232
Darmstadt, W.Ger. C 4 20
Dartford, Eng. J 8 11
Dartmouth, Mass. K 6 184
Dartmouth, N.S. E 4 100
Daru, P.N.G. B 7 82
Darwin, Aust. E 2 86
Dauphin, Man. B 3 110
Davao, Phil. H 4 83
Davenport, Iowa M 5 165
David, Pan. F 6 122
Davie, Fla. B 4 148
Davis (sea), Ant. C 5 88
Davis, Calif. B 8 140
Davis (str.), N.A. K 1 96
Davison, Mich. F 5 186
Davos, Switz. J 3 37
Dawson, Ga. D 7 152
Dawson, Yukon C 3 96
Dawson Creek, B.C. G 2 117
Dayton, Ky. T 2 173
Dayton, Ohio B 6 220
Dayton, Tenn. L 9 173
Daytona Beach, Fla. F 2 148
Dead (sea), Asia C 4 67
Deadwood, S.Dak. B 5 234
Dearborn, Mich. B 7 186
Dearborn Hts., Mich. B 7 186
Death Valley (depr.), Calif. H 7 140
Death Valley N.M., U.S. H-J 7 140
Deauville, France C 3 26
Debrecen, Hung. F 3 39
Decatur, Ala. D 1 130
Decatur, Ga. D 3 152
Decatur, Ill. E 4 158
Decatur, Ind. H 3 163
Deccan (plat.), India D 5-6 70
Decorah, Iowa K 2 165
Dedham, Mass. C 7 184
Dee (riv.), Scot. F 3, D 5 13
Deerfield, Ill. F 1 158
Deerfield Bch., Fla. F 5 148
Deer Park, N.Y. O 9 213
Deer Park, Ohio C 9 220
Deer Park, Tex. K 2 238
Defiance, Ohio B 3 220
Dehra Dun, India D 2 70
De Kalb, Ill. E 2 158
Delagoa (bay), Moz. N17 57
De Land, Fla. E 2 148
Delano, Calif. F 8 140
Delavan, Wis. J10 253
Delaware, Ohio E 5 220
Delaware (bay), U.S. C 5 209
Delaware (riv.), U.S. B 5 209
Delaware (state), U.S. 181
Delaware Water Gap N.R.A., U.S. C 1 209
Del City, Okla. L 4 225
Delft, Neth. E 4 25
Delgado (cape), Moz. P14 57
Delhi, India D 3 70
Deloraine, Man. B 5 110
Delphos, Ohio B 4 220
Delran, N.J. B 3 209
Delray Beach, Fla. F 5 148
Del Rio, Tex. D 8 238
Del Rosa, Calif. E10 140
Demarest, N.J. C 1 209
Demavend (mt.), Iran H 2 68
Deming, N.Mex. B 6 210
Demopolis, Ala. C 6 130
Denbigh, Wales D 4 11
Denham Sprs., La. L 1 175
Denison, Iowa C 4 164
Denison, Tex. H 4 238
Denmark 19
Denmark (str.) R 3 94
Dennis, Mass. O 5 184
Denton, Tex. G 4 238
Denver (cap.), Colo. K 3 145
Denville, N.J. E 2 209
De Pere, Wis. K 7 253
Depew, N.Y. C 5 212
Deptford, N.J. B 4 209
Derby, Aust. C 3 86
Derby, Conn. C 3 146
Derby, Eng. F 5 11
Derby, Kans. E 4 168
De Ridder, La. D 5 174
Derna, Libya L 5 54
Derry, N.H. E 6 204
Des Moines (cap.), Iowa G 5 164
De Soto, Mo. M 6 197
De Soto, Tex. G 2 238
De Soto N.Mem., Fla. D 4 148
Des Peres, Mo. O 3 197
Des Plaines, Ill. A 1 158
Dessau, E.Ger. E 3 20
Dessye, Eth. O 9 55
Detroit, Mich. B 7 186
Detroit Lakes, Minn. C 4 190
Deva, Rum. F 3 43
Deventer, Neth. J 4 25
Devils (isl.), Fr.Gui. K 2 90
Devils Lake, N.Dak. N 3 218
Devils Postpile N.M., Calif. F 6 140
Devils Tower N.M., Wyo. H 1 254
Devon, Alta. D 3 114
Devon (isl.), N.W.T. H 1 96
Dexter, Mo. N 9 197
Dezhnev (cape), U.S.S.R. T 3 47
Dhahran, Saudi Ar. E 4 60
Dhaulagiri (mt.), Nepal E 3 70
Dhofar (reg.), Oman F 6 60
Diamond (head), Hawaii C 5 155
Dickinson, N.Dak. E 6 218
Dickson, Tenn. G 8 172
Dickson City, Pa. L 3 231
Diego Garcia (isls.), B.I.O.T. L10 58
Diégo-Suarez, Mad. R14 57
Dien Bien Phu, Viet. D 2 81
Dieppe, France D 3 26
Dieppe, N.Br. F 2 102
Digby, N.S. C 4 100
Dijon, France F 4 26
Dili, Indon. H 7 83
Dillon, S.C. J 3 232
Dinaric Alps (mts.), Yugo. B 3 43
Dinosaur N.M., U.S. A 1 144
Dinuba, Calif. F 7 140
Diomede (isls.) E 1 133
Dire Dawa, Eth. Q10 55
Disappointment (cape), Wash. A 4 246
District Hts., Md. G 5 180
District of Columbia, U.S. F 5 180
Dixon, Ill. D 2 158
Dixon Entrance (str.), N.A. M 2 133
Diyarbakir, Turkey H 4 65
Djajapura, Indon. K 6 83
Djakarta (cap.), Indon. H 1 83
Djerba (isl.), Tun. J 5 54
Djibouti (cap.), Djibouti Q 9 55
Djokjakarta, Indon. J 2 83
Dnepropetrovsk, U.S.S.R. D 5 50
Dnieper (riv.), U.S.S.R. D 5 50
Dniester (riv.), U.S.S.R. C 5 50
Dobbs Ferry, N.Y. O 6 213
Dodecanese (isls.), Greece H 8 43
Dodge City, Kans. B 4 168
Dodoma, Tanz. O13 57
Doha (cap.), Qatar F 4 60
Dolgellau, Wales D 5 11
Dolomite Alps (mts.), Italy C 1 32
Dolton, Ill. B 2 158
Dominica G 4 125
Dominican Republic D-E 3 124
Domrémy-la-Pucelle, France F 3 26
Don (riv.), Eng. F 4 11
Don (riv.), Ont. J 4 109
Don (riv.), Scot. F 3 13
Don (riv.), U.S.S.R. F 5 50
Donaldsonville, La. K 3 175
Doncaster, Eng. F 4 11
Dondra (head), Sri Lanka E 7 70
Donegal, Ire. E 2 15
Donets (riv.), U.S.S.R. E 5 50
Donetsk, U.S.S.R. E 5 50
Dongola, Sudan M 8 54
Donna, Tex. F11 238
Donora, Pa. C 5 230
Doorn, Neth. G 4 25
Doraville, Ga. D 3 152
Dorchester, Mass. D 7 184
Dorchester Hts. N.H.S., Mass. D 7 184
Dordogne (riv.), France D 5 26
Dordrecht, Neth. F 5 25
Dormont, Pa. B 7 230
Dornbirn, Aus. A 3 38
Dortmund, W.Ger. B 3 20
Dothan, Ala. H 8 130
Douai, France E 2 26
Douala, Cameroon J11 54
Douglas, Ariz. F 7 134
Douglas, Ga. G 7 152
Douglas (cap.), I. of Man C 3 11
Douglasville, Ga. C 3 152
Douro (Duero) (riv.), Europe C 2 31
Dover (cap.), Del. R 4 181
Dover, Eng. J 6 11
Dover (str.), Europe J 6 11
Dover, N.H. F 5 204
Dover, N.J. D 2 209
Dover, Ohio G 4 220
Dovrefjeld (mts.), Nor. F 5 16
Dowagiac, Mich. D 6 186
Downers Grove, Ill. A 2 158
Downey, Calif. C11 140
Downingtown, Pa. L 5 231
Downpatrick, N.Ire. K 3 15
Doylestown, Pa. M 5 231
Dracut, Mass. J 2 184
Dragons Mouth (passage) F 5 124
Drake (passage) C15 88
Dráma, Greece F 5 43
Drava (riv.), Europe D 3 39
Dresden, E.Ger. E 3 20
Drumheller, Alta. D 4 114
Duarte, Calif. D10 140
Dubai, U.A.E. F 4 60
Dubbo, Aust. H 6 86
Dublin, Ga. G 5 152
Dublin (cap.), Ire. J 5 15
Du Bois, Pa. E 3 230
Dubrovnik, Yugo. C 4 43
Dubuque, Iowa M 3 165
Dudley, Mass. G 4 184
Duero (Douro) (riv.), Europe C 2 31
Dufourspitze (mt.), Switz. E 5 37
Duisburg, W.Ger. B 3 20
Duluth, Minn. F 4 190
Dumas, Tex. C 2 238
Dumbarton, Scot. B 2 13
Dumfries, Scot. E 5 13
Dumont, N.J. C 1 209
Dunbar, W.Va. C 6 248
Duncan, Okla. L 5 225
Duncanville, Tex. G 2 238
Dundalk, Ire. H 3 15
Dundalk, Md. N 3 181
Dundas, Ont. D 4 108
Dundee, Scot. F 4 13
Dunedin, Fla. B 2 148
Dunedin, N.Z. L 7 87
Dunellen, N.J. D 2 209
Dunfermline, Scot. D 1 13
Dunkirk (Dunkerque), France E 2 26
Dunkirk, N.Y. B 5 212
Dún Laoghaire, Ire. J 5 15
Dunmore, Pa. L 3 231
Dunn, N.C. M 4 217
Duquesne, Pa. C 7 230
Du Quoin, Ill. D 5 158
Durango, Colo. D 8 144
Durango, Mex. G 4 119
Durant, Okla. O 6 225
Durazno, Urug. J10 93
Durban, S.Afr. N17 57
Durham, Eng. F 3 11
Durham, N.H. F 5 204
Durham, N.C. M 2 217
Durrës, Alb. D 5 43
Duryea, Pa. L 3 231
Dushanbe, U.S.S.R. G 6 46
Düsseldorf, W.Ger. B 3 20
Dutch Harbor, Alaska E 4 132
Duxbury, Mass. M 4 185
Dvina, No. (riv.), U.S.S.R. F 2 50
Dvina, Western (riv.), U.S.S.R. C 3 50
Dyersburg, Tenn. C 8 172
Dzerzhinsk, U.S.S.R. F 3 50
Dzhambul, U.S.S.R. H 5 46
Dzungaria (reg.), China C 3 76

E

Eagle Pass, Tex. D 9 238
Ealing, Eng. G 6 11
Easley, S.C. B 2 232
East Alton, Ill. B 6 158
E. Aurora, N.Y. C 5 212
Eastbourne, Eng. H 7 11
E. Bridgewater, Mass. L 4 184
E. Brunswick, N.J. E 3 209
E. Chicago, Ind. C 1 163
E. Chicago Hts., Ill. B 3 158
East China (sea), Asia L 5 77
E. Detroit, Mich. B 6 186
Easter (isl.), Chile Q 8 89
Eastern Ghats (mts.), India D-F 4-6 70
East Flevoland (polder), Neth. H 4 25
E. Frisian (isls.), W.Ger. B 2 20
E. Grand Forks, Minn. B 3 190
E. Grand Rapids, Mich. D 6 186
E. Greenwich, R.I. H 6 184
E. Hampton, Conn. E 2 146
Easthampton, Mass. D 3 184
E. Hanover, N.J. E 2 209
E. Hartford, Conn. E 1 146
E. Haven, Conn. D 3 146
East Korea (bay), N.Korea D 4 74
Eastlake, Ohio J 8 220
E. Lansing, Mich. E 6 186
E. Liverpool, Ohio J 4 220
East London, S.Afr. M18 57
E. Longmeadow, Mass. E 4 184
E. Los Angeles, Calif. C10 140
E. Lyme, Conn. G 3 146
Eastman, Ga. F 6 152
E. Meadow, N.Y. R 7 213
E. Millcreek, Utah C 3 240
E. Moline, Ill. C 2 158
Easton, Md. O 5 181
Easton, Mass. K 4 184
Easton, Pa. M 4 231
E. Orange, N.J. B 2 209
E. Palestine, Ohio J 4 220
E. Peoria, Ill. D 3 158
E. Point, Ga. C 3 152
E. Providence, R.I. J 5 184
E. Ridge, Tenn. L11 173
E. Rochester, N.Y. F 4 212
E. Rutherford, N.J. B 2 209
E. St. Louis, Ill. B 6 158
East Siberian (sea), U.S.S.R. R 2 47
E. Stroudsburg, Pa. M 4 231
E. Windsor, Conn. E 1 146
Eaton, Ohio A 6 220
Eatontown, N.J. E 3 209
Eau Claire, Wis. D 6 253
Eboli, Italy E 4 32
Ebro (riv.), Spain G 2 31
Economy, Pa. B 4 230
Ecorse, Mich. B 7 186
Ecuador D-E 4 90
Edam, Neth. G 4 25
Eddystone (rocks), Eng. C 7 11
Ede, Neth. H 4 25
Eden, N.C. K 1 217
Eden Prairie, Minn. G 6 190
Edenton, N.C. R 2 217
Edgewater, Colo. J 3 145
Edgewater, N.J. C 2 209
Edgewater Park, N.J. D 3 209
Edgewood, Pa. B 7 230
Edina, Minn. G 5 190
Edinburg, Tex. F11 238
Edinburgh (cap.), Scot. D 1 13
Edirne, Turkey B 2 64
Edison, N.J. E 2 209
Edison N.H.S., N.J. A 2 209
Edmond, Okla. M 3 225
Edmonds, Wash. C 3 246
Edmonton (cap.), Alta. D 3 115
Edmundston, N.Br. B 1 102
Edna, Tex. H 9 238
Edward (lake), Afr. M12 57
Edwards (plat.), Tex. C 7 238
Edwards A.F.B., Calif. H 9 140
Edwardsville, Ill. B 6 158
Eel (riv.), Calif. B 4 140
Efate (isl.), New Hebr. G 7 89
Effigy Mounds N.M., Iowa L 2 165
Effingham, Ill. E 4 158
Eglin A.F.B., Fla. C 6 148
Egmont (mt.), N.Z. L 6 87
Egypt M 6 54, A 4 60
Eielson A.F.B., Alaska J 2 133
Eindhoven, Neth. G 6 25
El 'Alamein, Egypt M 5 54
Elath, Isr. D 5 67
Elba (isl.), Italy C 3 32
Elbe (riv.), Ger. C 2 20
Elbert (mt.), Colo. G 4 145
Elberton, Ga. G 2 152
El'brus (mt.), U.S.S.R. F 6 50
Elburz (range), Iran F-J 2 68
El Cajon, Calif. J11 140
El Campo, Tex. H 8 238
El Centro, Calif. K11 140
El Cerrito, Calif. J 2 140
El Dorado, Ark. E 7 139
El Dorado, Kans. F 4 168
Elephanta (isl.), India B 7 70
Elephant Butte (res.), N.Mex. B 5 210
Eleuthera (isl.), Bah. C 1 124
El Faiyûm, Egypt M 6 54
El Ferrol, Spain B 1 30
Elgin, Ill. E 1 158
Elgin, Scot. E 3 13
Elgon (mt.), Afr. N11 57
Elizabeth, Aust. D 7 86
Elizabeth, N.J. B 2 209
Elizabeth City, N.C. S 2 217
Elizabethton, Tenn. S 8 173
Elizabethtown, Ky. K 5 173
Elizabethtown, Pa. J 5 230
El Karnak, Egypt B 4 60
Elk City, Okla. G 4 224
Elk Grove Village, Ill. A 1 158
Elkhart, Ind. F 1 163
Elkins, W.Va. G 5 248
Elko, Nev. F 2 202
Elkton, Md. P 2 181
Ellensburg, Wash. E 3 246
Ellesmere (isl.), N.W.T. N 3 97
Ellwood City, Pa. B 4 230
El Mansûra, Egypt B 3 60
Elmendorf A.F.B., Alaska B 1 132
Elm Grove, Wis. K 1 253
Elmhurst, Ill. A 2 158
Elmira, N.Y. G 6 212
Elmont, N.Y. R 7 213
El Monte, Calif. D10 140
El Morro N.M., N.Mex. A 3 210
Elmwood Park, Ill. B 2 158
Elmwood Park, N.J. B 2 209
Eloy, Ariz. D 6 134
El Paso, Tex. A10 238
El Puerto de Sta. María, Spain C 4 30
El Rashid, Syria H 5 65
El Reno, Okla. K 3 225
El Salvador C 4 122
El Segundo, Calif. B11 140
El Seibo, Dom.Rep. E 3 124
Elsmere, Del. R 2 181
Elsmere, Ky. R 3 173
El Toro, Calif. E11 140
Elwood, Ind. F 4 163
Ely, Eng. H 5 11
Elyria, Ohio F 3 220
Emden, W.Ger. B 2 20
Emerson, Man. E 5 110
Emerson, N.J. B 1 209
Emeryville, Calif. J 2 140
Emilia-Romagna (reg.), Italy B-D 2 32
Emmaus, Pa. M 4 231
Emporia, Kans. F 3 168
Emporia, Va. N 7 243
Ems (riv.), W.Ger. B 2 20
Encino, Calif. B10 140
Endicott, N.Y. H 6 212
Enfield, Conn. E 1 146
Engadine (valley), Switz. J 3 37
England 11
Englewood, Colo. K 3 145
Englewood, N.J. C 2 209
Englewood, Ohio B 6 220
Englewood Cliffs, N.J. C 2 209
English (chan.), Europe A-D 2-3 26
Enid, Okla. L 2 225
Eniwetok (atoll), T.T.P.I. G 4 89
Enköping, Sweden G 1 16
Ennis, Tex. H 5 238
Enns (riv.), Aus. C 3 38
Enschede, Neth. K 4 25
Ensenada, Mex. A 1 118
Entebbe, Uganda N12 57
Enterprise, Ala. G 8 130
Enugu, Nig. H10 54
Ephrata, Pa. K 5 231
Ephrata, Wash. F 3 246
Epping, Eng. H 7 11
Equatorial Guinea H11 57
Erbil, Iraq D 2 68
Erfurt, E.Ger. D 3 20
Erie (lake), N.A. K 2 126
Erie, Pa. B 1 230
Eritrea (reg.), Eth. O 8 55
Erivan, U.S.S.R. F 6 50
Erlanger, Ky. R 3 173
Erne (lake), N.Ire. F 3 15
Er Roseires, Sudan N 9 54
Erzgebirge (mts.), Europe E 3 20
Erzurum, Turkey J 3 65
Esbjerg, Den. B 7 19
Escalante (des.), Utah A 6 240
Escanaba, Mich. C 3 186
Escondido, Calif. J10 140
Escuintla, Guat. B 3 122
Eskilstuna, Sweden K 7 16
Eskişehir, Turkey D 3 64
Esmeraldas, Ecua. D 3 90
Espiritu Santo (isl.), New Hebr. G 7 89
Essaouira, Mor. D 5 54
Essen, W.Ger. B 3 20
Essequibo (riv.), Guyana J 2 90
Essex, Md. N 3 181
Essex Jct., Vt. A 3 204
Es Suweida, Syria G 6 64
Estados (isl.), Arg. H14 93
Este, Italy C 2 32
Estevan, Sask. J 6 113
Estherville, Iowa D 2 164
Estonian S.S.R., U.S.S.R. C 1 51
Estremadura (reg.), Spain C 3 31
Esztergom, Hung. E 3 39
Ethiopia O 9 55
Etna (vol.), Italy E 6 32
Etna, Pa. B 6 230
Etosha (salt pan), S.W.Afr. J15 57
Euboea (isl.), Greece F 6 43
Euclid, Ohio J 9 220
Eufaula, Ala. H 7 130
Eugene, Oreg. D 3 226
Euless, Tex. F 2 238
Eunice, La. F 6 175
Eupen, Belg. J 7 25
Euphrates (riv.), Asia E 3 60
Eure (riv.), France D 3 26
Eureka, Calif. A 3 140
Europe 6-7
Eustis, Fla. E 3 148
Evans (mt.), Colo. H 3 145
Evansdale, Iowa J 4 164
Evanston, Ill. B 1 158
Evansville, Ind. C 9 163
Everest (mt.), Asia F 3 70
Everett, Mass. D 6 184
Everett, Wash. C 3 246
Everglades N.P., Fla. E 6 148
Evergreen Park, Ill. B 2 158
Evesham, Eng. F 5 11
Évora, Port. C 3 30
Ewa Beach, Hawaii A 4 154
Excelsior Sprs., Mo. R 4 197
Exeter, Eng. D 7 11
Exeter, N.H. F 6 204
Exuma (sound), Bah. C 1 124
Eyre (lake), Aust. F 5 86

F

Faenza, Italy D 2 32
Faerøe (isls.), Den. B 2 19
Fagersta, Sweden J 6 16
Fairbanks, Alaska J 2 133
Fairborn, Ohio B 6 220
Fairbury, Nebr. G 4 201
Fairfax, Calif. H 1 140
Fairfax, Va. O 3 243
Fairfield, Ala. E 3 130
Fairfield, Calif. K 1 140
Fairfield, Conn. B 4 146
Fairfield, Ill. E 5 158
Fairfield, Iowa J 6 164
Fairfield, Maine D 6 178
Fairfield, N.J. A 2 209
Fairfield, Ohio A 7 220
Fairhaven, Mass. L 6 185
Fair Haven, N.J. E 3 209
Fairhope, Ala. C10 130
Fair Lawn, N.J. B 1 209
Fairlawn, Ohio G 3 220
Fairmont, Minn. D 7 190
Fairmont, W.Va. F 2 248
Fairport, N.Y. F 4 212
Fairview, N.J. C 2 209
Fairview Hts., Ill. B 6 158
Fairview Park, Ohio G 9 220
Fairweather (mt.), N.A. L 1 133
Faizabad, Afgh. C 1 70
Faizabad, India E 3 70
Falaise, France C 3 26
Falcon (res.), N.A. E11 238
Falcon Hts., Minn. G 5 190
Falfurrias, Tex. F10 238
Falkirk, Scot. C 1 13

Falkland Islands H14 93
Fall River, Mass. K 6 184
Falls Church, Va. O 3 243
Falls City, Nebr. J 4 201
Falmouth, Eng. C 7 11
Falmouth, Maine C 8 178
Falmouth, Mass. M 6 185
Falun, Sweden J 6 16
Famagusta, Cyprus F 5 64
Famatina (mts.), Arg. G 9 93
Fanning (isl.), Gilb. Is. L 5 89
Fanwood, N.J. E 2 209
Farallon (isls.), Calif. B 6 140
Farewell (cape), Greenl. O 4 94
Fargo, N.Dak. S 6 219
Faribault, Minn. E 6 190
Farmers Branch, Tex. G 1 238
Farmingdale, N.Y. N 9 213
Farmington, Conn. D 2 146
Farmington, Maine C 6 178
Farmington, Mich. F 6 186
Farmington, Mo. M 7 197
Farmington, N.Mex. A 2 210
Faro, Port. B 4 30
Farrell, Pa. A 3 230
Fatehgarh, India D 3 70
Fatshan, China H 7 77
Fayetteville, Ark. B 1 139
Fayetteville, N.C. M 4 217
Fayetteville, Tenn. H10 172
Fear (cape), N.C. O 7 217
Feeding Hills, Mass. D 4 184
Fehmarn (isl.), W.Ger. D 1 20
Feldkirch, Aus. A 3 38
Fénérive, Madag. R15 57
Fenton, Mich. F 6 186
Fergana, U.S.S.R. H 5 46
Fergus Falls, Minn. B 4 190
Ferguson, Mo. P 2 197
Fernandina Bch., Fla. E 1 148
Ferndale, Mich. B 6 186
Fernie, B.C. K 5 117
Ferozepore, India C 2 70
Ferrara, Italy C 2 32
Ferriday, La. G 3 175
Festus, Mo. M 6 197
Fez, Mor. F 5 54
Fezzan (reg.), Libya J 6 54
Ffestiniog, Wales D 5 11
Fianarantsoa, Madag. R16 57
Fichtelgebirge (mts.), W.Ger. D3 20
Fifth Cataract (falls), Sudan N 8 54
Fiji H 8 89
Fillmore, Calif. G 9 140
Findlay, Ohio C 3 220
Finisterre (cape), Spain B 1 30
Finland 16
Finland (gulf), Europe P 7 16
Finlay (riv.), B.C. E 1 117
Finsteraarhorn (mt.), Switz. F 3 37
Fircrest, Wash. C 3 246
Fire I. N.Sea., N.Y. P 9 213
Firenze (Florence), Italy C 3 32
Fitchburg, Mass. G 2 184
Fitzgerald, Ga. F 7 152
Fiumicino, Italy F 7 32
Flagstaff, Ariz. D 3 134
Flaming Gorge (res.), U.S. C 4 254
Flanders (prov's), Belg. B-E 6-7 25
Flathead (lake), Mont. C 3 198
Flat Rock, Mich. F 6 186
Flattery (cape), Wash. A 2 246
Flatwoods, Ky. R 4 173
Flemington, N.J. D 2 209
Flensburg, W.Ger. C 1 20
Flin Flon, Man. H 3 110
Flint, Mich. F 6 186
Flora, Ill. E 5 158
Floral Park, N.Y. R 7 213
Florence, Ala. C 1 130
Florence, Italy C 3 32
Florence, Ky. R 3 173
Florence, S.C. H 3 232
Flores (isl.), Indon. G 7 83
Florham Park, N.J. E 2 209
Florianópolis, Braz. L 9 93
Florida (bay), Fla. F 7 148
Florida (straits), N.A. B 1 124
Florida (state), U.S. 148
Florida, Urug. J10 93
Florida City, Fla. F 6 148
Florissant, Mo. P 2 197
Florissant Fossil Beds N.M., Colo. J 5 145
Flossmoor, Ill. B 3 158
Flushing, Mich. F 5 186
Flushing, Neth. C 6 25
Fly (riv.), P.N.G. A 7 82
Foggia, Italy E 4 32
Foix, France D 6 26
Folcroft, Pa. M 7 231
Folkestone, Eng. J 6 11
Fongafale (cap.), Tuvalu H 6 89
Fond du Lac, Wis. K 8 253
Fonseca (gulf), C.A. D 4 122
Fontainebleau, France E 3 26
Fontana, Calif. E10 140
Foochow, China J 6 77
Forest Acres, S.C. F 3 232
Forest City, N.C. E 4 216
Forest Grove, Oreg. A 2 226
Forest Hill, Tex. F 2 238
Forest Hills, Pa. C 7 230
Forest Park, Ga. D 3 152
Forest Park, Ill. B 2 158
Forest Park, Ohio B 9 220
Forfar, Scot. F 4 13
Forlì, Italy D 2 32
Formosa, Arg. J 9 93
Formosa (Taiwan) (isl.), China K 7 77
Forrest City, Ark. J 3 139
Fortaleza, Braz. N 4 91
Fort Atkinson, Wis. J10 253
Ft. Belvoir, Va. O 3 243
Ft. Benning, Ga. B 6 152
Ft. Bliss, Tex. A10 238
Ft. Bowie N.H.S., Ariz. F 6 134
Ft. Bragg, N.C. M 4 217
Ft. Campbell, U.S. G 7 172
Ft. Caroline N.Mem., Fla. E 1 148
Ft. Clatsop N.Mem., Oreg. C 1 226
Ft. Collins, Colo. J 1 145
Ft. Davis N.H.S., Tex. D11 238
Ft-de-France (cap.), Mart. G 4 125
Ft. Dodge, Iowa E 3 164
Ft. Donelson N.M.P., Tenn. F 8 172
Ft. Erie, Ont. E 5 108
Ft. Frederica N.M., Ga. K 8 152
Ft. George G. Meade, Md. L 4 181
Forth (firth), Scot. F 4 13
Fort Jefferson N.M., Fla. C 7 148
Ft. Knox, Ky. K 5 173
Ft. Laramie N.H.S., Wyo. H 3 255
Ft. Larned N.H.S., Kans. C 3 168
Ft. Lauderdale, Fla. C 4 148
Ft. Lee, N.J. C 2 209
Ft. Lee, Va. O 6 243
Ft. Leonard Wood, Mo. H 7 197
Ft. Macleod, Alta. D 5 114
Ft. Madison, Iowa L 7 165
Ft. Matanzas N.M., Fla. E 2 148
Ft. McHenry N.M., Md. M 3 181
Ft. McMurray, Alta. E 1 114
Ft. Mitchell, Ky. S 3 173
Ft. Morgan, Colo. M 2 145
Ft. Myers, Fla. E 5 148
Ft. Necessity N.B.P., Pa. C 6 230
Ft. Payne, Ala. G 2 130
Ft. Peck Lake, (res.), Mont. K 3 198
Ft. Pierce, Fla. F 4 148
Ft. Point N.H.S., Calif. L 5 213
Ft. Providence, N.W.T. E 3 96
Ft. Pulaski N.M., Ga. L 6 152
Ft. Raleigh N.H.S., N.C. T 3 217
Ft. Richardson, Alaska C 1 132
Ft. Riley, Kans. F 2 168
Ft. Scott, Kans. H 4 169
Ft. Sill, Okla. K 5 225
Ft. Simpson, N.W.T. D 3 96
Ft. Smith, Ark. B 3 138
Ft. Smith, N.W.T. E 3 96
Ft. Smith N.H.S., Ark. B 3 138
Ft. Stanwix N.M., N.Y. J 4 212
Ft. Stockton, Tex. A 7 238
Ft. Sumter N.M., S.C. H 6 232
Ft. Thomas, Ky. S 2 173
Ft. Ticonderoga, N.Y. O 3 213
Ft. Union N.M., N.Mex. E 3 210
Ft. Union Trading Post N.H.S., N.Dak. B 3 218
Ft. Valley, Ga. E 5 152
Ft. Vancouver N.H.S., Wash. C 5 246
Ft. Walton Bch., Fla. C 6 148
Ft. Wayne, Ind. G 2 163
Ft. William, Scot. C 4 13
Ft. Worth, Tex. E 2 238
Forty Fort, Pa. L 3 231
Fostoria, Ohio D 3 220
Fountain Hill, Pa. L 4 231
Fountain Valley, Calif. D11 140
Fourth Cataract (falls), Sudan N 8 54
Foxboro, Mass. J 4 184
Foxe (basin), N.W.T. J 2 96
Fox Point, Wis. M 1 253
Frackville, Pa. K 4 231
Framingham, Mass. A 7 184
France 26
Francis Case (lake), S.Dak. L-M 6-7 234
Francistown, Botswana M16 57
Frankfort, Ind. E 4 163
Frankfort (cap.), Ky. M 4 173
Frankfurt-am-Main, W.Ger. C 3 20
Frankfurt-an-der-Oder, E.Ger. F 2 20
Franklin, Ind. E 6 163
Franklin, Ky. J 7 173
Franklin, La. G 7 175
Franklin, Mass. J 4 184
Franklin, N.H. D 5 204
Franklin, N.J. D 3 209
Franklin (dist.), N.W.T. E-J 1 96
Franklin, Ohio B 6 220
Franklin, Pa. C 3 230
Franklin, Tenn. H 9 172
Franklin, Va. P 7 243
Franklin, Wis. L 2 253
Franklin D. Roosevelt (lake), Wash. G 2 247
Franklin Lakes, N.J. B 1 209
Franklin Park, Ill. A 2 158
Franz Josef Land (isls.), U.S.S.R. E-G 1 46
Fraser (riv.), B.C. F 4 117
Fraser, Mich. B 6 186
Fredericia, Den. C 6 19
Frederick, Md. J 3 181
Frederick, Okla. H 6 225
Fredericksburg, Tex. E 7 238
Fredericksburg, Va. N 4 243
Fredericton (cap.), N.Br. D 3 102
Fredonia, N.Y. B 6 212
Freehold, N.J. E 3 209
Freeport, Ill. D 1 158
Freeport, N.Y. R 7 213
Freeport, Tex. J 9 238
Freetown (cap.), S.Leone D10 54
Freiburg, W.Ger. B 5 20
Freising, W.Ger. D 4 20
Fremantle, Aust. B 2 86
Fremont, Calif. K 3 140
Fremont, Nebr. H 3 201
Fremont, Ohio D 3 220
French Guiana K 3 90
Frenchman (riv.), N.A. E 1 126
French Polynesia L-N 8 89
Fresno, Calif. F 7 140
Fribourg, Switz. D 3 36
Fridley, Minn. G 5 190
Friedrichshafen, W.Ger. C 5 20
Friendswood, Tex. J 2 238
Friesland (prov.), Neth. H 2 25
Frio (cape), Braz. M 8 93
Friuli-Venezia Giulia (reg.), Italy D 1 32
Frobisher Bay, N.W.T. K 3 96
Front Royal, Va. M 3 243
Frostburg, Md. C 2 180
Frunze, U.S.S.R. H 5 46
Fuerteventura (isl.), Spain C 4 30
Fujairah, U.A.E. G 4 60
Fuji (mt.), Japan J 6 75
Fukien (prov.), China J 6 77
Fukui, Japan G 5 73
Fukuoka, Japan D 7 74
Fukushima, Japan K 5 75
Fulda, W.Ger. C 3 20
Fullerton, Calif. D11 140
Fulton, Mo. J 5 197
Fulton, N.Y. H 4 212
Fultondale, Ala. E 3 130
Funchal, Port. A 2 30
Fundy (bay), N.A. E 3 102
Fundy N.P., N.Br. E 3 102
Fürstenfeldbruck, W.Ger. D 4 20
Fürth, W.Ger. D 4 20
Fushun, China K 3 77
Füssen, W.Ger. D 5 20

G

Gabès (gulf), Tun. J 5 54
Gabon J12 57
Gaborone (cap.), Botswana L16 57
Gadsden, Ala. G 2 130
Gaeta, Italy D 4 32
Gaffney, S.C. D 1 232
Gafsa, Tun. H 5 54
Gahanna, Ohio E 5 220
Gainesville, Fla. D 2 148
Gainesville, Ga. E 2 152
Gainesville, Tex. G 4 238
Gaithersburg, Md. K 4 181
Galápagos (isls.), Ecua. J 9 94
Galaţi, Rum. H 3 43
Galax, Va. G 7 242
Galena Park, Tex. J 1 238
Galesburg, Ill. C 3 158
Galicia (reg.), Spain B-C 1 30
Galilee (reg.), Isr. C 2 67
Galion, Ohio E 4 220
Gallatin, Tenn. H 8 172
Galle, Sri Lanka D 7 70
Gallipoli, Turkey C 6 64
Gallipolis, Ohio F 8 220
Gällivare, Sweden M 3 17
Gallup, N.Mex. A 3 210
Galveston, Tex. L 3 238
Galway, Ire. C 5 15
Gambia C 9 54
Gambier (isls.), Fr. Poly. N 8 89
Gananoque, Ont. H 3 108
Gander, Newf. C 3 99
Gap, France G 5 26
Garanhuns, Braz. N 5 91
Ganges (riv.), Asia F 3 70
Gangtok, India F 3 70
Garda (lake), Italy C 2 32
Gardena, Calif. C11 140
Garden City, Ga. K 6 152
Garden City, Kans. B 4 168
Garden City, N.Y. R 7 213
Gardendale, Ala. E 3 130
Garden Grove, Calif. D11 140
Gardiner, Maine D 7 178
Gardner, Mass. G 2 184
Garfield, N.J. B 2 209
Garfield Hts., Ohio J 9 220
Garland, Tex. H 1 238
Garmisch-Partenkirchen, W.Ger. D 5 20
Garonne (riv.), France C 5 26
Garwood, N.J. E 2 209
Gary, Ind. C 1 163
Gas City, Ind. F 4 163
Gaspé (pen.), Que. D 2 105
Gastonia, N.C. G 4 216
Gateshead, Eng. J 3 11
Gatineau (riv.), Que. B 3 104
Gauhati, India G 3 70
Gävle, Sweden K 6 17
Gaya, India F 4 70
Gaza Strip, Egypt A 4-5 67
Gaziantep, Turkey G 4 64
Gdańsk, Pol. D 1 45
Gdynia, Pol. D 1 45
Geelong, Aust. K 2 87
Gelderland (prov.), Neth. H 4 25
Gelsenkirchen, W.Ger. B 3 20
General Grant Grove Park, Calif. G 7 140
Geneseo, Ill. C 2 158
Geneseo, N.Y. E 5 212
Geneva (lake), Europe C 4 36
Geneva, Ill. E 2 158
Geneva, N.Y. G 5 212
Geneva, Ohio J 2 220
Geneva, Switz. B 4 36
Genghis Khan Wall (ruins), Asia H 2 77
Genoa (Genova), Italy B 2 32
George Rogers Clark N.H.P., Ind. B 7 163
Georgetown (cap.), Cayman Is. A 3 124
Georgetown (cap.), Guyana J 2 90
Georgetown, Ky. M 4 173
George Town (Penang), Malaysia C 6 81
Georgetown, Mass. L 2 184
Georgetown, S.C. J 5 232
Georgetown, Tex. G 7 238
George Washington Birthplace N.M., Va. P 4 243
George Washington Carver N.M., Mo. D 9 196
Georgia (str.), B.C. E 5 117
Georgia (state), U.S. 152
Georgian (bay), Ont. C-D 2-3 108
Georgian S.S.R., U.S.S.R. F 6 50
Gera, E.Ger. E 3 20
Geraldton, Aust. A 5 86
Gering, Nebr. A 3 200
Gerlachovka (mt.), Czech. E 2 39
Germantown, Wis. K 1 253
Germany 20
Germiston, S.Afr. M17 57
Gerona, Spain H 2 31
Gettysburg, Pa. H 6 230
Gettysburg N.M.P., Pa. H 6 230
Gezira, El (reg.), Sudan N 9 54
Ghana F10 54
Ghazni, Afgh. B 2 70
Ghent, Belg. D 6 25
Gibraltar D 4 31
Gibraltar (str.) D 5 31
Gibson (des.), Aust. D 4 86
Gifu, Japan H 6 75
Gila (riv.), U.S. D 4 126
Gila Cliff Dwellings N.M., N.Mex. A 5 210
Gilbert (peak), Utah D 3 240
Gilbert Islands J 6 89
Gillette, Wyo. G 1 254
Gilroy, Calif. D 6 140
Girard, Ohio J 3 220
Gironde (riv.), France C 5 26
Gisborne, N.Z. M 6 87
Giza, Egypt B 4 60
Glace Bay, N.S. J 2 101
Glacier Bay N.M., Alaska M 1 133
Glacier N.P., B.C. J 4 117
Glacier N.P., Mont. B-C 2 198
Gladewater, Tex. K 5 238
Gladstone, Mich. C 3 186
Gladstone, Mo. P 5 197
Gladstone, Oreg. B 2 226
Glarus (canton), Switz. H 3 37
Glasgow, Ky. J 7 173
Glasgow, Scot. B 2 13
Glassboro, N.J. C 4 209
Glassport, Pa. C 7 230
Glastonbury, Conn. E 2 146
Glen Burnie, Md. M 4 181
Glen Canyon N.R.A., U.S. D 6 240
Glencoe, Ill. F 1 158
Glen Cove, N.Y. R 6 213
Glendale, Ariz. C 5 134
Glendale, Calif. C10 140
Glendale, Mo. P 3 197
Glendale, Wis. M 1 253
Glendive, Mont. M 3 199
Glendora, Calif. D10 140
Glen Ellyn, Ill. F 2 158
Glenolden, Pa. M 7 231
Glen Ridge, N.J. B 2 209
Glen Rock, N.J. B 1 209
Glens Falls, N.Y. M 4 213
Glenview, Ill. B 1 158
Glenwood, Ill. B 3 158
Glittertind (mt.), Nor. F 6 16
Gliwice, Pol. A 4 45
Globe, Ariz. E 5 134
Glomma (riv.), Nor. G 6 16
Gloucester, Eng. E 6 11
Gloucester, Mass. M 2 185
Gloucester City, N.J. B 3 209
Gloversville, N.Y. M 4 213
Goa (dist.), India C 5 70
Gobi (des.), Asia G 3 77
Godavari (riv.), India D 5 70
Godhavn, Greenl. N 3 94
Godthåb (cap.), Greenl. N 3 94
Godwin Austen (K2) (mt.), India D 1 70
Goffstown, N.H. D 5 204
Goiânia, Braz. L 7 90
Goiás (state), Braz. L 6 90
Golconda (ruins), India D 5 70
Gold Coast, Aust. J 5 86
Golden, Colo. J 3 145
Golden Gate (chan.), Calif. H 2 140
Golden Spike N.H.S., Utah B 2 240
Golden Valley, Minn. G 5 190
Goldsboro, N.C. O 4 217
Golf Manor, Ohio C 9 220
Gomel', U.S.S.R. D 4 50
Gómez Palacio, Mex. G 4 119
Gonâve (isl.), Haiti D 3 124
Gondar, Eth. O 9 54
Gonzales, Tex. G 8 238
Good Hope (cape), S.Afr. F20 57
Goodland, Kans. A 2 168
Goose (lake), U.S. G 5 226
Goose Bay, Newf. D 2 99
Gorham, Maine C 8 178
Gorizia, Italy D 2 32
Gor'kiy, U.S.S.R. F 3 50
Görlitz, E.Ger. F 3 20
Goshen, Ind. F 1 163
Goslar, W.Ger. D 3 20
Göta (canal), Sweden J 7 16
Göteborg, Sweden G 8 16
Gotha, E.Ger. D 3 20
Gotland (isl.), Sweden L 8 16
Göttingen, W.Ger. D 3 20
Gottwaldov, Czech. D 2 39
Gouda, Neth. F 4 25
Goulburn, Aust. J 7 86
Gozo (isl.), Malta E 6 32
Grafton, Aust. J 5 86
Grafton, Mass. H 4 184
Grafton, N.Dak. R 3 219
Grafton, W.Va. G 4 248
Grafton, Wis. L 9 253
Graham, N.C. L 2 217
Graham, Tex. F 4 238
Grahamstown, S.Afr. M18 57
Graian Alps (mts.), Europe G 5 26
Granada, Nic. E 5 122
Granada, Spain E 4 31
Granada Hills, Calif. B10 140
Granby, Conn. D 1 146
Granby, Mass. E 3 184
Granby, Que. E 4 105
Gran Canaria (isl.), Spain B 5 30
Gran Chaco (reg.), S.A. H 8-9 93
Grand (canal), China J 4 77
Grand (lake), Newf. B 3 99
Grand Bahama (isl.), Bah. B 1 124
Grand Bank, Newf. B 4 99
Grand Blanc, Mich. F 6 186
Grand Canyon N.P., Ariz. C 2 134
Grand Cayman (isl.), Cayman Is. B 3 124
Grand Centre, Alta. E 2 114
Grand Comoro (isl.), Comoros P14 57
Grand Coulee (dam), Wash. F 3 247
Grande (bay), Arg. G14 93
Grande (riv.), Bol. H 7 90
Grande, Rio (riv.), N.A. F 5 126
Grande Prairie, Alta. A 2 114
Grand Falls, Newf. C 3 99
Grand Forks, N.Dak. R 4 219
Grand Haven, Mich. C 5 186
Grand Island, Nebr. F 4 201
Grand Island, N.Y. B 5 212
Grand Junction, Colo. B 4 144
Grand Ledge, Mich. E 6 186
Grand Manan (isl.), N.Br. D 4 102
Grand'Mère, Que. E 3 105
Grand Portage N.M., Minn. G 2 190
Grand Prairie, Tex. G 2 238
Grand Rapids, Mich. D 5 186
Grand Rapids, Minn. E 3 190
Grand Teton N.P., Wyo. B 2 254
Grandview, Mo. P 6 197
Grandview Hts., Ohio D 6 220
Grandville, Mich. D 6 186
Granite City, Ill. B 6 158
Gran Paradiso (mt.), Italy A 2 32
Gran Quivira N.M., N.Mex. C 4 210
Grants, N.Mex. B 3 210
Grants Pass, Oreg. D 5 226
Granville, France C 3 26
Grapevine, Tex. F 1 238
Grasse, France G 6 26
Grass Valley, Calif. D 4 140
Graubünden (canton), Switz. H-K 3 37
Gravelbourg, Sask. E 6 113
Gravenhurst, Ont. E 3 108
Gravesend, Eng. H 6 11
Graz, Aus. C 3 39
Great (sound), Berm. G 3 124
Great Abaco (isl.), Bah. C 1 124
Gt. Australian (bight), Aust. D-E 6 86
Gt. Barrier (reef), Aust. H-J 2-3 86
Gt. Barrington, Mass. A 4 184
Gt. Bear (lake), N.W.T. D 2 96
Gt. Bend, Kans. D 3 168
Gt. Dividing (range), Aust. H-J 4-6 86
Gt. Eastern Erg (des.), Afr. H 5 54
Gt. Exuma (isl.), Bah. C 2 124
Gt. Falls, Mont. E 3 198
Gt. Inagua (isl.), Bah. D 2 124
Gt. Indian (des.), Asia C 3 70
Gt. Khingan (range), China K 1-2 77
Gt. Namaland (reg.), S.W.Afr. K17 57
Gt. Neck, N.Y. R 7 213
Gt. Salt (lake), Utah B 2-3 240
Gt. Salt Lake (des.), Utah A 2-3 240
Gt. Sand Dunes N.M., Colo. H 7 145
Gt. Sandy (des.), Aust. C 4 86
Gt. Slave (lake), N.W.T. E 3 96
Gt. Smoky (mts.), U.S. B-C 3 216
Gt. Smoky Mts. N.P., U.S. B-C 3 216
Gt. Victoria (des.), Aust. D-E 5 86
Gt. Wall (ruins), China G 4 77

Ionian (isls.), Greece D 6 43
Ios (isl.), Greece G 7 43
Iowa (state), U.S. 164-165
Iowa City, Iowa L 5 165
Iowa Falls, Iowa G 3 164
Iowa Park, Tex. F 4 238
Ipoh, Malaysia D 6 81
Ipswich, Aust. J 5 86
Ipswich, Eng. J 5 11
Ipswich, Mass. L 2 184
Iquique, Chile F 8 90
Iquitos, Peru F 4 90
Iráklion, Greece G 8 43
Iran 68-69
Irapuato, Mex. J 6 119
Iraq 68
Irbid, Jordan D 2 67
Ireland 15
Irish (sea), Europe B-D 4 11
Irkutsk, U.S.S.R. L 4 46
Irondequoit, N.Y. E 4 212
Iron Mountain, Mich. B 3 186
Ironton, Ohio E 8 220
Ironwood, Mich. F 2 186
Irrawaddy (riv.), Burma B 3 81
Irtysh (riv.), U.S.S.R. G 4 46
Irving, Tex. G 2 238
Irvington, N.J. B 2 209
Irvington, N.Y. O 6 213
Ischia (isl.), Italy D 4 32
Ise, Japan H 6 75
Isère (riv.), France F 5 26
Iserlohn, W.Ger. B 3 20
Isfahan, Iran G 4 68
Ishim, U.S.S.R. H 4 46
Ishpeming, Mich. B 2 186
Iskenderun, Turkey G 4 64
Islamabad (cap.), Pak. C 2 70
Island Park, N.Y. R 8 213
Islay (isl.), Scot. B 5 13
Isle Royale N.P., Mich. E 1 186
Islip, N.Y. O 9 213
Ismailia, Egypt N 5 54
Isparta, Turkey D 4 64
Israel 67
Issoudun, France D 4 26
Issyk-Kul' (lake), U.S.S.R. H 5 46
Istanbul, Turkey D 6 64
Itabuna, Braz. N 6 91
Italy 32
Itasca (lake), Minn. C 3 190
Ithaca, N.Y. G 6 212
Itháki (isl.), Greece E 6 43
Ivanovo, U.S.S.R. E 3 50
Ivindo (riv.), Afr. J11 57
Ivory Coast E-F 10 54
Iwo (isl.), Japan M 4 75
Iyo (sea), Japan E 7 74
Izhevsk, U.S.S.R. H 3 50
Izmir, Turkey B 3 64

J

Jabalpur, India D 4 70
Jacinto City, Tex. J 1 238
Jackson, Ala. C 8 130
Jackson, Mich. E 6 186
Jackson (cap.), Miss. D 6 192
Jackson, Mo. N 8 197
Jackson, Ohio E 7 220
Jackson, Tenn. D 9 172
Jackson, Wyo. B 2 254
Jacksonville, Ala. G 3 130
Jacksonville, Ark. F 4 139
Jacksonville, Fla. E 1 148
Jacksonville, Ill. C 4 158
Jacksonville, N.C. O 5 217
Jacksonville, Tex. J 5 238
Jaén, Spain E 4 31
Jaffna, Sri Lanka E 7 70
Jaipur, India D 3 70
Jalalabad, Afgh. B 2 70
Jalisco (state), Mex. H 6 119
Jamaica C 3 124
Jamaica, N.Y. N 9 213
Jamaica Plain, Mass. C 7 184
James (bay), Can. D 2 107
James (riv.), U.S. G 2 126
James (riv.), Va. O 6 243
Jamestown, N.Y. B 6 212
Jamestown, N.Dak. N 6 218
Jamestown (res.), N.Dak. N 6 218
Jamestown, Va. P 6 243
Jammu & Kashmir (state), India C-D 2 70
Jamshedpur, India F 4 70
Janesville, Wis. J10 253
Jan Mayen (isl.), Nor. D 1 6
Japan 74-75
Japan (sea), Asia S 6 58
Jars (plain), Laos D 3 81
Jarvis (isl.), Pacific K 6 89
Jasper, Ala. D 3 130
Jasper, Ind. D 8 163
Jasper, Tex. L 7 238
Jasper N.P., Alta. A-B 3 114
Java (isl.), Indon. G-L 2 83
Java (sea), Indon. D-E 6 83
Jeanerette, La. G 7 175
Jeannette, Pa. C 5 230
Jefferson, Pa. B 7 230
Jefferson, Wis. J10 253
Jefferson City (cap.), Mo. H 5 197
Jefferson Nat'l Expansion Mem., Mo. R 3 197
Jeffersontown, Ky. L 4 173
Jeffersonville, Ind. F 8 163
Jena, E.Ger. D 3 20
Jenkintown, Pa. M 5 231
Jennings, La. E 6 174
Jennings, Mo. P 2 197
Jerez de la Frontera, Spain C 4 31
Jericho, Jordan C 4 67
Jersey (isl.), Chan.Is. E 8 11
Jersey City, N.J. B 2 209
Jersey Shore, Pa. H 3 230
Jerseyville, Ill. C 4 158
Jerusalem (cap.), Isr. C 4 67
Jessore, Bang. F 4 70
Jesup, Ga. J 7 152
Jésus (isl.), Que. H 4 105
Jewel Cave N.M., S.Dak. B 6 234
Jewish Aut. Obl., U.S.S.R. O 5 47
Jhang Maghiana, Pak. C 2 70
Jhansi, India D 3 70
Jhelum (riv.), Asia C 2 70
Jidda, Saudi Ar. C 5 60
Jihlava, Czech. C 2 39
Jim Thorpe, Pa. L 4 231
João Pessoa, Braz. O 5 91
Jodhpur, India C 3 70
Johannesburg, S.Afr. M17 57
John Day (riv.), Oreg. G 2 226
John Muir N.H.S., Calif. K 1 140
Johnson City, N.Y. J 6 212
Johnson City, Tenn. S 8 173
Johnston (atoll), Pacific K 4 89
Johnstown, N.Y. M 4 213
Johnstown, Pa. D 5 230
Johor (state), Malaysia D 7 81
Joliet, Ill. E 2 158
Joliette, Que. D 3 105
Joncs (plain), Asia E 5 81
Jonesboro, Ark. J 2 139
Jonesboro, La. E 2 174
Jönköping, Sweden H 8 16
Jonquière, Que. F 1 105
Joplin, Mo. C 8 196
Jordan 67
Jordan (riv.), Asia D 3 67
Joshua Tree N.M., Calif. J10 140
Jost van Dyke (isl.), B.V.I. G 1 125
Juan de Fuca (str.), N.A. E 6 117
Juan Fernández (isls.), Chile 5
Juàzeiro do Norte, Braz. N 5 91
Juba (riv.), Somalia P11 57
Juchitán, Mex. M 8 19
Judaea (reg.), Asia B-C 4-5 67
Juiz de Fora, Braz. M 8 90
Jujuy, Arg. G 8 93
Julian Alps (mts.), Europe D 1 32
Julianehåb, Greenl. O 3 94
Jullundur, India D 2 70
Jumna (riv.), India E 3 70
Junagadh, India B 4 70
Junction City, Kans. E 2 168
Juneau (cap.), Alaska N 1 133
Jungfrau (mt.), Switz. E 3 37
Juquiá, Braz. L 8 93
Jura (mts.), Europe F-G 4 26
Jura (isl.), Scot. C 5 13
Justice, Ill. A 2 158

K

K2 (mt.), India D 1 70
Kabul (cap.), Afgh. B 2 70
Kachin (state), Burma C 1 81
Kaduna, Nig. H 9 54
Kaesŏng, N.Korea C 4 74
Kagoshima, Japan E 8 74
Kahoolawe (isl.), Hawaii H 3 155
Kahului, Hawaii J 2 155
Kaieteur (falls), Guyana J 3 90
Kaifeng, China J 5 77
Kailua, Hawaii F 2 155
Kairouan, Tun. H 4 54
Kaiserslautern, W.Ger. B 4 20
Kakinada, India E 5 70
Kalahari (des.), Afr. L16 57
Kalamazoo, Mich. D 6 186
Kalgoorlie, Aust. C 6 86
Kalimantan (reg.), Indon. D-F 5 83
Kalinin, U.S.S.R. E 3 50
Kaliningrad, U.S.S.R. B 4; E 3 50
Kalispell, Mont. B 2 198
Kalmar, Sweden K 8 16
Kalmuck A.S.S.R., U.S.S.R. F 5 50
Kaluga, U.S.S.R. E 4 50
Kamakura, Japan O 3 75
Kamchatka (pen.), U.S.S.R. Q 4 47
Kamloops, B.C. G 5 117
Kampala (cap.), Uganda N11 57
Kampot, Camb. E 5 81
Kananga, Zaire L13 57
Kanazawa, Japan H 5 75
Kanchenjunga (mt.), Asia F 3 70
Kandahar, Afgh. B 2 70
Kandy, Sri Lanka E 7 70
Kane, Pa. E 2 230
Kanem (reg.), Chad K 9 54
Kaneohe, Hawaii F 2 155
Kangaroo (isl.), Aust. F 7 86
Kanin (pen.), U.S.S.R. G 1 50
Kankakee, Ill. F 2 158
Kankan, Guinea E 9 54
Kannapolis, N.C. H 4 216
Kano, Nig. H 9 54
Kanpur, India E 3 70
Kansas (riv.), Kans. F 2 169
Kansas (state), U.S. 168-169
Kansas City, Kans. H 2 169
Kansas City, Mo. P 5 197
Kansu (prov.), China E-G 3-4 77
Kanye, Botswana L16 57
Kaohsiung, China J 7 77
Kaolack, Sen. C 9 54
Kaplan, La. F 6 175
Kara (sea), U.S.S.R. G 2 46
Kara-Bogaz-Gol (gulf), U.S.S.R. F 5 46
Karachi, Pak. B 4 70
Karaganda, U.S.S.R. H 5 46
Karakoram (mts.), Asia D 1 70
Karakorum (ruins), Mong. F 2 77
Kara-Kum (des.), U.S.S.R. F 5 46
Karamea (bight), N.Z. K 6 87
Karbala', Iraq C 4 68
Karelian A.S.S.R., U.S.S.R. D 2 50
Kariba (lake), Afr. M15 57
Karl-Marx-Stadt, E.Ger. E 3 20
Karlovy Vary, Czech. B 1 38
Karlskrona, Sweden K 8 16
Karlsruhe, W.Ger. C 4 20
Karlstad, Sweden H 7 16
Kárpathos (isl.), Greece H 8 43
Kars, Turkey K 2 65
Kasai (riv.), Afr. K12 57
Kashgar, China A 4 76
Kassala, Sudan O 8 54
Kassel, W.Ger. C 3 20
Kastamonu, Turkey F 2 64
Kastoría, Greece E 5 43
Katahdin (mt.), Maine F 4 178
Katanga (reg.), Zaire L-M 13 57
Katherina, Jebel (mt.), Egypt N 6 54
Katmai N.M., Alaska H 3 133
Kathmandu (cap.), Nepal E 3 70
Katowice, Pol. B 4 45
Kattegat (str.), Europe G 8 16
Kauai (isl.), Hawaii C 1 154
Kaukauna, Wis. K 7 253
Kaunas, U.S.S.R. C 3 51
Kavála, Greece G 5 43
Kawasaki, Japan J 6 75
Kayes, Mali D 9 54
Kayseri, Turkey F 3 64
Kaysville, Utah B 2 240
Kazakh S.S.R., U.S.S.R. F-J 5 46
Kazan', U.S.S.R. G 3 50
Kazbek (mt.), U.S.S.R. F 6 50
Keansburg, N.J. E 3 209
Kearney, Nebr. E 4 201
Kearny, N.J. B 2 209
Kecskemét, Hung. E 3 39
Kedah (state), Malaysia D 6 81
Keelung, China K 6 77
Keene, N.H. C 6 204
Keewatin (dist.), N.W.T. G-H 3 96
Kefar Sava, Isr. B 3 57
Kelantan (state), Malaysia D 6 81
Kelowna, B.C. H 5 117
Kelso, Wash. C 4 246
Kemerovo, U.S.S.R. J 4 46
Kemi (lake), Fin. Q 3 16
Kendall, Fla. B 5 148
Kendallville, Ind. G 2 163
Kenilworth, N.J. E 2 209
Kénitra, Mor. D 5 54
Kenmare, Ire. B 8 15
Kenmore, N.Y. C 5 212
Kennebunk, Maine B 9 178
Kenner, La. N 4 175
Kennesaw Mtn. N.B.P., Ga. C 3 152
Kennett, Mo. M10 197
Kennewick, Wash. F 4 246
Kenora, Ont. B 3 107
Kenosha, Wis. M 3 253
Kent, Ohio H 3 220
Kent, Wash. C 3 246
Kenton, Ohio C 4 220
Kentucky (lake), U.S. E 8 172
Kentucky (state), U.S. 172-173
Kentville, N.S. D 3 100
Kentwood, Mich. D 6 186
Kenya O11 57
Kenya (mt.), Kenya O12 57
Keokuk, Iowa L 8 165
Kerala (state), India D 6-7 70
Kerguélen (isls.) 5
Kérkira (isl.), Greece D 6 43
Kermadec (isls.), N.Z. J 9 89
Kerman, Iran K 5 68
Kermanshah, Iran E 3 68
Kermit, Tex. B 6 238
Kerrville, Tex. E 7 238
Kerulen (riv.), Asia H 2 77
Keta, Ghana G10 54
Ketchikan, Alaska N 2 133
Kettering, Ohio B 6 220
Kewanee, Ill. C 2 158
Keweenaw (pt.), Mich. B 1 186
Keyport, N.J. E 3 209
Keyser, W.Va. J 4 249
Key West, Fla. E 7 148
Khabarovsk, U.S.S.R. O 5 47
Khaniá, Greece G 8 43
Kharagpur, India F 4 70
Khârga (oasis), Egypt N 6 54
Khar'kov, U.S.S.R. E 5 50
Khartoum (cap.), Sudan N 8 54
Khemmarat, Thai. E 4 81
Kherson, U.S.S.R. D 5 50
Khíos (isl.), Greece G 6 43
Khorramshahr, Iran F 5 68
Khotan, China A 4 76
Khulna, Bang. F 4 70
Khyber (pass), Pak. C 2 70
Kiangsi (prov.), China J 6 77
Kiangsu (prov.), China K 5 77
Kiel, W.Ger. D 1 20
Kiel (canal), W.Ger. C 1 20
Kielce, Pol. E 3 45
Kiev, U.S.S.R. D 4 50
Kigali (cap.), Rwanda N12 57
Kigoma-Ujiji, Tanz. N12 57
Kilauea (crater), Hawaii H 6 155
Kildare, Ire. H 5 15
Kilgore, Tex. K 5 238
Kilimanjaro (mt.), Tanz. O12 57
Kilkenny, Ire. G 6 15
Killarney, Ire. C 7 15
Killeen, Tex. G 6 238
Killingley, Conn. H 1 147
Kimberley (plat.), Aust. D 3 86
Kimberley, B.C. K 5 117
Kimberley, S.Afr. L17 57
Kimberly, Wis. K 7 253
Kinabalu (mt.), Malaysia F 4 83
Kindersley, Sask. B 4 112
King (isl.), Aust. G 7 86
Kingman, Ariz. A 3 134
Kings Canyon N.P., Calif. G 7 140
Kingsford, Mich. A 3 186
Kings Mtn., N.C. G 4 216
Kings Mtn. N.M.P., S.C. E 1 232
Kings Point, N.Y. R 7 213
Kingsport, Tenn. R 7 173
Kingston (cap.), Jam. C 3 124
Kingston, Mass. M 5 185
Kingston, N.Y. M 7 213
Kingston (cap.), Norfolk I. G 8 89
Kingston, Ont. H 3 108
Kingston, Pa. K 3 231
Kingstown (cap.), St.Vincent G 4 125
Kingsville, Ont. B 6 108
Kingsville, Tex. G10 238
Kinloch, Mo. P 2 197
Kinnelon, N.J. E 2 209
Kinross, Scot. E 4 13
Kinsale, Ire. D 8 15
Kinshasa (cap.), Zaire K12 57
Kinston, N.C. O 4 217
Kioga (lake), Uganda N11 57
Kirgiz S.S.R., U.S.S.R. H 5 46
Kirin, China L 3 77
Kirkcaldy, Scot. D 1 13
Kirkcudbright, Scot. E 6 13
Kirkenes, Nor. Q 2 16
Kirkland, Wash. B 2 246
Kirkland Lake, Ont. D 3 107
Kirksville, Mo. H 2 197
Kirkuk, Iraq D 3 68
Kirkwall, Scot. E 2 13
Kirkwood, Mo. O 3 197
Kirov, U.S.S.R. D 4 50
Kirovabad, U.S.S.R. G 6 50
Kirovograd, U.S.S.R. D 5 50
Kirtland, Ohio H 2 220
Kiruna, Sweden L 3 16
Kisangani, Zaire M11 57
Kishinev, U.S.S.R. C 5 50
Kiska (isl.), Alaska J 4 133
Kismayu, Somalia P12 57
Kissimmee, Fla. E 3 148
Kistna (riv.), India D 5 70
Kita Iwo (isl.), Japan M 4 75
Kitakyushu, Japan E 6 74
Kitchener, Ont. D 4 108
Kitimat, B.C. C 3 116
Kittanning, Pa. D 4 230
Kittery, Maine B 9 178
Kitzbühel, Aus. B 3 38
Kiungchow (str.), China G 7 77
Kivu (lake), Afr. M12 57
Kizel, U.S.S.R. J 3 50
Kızılırmak (riv.), Turkey F 2 64
Kjölen (mts.), Europe J-N 2-4 16
Kladno, Czech. B 1 38
Klagenfurt, Aus. C 3 38
Klaipėda, U.S.S.R. A 3 51
Klamath Falls, Oreg. F 5 226
Kleve, W.Ger. B 3 20
Kloten, Switz. G 2 47
Kluane (lake), Yukon C 3 96
Knoxville, Iowa G 6 164
Knoxville, Tenn. O 9 173
Kobdo, Mong. D 2 77
Kobe, Japan H 7 75
Koblenz, W.Ger. B 3 20
Kobuk (riv.), Alaska G 1 133
Kodiak (isl.), Alaska H 3 133
Kokomo, Ind. E 4 163
Koko Nor (lake), China E 4 77
Kola (pen.), U.S.S.R. E 1 50
Kolar Gold Fields, India D 6 70
Kolguyev (isl.), U.S.S.R. G 1 50
Kolhapur, India C 5 70
Köln (Cologne), W.Ger. B 3 20
Kołobrzeg, Pol. B 1 45
Kolyma (range), U.S.S.R. Q 3 47
Komárno, Czech. D 3 39
Komi A.S.S.R., U.S.S.R. H 2 50
Kompong Chhnang, Camb. D 4 81
Kompong Thom, Camb. E 4 81
Komsomol'sk, U.S.S.R. O 4 47
Kongsberg, Nor. F 7 16
Königssee (lake), W.Ger. E 5 20
Konin, Pol. D 2 45
Köniz, Switz. D 3 37
Konstanz, W.Ger. C 5 20
Kontum (plat.), Viet. E 4 81
Konya, Turkey E 4 64
Kootenay (riv.), B.C. K 5 117
Koper, Yugo. A 3 43
Korçë, Alb. E 5 43
Korčula (isl.), Yugo. C 4 43
Kordofan (prov.), Sudan M 9 54
Korea 74
Koror, T.T.P.I. D 5 88
Korsakov, U.S.S.R. P 5 47
Koryak (range), U.S.S.R. R 3 47
Kos (isl.), Greece H 7 43
Kosciusko (mt.), Aust. H 7 86
Kosciusko, Miss. E 4 192
Košice, Czech. F 2 39
Kostroma, U.S.S.R. F 3 50
Koszalin, Pol. C 1 45
Kota Baharu, Malaysia D 6 81
Kota Kinabalu, Malaysia E 4 83
Kotka, Fin. P 6 16
Kotor, Yugo. D 4 43
Kowloon, Hong Kong H 7 77
Koyukuk (riv.), Alaska G 1 133
Kozhikode, India D 6 70
Kra (isth.), Thai. C 5 81
Kragujevac, Yugo. E 3 43
Krakatau (isl.), Indon. C 7 83
Krasnodar, U.S.S.R. E 6 50
Krasnovodsk, U.S.S.R. F 5 46
Krasnoyarsk, U.S.S.R. K 4 46
Krefeld, W.Ger. B 3 20
Kremenchug, U.S.S.R. D 5 50
Krishna (Kistna) (riv.), India D 5 70
Kristiansand, Nor. F 8 16
Kristiansund, Nor. E 5 16
Kristinehamn, Sweden H 7 16
Kristinestad, Fin. N 5 16
Krivoy Rog, U.S.S.R. D 5 50
Krk (isl.), Yugo. B 3 43
Kuala Lumpur (cap.), Malaysia D 7 81
Kuching, Malaysia E 5 83
Kufra (oasis), Libya L 7 54
Kuldja, China B 3 76
Kuma (riv.), U.S.S.R. G 5 50
Kumamoto, Japan E 7 74
Kumanovo, Yugo. E 4 43
Kumasi, Ghana F10 54
Kunlun (mts.), Asia B-D 4 76
Kunming, China F 6 77
Kuopio, Fin. Q 5 16
Kupang, Indon. G 8 83
Kura (riv.), U.S.S.R. G 6 50
Kurashiki, Japan F 6 75
Kŭrdzhali, Bulg. G 5 43
Kure, Japan F 6 75
Kurgan, U.S.S.R. G 4 46
Kuril (isls.), U.S.S.R. P 5 47
Kursk, U.S.S.R. E 4 50
Kuskokwim (riv.), Alaska G 2 133
Kutaisi, U.S.S.R. F 6 50
Kutch, Rann of (salt marsh), India B-C 4 70
Kutztown, Pa. L 4 231
Kuusamo, Fin. Q 4 16
Kuwait E 4 60
Kuybyshev, U.S.S.R. H 4 50
Kwajalein (atoll), T.T.P.I. G 5 89
Kwangju, S.Korea C 6 74
Kwangtung (prov.), China H 7 77
Kweichow (prov.), China G 6 77
Kweiyang, China G 6 77
Kwinana, Aust. B 2 86
Kyaukpyu, Burma B 3 81
Kyoto, Japan J 6 75
Kyushu (isl.), Japan E 7-8 74
Kyustendil, Bulg. F 4 43
Kyzyl, U.S.S.R. K 4 46
Kyzyl-Kum (des.), U.S.S.R. G 5 46

L

Laayoune, Morocco D 6 54
Labrador (dist.), Newf. D 1 99
Labuan (isl.), Malaysia E 4 83
Laccadive (isls.), India C 6 70
La Ceiba, Hond. D 3 122
La Chaux-de-Fonds, Switz. C 2 36
Lachine, Que. H 4 105
Lackawanna, N.Y. B 5 212
Lac-Mégantic, Que. G 4 105
Laconia, N.H. E 4 204
La Coruña, Spain B 1 30
La Crosse, Wis. D 8 253
Ladakh (reg.), India D 2 70
Ladoga (lake), U.S.S.R. D 2 50
Ladue, Mo. P 3 197
Ladysmith, S.Afr. N17 57
Lae, .N.G. B 7 82
Lafayette, Calif. K 2 140
La Fayette, Ga. B 1 152
Lafayette, Ind. D 4 163
Lafayette, La. F 6 175
La Follette, Tenn. N 8 173
Lagos (cap.), Nig. G10 54
La Grande, Oreg. J 2 227
La Grange, Ga. B 4 152
La Grange, Ill. A 2 158
La Grange Park, Ill. A 2 158
La Guaira, Ven. G 1 90
Laguna Beach, Calif. G10 140
La Habra, Calif. D11 140
Lahore, Pak. C 2 70
Lahti, Fin. O 6 16
La Junta, Colo. M 7 145
Lake Bluff, Ill. F 1 158
Lake Charles, La. D 6 174
Lake Chelan N.R.A., Wash. E 2 246
Lake City, Fla. D 1 148
Lake City, S.C. H 4 232
Lake Forest, Ill. F 1 158
Lake Havasu City, Ariz. A 4 134
Lakehurst, N.J. E 3 209
Lake Jackson, Tex. J 8 238
Lakeland, Fla. D 3 148
Lake Louise, Alta. B 4 114
Lake Mead N.R.A., U.S. G 6 202

M

Manitoulin (isl.), Ont. B 2 108
Manitou Sprs., Colo. J 5 145
Manitouwadge, Ont. C 3 107
Manitowoc, Wis. L 7 253
Manizales, Col. E 2 90

Mankato, Minn. E 6 190
Mannar (gulf), Asia D 7 70
Mannheim, W.Ger. C 4 20
Mansfield, Conn. F 1 146
Mansfield, Eng. K 2 11

Mansfield, La. C 2 174
Mansfield, Mass. J 4 184
Mansfield, Ohio F 4 220
Manteca, Calif. D 6 140
Mantiqueira (mts.), Braz. M 8 90

Mantua, Italy C 2 32
Manus (isl.), P.N.G. E 6 89
Manville, N.J. D 2 209
Manzanillo, Mex. G 7 119
Maple Grove, Minn. F 5 190

Maple Hts., Ohio H 9 220
Maple Shade, N.J. B 3 209
Maplewood, Minn. G 5 190
Maplewood, Mo. P 3 197
Maplewood, N.J. E 2 209

Maputo (cap.), Moz. N17 57
Maquoketa, Iowa M 4 165
Mar (mts.), Braz. L 9 93
Maracaibo, Ven. F 1 90
Maracay, Ven. G 1 90

Marajó (isl.), Braz. K 4 90
Maranhão (state), Braz. L 5 90
Marañón (riv.), Peru E 4 90
Maraş, Turkey G 4 64
Marblehead, Mass. E 7 184

March (riv.), Aus. D 2 39
Marche (reg.), Italy D 3 32
Mar del Plata, Arg. J11 93
Margarita (isl.), Ven. H 1 90
Margate, Fla. F 5 148

Margate City, N.J. E 5 209
Mari A.S.S.R., U.S.S.R. G 3 50
Mariana (isls.), T.T.P.I. E 4 89
Marianao, Cuba A 2 124
Marianna, Ark. J 4 139

Marianna, Fla. A 1 148
Maria van Diemen (cape), N.Z. L 5 87
Maribor, Yugo. B 2 43
Marie Byrd Land, Ant. B 12-13 88

Marie-Galante (isl.), Guad. G 4 125
Mariehamn, Fin. M 7 16
Marietta, Ga. D 3 152
Marietta, Ohio G 7 220
Marinette, Wis. L 5 253

Marion, Ill. E 6 158
Marion, Ind. F 3 163
Marion, Iowa K 4 165
Marion, Ohio D 4 220
Marion, S.C. J 3 232

Marion, Va. E 7 242
Maritime Alps (mts.), Europe G 5 25
Marken (isl.), Neth. G 4 25
Markham, Ill. B 2 158

Markham, Ont. J 4 109
Marlborough, Mass. H 3 184
Marlin, Tex. H 6 238
Marmara (sea), Turkey C 2 64
Marne (riv.), France E 3 26

Maroni (riv.), Fr.Gui. K 3 90
Marovoay, Madag. R15 57
Marquesas (isls.), Fr.Poly. M-N 6 89
Marquette, Mich. B 2 186

Marrakech, Mor. E 5 54
Marrero, La. O 4 175
Marseille, France F 6 26
Marshall, Mich. E 6 186
Marshall, Minn. C 6 190

Marshall, Mo. F 4 197
Marshall, Tex. K 5 238
Marshall (isls.), T.T.P.I. G 4 89
Marshalltown, Iowa G 4 164
Marshfield, Mass. M 4 185

Marshfield, Wis. F 6 253
Martha's Vineyard (isl.), Mass. M 7 185
Martin, Tenn. D 8 172
Martinez, Calif. K 1 140

Martinique G 4 125
Martinsburg, W.Va. K 4 249
Martins Ferry, Ohio J 5 220
Martinsville, Ind. D 6 163
Martinsville, Va. J 7 243

Mary, U.S.S.R. G 6 46
Maryland (state), U.S. 180-181
Marysville, Calif. D 4 140
Marysville, Mich. G 6 186
Marysville, Ohio D 5 220

Maryville, Mo. C 2 196
Maryville, Tenn. O 9 173
Masaya, Nic. D 5 122
Masbate (isl.), Phil. G 3 83
Mascara, Alg. G 4 54

Mascarene (isls.), Afr. R20 57
Mascoutah, Ill. D 5 158
Maseru (cap.), Lesotho M17 57
Mason, Mich. E 6 186
Mason, Ohio B 7 220

Mason City, Iowa G 2 164
Massa, Italy C 2 32
Massachusetts (state), U.S. 184-185
Massapequa, N.Y. O 9 213
Massapequa Pk., N.Y. O 9 213

Massawa, Eth. O 8 55
Massena, N.Y. L 1 212
Massillon, Ohio H 4 220
Masterton, N.Z. M 6 87
Masuda, Japan E 6 74

Matadi, Zaire J13 57
Matagalpa, Nic. E 4 122
Matagorda (isl.), Tex. H 9 238
Matamoros, Mex. L 4 119
Matane, Que. B 1 104

Matanzas, Cuba B 2 124
Matapan (Taínaron) (cape), Greece F 7 43
Matara, Sri Lanka E 7 70
Matarani, Peru F 7 90

Matautu (cap.), Wallis & Futuna J 7 89
Matawan, N.J. E 3 209
Mathis, Tex. G 9 238
Mato Grosso (plat.), Braz. K 7 90

Matra (mts.), Hung. E 3 39
Matrah, Oman G 5 60
Matsu (isl.), China K 6 77
Matsumoto, Japan H 5 75
Mattoon, Ill. E 4 158

Maturín, Ven. H 2 90
Maui (isl.), Hawaii J-K 2 155
Maumee, Ohio C 2 220
Mauna Kea (mt.), Hawaii H 4 155
Mauna Loa (mt.), Hawaii G 6 155

Maunawili, Hawaii F 2 155
Mauritania C-E 8 54
Mauritius S19 57
May (cape), N.J. D 6 209
Mayaguana (isl.), Bah. D 2 124

Mayagüez, P.R. F 1 124
Mayfield, Ky. D 7 172
Mayfield Hts., Ohio J 9 220
Maynard, Mass. J 3 184
Mayo, Yukon C 3 96

Mayotte P14 57
Maysville, Ky. O 3 173
Maywood, Calif. C10 140
Maywood, Ill. A 2 158
Maywood, N.J. B 2 209

Mazagan (El Jadida), Mor. D 5 54
Mazar-i-Sharif, Afgh. B 1 70
Mazaruni (riv.), Guyana H 2 90
Mazatlán, Mex. F 5 119
Mbabane (cap.), Swaz. N17 57

M'Banza Congo, Angola J13 57
McAlester, Okla. P 5 225
McAllen, Tex. F11 238
McComb, Miss. D 8 192
McDonald (isls.), Aust. 5

McGuire A.F.B., N.J. D 3 209
McKeesport, Pa. C 7 230
McKees Rocks, Pa. B 7 230
McKinley (mt.), Alaska H 2 133
McKinney, Tex. H 4 238

McLean, Va. O 3 243
M'Clintock (chan.), N.W.T. F 1 96
McLoughlin House N.H.S., Oreg. B 2 226
M'Clure (str.), N.W.T. E 1 96

McMinnville, Oreg. D 2 226
McMinnville, Tenn. K 9 173
McPherson, Kans. E 3 168
Mead (lake), U.S. A 2 134
Meadville, Pa. B 2 230

Mecca (cap.), Saudi Ar. C 5 60
Mechanicsburg, Pa. H 5 230
Mechanicville, N.Y. N 5 213
Mecklenburg (reg.), E.Ger. E 2 20
Medan, Indon. B 5 82

Medellín, Col. E 2 90
Medfield, Mass. B 8 184
Medford, Mass. C 6 184
Medford, Oreg. E 5 226
Media, Pa. L 7 231

Medicine Bow (range), Wyo. F 4 254
Medicine Hat, Alta. E 4 114
Medina, N.Y. D 4 95
Medina, Ohio G 3 220
Medina, Saudi Ar. D 5 60

Mediterranean (sea) G-N 4-5 54
Médoc (reg.), France C 5 26
Medway, Mass. J 4 184
Médenine, Tun. J 5 54
Meerut, India D 3 70

Mégantic (lake), Que. G 4 105
Megiddo, Isr. C 2 67
Meiningen, E.Ger. D 3 20
Meissen, E.Ger. E 3 20
Meknès, Mor. E 5 54

Mekong (riv.), Asia E 4 81
Melanesia (reg.), Pacific E-H 5-8 89
Melbourne, Aust. L 2 87
Melbourne, Fla. F 3 148

Melrose, Mass. D 6 184
Melrose, Scot. F 5 13
Melrose Park, Ill. A 2 158
Melville (isl.), Aust. D 2 86
Melville (isl.), N.W.T. E 1 96

Melville (pen.), N.W.T. H 2 96
Melville, Sask. J 5 113
Melvindale, Mich. B 7 186
Memphis, Tenn. B10 172
Memphremagog (lake), N.A C 1 204

Menasha, Wis. J 7 253
Mendocino (cape), Calif. A 3 140
Mendota, Ill. D 2 158
Mendota Hts., Minn. G 6 190
Mendoza, Arg. G10 93

Menlo Park, Calif. J 3 140
Menlo Park, N.J. E 2 209
Menominee, Mich. B 3 186
Menomonee Falls, Wis. K 1 253
Menomonie, Wis. C 6 253

Menton, France G 6 26
Mentor, Ohio H 2 220
Mentor-on-the-Lake, Ohio G 2 220
Menzel Bourguiba, Tun. H 4 54
Mequon, Wis. L 1 253

Merced, Calif. E 6 140
Mercedes, Tex. F12 238
Mercedes, Urug. J10 93
Mercer I., Wash. B 2 246
Mergui (arch.), Burma C 5 81

Mérida, Mex. P 6 119
Mérida, Spain C 3 31
Mérida, Ven. F 2 90
Meriden, Conn. D 2 146
Meridian, Miss. G 6 192

Meroe (ruins), Sudan N 8 54
Merriam, Kans. H 3 169
Merrick, N.Y. S 7 213
Merrill, Wis. G 5 253
Merrimack, N.H. D 6 204

Merritt I., Fla. F 3 148
Mersey (riv.), Eng. G 2 11
Merthyr Tydfil, Wales A 6 11
Mesa, Ariz. D 5 134
Mesa Verde N.P., Colo. C 8 144

Meshed, Iran L 2 69
Mesolóngion, Greece E 6 43
Mesopotamia (reg.), Iraq B-E 3-5 68
Mesquite, Tex. H 2 238

Messina, Italy E 5 32
Metairie, La. O 4 175
Methuen, Mass. K 2 184
Metropolis, Ill. E 6 158
Metuchen, N.J. E 2 209

Metz, France G 3 26
Meuse (riv.), Europe F 8 25; F 3 26
Mexia, Tex. H 6 238
Mexicali, Mex. B 1 118
Mexico 118-119

Mexico, Mo. J 4 197
Mexico (gulf), N.A. K 7 94
Mexico City (cap.), Mex. L 1 119
Miami, Fla. B 5 148
Miami, Okla. S 1 225

Miami Beach, Fla. C 5 148
Miamisburg, Ohio B 6 220
Miami Shores, Fla. B 4 148
Miami Sprs., Fla. B 5 148
Michigan (lake), U.S. J 2 126

Michigan (state), U.S. 186
Michigan City, Ind. C 1 163
Michoacán (state), Mex. H-J 7 119
Micronesia (reg.), Pacific E-H 4-6 89

Middleboro, Mass. L 5 184
Middleburg Hts., Ohio G10 220
Middlebury, Conn. C 2 146
Middlebury, Vt. A 3 204
Middlesboro, Ky. O 7 173

Middlesex, N.J. E 2 209
Middleton, Wis. G 9 253
Middletown, Conn. E 2 146
Middletown, N.J. E 3 209
Middletown, N.Y. L 8 213

Middletown, Ohio A 6 220
Middletown, Pa. J 5 230
Middletown, R.I. J 6 184
Midfield, Ala. E 4 130
Midland, Mich. E 5 186

Midland, Ont. D 3 108
Midland, Pa. A 4 230
Midland, Tex. C 6 238
Midland Park, N.J. B 1 209
Midlothian, Ill. B 2 158

Midvale, Utah B 3 240
Midway (isls.), Pacific J 3 89; A 5 154
Midwest City, Okla. M 4 225
Mikkeli, Fin. P 6 16
Míkonos (isl.), Greece G 7 43

Milan, Italy B 2 32
Milan, Tenn. D 9 172
Mildura, Aust. G 6 86
Miles City, Mont. L 4 199
Milford, Conn. C 4 146

Milford, Del. S 5 181
Milford, Mass. H 4 184
Milford, N.H. D 6 204
Millard, Nebr. H 3 201
Millbrae, Calif. J 2 140

Millburn, N.J. E 2 209
Millbury, Mass. H 4 184
Milledgeville, Ga. F 4 152
Mille Lacs (lake), Minn. E 4 190
Millersville, Pa. K 6 230

Millington, Tenn. B10 172
Millinocket, Maine F 4 178
Millis, Mass. A 8 184
Milltown, N.J. E 3 209
Mill Valley, Calif. H 2 140

Millville, N.J. C 5 209
Milpitas, Calif. L 3 140
Milton, Fla. B 6 148
Milton, Mass. D 7 184
Milton, Pa. J 3 230

Milwaukee, Wis. M 1 253
Milwaukie, Oreg. B 2 226
Minas (basin), N.S. D 3 100
Minas, Urug. K10 93
Minas Gerais (state), Braz. L 7 90

Mindanao (isl.), Phil. G-H 4 83
Minden, La. D 1 174
Mindoro (isl.), Phil. G 3 83
Mineola, N.Y. R 7 213
Mineral del Monte, Mex. K 6 119

Mineral Wells, Tex. F 5 238
Minersville, Pa. K 4 230
Mingo Jct., Ohio J 5 220
Minho (riv.), Port. B 2 30
Minneapolis, Minn. G 5 190

Minnesota (riv.), Minn. E 6 190
Minnesota (state), U.S. 190
Minnetonka, Minn. G 5 190
Minnetonka (lake), Minn. F 5 190
Miño (riv.), Spain B 1 30

Minorca (isl.), Spain J 2 31
Minot, N.Dak. H 3 218
Minsk, U.S.S.R. C 4 50
Minute Man N.H.P., Mass. B 6 184
Minya Konka (mt.), China F 6 77

Miramar, Fla. B 4 148
Miramichi (bay), N.Br. E 1 102
Mirim (lagoon), S.A. K10 93
Mirtóön (sea), Greece F 7 43
Mishawaka, Ind. E 1 163

Miskolc, Hung. F 2 39
Mission, Kans. H 2 169
Mission, Tex. F11 238
Mississippi (riv.), U.S. H 4 126
Mississippi (state), U.S. 192

Missoula, Mont. C 4 198
Missouri (riv.), U.S. H 3 126
Missouri (state), U.S. 196-197
Misti, El (mt.), Peru F 7 90
Misurata, Libya K 5 54

Mitchell (mt.), N.C. E 3 216
Mitilíni, Greece H 6 43
Mitla (ruin), Mex. M 8 119
Mittenwald, W.Ger. D 5 20
Miyazaki, Japan E 8 74

Moberly, Mo. G 4 197
Mobile, Ala. B 9 130
Moçambique, Moz. P15 57
Moçâmedes, Angola J15 57
Mocha, Y.A.R. D 7 60

Modena, Italy C 2 32
Modesto, Calif. D 6 140
Mogadishu (cap.), Somalia R11 57
Mogador (Essaouira), Mor. D 5 54
Mogilev, U.S.S.R. C 4 50

Mohács, Hung. E 4 39
Mohenjo Daro (ruins), Pak. B 3 70
Mojave (des.), Calif. H-K 9 140
Mokapu, Hawaii F 2 155
Moknine, Tun. J 4 54

Mokp'o, S.Korea C 6 74
Mola di Bari, Italy F 4 32
Mold, Wales D 4 11
Moldavian S.S.R., U.S.S.R. C 5 50
Moline, Ill. C 2 158

Molise (reg.), Italy E 4 32
Mollendo, Peru F 7 90
Molokai (isl.), Hawaii G-H 1 155
Moluccas (isls.), Indon. H-J 5-7 83
Mombasa, Kenya P12 57

Mona (passage), W.I. E 3 124
Monaca, Pa. B 4 230
Monaco G 6 26
Monaghan, Ire. G 3 15
Monahans, Tex. B 6 238

Mönchengladbach, W.Ger. B 3 20
Monclova, Mex. J 3 119
Moncton, N.Br. F 2 102
Monessen, Pa. C 5 230
Monett, Mo. E 9 196

Mongolia E-H 2 77
Monmouth, Ill. C 3 158
Monmouth, Oreg. D 3 226
Monmouth, Wales E 6 11
Monona, Wis. H 9 253

Monongahela, Pa. B 5 230
Monroe, Conn. C 3 146
Monroe, Ga. E 3 152
Monroe, La. F 1 175
Monroe, Mich. F 7 186

Monroe, N.C. J 5 216
Monroe, Wis. G10 253
Monroeville, Pa. C 7 230
Monrovia, Calif. D10 140
Monrovia (cap.), Lib. D10 54

Mons, Belg. E 8 25
Monson, Mass. E 4 184
Montague, Mass. E 2 184
Montague, P.E.I. F 2 100
Montana (state), U.S. 198-199

Montaña, La (reg.), Peru F 5-6 90
Mont Cenis (tunnel), Europe G 5 26
Montclair, Calif. D10 140
Montclair, N.J. B 2 209
Montebello, Calif. C10 140

Monte Carlo, Monaco G 6 26
Montecristi, Dom.Rep. D 3 124
Montecristo (isl.), Italy C 3 32
Montego Bay, Jam. B 3 124
Monterey, Calif. D 7 140

Monterey Park, Calif. C10 140
Monterrey, Mex. J 4 119
Montevideo, Minn. C 6 190
Montevideo (cap.), Urug. J11 93

Montezuma Castle N.M., Ariz. D 4 134
Montgomery (cap.), Ala. F 6 130
Montgomery, Ohio C 9 220
Monticello, Ark. G 6 139

Monticello, N.Y. L 7 213
Mont-Laurier, Que. B 3 104
Montmagny, Que. G 3 105
Montmorency, Que. J 3 105
Montoursville, Pa. J 3 230

Montpelier (cap.), Vt. B 3 204
Montpellier, France E 6 26
Montréal, Que. H 4 105
Montreux, Switz. C 4 36
Montrose, Colo. D 6 144

Mont-Royal, Que. H 4 105
Mont-St-Michel, France C 3 26
Montserrat G 3 125
Mont-Tremblant Prov. Pk., Que. C 3 105

Montvale, N.J. B 1 209
Montville, Conn. G 3 146
Montville, N.J. E 2 209
Monument (valley), Utah D-E 6 240
Moore, Okla. M 4 225

Moorea (isl.), Fr.Poly. L 7 89
Moores Creek N.M.P., N.C. N 6 217
Mooresville, Ind. E 5 163
Mooresville, N.C. H 3 216
Moorhead, Minn. B 4 190

Moosehead (lake), Maine D 4 178
Moose Jaw, Sask. F 5 113
Moosomin, Sask. K 5 113
Moradabad, India D 3 70
Morava (riv.), Czech. D 2 39

Morava (riv.), Yugo. E 3 43
Morawhanna, Guyana J 2 90
Moray (firth), Scot. J 4 13
Mordvinian A.S.S.R., U.S.S.R. G 4 50

Morehead, Ky. P 4 173
Morehead City, N.C. R 5 217
Morelia, Mex. J 7 119
Morena, Sierra (mts.), Spain D-E 3 31

Morgan City, La. H 7 175
Morgan Hill, Calif. L 4 140
Morganton, N.C. F 3 216
Morgantown, W.Va. G 3 248
Moro (gulf), Phil. G 4 83

Morocco E-F 5-6 54
Moroni (cap.), Comoros P14 57
Morrilton, Ark. E 3 139
Morris, Ill. E 2 158

Morris, Minn. C 5 190
Morris Plains, N.J. D 2 209
Morristown, N.J. D 2 209
Morristown, Tenn. P 8 173
Morristown N.H.P., N.J. D 2 209

Morrisville, Pa. N 5 231
Morro Bay, Calif. D 8 140
Morton, Ill. D 3 158
Moscow, Idaho B 3 156
Moscow (cap.), U.S.S.R. E 3 50

Mosel (riv.), Europe B 3 20
Moselle (riv.), France G 3 26
Moses Lake, Wash. F 3 246
Moshi, Tanz. O12 57
Mosquito (gulf), Pan. G 6 122

Mosquito Coast (reg.), C.A. E-F 3-4 122
Moss, Nor. D 4 16
Mossel Bay, S.Afr. L18 57
Moss Point, Miss. G10 192

Mostaganem, Alg. F 4 54
Mosul, Iraq C 2 68
Moulmein, Burma C 3 81
Moultrie, Ga. E 8 152
Mound, Minn. E 6 190

Mound City Group N.M., Ohio E 7 220
Mounds View, Minn. G 5 190
Moundsville, W.Va. E 3 248
Mountain Brook, Ala. E 4 130
Mountain Home, Idaho C 6 156

Mountainside, N. J. E 2 209
Mountain View, Calif. K 3 140
Mount Airy, N.C. H 1 216
Mount Carmel, Ill. F 5 158
Mount Carmel, Pa. K 4 230

Mount Clemens, Mich. G 6 186
Mount Ephraim, N.J. B 3 209
Mount Gambier, Aust. F 7 86
Mount Healthy, Ohio B 9 220
Mount Holly, N.C. H 4 216

Mount Isa, Aust. F 4 86
Mount Joy, Pa. K 5 230
Mount Kisco, N.Y. N 8 213
Mountlake Terrace, Wash. B 1 246
Mount Lebanon, Pa. B 7 230

Mount McKinley N.P., Alaska H 2 133
Mount Oliver, Pa. B 7 230
Mount Pleasant, Iowa L 7 165
Mount Pleasant, Mich. E 5 186

Mount Pleasant, Pa. D 5 230
Mount Pleasant, S.C. H 6 232
Mount Pleasant, Tex. K 4 238
Mount Prospect, Ill. A 1 158
Mount Rainier, Md. F 4 181

Mount Rainier N.P., Wash. D 4 246
Mount Rushmore N. Mem., S.Dak. B 6 234
Mount Sterling, Ky. N 4 173
Mount Vernon, Ill. E 5 158

Mount Vernon, Ind. B 9 163
Mount Vernon, N.Y. O 7 213
Mount Vernon, Ohio E 5 220
Mount Vernon, Va. O 3 243
Mount Vernon, Wash. C 2 246

Mozambique N-O 14-16 57
Mozambique (chan.), Afr. O16 57
Mtwara-Mikindani, Tanz. P14 57
Muğla, Turkey C 4 64
Mühlhausen, E.Ger. D 3 20

Muir Woods N.M., Calif. H 2 140
Mukalla, P.D.R.Y. E 7 60
Mukden, China K 3 77
Mulhacén (mt.), Spain E 4 31
Mülheim, W.Ger. B 3 20

Mulhouse, France G 4 26
Mull (isl.), Scot. C 4 13
Mullingar, Ire. G 4 15
Mullins, S.C. J 3 232
Multan, Pak. C 2 70

Muncie, Ind. G 4 163
Mundelein, Ill. E 1 158
Münden, W.Ger. C 3 20
Munhall, Pa. C 7 230
Munich (München), W.Ger. D 4 20

Munster, Ind. B 1 163
Münster, W.Ger. B 3 20
Muonio (riv.), Europe M 2 16
Mur (Mura) (riv.), Europe C-D 3 39
Murcia, Spain F 4 31

Mureş (riv.), Rum. E 2 43
Murfreesboro, Tenn. J 9 173
Murmansk, U.S.S.R. D 1 50
Murphysboro, Ill. D 6 158
Murray (riv.), Aust. G 6 86

Murray, Ky. E 7 172
Murray, Utah C 3 240
Murrumbidgee (riv.), Aust. G 6 86
Murzuk, Libya J 6 54
Muş, Turkey J 3 65

Musala (mt.), Bulg. F 4 43
Musandam, Ras (cape), Oman G 4 60
Muscat (cap.), Oman G 5 60
Muscatine, Iowa L 6 165

Muscle Shoals, Ala. C 1 130
Musgrave (ranges), Aust. E 5 86
Muskego, Wis. K 2 253
Muskegon, Mich. C 5 186
Muskegon Hts., Mich. C 5 186

Muskogee, Okla. R 3 225
Muskoka (lake), Ont. E 2 108
Musquodoboit (riv.), N.S. E 4 100
Musselshell (riv.), Mont. J 3 198
Muzaffarabad, India C 2 70

Muzaffarpur, India E 3 70
Muztagh (mt.), China B 4 76
Muztagh Ata (mt.), China A 4 76
Mwanza, Tanz. N12 57
Mweru (lake), Afr. M13 57

Myitkyina, Burma C 1 81
Mymensingh, Bang. G 4 70
Myrtle Beach, S.C. K 4 233
Mysore, India D 6 70
Mystic, Conn. H 3 147

N

Naas, Ire. H 5 15
Nablus (Nabulus), Jordan C 3 67
Nacogdoches, Tex. J 6 238
Nagaland (state), India G 3 71
Nagano, Japan J 5 75

Nagaoka, Japan J 7 75
Nagasaki, Japan D 7 74
Nagoya, Japan H 6 75
Nagpur, India D 4 70
Nagykanizsa, Hung. D3 39

Naha, Japan N 6 75
Nahariyya, Isr. C 1 67
Nahuel Huapi (lake), Arg. F12 93
Nairn, Scot. E 3 13
Nairobi (cap.), Kenya O12 57

Naivasha, Kenya O12 57
Najin, N.Korea D 2 74
Nakhichevan', U.S.S.R. F 7 50
Nakhon Ratchasima, Thai. D 4 81
Nakhon Si Thammarat, Thai. D 5 81

Nakskov, Den. E 8 19
Nakuru, Kenya O11 57
Namangan, U.S.S.R. H 5 46
Nam Dinh, Viet. E 2 81
Namib (des.), S.W.Afr. J 15-16 57

Nampa, Idaho B 6 156
Nampula, Moz. O15 57
Namsos, Nor. G 4 16
Namur, Belg. F 8 25
Nanaimo, B.C. J 3 117

Nanakuli, Hawaii D 2 155
Nanchang, China H 6 77
Nancy, France G 3 26
Nanda Devi (mt.), India D 2 70
Nandi, Fiji H 7 89

Nanga Parbat (mt.), India D 1 70
Nanking, China J 5 77
Nanning, China G 7 77
Nan Shan (mts.), China E 4 77
Nanterre, France A 1 26

Nantes, France C 4 26
Nanticoke, Pa. K 3 231
Nantucket (isl.), Mass. O 8 185
Napa, Calif. C 5 140
Naperville, Ill. E 2 158

Napier, N.Z. M 6 87
Naples, Fla. E 5 148
Naples, Italy E 4 32
Napoleon, Ohio B 3 220
Nara, Japan J 8 75

Narayanganj, Bang. G 4 70
Narberth, Pa. M 6 231
Narbonne, France E 6 26
Narmada (riv.), India D 4 70
Narragansett, R.I. J 7 184

Narragansett (bay), R.I. J 6-7 184
N.A.S.A. Space Ctr., Tex. K 2 238
Nasca, Peru F 6 90
Nashua, N.H. D 6 204
Nashville (cap.), Tenn. H 8 172

Nassau (cap.), Bah. C 1 124
Nässjö, Sweden J 8 16
Natal, Braz. O 5 91
Natal (prov.), S.Afr. N17 57
Natchez, Miss. B 7 192

Natchitoches, La. D 3 174
Natick, Mass. A 7 184
National City, Calif. J11 140
Natural Bridges N.M., Utah E 6 240

Naugatuck, Conn. C 3 146
Nauru G 6 89
Navajo N.M., Ariz. E 2 134
Navarin (cape), U.S.S.R. T 3 47
Navarra (reg.), Spain F 1 31

Navasota, Tex. J 7 238
Navojoa, Mex. E 3 118
Nawabganj, Bang. F 4 70
Náxos (isl.), Greece G 7 43
Nayarit (state), Mex. G 6 119

Nazaré, Braz. N 6 91
Nazareth, Isr. C 2 67
N'Djamena (cap.), Chad K 9 54
Ndola, Zambia M14 57
Neagh (lake), N.Ire. J 2 15

Nebo (mt.), Jordan D 4 67
Nebraska (state), U.S. 200-201
Nebraska City, Nebr. J 4 201
Neckar (riv.), W.Ger. C 4 20
Nederland, Tex. K 8 238

Needham, Mass. B 7 184
Needles, Calif. L 9 140
Neenah, Wis. J 7 253
Nefud (des.), Saudi Ar. C-D 4 60
Negaunee, Mich. B 2 186

Negev (reg.), Isr. D 5 67
Negombo, Sri Lanka D 7 70
Negro (riv.), S.A. H 4 90
Negros (isl.), Phil. G 4 83
Neisse (riv.), Europe F 3 20

Neiva, Col. F 3 90
Nejd (reg.), Saudi Ar. C-E 4-5 60
Nelson, B.C. J 5 117
Nelson (riv.), Man. J 2 111
Nelson, N.Z. L 6 87

Nenagh, Ire. E 6 15
Neosho, Mo. D 9 196
Nepal E-F 3 70
Neptune, N.J. E 3 209
Neptune City, N.J. E 3 209

Ness (lake), Scot. D 3 13
Netanya, Isr. B 3 67
Netherlands 25
Netherlands Antilles E 4, F 3 124
Neubrandenburg, E.Ger. E 2 20

Neuchâtel, Switz. C 3 36
Neuilly, France B 1 26
Neumünster, W.Ger. C 1 20
Neuquén, Arg. G11 93
Neuse (riv.), N.C. R 5 217

Neusiedler (lake), Europe D 3 39
Neuss, W.Ger. B 3 20
Neustadt, W.Ger. B 4 20
Neu-Ulm, W.Ger. D 4 20
Nevada, Mo. D 7 196

Nevada (state), U.S. 202
Nevada, Sierra (mts.), Spain E 4 31
Nevada, Sierra (mts.), U.S. E-G 4-7 140
Nevers, France E 4 26

Nevis (isl.), St.C.-N.-A. F 3 124
New Albany, Ind. F 8 163
New Albany, Miss. G 2 192
New Amsterdam, Guyana J 2 90
Newark, Calif. K 3 140

Newark, Del. P 2 181
Newark, Eng. G 4 11
Newark, N.J. B 2 209
Newark, N.Y. G 4 212
Newark, Ohio F 5 220

New Bedford, Mass. K 6 184
Newberg, Oreg. A 2 226
New Berlin, Wis. K 2 253
New Bern, N.C. P 4 217
Newberry, S.C. D 3 232

New Braunfels, Tex. F 8 238
New Brighton, Minn. G 5 190
New Brighton, Pa. B 4 230
New Britain, Conn. E 2 146
New Britain (isl.), P.N.G. F 6 89

New Brunswick (prov.), Can. 102
New Brunswick, N.J. E 3 209
Newburgh, N.Y. M 7 213
Newburyport, Mass. L 1 185
New Caledonia G 8 89

New Canaan, Conn. B 4 146
New Carlisle, Ohio C 6 220
New Castile (reg.), Spain D-E 2-3 31
Newcastle, Aust. J 6 86
New Castle, Ind. G 5 163

Newcastle, N.Br. E 2 102
Newcastle, N.Ire. J 3 15
New Castle, Pa. B 3 230
Newcastle-under-Lyme, Eng. E 5 11
Newcastle upon Tyne, Eng. F 2 11

New City, N.Y. N 8 213
New Cumberland, Pa. J 5 230
New Delhi (cap.), India D 3 70
New Fairfield, Conn. B 3 146
Newfoundland (prov.), Can. 99

Newfoundland (isl.), Newf. B 3 99
New Georgia (isl.), Sol. Is. F 6 89
New Glasgow, N.S. F 3 100
New Guinea (isl.), Pacific D-E 6 88

New Hampshire (state), U.S. 204
New Hanover (isl.), P.N.G. F 6 89
New Haven, Conn. D 3 146
New Haven, Ind. H 2 163
New Hebrides G 7 89

New Hyde Park, N.Y. R 7 213
New Iberia, La. G 6 175
Newington, Conn. E 2 146
New Ireland (isl.), P.N.G. F 6 89
New Jersey (state), U.S. 209

New Kensington, Pa. C 4 230
New London, Conn. G 3 147
New London, Wis. J 7 253
Newmarket, Ont. E3 108
New Martinsville, W.Va. E 3 248

New Mexico (state), U.S. 210
New Milford, Conn. B 2 146
New Milford, N.J. B 1 209
Newnan, Ga. C 4 152
New Orleans, La. O 4 175

New Paltz, N.Y. M 7 213
New Philadelphia, Ohio G 5 220
New Plymouth, N.Z. L 6 87
Newport, Ark. H 2 139
Newport, Ky. S 2 173

Newport, N.H. C 5 204
Newport, Oreg. C 3 226
Newport, R.I. J 7 184
Newport, Tenn. P 9 173
Newport, Vt. C 2 204

Newport, Wales D 6 11
Newport Beach, Calif. D11 140
Newport News, Va. P 6 243
New Port Richey, Fla. D 3 148
New Providence (isl.), Bah. C 1 124

New Providence, N.J. E 2 209
New Roads, La. G 5 175
New Rochelle, N.Y. P 7 213
Newry, N.Ire J 3 15
New Shrewsbury, N.J. E 3 209

New Siberian (isls.), U.S.S.R. O-Q 2 46
New Smyrna Bch., Fla. F 2 148
New South Wales (state), Aust. G-J 6 86

Newton, Iowa H 5 164
Newton, Kans. E 3 168
Newton, Mass. C 7 184
Newton, N.J. D 1 209
Newton, N.C. G 3 216

Newton Falls, Ohio J 3 220
Newtown, Conn. B 3 146
New Ulm, Minn. D 6 190
New Waterford, N.S. J 2 101
New Westminster, B.C. K 3 117

New York, N.Y. M 9 213
New York (state), U.S. 212-213
New Zealand M 7 87
Nez Perce N.H.P., Idaho A 3 156
Ngami (lake), Botswana L16 57

N'Gaoundéré, Cameroon J10 54
Niagara (riv.), N.A. B 4 212
Niagara Falls, N.Y. C 4 212
Niagara Falls, Ont. E 4 108
Niamey (cap.), Niger G 9 54

Nias (isl.), Indon. B 5 82
Niassa (dist.), Moz. O14 57
Nicaragua D-F 4 122
Nice, France G 6 26
Nicholasville, Ky. N 5 173

Nicobar (isls.), India G 7 71
Nicolet, Que. E 3 105
Nicosia (cap.), Cyprus E 5 64
Nicoya (gulf), C.R. E 6 122
Nidwalden (canton), Switz. F 3 37

Nieuw-Nickerie, Sur. J 2 90
Niğde, Turkey F 4 64
Niger G-J 7-9 54
Niger (riv.), Afr. G 9 54
Nigeria G-J 10 54

Nigríta, Greece F 5 43
Niigata, Japan J 5 75
Niihau (isl.), Hawaii A 2 154
Nijmegen, Neth. H 5 25
Nikolayev, U.S.S.R. D 5 50

Nile (riv.), Afr. N 7 54
Niles, Ill. A 1 158
Niles, Mich. C 7 186
Niles, Ohio J 3 220
Nîmes, France F 6 26

Ningpo, China K 6 77
Ningsia (Yinchwan), China F 4 77
Niort, France C 4 26
Nipawin, Sask. H 2 113
Nipigon (lake), Ont. C 3 107

Nipissing (lake), Ont. E 1 108
Niš, Yugo. E 4 43
Nishapur, Iran L 2 69
Nishinomiya, Japan H 8 75
Niterói, Braz. M 8 93

Nitro, W.Va. C 6 248
Niuafo'ou (isl.), Tonga J 7 89
Niue K 7 89
Nizhniy Tagil, U.S.S.R. G 4 46
Nkana, Zambia M14 57

Noblesville, Ind. F 4 163
Nogales, Ariz. E 7 134
Nome, Alaska E 2 133
Noranda, Que. B 3 106
Norco, Calif. E11 140

Nordhausen, E.Ger. D 3 20
Nordkyn (cape), Nor. Q 1 16
Nord-Ostsee (canal), W.Ger. C 1 20
Norfolk, Nebr. G 2 201
Norfolk, Va. R 7 243

Norfolk I. (terr.), Aust. G 8 89
Noril'sk, U.S.S.R. J 3 46
Normal, Ill. E 3 158
Norman, Okla. M 4 225
Normandy, Mo. P 3 197

Norman Wells, N.W.T. D 3 96
Normetal, Que. B 3 106
Norridge, Ill. B 1 158
Norristown, Pa. M 5 231
Norrköping, Sweden K 7 16

Norrtälje, Sweden L 7 16
North (sea), Europe E 3 6
North (isl.), N.Z. L 6 87
North (cape), Nor. P 1 16
North (chan.), U.K. D 3 8

North Adams, Mass. B 2 184
North America 94
Northampton, Eng. G 5 11
Northampton, Mass. D 3 184
Northampton, Pa. M 4 231

North Andover, Mass. K 2 184
N. Arlington, N.J. B 2 209
N. Attleboro, Mass. J 5 184
N. Augusta, S.C. C 5 232
N. Battleford, Sask. C 3 112

N. Bay, Ont. E 1 108
N. Bend, Oreg. C 4 226
N. Bergen, N.J. B 2 209
Northboro, Mass. H 3 184
North Braddock, Pa. C 7 230

N. Branford, Conn. E 3 146
Northbridge, Mass. H 4 184
Northbrook, Ill. A 1 158
North Brunswick, N.J. E 3 209
N. Caldwell, N.J. B 2 209

N. Canton, Ohio H 4 220
North Carolina (state), U.S. 216-217
North Cascades N.P., Wash. D 2 246
N. Chicago, Ill. F 1 158
N. College Hill, Ohio B 9 220

North Dakota (state), U.S. 218-219
No. Dvina (riv.), U.S.S.R. F 2 50
Northern Ireland F-K 2 15
No. Territory, Aust. E-F 3-4 86
Northfield, Ill. B 1 158

Northfield, Minn. E 6 190
Northfield, N.J. D 5 209
Northfield, Vt. B 3 204
N. Frisian (isls.), Europe C 1 20
Northglenn, Colo. K 3 145

North Haledon, N.J. B 1 209
N. Haven, Conn. D 3 146
N. Highlands, Calif. B 8 140
N. Kansas City, Mo. P 5 197
N. Kingstown, R.I. J 6 184

North Korea D 3-4 74
Northlake, Ill. A 2 158
N. Las Vegas, Nev. F 6 202
N. Little Rock, Ark. F 4 139
N. Magnetic Pole, N.W.T. F 1 96

N. Manchester, Ind. F 3 163
N. Mankato, Minn. D 6 190
N. Miami, Fla. B 4 148
N. Miami Bch., Fla. C 4 148
N. Ogden, Utah C 2 240

N. Olmsted, Ohio G 9 220
N. Palm Bch., Fla. F 5 148
N. Pelham, N.Y. O 7 213
N. Plainfield, N.J. E 2 209
N. Platte, Nebr. D 3 201

N. Platte (riv.), U.S. F 2 126
North Pole 5
Northport, Ala. C 4 130
Northport, N.Y. O 9 213
N. Providence, R.I. J 5 184

N. Reading, Mass. C 5 184
North Rhine-Westphalia (state), W.Ger. B-C 3 20
N. Richland Hills, Tex. F 1 238
N. Ridgeville, Ohio F 3 220

N. Riverside, Ill. B 2 158
N. Royalton, Ohio H10 220
N. St. Paul, Minn. E 5 190
N. Saskatchewan (riv.), Can. E-F 5 96

N. Syracuse, N.Y. H 4 212
N. Tarrytown, N.Y. O 6 213
N. Tonawanda, N.Y. C 4 212
Northumberland (str.), Can. D 2 100
Northvale, N.J. F 1 209

N. Vancouver, B.C. K 3 117
Northville, Mich. F 6 186
North West (cape), Aust. A 4 86
Northwest Territories, Can. E-J 2 96

Northwoods, Mo. P 2 197
Norton (sound), Alaska E-F 2 133
Norton, Mass. K 5 184
Norton, Ohio G 3 220
Norton, Va. C 7 242

Norton Shores, Mich. C 5 186
Norwalk, Calif. C11 140
Norwalk, Conn. B 4 146
Norwalk, Ohio E 3 220
Norway 16

Norwegian (sea), Europe D-E 2 6
Norwell, Mass. F 8 184
Norwich, Conn. G 2 147
Norwich, Eng. J 5 11
Norwich, N.Y. J 5 212

Norwood, Mass. B 8 184
Norwood, Ohio C 9 220
Norwood, Pa. M 7 231
Nossi-Bé (isl.), Madag. R14 57
Notre Dame, Ind. E 1 163

Nottingham, Eng. F 5 11
Nouadhibou, Mauritania C 7 54
Nouakchott (cap.), Mauritania C 8 54
Nouméa (cap.), New Cal. G 8 89

Nouveau-Québec (crater), Que. F 1 106
Nova Lisboa, Angola K14 57
Novara, Italy B 2 32
Nova Scotia (prov.), Can. 100-101

Novato, Calif. H 1 140
Novaya Zemlya (isls.), U.S.S.R. F-G 2 46
Novgorod, U.S.S.R. D 3 50
Novi, Mich. F 6 186

Novorossiysk, U.S.S.R. E 6 50
Novosibirsk, U.S.S.R. J 4 46
Nubia (lake), Sudan N 7 54
Nubian (des.), Sudan N 7 54
Nueces (riv.), Tex. F 9 238

Nueva San Salvador, El Sal. C 4 122
Nuevo Laredo, Mex. J 3 119
Nuevo León (state), Mex. K 4 119
Nuku'alofa (cap.), Tonga J 8 89
Nullarbor (plain), Aust. D-E 6 86

Nunivak (isl.), Alaska E 3 132
Nuremberg (Nürnberg), W.Ger. D 4 20
Nutley, N.J. B 2 209
Nyack, N.Y. N 8 213

Nyasa (lake), Afr. N14 57
Nyborg, Den. D 7 19
Nykøbing, Den. E 6; E 8 19
Nyköping, Sweden K 7 16
N'Zérékoré, Guinea E10 54

O

Oahe (lake), U.S. G 1 126
Oahu (isl.), Hawaii E 2 155
Oak Creek, Wis. M 2 253
Oakdale, Calif. E 6 140
Oakdale, La. E 5 174

Oak Forest, Ill. B 2 158
Oak Harbor, Wash. C 2 246
Oakland, Calif. J 2 140
Oakland, N.J. B 1 209
Oakland Park, Fla. B 3 148

Oak Lawn, Ill. B 2 158
Oakmont, Pa. C 6 230
Oak Park, Ill. B 2 158
Oak Park, Mich. B 6 186
Oak Ridge, Tenn. N 8 173

Oakville, Ont. E 4 108
Oakwood, Ohio B 6 220
Oamaru, N.Z. L 7 87
Oaxaca, Mex. L 8 119
Ob' (riv.), U.S.S.R. G 3 46

Oban, Scot. C 4 13
Oberammergau, W.Ger. D 5 20
Oberhausen, W.Ger. B 3 20
Oberlin, Ohio F 3 220
Óbidos, Braz. J 4 90

Obwalden (canton), Switz. F 3 37
Ocala, Fla. D 2 148
Ocean (isl.), Gilb. Is. G 6 89
Ocean City, N.J. D 5 209
Oceanport, N.J. F 3 209

Oceanside, Calif. H10 140
Oceanside, N.Y. R 7 213
Ocean Sprs., Miss. G10 192
Ocmulgee N.M., Ga. F 5 152
Oconomowoc, Wis. H 1 253

Ocumare, Ven. G 1 90
Odense, Den. D 7 19
Odenwald (for.), W.Ger. C 4 20
Oder (riv.), Europe F 3 6
Odessa, Tex. B 6 238

Odessa, U.S.S.R. D 5 50
Oelwein, Iowa K 3 165
O'Fallon, Ill. B 6 158
O'Fallon, Mo. N 2 197
Offenbach, W.Ger. C 3 20

Offenburg, W.Ger. B 4 20
Ogaden (reg.), Eth. Q-R 10 55
Ogallala, Nebr. C 3 200
Ogbomosho, Nig. H10 54
Ogden, Utah C 2 240

Ogdensburg, N.Y. K 1 212
O'Higgins (lake), Chile F13 93
Ohio (riv.), U.S. J 3 126
Ohio (state), U.S. 220
Ohrid (lake), Europe E 5 43

Oil City, Pa. C 3 230
Oise (riv.), France E 3 26
Oita, Japan E 7 74
Ojai, Calif. F 9 140
Ojos del Salado (mt.), S.A. G 9 93

Okanagan (lake), B.C. H 5 117
Okayama, Japan F 6 75
Okeechobee (lake), Fla. F 5 148
Okefenokee (swamp), U.S. H 9 152
Okhotsk (sea), U.S.S.R. P 4 47

Okinawa (isl.), Japan N 6 75
Oklahoma (state), U.S. 224-225
Oklahoma City (cap.), Okla. L 4 225
Okmulgee, Okla. O 3 225

Okovango (riv.), Afr. K15 57
Öland (isl.), Sweden K 8 16
Olathe, Kans. H 3 169
Olbia, Italy B 4 32
Old Bridge, N.J. E 3 209

Oldenburg, W.Ger. C 2 20
Old Forge, Pa. L 3 231
Old Orchard Bch., Maine C 9 178
Olds, Alta. D 4 114
Old Saybrook, Conn. F 3 146

Old Sturbridge Vill., Mass. F 4 184
Old Town, Maine F 6 178
Olean, N.Y. D 6 212
Olenek (riv.), U.S.S.R. M 3 46
Olinda, Braz. N 5 91

Olivette, Mo. P 3 197
Olney, Ill. E 5 158
Olomouc, Czech. D 2 39
Olsztyn, Pol. E 2 45
Olt (riv.), Rum. G 3 43

Olten, Switz. E 2 37
Olympia (cap.), Wash. C 3 246
Olympic (mts.), Wash. B 3 246
Olympic N.P., Wash. B 3 246
Olympus (mt.), Greece F 5 43

Olyphant, Pa. L 3 231
Omagh, N.Ire. G 2 15
Omaha (beach), France C 3 26
Omaha, Nebr. J 3 201
Oman G 4-6 60

Oman (gulf), Asia G 5 60
Omdurman, Sudan N 8 54
Omsk, U.S.S.R. H 4 46
Omuta, Japan E 7 74
Ondangua, S.W.Afr. K15 57

Onega (lake), U.S.S.R. E 2 50
Oneida, N.Y. J 4 212
Oneonta, N.Y. K 6 212
Onitsha, Nig. H10 54
Onon (riv.), Asia H 2 77

Onslow, Aust. B 4 86
Ontario, Calif. D10 140
Ontario (prov.), Can. 107,108-109
Ontario (lake), N.A. D-G 3 212
Ontario, Oreg. K 3 227

Ontong Java (atoll), Sol. Is. G 6 89
Ootacamund, India D 6 70
Opa-locka, Fla. B 4 148
Opava, Czech. D 2 39
Opelika, Ala. H 5 130
Opelousas, La. G 5 175
Opole, Pol. C 3 45
Oporto, Port. B 2 30
Opp, Ala. F 8 130
Oradea, Rum. E 2 43
Oradell, N.J. B 1 209
Oran, Alg. F 4 54
Orange (riv.), Afr. K17 57
Orange, Aust. H 6 86
Orange, Calif. D11 140
Orange, Conn. C 3 146
Orange, France F 5 26
Orange, Mass. E 2 184
Orange, N.J. B 2 209
Orange, Tex. L 7 238
Orangeburg, S.C. F 4 232
Orange Free State (prov.), S.Afr. M17 57
Orange Park, Fla. E 1 148
Orangeville, Ont. D 4 108
Orange Walk Town, Belize C 1 122
Oranjestad, Neth. Ant. D 4 124
Orava (riv.), Czech. E 2 39
Ord (riv.), Aust. D 3 86
Ordos (des.), China G 4 77
Ordzhonikidze, U.S.S.R. F 6 50
Örebro, Sweden J 7 16
Oregon, Ohio D 2 220
Oregon (state), U.S. 226-227
Oregon Caves N.M., Oreg. D 5 226
Oregon City, Oreg. B 2 226
Öregrund, Sweden L 6 16
Orel, U.S.S.R. E 4 50
Orem, Utah C 3 240
Orenburg, U.S.S.R. J 4 50
Orense, Spain C 1 30
Organ Pipe Cactus N.M., Ariz. C 6 134
Orillia, Ont. E 3 108
Orinoco (riv.), S.A. G 2 90
Orissa (state), India E-F 4-5 70
Oristano (gulf), Italy B 5 32
Orizaba, Mex. P 2 119
Orkney (isls.), Scot. E-F 1 13
Orlando, Fla. E 3 148
Orland Park, Ill. A 2 158
Orléans, France D 3 26
Orléans (isl.), Que. F 3 105
Orly, France B 2 26
Ormond Bch., Fla. E 2 148
Orne (riv.), France C 3 26
Oromocto, N.Br. D 3 102
Orono, Maine F 6 178
Orono, Minn. F 5 190
Orontes ('Asi) (riv.), Syria G 5 64
Oroville, Calif. D 4 140
Orrville, Ohio G 4 220
Orsk, U.S.S.R. J 4 50
Oruro, Bol. G 7 90
Osaka, Japan J 8 75
Osceola, Ark. K 2 139
Osh, U.S.S.R. H 5 46
Oshawa, Ont. F 4 108
Oshkosh, Wis. J 8 253
Oshogbo, Nig. H10 54
Oskaloosa, Iowa H 6 164
Oskarshamn, Sweden K 8 16
Oslo (cap.), Nor. D 3 16
Osnabrück, W.Ger. C 2 20
Osorno, Chile F12 93
Osoyoos, B.C. H 5 117
Ossining, N.Y. N 8 213
Ostend, Belg. B 6 25
Ostrava, Czech. E 2 39
Oswego, N.Y. G 4 212
Oświęcim, Pol. D 3 45
Otago (pen.), N.Z. L 7 87
Otaru, Japan K 2 75
Otavalo, Ecua. E 3 90
Otranto (str.), Europe D 5-6 43
Otsu, Japan J 7 75
Ottawa (cap.), Can. J 2 109
Ottawa (riv.), Can. J 6 96
Ottawa, Ill. E 2 158
Ottawa, Kans. G 3 169
Ottumwa, Iowa J 6 164
Ötztal Alps (mts.), Europe A 3 38
Ouachita (mts.), U.S. C 4 138
Ouagadougou (cap.), Upper Volta F 9 54
Ouahigouya, Upper Volta F 9 54
Ouargla, Alg. G 5 54
Oudtshoorn, S.Afr. L18 57
Ouezzane, Mor. E 5 54
Oujda, Mor. F 5 54
Oulu, Fin. O 4 16
Our (riv.), Europe J 8-9 25
Ouro Prêto, Braz. M 8 90
Ouse (riv.), Eng. G 4, G 6 11
Outer Hebrides (isls.), Scot. A 1 13
Outremont, Que. H 4 105
Ovalle, Chile F10 93
Ovamboland (reg.), S.W.Afr. J-K 15 57
Overijssel (prov.), Neth. J 4 25
Overland, Mo. P 3 197
Overland Park, Kans. H 3 169
Oviedo, Spain C 1 31
Owatonna, Minn. E 6 190
Owego, N.Y. H 6 212
Owensboro, Ky. G 5 172
Owen Sound, Ont. D 3 108
Owosso, Mich. E 5 186
Oxford, Eng. F 6 11
Oxford, Mass. G 4 184
Oxford, Miss. F 2 192
Oxford, N.C. M 2 217
Oxford, Ohio A 6 220
Oxnard, Calif. F 9 140
Oyapock (riv.), S.A. K 3 90
Oyo, Nig. G10 54
Oyster Bay, N.Y. S 6 213
Ozark, Ala. G 8 130
Ozark (mts.), U.S. H 3 126
Ozarks, Lake of the, Mo. G 6 197

P

Paarl, S.Afr. G19 57
Pabna, Bang. F 4 70
Pachuca, Mex. K 6 119
Pacifica, Calif. H 2 140
Pacific Grove, Calif. C 7 140
Pacific Islands, Territory of the D-G 5 88-89
Pacific Ocean 88-89
Pacific Palisades, Hawaii E 2 155
Padang, Indon. B 6 82
Paderborn, W.Ger. C 3 20
Padre I. N.Sea., Tex. G 10-11 238
Padua, Italy C 2 32
Paducah, Ky. D 6 172
Pagalu (isl.), Eq.Guin. G12 57
Pagedale, Mo. P 3 197
Pago Pago (cap.), Amer.Samoa J 7 89
Pahang (riv.), Malaysia D 7 81
Pahlevi, Iran F 2 68
Pahokee, Fla. F 5 148
Painesville, Ohio H 2 220
Painted (des.), Ariz. D-E 2-3 134
Paisley, Scot. B 2 13
Pakistan 70
Palatine, Ill. E 1 158
Palatka, Fla. E 2 148
Palau (isls.), T.T.P.I. D 5 88
Palawan (isl.), Phil. F 3-4 83
Palembang, Indon. D 6 83
Palencia, Spain D 2 31
Palenque, Mex. O 8 119
Palermo, Italy D 5 32
Palestine, Tex. J 6 238
Palisades Park, N.J. C 2 209
Palk (str.), Asia D 7 70
Palma, Spain H 3 31
Palmas (cape), Lib. E11 54
Palm Bay, Fla. F 3 148
Palm Beach, Fla. G 4 148
Palmdale, Calif. G 9 140
Palmer, Mass. E 4 184
Palmerston North, N.Z. M 6 87
Palmetto, Fla. D 4 148
Palm Sprs., Calif. J10 140
Palm Sprs., Fla. F 5 148
Palmyra, N.J. B 3 209
Palmyra, N.Y. F 4 212
Palmyra, Pa. J 5 230
Palmyra (Tadmor), Syria H 5 64
Palo Alto, Calif. K 3 140
Palos (cape), Spain F 4 31
Palos Hts., Ill. A 2 158
Palos Hills, Ill. A 2 158
Palos Verdes Estates, Calif. B11 140
Pamir (plat.), Asia K 2 61
Pampa, Tex. D 2 238
Pampas (plain), Arg. H 10-11 93
Pamplona, Spain F 1 31
Pana, Ill. D 4 158
Panama F-J 6 122-123
Panamá (cap.), Pan. H 6 123
Panamá (gulf), Pan. H 7 123
Panama City, Fla. C 6 148
Panay (isl.), Phil. G 3 83
P'anmunjŏm, Korea C 5 74
Pánuco, Mex. K 6 119
Papeete (cap.), Fr. Poly. M 7 89
Papillion, Nebr. J 3 201
Papua New Guinea B 7 82; E 6 89
Pará (state), Braz. K 4 90
Paradise, Nev. F 6 202
Paradise Valley, Ariz. D 5 134
Paragould, Ark. J 1 139
Paraguana (pen.), Ven. F 1 90
Paraguarí, Par. J 9 93
Paraguay H-J 8 90,93
Paraguay (riv.), S.A. J 8 93
Paraíba (João Pessoa), Braz. O 5 91
Paramaribo (cap.), Sur. K 2 90
Paramount, Calif. C11 140
Paramus, N.J. B 1 209
Paraná, Arg. J10 93
Paraná (riv.), S.A. J 9 93
Paranaíba, Braz. K 7 90
Pardubice, Czech. C 1 39
Paria (gulf) G 5 125
Parima (mts.), S.A. H 3 90
Paris (cap.), France B 2 26
Paris, Ill. F 4 158
Paris, Ky. N 4 173
Paris, Ont. D 4 108
Paris, Tenn. E 8 172
Paris, Tex. J 4 238
Park (range), Colo. F-G 1-4 145
Parker (dam), U.S. A 4 134
Parkersburg, W.Va. D 4 248
Parkes, Aust. H 6 86
Park Forest, Ill. B 3 158
Park Ridge, Ill. A 1 158
Park Ridge, N.J. B 1 209
Parkville, Md. M 3 181
Parma, Italy C 2 32
Parma, Ohio H 9 220
Parma Hts., Ohio G 9 220
Parnaíba, Braz. M 4 91
Parnassus (mt.), Greece F 6 43
Pärnu, U.S.S.R. C 1 51
Paro Dzong, Bhutan F 3 70
Paropamisus (mts.), Afgh. A 2 70
Páros (isl.), Greece G 7 43
Parramatta, Aust. L 3 87
Parris I. Marine Base, S.C. F 7 232
Parry (chan.), N.W.T. E-H 1 96
Parry Sound, Ont. E 2 108
Parsippany, N.J. E 2 209
Parsons, Kans. G 4 169
Pasadena, Calif. C10 140
Pasadena, Tex. J 2 238
Pascagoula, Miss. G10 192
Pasco, Wash. F 4 246
Pas-de-Calais (dept.), France D-E 2 26
Paso de los Toros, Urug. J10 93
Paso Robles, Calif. E 8 140
Passaic, N.J. E 2 209
Passamaquoddy (bay), N.A. C 3 102
Passau, W.Ger. E 4 20
Passo Fundo, Braz. K 9 93
Pasto, Col. E 3 90
Patagonia (reg.), Arg. F-G 12-14 93
Patapédia (riv.), Can. B 2 104
Patchogue, N.Y. P 9 213
Paterson, N.J. B 2 209
Patiala, India D 2 70
Pátmos (isl.), Greece H 7 43
Patna, India F 3 70
Patos (lagoon), Braz. K10 93
Pátrai, Greece E 6 43
Pau, France C 6 26
Paulsboro, N.J. C 4 209
Pauls Valley, Okla. M 5 225
Pavia, Italy B 2 32
Pavlodar, U.S.S.R. H 4 46
Pawcatuck, Conn. H 3 147
Pawtucket, R.I. J 5 184
Paysandú, Urug. J10 93
Pazardzhik, Bulg. F 4 43
Peabody, Mass. E 5 184
Peace (riv.), Can. E 4 96
Peace River, Alta. B 1 114
Pea Ridge N.M.P., Ark. B 1 138
Pearl (hbr.), Hawaii A 3 154
Pearland, Tex. J 2 238
Pearl City, Hawaii B 3 154
Pearl River, N.Y. M 8 213
Pearsall, Tex. E 9 238
Peary Land (reg.), Greenl. P 1 94
Peć, Yugo. E 4 43
Pechora (riv.), U.S.S.R. H 1 50
Pecos, Tex. D10 238
Pecos (riv.), U.S. F 4 126
Pecos N.M., N.Mex. D 3 210
Pécs, Hung. E 3 39
Pedernales (riv.), Tex. F 7 238
Peebles, Scot. E 5 13
Peekskill, N.Y. N 8 213
Peel, Isle of Man C 3 11
Pegasus (bay), N.Z. L 7 87
Pegu, Burma C 3 81
Peipus (lake), U.S.S.R. D 1 51
Pekin, Ill. D 3 158
Peking (cap.), China J 3 77
Pelée (vol.), Mart. G 4 125
Pelée (pt.), Ont. B 6 108
Pelham, N.H. E 6 204
Pelham Manor, N.Y. O 7 213
Pella, Iowa H 6 164
Pell City, Ala. F 3 130
Pelly (riv.), Yukon C 3 96
Pelotas, Braz. K10 93
Pemba (isl.), Tanz. P13 57
Pembroke, Mass. L 4 185
Pembroke, Ont. G 2 108
Pembroke, Wales C 6 11
Pembroke Pines, Fla. B 4 148
Pendembu, S. Leone D10 54
Pendleton, Oreg. J 2 227
Pend Oreille (lake), Idaho B 1 156
Penetanguishene, Ont. D 3 108
Penghu (isls.), China J 7 77
Penibética (mts.), Spain E 4 31
Pennine Alps (mts.), Europe D 5 37
Pennsauken, N.J. B 3 209
Penns Grove, N.J. C 4 209
Pennsylvania (state), U.S. 230-231
Penn Yan, N.Y. F 5 212
Penonomé, Pan. G 6 123
Penrhyn (Tongareva) (atoll), Cook Is. L 6 89
Penrith, Aust. K 3 87
Pensacola, Fla. B 6 148
Penticton, B.C. H 5 117
Pentland (firth), Scot. E 2 13
Penza, U.S.S.R. F 4 50
Penzance, Eng. B 7 11
Peoria, Ill. D 3 158
Peoria Hts., Ill. D 3 158
Pepperell, Mass. H 2 184
Pepper Pike, Ohio J 9 220
Pequannock, N.J. B 1 209
Perak (state), Malaysia D 6 81
Percé, Que. D 1 105
Perche (reg.), France D 3 26
Pereira, Col. E 3 90
Pergamino, Arg. M11 93
Péribonca (riv.), Que. C 3 106
Périgueux, France D 5 26
Perim (isl.), P.D.R.Y. D 7 60
Perkasie, Pa. M 5 231
Perlas (arch.), Pan. H 6 123
Perlis (state), Malaysia D 6 81
Perm', U.S.S.R. J 3 50
Pernambuco (Recife), Braz. O 5 91
Perpignan, France E 6 26
Perry, Fla. C 1 148
Perry, Ga. E 6 152
Perry, Iowa E 5 164
Perry, Okla. M 2 225
Perrysburg, Ohio C 2 220
Perry's Victory & Int'l Peace Mem. N.M., Ohio E 2 220
Perryton, Tex. D 1 238
Perryville, Mo. N 7 197
Persia (Iran) 68-69
Persian (gulf), Asia E-F 4 60
Perth, Aust. B 2 86
Perth, Ont. H 3 108
Perth, Scot. E 4 13
Perth Amboy, N.J. E 2 209
Perth-Andover, N. Br. C 2 102
Peru E-F 5-6 90
Peru, Ill. D 2 158
Peru, Ind. E 3 163
Perugia, Italy D 3 32
Pesaro, Italy D 3 32
Pescadores (Penghu) (isls.), China J 7 77
Pescara, Italy E 3 32
Peshawar, Pak. C 2 70
Petah Tiqwa, Isr. B 3 67
Petaluma, Calif. H 1 140
Petén-Itzá (lake), Guat. B 2 122
Peterborough, Eng. G 5 11
Peterborough, Ont. F 3 108
Peterhead, Scot. G 3 13
Petersburg, Alaska N 2 133
Petersburg, Va. N 6 243
Petitcodiac, N.Br. E 3 102
Petoskey, Mich. E 3 186
Petra (ruins), Jordan D 5 67
Petrified Forest N.P., Ariz. F 4 134
Petrolina, Braz. M 5 91
Petropavlovsk, U.S.S.R. G 4 46
Petrópolis, Braz. M 8 93
Petrozavodsk, U.S.S.R. D 2 50
Pforzheim, W.Ger. C 4 20
Phan Rang, Viet. F 5 81
Pharr, Tex. F11 238
Phenix City, Ala. H 6 130
Phet Buri, Thai. C 4 81
Phichit, Thai. D 3 81
Philadelphia, Miss. F 5 192
Philadelphia, Pa. N 6 231
Philippines H 3 83
Phillipsburg, N.J. C 2 209
Phnom Penh (cap.), Camb. E 5 81
Phoenix (cap.), Ariz. C 5 134
Phoenix (isls.), Gilb. Is. J 6 89
Phoenixville, Pa. L 5 231
Phsar Oudong, Camb. E 5 81
Phu Tho, Viet. E 2 81
Piacenza, Italy B 2 32
Piatra Neamţ, Rum. G 2 43
Piauí (state), Braz. M 5 90
Piave (riv.), Italy D 2 32
Picayune, Miss. E 9 192
Pico Rivera, Calif. C10 140
Picton, N.Z. L 6 87
Picton, Ont. G 3 108
Pictou, N.S. F 3 100
Pictured Rocks N.Lak., Mich. C 2 186
Piedmont, Ala. G 3 130
Piedmont, Calif. J 2 140
Piedmont (reg.), Italy A-B 2 32
Piedras Negras, Mex. J 2 119
Pierre (cap.), S.Dak. J 5 234
Pierrefonds, Que. H 4 105
Pietermaritzburg, S.Afr. N17 57
Pietersburg, S.Afr. N16 57
Pigeon (riv.) G 2 190
Pikes (peak), Colo. J 5 145
Pikesville, Md. M 3 181
Pikeville, Ky. S 6 173
Pilcomayo (riv.), S.A. H 8 93
Pinang, Malaysia C 6 81
Pinar del Río, Cuba A 2 124
Pindus (mts.), Greece E 6 43
Pine Bluff, Ark. F 5 139
Pine Hill, N.J. D 4 209
Pine Lawn, Mo. P 3 197
Pinellas Park, Fla. B 3 148
Pines, Isle of, Cuba A 2 124
Pines, Isle of, New Cal. G 8 89
Pineville, La. F 4 175
Pingsiang, China H 6 77
Pingtung, China K 7 77
Pinnacles N.M., Calif. D 7 140
Pinole, Calif. J 1 140
Pinsk, U.S.S.R. C 4 50
Piombino, Italy C 3 32
Piotrków, Pol. D 3 45
Pipe Spr. N.M., Ariz. C 2 134
Pipestone, Minn. B 7 190
Pipestone N.M., Minn. B 6 190
Piqua, Ohio B 5 220
Piraiévs, Greece F 7 43
Pírgos, Greece E 7 43
Pirmasens, W.Ger. B 4 20
Pisa, Italy C 3 32
Piscataway, N.J. D 2 209
Pisco, Peru E 6 90
Pistoia, Italy C 2 32
Pitcairn (isl.), Pacific O 8 89
Piteşti, Rum. G 3 43
Pitman, N.J. C 4 209
Pittsburg, Calif. L 1 140
Pittsburg, Kans. H 4 169
Pittsburgh, Pa. B 7 230
Pittsfield, Mass. A 3 184
Pittston, Pa. L 3 231
Piura, Peru D 5 90
Placentia, Calif. D11 140
Placentia, Newf. D 4 99
Placerville, Calif. C 8 140
Plainfield, Conn. H 2 147
Plainfield, Ind. E 5 163
Plainfield, N.J. E 2 209
Plainview, N.Y. O 9 213
Plainview, Tex. C 3 238
Plainville, Conn. D 2 146
Plano, Tex. H 4 238
Plantation, Fla. B 4 148
Plant City, Fla. D 3 148
Plaquemine, La. J 2 175
Plasencia, Spain C 2 31
Plata, Río de la (est.), S.A. J11 93
Platte (riv.), Nebr. E 4 201
Platteville, Wis. F10 253
Platt N.P., Okla. N 6 225
Plattsburgh, N.Y. O 1 213
Plattsmouth, Nebr. J 3 201
Plauen, E.Ger. E 3 20
Pleasant Grove, Utah C 3 240
Pleasant Hill, Calif. K 2 140
Pleasant Hills, Pa. B 7 230
Pleasanton, Calif. L 2 140
Pleasanton, Tex. F 9 238
Pleasantville, N.J. D 5 209
Pleasantville, N.Y. N 8 213
Pleasure Ridge Pk., Ky. J 4 173
Pleiku, Viet. E 4 81
Plenty (bay), N.Z. M 5 87
Plessisville, Que. F 3 105
Pleven, Bulg. G 4 43
Płock, Pol. D 2 45
Ploieşti, Rum. H 3 43
Plovdiv, Bulg. G 4 43
Plum, Pa. C 5 230
Plymouth, Conn. C 2 146
Plymouth, Eng. C 7 11
Plymouth, Ind. E 2 163
Plymouth, Mass. M 5 185
Plymouth, Mich. F 6 186
Plymouth, Minn. G 5 190
Plymouth (cap.), Montserrat F 3 124
Plymouth, Pa. K 3 231
Plymouth, Wis. L 8 253
Plzeň, Czech. B 2 38
Po (riv.), Italy C 2 32
Pobeda (peak), Asia J 5 46
Pocatello, Idaho F 7 156
Podol'sk, U.S.S.R. E 3 50
Pointe-à-Pitre, Guad. G 3 125
Pointe-Claire, Que. H 4 105
Pointe-Noire, Congo J12 57
Point Mugu Pacific Missile Range, Calif. F 9 140
Point Pelée N.P., Ont. B 6 108
Point Pleasant, N.J. E 3 209
Point Pleasant, W.Va. B 5 248
Point Reyes N.Sea., Calif. B 5 140
Poitiers, France D 4 26
Pokhara, Nepal E 3 70
Pola (Pula), Yugo. A 3 43
Poland 45
Poltava, U.S.S.R. D 5 50
Polynesia (reg.), Pacific J-M 3-8 89
Pomerania (reg.), Europe E-F 2 20
Pomona, Calif. D10 140
Pompano Bch., Fla. F 5 148
Pompeii (ruins), Italy F 4 32
Pompton Lakes, N.J. A 1 209
Ponape (isl.), T.T.P.I. F 5 89
Ponca City, Okla. M 1 225
Ponce, P.R. G 1 125
Pondicherry, India E 6 70
Ponta Grossa, Braz. K 9 93
Pontchartrain (lake), La. K 6 175
Pontecorvo, Italy D 4 32
Pontevedra, Spain B 1 30
Pontiac, Ill. E 3 158
Pontiac, Mich. F 6 186
Pontianak, Indon. D 6 83
Pontic (mts.), Turkey H-J 2 64
Pontine (isls.), Italy D 4 32
Pontoise, France E 3 26
Poona, India C 5 70
Poopó (lake), Bol. G 7 90
Popayán, Col. E 3 90
Poplar Bluff, Mo. L 9 197
Popocatépetl (mt.), Mex. M 1 119
Poquoson, Va. R 6 243
Porbandar, India B 4 70
Porcupine (riv.), N.A. B 2 96
Pordenone, Italy D 2 32
Pori, Fin. M 6 16
Porrentruy, Switz. C 2 36
Porsanger (fjord), Nor. O 1 16
Porsgrunn, Nor. G 7 16
Portage, Ind. C 1 163
Portage, Mich. D 6 186
Portage, Wis. G 8 253
Portage la Prairie, Man. D 4 110
Port Alberni, B.C. H 3 117
Portales, N.Mex. F 4 210
Port Allen, La. J 2 175
Port Angeles, Wash. B 2 246
Port Antonio, Jam. C 3 124
Port Arthur, China K 4 77
Port Arthur, Tex. K 8 238
Port Augusta, Aust. F 6 86
Port au Port (pen.), Newf. A 3 99
Port-au-Prince (cap.), Haiti D 3 124
Port Blair, India G 6 71
Port-Cartier, Que. D 2 106
Port Charlotte, Fla. D 5 148

Port Chester, N.Y.	P 7	213
Port Clinton, Ohio	E 2	220
Port Elizabeth, S.Afr.	M18	57
Porterville, Calif.	G 7	140
Port Everglades (hbr.), Fla.	C 4	148
Port Fairy, Aust.	G 7	86
Port-Francqui, Zaire	L12	57
Port-Gentil, Gabon	H12	57
Port Harcourt, Nig.	H11	54
Port Hawkesbury, N.S.	G 3	100
Port Hedland, Aust.	B 3	86
Port Hueneme, Calif.	F 9	140
Port Huron, Mich.	G 6	186
Port Jefferson, N.Y.	P 9	213
Port Jervis, N.Y.	L 8	213
Port Kembla, Aust.	L 4	87
Portland, Conn.	E 2	146
Portland (pen.), Eng.	E 7	11
Portland, Ind.	H 4	163
Portland, Maine	C 8	178
Portland, Oreg.	B 2	226
Portland, Tex.	G10	238
Portlaoighise, Ire.	G 5	15
Port Lavaca, Tex.	H 9	238
Port Lincoln, Aust.	E 6	86
Port Louis (cap.), Mauritius	S19	57
Port-Lyautey (Kénitra), Mor.	E 5	54
Port Macquarie, Aust.	J 6	86
Port Maria, Jam.	C 3	124
Port Melbourne, Aust.	K 2	87
Port-Menier, Que.	E 3	106
Port Moody, B.C.	L 3	117
Port Moresby (cap.), P.N.G.	B 7	82
Port Neches, Tex.	K 7	238
Port Nolloth, S.Afr.	K17	57
Porto (Oporto), Port.	B 2	30
Pôrto Alegre, Braz.	K10	93
Porto Amélia, Moz.	P14	57
Portofino, Italy	B 2	32
Port-of-Spain (cap.), T.&T.	G 5	125
Portola Valley, Calif.	J 3	140
Porto-Novo (cap.), Benin	G10	54
Portoviejo, Ecua.	D 4	90
Port Pirie, Aust.	F 6	86
Port Said, Egypt	N 5	54
Port Shepstone, S.Afr.	N18	57
Portsmouth, Eng.	G 7	11
Portsmouth, N.H.	E 5	92
Portsmouth, Ohio	D 8	220
Portsmouth, R.I.	J 6	184
Portsmouth, Va.	N 7	243
Port Sudan, Sudan	O 8	55
Port Swettenham, Malaysia	D 7	81
Port Talbot, Wales	D 6	11
Port Townsend,	C 2	109
Wash.	C 2	246
Portugal		30
Port-Vendres, France	E 6	26
Port Vue, Pa.	C 7	230
Port Washington, Wis.	L 9	253
Port Weld, Malaysia	D 6	81
Posadas, Arg.	J 9	93
Poschiavo, Switz.	J 4	37
Posen, Ill.	B 2	158
Potchefstroom, S.Afr.	M17	57
Poteau, Okla.	S 4	225
Potenza, Italy	F 4	32
Potomac (riv.), U.S.	M 8	181
Potosí, Bol.	G 7	90
Potsdam, E.Ger.	E 2	20
Potsdam, N.Y.	K 1	212
Pottstown, Pa.	L 5	231
Pottsville, Pa.	K 4	231
Poughkeepsie, N.Y.	N 7	213
Povungnituk, Que.	E 1	106
Powder (riv.), U.S.	E 2	126
Powell (lake), U.S.	D 6	240
Powell River, B.C.	E 5	117
Poyang (lake), China	J 6	77
Poznań, Pol.	C 2	45
Prague (Praha) (cap.), Czech.	C 1	38
Prairie du Chien, Wis.	D 9	253
Prairie Village, Kans.	H 2	169
Pratt, Kans.	D 4	168
Prattville, Ala.	E 6	130
Prescott, Ariz.	C 4	134
Prescott, Ont.	J 3	109
Presidente Prudente, Braz.	K 8	90
Presidio, Tex.	C12	238
Prespa (lake), Europe	E 5	42
Presque Isle, Maine	H 2	178
Preston, Aust.	L 1	87
Preston, Eng.	E 4	11
Prestwick, Scot.	D 5	13
Pretoria (cap.), S.Afr.	M17	57
Préveza, Greece	E 6	43
Prey Veng, Camb.	E 5	81
Pribilof (isls.), Alaska	D 3	133
Příbram, Czech.	B 2	38
Price, Utah	D 4	240
Prichard, Ala.	B 9	130
Prilep, Yugo.	E 5	43
Prince Albert, Sask.	F 2	113
Prince Charles (isl.), N.W.T.	J 2	96
Prince Edward (isls.), S.Afr.		5
Prince Edward Island (prov.), Can.	E-F 2	100
Prince George, B.C.	F 3	117
Prince of Wales (isl.), N.W.T.	G 1	96
Prince Patrick (isl.), N.W.T.	M 3	97
Prince Rupert, B.C.	B 3	116
Princeton, B.C.	G 5	117
Princeton, Ill.	D 2	158
Princeton, Ind.	B 8	163
Princeton, Ky.	F 6	172
Princeton, N.J.	D 3	209
Princeton, W.Va.	D 8	248
Príncipe (isl.), São T.&P.	H11	57
Priština, Yugo.	E 4	43
Prizren, Yugo.	E 4	43
Progreso, Mex.	P 6	119
Prokop'yevsk, U.S.S.R.	J 4	46
Promontory, Utah	B 2	240
Proserpine, Aust.	H 4	86
Prospect, Conn.	D 2	146
Prospect Park, N.J.	B 1	209
Prospect Park, Pa.	M 7	231
Prostějov, Czech.	D 2	39
Providence (cap.), R.I.	H 5	184
Providencia (isl.), Col.	B 4	124
Provincetown, Mass.	O 4	185
Provo, Utah	C 3	240
Prudhoe (bay), Alaska	J 1	133
Prudhoe Land (reg.), Greenl.	M 2	94
Pruszków, Pol.	E 2	45
Prut (riv.), Europe	J 2	43
Pryor, Okla.	R 2	225
Przemyśl, Pol.	F 4	45
Pskov, U.S.S.R.	C 3	50
Puebla, Mex.	N 2	119
Pueblo, Colo.	K 6	145
Puente-Genil, Spain	D 4	31
Puerto Aisén, Chile	F13	93
Puerto Ángel, Mex.	L 9	119
Puerto Ayacucho, Ven.	G 2	90
Puerto Barrios, Guat.	C 3	122
Puerto Cabello, Ven.	G 1	90
Puerto Colombia, Col.	E 1	90
Puerto Cortés, Hond.	D 2	122
Puerto de Hierro, Ven.	H 1	90
Puerto Deseado, Arg.	G13	93
Puerto La Cruz, Ven.	H 1	90
Puertollano, Spain	D 3	31
Puerto Montt, Chile	F12	93
Puerto Peñasco, Mex.	C 1	118
Puerto Plata, Dom.Rep.	D 3	124
Puerto Princesa, Phil.	F 4	83
Puerto Real, Spain	D 4	31
Puerto Rico	F-G 1	125
Puerto Suárez, Bol.	J 7	90
Puget (sound), Wash.	C 3	246
Pukapuka (atoll), Cook Is.	K 7	89
Pula, Yugo.	A 3	43
Pulaski, Tenn.	G10	172
Pulaski, Va.	G 6	242
Pulicat (lake), India	E 6	70
Pullman, Wash.	H 4	247
Punakha, Bhutan	G 3	70
Punjab (state), India	C-D 2	70
Punjab (reg.), Pak.	C 2-3	70
Puno, Peru	F 7	90
Punta Arenas, Chile	F14	93
Puntarenas, C.R.	E 6	122
Punxsutawney, Pa.	E 4	230
Puri, India	F 5	70
Pursat, Camb.	D 4	81
Purulia, India	F 4	70
Purus (riv.), S.A.	H 5	90
Pusan, S.Korea	D 6	74
Pushkin, U.S.S.R.	C 3	50
Putnam, Conn.	H 1	147
Puttalam, Sri Lanka	D 7	70
Putumayo (riv.), S.A.	F 4	90
Puyallup, Wash.	C 3	246
Puy-de-Dôme (mt.), France	E 5	26
Pye, Burma	B 3	81
P'yŏngyang (cap.), N.Korea	C 4	74
Pyramid (lake), Nev.	B 2	202
Pyrenees (mts.), Europe	F-H 1	31
Pyuthan, Nepal	E 3	70

Q

Qatar	F 4	60
Qattâra (depr.), Egypt	M 6	54
Qena, Egypt	N 6	54
Qiryat Gat, Isr.	B 4	67
Qiryat Motzkin, Isr.	C 2	67
Qiryat Shemona, Isr.	C 1	67
Qiryat Yam, Isr.	C 2	67
Qishm (isl.), Iran	J 7	68
Qishn, P.D.R.Y.	F 6	60
Quakertown, Pa.	M 5	231
Quang Ngai, Viet.	F 4	81
Quang Tri, Viet.	E 3	81
Quantico M.C.A.S., Va.	O 4	243
Qu'Appelle (riv.), Sask.	J 5	113
Québec (prov.), Can.		104-105, 106
Québec (cap.), Que.	H 3	105
Queen Charlotte (isls.), B.C.	B 3-4	116
Queen Elizabeth (isls.), N.W.T.	M 2	97
Queens (borough), N.Y.	N 9	213
Queensland (state), Aust.	G 4	86
Queenstown, Aust.	G 8	86
Queenstown (Cóbh), Ire.	E 8	15
Quelimane, Moz.	O15	57
Quemoy (isl.), China	J 7	77
Querétaro, Mex.	K 6	119
Quesnel, B.C.	F 4	117
Quetico Prov. Pk., Ont.	B 3	107
Quetta, Pak.	B 2	70
Quezaltenango, Guat.	B 3	122
Quezon City (cap.), Phil.	G 3	83
Quibdó, Col.	E 2	90
Quiberon, France	B 4	26
Quillacollo, Bol.	G 7	90
Quilon, India	D 7	70
Quimper, France	A 4	26
Quincy, Fla.	B 1	148
Quincy, Ill.	B 4	158
Quincy, Mass.	D 7	184
Qui Nhon, Viet.	F 4	81
Quintana Roo (state), Mex.	P 7	119
Quirindi, Aust.	H 6	86
Quito (cap.), Ecua.	E 3	90
Qum, Iran	G 3	68

R

Raahe, Fin.	O 4	16
Rabat (cap.), Mor.	E 5	54
Rabaul, P.N.G.	F 6	89
Race (cape), Newf.	D 4	99
Rach Gia, Viet.	E 5	81
Racibórz, Pol.	C 3	45
Racine, Wis.	M 3	253
Radcliff, Ky.	K 5	173
Radford, Va.	G 6	242
Radium Hill, Aust.	G 6	86
Radom, Pol.	E 3	45
Radville, Sask.	G 6	113
Rae-Edzo, N.W.T.	E 3	96
Ragusa, Italy	E 6	32
Ragusa (Dubrovnik), Yugo.	C 4	43
Rahway, N.J.	E 2	209
Raiatea (isl.), Fr.Poly.	L 7	89
Rainbow Bridge N.M., Utah	C 6	240
Rainier (mt.), Wash.	D 4	246
Rainy (lake), N.A.	E 2	190
Rainy (riv.), N.A.	D 2	190
Raivavae (isl.), Fr.Poly.	M 8	89
Rajahmundry, India	E 5	70
Rajasthan (state), India	C 3	70
Rajkot, India	C 4	70
Rajpur, India	F 2	70
Rajshahi, Bang.	F 4	70
Raleigh (cap.), N.C.	H 3	217
Ramallah, Jordan	C 4	67
Ramat Gan, Isr.	B 3	67
Rambouillet, France	D 3	26
Ramla, Isr.	B 4	67
Ramsey, Isle of Man	C 3	11
Ramsey, N.J.	B 1	209
Ramsgate, Eng.	J 6	11
Rancagua, Chile	F10	93
Ranchi, India	F 4	70
Rancho Cordova, Calif.	C 8	140
Randallstown, Md.	L 3	181
Randers, Den.	C 5	19
Randolph, Mass.	D 8	184
Randwick, Aust.	L 3	87
Rangoon (cap.), Burma	C 3	81
Rantoul, Ill.	E 3	158
Rapa (isl.), Fr.Poly.	M 8	89
Rapallo, Italy	B 2	32
Rapa Nui (Easter) (isl.), Chile	Q 8	89
Rapidan (riv.), Va.	M 4	243
Rapid City, S.Dak.	C 5	234
Rappahannock (riv.), Va.	P 4	243
Raritan, N.J.	D 2	209
Raritan (riv.), N.J.	D 2	209
Raroia (atoll), Fr.Poly.	M 7	89
Rarotonga (isl.), Cook Is.	K 8	89
Ras Dashan (mt.), Eth.	O 9	55
Ras Tanura, Saudi Ar.	F 4	60
Raton, N.Mex.	E 2	210
Ravenna, Italy	D 2	32
Ravenna, Ohio	H 3	220
Ravensburg, W.Ger.	C 5	20
Ravi (riv.), Asia	C 2	70
Rawalpindi, Pak.	C 2	70
Rawlins, Wyo.	E 4	254
Ray (cape), Newf.	A 4	99
Raymondville, Tex.	G11	238
Rayne, La.	F 6	175
Raynham, Mass.	K 5	184
Raytown, Mo.	P 6	197
Ré (isl.), France	C 4	26
Reading, Eng.	G 8	11
Reading, Mass.	C 5	184
Reading, Ohio	C 9	220
Reading, Pa.	L 5	231
Readville, Mass.	C 8	184
Real (mts.), S.A.	G 7	90
Recife, Braz.	O 5	91
Recklinghausen, W.Ger.	B 3	20
Reconquista, Arg.	H 9	93
Red (sea)	B-D 4-7	60
Red (riv.), Asia	E 2	81
Red (riv.), U.S.	H 4	126
Red Bank, N.J.	E 3	209
Red Bank, Tenn.	L10	173
Red Bluff, Calif.	C 3	140
Red Deer, Alta.	D 3	114
Red Deer (riv.), Alta.	D 4	114
Redding, Calif.	C 3	140
Redding, Conn.	B 3	146
Red Hill (mt.), Hawaii	J 2	155
Red Lake (riv.), Minn.	B-C 2	190
Redlands, Calif.	H 9	140
Red Lion, Pa.	J 6	230
Redmond, Wash.	B 1	246
Red Oak, Iowa	C 6	164
Redondo Bch., Calif.	B11	140
Red River of the North (riv.), U.S.	A 2	190
Red Volta (riv.), Afr.	F 9	54
Red Wing, Minn.	F 6	190
Redwood City, Calif.	J 3	140
Redwood N.P., Calif.	A 2	140
Ree (lake), Ire.	F 5	15
Reedley, Calif.	F 7	140
Regensburg, W.Ger.	E 4	20
Reggio, Italy	C 2, E 5	32
Regina (cap.), Sask.	G 5	113
Registan (des.), Afgh.	A-B 2	70
Rehoboth, Mass.	K 5	184
Rehovot, Isr.	B 4	67
Reidsville, N.C.	F 2	217
Reigate, Eng.	H 8	11
Reims, France	E 3	26
Reindeer (lake), Can.	N 3	113
Remagen, W. Ger.	B 3	20
Remscheid, W.Ger.	B 3	20
Renfrew, Ont.	H 2	108
Renfrew, Scot.	C 2	13
Rennes, France	C 3	26
Reno, Nev.	B 3	202
Rensselaer, N.Y.	N 5	213
Renton, Wash.	B 2	246
Republican (riv.), U.S.	F 2	126
Repulse Bay, N.W.T.	H 2	96
Reseda, Calif.	B10	140
Resht, Iran	F 2	68
Resistencia, Arg.	H 9	93
Reşiţa, Rum.	E 3	43
Resolute Bay, N.W.T.	G 1	96
Resolution (isl.), N.W.T.	K 3	96
Restigouche (riv.), Can.	C 1	102
Reston, Va.	O 3	243
Retalhuleu, Guat.	B 3	122
Réunion	R20	57
Reutlingen, W.Ger.	C 4	20
Revelstoke, B.C.	J 5	117
Revere, Mass.	D 6	184
Revillagigedo (isls.), Mex.	C 7	118
Rewa, India	E 4	70
Rexburg, Idaho	G 6	156
Reykjavík (cap.), Ice.	B 1	19
Reynoldsburg, Ohio	E 6	220
Reza'iyeh, Iran	D 2	68
Rhaetian Alps (mts.), Europe	J-K 3-4	37
Rheydt, W.Ger.	B 3	20
Rhine (riv.), Europe	E 4	6
Rhinelander, Wis.	H 4	253
Rhineland-Palatinate (state), W.Ger.	B 4	20
Rhode Island(state),U.S.		184
Rhodes (Ródhos), Greece	J 7	43
Rhodesia	M15	57
Rhodope (mts.), Europe	G 5	43
Rhön (mts.), Ger.	D 3	20
Rhondda, Wales	A 6	11
Rhône (riv.), Europe	E 4	6
Rialto, Calif.	E10	140
Riau (arch.), Indon.	C 5	83
Ribeirão Prêto, Braz.	L 8	90
Riberalta, Bol.	G 6	90
Rice Lake, Wis.	C 5	253
Richardson, Tex.	G 1	238
Richfield, Minn.	G 6	190
Richibucto, N.Br.	E 2	102
Richland, Wash.	F 4	246
Ricland Ctr., Wis.	F 9	253
Richland Hills, Tex.	F 2	238
Richmond, Aust.	L 2	87
Richmond, Calif.	J 1	140
Richmond, Ind.	H 5	163
Richmond, Ky.	N 5	173
Richmond, Tex.	J 8	238
Richmond (cap.), Va.	O 5	243
Richmond Hts., Mo.	P 3	197
Richmond Hts., Ohio	H 9	220
Richmond-upon-Thames, Eng.	H 8	11
Rideau (riv.), Ont.	J 3	109
Ridgecrest, Calif.	H 8	140
Ridgefield, Conn.	B 3	146
Ridgefield, N.J.	B 2	209
Ridgefield Park, N.J.	B 2	209
Ridgewood, N.J.	B 1	209
Ridgway, Pa.	E 3	230
Riding Mtn. N.P., Man.	B 4	110
Ridley Park, Pa.	M 7	231
Ried, Aus.	B 2	38
Riehen, Switz.	E 1	37
Rieti, Italy	D 3	32
Riga, U.S.S.R.	C 2	51
Rigi (mt.), Switz.	F 2	37
Riihimäki, Fin.	O 6	16
Rijeka, Yugo.	B 3	43
Rimini, Italy	D 2	32
Rimouski, Que.	J 1	105
Ringwood, N.J.	E 1	209
Riobamba, Ecua.	E 4	90
Río Caribe, Ven.	H 1	90
Rio de Janeiro, Braz.	M 8	93
Río de Oro (reg.), Sp.Sahara	D 7	54
Rio Grande, Braz.	K10	93
Rio Grande (riv.), N.A.	F-G 5	126
Riohacha, Col.	F 1	90
Río Muni (reg.), Eq.Guin.	J11	57
Río Negro (prov.), Arg.	G12	93
Rio Tinto, Braz.	O 5	91
Ripon, Wis.	J 8	253
Rishon Le Ziyyon, Isr.	B 4	67
Rittman, Ohio	G 4	220
Rivas, Nic.	E 5	122
Rivera, Urug.	J10	93
Riverdale, Ill.	B 2	158
Riverdale, Md.	F 4	180
River Edge, N.J.	B 1	209
River Falls, Wis.	A 6	253
River Forest, Ill.	B 2	158
River Grove, Ill.	A 2	158
Riverhead, N.Y.	P 9	213
River Oaks, Tex.	E 2	238
River Rouge, Mich.	B 7	186
Riverside, Calif.	E11	140
Riverside, Conn.	A 4	146
Riverside, Ill.	B 2	158
Riverton, Wyo.	D 2	254
Riverview, Mich.	B 7	186
Riviera (reg.), Europe	G 6	26
Riviera Bch., Fla.	G 5	148
Rivière-du-Loup, Que.	H 2	105
Road Town (cap.), B.V.I.	H 1	125
Roanoke, Ala.	H 4	130
Roanoke (isl.), N.C.	T 3	217
Roanoke, Va.	H 6	242
Roanoke Rapids, N.C.	K 2	217
Robbins, Ill.	B 2	158
Robbinsdale, Minn.	G 5	190
Robertsport, Lib.	D10	54
Roberval, Que.	E 1	105
Robinson, Ill.	F 5	158
Robstown, Tex.	G10	238
Rocha, Urug.	K10	93
Rochefort, France	C 4	26
Rochelle, Ill.	D 2	158
Rochelle Park, N.J.	B 2	209
Rochester, Eng.	J 8	11
Rochester, Mich.	F 6	186
Rochester, Minn.	F 6	190
Rochester, N.H.	E 5	204
Rochester, N.Y.	E 4	212
Rock (riv.), Wis.	J 9	253
Rockall (isl.), Scot.	C 3	6
Rockaway, N.J.	D 2	209
Rockcliffe Park, Ont.	J 2	109
Rockdale, Aust.	L 3	87
Rock Falls, Ill.	D 2	158
Rockford, Ill.	D 1	158
Rockhampton, Aust.	J 4	86
Rock Hill, Mo.	P 3	197
Rock Hill, S.C.	E 2	232
Rockingham, N.C.	F 5	217
Rockingham, Vt.	C 5	204
Rock Island, Ill.	C 2	158
Rockland, Maine	E 7	178
Rockland, Mass.	L 4	184
Rockledge, Fla.	F 3	148
Rockport, Mass.	M 2	185
Rock Sprs., Wyo.	C 4	254
Rockville, Md.	K 4	181
Rockville Centre, N.Y.	R 7	213
Rockwood, Tenn.	M 9	173
Rocky (mts.), N.A.	F-H 4-6	94
Rocky Hill, Conn.	E 2	146
Rocky Mount, N.C.	K 3	217
Rocky Mtn. House, Alta.	C 3	114
Rocky Mtn. N.P., Colo.	H 2	145
Rocky River, Ohio	G 9	220
Rodez, France	E 5	26
Ródhos, Greece	J 7	43
Rodrigues (isl.), Mauritius	K11	58
Roeland Park, Kans.	H 2	169
Roeselare, Belg.	C 7	25
Rogers, Ark.	B 1	138
Roger Williams N.Mem., R.I.	J 5	184
Rogue (riv.), Oreg.	C 5	226
Rohnert Park, Calif.	C 5	140
Rolla, Mo.	J 7	197
Rolling Hills Estates, Calif.	B11	140
Rolling Meadows, Ill.	A 1	158
Roma, Aust.	H 5	86
Romanshorn, Switz.	H 1	37
Rome, Ga.	B 2	152
Rome (cap.), Italy	F 6	32
Rome, N.Y.	J 4	212
Romeoville, Ill.	E 2	158
Ronda, Spain	D 4	31
Rondeau Prov. Pk., Ont.	C 5	108
Rondônia (terr.), Braz.	H 6	90
Rønne, Den.	F 9	19
Roosevelt (riv.), Braz.	H 5	90
Roosevelt (isl.), Ant.	A10	88
Roosevelt Campobello Int'l Pk., N.Br.	D 4	102
Roraima (terr.), Braz.	H 2	90
Rorschach, Switz.	H 2	37
Rosa (mt.), Europe	A 1	32
Rosario, Arg.	H10	93
Rosario, Mex.	G 5	119
Roscommon, Ire.	E 4	15
Roseau (cap.), Dominica	G 4	125
Roseburg, Oreg.	D 4	226
Roseland, N.J.	A 2	209
Roselle, Ill.	E 1	158
Roselle, N.J.	B 2	209
Roselle Park, N.J.	A 2	209
Rosemead, Calif.	D10	140
Rosenberg, Tex.	J 8	238
Rosetown, Sask.	D 4	113
Rosetta, Egypt	B 3	60
Roseville, Calif.	B 8	140
Roseville, Mich.	G 6	186
Roseville, Minn.	G 5	190
Rosignol, Guyana	J 2	90
Roslyn, N.Y.	B 2	95
Ross (sea), Ant.	B10	88
Ross (lake), Wash.	D 2	246
Rossford, Ohio	C 2	220
Ross Lake N.R.A., Wash.	E 2	246
Rossland, B.C.	H 6	117
Rosso, Mauritania	C 8	54
Rosthern, Sask.	E 3	113
Rostock, E.Ger.	E 1	20
Rostov, U.S.S.R.	E 3	50
Roswell, Ga.	D 2	152
Roswell, N.Mex.	E 5	210
Rothenburg, W. Ger.	D 4	20
Rothesay, Scot.	A 2	13
Roti (isl.), Indon.	G 8	83
Rotorua, N.Z.	M 6	87
Rotterdam, Neth.	E 5	25
Rottweil, W.Ger.	C 4	20
Rotuma (isl.), Fiji	H 7	89
Roubaix, France	E 2	26
Rouen, France	D 3	26
Rouyn, Que.	B 3	106
Rovaniemi, Fin.	O 3	16

Rovereto, Italy C 2 32
Rovigo, Italy C 2 32
Rovno, U.S.S.R. C 4 50
Roxboro, N.C. H 2 217
Roxbury, Mass. C 7 184

Roxbury, N.J. D 2 209
Roy, Utah C 2 240
Royale, Isle, Mich. E 1 186
Royal Gorge (canyon), Colo. J 6 145
Royal Oak, Mich. B 6 186

Ruapehu (mt.), N.Z. L 6 87
Rub' al Khali (des.), Asia E-F 5 60
Ruda Śląska, Pol. B 4 45
Rudolstadt, E.Ger. D 3 20

Rufiji (riv.), Tanz. O13 57
Rufisque, Sen. C 9 54
Rufus Woods (lake), Wash. F 2 246
Rugby, Eng. F 5 11
Rügen (isl.), E.Ger. E 1 20

Ruhr (riv.), W. Ger. B 3 20
Rukwa (lake), Tanz. N13 57
Rum (cay), Bah. C 2 124
Rum (isl.), Scot. B 3 13
Rumania F-J 3 43

Rumford, Maine B 6 178
Rum Jungle, Aust. E 2 86
Rumson, N.J. F 3 209
Runnemede, N.J. C 4 209
Rupert (riv.), Que. B 2 106

Rupununi (riv.), Guyana J 3 90
Ruse, Bulg. H 4 43
Rushville, Ind. G 5 163
Russell, Kans. D 3 168
Russell Cave N.M., Ala. G 1 130

Russellville, Ala. C 2 130
Russellville, Ark. D 3 138
Russellville, Ky. H 7 172
Russian S.F.S.R., U.S.S.R. D-S 3-4 46

Ruston, La. E 1 174
Rutherford, N.J. B 2 209
Rutland, Vt. B 4 204
Ruvuma (riv.), Afr. O14 57
Ruwenzori (mts.), Afr. N11 57

Rwanda N12 57
Ryazan', U.S.S.R. E 4 50
Rybinsk, U.S.S.R. E 3 50
Ryde, Aust. L 3 87
Rye, N.Y. P 7 213

Ryukyu (isls.), Japan K-O 5-7 75
Rzeszów, Pol. E 3 45
Rzhev, U.S.S.R. D 3 50

S

's Gravenhage (The Hague) (cap.), Neth. E 4 25
's Hertogenbosch, Neth. G 5 25
Saale (riv.), E.Ger. D 3 20
Saar (riv.), Europe B 4 20

Saarbrücken, W.Ger. B 4 20
Saaremaa (isl.), U.S.S.R. B 1 51
Saarland (state), W.Ger. B 4 20
Saba (isl.), Neth.Ant. F 3 124
Sabadell, Spain H 2 31

Sabah (state), Malaysia F 4 83
Sabinas, Mex. J 3 119
Sabine (riv.), U.S. L 7 238
Sable (cape), Fla. E 6 148
Sable (cape), N.S. C 5 100

Sable (isl.), N.S. J 5 101
Sabzawar, Afgh. A 2 70
Sabzawar, Iran K 2 68
Sacajawea (lake), Wash. G 4 247
Sackville, N.Br. F 3 102

Saco, Maine C 8 178
Sacramento (cap.), Calif. B 8 140
Sacramento (riv.), Calif. D 5 140
Sacramento (mts.), N.Mex. D 6 210

Saddle Brook, N.J. B 1 209
Safford, Ariz. F 6 134
Safi, Mor. E 5 54
Saga, Japan E 7 74
Sagaing, Burma B 2 81

Sagamore Hill N.H.S., N.Y. S 6 213
Sagar, India D 4 70
Saginaw, Mich. F 5 186
Sagua la Grande, Cuba B 2 124
Saguaro N.M., Ariz. E 6 134

Saguenay (riv.), Que. G 1 105
Saguia el Hamra (reg.), Sp.Sahara D-E 6 54
Sagunto, Spain F 3 31
Sahara (des.), Afr. E-M 7 54

Saharanpur, India D 3 70
Sahuaripa, Mex. E 2 118
Saigon (Ho Chi Minh City), Viet. E 5 81
Saint Albans, Eng. H 7 11

St. Albans, Vt. A 2 204
St. Albans, W.Va. C 6 248
St. Albert, Alta. D 3 114
St. Andrews, N.Br. C 3 102
St. Andrews, Scot. F 4 13

St. Ann, Mo. O 2 197
St. Anthony Falls, Minn. G 5 190
St. Arnaud, Aust. G 7 86
St. Augustine, Fla. E 2 148
St. Austell, Eng. C 7 11

St-Barthélémy (isl.), Guad. F 3 124
St. Bernard, Ohio B 9 220
St. Boniface, Man. F 5 110
St. Catharines, Ont. E 4 108
St. Charles, Ill. E 2 158

St. Charles, Mo. O 2 197
St. Christopher (isl.), St.C.-N.-A. F 3 124
St. Christopher-Nevis-Anguilla F 3 124

St. Clair (lake), N.A. G 6 186
St. Clair Shores, Mich. G 6 186
St. Cloud, Fla. E 3 148
St-Cloud, France A 2 26
St. Cloud, Minn. D 5 190

St. Croix (isl.), V.I. H 2 125
St. Croix (riv.), U.S. A 4 253
St. Croix I. N.M., Maine J 5 178
St-Denis, France B 1 26
St-Denis (cap.), Réunion P20 57

Ste-Agathe, Que. C 3 105
Ste-Anne-de-Beaupré, Que. F 2 105
Ste-Foy, Que. H 3 105
Ste-Geneviève, Que. H 4 105
St. Elias (mt.), N.A. K 2 133

Ste-Marie (cape), Madag. P17 57
Ste-Marie (isl.), Madag. S15 57
Ste-Mère-Église, France C 3 26
Ste-Scholastique, Que. C 4 105
Ste-Thérèse, Que. H 4 105

St-Étienne, France F 5 26
St. Eustatius (isl.), Neth.Ant. F 3 124
St-Florent (gulf), France B 6 26
St. Francis, Wis. M 2 253

St. George, Berm. H 2 125
St. George (cape), Newf. A 3 99
St. George, Utah A 6 240
St. George's (chan.), Europe B 5 11
St. George's (cap.), Grenada F 5 124

St-Germain, France D 3 26
St. Gotthard (tunnel), Switz. G 3 37
Saint Helena 5
St. Helena (isl.), S.C. F 7 232
St. Helens, Eng. G 2 11

St. Helens, Oreg. E 2 226
St. Helens (mt.), Wash. C 4 246
St. Helier (cap.), Chan.Is. E 8 11
St-Hyacinthe, Que. D 4 105
St. James, Man. E 5 110

St-Jean, Que. D 4 105
St-Jean (lake), Que. E 1 105
St-Jérôme, Que. H 4 105
St. John, Mo. P 2 197
Saint John, N. Br. E 3 102

St. John (riv.), N.A. C 2 102; G 1 178
St. John (isl.), V.I. H 1 125
St. Johns (cap.), Antigua G 3 125
St. Johns (riv.), Fla. E 2 148
St. Johns, Mich. E 6 186

St. John's (cap.), Newf. D 4 99
St. Johnsbury, Vt. D 3 204
St. Joseph, Mich. C 6 186
St. Joseph, Mo. C 3 197
St-Joseph, Que. D 3 105

St. Kilda, Aust. L 2 87
St. Kitts (St. Christopher) (isl.), St.C.-N.-A. F 3 124
St-Laurent, Que. H 4 105
St. Lawrence (isl.), Alaska D 2 132

St. Lawrence (gulf), Can. K 6 97
St. Lawrence (riv.), N.A. K 6 97
St-Lô, France C 3 26
St. Louis, Mo. P 3 197
St-Louis, Sen. C 8 54

St. Louis Park, Minn. G 5 190
Saint Lucia G 4 125
St-Malo, France B 3 26
St. Martin (isl.), Guad. & Neth. Ant. F 3 124

St. Martinville, La. G 6 175
St. Marys, Ohio B 4 220
St. Marys, Pa. E 3 230
St. Matthews, Ky. K 4 173
St-Maurice (riv.), Que. E 2 105

St-Mihiel, France F 3 26
St. Moritz, Switz. J 3 37
St-Nazaire, France B 4 26
St. Paul (cap.), Minn. G 6 190
St. Paul Park, Minn. G 6 190

St. Peter, Minn. E 6 190
St. Peter Port (cap.), Chan.Is. E 8 11
St. Petersburg, Fla. B 3 148
St. Petersburg Bch., Fla. B 3 148

St. Pierre & Miquelon B 4 99
St-Quentin, France E 3 26
St. Simons Isl., Ga. K 8 152
St. Stephen, N.Br. C 3 102
St. Thomas, Ont. C 5 108

St. Thomas (isl.), V.I. G 1 125
St-Tropez, France G 6 26
Saint Vincent G 4 125
St. Vincent (gulf), Aust. D 7 86
St. Vincent (cape), Port. B 4 30

Saipan (isl.), T.T.P.I. E 4 89
Sakakawea (lake), N.Dak. G 5 218
Sakarya (riv.), Turkey D 2 64
Sakhalin (isl.), U.S.S.R. P 4 47
Sakishima (isls.), Japan K-L 7 75

Salado (riv.), Arg. G11, H 9 93
Salamanca, Mex. J 6 119
Salamanca, N.Y. C 6 212
Salamanca, Spain D 2 31
Sala y Gómez (isl.), Chile Q 8 89

Salé, Mor. E 5 54
Salekhard, U.S.S.R. G 3 46
Salem, Ill. E 5 158
Salem, India D 6 70

Salem, Ind. E 7 163
Salem, Mass. E 5 184
Salem, N.H. E 6 204
Salem, N.J. C 4 209
Salem, Ohio J 4 220

Salem (cap.), Oreg. A 3 226
Salem, Va. H 6 242
Salem Maritime N.H.S., Mass. E 5 184
Salerno, Italy E 4 32

Salford, Eng. H 2 11
Salina, Kans. E 3 168
Salina Cruz, Mex. M 9 119
Salinas, Calif. D 7 140
Salinas, Ecua. D 4 90

Salisbury, Aust. D 7 86
Salisbury, Eng. F 6 11
Salisbury, Md. R 7 181
Salisbury, N.C. H 3 216
Salisbury (cap.), Rhod. N15 57

Salmon (riv.), Idaho B 4 156
Salonika (Thessaloníki), Greece F 5 43
Salta, Arg. G 8 93
Saltillo, Mex. J 4 119

Salt Lake City (cap.), Utah C 3 240
Salto, Urug. J10 93
Salton Sea (lake), Calif. K10 140
Saluda (riv.), S.C. D 3 232
Salûm, Egypt M 5 54

Salvador, Braz. N 6 91
Salween (riv.), Asia C 3 81
Salzach (riv.), Europe B 2-3 38
Salzburg, Aus. B 3 38
Salzgitter, W.Ger. D 2 20

Samaná (bay), Dom.Rep. E 3 124
Samar (isl.), Phil. H 3 83
Samaria (reg.), Jordan C 3 67
Samarinda, Indon. F 6 83
Samarkand, U.S.S.R. G 5 46

Sambhar (lake), India C 3 70
Samnan, Iran H 3 68
Sam Neua, Laos E 2 81
Sámos (isl.), Greece H 7 43
Samothráki (isl.), Greece G 5 43

Samsun, Turkey F 2 64
Samut Sakhon, Thai. D 4 81
San, Mali F 9 54
San (riv.), Pol. F 3 45
San'a (cap.), Y.A.R. D 6 60

San Andrés (isl.), Col. D 1 90
San Andrés Tuxtla, Mex. M 7 119
San Angelo, Tex. D 6 238
San Anselmo, Calif. H 1 140
San Antonio, Tex. F 8 238

San Benito, Tex. G12 238
San Bernardino, Calif. E10 140
San Bernardino (mts.), Calif. J10 140
San Bernardino, Switz. H 4 36

San Blas (gulf), Pan. H 6 123
San Bruno, Calif. J 2 140
San Carlos, Calif. J 3 140
San Carlos, Nic. E 5 122
San Carlos, Ven. G 2 90

San Carlos de Bariloche, Arg. F12 93
Sánchez, Dom.Rep. E 3 124
San Clemente, Calif. H10 140
San Clemente (isl.), Calif. G11 140

San Cristobal (isl.), Solomon Is. G 7 89
San Cristóbal, Ven. F 2 90
Sancti-Spíritus, Cuba B 2 124
Sandakan, Malaysia F 4 83

Sandersville, Ga. G 5 152
Sandgate, Aust. J 5 86
Sandia (peak), N.Mex. C 3 210
San Diego, Calif. H11 140
San Dimas, Calif. D10 140

Sandoway, Burma B 3 81
Sand Sprs., Okla. O 2 225
Sandusky, Ohio E 3 220
Sandwich, Ill. E 2 158
Sandwich, Mass. N 5 185

Sandy, Utah C 3 240
Sandy Hook (spit), N.J. F 3 209
San Felipe, Mex. J 6 119
San Fernando, Calif. C10 140
San Fernando, Chile F10 93

Sanford, Fla. E 3 148
Sanford, Maine B 9 178
Sanford, N.C. L 4 217
San Francisco, Calif. H 2 140
San Francisco (bay), Calif. J 2 140

San Francisco de Macorís, Dom.Rep. E 3 124
San Francisco del Oro, Mex. F 3 119
San Gabriel, Calif. C10 140
San Gabriel, Mex. K 7 119

Sanger, Calif. F 7 140
San Germán, P.R. F 1 124
Sangre de Cristo (mts.), U.S. H-J 6-8 145; D 2-3 210
San Joaquin (riv.), Calif. E 6 140

San Jose, Calif. L 3 140
San José (cap.), C.R. F 5 122
San José, Guat. B 4 122
San José, Urug. J10 93
San José de Chiquitos, Bol. H 7 90

San Juan, Arg. G10 93
San Juan (riv.), C.A. E-F 3 122
San Juan (cap.), P.R. G 1 125
San Juan, Tex. F11 238
San Juan (riv.), U.S. E 3 126

San Juan del Norte, Nic. F 5 122
San Juan I. N.H.P., Wash. B 2 246
San Juan Pueblo, N.Mex. C 2 210
Sankt Gallen, Switz. H 2 37
Sankt Pölten, Aus. C 2 39

San Leandro, Calif. J 2 140
San Lorenzo, Calif. K 2 140
San Lorenzo de El Escorial, Spain E 2 31
San Lucas (cape), Mex. E 5 118

San Luis, Arg. G10 93
San Luis Obispo, Calif. E 8 140
San Luis Potosí, Mex. J 6 119
San Marcos, Tex. F 8 238
San Marino D 3 32

San Marino, Calif. D10 140
San Marino (cap.), San Marino D 3 32
San Mateo, Calif. J 3 140
San Miguel, El Sal. C 4 122

San Martín Texmelucan, Mex. M 1 119
San Nicolas (isl.), Calif. F10 140
San Pablo, Calif. J 1 140
San Pedro, Calif. C11 140

San Pedro, Par. J 8 93
San Pedro Sula, Hond. C 3 122
San Rafael, Arg. G10 93
San Rafael, Calif. J 1 140
San Remo, Italy A 3 32

San Salvador (isl.), Bah. D 1 124
San Salvador (cap.), El Sal. C 4 122
San Sebastián, Spain E 1 31
Santa Ana, Calif. D11 140
Sta. Ana, El Sal. C 4 122

Sta. Barbara, Calif. F 9 140
Sta. Barbara (isls.), Calif. F10 140
Sta. Bárbara, Hond. C 3 122
Sta. Bárbara, Mex. F 3 119
Sta. Catalina (isl.), Calif. G10 140

Sta. Catarina (isl.), Braz. L 9 93
Sta. Clara, Calif. K 3 140
Sta. Clara, Cuba B 2 124
Sta. Cruz, Arg. G14 93
Sta. Cruz, Bol. H 7 90

Sta. Cruz (isls.), Sol. Is. G 6 89
Sta. Cruz, Calif. K 4 140
Sta. Cruz de Tenerife, Spain B 4 30
Sta. Elena, Ecua. D 4 90

Sta. Fe, Arg. H10 93
Sta. Fe (cap.), N.Mex. C 3 210
Sta. Fe Sprs., Calif. C11 140
Sta. Isabel (isl.), Sol. Is. F 6 89
Sta. Maria, Braz. K 9 93

Sta. Maria, Calif. E 9 140
Sta. Maria, Italy E 4 32
Sta. María (riv.), Mex. F 1 119
Sta. Marta, Col. F 1 90
Sta. Monica, Calif. B10 140

Santana do Livramento, Braz. K10 93
Santander, Col. E 3 90
Santander, Spain D 1 31
Sta. Paula, Calif. F 9 140

Santarém, Braz. J 4 90
Santarém, Port. B 3 30
Sta. Rosa, Arg. H11 93
Sta. Rosa, Calif. C 5 140
Sta. Rosa de Copán, Hond. C 3 122

Sta. Rosalía, Mex. C 3 118
Santee (riv.), S.C. H 5 232
Santiago (cap.), Chile F10 93
Santiago, Dom.Rep. D 3 124
Santiago, Pan. G 6 122

Santiago, Spain B 1 30
Santiago (mts.), Tex. A 8 238
Santiago de Cuba, Cuba C 3 124
Santiago del Estero, Arg. H 9 93

Säntis (mt.), Switz. H 2 37
Sto. Ângelo, Braz. K 9 93
Sto. Domingo (cap.), Dom.Rep. E 3 124

Santos, Braz. L 8 93
San Vito, Italy D 2 32
São Bernardo do Campo, Braz. L 8 93
São Francisco (riv.), Braz. N 5 91

São João da Bôa Vista, Braz. L 8 90
São José do Rio Prêto, Braz. K 8 90
São Leopoldo, Braz. K 9 93

São Luís, Braz. M 4 90
Saône (riv.), France F 4 26
São Paulo, Braz. L 8 93
São Roque (cape), Braz. O 5 91

São Tomé (cap.), São T.&P. H11 57
São Tomé e Príncipe G11 57
Sapporo, Japan K 2 75
Sapulpa, Okla. O 3 225
Saragossa, Spain F 2 31

Sarajevo, Yugo. D 4 43
Saraland, Ala. B 9 130
Saranac Lake, N.Y. M 2 213
Saransk, U.S.S.R. G 4 50
Sarasota, Fla. D 4 148

Saratoga, Calif. K 4 140
Saratoga N.H.P., N.Y. N 4 213
Saratoga Sprs., N.Y. N 4 213
Saratov, U.S.S.R. G 4 50
Sarawak (state), Malaysia E 5 83

Sardinia (isl.), Italy B 4 32
Sardis (lake), Miss. E 2 192
Sargodha, Pak. C 2 70
Sark (isl.), Chan.Is. E 8 11
Sarnath, India E 3 70

Sarnia, Ont. B 5 108
Sarthe (riv.), France D 4 26
Sasebo, Japan D 7 74
Saskatchewan (prov.), Can. 112-113
Saskatchewan (riv.), Can. F 5 96

Saskatoon, Sask. E 3 113
Sassandra, I.C. E11 54
Sassari, Italy B 4 32
Satellite Bch., Fla. F 3 148
Satpura (range), India D 4 70

Satu Mare, Rum. F 2 43
Saudi Arabia C-E 4-5 60
Sauer (riv.), Europe J 9 25
Sauerland (reg.), W.Ger. B 3 20
Saugus, Mass. D 6 184

Saugus Iron Works N.H.S., Mass. D 6 184
Sauk Rapids, Minn. D 5 190
Sauk Village, Ill. F 2 158
Sault Ste. Marie, Mich. E 2 186

Sault Ste. Marie, Ont. J 5 109
Saumur, France D 4 26
Sausalito, Calif. H 2 140
Sava (riv.), Yugo. D 3 43
Savai'i (isl.), W.Samoa J 7 89

Savannah, Ga. L 6 152
Savannah, Tenn. E10 172
Savannah (riv.), U.S. E 6 232
Savannakhet, Laos E 3 81
Savanna la Mar, Jam. B 3 124

Save (riv.), Moz. N16 57
Savoie (dept.), France G 5 26
Savona, Italy B 2 32
Savonlinna, Fin. Q 6 16
Sawatch (range), Colo. G 4-5 145

Sawtooth (range), Idaho C 6 156
Sawu (isls.), Indon. G 8 83
Saxony (reg.), E.Ger. E 3 20
Sayre, Pa. K 2 230
Sayreville, N.J. E 3 209

Scapa Flow (chan.), Scot. E 2 13
Scarborough, Eng. G 3 11
Scarborough, Maine C 8 178
Scarborough, Ont. K 4 109
Scarborough, T.&T. G 5 125

Scarsdale, N.Y. P 7 213
Schaffhausen, Switz. G 1 37
Schaumburg, Ill. E 1 158
Schefferville, Que. D 2 106
Scheldt (riv.), Belg. C 7 25

Schenectady, N.Y. M 5 213
Scheveningen, Neth. E 4 25
Schiedam, Neth. E 5 25
Schiller Park, Ill. A 1 158
Schleswig, W.Ger. C 1 20

Schleswig-Holstein (state), W.Ger. C 1 20
Schofield Barracks, Hawaii E 2 155
Schuylkill (riv.), Pa. M 5 231
Schuylkill Haven, Pa. K 4 231

Schwäbisch Gmünd, W.Ger. C 4 20
Schwarzwald (Black) (for.), W.Ger. C 4 20
Schweinfurt, W.Ger. D 3 20
Schwerin, E.Ger. D 2 20

Schwyz, Switz. G 2 37
Scilly (isls.), Eng. A 7 11
Scioto (riv.), Ohio D 8 220
Scituate, Mass. F 8 184
Scotch Plains, N.J. E 2 209

Scotia (sea), Ant. D 16-17 88
Scotia, N.Y. N 5 213
Scotland 13
Scotlandville, La. J 1 175
Scottdale, Pa. C 5 230

Scottsbluff, Nebr. A 3 200
Scotts Bluff N.M., Nebr. A 3 200
Scottsboro, Ala. F 1 130
Scottsdale, Ariz. D 5 134
Scranton, Pa. L 3 231

Scutari (lake), Europe D 4 43
Sea (isls.), U.S. K-L 7-9 152
Sea Cliff, N.Y. R 6 213
Seaford, Del. R 6 181
Seal Beach, Calif. C11 140

Searcy, Ark. G 3 139
Seaside, Calif. D 7 140
Seat Pleasant, Md. G 5 180
Seattle, Wash. A 2 246
Sebha, Libya J 6 54

Sebring, Fla. E 4 148
Secaucus, N.J. B 2 209
Secunderabad, India D 5 70
Sedalia, Mo. F 5 197
Sedan, France F 3 26

Seekonk, Mass. J 5 184
Ségou, Mali E 9 54
Segovia, Spain D 2 31
Segre (riv.), Spain G 2 31
Seguin, Tex. G 8 238

Seine (riv.), France D 3 26
Sekondi, Ghana F11 54
Selangor (state), Malaysia D 7 81
Selenga (riv.), Asia G 1 77
Selinsgrove, Pa. J 4 230

Selkirk (mts.), B.C. H-J 4-5 117
Selkirk, Man. F 4 117
Selkirk, Scot. F 5 13
Selma, Ala. E 6 130
Selma, Calif. F 7 140

Semarang, Indon. J 2 83
Semeru (mt.), Indon. K 2 83
Seminole, Okla. N 4 225
Seminole, Tex. B 5 238
Semipalatinsk, U.S.S.R. H 4 46

Sendai, Japan K 4 75
Seneca (lake), N.Y. G 5 212
Seneca, S.C. A 2 232
Seneca Falls, N.Y. G 5 212
Senegal C-D 8-9 54

Senegal (riv.), Afr. D 8 54
Sennar, Sudan N 9 54
Sens, France E 3 26
Seoul (cap.) S.Korea C 5 74
Sepik (riv.), P.N.G. B 6 82

Sept-Îles, Que. D 2 106
Sepulveda, Calif. B10 140
Sequoia N.P., Calif. G 7 140
Serbia (rep.), Yugo. D-E 3-4 43
Sergipe (state), Braz. N 6 91

T

Tabasco (state), Mex. N-O 7-8 119
Taber, Alta. E 5 114
Table (bay), S.Afr. P19 57
Tabor (mt.), Isr. C 2 67
Tabora, Tanz. N12 57

Tabriz, Iran D 2 68
Tacna, Peru F 7 90
Tacoma, Wash. C 3 246
Taconic (mts.), U.S. A 1-3 184
Tacuarembó, Urug. J10 93

Tadmor, Syria H 5 64
Tadoussac, Que. H 1 105
Tadzhik S.S.R., U.S.S.R. G-H 6 46
Taegu, S.Korea D 6 74
Taejŏn, S.Korea C 5 74

Taganrog, U.S.S.R. E 5 50
Tagus (riv.), Europe B 3 30
Tahiti (isl.), Fr.Poly. L 7 89
Tahlequah, Okla. R 3 225
Tahoe (lake), U.S. A 3 202

Tahquamenon (riv.), Mich. D 2 186
Taichung, China J 7 77
Tainan, China J 7 77
Taipei (cap.), China K 7 77
Taiwan (isl.), China K 7 77

Taiyüan, China H 4 77
Ta'izz, Y.A.R. D 7 60
Tajo (Tagus) (riv.), Spain D 3 31
Taklamakan (des.), China A-C 4 76

Takoma Park, Md. F 4 180
Takoradi, Ghana F11 54
Taku (glacier), Alaska N 1 133
Talara, Peru D 4 90

Talbot (isl.), Fla. E 1 148
Talca, Chile F11 93
Talcahuano, Chile F11 93
Talladega, Ala. F 4 130
Tallahassee (cap.), Fla. B 1 148

Tallinn, U.S.S.R. C 1 51
Tallmadge, Ohio H 3 220
Tallulah, La. H 2 175
Tamanrasset, Alg. H 7 54
Tamaqua, Pa. L 4 231

Tamarac, Fla. B 3 148
Tamatave, Madag. R15 57
Tamaulipas (state), Mex. K 4-5 119
Tambov, U.S.S.R. F 4 50

Tamiami (canal), Fla. E 6 148
Tampa, Fla. C 2 148
Tampa (bay), Fla. C 2 148
Tampere, Fin. N 6 16
Tampico, Mex. L 5 119

Tana (lake), Eth. O 9 55
Tanana (riv.), Alaska J 2 133
Tandil, Arg. J11 93
Tanezrouft (des.), Afr. F-G 7 54

Tanga, Tanz. O12 57
Tanganyika (lake), Afr. N13 57
Tangier, Mor. E 4 54
Tangier (sound), U.S. P 8 181
Tangshan, China J 4 77

Tanta, Egypt N 5 54
Tanzania N-O 13 57
Taormina, Italy E 6 32
Taos, N.Mex. D 2 210
Tapachula, Mex. N 9 119

Tapajós (riv.), Braz. J 5 90
Tar (riv.), N.C. O 3 217
Tarabulus, Leb. F 5 64
Taranto, Italy F 4 32
Tarascon, France F 6 26

Tarawa (atoll), Gilb. Is. H 5 89
Tarboro, N.C. O 3 217
Tarentum, Pa. C 4 230
Tarija, Bol. H 8 90
Tarim (riv.), China C 3 76

Tarnów, Pol. E 3 45
Tarpon Sprs., Fla. D 3 148
Tarragona, Spain G 2 31
Tarrant, Ala. E 3 130
Tarrytown, N.Y. O 6 213

Tarsus, Turkey F 4 64
Tartu, U.S.S.R. D 1 51
Tarzana, Calif. B10 140
Tashkent, U.S.S.R. G 5 46
Tasman (sea), Pacific F-G 9 89

Tasmania (state), Aust. H 8 86
Tata, Hung. E 3 39
Tatar (str.), U.S.S.R. P 4 47
Tatar A.S.S.R., U.S.S.R. G 3 50
Tatra, High (mts.), Europe D 4 45

Taubaté, Braz. L 8 93
Taunton, Eng. D 6 11
Taunton, Mass. K 5 184
Taunus (mts.), W.Ger. C 3 20
Taupo (lake), N.Z. M 6 87

Taurus (mts.), Turkey D-F 4 64
Taxco, Mex. K 7 119
Taxila (ruins), Pak. C 2 70
Tay (firth), Scot. F 4 13
Taylor, Mich. B 7 186

Taylor, Pa. L 3 231
Taylor, Tex. G 7 238
Taylorsville, Utah B 3 240
Taylorville, Ill. D 4 158
Taymyr (pen.), U.S.S.R. L 2 46

Tay Ninh, Viet. E 5 81
Tbilisi, U.S.S.R. F 6 50
Tczew, Pol. D 1 45
Teaneck, N.J. B 2 209
Tecumseh, Mich. E 7 186

Tees (riv.), Eng. F 3 11
Tegucigalpa (cap.), Hond. D 3 122
Tehran (cap.), Iran G 3 68
Tehuantepec, Mex. M 8 119
Tejo (Tagus) (riv.), Port. C 3 30

Tel Aviv-Jaffa, Isr. B 3 67
Tema, Ghana G10 54
Tempe, Ariz. D 5 134
Temple, Tex. G 6 238
Temple City, Calif. D10 140

Temple Terrace, Fla. C 2 148
Templeton, Mass. F 2 184
Temuco, Chile F11 93
Tenafly, N.J. C 1 209
Tenasserim, Burma C 5 81

Tenerife (isl.), Spain B 5 30
Tenkiller Ferry (res.), Okla. S 3 225
Tennessee (riv.), U.S. J 3 126
Tennessee (state), U.S. 172-173

Ten Thousand (isls.), Fla. E 6 148
Ten Thousand Smokes (valley), Alaska G 3 133
Teófilo Otôni, Braz. M 7 90
Teotihuacán, Mex. L 1 119

Tepic, Mex. G 6 119
Teplice, Czech. B 1 38
Teresina, Braz. M 4 91
Termini Imerese, Italy D 6 32
Ternate, Indon. H 5 83

Terni, Italy D 3 32
Terrace, B.C. C 3 116
Terra Nova N.P., Newf. D 3 99
Terrebonne (bay), La. J 8 175
Terrebonne, Que. H 4 105

Terre Haute, Ind. C 6 163
Terrell, Tex. H 5 238
Terrell Hills, Tex. F 8 238
Teruel, Spain F 2 31
Teslin (lake), Canada C 3 96

Tete, Moz. N15 57
Teton (range), Wyo. B 2 254
Teutoburger Wald (for.), W.Ger. C 2-3 20
Tewksbury, Mass. K 2 184

Texarkana, Ark. C 7 138
Texarkana, Tex. L 4 238
Texas (state), U.S. 238
Texas City, Tex. K 3 238
Texcoco, Mex. M 1 119

Texel (isl.), Neth. F 2 25
Thailand 81
Thai Nguyen, Viet. E 2 81
Thames (riv.), Conn. G 3 147
Thames (riv.), Eng. H 6 11

Thames (riv.), Ont. B 5 108
Thásos (isl.), Greece G 5 43
The Dalles, Oreg. F 2 226
Theodore Roosevelt (lake), Ariz. D 5 134

Theodore Roosevelt N.M.P., N.Dak. D 4-6 218
The Pas, Man. H 3 111
Thessaloníki, Greece F 5 43

Thetford Mines, Que. F 3 105
The Village, Okla. L 3 225
Thibodeaux, La. J 7 175
Thief River Falls, Minn. B 2 190
Thiès, Sen. C 9 54

Thimphu (cap.), Bhutan F 3 70
Third Cataract (rapids), Sudan M 8 54
Thisted, Den. B 4 19
Thívai, Greece F 6 43

Thomaston, Conn. C 2 146
Thomaston, Ga. D 5 152
Thomasville, Ga. E 9 152
Thomasville, N.C. J 3 217
Thompson, Conn. H 1 147

Thomson, Ga. H 4 152
Thonburi, Thai. D 4 81
Thornton, Colo. K 3 145
Thorold, Ont. E 4 108
Thousand (isls.), N.A. H 2 212

Thousand Oaks, Calif. G 9 140
Three Rivers, Mich. D 7 186
Thule, Greenl. M 2 94
Thun, Switz. E 3 37
Thunder Bay, Ont. C 3 107

Thurgau (canton), Switz. G-H 1 37
Thüringer Wald (for.), E.Ger. D 3 20
Thuringia (reg.), E.Ger. D 3 20
Thursday Island, Aust. G 2 86

Thurso, Scot. E 2 13
Tiber (riv.), Italy D 3 32
Tiberias, Isr. C 2 67
Tibesti (mts.), Chad K 7 54
Tibet (reg.), China B-D 5 76

Tiburon, Calif. J 2 140
Ticino (canton), Switz. G 4 37
Tien Shan (mts.), Asia A-B 3 76
Tientsin, China J 4 77
Tierra del Fuego (isl.), S.A. G14 93

Tiffin, Ohio D 3 220
Tifton, Ga. F 8 152
Tigard, Oreg. A 2 226
Tigris (riv.), Asia E 4 68
Tihama (reg.), Asia C-D 5-7 60

Tijuana, Mex. A 1 118
Tilburg, Neth. G 5 25
Timaru, N.Z. L 7 87
Timbalier (bay), La. K 8 175
Timbuktu, Mali F 8 54

Timiskaming (lake), Can. E 3 107
Timişoara, Rum. E 3 43
Timmins, Ont. D 3 107
Timor (isl.), Asia H 7 83
Timor (sea) D 2 86

Timpanogos Cave N.M., Utah C 3 240
Tinian (isl.), T.T.P.I. E 4 89
Tinley Park, Ill. B 2 158
Tioga (riv.), U.S. H 1 230
Tipp City, Ohio B 6 220

Tippecanoe (riv.), Ind. E 2 163
Tipperary, Ire. E 7 15
Tipton, Ind. F 4 163
Tiranë (Tirana) (cap.), Alb. E 5 43
Tîrgovişte, Rum. G 3 43

Tîrgu Neamţ, Rum. G 2 43
Tirich Mir (mt.), Pak. C 1 70
Tirol (reg.), Aus. A-B 3 38
Tiruchchirappalli, India D 6 70
Tisza (riv.), Europe E 3 43

Titicaca (lake), S.A. F 7 90
Titograd, Yugo. D 4 43
Titusville, Fla. F 3 148
Titusville, Pa. C 2 230
Tiverton, Eng. D 7 11

Tiverton, R.I. K 6 184
Tizi-Ouzou, Alg. G 4 54
Tjirebon, Indon. H 2 83
Tlaxcala, Mex. M 1 119
Tlemcen, Alg. F 5 54

Toba (lake), Indon. B 5 82
Tobago (isl.), T.&T. G 5 125
Tobol'sk, U.S.S.R. G 4 46
Tobruk, Libya L 5 54
Tocantins (riv.), Braz. L 4 90

Toccoa, Ga. F 1 152
Tocopilla, Chile F 8 90
Toggenburg (dist.), Switz. H 2 37
Togo G10 54
Toiyabe (range), Nev. D 3-4 202

Tokaj, Hung. F 2 39
Tokelau Islands J 6 89
Tokushima, Japan G 7 75
Tokyo (cap.), Japan O 2 75
Tokyo (bay), Japan O 2 75

Toledo, Ohio D 2 220
Toledo, Spain D 3 31
Tolima (mt.), Col. E 3 90
Tolland, Conn. F 1 146
Tolosa, Spain F 1 31

Toluca, Mex. K 7 119
Tomah, Wis. F 8 253
Tombigbee (riv.), U.S. B 7 130
Tombstone, Ariz. F 7 134
Tomsk, U.S.S.R. J 4 46

Toms River, N.J. E 4 209
Tonawanda, N.Y. B 4 212
Tonga J 8 89
Tongareva (atoll), Cook Is. L 6 89
Tongatapu (isls.), Tonga J 8 89

Tongue (riv.), U.S. K 5 198
Tonkin (gulf), Asia E 3 81
Tonle Sap (lake), Camb. D 4 81
Tonto N.M., Ariz. D 5 134
Tooele, Utah B 3 240

Topeka (cap.), Kans. G 2 169
Toppenish, Wash. E 4 246
Topsfield, Mass. L 2 184
Topsham, Maine D 8 178
Torbay, Eng. D 7 11

Torino (Turin), Italy A 2 32
Toronto, Ohio J 5 220
Toronto (cap.), Ont. K 4 109
Torrance, Calif. C11 140
Torre Annunziata, Italy E 4 32

Torreón, Mex. H 4 119
Torres (str.) G 1 86
Torrington, Conn. C 1 146
Tórshavn, Faerøe Is. A 3 19
Tortola (isl.), B.V.I. H 1 125

Tortuga (isl.), Haiti D 2 124
Toruń, Pol. D 2 45
Totowa, N.J. B 1 209
Toul, France F 3 26
Toulon, France F 6 26

Toulouse, France D 6 26
Toungoo, Burma C 3 81
Tournai, Belg. C 7 25
Touro Synagogue N.H.S., R.I. J 7 184

Tours, France D 4 26
Townsville, Aust. H 3 86
Towson, Md. M 3 181
Toyama, Japan H 5 75
Toyohashi, Japan H 6 75

Trabzon, Turkey H 2 65
Tracy, Calif. D 6 140
Trafalgar (cape), Spain C 4 31
Trail, B.C. J 6 117
Tralee, Ire. B 7 15

Tranquebar, India E 6 70
Trans-Himalayas (mts.), China B-C 5 76
Transkei (prov.), S.Afr. M18 57
Transvaal (prov.), S.Afr. M17 57

Transylvanian Alps (mts.), Rum. F-H 3 43
Trapani, Italy D 5 32
Travancore (reg.), India D 7 70
Traverse City, Mich. D 4 186

Treasure Island, Fla. B 3 148
Treinta y Tres, Urug. K10 93
Trelleborg, Sweden H 9 16
Tremadoc (bay), Wales C 5 11
Trent (riv.), Eng. G 4 11

Trentino-Alto Adige (reg.), Italy C 1-2 32
Trento, Italy C 1 32
Trenton, Mich. B 7 186
Trenton, Mo. E 2 197

Trenton (cap.), N.J. D 3 209
Trenton, Ohio B 7 220
Trenton, Ont. G 3 108
Trier, W.Ger. B 4 20
Trieste, Italy D 2 32

Tríkkala, Greece E 6 43
Trincomalee, Sri Lanka E 7 70
Trinidad, Bol. H 6 90
Trinidad, Colo. L 8 145
Trinidad (isl.), T.&T. G 5 125

Trinidad, Urug. J10 93
Trinidad & Tobago G 5 125
Trinity (riv.), Calif. B 3 140
Trinity (bay), Newf. D 3 99
Trinity (riv.), Tex. H 5 238

Tripoli (Tarabulus), Leb. F 5 64
Tripoli (cap.), Libya J 5 54
Trípolis, Greece F 7 43
Tripolitania (reg.), Libya J-K 6 54
Tripura (state), India G 4 70

Tristan da Cunha (isl.), St. Helena 5
Trivandrum, India D 7 70
Trois-Rivières, Que. E 3 105
Trombay, India B 7 70

Tromsø, Nor. L 2 16
Trondheim, Nor. F 5 16
Troy, Ala. G 7 130
Troy, Mich. B 6 186
Troy, N.Y. N 5 213

Troy, Ohio B 5 220
Troyes, France F 3 26
Truckee (riv.), U.S. B 3 202
Trujillo, Hond. D 3 122
Trujillo, Peru E 5 90

Trujillo, Ven. F 2 90
Truk (isls.), T.T.P.I. F 5 89
Trumann, Ark. J 2 139
Trumbull, Conn. C 4 146
Truro, Eng. B 7 11

Truro, N.S. E 3 100
Truth or Consequences, N.Mex. B 5 210
Tsingtao, China K 4 77
Tsitsihar, China K 2 77

Tuamotu (arch.), Fr.Poly. M 7 89
Tübingen, W.Ger. C 4 20
Tubuai (Austral) (isls.), Fr.Poly. M 8 89
Tuckahoe, N.Y. O 7 213

Tucson, Ariz. D 6 134
Tucumán, Arg. H 9 93
Tucumcari, N.Mex. F 3 210
Tujunga, Calif. C10 140
Tula, U.S.S.R. E 4 50

Tulare, Calif. F 7 140
Tulia, Tex. C 3 238
Tullahoma, Tenn. J10 173
Tulsa, Okla. O 2 225
Tumacacori N.M., Ariz. E 7 134

Tumwater, Wash. B 3 246
Tunis (cap.), Tun. J 4 54
Tunisia H 4-5 54
Tunja, Col. F 2 90
Tupelo, Miss. G 2 192

Tupelo N.B., Miss. G 2 192
Turin, Italy A 2 32
Turkana (lake), Africa O11 55
Turkestan, U.S.S.R. G 5 46
Turkey 64-65

Turkey (riv.), Iowa K 2 164
Turkmen S.S.R., U.S.S.R. F-G 6 46
Turks (isls.), T.&C.Is. D 2 124
Turks & Caicos Is. D 2 124
Turku, Fin. N 6 16

Turlock, Calif. E 6 140
Turneffe (isls.), Belize D 2 122
Turnhout, Belg. F 6 25
Turnu Măgurele, Rum. G 4 43
Turnu Severin, Rum. F 3 43

Turtle (mts.), N.Dak. K-L 2 218
Turtle Creek, Pa. C 7 230
Tuscaloosa, Ala. C 4 130
Tuscany (reg.), Italy C 3 32
Tuscarawas (riv.), Ohio H 5 220

Tuscumbia, Ala. C 1 130
Tuskegee, Ala. G 6 130
Tustin, Calif. D11 140
Tuvalu H 6 89
Tuvinian A.S.S.R., U.S.S.R. K 4 46

Tuxtla Gutiérrez, Mex. N 8 119
Tuzigoot N.M., Ariz. D 4 134
Tweed (riv.), Eng. E 2 11
Tweedsmuir Prov. Pk., B.C. D 3 117

Twin Falls, Idaho D 7 156
Twinsburg, Ohio J10 220
Two Rivers, Wis. M 7 253
Tyler, Tex. J 5 238
Tyne (riv.), Eng. F 3 11

Tyre (Sur), Leb. F 6 64
Tyrone, Pa. F 4 230
Tyrrhenian (sea), Italy C-E 4-5 32
Tzepo, China J 4 77

U

Ubangi (riv.), Afr. K11 57
Uberaba, Braz. L 7 90
Ucayali (riv.), Peru E 5 90
Udine, Italy D 1 32
Udjung Pandang, Indon. F 6 83

Udmurt A.S.S.R., U.S.S.R. H 3 50
Ufa, U.S.S.R. J 4 50
Uganda N11 57
Uhrichsville, Ohio H 5 220
Uinta (mts.), Utah D-E 3 240

Uitenhage, S.Afr. M18 57
Ukiah, Calif. B 4 140
Ukrainian S.S.R., U.S.S.R. B-D 5 50
Ulan Bator (cap.), Mong. G 2 77
Ulan-Ude, U.S.S.R. L 4 46

Uliassutai, Mong. E 2 77
Ulm, W.Ger. C 4 20
Ul'yanovsk, U.S.S.R. G 4 50
Umbria (reg.), Italy D 3 32
Umeå, Sweden M 5 16

Umpqua (riv.), Oreg. D 4 226
Umtali, Rhod. N15 57
Unalaska, Alaska E 4 132
Ungava (pen.), Que. E 1 106
Union, Mo. L 6 197

Union, N.J. A 2 209
Union, S.C. D 2 232
Union Beach, N.J. E 3 209
Union City, Calif. K 2 140
Union City, N.J. C 2 209

Union City, Tenn. C 8 172
Union of Soviet Socialist Republics 46-47, 50-51
Uniontown, Pa. C 6 230
United Arab Emirates F-G 5 60

United Kingdom 8
United States 126-127
University City, Mo. P 3 197
University Hts., Ohio H 9 220
University Park, Tex. H 2 238

Unterwalden (dist.), Switz. F 3 37
Upernavik, Greenl. L 1 96
Upland, Calif. E10 140
Upolu (isl.), W.Samoa J 7 89
Upper Arlington, Ohio D 6 220

Upper Darby, Pa. M 6 231
Upper Klamath (lake), Oreg. E 5 226
Upper Saddle River, N.J. B 1 209
Upper Sandusky, Ohio D 4 220

Upper Tunguska (riv.), U.S.S.R. K 4 46
Upper Volta F-G 9 54
Uppsala, Sweden L 7 16
Ural (mts.), U.S.S.R. J-K 1-4 50

Ural (riv.), U.S.S.R. H 5 50
Urbana, Ill. E 3 158
Urbana, Ohio C 5 220
Urbandale, Iowa F 5 164
Uri (canton), Switz. G 3 37

Urmia (lake), Iran D 2 68
Uruguay J10 93
Uruguay (riv.), S.A. J 9 93
Urumchi, China C 3 76
Ushuaia, Arg. G14 93

Ussuri (riv.), Asia M 2 77
Ustí nad Labem, Czech. C 1 38
Utah (state), U.S. 240
Utica, N.Y. K 4 212
Utrecht, Neth. G 4 25

Uttar Pradesh (state), India D 3 70
Uvalde, Tex. E 8 238
Uxbridge, Mass. H 4 184
Uxmal (ruins), Mex. P 6 119
Uzbek S.S.R., U.S.S.R. G 5-6 46

V

Vaal (riv.), S.Afr. M17 57
Vaasa, Fin. M 5 16
Vacaville, Calif. D 5 140
Vaduz (cap.), Liecht. H 2 37
Valais (canton), Switz. D-F 4 37

Valdez, Alaska D 1 132
Valdivia, Chile F11 93
Val-d'Or, Que. B 3 106
Valdosta, Ga. F 9 152
Valencia, Spain F 3 31

Valencia, Ven. G 2 90
Valladolid, Spain D 2 31
Vallejo, Calif. J 1 140
Valletta (cap.), Malta E 7 32
Valley City, N.Dak. P 6 219

Valley Sta., Ky. K 4 173
Valley Stream, N.Y. N 9 213
Valparaíso, Chile F10 93
Valparaiso, Fla. C 6 148
Valparaiso, Ind. C 2 163

Van Buren, Ark. B 3 138
Vancouver, B.C. K 3 117
Vancouver (isl.), B.C. D-E 5 117
Vancouver, Wash. C 5 246
Vandalia, Ill. D 5 158

Vandalia, Ohio B 6 220
Vandenberg A.F.B., Calif. E 9 140
Vandergrift, Pa. D 4 230
Vänern (lake), Sweden H 7 16
Van Nuys, Calif. B10 140

Vanua Levu (isl.), Fiji H 7 89
Van Wert, Ohio A 4 220
Varanasi, India E 3 70
Vardar (riv.), Europe E 5 43
Varna, Bulg. J 4 43

Västerås, Sweden J 7 16
Vatican City B 6 32
Vättern (lake), Sweden J 7 16
Vaud (canton), Switz. B-D 3-4 36
Vendée (dept.), France C 4 26

Venetia (reg.), Italy C-D 2 32
Venezuela F-H 2 90
Venice, Calif. B11 140
Venice, Fla. D 4 148
Venice, Italy D 2 32

Ventnor City, N.J. E 5 209
Ventura, Calif. F 9 140
Veracruz, Mex. Q 1 119
Vercelli, Italy B 2 32
Verde (cape), Sen. C 9 54

Verdun, France F 3 26
Vermilion, Alta. E 3 114
Vermilion, Ohio F 3 220
Vermillion, S.Dak. R 8 235
Vermont (state), U.S. 204